Financial Institutions and Capital Markets

• ***Tim S. Campbell*** •

University of Southern California

• ***William A. Kracaw*** •

Pennsylvania State University

HarperCollins*CollegePublishers*

Acquisitions Editor: Kirsten D. Sandberg
Developmental Editor: Pamela Wilkie
Project Coordination and Text Design: Ruttle, Shaw & Wetherill, Inc.
Cover Design: Jill Yutkowitz
Cover Illustration: Barry Jackson
Production Administrator: Hilda Koparanian
Compositor: Ruttle Graphics, Inc.
Printer and Binder: R. R. Donnelley & Sons Company
Cover Printer: The Lehigh Press, Inc.

Financial Institutions and Capital Markets
Copyright © 1994 by HarperCollins*CollegePublishers*
All rights reserved. Printed in the United States of America. No part of this book may be used or reproduced in any manner whatsoever without written permission, except in the case of brief quotations embodied in critical articles and reviews. For information address HarperCollins*College Publishers,* 10 East 53rd Street, New York, NY 10022.

Library of Congress Cataloging-in-Publication Data
Campbell, Tim S.
Financial institutions and capital markets / Tim S. Campbell, William A. Kracaw.
p. cm.
Includes index.
ISBN 0-673-46330-3
1. Financial services industry. 2. Securities. 3. Capital market.
4. International finance. I. Kracaw, William Allen, 1947-. II. Title.
HG173.C268 1994
332.1–dc20
94-42519
CIP

Brief Contents

Contents

Preface

One of the great challenges inherent in designing the finance curriculum of any business school is structuring the course or sequence of courses most commonly referred to as "financial markets and institutions." You may find it in your own course catalog under any number of titles: money and capital markets, financial service organizations, the financial marketplace, the financial system, or even financial intermediation. Depending on the instructor's area of interest and the prerequisites to the course, it may cover a wide array of topics—the structure of interest rates and the pricing of fixed income securities, the structure and operation of various types of financial institutions, the regulation of financial markets, the regulation of banks and the conduct of monetary policy, the globalization of financial markets, and increasingly, the creation and use of derivative securities and financial risk management—a daunting list indeed. What should such a course cover? What should its focus be? What is the best blend of specific items that will make for a challenging and informative course?

When we began to write this book, we decided that rather than address these traditional concerns, we would ask ourselves some very different questions: What does the marketplace expect from a finance professional today? What about tomorrow? What will our students really need to know to compete for jobs or promotions? Since we believe that course design should address these concerns, we wrote this book from a competitive point of view, to incorporate those skills that students must develop to become effective finance professionals, whether they position themselves in financial or nonfinancial firms.

What do students need to know? Walter Wriston, former CEO and chairman of Citicorp, provided an answer, "Bankers are in the business of managing risk. Pure and simple, that is the business of banking." Considering the broad area of financial institutions and capital markets in this light, we decided to emphasize two important topics in this book:

Financial Innovation

Financial Risk Management

To be able to create a competitive advantage in the financial marketplace, students should understand the process of innovation *and* learn how to use the modern tools of risk management. We wrote this book not only to persuade our students that these two areas—financial risk management and financial innovation—are critical to business success, but, even more importantly, to train them sufficiently in these areas so that they can achieve their career goals.

We want to show students how to use what we call the risk management product set—not just forwards, futures, and options, but also caps, collars and swaps—to solve various financial risk management problems related to interest rates and foreign exchange rates. In this fast-paced world, students will benefit from practical material, that which truly prepares them for choosing among all these products to manage the various forms of risk exposure.

Even though we emphasize risk management and innovation, we have not abandoned those long-time staples of the financial institutions and markets curriculum. As you inspect the table of contents of our book, you will see that we do describe the structure of financial institutions and markets, and we build a framework for understanding interest rates and the pricing of fixed income securities. We also cover the regulation of financial markets and institutions as well as the basics of monetary policy, and we examine global financial markets and the forces driving foreign exchange rates. However, we discuss these topics only to the extent that they expedite a student's mastery of the skills that will become a valuable asset to the student's current or future firm of employment. Therefore, we downplay some of these topics perhaps more so than other books on financial markets and institutions.

We have developed and taught this material over the last several years in both university and business settings. Our audience has ranged from the typical finance major and MBA student to the emerging finance professional, whose backgrounds are broad and varied. Consequently, we have made the text as accessible as possible through clear exposition and use of numerous practical examples. We have avoided the use of complicated equations so that interested readers who lack a high level of technical skill and experience might also become sophisticated users of this information. Simply, we wanted to blend theory and application, to avoid theory for its own sake, but when we did present it, to do so in a simple and interesting way. To be certain that readers grasp risk management and innovation in terms of financial service organizations, we crafted a number of other pedagogical features:

Key Concepts to Learn—A list of key concepts begins each chapter so that students know exactly what they should be getting from their reading assignment.

Practical inserts—Throughout the book, specially marked examples highlight current events or demonstrate the point at hand. Since some chapters lended themselves more to these inserts than did others, we put them where most appropriate to aid the learning process.

Current examples—To keep content as up to date as possible, we used the most recent examples and illustrations from the financial news.

Applications—We have also included detailed illustrations, especially in the chapters dealing with risk management, so that students can see how risk management products actually work.

In addition to these features in the book, we are proud to include several other supplementary items to facilitate the teaching as well as the learning process.

Instructor's Manual and Test Bank

Prepared by the authors and Stacey L. Suydam, Eastern Montana College.

To give instructors alternative material for lecture presentations and examinations, the Instructor's Manual includes a new Test Bank, supplemental overhead transparency masters, which can also serve as classroom handouts, and solutions to end-of-chapter questions and problems. Instructors who need the Test Bank in electronic form should contact their publisher's representative for more information.

Study Guide
Created by Subhrendu P. Rath, Washington State University, and John W. Byrd, Fort Lewis College, Colorado.

To save students valuable time in preparing for examinations, each chapter features the following sections: a summary of key chapter points and definitions, a list of learning objectives, a chapter outline with equations, multiple choice and true-false test items, and review questions; all answers include an explanation for reinforcement. Instructors should ask their HarperCollins representative for a copy, because bookstores will no doubt want to make it available for students who really need help outside the classroom.

Acknowledgments

A number of people have helped us in this effort. We are grateful to them all, especially to those colleagues who contracted with HarperCollins to add value to the supplements package and to critique the earlier work titled *Money and Capital Markets,* our recently published *Financial Risk Management,* and, finally, the manuscript for this new book. They are as follows:

Nasser Arshadi, University of Missouri - St. Louis
David F. Babbel, University of Pennsylvania
James C. Baker, Kent State University
W. Brian Barrett, University of Miami
John W. Byrd, Fort Lewis College
John W. Cooney, Washington State University
Dale L. Domian, Michigan State University
Joseph Friedman, Temple University
Joseph Fuhrig, Golden Gate University
James F. Gatti, University of Vermont
Bruno Gerard, University of Southern California
Gerardo Jacobs, Vanderbuilt University
Ronnie M. Karanjia, Fordham University
John L. Kling, Washington State University
Paul A. Leonard, SUNY - Albany
Coleen C. Pantalone, Northeastern University
Douglas K. Pearce, North Carolina State University
Subhrendu P. Rath, Washington State University
Ehud I. Ronn, University of Texas - Austin
Todd Shank, University of Portland
Donald G. Simonson, University of New Mexico
John S. Strong, College of William and Mary
Stacey L. Suydam, Eastern Montana College
Lawrence J. White, New York University
David A. Yamoah, Kean College of New Jersey

Each did an excellent job, and we incorporated many of their suggestions throughout the book to make it the most customer-driven product available. Special thanks to Heather Hulburt, who meticulously doublechecked the manuscript for accuracy and consistency. We also want to thank the staff at HarperCollins, especially our developmental editor Pamela Wilkie, our sales representatives Jennifer Hurwitz and Vince Straub, and our sponsor Kirsten Sandberg, for their encouragement in moving this project forward. Finally, but most importantly, many thanks to our families for providing support and understanding throughout the development and production process.

Tim S. Campbell
William A. Kracaw

• Chapter 1

Introduction

This book is about financial markets and financial institutions or financial services firms. Of all the markets in the world, financial markets are among the most interesting and the most important. They are complicated, and it is a challenge to figure out how they work. Financial markets are intimately linked to every other market and every individual in the economy. They provide an important mechanism by which business firms raise funds to carry out their operations. As consumers, we all use financial markets to improve our personal well-being. The returns we earn in other markets can be stored in financial markets for future use. The importance of financial markets, therefore, lies in their linkage with all our spending decisions, both in our personal lives and in the business world.

The financial marketplace has been a tremendously interesting place over the last decade. The pace of innovation in financial markets has been fantastic. We have seen a wide array of new financial instruments evolve and grow and new marketplaces thrive. At the same time we have witnessed some financial institutions rise and then fall. The last decade has made average U. S. citizens more aware than they may have been for many years of the importance of financial markets in our everyday lives. For example, the debacle in the savings and loan industry, which we discuss in later chapters, is probably the largest and most conspicuous event in the financial marketplace that has affected all of us. In this book we want to explore some of the big stories in financial markets in the last decade and, hopefully, anticipate some of the big ones of the next decade. But most important, we want to provide you with enough understanding of how the financial marketplace works so that you can become an informed market participant or financial professional.

In this chapter our objective is to develop a basic understanding of the organization and structure of financial markets and to develop a few key ideas about what financial markets do. The key concepts to be learned in this chapter are listed below.

• *Concepts to Learn in Chapter 1* •

- Services that financial markets provide
- Characteristics of how financial information is produced, distributed, and used
- Characteristics of auction, over-the-counter, and intermediated financial markets
- Key issues we will address throughout this book

The Role of Financial Assets and Markets

A financial asset is a claim on some future cash flow. The asset might be as simple as a Treasury bill, which represents a promise by the U.S. Treasury to pay a certain amount, say $10,000, at a specified future date. It might be as complicated as a share of stock in a corporation. This is a promise to pay the shareholder a portion of the profits that the company earns and does not retain for its own investments. A financial market is the place or mechanism whereby financial assets are exchanged and prices of these assets are set. We believe it is important to start by developing some understanding of the functions that financial assets and markets serve in our economy.

Two Principal Functions of Financial Assets

Financial assets provide the economy with two services. First, they provide a means by which funds can be transferred from those who have a surplus to those who have profitable investments for those funds. Second, they provide the means to transfer risk from those who undertake investments to those who provide funds for those investments. Therefore, financial assets are the record or the claim that facilitates an exchange of funds and a shift of risk. These two functions are summarized in Figure 1-1.

The first function of financial assets is probably the most obvious. A competitive economy is composed of a number of businesses and individuals that have productive uses for more financial resources than they have on hand at any given time. The variety of these uses is enormous, ranging from high-technology investments by large corporations to investments in homes by individuals. In both examples, if there were no way to obtain funds from other sources the investment would be impossible to undertake. Thus, the availability of outside resources is crucial to the level of investment, and therefore to the level of employment and income in the economy.

Funds are supplied by those in the economy who have fewer profitable investments than resources. These entities can profitably lend to those with productive investments if they can receive a reliable promise to share in the investment's returns. The financial asset represents that promise. It is issued by the user or borrower of funds to the supplier of funds, and it represents a claim on the user or on the investment he or she is undertaking. The fact that such assets exist and are exchanged raises the level of income and wealth of the entire economy because more productive investment may be undertaken.

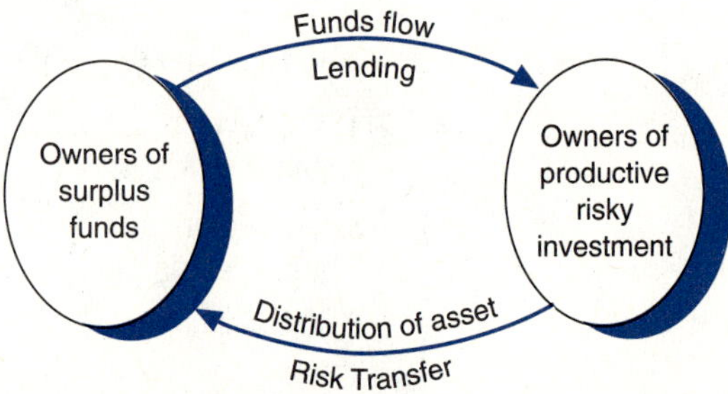

Figure 1-1
Principal functions of financial assets. Funds flow from those with a surplus to those who can make productive investments. Those who undertake risky investments transfer risk to those who supply funds.

Unfortunately, the return on most productive investments is risky. The incentive to undertake risky investments hinges on how the returns will be distributed or who bears the investment risk. If a party who considers undertaking an investment bears all the risk, then her incentive to undertake that investment may be limited. If, however, that risk can be redistributed or shared with the suppliers of funds, then the incentive to go through with the investment is enhanced. Financial assets provide the mechanism through which this risk sharing takes place.

Two Principal Functions of Financial Markets

Financial assets can be created and exchanged between a supplier and a user of funds without ever utilizing an organized financial market, but in a developed economy that is more the exception than the norm. Most assets are exchanged through some kind of financial market. These markets assume widely diverse forms, from public auction markets like the New York Stock Exchange to highly diffuse markets like the market for savings deposits from financial intermediaries. Both of these examples are financial markets where financial assets are exchanged. The markets serve two useful functions above and beyond those served by the assets exchanged in those markets. The first function is that a market affords the holder of an asset liquidity. The second is that the market collects and aggregates information about the returns on assets. The two principal functions of a financial market are summarized in Figure 1-2, which depicts the same sort of exchange process illustrated in Figure 1-1, except that now the exchange passes through an organized market.

A market provides *liquidity* by offering a place or mechanism through which financial assets can be resold or liquidated. Liquidity is an extremely valuable feature for an asset. If an asset is not liquid, that is if it cannot be sold easily and quickly, then the only way to receive the value of the asset is to wait to receive the future cash flow promised by the asset. The future income is what makes the asset valuable. Because of contingencies, often a particular owner of an asset would find it advantageous to pass on title to that future income to someone else in order to collect and use today's value of that future income. Most of us can think of events that might cause us to want to sell assets. Some are not very pleasant, like losing a job or becoming ill. On the more positive side we might want to purchase something expensive that

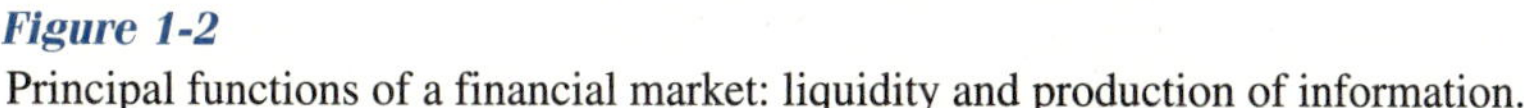

Figure 1-2
Principal functions of a financial market: liquidity and production of information.

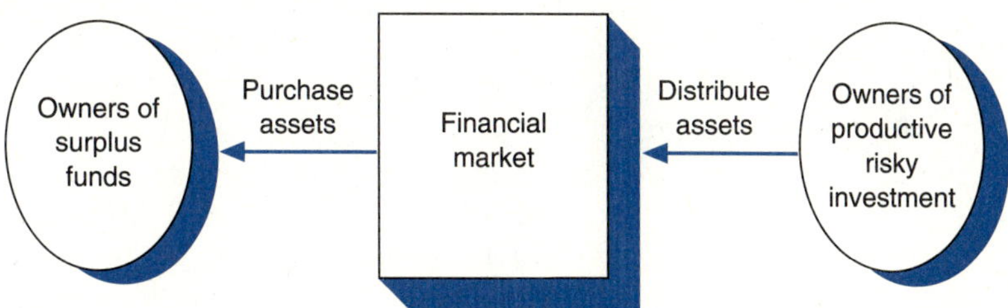

we cannot finance from our current income, or we might want to get married (something that is especially expensive). The existence of a market where assets can readily be bought and sold increases the flexibility of all market participants. They can either sell or wait, depending on which option promises the greater personal benefit.

The market can also reduce the cost of collecting information about the future returns on financial assets and about the activities of those who are undertaking productive investments, to ensure that they are acting in your interests. The market actually acts as a producer of information, when the various types of participants in the market search out information about the future returns on traded assets and distribute or sell that information in a variety of ways. The industry that produces financial information in the world's financial markets is diverse and complicated. At least four distinct types of information producers can be identified. They differ not so much by the nature of the production process used as in the way they market the product produced. Each type of producer is discussed briefly below.

Information Production for Direct Sale. The most obvious type of information producer is the company that seeks information relevant to economic conditions, and, therefore, investment decisions, and publishes that information for direct distribution to investors. Probably the best-known organization of this kind in the United States is Dow Jones & Company, Inc., publisher of the *Wall Street Journal* and other business-oriented publications. Other examples of the same type of publication are *Value Line, Standard & Poor's Stock Report,* and *Fortune.* Of course, much of the material found in more general publications such as the *New York Times* is directly relevant to investment decision making. In addition, there are newsletters, consulting services, credit reporting services such as TRW, and a large number of graduate schools of business administration whose primary business is directly distributing information and technically assessing information about investment decisions.

Sales of a Judgment about an Asset's Value. Some information producers do not distribute their information directly but use it to produce an estimate of an asset's value and then sell the assessment of value. Examples are the rating services provided by Moody's and Standard & Poor's. These organizations continually collect information about the riskiness of the debt obligations of corporate and municipal borrowers and distribute the conclusions they draw from this information to investors in the form of ratings. The borrowers being evaluated find it profitable to pay for the service. Other examples of this type of information producer are real estate appraisers and film, music, and drama critics.

Information Production Bundled with the Sale of an Asset. A number of firms produce information as a major part of their business but only rarely sell it directly to any of their customers. An interesting example outside of financial markets is the medical profession. Physicians are in the business of diagnosing illness and providing treatment, but they generally tie in the diagnosis with the treatment and do not sell the products separately. Only with increased demand for second and third opinions is the diagnosis becoming known as a distinct product. The analogy with the securities brokerage industry is quite close. Securities brokers are in the business of producing information about securities to facilitate the sale of shares; however, information normally has not been sold as a distinct product. Instead, it is tied in with the service of executing a trade, so that the broker's fee pays for both the transaction and the cost of the information.

Information Production Bundled with Investment of Funds. Financial institutions, such as commercial banks, savings and loan associations, savings banks, insurance companies, and mutual funds, largely provide information bundled with the management of funds. These institutions are in the business of investing funds for their customers. They produce information about the investments they may make and return a share of the profits from the investments they undertake to those whose funds they manage. The profits they receive on their investments may be viewed as a return on their production of information.

Efficient Use of Financial Information

Because one of the key functions of financial markets is to produce information, we believe it is appropriate to introduce you rather early in this book to the concept of efficient use of information in financial markets. We limit ourselves to a brief overview of this idea in this chapter, but we will encounter this topic in various places throughout the book. The idea that financial markets use information efficiently has come to be known as the *efficient markets hypothesis.* The hypothesis states that the market does not waste information or that it efficiently uses all of a specified set of information. An important implication of this hypothesis is that we should not expect to be able to make a profit on a specific set of information based on the market prices that prevail *after* the information becomes available. The reason for this is that the market quickly and efficiently adjusts the prices of assets to reflect new information as soon as it becomes available. Therefore, if we examine the price of an asset after the emergence of important information affecting the future cash flows flowing to that asset, the price should already reflect that information.

The degree of efficiency of a market is often divided into three forms, according to the set of information that is used: weak-, semistrong-, or strong-form market efficiency. These three forms of efficiency are summarized briefly below.

• *The Three Levels of Market Efficiency* •

1. **Weak-Form Efficiency.** In this form of the efficient market hypothesis the information set that the market is able to use efficiently comprises all of the history of the prices of a security.
2. **Semistrong-Form Efficiency.** In this form the information set comprises all publicly available information about a security (i.e., it is not restricted to price alone). For example, this might include the history of dividend payout rates or bond ratings in a recent *Wall Street Journal* article about a company.
3. **Strong-Form Efficiency.** In this form the hypothesis includes what is called *insider information.* This includes information that, at least initially, is known only to the managers of the company.

The weak-form efficient market hypothesis says that, based solely on the past behavior of the price of a security, its current price is the best possible forecast of the future price. Additional information, other than the security's price history, might well improve the forecast, but such information is not included in the set of information relevant to the weak-form efficient market hypothesis. It is important to emphasize what this hypothesis does not say: it does not say that the best forecast of the next period's price of a security is this period's price. This statement is unconditional; it makes no reference to a set of information.

One way to appreciate the differences between the forms of market efficiency pertains to the cost of information. The weak- and semistrong-form categories refer to information for which the costs of acquisition are relatively low. This kind of information should be readily incorporated into market prices. A much stronger argument is that even information that is difficult or costly to acquire and that may be known only to insiders will very quickly work its way into the market and be incorporated into prices. The implicit argument here is that the incentives to use this information profitably are so strong that it will be disclosed rapidly to the market and incorporated into prices. This argument relies on the incentives for corporate insiders to disclose information rather than the incentives for outsiders to discover or collect information. Both kinds of forces are constantly at work to contribute to the efficiency of markets.

The real message that the efficient markets hypothesis seeks to communicate pertains to the state of competition in financial markets. That message is that one cannot expect to earn *monopolistic* or *excess returns* from collecting information and trading on it. The hypothesis contends that financial markets are highly competitive. This does not mean that, ex post, some participants in the market will not make exceptionally large returns. Some will, just as some others will earn very low returns. The hypothesis means that one cannot *expect* to earn such returns ex ante. Without barriers to competition, such excess returns will be eliminated in an efficient capital market.

Now that we have some understanding of the role of liquidity and information in financial markets, we want to turn our attention to the organizational structure of financial markets. Throughout this book we examine various specific financial markets, as well as the institutions that operate in those markets. It will prove very useful if we begin our analysis of them with an outline or taxonomy for organizing them. This is the task we turn to next.

The Alternative Forms of Market Organization

Probably the most obvious way to classify financial markets corresponds to the types of securities traded in those markets. Equities, mortgages, bonds, short-term debt instruments, deposits, and the like are often treated as having distinct markets. We will be discussing these various instruments throughout this book. Another extremely useful way to classify markets is according to who wants to borrow and who wants to lend. But both of these ways of organizing financial markets fail to emphasize the mode of operation of the market, and that is what we will explore here.

We can identify three distinct types of markets: auction, over-the-counter, and intermediated markets. An auction market involves some kind of centralized facility where buyers and sellers or their commissioned agents come together (possibly electronically) to execute trades. Over-the-counter markets have no centralized mechanism or facility for trading. Instead, they are composed of dealers who stand ready to buy and sell assets with anyone who chooses to trade. In an intermediated market financial intermediaries function like dealers, but they also change the nature of the asset they acquire. Financial intermediaries issue one class of claims to fund their purchases or acquisitions of another class of claims. Financial intermediaries are by no means restricted to dealing solely in this manner. They also purchase from public auction or over-the-counter markets. Next we want to consider the basic characteristics of each of these three forms of markets and how and why markets may change or evolve from one form into another.

Auction Markets

The essence of an auction market is that it involves some kind of a centralized facility through which exchanges are made and does not allow private exchanges between individual parties or traders off the centralized exchange. When trading off the central exchange becomes significant, we have an over-the-counter market. Auction markets can be further divided into two types of auctions, referred to as "call" and "continuous" markets. A call market operates with simultaneous offers to buy and sell, all placed at one time. All the bids and offers are then collected, and exchanges take place at once. The market then ceases to function until there is sufficient demand for another round of exchanges, at which time the market operates again. The alternative type of auction market is a continuous market, in which offers to buy or sell can be placed at any time the market is in operation, and exchanges take place on a continuous basis. The continuous market increases the flexibility of the market participants so that they are not constrained to wait until the times when the market operates, as in a call market. However, in a continuous market the offers to buy or sell may be quite spread out over time. As a result, there will be opportunities for imbalances between offers to buy and sell, called trading imbalances, to develop. The market price can rise or fall as excesses of buy or sell offers develop. For example, the New York Stock Exchange is a hybrid of a continuous and a call market in that it functions as a continuous market during the trading hours it is open but then shuts down part of each trading day and on weekends and holidays.

A centralized exchange process cannot operate successfully in every financial market. Three basic requirements are generally necessary for such an auction market to be viable. We will examine each of these in turn.

• *The Three Requirements for an Auction Market* •

1. A central trading facility
2. Homogeneous assets
3. A minimum volume of buy and sell offers

Central Trading Facility

At one time it might have been relatively simple to picture exactly what a central trading facility would look like: one large room where buyers and sellers of assets or their representatives could meet to make their bids and exchange assets. In some cases technology has rendered this concept obsolete. A centralized trading facility no longer need be a central *physical* location where people who want to trade or their representatives congregate, like, say, the New York Stock Exchange. Instead it can be a computerized trading facility where all trades are processed though no traders are physically present. The essence of today's central trading facility is that all trades must be executed through a mechanism that preserves ready access. The central trading facility makes all trades and prices known to all market participants on an ongoing basis, and no trades are priced and executed away from the central facility. The central facility relieves the market participants of the burden of searching for individual prices. All the market's information about prices and exchanges is centralized in one location.

Homogeneous Assets

The second requirement for an auction market to operate successfully is that assets must be reasonably homogeneous. The centralized trading facility in an auction market collects information about bids and prices of assets. If each asset is so distinct that it cannot be succinctly described, a central market cannot successfully collect and communicate the necessary information to potential buyers and sellers. But, if assets are homogeneous, the cost of collecting information can be spread over a number of such assets, so that central distribution of this information becomes economical. For example, consider the market for mortgages on residential real estate. Mortgages on residential property traditionally have not been distributed through an auction market. The principal reason is that each mortgage contract is so peculiar, owing to the credit risk of the individual borrower and the collateral of the underlying property. A centralized auction market could not economically process all the information necessary to describe each mortgage offered for sale. Of course, if it is possible to impose standard requirements for structuring mortgages, so that many mortgages can become highly homogeneous, then it is possible to transform the mortgage market into something close to an auction market. We will learn in later chapters that this is precisely what has been happening in recent years. For another example, consider equity shares in corporations. The homogeneity of these assets depends on the feature of equity known as limited liability. Limited liability means that the value of a share of equity stock is independent of its holder. If liability were not limited in this way, the value of the security would change if a rich person sold it to a poor person simply because the personal assets standing behind the security would be reduced. Limited liability has meant that all equity claims on a particular company are homogeneous assets.

Minimum Volume

A closely related requirement to that of homogeneity is that the market not be too "thin" in an asset. There must be some minimum volume of transactions in the asset and a desire to exchange the asset. If there are too few shares of a homogeneous asset or if most of the shares are held by individuals who choose not to trade in the asset, then the centralized facility does not work efficiently. The costs of collecting and maintaining access to an asset in a centralized facility are largely fixed, in that they do not rise and fall with the volume of trading. Therefore, it is difficult to maintain a centralized market in an asset that is traded only infrequently.

Over-the-Counter Markets and the Roles of Brokers and Dealers

There are two important features of an over-the-counter market. First, there is no central exchange facility, as in an auction market. Second, the market operates through middlemen (or women) who stand ready to buy or sell a given security on request. These middlemen are referred to as *dealers*. Dealers are distinguished from brokers on the one hand and from financial intermediaries on the other. Brokers do not buy and sell assets on their own. Rather, they act as salespersons and receive commissions. Dealers are principally engaged in selling the same securities they buy, whereas financial intermediaries create and sell new claims on themselves to fund their holdings of the securities they purchase. Dealers' holdings of securities are small relative to their turnover of those securities. In this sense they operate like the typical retailer: they buy assets not to hold them for long periods but to sell them quickly, so that the stock of assets they hold at any one time is an inventory maintained for resale.

In many respects, an auction market and an over-the-counter market can be quite similar. Over-the-counter and auction markets function better the more homogeneous are the assets and the larger the volume of trades. In addition, dealers may perform a useful function in either market. In a continuous auction market, dealers will be able to operate profitably if there are periodic imbalances between orders to buy and sell and if market participants are willing to pay to reduce the impact of those imbalances on prices. The reason an auction market arises in one instance and an over-the-counter market in another hinges on the benefits perceived by the participants in the market of a centralized exchange facility. Such a facility serves essentially as a collector of information and a means of economizing on the costs of searching for alternative prices from dealers. Therefore, if communication among dealers and participants in a market is good enough and competition is intense, a centralized facility may be a luxury.

The important feature of an over-the-counter market involves the nature of the service provided by dealers, though this service may be rendered in auction markets as well. The service provided by dealers has been referred to as *immediacy*.[1] The dealer allows the buyer or seller of an asset to make the exchange when he or she desires, rather than waiting to locate a party who wants to do business. It is important to emphasize the distinction between services provided by a dealer and by a broker. A broker acts as an agent in executing a transaction and collects a commission. The broker goes hunting for the party on the other side of the transaction. Her incentive to hunt efficiently is improved if her fee is tied to the outcome, so it is

[1] The concept of immediacy was articulated in Demsetz, Harold. "The Cost of Transacting." *Quarterly Journal of Economics* 82 (February 1968), pp. 33–53.

usually stated as a percentage of the sale price. On the other hand, a dealer holds an inventory of the assets in which she deals and, so, stands ready to execute the transaction when the buyer or seller desires.

Whether in an auction market or an over-the-counter market, dealers must be able to operate profitably while providing the service of immediacy. The costs that the dealer faces can be broken down into three components: holding costs, order costs, and information costs. Holding costs are the costs the dealer bears for holding a portfolio of assets that is risky. In order to make a market in a particular asset, a dealer must hold an inventory larger than she would hold if she were investing in the asset on her own. Dealers demand compensation for holding an excess amount of such assets. In contrast, order costs are costs of transacting. These are all the costs of handling securities and the fixed costs of office and staff, record keeping, and so forth, involved in executing transactions. Finally, information costs arise because some investors trade with a dealer based on special information that is not available to the dealer. The dealer knows that some portion of his or her transactions are with parties who have superior information, and the dealer expects to lose on such transactions.

The dealer earns returns from a spread between offers to buy or the *bid price* and offers to sell or the *asked price*. This simply means that the dealer attempts to buy low and sell high, on average. The difference between the price paid for assets and the price received is the bid-ask spread. In markets where dealers are involved, the bid-ask spread is a function of the dealer's costs and the degree of competition in the market.

• *The Over-The-Counter Market in Treasury Obligations* •

A good example of an over-the-counter market where dealers demand a bid-ask spread is the market for U. S. Treasury securities. One type of Treasury security is a long-term bond that promises to pay a coupon payment, or make an interest payment every six months. A variety of firms act as dealers in this market and are ready to trade Treasury securities of various maturities and various coupon rates with the public. We discuss this market in some detail in Chapter 2, but at this point let us simply examine the bid-ask spread in this market. Table 1-1 shows the prices quoted in the *Wall Street Journal* for September 14, 1992 for a selection of various Treasury bonds in the market on 11 September, 1992 (14 September was a Monday, so the prices are quoted for the previous Friday). The table states the bid and ask prices of Treasury bonds, for various coupon rates available, in terms of the cost of the bond per $100 to be paid on that bond by the Treasury at its maturity. The coupon interest rate determines the cash flow paid by the Treasury to the owner of the bond over its life. The Treasury makes payments every six months, so that on an 8 1/2 percent coupon bond it would pay 4 1/4 percent interest every six months. The table indicates that, for example, the January 1998 bond with a coupon of 7 7/8 percent has a bid price of $110 27/32 and an asked price of $110 29/32. This means that the bid-ask spread is 2/32 of a dollar. Notice that a few of the bonds (specifically the February 1995 with a coupon of 3 percent) have a much larger bid-ask spread. The February 1995 bond has a bid-ask spread of $1. This seems to be because there are few of these particular bonds available, so dealers charge a higher price or bid-ask spread to make a market in them.

Table 1-1
Bid-Ask Spread On Treasury Securities

Coupon	Maturity	Bid*	Asked*
8 1/4	Nov 94	108:26	108:28
3	Feb 95	99:04	100:04
8 1/2	Jul 97	113:10	113:12
7 7/8	Jan 98	110:27	110:29
15 3/4	Nov 2001	164:25	164:29

*Prices are listed in 1/32s of a dollar.
Source: *Wall Street Journal,* September 14, 1992

Primary and Secondary Markets

Primary markets are the markets where new securities are bought and sold. This does not mean that other securities like the new ones being sold cannot already exist. It simply means that the particular securities being distributed have not been owned before. For example, a primary market exists in the stock of a particular company when it issues new shares, despite the fact that it may already have shares outstanding. We think of the primary market as the market for the *new* shares, not the often virtually identical old shares. Thus, primary markets essentially act as the conduit through which new capital or funds are acquired. These markets operate in whatever method is best suited to the purpose of collecting information and facilitating this initial distribution. A secondary market is a market where old (used) securities are traded. For example, all IBM shares sold in the secondary market would not be offered for sale by IBM. They would be sold by the parties who own them. The difference between the two forms of markets is that the exchange opportunities offered by a secondary market provide liquidity for those who hold the security as well as a mechanism for valuing the outstanding stock of assets. In other words, the outstanding stock of assets has some market value that is determined through the secondary market. The asset need not actually change hands in order for the asset to be valued, as long as there is a secondary market where similar assets are traded. Thus, the market serves even those who do not directly use it.

Intermediated Markets and the Concept of Intermediation

To understand the differences between the two types of markets discussed above and an intermediated market, it is useful to begin by comparing a financial intermediary with a dealer. A dealer buys and sells assets but does not acquire assets for the long term. Rather, assets are held only for the purpose of providing an inventory, though dealers may also speculate for themselves and hold some assets for such purpose. As a result, the dealer's role as a middleman does not involve any change in an asset or the creation of any new or distinctly different types of assets. Precisely the opposite is true with financial intermediaries such as commercial banks or insurance companies. Intermediaries purchase most assets as investments for a specific intended holding period. This means that intermediaries' holdings of assets do not serve essentially as inventory. Instead of reselling the assets they purchase, they create new assets and sell them to the market. The new assets constitute a financial claim on the intermediary rather than on the party who originally issued the asset purchased by the intermediary. Therefore, unlike the dealer, the intermediary does more than provide immediacy or absorb temporary trading imbalances; it creates and distributes new financial claims upon itself. This alteration of the nature of the financial claim distributed to the market is the concept behind the word "intermediation." For example, a commercial bank traditionally makes loans to a business and funds those loans, not by selling the loans directly, but by issuing another type of instrument, generally a deposit, which is a direct claim on the overall assets of the bank. This is illustrated in Figure 1-3. We will see that, increasingly, banks and other financial intermediaries are finding that they have the option to sell loans rather than hold them to maturity and fund them with deposits. This change in the way the market works is threatening to transform the financial intermediation industry. We will have much more to say about this later in this book.

While the distinction between a dealer and an intermediary is relatively clear cut, the distinction between an intermediated market and either an auction market or an over-the-counter market is not quite as straightforward. An intermediary may participate in either an auction or an over-the-counter market. For example, commercial banks buy and sell Treasury securities on a regular basis, so, depending on whether they use the primary or secondary market, they are participating in an auction or an over-the-counter market. Commercial banks also participate in a private loan market. That is, they stand ready to make loans to business customers out of the funds they raise by offering various types of deposit accounts. This private loan market is certainly not an auction market; it operates much like an over-the-counter market. The important difference between this market and an over-the-counter market is that the suppliers of loans are intermediaries rather than dealers. The same distinction applies to the liabilities offered by intermediaries. The market for the liabilities of an intermediary operates like an over-the-counter market, but the suppliers are intermediaries—that is, institutions that create new and distinct liabilities to fund their assets. Therefore, we call these intermediated markets. The important concept here is that financial intermediaries are distinct entities because they create new financial claims, but they may participate in all the types of markets we have identified. Thus, they create a distinct or new type of market but they also bridge the gaps between markets.

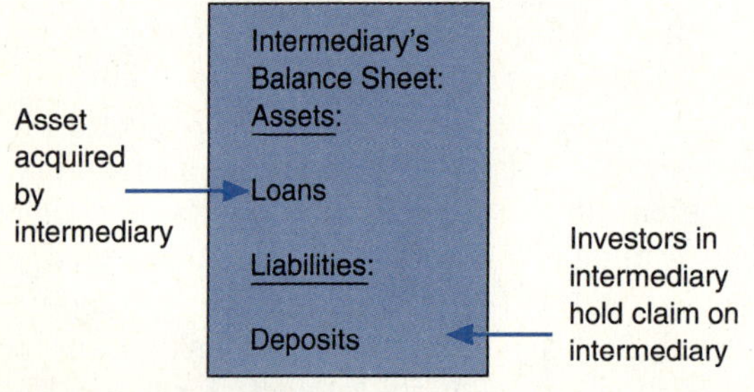

Figure 1-3
Illustration of the operation of an intermediated market.

Overview Of This Book

This book addresses four major topics. They can be stated most succinctly as simple questions:

1. What are the major types of financial institutions and markets in the U. S. economy and how does the U. S. system differ from those of the rest of the world?
2. How are interest rates and exchange rates between currencies determined in competitive global financial markets?
3. What are the major innovations in financial products and services in recent years and how do these new products work?
4. How can modern financial institutions be managed to add value for their shareholders?

The book is divided into four parts, which correspond to these four questions.

The chapters in Part I provide a survey of the various types of financial markets and institutions that are found in the United States and contrast this structure with markets and institutions around the world. Chapter 2 presents a summary of money and bond markets and focuses on the various types of instruments traded in these markets and the basic structure and operation of the markets. Chapter 3 concentrates on the capital markets—or the markets for equity securities, including venture capital and initial public offerings. Chapter 4 contains a summary of the operations of depository institutions in the United States including principally commercial banks and savings and loans. Chapter 5 describes the basic features of the system for government regulation of depository institutions. Chapter 6 continues the description of the regulatory system by chronicling major reforms instituted in recent years. Chapter 7 deals with nondepository financial institutions, including pension funds, investment and brokerage firms, and insurance companies. Finally, Chapter 8 deals with the global financial system. This chapter presents a brief overview of the structure of financial markets and institutions in Europe and Asia and a description of multinational banks and foreign banks in the United States.

In Part II the chapters deal with the determinants of interest rates and exchange rates in a competitive global economy. Chapter 9 concentrates on interest rates in a market economy, explaining the basic theory of interest rate determination and presenting an introduction to the various forms of interest rate risk. Chapter 10 deals with the term structure of interest rates. It presents both classical and more modern theories of the term structure and explains the forward rates and the yield curve. Chapter 11 concentrates on exchange rates between currencies and capital flows between countries. This chapter explains the balance of payments and the economic significance of current and capital account surpluses and deficits. It also explains the determinants of foreign exchange rates and various parity relationships in foreign exchange. Chapters 12 and 13 deal with the impact of monetary policy on interest rates. These chapters present material on the operation of the Federal Reserve and the conduct of monetary policy, but they focus on the links between monetary policy, interest rates, and exchange rates in a competitive global economy.

Part III deals with innovation. In this part of the book we introduce various types of contingent claims or derivative securities and their markets. We also explain the evolution of securitization of financial markets. Chapter 14 deals with futures and forward markets. The structure and operation of these markets are explained and the determinants of futures and forward prices are explained. Chapter 15 deals with options and options markets. This chapter emphasizes how options work and how to compute the payoffs on positions taken with options. It also explains various ways that options may be used. It does not emphasize pricing of options. Chapter 16 presents interest rates and currency swaps. This chapter explains the evolution of the swaps market and the various forms of swaps that are used in the modern marketplace. It also provides an introduction to the pricing of swaps. Chapter 17 deals with strategies for managing risk using the derivative securities introduced in the preceding chapters. Chapter 18 deals with securitization. This chapter explains the origins of securitization and provides a framework for comparing the costs and benefits of securitizing a particular class of assets. It also discusses in some detail the securitization of mortgages and credit card-backed receivables.

The material in Part IV deals with the management of financial firms. This part of the book reflects the view that financial institutions are principally in the business of managing three types of risk: credit risk, interest rate risk, exchange rate risk. Therefore, this part of the book concentrates on these three sources of risk. Chapter 19 begins with a discussion of the process of value creation and the establishment of competitive advantage. Like other firms in competitive markets, financial institutions must seek strategies that create value for their shareholders. This chapter evaluates the alternative ways companies can establish competitive advantage and assesses how effective these may be in the financial services marketplace. Then the chapter develops the concept of a value chain for companies operating in markets that face securitization. The strategies employed recently by a selection of major commercial banks are then critically evaluated. Chapter 20 focuses on management of credit risk. This chapter describes procedures for assessing credit risk and discusses problems of effective management and pricing of credit risk. Chapters 21 and 22 deal with strategies for managing interest rate risk. These chapters extend the material related in Part III. The book's final chapter, Chapter 23, deals with foreign exchange risk.

SUMMARY

We began this chapter with a discussion of the basic functions of financial assets and markets. We indicated that financial markets provide liquidity to holders of assets and produce information about the returns on assets. We emphasized that there is a large industry that produces information about financial assets. The information is distributed in a number of different ways. Some, like many business publications, is produced for direct sale. Sometimes it is tied in with an estimate of the impact of that information on particular firms, like that produced by rating agencies for bonds. Sometimes it is tied in with the sale of an asset, as in the brokerage industry, and sometimes it is tied in with the management of funds. We also described efficient use of information in a financial market. We identified three levels of efficiency distinguished by the set of information used in the market.

Then we identified three distinct types of market organization: auction, over-the-counter, and intermediated markets. The important distinction between auction and over-the-counter markets is that all trades or exchanges take place in an auction market through some kind of centralized facility. At one time this meant that all buyers and sellers or their brokers had to meet in one location to trade in a competitive bidding process. But with modern computer technology an auction market now requires only that there be a single facility through which all trading takes place or all transactions are recorded.

The alternative to the auction market is an over-the-counter market. The name is used to describe the operation method of any market that has no centralized trading or exchange facility but instead has all trades handled by dealers. Dealers can also operate in an auction market. A dealer is a person who maintains an inventory of a particular security and buys and sells for that inventory with anyone who enters the market. The dealer provides immediacy to the market by offsetting imbalances between supply and demand. This service can be valuable in both auction and over-the-counter markets. In an auction market all trading with dealers takes place through a centralized facility; in an over-the-counter market trading is decentralized.

We enumerated three requirements for a market to become centralized like an auction market. First, the market must have an economical, centralized facility for conducting exchanges. Second, the assets traded must be homogeneous so that a centralized trading facility is feasible. Third, trading volume in the assets must be great enough to make it efficient to operate the centralized facility. All of these requirements derive from the function of a market as an information collector and processor. If the assets traded in a market are homogeneous and trading volume large, the process of collecting information and bringing it together can be centralized efficiently.

We also considered the distinction between primary and secondary markets. Primary markets are markets for new securities, and secondary markets are for used securities. There is no necessary connection between the primary versus secondary classification and the auction versus over-the-counter classification for markets; both primary and secondary markets can operate as either auction or over-the-counter markets.

An intermediated market is one in which financial intermediaries play a dominant role. A financial intermediary differs from a dealer in that an intermediary purchases assets and holds them as an investment rather than purchasing for resale and holding only an inventory. The intermediary acquires funds for these investments by selling claims on itself to the public. Therefore, unlike a dealer, the intermediary creates a new security and sells it to the market rather than reselling the securities it purchases.

Finally, we provided an overview of the organization of this book.

QUESTIONS

1. What are the important characteristics of an auction market? Why is the auction market held out as economists' ideal of a market organization?
2. What is an over-the-counter market? Compare it to an auction market.
3. What service does a dealer provide? Explain the costs incurred by a dealer in providing the service.
4. Distinguish between a continuous market and a call-auction market.
5. Distinguish between a primary and a secondary market. Can primary and secondary markets be either over-the-counter or auction markets? Why?
6. What is an efficient market? Distinguish between the three types or forms of market efficiency.
7. What does the efficient markets hypothesis suggest to you about how much energy you should expend trying to forecast market interest rates?

REFERENCES

Arrow, Kenneth J. "Insurance, Risk and Resource Allocation," Arrow, Kenneth J. ed. *Essays in the Theory of Risk-Bearing.* New York: Markham, 1971.

Demsetz, Harold. "The Cost of Transacting," *Quarterly Journal of Economics* 82 (February 1968), pp. 33–53.

Fama, Eugene F. "Efficient Capital Markets: A Review of Theory and Empirical Work." *Journal of Finance* 25 (1970), pp. 383–417.

———. "Efficient Capital Markets: II." *Journal of Finance* 46 (December 1991), pp. 1575–1618.

Garbade, Kenneth D., and William L. Silber. "Structural Organization of Secondary Markets: Clearing Frequency, Dealer Activity and Liquidity Risk." *Journal of Finance* 34 (June 1979), pp. 577–594.

Stoll, Hans R. "The Supply of Dealer Services in Securities Markets." *Journal of Finance* 33 (September 1978), pp. 1133–1151.

• *Part I* •

Survey of Financial Institutions and Markets

Money and Bond Markets

Equity Markets

Overview of Depository Financial Institutions in the United States

Government Regulation of Depository Financial Institutions

The Dynamics of Regulatory Reform

Nondepository Financial Intermediaries

Global Financial Markets

• Chapter 2

Money and Bond Markets

In this chapter we examine the operation of money and bond markets in the United States. We focus on spot markets, or cash markets, as opposed to futures markets, or markets for contingent claims or derivative securities. *Spot* (cash) markets are markets where debt instruments or claims on money lent immediately are traded. *Futures* and *options* refer to claims on assets in the future where the payoff depends on the value of another underlying asset. We organize our survey of fixed-income or debt instruments both by the maturity of the instrument and by its issuer. We start by explaining the various interest rates that we can observe in the marketplace for bonds and money market instruments. Then we discuss the money market, the market for short-term (one year or less) debt instruments. Then we examine longer-term debt issues sold by the U.S. Treasury and agencies of the federal government by state and local governments in the United States, and by corporations. To develop an understanding of the basic definitions of various forms of interest rates that we will begin using in this chapter, we start with a summary of alternative interest rates. The key learning concepts in this chapter are listed below.

• *Concepts to Learn in Chapter 2* •

- Characteristics of instruments traded in the money market
- Definitions of different interest rates
- Method of operation of the market for U. S. Treasury securities
- Characteristics of agency- and mortgage-backed securities
- Characteristics of municipal and corporate bonds

Distinguishing Among Interest Rates

The interest rate can be defined in a number of ways. Let us examine a few. We start with a very basic idea of the interest rate and quickly cover nine specific types (Table 2-1).

The Simple Interest Rate

The *simple interest rate,* truly simple, is defined with reference to a bond or a loan contract. Suppose the amount of the loan or the initial value of the bond is represented by P_0, and the amount of the loan or the value of the bond due at the end of one period is represented by P_1. Then the interest rate, represented by r and measured as a decimal, is defined as

$$1 + r = \frac{P_1}{P_0} \tag{2.1}$$

This equation can be manipulated in either of two ways: If we know the initial value of the loan and the interest rate, we can solve for the amount due. Or, if we know the amount due and the interest rate, we can solve for the current value of the loan. If, for example, the interest rate is 9 percent and the amount due at the end of the period is \$1200, then $P_0 = \$1200/1.09 = \$1100.92$.

Compound Interest

When we deal with bonds or loans that are longer than one period, we must distinguish between simple and compound interest. To see the distinction, suppose we examine a bond with an initial value of P_0 as in equation 2.1, and a value of P_4 four periods later. What is the single-period interest rate earned by this bond, or the yield per period on this bond? One way to determine this rate is simply to divide the percentage price increase by the number of periods involved, in this case four. This is the *average simple interest rate:*

$$\frac{(P_4/P_0) - 1}{4} = r \tag{2.2}$$

For example, if P_0 and P_4 assume the values of 100 and 220, respectively, the average simple interest rate is

$$\frac{(220/100) - 1}{4} = 30\%$$

Table 2-1

Summary of Alternative Interest Rates

Simple interest	Rate of growth of value of an asset in a single period.
Compound interest	Rate of growth of value of an asset over many periods, taking into account compounding over time.
Discount interest	Interest applied to the amount due on a loan to determine the amount lent.
Coupon interest	The periodic cash flow paid out to the holder of a bond.
Real and nominal interest	The nominal rate is the rate that includes the market's expected rate of inflation. The real rate is expressed net of inflation.
Before- and after-tax interest	The after-tax rate is equal to the before-tax rate less the tax on interest.
Yield to maturity	The single interest rate or internal rate of return on a bond that would be earned if the bond were held to maturity.
Holding-period yield	The internal rate of return actually earned given the price received when a bond is sold and the time at which it is sold.
Zero-coupon yield or discount rate	The yield to maturity for a zero-coupon bond.

This method does not provide a completely satisfactory measure of the interest actually earned by the asset in each period. It ignores the fact that interest earned in early periods increases the base on which interest is paid in later periods. In effect, it ignores the fact that interest compounds. We therefore refer to the appropriate measure of the interest rate as the *compound* rather than the simple interest rate. To see how to define the compound interest rate, we can trace the growth of the value of the asset in each period from 0 to 4. If we buy a bond that increases in value at an interest rate of r per period, then the relationship between its value in period 1 and its value in period 0 is defined as in equation 4.1:

$$P_1 = P_0(1 + r) \tag{2.3}$$

The relationship between the values in periods 2 and 1 can be defined in the same way:

$$P_2 = P_1(1 + r) \tag{2.4}$$

By substituting from equation 2.3 for the value of P_1, this yields

$$P_2 = P_0(1 + r)(1 + r) = P_0(1 + r)^2 \tag{2.5}$$

This substitution process can be continued until we derive an expression for P_4:

$$P_4 = P_0(1 + r)^4 \tag{2.6}$$

We can now easily use this expression to solve for the compound (as opposed to the simple) interest rate. We merely divide through both sides of equation 2.6 by P_0 and take the fourth root:

$$r = \sqrt[4]{\frac{P_4}{P_0}} - 1 \tag{2.7}$$

In the previous example, where P_4 and P_0 are 220 and 100, respectively, the compound interest rate is 22 percent as compared to 30 percent for the average simple interest rate. Note that whenever we refer to the interest rate, it is the compound rather than the simple interest rate.

The Interest Rate on a Discount Loan

The typical loan contract is usually stated in the following terms: For a single-period loan, the initial amount of the loan is P_0 and the interest rate is equal to r. Thus, at the end of the period the amount owed to the lender is $P_1 = P_0(1 + r)$. This is identical to our statement of simple interest. The loan may instead be made on a discount basis. The amount of the discount loan is stated in terms of the amount to be repaid rather than the amount loaned, that is, in terms of P_1 rather than P_0. In addition, the quoted interest payment is based on P_1 rather than P_0; that is, P_0 is determined as follows: $P_0 = (1 - r_d)\,P_1$, where r_d is the stated interest rate on a discount basis. This has the effect of understating the true interest rate that is paid, for one plus the true interest rate is still equal to $P_1/P_0 = 1/(1 - r_d)$. If, for example, the amount that is owed at the end of the period is $1000, and the stated interest rate for the discount loan is 10 percent, then the amount actually loaned is \$900, and the actual interest rate on this loan is (\$1000/\$900) − 1 = 11.11 percent.

The Coupon and the Market Interest Rate

Many bonds have both a coupon and a market interest rate or yield. We will encounter some later in this chapter. To distinguish between these two interest rates we must understand the terms of a coupon bond. Most coupon bonds have maturities longer than one period. For example, a Treasury bond (T bond) may have ten years to maturity and a payment of coupon interest every six months. If the bond pays \$10,000 at maturity and the coupon interest rate is 8 percent, then \$400 is paid to the holder of the bond every six months. To explain this in a little more detail let's deal with a very simple coupon-bearing bond that has only one period to maturity. A coupon bond has what is termed *face value,* and the face value along with the coupon rate determine the amount that will be paid to the lender at the bond's maturity. For example, a single-period bond with a \$1000 face value and 6 percent coupon interest rate (paid annually) will pay \$1060 at maturity. That is,

$$P_1 = (1 + r_c)\mathrm{F} \tag{2.8}$$

where r_c is the coupon interest rate and F is the face value of the bond. Now that we know how P_1 is determined we still can return to equation 2.1 for the determinants of either the market value of the bond, P_0, or the market interest rate on the bond, r. If we know the market interest rate we can solve for the market value of the bond as follows:

$$P_0 = P_1/(1 + r) \tag{2.9}$$

Conversely, if we know the market value of the bond, we can solve for the market interest rate:

$$r = P_1/P_0 - 1 \tag{2.10}$$

For example, for the bond with a face value of \$1000 and a coupon interest rate of 6 percent, if the market interest rate is 10 percent, then the price of the bond must be \$1060/1.1 = \$963. Only at this price will the bond have a yield that is the same as the one prevailing in the market. Therefore, the coupon rate merely defines the payment that will be made to the lender. It need not be the same as the interest rate that the market demands for lending funds.

Real and Nominal Interest Rates

In our discussion of interest rates thus far we have not mentioned the possibility that the general price level, that is, the price of goods and services, will change during the period covered by a bond or a loan. If the price level changes, then the real return received by the lender and the real cost paid by the borrower will change. This is clear from examining the value of the contract at its beginning and termination—P_0 and P_1. Both values are expressed in dollars, but if the general level of prices changes from period 0 to period 1, then the ex post real interest rate, the actual interest rate net of observed inflation, is altered. To make this statement more specific we define the ex post real interest rate that is received by the lender, r_R, as being approximately equal to

$$r_R \approx \left(\frac{P_1}{P_0} - 1\right) - \text{Observed inflation rate}$$

$$\approx r_N - \text{Observed inflation rate} \quad (2.11)$$

where r_N is the nominal interest rate used in the previous equations. For example, when the nominal interest rate is 10 percent, and the inflation rate is 6 percent, the real rate is 4 percent. We return to this topic in Chapter 9 and develop the difference between real and nominal rates in more detail.

Before-Tax and After-Tax Interest Rates

Most types of interest income are subject to income tax from both federal and state governments, but we will learn in this chapter that municipal bonds are an important exception. Thus, it is important to distinguish between interest rates before taxes and after taxes. For any individual, this distinction depends on that person's *marginal tax rate,* that is the tax rate paid on the marginal amount of income that the interest payment represents. If this marginal tax rate is represented by t, the relationship between the before-tax and after-tax nominal interest rates for a particular individual can be expressed as follows:

$$r_A = r_N(1 - t) \quad (2.12)$$

where r_A is the after-tax nominal interest rate, and r_N is the before-tax nominal interest rate.

Equation 2.12 indicates that the after-tax interest rate is equal to the before-tax interest rate reduced by the marginal tax rate of the individual in question. For example, if the nominal interest rate is 16 percent, then the after-tax nominal rate for a person in the 28 percent tax bracket is 11.5 percent.

We can combine the adjustments we have made for taxes and inflation rates to arrive at the after-tax real interest rate of an individual in the market. If we represent the after-tax real interest rate by r_{RA}, then its relationship to the nominal interest rate can be defined as follows:

$$r_{RA} = r_N(1 - t) - \text{Inflation rate} \quad (2.13)$$

For example, for an individual with a 28 percent marginal tax rate who receives a nominal interest rate of 16 percent while inflation is 10 percent, the real after-tax return is $0.115 - 0.10 = 1.5$ percent. The discrepancy between the real after-tax interest rate and the nominal interest rate is substantial. This highlights how misleading it can be to examine nominal interest rates without carefully considering taxes and inflation. As the example shows, a 16 percent interest rate is not particularly high with 10 percent inflation and a 28 percent tax rate.

Yield to Maturity

We often hear reference to the *yield* on some security, like a Treasury bill or bond. This usually refers to the observed nominal yield to maturity. To see more specifically what is meant by observed nominal yield to maturity, we can examine a diagram that plots the levels of various yields in the United States over a specific historical period. Figure 2-1 shows the average annual yield on a collection of long-term instruments from 1981 to 1991, including bonds issued by private corporations, the U.S. government, and state and local governments (municipal bonds). Municipal bonds generally had the lowest yield of all the debt securities indicated, owing to their tax treatment, which we discuss later in this chapter. The yields on corporate bonds were consistently higher than the yields on Treasury or municipal bonds.

In order to understand the various nominal yields quoted in financial markets, let's compute the market yield or yield to maturity on a T bill and then on a T bond. A T bill is a pure *discount instrument,* which means that it has no coupon payments. In the *Wall Street Journal*, yields are quoted on T bills in a specific format. For example, the *Wall Street Journal* of November 18, 1991 listed the following information on a specific T bill in the section that shows current T-bill prices:

Maturity	Number of Days	Bid	Asked	Yield
2-13-92	86	4.59	4.57	4.68

The first column indicates the date on which this particular bill will mature. The second column indicates the number of days between the settlement date for purchase of the security and the maturity date. The third indicates the annualized discount interest rate that determines the price a dealer would pay for this bill. The fourth column indicates the discount interest rate that determines the price at which a dealer would sell this bill. The final column indicates the yield you would earn if you bought this bill at the asked price and held it until maturity, the *yield to maturity.* Before we go any farther we will decipher how to compute the yield to maturity for this bill.

By convention, for the T-bill market the year is 360 days long. As a result, the time to maturity for this bill is expressed as a fraction of a 360-day year or $t/360$, $t = 86$. To compute the price the dealer is asking for this bill it is necessary to multiply this fraction by the asked discount interest rate ($r_d = 4.57$) and to discount the future value to received ($FV = 100$):

$$B = FV\left(1 - \frac{r_d \times t}{360}\right)$$

Then, substituting the values we specified,

$$98.9083 = 100\left(1 - \frac{0.0457 \times 86}{360}\right)$$

This bill commands a price of \$98.9083 per \$100 of maturity value of the bill. Now we can use this price to determine the yield to maturity. We simply need to ask, What is the yield on an investment for which we pay \$98.9083 today and receive \$100 in 86 days?

$$\text{Yield to maturity} = \left(\frac{100}{98.9083} - 1\right)\frac{365}{86} = 4.68\%$$

To compute the true yield to maturity, we must correct for the fact that the discount asked interest rate was based on a 360-day, rather than the 365-day, year on which the *actual* market yield to maturity is based.

Now let's consider a bond that has coupon payments, a coupon bond. We discussed the distinction between a coupon and market interest rate earlier. Coupon interest is the promised interest payment paid periodically on a bond. It is generally stated as some percentage of the face or maturity value of the bond. For example, a 5 percent coupon bond with a face value of \$100,000 would pay \$5000 every year to the bond owner until the bond matured. At maturity the bondholder would receive the face value of \$100,000.

To see how the market prices a coupon bond, let's consider an example of a T bond with the following characteristics. The bond has a maturity value of \$100,000 and 5 percent coupon interest paid semiannually. The bond was originally issued with a maturity of 20 years; now exactly 10 years remain to maturity, and the current date is 1 January 1993. We want to ask two questions about this bond. First, we want to know what the market price of this bond would be, given the prevailing yield on 10-year bonds. Then we want to know what the yield would be if we know the bond price. The market computes the value of a bond in terms of both a dollar price and a market yield. Given one, we can determine the other, and we want to see how this is done in our example.

To determine the price or the yield for the bond we must first carefully define the income stream that will accrue to it. With a 5 percent coupon rate, the bondholder will receive \$5000 per year in interest. But because this bond stipulates semiannual payments, \$2500 will be received every six months. In addition, at the end of ten years, or on 31 December 2002, the bondholder will receive the \$100,000 maturity value. The cash flows received on each future date are shown below.

Cash Flow on a 5% Coupon \$100,000 Treasury Bond

Date	**June 93**	**Dec. 93**	**June 94**	**...**	**June 02**	**Dec. 02**
Cash Flow	\$2500	\$2500	\$2500	\$2500	\$2500	\$100, 000 + \$2500

To determine either market price or yield we need to set up the present value equation for this bond. From the time path of future payments to the bondholder we know that there are 19 periods, each six months long, when the bondholder will receive \$2500 per period. In the twentieth period the bondholder will receive \$102,500. The present value equation therefore can be written as:

$$PV = \sum_{t=1}^{19} \frac{\$2500}{(1 + r/2)^t} + \frac{\$102{,}500}{(1 + r/2)^{20}}$$

We have to divide the annual interest rate by two because we are compounding every six months rather than annually, owing to the fact that coupon payments are made every six months.

We can use this equation to solve for either the market price of the bond or the yield, given the other value. Some combinations of price and yield that satisfy our pricing equation are shown below. You should notice that as the price rises, the yield to maturity falls. The yield to maturity is equivalent to the internal rate of return; that is, it is the single or unique interest rate such that if you discount all the promised cash flows at that rate, you get the price of the bond. Another way to understand yield to maturity is as the yield you would actually earn, after the fact, if you held the bond to maturity. This leads us right up to an explicit consideration of holding-period yield.

Price and Yield on a 10-Year 5 Percent Coupon Bond of $100,000

Price	$108,176	$103,991	$100,000	$96,193	$92,561
Yield	4.00%	4.50%	5.00%	5.50%	6.00%

Holding-Period Yield

The holding-period yield is the yield you actually earn, after the fact, for a time you hold a security. This means the yield to maturity will also be your *holding-period yield* if you hold this security to maturity. Suppose, however, you were to buy a security, say a T bill with six months to maturity, and sell it when it had three months to maturity. The yield to maturity on that bill when you bought it would not turn out to be your holding-period yield, unless by chance. The key problem here is that holding-period yield depends on the price of the security when it is sold.

To see how to compute the holding-period yield in this situation, consider another example. Suppose that on 30 June 1993 you purchased a T bill that matured on 26 December 1993. The asked discount rate on that bill when you bought it would have been 7.21 percent, and the corresponding asking price would have been $96.415. If you had sold that bill on 30 September 1993, when it still had approximately three months to maturity, the bid price would have been $98.375. Therefore, the holding period would have been 91 days, and the holding-period yield can be computed:

$$\text{Holding-period yield} = \left(\frac{98.357}{96.415} - 1\right)\frac{365}{91} = 8.08\%$$

The holding period yield in this situation cannot be known with certainty when the Treasury bill is purchased because the price of the three-month bills prevailing three months in the future cannot be known. Only if the bill is held to maturity will the holding-period yield and the yield to maturity be equivalent.

We can also compute the holding-period yield on a long-term bond. For example, suppose that the bond described above that carried a 5 percent coupon were sold at a price of $103,000 after it had been held exactly five years. Then the holding-period yield would be the internal rate of return over those five years, the value at the end of the fifth year being $103,000, rather than the $100,000 after ten years if the bond were held to maturity. The holding-period yield is the internal rate of return over five years with cash flows of $2500 every six months and $105,500 at the end of the five years, in this case 6 percent. You have to determine this either by experimenting with different interest rates that solve the present-value problem or by relying on your friendly calculator. We strongly recommend the latter.

Zero-Coupon Yield or Discount Rate

The zero-coupon yield or discount rate is simply an example of the yield to maturity, but it is a very special yield to maturity that we will use throughout the rest of this book. It is the yield to maturity on a bond with one cash flow at a specific date, or a *zero-coupon bond.* The following basic present-value relationship holds for a zero-coupon bond with a specific cash flow M, received N years in the future:

$$\text{Price of bond} = \frac{M}{(1 + {}_0r_N)^N}$$

Here, ${}_0r_N$ refers to the yield to maturity prevailing at time 0, today, on a bond with a cash flow at time N, or N years in the future. For example, if M is $10,000, N is 10, and the price of the bond $4224, then ${}_0r_N$ is 9 percent. Often, the yield on a zero-coupon bond is expressed in what is called a *bond-equivalent basis,* in order to make it comparable to bonds with coupon payments. This means that the present-value equation is written to reflect semiannual compounding. If we use semiannual compounding in our example where M is $10,000 and the price of the bond is $4224, then the bond-equivalent yield is 8.81 percent. The set of zero-coupon yields or discount rates for single cash flows of different maturity are the fundamental ingredients of our basic approach to valuation of fixed-income securities, to which we turn next.

Now that we have some understanding of the various interest rates used in money and bond markets, we can turn our attention to a survey of the operation of those markets.

The Money Market

We can observe a wide variety of distinct types of financial instruments and forms of market organization in the money markets. Actually, money markets consist of a collection of markets where distinct types of short-term financial instruments are traded, such as T bills, commercial paper, and federal funds. Some of the money market instruments exist largely because regulations created them. This is particularly true of the federal funds market, which grew out of bank trading in excess reserves. Were it not for bank reserve requirements, there simply would be no federal funds as we know them. In other cases an over-the-counter market has developed in a particular type of instrument because it was exempted from some kind of regulation. For instance, debt instruments with maturities shorter than 270 days are exempt from Securities and Exchange Commission (SEC) registration. Because of this rule, commercial paper has a maturity of less than 270 days.

Overview of Money Market Instruments

In one sense the name *money market* is a misnomer because money, per se, is not traded in this market. Money is composed essentially of cash or currency and demand deposits or checking account balances, and these items are not traded in the money market. In the money market are traded the closest money substitutes that thc financial markets have to offer. As a result, it is useful to think of the money market as determining yields on these close money substitutes, and thus, indirectly, on money itself.

The money market refers to the market for a wide variety of short-term debt instruments, where short term generally means that securities have maturities of one year or less. Since the instruments in the money market are relatively close substitutes, their yields move quite closely together. Figure 2-1 shows recent yields on some of the most important money market instruments. The money market is a combination of primary and secondary markets. A primary market is one where securities are traded that have just been issued: *seasoned,* or already-issued, instruments are traded in a secondary market. The important feature in the money market is that the asset must be relatively liquid, so it can be turned over quickly at low cost. For assets with very short maturities, however, an active secondary market may not be all important, as long as there is little probability of default. As a result, the money market is composed of assets perceived to be liquid, either because they have short maturities with low default risk or because there are active secondary markets in those assets. To qualify under either of these accounts, an asset must be

Figure 2-1, Panel A

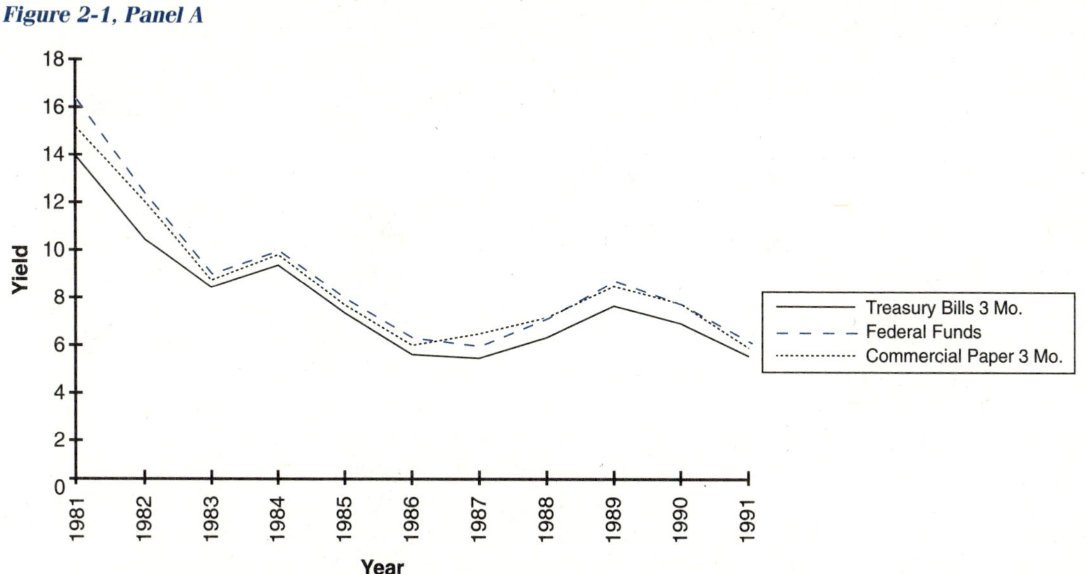

Figure 2-1, Panel B

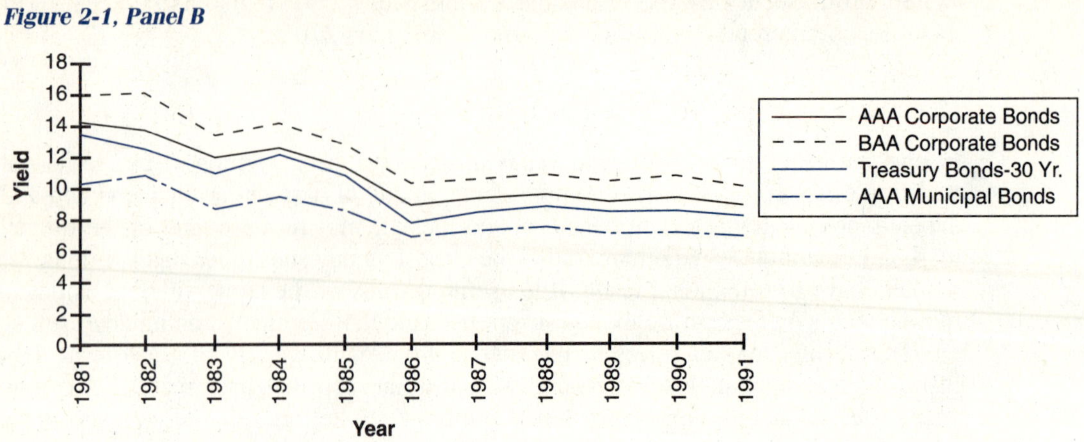

reasonably homogeneous or standardized and have sufficient trading volume to make it profitable for dealers to hold it in their inventories. To understand the money market we have to understand the nature of the securities traded in it.

Treasury Bills

The most important type of security in the money market, in terms of volume of securities outstanding, is U.S. T bills. These bills are available in denominations as small as $10,000, though most T-bill trading occurs in larger denominations. The maturities available on new bills issued by the Treasury range from three months to one year. The interest rates in the secondary market are closely related to the rates on new issues of T bills, because bills of the same maturity are perfect substitutes, regardless of when they might have been issued.

Commercial Paper

Commercial paper is an unsecured short-term financial obligation sold to the market by corporations or financial institutions. Trading in commercial paper is principally a primary rather than a secondary market. Commercial paper is generally issued with denominations of at least $100,000 and may have a maturity of up to 270 days. As we have already mentioned, publicly issued securities with longer maturities must be registered with the SEC, a costly process that would raise the cost of these short-term debt instruments. The market for commercial paper is generally limited to the more creditworthy corporations and financial institutions. As a result, commercial paper is thought to be a relatively low-risk investment.

However, defaults on commercial paper are not unknown. As long ago as 1970, in the relatively early days of the commercial paper market, the Penn Central Railroad defaulted on $82 million worth of commercial paper. The market did not suffer any serious long-term difficulties from this default by a major borrower, though it did encourage lenders to analyze the risks carefully. One mechanism used to limit the amount of risk is for borrowers to have their commercial paper backed by commitments from commercial banks to extend loans, if necessary, at the time the commercial paper matures. Commercial paper backed in this way is called *prime commercial paper.*

Certificates of Deposit

Certificates of deposit (CDs) are a marketable type of time deposit originally issued by commercial banks. They are issued with a specific maturity and have a minimum denomination of $100,000. The market for CDs began to develop in the early 1960s as a secondary market where existing CDs could be resold. Before that time, investors were reluctant to commit large amounts of funds to bank time deposits because of the penalty if funds were withdrawn before maturity. With the advent of a secondary market, this problem was essentially eliminated. Still, CDs, like other bank deposits, were for many years subject to restrictions on maximum interest rates. They were therefore unattractive in periods when interest rates on other money market securities were above these limits. Between 1970 and 1973, the Federal Reserve phased out the interest rate restrictions paid on deposits larger than $100,000 or on CDs. With this change, CDs became an important part of the money market when interest rates were both high and low. Negotiable CDs have become less important in very recent years as interest rates on bank deposit accounts have been deregulated.

Bankers' Acceptances

Historically, bankers' acceptances were one of the first short-term highly marketable assets. They have been used for virtually hundreds of years. A banker's acceptance is created to finance goods that have not yet been transported from seller to buyer. The buyer of the goods promises to pay a prespecified amount of money within a limited period of time, say 90 days. The promise is given credibility if the bank "accepts" it because the bank then commits itself to make the payment should the buyer default. The banker's acceptance is therefore a commitment from a merchant and from a bank to pay a specified amount at a particular time. This means these securities have rather low risk. Bankers' acceptances have functioned as a highly liquid short-term asset for many years.

Federal Funds and Repurchase Agreements

Federal funds and repurchase agreements constitute probably the most liquid and the shortest-maturity assets available in the money market. The federal funds market started as a market where commercial banks that were members of the Federal Reserve System could borrow and lend excess reserves to one another. Reserves are funds that banks hold on deposit with the Federal Reserve to satisfy its reserve requirements. If one bank finds it has an excess in deposits at the Federal Reserve, it can lend these funds to another bank, and the exchange is made by the Federal Reserve through its wire transfer service, an electronic mechanism whereby funds are transferred instantly from one bank to another. There is no delay for a check to clear as with other types of transactions. As a result, it became possible to have virtually overnight maturities on federal funds. The market for federal funds has gradually grown to be much broader than merely the borrowing and lending of excess reserves between a set of commercial banks who then were members of the Federal Reserve System. The federal funds market now involves borrowing and lending among a variety of financial institutions. The fundamental characteristic of the market is that it deals in immediately available funds, or funds cleared through the Federal Reserve's wire transfer service.

A closely related market is the market for repurchase agreements (RPs). An RP involves the sale of a security, usually a T bill, with the simultaneous agreement by the seller to repurchase the security at a prespecified later date. An RP is therefore similar to a collateralized loan. The seller of the T bill is borrowing funds for a prespecified period. RPs generally have a very short maturity, sometimes one day, but most often 3 to 14 days. Because of this, they are very similar to federal funds, but RPs involve a larger market. In addition, RPs are used as a substitute for federal funds because of the flexibility of negotiating maturities. Financial and nonfinancial corporations, as well as governments, borrow and lend through repurchase agreements.

Eurodollars

Eurodollars are simply U.S. dollar–denominated assets deposited overseas in foreign banks or in branches of U.S. banks located offshore. More generally, a Eurocurrency is any asset denominated in the currency of one country but held outside that country. The Eurodollar and broader Eurocurrency markets have grown tremendously in the postwar era. The short-term market in dollar-denominated assets outside the United States represents a growing alternative source of short-term borrowing and investing for individuals and firms in the United States.

Most of the money market is an over-the-counter market. An over-the-counter market is a market without a centralized exchange, so trading takes place through dealers who maintain inventories of the security. The exception is the primary market in T bills. The money market operates over the telephone, and most transactions are carried out by large institutions or corporations so that transactions are relatively large. Because the market's central purpose is to provide highly liquid short-term borrowing and investment opportunities to corporations and financial institutions, it is particularly concerned with executing fast and efficient transactions.

An order is placed in this market through a dealer, who quotes a bid or asked price. An order can be placed immediately with a dealer, or a customer may shop around for quotations from other dealers. Once an order is placed, the dealer arranges for transfer of title to the securities and an exchange of funds through the customer's bank. Some of the dealers in this market are commercial banks and others are brokerage firms. In either case, they stand ready to quote a price and execute the transaction over the telephone.

In terms of the volume of securities outstanding, the largest component of the money market is T bills. Moreover, because RPs are often collateralized by T bills and federal funds are closely related to T bills, government securities are the dominant portion of the market. Because of the predominance of government securities in the money market, the over-the-counter market in these assets is closely tied to the secondary market in government securities, not just the secondary market in T bills.

The money market differs from other markets. It is a conglomeration of markets for distinct securities that have some common characteristics—short maturities, low default risk, and high degree of liquidity. The securities are similar enough that a dealer in one can be a dealer in all, yet they are not sufficiently homogeneous to make an auction market an efficient trading method. As a result, they have come to be traded in what operates like a single over-the-counter market.

Though the money market operates much like a single over-the-counter market for a variety of different money market instruments, it is still useful to examine one of these markets in a little more detail. We will look next at the broader class of Treasury obligations, of which T bills are a part.

The Market For Treasury Obligations

One of the largest markets in the world is the market for obligations of the U.S. Treasury—Treasury bills, Treasury notes, and Treasury bonds. These three distinct marketable securities differ by their original maturities and their cash flow structure. As we have already noted, bills have a maturity of one year or less and carry no coupon payments. Notes have maturities of one to ten years; bonds carry initial maturities longer than seven years. Oftentimes, notes and bonds are lumped together and called *bonds*. The U.S. Treasury also sells a significant volume of savings bonds and other nontraded interest-bearing instruments.

Treasury financing has been a growth industry in the last decade, as the size of the total outstanding debt of the U.S. government has increased dramatically. Figure 2-2 shows the total debt of the U.S. Treasury and the volume of bills, notes, bonds, and other Treasury obligations outstanding for the years from 1981 to 1991. The figure illustrates that all forms of Treasury financing increased over this decade. It also shows the relative proportions of the total marketable debt made up by bills, notes, and bonds.

Figure 2-2

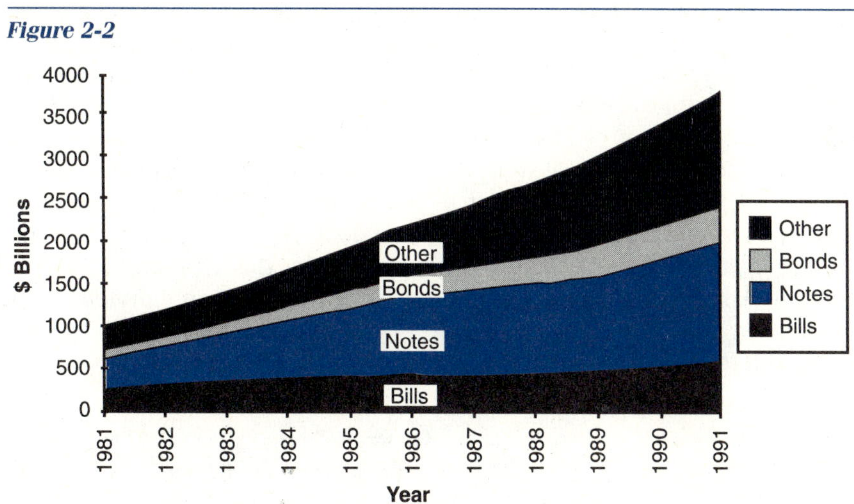

The primary and secondary markets for Treasury debt are organized in very different ways. The primary market, where the Treasury sells new securities, involves an auction by the Treasury to authorized dealers. New T bills are auctioned weekly. Every month the Treasury sells two-year and five-year notes, and once a quarter it sells bonds. The secondary market is an over-the-counter market where so-called dealers who buy securities in the primary market offer to buy and sell Treasury obligations on an ongoing basis. We concentrate on describing the operation of the market for T bills in some detail, and much of this pertains to bonds as well.

The Treasury-Bill Market

The primary T-bill market is one of the few pure call auction markets for financial assets in operation. Auctions are conducted by the U.S. Treasury at regular weekly intervals. The Treasury decides ahead of time what volume of bills it intends to issue and then auctions them to the highest bidders. At one time the Treasury operated in the reverse manner, by setting a price and then seeking buyers, but this was abandoned some years ago in favor of the auction procedure.

Two types of offers to purchase bills are entertained by the Treasury. *Competitive tenders* constitute an offer to buy a specific volume of T bills at a specific price. Buyers who make such offers are dealers in the secondary market in government securities. If they bid high, they will be assured of securing their bids. If they bid low, there may be sufficient offers at higher prices to exhaust the Treasury's issue. *Noncompetitive tenders* contain no specific offer of a price; instead, they constitute an offer to buy a specific volume of securities at the average price prevailing in that auction, whatever it might be. The Treasury places maximum limits on the size of noncompetitive tenders for bills.

In the T-bill auction, the procedure used to determine what orders will be accepted is as follows: The Treasury accepts all noncompetitive tenders first and then turns to the competitive tenders. It proceeds through the competitive tenders from highest to lowest bid until all available bills have been sold or the issue is fully subscribed. It then computes the average price of all competitive tenders and applies that price to the noncompetitive tenders. This means that the low bidders go without. They can then wait for the next primary auction, or they can turn to a dealer in the secondary T-bill market.

While neither the Treasury nor the Federal Reserve has collected historical data on the composition of noncompetitive tenders, the Federal Reserve Bank of New York did conduct a special study of those making noncompetitive tenders in the New York Federal Reserve district for the auction on 20 July 1978. In that auction more than 85 percent of the total number of noncompetitive tenders came from individuals rather than financial institutions or corporations; this represented 70 percent of the total dollar volume of such tenders. Of these tenders from individuals, more than 40 percent of the volume came in amounts greater than $100,000, though many of these large offers came from estates or trust accounts managed by commercial banks.[1]

---

[1]See Sivesind, Charles M. "Noncompetitive Tenders in Treasury Auctions: How Much Do They Affect Savings Flows?" *Quarterly Review* [Federal Reserve Bank of New York] 3 (Autumn 1978), pp. 34–38.

The secondary market in Treasury securities is an over-the-counter market because there is no centralized exchange facility. Trading in the market is generally broken down into the interdealer market and the customer market. The customer market includes trading with all other nondealer participants. The interdealer market includes trades directly between dealers and trades between dealers arranged through a broker. Brokers are used in the interdealer market to maintain confidentiality or anonymity about the other trading party's identity.

In the early 1960s and 1970s the market operated over the telephone. The traders working for each dealer firm would quote prices and make exchanges with other dealers, with brokers, or with other types of customers. Customers would have to search for the best price to buy or sell by calling separate firms and asking for quotes. There was no centralized facility for exchange or for displaying quotations of bid or ask prices. In the mid-1970s this system began to change. Dealer firms began to implement automated quotation systems as a result of private entrepreneurial activity. The automated quotation system involved two separate systems, one used in the interdealer market and one available to dealers and nondealer customers of brokers. The system, used exclusively in the interdealer market, facilitates automated quotation of bid and ask prices as well as automated execution of trades. It eliminates the need for dealers to search for the best prices among themselves.

The billboard system used outside the interdealer market displays only bid and ask prices. Actual exchanges cannot be conducted through it. A dealer displays his or her price on the quotation system, and a customer interested in an exchange at that price must call the dealer to conduct the exchange. These billboard systems can be rented by anyone interested in the market. A billboard system like this is essentially an advertising device; it reduces the cost of searching for alternative prices that is borne by the customers in an over-the-counter market. This billboard system is most economical for securities that are very actively traded.

Dealers in the Treasury Market

The primary dealers in Treasury securities are firms recognized by the Federal Reserve Bank of New York (FRBNY). As of late 1991, 39 primary dealers were so recognized. The FRBNY has a central position in this market because it conducts all trades in Treasury securities for the Federal Reserve System. The principal mechanism by which the Federal Reserve implements monetary policy is by purchase and sale of Treasury securities. Most dealers in the T-bill market also act as dealers in at least a selection of other instruments. The system of primary dealers was created by the Federal Reserve ("The Fed") and Treasury for the apparent purpose of ensuring continual smooth operation and low cost of the Treasury's funding operations and the conduct of the Fed's open market operations. In fact, a committee of representatives of the primary dealers, known as the Treasury Borrowing Advisory Committee, meets regularly with Fed and Treasury officials to help them monitor the market and plan Treasury operations. The FRBNY receives daily statistical reports from all dealers it recognizes and trades with. In addition, it maintains daily phone contact with these dealers and visits the firms periodically. A firm is invited to join the official list when the FRBNY concludes that it has sufficient business volume across the maturity spectrum of available securities and is adequately capitalized and managed. The FRBNY has defined a number of requirements that must be met by primary dealers. According to the FRBNY, primary dealers

must have at least $50 million in capital;

must evidence "management depth, a reasonable profitability record, and good internal controls";

must "freely and candidly supply the Fed with information" pertaining to financial conditions;

are free from a 5 percent deposit requirement for nonprimary dealers; and

must make a market in the full range of U.S. government securities.

Dealers in this market earn their profits, in part, from the spread between bid and asked prices on the securities they trade and from the gains or losses in particular securities. In addition, dealers attempt to earn a higher interest rate on their securities inventory than they must pay for funds to support that inventory. When this yield spread is favorable to the dealer it is referred to as "positive carry." Their ability to generate a positive carry hinges on the level of yields at different maturities, because their investments tend to be spread across the maturity spectrum while their funding is obtained with a very short maturity. The profit earned from trading depends on the magnitude of the market spread and how successfully dealers have managed their positions. As the volatility of Treasury yields increased in the late 1970s and early 1980s, dealers became particularly interested in using T-bill futures and other futures and options to hedge the risks of their positions. Such hedging activities are now an integral part of the dealer's risk management.

The system of primary dealers and the related trading process used in the primary Treasury market have received substantial criticism in recent years. The criticism centers on the contention that primary dealers act as a "cartel," limiting access of investors from around the globe to one of the world's largest financial markets. In addition, it is contended that, in deference to the cartel, the Treasury has not implemented modern trading practices that would afford easy access to many investors. For example, the practice as of the end of 1991 was for primary dealers to accept orders for new issues of Treasury obligations and submit those in writing to the Fed. The Fed has no system to accept orders electronically. Instead, they must be submitted to an order taker who records them by hand. Only primary dealers can submit bids for other customers or for their own account. Furthermore, only primary dealers can submit specific bids of prices they will pay for securities without depositing funds up front. Any other bids from nonprimary dealers are not allowed to specify the prices they will pay. Rather, they must accept the average price of all bids from primary dealers.

Many observers of the market contend that the primary dealers have actively sought to prevent the introduction of innovative practices that might hamper their own strategic position. One contention is that the dealers have discouraged the development of automated trading practices that would allow any mutual fund or pension fund that wants to purchase Treasury securities to place orders directly with the Treasury for such issues. Another interesting contention is that the dealers dissuaded the Treasury from developing its own zero-coupon bond offerings. (See Chapter 9 for a discussion of zero-coupon bonds.) Such issues by the Treasury would directly compete with the zero-coupon bonds created by investment banks, many of them primary dealers, who have stripped off coupon payments to develop "synthetic" zero-coupon bonds. We discuss this in some detail in Part III.

Several episodes over the years have focused attention on possible reform of the primary dealer system. In 1985 a U.S. government securities dealer known as E.S.M. Government Securities, Inc. of Fort Lauderdale, Florida, went into bankruptcy. E.S.M. was not a primary dealer; however, a number of other financial institutions took sizable losses as a result of the E.S.M. collapse, causing considerable attention to be focused on the operations of Treasury dealers and their regulation. It also caused market participants to take new precautions to limit their loss exposure with individual dealers. In 1991 a much larger scandal erupted involving the most important of the primary dealers, Salomon Brothers, Inc. We examine this next.

• *Anatomy of a Short Squeeze* •

In May 1991 one of the largest scandals in the history of the Treasury securities markets began to unfold. This scandal involved Salomon Brothers' acquisition of an unusually large portion of the 22 May auction of $12.26 billion in 2-year notes. It is alleged that Salomon Brothers' strategy was to create a short squeeze in the market for these notes. To understand this episode it is essential to begin by understanding how a short squeeze works.

Each month the government sells two- and five-year notes in an auction. Since the early 1980s, what is called a *when-issued market* for the new notes operates before the auction takes place. Here the notes are traded among dealers and customers before they are actually issued. A dealer who commits to selling a note in the when-issued market must purchase that note in the auction or purchase it from some other source. It stands to lose if it cannot obtain the note at a price below that at which it promised to sell in the when-issued market. It has been observed for some time that prices of notes to be issued at auction rise before the auction and fall right after the auction. In an effort to earn an arbitrage profit off this pattern, many traders have sold notes short ahead of the auction. Thus, they borrow the securities and sell them in the when-issued market, hoping to replace them with cheaper securities after the auction. Of course, if someone could corner the market on the actual notes when they are issued, when many traders need them to cover their short positions, and so drive the price up rather than down, that person would stand to make a large profit, a profit at the expense of all the short traders. This is precisely what Salomon Brothers is alleged to have accomplished in the 22 May auction. On May 30, a week after the auction, the two-year notes were quoted at a price of 100 5/32, which represents a yield of 6.60 percent. The average auction price, one week earlier was $99 29/32, yielding 6.81 percent. This represents a $30.6 million appreciation on the $12.26 billion in notes in only a week.

There is one very serious problem with this strategy of creating a short squeeze. The rules enforced by the Treasury and the Fed require that primary dealers never purchase, directly through their own account or indirectly through accounts of others indirectly pledged to themselves, more than 35 percent of any issue at auction. Somewhat belatedly, Salomon admitted to having purchased at least 57 percent of the 22 May issue, and it was alleged in the subsequent investigation that the actual proportion may have been 85 percent. Furthermore, investigations carried out internally at Salomon and externally by various government offices reveal that Salomon apparently had violated the rule on several previous occasions, including December 1990 and February and April 1991. It was also revealed that managers in the firm knew of at least part of these actions and failed to report them to the proper regulatory authorities. As a result, Salomon chairman John Gutfreund and several other key officers of the firm were forced to resign.

This incident put the entire U.S. government securities market under intense scrutiny. The central question is whether there are such serious flaws in the whole system for trading government securities that wholesale reform is needed. Alternatively, it may be that Salomon Brothers simply engaged in unethical and illegal behavior that deserves appropriate punishment. Some observers have argued that the real culprit here is the 35 percent rule that Salomon violated.[2]

Those who criticize the 35 percent rule argue that it creates incentives for strategic behavior that lowers the prices and increases the yields the government pays to borrow funds. Because dealers must share the individual securities in any auction, they do not have an incentive to bid the highest price. They know that an entire range of prices will receive part of the issue. One view is that a better solution would be to abandon the rule but have the Treasury make the amount of the issue flexible, so that it could expand or contract the volume depending on price bid. Another solution is to curtail the primary dealer system and move toward easier and more efficient access by a larger set of market participants to direct purchases from the Fed or the Treasury. Either of these solutions, so it is argued, would be preferred to punitive action against dealers whose behavior is inspired, in part, by inappropriate regulations.

Many of the news accounts of these events portrayed the short squeeze allegedly perpetrated by Salomon Brothers as behavior that was unprecedented in the marketplace. Actually, there were apparent short squeezes before the one involving Salomon Brothers, or so it is reported by scholars who have studied the market.[3]

It may even seem ironic that the incident of a short squeeze reported in the academic literature was allegedly perpetrated by Japanese investors who were not primary dealers. Apparently, in June 1986 some Japanese investors who had much the same strategic intent later pursued by Salomon Brothers acquired a large position in T bonds. Moreover, it is reported that this short squeeze was successful. Of course, the key difference between the two episodes is that the Japanese were customers of primary dealers rather than primary dealers themselves. Thus, they did not violate the rules for dealers by bidding, through dealers, for such a large portion of the market. The irony seems to be that the U.S. primary dealers must have watched this process with envy. Their envy may eventually have become so great that they violated rules that cost them their positions. Moreover, some have alleged that the primary dealers actively sought to keep the Japanese out of the primary dealer network, so as to limit their participation in the cartel. One part of the price of membership was the illegality of acquiring enough of a position in a single issue to accomplish a squeeze successfully. The top officers of Salomon apparently could not resist the temptation.

---

[2]See Macey, J. R. "Don't Blame Salomon, Blame the Regulators." *Wall Street Journal* August 19, 1991, p. A14.

[3]Cornell B., and A. Shapiro. "The Mispricing of U.S. Treasury Bonds: A Case Study." *Review of Financial Studies* 2 (1990), pp. 297–310.

Agency Debt and Mortgage-Backed Securities

Agency securities are the securities issued by a number of institutions that are either part of the federal government or are privately owned quasigovernmental institutions. Each of these institutions was created under federal law to serve an explicit purpose and authorized to issue their own securities. Some of these agencies have remained part of the federal government; others have become private institutions subject to some government control or regulation. There is a general perception in the marketplace that the federal government would not permit these agencies to default on their obligations. The agency security market is now a large market for debt securities and has active secondary trading.

Agency securities serve a somewhat different purpose than Treasury securities. Treasury obligations are issued essentially to fund the deficit of the U.S. government. Therefore, the larger the gap between federal expenditures and revenues, the larger the volume of Treasury securities that must be issued. But the volume of agency financing does not represent any accumulated deficit. Instead, most of the institutions that offer agency securities act essentially like private financial intermediaries. They issue securities of their own to the public and utilize the proceeds of those securities to purchase various other types of assets. Moreover, at least one agency, the Government National Mortgage Association, (GNMA), merely provides a guarantee against default on securities issued by private mortgage brokers. Thus, the obligations they guarantee are not really securities issued by a government agency. Yet the agency guarantee means they are perceived to have very little or no credit risk, so they trade close to the yield of Treasury obligations.

There is such a variety of institutions issuing securities in the agency market that it is difficult to give a complete characterization of each. Table 2-2 lists the

Table 2-2

The Borrowers in the Agency Security Market and their Acronyms

Federally Sponsored Agencies	Acronyms
Banks for Cooperatives	BC or COOP
Federal Farm Credit Banks	FFCB
Federal Home Loan Banks	FHLB
Federal Home Loan Mortgage Corporation	FHLMC
Federal Intermediate Credit Banks	FICB
Federal Land Banks	FLB
Federal National Mortgage Association	FNMA
Student Loan Marketing Association	SLMA
Export-Import Bank	EXIM
Farmers Home Administration	FmHA
General Services Administration	GSA
Government National Mortgage Association	GNMA
Postal Service	PS
Tennessee Valley Authority	TVA

Figure 2-3, Panel A

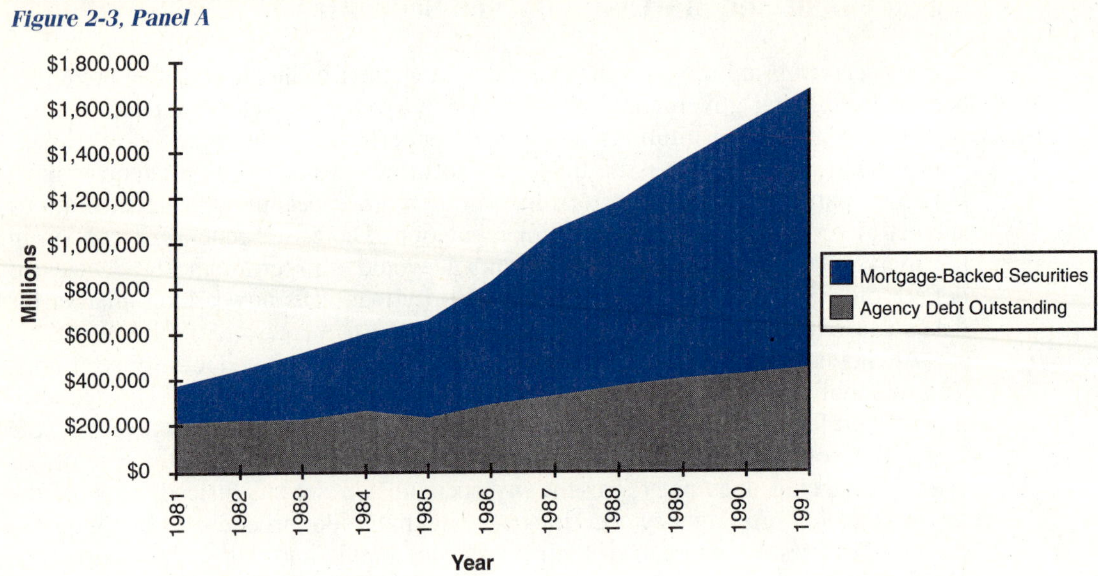

names of the principal agencies along with the acronyms by which they are known. The largest portion of the agency security market provides financing for residential construction; that is, most agency securities are collateralized by mortgages and are issued or guaranteed by government-sponsored institutions that purchase mortgages in the secondary mortgage market. The other important purpose served by the federally sponsored agencies is to provide funding for agriculture.

Figure 2-3 documents the total outstanding liabilities of the agencies of the U.S. government from 1981 to 1991. Panel A shows outstanding bonds, or traditional forms of debt, by the various agencies, as well as mortgage-backed securities issued or guaranteed by the mortgage-related agencies. Though there has been growth in regular bonds or traditional debt, the real, more important, story lies in mortgage-backed securities. Panel B of Figure 2-3 shows the total volume of residential mortgages held and mortgage-backed securities issued or guaranteed by the various housing-related agencies relative to total residential mortgages outstanding. It is apparent from these figures that mortgage-backed securities have grown in volume and as a proportion of total single-family mortgage financing in the United States.

One of the reasons the mortgage-backed securities market has grown so rapidly is the significant innovations in the types of securities offered. Two basic types of securities have been important. The first is the *pass-through security.* The second and more recent innovation is the *collateralized mortgage obligation* (CMO). We provide a brief description of the pass-through security in this chapter, but we postpone our discussion of CMOs and other forms of restructuring cash flows until Chapter 21.

Figure 2-3, Panel B

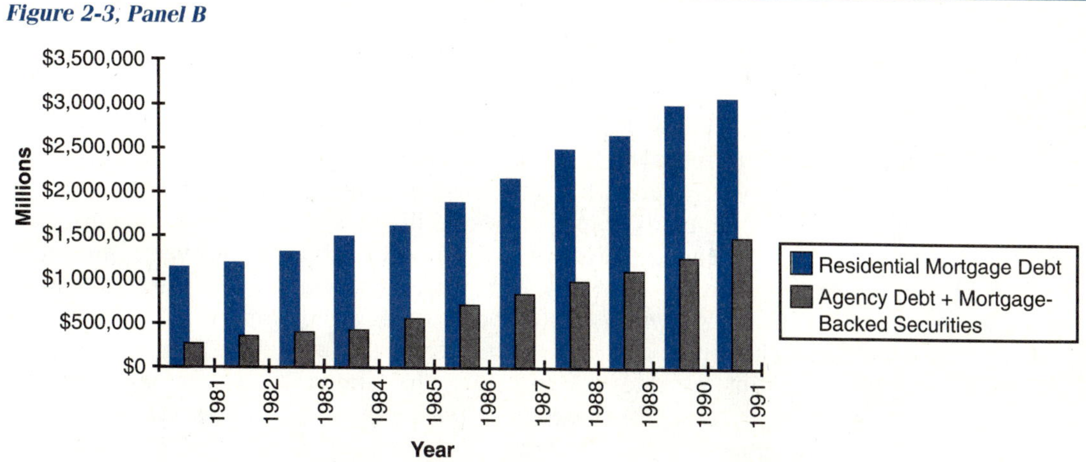

Growth of the Pass-Through Security

Beginning in 1970, GNMA began to guarantee timely payment of principal and interest on securities issued by private mortgage institutions and backed by pools of government-insured or government-guaranteed mortgages. The pass-through security is a claim on a share of the income from a specific mortgage pool. The private originators of the individual mortgages generally continue to service the mortgages in the pools, collecting the principal and interest payments and passing them through to the security holders. A loan originator may also sell the servicing function to another firm. Currently issued GNMA-guaranteed certificates are termed *fully modified.* This means that scheduled payments of principal and interest are provided to the security holders, whether or not collected by the mortgage servicer, plus a pro rata share of any prepayments made on the pool of mortgages.

As the market for GNMA pass-throughs expanded in the early 1970s, the Federal Home Loan Mortgage Corporation (FHLMC) introduced its own pass-through, known as a *participation certificate,* or PC. The PCs differ from GNMA pass-throughs guaranteed by GNMA in a number of respects. Probably the most important is that mortgages in the pools backing PCs are conventional mortgages; that is, they are not guaranteed against default by some U.S. government agency. The second is that FHLMC does not simply provide a guarantee of timely payments on securities issued by private firms but rather buys mortgages from originators, forms mortgage pools, issues its own securities, and guarantees timely payment of interest. Unlike GNMA, however, it does not guarantee timely payment of principal in the event of delinquency or default. As a result, FHLMC is an integrated firm that creates mortgage-backed securities. The extent of vertical integration is limited by the fact that FHLMC does not originate its own mortgages, and it relies on independent dealers to maintain a market in PCs. Federal National Mortgage Association (FNMA) now also issues its own pass-through securities, though it was the last of the three agencies to do so. A number of private institutions have also sold pass-throughs, but the volume of these security issues is small compared with those of the three quasifederal agencies. The total volume of outstanding mortgage-backed securities issued or guaranteed by the three agencies as of the end of 1990 was as follows: GNMA, $403.613 billion; FHLMC, $316.359 billion; FNMA, $299.833 billion.

It is important to see why the pass-through security has become such a popular instrument in the mortgage market. In principle, it would be possible to utilize the cash flow pattern commonly found in a bond that has a well-defined maturity and coupon interest payments promised over the life of the bond. However, if mortgage-backed securities were issued in this form, the issuer would accept the risk of mortgage prepayments. *Prepayment risk* is the risk that a mortgage will be paid off by the borrower prior to its maturity. This happens either when the borrower sells the property or when interest rates fall relative to the rate on the outstanding mortgage, making it attractive for the borrower to refinance the loan. We discuss prepayment risk in some detail in Chapter 9 and in several chapters in Parts III and IV. With a pass-through security, prepayment risk is transferred to the security holder. This has worked reasonably well for institutional investors who understand prepayment risk and are willing to accept it. Many institutions, however, originally principally insurance companies and pension funds, avoided investing directly in mortgages to any great extent because they preferred the stable and predictable cash flow streams available from corporate bonds and others. These institutions were ready for new types of mortgage-backed securities that used innovative ways of dealing with prepayment risk. We discuss the securities that have met this need, the CMOs, later.

The Municipal Bond Market

Characteristics of Municipal Debt

The municipal bond market is the market for obligations of state and local governments in the United States. The distinguishing feature of this market is the tax treatment of municipal bonds. In recognition of a general principle that one level of government should not interfere with another, and in an effort to reduce the cost of borrowing for state and local governments across the country, the U.S. government made the interest income on municipal bonds exempt from federal income taxes. In addition, each state declared that the interest income on its own bonds will be exempt from its state income taxes. Finally, some states and localities have given tax-exempt status to bonds issued by other states on a reciprocal basis.

The tax-exempt feature of the interest income on municipal bonds has made them attractive to individuals and institutions whose tax rates are high. Individuals who have historically faced a progressive income tax schedule have found that the higher the tax bracket, the more advantageous is the tax-exempt feature of municipal bonds. Corporations with a constant marginal tax rate (as long as their taxable income exceeds $25,000) have not found that the attractiveness of municipal securities varies directly with their income level in the same way that individuals have. In addition, some institutions with sizable amounts of funds to invest, such as pension funds and tax-exempt foundations, do not pay taxes and so find the tax-exempt feature of municipals totally unattractive.

Before the enactment of the 1986 tax law, the tax treatment of municipal bonds was relatively straightforward. The 1986 law made the situation much more complicated. The general thrust of the 1986 tax law was to limit the ability of municipal governments to sell tax-exempt bonds. This limitation was motivated by the perception that municipal governments were abusing the privilege granted to them through the tax exemption feature.

Two principal types of abuses were perceived. One pertains to the growth of industrial revenue bonds used to finance a wide variety of projects that were not deemed essential services of state and local governments. It was relatively common practice for state and local governments to issue bonds to fund private ventures. This was used extensively in campaigns to provide incentives for corporations to locate facilities in a particular town or region. The local government would fund the development of the new facility and related capital expenditures in order to provide an incentive for the firm to locate in that area. This reduced the cost to the corporation, which was able to finance its project at the tax-exempt rate.

The second perceived abuse was that some state and local governments sold municipal bonds in order to reinvest the proceeds in higher-yield instruments. Though the practice was expressly prohibited by the Internal Revenue Service (IRS), it was very difficult to prove that was the purpose of a specific bond issue. As a result, Congress chose to limit the ability of state and local governments to engage in such transactions.

The 1986 tax law defines four classes of municipal debt:

Class I consists of public-purpose bonds. These are issued by state and local governments or their agencies to meet essential government functions, such as highway construction and school financing. These bonds retained their tax-exempt status.

Class II includes bonds issued to finance what the tax law calls *nongovernmental purposes,* like housing and student loans. States have a ceiling on the amount of Class II bonds they can issue. Moreover, taxpayers who purchase such bonds have to treat interest earned on them as a preference item on their tax returns; it is added to taxable income if the taxpayer is liable for the minimum tax mandated in the law.

Class III includes taxable municipals, issued for purposes that Congress deemed nonessential, such as upgrading of pollution control facilities or building a sports stadium. The tax exemption on these bonds is restricted.

Class IV consists of bonds issued prior to 7 August, 1986, which continue to provide tax-free income.

The 1986 tax law had a clearly discernible impact on the total volume of municipal bond financing. Figure 2-4 shows the total volume of municipal bonds issued, including refundings and new issues, from 1981 to 1991. The data is broken down

Figure 2-4

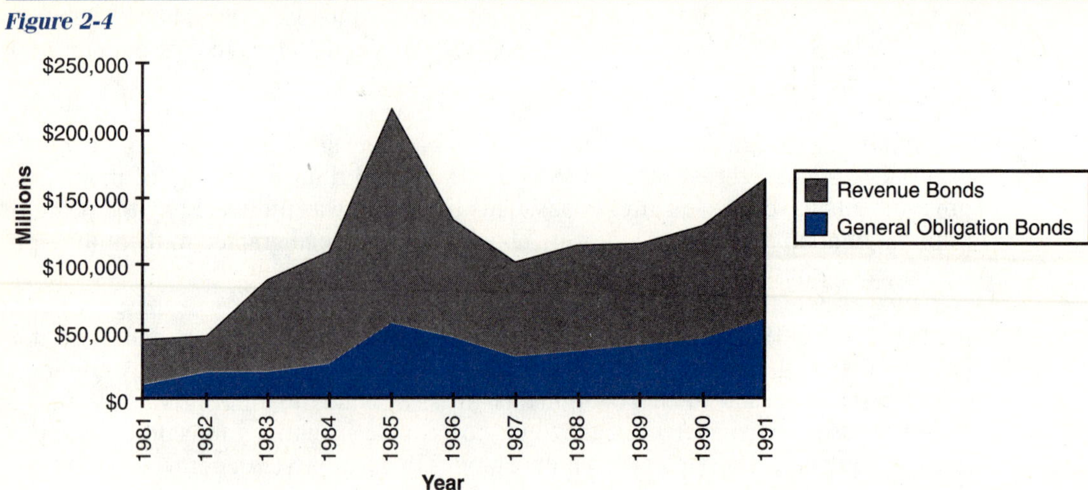

by general obligation bonds and revenue bonds. General obligation bonds represent obligations of the taxpayers of the state or local government. Revenue bonds are supported by revenues of specific public projects such as airports, toll roads, and bridges. There was a significant increase in revenue bond financing in the early 1980s and a large bulge in 1985, in anticipation of the new law. The volume of such issues declined significantly after the law was passed.

The Effect of Taxes on Municipal Bond Yields

The attractiveness of tax-exempt municipal bonds hinges on the difference in yields between the municipal security and an otherwise comparable security that is fully taxable. For example, suppose that a municipal bond and a corporate bond are identical in every respect except the tax-exempt status of the municipal bond. Suppose the yield on the corporate bond is 10 percent, and the yield on the municipal 8 percent. At what marginal tax rate will it be profitable for an investor to hold the municipal rather than the corporate bond? To answer this question we must emphasize that investors are interested in after-tax returns. The problem facing investors is to determine the yield they will receive after taxes on a taxable bond that pays 10 percent. We learned in equation 2.12 that the corporate and municipal bonds yield identical after-tax returns if

$$r_C(1 - t) = r_M$$

where t is the tax rate, r_M the yield on the municipal bond, and r_C the yield on an otherwise equivalent taxable corporate bond

For a given yield on both the municipal and corporate bonds, we can solve for the minimum marginal tax rate where the municipal bond produces the higher after-tax yield:

$$t = 1 - \frac{r_M}{r_C}$$

Now we can answer the question in our example:

$$1 - \frac{0.08}{0.10} = 0.20$$

This means that, in the example, anyone whose tax rate is higher than 20 percent will find the municipal bond to be a better investment than the corporate bond.

From the observed yields on municipals and roughly comparable securities that are taxable it is possible to compute the implied marginal tax rate, as in this example. Panel A of Figure 2-5 shows the yields on high-quality long-term municipal bonds. It also shows the yield on high-quality long-term corporate bonds over the same period. Using the corporate bonds as the comparable security, it is possible to compute the marginal tax rate at which the municipal security becomes preferable, over the same historical period. The marginal tax rates are shown in panel B of the figure. While, historically, there has been considerable fluctuation in the computed marginal tax rate, it was fairly stable in the late 1980s—roughly 24 percent—whereas the maximum federal tax rate since 1986 has been 33 percent.

It is not obvious why this yield spread has been around 76 percent rather than some higher or lower amount. The size of the spread depends largely on who is attracted to hold municipals and who is not. For many years, until the mid-1980s, commercial banks were the dominant purchaser of municipal bonds. Other purchasers included property and casualty insurance companies and individuals in high tax brackets. Because commercial banks historically had the largest position in the municipal bond market, it has been argued that their decisions to buy or sell municipals are an important, if not the most important, determinant of the marginal tax rate. It was argued that as banks, which are subject to the corporate tax rate, move

Figure 2-5, Panel A

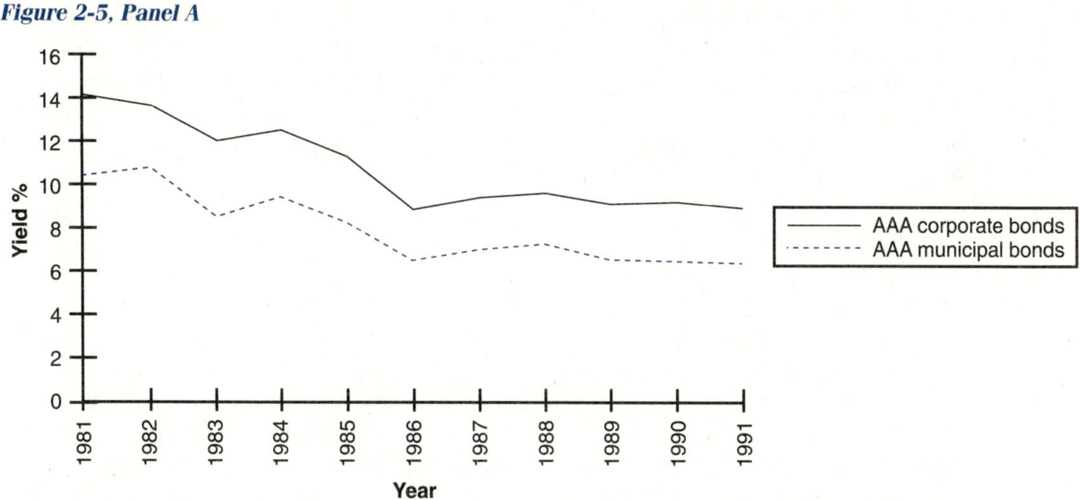

Figure 2-5, Panel B

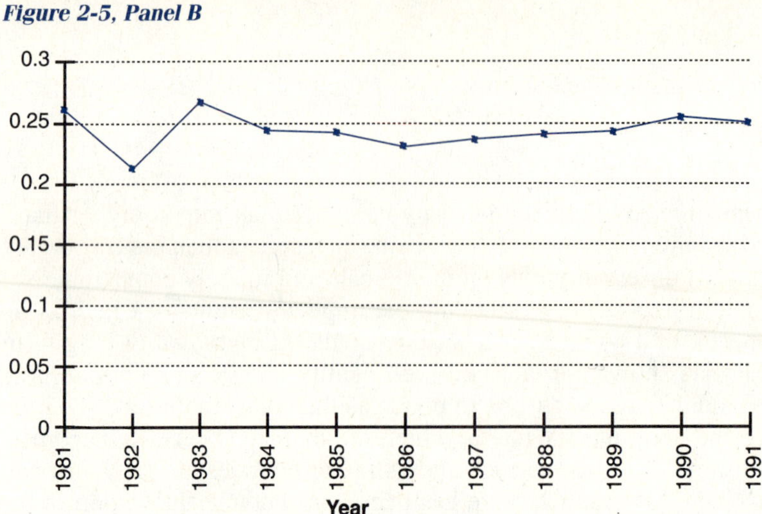

into or out of the market, they increase or decrease the total demand for municipals. The slack was taken up by individuals who faced a progressive tax schedule. Therefore, when they must pick up additional slack, the marginal tax rate must fall to induce more individual investors to buy municipals.

Demand for municipal bonds by commercial banks declined during the late 1970s and 1980s, largely because banks had plentiful tax deductions from other sources such as foreign tax credits and leasing operations. An increase in municipal bond rates relative to other taxable rates roughly coincided with this change in bank demand, but it is difficult to determine whether this was the principal cause of the shift in yields. Moreover, the commercial banks became a less important force in the market in the late 1980s as municipal bond mutual funds made it easier for high–tax bracket investors to invest directly in the market on their own. The change in ownership patterns of municipal bonds is documented in Figure 2-6, which shows the proportion of municipal bonds owned by households, banks, insurance companies, and other institutions in 1982 and in 1992. Notice that both bank and insurance company proportional holdings decreased while household and others increased significantly.

Corporate Bonds

Corporate bonds are another major category of fixed-income securities. Corporate bonds include all long-term (longer than one year to maturity) obligations of corporations. Most corporate bonds have stated coupon payments that are close to the market interest rate when they are issued. Thus, they constitute an obligation to pay the coupon payments and the principal at maturity or through a sinking fund provision of gradual principal payments. The total volume of corporate bond issues from 1981 to 1991 is shown in Figure 2-7. For the later years of the period, the data are

Figure 2-6
Source: Public Securities Association

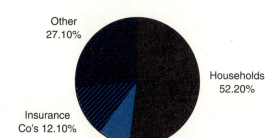

MUNICIPAL OWNERSHIP 1992

Other 27.10%
Households 52.20%
Insurance Co's 12.10%
Banks 8.60%

MUNICIPAL OWNERSHIP 1982

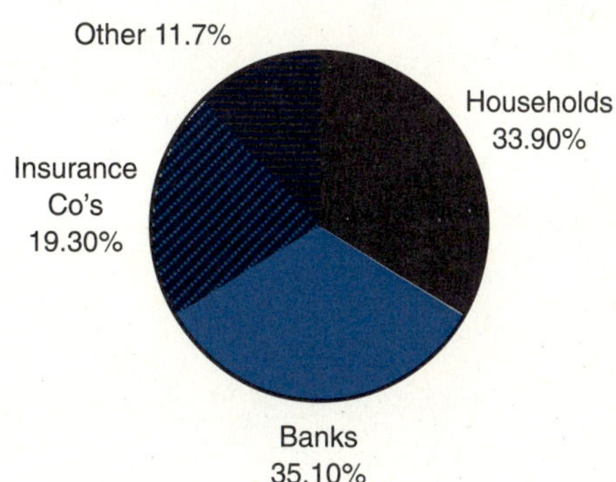

broken down into three major categories: domestic public offerings, private placements, and sold abroad. The domestic versus foreign components are not available for the first half of the period. Notice that the domestic public offering is consistently the most popular form of bond issue. Publicly issued bonds tend to be larger and more standardized than privately issued bonds, and, historically, they were generally issued by well-known companies. Privately placed bonds generally have more complicated covenants than publicly distributed bonds. This often means that the issuer will renegotiate the terms of the bond over its life with the purchaser. Insurance companies are the predominant purchasers of privately placed bonds. This is so in large part because of the long-term maturity structure of insurance companies' liabilities, at least compared to those of commercial banks, which are the more common source for private short-term borrowing by corporations.

Historically, nearly all of the publicly distributed corporate bonds are rated for credit quality by either Moody's or Standard & Poor's. The expense of preparing the rating is paid by the companies being rated rather than by the users of the service. The ratings provide a qualitative judgment of the risk of each bond. The various rating categories employed by the agencies are shown in Table 2-3. The highest rating is AAA or Aaa. Rating agencies not only provide ratings for newly issued bonds; they also update ratings on bonds already issued when they perceive that the riskiness of these bonds is changing.

Innovations in Corporate Bonds: Hybrids and Junk

One of the most important growth areas of the capital markets in the late 1980s were securities that are hybrids of debt and equity. One of the most common and long-standing of such securities is the convertible bond, which carries an option to convert into a company's stock. Convertible bonds are particularly attractive to companies that face severe obstacles to directly issuing equity. If their stock prices

Figure 2-7

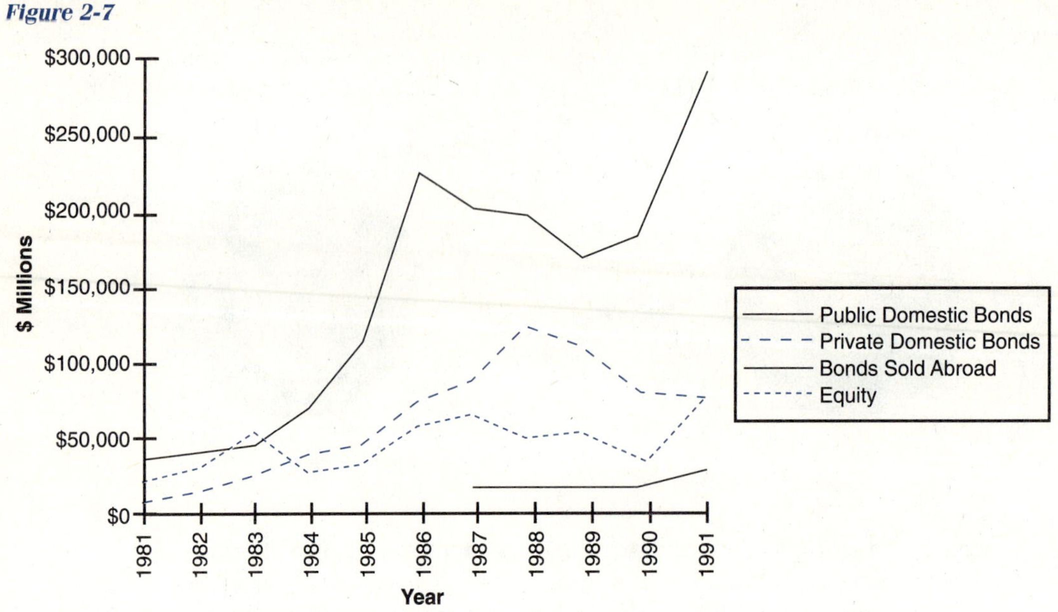

increase, convertible bonds can be converted into equity so that the company will eventually end up with equity financing. Moreover, the valuable conversion feature provides an inducement to bondholders to purchase the bonds without having to raise the promised interest rate to an extremely high level. Thus, companies viewed as highly risky or volatile often find convertible financing more attractive than straight debt. The convertible feature provides what is termed an "equity sweetener," so that the bond has some features of equity and some features of debt.

A very interesting development in the bond markets during the 1980s was the so-called junk bond market. Junk or high-yield bonds are publicly distributed bonds rated below investment grade by Moody's or Standard & Poor's. (*Investment grade* usually means Baa or higher, according to Moody's rating category.) For many years there were relatively few publicly distributed bonds that did not receive an investment-grade rating or that received no rating at all. Potential issuers of low-rated bonds simply did not distribute their bonds in the public markets. Instead, they went to an insurance company for a private placement of debt or to a bank for a private loan. But in the 1980s the new phenomenon of the public distribution of low-rated, or high-yield bonds developed.

To a large degree the junk bond market is the invention of the now defunct investment banking firm of Drexel Burnham Lambert and its star performer Michael Milken. Drexel Burnham Lambert developed a group of investors who were willing to invest in junk bonds if they carried a high enough yield to maturity, or spread over the yield to maturity on bonds with substantially higher rating. The question was then, and still is, whether the higher promised yield on these low-rated bonds is worth the risk. This issue has attracted considerable attention in the last

Table 2-3
Bond Ratings Produced by Moody's and Standard & Poor's

Moody's	Explanation
Aaa	Best quality
Aa	High quality
A	Higher medium grade
Baa	Medium grade
Ba	Possesses speculative elements
B	Lacks characteristics of desirable investment
Caa	Poor standing; may be in default
Ca	Speculative in a high degree; often in default
C	Lowest grade
Standard & Poor's	**Explanation**
AAA	Highest grade
AA	High grade
A	Upper medium grade
BBB	Medium grade
BB	Lower medium grade
B	Speculative
CCC-CC	Outright speculation
C	Reserved for income bonds
D	In default

few years, in part because junk bonds have been so controversial. Part of the controversy arises from the fact that junk bonds were used to finance many of the actual and threatened takeovers of corporations common in the 1980s. Many people who believe takeovers should be regulated or that significant abuses have occurred in the takeover process have also argued that junk bonds are excessively risky. Those who defend the use of junk bonds, particularly the issuers and the investment banks that developed the market, argue that the relatively high promised yield to maturity on junk bonds make them very attractive investments. They contend that the high yield is at least a fair compensation for the risk involved.

Figure 2-8 documents the total volume of new issues of junk or high-yield bonds from 1985 through 1991. Notice that the volume of new issues peaked in 1986 but continued strong until the onset of the 1990 recession and the demise of Drexel Burnham Lambert. To a substantial degree the junk market then rebounded in 1991, as market interest rates fell and it became attractive for firms with outstanding junk bonds to refinance their debt at the new lower interest rates.

Eurobonds

In many respects Eurobonds are similar to corporate or even T bonds sold in the domestic U.S. market, in that they are long-term obligations of both companies and governments around the world. The key distinguishing feature of Eurobonds is that

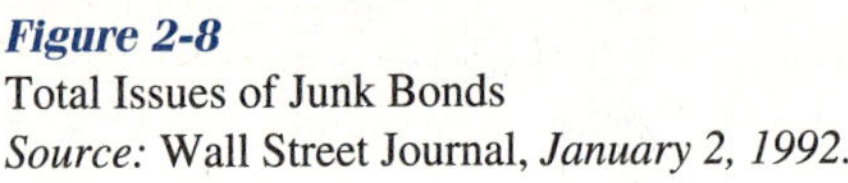

Figure 2-8
Total Issues of Junk Bonds
Source: Wall Street Journal, *January 2, 1992.*

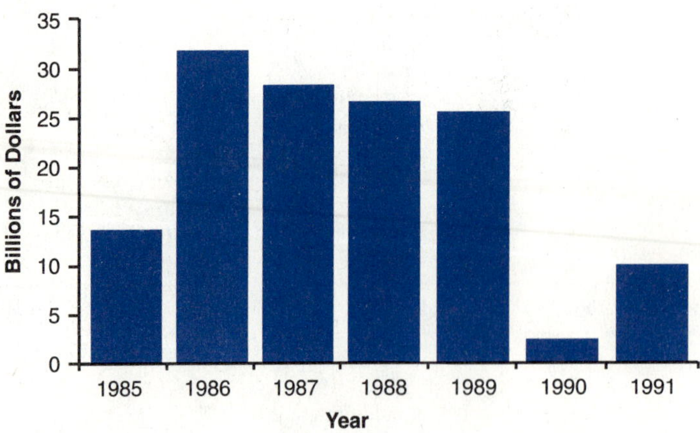

they are sold outside the country in whose currency they are denominated. For example, any U.S. dollar–denominated bonds sold outside the United States are Eurobonds. The driving force behind the Eurobond market is that, by selling outside the country of origin, a company or government can often escape local regulation and securities law. For companies in the United States, Eurobond issues are not subject to SEC registration and disclosure requirements. Therefore, the issuing company does not have to incur the costs of complying with SEC requirements. In addition, the Eurobond market is largely a "name" market, where only the most creditworthy borrowers can issue securities.

Another advantage of Eurobonds is that they are bearer bonds, which means the ownership of the bond is not recorded, especially for tax purposes. Hence Eurobonds are effectively tax free. Because of their tax advantages, Eurobonds have been popular with high–tax bracket investors around the world who invest in bonds held outside of their country of residence, often in Switzerland or Luxembourg. These countries have been particularly cooperative by not withholding tax payments from the interest payments on these bonds. This tax treatment of Eurobonds was especially attractive to investors in the United States prior to 1984, when the IRS required withholding on interest paid to foreign bondholders. This provided a strong disincentive for such investors to hold dollar-denominated bonds in the United States. However, the United States eliminated such withholding in 1984, which had a dampening influence on volume in the Eurobond market. But the growth of the swaps market provided additional demand for Eurobonds, as bond issuers who would not otherwise have had access to the Eurobond market gained indirect access by swapping their domestic obligations with firms that could sell obligations in this market.

It is important not to confuse Eurobonds with Eurocurrencies such as the Eurodollars discussed earlier. Eurocurrencies represent bank deposits in banks outside the country in whose currency the deposit is denominated. Moreover, these are generally short-term claims on those intermediaries. Eurobonds are long-term bonds sold in many countries by securities dealers or underwriters.

SUMMARY

This chapter surveyed the various markets for fixed income securities. We began with a description of the various interest rates we observe in money and bond markets, summarized in Table 2-1. Then we moved on to a discussion of the money market: a collection of markets for various short-term debt instruments that are viewed as close substitutes for cash. Most of these instruments are traded in over-the-counter markets by dealers or by commercial banks: T bills, commercial paper, certificates of deposit, bankers' acceptances, federal funds, and repurchase agreements.

Next we focused in some detail on one of the markets for Treasury securities—bills, notes, and bonds. There are two distinct markets for Treasury obligation, primary and secondary markets. The primary market is an auction market where the Treasury auctions securities to the highest bidders. The Treasury relies on a group of primary dealers who meet certain requirements mandated by the Federal Reserve Bank of New York. These dealers place specific bids on securities auctioned by the Treasury and they provide a secondary market in the issued securities. There has been increasing criticism of the system of primary dealers spawned by an incident where Salomon Brothers violated rules regarding the maximum proportion of the securities sold in an auction that can be acquired by any single primary dealer.

Next we examined the market for agency debt, especially mortgage-backed securities. Unlike Treasury securities, agency securities are not sold to fund the deficit of the U.S. government or of specific agencies. Instead, they are sold to fund the activities of specific agencies of the U.S. government and privately owned companies with specific ties to the government. The majority of these securities provide financing for housing and agriculture. We described some of the principal institutions that sell agency securities and noted that agency debt is usually priced close to comparable Treasury debt, owing to a perception that the U.S. Treasury will not allow defaults by the institutions that sell agency securities. The largest component of growth in the agency security market has been mortgage-backed securities, specifically one form or another of mortgage pass-throughs. These securities pass through the cash flows from mortgages, including prepayments, directly to the security holders. This means that pass-throughs do not have the stability of timing of cash flows that are common to traditional bonds. This has led to the development of various means to manage this added element of uncertainty. We take this up in some detail in Part IV.

Next we examined the market for municipal bonds. The principal distinguishing feature of municipal debt is its exemption from federal taxation of interest income. This feature has made municipal debt an attractive alternative for investors in relatively high tax brackets. The 1986 tax law provided some major reforms of the ability of state and local governments to sell tax-exempt debt. The law restricted the ability of these governments to sell such revenue bonds for nonpublic purposes. This led to a bulge in the total volume of such funding, in anticipation of the 1986 law, and then to a decline in that funding after the enactment of the law in 1986.

Finally, we provided an overview of the market for corporate bonds. This market includes a wide variety of different types of instruments, including hybrids of debt and equity. We documented the relative proportion of public and privately distributed corporate bonds and the volume of corporate bonds sold abroad. We also briefly explained the development of the junk bond market and documented the volume of junk bond financing from 1985 to 1991. Finally, we briefly examined the Eurobond market, which is composed of bonds sold outside the country in whose currency they are denominated. To a large degree this market has prospered because issuers can avoid domestic regulation and investors can avoid domestic taxation.

QUESTIONS

1. Provide concise definitions of T bills, CDs, bankers' acceptances, federal funds, repurchase agreements, and Eurodollars.
2. Describe how the auction price for T bills is determined.
3. What distinguishes primary dealers in Treasury obligations from nonprimary dealers?
4. Discuss the pros and cons of regulating the total portion of a Treasury offering that a primary dealer may obtain in an auction.
5. What is a pass-through security? Why have they become so popular?
6. What is the implied marginal tax rate on a municipal bond? How would you use it to decide whether to purchase municipal bonds?
7. What are the principal factors that would motivate a U.S. company to consider selling Eurobonds?
8. The volume of junk bond financing bounced back in late 1990 and 1991 from earlier low levels. Why did this happen?
9. What are hybrids of debt and equity? Explain how they work.
10. Discuss the difference between holding period yield and yield to maturity. When will they be the same?

REFERENCES

Cornell, B., and A. Shapiro. "The Mispricing of U.S. Treasury Bonds: A Case Study." *Review of Financial Studies* 2 (1990), pp. 297–310.

Macey, J. R. "Don't Blame Salomon, Blame the Regulators." *Wall Street Journal* August 19, 1991, p. A14.

Stigum, Marcia. *The Money Market.* Homewood, IL: Irwin, 1990.

• *Chapter 3*

Equity Markets

In this chapter, we describe and discuss the market for equity securities. In the U.S. economy, equity markets take on a level of particular importance that is, perhaps, unparalleled elsewhere in the world. For most of us, few days pass by without hearing some mention of or reference to the general condition of the stock market—The market is up today; the Dow broke 3500. Certainly, the opinion of the stock market is regularly assessed when economic news is released. Frequent news report cite the "market's reaction" to various economic reports and statistics.

For corporations that issue stock, equity values take on a special significance, as well. A company's stock price is in many ways a scorecard of its performance. An increase in the price of the firm's stock indicates increased demand for the firm's shares in the capital markets and reflects a favorable evaluation of the firm's prospects as an investment. Higher share prices make it more attractive for the firm to raise capital and to expand and extend its business activities. Moreover, as an ownership claim against the firm's assets, the value of the firm's common stock should be the focal point of corporate policy. It is generally accepted in finance that the appropriate objective of corporate management is to maximize owners' wealth (i.e., the value of equity). Indeed, the current trend in design of executive compensation contracts is to tie the compensation of top management to the performance of the firm's stock, for example, through performance-based bonus plans or stock options.

This chapter explains the major forms of securities traded in U.S. equity markets and the major differences between equity and debt securities. The organization of U.S. equity markets is broken down into two parts, the primary and secondary markets for equity. We deal with the primary market first. We focus on the issuance of new securities and the role of investment banks in bringing new issues to the market. Markets for Initial Public Offerings (IPOs) and venture capital are also discussed.

The secondary market, or market for trading existing securities, is explained next. The two major organizational forms of trading U.S. equities are described. The organized exchanges are dealt with first, and particular emphasis is placed on the New York Stock Exchange (NYSE) and the unique role of the specialist on the NYSE. The over-the-counter (OTC) market is also explained and the role of the National Association of Securities Dealers Automatic Quotation (NASDAQ) system in centralizing trading information is discussed. Additionally, the role of the "third and fourth markets" in large block trades is explained.

We also describe the major stock market indices that represent broad-based indications of stock prices. The Dow Jones Industrial Average (DJIA), the most familiar of these, is often used as a general barometer of economic conditions. Finally, we examine the important role of diversification in determining the organization of equity markets. The fact that diversification reduces the risk of investments in equities means that most investors hold diversified portfolios of securities. This heightens the importance of the market indices of the performance of portfolios of stocks. Moreover, the demand for diversification has led to the growth of numerous mutual funds that provide diversification to investors. We discuss these funds in Chapter 7. The key concepts to learn in this chapter are listed below.

• *Concepts to Learn in Chapter 3* •

- Characteristics of equity securities and the trends in the issuance of equity
- How the primary market for equities operates
- How the exchanges and over-the-counter equity markets operate
- How diversification affects the risk of investments in equity securities

Characteristics of Equity Securities

There are two general categories of equity securities: preferred stock and common stock. While the word "equity" generally implies ownership interest in a firm, only common stock conveys the full range of rights and obligations associated with an ownership position. As we will detail below, the rights and obligations associated with preferred stock are different in that these securities combine some of the attributes of common stock and some of corporate bonds. A distinguishing feature of equity securities generally is that payments to equityholders are subordinated to the obligations to debtholders and other creditors. In other words, payments to equityholders cannot be made until all outstanding obligations to debtholders are satisfied.

Preferred Stock

Preferred stock is usually issued with a par value (e.g., $100) and pays a fixed dividend expressed as a percentage of the par value. For example, 8 percent preferred stock promises an annual dividend of $8 per $100 par value. Because preferred stock combines some of the basic attributes of bonds and common stock it is often referred to as a *hybrid security.* In particular, the fixed-dividend payment promised by preferred stock is similar to the fixed-interest payment associated with a bond. At the same time, preferred stock has no maturity date and is generally subordinate to corporate debt securities, both attributes of common stock. Also, like many bonds, some preferred issues have a call provision, which allows the issuer to call (buy back) the stock at a pre-specified call price.

Preferred stock holds a claim against the firm's cash flows that is superior to that of common stock. In other words, preferred stockholders receive promised dividends before cash flows accrue to common stockholders either as dividends or retained earnings. At the same time, preferred stock dividends are paid after all obligations to debtholders. Under most circumstances, dividends to preferred stockholders are cumulative, in which case the stock is called *cumulative preferred stock.* The word "cumulative" refers to the provision that when a scheduled dividend payment is not made, the unpaid dividend is carried forward to the next dividend date. Cumulative dividends to preferred stockholders must be paid before common stockholders can be paid dividends. For example, if a firm issued $10 million in 8 percent cumulative preferred stock, the annual dividend payment to preferred stockholders is $800,000.[1] Suppose that during the year, the issuing firm earned after-tax income of $500,000, which was paid to satisfy part of the obligation to preferred shareholders. Because preferred dividends are not met with current earnings, no dividend payment is made to common stockholders, and $300,000 in accrued dividends payable are carried forward. During the next year, the firm would have to generate after-tax earnings of $1,100,000 to meet its obligation to preferred shareholders and more than $1,100,000 to be able to make a dividend payment to common stockholders.

An important difference between preferred stock and corporate debt is that, while corporate interest payments are deductible for computing taxable earnings, preferred dividends are not tax deductible. This aspect of preferred stock is often given as an important disadvantage of preferred stock as compared to debt. All else the same, the tax treatment of preferred dividends makes it more costly to finance a company with preferred stock than with corporate debt. On the other hand, preferred stock has one important advantage over corporate debt—the ability to partially suspend dividend payments without forcing the firm into financial distress or bankruptcy. When a firm fails to meet scheduled debt payment, the firm is technically in default and may be forced into bankruptcy; when a firm fails to meet a scheduled dividend to preferred stockholders, the dividend can be accrued and paid later.

Probably the most important difference between preferred stock and common stock is voting control. Unlike most issues of common stock, preferred stock seldom confers voting rights.[2] Voting rights entitle shareholders to participate in many decisions that affect the management of the firm and the selection of top managers. New issues of common stock have the potential to dilute the voting power of outstanding common shares. Therefore, the preservation of voting control of existing shareholders is often given as an important advantage in favor of issuing nonvoting preferred stock.

Common Stock

Common stock represents an ownership claim against the assets of the firm. Payoffs to common shareholders, who are owners of the firm, are subordinate to those of all other stakeholders—employees, suppliers, taxing authorities, preferred shareholders,

---

[1]Preferred dividends are most often paid quarterly. Annual dividends are used here to simplify the example.
[2]Voting preferred stock often provides voting power that is limited compared to that of common stock. In some circumstances preferred shareholders are allowed to vote only when the firm is in extreme financial distress.

bondholders, and other debt holders. Because it is last in priority for claims against the firm's cash flows, common stock is often referred to as the *residual claim.* Common shareholders have the right to all residual cash flows accruing to the firm after all other claims and obligations are satisfied. As the residual claim against the firm's assets, common stock is inherently the riskiest of the firm's securities.

The riskiness of common stock compared to debt and preferred stock is illustrated by the example in Table 3-1. A company with $100 million in assets is financed by $50 million in 6 percent 20-year bonds, $20 million in 8 percent nonvoting preferred stock, and $30 million in equity. Earnings before interest and taxes (EBIT) varies according to four possible economic scenarios: boom, normal economy, mild downturn, and severe recession. The firm's annual obligations to bondholders and preferred shareholders are $3.0 million and $1.6 million in bond interest and preferred dividends, respectively. Assuming a 30 percent income tax rate, the cash flows available to each category of the firm's securityholders are given in Table 3-1 for the four different economic scenarios.

As Table 3-1 shows, the returns to common stock are the most variable, or the most risky, of the three types of securities. In an economic boom equity holders receive $6.8 million; in a severe recession, they receive nothing. Debt holders receive full payment regardless of the economic outcome, and debt is therefore the least risky of the three categories of securities. The riskiness of preferred stock falls somewhere between common stock and debt. Preferred shareholders receive full dividends of $1.6 million in all economic scenarios except severe recession, when they receive $700,000, and in that circumstance the unpaid amount of $900,000 million is carried forward to the next dividend payment date. Future returns would not accrue to common stockholders until cumulative dividends owed to preferred shareholders were paid.

Though common stock is the riskiest class of the three classes of claims, the risk is limited on the down side to be no less than zero. That is, even in circumstances where the firm would generate insufficient earnings to meet more senior obligations, equity holders cannot be held personally liable. This is the property of limited liability associated with corporate organizations. Limited liability ensures

Table 3-1

Claims Against the Firm's Cash Flows from Debt, Preferred, and Common Stock ($ million)

	Economic Boom	**Normal Economy**	**Economic Downturn**	**Severe Recession**
EBIT	$15.0	$10.0	$6.0	$4.0
Debt interest	*3.0*	*3.0*	*3.0*	*3.0*
Taxable earnings	12.0	7.0	3.0	1.0
Tax	*3.6*	*2.1*	*0.9*	*0.3*
After-tax earnings	8.4	4.9	2.1	0.7
Preferred dividends	*1.6*	*1.6*	*1.6*	*0.7*
Available to common	6.8	3.3	0.5	0

that investors in the firm's securities will not lose more than the value of their initial investment, and if the firm is forced into bankruptcy, the personal assets of firm's shareholders are not subject to the claims of creditors.

Notice, also, that contractual priority serves not only to define the difference between corporate debt and equity but also to manifest a powerful conflict of interest between the two classes of corporate claimants over the policies and decisions of the firm. With regard to the investment strategy of the firm, it is generally beneficial to debt holders for investments to be less risky, to increase the chances that sufficient returns will be available to meet interest and principal payments to debt holders. As it turns out, this is precisely the case in Table 3-1, as, under all economic scenarios, earnings are more than sufficient to meet obligations to bondholders. The interests of equity holders, the most junior claimholders against the firm's assets, are enhanced by riskier investments because riskier investments generally increase potential up side residual earnings, while on the downside, equity holders are still protected by limited liability.

To see this more clearly, reconsider the example outlined in Table 3-1. Let the value of EBIT under conditions of economic boom increase by $3 million and the value of EBIT under severe recession decrease by $3 million. Let EBIT under the other two economic outcomes remain unchanged. This increases the variability, or risk, of the firm's earnings. This clearly works against debt holders and preferred shareholders while helping common shareholders. Debt holders who formerly would stand to receive full payment of $3 million in *all four* states of the economy now stand to receive only $1 million in a severe recession. Additionally, preferred shareholders who formerly would receive $700,000 in a severe recession stand to receive nothing in the higher-risk scenario. Notice also that because both debt holders and preferred stockholders already stand to receive full payment in an economic boom there is no benefit to them as EBIT increases from $15 million to $18 million. On the other hand, equity holders will be no worse off under a severe recession, receiving nothing in either risk scenario. Equityholders receive $2.1 million *more* in an economic boom as a result of the increased risk.

As owners of the firm, common shareholders enjoy certain rights not generally enjoyed by other security holders. In particular, common shareholders generally have the right to vote on matters of corporate policy and management. Voting rights also enable shareholders to participate in the election of the board of directors of the firm. Even though most common stock issues entitle the shareholders to vote, there are some issues of common stock that do not carry voting rights. In fact, some firms issue two classes of common stock. Class A stock refers to common stock that carries voting rights. Class B stock refers to nonvoting stock. Generally, the incentive for a firm to issue Class B stock is to keep control of the firm in the hands of existing shareholders. Class B stock issued to new shareholders does not dilute the voting power of old shareholders. On the other hand, the value of Class B stock is normally lower than the price of Class A stock. The difference in the price of the two can be viewed as the value of control associated with voting rights. Thus, while firms issuing Class B stock avoid diluting the control of existing shareholders, they receive less money for the shares. In effect, new shareholders "discount" the price they are willing to pay for Class B stock by the value of voting rights.[3]

Equity and the Capital Acquisition Process

The appropriate balance of debt and equity in funding capital investments has been a topic of considerable study and debate in finance for decades. Early theories espoused the idea of an optimal capital structure in which the average cost of capital raised from debt and equity is minimized. This view emphasized the tradeoff between the tax advantage of debt finance on the one hand and the costs of financial distress associated with debt on the other. The tax deductibility of interest affords debt finance a natural advantage over equity, which implies that debt should be the preferred alternative with which to finance investment. However, as leverage increases and the firm's interest obligations increase, it becomes more prone to financial distress or bankruptcy. If there are real costs associated with liquidating the firm, such as lawyers' fees and other real liquidation costs, the firm may reach a point where further increases in leverage will increase the expected financing cost of the firm. The tradeoff between the tax benefit of interest deductions and the cost of financial distress implies that at some level of debt an optimum is reached.

The relative importance of debt and equity in financing corporate investment has changed steadily over the past several decades. A recent study of the funding sources for U.S. nonfinancial corporations during the period 1952 to 1988 showed a rather striking trend in the relative use of debt and equity as sources of finance. During that period, the proportion of funds raised from loans, corporate bonds, and notes increased from 19.1 percent of total funding in 1952, to 33.3 percent of total funding in 1988. Over the same time period, the proportion of total funding raised through common stock steadily decreased, from 7.1 percent in 1952, to *negative* 14.7 percent in 1988. These results indicate two things: (1) equity as a source of corporate funding has decreased significantly over the 36 years from 1952 to 1988, and (2) by 1988, nonfinancial corporations were actually decreasing equity (i.e., retiring more equity than they were issuing).[4]

The tax advantage of debt finance has often been emphasized as an important reason for the long-term increase in corporate leverage observed above. At the same time, however, economists point to several other factors that contribute to the increased use of debt finance, particularly during the 1980s. One source of the increase in debt finance came from the proliferation of leveraged mergers and acquisitions for which the 1980s are particularly well-known. A firm seeking to take over another firm would

---

[3]Because most shareholders do not attend shareholder meetings to exercise their voting rights by casting their votes, it can be argued that most shareholders attach little value to voting shares, which accounts for the normally small difference between the prices of Class A and Class B stock for dual class firms. In fact, voting rights are often delegated to management or another voting shareholder through a proxy, which is a legal transfer of voting rights by voting shareholders. Often, management solicits the proxies of voting shareholders to try to ensure the outcome of important votes. If an opposing group of shareholders solicits the same proxies, the result is called a *proxy fight.* Management generally has a clear advantage in such situations, since it is often the case that shareholders fail to return their proxies. When proxies are not returned, their votes usually revert to management.

[4]See Kopke and Rosengren (1990) for a more complete discussion.

Figure 3-1

Net Equity Issuance by U.S. Corporations. *Source: Board of Governors of the Federal Reserve System. Flow of funds data: Federal Reserve Bank of New York staff estimates. Reprinted from Remolona et. al., "Corporate Refinancing in the 1990s," Federal Reserve Bank of New York* Quarterly Review, *Winter 1992–1993.*

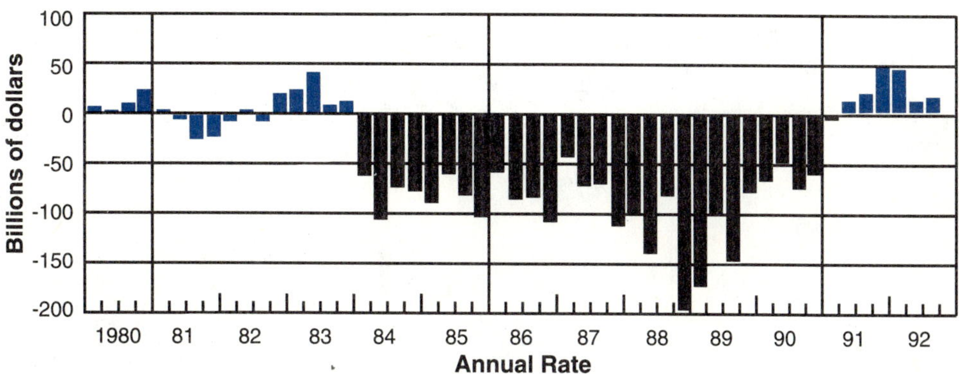

often go to the debt markets to raise cash to buy up target stock. In many instances the acquiring firm would issue junk bonds to finance the acquisition. Leveraged buyouts (LBOs) and management buyouts (MBOs) were common transactions during the same period. In these deals, a small group of persons generally issues a large amount of debt to purchase the shares of the company. Between 1984 and 1990, more than 18,000 U.S. nonfinancial corporations underwent LBOs. The dollar value of equity purchased in these deals exceeded $250 billion, of which $165 billion (about two thirds) was replaced with debt.[5] Another important cause of the increase of debt relative to equity was the attempt by firms to resist takeover attempts from potential acquirers. In these transactions, sometimes called "defensive repurchases," a firm would issue debt and use the proceeds to repurchase its own shares, making it more difficult for a potential acquirer to obtain a controlling interest in the firm.[6]

Figures 3-1 and 3-2 provide additional perspective on this issue. Figure 3-1 shows the net equity issued by nonfinancial corporations from 1980 through 1992. Notice that from about 1984 through 1990 the volume of net equity issued was negative. This demonstrates that equity retired during that period was greater than equity issued. Figure 3-2 breaks down the net issuance of equity into four parts: gross issuance of equity, stock repurchases, LBOs, and other mergers and acquisitions. Gross issuance involves an increase in the quantity of equity outstanding, the other three categories of transactions involve retirement of equity. Added together, all four categories of equity transactions give the total net equity issuance documented in Figure 3-2.

[5]See Remolona, et. al, (1992).

[6]Additionally, product developments contributed to increases in corporate leverage. Innnovations in bond markets, contingent debt instruments, the growth of the high-yield bond market, and other developments in financial markets during the 1980s contributed to the greater reliance on debt as a more important form of finance. In particular, the development of interest rate options, swaps, and futures markets made the management of financial risks associated with debt instruments possible. We take these up in some detail in later chapters.

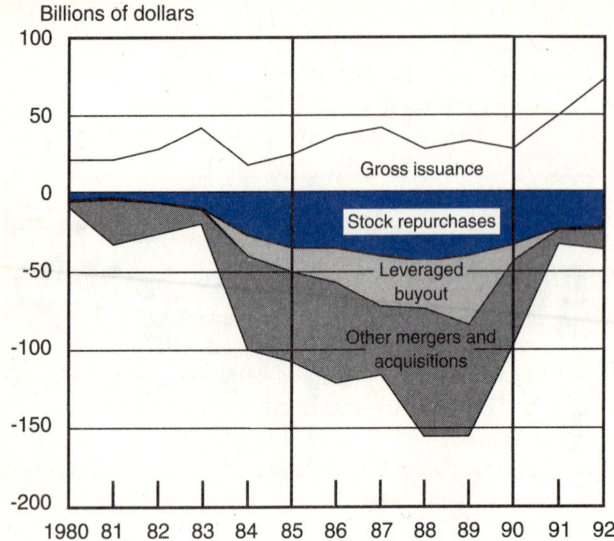

Figure 3-2
Components of Net Equity Issuance by U.S. Nonfinancial Corporations. *Sources: Margaret Pickering, "A Review of Corporate Restructuring Activity, 1980-90," Board of Governors of the Federal Reserve System, Staff Study no. 161, May 1991, Board of Governors of the Federal Reserve System. Reprinted from Remolona et. al., "Corporate Refinancing in the 1990s," Federal Reserve Bank of New York* Quarterly Review, *Winter 1992–1993.*

Figures 3-1 and 3-2 also indicate that net equity issued has rebounded during more recent years, becoming positive during 1991 and 1992. This coincides with the dramatic decrease in LBOs and other mergers and acquisitions. By 1992, LBO activity was almost nil and other takeover and merger activity was less than one fifth that during its heyday of 1988–1989. The increase in net equity issuance is also connected to the economic slowdown and recession that set in during the late 1980s. During the recent recession, heavily leveraged firms have found it necessary to trim back the debt levels and the higher interest burdens built up during the mid-1980s. Equity issues have been used to a large extent to refinance bank debt, corporate bonds, and notes.

While the role of equity finance in funding capital expenditures has changed over time, there has been a fundamental shift in the importance of corporate equities among investors as well. That is, direct investment in corporate equity by individual investors has decreased as a proportion of total assets over the past three decades. Over the same period the proportional investment by institutional investors in equities has increased. Figure 3-3 shows the composition of investment by U.S. households in equities, deposits and open market paper (debt), and life insurance and pension reserves from 1952 to 1988. Notice that in 1952 equity accounted for almost 60 percent of total financial assets of U.S. households. By 1987 that proportion had fallen to less than 40 percent of total financial assets. At the same time, the proportion of financial assets represented by debt and life insurance and pension reserves increased substantially.

The trend of decreasing *direct* investment by individual investors in equity markets identified in Figure 3-3 has been documented extensively in recent years. Individual investors increasingly have relied on financial institutions such as mutual funds as a form of *indirect* investment in equity markets. Figure 3-4 shows corporate equity as a percentage of total assets for pension funds, government retirement funds, and life insurance companies over the period 1952–1987. The figure shows that proportional investment in equity by total institutional investors has steadily increased over the period. In particular, the proportion of private pension fund assets invested in equity securities increased from less than 20 percent in 1952 to almost 50 percent in 1987. This clearly reflects the withdrawal of individual investors from U.S. equity markets and the growing importance of institutional investors.

The Primary Market for Equities

As we first explained in Chapter 1, the primary market for equity securities is the market in which new issues of securities are sold and the secondary market is the market in which existing securities are traded. The primary markets depend in an important way on the existence of an active secondary market. Secondary markets provide liquidity to investors who buy assets in the primary market. *Liquidity* is the ability to sell an asset or convert the asset to cash without losing value. A liquid asset is one that can be sold quickly, without absorbing a significant price decrease or transactions cost.

The distinction between primary and secondary markets and the notion of liquidity is apparent in many markets, including markets for real assets and consumer

Figure 3-3

Assets Held by Households. *Sources: Board of Governors of the Federal Reserve System, Flow of Funds Macro Data Library. Kopke/Rosengren, "Are the Distinctions Between Debt and Equity Disappearing?" Federal Reserve Bank of Boston,* New England Economic Review, *March/April 1990.*

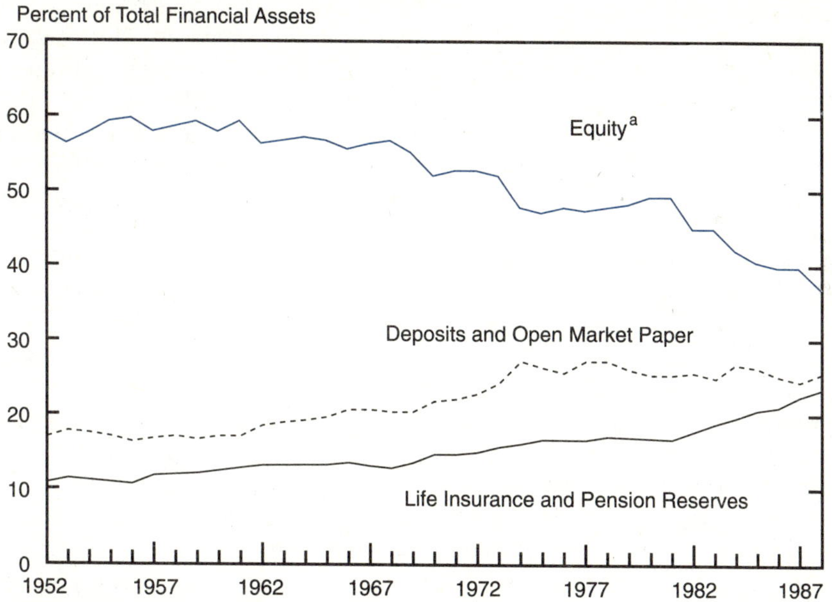

[a]Equity: sum of corporate equities held by households and equity in noncorporate business held by households less credit market instruments held by open-end investment companies (mutual funds).

Figure 3-4

Institutional Holdings of Corporate Equity. *Sources: Board of Governors of the Federal Reserve System, Flow of Funds Macro Data Library. Kopke/Rosengren, "Are the Distinctions Between Debt and Equity Disappearing?" Federal Reserve Bank of Boston,* New England Economic Review, *March/April 1990.*

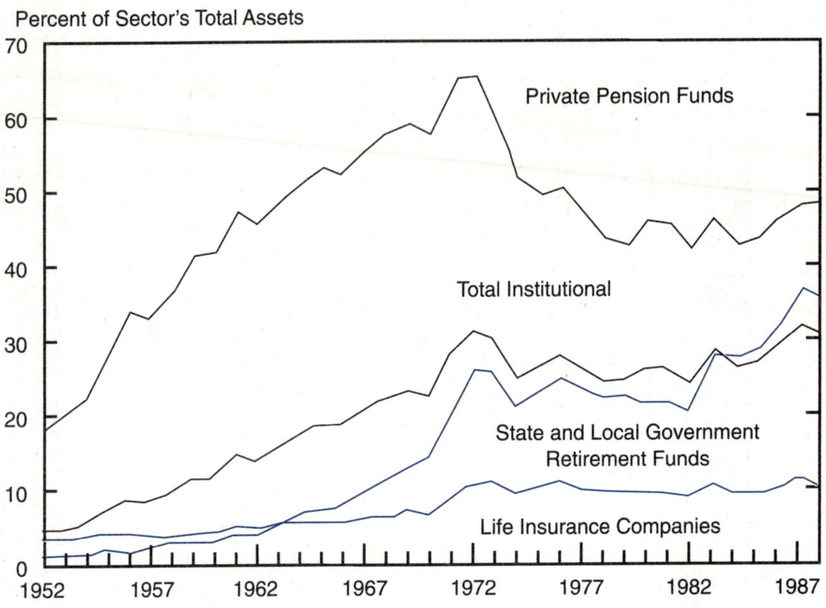

products. A useful example is the market for automobiles. The new car market is an example of a primary market, that is, the market in which automobiles are purchased for the first time. The used car market is a secondary market for automobiles that provides a source of liquidity to the automobile market. If the owner of an automobile needs to convert his or her investment in an automobile into cash, either to buy another car or to make another expenditure, the owner can sell the car to a used car dealer or directly to a new owner. When buying a new car, many buyers trade in their old car, receiving credit for the value of the trade-in toward the new car purchase price. Thus, new car dealers help "make" the secondary market for used cars by taking trade-ins and reselling those cars to other buyers.

The importance of the secondary market and the liquidity provided to the primary market for automobiles is clear if you first imagine there were no secondary market for used cars—no opportunities to resell newly purchased cars. Original buyers would be more reluctant to purchase a new car if they knew that there would be no opportunity to sell it later on. This would obviously have a detrimental effect on the volume of original new car sales. An active and liquid secondary market ensures that if the buyer decides a different car is more suitable later on, the value of the existing automobile can be recovered with a minimal loss and another new car can be purchased. The same principle applies in security markets. When an active secondary market exists for a security, the sale of original issues is enhanced. Investors know that if cash is needed later on their investment can be resold for cash in the secondary market. Thus, the operation of a secondary market provides liquidity to the securities market, which is often necessary to generate demand for primary sales.

In the primary market there are two different types of offerings: public offerings and private placements. In a public offering, the issue is sold to the general public. In a private placement, the issue is sold to a specific investor or group of investors. Private placements are generally arranged to protect the interests of existing security holders, in particular by protecting private information and avoiding public disclosure associated with public offerings. Public placements are regulated by the Securities and Exchange Commission (SEC), which imposes registration requirements and mandates disclosure of information to public investors. The cost associated with SEC compliance is also cited when private placement is sometimes chosen over public offering to bring a new issue to the market.

The Role of Investment Banks

Under most circumstances, new issues of equity securities are organized with the help of an investment bank. The investment bank is involved in a number of activities required in the process of a new issue: advisory services, distribution services, and underwriting services.

Investment banks offer a variety of advisory services to the issuing firm. In a public issue, in its advisory role the investment bank provides needed assistance in meeting SEC requirements for registering the issue and preparing the necessary materials to satisfy public disclosure rules. One such requirement is the prospectus, the document that officially offers the securities for sale. It also provides required information to potential investors, including a business plan, the current financial condition of the issuing firm, and details about the firm's officers and ownership. The prospectus is the major instrument of public disclosure required by the SEC to inform investors about the impending issue. One of the advantages of employing the advisory services of an investment bank is that investment bankers are experienced in the preparation of materials to satisfy public disclosure requirements. An error in or omission of important information from the prospectus could lead to a lawsuit against the firm and its management by new security holders.

Another advisory function of the investment bank is to determine the price at which the new issue should be sold. This price is generally referred to as the *offer price*. The investment bank has experience in assessing the condition of the equity market and determining the demand for the issuing firm's securities. The objective of the investment bank is to set the price as high as possible while still allowing the issue to be sold in an acceptable period of time. The investment bank sets the offer price slightly below the market price (say, about 0.5 percent) to ensure the issue will be placed within a reasonable period. The price concession given by the issuer is apparent when the issuer already has publicly traded securities outstanding and the market price can be readily observed. When a firm's stock has not previously been publicly traded it is more difficult to determine the market value of the issue and what the appropriate offer price should be. We discuss this problem more carefully later, in the section on initial public offerings.

Investment banks are also involved in the process of placing the securities with investors. This is the service known as distribution of the securities. Generally, the issuing firm organizes its issue through one or two lead investment banks. Depending on the size of the issue, the lead bank will organize a group of other investment banks to participate in the distribution of the issue. The group is generally referred to as a *syndicate.* Members of the syndicate are mostly other large investment banks that deal regularly with each other and with a number of smaller investment firms that ultimately broker the securities to investors. The network in this process can be quite large. Larger issues require a larger distribution network to distribute securities to final buyers. Syndication not only facilitates the placement of securities with a broad-based group of investors but also enables the investment banks involved to diversify the risk associated with underwriting the issue.

An announcement in the *Wall Street Journal* (May 24, 1993) of an issue of common stock by Titan Wheel International, Inc. provides an example of an underwritten issue distributed through a syndicate of investment banks. The announcement, commonly called a *tombstone,* is shown in Figure 3-5. The tombstone is essentially an advertisement and not an offer to sell securities. The announcement gives information about the size of the issue (2.7 million shares), the offer price ($15 per share), and the syndicate of investment banks involved in the distribution. In this case, there are two lead banks in the syndicate: Smith Barney, Harris Upham & Co., Inc., and Paine Webber, Inc. Other members of the syndicate are listed below the two lead banks.

The process of underwriting a new issue is another important service provided by investment banks for bringing new issues to the market. Underwriting is one of two ways in which an issue may be distributed to investors. When an issue is *underwritten* by the investment bank, the bank essentially buys the issue from the issuing firm and attempts to resell it at a profit. This method of placement transfers the price risk associated with the issue from the issuing firm to the underwriting investment bank. The issuing firm receives a *firm commitment* from the investment bank for its securities. This represents a guarantee that the investment bank and its syndicate will buy the entire issue at one price, the *bid price.* The bank then attempts to sell the securities at a higher price, the *offer price,* through its distribution network. The difference between the bid price and the offer price is called the *underwriter's spread.* The spread compensates the underwriter for bearing the price risk associated with reselling the issue. The size of the spread depends on the size of the issue, the risk of price fluctuations, market conditions, and other factors that affect demand for the securities. The other method of placement involved in investment banking relationships is called a *best efforts basis.* Under the best efforts method of placement the issuing firm retains the price risk associated with selling the securities. The investment bank attempts to sell the securities at the best price available in the market. By the best efforts arrangement the bank receives compensation in the form of a fee. The bank's incentive to find the best available price is the prospect for return business and its reputation in the investment banking community.

Figure 3-5

A "Tombstone" Announcement. *Source:* Wall Street Journal, *May 24, 1993. Reprinted with permission of* The Wall Street Journal, *© 1993 Dow Jones and Company, Inc. All Right Reserved Worldwide.*

This announcement constitutes neither an offer to sell nor a solicitation of an offer to buy these securities. The offering is made only by the Prospectus, copies of which may be obtained in any State from such of the undersigned and others as may lawfully offer these securities in such State.

May 24, 1993

2,700,000 Shares

Common Stock

Price $15 per Share

Smith Barney, Harris Upham & Co. Incorporated
PaineWebber Incorporated

Bear, Stearns & Co. Inc.
The First Boston Corporation
Alex. Brown & Sons Incorporated
Dillon, Read & Co. Inc.
Donaldson, Lufkin & Jenrette Securities Corporation
A.G. Edwards & Sons, Inc.
Kidder, Peabody & Co. Incorporated
Lehman Brothers
Morgan Stanley & Co. Incorporated
Oppenheimer & Co., Inc.
Prudential Securities Incorporated
Salomon Brothers Inc
Wertheim Schroder & Co. Incorporated
Dean Witter Reynolds Inc.
Dain Bosworth Incorporated
Kemper Securities, Inc.
Legg Mason Wood Walker Incorporated
Piper Jaffray Inc.
The Robinson-Humphrey Company, Inc.
Wheat First Butcher & Singer Capital Markets
Robert W. Baird & Co. Incorporated
The Chicago Corporation
First of Michigan Corporation
McDonald & Company Securities, Inc.
The Ohio Company
Stifel, Nicolaus & Company Incorporated
Cleary Gull Reiland & McDevitt Inc.
Roney & Co.

Initial Public Offerings

Initial public offerings (IPOs) are offerings of securities that are made for the first time. Primary equity offerings by established public companies are not usually IPOs since these firms have issued stock before. IPOs generally involve smaller firms that have grown to the point that they are unable to sustain their growth with internal capital and must finance further growth through the external capital market. In many cases IPOs are organized in conjunction with venture capital financing of new firms.

Table 3-2 documents the volume of IPOs during the period 1978–1988. Notice the bulk of the IPO activity occurred during the last three years of that period, when more than $70 billion of IPOs were issued. Of that volume, about half involved industrial companies and half financial firms. Also during that period, Table 3-2 shows that most of the industrial IPOs involved manufacturing companies (about $10.5 billion), followed by service companies (about $9 billion). Activity in IPOs tends to fluctuate with market conditions, which dictate optimal timing of a public offering. There were two periods during the 1980s when IPO activity was high, as indicated by the number of new issues: from 1980 to 1983, and during 1986 and 1987.

One of the more interesting aspects of IPOs is the fact that issuers and investment banks involved in setting the offer price cannot observe the market price of the firm's equity because it was not previously traded in the market.[7] It is widely accepted that IPOs are underpriced: the offer price is set significantly below the market value of the issue. For example, if the underwriter's bid for a new issue is $12.00 per share and the offer price is $12.25, the underwriter's spread is 25 cents per share. Again, the spread itself represents no underpricing, but fair compensation to the underwriter for bearing the price risk associated with the issue. If, however, the issue trades at $14.00 shortly after it is sold, the issue has been underpriced by $1.75 per share. The conclusion of many economists that IPOs are underpriced at the initial offering is based on considerable empirical evidence that IPO prices at the initial offering are anywhere from 5.6 percent to 48.4 percent lower, on average, than the market price one week after the offering.

Several reasons for this apparent underpricing have been cited in the academic literature. One is that investment banks enjoy some monopoly power in the securities business. Proponents argue that lack of competition from other banks allows the underwriting firm to set the offer price low, to minimize the underwriting risk it bears. They blame regulations that prohibit commercial banks from underwriting equity securities (the Glass-Steagall Act, discussed in Chapter 6) for leaving the

---

[7]An exception is a reverse LBO. An LBO is used to buy publicly traded shares of a company. Once publicly traded shares are purchased in the LBO the firm becomes a private company. LBOs are often used by an investor or group of investors to gain control of the firm in order in reorganize management and/or institute changes in policy or in the business strategy of the firm. Once these investors implement their intended changes, they sometimes "reverse" the LBO by reissuing publicly traded securities. In this case, both the firm and the lead investment bank have access to the price history of the firm's stock during the pre-LBO period. This information can be of some use in determining the offer price of the new public issue, even though the LBO likely has caused changes in the business and financial structure of the firm that will have an important impact on how the market receives the new public issue.

Table 3-2

Initial Public Equity Offerings, 1978 to 1988[a]

Breakdown for Industrial Companies

	Total[b]	Industrial Companies	Financial Companies[c]	Utilities	Manufacturing	Services	Retail Trade	Natural Resources	Other[d]
A. Number of issues									
1978	18	16	1	1	13	0	1	0	2
1979	61	46	13	2	29	9	1	5	2
1980	152	134	18	0	63	29	3	34	5
1981	355	336	17	2	145	117	7	51	16
1982	124	112	12	0	50	53	1	2	6
1983	687	583	104	0	243	234	46	4	56
1984	354	295	57	2	132	120	15	2	26
1985	360	272	87	1	100	112	28	8	24
1986	721	498	222	1	188	217	51	6	36
1987	551	407	142	2	165	162	43	12	25
1988	279	165	109	3	73	54	17	7	14
Total	3662	2864	782	14	1201	1107	213	131	212
B. Billions of dollars									
1978	.214	.154	.010	.050	.093	0	.026	0	.035
1979	.408	.283	.076	.049	.170	.068	.003	.022	.020
1980	1.404	1.165	.239	0	.662	.139	.018	.295	.050
1981	3.180	2.952	.215	.013	1.199	1.103	.028	.463	.160
1982	1.351	1.088	.263	0	.566	.474	.004	.004	.041
1983	12.499	9.449	3.049	0	4.773	2.724	.948	.129	.875
1984	3.892	2.750	.859	.283	1.322	.970	.146	.118	.194
1985	8.650	4.053	4.564	.034	1.110	1.125	.647	.896	.274
1986	22.461	11.487	10.654	.320	4.218	5.279	1.000	.437	.553
1987	24.191	11.674	12.409	.108	4.495	3.163	.955	1.014	2.047
1988	23.749	4.599	18.875	.252	1.993	.885	.225	.746	.750
Total	101.999	49.655	51.213	1.108	20.602	15.931	4.001	4.123	4.999

[a]Firm commitment offerings only.

[b]Includes limited partnerships. Government agencies (two issues valued at $22 million in 1988) are included in the total but are not included in any other category.

[c]Includes closed-end funds.

[d]Includes hospitals and health care (111 issues valued at $1.351 billion from 1978 to 1988), transportation (66 issued values at $884 million), unregulated phone (21 issues valued at $951 million), and railroads and shipping (14 issues valued at $1.813 billion.)

Sources: IDD Information Services. Y.K. Henderson, "The Emergence of the Venture Capital Industry" Federal Reserve Bank of Boston, *New England Economic Review,* July/August 1989.

investment banking industry with insufficient competition to ensure that the offer price is competitively set.

The second reason often cited for underpricing of IPOs is that the underwriter builds in some protection against lawsuits that might be brought against it for overpricing the issue. This argument essentially says that the bank sets the price low to keep investors in the issue happy. An investor who buys an issue that is overpriced might sue the underwriting firm for not exercising due diligence in determining the initial offer price.

Yet another reason why IPOs may be underpriced is based on the assumption that there are two types of investors—informed investors and uninformed investors. According to this view, underpricing occurs because both good and bad securities are being issued at the same time. Informed investors invest only in good securities, whereas uninformed investors cannot distinguish good from bad. Thus, when a good issue comes along, both types of investors buy the securities, making it likely that the issue will be oversubscribed. This implies that both types of investors may receive only part of their intended allotment of securities. When a bad issue comes to the market, informed investors do not buy, uniformed investors buy and are more likely to receive their full allotment of (bad) securities. This outcome is commonly referred to as the "winner's curse." Uninformed investors receive their full allotment of securities only when the securities are bad. This could cause uninformed investors to exit the market and cause the issue to be undersubscribed. Some economists argue that IPOs are deliberately underpriced to provide incentives for uninformed investors to buy securities and to overcome the destructive incentive effect of the winner's curse.

Venture Capital Markets

Venture capital is another important source of equity financing for small businesses. Traditionally, small businesses have been financed in their early stages of growth through funding from the firm's founders and friends. Later, the firm might turn to bank funding or public capital markets to support additional growth. Venture capital refers to another form of equity funding. Typically, venture capital is provided by investors who take a more active role in the management of relatively new firms. Once a new firm reaches the point where internal sources of capital are exhausted, venture capital is often obtained to finance the next stage of growth. At the same time, the venture capitalist often specializes in the development of small businesses in particular industries and can also provide valuable management expertise and advice.

Venture capital investors generally provide investment capital in stages. That is, rather than making one lump-sum investment, capital is committed as the firm successfully reaches succeeding stages of expansion. For example, suppose a venture capitalist is sought to help finance an expansion project for a small manufacturing firm. An amount of $10 million is needed to fund the project, which will be developed over a period of 4 years. During the first six months the venture capitalist may commit $1 million toward the development of a business plan, product and market research, and establishing a management team. Once the first stage is complete, venture capital would be committed over the following year for the next stage of development, say $2 million for the development of a new pilot plant or prototype. If development during the first two stages is successful, an additional $7 million might be invested over the remaining 2 1/2 years for permanent production facilities. In effect, the total $10 million venture capital investment would occur in three stages. This affords venture capital investors some degree of protection against down side risk because they have the option to terminate the investment before the full $10 million is committed, if, for instance, project development went poorly during the earlier stages.

Venture capital investors generally retain substantial control over management decisions and some degree of ownership in the firm. In many cases, venture capitalists receive convertible preferred stock in return for their investment. Convertible preferred provides investors priority of claim over common stockholders in the event the firm becomes insolvent. At the same time, the conversion feature allows investors to participate in large gains associated with a successful firm. If the firm does well, the venture capital investors can convert their preferred stock to common stock and share in the appreciation of the firm's equity. When venture capital is raised in the form of debt, the venture capitalist usually receives some form of option to convert debt into equity.

Venture capital investment generally takes one of three organizational forms. Figure 3-6 shows the growth in venture capital financing provided by each type of investor over the period from 1977 to 1988.[8] Private independent venture capital funds are the largest and fastest growing providers of venture capital, followed by corporate subsidiaries, and small business investment companies. During 1988 more than 800 private independent venture capital funds provided more than $25 billion of the total of nearly $32 billion in venture capital raised from these three major sources.[9] Of the total amount of funding provided through independent funds, about 67 percent was raised from financial intermediaries such as private pension funds, insurance companies, and private endowments and foundations. The other 33 percent originated from individual investors, corporations, and various sources of foreign capital. Individual funds commonly manage around $50 to $60 million in venture capital investments, though some of the larger funds manage in excess of $500 million.

Corporate subsidiaries specializing in venture capital investments were an important source of venture capital finance during the late 1970s, but their relative importance has diminished (Figure 3-4). During 1988, subsidiaries accounted for about $5 billion in venture capital funding, about 16 percent of the total. Major financial corporations like large commercial banks and insurance companies operate venture capital subsidiaries primarily to diversify their business activities; however, these subsidiaries also help provide information about industries and technologies that can benefit other operations, such as commercial lending or business risk underwriting. A bank, for example, could develop expertise in a particular emerging technology through its venture capital activities. This knowledge could provide the understanding of the industry necessary to identify better quality commercial clients for other bank services such as lending.

Small Business Investment Companies (SBICs), authorized under the Small Business Investment Company Act of 1958, are often organized as subsidiaries of financial institutions. The major benefit enjoyed by this form of venture capital enterprise is the ability to borrow from the Small Business Administration. The reliance on debt finance to fund venture capital investments makes these organizations unique

---

[8]See the article by Henderson (1989) for an in depth discussion of the venture capital process and the development of venture capital firms.

[9]These figures omit venture capital contributed by large corporations not operating through a venture subsidiary and individual investors.

Figure 3-6

Venture Capital Pool. *Source: Poterba (1988), Ventura Economics, Inc. and* Economic Report of the President, *1989. Y.K. Henderson, "The Emergence of the Venture Capital Industry" Federal Reserve Bank of Boston,* New England Economic Review, *July/August 1989.*

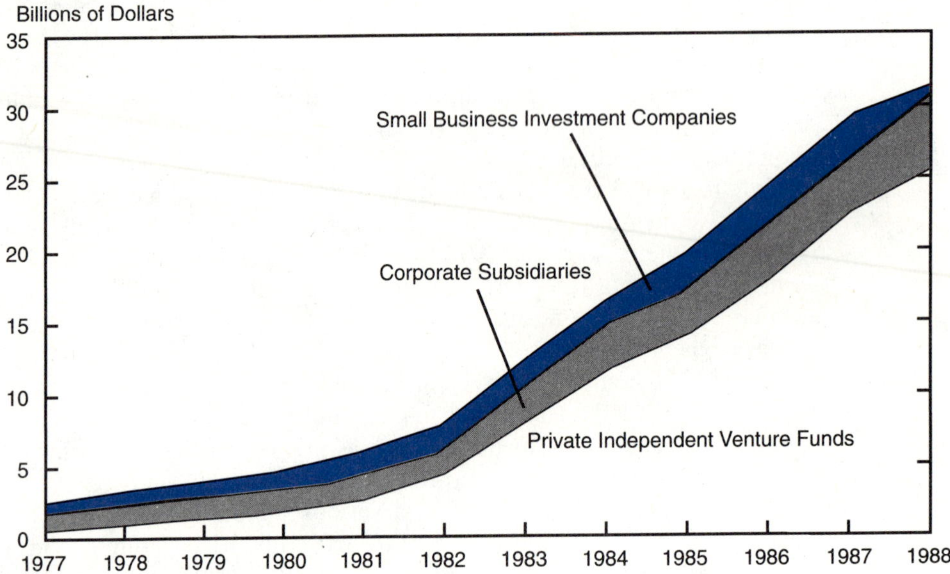

among venture capital firms, which generally rely on equity funding. The dependence of SBICs on the federal budget for funding in many cases, and the effect of changes in government policies toward small business development, has caused the importance of these organizations to fluctuate over time and generally diminish as compared to independent funds and corporate subsidiaries.

Secondary Markets for Equity

The secondary market for U.S. equity securities encompasses a number of systems and facilities that permit trading in equity securities. Trades in the secondary market represent a different kind of transaction from the original issue of securities accomplished in the primary market. The primary market is the market for new issues. Once new issues are sold to investors, subsequent trades in those issues are secondary transactions. Generally, the secondary market includes four categories of trading:

1. The *first market,* is trading of exchange-listed issues though an exchange.
2. The *second market* is trading in the over-the-counter market.
3. The *third market* is brokered trading in exchange-listed issues that takes place off the exchange.
4. The *fourth market* is trading in exchange-listed issues that takes place off the exchange and without the involvement of a broker.

Organized Stock Exchanges

Probably the most visible and familiar facilities in the market for equities are the New York Stock Exchange (NYSE) and the American Stock Exchange (AMEX). Often referred to as "national exchanges," these institutions are responsible for most of the secondary transactions of equity securities of the largest U.S. companies. There are also a number of regional exchanges, which originally evolved to trade securities of companies that operated primarily in one region of the country. Major regional exchanges in the United States include the Midwest Stock Exchange in Chicago, the Philadelphia Stock Exchange, and the Pacific Stock Exchange, which has trading facilities in Los Angeles and San Francisco.

An *exchange* is a facility for trading assets, commodities, or financial contracts. The primary purpose of the exchange is to bring together offers to buy and sell in a central location. Centralization of orders increases the opportunity to locate compatible (matching) offers to buy and sell and decreases search costs for market participants. The greater the flow of orders to buy and sell to the exchange, the more likely it is that matching orders to buy and sell will arrive within a reasonable period of time. If an exchange is to be an efficient alternative to the process of direct search, in which buyers and sellers attempt to locate each other directly, sufficient order flow is necessary.

The organization and microstructure of the various U.S. stock exchanges are quite similar, though differences do exist. In this chapter we concentrate on the NYSE, partly because it is the largest and most important stock exchange in the United States, and because its organization fairly describes that of other major U.S. stock exchanges. The NYSE is actually a corporation that is owned by a group of *members*. Members of the NYSE are either individuals or member firms who own *seats* on the exchange. The exchange is governed by a board of directors much as any other corporation is. Ownership of a seat on the exchange entitles a member to conduct business on the floor of the exchange. Seats on the exchange can be bought, sold, or leased by individuals or firms. The value of a seat reflects the value of trading privileges on the floor. Though the NYSE trades primarily common stock, preferred stock, warrants, and American Depository Receipts (ADRs) are also traded. Some of the stocks traded over the NYSE are also traded in the over-the-counter (OTC) market. Very few issues are traded over both the NYSE and the AMEX.

In order to have its stock listed for trading on the NYSE, a company must be of sufficient size and quality and must generate sufficient interest among investors to make trading over the exchange economical. The exchange imposes several specific requirements along these lines for a corporation's stock to be listed. As of the end of 1992, they were these:

1. $18 million or more in net tangible assets.
2. 1.1 million or more in publicly held shares.
3. $18 million or more market value of publicly held shares.
4. Two thousand shareholders each owning 100 shares or more.

5. Current pretax earnings of $2.5 million or more.
6. Pretax earnings in previous 2 years of $2 million or more.[10]

Exchange members who operate on the trading floor of the exchange consist of brokers, traders, and specialists. Brokers trade, not for their own account, but on behalf of nonmember clients who want to buy or sell stock. A broker receives orders from outside the exchange and executes those orders for a fee called a "commission." As a result, these participants are often called "commission brokers." Commission brokers are employed by brokerage houses to process orders for their clients. Operating from the borders of the trading floor, commission brokers provide the principal link between the major brokerage firms and the trading floor. There are other brokers, traditionally called "two-dollar brokers," who complement the activities of commission brokers. These members are not employed by the brokerage firms but, for a commission, help execute orders that are too large for commission brokers to execute by themselves. Traders (sometimes called "registered traders") are a general category of members of the exchange who trade for their own accounts. These members can also act as brokers, or even as specialists (discussed below). Generally, however, traders are forbidden to act as agent (broker) *and* principal (trading on their own account) in a given stock on the same day.

Specialists are members who are designated by the exchange to trade in a particular stock or stocks. The specialist is a key participant in the operation of the exchange, because it is his or her responsibility to "make a market" in the assigned security. As a result, the specialist operates as both a broker and a dealer in the stock. As a broker, the specialist serves as the mechanism through which outside orders are matched up. As a dealer, the specialist also trades on his or her own account, within certain restrictions set forth by the exchange.

The specialist maintains what is called the *limit order book.* An understanding of the limit order book is key to understanding the function of the specialist. A limit order is an order to buy or sell stock at a particular price. For example, a limit buy order for 100 shares at $99.50 represents a bid for 100 shares of stock at $99.50 per share. When the specialist receives a limit order he or she records the order in the book. At any point in time the limit order book holds a number of standing orders to buy and sell at different prices. The specialist makes available to potential customers the highest bid and the lowest ask prices in the book. Other prices in the specialist's book are not publicly available. For example, the specialist may have orders to buy at $99, $99.50, and $100 and orders to sell at $101, $101.50, and $102. The specialist reveals the bid of $100 and the ask of $101 to potential customers.[11] As market orders arrive, these prices receive first priority in filling orders. In order

[10]A company can delist its stock from the NYSE if three basic conditions are met: (1) owners of 67% of the firm's shares vote to delist; (2) no more than 10% of owners vote against delisting; (3) delisting is approved by more than half the firm's board of directors.

[11]Access to the limit order book provides a significant trading advantage to the specialist. By knowing the volume of limit buy orders at various prices, the specialist has an advantage in determining the potential for a decrease in the market price (large buy orders provide resistance to decreases in the price). In addition, knowlege of standing sell orders provides information about the potential for increases in the price. This gives the specialist an advantage in structuring his or her inventory in anticipation of a price change.

for the specialist to trade on his or her own account, he or she must buy or sell within the spread, $100 to $101. That is, the specialist must bid (buy) at a price higher than $100 and offer (sell) at a price lower than $101.[12]

As a broker, the specialist receives a commission for executing compatible trades. An incoming order to sell at $100 is crossed with the $100 limit buy order in the book and the specialist receives a fee, usually around 2 cents per share. As a dealer, the specialist quotes her own bid and ask prices and profits from the spread. For example, the specialist might bid at $99 and ask at $101.50. For the most part, the specialist acts as a broker in facilitating trades of brokers. Fewer than 25 percent of all trades over the NYSE represent specialists trading on their own accounts.

In additon to certain restrictions imposed to ensure priority of public orders, the exchange imposes other responsibilities on the specialist. Chief among these is the obligation to make a fair and orderly market in their assigned stock. If new orders are not forthcoming to accomodate outstanding orders in the book the specialist has the obligation to trade. The specialist also has the obligation to stabilize prices. This means the specialist is expected to buy into a falling market and sell into a rising market in order to moderate large swings in the price. Finally, the specialist is expected to provide "price continuity." Continuity implies there are not large differences between bids and asks. If, for example, there were a large difference between the highest bid and the lowest ask price in the limit order book, the specialist would establish his or her own bid and ask prices within that range to narrow the gap. This would encourage trading in the stock and provide greater liquidity for investors.

The specialist occupies a particular location on the floor of the exchange called the "specialist's post." Orders received at the exchange are handled in one of two ways. First, if the order involves a small number of shares in an actively traded stock, say 100 shares of General Motors, it is processed electronically through the exchange's SuperDOT (Designated Order Turnaround) System. SuperDOT transmits the order to the specialist electronically and it is executed immediately, without the aid of a commission broker. If the order is large, it is given to the broker for execution, who takes it to the specialist. The broker has some latitude in managing a large order. For example, he may execute the order gradually to get the best price for the client. In particular, free-lance, or two-dollar, brokers have the incentive to get the best execution they can, in order to get future orders.

Once an order is executed the transaction is reported to the customer and to the exchange. The exchange records the transaction by computer and it appears within seconds on the consolidated tape, an electronic record of trades that is sent to subscribers all over the world. The tape consolidates transactions that occur over a number of exchanges. In additon to transactions executed over the NYSE, the consolidated tape reports transactions in NYSE-listed stocks that are executed over other exchanges as well. Once the exchange makes public information on trading it appears in a variety of forms in the financial press. Figure 3-7 shows price and volume information for a selected group of securities traded over the NYSE on 11 Aug 1993, as reported by

---

[12]In addition, exchange rules prohibit the specialist from taking priority over public orders at the same price.

Figure 3-7

Price and Volume Information for a group of securities traded over the NYSE. *Source:* Wall Street Journal, *August 12, 1993. Reprinted with permission of* The Wall Street Journal, *© 1993 Dow Jones and Company, Inc. All Right Reserved Worldwide.*

NEW YORK STOCK EXCHANGE COMPOSITE TRANSACTIONS

Quotations as of 5 p.m. Eastern Time
Wednesday, August 11, 1993

-A-A-A-

	52 Weeks Hi	52 Weeks Lo	Stock	Sym	Div	Yld %	PE	Vol 100s	Hi	Lo	Close	Net Chg
	14⅝	10¾	AAR	AIR	.48	3.6	cc	95	13¾	13½	13½	...
	12	10¾	ACM Gvt Fd	ACG	.96	8.7	...	2173	11¼	11	11	– ¼
	10⅛	9	ACM OppFd	AOF	.80	8.1	...	144	10	9⅞	9⅞	– ⅛
	11⅞	9⅞	ACM SecFd	GSF	.96	8.7	...	1958	11	10¾	11	+ ⅛
	9⅞	8⅝	ACM SpctmFd	SI	.80	8.8	...	683	9¼	9⅛	9⅛	...
	11⅝	9⅜	ACM MgdIncFd	AMF	1.08	9.5	...	919	11½	11¼	11⅜	– ⅛
	11¼	8⅝	ACM MgdMultFd	MMF	.81e	8.8	...	127	9¼	9⅛	9¼	...
n	15⅛	13½	ACM MuniSec	AMU	.90	6.3	...	63	14¼	14	14¼	+ ⅛
	10⅛	6⅜	ADT	ADT		...	...	6058	9⅞	9⅝	9¾	– ¼
	1⅞	⅞	ADT wt			...	...	917	1½	1⅜	1½	– ⅛
s	32⅛	23	AFLAC	AFL	.40	1.3	15	1055	31⅜	30⅞	31⅛	...
	29⅝	13¾	AL Labs A	BMD	.18	1.0	24	424	17½	17¼	17½	...
	65⅞	52¾	AMP	AMP	1.60	2.4	23	799	65⅝	65⅜	65½	– ⅛
	72⅞	54⅜	AMR	AMR		...	dd	4465	66¼	64¾	65	–1¼
	47¼	39¼	ARCO Chm	RCM	2.50	6.2	18	108	40⅝	40½	40⅝	+ ⅛
	2¾	**1⅜**	**ARX**	**ARX**		**...**	**15**	**50**	**2⅜**	**2⅜**	**2⅜**	**– ⅛**
	51½	29¾	ASA	ASA	2.00	4.4	...	515	45¾	45⅜	45½	– ⅝
n	27⅞	23⅛	ATT Cap	TCC		...	...	1772	27¾	27¼	27⅜	+ ⅜
	33	22⅝	AbbotLab	ABT	.68	3.0	15	20303	24⅛	23	23	– ¾
	8	3½	Abex	ABE		...	dd	171	3⅝	3½	3½	...
	13⅜	9⅞	Abitibi g	ABY	.38j	...	...	3	10⅜	10⅜	10⅜	...
s	15	6	AcceptIns	AIF		...	dd	160	14	14	14	...
n	4⅝	2¼	AcceptIns wt			...	...	223	3⅞	3¾	3⅞	+ ⅛
n	33	25½	ACE Ltd	ACL	.20e	.6	...	712	32⅜	32⅛	32⅜	+ ⅛
	12⅜	6¼	AcmeCleve	AMT	.44f	4.0	15	417	11⅜	11	11⅛	+ ¼
	9¼	3¾	AcmeElec	ACE		...	dd	26	7½	7½	7½	– ⅛
n	24⅞	15⅛	Acordia	ACO	.29e	1.2	...	668	24⅝	24⅛	24⅝	– ⅛
	14½	7⅞	ActavaGp	ACT	.36	4.4	27	128	8⅜	8⅛	8¼	...
	18¾	10⅜	Acuson	ACN		...	33	531	11⅞	11⅝	11⅞	+ ⅛
	22¼	18⅝	AdamsExp	ADX	1.62e	8.0	...	110	20¼	20⅛	20⅛	...
	32⅞	8⅜	AdvMicro	AMD		...	12	18924	30¼	29¼	29⅝	+1¼
	66	34¾	AdvMicro pf		3.00	4.9	...	587	62	60½	61¾	+1⅞
	7¾	4⅞	Advest	ADV		...	11	284	6½	6¼	6⅜	+ ⅛
s	24¾	16¼	Advo	AD	.04e	.2	17	86	16⅝	16¼	16¼	– ¼
	49⅜	36¾	Aegon	AEG	2.15e	4.6	...	25	46⅞	46⅞	46⅞	+ ⅛
	60	37¼	AetnaLife	AET	2.76	4.7	22	3930	59⅛	58⅛	58⅝	– ⅝
	14½	10	AffilPub	AFP	.26	1.8	31	4965	14⅜	14¼	14⅜	...
	25⅜	20⅝	AgriMinl	AMC	2.42	9.7	10	139	25	24½	24⅞	– ⅛
	22⅛	13	Ahmanson	AHM	.88	4.6	dd	1251	19⅜	19⅛	19¼	...
n	26¾	24¾	Ahmanson pfC		2.10	8.1	...	78	26	25⅞	26	...
	28½	25⅛	Ahmanson pf		2.40	8.8	...	55	27⅜	27¼	27¼	– ⅛
	10⅜	4	Aileen	AEE		...	dd	161	4⅜	4¼	4⅜	...
	49⅛	37½	AirProduct	APD	.92f	2.2	17	2812	42¼	41⅞	42	– ⅛
	27	12½	AirbornFrght	ABF	.30	1.5	27	2291	20½	20	20⅜	+ ½
s▲	37⅛	13½	Airgas	ARG		...	42	184	37½	36⅝	37½	+ ¾
	15⅜	10¼	Airlease	FLY	1.60	10.5	12	148	15¼	15	15¼	+ ¼
	26⅞	24⅛	AlaPwr pfA		1.90	7.2	...	85	26⅞	26½	26½	– ⅛
n	27	24	AlaPwr pfH		1.90	7.2	...	11	26¾	26½	26½	– ¼
	18¾	12¼	AlaskaAir	ALK	.05j	...	dd	515	12½	12¼	12⅜	– ⅛
	19	11¼	AlbanyInt	AIN	.35	1.9	62	104	18¾	18⅝	18¾	...
	28¼	21	AlbertoCl	ACV	.26	1.2	15	174	21¾	21⅛	21⅜	– ⅜
	25¼	17	AlbertoCl A	ACVA	.26	1.5	13	259	17⅞	17½	17½	...
	59⅜	39¼	Albertsons	ABS	.72	1.4	22	1344	53¾	53¼	53¼	– ⅛
	21⅝	15¼	Alcan	AL	.30	1.4	dd	4792	21⅜	20⅞	21	– ½
	27⅛	21⅝	AlcatelAsthom	ALA	.81e	3.5	...	1479	23⅜	23	23⅜	+ ½
	50⅝	33¼	AlcoStd	ASN	.96	2.1	22	2019	46⅝	46	46½	+ ⅜
n	64¼	56¾	AlcoStd pf		.59p	1.0	...	8	60⅞	60⅞	60⅞	+ ¼
▲	26⅝	14½	AlexBrown	AB	.60f	2.3	7	815	27¼	26⅛	26⅜	– ¼
	28⅞	23⅜	Alex&Alex	AAL	1.00	4.0	dd	236	25⅛	24¾	24⅞	– ¼
	59¾	18½	vjAlexanders	ALX		...	...	15	57¼	57	57⅛	...
n	15¼	14⅛	AllAmTerm	AAT	1.26	8.4	...	303	15	14⅞	15	...
	148½	115⅛	AlleghanyCp	Y	2.63t	1.8	11	5	146	144¼	144¼	–1¼
s	23⅛	14¾	AllegLud	ALS	.48	2.3	22	841	21	20¾	21	+ ¼
	54⅞	45⅞	AllegPwr	AYP	3.24	6.0	15	219	54¼	53⅞	53⅞	– ¼
	49½	21¾	AllenGp	ALN	.24	.5	34	1542	48⅝	48¼	48⅝	+ ⅜
	27	21¼	Allergan	AGN	.40	1.8	14	615	23⅛	22⅝	22¾	– ¼
s	23¼	14⅜	AllncCapMgt	AC	.69e	3.2	25	694	21¾	21⅜	21⅝	+ ¼
	10¼	8⅞	AllncGlblEnv	AEF		...	...	141	9¼	9⅛	9¼	...
n	15⅛	15	AllianceWrld II	AWF		...	...	1118	15⅛	15	15	– ⅛
n	19½	14⅛	AllianceWrld	AWG	1.68	8.7	...	443	19½	19¼	19¼	– ¼
	31	19⅛	AlliantTech	ATK		...	dd	95	29⅜	29⅛	29⅜	+ ¼
	24¾	16¼	AlldIrishBk	AIB	.94e	3.8	...	5	24¾	24½	24¾	...
	28⅝	25⅜	AlldIrishBk pf		2.97e	10.6	...	63	28¼	28	28	+ ⅛
	15⅞	1½	AlliedPdts	ADP		...	dd	241	11	10⅝	10⅞	+ ¼
▲	73⅞	50	AlliedSgnl	ALD	1.16	1.6	17	3166	74⅜	73⅜	73⅝	+ ½
	62½	38	AllmrPC	APY	.44	.8	5	192	57⅞	57⅞	57⅞	...
	10⅛	9⅝	AllmonTr	GSO	.43e	4.4	...	128	10	9⅞	9⅞	...
n	31¾	27⅛	Allstate	ALL		...	...	1687	30⅞	30⅜	30½	– ⅛
s	28⅜	19½	ALLTEL	AT	.80	2.9	21	2580	27⅞	27⅜	27½	+ ⅛
	7¾	4	Allwaste	ALW		...	13	1236	4¼	4	4⅛	...
	78⅜	59	Alcoa	AA	1.60a	2.2	cc	2142	73⅛	72⅜	72½	– ⅛
▼	49½	19¾	Alza	AZA		...	21	5900	20⅛	19¼	19⅜	– ¾
	25¼	15	Amax	AMX	.30j	...	dd	1020	24⅞	24½	24⅝	– ⅛
	50	40½	Amax pf		3.00	6.0	...	7	49⅝	49⅝	49⅝	– ⅜
	10½	6⅞	AmaxGold	AU	.08	1.0	dd	995	8⅜	8¼	8⅜	– ⅛
	48⅜	34¾	Ambac	ABK	.44	1.0	10	578	43½	43¼	43⅜	...
	22½	11⅝	AmcastInd	AIZ	.48	2.7	dd	148	17⅞	17⅝	17⅞	...
	3¾	1⅞	Amdura	ADU		...	...	402	2⅜	2⅛	2¼	...
	56⅜	43½	AmerHess	AHC	.60	1.2	dd	1833	48⅞	48¼	48⅞	+ ⅝
	10⅝	9¾	AmAdjTerm95	ADJ	.60e	6.2	...	402	9⅞	9¾	9¾	...
	10⅜	9⅜	AmAdjTerm96	BDJ	.62e	6.4	...	255	9¾	9½	9⅝	– ⅛

-B-B-B-

	52 Weeks Hi	52 Weeks Lo	Stock	Sym	Div	Yld %	PE	Vol 100s	Hi	Lo	Close	Net Chg
	39¼	32	BCE Inc g	BCE	2.64	...	...	1091	34½	34⅛	34¼	– ¼
	19	12½	BetHldg	BTV		...	27	22	16⅝	16½	16½	– ⅛
	9½	5⅛	BET	BEP	.26e	3.3	...	157	8	7⅞	7⅞	+ ¼
	31⅝	13⅝	BJ Svc	BJS		...	31	307	27¼	26	27¼	+1¼
	14⅛	7	BMC	BMC		...	10	52	13¾	13½	13¾	+ ¼
	32¼	26⅛	BP Prudhoe	BPT	2.67e	9.2	...	249	29	28½	28⅞	+ ¼
	39⅞	31	BRE Prop	BRE	2.40	6.9	11	142	35⅛	34¾	35	+ ½
	4¼	2⅛	BRT RltyTr	BRT		...	dd	118	4⅛	3⅞	4	...
	8½	4¾	Bairnco	BZ	.20	3.8	8	249	5⅜	5¼	5¼	+ ⅛
	29⅝	17¾	BakrHughs	BHI	.46	1.8	89	3997	25⅞	25⅝	25¾	...
	19⅛	16⅝	BakrFentrs	BKF	1.81e	9.8	...	147	18½	18¼	18½	+ ¼
s	25⅝	17½	BaldorElec	BEZ	.40	1.7	20	76	23½	23⅛	23⅛	– ⅜
s	33⅞	24⅜	Ball Cp	BLL	1.24	4.1	14	887	30½	30¼	30½	+ ⅛
	12¾	4¼	BallyMfg	BLY		...	dd	1122	9⅛	8⅞	9	...
▲	12	6	BaltimrBcp	BBB		...	15	2422	12⅛	11¾	11⅞	...
	26⅝	21½	BaltimrGE	BGE	1.48	5.6	15	1465	26½	26¼	26⅜	+ ⅛
	61½	42⅛	BancOne	ONE	1.40	2.6	15	3693	54⅜	52⅞	53	–1¼
n			BancOne wi			...	...	4	43	43	43	...
	23	8⅜	BancFla	BFL		...	8	91	21½	21	21¼	+ ½
	29⅜	24⅞	BancoBilV pf		2.44	8.4	...	143	29⅛	28⅞	29⅛	+ ⅛
n▲	26⅛	24⅞	BancoBilV pfC			...	...	81	26⅜	25⅝	26	+ ¼
	27¼	18⅞	BancoBilV	BBV	1.44e	6.3	...	235	23	22¾	23	+ ¼
n▲	27⅞	24½	BancoBilV pfB		1.23e	4.4	...	65	28	27⅝	28	+ ¼
	17½	12⅜	BancoCentrl	BCM	.89e	6.7	...	19	13¼	13	13¼	+ ¼
s	14¼	10½	BanComercial	BPC		...	...	5	11⅛	11⅛	11⅛	– ⅛
	47⅜	33	BancoSantdr	STD	2.78e	6.1	...	239	45⅞	45⅜	45½	...
n▲	37⅞	20⅛	BancoLatin	BLX	.40p	1.1	...	103	38⅛	37⅞	38	+ ⅛
	53⅞	40¼	BcpHawii	BOH	1.38	3.2	10	692	42⅞	42⅝	42⅞	+ ⅛
	3	1	BancTexas	BTX		...	35	80	1⅞	1¾	1¾	...
	72	44¾	Bandag	BDG	.65	1.3	18	123	51¾	51¼	51¼	– ¼
	68⅜	44¼	Bandag A		.65	1.3	17	260	49¾	49½	49¾	...
	24⅛	17⅞	BangorHyd	BGR	1.32	6.0	12	82	22	21¾	21⅞	+ ⅛
	29⅛	18¾	BankBost	BKB	.40	1.6	11	3305	24¾	24¼	24⅝	+ ⅛
	50⅛	40	BankBost pfA		3.01e	6.2	...	20	48½	48¼	48¼	– ⅜
	49	38¾	BankBost pfB		3.01e	6.4	...	19	47¾	47	47	+ ⅛
	91	69	BankBost pfC		5.51e	6.3	...	10	88	87½	88	–1
n	27⅛	23⅞	BankBost pfE		2.15	8.1	...	169	26½	26¼	26½	...
▼▲	25¾	25⅜	BankBost pfF		.41p	1.6	...	490	26⅜	25⅛	25⅛	– ¼
	62½	39⅝	BankNY	BK	1.80f	3.3	10	1316	54⅞	54½	54⅝	– ⅛
	50	43½	BankNY pfA		3.25	6.5	...	4	49¾	49¾	49¾	...
n	28	25¼	BankNY pfB		2.15	8.0	...	46	26¾	26⅝	26¾	+ ¼
n	27¾	24¾	BkUtdTex pf	BKUA	2.53	9.4	...	34	26⅞	26¾	26⅞	...
	55½	40½	BankAmer	BAC	1.40	3.0	10	9631	47⅛	46¾	47	+ ½
	50	42¼	BankAmer pfA		3.25	6.6	...	51	49¼	48⅞	49	– ⅛
	89¾	74¼	BankAmer pfB		6.00	6.8	...	12	88	87⅜	87⅞	+ ¼
	28½	25¾	BankAmer pfF		2.41	8.8	...	104	27½	27⅛	27⅜	+ ¼
	70	55½	BankAmer pfG		3.25	5.4	...	1073	60¾	59½	60⅛	– ½
	28⅛	24½	BankAmer pfH		2.25	8.3	...	73	27¼	26⅞	27	...
	31	28⅜	BankAmer pfI		2.75	9.2	...	33	30	29⅞	29⅞	...
	30⅞	28¼	BankAmer pfJ		2.75	9.1	...	73	30⅜	30⅛	30¼	+ ⅛
	27⅛	23¾	BankAmer pfK		2.09	8.0	...	200	26	25¾	26	+ ¼
	27⅛	23½	BankAmer pfL		2.04	7.9	...	157	25⅞	25⅝	25¾	+ ⅛
n	26⅝	22⅞	BankAmer pfM		1.97	7.8	...	267	25½	25⅜	25⅜	...
n	27½	25	BankAmer pfN		2.13	8.1	...	87	26⅜	26⅛	26⅜	+ ⅛
n	25½	17	BkrsLife	BLH	.04e	.2	...	836	23⅝	23⅛	23½	+ ¼
▲	79¼	58⅞	BankTrst	BT	3.12	3.9	8	2337	80	79⅛	79⅝	+ ¾
	27¼	24⅞	BankTrst un		2.14	8.2	...	15	26½	26¼	26¼	– ⅛
	6⅛	4	BannerAero	BAR		...	dd	16	5⅜	5⅜	5⅜	...
	⅞	11/32	BanyanMtgInv	VMG		...	dd	284	11/16	⅝	11/16	...
	30⅜	20⅛	Barclays	BCS	1.35e	4.5	...	7	29⅞	29⅝	29¾	...
	27¾	24⅝	Barclays pr		2.78	10.4	...	113	26⅞	26⅝	26¾	...
	27⅝	25	Barclays prB		2.72	10.2	...	59	27	26⅝	26⅝	– ¼
	30½	25¾	Barclays pfD		2.88	9.7	...	58	29⅞	29½	29⅝	– ⅛
n	25⅞	24	Barclays prE		.18e	.7	...	805	25	24¾	24⅞	...
	30	25¾	Barclays unC		2.81	9.6	...	93	29⅝	29¼	29¼	...
▼	35⅞	21¼	Bard CR	BCR	.56f	2.6	13	3313	21¾	20½	21¾	+ ⅜
	33	28¼	BarnesGp	B	1.40	4.4	32	2	31⅞	31⅞	31⅞	+ ¼
	50⅜	34¼	BarnettBks	BBI	1.44f	3.0	18	1109	47⅝	47¼	47⅝	+ ⅜
	99	75	BarnettBks pfA		4.50	4.6	...	77	98¾	98⅜	98½	+ ½
	72¾	57⅜	BarnettBks pfC		4.00	5.6	...	20	72	71	71⅛	– ⅝
	8¼	5	BaroidCp	BRC	.20	2.7	28	1063	7½	7⅛	7½	+ ¼
	20⅛	13½	Bass	BAS	.76e	5.2	...	21	14¾	14⅜	14½	+ ⅛
	11	4½	BattleMtn	BMG	.05	.5	dd	4680	9⅝	9⅜	9⅝	– ⅛
n	66	52	BattleMtn pf		.81p	1.3	...	135	62	61¼	61½	– ½
	59¼	43⅞	BauschLomb	BOL	.88	1.9	15	3014	45⅞	45½	45½	– ½
s	35⅛	25⅝	BaxterInt	BAX	1.00	3.8	13	8900	26	25¾	26	+ ⅛
	29⅞	23⅞	BayStGas	BGC	1.42	5.0	15	42	28½	28¼	28¼	– ⅛
x	23⅝	12¾	BearStearns	BSC	.60b	2.6	8	2919	23⅛	22⅝	22⅞	+ ¼
n	25⅝	24	BearStearns pfB		1.97	7.8	...	359	25¼	25⅛	25⅛	...
n	25	24½	BearStearns pfC		.44p	1.8	...	217	24¾	24⅝	24¾	...
	24¾	16¾	BearingsInc	BER	.64	2.9	18	44	22¼	21⅞	22¼	+ ¼
	25½	19⅛	BeckmanInstr	BEC	.36	1.6	14	816	22¾	22¼	22¾	+ ⅜
s	42⅛	32⅝	BectonDksn	BDX	.66	1.9	13	2143	35	34⅝	34¾	– ¼
	5	2⅝	BedfdPrpty	BED	.05e	1.1	dd	18	4½	4½	4½	– ⅛
	60⅛	44½	BellAtlantic	BEL	2.68	4.6	17	1688	59⅛	58⅝	58¾	– ¼
	14⅞	9¼	BellIndus	BI	.40b	2.7	dd	50	14⅞	14¾	14¾	– ⅛
	58⅞	46¾	BellSouth	BLS	2.76	4.9	18	2105	56⅝	56¼	56⅜	...
	49⅝	38¾	Belo AH A	BLC	.56	1.2	23	43	48	47½	48	+ ½
	29⅝	19⅞	Bemis	BMS	.50	2.4	19	366	21½	20⅝	21	– ¼
	77⅜	56⅝	Beneficial	BNL	2.80	3.7	13	526	76¼	75	75¼	– ¾
	63¾	51	Beneficial pfB		4.30	6.9	...	1	62¼	62¼	62¼	...
▲	338	262	Beneficial pfC		5.50	1.6	...	z240	339¾	339¾	339¾	+1¾
▲	26⅞	17¾	Benetton	BNG	.42e	1.6	...	4	27	26¼	26¼	+ ¼

the *Wall Street Journal.* Looking across the columns of information for each stock, the *Wall Street Journal* first reports the 52-week high (Hi) and low (Lo) prices. Next, the name of the stock and the ticker symbol (Sym) for each listed stock. Along with the dividend, the percentage dividend yield on the stock, and its price to earnings ratio (PE), the *Wall Street Journal* reports the number of shares traded during the day in 100s of shares (Vol 100s). Next, the highest (Hi) and lowest (Lo) transactions price in the stock for the trading day are reported. Then are listed the closing price (Close) and the change in the closing price (Net Chg) from the previous day.

The Over-the-Counter Market

The Over-the-Counter Market (OTC) is the thousands of securities firms across the United States that are linked by telephone and electronic information systems. The term "over-the-counter" refers to a much earlier time, when securities were commonly purchased and sold at banks and certificates were physically handed over the counter. Today, OTC refers to any trading that takes place off the organized securities exchanges. The most important differences between the OTC market and the organized exchanges are that (1) trading does not take place in a central location, as in the major exchanges, and (2) the OTC market is operated by dealers rather than specialists.

The difference between the dealer operating in the OTC market and the specialist on the NYSE is that, whereas the specialist operates principally as a broker (about 75 percent of all transactions over the NYSE do not involve a trade with the specialist), a dealer in the OTC market makes money *primarily* from buying and reselling securities. Dealers normally maintain an inventory of securities. The inventory is generally financed by the dealer's equity and by a credit line from a bank. For the most part, the dealer's profit is generated by the bid-ask spread (i.e., the difference between the price at which the dealer buys the inventory, and the price at which he or she sells it). In addition, the dealer can receive additional earnings from a positive carry. The *carry* is the difference between the income earned from the inventory, generally in the form of dividends, and the interest cost paid to finance the inventory. Depending on the magnitude of cash flows from inventory and financing rates, the carry can be positive or negative.

The bid-ask spread quoted by the dealer can be different for different securities. Generally, as we first explained in Chapter 1, three factors determine the magnitude of the bid-ask spread. The first is the cost of holding inventory, the opportunity cost of capital invested by the dealer in the inventory. By its nature the dealer's inventory is a portfolio of risky assets. The bid-ask spread is set in part to compensate the dealer for bearing the risk associated with his or her inventory. The second factor that has an impact on the magnitude of the spread is transactions costs associated with transferring securities to and from customers and with processing information. The third factor is the cost imposed on the dealer by informed traders. *Informed traders* are traders who have more information about the dealer's securities than the dealer does. For example, a trader may have inside information that the dealer's stock will increase in value in the near future. Selling to the informed trader causes the dealer to trade before the price goes up, and the dealer misses out on increasing value of his inventory. By the same token, if the informed trader knows the price of the dealer's stock will go down and sells to the dealer, the dealer suffers a loss on the securities purchased from an informed trader. When they receive an order dealers recognize that there is always a chance they are trading with an informed trader. In anticipation of encountering an informed trader, the dealer increases the spread, lowering the bid price so as not to pay too much for the stock and raising the ask so as not sell the stock too low. The greater the opportunity for encountering an informed trader in a particular stock, the larger will the dealer set the spread.

To trade in the OTC market securities dealers must be members of the NASD, an industry group that serves as the regulator of the OTC market. Like exchange specialists, OTC dealers may specialize in certain stocks they handle, and they are referred to as "market makers" in those stocks. Unlike specialists, however, dealers are not assigned specific securities but can choose the stocks in which they want to specialize. In addition, they are not required to maintain a fair and orderly market in the stocks they deal in. Under the NASD, however, the dealer must maintain a bid and an ask price in their securities on a continuing basis (i.e., they must always make a market in the security). The number of dealers who make the market in a particular stock depends mainly on the volume or activity of that stock. For most stocks, generally between two and 25 dealers specialize in the stock.

Stocks traded in the OTC market often have regional rather than national appeal and are typically issued by smaller companies than those traded over the NYSE. The OTC market also serves as the major market for securities that do not meet the listing requirement of the major exchanges. At the same time, however, some firms elect to have their stock traded OTC even though they qualify for listing on the NYSE or AMEX.

The NASDAQ and National Market Systems

The most actively traded OTC stocks are those quoted on the NASDAQ system, a nationwide electronic quotation system that displays dealer quotes on terminals to securities firms across the country. The terminal shows the best available quotes in traded stocks continuously to participating dealers. In effect, the NASDAQ system allows several thousand NASD dealers instantaneously to learn the best available bid and ask prices for participating securities. You will recall that the efficiency derived from operating an exchange comes from centralizing offers to buy and sell and economizing on the cost of search. The NASDAQ system performs a similar service by electronically "centralizing" orders to buy and sell among participating dealer firms. When dealers locate compatible offers displayed over the terminal they contact each other directly to make the trade.

To be linked to the NASDAQ system a securities firm must meet certain requirements, including a minimum capital requirement that depends on the number of securities in which they specialize, disclosure of trading information (volume, etc.), and maintenance of continuous bid and ask quotes through the NASDAQ system.

For stocks to be included in the NASDAQ system the issuer must also satisfy certain minimum requirements. These include minimum assets of $2 million, minimum capital of $1 million, minimum of 300 shareholders, minimum of 100,000 publicly held shares, and at least two market makers in the stock. Though the OTC market as a whole trades more than 15,000 stocks, only about 4,000 have qualified to be quoted over the NASDAQ system.

The National Market System (NMS) is a more extensive reporting system for about 2700 of the larger and more actively traded stocks in the NASDAQ system. The objective of the NMS is to provide more extensive and more timely information about trading in this subset of more important securities. Generally, the NASDAQ requires dealers only to enter their bid-ask quotes in the computer and to report daily trading volume in each stock at the end of the trading day. Under the NMS dealers immediately report the price and size of a given trade after the transaction takes place. The *Wall Street Journal* reports information about trading in NMS stocks on a daily basis. Figure 3-8 shows an excerpt from the data provided on NMS stocks for transactions that took place on 11 August 1993. The type of information reported for NMS issues is similar to that provided for NYSE trades presented in Figure 3-7.

The Third and Fourth Markets

The third and fourth markets trade very large numbers of shares in what are called "blocks." A *block* is a trade of 10,000 shares or more. Several thousand block trades, involving billions of dollars, occur daily. Though a substantial volume of block trading takes place over the organized exchanges, a growing volume of block trading takes place off of the exchanges. It is this trading that is identified with the third and fourth markets.

The third market involves large block trading among large investors, generally pension funds, mutual funds, and other institutional investors. In this market brokers play a role in bringing institutional investors together. The fourth market involves trading among institutional investors without the assistance of a broker. Whereas the third market evolved to avoid large commissions charged by brokers in trading over the organized exchanges, the fourth market has more recently evolved to avoid the commissions charged by third market brokers. Fourth market transactions involve large institutional investors trading large blocks of securities among themselves, without the assistance of a broker.

Stock Market Indices

Probably the most visible and widely cited indicator of business activity in the United States is the Dow Jones Industrial Average (DJIA). The Dow, as it is sometimes called, is an index of value of a group of 30 of the largest industrial stocks traded over the NYSE. The Dow is not a true average of the prices of these 30 stocks but represents a summation of the prices that is adjusted for occasional changes in the securities that are included in the index. Increases in the Dow reflect general increases in the prices of the 30 stocks in the index. Because these stocks

Figure 3-8

Data provided on NMS stocks. *Source:* Wall Street Journal, *August 12, 1993. Reprinted with permission of* The Wall Street Journal, *© 1993 Dow Jones and Company, Inc. All Right Reserved Worldwide.*

NASDAQ NATIONAL MARKET ISSUES

Quotations as of 4 p.m. Eastern Time
Wednesday, August 11, 1993

-A-A-A-

	52 Weeks Hi	52 Weeks Lo	Stock	Sym	Div	Yld %	PE	Vol 100s	Hi	Lo	Close	Net Chg
s	25¾	15	A&W Brands	SODA	.32	1.7	16	1016	18½	17¾	18½	+ ½
s	13¼	5⅝	ABS Ind	ABSI	.20	1.7	21	22	12¼	11½	12	...
n	19⅝	15	ABT BldgPdt	ABTC		...	...	129	18¼	17¾	18	− ¼
s	17⅞	9¾	ACC	ACCC	.12	.8	55	281	15¾	14¾	15½	− ⅛
n	46¾	10¾	ACX Tch	ACXT		...	...	63	41¼	40¼	41¼	+1
s	33½	16⅛	ADC Tel	ADCT		...	31	406	33	31¾	32¼	− ⅛
▲	14¼	4⅞	ADESA	SOLD		...	25	275	14½	14	14½	+ ½
	7½	5	AEL Ind A	AELNA		...	dd	11	5⅞	5⅞	5⅞	− ¼
	17¾	9¾	AEP Ind	AEPI	.03p	.2	18	28	16¾	16¼	16¾	+ ⅛
n	9¼	7	AER EngyRes	AERN		...	...	165	9	8¼	9	...
	32¼	18½	AES Cp	AESC	1.00f	3.1	20	31	32¼	31½	32¼	+ ¾
	23¼	5	AGCO Cp	AGCO	.04	.2	24	1842	23¼	22¼	22¼	− ⅝
n	34	24½	AGCO pf		.46p	1.4	...	10	33¼	33¼	33¼	− ½
	18	9¾	AgSvcAm	AGSV		...	16	1	15½	15½	15½	...
n	24⅞	20⅛	AMCOR Ltd	AMCRY		...	...	73	23⅞	23¾	23⅞	+ ⅛
	6	1⅞	**ARI Netwk**	**ARIS**		...	dd	272	2¾	2½	2½	− ¼
	28⅛	9½	ASK Grp	ASKI		...	dd	626	11¼	10⅞	11	...
	24¼	11¼	AST Rsrch	ASTA		...	dd	3474	15½	15	15¼	+ ¼
	9	5¾	ATSMed	ATSI		...	dd	33	6⅛	5¾	6	+ ¼
	6⅛	2⅝	AW Cptr A	AWCSA		...	9	58	4	3¾	3¾	− ⅛
s	13⅛	5⅛	AamesFnl	AAMS	.30	2.6	10	116	11¾	11¼	11¾	+ ½
s	12¾	7¼	AaronRents	ARONA	.06	.5	12	172	11⅛	11	11⅛	+ ⅛
n	11½	7	AaronRents B		.08	.8	...	388	10¾	10	10½	− ¼
	7¾	3¾	**Abaxis**	**ABAX**		...	...	24	5½	5⅛	5½	+ ⅜
	24¾	11	**AbbeyHlthcr**	**ABBY**		...	17	1103	24	22	22¾	−1¼
	11¾	5¾	AbingtnSav	ABBK		...	12	20	9⅞	9¾	9⅞	+ ⅛
	15½	7	**Abiomed**	**ABMD**		...	dd	178	9½	7½	9	+ ¾
	6	3¾	AbramsInd	ABRI	.08	1.4	10	10	5¾	5¾	5¾	+ ¼
n	16½	4½	AbsolutEntn	ABSO		...	...	238	5⅛	4⅞	4⅞	− ⅛
	4¾	2¾	AccelInt	ACLE		...	dd	1	2⅞	2⅞	2⅞	...
	12⅛	3¼	AccessHlth	ACCS		...	39	72	8⅞	8½	8⅝	...
s	34⅞	7⅝	AcclmEntn	AKLM		...	46	7304	35¾	34⅝	35⅝	+ ⅞
n	17½	6¾	**AceCashExp**	**AACE**		...	22	61	9	8¼	9	+ ¾
s	17½	12⅝	Aceto	ACET	.28	2.0	42	12	14	14	14	...
	20¾	11	AcmeMetals	ACME		...	cc	728	18	17½	17¾	...
n	15½	10½	Actel	ACTL		...	...	2221	15½	14¾	15¼	+ ⅜
n	7	4½	**ActionPerf**	**ACTN**		...	...	948	5¼	4½	5 1/16	+ 9/16
n	1¾	23/32	ActionPerf wt			...	...	274	15/16	11/16	15/16	+ 7/32
s	20¼	8⅝	Acxiom	ACXM		...	30	185	18	17½	18	...
s	16⅞	9 3/16	AdacLabs	ADAC	.48	3.5	13	425	14½	13¾	13¾	− ⅜
	6⅛	3¼	Adage	ADGE		...	24	30	4⅜	4⅜	4⅜	+ ⅛
	31¾	18½	**Adaptec**	**ADPT**		...	15	11313	30⅝	28⅞	30⅜	+1½
	17¼	10⅝	AddintnRes	ADDR		...	cc	482	17	16½	17	+ ¼
	22	11½	AdelphiaComm	ADLAC		...	dd	157	16½	15¾	15¾	+ ¼
	26½	13¾	AdiaSvcs	ADIA	.16	.7	19	13	25½	24½	24½	...
s	37	12⅝	**AdobeSys**	**ADBE**		...	29	19408	29	26½	28¾	+1⅞
	10¼	1¼	AdvaCare	AVCR		...	dd	516	2⅞	2¾	2 13/16	− 1/16
	15	5⅜	AdvCircuit	ADVC		...	9	275	10	9⅝	9⅞	+ ⅛
	19½	9½	AdvRoss	AROS		...	22	11	18¾	18¾	18¾	− ¾
	5⅞	2⅛	AdvIntrvnt	LAIS		...	dd	213	2⅝	2⅜	2⅜	...
	5 9/16	2½	AdvLogicRsrch	AALR		...	dd	121	3¼	3	3	− ⅛
	9¾	4⅞	AdvMktg	ADMS		...	12	707	6⅝	6¼	6⅝	+ ¼
	11⅞	5¼	AdvPolymer	APOS		...	dd	884	6½	6¼	6½	+ ⅛
	13⅛	4⅞	AdvPromoTch	APTV		...	...	545	10	9½	9⅞	− ⅜
	1¾	⅝	AdvSemi	ASMIF		...	...	52	1⅜	1¼	1⅜	+ ⅛
	24½	14½	AdvTchLab	ATLI		...	30	731	17¼	17	17	− ⅛
▼	14½	7⅜	**AdvTissue**	**ATIS**		...	...	3515	7⅝	6¾	7	− ⅝
▲	54½	15½	Advanta A	ADVNA	.25f	.5	21	1054	55¼	54	55¼	+1½
▲	46⅝	14	Advanta B	ADVNB	.30f	.6	20	1273	48½	46	48	+1⅝
	24¼	15¾	AdvntgBcp	AADV		...	11	77	23¾	23⅝	23¾	...
	20¾	9⅜	AdvntgHlth	ADHC		...	12	69	13	12½	13	...
	3⅞	1¾	Aequitron	AQTN		...	11	93	2 3/16	2⅛	2⅛	...
	10	4¼	**Aerovox**	**ARVX**		...	29	161	9¼	8⅝	9¼	+ ⅝
n	[illegible]	9	Aetrium	ATRM		...	...	1935	9½	9	9	− ¼
	22½	11½	Affymax	AFMXF		...	dd	98	13¼	12¼	12¾	− ½
	10	6⅞	**AgncyRent**	**AGNC**		...	14	250	9	8½	9	+ ½
	13⅝	3¾	**AgnicoEgl**	**AEAGF**	.10f	1.1	...	10298	10⅜	9⅛	9⅜	−1
	15¼	6¾	AgouronPhrm	AGPH		...	dd	132	9	8¼	8¼	...
	7⅛	3⅜	AgridyneTch	AGRI		...	dd	333	4⅜	3¾	4 1/16	+ 1/16
	53½	41⅜	Ahold	AHLDY	.55r	1.1	...	59	49¼	49	49⅛	− ¼
▲	7⅛	2⅛	AirMethod	AIRM		...	...	1933	7¼	6⅜	6¾	− ⅛
s	10½	3	**AirSensor**	**ARSN**		...	31	167	9½	9	9½	+ ½
n	2 5/16	¼	AirSensor wt			...	...	342	2	1¾	2	+ ¼
	14½	6¾	AirtranCp	ATCC	.12	1.3	13	71	10¼	9⅜	9⅜	− ⅛
	3⅛	1½	**Akorn**	**AKRN**		...	14	452	2 11/16	2¼	2⅜	− ⅛
	45¼	35⅝	Akzo	AKZOY	1.71e	3.9	...	655	44⅛	43½	43⅞	+ ¾
n	18¼	11⅜	AlamoGp	ALMO	.32	2.1	...	42	15½	14¾	15⅛	+ ½
x	24¼	20½	AlatennRes	ATNG	1.20	5.3	6	17	22½	22¼	22½	+ ⅞
	18¾	12⅛	AlbankFnl	ALBK		...	...	57	18¼	18	18¼	...
s	10¾	4 11/16	Alcide	ALCD		...	22	45	9¾	9	9½	+ ¼
n▲	32¾	19	**Aldila**	**ALDA**		...	...	4286	35¼	33¼	34½	+2¼
	20¾	10¼	Aldus	ALDC		...	64	545	17	16¼	16⅝	− ⅛
	26	21½	Alex&Bldwn	ALEX	.88	3.6	15	641	25½	24¾	24¾	...
	16	12	AlliedCap	ALLC	.80a	6.0	...	54	13¾	13	13¼	− ⅛
	19½	16	AlliedCapII	ALII	1.00a	6.0	...	95	16¾	16	16¾	+ ¾
	37½	15	AlliedClinLab	ACLB		...	20	320	23¼	23	23	...
s	30¼	16½	AlliedGp	ALGR	.52	1.8	6	1512	29¼	27¾	28¾	+ ⅝
	12	6⅞	AlldHlthcr	AHPI	.18e	1.8	11	701	10	9½	10	+ ⅛
	6⅞	4	AlliedWaste	AWIN		...	27	423	4 9/32	4⅛	4⅛	...
	19¼	.6	AllstFnl	ASFN		...	10	645	7	6½	6⅝	− ⅛
n	19¼	12	Alltrista	JARS		...	...	222	15¾	15¼	15¾	+ ½
	7½	4¾	**AloetteCosm**	**ALET**	.32	5.3	15	10	6	6	6	+ ⅝
	16¼	8	AlphOneBio	ALBM		...	...	24	11¼	10¾	11¼	+ ½
n	3⅞	1⅝	AlphOneBio wtC			...	...	10	2⅞	2⅞	2⅞	− ⅛
n	27½	8	AlphaBetaTch	ABTI		...	...	37	25¾	24¾	25¼	...
	4⅛	1	**AlphaMicSys**	**ALMI**		...	dd	31	2¾	2⅝	2⅝	− ⅜
	2 9/16	1⅛	Alpharel	AREL		...	32	127	2⅛	1 13/16	1 15/16	− 1/16
	7¼	3¼	AlpineLace	LACE		...	dd	9	3⅞	3⅝	3⅞	...
	2⅜	13/32	AltaGold	ALTA		...	dd	784	1¾	1 11/16	1 23/32	− 1/32
	4	2⅝	Altai	ALTI		...	92	1	2¾	2¾	2¾	...
▼	15¾	8¼	Alteon	ALTN		...	...	254	8¾	8	8	− ¼
	28¼	8⅛	AlteraCp	ALTR		...	52	2831	27⅝	27⅛	27⅜	...
▲	28¾	4	**Altron**	**ALRN**		...	37	4476	30½	27¾	30	+2¼
n	18½	6½	**AmbersStr**	**ABRS**		...	12	11	7	6½	7	+ ½
	28¼	18¼	AmcoreFnl	AMFI	.64	2.6	11	38	25	24¼	24¼	+ ½
	23½	16½	AmerianaBcp	ASBI	.80f	3.9	10	16	21	20¼	20⅝	− ⅜
	2	⅝	AmeribcInv	AINVS	j	...	32	270	1 9/32	1¼	1 9/32	...
	30	22	AmFstFnlFd	AFFFZ	1.60	5.5	...	75	29	27¾	29	+1¼
	11¾	9½	AmFstPfFd	AFPFZ	1.06	9.9	...	93	10¾	10⅝	10¾	+ ⅜
s▲	7½	5½	AmFstTxEx	AFTXZ	.54b	7.1	...	181	7⅝	7⅛	7⅝	+ ⅛
	9¾	7¾	AmFstTxEx2	ATAXZ	.75	7.7	...	102	9¾	9¼	9¾	...
▲	47¼	12¼	**AmOnline**	**AMER**		...	cc	3049	50½	45¾	49¾	+3⅝
	7½	3⅝	**AmSvcGp**	**ASGR**		...	12	64	4 11/16	4½	4½	− ¼
	5	3¾	AmAllSeasFd	FUND	.38e	9.4	...	317	4 3/16	4	4 1/16	+ 1/16
	30⅜	18½	AmBkrsIns	ABIG	.68	2.6	10	235	26¼	26	26	− ⅛
	7½	3½	**AmBiogen**	**MABXA**		...	...	841	5⅞	5¼	5½	− ⅜
	18½	10½	AmBusnInfo	ABII		...	15	6	11¼	11	11	...
	25	15	AmCtyBsJnl	AMBJ		...	30	103	25	23¾	24	+ ¼
	7¾	2½	AmClaimEval	AMCE		...	12	18	2⅞	2¾	2⅞	+ ⅛
s	18¾	4⅞	AmColloid	ACOL		...	27	1456	18¾	17¾	18½	+ ¼
	6⅛	3	AmConsumr	ACPI		...	10	50	4⅝	3¾	4⅝	+ ⅞
	13½	2¾	AmDentalTcn	ADLI		...	dd	145	3⅞	3⅝	3⅝	...
	16	6	AmEcology	ECOL		...	7	183	8	7¼	8	+ ¼
	7½	3⅞	**AmEducation**	**AMEP**		...	20	65	6¼	5⅞	6¼	+ ⅜
	12¼	6	AmFedBank	AMFB	.20	1.8	7	355	11¾	11	11¼	+ ¼
	2⅜	9/32	AmFilmTech	AFTI		...	dd	1058	⅞	23/32	¾	− 1/16
s	20½	8⅝	AmFrtways	AFWY		...	31	73	18¼	17½	18¼	...
▲	59½	40⅞	AmGreetgs	AGREA	1.00f	1.7	19	1621	59⅝	59¼	59½	...
	26¼	15½	AmHlthcp	AMHC		...	20	99	19	18½	19	...
	3¼	1⅝	AmHldg	HOLD		...	13	323	2	1⅞	1⅞	− 1/16
▲	15¾	4¾	AmIndemFnl	AIFC	.12f	.7	5	1	16	16	16	+ ½
	3⅛	⅝	AmIntPetrol	AIPN		...	dd	6262	¾	21/32	11/16	...
n	26½	23½	Am Life pf	ALHCP	2.16	8.2	...	38	26⅜	26⅛	26⅜	+ ⅛
	23¾	14⅞	**AmMgtSys**	**AMSY**		...	17	1284	18⅜	17	18⅜	+1¼
	14¾	5½	AmMedElec	AMEI		...	16	170	7¾	7¼	7¾	+ ¼
	9	2¼	AmMobSys	AMSE		...	...	649	7⅞	7½	7 11/16	+ 3/16
	61	39	AmNatlIns	ANAT	2.04	3.6	7	207	56¼	55	56¼	+ ¼
	1 15/16	⅛	AmNuclear	ANUC		...	dd	542	9/16	7/16	15/32	...
n▲	10½	9¼	AmOilField	DIVE		...	...	295	10¾	10	10½	...
	37¼	11¼	AmPacCorp	APFC		...	33	363	16	15½	15¾	− ¼
	4	1¼	AmPhysnSvc	AMPH		...	12	110	2⅞	2 25/32	2⅞	+ ⅛
s	48	15	AmPwrConv	APCC		...	58	4983	46½	45½	45⅞	− ¼
▲	7½	5½	AmRecCtrs	AMRC	.22	2.8	20	98	7¾	7¼	7¾	+ ¼
n	24½	13	AmResident	AMRS		...	8	584	20	19	19	− ½
n	12¼	10½	AmSaftyRazr	RAZR		...	...	242	11¼	11	11	...
s	16⅜	5⅝	AmSavFla	ASFL		...	4	153	15⅛	14⅝	15⅛	+ ½
	13⅞	5½	**AmSftwr A**	**AMSWA**	.32	4.1	34	542	7⅞	7	7⅞	+ ½
sn	21¼	6	AmStudios	AMST	.08	1.2	...	452	7	6½	6½	...
	27¾	12	AmSuprcnd	AMSC		...	...	222	25½	24¾	24¾	− ¼
▲	12½	5	AmTrvlrs	ATVC		...	11	1330	13¼	12¾	13	+ ½
	6⅜	3½	AmUtdGlbl	AUGI		...	...	277	5⅝	5 7/16	5 7/16	− 3/16
	15¼	7¼	AmVngrd	AMGD		...	cc	10	11¾	10½	11¼	− ½
	33¾	16¾	AmeriFed	AFFC	.60a	1.9	11	282	32½	32	32¼	...
	12¼	4	AmhostProp	HOST		...	23	212	5	4½	4¾	− ⅛
s	13½	8	**Ameriwood**	**AWII**		...	7	69	11⅞	11½	11½	− ¾
n▲	23¼	11¾	AMFED Fnl	AMFF	.05r	.2	...	2119	23⅞	23	23½	+ ¼
	78	31½	Amgen	AMGN		...	12	16231	32¾	31¾	32	− ⅝
	43	15¼	Amoskg	AMOS		...	16	51	42	40¾	40¾	...
	8⅛	3½	**Ampex**	**AMPX**		...	dd	31	4	4	4	− ¼
s	32	12⅜	AmtechCp	AMTC		...	50	4900	31¼	28¾	29¾	+ ¾
n▼	16½	11¾	**Amtran**	**AMTR**		...	...	1012	12½	11½	11½	− ⅝
n	20½	14½	AMTROL	AMTL	.10e	.5	...	93	19¼	18½	19¼	+ ¼
s	16⅞	5 15/16	AmvstrFnl	AVFC		...	3	629	10¼	9¾	10	− ½
	15½	5¾	AmylinPharm	AMLN		...	...	49	9¾	9¼	9½	+ ¼
	16¾	10¼	**Analogic**	**ALOG**		...	14	652	14½	13⅝	13½	− ¾
▲	14½	9¾	Anly&Tech	AATI	.22f	1.6	17	9	14¾	13¾	13¾	− ½
	35¾	16¼	AnlyInt	ANLY	.60	1.9	20	69	31	31	31	+ ⅝
	18	10⅞	Anangel	ASIPY	1.00e	6.1	...	241	16½	16⅛	16½	+ ⅛
	15	5⅝	AnchrBcp	ABKR		...	6	965	14⅝	14½	14½	...
	24¾	13⅛	AnchrBcpWis	ABCW	.18e	.8	...	42	23	22¼	23	+ ¼
▲	14¾	5¾	AndovrBcp	ANDR	.05e	.3	6	451	14⅞	14¼	14⅞	+ ⅝

represent the largest and most established group of industrial companies in the United States, the so-called blue-chip stocks, movements in the Dow are generally associated with changes in the market as a whole.

Figure 3-9 provides information on recent movements in the DJIA from the *Wall Street Journal,* of August 11, 1993. The upper panel shows the general pattern of the DJIA during the previous 6 months and the range of the index for each trading day in that period. Each of the vertical bars shows the range of the DJIA for a particular day. The small dot in each of those ranges indicates the closing value of the index. Over the previous six months the Dow generally increased from a value around 3300 in early March 1993 to about 3550 during early August 1993. A variety of other information is provided by the lower panel of Figure 3-9, giving the closing value of the DJIA, the change in the index from the previous close, the 12-month high and low, and the percentage change in the index during the past 12 months and since the previous year's-end.

Notice that several other indices of stock market activity are indicated in the lower portion of Figure 3-9. In particular, information on the NYSE Index, the Standard & Poor's (S&P) 500 Index, and the NASDAQ Composite is tabulated. Each of these indices is based on a different group of stocks and may employ a different procedure for computing the index. The S&P 500 is another commonly used barometer of general movements in equity prices. While the interpretation of movements in the S&P 500 and the DJIA are generally similar, two major differences in the two should be noted. One difference is in the way the two indexes are computed. The DJIA represents a summation of prices for 30 of the largest industrial stocks. The S&P 500, however, is a value-weighted index of the value of 500 stocks from various industries. In a value-weighted index, changes in the prices of larger firms have a proportionally greater effect on the value of the index than changes in the prices of smaller firms.

Another important difference is that the S&P 500 is a much broader index than the DJIA. For the most part, the S&P 500 includes stocks traded over the NYSE, but some larger OTC stocks are included as well. Stocks in the S&P 500 account for more than 80 percent of the market value of all shares traded over the NYSE. A still broader index is the NYSE index, which includes all stocks traded over the NYSE. The NASDAQ Composite includes securities quoted on the NASDAQ system.

Diversification of Asset Risk

One of the major reasons that the various indices of market performance have become so important is that most investors in equities hold diversified portfolios rather than concentrating their investments in just a few securities. The demand for diversification has spawned the growth of a variety of mutual funds that offer both diversification and management of an investors funds. We discuss the mutual fund industry along with other forms of financial intermediaries in Chapter 7. Here, we want to explain the basic elements of diversification, with an emphasis on how diversification reduces risk.

Figure 3-9

Recent movements in the Dow Jones Industrial Average. *Source:* Wall Street Journal, *August 11, 1993. Reprinted with permission of* The Wall Street Journal, © *1993 Dow Jones and Company, Inc. All Right Reserved Worldwide.*

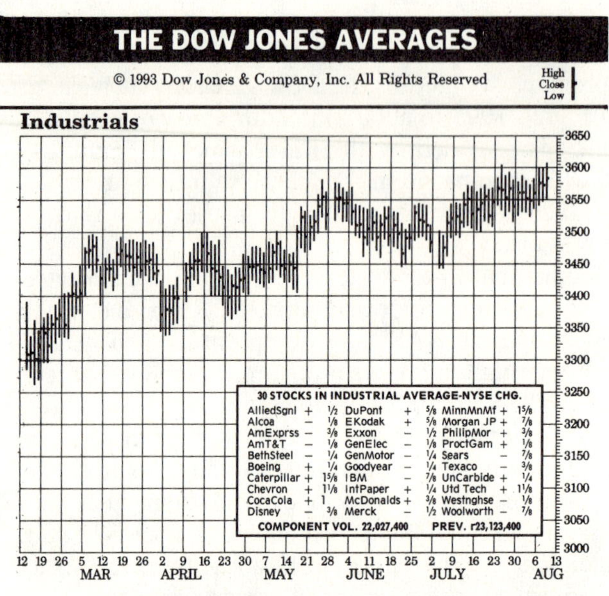

STOCK MARKET DATA BANK 8/11/93

MAJOR INDEXES

HIGH	LOW (†365 DAY)		CLOSE	NET CHG	% CHG	†365 DAY CHG	% CHG	FROM 12/31	% CHG
DOW JONES AVERAGES									
3583.35	3136.58	**30 Industrials**	3583.35	+ 10.62	+ 0.30	+ 262.52	+ 7.91	+ 282.24	+ 8.55
1683.08	1204.40	**20 Transportation**	1620.01	− 10.26	− 0.63	+ 370.39	+ 29.64	+ 170.80	+ 11.79
252.04	214.76	**15 Utilities**	251.05	+ 1.05	+ 0.42	+ 31.60	+ 14.40	+ 30.03	+ 13.59
1329.04	1107.47	**65 Composite**	1329.04	+ 0.33	+ 0.02	+ 174.32	+ 15.10	+ 124.49	+ 10.33
432.78	380.79	**Equity Mkt. Index**	428.24	+ 1.01	+ 0.24	+ 34.90	+ 8.87	+ 14.95	+ 3.62
NEW YORK STOCK EXCHANGE									
251.36	222.11	**Composite**	249.99	+ 0.36	+ 0.14	+ 20.00	+ 8.70	+ 9.78	+ 4.07
303.91	273.18	**Industrials**	295.61	+ 0.38	+ 0.13	+ 11.58	+ 4.08	+ 1.22	+ 0.41
236.58	198.98	**Utilities**	236.58	+ 0.84	+ 0.36	+ 30.60	+ 14.86	+ 26.92	+ 12.84
250.70	182.66	**Transportation**	250.06	− 0.64	− 0.26	+ 59.24	+ 31.04	+ 35.34	+ 16.46
225.16	175.49	**Finance**	225.16	+ 0.19	+ 0.08	+ 42.94	+ 23.56	+ 24.33	+ 12.11
STANDARD & POOR'S INDEXES									
456.33	402.66	**500 Index**	450.46	+ 1.01	+ 0.22	+ 32.68	+ 7.82	+ 14.75	+ 3.39
524.99	471.36	**Industrials**	508.63	+ 1.41	+ 0.28	+ 18.30	+ 3.73	+ 1.17	+ 0.23
405.65	307.94	**Transportation**	397.52	− 2.04	− 0.51	+ 77.86	+ 24.36	+ 33.77	+ 9.28
179.48	148.88	**Utilities**	179.48	+ 0.57	+ 0.32	+ 22.94	+ 14.65	+ 21.02	+ 13.27
46.88	34.58	**Financials**	46.84	− 0.04	− 0.09	+ 10.57	+ 29.14	+ 5.95	+ 14.55
169.92	140.50	**400 MidCap**	169.72	− 0.20	− 0.12	+ 25.96	+ 18.06	+ 9.16	+ 5.71
NASDAQ									
718.77	554.22	**Composite**	718.77	+ 1.69	+ 0.24	+ 147.92	+ 25.91	+ 41.82	+ 6.18
757.05	586.01	**Industrials**	732.84	+ 1.09	+ 0.15	+ 128.76	+ 21.32	+ 7.90	+ 1.09
905.73	665.44	**Insurance**	900.47	− 3.10	− 0.34	+ 216.58	+ 31.67	+ 96.56	+ 12.01
652.95	451.08	**Banks**	652.93	− 0.02	− 0.00	+ 187.76	+ 40.36	+ 120.00	+ 22.52
317.70	245.36	**Nat. Mkt. Comp.**	317.70	+ 0.71	+ 0.22	+ 64.95	+ 25.70	+ 17.14	+ 5.70
303.87	234.80	**Nat. Mkt. Indus.**	292.94	+ 0.40	+ 0.14	+ 50.90	+ 21.03	+ 1.54	+ 0.53
OTHERS									
440.95	364.85	**Amex**	438.87	− 0.32	− 0.07	+ 52.41	+ 13.56	+ 39.64	+ 9.93
281.64	238.81	**Value-Line**(geom.)	281.49	+ 0.48	+ 0.17	+ 32.52	+ 13.06	+ 14.81	+ 5.55
229.96	186.50	**Russell 2000**	239.96	c+ 0.33	+ 0.14	+ 47.58	+ 24.73	+ 18.95	+ 8.57
4477.53	3899.31	**Wilshire 5000**	4477.44	+ 8.17	+ 0.18	+ 452.13	+ 11.23	+ 187.70	+ 4.38

Diversification of risk is a fundamental concept in finance. Basically, diversification occurs when invested wealth is spread out among a number of assets rather than being concentrated in relatively few. A simple example will help to illustrate the effect of diversification using two assets that we will call Asset Y and Asset Z. Assume the assets have probability distributions for their rate of return as defined by Table 3-3. There are four possible outcomes with the indicated probabilities. For each outcome, the percentage rates of return jointly available on Asset Y and Asset Z are shown.

For each asset, the expected, or mean rate of return is calculated as the probability-weighted sum of the possible rates of return across the four possible outcomes, or,

$$E(R) = \sum_i p_i(R_i) \tag{3.1}$$

As a measure of risk, the variance of the return distribution is calculated as the probability-weighted sum of the squared deviation of each outcome from the mean of the distribution, or,

$$\sigma^2 = \sum_i p_i[R_i - E(R_i)]^2 \tag{3.2}$$

As an equivalent measure of risk, the standard deviation of the distribution is the square root of the variance, or,

$$\sigma = \sqrt{\sigma^2} \tag{3.3}$$

Notice that, because of the symmetry of these particular distributions, the expected return and variance for Asset Y and Asset Z are equal. That is,

$$E(R_Y) = E(R_Z) = (0.2)(-4\%) + (0.3)(+1\%) + (0.3)(5\%) + (0.2)(10\%)$$
$$= +3\%,$$

$$\sigma_Y^2 = \sigma_Z^2 = (0.2)(-0.04 - 0.03)^2 + (0.3)(0.01 - 0.03)^2 + \ldots$$
$$\ldots + (0.3)(0.05 - 0.03)^2 + (0.2)(0.10 - 0.03)^2 = 0.0022$$

and,

$$\sigma_Y = \sigma_Z = \sqrt{\sigma^2} = 0.0469 = 4.69\%$$

Individually, Asset A and Asset B have the same expected return and the same risk. An investment in either asset would be expected to yield net returns of 3 percent

Table 3-3

Probability Distributions of Rate of Return for Assets Y and Z

Probability	**Return on Asset Y (%)**	**Return on Asset Z (%)**
0.20	−4	+10
0.30	+1	+5
0.30	+5	+1
0.20	+10	−4

after one year. The standard deviation of possible (annual) returns on both investments is 4.69 percent. At first glance, it doesn't seem to matter how invested capital is distributed between the two assets, as, individually, the assets look the same. There is, however, a difference between the two assets; knowing this is important in understanding the effects of diversification. That difference is that the patterns of return distributions are opposites. When Asset A has its highest outcome, Asset B has its lowest. When Asset A has its second highest outcome, Asset B has its second lowest, and so on. The statistical definition of this property is that the return distributions are negatively correlated—in fact, in this case, they are *perfectly* negatively correlated.[13]

Consider an investment strategy in which X_Y is the percentage of total wealth invested in Asset Y and $(1 - X_Y)$ is the percentage of wealth invested in Asset Z. Under any of the four outcomes, the overall return from a portfolio composed of Asset Y and Asset Z is,

$$R_P = (X_Y)(R_Y) + (1 - X_Y)(R_Z) \tag{3.4}$$

For joint distribution of return for Assets Y and Z in Table 3-3, the return distributions for three portfolios are computed using equation 3.4 and the values are presented in Table 3-4. In the table, distributions of portfolio returns are calculated for $X_Y = 0.25$, $X_Y = 0.5$, and $X_Y = 0.75$.

Notice that the expected portfolio return is the same across the three different portfolio configurations, but the standard deviation is not. In each of the three portfolios, the portfolio standard deviation, σ_p is lower than that of the respective Assets Y and Z. This is due to the effect of diversification. Because the individual return distributions are not positively correlated, combinations of the two assets, as in a portfolio of the two, reduces risk. Intuitively, inspection of the return distributions shows why this is the case. Because of the negative correlation between asset return distributions, in combination with each other, high rates of return on one asset are matched by lower rates of return on the other asset. In other words, the outcomes on the respective asset return distributions moderate or stabilize each other. It is this stabilizing effect that lowers the variance of the portfolio as compared to the variance of the respective assets. This is the effect of diversification that is achieved by dividing invested wealth among many assets that have different payoff patterns.

---

[13]For the mathematically inclined, the Pearson correlation coefficient is defined as,

$$\rho = \frac{\sigma_{yz}}{\sigma_y \sigma_z},$$

where $\sigma_{y,z}$ is the covariance of the distributions with each other, or,

$$\sigma_{yz} = \sum_i p_i[R_Y - E(R^Y)]_i [R_Z - E(R_Z)]_i.$$

In the example above, the correlation coefficient is equal to -1.0. A correlation coefficient of -1.0 indicates perfect negative correlation between two random variables. Intuitively, a negative correlation coefficient means the probability distributions underlying the two random variables have opposite patterns of payoffs.

Table 3-4
Distribution of Portfolio Returns for Alternative Two-Asset Portfolios

Portfolio Rate of Return (R_p)			
Probability	$X_Y = .25$ (%)	$X_Y = .5$ (%)	$X_Y = .75$ (%)
0.20	5.5	3	−0.5
0.30	4.0	3	2.0
0.30	2.0	3	4.0
0.20	−0.5	3	5.5
Expected return $E(R_p)$	3	3	3
σ_p	3.81	0	3.81

Note also that our example is designed to produce fairly dramatic results. In fact, for the fifty-fifty portfolio, where half of the investment allocation is made in Asset Y and half in Asset Z, portfolio variance is reduced to zero. This implies that by combining these risky assets together in an equally-weighted portfolio, a risk-free portfolio is created that provides a 3 percent expected return, the same expected return as the individual assets! Perfect negatively correlated return distributions are a rare opportunity indeed, but even though opportunities to combine assets as efficient as those seldom arise, dividing invested wealth among a large number of assets generates diversification effects similar to, though not as dramatic as, those illustrated above.

SUMMARY

In this chapter we covered the basic types of equity securities that are traded in the capital markets. Important distinctions between common and preferred stock were discussed. Preferred stock is most easily described as a hybrid security, having some of the characteristics of a bond (i.e., fixed dividend payments) and some of the characteristics of common stock. Common stock is the security that most fairly represents an ownership interest in the firm, and a residual claim against the firm's earnings. Two classes of common stock exist. They are usually referred to as Class A and Class B. Class A stock affords shareholders voting privileges; class B does not.

Two general types of equity markets were discussed: the primary market and the secondary market. The primary market is the market for original issues of securities; the secondary market trades in preexisting securities, those that have already been issued. The market for primary issues was discussed and the role of investment banks in bringing new issues to the market was described. Additionally, the markets for IPOs and for venture capital were described.

Secondary markets for equities were also covered, emphasizing the operation of the NYSE. The NYSE is the largest and most active exchange in the United States and is representative of many of the characteristics and procedures of other national and regional exchanges in the United States and the world. The process of trading over the NYSE was explained in some detail. The most important figure in the trading process is the specialist, who is responsible for making a market in his or her assigned securities. The role of the specialist as both broker and dealer in securities was explained. Next, we described the OTC market, the secondary market trading that takes place among securities dealers and not over an organized exchange. While trading takes place in a highly decentralized fashion, the NASDAQ system has centralized information on offers to buy and sell securities so that the market operates in many ways like an organized exchange. Some of the organizational and regulatory aspects of the NASDAQ and the National Market System were described and discussed.

We explained the major indices of equity market values. Representing measures of general movements in the values of equity securities, these indices are often used as indicators of economic health and business conditions. The major indices published in the financial press were briefly discussed. In particular, the most commonly quoted index, the DJIA , or the Dow, was explained and illustrated. Finally, we showed how diversification of investments in equities to create portfolios reduces the risk to which an investor is exposed.

QUESTIONS

1. Explain the major differences between preferred stock and common stock. Why is preferred stock often referred to as a hybrid security?
2. Why is common stock often referred to as the residual claim? Explain why the residual claim is riskier than other claims against a firm's assets?
3. Explain the difference between a primary and a secondary market. Why is the existence of a secondary market in an asset important to the performance of the primary market in the asset?
4. Outline the role of the investment bank in a primary issue of equity securities. What are the major services provided by the bank?
5. When new issues are brought to the market, the investment bank places the issue on either a underwritten or a best efforts basis. Explain the difference between underwritten and best efforts placement.
6. It is well-documented in the finance literature that IPOs are underpriced. Explain the nature of this underpricing and outline the reasons for this phenomenon.
7. Describe the major forms of venture capital investment. How is the process of raising venture capital different from other kinds of financing?
8. Explain how the exchange specialist acts as both broker and dealer in particular stocks. What are the specialist's affirmative responsibilities in his assigned stocks?
9. What are the determinants of the dealer's bid-ask spread?

REFERENCES

Henderson, Y.K. "The Emergence of the Venture Capital Industry." *New England Economic Review* (July/August, 1989), pp. 64–79.

Kopke, R.W., and E.S. Rosengren. "Are the Distinctions between Debt and Equity Disappearing? An Overview." *New England Economic Review* (March/April, 1990), pp. 3–32.

Mulherin, J.H. "Market Transparency: Pros, Cons, and Property Rights." *Journal of Applied Corporate Finance* 5–4 (Winter, 1993), pp. 94–98.

Muscarella, C.R., and M.R. Vetsuypens. "Initial Public Offerings and Information Asymmetry," Working Paper, Southern Methodist University.

Remolona, E.M., R.N. McCauley, J.S. Ruud, and F. Iacono. "Corporate Refinancing in the 1990s." *Quarterly Review* [Federal Reserve Bank of New York] 17–4 (Winter, 1992), pp. 1–27.

Ritter, J. "The 'Hot Issue' Market of 1980." *Journal of Business* 57 (1984), pp. 215–240.

Rock, K. "Why New Issues are Underpriced." *Journal of Financial Economics* 15 (1986), pp. 187–212.

Sahlman, W.A. "Aspects of Financial Contracting in Venture Capital." *Journal of Applied Corporate Finance* 1–1(Spring 1988), pp. 23–36.

Schwartz, R.A. *Equity Markets: Structure, Trading, and Performance* (1988), Harper & Row, Inc., New York.

Stoll, H.R. "Organization of the Stock Market: Competition or Fragmentation?" *Journal of Applied Corporate Finance* 5–4 (Winter, 1993), pp. 89–93.

• *Chapter 4*

Overview of Depository Financial Institutions in the United States

In this chapter we provide an overview of the operation of depository financial intermediaries, or intermediaries that accept deposits—principally commercial banks and savings and loan associations. As we proceed through this book we will focus on understanding how financial firms compete and attempt to earn a profit in the competitive and global financial markets now emerging in the United States. In this chapter we want to lay a foundation for our analysis of issues in managing financial firms by laying out the fundamental structure of the banking industry in the United States. When we use the word "banking," we generally use it in a broad sense. The best definition we know of for a bank is any institution that *both* accepts deposits and makes loans. At one time, the U. S. regulatory system created strong divisions between different classes of financial firms that fit this definition. These included commercial banks, savings and loans, and mutual savings banks. The latter two categories, and sometimes just savings and loans, are often referred to as "thrifts." As we will learn, as the legal distinctions between these institutions have evolved over time it now seems more appropriate to refer to all of these institutions as banks. We will point out the key legal distinctions as we proceed. Our discussion in this chapter focuses principally on commercial banks, and to a lesser extent on savings and loans. Part of our description of savings and loans is contained in Chapter 5, which deals with regulation. Banks and savings and loans are distinguished almost entirely by government regulations. We start this chapter by describing the types of depository financial intermediaries in the United States and the services they provide. Then we describe the basic features of commercial banks in the United States, focusing on the structure of their balance sheets. Finally, we describe the basic structure of savings and loans. The key concepts to be learned in this chapter are listed below.

• *Concepts to Learn in Chapter 4* •

- Types of financial intermediaries in the United States
- Key services provided by financial intermediaries
- How the balance sheets and income statements of commercial banks and savings and loans are structured
- How commercial banks have performed in recent years
- Basic structure of savings and loans

Types of Financial Intermediaries in the United States

We can divide the many specific varieties of financial institutions in the United States into three broad categories: depository intermediaries, investment companies and contractual intermediaries. Depository intermediaries accept deposits—usually demand deposits or savings deposits—from customers and invest those funds in loans or securities. Investment companies raise funds from investors without issuing deposits and invest those funds in various classes of securities. Finally, contractual intermediaries bundle the provision of some other contractual service, usually insurance, with the investment of funds. In part, the wide variety of institutions we observe is a response to the market's demand for varied financial services, but it is also due to government regulation, which has fostered the growth of distinct or segmented financial institutions. The basic characteristics of each type of intermediary are described next.

Commercial Banks. Commerical banks are probably the oldest, largest, and most diversified of financial intermediaries, and they have been the dominant source of credit throughout the history of the United States, where commercial banking was a large and important enterprise even before the NYSE was founded. Commercial banks have provided mainly short-term debt financing to business borrowers. This traditional role limited the risk of intermediating across time. Risk is potentially significant for commercial banks, because most of their funds are obtained through highly liquid deposits. Banks offer demand deposits and savings deposits, the latter being interest-bearing accounts with prespecified maturities. Historically, banks have been differentiated from other financial intermediaries by the fact that only banks could offer demand deposits. As a result, they alone were involved in managing the payments mechanism. However, recent changes in regulations have placed commercial banks and savings and loans on more equal footing vis à vis both asset and liability sides of their balance sheets.

Savings and Loans. Savings and loans are depository institutions that specialize in making mortgage loans. They obtain funds through deposit accounts of various maturities and they extend loans principally to finance real estate. Savings and loans have historically held a small volume of highly liquid nonmortgage investments, principally to maintain some flexibility in their balance sheet. For many years savings and loans were compelled by regulation to invest almost exclusively in fixed-rate, fully amortizing, long-term residential mortgages, yet most of their deposits had short maturities. As a result, they historically provided the market with the service of intermediating across time. Until the passage of the Garn-St. Germain Act of 1982, savings and loans were prevented from extending either commercial or nonmortgage consumer loans to any great extent and from accepting demand deposits. Garn-St. Germain liberalized these restrictions on savings and loans so that their powers are now comparable in many respects to those of commercial banks. Some important differences in regulatory treatment of the two types of intermediaries remain, however. These include the treatment of holding companies and the funding of savings and loans through advances provided by the regulators, specifically through the Federal Home Loan Banks. We discuss this in detail later.

Credit Unions. Credit unions are generally mutual organizations (i.e., they are owned by their depositors). They provide an alternative to commercial banks where consumers can save money and obtain loans. Credit unions do not invest heavily in first mortgages because they are generally restricted from doing so, but they do often finance most other types of consumer purchases. Credit unions got their start early in the twentieth century and by 1934 existed in 38 states. Their largest growth occurred after World War II; since then, they have had the highest growth rate of any financial intermediary in the country. There is usually some common affiliation among the members of a credit union, often as a result of sponsorship of credit unions by employers. In addition, credit unions often enjoy special tax treatment that other financial intermediaries do not.

Investment Companies and Securities Brokers. Investment companies and security brokers act as managers of investment portfolios and underwriters and distributors of securities. They sell individual securities as well as a variety of mutual funds. An increasingly important type of investment company is the pension fund. Pension funds accept funds from workers during their working lifetime, invest those funds, and provide benefits after retirement. Like other intermediaries, they channel funds from lenders to borrowers, but with the special contingency that retirement triggers access to those funds. Investment companies are registered with and regulated by the Securities and Exchange Commission (SEC); pension funds are regulated by the U. S. Department of Labor.

Insurance Companies. It is not always obvious that insurance companies perform a financial intermediation function similar to that of commercial banks, but they do. There are two basic types of insurance companies: those that sell life insurance and those that sell property and casualty insurance. These institutions insure different types of risk and make different types of investments, but they serve the same basic function. Insurance companies accept premiums and stand ready to pay off on the risks they insure. They also invest funds they receive, so acting as lenders. Insurance companies are regulated, not at the federal level, but by each state where they operate.

Finance Companies. Finance companies raise funds like any other type of nonfinancial firm, by issuing both debt and equity securities. They then use the funds they raise to make loans, fund leases, invest in securities of a variety of corporations, and make loans to purchasers of consumer products. Many finance companies are subsidiaries of or are affiliated with nonfinancial firms. Principal examples include Ford Credit Corporation, General Motors Acceptance Corporation, and General Electric Credit Corporation. These types of financial institutions have become an increasingly important part of the U. S. financial system in recent years.

In this chapter and the next two we concentrate on depository financial intermediaries; we take up the various forms of nondepository intermediaries in Chapter 7.

Services Provided by Financial Intermediaries

Financial intermediaries provide six services for the financial markets:

Risk reduction through diversification,

Maturity intermediation,

Reduction in the cost of contracting,

Information production,

Management of the payments system, and

Insurance.

Almost all intermediaries provide some reduction of risk through diversification, but the other five services are more specialized. Some intermediaries provide two or more of these additional services; others are more narrow.

Risk Reduction Through Diversification

All financial market participants are interested in reducing risk through diversification. We discussed the idea of diversification in Chapter 3, where we focused on equity securities, though diversification is valuable for investments in either debt (loans) or equity instruments. As we emphasized in Chapter 3, by choosing a portfolio of investments, rather than investing all one's resources in a single asset, individuals can reduce the total risk to which they are exposed. The concept behind constructing a diversified portfolio is illustrated in Figure 4-1, which shows a hypothetical combination of expected return and risk measured by the standard deviation of the rate of return on a portfolio of securities. Various portfolios may be selected by allocating one's wealth in different proportions across the assets available in the market. Each such selection corresponds to a point along the curve labeled DD′. Any combination

Figure 4-1
Efficient frontier of portfolios of risky assets.

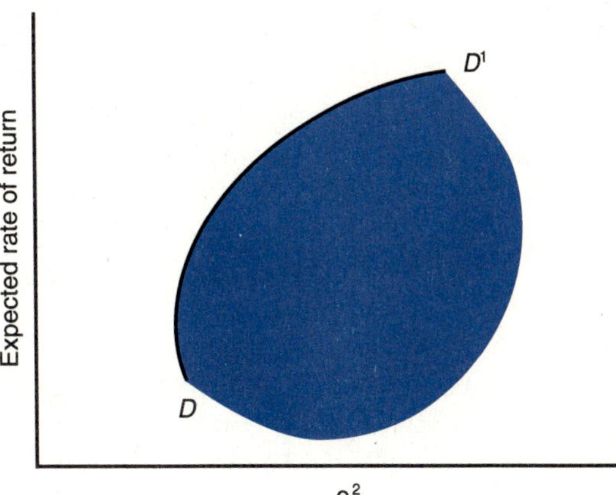

of available assets that does not plot on that curve is inferior to some portfolio that does plot on the curve, because not enough risk has been diversified. The implication is that any risk-averse person will find it optimal to choose a portfolio of assets from the set of portfolios on this line. The optimal portfolio for any individual to choose is the one that provides what that individual perceives to be the best combination of expected return and risk from those combinations that plot on line DD′.

Though this is a very useful representation of what constitutes any optimal portfolio and the impact of diversification, it is not necessarily a very practical guide for choosing investments. To use it as a practical guideline, one must estimate the risk and return on each asset one might choose and the relationships between these assets, or between individual assets and some representative market portfolio. As a result, portfolio theory recommends that individuals who have no special knowledge should choose a portfolio that closely approximates the market as a whole. As a practical matter, if one randomly chooses 20 or more equity securities from the market and spreads available funds across these securities, the resulting portfolio will be a close approximation of the return on the market as a whole. As one adds more randomly chosen securities to the portfolio, the benefits from diversification increase slightly. In the extreme case, one could choose to invest a small amount in virtually all securities in the market and thus have a completely diversified portfolio.

There is one difficulty with following this advice directly: it does not account for the fact that it is costly to buy and sell securities in order to construct such a diversified portfolio. To illustrate the nature of the problem, suppose an individual had $10,000 to invest and wanted a highly diversified portfolio. In order to accomplish this, suppose that the person went to a broker with an order to purchase equal shares in each of the largest 100 corporations in the United States. Suppose the broker said that the brokerage fee would be $5 per share. The investor would then be able to purchase $95 worth of stock from each company, and the total cost for conducting the transaction would be $500. If the investor wanted to liquidate half of these holdings six months later yet maintain the same degree of diversification, additional large transactions costs would be incurred.

Financial intermediaries can economize on such transactions costs by providing diversified portfolios for customers. That is, anyone can diversify, but intermediaries offer an efficient means to reduce transactions costs. The financial intermediary pools the funds of a number of investors and acquires a large diversified portfolio, then it sells claims on the entire portfolio of assets to individual investors. In this way, an individual who has $10,000 to invest and desires a diversified portfolio can purchase a portion of the larger portfolio of the intermediary. The intermediary does not have to buy small portions of each asset when individuals add to or withdraw their claims on the intermediary. Instead, the intermediary holds an inventory of assets that can be liquidated at low cost and uses these to provide funds to individuals when they withdraw. Similarly, it adds to this pool of low–transaction cost assets when new funds are provided to it. As long as there is some balance between the inflow and outflow of funds, the intermediary can reduce the costs of transacting for all market participants who seek diversified portfolios.

Maturity Intermediation and Provision of Liquidity

Many financial intermediaries currently provide the service of intermediating across maturities, or borrowing short and lending long. This means that they accept funds from investors who desire to lend their funds with a short maturity, and they lend those funds out to borrowers who desire a long maturity. Borrowers and lenders who have different preferred maturities are thus not compelled to agree on a common maturity. But as we will learn as we proceed through this book, this cannot be accomplished without cost. By intermediating across maturities, financial intermediaries bear the risk of fluctuations in interest rates. Lenders who supply funds to the intermediaries at short maturities are provided with liquidity that they would otherwise have to forego or else purchase directly from borrowers without an intermediary in the transaction. When lenders deal with an intermediary, they still have to pay a price for this liquidity. Moreover, the risk involved is not a risk that can be reduced by diversification. Diversification is beneficial when assets can be combined that have probability distributions on returns that are less than perfectly correlated. The risk borne by an intermediary that borrows short and lends long is the risk that nominal short-term interest rates will rise and its costs will increase while its revenues will not. If these rates rise above the rate of return on outstanding long-term loans, the intermediary loses money. The risk of an increase in short-term rates is not a risk that can be diversified.

Such risk can be transferred or sold off to another party and reduced in that way. As we will learn in Part III of this book, futures and options markets can be utilized to hedge the risk of these changes. But whether the risk is sold or held, a price will be charged as compensation for bearing it. In spite of the fact that the intermediary cannot reduce the underlying risk involved in bridging the gap between preferred maturities, it can often perform this function more efficiently than other forms of market organizations. The intermediary must be able to generate some kind of economies by specializing in lending long and borrowing short for large numbers of borrowers and lenders. These economies come from two sources. First, individuals who supply funds in small amounts cannot easily estimate the risk involved in arranging long-term contracts. By specializing in this function, intermediaries are better able to assess these prospects. Second, they are able to package short-term liabilities and long-term loans in economical units. A borrower who is not large enough to sell debt claims effectively in an over-the-counter market but who is large enough to require funds from a sizable number of lenders will find it efficient to use an intermediary's services.

Reduction in the Cost of Contracting

In almost all of the financial arrangements they engage in, financial intermediaries reduce the cost of contracting. Two distinct types of costs are included under the label of contracting costs. The first is simply the cost of writing and understanding a financial contract. The second is the cost of monitoring the contracting parties' activities to ensure that contract terms are observed (and enforcing them if they are not).

Sometimes financial intermediaries are able to reduce the costs of writing contracts in cases where lenders or borrowers find highly standardized contracts unsuitable. In some instances, the intermediary is able to write a contract tailored to the needs of individual borrowers at a lower cost than would be possible in an auction or over-the-counter market. In these markets contracts are usually highly standardized and lack special provisions tailored to individual borrowers. To some extent, such special provisions make it difficult for the market as a whole to evaluate the financial instrument. Moreover, when specialized contracts are written with an intermediary, the borrower is also able to renegotiate the terms of the contract with relative ease, whereas this would be costly and difficult if financial claims were widely distributed to the public.

The financial intermediary can reduce the costs of monitoring and enforcement by centralizing these functions in one agent rather than distributing them across all bondholders. This centralization can be efficient because, acting on his own, each bondholder has a limited incentive to expend effort in monitoring and enforcement activities. The same advantage in centralization leads to the use of trustees in public distributions of bonds who are given certain monitoring and enforcement tasks. Moreover, as long as the intermediary's own return is tied to the success of monitoring and enforcement activities there is an incentive to perform those duties reliably. A trustee could also be compensated in a way that provides such an incentive, but the fact that the intermediary's return comes from the asset and is not sold off as a dealer would sell it accomplishes this as well.

Finally, the intermediary can provide a service for lenders if they are relatively unsophisticated compared to borrowers. The intermediary is interposed between a sophisticated party, usually the borrower, and an unsophisticated party, usually the lender. The intermediary is therefore in a position to write, monitor, and enforce contracts with greater skill than the individual lender. In effect, lenders find it profitable to pool their resources and hire a financial intermediary in the same way they would hire a lawyer.

Information Production

An important service provided by financial intermediaries is the production of information about the value of assets. Intermediaries certainly are not the only type of information producer in the financial markets. As we emphasized in Chapter 1, the news media, brokerage houses, bond rating agencies, and other entities all produce information, and so do intermediaries. Intermediaries expend considerable resources collecting, processing, analyzing, and interpreting facts and opinions about the future profits of the firms they finance. Investors could do this on their own, and to a certain extent, they do. It is as efficient to hire specialists in the production of information as it is to hire specialists to monitor the terms of contracts. The unique aspect of the financial intermediary as an information producer is that the intermediary generally does not redistribute information to the market as a whole. In other words, the intermediary does not collect information for direct resale to the market, as the *Wall Street Journal* does. Instead, the intermediary collects information and uses it to guide investment decisions it makes for those who supply it with funds. Therefore, it can be thought of as tying in the production of information with the management of investments.

One of the major concerns about financial intermediaries as information producers is whether they perform this function reliably. The investor never directly sees the information produced by most intermediaries and therefore needs some assurance that the intermediary is not in effect being bribed to invest in firms at too high prices. In this case, a "bribe" is some kind of extra payment paid to owners or managers of an intermediary to induce them to lend funds to a firm that might not qualify or to provide funds on terms that are not in the interest of the intermediary's suppliers of funds. The principal insurance the investor has that the intermediary will perform reliably is the stake the owners and/or managers of the intermediary have in the investments they choose for the intermediary's customers. The larger the amount of capital the intermediary's owners and managers contribute to the intermediary, the more the owners have to lose if they place investments where they know they will not pay off. The market is therefore able to judge by the size of the intermediary's capital stock, and by the personal stake of its managers, the extent of its reliability in gathering information and using it to guide investment decisions.

Intermediaries provide another service to the market that goes hand in hand with information production. They often receive information from corporate borrowers who seek to protect the confidentiality of their information. Firms that seek to protect such confidential information find it advantageous to finance their activities from internal funds if and when they can. When they can't, they find it advantageous to go to sources of financing to whom they can reveal the information in order to secure financing but who will protect its confidentiality. Financial intermediaries provide this option.

Management of the Payments System

The services discussed thus far are provided by almost all intermediaries engaged in the management of investments. Now we will examine two important but more specialized services. The first, management of the payment mechanism, has long been provided by commercial banks. Banks provide the bookkeeping function of keeping track of receipts and disbursements for their customers as well as handling the exchange of funds. There is no reason why the management of payments has to be handled by a financial intermediary that also manages funds. For example, some European countries have payments systems, referred to as *giro,* that are not linked to commercial banks. Although these systems are not all alike, such systems allow individuals to authorize payments to a number of parties through the giro. Usually the giro system allows a user to specify a list of payments to be made and a bank account number from which the funds can be drawn. The bank is then notified of the total funds used. Automated giro systems are sometimes more closely related to the postal system in such countries than to commercial banks. The postal system handles the exchange of funds and provides the customer with a record of these exchanges, and the commercial bank merely maintains the balances of funds for the customer.

Management of the payments mechanism became tied in with the banking industry early in U.S. history. In the first half of the nineteenth century the banking industry issued bank notes that were like a bank's own currency. These notes did not always trade at the same value. That is, the notes issued by a very strong and reputable bank would exchange at a higher value than notes issued by a weak and risky bank. Each bank was willing to accept the notes of other banks at what they thought was a fair rate of exchange, and this constituted the payments mechanism. In the latter part of the century notes were replaced by demand deposits or checking accounts. Banks then began to keep records of transactions from demand deposit accounts, and they had to establish procedures for clearing checks back and forth. Banks set up clearinghouses to handle these exchanges, and large urban banks began to provide many of the collection and record-keeping services for smaller banks. In the twentieth century, after the Federal Reserve System was created, it began to provide many check-clearing services for the banking industry.

More recently, innovations have dramatically changed the economics of the payments system. These changes continue at a rapid pace. First of all, credit and debit cards are actively competing with checks as efficient means of making payments. Credit and debit cards provide the customer with a direct link to a source of credit, but it also alters the method of recording and accounting for transactions. It increases reliance on automated record keeping and seeks to economize on the amount of paper that must change hands. Probably the most significant change in the payments mechanism is the prospect of an electronic funds transfer system. Such a system further minimizes the amount of paper that changes hands in the payments system while relying on electronic record-keeping to the greatest extent possible. There are large potential economies in such a system, but it is difficult to estimate how rapidly we will progress toward a completely electronic system of funds transfer.

Insurance

Another service provided by some financial intermediaries is insurance. Insurance is a service that, like management of the payments mechanism, is easily tied in with the function of managing investments. In the process of insuring various contingencies, insurance companies receive premiums, which they invest, just as commercial banks invest the funds they receive in the course of managing payments for their depositors. While it might be possible to utilize a separate investment manager for funds collected by an insurance company, this is a less efficient means of insuring than is combining the two services.

The basic idea behind insurance is essentially similar to the idea of diversifying risk in the stock market. Individuals and corporations are subject to risks that they would like to be able to avoid or shift to other parties. The risk may be the economic hardship imposed on a family by a death or the loss incurred by damage to property. People who are exposed to these risks are generally willing to pay a fee to have someone else bear at least part of that risk. This shifting of risk becomes economical when the risk can be diversified. For instance, consider the case of a company exposed to the risk of a fire. A company that is interested in insuring against a fire faces a small probability that a fire will occur, which would result in a large loss, and a large probability that no fire will occur, which means no loss at all. A company that insures other companies against fire knows that there will always be some fires, but it knows that the probability that a large number of fires will occur at once is exceptionally small. As long as the insurance company has a large number of customers spread out geographically, it diversifies the risk of fire facing each customer. Therefore, the insurance company can offer customers a price for insurance that the consumer values higher than the prospect of no cost as long as no fire occurs but a large loss if it does.

From the standpoint of the economy, this kind of risk shifting is beneficial because it induces people to undertake productive activities they otherwise would perceive as too risky. The owners of a company might well be averse to constructing an expensive manufacturing plant if they alone had to bear the risk of its burning down. Therefore, risk shifting in general, and insurance in particular, serve a socially useful function.

Now that we have some idea of the basic services provided by financial institutions, we can turn our attention more specifically to the major classes of depository intermediaries. We will discuss commercial banks first and then move on to savings and loans or thrifts.

Commercial Banking

To understand the banking industry in the United States it is essential to recognize that banking, like the entire United States, evolved in an atmosphere infused by populism and states' rights. By this we mean that banking was locally controlled throughout the United States and, even to this date, no national banking firms have emerged. For most of the history of this country, most banks could operate in only one state, and in many states banks were restricted to operating out of only one physical location. While many of these legal barriers to interstate and branch banking are in the process of crumbling, the structure of banking that we see in the United States is still largely a result of the historical barriers to geographic expansion. This is readily apparent from the data in Table 4-1, which shows the distribution of banks by asset size. It is extremely important to recognize that the distribution of banks documented in Table 4-1 may or may not be very efficient, and it may not stay like this very long. The current structure of the banking industry is a result of a long process involving considerable government protection and regulation. Competitive forces in our current economy may well change banking radically in the years ahead. We will be discussing this throughout the book.

The best place to start to understand contemporary commercial banks is to examine the structure of their balance sheets and the nature of their lending activities. We will also examine some of the market characteristics of specific types of bank loans, including loan commitments.

Table 4-1
Size Distribution of Commercial Banks (Based on Total Assets for 1991)

Total Assets ($Millions)	Number of Banks
<10	570
10–25	2,557
$25–50	3,105
$50–100	2,783
$100–500	2,610
$500–5,000	617
$5,000–10,000	70
>10,000	47
TOTAL	12,359

Source: American Bankers Association.

Defining the Commercial Bank Product Set

We think that the way to start to develop an understanding of commercial banking is to make a list of the product and/or services that banks sell to their customers. Table 4-2 presents a list that was originally outlined by the chief economist of Chase Manhattan Bank, of the various types of financial services in a modern economy. This list includes five broad categories of services that encompass all of the assets and liabilities on a bank's balance sheet and all of the various activities that generate noninterest income for a bank. Regulations imposed on banks, which we will discuss in some detail in the next two chapters, restrict banks from engaging in some of the activities on this list. Two major categories of activity are currently restricted or not open to banks; they cannot underwrite life (except credit life), casualty, and fidelity or financial-related insurance and they are restricted in the extent of their securities activities. Table 4-3 provides a list of the major market segments of the securities business and the relevant restrictions on commercial banks in those segments. The table shows whether, as of the end of 1992, banks, bank subsidiaries, or affiliates of bank holding companies were allowed by regulation to operate in each market segment. Further, the table indicates whether there are restrictions on the total gross revenue that can be generated from each activity as a percentage of the total revenue of the bank. (We discuss the regulations as well as bank holding companies in Chapters 5 and 6.) While bank regulators have allowed banks to expand securities activities through holding company affiliates, they have placed restrictions on the scale of those operations. A bank or other financial services firm that hopes to create value for its shareholders must carefully choose which of the market segments identified in Table 4-2 it wants to compete in and how it may do so successfully.

An Overview of the Bank Balance Sheet

To understand how commercial banks operate it is essential to start with the basic structure of the balance sheet of a bank. Table 4-4 presents a simple statement of the balance sheet for a hypothetical bank that we will call the Completely Reliable

Table 4-2
Classes of Finance-Related Services

1. Transactions
   a. Funds transfers
   b. Payments processing
   c. Clearing
   d. Loan servicing
   e. Securities purchases and sales
   f. Foreign exchange purchases and sales
2. Investment and liquidity vehicles
   a. Deposits
      - Immediately transferable
      - Term maturities
   b. Direct issues of fixed-income instruments
      - Short-term maturities
      - Long-term maturities
   c. Equities
   d. Commingled funds
   e. Futures and options
   f. Swaps
3. Fund raising
   a. Borrowing
   b. Equity issuance
   c. Facilitating
      - Origination
      - Underwriting
      - Distribution
4. Insurance
   a. Life
   b. Casualty
   c. Fidelity
   d. Credit protection or enhancement
   e. Market valuation
      - Interest rate
      - Foreign exchange
5. Fiduciary activities
   a. Investment management
   b. Trust
   c. Agency
   d. Safekeeping
   e. Advice

Source: Richard Aspinwall, "The Erosion of the Banking Franchise." *Journal of Commercial Lending*, January 1992, p. 23. Copyright © 1992 by Robert Morris Associates. Reprinted with permission from *The Journal of Commercial Lending*.

Bank. Notice that many banks choose names that communicate to their customers that they can be trusted. Completely Reliable Bank has total assets of $1 billion. These assets are divided into three broad categories. The largest category is loans. Completely Reliable bank has $600 million in loans outstanding. These include loans to consumers and corporations. Loans to corporations are generally referred to

Table 4-3
Status of Major Domestic Securities Activities for Banks and Bank Affiliates

	Banks or Bank Subsidiaries[a]		Nonbank Holding Company Affiliates	
	Underwriting and Dealing[b]	**Investment**	**Underwriting and Dealing**	**Revenue Limits (if any)**
1. U.S. government securities and securities of agencies guaranteed by the U.S. government	Yes	Yes	Yes	None
2. General-obligation securities issued by state and municipal entities	Yes	Yes	Yes	None
3. Other securities issued by state and municipal entities	No[c]	Yes[d]	Yes	10% of gross revenues
4. Corporate debt a. Commercial paper b. Other debt	No	Yes[d]	Yes	10% of gross revenues
5. Mortgage-backed securities a. Secured by federally insured mortgages b. Secured by other mortgages	No[e]	Yes[d]	Yes	10% of gross revenues
6. Securities backed by non-mortgage securities	No[e]	Yes[d]	Yes	10% of gross revenues
7. Corporate equities	No	No	Yes (subject to infrastructure review)	10% of gross revenues

	Permitted for Banks or Bank Subsidiaries	**Permitted for Nonbank Holding Company Affiliates**
8. Mutual funds		
a. Underwriting and distribution	No[b]	No
b. Investment adviser	Yes	Yes
c. Brokerage	Yes	Yes
9. Futures, options, and swaps (brokerage and advice)	Yes	Yes
10. Brokerage		
a. Discount	Yes	Yes
b. Full service	Yes	Yes
11. Private placements	Yes	Yes
12. Advisory services	Yes	Yes

[a]This table generally refers to the powers of national and state member banks of the Federal Reserve System. State nonmember banks may have broader powers under state laws.
[b]Nonmember banks may engage in underwriting through a bona fide subsidiary pursuant to FDIC regulations (12 C.F.R 337.4).
[c]National banks may underwrite certain state housing, hospital, and dormitory securities.
[d]Subject to limitation of 10% of the bank's capital and surplus.
[e]National banks may underwrite their own securitized assets.

Source: Richard Aspinwall, "The Erosion of the Banking Franchise," *Journal of Commercial Lending,* January 1992, p. 25. Copyright © 1992 by Robert Morris Associates. Reprinted with permission from *The Journal of Commercial Lending.*

Table 4-4
Completely Reliable Bank Balance Sheet

Assets	***$ Millions***
Cash	10
Loans	
Commercial and industrial	180
Consumer	
Revolving	110
Installment	80
Real estate	230
Total loans	600
Investments	
Treasury obligations	220
Municipal obligations	60
Total investments	280
Non–Interest-bearing assets	110
Total assets	1,000
Liabilities	
Savings and time deposits	430
Demand deposits	160
Federal funds	80
Commercial paper	250
Loan loss reserves	15
Equity capital	65
Total liabilities and equity	1,000

as commercial and industrial loans. Loans to individuals fall into the categories of credit card loans and installment loans. Installment loans have some regular payments schedule, like an automobile loan; credit card loans generally require only a minimum payment on the outstanding balance. The other major type of loans is real estate or mortgage loans. In some parts of the country the largest component of bank loans may be agricultural loans. These may be listed separately or included in other loans categories. Many banks whose loans are concentrated in agriculture are called agricultural banks. Historically, banks have generated much of their income from the interest rates they charge on loans. This is why loans are counted as bank assets. Notice that these loans are liabilities of the bank's customers, but they are assets on the bank's balance sheet.

The second major category on the bank's balance sheet is investments. Investments include any holdings of marketable securities, principally obligations of the United States Treasury and of state and local governments (municipal bonds). Historically, banks invested funds in marketable securities when they had an excess of liabilities relative to loans. Then, if loan demand were to pick up in the future, they could liquidate or sell their securities to fund the demand for loans. Thus, these investments serve as a kind of secondary reserve to provide extra liquidity. This process of managing the funding of loans was referred to as *asset management* because it involved a tradeoff between these two components of the asset side of the bank's balance sheet. Completely Reliable has $280 million in investments. The third category on the asset side of the balance sheet is non–interest-bearing assets. Completely Reliable has $110 million in such assets. It would be nice if a bank could drive such assets to zero, since this might improve its return on total assets as assets would be less. But banks need office buildings and computers and other equipment to operate. Non–interest-bearing assets include these sorts of things. They also include reserves that Completely Reliable is compelled to hold with the Federal Reserve. These reserves do not earn interest with the Fed, so they show up in this category of the asset side of the balance sheet. In fact, Completely Reliable would like to avoid holding reserves altogether, since they amount to a tax on Completely Reliable's earnings. Finally, Completely Reliable has $10 million in cash.

On the liability side of Completely Reliable's balance sheet we see a variety of different types of deposit and nondeposit sources of funds. The deposits that a customer of Completely Reliable holds are assets from the vantage point of that customer, but they are liabilities from the standpoint of Completely Reliable. The largest source of funds for Completely Reliable is savings and time deposits of $430 million. Completely Reliable also has federal funds of $80 million. These are essentially short-term loans from other banks. Finally, it has demand deposit accounts of $160 million that do not earn interest. Of course Completely Reliable has to handle the check processing for these demand deposit accounts and charges a fee for this service. The next category of liabilities goes outside the realm of deposits. Completely Reliable issues short-term debt securities, commercial paper, just as do industrial firms. This constitutes $250 million. Completely Reliable, consistent with its name, holds reserves for losses of $15 million. These should not be confused with reserves (assets) held with the Federal Reserve. Reserves against losses provide a cushion against future losses from bad loans.

Finally, the residual category on the liability side of the balance sheet is the equity of Completely Reliable. Notice that Completely Reliable has equity of only $65 million. If you were comparing this equity position to the equity of most industrial companies, you would come to the conclusion that Completely Reliable operates on an astonishingly thin margin of equity compared to the size of its assets. That is, this company uses a lot of debt to fund its assets or it is very heavily levered. This is characteristic of all commercial banks; they are very heavily levered institutions. Also, like the accounting statements of other types of firms, the accounting statements of commercial banks show the historical value of most assets and liabilities rather than their current market value. This includes equity, or net worth. The market value of Completely Reliable's stock could have any value, relative to the value shown on the balance sheet in Table 4-4. That market value will be determined by what the market think's Completely Reliable is going to be able to generate in the way of profits in the years ahead. The accounting balance sheet gives us no clue about Completely Reliable's earning capacity.

We have introduced the structure of commercial banking with a hypothetical example of an individual bank. Now we want to turn to the structure of the real financial statements of commercial banks in the United States.

Recent Structure of Commercial Bank Balance Sheets

As of the end of 1991, total bank assets for all United States banks stood at $3,545 billion. The structure of aggregate bank balance sheets is summarized in Tables 4-5 and 4-6. These tables show the rate of growth and the percentage composition of the major categories of bank assets for all United States banks from 1985 through 1991. The tables illustrate that, as of 1991, banks had nearly 88 percent of their total assets invested in some interest-bearing category. The remainder was invested in all of the plant and equipment (buildings, computers, etc.) necessary to operate a bank. Approximately 60 percent of all bank assets were loans, of which the largest single category was real estate. Notice that in 1985 the largest category of bank loans was loans to corporations, or commercial and industrial loans. However, these loans declined steadily, as a percentage of total assets, over the seven years ending in 1991, just as real estate loans increased. This pattern is evident in Table 4-6 as well, where the growth rates in real estate loans have been substantial and the growth rates in commercial and industrial loans have been small or negative. By contrast, consumer lending has remained a roughly stable percentage of total assets over the

Table 4-5

Portfolio Composition of Insured Commercial Banks, 1985–91[1]

Item	1985	1986	1987	1988	1989	1990	1991
	Balance sheet items as a percentage of average consolidated assets including loss reserves						
Interest-earning assets	86.59	86.98	87.43	87.94	87.86	87.71	87.95
Balances due from depositories	5.53	5.14	5.25	4.98	4.35	3.54	3.04
Loans	59.88	59.49	59.75	60.59	61.32	61.16	60.07
Commercial and industrial	22.02	20.80	19.92	19.41	19.06	18.49	17.34
U.S. addressees	17.29	16.80	16.51	16.44	16.48	15.98	14.98
Foreign addressees	4.72	4.00	3.41	2.97	2.58	2.51	2.35
Consumer	10.88	11.18	11.11	11.32	11.44	11.23	10.84
Credit card	2.56	2.88	2.98	3.14	3.30	3.31	3.31
Installment and other	8.31	8.30	8.13	8.18	8.14	7.92	7.53
Real estate	15.70	16.69	18.69	20.56	22.18	23.51	24.39
Construction and land development	3.20	3.49	3.87	4.01	4.14	3.97	3.37
Farmland	.41	.43	.46	.49	.51	.51	.53
One- to four-family residential	7.19	7.30	8.00	9.18	9.93	10.95	11.96
Home equity	n.a.	n.a.	n.a.	1.17	1.41	1.64	1.90
Other	n.a.	n.a.	n.a.	8.01	8.52	9.30	10.06
Multifamily residential	.44	.49	.56	.58	.59	.61	.64
Nonfarm nonresidential	4.00	4.42	5.21	5.77	6.29	6.72	7.12
Booked in foreign offices	.46	.55	.59	.52	.72	.76	.77
Depository institutions	2.88	2.53	2.39	2.17	1.90	1.66	1.50
Foreign governments	1.56	1.42	1.34	1.23	1.03	.79	.76
Agricultural production	1.51	1.21	1.03	.99	.96	.96	1.02
Other	4.51	4.75	4.30	3.85	3.64	3.41	3.16
Lease financing receivables	.84	.91	.97	1.07	1.11	1.11	1.07

Table 4-5 (continued)

Portfolio Composition of Insured Commercial Banks, 1985–91[1]

Item	1985	1986	1987	1988	1989	1990	1991
	Balance sheet items as a percentage of average consolidated assets including loss reserves						
Securities	15.52	16.09	16.67	16.84	16.73	17.25	18.66
U.S. government and other debt	10.58	10.79	12.33	13.15	13.38	14.35	16.08
U.S. government securities	9.49	9.24	10.03	10.35	10.77	11.85	13.59
U.S. Treasury	4.53	4.31	5.91	5.47	4.75	4.34	4.88
U.S. government agency and corporation obligations	4.96	4.93	4.12	4.88	6.03	7.51	8.70
Government-backed mortagage pools	.95	1.16	2.07	2.59	3.27	4.07	4.46
Collateralized mortgage obligations	n.a.	n.a.	n.a.	n.a.	n.a.	1.34	2.07
Other obligations	4.01	3.77	2.05	2.30	2.76	2.10	2.17
Other debt securities	1.08	1.55	2.29	2.80	2.61	2.50	2.49
State and local government	4.94	5.31	4.29	3.63	3.06	2.57	2.23
Taxable	n.a.	n.a.	.06	.06	.08	.08	.07
Tax-exempt	4.94	5.31	4.34	3.69	3.14	2.65	2.30
Equity[2]	n.a.	n.a.	n.a.	n.a.	.26	.25	.28
Trading account assets	1.24	1.55	1.32	1.27	1.25	1.44	1.78
Gross federal funds sold and reverse repurchase agreements	4.42	4.71	4.43	4.26	4.20	4.33	4.40
Non–interest earning assets	12.61	12.09	11.20	10.51	10.63	10.73	10.47
Interest-bearing liabilities	72.16	72.31	72.87	73.91	74.59	75.09	75.11
Deposits	60.89	59.90	60.27	61.17	61.68	62.50	63.47
In foreign offices	12.18	11.17	10.94	10.46	9.65	9.16	8.59
In domestic offices	48.72	48.72	49.34	50.74	52.03	53.34	54.88
Transaction accounts	4.56	5.20	6.01	6.27	6.16	6.22	6.76
Savings deposits (including MMDAs)	16.35	17.41	18.22	17.52	16.36	16.56	17.95
Large-denomination time deposits	11.47	10.78	10.60	11.09	11.69	11.18	9.63
Small-denomination time deposits	16.33	15.33	14.63	15.86	17.82	19.38	20.55
Gross federal funds purchased and repurchase agreements	7.68	8.26	8.06	7.72	7.95	7.75	6.86
Other interest-bearing liabilities	3.59	4.15	4.54	5.02	4.96	4.85	4.79
Non–interest-bearing liabilities	21.66	21.48	21.08	20.00	19.14	18.65	18.34
Demand deposits	15.61	16.02	15.41	14.34	13.63	12.98	12.77
MEMO							
Money market liabilities	35.23	34.68	34.50	34.61	34.58	33.26	30.19
Loss reserves	.80	.93	1.37	1.55	1.51	1.55	1.58
Equity capital[3]	6.18	6.21	6.05	6.09	6.27	6.26	6.55

Source: *Federal Reserve Bulletin,* July 1992.

1. Numbers in table have been revised from previous years using uniform definitions across time and incorporating updated Call Report information.
2. Before 1989, "equity" securities were combined with "other debt securities."
3. Includes banks with negative as well as positive equity.

n.a. not available

Table 4-6

Annual Rate of Growth of Balance Sheet Items, All Insured Commercial Banks, 1985–91[1]

Percent

Item	1985	1986	1987	1988	1989	1990	1991
Total assets	8.5	7.7	2.0	4.4	5.9	2.8	2.6
Interest-earning assets[2]	9.3	8.0	3.9	4.1	6.3	2.4	3.3
Loans	7.5	7.5	4.1	6.0	6.8	2.4	-1.4
Commercial and industrial	2.2	4.3	-1.5	2.4	3.4	-.3	-7.8
Consumer	14.4	7.4	3.3	6.3	5.7	.4	-2.0
Credit card	22.9	12.8	6.7	8.7	10.2	.6	4.0
Installment and other	11.8	5.6	2.1	5.4	3.9	.3	-4.6
Real estate	13.1	17.7	16.6	13.8	13.6	9.1	4.7
Other	5.1	-.2	-4.7	-2.9	-.2	-6.6	-3.5
Securities	13.9	10.2	7.2	1.9	4.9	8.9	15.8
U.S. government	2.5	17.2	9.9	5.0	10.2	16.4	23.4
State and local government	33.0	-12.6	-13.7	-12.0	-9.8	-11.9	-11.9
Non–interest-earning assets	8.1	9.5	-5.5	1.9	5.5	-.5	-.3
Total liabilities	8.5	7.8	2.3	4.2	6.0	2.6	2.4
Deposits	7.7	7.9	2.3	4.2	5.4	4.1	3.0
Demand	9.0	14.0	-10.4	1.4	.7	1.0	-.8
Other checkable	17.8	33.3	8.3	8.1	2.7	6.7	16.4
Savings	23.8	13.4	39.9	1.2	1.0	6.6	16.0
Small-denomination time	2.8	-1.3	7.9	15.6	17.7	14.3	1.6
Large-denomination time	3.9	-2.0	11.5	8.8	7.4	-4.7	-19.0
Subordinated notes and debentures	43.7	14.6	3.5	-.5	15.4	21.1	6.9
Equity capital[3]	8.8	7.1	-1.4	8.4	3.7	6.1	6.2
Memo							
Loss reserves	24.2	24.8	74.5	-4.6	17.7	3.6	2.7

Source: *Federal Reserve Bulletin,* July 1992.

1. Growth rates calculated from year-end to year-end.
2. Includes trading account assets, federal funds sold, and interest-bearing balances.
3. Includes banks with negative as well as positive equity.

period. Investments in securities have increased from roughly 16 percent to 18 percent of total assets. However, two opposite trends are embedded in these numbers. Investments in obligations of the U.S. government and in mortgage-backed securities have increased significantly while investments in municipal bonds have declined. Municipal bonds are free of corporate income taxes, a feature attractive to commercial banks, which, unlike such investors as pension funds, are subject to income taxes. In fact, historically, commercial banks and insurance companies were once the largest holders of municipal bonds in the economy, though in the last few years holdings of municipal bonds by individual investors and mutual funds have been increasing dramatically. The decrease in municipal investments by commercial banks reflects changes in the tax law passed in 1986, which made municipal securities less attractive to banks (see Chapter 2). At the same time, as loan demand from corporations declined in recent years, banks were compelled to invest in other marketable securities. This shift in investment patterns is clearly evident in these data.

Most of the commercial and industrial loans extended by commercial banks are short-term as opposed to long-term loans. Short-term loans generally average less than two months in maturity, and most short-term loans are made at fixed rates. By contrast, most long-term loans are made with floating interest rates. The long-term floating rate loans were most commonly based on or tied to the prime interest rate. The prime interest rate was once thought to be the rate charged to a bank's most creditworthy customers; however, a sizable portion of total loan volume is made at interest rates below prime. Below-prime lending has become commonplace in response to increased competition for lending to high-quality borrowers. These borrowers can now issue commercial paper at very tight spreads over the Treasury bill rate. (See Chapter 2 for discussions of commercial paper and Treasury bills). As a result, it has been necessary for banks to reduce the rates they charge to the high-quality segment of the commercial and industrial loan market. Rather than being the rate charged to the highest-quality borrower, the prime interest rate is now an index rate used as the base in pricing many floating rate loans. Thus, what matters to a borrower is the spread charged over or under the prime rate and the extent to which a bank's prime rate moves with other market interest rates. Most prime interest rates charged by banks are now closely indexed to market rates, which reflect the cost of specific sources of funds for the bank. Banks have some incentive to attempt to hold the prime up when market interest rates are falling. If bank customers can without cost move from bank to bank in their borrowing, then this incentive is limited. If there are significant costs in such adjustments, there may tend to be some "stickiness" in the prime, at least on the way down.

Another interesting feature of bank lending is the importance of commitments in determining bank lending. The majority of commercial and industrial loans are made under loan commitments. The purpose of the commitment is to provide some assurance to the borrower that funds will be available if and when they are needed. Two major types of commitments may be agreed upon by borrowers and commercial banks. One, referred to as a line of credit, is an informal agreement between borrower and lender to provide funds up to a prespecified amount over a prespecified interval. Most lines of credit stipulate that the interest rate will float with the prime rate; thus, they are referred to as *floating rate agreements.* Lines of credit that commit a bank to a specific rate in the future, or fixed rate agreements, are now less common than floating rate agreements. Lines of credit are informal agreements, as they are not legally binding on the bank. Banks scrupulously try to honor most such agreements because their reputation for reliability is at stake, but this type of agreement is not enforceable in court and banks can legally refuse to honor it. Historically, banks generally required that borrowers with a line of credit maintain balances with the bank as a means of compensating for a line of credit; today, however, banks are increasingly emphasizing fees over balances as compensation for commitments. The alternative type of commitment is a revolving credit agreement. Unlike the line of credit, the revolving credit agreement is a legally binding commitment to provide

Table 4-7
Income and Expense as Percentages of Total Assets for All Insured Commercial Banks

Item	1987	1988	1989	1990	1991
Net income			0.49	0.49	0.54
Gross interest income	8.34	8.95	10.0	9.57	8.59
Gross interest expense	4.95	5.42	6.46	6.13	4.98
Net interest margin	3.40	3.53	3.54	3.44	3.61
Less loss provisions	1.27	0.54	0.95	0.93	0.98
Noninterest income	1.41	1.47	1.57	1.63	1.73
Noninterest expense	3.30	3.33	3.4	3.45	3.69
Net noninterest margin	−1.89	−1.86	−1.83	−1.82	−1.96
Securities gain or loss	0.05	0.01	0.03	0.02	0.09
Income before taxes	0.28	1.14	0.78	0.70	0.76
Taxes and extraordinary items	0.18	0.33	0.29	0.21	0.22
Cash dividends	0.36	0.44	0.44	0.42	0.43
Retained income	−0.24	0.4	0.05	0.07	0.11

Source: *Federal Reserve Bulletin,* various issues.

funds on prespecified terms. As a result, revolving credit agreements often include more detailed terms for the borrower than do lines of credit.

On the liability side of the balance sheet, commercial banks derive most of their funds from various types of deposit accounts. The percentage composition of total assets of the various types of deposit accounts that appear on the books of commercial banks are shown in Table 4-5. The growth rates are shown in Table 4-6. The largest single source of deposits is small-denomination time deposits. The cutoff between small and large denomination is generally $100,000. The growth in this category of deposits in the last few years apparently reflects an effort on the part of banks to emphasize retail deposits at the expense of more costly deposits that are more price sensitive, such as large-denomination time deposits and foreign deposits. Deposits in foreign branches or Eurodollar deposits have been declining and are now the smallest fraction of the total. Eurodollar deposits represent overseas liabilities held in foreign branches of U.S. banks and denominated in U.S. dollars. Overall, banks were not as willing to compete intensively for deposits in the last few years as interest rates have fallen and their investments in government securities have been increasing. This reflects the relatively small profit that is available for a bank in the long run from investing deposits in Treasury obligations.

Profitability of Commercial Banks

Table 4-7 presents data that tell an interesting story about the performance of the commercial banking industry from 1987 to 1991. This table presents basic income statement information for commercial banks as a percentage of total assets. The first line is net income or return on assets. The next two lines in this table report gross interest income and interest expense for insured banks. Notice that both hit their peak in 1989, when short-term market interest rates hit their peak as well. This is evidenced in Figure 4-2, which shows the level of 90-day Treasury bill interest rates over the period from 1981 to 1991. By contrast, net interest margin, which is the difference between interest income and expense, was increasing slightly during most of this period, though the change was not particularly dramatic. The next few lines in the table document some important changes in the performance of commercial banks. Noninterest or fee income (that is, income that banks charge for various services that they provide) was increasing. The increase in noninterest income, especially pronounced at relatively large commercial banks, was less significant at smaller banks. Most commercial banks are placing significant emphasis on generating a greater portion of total income from fees for services. However, noninterest expense has also been increasing, so the difference between these two items, or the noninterest margin, has fluctuated, depending on which item experienced the stronger growth. Moreover, as many banks were forced to restructure and take significant charges against earnings associated with restructuring, this shows up in noninterest expense. The other major determinant of net income or return on assets is loss provisions on loans. Loss provisions were very high early in this period but stabilized somewhat in the last few years. Moreover, many large commercial banks had substantial losses resulting from defaults and write-downs of loans to less developed countries (LDC debt).

It is particularly interesting to break down this profitability data by size class of bank. Table 4-8 shows income and expense categories for the years 1989 to 1991 for banks of four size classes. These data tell a very interesting story about the

Figure 4-2

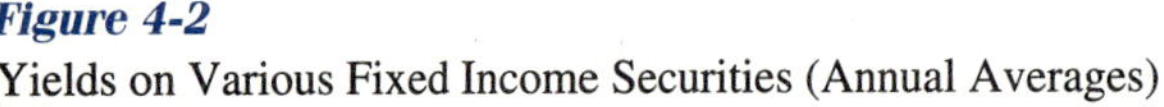
Yields on Various Fixed Income Securities (Annual Averages)

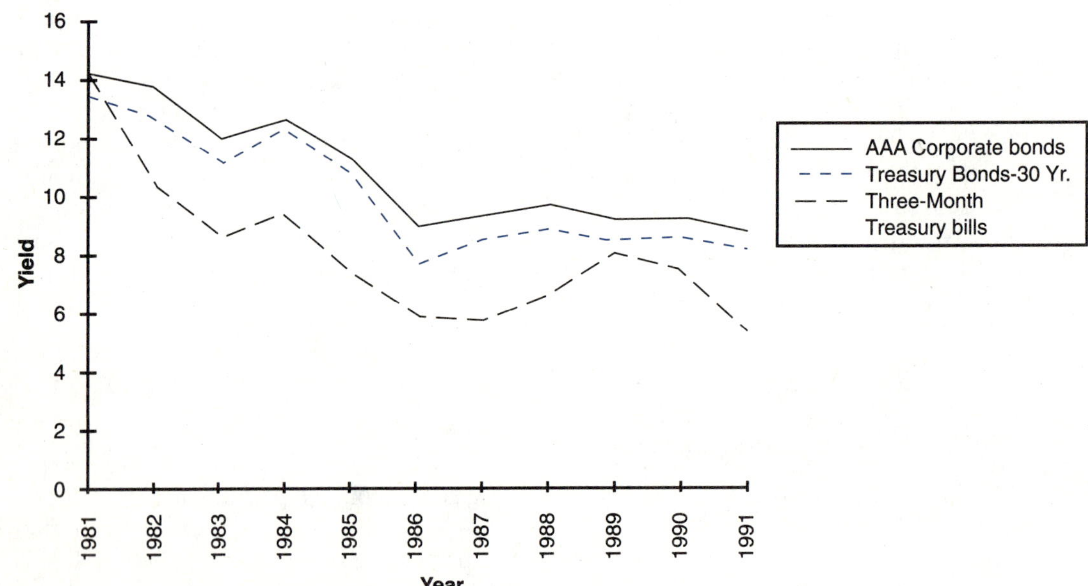

Table 4-8

Income and Expense Items as a Percentage of Average Net Consolidated Assets, Insured Commercial Banks, by Size of Bank, 1989–1991

Year and size of bank	Net interest margin (taxable equivalent)[1]	Net noninterest margin	Loss provisions	Net income (return on assets)
1991				
All banks	3.71	-1.96	.98	.54
Small	4.25	-2.52	.47	.82
Medium	4.08	-2.18	1.05	.53
Large, excluding ten largest	3.58	-1.81	1.09	.58
Ten largest	2.96	-1.42	1.20	.21
1990				
All banks	3.55	-1.82	.93	.49
Small	4.25	-2.48	.49	.79
Medium	4.02	-2.04	1.11	.53
Largest, excluding ten largest	3.31	-1.63	1.20	.28
Ten largest	2.73	-1.26	.76	.47
1989				
All banks	3.68	-1.83	.95	.49
Small	4.35	-2.49	.47	.85
Medium	4.10	-2.10	.76	.74
Large, excluding ten largest	3.49	-1.57	1.06	.55
Ten largest	2.82	-1.23	1.49	-.22

[1]For each bank with profits before tax greater than zero, income from tax-exempt state and local obligations was increased by $[t/(1 - t)]$ times the lesser of profits before tax or interest earned on tax-exempt obligations, where t is the marginal federal income-tax rate. This adjustment approximates the equivalent pretax return on tax-exempt obligations. Source: *Federal Reserve Bulletin,* July 1992.

performance of U.S. banks. First, smaller banks have a consistently higher net interest margin than larger banks. This means smaller banks seem to be able to charge higher interest rates on loans or attract deposits with lower rates than do larger banks. In addition, large banks have relied more on so-called hot money, or deposits purchased in large denominations. These are generally more expensive than deposits raised through a banks consumer and small business customer base. Moreover, in two of the three years shown, smaller banks had smaller loss provisions than did larger banks. However, smaller banks had lower noninterest margins than larger banks. This primarily reflects the fact that smaller banks have been less effective than larger banks in generating fee or noninterest income. When all three considerations are combined, smaller banks generally have a higher return on assets or net income, as a percentage of assets, than do larger banks. In fact, the ten largest banks have performed rather poorly in return on assets in recent years.

Another way to evaluate the performance of commercial banks is to examine their stock price performance. The stock price is a measure that tells us how much potential for future profitability the market places on commercial banks. That is, for a given level of current and historical earnings, a high stock price suggests the market has a high degree of confidence that earnings will increase significantly in the future, whereas a low price suggests just the opposite. Another way to draw an inference about the market's judgment of future bank performance is to examine the spread charged when banks sell debt (specifically subordinated debt) to the marketplace. Figure 4-3 presents data on both bank stock prices and the spread commanded in the market on subordinated debt issues, broken down by money center and regional banks. Notice that bank stocks hit their bottom and the spreads on subordinated debt hit their peak in late 1990. From that point through mid-1992, bank stock prices climbed and spreads on subordinated debt fell. This seems to reflect increased optimism about the profit potential of commercial banks. Much of this is due to the decline in market interest rates that roughly coincides with these changes, and part is due to an assessment that loan losses and charges for restructuring may be declining.

• *The "Bigger Is Better" Syndrome in Commercial Banking* •

One of the most important big stories in the commercial banking business in the early 1990s pertains to the mergers that have taken place between some of the largest commercial banks in the United States. The mergers have combined some of the largest institutions in specific regions of the country resulting in some much larger banks. To see how dramatic some of these changes have been we simply need to examine Table 4-9, which shows the 12 largest commercial banks as of 31 March 1991. The table also shows the same 12 banks after the combinations that took place roughly in the next two years. Note that the total assets shown are all for the same date, 21 March 1991. Six of the top 12 banks were involved in mergers with each other. Moreover, these banks and many other relatively large banks (but smaller than the top 12) are actively acquiring many smaller banks. Mergers took place between the following banks: Chemical and Manufacturers Hanover (now known as Chemical), BankAmerica and Security Pacific (now known as BankAmerica), and NCNB and C&S/Sovran (now known as NationsBank).

There are a number of reasons for these mergers. Probably the most important reason is the perception that bigger is better because of economies of scale in operations, the ability to eliminate duplication between competing banks, and the ability to generate higher margins with less competition in regional markets. Notice that none of these three mergers among the top 12 banks involved major banks in one region of the country acquiring a major bank in a distant region. We have not (yet) seen something like a top New York bank acquiring a top California bank. These mergers were aimed more at increasing market power and reducing costs among competitors in a given market.

It is important to recognize that it may well not be essential to be big in order to be successful. A number of very well-run institutions have chosen not to get involved in major mergers.

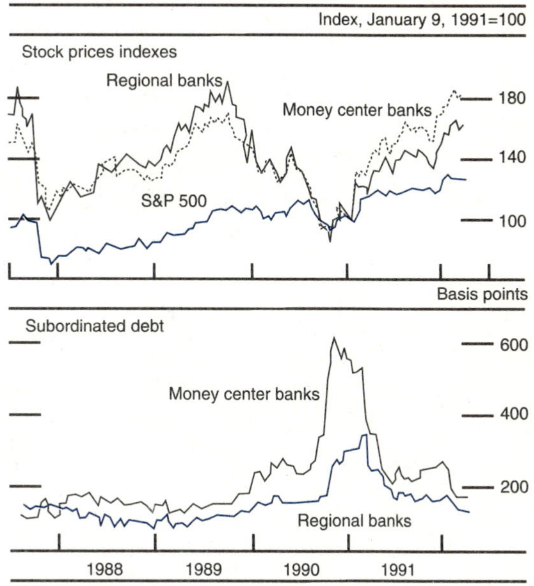

Figure 4-3

Stock price indexes, and spread of interest rates paid on bank subordinated debt over rates on comparable Treasury Securities, 1987–92[1]

Source: Federal Reserve Bulletin, *July 1992.*

[1] Data in top panel are for eleven money center and twenty-four regional banks as defined by Salomon Brothers. Data in lower panel are for a subset of banks in each of these groups. Yields on Treasury securities and subordinated debt are based on actively traded issues adjusted to a ten-year constant maturity.

One good reason may be a judgment that the price an acquirer has to pay to acquire another bank may be too large. One example of a bank that has been very successful in the early 1990s, though it has avoided acquisitions while its major competitors have been heavily involved in mergers, is Sun Trust Banks. Sun Trust has avoided acquisitions, reportedly because it has not felt that prices have been attractive enough to generate the return it has been able to obtain from its own assets. As of the end of 1992 Sun Trust had roughly $37 billion in assets and earned a rate of return on assets of 1.21 percent for 1992, the fifth highest return among the 25 largest U.S. banks. Sun Trust appears to concentrate on conservative lending policies and on profitable trust operations.[1] This policy has worked at the same time that many of Sun Trust's competitors have sought profits through aggressive acquisition growth.

The Structure of the Savings and Loan Industry

Savings and loans have received much attention from the public in the United States in recent years owing to the large cost of the government bailout of depositors in savings and loans and to the prosecution of some highly visible former savings and loans executives. We will deal with the regulatory issues in this industry in the next two chapters, but here we want to describe the basic features of the savings and

[1] See Brannigan, Martha. "Sun Trust Banks Plods Its Way Along to Strong Results." *Wall Street Journal,* March 31, 1993, p. B4.

Table 4-9
Top U. S. Banks by Total Assets Before and After Major Mergers (Billions of Dollars as of 31 March 1991)

Before Mergers		After Mergers	
1. Citicorp	$217	1. Citicorp	$217
2. BankAmerica	112	2. BankAmerica	173
3. Chase Manhattan	98	3. Chemical	135
4. J. P. Morgan	94	4. NationsBank	113
5. Chemical	74	5. Chase Manhattan	98
6. Manufacturers Hanover	61	6. J. P. Morgan	94
7. Security Pacific	61	7. Bankers Trust	57
8. NCNB	63	8. Wells Fargo	56
9. Bankers Trust	57	9. First Interstate	50
10. Wells Fargo	56		
11. First Interstate	50		
12. C&S/Sovran	50		

loan industry. In order to understand savings and loan institutions, the other major form of depository institution, we need to focus on the mortgage industry. Historically, savings and loans were restricted to investing almost exclusively in mortgages, and mortgage finance is still their primary business. Mortgage finance is a big topic, however, and we can only scratch the surface in the remainder of this chapter. But we will be dealing with mortgage finance in many places throughout the rest of this book.

The best place to start is with a clear understanding of what mortgages actually finance. It is easy to get the impression that people take out home mortgage loans almost exclusively for the purpose of acquiring homes. But it is necessary to look back to the late 1960s to find a time when this was the case. In the early part of the postwar era mortgage debt was consistently less than the volume of new construction. During this period mortgage debt was used to finance the acquisition of new housing, but by the early 1970s the volume of new mortgage financing outstripped the increase in new residential property. Mortgage debt was being used for all sorts of purposes, from financing education to funding vacations. It had become a source of consumer financing. This is evident in the recent data on new residential mortgage debt and residential construction (Fig. 4-4). During most of the years since 1985 new mortgage debt substantially exceeded residential construction, as consumers used mortgage financing for a variety of purposes.

This change did not occur simply because the United States emerged from a time of tremendous unsatisfied demand for housing, as was the case in the early 1950s, but also because of a significant increase in the value of real property coupled with a decline in the real cost of existing mortgages. In other words, in the 1970s residential property owners found that the market value of their property increased while their mortgage payments remained fixed. The fixed terms of the

Figure 4-4
New Residential Construction and New Residential Mortgage Debt

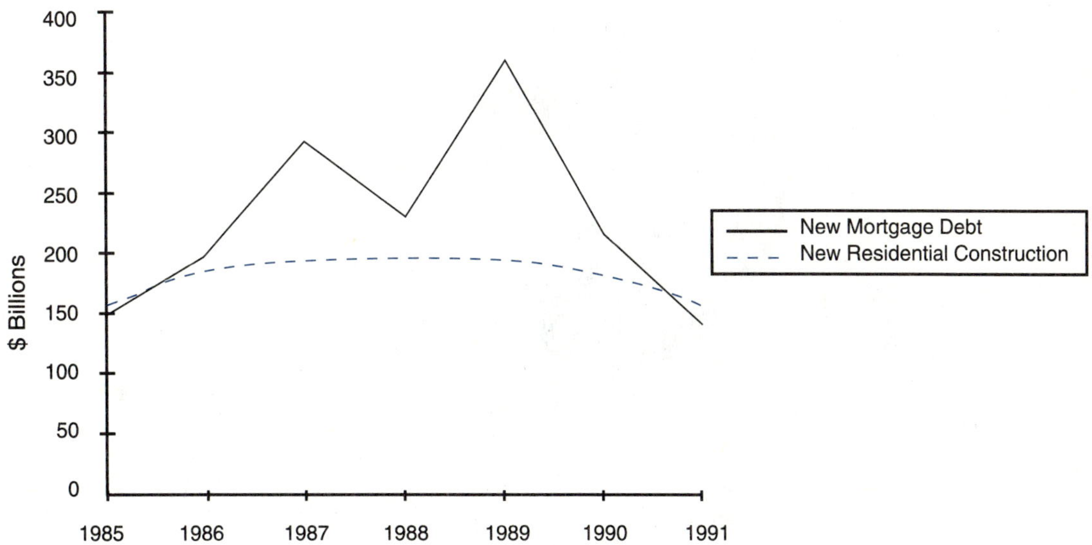

mortgage at interest rates that proved, with hindsight, to be quite low meant that the real cost of the mortgage was declining. As a result, homeowners chose to borrow against the increased value of their property and use the funds to finance other expenditures. Such loans are often called home equity loans. For most individuals in the 1970s and much of the 1980s, their homes turned out to be the best investment they ever made. Unfortunately, this was not the case in the late 1980s and the early 1990s in many parts of the country. Figure 4-4 shows the extent to which they have borrowed against that value. Using mortgage debt for a variety of purposes was reinforced by the 1986 tax law, which stipulated that mortgage interest up to the limit of the initial purchase price of a home plus improvements was tax deductible while other forms of consumer interest were no longer deductible.

What was good for the borrower was not necessarily good for either the ultimate supplier of funds or for private institutions that act as intermediaries between borrowers and lenders. With the advent of high inflation rates in the 1970s, which were to a large degree unanticipated, wealth was transferred from lenders to borrowers. Those who borrowed at fixed rates early in the inflationary process benefited, those who lent were hurt. As inflation declined in the early 1980s, financial intermediaries continued to experience financial difficulties owing to high default rates on mortgages and poor credit quality of many loans. To understand the nature of the difficulties we have to examine the industry that funds mortgages in the United States.

The single most important type of institution that originates and invests in home mortgages is the savings and loan. This is apparent from inspection of Figure 4-5,

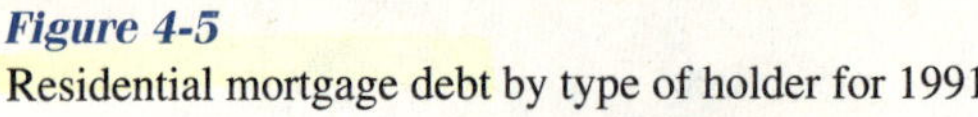

Figure 4-5
Residential mortgage debt by type of holder for 1991

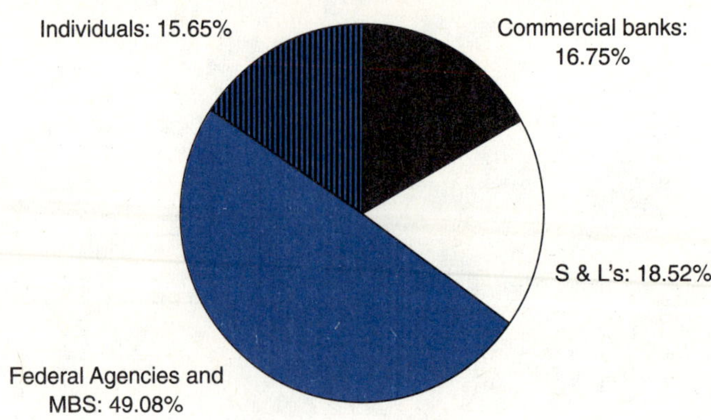

which shows the total amount of single-family (actually one- to four-family) home mortgage debt directly held by various types of institutions and the amount held by the federal mortgage agencies and issued in the form of mortgage-backed securities in 1991. (Note that life insurance companies, which comprise a very small portion of the total, are included in mortgage-backed securities.) The figure also shows that commercial banks ranked second after savings and loans. But commercial banks have a total portfolio, including nonmortgage loans, that is much more diversified than the portfolio of savings and loans. Savings and loans, on the other hand, historically were constrained by regulation to invest almost exclusively in residential mortgages. Only since 1982, with the passage of the Garn-St. Germain Act, have savings and loans been allowed to diversify to any great extent. We discuss this act in more detail in Chapter 6.

The role of savings and loans in the mortgage finance system is also apparent from an inspection of their balance sheets. Panel A of Figure 4-6 shows the proportion of total assets in various categories of loans and investments for all savings and loans; Panel B shows the level of total assets in savings and loans from 1985 to 1991. Notice that the vast majority of assets are still in mortgages or mortgage-backed securities. Notice also that the total assets in savings and loans has been shrinking as large numbers of savings and loans have failed and have been taken over by the regulators in recent years.

The savings and loan industry has been the focal point of tremendous attention from the American public in recent years, as a result of the large losses in this industry and the absorption of those losses by U.S. taxpayers as a result of deposit insurance. To understand how this problem developed and how it has affected the savings and loan industry we need to develop a more detailed understanding of the entire regulatory system for depository financial intermediaries. We turn to this topic in the next chapter.

Figure 4-6
Panel A: Components of 1991 S&L Assets
Panel B: Total S&L Assets, 1985–1991

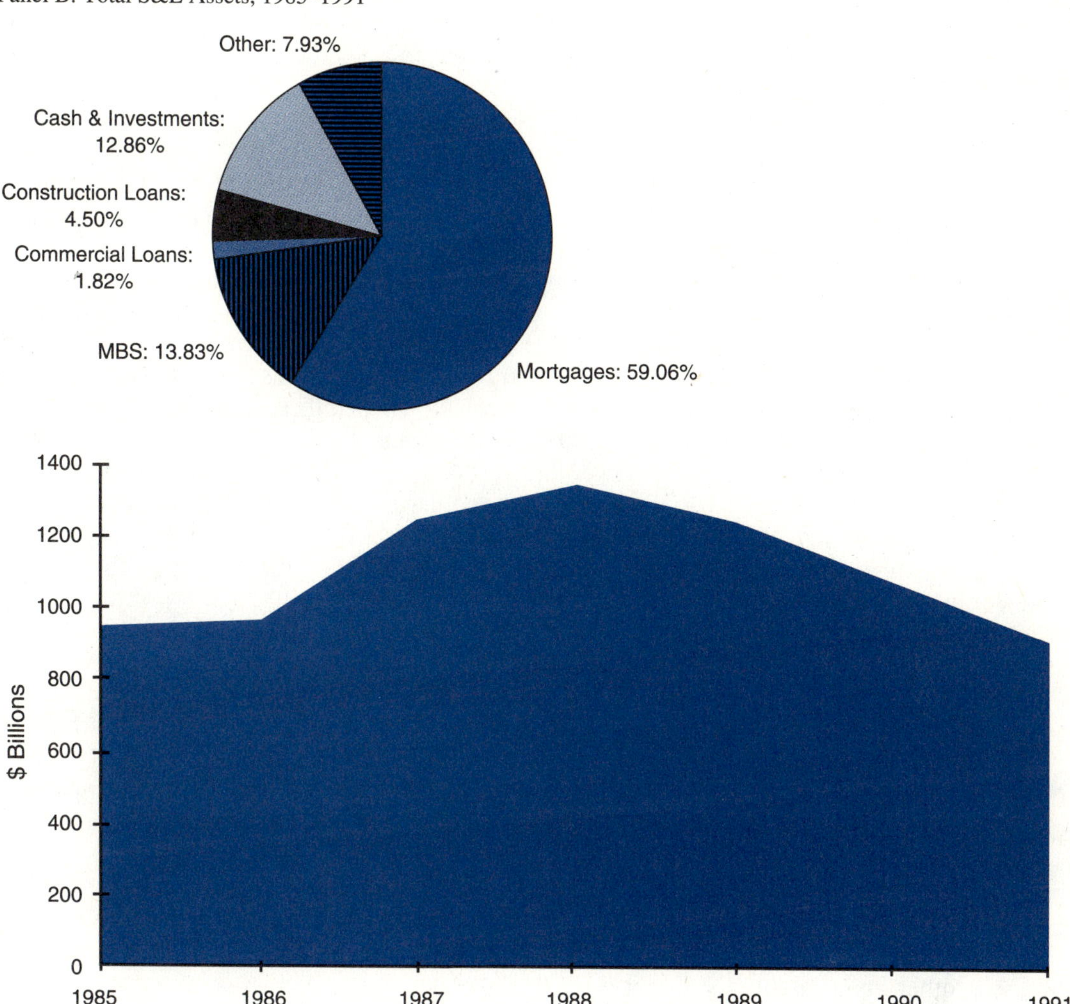

SUMMARY

We began this chapter by describing the various types of financial intermediaries that operate in the United States. Then we examined six services financial intermediaries provide to financial markets. The first few services are provided by almost all intermediaries; the latter ones are more specialized.

Risk reduction through diversification. Financial intermediaries construct diversified portfolios of securities and sell claims on themselves to the market. In this way, they provide diversification for the investor. This is profitable because intermediaries find it less costly to construct a large diversified portfolio and sell small portions of it than individual investors would if they had to construct their own small, diversified portfolios.

Maturity intermediation and provision of liquidity. Many intermediaries acquire assets with long maturities and sell claims with very short maturities. This is referred to as intermediating across time, or maturity intermediation. The intermediaries demand a price that compensates them for the risk they bear in bridging the gap between desired maturities.

Reduction in the cost of contracting. Two principal costs are involved in utilizing financial contracts. The first is the cost of constructing the contract, including the expertise required to know how best to structure the contract. The second is the cost of monitoring the parties' behavior to be sure the contract terms are observed. Investors who supply funds to financial intermediaries would find these costs to be quite large if they had to write, monitor, and enforce contracts with borrowers themselves. Financial intermediaries can lower these costs by specializing in financial contracting.

Information production. Financial intermediaries produce information about the borrowers who are supplied with funds. They differ from other types of information producers because they do not directly distribute this information to the market. Thus, much of the information they receive is confidential.

Management of the payments system. A service historically provided by commercial banks is keeping records and providing for exchange of funds through demand deposits. Today, other types of intermediaries are competing with commercial banks in providing this service in the United States. This service is tied in with other services involved in managing investments for individuals and companies.

Insurance. Many types of financial intermediaries provide insurance against particular contingencies, such as life insurance and property and casualty insurance companies. These companies invest the funds received as premium income and repay these funds in the event of some event, such as fire, accident, or death. Though the management problems of insurance intermediaries are quite different from those of deposit intermediaries, they serve as a market for borrowing and lending, just as other financial intermediaries do.

Next we turned our attention to the commercial banking industry. We started by examining the balance sheets of commercial banks. An examination of the balance sheets of commercial banks shows that the largest component of bank loans is business or commercial and industrial loans, followed by mortgage loans. Banks' investments consist largely of holdings of Treasury and municipal debt instruments. Banks invest in Treasuries when they want very liquid investments and in municipals when they want tax-sheltered income. Banks finance their loans and investments principally with deposit accounts. The most important source of deposits in the 1980s was small time deposits. Various types of transaction accounts, including demand deposits, are second in importance.

Most commercial and industrial loans are short term rather than long term, and most short-term loans have fixed rates. On the other hand, the vast majority of the longer-term loans are made at floating rates tied to the prime interest rate or some market rate. A majority of loans are made under loan commitments of one kind or another, though small loans are less likely than large ones to be made under commitments.

Banks experienced a general decline in the relative importance of commercial and industrial loans as a percentage of total assets while real estate loans grew in importance. Moreover, growth of banks' investments in Treasury obligations added to the liquidity of bank balance sheets. Banks have had difficulties maintaining profitability during much of the 1980s; however, banks generated larger profits in the early 1990s, as interest rates declined and bank stock prices moved up as well. Smaller banks were generally more profitable than larger ones. Problems with profitability were most severe for the 10 largest banks in the United States.

Finally, we examined the basic structure of the savings and loan industry. Savings and loans, historically and currently, are principally engaged in mortgage finance. But we emphasized that mortgages are now used to finance a wide variety of different consumer expenditures. We also briefly discussed how regulation has compelled the savings and loan industry to adopt the structure that we observe today. We will look more closely at savings and loan regulation in the next chapter.

QUESTIONS

1. Without the aid of an intermediary investors can diversify portfolios and purchase securities with different maturities. Under what circumstances would they seek to use intermediaries to do this for them?
2. What does it mean to say that intermediaries can reduce the cost of contracting? What is included in the cost of contracting? What is the difference between an intermediary and the trustee of a bond?
3. What incentive does a financial intermediary have to produce reliable information? How does the market deal with the problem of unreliable information produced by financial intermediaries?
4. What is the payment system? How do commercial banks in the United States manage the payment system? Can you imagine an alternative, equally efficient system?
5. Insurance leads to a redistribution of risk. How can such a redistribution be socially beneficial?
6. Describe the patterns in the early 1990s in the composition of bank assets and liabilities. What percentage of bank assets were loans of various types? How did this percentage change over time?
7. Of what significance is the prime interest rate in modern pricing of bank loans? How has the use of the prime rate changed over time?

8. What are lines of credit and revolving credit agreements? How important are they in bank lending in the 1980s?
9. Explain the basic trends in bank profitability in the 1980s. How has the relative importance of interest income versus fee income changed over this period?
10. How did banks of different sizes perform during the 1980s, in both return on assets and return on equity? How can the differences in performance be explained?

REFERENCES

Brady, Thomas F. "Changes in Loan Pricing and Business Lending at Commercial Banks." *Federal Reserve Bulletin* (January 1985), pp. 1–13.

Brannigan, Martha. "Sun Trust Banks Plods Its Way Along to Strong Results." *Wall Street Journal,* March 31, 1993, p. B4.

Brunner, Allan D., Diana Hancock, and Mary M. McLaughlin. "Recent Developments Affecting the Profitability and Practices of Commercial Banks." *Federal Reserve Bulletin* (July 1992) pp. 459–483.

Diamond, D.W. "Financial Intermediation and Delegated Monitoring." *Review of Economic Studies* 51 (1984), pp. 393–414.

Fama, Eugene F. "Banking in the Theory of Finance." *Journal of Monetary Economics* 6 (1980) pp. 39–57.

Leland, Hayne E., and David H. Pyle. "Information Asymmetries, Financial Structure and Financial Intermediation." *Journal of Finance* 32 (May 1977), pp. 371–387.

Mayer, Martin. *The Bankers.* New York: Weybright and Talley, 1974.

• *Chapter 5*

Government Regulation of Depository Financial Institutions

This chapter deals with the regulation of depository financial institutions. Recall that depository financial institutions accept deposits *and* make loans. The regulatory system that governs financial institutions of all types is complicated and often confusing. It is difficult to imagine, if we could start over to build a new regulatory system, that we would create something exactly like what we have today. The system we have now evolved only gradually, in response to crises. Regulations that dealt with these crises were preserved, and the government institutions in charge of implementing those regulations grew. Oftentimes, however, institutions and regulations that were hard to justify were also preserved. So today's system is a bit of a mixed bag. In order to try to make some sense of the existing regulatory system we begin this chapter with a discussion of the basic problem of liquidity and solvency, which has plagued depository financial institutions throughout history. Then we outline two alternative approaches or explanations for why we have regulation. Under the first approach, which we call the positive approach, we describe three positive reasons why regulation of financial institutions may be justified. The second approach is often referred to as the capture theory of regulation. The capture theory essentially says that many regulations are enacted to protect entrenched interests of those who are being regulated. We believe that the regulatory system we see around us is the result of a tension between the positive approach and the capture theory.

After we explain the foundations for financial regulation, we move on to describe the key features of the current regulatory system for the banking industry. Much of the current system is oriented toward controlling the riskiness in the banking industry to limit the risk exposure of the government guarantor of bank deposits, the Federal Deposit Insurance Corporation (FDIC). Therefore, we focus on describing the various ways in which our regulatory system attempts to control bank risk taking.

It is important to recognize that the current regulatory system is a "moving target": it is constantly changing. Moreover, the pace of change was very rapid during the 1980s, and that pace may well continue in the late 1990s. To highlight understanding of this process of change we have broken our treatment of regulation of depository institutions and a few of their close competitors into two chapters. In this chapter we outline the basic structure of regulation, and in Chapter 6 we focus on the process of regulatory reform and on a potential competitor of depository institutions, finance companies. The key concepts to learn in this chapter are listed below.

• ***Concepts to Learn in Chapter 5*** •

- Fundamental justification for regulation of financial markets and institutions
- Key features of contemporary bank regulation
- Historical evolution of bank regulation
- Basic problems with the deposit insurance system

Why Do We Regulate Depository Financial Institutions?

We think it is essential to begin a discussion of the regulation of depository institutions with a careful consideration of the basic problems that have long plagued this industry. We think these basic problems are best described under the label of liquidity and solvency.

The Underlying Issue in Bank Regulation: Liquidity and Solvency

The banking industry has historically faced two fundamental, interrelated problems that have made regulation necessary. The problems arise from the basic structure of the bank balance sheet: banks are highly leveraged with short-term, highly liquid debt known as *deposits.* (Recall the example bank in Chapter 4.) The first problem is that the short maturity or highly liquid nature of deposits means that banks are constantly exposed to the prospect that some depositors could withdraw their funds. In the extreme case, a large number of depositors could run on the bank and so force it to attempt to liquidate large amounts of its assets or loans. This liquidation can result in losses that end up driving the bank into insolvency. The second problem is that their high leverage creates an incentive for banks to take on very risky assets, or loans, that could also drive the bank into insolvency. Let's discuss the liquidity problem first.

The fundamental problem of instability facing depository institutions, virtually throughout history, results from the fact that deposits can be converted to cash upon demand. In the broadest sense, deposits are simply another type of debt claim, such as a bond or loan. One of the problems with any debt claim, including deposits, is the opportunity for the issuer of the debt claim, in this case the commercial bank, to engage in activities that tend to expropriate the claim holder. The most obvious kind of expropriation is for a borrower to take a lender's funds, issue a promise to repay, and simply disappear or spend the money and then claim bankruptcy. Another way is for the bank to take on more risky assets or loans than the depositor perceives to be the case, or to gamble with depositors' funds. We will explore this incentive in detail shortly. To prevent such problems, debt contracts issued by corporations often include covenants that constrain the borrower or require collateral the lender can claim if expropriation is attempted. The covenants restrict such things as future dividends and debt issues in order to limit the borrower's ability to divert funds from the corporation to equity owners, or to increase the company's debt and therefore the risk to which existing debtholders are exposed.

But with depository institutions it is exceedingly difficult to construct covenants that adequately protect against future increases in the debt issued by the institution because the business of a bank is to issue deposits. In order to function effectively banks must have the freedom to increase or decrease deposits as the need arises. It would be totally infeasible for the initial depositors to restrict the bank's ability to issue additional deposits. The volume of deposits fluctuates from day to day and must do so if the bank is to serve its customers effectively. Moreover, this same flexibility makes it impossible to assign collateral to specific deposits. Thus, an opportunity for expropriation is created. It is important to see that much the same problem would face any kind of corporation that attempted to finance itself largely with highly liquid short-maturity debt. In fact, precisely because of these kinds of difficulties, most corporations avoid this kind of financing. But it is inherently a part of the banking business.

One method that was once used to attempt to deal with this problem was for banks to back their deposits, or the antecedents of deposits called notes, with gold. Under such a system banks promised to redeem their notes or deposits in gold at a prespecified price. As a result, notes or deposits were titles to gold, and gold essentially fulfilled the role of collateral. But banks invested only a small portion of their funds in gold, as most funds were committed to loans and other investments. As a result, the commitment to convert deposits to gold could be honored only if a small portion of the total volume of deposits was presented for conversion at a given time. In essence, banks held gold as a reserve to satisfy the volume of conversions anticipated, plus some amount as a cushion. But because banks earned their profits from loans, the more gold they held in reserve, the less profitable they could expect to be. The same thing is true today, though other types of assets now play the role of gold as a cushion to satisfy demands for funds.

This problem of balancing liquidity against profitability has always been the fundamental choice facing commercial banks. Throughout the history of the U.S. banking industry, panics developed when the public perceived either that banks were trying to expropriate them or that they had become too illiquid or were running too short on gold. If the panic became serious enough, it virtually guaranteed that the existing liquidity would be insufficient and the system would become unstable.

The principal form of regulation that has evolved to deal with this problem involves a fundamental change in the nature of the financial contract that individuals agree to when they deal with a financial intermediary. The most important single feature of the current regulatory system is insurance of deposits. Deposits with commercial banks and with savings and loans are now insured by the federal government up to a maximum of $100,000. Individual depositors at commercial banks need not fear, as they once did, that their funds will be misused when they deal with a financial institution that has vastly superior knowledge about financial markets and financial contracts. A depositor no longer needs to withdraw bank funds because he or she distrusts the banker's incentive to act in the depositor's interest. The government guarantees the banker's performance so that the underlying problem that historically threatened the viability of the entire system is, at least in part, eliminated.

Unfortunately, there is an additional problem, beyond the highly liquid nature of bank deposits, that is fundamental to banking. This is the incentive of a highly leveraged bank to take on excessive risk. To some extent this problem may well be accentuated rather than alleviated by deposit insurance. To explain the nature of this problem we have constructed as an example a fictitious bank or savings and loan. The specific institution, Roll It Federal, is fictitious, but unfortunately the story in this example is all too real.

• *So You Want to Gamble with Other Peoples' Money?* •

At one time Roll It Federal had positive real or economic net worth in the amount of $10 million. Let's suppose that it had total assets of $100 million and total deposit liabilities of $90 million. We will suppose that the government accounting system recorded the same values, so that it also had accounting net worth of $10 million, and that capital requirements are five percent of total assets, so it has excess capital.

Now let's suppose some kind of disaster comes along, such as high interest rates or a decline in the value of its assets for some other reason, so that Roll It's assets are now worth only $60 million. This means that Roll It's economic net worth is now −$30 million, because the company still owes depositors $90 million. It is very important, however, to recognize that Roll It's stockholders will never actually have to pay the depositors any negative amount, because they have limited liability. If the depositors ever had to be paid off and the company closed down, it is the government guarantor that would step in and be liable for the $30 million needed to pay off the depositors. If the government did close down Roll It, its stockholders would lose the opportunity to engage in any future investments and to reap any gains out of these investments. So the stockholders' loss is the loss of future opportunities rather than the direct financial obligation to depositors.

Now let's suppose that the stockholders of Roll It calculate that, if they keep going as they are now with the same kind of investments they currently have in place, things have no chance of getting better and eventually the government accounting system will (however slowly) catch up with them and close their institution down. Now some entrepreneur comes along, let's call this company Build the Hills Developers (BHD). BHD provides an opportunity for Roll It to participate in a new real estate venture. When Roll It carefully scrutinizes this venture it concludes that it would require an investment of $100 million and has a 75 percent chance of being a total bust and returning zero. On the other hand, it has a 25 percent chance of succeeding fantastically and generating a payoff of $200 million. We hope it is clear that Roll It should not participate in this investment by any criteria we can think of that take into account the total cost and return of the project. That is, this venture has an expected return of $50 million ($0.75 \times 0 + 0.25 \times \$200$) and a cost of $100 million, for a negative value (ignoring discounting for the time value of money) of $50 million. This venture is clearly one to avoid, but it is very attractive to the stockholders of Roll It. The reason is that they can borrow the needed $100 million (because the government guarantees deposits) and invest the borrowed money in the project. They can borrow more because they have sufficient excess regulatory capital of $5 million.

Now let's see what happens. Suppose, as is likely, that the project generates a return of zero. Now Roll It has a negative net worth of $130 million—$60 million in assets minus $190 million in deposits. That is, its negative net worth has increased by $100 million. But since the stockholders are protected by limited liability, they are no worse off than they were before Roll It got involved with BHD, since all of this negative net worth is a liability of the deposit insurer. This is a no-loss situation for the stockholders.

If the project were to succeed, the Roll It stockholders would do very nicely. They would have the old assets worth $60 plus the $200 million from the venture with BHD, or $260 million. They owe depositors $190 million. This means they now have economic net worth of $70 million. Now the stockholders of Roll It once again have some real or economic capital. They also have even more accounting net worth if the government accounting system has not changed the value of their initial assets. In fact, they have to choose whether to pay out their profits in the form of dividends or keep them in the company. They are likely to pay them out in dividends up to the limit imposed by any capital requirements.

We hope you see that this kind of situation is very dangerous for the deposit insurer, and ultimately for the taxpayer. The deposit insurers can never afford to let large numbers of insured institutions be in the position of Roll It, where they can continue to gamble with the government's guarantee. Moreover, we hope you also see that the stockholders of Roll It in our example did not do anything illegal. They played by the rules of the game. The rules themselves created incentives to take gambles that did not have attractive expected returns.

Now that we have described the basic problems pertaining to liquidity and solvency of commercial banks we want to outline a simple approach toward regulation that should allow you to evaluate the merits of specific current regulations and to acquire a better understanding of how and why we inherited this system.

The Positive Rationale for Regulation

We believe there are two basic approaches that are both necessary ingredients in building a complete understanding of current regulation of financial institutions. The first approach, which we label the *positive approach* to regulation, essentially asks us to identify the problems that could arise in an unregulated system that could cause rational observers of that system to want the government to intervene in the market and impose regulations. In other words, here we are looking for defensible reasons for government regulation of the private market that promotes the welfare of the society as a whole. The alternative approach is somewhat more cynical; it says that regulation is largely a result of efforts by members of the industry being regulated to protect themselves against forces that threaten their profitability or survival. This is often call the *capture theory* of regulation. We think it is important for you to recognize that both approaches can be applied to any form of government regulation, from the trucking industry to pharmaceuticals, though in this chapter we examine regulation of financial institutions.

We believe there are four important and specific positive rationales for regulation of financial institutions. Most of them follow directly from our discussion of the basic problem of liquidity and stability that we described above. They are

To prevent or limit expropriation,

To monitor risk taking,

To prevent system failure, and

To promote competition and prevent monopolistic practices.

These four basic rationales for regulation, the problems they create, and the types of regulation they have spawned are briefly summarized in Table 5-1, which provides a useful frame of reference for the discussion of regulation throughout the rest of the book.

Regulation and the Problem of Expropriation

You will recall that we began using the word "expropriation" in our discussion of the ways in which a firm might take actions that would impose some kind of financial loss on its debt holders, such as by paying themselves excessive dividends. This action increases the likelihood that the firm will be unable to meet its contractual obligation to debtholders and thereby expropriates their value. We can think of expropriation in a broader sense as actions that tend to impose a loss on any of the stakeholders of a firm, such as customers, suppliers, or even the government. The unregulated market has methods for dealing with these expropriation activities, but the market's methods are costly and complicated, even when parties to contracts are sophisticated and have a thorough understanding of how the market operates. But if some potential parties to financial contracts are unsophisticated or naive the opportunities for expropriation are

Table 5-1
Summary of Positive Rationales for Regulation

Motive for Regulation	Nature of Problem	Regulation to Deal with Problem
Limit opportunities for expropriation where there is a difference in information between contract parties	Unsophisticated parties, generally consumers, may be unable to protect themselves adequately against expropriation.	Limit allowable contracts and require disclosure of information.
Monitor the risks undertaken by financial institutions	High leverage provides an incentive to take on excessive risk.	Empower regulators to inspect and control investments of financial institutions.
Avoid system failure	With unregulated financial intermediaries, depositors periodically withdraw from the market if they fear for the safety of their funds.	Provide insurance on deposits and control the risk of financial intermediaries.
Limit monopoly power and promote competition	Concentration of power and cartel behavior raise prices and reduce services.	Promote and enforce rules designed to prevent monopolistic practices.

enhanced. In contracts between corporate representatives, the general presumption is that parties are sophisticated, or at least should be. But in consumer contracts this is not the case. Consumers engage in financial contracts on a relatively infrequent basis and therefore do not often have the opportunity to learn ways in which they could be expropriated and methods to protect themselves. This possibility can provide a motivation for regulation that directly protects the consumer or helps him to be self-protecting.

The desire to protect consumers of financial services has led to two general types of regulations. One involves restrictions on the allowable contracts that are legally binding so that some contract provisions may be completely prohibited. The second type of regulation is to impose requirements of disclosure on the relatively sophisticated party. Both of these are supplements to the methods utilized by the private market to deal with expropriation opportunities in contracts. In recent years there has been a trend toward regulations that improve access to information rather than restrict the kinds of contracts to which people are allowed to agree. Principal among these regulations is truth in lending. Significant truth-in-lending legislation was first adopted by the U.S. Congress in the early 1970s. It requires that any firm that lends to consumers must comply with federal regulations regarding disclosure of the loan terms. In particular, the legislation requires that lenders present the true cost of the loan in what is purported to be a simple and understandable manner. The drawback is that such disclosure is costly. Many economists argue that in most instances the market generates the optimal amount of disclosure when left to its own devices. When relatively uninformed consumers are involved this argument may well be weak. Yet the opposite extreme, extensive disclosure requirements, is also socially suboptimal, for truth-in-lending legislation raises the cost of providing credit, and all borrowers bear that additional cost.

Another example of a tradeoff between the costs and benefits of disclosure pertains to disclosure of financial information about the ongoing operations of a company or about the issuance of new securities. Such disclosure regulation, which is monitored by the Securities and Exchange Commission, has long been a hot topic of debate. Those who argue against such disclosure requirements contend that the mandated disclosure raises the cost of issuing securities and often does not actually result in more real information being provided to the market than would be otherwise. Such opponents of required disclosure often argue that there are strong incentives for most important information to be distributed to the market in one form or another, regardless of government requirements, or that the markets are highly efficient at gathering such information and incorporating it into the prices of securities. One interesting area in which this type of disclosure issue has become important in depository financial institutions pertains to whether such institutions should be required to report the market values of their assets on their accounting statements and whether such measures of value will be used in the regulatory process. Historically, banks have generally been required to report only historical costs of assets rather than current market values or estimates of such values. Proponents of reporting market values argue that disclosure of market values, rather than historical costs of assets, puts depositors and other security holders of banks in a better position to evaluate the worth of their holdings and ultimately leads to diminished problems with the liquidity and solvency of such institutions. We will have more to say about this topic in later chapters.

Regulation to Monitor Risk Taking

As we hope our example of Roll It Federal made clear, highly leveraged companies, both banks and others, that have little real or economic equity have an incentive to undertake very poor and risky investments, to the detriment of the economy as a whole. Therefore, in all markets there is a need for some kind of monitoring of the activities of the managers of relatively highly leveraged companies. In the private marketplace, an important part of this monitoring activity is performed by private rating agencies, principally Moody's and Standard & Poor's. They keep track of the cash flows and investment decisions of companies and provide debt holders with information about the perceived riskiness of those companies' securities.

One rationale for regulation is that regulators perform a monitoring function much like that performed by private rating agencies. Moreover, in the banking and savings and loan industries, where much of the information acquired by these institutions about their customers is often treated as confidential, government regulators have unique access to this confidential or proprietary information. Such access is often essential to being able to perform a monitoring function. Therefore, government regulators may serve as monitors even if they do not necessarily also provide insurance to depositors at the same time. They will be preferred to private monitors if they are inherently more efficient, or if better incentives can be structured for government than private monitors, or if confidentiality of information held by banks leads to a preference for government monitoring. If, as is the case in the United States today, the government also provides deposit insurance, then it is the government that is also exposed to loss if the monitoring function is performed poorly. It is important to recognize that the fact that the government provides deposit insurance does not necessarily mean that it should perform the monitoring function. This issue still should turn on who can monitor more accurately or efficiently and at what total cost to the system as a whole. The current system in the United States relies largely on government monitoring, but that does not necessarily mean it is the most effective approach to the problem.

Regulation to Limit System Failure

The prospect of a significant collapse of financial markets has been one of the prime reasons for market regulation in the United States for more than 150 years. During most of this period, such concerns centered around the banking industry because banks were involved, in one way or another, in almost all financial transactions. The country did not have the very diverse types of markets and financial institutions that exist today. The problem that plagued commercial banks throughout the nineteenth century and into the early twentieth century was periodic financial panics. Depositors who often had little information about the value of a bank's assets and who feared that their deposits would be lost, withdrew their funds and hoarded them. Once the withdrawals began, the stability of the banks was threatened and the incentive to withdraw funds increased. This kind of panic could, and in the early 1930s did, lead to the breakdown of the entire system—to system failure. Many observers believe that it was really a fear of widespread runs or system failure that spawned much of the existing bank and savings and loan regulation system. We will present a brief overview of the events of 1930 shortly.

Regulation and Monopoly Power in Financial Markets

One of the most important goals of regulation of any kind of market, financial or otherwise, should be to promote competition or restrict practices that are perceived to be monopolistic. In some cases it may be possible for a single firm operating in a particular small regional market to establish substantial monopoly power, but increasingly few financial markets are so dominated by a single firm that it is possible without the cooperation of competitors to create a monopoly. If a group of firms cooperate to act like a monopolist we often call it a "cartel." In order for a cartel to be successful in the long run, it usually requires some kind of legal sanction or support from government policy. Thus, government policy is a particularly crucial element in striving to prevent monopolies from being formed.

The prospect that a monopoly might exist in U.S. financial markets has long been viewed as exceptionally pernicious, maybe more so than in most nonfinancial markets. The reason is probably that an important part of the structure of any democratic society is the concept that no citizen should be arbitrarily restricted from access to capital. A monopoly in the market for capital holds out the prospect that capital may be distributed in an arbitrary manner or, even if access is not restricted, that prices will be set at monopolistic levels. As a result, it has been a strong part of the democratic tradition for the government to take actions that ensure access to financial resources and to explicitly forbid practices that are clearly monopolistic.

In the banking and savings and loan industries the promotion of competition has a particularly troubling side effect, as many actions that tend to increase competition and lower prices also tend to interfere with the regulatory system that is designed to prevent system failure. A competitive market is one in which weak and inefficient firms fail to survive, but in banking such failure has often come all at once for a large number of institutions in response to a financial panic. Such failures threaten the stability of the whole industry and the economy. The regulatory system that has evolved to deal with this problem tends to ensure the survival of at least some banks that would not be profitable in a more competitive environment. This tradeoff between the desirable effects on prices of increased competition and the undesirable effects on bank stability—and ultimately on the increased chance of system failure—lead us right up the alternative view of bank regulation, the so-called capture theory of regulation.

The Capture Theory of Regulation

The essence of the capture theory of regulation is that regulation is intended more to protect the often entrenched interests of managers and shareholders in established firms rather than to promote social welfare. While we do not want you to discount the positive approach to regulation, we believe that much of the specific regulatory structure that we observe in the United States can be explained to a large degree by the capture theory. Let's consider a few conspicuous examples.

For many years many states in the United States had extensive prohibitions restricting the branching of banks operating in those states. For example, Illinois long had a law that essentially allowed individual banks to offer complete banking services in only one physical location in the state. It is possible to make a case that such restrictions are motivated by a desire not to have too many banks in an area competing so fiercely that none of them is stable. This would be a positive argument for such regulatory restrictions, but we feel that such an explanation has little merit. An alternative explanation is that bankers throughout the state of Illinois wanted to protect themselves from competition from large rivals located in Chicago. Thus, they supported the enactment of laws that limited the ability of the large Chicago banks to set up offices in other parts of the state where smaller banks operated. This view says that the smaller banks essentially "captured" the political process to promote regulations that protected their vested interests. We think this explanation, though more cynical, is probably more accurate.

Consider, also, something as historically important as the enactment of deposit insurance. As we will explain in more detail shortly, deposit insurance was enacted in the early 1930s in response to the largest, most thorough going system-wide failure of banks ever experienced in this country. The positive explanation for deposit insurance is that it provided the kind of guarantee necessary to limit the incentives of individual depositors to run on banks and thereby promoted the stability of the entire system. The capture theory argues that the bankers that were still in business by 1933, after four years of watching many other banks become insolvent, became keenly interested in finding ways to protect themselves from a similar fate and thus encouraged and supported enactment of new laws that authorized the government to provide a new guarantee to their customers that they could not lose their money if they deposited it in their traditional commercial bank. This greatly increased the chances that the existing structure of bank ownership would survive.

The same tension between positive and capture explanations for important regulations goes on today and will undoubtedly persist. For example, an important current issue pertains to whether banks will be allowed to sell and underwrite (that is bear the risk of) insurance products such as life, auto, and health insurance. They are currently prohibited from underwriting such products and face several restrictions on selling them. The positive argument is that underwriting insurance products is a risky business. Because banks have the benefit of deposit insurance they should not be allowed to enter such risky businesses as insurance underwriting lest this expose the FDIC to undue risk. The capture argument holds that the insurance industry is opposed to allowing new competitors into *their* marketplace that might acquire market share from them and might make it harder for them to generate high rates of return for their shareholders. The insurance industry wants to limit competition by controlling government regulation.

It is often impossible to determine unequivocally whether a particular regulation can be entirely explained by one approach or the other. As we have already said, there is constant tension between the two forces that drive regulation, and we do not expect that one or the other will ever come to dominate. As you examine the specific types of regulation that are operating today or as you watch the system evolve in the future you will do well to keep both views in mind.

Overview of the Bank Regulation System

Now we turn our attention to a description of the key features of regulations governing both banks and savings and loans. We will try, as we go along, to make the positive case for regulation as best we can, where we think we can.

Key Features of Bank Regulation

The problems that have led to regulation of financial intermediaries are not strictly a matter of recent history. Instead, they have been with this country virtually since its birth. Various methods have been instituted by the government over the years to deal with the crises that have developed in banking. With each additional approach to the problem the regulatory system became more complex. To appreciate the complexity of the current system for regulating commercial banks and savings and loans it is helpful to outline the major current regulations. Then we can turn to the rationale behind them. The regulations are listed roughly in the sequence in which they came into existence and in an order that facilitates a logical explanation of their purpose. After we list the key features of the regulatory system we briefly turn our attention to the historical development of this system.

• *Bank Regulation in a Nutshell* •

Fractional Reserve Banking and National Currency. The National Banking Act of 1863 created a system of government-required reserves for nationally chartered banks, though no provision was made for expansion or contraction of those reserves. The legislation that followed shortly after led to the extinction of the multiple currencies issued by state banks that existed throughout the early nineteenth century.

Elastic Currency. In 1913 the Federal Reserve System came into existence and with it a provision for government control of the volume of currency and bank reserves. The Federal Reserve was designed to serve as a lender of last resort for commercial banks experiencing liquidity difficulties, or to provide an *elastic currency.*

Restriction of Interest Payments on Deposits. Beginning with the Banking Acts of 1933 and 1935, the federal government imposed limits on the interest rates that could be paid on demand, savings, and time deposit accounts, in order to limit competition. Interest payments on demand deposit accounts were entirely prohibited, and the Federal Reserve periodically adjusted interest rate ceilings on saving and time deposits. These ceilings were eliminated in 1982.

Deposit Insurance. Since the Great Depression, deposits at commercial banks, and savings and loans, have been insured by agencies of the U. S. government. This insurance is provided by the FDIC and is limited to $100,000 per account. Deposit insurance has succeeded in eliminating the incentive to run on banks in anticipation of possible problems for that bank.

Restrictions on Permissible Activities. Banks and savings and loans are restricted as to what activities they can engage in and what investments they can make. These restrictions were imposed in the 1930s and have since been revised. The restrictions have also been imposed on bank holding companies.

Capital Requirements. The government imposes minimum capital requirements on all depository institutions. As of 1992, these capital requirements were based on international agreements for common capital requirements around the world, and the requirements are related to the riskiness of a bank's investments and loans.

Entry Restrictions. Permission must be obtained from the appropriate regulators to create a new bank, savings and loan, or (in some states) branch of an existing institution. Each state has the right to determine whether banks will be permitted to have branch offices and whether banks from another state can accept deposits in that state.

Inspection and Control of Riskiness. The government examines depository institutions to assess the riskiness of their deposits and investments and can compel management to alter risky policies.

Segmentation of Financial Services. Separate regulatory agencies deal with regulation of distinct types of financial firms. Even among depository institutions, there are multiple federal regulators of banks and separate regulators of savings and loans. Moreover, legal restrictions have separated the commercial banking, investment banking, and insurance industries.

Early History of Bank Regulation

To fully grasp the current system of bank regulation it is essential to have some sense of how it developed. Much of it was put in place during the Great Depression of the 1930s. We provide a brief overview of this history beginning with the period just before the Civil War. For several decades before that war, during a time known as the "wildcat banking era," the banking industry was virtually unregulated at the national level (regulations were imposed in some states). During this period there was virtually no national currency as we know it today. Each bank issued its own notes or currency, and the only common denominator was their link to gold. The price of gold was fixed in dollars, but individual notes often exchanged at values well below $1. Notes often deteriorated in value with distance from the issuing bank because the perceived risk of convertibility to gold increased. This system of competing monies came to an end with the onset of the Civil War.

By 1863 the United States had experienced nearly 30 years of what some people thought was virtual chaos in the banking industry. There was, therefore, considerable support for the position that the system was ripe for reform. Had it not been for the Civil War, this sentiment might not have been sufficient to bring about any significant changes. The government found banking reform to be a convenient way to create a market for the government bonds needed to finance the war. As a result, the National Banking Act was passed in 1863 and was amended in the next few years.

The most important and permanent accomplishment of the National Banking Act was to create a national currency and to eliminate competing monies. But this was not accomplished by directly distributing a government-produced currency as we have today. Instead, the National Banking Act provided for the federal chartering of banks, which could issue notes backed by government bonds. The act as it was amended in 1866 also imposed a 10 percent tax on the notes of state banks, which virtually eliminated state bank notes. As a result, the notes of the nationally chartered banks became the national currency. Unlike the notes of state banks issued during the

Wildcat banking era, national bank notes always traded at par because they were not really backed by the promises of individual issuing banks. Instead, the volume of these notes was directly linked to the bank's holdings of government securities, bearing what was called a "circulation privilege." Thus, the national bank notes were really an indirect form of government-issued money. With this system the government created, at one time, both a ready market for its bonds and a uniform currency.

In addition to establishing a national currency, the National Banking Act created the basic banking regulation structure that we have today. First, it required nationally chartered banks to hold reserves behind their deposits in a fixed proportion that depended on the size and location of the bank. This is why it is called a *fractional reserve* banking system. These reserves were maintained in the form of cash or deposits with other banks. The major difficulty with the system was that these reserves were virtually unavailable when problems of liquidity arose, because there was no provision for adjusting reserve requirements or for extending loans to banks. Large banks often acted as lender for smaller banks, but when liquidity problems spread to the larger banks the system did not work well. The National Banking Act also created the office of the Comptroller of the Currency, which still exists today. The Comptroller was empowered to maintain minimum capital requirements for national banks and to inspect and restrict their activities and investments. This laid the foundation for the more elaborate regulatory structure we have today.

The banking system created by the National Banking Act operated without major changes until the panic of 1907, when the solvency of the financial system came into serious question. This crisis in financial markets led to a major reexamination of the banking system that culminated in the passage of the Federal Reserve Act of 1913. The Federal Reserve was created out of dissatisfaction with the existing mechanism for ensuring banking system stability. The nineteenth century witnessed a number of banking panics in which people would run on the banks demanding redemption, first of their notes in gold, and later of their deposits in either gold or currency. But if the run on virtually any bank is large enough, that bank will be unable to satisfy the demand for conversion, regardless of how sound its loans may be. Even the strongest bank does not hold nearly enough highly liquid assets to satisfy its depositors' demands to convert deposits to currency if enough of them show up at once. Such liquidity problems surfaced every few years throughout the nineteenth century and were particularly severe in 1907.

The important feature of the Federal Reserve System was its power to control the supply of reserves, and therefore the liquidity of commercial banks. As it has developed since 1913 the most important method for exercising this control is through the purchase and sale of United States Treasury securities by the Federal Reserve. But the other method, which was of critical importance at that time, was the ability of the Federal Reserve to extend loans or discounts to member commercial banks. The Federal Reserve had the ability to increase or decrease the liquidity of member commercial banks by extending or contracting its loans to these banks. Banks did not, and do not now, rely on the Federal Reserve as a major source of funds. Rather, this discounting function of the Federal Reserve provided flexibility in the amount of currency outstanding or in the liquidity of the banking system, as the Federal Reserve was able to act as a lender of last resort.

Unfortunately, for reasons we cannot ever know for sure, the Federal Reserve chose not to provide the banking system with sufficient liquidity to avoid the onset of the Great Depression during the early 1930s. Between 1929 and 1933 approximately 9000 banks failed, roughly half the banks in the United States at the time. This was virtually unprecedented in the history of the country. While there were a number of banking panics throughout the nineteenth century, a general suspension of all banking business for a period as long as a week had never before taken place. Such a banking holiday was declared on March 6, 1933, however, and all banks, including the Federal Reserve, closed down for a week. The banking system collapse developed in stages between 1930 and 1933. At each stage confidence in the system was further shaken and the crisis became more severe. The initial bank failures were probably due to bad loans as much as anything else. But as the crisis deepened, the demand for conversion of demand deposits into cash intensified at a time when the bond market collapse made the current market value of a large portion of bank assets unusually low. This did not necessarily mean there would be default if those bonds were held to maturity; however, many banks would become insolvent if they had to liquidate those bonds at current low market prices to satisfy demands for conversion of demand deposits to currency. The Federal Reserve could have extended loans on a massive scale to banks facing this difficulty, but it did not. A prominent view is that this failure was due to a lack of understanding of the situation, and it seems difficult to come to any other conclusion.

Banking Regulation Spawned by the Great Depression

The banking crisis of the early 1930s led to significant reform legislation that altered the nature of the regulation of the depository institutions industry in fundamental ways. The major piece of legislation adopted at that time is the Banking Act of 1933. The most important element of this act was the provision of federal insurance of deposits. Under this law, the federal government provided insurance of deposits, originally up to $2500 and today up to $100,000, for commercial banks that became members of a new agency, the FDIC. The FDIC became the third federal regulatory agency, in addition to the Comptroller of the Currency and the Federal Reserve, that dealt with commercial banks. Only federally chartered banks were required to join the FDIC, but nearly 97 percent of all (state as well as federal) commercial banks became insured by the FDIC. This percentage has increased to nearly 100 percent in the intervening years.

In addition to the legislation directed toward the commercial banking industry, in 1934 Congress passed the Home Owners Loan Act, which established Federal Home Loan Banks to regulate and insure savings and loans. While there were many similarities between the regulation of savings and loans and commercial banks, there was a philosophical objective guiding savings and loan regulation that had no parallel in commercial bank regulation. Savings and loans were government regulated and protected for the purpose of promoting and stimulating housing. Because of this objective, a separate class of depository institutions was created and restricted to serve the home mortgage industry. That purpose has been maintained to this day, though the regulatory system for savings and loans has been altered significantly so that they now have many powers that originally were reserved for commercial banks. We will focus on the savings and loan industry in Chapter 6.

In one sense, the deposit insurance system created for commercial banks and savings and loans has been tremendously successful in that the recurring panics of the nineteenth century have been virtually nonexistent since the provision of deposit insurance. This was especially apparent during the 1980s, as the rate of failure of savings and loans and banks increased dramatically and the media were awash in publicity of the debacle in the savings and loan, or thrift, industry.

At least four other important changes were instituted in the 1930s. The first was the Glass-Steagall Act, a law that compelled commercial banks to divest themselves of underwriting and distribution of, and investment in, marketable securities such as stocks and bonds. Prior to that time, commercial banks were very broad institutions empowered to engage in nearly all types of financial transactions. It was perceived that there was a conflict of interest between the responsibility to manage depositors' funds and the activities of the securities business. Indeed, it was argued, and widely believed, that this conflict was in part responsible for the stock market crash of 1929 and the Great Depression that followed. The solution was a fundamental restructuring of the banking industry with the creation of a separate class of investment banks that are legally separate from commercial banks. We will return to the question of whether this division is sensible for our current globally competitive marketplace.

The second change was prohibition of interest payments on demand deposits and time deposits above a ceiling set by the Federal Reserve. This prohibition was instituted to prevent what many perceived as dangerous competition among banks for depositors' funds. When allowed to compete with interest payments, many believed banks would seek highly risky investments to earn enough return to compensate their depositors. The increased competition was therefore perceived to be the source of excessive risk taking. By restricting payment of interest on deposits, it was believed risk would be reduced.

Third, the government completely phased out national bank notes, which originally came into existence with the National Banking Act of 1863. This was accomplished by retiring the remaining U.S. bonds, which when held by nationally chartered commercial banks gave them the authority to issue notes. National bank notes had gradually come to be replaced by Federal Reserve notes anyway, which are still used in the United States. With this change the evolution was complete—from a currency produced by private institutions, as during the first half of the nineteenth century, to a government monopoly currency.

A final and very important change that took place at that time was that of the role of gold in the banking system. Throughout U.S. history, banking system stability hinged on the believability of the promise to redeem notes or deposits in gold. In the nineteenth century banks converted notes directly to gold on demand. But by the late 1920s most conversions were actually from deposits to currency, and the government stood ready to convert currency to gold if the demand was made. In 1933 President Franklin Roosevelt essentially nationalized gold by making it illegal, through the power of existing statutes, for private citizens and institutions in the United States to hold gold. All gold was turned over to the U.S. Treasury at the legal price at that time, $20.67 per ounce.

The implications of the nationalization of gold and the enactment of deposit insurance were substantial. The backing behind the bank's deposits became a government promise rather than essentially a promise of the individual bank. Individual banks no longer backed their deposits with gold. Rather, they were compelled to maintain convertibility of their deposits into government-issued currency, which in turn was backed by the good will of the government. But because depositors were insured if private banks reneged on that promise, depositors no longer had an incentive to carefully assess the promises made by individual banks. That responsibility now lay with the government, and in order to fulfill it a more elaborate system of regulation and control of risk was necessary.

The regulatory system put in place in the 1930s remained largely intact until the 1980s, when major reform of the regulatory system began. We examine the process of regulatory reform in the 1980s and 1990s closely in Chapter 6. The current regulatory system relies heavily on two basic mechanisms to prevent bank failures: direct control of risk, through restrictions on bank activities and monitoring of banks to enforce those restrictions, and imposition of minimum capital requirements, to provide a cushion for the government guarantor of deposits and for uninsured depositors. We discuss these methods next.

Regulation to Limit Risk

With government deposit insurance must come government control of risk. There are essentially three methods of direct regulatory control over risk taking in banks:

1. The government directly audits bank loans and investments to be sure that they are accurately reported and that they comply with regulations on allowable bank activities.
2. There is direct control over the extent of competition in banking markets.
3. There are restrictions on banks and bank holding companies to limit the lines of business in which they may engage.

Bank Examination

Examination of various classes of commercial banks is carried out by the three federal regulatory agencies—the Comptroller of the Currency, the Federal Reserve, and the FDIC—plus state regulators. All of these bank examiners are looking for problems in loans and investments that threaten bank stability and the value of depositors' claims. Such problems may result from fraud, but more frequently they are due to mismanagement. The FDIC, in cooperation with the other two federal regulators, maintains a list of banks it judges may become insolvent. This list of problem banks is used to assess the probability that FDIC insurance will have to be used. The agencies utilize the examination procedure to try to spot difficulties early enough to take corrective action. When examiners discover loans or investments that violate the law or that they consider unsound, they meet with bank management and the board of directors and insist on changes. The ultimate penalty the regulators wield is to prosecute managers or bank owners for explicit law violations or to take over the bank if they judge that it is becoming insolvent.

Restriction of Competition

The second mechanism used to limit the riskiness of commercial banks has been to limit competition within the banking industry through regulation at both federal and state levels. The simultaneous existence of banks with federal charters and banks with state charters, and thus both state and federal regulators, persists to this day and is generally referred to as the *"dual banking system."* This system has evolved so that each state has the authority to determine what its banking industry will look like. The system is enhanced by the fact that in 1926 Congress passed the McFadden Act, which permits each state to set its own laws on intrastate branch banking and regulate entry of banks from other states. As a result, each state has a separate banking industry and the rules for creation or expansion vary from state to state. Some states, such as Illinois, have been unit banking states where banks cannot branch statewide; in other states, such as California, statewide branch banking is permitted. Some states have recently allowed out-of-state banks to enter. For instance, a law California passed in 1986 allowed banks from other states to enter the California market in 1991. Much of the relaxation of interstate banking restrictions has occurred as a result of actual or potential bank failures in a particular state that have compelled those states to seek assistance from banks in other states that have the capital to acquire a troubled bank. Important recent examples include Arizona and Texas, where economic recessions lead to large losses for local banks, which in turn induced local legislatures to permit out-of-state banks to acquire banks in those states.

The traditional laws on branching and the prohibition on banks operating in more than one state are viewed by many as exceptionally archaic restrictions. These observers contend that commercial banking has been regulated so that it has evolved like a large number of mom-and-pop stores and is inefficient as a result. Advocates point to the size distribution of banks and argue that the large number of small banks simply cannot be justified on economic grounds. The majority of banks have less than $25 million in deposits; only a very small portion of all banks have total deposits of $1 billion. However, the large banks hold most of the deposits in the entire banking system. The top 0.2 percent of the banks hold 37 percent of all deposits. To many people who have examined this question, it seems that many small banks would not exist were it not for regulatory restrictions, particularly about branching. This view suggests that the branching laws work to protect the entrenched monopoly position, an example of the capture theory realized.

Bank Holding Company Regulation

The third mechanism used to control risk is to enforce restrictions on bank holding companies. According to the Bank Holding Company Act of 1956 and its amendments in 1966 and 1970, all bank holding companies are subject to Federal Reserve Board regulation. The Fed restricts the amount of direct control a holding company can exercise on an individual bank, and the law stipulates that bank holding companies can be engaged only in activities deemed "closely related to banking."

The Federal Reserve Board has been concerned about the diversification of bank holding company activities because it perceives that it may increase the risk to which deposits are exposed. As a result, the Federal Reserve has exercised strict control over the lines of business in which bank holding companies are allowed to engage. These restrictions initially were included in the Bank Holding Company Act of 1956, which gave the Federal Reserve Board the power to approve requests to engage in traditionally "nonbanking" businesses. But the original law had a number of loopholes, and significant amendments were added in 1970. One loophole was that the law was worded to restrict multibank holding companies; this left holding companies with only one bank unrestricted. This encouraged a large number of banks to form single-bank holding companies so that they could engage in other businesses as they pleased. It also meant that nonbanking firms could seek to acquire banks. This loophole was closed in 1970.

Today, the Federal Reserve maintains a list of activities permissible for bank holding companies and a list of those that are specifically forbidden. Many of the permissible activities are in the general financial area, such as mortgage banking, leasing, financial advisory services, credit cards, and data processing services. The restrictions placed on allowable bank activities under the bank holding company statutes can be viewed in conjunction with the restrictions of the Glass-Steagall Act on investment banking activities of commercial banks. In total, these restrictions define a fairly narrow range of businesses that are permissible for commercial banking. Moreover, the contrast is particularly vivid between the restriction on U.S. banks and those on banks in many European countries and in Asia, where there is no historical episode of financial reform and tightening of regulations such as that which occurred in the 1930s. Moreover, these countries generally did not evolve with a system that emphasized dispersed financial power with banks regulated and chartered at the state level. Instead, most European countries have relatively few banks compared to the United States, and more diversified ones. We discuss the systems in other countries in Chapter 8 and the Glass-Steagall Act in more detail in Chapter 6.

The geographic restrictions on banks and the product line restrictions imposed on bank holding companies face severe challenges in today's marketplace. Large banks such as BankAmerica would like to become nationwide providers of consumer financial services, and regional banks are attempting to expand their territories and to limit the expansion of their larger competitors. Moreover, large industrial firms such as General Electric and Ford have very efficient finance companies that provide many of the services offered by commercial banks. The nature of competition in the financial services market is changing rapidly. We will look closely at the evolving nature of competition in this market in the next chapter and at various points throughout this book.

Capital Regulation

The principal alternative regulatory tool that is used to limit the risk exposure of the government guarantor is to require that banks maintain a minimum level of equity. We learned from our example of Roll It Federal that equity is an important key to controlling the incentive of banks to take on excessive risk. The insidious incentive to seek excessive risk is directly related to the amount of leverage the bank has and, therefore, is inversely related to the amount of its real equity.

Historically, bank regulators did not attempt to enforce a standard capital requirement across all U. S. banks; that is, they did not require that all banks finance, say, 10 percent of the total assets through equity capital. Rather, they tried to see that capital was adequate, given the risk of a bank or of a particular class of banks. This resulted in a system where banks governed by different regulators and banks of different sizes were subject to different capital requirements. In June, 1983, the Federal Reserve and the office of the Comptroller of the Currency agreed to apply common capital requirements to all commercial banks. This minimum capital requirement was 6 percent of adjusted total assets.

As of the end of 1992, banks had to comply with a new set of capital requirements that are related to the perceived risk of alternative types of loans and investments. There are two tiers of capital. *Tier 1 capital,* mainly common equity and perpetual preferred stock, must account for at least 4 percent of total assets, when these assets are weighted by measures of risk. We will explain weights for risk shortly. Second, total capital, which includes Tier 1 capital plus Tier 2 capital must equal 8 percent of risk-weighted assets. *Tier 2 capital* includes other types of preferred stock, subordinated debt, loan loss reserves (up to 1.25 percent of risk-based assets), and mandatory convertible debt.

Risk-weighted assets are calculated by multiplying the amount of assets in various asset categories by a factor determined by the perceived credit risk of that category. Riskier assets have higher weights, so they require more capital. At the time of this writing the weights are: 0 percent weight for U. S. Treasury securities, government-backed mortgages, and mortgage-backed securities guaranteed by the Government National Mortgage Association (which guarantees mortgage-backed securities against default); a 20 percent weight to other mortgage-backed securities and securities of other agencies of the U. S. government; a 50 percent weight to qualifying one-family to four-family–home conventional mortgages; and a 100 percent weight to most other loans, including commercial and industrial, consumer, and commercial real estate loans.

As a result of the problems banks faced during the 1980s, many had to scramble to raise enough capital or dispose of enough assets to meet these new capital requirements. The fact that interest rates were falling and bank stock prices were rising during late 1990 and 1991 made it more feasible for a larger number of banks to satisfy the requirements. Figure 5-1 shows the level of Tier 1 and Tier 2 capital as percentages of total assets in 1990 and 1991 for banks of various asset size categories. It is apparent from these data that, in the aggregate, each size class of banks satisfies these requirements. It also apparent that the ten largest banks were having the greatest difficulty meeting the new standard. These data indicate that the smaller banks, which are much more numerous, have much higher capital ratios than the larger banks. Recall that smaller banks also have a higher return on assets than larger banks. Moreover, within each category there are a number of banks that were having difficulty raising enough capital. As a result of these pressures, banks sold a total of 26.8 billion in new debt and

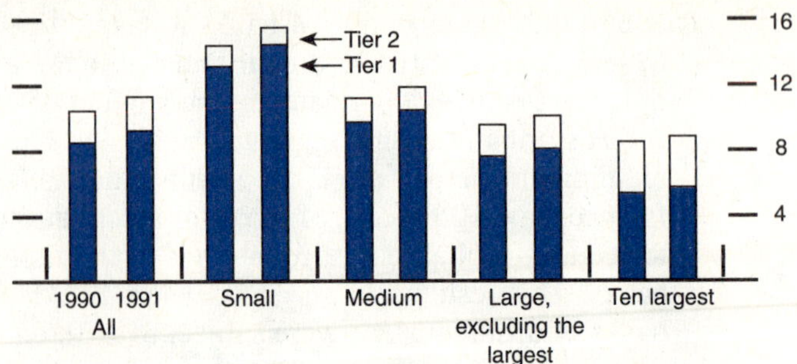

Figure 5-1
Risk-based capital ratios at insured commercial banks, by size of bank, fourth quarter, 1990 and 1991
Source: Federal Reserve Bulletin, *July 1992.*

equity securities in 1991 and followed that up with 30.8 billion through August of 1992. This was substantially more than had been raised in any previous year.[1]

What constitutes an adequate or optimal supply of capital for a bank? This is an exceptionally difficult question. We do not even have a clear understanding of what constitutes an optimal capital structure, or mix of debt and equity, for a nonfinancial firm. But for banks, whose failure in large numbers exacts a substantial social cost, the problems are even more difficult. In a competitive capital market, all securities are priced to reflect the market's perception of risk and return. As a result, the market extracts a premium from firms that use more risky debt and prices the equity capital of the firm to reflect that risk. But the elements of secrecy surrounding commercial banks, insurance of deposit liabilities, and restrictions and examinations of riskiness make assessment of such premiums a difficult task for the marketplace. As a result, government regulators seek to use capital to provide an additional cushion of protection for the FDIC and uninsured depositors against mismanagement, conflicts of interest, and fraud committed by commercial bankers. As such, capital requirements are one more tool used by the regulators to minimize the prospect of major instability in the banking system.

Structural Problems with Deposit Insurance

We have emphasized several times that a key feature of our current regulatory system is deposit insurance. The current deposit insurance system is widely believed to have serious structural problems. Two of the keys to understanding this system pertain to the incentive effects of pricing of deposit insurance and the lack of diversification of risk of the government insurer, the FDIC.

Pricing of Deposit Insurance

The basic idea behind deposit insurance is that an agency of the U.S. government assumes the risk-bearing function for individual depositors. Once this function has been transferred to a government agency, that agency must undertake the kinds of

[1]See "Banks Slake Thirst for Capital in Debt, Equity Markets." *Wall Street Journal,* September 2, 1992, p. B3.

activities that a private lender would take to limit its risk exposure. A private debt holder would impose restrictions or covenants on the borrower to limit the borrower's opportunities to impair the interests of the lender. In addition, a private lender would charge a price for a debt that reflected the perceived risk of loss from insolvency or bankruptcy. An important determinant of the price or interest rate the lender would charge is the amount of capital maintained by the borrower. The more capital the borrower maintains, the smaller is the likelihood of insolvency, and therefore, the lower the loan cost.

While these basic finance principles guide pricing decisions for most private debt contracts throughout the world, they have not been the basis for the operation of the FDIC. Historically, the FDIC has not attempted to assess the risk of insolvency for the institutions they insure so that it could use this assessment to determine the price of deposit insurance. Instead, they have set a flat price for deposit insurance for all banks and savings and loans, regardless of the riskiness of that institution. For many years the FDIC charged an insurance premium nominally set at one-twelfth of 1 percent of a bank's total domestic deposits. This is the nominal rate because the FDIC can allow a credit on this amount so for a number of years the effective rate was roughly half of this. The premiums collected by the FDIC build a fund of investments that can be drawn upon if a bank fails.

The fact that the FDIC historically charged a flat rate rather than risk-adjusted premiums for deposit insurance has immense implications for how the entire regulatory system for banks and savings and loans must operate. First, the regulators have been forced to lean more heavily on direct control of the risk of the loans and investments of depository institutions as a way of limiting their risk exposure. Second, there is an incentive for excessive risk taking.

When risk is priced fairly, as in most private contracts, it not only provides appropriate compensation to the lender but it also has an incentive effect for the borrower. The borrower knows that if he undertakes a relatively risky investment, lenders will demand higher compensation for accepting that risk. As a result, the borrower has an incentive to evaluate the risk and return of projects based on their overall payoffs. That is, part of the potential gain for the borrower does not come from a loss that he or she can expect to inflict on the lender. Fair and efficient pricing provides an incentive for borrowers not to undertake projects fraught with excessive risk.

In a system where the price of debt instruments is not related to the inherent risk, borrowers have a strong incentive to attempt to expropriate lenders. This incentive becomes particularly strong when the borrower is highly leveraged, as we hope our example of Roll It Federal earlier in this chapter made clear. The problem is simply that managers and owners of depository institutions, who do not have to compensate the FDIC for the riskiness of the ventures they undertake, will have a strong incentive to make very risky investments if the institutions have very little capital. In this case they are not playing with their own money. If the guarantor of deposits cannot provide an incentive to avoid very risky projects by changing the price of deposit insurance as the nature of the bank's investments changes, then it is compelled to attempt to place direct controls on the riskiness of the institution's investment. Fortunately, in 1992 the FDIC took initial steps toward implementation of some risk adjustment in deposit insurance pricing. This issue is being hotly debated, and the extent to which such a system may actually be used in the future is not clear at this time.

Diversification of FDIC Risk

A second fundamental problem facing the deposit insurance agency is that it is insuring a risk that is not well-diversified. Financial institutions tend to experience serious difficulties at the same time because they mirror the financial health of the economy. When significant sectors of the economy are in financial difficulty, the banking industry is threatened with serious losses. When the banking industry as a whole experiences serious losses, the guarantors who insure the debt of these industries are threatened. This risk has a significant systematic element. A *systematic risk* is a risk that cannot be reduced through diversification. We know that systematic risks are priced in the capital markets on a regular basis; however, if the outcome of a systematic risk is sufficiently bad, the guarantor can become insolvent. Precisely because of this, deposit insurance is provided by a government agency rather than a private firm. No private guarantor could provide a credible complete guarantee for significant systematic risk. Only a government guarantor, which places the ultimate liability with the U. S. Treasury, has the ability to provide a credible guarantee.

When the underlying risk accepted by the FDIC is not well-diversified, there can be circumstances when large numbers of institutions have to close simultaneously. Under these conditions a government insurer can have a strong incentive to seek to protect a (finite) insurance fund and fail to close institutions that it determines have negative net worth. One way to accomplish this is to change the regulatory or accounting definitions for solvency. As we will explain in the next chapter, this is what occurred in the savings and loan industry in the early 1980s. The savings and loan regulators adopted more liberal rules to account for the net worth of savings and loans. As a result, lower levels of capital were required to remain solvent. In an economic environment where there are many failing institutions, the regulators presumably take into account the perceived social cost of closing institutions on a large scale. The ability to use discretion about the magnitude of this social cost is a critical element of the federal deposit insurance system. It is apparent that the social cost of a complete failure of the financial system, owing to widespread withdrawals, is intolerably large. It does not seem that the failure of modest or even large numbers of institutions generates a large social cost, if those institutions are closed promptly without allowing large negative economic net worth to accumulate. More extensive coverage or more liberal rules for determining closure result in de facto insurance protection for equity owners or for entrenched management. In effect, this means insurance for the existing market and ownership structure of the depository institutions industry. If this view is correct, then the social cost involved in deposit insurance is the cost of avoiding large-scale concentration of firms in the financial services industry.

The way deposit insurers enforce a closure rule in a circumstance where a large number of institutions are experiencing financial difficulty is likely to affect the way those institutions evaluate risk. If managers of institutions perceive that their risk of being closed by the guarantor is minimal as long as they all experience the same risk, then there will be an incentive to collectively take on large risks and underprice those risks.

The problems faced by the current system for deposit insurance grow as much out of problems in other aspects of the regulatory system for commercial banks as out of deficiencies in deposit insurance per se. The basic problem is that the market for financial services is changing dramatically and is threatening the traditional organization and operation of the banking industry. This change in the financial services marketplace is a central feature of Parts III and IV of this book.

SUMMARY

We began this chapter with a discussion of the Achilles' heel of the banking system, the problem of liquidity and solvency. We also examined the fundamental incentive problem created by high leverage and government deposit insurance, the incentive of banks with little equity to undertake excessively risky investments. Next, we described the two basic approaches to understanding the regulatory system, the positive theory of regulation and the capture theory. We emphasized that the existing regulatory system is a result of a constant tension between these two approaches to regulation. We identified four distinct positive rationales for regulation: limit the opportunities for expropriation, control risk taking, prevent system failure, and promote competition and limit monopolistic practices.

Next, we examined the regulatory system for commercial banks. We began with a brief summary of the historical evolution of the current bank regulatory system. Next we emphasized that the current system of bank regulation relies heavily on restrictions on the riskiness of bank loans and investments and auditing of bank observance of these restrictions and on capital requirements. Capital requirements provide a cushion to protect the FDIC against losses incurred by the bank. They also provide an incentive for banks to act wisely because they are betting their own resources first, rather than the depositors'. As of 1992, banks had to comply with a new system of capital regulation that weights various types of loans and investments according the their perceived risk. Total capital must equal 8 percent of such risk-weighted assets.

Finally, we turned our attention to the deposit insurance system. We emphasized two important issues about deposit insurance. First, we examined the pricing of deposit insurance. In principle, deposit insurance should be priced like any other form of insurance in that the price should be tied to the perceived risk. However, historically, premiums for deposit insurance have not been related to risk, just as capital requirements have not been related to risk. This creates an insidious incentive for institutions that are experiencing difficulty to attempt to gamble their way out of their problems. We also discussed the fact that much of the risk exposure of the government insurer is systematic risk that is not insurable in a private market.

QUESTIONS

1. What is expropriation? Should we attempt to limit opportunities for expropriation with government regulation? Is this a good idea or simply government interference?
2. What does convertibility mean? Explain the nature of the convertibility problem that faced banks throughout most of the nineteenth century.
3. Deposit insurance and regulatory control of risk are said to go hand in hand. Why is this so?
4. Summarize the various ways that the regulatory system tries to limit bank risk taking? What do you think of these mechanisms to control risk? Which do you think is likely to be most effective and which most costly?
5. In 1992 a new set of bank capital requirements went into effect. Summarize the basic features of these requirements.
6. Bank solvency is determined by accounting or book measures of net worth rather than market measures of net worth. Do you think we would be better off if we required banks to report the market values of the various assets on their balance sheets and used market values to determine solvency?
7. How does the choice of a system for pricing deposit insurance affect the risk taking of commercial banks? Would we be better off with a system of risk-based deposit insurance prices?

REFERENCES

Black, Fischer, Merton H. Miller, and Richard A. Posner. "An Approach to the Regulation of Bank Holding Companies." *Journal of Business* 51 (1978), pp. 379–412.

Boot, Arnoud W. A., and Anjan V. Thakor. "Self-Interested Bank Regulation." *American Economic Review* 83 (May 1993) pp. 206–212.

Calomiris, Charles W., and Charles M. Kahn. "The Role of Demandable Debt in Structuring Optimal Banking Arrangements." *American Economic Review* 81 (June 1991) pp. 497–513.

Campbell, Tim S., Yuk-Shee Chan, and A. Marino. "An Incentive-Based Theory of Bank Regulation." *Journal of Financial Intermediation* 2 (Sep 1992), pp. 255–276.

Chan, Yuk-Shee, Stuart I. Greenbaum, and Anjan V. Thakor. "Is Fairly Priced Deposit Insurance Possible?" *Journal of Finance* 47 (March 1992) pp. 227–245.

Diamond, Douglas W., and Philip H. Dybvig. "Bank Runs, Deposit Insurance, and Liquidity." *Journal of Political Economy* 91 (1983), pp. 401–419.

Kareken, John H. "Federal Bank Regulatory Policy: A Description and Some Observations." *Journal of Business* 19 (January 1986), pp. 3–48.

White, Lawrence J. "The Reform of Federal Deposit Insurance." *Journal of Economic Perspectives* 3 (Fall 1989), pp. 11–29.

• Chapter 6

The Dynamics of Regulatory Reform

In this chapter our purpose is to understand why and how the regulatory system for financial institutions is changing and how this process of change is reshaping financial firms and markets in the United States. Our purpose is also to see how the regulatory system responds to and fosters innovation in financial markets. Ultimately, we are interested in being able to formulate and execute strategies for managing financial firms. This requires a clear understanding of the current nature and probable evolution of the regulatory system.

In the 1980s there was considerable movement toward complete reform of the regulatory system for financial institutions. At the peak of the crisis in the savings and loan industry in the late 1980s, it appeared that the changes might be massive, but as that crisis became old news, and as it became apparent that the banks would not immediately follow the path of the savings and loans, the pressure for immediate reform lessened. As a result, it is difficult to predict how extensive the reform of the next few years may be. What is certain is that we cannot significantly undo what has already been done. To a large degree, the U.S. financial system that prevailed from the late 1930s until the early 1980s is gone. While some features of the system now being formed are becoming clear, there is considerable uncertainty about how the regulatory system may evolve in the future.

In this chapter we try to look both backward and forward at the process of change. By that we mean we examine the key changes in the regulatory system in the last few decades and we synthesize the reasons for those changes. We also look forward and discuss a few examples of the kind of change in the regulatory system we might expect to see in the future. We begin with a synthesis of the important characteristics of the regulation of banks and savings and loans in the 1960s and 1970s. Then we examine how increased inflation and technological progress impaired the effective operation of that regulatory system. Next we examine the principal legislative actions taken to reform that regulatory system. Finally, we examine several outstanding issues of regulatory reform still being debated: interstate banking, the possible repeal of the Glass-Steagall Act, and the competition between banks and finance companies. To explain the current level of competition between banks and finance companies we need to describe the operations of finance companies. This also provides a transition into Chapter 7, where we deal with nondepository financial institutions, including insurance and investment companies. The key concepts to learn in this chapter are listed below.

• Concepts to Learn in Chapter 6 •

- Why reform of bank and savings and loan regulation has been needed
- Key characteristics of regulatory reform of the 1980s and 1990s
- Remaining unsolved problems in bank regulation
- Issues of regulation and competition among finance companies

The Background for Regulatory Reform

Features of the Regulatory System that Created Vulnerability

We think it is extremely important to begin this chapter by identifying the features of the regulatory system of the 1960s and 1970s that ultimately became its Achilles heel. We proceed by discussing the problems in the overall regulatory system for both banks and savings and loans, and then we focus directly on savings and loans. A list of five features of the regulatory system that made it vulnerable during a period of high inflation and rapid technological progress is followed by a brief description of each point.

- Geographic and product line segmentation of financial services
- Competing and overlapping regulatory agencies for various types of financial service firms
- Creation of a barter system through restriction on competition with interest rates
- Selective use of reserve requirements tax and deposit insurance subsidy
- Monetary policy directed toward insuring the stability of interest rates

Segmentation of Services and Overlapping Regulation

As we discussed in the last chapter, an important feature of regulatory policy for financial institutions has been the restriction of competition to ensure stability. These restrictions have taken two basic forms. Each state has the right (1) to regulate entry by commercial banks domiciled in other states and (2) to determine its own laws governing branch banking. This system led to geographically segmented institutions and prevented the development of nationwide distribution systems for commercial banking services. While very rigid geographic restrictions were applied to commercial banks and savings and loans, no comparable restrictions were placed on either Securities and Exchange Commission (SEC)–regulated investment and brokerage firms or insurance companies (see Chapter 7). The system of geographic restrictions was accompanied by a system of product line restrictions that created separate classes of institutions for different financial products or services, principally banks, savings and loans, insurance companies, and investment companies and securities brokers.

The regulatory system itself is virtually as segmented as the institutions it is intended to regulate. Commercial banks have multiple federal regulators, including the Federal Reserve, the Comptroller of the Currency, and the Federal Deposit Insurance Corporation (FDIC), as well as a state bank regulator in each state. Investment companies and securities brokers are regulated by the SEC and by state agencies, whereas insurance companies are subject solely to state regulations. There are two alternative views of the virtues of the current overlapping regulatory system for financial institutions. One view is that multiple regulatory agencies for the same institutions, specifically commercial banks, or for competing institutions such as commercial banks and savings and loans, promotes efficient regulation. The basis for this view is that multiple regulators compete with each other and this helps to keep them both honest and efficient. This competition is particularly evident among the various regulatory agencies for commercial banks, which often differ on the merits of specific regulations. The alternative view is that multiple regulatory agencies constitute wasteful duplication of effort. In addition, a system of separate regulatory agencies for specific industries creates a greater opportunity for the regulators to become captured by the institutions they are regulating.

The Barter System

The third characteristic of the regulatory system of the 1960s and 1970s was the barter system—the practice of exchanging services for balances—created through restrictions on competition with interest rates by commercial banks and savings and loans. This system resulted from two factors. The first was the restriction of interest payments on deposit accounts through Regulation Q, which prevented banks and savings and loans from competing for deposit balances by offering higher interest rates. As a result, they attempted to attract those deposits by offering services, including convenience, to their customers. For example, there was no direct charge for processing transactions through a checking account. This system was like the one between commercial banks and the Federal Reserve.

The second factor was the Federal Reserve's policy requiring that banks hold reserves that do not earn interest and its provision of Federal Reserve services in exchange. Since its inception the Federal Reserve has imposed reserve requirements on commercial banks that are members of the Fed. Because the Federal Reserve pays no interest on them these reserves amount to a tax on the bank. The banks could invest the funds in Treasury bills or other securities and earn a rate of return if they were not held in reserve. In exchange for these reserves, the Federal Reserve provided services to commercial banks without charge, including check clearing and electronic transfer of funds on which the federal funds market is based.

Reserve Taxes and Insurance Subsidies

The next characteristic of the regulatory system of the 1960s and 1970s was the selective use of the reserve requirements tax and the deposit insurance subsidy. Government deposit insurance was provided to banks and savings and loans at prices that were not related to the risk taken on by the government. The insurance prices appear to have included a significant subsidy relative to the price a bank would have to pay to obtain funds without government insurance. When required reserves do not earn interest, this acts as a tax on institutions that face this requirement. The total cost of regulation for a specific type of financial institution is determined by the aggregate subsidy and tax imposed by various regulations. The important feature of the regulatory system that prevailed in the 1960s and 1970s (and in part still applies today), is that these taxes and subsidies were applied in different degrees to different classes of institutions. For example, banks of different sizes had different reserve requirements, and banks that were not Federal Reserve members had lower reserve requirements, and therefore a lower imposed tax. Savings and loans had no reserve requirements imposed by the Fed and so escaped this tax altogether. At the same time, banks and savings and loans had access to deposit insurance but investment companies did not. This created opportunities for regulatory arbitrage: institutions had an incentive to change their structure to minimize the total cost of regulation or to shift from one type of regulatory treatment to another as the regulation costs and benefits changed.

Monetary Policy and Stable Interest Rates

The final important characteristic of the U.S. regulatory system is a monetary policy directed toward insuring the stability of interest rates. From the early 1950s through the late 1970s, the Fed conducted monetary policy by attempting to control the federal funds rate (see Chapter 13). This policy had a very important implication for the operation of financial intermediaries such as banks and savings and loans. It meant the Fed was implicitly attempting to guarantee a market environment of stable interest rates. If the Fed could maintain this guarantee, then individual financial institutions could, in turn, offer financial instruments that provided interest rate guarantees to their customers. Principal among these instruments were such things as long-term fixed-rate loans. One of the main services that many financial institutions offered their customers was intermediation across time so that the financial institution, rather than that institution's customer, was accepting the risk of fluctuations in market interest rates. This service could be provided with relatively low risk as long as the Fed was able and willing to live up to its implicit commitment to maintain stable interest rates.

The Role of the Regulatory System for Savings and Loans

A crucial problem with the regulatory system that was in place in the 1970s derived from the structure of savings and loan regulation. Before we can describe how savings and loan regulation has been reformed we need to spell out the key features of the old system and explain why they created special problems. Before the enactment of major reforms in 1989 (described below) the savings and loan industry was regulated by the Federal Home Loan Bank Board (FHLBB) and insured by the Federal Savings and Loan Insurance Corporation (FSLIC), which was separate from the FDIC. While some of the regulations imposed upon savings and loans prior to the Garn-St. Germain Act of 1982 were nearly identical to similar regulations for commercial banks, there were some very important differences, which grew out of the long-standing intent of the federal government to support housing finance. These are listed below.

• *The Old Savings and Loan Regulatory System in a Nutshell* •

- Savings and loans were required to place all but a small portion of their assets into residential mortgages.
- Savings and loans were authorized to pay higher interest rates (historically ranging up to one half of 1 percent) than commercial banks on deposit accounts.
- The FHLBs still provide a continuing source of funds to savings and loans in the form of advances. A comparable source of funds is not available to commercial banks.
- The Congress granted special tax treatment to savings and loans.
- The FHLBB restricted the type of mortgage contracts savings and loans could offer.

The requirement that savings and loans invest only in residential mortgages, aside from some holdings of liquid assets such as Treasury bills, was one of the most direct steps taken by the government to support housing construction. This was accomplished through both direct restrictions on permissible nonmortgage investments and significant tax advantages to institutions with portfolios concentrated in qualifying mortgage investments, which we discuss below. The restrictions limiting investments in nonmortgage assets were relaxed in the Garn-St. Germain Act of 1982, but many of the tax advantages of mortgage investments remain. These restrictions have meant that roughly 80 percent of all savings and loan assets have been—and still are—invested in mortgages.

By establishing a lender restricted to investing almost exclusively in mortgages, it was hoped more funds would flow into home mortgages than would otherwise be the case. But the problem with this kind of restriction is that a private institution so constrained is unlikely to be able to compete effectively in the long run with institutions not so restricted. To offset this disadvantage, Congress permitted savings and loans to pay higher interest rates than banks on comparable regulated deposit accounts. In addition, the regional FHLBs came to assume a supportive role to savings and loans that the bank regulatory agencies never provided for commercial banks. The FHLBs are direct suppliers of funds to savings and loans through a form of loan called an "advance," which has come to represent a sizable portion of the total source of funds for savings and loans. The Fed provides a service that is in some respects similar through what is called the "discount window," but loans extended to commercial banks in this way are intended as temporary sources of funds to be used only when a bank has a short-term liquidity problem. Continued reliance on the discount window is a sign of trouble that attracts bank examiners, but the same cannot be said of use of advances by savings and loans. Advances have been a more permanent source of funds, and therefore, in effect, a way of providing federal support for mortgage loans. Total Fed advances were $192 million in December 1991; total FHLBs advances were $65.8 billion in the same month. As part of the Garn-St. Germain Act of 1982 savings and loans were given access to loans through the Federal Reserve discount window.

Savings and loans are also regulated through the tax laws. For many years, savings and loans were able to avoid almost all federal income taxes through liberal use of bad-debt reserves, funds set aside to cover possible defaults on loans. Income is tax deductible when it is placed in the bad-debt reserve rather than when a bad debt is actually realized. Therefore, by diverting funds to bad-debt reserves these institutions were able to offset almost all taxable income. In 1969 a law was passed that stipulated that savings and loans must have 82 percent of their assets in residential mortgages, cash, government securities, and passbook loans if they were to continue to receive favorable tax treatment of bad-debt reserves. This feature of the tax law had crucial and lasting impact on this industry. It confined them to a such a narrow range of investments that they were unable to adapt to the changing financial conditions of the 1980s.

The last unique feature of the savings and loans regulatory system was that the FHLBB restricted the types of mortgages federally chartered institutions could offer, and state regulators restricted the allowable contracts for state-chartered institutions. It is somewhat difficult to pin down the exact motive for such a restriction. In part it was a desire to control the risk assumed by insured institutions, and in part it was designed to prevent exploitation of unwary consumers. Specifically, savings and loans were allowed to invest mainly in fixed-rate mortgages. In 1981, the FHLBB eliminated these restrictions, and since then a number of alternative mortgages have become popular in the marketplace.

Weaknesses in the Regulatory System

The regulatory system we have been describing was reasonably well-suited to an economy where the market for financial services was highly segmented, both by geography and by the characteristics of the financial services being provided. It was also well-suited to an economy with low rates of inflation, and therefore relatively low and stable interest rates. But in the 1970s both of these conditions changed: inflation reached unprecedented levels, and rapid technological progress in both computers and communications transformed a collection of regional markets for financial services into a national, if not a global, market. To see how vulnerable the old regulatory system was to these basic changes in the U.S. economy we need to examine its specific weaknesses.

The Impact of Inflation

Probably the most important weakness in the system is that, in a time of high inflation the Federal Reserve's implicit commitment to provide stable interest rates becomes unworkable. As we will learn in Part II, market interest rates are determined by the real interest rate and by the market's expectation of the future rate of inflation. If the Fed tries to hold down market interest rates in the face of expectations of increasing inflation rates, its efforts will be futile. By concentrating on attempting to maintain low market interest rates, it would lose control of the supply of money and thus exacerbate the inflation problem. The Fed faced precisely this type of situation during the late 1970s. In October, 1979, Chairman Paul Volcker renounced the Fed's long-standing policy of attempting to control market interest rates, in effect, abandoning its implicit commitment to maintain stable rates.

Many financial institutions had based much of their business strategy, either explicitly or implicitly, on the Fed's commitment to maintain stable interest rates. Once this commitment was broken, it was no longer feasible for many financial intermediaries to assume significant amounts of interest rate risk. As a result, banking firms moved away from fixed-rate to floating-rate loans in both commercial and mortgage lending. Market participants came to rely more heavily on new instruments such as futures and options (which we discuss in Part III) as mechanisms for limiting interest rate risk. In addition, institutions that had not anticipated the changes that inflation would create became unstable and unprofitable.

The difference in performance of Citicorp and Bank of America in the early 1980s illustrates the results, respectively, of anticipating and failing to anticipate change. Possibly more than any other large financial intermediary, Citicorp anticipated changes in the economic and regulatory environment that occurred in the early 1980s. Its chairman during the late 1970s and early 1980s, Walter Wriston, is highly regarded for his anticipation and planning of these changes. To a large degree, Citicorp was very profitable during the early 1980s because it bet correctly on how the economic environment would change. Bank of America made precisely the opposite bet. Even as inflation accelerated and the Fed backed away from its commitment to stabilize interest rates, Bank of America continued to conduct business in the same ways it always had. It continued to make a large volume of fixed-rate mortgage loans and persisted in making business loans at home and abroad as if inflation meant a prolonged era of continued prosperity. Furthermore, once it became apparent that it had made the wrong bet, Bank of America still seemed not to understand the degree to which the market environment had changed. As a result, Bank of America's performance deteriorated in the early 1980s while Citicorp prospered. Of course, the performance of these two banking giants completely reversed itself in the late 1980s as Bank of America successfully restructured and Citicorp began to stumble.

The advent of relatively high and volatile interest rates and the elimination of Regulation Q meant that depository institutions had to change the way they sought to attract deposit balances. They had to compete with interest rates, where they had been prohibited from doing so before. The methods they had previously used to attract deposits were no longer so valuable. Some, such as prizes and gifts for new deposits, were easy to abandon, but many institutions had used convenience as their means of competition. And convenience generally meant the development of an expensive branch system for delivering financial services. With the demise of Regulation Q and the increasing changes in the nature of the financial services market toward a national one, the branch systems needed to be overhauled dramatically. In a sense, the barter system, which had been used for so long, was destroyed and a new system with a much larger role for price competition had to replace it.

The barter system between the banks and the Fed was fundamentally altered at the same time, though the nature of the change was quite different. Under the barter system, the Fed provided services in exchange for reserves that earned no interest. When interest rates were relatively low, these services were not very expensive, but the increase in interest rates, which reached its peak in 1981, drove up the cost of holding reserves, while the benefit the commercial banks derived from these services did not match those increases. Member banks therefore simply chose, in increasing numbers, to withdraw from the Federal Reserve system. They no longer received the services, but they also did not have to hold reserves that earned no interest. The incentive of banks to withdraw from the Federal Reserve system came to be referred to, somewhat euphemistically, as the "membership problem." The solution to the membership problem adopted by Congress in 1982 was to require all financial intermediaries that offered transactions accounts, including both banks and savings and loans, to be subject to common reserve requirements. These reserves would still not earn interest, however. This was a step toward uniformity in regulation or away from imposing significantly different levels of implicit taxation on different classes of institutions. Nonetheless, the tax itself was not eliminated.

The Impact of Technological Progress

At the same time that high inflation rates were rendering Regulation Q obsolete, the rapid pace of change in the technology of delivering financial services was also leading to significant changes in the U.S. financial system. The pace of technological progress in communications and computers altered the working definition of what constituted a market for financial services. In the 1950s, and even in the 1960s, it was reasonable to argue that the market for financial services in one part of the country, say Pittsburgh, was distinct from the market for the same service in another part of the country, say Dallas. There were real obstacles, or at least few economies to be generated, for any firm that attempted to offer banking services in both cities. But as it became possible to computerize an increasingly large portion of bank operations, and as the cost of transferring computer information from one part of the country to another declined, the gains in efficiency from geographic expansion of banking firms increased. Furthermore, as the emphasis on both price and quality of service increased with the demise of Regulation Q, brand-name identification and brand loyalty began to become as valuable in banking as it is in many other lines of business. In the post–Regulation Q era, marketing had become an important part of banking, and an important part of marketing was the penetration of new markets with a brand name and a reputation for quality. The geographic segmentation that had been an essential ingredient of the regulatory system was becoming increasingly costly and was a barrier to development of a more efficient financial system. The same changes in technology and marketing affected the segmentation between product lines enforced by regulation. As we have seen, the U.S. financial system had maintained a separation between broad classes of financial services by erecting barriers that prohibited institutions that specialized in one class from invading the turf of specialists in other classes. Technological progress has blurred the distinctions between the actual processes of producing the services in each of these categories.

Special Problems with Savings and Loan Regulation

The basic problem historically faced by savings and loans is that they "borrowed short and lent long". That is, the average maturity of their loans has been considerably longer than the average maturity of their deposit liabilities. Savings and loans have historically performed the task of intermediating across time. When they extend mortgage loans with maturities of 30 years at a fixed interest rate, they are making a commitment to provide insurance to the borrower against future changes in interest rates. If the lender's liabilities had the same maturity as its mortgage loans, it would bear no risk in providing that insurance. But when its funds are obtained with an average maturity substantially shorter than the maturity of its loans, it bears the risk that the cost of its funds will increase while the return on its mortgages remains unchanged. In a time when inflation is accelerating, short-term interest rates tend to increase and the rates of return on existing long-term mortgages remain unchanged. If this kind of development persists long enough, it can mean disaster for financial intermediaries that invest almost exclusively in fixed-rate mortgage loans. This problem is illustrated in Figure 6-1, which shows the return for a lender that makes a fixed-rate loan and funds that loan with shorter-maturity funds. The flat horizontal line through the figure represents the fixed interest rate on the loan; the irregular line represents the current cost of funds, reflecting short-term interest rates. In the earlier years of this loan, the lender experienced a gain, but the gain turned into a loss as interest rates rose above the rate on the fixed-rate long-term loan.

It is precisely this problem that afflicted the savings and loan industry in the 1980s. As interest rates rose to unprecedented levels in the early 1980s, savings and loans incurred significant losses, owing to the negative spread between the rate of return on their existing loan portfolios and the cost of funding those new loans in the marketplace. It has been estimated that during 1982, when the negative spread between the return on their loan portfolios and the cost of funding those portfolios was at its peak, the accumulated negative net worth of the savings and loan industry rose to between $100 billion and $175 billion. This represents the difference between the value of their assets and the value of outstanding liabilities of these institutions.

Under the current regulatory system, savings and loans can operate with negative real or economic net worth, as measured by the market value of their assets, as

Figure 6-1
Gains and losses on funding long-term loans with short-term deposits.

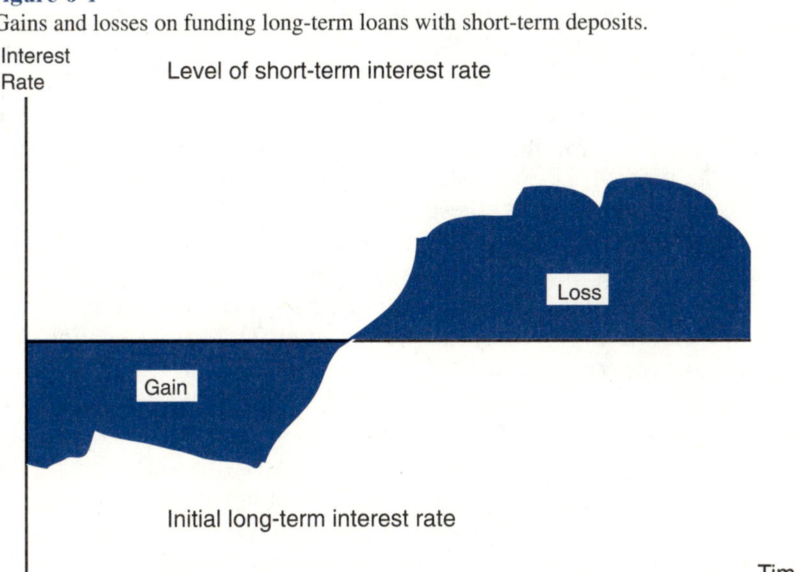

long as they maintain positive accounting net worth as measured by the book value of assets. Unlike investment companies regulated by the SEC (see Chapter 7), savings and loans and commercial banks do not have to record the market value of the assets they manage, though movement toward reform of this point is proceeding as this is written. A savings and loan carries its mortgage portfolio on its books at its value when the mortgage loans in the portfolio were originated (less repayments of principal). As a result, there can be a considerable spread between the book value and the market value of the assets for a savings and loan. When interest rates rise, as they did in the late 1970s and early 1980s, the market value of outstanding loans can decline significantly below their book value. This means that savings and loans can have significant negative net worth as measured by the market value of their assets and liabilities and still have positive net worth as measured by book or accounting values. Furthermore, because regulators define the solvency of savings and loans according to their accounting rather than their market net worth, these institutions can continue to operate with negative market net worth unless negative earnings cause their accounting net worth to fall below regulatory limits.

By the middle 1980s a large number of savings and loans had experienced sufficiently severe losses that their accounting net worth had declined below limits considered minimally acceptable by the FHLBB. In fact, the problem had become sufficiently widespread that the FSLIC found it difficult to deal with the situation effectively. The FSLIC had a limited amount of reserves to deal with failed savings and loans. We already mentioned that the estimated negative net worth in the early 1980s reached as high as $175 billion, but the assets of the FSLIC were never as much as $10 billion. This meant that if the government was going to admit that large numbers of institutions were actually bankrupt it would have to explain to the taxpayers that they would have to recognize a very large loss. Furthermore, the savings and loan industry had considerable influence and power in the U. S. Congress. This made aggressive action to close down large numbers of institutions an extremely unattractive alternative. A completely different approach to the problem entailed reducing capital requirements so that many thrifts could remain legally solvent and hoping that economic growth and lower interest rates in the future would solve the problem.

The regulators chose the alternative of altering accounting standards to try to camouflage the serious situation in the industry. In addition, they lowered capital requirements for savings and loans from 5 percent of assets in 1980 to 3 percent in 1982. They apparently took these actions hoping that a booming economy and changes in interest rates would bail them out of their problems. Unfortunately, this approach did not succeed. The problems created by high interest rates described above were exacerbated by the regulatory policy that allowed savings and loans to continue to operate even if they had little capital. This created an incentive for managers of these firms to invest funds in highly risky real estate investments, in the hope that they could grow their way out of their problems. Far too many institutions pursued unsound policies and some engaged in substantial fraud. This led to the collapse of the existing system for regulating savings and loans and the enactment of major reform of the system, including the dismantling of the FHLBB and the FSLIC.

The losses that resulted from the thrift debacle have become a widely discussed item throughout the United States as it has become apparent that these losses will be incurred by U. S. taxpayers. The government estimated in 1991 that the present value of the total losses from the thrift bailout would be $130 billion to $176 billion. Much larger numbers are sometimes quoted in the press. It is difficult to reconcile seemingly disparate quotes of the bailout costs as often estimates are used that add up costs incurred over many years without calculating their present values. Such a mistake is not included in the estimate of up to $176 billion,[1] but any estimate depends on the future prices that assets of bankrupt thrifts will command and on the incidence of failures in the future. Therefore, there is considerable uncertainty in any estimate, and the total cost could far exceed the 1991 estimate.

By now it should be apparent that the regulatory system put in place in the 1930s is not very well-suited to the economic environment that will obtain in the United States in the decades ahead. Some reform of the old system has already taken place, and more will probably be forthcoming.

Reform of the U.S. Financial System in the 1980s and 1990s

The reform of the regulatory system thus far has come in three forms: new laws enacted by the Congress and by state legislatures, changes in regulatory policy by regulators within the scope of existing laws, and reinterpretation of existing laws by the courts. The biggest changes have taken the form of new federal legislation, but that does not mean that the other types of changes have been unimportant. In Chapter 5 we provided an overview of four major pieces of federal legislation, enacted in 1980, 1982, 1989, and 1991. Now we want to delve more carefully into how this reform developed.

The Deregulation Legislation of the 1980s

The first important piece of federal reform legislation enacted during the 1980s was the Depository Institutions Deregulation and Monetary Control Act of 1980. This legislation, passed by Congress and signed by President Jimmy Carter in March, 1980, involved four principal changes in the regulatory system. These are spelled out in Panel A of Table 6-1.

The Deregulation Act of 1980 focused on two basic issues. First, it attempted to mandate gradual deregulation of the liability side of the balance sheets of depository institutions. It indicated that banks and savings and loans should eventually be allowed to compete with interest rates for deposits. Second, it attempted to solve the membership problem of the Federal Reserve by making the reserve requirements tax uniform across all types of institutions that offered transactions accounts. While these changes seemed extraordinarily significant at the time, with hindsight it seems remarkable that they could be viewed as being adequate to deal with the problems in the regulatory system. It also seems remarkable, with the benefit of hindsight, to have expected that the market would allow gradual phasing out of Regulation Q over six years.

---

[1]See *Economic Report of the President.* Washington, DC, U. S. Government Printing Office, February, 1991, p. 173.

Table 6-1
Key Features of 1980 and 1982 Banking Legislation

**Panel A:
Principal features of the Depository Institutions Deregulation and Monetary Control Act of 1980**

1. All depository institutions that offer transactions accounts, not simply commercial banks that are members of the Federal Reserve System, must maintain reserves. The law stipulates that banks that were Federal Reserve members in 1980 cannot escape current reserve requirements by withdrawing from the system. It also defines a gradual phasein for reserve requirements on depository institutions that were not previously subject to reserve requirements—that is, they were not member banks in 1980.
2. The Federal Reserve must directly price those services provided to commercial banks and make them available to all depository institutions.
3. It provided for what amounts to payment of interest on demand deposits by authorizing automatic transfer accounts, NOW accounts, and share drafts. Automatic transfer accounts provide for automatic transfer from savings to checking accounts. NOW accounts are essentially interest-bearing accounts on which checks can be written, as are share drafts at credit unions. It further specified that all of these accounts will be subject to reserve requirements.
4. It required the gradual elimination of interest rate restriction on deposit accounts over a 6-year period.

**Panel B:
Principal Features of the Garn St. Germain Act of 1982**

1. Within 60 days, the regulatory agencies for each distinct type of depository institution must authorize those institutions to offer a deposit account fully competitive with accounts available from money market funds.
2. All regulations on interest rates on specific accounts are eliminated, which permits savings and loans to pay a higher interest rate than commercial banks, the interest differential.
3. Savings and loans have the authority to make commercial loans. They may make no loan to a single borrower in an amount greater than would be permitted for a national bank with equivalent capital. After January 1, 1984, such loans could comprise as }uch as 10 percent of an institution's total assets.
4. Savings and loans may make consumer loans. These loans may not comprise more than 30 percent of the total assets of an institution.
5. Savings and loan holding companies have authority to engage in or acquire insurance underwriting firms. No such authority is granted to bank holding companies.

To understand why the intended six-year phaseout of Regulation Q became impractical, it is necessary only to examine the prime new competitor of banks and savings and loans for consumer deposits, the money market mutual funds (MMMFs). MMMFs are mutual funds that invest exclusively in short-term debt instruments and generally provide check-writing privileges to their customers. MMMFs began to grow in the late 1970s as market interest rates increased substantially above the Regulation Q interest rate ceilings on regulated deposit accounts at banks and savings and loans. At the end of 1977 MMMF had total assets of $3.8 billion. By the end of 1979, when the 1980 legislation was in preparation, MMMFs assets had increased to $43.6 billion. (Total assets in MMMFs exceeded $200 billion in 1991.) While this increase was sizable, it was still not enough to render infeasible the planned gradual elimination of Regulation Q. In the next two years, however, total MMMFs assets increased another four times, to a total of $190 billion. During this same period interest rates in the United States had reached their historical peak. The combination of unprecedented high interest rates and decreasing market share of consumer savings for traditional depository institutions threatened to completely restructure the existing financial system. Regulators and Congress were virtually compelled to take some action to speed up the phaseout of Regulation Q. They responded with the Garn-St. Germain Act of 1982.

The Garn-St. Germain Act is a long, detailed piece of legislation that produced numerous important changes in regulations. Its principal features are summarized in Panel B of Table 6-1. The 1980 and 1982 acts gave banks and savings and loans distinct but roughly similar authority to offer transactions accounts. The 1980 act—specifically, the Consumer Checking Account Equity Act—enabled Negotiable Order of Withdrawal (NOW) accounts, which pay interest, to be used to effect transfers to third parties. NOW accounts pay interest and may require notice of intention to withdraw; thus, they are different from demand deposits, which then paid no interest and are payable upon demand. Section III of the Garn-St. Germain Act (known as the Thrift Institution Restructuring Act) allowed savings institutions to accept demand deposits from individuals, if they were used for business purposes, and from corporations. This law did not give savings and loans the authority to accept individual, nonbusiness demand deposits.

Reform Spawned by the Thrift Crisis

As we discussed above, the savings and loan or thrift industry of the early 1980s had accumulated negative net worth far beyond the capacity of the Federal Savings and Loan Insurance Corporation to offset it. In the early 1980s the thrifts' negative net worth was principally a result of significant increases in interest rates, which raised the cost of funding portfolios of fixed-rate mortgages. The 1980 and 1982 laws attempted to help the savings and loans by expanding their powers to make a wide variety of types of loans to consumers and corporations and allowed them to offer competitive interest rates on liabilities to attract funds. One observer of the system quipped that the 1980 act, which focused largely on the liability side of the balance sheet, was based on the following philosophy: Suppose you see a person drowning. You might consider throwing him a large rock, on the premise that if he swims long enough with that rock he will develop the strength to swim ashore and save himself. The historical record of the 1980s has made clear that the thrifts were not able to bail themselves out by engaging in new types of lending. Indeed, their capital levels were so low that they had little incentive to invest depositors' funds in the best projects they could find. Instead, they had an incentive to invest in very risky projects. If those projects generated large returns, they would be saved. If they turned out to be disasters, it would be the taxpayers' problem. Indeed, it has turned out to be the taxpayers' problem. (Recall our example of Roll It Federal from Chapter 5.)

Congress responded to this situation in 1989 with the Financial Institutions Reform, Recovery and Enforcement Act (FIRREA). The essential features are described below, and Table 6-2 outlines the basic structure of the regulatory system before and after FIRREA.

• FIRREA in a Nutshell •

1. FIRREA created the Resolution Trust Corporation (RTC) and empowered it to administer the closure and disposition of insolvent savings and loans. Congress authorized both the Treasury and the RTC to borrow an initial $50 billion to cover the cost of thrift insolvencies. Additional funds have been requested each year as the size of the problem has increased.
2. FIRREA consolidated bank and savings and loan insurance agencies within the FDIC. The FSLIC, formerly under the jurisdiction of the FHLBB, was replaced by the Savings Association Insurance Fund (SAIF) and placed under the control of the FDIC. A separate fund (within the FDIC) for commercial banks called the Bank Insurance Fund (BIF) was established. Deposit insurance prices charged to banks and savings and loans were altered with the intent of replenishing the resources of the two funds over a long-term horizon.
3. FIRREA restructured the regulation of savings and loans. It abolished the FHLBB and transferred most of its responsibilities to a new Office of Thrift Supervision (OTS). The regional FHLBs are governed by a new Federal Housing Finance Board. This meant that regulation and insurance of savings and loans would be split between two agencies as it is for commercial banks.
4. FIRREA tightened restrictions on savings and loan activities and raised their capital requirements to be no more lax than those imposed on commercial banks. The Act also tightened controls on savings and loan practices, including investments in junk bonds, the size of loans made to one borrower, allowable equity investments, and the use of brokered deposits for institutions with insufficient capital. The act also reinstituted controls that focus savings and loans on housing-related assets. An savings and loan that fails to have 70 percent of its portfolio in qualifying housing-related investments loses access to advances from the FHLBs. Recall that these advances totaled roughly $60 billion in 1991.
5. FIRREA increased the legal enforcement powers of the regulators and imposed new penalties for banking law violations. The law authorized regulators to close institutions more swiftly than they could previously and increased their ability to recover losses from other institutions owned by the parent of a failed savings and loan. It also increased civil and criminal penalties for a broader set of officials of savings and loans.

Another important piece of reform legislation was passed in November 1991, the Federal Deposit Insurance Corporation Improvement Act (FDICIA). The basic thrust of this law is to increase (1) the authority of the FDIC to make examinations of banks and (2) its responsibility for the thoroughness of such examinations. All federal bank regulators are instructed by the law to conduct full-scope on-site examinations every 12 months. Only small institutions with very high capital and prior good examinations are exempt. This substantially increased the frequency of examinations. In addition, there

Table 6-2

Regulation Before and After FIRREA

Old Regulatory Structure

Treasury Department

Office of the Comptroller of the Currency

—Charters national banks

—Supervises and regulates national banks

FDIC

—Insures deposits at commercial and savings banks

—Manages assets and liabilities of insolvent banks

—Supervises and regulates state-chartered banks that are not members of the Federal Reserve System

Federal Home Loan Bank Board

—Charters federal savings and loans

—Regulates and supervises federal savings and loans

—Oversees the FSLIC

—Oversees the 12 regional FHLBs

FSLIC

—Insures deposits at savings and loans

—Manages assets and liabilities of insolvent savings and loans

Federal Home Loan Banks

—Lend (make advances) to member savings and loans

—Examine savings and loans

Federal Reserve

—Supervises and regulates state-chartered member banks, bank holding companies and their nonbank subsidiaries, the international activities of banks and bank holding companies, and the U.S. banking and nonbanking operations of foreign banks

—Sets reserve requirements for all banks, savings and loans, and credit unions

—Through the 12 regional Federal Reserve Banks, provides discount-window loans to depository institutions

New Regulatory Structure

Treasury Department

Office of the Comptroller of the Currency

—No major change in duties

Office of Thrift Supervision

—Charters federal savings and loans

—Establishes savings and loans regulations

—Supervises both federal and state-chartered savings and loans, and savings and loans holding companies

FDIC

—FDIC's Board of Directors expanded from three to five members and will include the Director of the Office of Thrift Supervision

Bank Insurance Fund (BIF—same as original FDIC fund)

—Insures deposits of commercial and savings banks

—Manages assets and liabilities of insolvent banks

Savings Association Insurance Fund (SAIF) replaces FSLIC

—Insures deposits of savings and loans

—Manages assets and liabilities of insolvent savings and loans *after 1992*

FSLIC Resolution Fund

—Manages the remaining assets and liabilities of some 200 savings and loans taken over by the FSLIC prior to 1989

Table 6-2 (continued)
Regulation Before and After FIRREA

New Regulatory Structure

Resolution Trust Oversight Board
—Oversees the Resolution Trust Corporation
—Chaired by the Secretary of the Treasury. Includes the Federal Reserve Board Chairman, the Secretary of Housing and Urban Development, and two others appointed by the President

Resolution Trust Corporation (managed by the FDIC)
—Manages the assets and liabilities of savings and loans that become insolvent between 1989 and August 1992
—Can use $50 billion that will be raised by the Treasury and the Resolution Funding Corporation to resolve savings and loan problems
—Ceases to operate after 1996, when its responsibilities are shifted to the FDIC's SAIF

Resolution Funding Corporation
—Issues up to $30 billion of long-term bonds to finance the activities of the Resolution Trust Corporation

Federal Housing Finance Board
—Oversees the 12 regional Federal Home Loan Banks

Federal Home Loan Banks
—Lend (make advances) to member institutions, which may include banks and credit unions as well as S&Ls

Federal Reserve
—No major change in duties

must be more extensive private auditing of the management and financial controls of regulated institutions. Regulators are instructed to revise risk-based capital rules to include interest rate risk and credit concentration exposures. The law instructs bank regulators and examiners to take what actions they deem prudent and necessary in the process of examining a bank. This places an increased burden on the bank examiners to anticipate problems in commercial banks and thrifts. This law clearly reflects a desire on the part of the Congress to avoid a repeat of the 1980s disaster in the thrift industry.

The general philosophy behind FIRREA and FDICIA is almost directly the opposite of the philosophy that guided the Garn-St. Germain Act of 1982. In the more recent laws, savings and loans were forced to return toward a more narrow definition of their role in the U. S. financial markets, and they are now subject to more stringent capital requirements and regulatory scrutiny than during most of the 1980s. It is important to recall that part of the justification for the approach taken toward the savings and loan problem early in the early 1980s was the recognition that it was politically untenable to close large numbers of savings and loans that were bankrupt on an economic, though not a legal, basis. Over the decade, the politics changed, as numerous scandals involving key savings and loan figures and politicians awakened the public to the fact that there was a serious problem. The real implication of the recent FIRREA legislation may turn out to be not much different than if most savings and loans had been closed in the early 1980s, though the cost will probably be greater. FIRREA effectively mandates that savings and loans must find a way to be profitable as providers of housing-related financial services and they must maintain their capital levels as they do so. It seems difficult to imagine that large numbers of institutions can successfully accomplish this mission without government subsidies and protection like that they enjoyed in the 1960s and 1970s. If this gloomy prediction turns out to be accurate, we will still have to manage the process of closing and liquidating many billions of dollars of assets in failing thrifts, which will surely be a difficult and expensive process. As we proceed through the rest of this book and focus on the management issues that must be dealt with in running a financial firm, it might be a good idea to keep in the back of your mind the question of how the thrifts can find a strategy for generating a profit.

Unresolved Problems in Bank Regulation

The reform legislation of the 1980s and early 1990s leaves unresolved a number of issues surrounding the future regulation of banks and savings and loans. The list of such issues is rather long, but we have selected a few we believe are especially important and deserve attention here. They include interstate banking, Glass-Steagall, and restructuring of the bank holding company laws.

Interstate Banking

An important question not addressed by recent federal legislation is whether interstate banking should be permitted. By 1992 many restrictions on interstate banking had been eliminated, largely owing to piecemeal changes made by individual states rather than enactment of federal legislation permitting interstate banking. Once again, the change is, not the result of some rational deliberation about how to improve the regulatory system, but a response to a crisis. The crisis has two elements to it. The first is that a number of banks and savings and loans have become insolvent or were threatened with insolvency. When a bank gets into trouble, part of the solution is to attract new capital. If interstate banking is prohibited, and a merger or a takeover is required to inject new capital, then the only sources of new capital are banks in the same state. Even in times when other banks are doing well, this kind of merger can decrease competition in a given region, but when a number of financial institutions in the region are simultaneously experiencing financial difficulties, it can be very difficult to attract capital from within a state. The option of going outside the state to attract capital becomes attractive.

This option was pursued in both the banking and the savings and loan industry in the 1980s. The savings and loan regulators were willing to sell failing thrifts to healthy commercial banks or industrial firms, regardless of where they were domiciled. Through this process of auctioning failed institutions Citicorp, for example, was able to acquire savings and loans in California and Florida. This provided the only vehicle available at the time for Citicorp to acquire the rights to deliver financial services to consumers in these states. With the enactment of the Garn-St. Germain Act and the enhanced powers for savings and loans it provided, these franchises became nearly as valuable as the right for Citicorp to operate a bank in these states.

The second feature of the crisis, which has hastened the approach of interstate banking, is the fear of smaller regional banks and savings and loans that a few institutions will become national distributors of financial services. Smaller institutions have developed a legitimate concern that they will fall too far behind if Bank of America, for example, can successfully use mechanisms like the acquisition of failing institutions to build a national market. At the urging of smaller banks, many states have passed laws that allow acquisition of banks in other cooperating states by banks in a given region, but not by banks from other states, specifically New York and California. This arrangement has been used extensively in the southeastern United States to allow state banks to merge into regional banks, which may then prepare to be more effective competitors of large institutions such as Citicorp, if and when they eventually enter that region.

A few states have completely opened their doors to banks from other states. In 1986 Arizona passed a law permitting other banks to enter that state and acquire banks there. Banks from other states, particularly California, were quick to take advantage of the opportunity. In 1986 California passed a law stipulating that banks from other states would be allowed to enter California in 1991. Texas has also welcomed out-of-state banks, but the situation there is rather special. In 1985 and 1986 Texas banks experienced severe losses because of the decline in the energy business. As a result, they were hungry for new capital. Because these problems are reasonably widespread in Texas banks, Texas opted to allow outside banks to enter the state.

The interstate banking issue is intimately tied in with the question of how to regulate bank holding companies, and even how to define a bank. Existing law regarding bank holding companies restricts these firms to lines of business "closely related to banking." In effect, firms engaged in most lines of commerce cannot be in the banking business or cannot acquire banks; however, no equivalent restrictions apply to *unitary* savings and loan holding companies, that is, to companies that now own only *one* savings and loan. Any firm, as long as it is approved by the regulators, can acquire a savings and loan. For example, in 1985 Ford Credit Corporation, a subsidiary of Ford Motor Company, acquired First Nationwide Savings and Loan. Ford did not necessarily acquire a savings and loan because it preferred that to acquiring a bank. It was precluded from acquiring a bank by the bank holding company laws. There appears to be no logical reason for the distinction in treatment of bank and savings and loan holding companies. Instead, there is a long history of separation of banking and commerce, but there is no comparable history with savings and loans. As banks attempt to diversify their financial products and expand their geographic areas of operation, the bank holding company laws that restrict their ability to move out of financial services will come under increasing pressure.

The issue of bank holding companies has been complicated by the debate surrounding the appropriate legal definition of a bank. The bank holding company statutes state that, for the purposes of the bank holding company law, a commercial bank engages in two activities: it accepts deposits and makes loans. A bank holding company that would otherwise find it difficult to acquire banks in other states, as well as investment companies that would not be able to acquire a bank at all, could then acquire a bank and curtail its lending. They would then be able to accept deposits and have them insured by the FDIC, but they would not violate the bank holding company statutes because the bank they would operate would be what has been called a "nonbank bank." Alternatively, a bank could acquire a bank in another state solely for the purpose of making loans in that state and not accept deposits. The office of the Comptroller of the Currency, which has the authority to grant federal charters for nonbank banks, has chosen to give a liberal interpretation to the statutes. As a result, it has granted charters for limited-service banks, which to a certain degree circumvents the bank holding statutes.

In our view, one of the most compelling reasons to allow interstate banking throughout the United States is that it tends to diversify the risk of individual institutions. One of the central problems of regionally segmented financial institutions is that they cannot achieve geographic diversification of their credit risk. Thus, when a region of the country experiences serious difficulties, as happened in several parts of the country in recent years, the banks in that region often get into trouble. If the banks' losses are sufficient to render them insolvent, then the FDIC is compelled to step in. If such institutions were able to diversify their credit exposure beyond one geographic area, the loss exposure of the taxpayers would be significantly reduced.

The Glass-Steagall Act

One of the most important pieces of legislation affecting the current structure of financial institutions in the United States is the Glass-Steagall Act. In the 1930s this new law forced banking firms to divest themselves of their securities operations and limit future activities to what is now called "commercial banking," as opposed to investment banking. The motivations for this separation were principally to prevent conflicts of interest between those who handle depositors' funds and those who underwrite securities, as well as to limit the riskiness of the activities of commercial banks.

Tremendous pressure is now building in the U.S. financial system to repeal the Glass-Steagall Act. A consensus seems to be growing that better methods are available to limit the kinds of conflict of interest that much concerned Congress when Glass-Steagall was passed. Moreover, there is also a consensus emerging that the commercial banking business is changing to such an extent that an inherent part of its business is the underwriting of some types of securities. This change in the banking business is the process of securitization, which we discuss in detail in Chapter 18. It is probably no longer sufficient for large banks to act simply as portfolio lenders, that is to accept deposits and use those deposits to fund loans they hold on their books. Many financial markets that have been dominated by financial intermediaries are now being transformed into over-the-counter markets. This means banks have to act less like portfolio lenders and more like dealers and guarantors of securities. Unfortunately, Glass-Steagall stands directly in their path as they attempt to change.

Rather than take on all of the restrictions incorporated in Glass-Steagall in a head-on assault, the major money center banks, such as Bankers Trust, Citicorp, Morgan Guaranty, and Chase, first pursued authority to act as dealers only for specific types of securities. They have sought this authority for commercial paper, mortgage-backed and consumer paper–backed securities, and municipal revenue bonds. They have always had the authority to operate subsidiaries that act as dealers in U.S. Treasury securities. Therefore, they contend that the movement into trading and underwriting these additional types of issues is a natural extension of their existing authority and their normal lending and investment activities. Commercial paper and mortgage and consumer paper–backed securities essentially constitute securitized bank loans, and banks historically have been active in these types of loans. Banks have also been active investors in municipal bonds and have underwritten general obligation municipal bonds in the past.

To obtain approval for underwriting securities, a number of bank holding companies that operate in large money center banks have sought approval from the Federal Reserve to establish subsidiaries specifically to conduct such activities. In the spring of 1987, the Federal Reserve granted authority first to three large New York bank holding companies and then to four other large bank holding companies to underwrite and distribute commercial paper, municipal revenue bonds, and mortgage-backed securities issued by other companies through such a subsidiary. The Fed placed restrictions on such subsidiary activities that stipulated that gross revenue from each activity cannot exceed 5 percent of the unit's total gross revenue and that its share of the total market in each type of security cannot exceed 5 percent. In September, 1989, the Federal Reserve Board expanded the gross revenue limitation for a subsidiary to 10 percent.

Also, in December, 1986, the New York State Banking Department ruled that state-chartered banks could set up subsidiaries to underwrite corporate and other securities. Because many large money center banks that are owned by holding companies and regulated by the Federal Reserve are state-chartered New York banks, this creates a significant conflict between the state and federal regulatory agencies on this issue. This decision by the New York State Banking Department was made in response to a request from Bankers Trust New York Corp. and J. P. Morgan & Co. for an interpretation of what is known as the "little Glass-Steagall Act," a New York state law that is nearly identical to the federal statute of the same name. The state regulatory agency interpreted the law as stipulating that a state-chartered bank can be affiliated with a securities firm as long as underwriting activities that were previously disallowed, such as underwriting municipal revenue bonds, do not exceed 25 percent of total underwriting activities.

This decision on the part of the New York State Banking Department is an example of the way multiple regulatory agencies can be used to move the current regulatory system toward reform. New York banks have had an incentive to pressure the state agency to take a position contrary to the existing position of the Fed. This puts additional pressure on the Fed and on Congress to offer a more liberal interpretation of Glass-Steagall; however, as the economy slowed down in the early 1990s and as the public became increasingly disenchanted with the savings and loan crisis, the attractiveness of further relaxation of restrictions on commercial banks became dubious, at best. This has stalled the process of reform, particularly regarding Glass-Steagall.

Reform of the Bank Holding Company Laws

Closely related to the question of whether there should be complete repeal of Glass-Steagall is that of whether there should be substantial reform of the bank holding company laws that separate banking and commerce. It is important to note that few other countries have statutes resembling our bank holding company laws that restrict banks from engaging in other business activities or from having affiliations with industrial firms. In fact, such affiliations are common practice in many European countries and in Japan. Some interpret U.S. history as a rejection of such close relationships between commerce and finance, for political and social as much as economic reasons, but as the world's capital markets become more integrated, it may prove difficult or costly to attempt to maintain the degree of separation we have had in the United States in recent decades.

One of the most important practical forces that is creating pressure for reductions in the barriers between banking and commerce is the growth of finance companies, many of which are wholly owned subsidiaries of major industrial firms. Because these finance companies cannot act as banks, they cannot accept government-guaranteed deposits, but this does not mean that they cannot compete with commercial banks and savings and loans in many of their main markets. Indeed, banks are increasingly finding that their competition is coming from nontraditional sources, often from finance companies. Because this question of how we organize both our industrial and financial firms is likely to be so important in the years ahead, as financial markets become more globalized we think it is crucial to spend some time analyzing the relative competitive positions of traditional commercial banks and finance companies. Therefore, we devote the remainder of this chapter to an assessment of the operation of finance companies as competitors of commercial banks and to the regulatory issues this competition creates. This provides a transition into Chapter 7, which deals with a variety of different types of other financial institutions.

Competition Between Finance Companies and Banks

Finance companies and commercial banks are similar in many respects, particularly in their lending activities. They compete with each other most directly in commercial and consumer loan markets. The major difference between finance companies and commercial banks is their sources of funding. Commercial banks raise funds primarily through deposits, often small accounts. Finance companies raise funds primarily in the money and capital markets, with large denomination issues. A convenient way to characterize the difference is that banks pool funds from many small accounts to make larger commercial loans; finance companies raise money in large amounts through security issues and then break the proceeds up into investments in a number of smaller commercial loans.

Another important difference between these two types of intermediaries is that, while finance companies lend directly to many of the same household and business customers commercial banks lend to, their activities are not as restricted by regulations. For example, finance companies need not comply with loan limits to single borrowers, capital requirements, reserve requirements on deposits, or limits on transactions with a parent company. Thus, in many respects finance companies function a lot like banks but without the costs of compliance with bank regulations.

During the 1980s domestic finance companies more than tripled in size, from a total asset base of $242 billion in 1980 to $790 billion in 1990. The growth of finance companies is more extraordinary when compared with that of commercial banks. For example, in 1980 total assets of U.S. finance companies were only 16 percent of total assets for U.S. commercial banks. By 1990 finance company assets had grown to 26 percent of total commercial bank assets. Some observers point to the regulatory advantages enjoyed by domestic finance companies as a key to their rapid growth in credit markets that traditionally were dominated by banks. Besides regulatory advantages, the rapid growth of finance companies during the 1980s can be attributed to the growth of MMMFs. Without a doubt, the most visible effect of the advent of MMMFs was their devastating effect on regulated depository intermediaries. The high interest rates offered by MMMFs during the early 1980s drew billions in deposit dollars away from traditional savings institutions, including commercial banks and savings and loans. At the same time, there was an important side effect to the growth of MMMFs, the growth of the commercial paper market. Commercial paper is one of the most important sources of funding for domestic finance companies, and one of the most important investments for MMMFs. In fact, domestic finance companies sell the bulk of their commercial paper to MMMFs. As MMMFs grew during the early 1980s, billions of dollars in household savings were redirected from banks and thrift institutions toward finance companies, MMMFs acting as the intermediaries. MMMFs accepted deposits from savers and reinvested the funds in a variety of money market instruments, including commercial paper issues of consumer and diversified finance companies. In effect, the advent of MMMFs provided domestic finance companies with a conduit through which they could compete (however indirectly) with savings institutions for deposit dollars.

Organization of Finance Companies

Compared with commercial banks, finance companies are a somewhat more diverse group of intermediaries. One way to characterize differences among domestic finance companies is by their major lending activities, or concentration of business. In that regard, there are two major categories of finance companies: consumer finance companies and diversified finance companies. Generally, *consumer finance companies* concentrate on lending to individuals, or consumers. These are personal loans to purchase goods and services. Consumer loans are often made on installment terms, as in the case of an automobile loan, where the credit is paid off with a sequence of installment payments. *Diversified finance companies* engage in a variety of financial services, including both consumer and commercial lending.[2] Commercial loans are loans to businesses that are often secured by collateral. Leasing is another important form of business financing provided by finance companies. Rather than borrowing money to purchase equipment, firms may choose to lease the equipment from a finance company. Under most leasing contracts, the finance company actually owns the equipment, which it leases for the business firm's use. This form of equipment financing has been a growing source of business lending to finance companies.

Consumer lending is the traditional activity of many finance companies. Most finance companies are significantly involved to some extent in consumer finance; but business finance has become an increasingly important activity for many finance companies. In fact, during recent years business lending has been the most important source of growth for finance companies. Over the decade of the 1980s finance company credits to businesses grew from $88 billion in 1980 to $294 billion in 1990. Figure 6-2 illustrates the growing importance of finance companies in the

---

[2]By convention, finance companies are considered to be diversified if they hold at least 35 percent of their loans in the form of business credits.

business loan market, showing finance companies' market share of the short-term business credit market over the past four decades. The market share held by finance companies increased over the decade of the 1980s, a period that saw parallel growth in the commercial paper market and MMMFs.

In another dimension, finance companies can also be classified according to organizational form, or parent affiliation. It is useful to think about a spectrum of organization forms of domestic finance companies. At one end of the spectrum are firms called "captive" finance companies. Captives are subsidiaries of retail or manufacturing firms that principally finance the sales and leases of the parent company. The major automobile manufacturers are the best examples of captives. General Motors Acceptance Corporation (GMAC), Ford Motor Credit, and Chrysler Financial are captive subsidiaries designed to finance sales and leases of automobiles manufactured by the parent firms. An important reason for the formation of a captive finance subsidiary is to stimulate sales of the primary product. When financing is readily available product sales are easier to accomplish. In addition, captive subsidiaries may be more efficient lenders of certain kinds of products. For example, captive finance subsidiaries are often in a better position to assess the collateral value of the asset being financed. This enables them to design loan terms more efficiently. In the event the borrower defaults and the asset is repossessed, a captive is generally in a better position to recondition and dispose of the asset.

Figure 6-2

Finance companies' share of business borrowing.

Source: Flow of Funds, Board of Governors of the Federal Reserve System. "Are Bank Loans Still Special?" by S. Becketti and C. Morris, Economic Review, *Federal Reserve Bank of Kansas City, 3rd Quarter 1992, p. 71.*

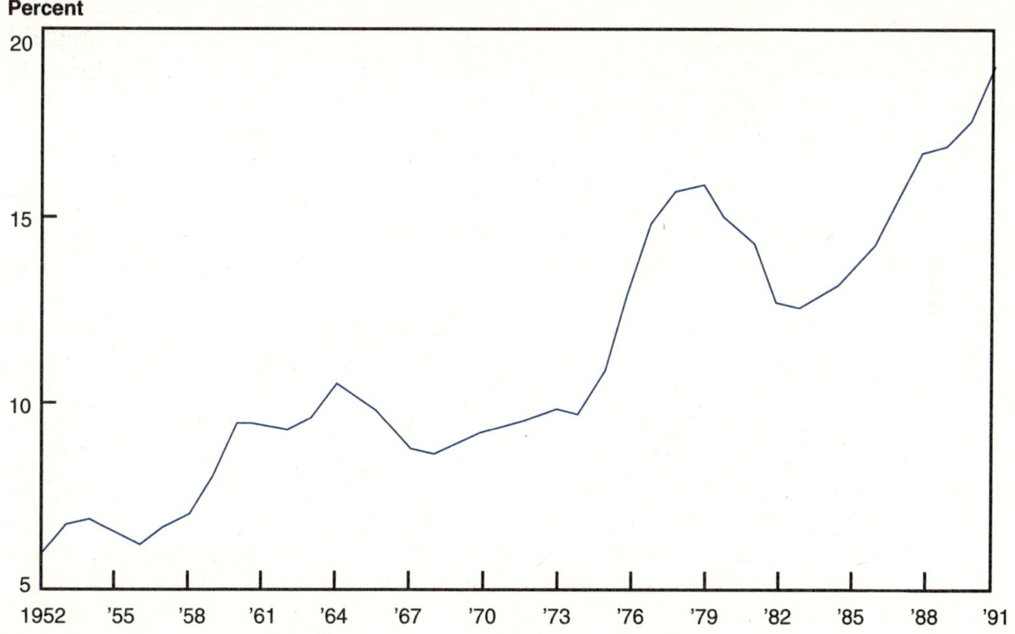

Note: Finance company loans to nonfinancial corporations as a share of short-term borrowing.

At the other end of the spectrum are independents. Independent finance companies are not affiliated with any parent organization. Typically, independent finance companies are oriented toward providing consumer finance. Examples of independent finance companies are Household Finance and Beneficial Finance Company, traditional providers of personal financial services. Between the extremes of captive finance subsidiaries and independent finance companies, there are a variety of companies operating as subsidiaries of major bank holding companies, nonbank financial companies, and nonfinancial companies. These companies are engaged in a mixture of activities, some related to the parent's principal line of business and some not. In some cases finance subsidiaries operate as in-house banks to raise capital for the parent corporation. General Electric Capital Corporation and ITT Financial Services are examples of financial subsidiaries of major nonfinancial firms. CIT Group and Heller Financial are examples of finance subsidiaries of major (foreign) bank holding companies. CIT Group is a wholly owned subsidiary of Dai-Ichi Kangyo Bank and Heller Financial is owned by Fuji Bank.

Table 6-3 lists the 20 largest finance companies according to asset size as of year's end 1990. The first column indicates the size of the company by total assets. The second and third columns give the parent relationship and concentration of business, respectively. The 20 companies listed in Table 6-3 held $426 billion in assets, accounting for more than 80 percent of total assets for all domestic finance companies. By far the largest domestic finance company is GMAC, the captive subsidiary of General Motors Corporation, with more than $105 billion in total assets. Three of the largest four companies are captive finance subsidiaries of the big three auto makers, GM, Ford, and Chrysler. Notice also that seven of the top ten are diversified companies. This emphasizes the fact that the fastest-growing companies in the industry during recent years are those that have expanded in the markets for business credit rather than consumer finance. Moreover, of the top 20 companies listed in Table 6-3, 12 are diversified companies that collectively hold almost 80 percent of total assets of the group.

Financial Structure of Finance Companies

There are four major categories of receivables for finance companies: leasing, other business lending, real estate, and consumer credit. Receivables are essentially loan credits purchased by the company. Figure 6-3 shows the growth and composition of finance company receivables over the past decade. The expansion of finance companies into business lending is again highlighted by Figure 6-2, showing the growth over the decade of the 1980s. While gross receivables grew from about $160 billion in 1980 to about $480 billion in 1990, business credits—leasing and other business credits—grew from about $100 billion to about $280 billion. Leasing is responsible for much of the growth in business credits held by finance companies during the 1980s, accounting for more than $100 billion in assets during 1990. At the same time, growth in consumer credit leveled off around 1986 at about $140 billion and has actually decreased somewhat during recent years. The decrease in finance companies' share of the consumer finance market has been due, in large part, to increased competition by commercial banks in that area.

Table 6-3
The Twenty Largest Finance Companies

(Assets in Millions of Dollars End 1990)

Bank	Total Assets	Parallel Relationship Type of Parent	Concentration of Business
1 General Motors Acceptance Corp.	105,103	Captive	Diversified
2 General Electric Capital Corp.	70,385	Nonfinancial firm	Diversified
3 Ford Motor Credit	58,969	Captive	Diversified
4 Chrysler Financial	24,702	Captive	Diversified
5 Household Financial	16,898	Independent	Consumer
6 Associates Corp. of North America	16,595	Nonfinancial firm	Diversified
7 Sears Roebuck Acceptance Corp.	15,373	Captive	Consumer
8 American Express Credit	14,222	Captive	Consumer
9 ITT Financial Corp.	11,665	Nonfinancial firm	Diversified
10 CIT Group	11,374	Bank holding company	Diversified
11 I.B.M. Credit	11,132	Captive	Diversified
12 Westinghouse Credit	10,336	Nonfinancial firm	Diversified
13 Security Pacific Financial Services System	9,928	Bank holding company	Diversified
14 Beneficial Corp.	9,270	Independent	Consumer
15 Transamerica Finance	8,501	Financial nonbank	Diversified
16 Heller Financial	7,512	Bank holding company	Diversified
17 Commercial Credit Corp.	7,138	Financial nonbank	Consumer
18 American General Finance	5,933	Financial nonbank	Consumer
19 Toyota Motor Credit	5,579	Captive	Consumer
20 Avco Financial	5,084	Nonfinancial firm	Consumer

Sources: *American Banker,* December 11, 1991, First National Bank of Chicago: annual reports. Reprinted from Eli M. Remolona and Kurt C. Wulfekuhler, "Finance Companies, Bank Competition, and Niche Markets," Federal Reserve Bank of New York *Quarterly Review*, Summer 1992.

The major sources of funding for domestic finance companies are commercial paper, long-term debt, and bank loans. Growth and changes in the sources of funding during the past decade are illustrated in Figure 6-4. The importance of the commercial paper market to the growth of finance companies during the 1980s is clear. The volume of commercial paper outstanding in 1990 was about $150 billion, roughly three times its volume a decade earlier. At the same time, there has been parallel growth in funding from long-term debt, which constituted more than $180 billion in outstanding liabilities by 1990. The growth of long-term debt is due, in large part, to subordinated debt issued by captive subsidiaries to the parent companies. Notice also that a small portion of funding is due to bank loans. This source of funding is due mainly to smaller companies that have more limited access to money and capital markets, and it has not grown appreciably over the past decade.

Consumer Installment Credit

One area of lending in which commercial banks continue to enjoy a comparative advantage over finance companies is consumer credit. During the 1980s consumer credit was the most significant market in which finance companies lost ground to

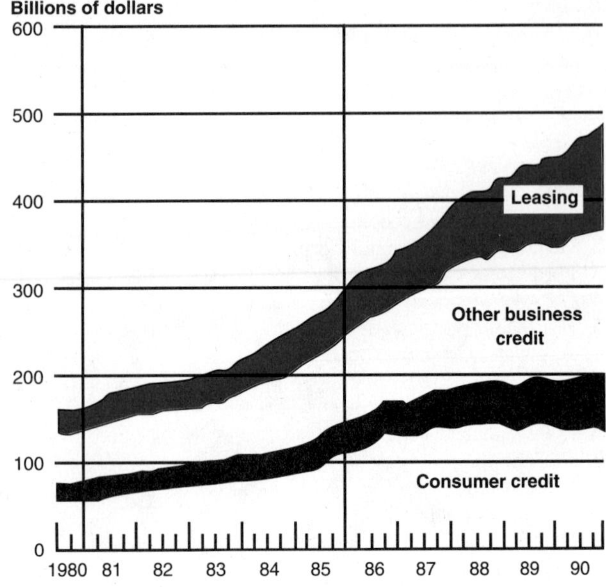

Figure 6-3

Finance Company Gross Receivables.
Sources: Board of Governors of the Federal Reserve System, Federal Reserve Bulletin, *as reprinted in* FRBNY Quarterly Review *(Summer 1992) p. 27. Reprinted from Eli M. Remolona and Kurt C. Wulfekuhler, "Finance Companies, Bank Competition, and Niche Markets," Federal Reserve Bank of New York* Quarterly Review, Summer 1992.

**Federal Reserve Bulletin* data for long-term debt end in 1987. Data after 1987 are based on Flow of Funds data for corporate bonds.

banks. This trend is emphasized more clearly in Figure 6-5 below. Figure 6-5 shows the volume of installment consumer credit outstanding for domestic finance companies and insured commercial banks over the past decade. As the figure shows, growth in this market has been primarily due to installment credit issued by commercial banks rather than finance companies. Over the decade of the 1980s, consumer installment credit extended by banks grew from $145 billion to $340 billion.

Many observers attribute the phenomenon illustrated in Figure 6-5 to advantages held by banks in data processing technology associated with the development of credit card finance. Banks have established economies of scale in processing large numbers of small installment credit accounts associated with their credit card business, which makes additional installment lending efficient. However, both traditional finance companies and new entrants such as American Telephone and Telegraph are now moving into this market.

The Market for Lease Financing

Banks appear to have an advantage in the area of installment credit, and finance companies have a similar advantage in the leasing market. Figure 6-6 compares the growth of lease financing provided by finance companies and by commercial banks over the 1980s. Leasing receivables of finance companies have grown over the decade from less than $30 billion in 1980 to more than $130 billion in 1990, an increase in market share from 66 percent to 78 percent. As noted earlier, the growth in lease finance is an important component of the overall growth in business credits issued by finance companies during the 1980s.

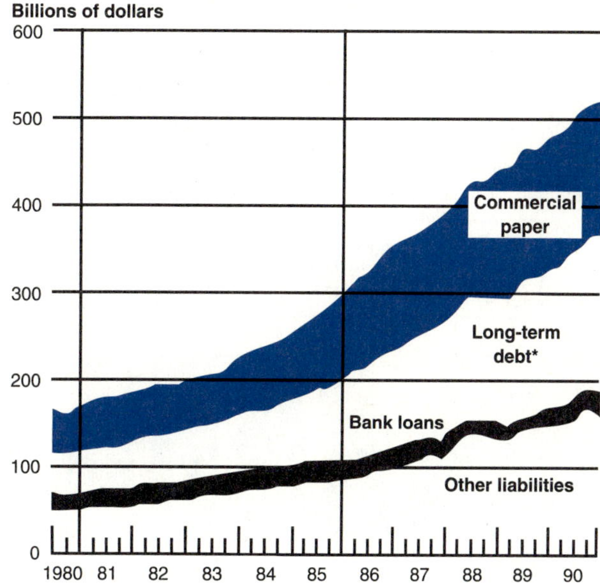

Figure 6-4

Finance Company Liabilities.

Sources: Board of Governors of the Federal Reserve System, Federal Reserve Bulletin, and *Flow of Funds Data, as reprinted in* FRBNY Quarterly Review *(Summer 1992) p. 28. Reprinted from Eli M. Remolona and Kurt C. Wulfekuhler, "Finance Companies, Bank Competition, and Niche Markets," Federal Reserve Bank of New York* Quarterly Review, Summer 1992.

**Federal Reserve Bulletin* data for long-term debt end in 1987. Data after 1987 are based on Flow of Funds data for corporate bonds.

The expansion by finance companies in the leasing market during this time period is due to at least two advantages finance companies have over commercial banks in this market. The first is the informational advantage enjoyed by finance subsidiaries in designing leases on equipment made by their parent companies. Profits on lease contracts depend in an important way on having reliable estimates of residual value of equipment at the end of the contract. Finance subsidiaries have a "natural" expertise in equipment produced by the parent, which enables them more accurately to estimate the future value of leased equipment. In particular, the residual value of leased equipment depends crucially on the introduction of new models currently under development. This is particularly true of leases on computer equipment, where the introduction of a new, more powerful line of computers can render existing equipment virtually obsolete. Knowledge of ongoing research and development enables a captive finance subsidiary such as IBM Credit to better anticipate the future value of leased equipment. Independent leasing companies and commercial banks are at an extreme disadvantage compared to a captive finance company when writing leases on equipment produced by the captive's parent.

A second reason for the dominance of finance companies in the leasing market is that during the 1980s commercial banks were prohibited under Regulation Y from writing nonoperating leases. It turns out that most of the growth experienced by finance companies occurred as the result of writing non-operating lease contracts. Under the Economic Recovery Tax Act of 1981, non-operating leases enabled finance companies to take advantage of substantial tax benefits associated with rapid depreciation of leased equipment. An operating lease, the near equivalent of a loan contract, afforded banks no such tax advantage. The tax advantage associated with nonoperating leases gave finance companies a powerful pricing advantage over commercial banks during the 1980s.

Figure 6-5

Consumer Installment Credit.

Sources: Board of Governors of the Federal Reserve System, Federal Reserve Bulletin *as reprinted in* FRBNY Quarterly Review *(Summer 1992) p. 32. Reprinted from Eli M. Remolona and Kurt C. Wulfekuhler, "Finance Companies, Bank Competition, and Niche Markets," Federal Reserve Bank of New York* Quarterly Review, *Summer 1992.*

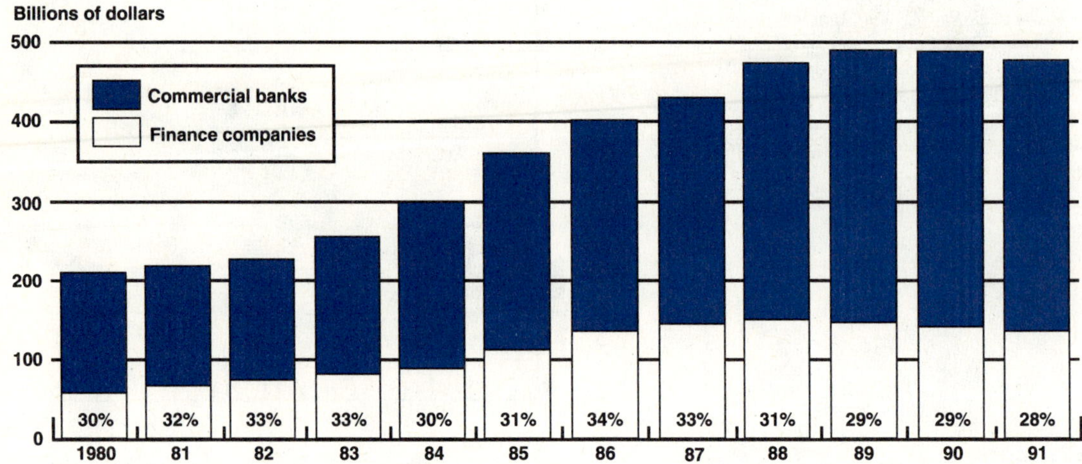

Note: Percentages appearing in the bars indicate finance company share of total consumer installment credit extended by banks and finance companies.

Alternative Views of the Future Role of Finance Companies

There are at least two alternative views of the recent growth of finance companies. Some observers see the competition between finance companies and banks as simply another example of regulatory arbitrage. Under this view, the regulatory system imposed on banks, particularly after FDICIA, has made it too expensive for banks to compete with unregulated finance companies in many loan and leasing markets. Thus, the more efficient forms of organizations either drive the market share of banks down appreciably farther or compel the Congress to reform the regulatory system to improve the competitive position of banks. Another view, however, sees the rapid growth of less regulated industry as a threat to the stability of the financial system. In particular, there is some concern that the growing influence of finance companies in traditional bank lending markets may impede the conduct of effective monetary policy, which is channeled through bank credit markets. There is concern, too, that the effects of widespread default among finance companies would have ripple effects in the banking industry. To obtain investment grade ratings on commercial paper issues, finance companies often obtain bank guarantees on the issue through backup lines of credit. In the event the issuer is unable to make payment on its primary obligation (commercial paper), the backup credit line can be drawn on to avoid default. The widespread use of backup lines of credit and other bank guarantees by finance companies represents a substantial transfer of (default) risk to an already fragile banking industry. If this second view prevails this may lead to increased regulation of finance

Figure 6-6

Leasing Receivables.

Sources: Board of Governors of the Federal Reserve System, Federal Reserve Bulletin *as reprinted in* FRBNY Quarterly Review *(Summer 1992) p. 32. Reprinted from Eli M. Remolona and Kurt C. Wulfekuhler, "Finance Companies, Bank Competition, and Niche Markets," Federal Reserve Bank of New York* Quarterly Review, *Summer 1992.*

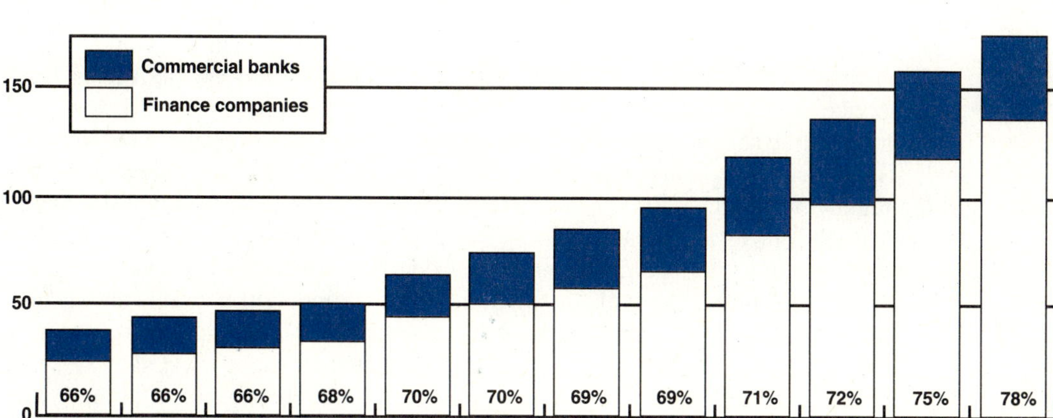

Notes: Because leasing data for commercial banks are reported on a net basis, the data are increased by 20 percent to approximate gross amounts. Percentages appearing in the bars indicate finance company share of total leasing activities by banks and finance companies.

companies, with the objective of insuring the stability of the financial system. We are not sure how the future competition between finance companies and banks will work out but we do think that this will be one of the more important regulatory issues the financial system will confront in years to come.

SUMMARY

This chapter has been concerned with the reform of the regulatory system for financial institutions in the United States, a process that has been referred to as "deregulation." Desegmentation may be a more appropriate word. Since the Great Depression, when the major pieces of regulation legislation were enacted, the United States has had a set of highly segmented financial firms, both by geography and by product line. Because the barriers that created separate geographic and product markets are now breaking down, the financial institutions of the very near future may be quite different from the ones of the 1960s and 1970s. Two principal changes in the economic environment of the United States have precipitated regulatory system reform: (1) the high rate of inflation and the high interest rates that accompanied it and (2) tremendous technological progress in communications and computers.

Five features of the existing regulatory system made it vulnerable to high inflation and technological progress. The first was the geographic and product line segmentation of financial services. The geographic segmentation has been particularly evident in the commercial banking industry, where the McFadden Act (1926) gives each state the right to determine whether banks from another state may enter. Historically, most states chose to restrict entry of other states, and some restricted competition within the state by limiting or prohibiting branch banking. Product line segmentation is also evident where bank holding company laws and the Glass-Steagall Act restrict commercial banks to a specific set of activities and prohibit other firms from owning commercial banks. As the technology for delivering financial services evolved in the last decade, the rationale for maintaining both geographic and product line segmentation of financial services became increasingly tenuous.

The second characteristic of the regulatory system was the competing and overlapping regulatory agencies for specific financial institutions. We learned that this system has both advantages and disadvantages. The duplication involved is costly, and it creates the opportunity for specific regulatory agencies to be captured by the institutions they regulate. An advantage of this system is that competition between the agencies tends to encourage change and reform. Regulated institutions use this structure to try to encourage reform, which we have seen in the recent attempts to reform Glass-Steagall.

The third feature of the regulatory system was the creation of a barter system between depository institutions and those who placed deposits in those institutions as well as between commercial banks and the Federal Reserve. The barter system between banks or savings and loans and depositors was fostered by Regulation Q, which restricted banks and savings and loans from competing for deposits with higher interest rates. These institutions were forced to compete with convenience and other "nonprice" means to attract customers. At the same time the Fed required banks to hold reserves but did not pay interest on them; instead, it offered services to the banks. This worked well as long as the opportunity cost to the banks of holding reserves remained stable, but as interest rates rose with inflation during the 1970s, the opportunity cost of reserves went up accordingly. This meant banks were incurring what amounted to a large tax for being Federal Reserve members.

The fourth feature of the regulatory system was the selective use of this reserve requirement tax and the subsidy implicit in deposit insurance. These two items are important parts of the total cost of regulation imposed on financial firms. If the cost of regulation for one type of firm, say commercial banks who are Federal Reserve members, becomes too high relative to some other type of regulated institution, the institutions go to great lengths to change the situation.

The final characteristic of the regulatory system was the implicit commitment made by the Federal Reserve to maintain stable interest rates. For most of the post–World War II era the Fed had conducted monetary policy by attempting to control and stabilize interest rates. As a result, many financial institutions found it profitable to pass on the Fed's implicit commitment to stable interest rates to other participants in financial markets. As inflation increased and persisted, however, the Fed abandoned its long-standing policy of attempting to control interest rates. This made it untenable for financial institutions to continue to offer implicit as well as explicit commitments to the market. As a result, one of the principal services offered by financial institutions was threatened.

A number of major reforms in the regulatory system have been instituted in the last few years. Two pieces of federal reform legislation are the Financial Institutions Deregulation and Monetary Control Act of 1980 and the Garn-St. Germain Act of 1982. The earlier piece of legislation mandated that Regulation Q be phased out over six years, that all financial institutions offering transactions accounts be subject to equivalent reserve requirements, and that the Federal Reserve begin to charge explicit prices for the services it offered to commercial banks.

As it turned out, a planned six-year phaseout of Regulation Q was simply not fast enough, leading Congress to pass the Garn-St Germain Act. This law directed the regulators to implement deposit accounts promptly with terms fully competitive with those offered by money market funds. The law also granted much expanded lending and investment powers to savings and loans and unitary savings and loan holding companies.

In 1989, the government changed its course in the regulation of banks and savings and loans when it adopted FIRREA. This law abolished the previous agencies for insuring and regulating savings and loans and created a new system for administering the closure of bankrupt institutions. It also mandated higher capital requirements and more scrutiny of loans and investments of insured savings and loans. This act, combined with FDICIA, in 1991, changed the focus from desegmentation of the financial system to tight control of and protection against excessive risk in banking.

Three important, and still not fully resolved, issues of regulatory reform are interstate banking, the Glass-Steagall Act, and bank holding companies. There has been fairly rapid movement toward interstate banking in recent years, as many states have changed laws to allow banks from outside to enter their markets, at least under some conditions. Some states have allowed such entry for reciprocating states, thus preventing entry of large money center banks. But no action has been taken on the issue at the federal level.

The movement toward repeal of the Glass-Steagall Act has included both a frontal assault and attempts to circumvent it. Money center banks have acquired limited authority to underwrite various securities, particularly commercial paper, mortgage-backed and consumer paper–backed securities, and municipal revenue bonds. Whether or not Glass-Steagall will be repealed or effectively circumvented in the near future is difficult to determine.

Finally, we examined the operation of finance companies and how they are competing with commercial banks. We noted that finance companies are not regulated to the same degree as commercial banks and thus have the potential to compete effectively if regulatory costs borne by banks are large. Finance company lending to businesses has been increasing significantly in recent years as many commercial banks have found it increasingly difficult to compete in the business lending market. We also noted that many finance companies are subsidiaries of larger industrial firms and that this affiliation may afford a competitive advantage. We expect the state of competition in this market to be an important force shaping the regulatory system of the future.

QUESTIONS

1. How do the two major pieces of federal legislation enacted in 1980 and 1982 differ? In what ways did the 1982 act speed up the provisions of the 1980 act?
2. Why was a barter system in operation under the regulatory structure for commercial banks that operated during the 1960s and 1970s? What was the Fed's membership problem? How was it solved? Discuss the advantages and disadvantages of the solution.
3. What is the difference between deregulation and desegmentation? Why and how has our financial system been segmented?
4. Why and how was our regulatory system for financial institutions vulnerable in a period of high inflation? How did inflation hurt the system?
5. How did the Garn-St. Germain Act change the powers of savings and loans versus those of commercial banks? What is the significance of these changes?
6. How much progress had been made toward interstate banking? Who is hurt and who is helped by interstate banking?
7. What is a nonbank bank? Why have these been important in the evolution of a new form of financial institution?
8. Who would be hurt and who would be helped by repeal of the Glass-Steagall Act?
9. How do you think we should seek to regulate finance companies? Should we reform the regulation of commercial banks to allow them to compete more directly with finance companies? Would this compromise the deposit insurance system? If so, how?

REFERENCES

Aguilar, L. "Still Toe-to-Toe: Banks and Nonbanks at the End of the '80s." *Economic Perspectives* Federal Reserve Bank of Chicago 14 (Jan-Feb 1990), pp. 12–23.

Becketti, S., and C. Morris. "Are Bank Loans Still Special?" *Economic Review* Federal Reserve Bank of Kansas City 77 (3rd Q 1992) pp. 71–84.

Kane, Edward J. "Technological and Regulatory Forces in the Developing Fusion of Financial-Services Competition." *Journal of Finance* 32 (July 1984), pp. 759–72.

Kaufman, George G., Larry R. Mote, and Harvey Rosenblum. "Consequences of Deregulation for Commercial Banking." *Journal of Finance* 32 (July 1984), pp. 789–802.

Kaufman, George G., and Larry R. Mote. "Glass-Steagall: Repeal by Regulatory and Judicial Interpretation." *Banking Law Journal* (Sep-Oct 1990) pp. 388–421.

Lang, Richard W., and Timothy G. Schiller. "The New Thrift Act: Mending the Safety Net." *Business Review* Federal Reserve Bank of Philadelphia (Nov-Dec 1989) pp. 3–8.

Remolona, E.M., and K.C. Wulfekuhler. "Finance Companies, Bank Competition, and Niche Markets." *Quarterly Review* Federal Reserve Bank of New York (Summer 1992) pp. 25–38.

Smith, Brian P. "The Scope of the New Banking Law is Anything but Narrow." *Savings Institutions* (February 1992) pp 34–35.

Zweig, Phillip L., "New York Rules State-Chartered Banks Can Form Units to Underwrite Securities." *Wall Street Journal* December 31, 1986.

• Chapter 7

Nondepository Financial Intermediaries

This chapter describes three important classes of nondepository intermediaries: insurance companies, investment companies, and pension funds. Nondepository intermediaries are those that do not issue deposit liabilities. This is the most important distinction between the organizations discussed in this chapter and depository firms like commercial banks and savings institutions. While the issuance of deposits is the major difference between the two major categories of institutions, non-depository institutions have become increasingly competitive in attracting the savings of individual citizens over recent years. This is due largely to two factors. The first is deregulation of financial markets, which has left traditional depository institutions more vulnerable to new competition for savings dollars from financial and nonfinancial firms. The second is the rapid advance of technological and product innovation, which has created an expanded menu of savings and investment alternatives for individuals. A little more than a decade ago, most individual "investments" were confined largely to deposit and savings accounts at their local banks, savings and loans, or credit unions.

In the discussion that follows we provide an overview and description of each of the three major types of nondepository firms. First, the activities of the two major categories of insurance companies are described: life and health insurance companies and property and casualty companies. The primary activity of risk underwriting and the efficiency of risk pooling are explained in the context of a simple example. We also discuss the more recent expansion of major insurance firms into investment products. Next, we discuss the major characteristics and activities of investment companies. The primary service of an investment company is diversification of investment risk. Closed- and open-end companies are explained, and the pricing and sales distribution of mutual fund shares is explained. Finally, we describe the major characteristics of pension funds and retirement plans. Pension plans and retirement accounts provide individuals with important sources of income to supplement social security and other savings during retirement years. Two major categories of pension plans are discussed: defined-benefit plans and defined-contribution plans. Regulation of pension funds is discussed, and the effect of Employee Retirement Income Security Act (ERISA) on defined benefit plans is explained.

> **• Concepts to Learn in Chapter 7 •**
>
> - The economic efficiency of insurance and the major products offered by insurance companies to spread risk
> - The growing emphasis in life insurance companies on selling investment products and the effects of these activities on the companies' stability
> - The role of investment companies in channeling small savings into major capital markets, and the competition between investment funds and traditional savings institutions
> - The increasing importance of pension funds among non-traditional intermediaries of individual savings. The role of regulation in protecting employee pension plans.

Insurance Companies

Insurance companies are financial intermediaries that provide the service of underwriting economic risks associated with death, illness, damage or loss of property, and other exposures to loss. Insurance companies issue contingent liabilities against themselves in the form of insurance policies. Insurance policies are "contingent" liabilities in that they become payable by the issuer *contingent* on the event that is insured, such as death in the case of a life insurance policy, or fire in case of fire insurance. The funds raised from issue of these liabilities, through the collection of policy premiums, are invested by the company in securities, commercial loans, mortgages, and other financial instruments. These investments provide the funds necessary to meet financial obligations to outstanding policy holders.

Insurance companies are organized as either stock or mutual organizations. Under the stock form of organization, an insurance company operates as a corporation owned by stockholders, who participate in the profits of the firm as the residual claimants. Stockholders also exert control over the management of the company through the voting privileges associated with common stock. In particular, stockholders elect the firm's board of directors and vote on major policy decisions. Under a mutual form of organization, an insurance company is owned by policyholders. Policyholders participate in the profits of the company by receiving dividends based on the company's performance. The dividend associated with a mutual insurance policy constitutes a kind of rebate paid pro rata to policyholders. In effect, the company refunds part of the policyholder's premium when claims against the company are fewer than expected. Unlike stockholder dividends, dividends paid to mutual policyholders are not taxed as income to the policyholder.

Insurance companies can be classified into two major categories according to the kinds of risks they insure: (1) life and health insurance companies and (2) property and liability companies. Life and health insurance companies specialize in offering insurance against economic loss from death or illness, whereas property and liability companies offer protection against economic losses to property or from legal liability. Within each of these general categories are numerous more specific risks in which particular insurance companies may specialize. For example, some life insurance companies provide a special type of life insurance called key-man insurance, through which the lives of key executives in a business may be insured on behalf of the firm's owners and other constituents. Some property and liability companies provide insurance against loss due to negligence, as in malpractice insurance for medical doctors.

Life and Health Insurance Companies

Life insurance contracts, or life insurance policies, generally involve three parties: the insurer, the insured, and the beneficiary. The insurer is the company that issues (or sells) the policy and to which the policy represents a contingent liability. Usually, life insurance is designed to protect the economic well-being of the family or dependents in the event of the insured's premature death. In this case, the dependents are designated as beneficiaries. In the event of premature death, the life insurance contract pays a cash benefit to the family, replacing the lost income stream of the insured. While immediate family members are generally designated as beneficiaries, the benefits of a life policy may be assigned to parties other than the family of the insured.

The largest life and health insurance companies in the United States are Prudential Insurance Company of America and Metropolitan Life Insurance Company. The combined value of assets controlled by these two companies exceeded $250 billion in 1991, accounting for more than 40 percent of the total asset value of the top ten life and health insurance companies in the United States. The size of these two companies is to a large extent the result of a decade of substantial growth for life insurance underwriters—the 1980s. All together, U.S. life insurance companies provided slightly under $4 trillion in insurance (at insured value) as of 1982. By 1992 they provided more than $9 trillion. In 1982 the average insured value of outstanding life insurance policies was less than $50,000. By 1992, the average insured value of outstanding policies exceeded $100,000.

The financial structure of U.S. life insurance companies is described in Table 7-1. In 1990, total assets for U.S. life and health insurance companies were $1.41 trillion. Most of the investments made by life insurance companies (almost 70 percent) were in corporate securities (stocks and bonds), and mortgages. About 15 percent of total assets was invested in cash and government securities. On the other side of the balance sheet, almost 25 percent of liabilities were due to life insurance reserves, resources set aside within the company to back outstanding policies. As in most lines of insurance, life insurance reserves represent only a fraction of the insured value of outstanding policies, owing to the nature of insurance underwriting and the ability of the underwriter to diversify insured risks. With large numbers of policies, claims against the underwriter become highly predictable, allowing the level of reserves to be much less than the insured value of policies outstanding. A more detailed discussion of risk underwriting and diversification is provided later in the chapter. Notice that the

Table 7-1

Financial Structure of U.S. Life Insurance Companies, 1990

Assets	
Cash and government securities	14.9%
Corporate securities	50.5%
Mortgages	19.2%
Real estate	3.1%
Policy loans	4.5%
Other assets	7.8%
	100%
Liabilities and net worth	
Life insurance reserves	24.8%
Health insurance reserves	2.3%
Annuities	56.7%
Supplementary contracts	1.2%
Other liabilities	8.5%
Net worth	6.5%
	100%

Source: *Insurance Information Institute, 1991 Fact Book.*

largest source of funding for life insurance companies was annuities. More than 56 percent of liabilities and net worth represented outstanding annuity contracts. Additionally, only 6.5 percent of total assets was funded by equity.

Individuals usually acquire life insurance as what is called "*ordinary life insurance.*" These policies are sold directly to individuals, ordinarily through insurance agents who operate in a local market area. To qualify for coverage under most ordinary life policies, the insured party often must pass certain screening requirements to establish insurability, sometimes including a medical examination. Individuals can also buy life insurance as a part of a "*group life insurance plan.*" A group plan is an insurance plan sold directly to a corporation or other organization to cover its employees. Often, group insurance is a component of a standard package of employee benefits for which employees automatically qualify without prescreening or medical examination. There are three broad categories of ordinary life insurance contracts: whole life insurance, universal life insurance, and term life insurance.

Term Insurance

Term insurance is the simplest form of life insurance. Other forms of insurance incorporate some form of savings benefit, and the savings component can be quite involved and complicated. Term insurance, on the other hand, provides *only* insurance. As the name implies, term insurance is not permanent and remains in force for a prespecified period, called the term or duration of the policy. Typically, term insurance policies are written for periods from one to ten years. If the insured party dies during the term, the policy pays a specified death benefit. If the term of the policy runs out before the insured party dies, the policy pays nothing. In contrast to some other forms of insurance, policy premiums are dedicated to underwriting risk and not saving.

Under a "*straight term*" policy, the death benefit remains constant over the entire term. Other available policies vary the benefit over the term of the contract.

Decreasing term insurance carries a death benefit that decreases over the term of the policy. This form of insurance is often used when the beneficiaries would need more financial protection during the early years of the policy but will have other sources of financial support during the later years of the policy, say from pension benefits or long-term investments. Another form of insurance, "*increasing term*" insurance, provides a death benefit that increases over the term of the policy. Increasing term policies are sometimes purchased to offset the effects of inflation and to maintain the real value of the death benefit over the term of the policy.

Because term insurance is normally issued for a period of less than ten years, term policies often provide mechanisms for renewal. "*Renewable term*" insurance may be renewed at the end of the policy term without undergoing screening or providing additional evidence of insurability. At the same time, however, renewal gives the insurer the opportunity to reprice the insurance in accordance with the age and occupation of the insured. "*Convertible term*" insurance allows the insured to convert the insurance to another form when the term runs out. When the term policy expires, the insured may be given the opportunity to convert the policy to an equivalent amount of whole life insurance. Usually conversion privileges may be utilized during a certain period following the expiration of the term policy and without additional screening or proof of insurability.

The level premiums associated with term life insurance are set to reflect three factors: (1) anticipated operating and administrative costs over the term of the policy, (2) expected value of claims from the policy over its term, and (3) an acceptable expected profit comensurate with the risk associated with the policy. The second feature deserves further explanation. Consider a simple example of a 45-year-old man who purchases a $500,000, one-year term policy. Assume the company computes the annual charge for adminstrative cost and profit contribution to be $40 on this policy. The additional charge for expected losses from claims is computed as follows. First, the probability of death during the next year for a 45-year-old man in good health is determined from actuarial statistics to be .00125. If the cost of funds to the company during the next year is 10 percent, the present value of the expected loss on the policy is given as

$$E\{L\} = \frac{(\$500{,}000)\ (.00125)}{1.10} = \$568.18$$

where E{L} is the value of the expected death benefit on the policy over the next year. Thus, the total premium for the one-year policy is $40 + $568.18, or $608.18. Premiums for longer-term policies are determined in a similiar way. Each year, as the insured individual grows older the probability of death increases. Most renewable term insurance policies are written for five to ten years. During that time the premium is adjusted according to the probability of loss. Once the value of the expected loss for the year is determined, the policy premium is determined by adding on the components for administrative costs and risk-adjusted profit. In some other types of policies, the premiums may be fixed over several years, even though the risk of loss increases as the insured individual ages. That is, during each policy year, the actuarial probability of death is generally different. In the case of a five-year policy with a level premium, there would be a sequence of five values for expected loss, one for each year. The level of the premium charged on the five-year policy is determined as the value of an ordinary annuity equal to the present value of the stream of expected losses over the five years of the policy.

Whole Life Insurance

Whole life insurance is designed to provide long-term life insurance protection. As the name implies, these policies remain in force over the policyholder's entire life. The most popular such policy is "level-premium whole life." Premiums on level-premium whole life policies are determined in a manner similar to those on term insurance. A fixed annual premium is determined from the stream of expected death benefits paid on the policy over the life of the insured. Because the probability of death generally increases over the term of the policy, expected losses are generally greater during the later years. This results in the insured paying more than the expected cost of the insurance during the early years of the policy and less than the expected cost during the later years.

The amount by which the premium exceeds the actual cost of insurance during the early years of the policy contributes toward what is called the "cash value" of the policy. The cash value accumulates from "overpayments" during the early years of the policy, that are invested by the company and earn interest.[1] The cash value feature of whole life policies is often given as an advantage of this type of insurance. It constitutes an embedded savings instrument that earns interest and an amount the policyholder can borrow against. During the early years of the policy, when insurance against loss of income is most needed, whole life provides protection through the policy's death benefit. During the later years, when the insured reaches retirement, there is less need for insurance against income loss. At the same time, the cash value of the insurance policy can be used to supplement retirement income. Finally, the interest earned on the cash value of the policy is tax deferred, which is another advantage of whole life policies as a savings vehicle.

While whole life insurance has traditionally been the most popular form owing to the long-term coverage and the savings attributes, term insurance is deemed a more sensible alternative by those who think individuals can buy the same insurance protection at a lower premium with a term policy and invest the difference on their own, perhaps at a higher rate than the insurer. This was a popular recommendation during the 1970s and 1980s. Proponents of the strategy believed that insureds could earn a higher return by managing their own money (cash value) than by letting the insurance company do it for them. The disadvantages of this strategy are that the premiums on term life increase with age and the earnings from personally managed savings are under most circumstances taxable as income.

---

[1]Cash value is also accumulated through what are called survivorship benefits. These benefits accumulate to policyholders who survive longer than others. As policyholders die, and the death benefits are paid out to beneficiaries, the remaining cash value of their policies is distributed to surviving policyholders in the company.

Universal Life Insurance

Other long-term insurance products have become popular in recent years. A new product, "universal life insurance," is structured to have two separate accounts for insurance and cash value. The policy was originally designed to combine some of the attributes of term insurance and some of whole life. In particular, the insurance portion of the plan functions as term insurance whose premiums are adjusted each year according to the age of the insured. At the same time, the policy stays in force over the whole life of the insured. With regard to cash value, the insured can contribute to the savings portion of the plan at any time and the interest earned on the account is not taxed until it is withdrawn from the account.

Annuities

Annuities have become increasingly important during recent years. Whereas the purpose of life insurance is to provide financial security in the event of premature death, in many circumstances the purpose of an annuity is to provide security in the event one survives longer than expected. Annuities provide a level payment to the holder, the "annuitant," for a prespecified number of years, or in some cases until death. As was mentioned above, owners of whole life policies who reach retirement age and no longer need the protection provided by life insurance often liquidate the cash value of their policy to purchase an annuity. Payments from the annuity are used to augment retirement income from Social Security and other savings for retirement.

Annuity contracts can be designed in a number of ways. The most common forms are "*fixed period annuities*" and "*life annuities.*" The major difference is that fixed period annuities are designed to pay a level annuity to the annuitant for a fixed number of years. Usually the annuitant will make a sequence of payments, or a single payment, to the insurer. Then, at a later time, the annuitant will receive the sequence of prespecified payments. The annuitant of a life annuity receives a series of annuity payments until death. The life annuity holds the advantage of providing benefits until the annuitant dies, which avoids the risk of running out of annuity income prematurely. The fixed-period annuity has the advantage of being assigned to a beneficiary in the event the annuitant dies before the annuity expires.

The importance of annuities in the product mix of life insurers is apparent in Table 7-1. Annuities comprised about 57 percent of total liabilities for U.S. life insurance companies at year's end 1990. In fact, over the past 30 years, and especially during the past decade, the volume of business by life insurer's due to annuities has surpassed that of their traditional life insurance products. This pattern is clearly illustrated by Figure 7-1 showing the premium income received by U.S. life insurance companies from 1970 to 1990. In 1970, premiums from annuities were only a fraction of those from life policies. By the mid-1980s, however, premium income from annuities surpassed premium income from life insurance. By 1990, premium income from annuities was about $130 billion, whereas premium income from life insurance was around $75 billion.

The growth in the importance of annuities reflects a shift in the orientation of the insurance industry from insurance products toward investments. The major innovations responsible for this change are "*single-premium deferred annuities*"

Figure 7-1

The Growing Dominance of Annuities in Life Insurers' Premium Income Annually, 1970–90.

Source: American Council of Life Insurance 1991, p. 34. "SPDAs and GICs: Like Money In the Bank," Quarterly Review, *Federal Reserve Bank of Minneapolis, Summer (1992), pp. 2–15.*

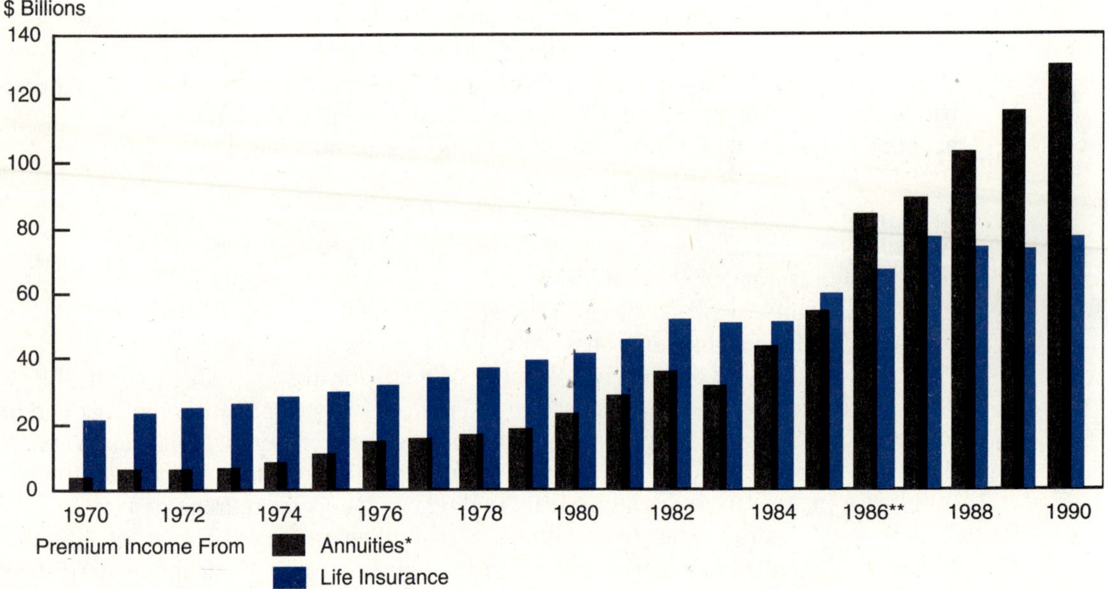

*This category includes not only traditional annuities but also investment-oriented products like SPDAs and GICs.

**The 1986 jump in annuity premiums partly reflects improved data collection on GICs, which some companies had not been previously reporting.

(SPDAs) and "*guaranteed investment contracts*" (GICs). SPDAs are contracts in which the purchaser, typically an individual, pays a single premium in return for a payment some years later. SPDAs are not annuities per se, they are more like zero-coupon bonds in that they pay a lump sum at maturity. Generally, when the contract matures it offers the owner an option of receiving a cash payment or rolling the payment over into a multiyear annuity at a predefined interest rate. The annuity option, which gives the contract its name, provides the owner with what might be called "annuity insurance." Certainly, the owner could elect to receive a lump sum payment at maturity and purchase an annuity, perhaps from another company; though the available terms on annuities may be less favorable by the time the SPDA matures. Thus, by locking in the terms of the annuity in advance, the buyer of the SPDA can avoid the risk of market changes in the terms of multiyear annuities.

GICs are also similar to zero-coupon bonds. The insurance company that issues the contract promises to pay a fixed interest rate over the term of the contract, ordinarily a period of three to seven years. In many cases the annual interest rate on the GIC is adjusted to market levels each year, causing the contract to operate much like a variable-rate deposit with a fixed maturity. The major difference between GICs and SPDAs is that, though SPDAs are normally sold to individuals, GICs are normally sold to institutions, in particular, to pension funds. And even though GIC uses the word "guaranteed," normally no third party guarantee is associated with the contract, as is the case with an insured deposit. Ordinarily, the only guarantee involved in a GIC is the promise of the issuer to make contractual payments of interest and principal. A sample of rates on GICs published in the *Wall Street Journal* (May 13, 1993) is shown in Table 7-2. Rates are given for contracts with one to five years to maturity in investment-grade GICs. Notice that generally GICs trade at rates from about 1/4 percent to 1/2 of one percent above Treasury securities with comparable maturities.

The rapid growth of SPDAs and GICs during the 1980s accounts for much of the growth in annuity premiums collected by U.S. life insurers. The annual sales of GICs grew from almost nothing in 1980 to $75 billion in 1987. This growth is due in large part to the increased use of defined-contribution pension plans. As we will explain more carefully later in this chapter, defined-contribution pension plans are pension plans in which individuals contribute a defined amount to be invested on their behalf into an investment fund until retirement. On retirement, the amount of retirement benefit available depends directly on the performance of the investment fund. GICs became popular investments for pension funds because they provided high fixed-rate investments that were attractive to pension contributors. Over the 1980s, the growth of SPDAs was almost as dramatic as that of GICs: from a negligible volume in 1980, annual sales of SPDAs grew to $54 billion in 1990. The reasons most commonly given for the rapid growth in SPDAs are (1) the high interest rates given on the contracts and (2) favorable tax treatment of interest earnings. Especially during the early 1980s, with higher interest rates and higher marginal tax rates, SPDAs provided an attractive opportunity for individuals to earn tax-deferred interest at a competitive rate.

Health Insurance

Health insurance policies provide protection against the cost of illness or injury. Medical costs associated with an unexpected illness or injury can be as economically devastating to a family as the death of the major income producer. Besides

Table 7-2
Guaranteed Investment Contracts

	1 Year		2 Years		3 Years		4 Years		5 Years	
	Rate	**Chg**	**Rate**	**Chg**	**Rate**	**Chg**	**Rate**	**Chg**	**Rate**	**Chg**
High	3.45%	+ 0.01	4.47%	+ 0.02	5.02%	+ 0.08	5.51%	unch	5.85%	unch
Low	2.72	unch	3.48	+ 0.06	4.06	+ 0.06	4.22	unch	4.87	+0.04
Index	3.20	+ 0.01	4.02	+ 0.02	4.60	+ 0.04	5.03	+ 0.03	5.52	+0.01
Top Quartile Range	3.45%	−3.45%	4.47%	−4.18%	5.02%	−4.85%	5.51%	−5.19%	5.85%	−5.70%
Spread vs. Treasuries	− 0.04		+ 0.21		+ 0.28		+ 0.27		+ 0.46	

GIC rates quoted prior to 10:30 am (Eastern) net of all expenses, no broker commissions. Rates represent best quote for a $2-$5 million immediate lump sum deposit with annual interest payments. Yield spreads based on U.S. Treasury yields, as of 10:30 am (Eastern), versus the Index rate unadjusted for semi vs. annual interest payments. CHG reflects change in rate from previous day. INDEX is average of all rates quoted. Universe is investment grade.

Source: *Wall Street Journal* May 12, 1993, p. C18. T. Rowe Price GIC Index. Reprinted by permission of *The Wall Street Journal*, ©1993 Dow Jones & Company, Inc. All Right Reserved Worldwide.

the major life insurance companies, health insurance is provided through Blue Cross/ Blue Shield Organizations, Preferred Provider Organizations (PPOs), and Health Maintenance Organizations (HMOs). The benefits provided under most health plans encompass expenses incurred during hospitalization, surgery, emergency care, and in many cases for health maintenance. Insurance companies also provide policies that provide Medicare supplements, income lost owing to disability, and costs of long-term care.

While individual health policies are available, it is more common for individuals to obtain health insurance through group plans provided through employers. Group policies are usually cheaper for the employee, and it is often easier for the employee to qualify for coverage. Individual health policies often require people to pass a physical examination in order to be insured, whereas group plans often require less rigorous screening.

Property and Casualty Insurance Companies

Property and casualty insurance companies provide protection against losses from natural disasters, fire, theft, injury, and other events that result in damage to property or injury to persons. Property and casualty policies are of two general types. First, there are policies that insure against specific risks, such as fire or flood. More often, however, policies provide protection against multiple risks, like a homeowner's insurance policy, which can be tailored to insure the house and its occupants against fire, weather, theft, and liabilities arising from negligence or injury. Personal auto policies provide protection against multiple risks associated with owning and operating an automobile.

There were about 3900 property and casualty insurance companies in the United States in 1990. The financial structure for the property-casualty insurance industry is described in Table 7-3 for 1990, when the industry had a total of around $560 billion in assets. As shown in Table 7-3, the assets of property-casualty companies are

Table 7-3

Financial Structure of U.S. Property and Casualty Insurance Companies, 1990

Assets	
Cash and government securities	23%
Municipal and corporate bonds	29%
Special revenue bonds	26%
Corporate stocks	19%
Other assets	3%
	100%
Liabilities and Net Worth	
Policy Liabilities	75%
Net worth	25%
	100%

Source: *Insurance Information Institute, 1991 Fact Book.*

concentrated in fixed-income securities, primarily government, corporate, and municipal bonds. On the other side of the balance sheet, the primary source of financing is policy liabilities, at 75 percent of total assets. Equity financing accounts for about 25 percent of total financing.

One of the most apparent differences between the financial structure of property-casualty companies and life-health companies is the higher level of net worth as a proportion of assets employed by the property and casualty industry. Recall from Table 7-1 that the proportion of life insurance assets financed by equity during 1990 was 6.5 percent, compared to 25 percent from Table 7-3 for property-casualty companies during the same year. The difference is due in large part to the nature of the risks that are underwritten by each type of insurer. In particular, the mortality rates of the pools of individuals underwritten by life insurance companies are much more predictable than is the risk of a major storm or flood that is underwritten by a property-casualty company. In other words, it is very unlikely that claims against a life insurance company will be much larger (or smaller) than expected when insurance is priced and reserves for losses are established. Death rates don't change dramatically unless there is a catastrophe of enormous proportions, but exposure to loss from a major storm or earthquake is difficult to predict. The enormous losses experienced recently by major property and casualty insurers from hurricane Andrew and the floods along the Mississippi provide evidence to that effect (see inset below). Because property and casualty insurers can experience scenarios with such extreme losses, they must be better capitalized than their counterparts in the life insurance industry.

The financial performance of property-casualty companies is driven by two major sources of income. The first is income from their primary business of underwriting various lines of property and casualty risks. When premium income exceeds losses from claims plus administrative expenses, the underwriting business makes a profit. The second source of income comes from the securities portfolio maintained by the company. As indicated above, most of the assets of property-casualty companies are invested in fixed-income securities. When interest rates decrease, as they did during the early 1990s, the securities portfolio generates significant capital gains.

The years 1992 and 1993 were particularly difficult for U.S. property-casualty insurers. There were a record number of tornadoes, the Los Angeles riots, a flood in Chicago, hurricane Iniki, and the most devastating of all, hurricane Andrew. Hurricane Andrew alone stands to cost the insurance industry in the neighborhood of $16 billion. For 1992, the insurance industry paid $1.56 in claims for every $1 paid in premiums on homeowner's insurance policies. State Farm Fire and Casualty Co., the nation's largest home insurer, announced a $1.2 billion loss for 1992. In spite of these losses, the financial position of many insurers has remained stable, and in some cases has improved. There are two reasons. The first is that property-liability companies have reaped substantial capital gains from their securities portfolios owing to falling interest rates over the past few years. The second reason is that the substantial losses of 1992 may in fact provide justification to raise premiums in the near future. Anticipation of future rate hikes has added strength to the stock prices of many property insurers who were hard hit by claims in the Florida market following hurricane Andrew.

• *Hurricane Andrew Scares Major Property Insurers Out of Florida* •

The losses incurred by major property insurers due to hurricane Andrew during March 1992 continue to mount. The experience with this storm has caused major property insurers to generally revise their estimates of their loss exposures to tropical storms. Recently, industry experts estimated that, primarily owing to rapidly rising property values in the South Florida area, losses of up to $75 billion are possible from a single storm. This figure represents more than half the net worth of the property-liability insurance *industry.*

Many companies are taking steps to avoid storm-prone areas in the future. For example, shortly after hurricane Andrew, State Farm Insurance stopped writing new policies in the South Florida area, and it is considering similar action in other Gulf states. Allstate Insurance and Traveler's Insurance implemented similar policies in Florida and are considering actions to limit risk in other storm-prone states. Prudential Insurance announced an 18-month moratorium on new policies in the Florida area and is not renewing others.

The retreat by major underwiters from storm-prone markets has left many residents in South Florida and other areas without insurance and understandably unhappy. Consumer activists complain that the actions by these companies is the counterpart to "redlining" in the mortgage lending business and argue the practice should be illegal.[2] On the other hand, if insurers were to resume writing policies in storm-prone areas, it is very likely insurance rates would end up being much higher than before. Either way, it looks as if South Florida homeowners are in for more bad news.

Basic Principles of Insurance

Insurance provides a device by which insured parties transfer risks they are unable or unwilling to bear to insurers who are in better position to bear and manage those risks. Under many circumstances, insurance provides a more efficient means of managing exposures to risk than the alternative of self-insurance. To understand why insurance is usually a more efficient alternative to manage risk, consider the problem faced by an individual homeowner. Perhaps the greatest threat to the value of the home comes from risk of loss due to fire, flood, severe weather, or some other form of calamity. Imagine a simple scenario in which the loss from a single catastophic event would be $100,000. Assume that, during any one year such events are forecast

[2]Redlining refers to a practice formerly used by some mortgage lenders to identify specific geograpical areas at high risk for purposes of granting residential mortgage credit. Borrowers seeking mortgage credit in these areas were often denied credit based soley on fact that the property fell within the "redlined" area and not the strengths (or weaknesses) of their individual credit records. Because redlining generally excudes residents of low-income areas from being eligible for mortgage credit, it has been ruled as discriminatory and banned by regulators.

to have a probability equal to 0.01. To keep the example simple, we will assume that this is the only possible loss event. Thus, the homeowner knows that he or she will lose exactly $100,000 with probability 0.01 or nothing with probability 0.99. Under this assumption, the expected loss is (0.01)($100,000) + (0.99) ($0), or $1000.

Self-Insurance

To completely self-insure this risk, the homeowner would need to set aside cash or other liquid assets in the amount of $100,000. For most homeowners, an emergency fund of $100,000 is difficult, if not impossible, to establish. At the very least, saving an amount of this size would require the homeowner to forego other expenditures and opportunities. Moreover, since the money might be more productively used in other ways, perhaps in higher-yielding investments, dedication of $100,000 toward self-insurance may be quite costly, especially since the chance that the cash will actually be needed during any one year is only one in one hundred. While some individuals and corporations choose to self-insure certain risks, the opportunity to transfer risk through the purchase of insurance is often more economical and efficient. In the example above, an underwriter might provide the homeowner nearly complete insurance for a price slightly greater than the expected loss. For example, the premium might be set at $1200—$1000 to cover the expected loss of writing the insurance, plus $200 to cover administrative expense and provide a competitive profit. Buying the insurance policy allows the homeowner to reallocate the $100,000 self-insurance fund toward more productive investment, perhaps in long-term securities or real assets.

Underwriting and Diversification

It is generally more efficient to manage exposures to most risks through insurance than with self-insurance. The efficiency afforded by insurance derives from the underwriter's ability to diversify individual risk exposures by forming large groups, or pools, of insured risks. That is, by insuring a large number of homeowners with similar risks, the insurance company is able to reduce exposure to loss. In so doing, the insurer is able to maintain lower loss reserves, and provide more economical coverage to insureds, than would self-insurance. To illustrate the efficiency provided through diversification of individual risks, consider a problem involving two homeowners who must insure their homes, Homeowner A and Homeowner B. Assume the loss exposures and loss probabilities for both homeowners are as in the example above. That is, the probability of loss for each is 0.01 and the loss exposure is $100,000. The expected loss is equal to $1000 for each homeowner, or a combined expected loss of $2000. As before, either of two outcomes is possible for each homeowner: a loss of $100,000 or nothing. Further, we will assume the risks are independent. This means there is no correlation between outcomes realized by the two insured homeowners. This assumption is reasonable, especially if the homeowners do not live in the same city or region where they might be exposed to the same risks from storms or earthquakes.

Table 7-4 compares the possible loss outcomes under two insurance arrangements. The first is a simple self-insurance arrangement by which each individual underwrites his or her own risk. Under the second arrangement, the two homeowners form a "mutual" organization to share risk. The sharing arrangement works as follows. The two homeowners agree to group their losses and to share in the group loss on a fifty-fifty basis. Under the mutual arrangement, there are four possible outcomes: (1) A and B both lose \$100,000; (2) A loses \$100,000 and B loses nothing; (3) B loses \$100,000 and A loses nothing; and (4) both A and B lose nothing. Under the fifty-fifty sharing rule, the individual, or pro rata loss under the mutual arrangement is the total loss divided by two. Since the outcomes are from independent risks, the probability of both homeowners losing at once is (0.01) (0.01), or 0.0001. The probability of one homeowner losing \$100,000 and the other homeowner losing nothing is (0.01)(0.99), or 0.0099. And the probability of both homeowners losing nothing is (0.99)(0.99), or 0.9801. Table 7-4 provides the pro rata losses (probabilities in parentheses) for each possible outcome under each insurance arrangement.

Inspection of Table 7-4 shows that under both arrangements the expected loss to each homeowner is the same. The expected loss, which is the probability-weighted sum of the loss outcomes, is calculated as \$1000, the same as under self-insurance. The variances of the loss outcomes under the two arrangements, however, are quite different. Recall that variance, a measure of risk, is the probability-weighted sum of squared deviations of each outcome from the mean outcome. For the self-insurance arrangement, the variance is

$$\sigma^2 = (0.01)\ (\$100{,}000 - \$1{,}000)^2 + (0.99)\ (\$0 - \$1{,}000)^2 = \$99 \text{ million}$$

For the mutual arrangement the variance is

$$\sigma^2 = (0.0001)\ (\$100{,}000 - \$1{,}000)^2 + (2)\ (0.0099)\ (\$50{,}000 - \$1{,}000)^2 + \ldots + (0.9801)\ (\$0 - \$1{,}000)^2 = \$49.5 \text{ million}$$

Table 7-4

Risk Exposure to Loss Under Self-Insurance versus a "Mutual" Arrangement

		Loss	**No Loss**
Self-insurance			
Homeowners A and B		\$100,000 (0.01)	0 (0.99)

		Loss	**No Loss**
Mutual insurance organization		Homeowner B	
Homeowner A		Loss	No Loss
	Loss	\$100,000 (0.0001)	\$50,000 (0.0099)
	No Loss	\$50,000 (0.0099)	0 (0.9801)

By pooling their independent risks, A and B are able to cut the risk of their individual exposures in half.[3] By sharing risk, the extreme outcomes $100,000 loss and zero loss become less likely, tending to concentrate the distribution of outcomes more toward the expected loss of $1000.

Of course, modern insurance arrangements are seldom worked out in the bilateral manner described above, but the concept of a mutual risk-sharing arrangement has its counterpart in the insurance industry in mutual insurance companies. When large numbers of independent risks are pooled in a manner similar to our pooling arrangement, the variance of loss exposures to individual participants is much reduced, causing actual losses to the mutual organization to be very predictable. This allows the association to charge a premium equal to the expected loss per insured risk, plus an allowance for administrative costs, risk reserves, and profit.

Regulation of Insurance Companies

Insurance companies are regulated by individual state insurance commissions. Commissions generally exist to enforce licensing requirements and ensure that insurance firms satisfy minimum capital requirements. In many states, commissions control prices (premiums) and restrict exposure to certain investments, such as real estate. Insurance commissions generally conduct examinations of the operation of individual life companies. In addition, insurance commissions generally supervise the liquidation of failed insurance companies in their jurisdiction. The National Association of Insurance Commissioners (NAIC) provides a unifying influence over the 50 different state insurance commissions. Possibly the chief influence the NAIC exerts over the state regulatory commissions is to propose model legislation to be considered by individual state legislatures.

The system of regulation in the insurance industry is somewhat different from that in the banking industry, where the Federal Deposit Insurance Corporation (FDIC), a federal regulatory agency, provides oversight for most U.S. commercial banks and insures depositors against failure. Insurance policyholders in most states are covered by some form of state guarantee fund that guarantees their claims against a participating insurance company, up to certain limits. Unlike the banking industry, state guarantee funds don't assess premiums to provide reserves against the failure of member companies. Instead, when a company fails, the guarantee fund assesses other member companies to pay the shortfall on the failed company's obligations, or to assist in funding a bailout. Assessments are generally limited, however, to a fixed percentage of the assessed company's premium income for the year.

There are some close similarities between recent failures in the insurance industry and the the massive collapse of the savings and loan industry during the 1980s. Reacting to a sluggish market for traditional insurance products, many insurance companies grew rapidly through the issuance of annuities, in particular GICs. The shift by

[3]The standard deviation of loss outcomes for Homeowners A and B is calculated as the square root of the variance: $9949.87 and $7035.62, respectively. Standard deviation is an alternative measure of the risk associated with the distribution of loss outcomes.

many insurance companies toward investment-oriented products responded to a growing demand for such products from pension funds. High fixed rates offered GICs were attractive investments to pension funds while they provided a means of rapid expansion to insurance companies. This led many companies into an increasingly precarious position that in many ways was similar to that of failed savings and loans of the 1980s. The high long-term rates promised on outstanding GICs caused many insurance companies to seek higher-yielding investments. Rather than invest in Treasury or high-grade corporate securities, many turned to higher-yielding junk bonds or mortgage-backed securities such as Collaterized Mortgage Obligations (CMOs, see Chapter 21), investments that were much riskier than those traditionally associated with highly rated insurance firms.

The failure of several large insurance companies during the late 1980s and early 1990s has focused attention on the regulation of the insurance industry and on the manner in which state regulators deal—or fail to deal—with troubled institutions. The regulatory safety net provided by state insurance funds has been criticized for causing the same moral hazard problem that the Federal Savings and Loan Insurance Corporation (FSLIC) caused during the saving and loan calamity. In particular, blanket protection provided by the states to many failed insurance companies creates an incentive for insurers to take risks that afford faster growth. If risk taking pays off, the company receives large gains. If not, the insurance guarantee fund provides a bailout financed by the rest of the industry.

The failure of Executive Life Insurance Company of California and New York is an example of the phenomena described above. In particular, regulators were reportedly concerned, years before the company failed, over the high concentration of junk bonds in Executive Life's investment portfolio. Warnings to the company went unheeded, as it built its junk bond investments to 75 percent of total assets by 1987. Financing for this growth came largely from guaranteed investment contracts sold by Executive Life, principally to pension funds. The pension funds were not overly concerned about the risk of Executive Life's investment portfolio, owing to explicit, and sometimes implicit, guarantees made by state regulators about both insurance and investment-oriented products. Thus, the pension funds paid little attention to the rate at which Executive Life built its investment portfolio in junk bonds. State regulators, concerned with the level of risk undertaken by Executive Life (and other insurers), lacked the legal authority to prohibit the company from investing further in junk bonds. Moreover, attempts to pass legislation that would control the risk-taking activities of insurers were met by powerful opposition from the junk bond lobby. Led by Drexel, Burnham, Lambert, this opposition was able to thwart most efforts to regulate insurance companies' use of junk bonds. When the junk bond market went sour toward the end of the 1980s, Executive Life was unable to continue meeting the fixed-rate obligations owed on its investment-oriented liabilities (GICs). In April 1991 the newly formed insurance commission in California seized Executive Life.

Another example of how regulation has failed to keep pace with the new and riskier investment strategies of insurance companies is the case of a smaller company called Coastal States Life Insurance Company. Coastal States Life was seized by Georgia state regulators in December, 1992 because of concern over Coastal's heavy investment in CMOs. Of its $128 million in assets at the time, $120 were investments in CMOs. Though CMOs don't carry the credit risk associated with junk bonds, they are prone to large swings in value in response to changes in interest rates. While the company has recently taken legal action of its own in an attempt to block the seizure, the Coastal States case has taken on special significance in the industry as an indicator of where regulations on CMOs will lead.

To most regulators in the insurance industry CMOs were relatively new, and the AAA rating most carried was regarded as proof against risk. Though the credit risk associated with CMOs is indeed relatively small, the interest rate risk of these securities can be extraordinarily high. The interest rate risk associated with CMOs, which is be discussed in some detail in Chapter 22, stems from two effects: market risk and prepayment risk. Market risk is common to fixed-income securities. Prepayment risk, however, which comes from the option of mortgage borrowers to refinance their debt, can exacerbate the volatility of CMO values in response to shifts in market rates. When CMOs are financed with fixed-rate instruments like GICs, which have no prepayment options, large exposure to loss can attend unexpected shifts in interest rates. Unexpected losses from CMOs experienced by some insurance companies have recently caused the NAIC to begin studying new rules for valuing CMOs. Until the states respond with new rules regarding investment in, and valuation of, CMOs, the ability of regulatory commissions to understand and deal with CMOs will continue to lag behind the more sophisticated strategies to invest in these securities.

• *Executive Life Insurance Company: A Bailout Gone Bad?* •

In April, 1991, John Garamendi, newly elected California Insurance Commissioner, seized nearly insolvent Executive Life Insurance Company. Executive Life's difficulties were due largely to rapid growth in junk bond investments financed by guaranteed investment contracts that were issued to fund issues of municipal debt. These contracts, often called muni-GICs, carried high fixed rates of interest. When the junk bond portfolio deteriorated Executive Life found it increasingly difficult to handle its fixed obligations.

By March, 1991, Garamendi arranged a bid for Executive Life involving Altus Finance, which agreed to buy $9 billion in junk bonds for $3.25 billion, and a French insurance company called Mutuelle Assurance Artisanale de France (MAAF). MAAF agreed to buy the insurance operations and infuse $300 million in new capital into the company. While this arrangement would have left policyholders almost whole (receiving 95 cents on the dollar), Garamendi's deal would have left muni-GIC holders with significant losses (about 50 cents on the dollar).

When Executive Life's junk bond portfolio rebounded, by about $1.3 billion since April 1991, the deal began to unravel. Many questioned Garamendi's competence, if not his motives, since Altus Finance—not the policyholders or GIC investors—stood to gain the windfall gains in the junk bond portfolio. At the same time, holders of $1.8 billion in muni-GICs sued to block the sale of the insurance operation to MAAF. The California Court of Appeals found in favor of bondholders and nullified the sale, ruling that bondholders should be treated equally with policy holders. This angered policyholders, who consequently would stand to receive less, and encouraged GIC holders to file suit again, this time to block the junk bond sale. As the legal wrangling dragged on, it seemed ironic that the the major cause of Executive Life's difficulties, its portfolio of junk bonds, became the most coveted prize.

Investment Companies and Pension Funds

In general, households have three alternative means of savings. The first is through the direct purchase of financial securities like stocks and bonds. The second is by holding liabilities of traditional savings intermediaries like banks, savings and loans, and life insurance companies. The third is through intermediaries like mutual funds and pension plans. One of the most important changes in the U.S. financial system over the past several decades has been the increased importance of investment companies and pension funds as financial intermediaries of household savings. In fact, the growth of pension and mutual funds accounts for much of the decrease in both direct purchases of stocks and bonds by household savers and indirect investment through traditional intermediaries. Figure 7-2 shows the three major categories of household savings as percentages of total household financial assets. Since 1952, direct purchases of stocks and bonds have decreased from over 50 percent of household financial assets to about 35 percent in 1991. The percentage of total household financial assets represented by claims against traditional intermediaries decreased from about 40 percent in 1952 to less than 30 percent in 1991. Over the same period, intermediation of household savings by pension and mutual funds increased from less than 10 percent of total household financial assets in 1952 to almost 40 percent in 1991.

The trends illustrated in Figure 7-2 are the combination of two phenomena. The first is the the growth in the importance of institutional investors, chiefly pension and mutual funds, channelling investments by small savers to the money and capital markets. In 1952, small savers were effectively limited to investments in savings deposits at banks and thrift institutions, or low-interest investments via whole life insurance policies. Investments in stocks and bonds were largely limited to wealthier persons. By the 1990s, pension and mutual funds evolved to provide access to stock and bond markets for small investors. The second effect demonstrated by Figure 7-2 is the increased competition between traditional and nontraditional savings intermediaries. Especially since the late 1970s, banks and savings and loans have come under increased competitive pressure from a variety of nondepository institutions, including mutual funds and pension funds. To some extent, the inroads made by nontraditional intermediaries into traditional markets has been stimulated by the deregulation and reregulation of financial markets that took place during the late 1970s and 1980s. In addition, however, nontraditional intermediaries became attractive alternatives to traditional savings institutions owing to greater flexibility and innovation that allow savers to better tailor their investments to personal investment objectives.

Figure 7-2
Intermediation of Household Saving

Source: "Changes in Financial Intermediation: The Role of Pension and Mutual Funds" by G. Sellon, Jr., Economics Review, *Federal Reserve Bank of Kansas City, 3rd Quarter 1992, pp. 53–70.*

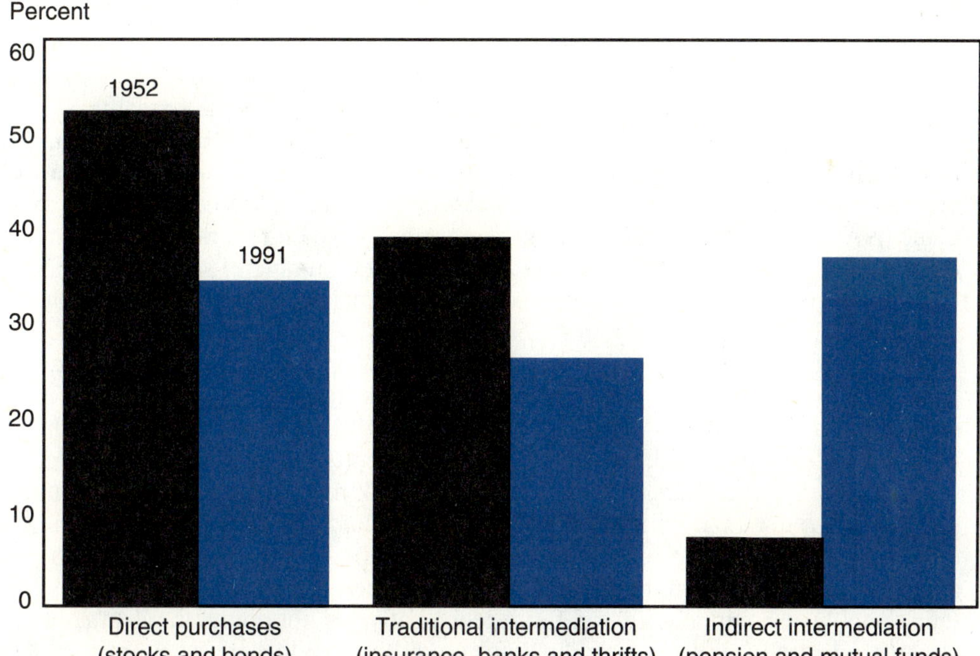

Note: The chart shows each category as a percent of household financial assets.

Investment Companies

Investment companies are organizations that invest the pooled funds of shareholders in securities that meet the objectives of the fund. The most important benefits of investment companies to their shareholders are diversification and professional management. The benefits of diversification are particularly important for small investors. Spreading investments among a number of securities significantly reduces risk. Typically, to achieve a reasonable level of diversification, say in the stock market, investors would need to spread their money over investments in 20 to 25 different stocks. This poses two problems for the small investor. First, it would be impractical for very small amounts of money to be divided among that many securities. For example, it is more difficult (and more costly) for individuals to buy individual stocks in quantities less than 100-share round lots. A 100-share transaction in a particular stock could involve thousands of dollars by itself. Many small investors just don't have enough money to divide up among 20 or more securities.

The second reason why sufficient diversification is difficult for small investors is transactions costs. Because most brokered transactions involve a commission, purchasing 20 to 30 securities would cost a significant brokerage fee. Investment companies are able to pool transactions into large blocks of shares, for which the unit transactions costs are much smaller.

Types of Investment Companies

There are two general types of investment companies. "Mutual funds," or "open-end investment companies," are the most popular type of investment company. Mutual funds invest in a variety of securities, including stocks, bonds, and money market instruments. A shareholder in a mutual fund owns a pro rata share of the assets of the fund. The fund stands ready to buy back, or redeem, its shares at their net asset value (NAV). The NAV of mutual fund shares equals the current market value of the fund's securities, minus liabilities, divided by the total number of shares outstanding. When new investors buy into the fund, the fund merely issues new shares at the current NAV. Thus, there is no limit to the number of shares the fund may issue.

The second general category of investment company is called a "closed-end fund." Closed-end funds are investment companies that issue a limited number of shares that are traded in public equity markets. When investors, or shareholders, invest in a closed-end fund, they do so by purchasing the company's publicly traded stock. The price of a share of closed-end fund stock reflects the NAV of the fund's securities, but not exactly. Shares in a closed-end fund can trade at a premium or a discount relative to the NAV. When the shares of the fund trade at a premium, the share price is greater than the NAV. When shares trade at a discount, the price is less than the NAV. Though closed-end funds technically are not mutual funds, the popular press generally uses the term "mutual fund" to refer to both categories. In this chapter, we will also make general references to mutual funds, so as to include both categories of investment companies. We will use the terms "open-" and "closed-end" to distinguish between the two types of investment companies specifically.

Investors in mutual funds can realize profits from their investment in three ways. First, income from the fund's assets, in the form of either dividends or interest, can be passed on to the shareholders in the fund. Second, increases in the value of the fund's assets, or capital gains, can be passed on to shareholders as well in what is called capital gain distribution. Third, if capital gains are not distributed to shareholders, the gains will be reflected by an increase in the value of investor's shares in the fund. The form in which investors realize profits on their investments reflects, to a large extent, the overall strategy of the fund. For example, an income fund invests in securities that will generate high current income (either as dividends or interest) that will be passed on to shareholders. Growth funds emphasize investments in securities with high capital gains. Other differences in funds by investment orientation are described later in this chapter.

Investors can buy mutual fund shares in two basic ways. First, some funds market their shares directly to investors, via direct mail and advertising. These shares are generally sold with no sales commission, or a very low commission. In some circumstances the fund charges what is called a 12b-1 fee to pay for distribution costs.[4] The second way in which fund shares are marketed is through a sales force of brokers, insurance agents, financial planners, and in some cases a captive, or dedicated, sales force employed by the fund. In most cases, sales people are paid a direct sales commission, called a "load," which is included in the price of the shares. "Front-end load" funds charge a sales commission when mutual fund shares are originally sold to the investor. "No-load" funds do not charge a sales commission when share are originally sold, but distribution costs for no-load funds are often covered by "back-end" fees, a charge applied when shares are redeemed. Alternatively, sales commissions are sometimes accomplished through a 12b-1 fee rather than a front-end load.

Table 7-5 provides an excerpt from the *Wall Street Journal* of market information for a selected number of (open end) mutual funds reported for 9 July 1993. The first column gives the name of the fund. Lowercase letters following the fund name indicate special characteristics, including whether distribution costs apply (p), or whether a redemption charge or back-end fee (r) is applied to the sale of shares. The second column provides the advertised investment objective of the fund, as indicated in the fund's prospectus. Investment objectives are discussed in more detail below. The third column gives the current NAV per share, and the fourth column provides the most recent offer price as given by the National Association of Securities Dealers (NASD) through its quotation system (Nasdaq). The offer price represents the cost of fund shares to prospective investors and it is generally equal to the NAV plus any sales commission, or load fee. The last column indicates the change in the offer price from the previous day's quotation.

Table 7-6 provides market information for selected closed-end funds for 9 July 1993. Information on these funds is categorized by investment orientation. The name of the fund is given in the left-hand column and the stock exchange on which the fund's shares are traded is listed in the second column. In the next column, the NAV of the fund's shares is given, followed by the market price of the shares. The quoted share price is the closing price for shares traded over an exchange or the dealer-to-dealer ask price for shares traded over the counter. The right-hand column in Table 7-6 provides the 52-week rate of return (capital gains plus dividends) on shares of equity funds and the dividend yield from income on shares of bond funds.

Investment Objectives of Mutual Funds

There are numerous types of mutual funds which are defined by a particular investment orientation. Regulation of the mutual fund industry requires funds to advertise the major objective in their prospectus. The different types of funds that are offered ultimately are determined by the preferences of individual investors, that is, by consumer demand. The major categories of mutual fund objectives or orientations are listed in Figure 7-3. The number of funds in each category is given for the years 1987

---

[4]The term "12b-1" fee derives from a Securities and Exchange Commission (SEC) rule that permits funds to deduct the fee.

Table 7-5

Mutual Fund Quotations

Friday July 9, 1993

Ranges for investment companies, with daily price data supplied by the National Association of Securities Dealers and performance and cost calculations by Lipper Analytical Services, Inc. The NASD requires a mutual fund to have at least 1,000 shareholders or net assets of $25 million before being listed. Detailed explanatory notes appear elsewhere on this page.

	Inv. Obj.	NAV	Offer Price	NAV Chg.	% Ret YTD	Max Initl Chrg.	Total Exp Ratio R
AAL Mutual:							
Bond	BND	10.62	11.15	+ 0.01	+ 7.0	4.750	1.030 ..
CaGr	GRO	14.78	15.52	− 0.03	+ 2.2	4.750	1.280 ..
MuBd	GLM	11.13	11.69	+ 0.01	+ 6.6	4.750	0.950 ..
AARP Invst:							
CaGr	GRO	33.62	NL	+ 0.06	+ 4.48	0.000	1.130 ..
GiniM	BND	16.10	NL	+ 0.01	+ 5.0	0.000	0.720 ..
Gthinc	G&I	31.40	NL	− 0.04	+ 7.4	0.000	0.910 ..
HQBd	BND	16.82	NL	+ 0.03	+ 7.8	0.000	1.130 ..
TxFBd	ISM	18.53	NL	...	+ 7.9	0.000	0.740 ..
ABT Funds:							
Emrg	CAP	13.15	13.81	+ 0.08	+ 2.8	4.750	1.440 ..
FL HI	MFL	NA	NA	NA	NA	4.750	NA ..
FL TF	MFL	NA	NA	NA	NA	4.750	0.410 ..
Gthin	G&I	10.89	11.43	...	+ 2.5	4.750	1.230 ..
Utilln	SEC	14.16	14.87	− 0.01	+ 13.2	4.750	1.170 ..
Acc Mortg	BND	12.38	NL	+ 0.01	+ 5.4	0.000	0.840 ..
Acc Sht Int	BST	12.44	NL	+ 0.01	+ 4.4	0.000	0.830 ..
AHA Funds:							
Balan	S&B	12.73	NL	...	+ 6.3	0.000	0.380 ..
Full	BND	10.78	NL	+ 0.01	+ 8.1	0.000	0.420 ..
Lim	BST	10.52	NL	...	+ 3.6	0.000	0.290 ..
AIM Funds:							
AdjGv p	BST	9.89	10.20	...	+ 2.6	3.000	0.140 ..
Agrsv p	SML	20.59	21.79	+ 0.14	+ 11.2	5.500	1.250 ..
Chart p	G&I	8.95	9.47	+ 0.01	+ 5.4	5.500	1.170 ..
Const p	CAP	15.75	16.67	+ 0.07	+ 5.6	5.500	1.200 ..
CvYld p	S&B	15.17	15.93	+ 0.06	+ 7.8	4.750	2.120 ..
GoSc p	BND	10.38	10.90	+ 0.01	+ 5.3	4.750	0.980 ..
Grth p	GRO	12.04	12.74	+ 0.04	− 2.0	5.500	1.170 ..
HiYld p	BHI	5.94	6.24	+ 0.01	+ 10.7	4.750	1.530 ..
HYldC p	BHI	10.00	10.50	+ 0.03	+ 12.1	4.750	1.150 ..
Inco p	BND	8.59	9.02	+ 0.01	+ 10.9	4.750	0.990 ..
IntlE p	ITL	10.27	10.87	− 0.03	+ 14.6	5.500	1.800 ..
LimM p	BST	10.22	10.32	...	+ 2.8	1.000	0.480 ..
MuB p	GLM	8.59	9.02	...	+ 7.0	4.750	0.900 ..
Sumit	GRO	9.84	NA	+ 0.01	+ 2.1	8.500	0.760 ..
TeCt p	SSM	11.12	11.67	...	+ 7.5	4.750	0.250 ..
TF Int	IDM	10.87	11.21	...	+ 5.1	3.000	0.020 ..
Util p	SEC	14.65	15.50	− 0.01	+ 12.5	5.500	1.170 ..
Valu p	G&I	20.07	21.24	+ 0.09	+ 10.0	5.500	1.160 ..
Weing p	GRO	16.68	17.65	...	− 3.8	5.500	1.100 ..
AMF Funds:							
AdjMtg	BST	10.02	NL	...	+ 2.9	0.000	0.440 ..
IntMtg	BND	10.00	NL	+ 0.01	+ 6.1	0.000	0.430 ..
IntlLiq	BST	10.92	NL	...	+ 4.1	0.000	0.500 ..
MtgSc	BND	11.39	NL	...	+ 3.9	0.000	0.530 ..
ASM Fd	G&I	9.68	NL	+ 0.01	+ 6.9	0.000	0.750 ..
ASO Funds:							
Balance	S&B	11.81	12.37	...	+ 8.7	4.500	0.830 ..
Bond	BND	11.37	11.91	+ 0.02	+ 7.8	4.500	0.820 ..
Equity	CAP	14.21	14.88	− 0.01	+ 9.9	4.500	1.010 ..
LtdMat	BST	10.85	11.13	+ 0.01	+ 5.1	2.500	0.680 ..
RegEq	CAP	16.48	17.26	+ 0.03	+ 0.07	4.500	0.910 ..
AcornIn	ITL	12.72	12.72	− 0.06	+ 19.0	0.000	NA ..
AcornF	SML	64.52	64.52	+ 0.16	+ 16.7	0.000	0.670 ..
AdsnCa p	G&I	21.56	22.23	...	+ 8.6	3.000	2.120 ..
AdvCaplBal	S&B	10.37	NL	− 0.01	+ 1.4	0.000	1.130 ..
AdvCaplRet	BND	10.66	NL	+ 0.01	+ 10.5	0.000	NA ..
Advest Advant:							
Govt	BND	10.14	10.14	+ 0.03	+ 13.3k	0.000	1.390 ..
Gwth	GRO	16.63	16.63	+ 0.02	+ 1.9	0.000	2.150 ..
HY Bd	BHI	9.74	9.74	+ 0.02	+ 12.2k	0.000	1.500 ..
Inco	BND	12.96	12.96	...	+ 9.6	0.000	2.020 ..
Spcl	SML	18.07	18.07	+ 0.02	+ 3.9	0.000	2.840 ..
Aetna Funds:							
Aetna	S&B	10.45	NL	+ 0.01	+ 4.3	0.000	0.070 ..
Bond	BND	10.40	NL	+ 0.01	+ 7.9	0.000	0.050 ..
GrwIncm	G&I	10.52	NL	− 0.01	+ 0.9	0.000	0.330 ..
IntlGr	ITL	9.94	NL	− 0.03	+ 11.9	0.000	0.500 ..
Alger Funds:							
Growth	GRO	19.99	19.99	+ 0.09	+ 4.3	0.000	2.320 ..
IncGr	G&I	13.71	13.71	+ 0.01	+ 3.5	0.000	3.090 ..
SmCap	SML	22.91	22.91	+ 0.09	− 2.2	0.000	2.170 ..
Alliance Cap:							
Alian p	GRO	7.09	7.50	...	+ 6.4	5.500	0.180 ..
Balan p	S&B	14.06	14.88	+ 0.01	+ 5.7	5.500	1.400 ..
Canad p	ITL	5.44	5.76	...	+ 12.6	5.500	2.690 ..
CpBdA p	BND	14.23	14.67	+ 0.03	+ 19.1k	3.000	1.480 ..
CpBdB p	BND	14.23	14.23	+ 0.04	NS	0.000	NA ..
Count p	G&I	19.08	20.19	+ 0.01	− 1.0	5.500	1.620 ..
GlbSA p	WOR	10.44	11.05	...	+ 7.9	5.500	2.340 ..
GovtA p	BND	8.65	8.92	+ 0.01	+ 7.2k	3.000	1.120 ..
GovtB p	BND	8.65	8.65	+ 0.01	+ 6.8k	3.000	1.800 ..
GovtC p	BND	8.65	8.65	+ 0.01	NS	0.000	NA ..
Grinc p	G&I	2.49	2.63	...	+ 4.6	5.500	1.090 ..
GrincB p	G&I	2.48	2.48	...	+ 4.2	0.000	1.900 ..
ICalTA p	ISM	13.97	14.63	...	+ 7.3k	4.500	0.780 ..
InsMuA p	ISM	10.60	11.10	+ 0.01	+ 8.0k	4.500	0.810 ..
IntlA p	ITL	16.00	16.93	+ 0.02	+ 15.3	5.500	1.820 ..
MrtgA p	BND	9.41	9.70	+ 0.01	+ 7.8k	3.000	1.180 ..
MrtgB p	BND	9.41	9.41	+ 0.01	+ 7.4k	0.000	1.870 ..
MrtgTrA p	BST	10.01	10.32	...	+ 4.4k	3.000	1.440 ..
MrtgTrB p	BST	10.02	10.02	+ 0.01	+ 4.1k	0.000	2.130 ..
MrtgTrC	BST	10.02	10.02	+ 0.01	NS	0.000	NA ..
MltIG	SEC	10.27	10.37	...	+ 5.6k	1.000	2.330 ..
Mltln p	WBD	1.90	1.90	...	+ 2.4	0.000	1.810 ..
MMSA p	WBD	8.92	9.20	− 0.01	+ 6.9k	3.000	2.530 ..
MMSB p	WBD	8.92	8.92	− 0.01	+ 6.5k	0.000	3.240 ..
MuCA A p	MCA	10.71	11.21	...	+ 7.5k	4.500	0.590 ..
MuCA B p	MCA	10.71	10.71	+ 0.01	+ 7.0k	0.000	NA ..
MuCA C p	MCA	10.71	10.71	+ 0.01	NS	0.000	NA ..
MuNYA p	DNY	10.04	10.51	...	+ 7.7k	4.500	0.700 ..
MuNYB p	DNY	10.04	10.04	+ 0.01	+ 7.0k	0.000	NA ..
NtlMuA p	GLM	10.91	11.42	+ 0.01	+ 7.8k	4.500	0.830 ..
NtlMuB p	GLM	10.91	10.91	+ 0.01	+ 7.5k	0.000	NA ..
NatlMuC p	GLM	10.90	10.90	...	NS	0.000	NA ..
NEur p	ITL	10.35	10.95	− 0.01	+ 12.5	5.500	2.240 ..
NAGvA	WBD	10.13	10.44	+ 0.02	+ 9.7k	3.000	2.450 ..
NAGvB	WBD	10.13	10.13	+ 0.02	+ 9.2k	0.000	3.130 ..
NAGvC	WBD	10.13	10.13	+ 0.02	NS	0.000	NA ..
PrGrthA p	GRO	11.23	11.58	+ 0.02	+ 2.8	3.000	NA ..
PrGrthB p	GRO	11.19	11.19	+ 0.02	+ 2.6	0.000	NA ..
QusrA p	SML	22.43	23.74	+ 0.07	5.7	5.500	1.620 ..
ST Mla p	WBD	9.29	9.58	− 0.01	+ 5.3k	3.000	1.100 ..
ST Mlb p	WBD	9.29	9.29	− 0.01	+ 4.9k	0.000	1.810 ..
Tech p	SEC	30.66	32.44	+ 0.16	+ 8.7	5.500	1.610 ..
Wldln	WBD	1.91	1.91	− 0.01	+ 2.6k	0.000	1.590 ..
AmanaIncome	EQL	12.71	NL	− 0.01	+ 5.1	0.000	1.580 ..

Source: *Wall Street Journal,* July 12, 1993, C-15. Reprinted by permission of *The Wall Street Journal,* © 1993 Dow Jones & Company, Inc. All Right Reserved Worldwide.

Table 7-6

Closed End Funds

Friday, July 9, 1993.

Unaudited Net Asset Values (NAV) of closed end funds, reported by the companies as of Friday's close. Each quote includes the closing stock exchange price or dealer-to-dealer asked price of each fund's shares, with the percentage of difference. For equity funds, the final column shows the 52-week percentage change in stock market price plus dividends. For bond funds, the final column shows dividends paid from income in the last 12 months, as of the prior month-end, as a percentage of the stock market price. The figure doesn't include capital gains distributions. N-New York Stock Exchange. O-Over-the-Counter. A-American. C-Chicago.

Fund Name	Stock Exch	NAV	Market Price	Prem /Disc	52 week Market Return
General Equity Funds					
Adams Express	N	20.66	20 3/4	+ 0.4	20.1
Baker Fentress	N	21.74	18 1/8	− 16.6	8.5
Bergstrom Capital	A	88.92	95	+ 6.8	− 8.2
Blue Chip Value	N	8.04	8 3/8	+ 4.2	13.7
Central Securities	A	16.46	14 7/8	− 9.6	57.4
Charles Allmon Tr	N	10.58	10	− 5.5	8.4
Engex	A	11.70	9 5/8	− 17.7	20.3
Gabelli Equity Tr	N	11.36	11 3/8	+ 0.1	16.7
General American	N	25.03	23 1/8	− 7.6	− 6.0
Inefficient Mkt	A	11.20	9 5/8	− 14.1	3.2
Jundt Growth	N	15.04	14 3/8	− 4.4	7.5
Liberty All-Star	N	10.52	11 1/8	+ 5.8	20.3
Morgan Gren Sm Cap	N	11.77	10 7/8	− 7.6	7.5
NAIC Growth	O	N/A	11 1/4	N/A	16.4
Royce Value Trust	N	13.51	13 1/8	− 2.8	26.7
Salomon SBF	N	N/A	13 3/8	N/A	6.6
Source Capital	N	41.61	48 1/8	+ 15.7	13.4
Spectra	O	19.03	16 1/2	− 13.3	25.5
Tri-Continental	N	28.08	24 1/2	− 12.7	− 0.1
Z-Seven	O	15.63	16 1/2	+ 5.6	− 1.5
Zweig	N	a11.32	13	+ 14.8	11.4
Specialized Equity Funds					
ASA Limited	N	cvN/A	48 3/8	N/A	22.5
Alliance Glob Env	N	10.61	9 1/8	− 14.0	− 9.9
Anchor Gold & Curr	C	6.23	6 3/8	+ 2.3	43.6
BGR Prec Metals	T	cy14.09	13 1/2	− 4.2	89.5
C&S Realty Income	A	8.81	9 1/2	+ 7.8	35.7
Central Fd Canada	A	c5.02	5 5/8	+ 12.1	45.4
Counsellors Tandem	N	18.27	15 7/8	− 13.1	25.5
Delaware Gr Div	N	14.46	14 3/8	− 0.6	N/A
Dover Regional Fin	O	N/A	6 1/2	N/A	52.9
Duff Phelps Ut Inc	N	N/A	10 7/8	N/A	12.3
Emerging Mkts Tel	N	15.74	16 7/8	+ 7.2	14.2
First Financial	N	17.29	15 1/4	− 11.8	45.6
Global Health Sci	N	11.20	10	− 10.7	− 17.8
H&Q Healthcare Inv	N	17.39	17 1/4	− 0.8	− 14.8
H&Q Life Sci Inv	N	12.80	12 1/4	− 4.3	− 18.3
Patriot Global Dvd	N	15.23	14 3/4	− 3.2	N/A
Patriot Pre Dvd II	N	13.60	12 1/2	− 8.1	19.1
Patriot Pref Div	N	13.99	15	+ 7.2	N/A
Patriot Prem Divd	N	11.17	10 3/4	− 3.8	19.5
Patriot Select Dvd	N	17.43	18 1/4	+ 4.7	17.9
Petroleum & Res	N	31.24	28	− 10.4	13.7
Pilgrim Reg Bk Shs	N	N/A	12	N/A	18.2
Preferred Inc Mgt	N	14.35	14 3/4	+ 2.8	N/A
Preferred Inc Opp	N	13.19	13 3/4	+ 4.2	14.7
Preferred Income	N	18.38	19 3/8	+ 5.4	15.7
Putnam Divd Income	N	N/A	12	N/A	4.6
5thEastern ThriftBk	O	18.54	16 1/2	− 11.0	37.5
Templeton Gl Util	A	a14.22	15	+ 5.5	14.4
Amer Adj Rate '98	N	c9.64	9 5/8	− 0.2	7.0
Amer Adj Rate '99	N	c9.61	9 5/8	+ 0.2	N/A
Amer Govt Income	N	c8.72	9 1/4	+ 6.1	8.9
Amer Govt Port	N	c10.97	11 3/4	+ 7.1	9.6
Amer Govt Term Tr	N	c9.71	10 1/4	+ 5.6	8.8
Amer Oppty Income	N	c10.78	11 1/2	+ 6.7	9.8
Amer Str Income	N	c15.59	16 1/4	+ 4.2	8.3
Amer Strat Inc II	N	c14.80	15 1/2	+ 4.7	N/A
Amer Strat Inc III	N	c14.38	15 1/4	+ 6.1	N/A
American Cap Bond	N	b21.17	20 3/8	− 3.8	7.9
American Cap Inc	N	8.20	8 1/4	+ 0.6	10.1
BickRk 1998 Term	N	c10.32	10	− 3.1	7.5
BlckRk 1999 Term	N	c9.56	10	+ 4.6	N/A
BlckRk 2001 Term	N	c9.64	9 3/8	− 2.7	N/A
BlckRk Adv Term	N	c10.81	10 3/8	− 4.0	8.2
BlckRk Income Tr	N	c8.95	9 1/8	+ 2.0	9.6
BlckRk Inv Gr 2009	A	c14.16	15	+ 5.9	N/A
BlckRk Inv Qual Tm	N	c9.91	9 5/8	− 2.9	8.4
BlckRk Strat Term	N	c9.80	10	+ 2.0	8.6
BlckRk Target Term	N	c10.79	10 1/4	− 5.0	8.1
Bunker Hill Income	N	16.93	15 3/4	− 7.0	8.6
CIGNA High Income	N	7.61	8 3/4	+ 15.0	11.0
CIM High Yld Secs	N	8.16	8 3/8	+ 2.6	9.9
CNA Income Shares	N	c10.87	12 1/4	+ 12.7	9.6
Circle Income	O	c12.40	11 1/2	− 7.3	8.1
Colonial Int High	N	6.84	7 1/8	+ 4.2	10.3
Colonial Intrmkt I	N	a11.92	12	+ 0.7	9.2
Corporate High Yld	N	14.17	N/A	N/A	N/A
Current Inc Shares	N	14.18	13 1/2	− 4.8	7.3
Dean Witter Govt	N	9.58	9 1/8	− 4.7	7.6
Dreyfus Str Govt	N	10.99	11 5/8	+ 5.8	7.8
Duff&PhelpsUtilCor	N	a14.93	15 1/4	+ 2.1	N/A
Excelsior Income	N	c19.64	18 3/8	− 6.4	7.2
First Boston Inc	N	8.92	9 3/8	+ 5.1	9.9
First Boston Strat	N	10.33	10 1/2	+ 1.6	10.2
Fortis Securities	N	10.27	11 1/4	+ 9.5	9.2
Franklin Multi-Inc	N	c11.35	10 1/2	− 7.5	8.9
Franklin Princ Mat	N	c9.25	8	− 13.5	7.3
Franklin Univ Tr	N	c9.68	9 1/4	− 4.4	8.0
Ft Dearborn Income	N	17.33	17 1/8	− 1.2	7.2
Hatteras Income	N	16.83	18 3/4	+ 11.4	8.5
High Inc Adv III	N	7.14	7 5/8	+ 6.8	12.1
High Income Adv II	N	6.58	6 5/8	+ 0.7	14.0
High Income Adv Tr	N	5.94	6 1/4	+ 5.2	13.1
High Yield Income	N	7.79	8 1/2	+ 9.1	10.8
High Yield Plus	N	8.82	8 7/8	+ 0.6	9.5
Hyperion 1997 Tm	N	ac8.97	9 1/2	+ 5.9	N/A
Hyperion 1999 Tm	N	ac7.90	8 3/4	+ 10.8	8.3
Hyperion 2002 Tm	N	ac8.93	9 1/8	+ 2.2	N/A
Hyperion 2005 Inv	N	ac9.45	9 1/8	− 3.4	N/A
Hyperion Total Rtn	N	c10.72	11 3/8	+ 6.1	10.1
INA Investments	N	19.90	18 1/4	− 8.3	7.5
Inc Opp 1999	N	9.51	9 1/2	− 0.1	N/A
Inc Opp 2000	N	10.11	9 1/2	− 6.0	N/A
Independence Sq	O	18.66	18 1/2	− 0.9	7.8
InterCap Income	N	18.87	20 3/8	+ 8.0	8.3
J Hancock Income	N	17.16	17 1/2	+ 2.0	7.8
J Hancock Invest	N	22.75	23 3/4	+ 4.4	7.6
Kemper High Inc Tr	N	a9.21	9 7/8	+ 7.2	9.7
Kemper Int Govt Tr	N	a8.86	8 1/2	− 4.1	8.6
Kemper Multi Mkt	N	a11.21	11 3/8	+ 1.5	9.4
Liberty Tm Tr 1999	N	9.39	9 1/2	+ 1.2	8.6
Lincoln Nat Income	N	c30.99	30 1/4	− 2.4	8.5
MFS Charter Income	N	a10.62	10 1/8	− 4.7	8.6
MFS Govt Mkts Inc	N	a7.86	7 1/4	− 7.8	7.4
MFS Intmdt Inc Tr	N	a8.09	7 1/2	− 7.3	7.7
MFS Multimkt Inc	N	a7.75	7 1/4	− 6.5	8.2

Fund Name	Stock Exch	NAV	Market Price	Prem /Disc	12 mo Yield 6/30/93
Nuveen Muni Adv	N	a16.05	17	+ 5.9	7.4
Nuveen Muni Inco	N	a12.38	13 1/2	+ 9.0	6.2
Nuveen Muni Mkt Op	N	a16.36	17	+ 3.9	7.2
Nuveen Muni Value	N	a10.84	11 1/4	+ 3.8	6.1
Nuveen Perf Plus	N	a15.73	16 5/8	+ 5.7	7.2
Nuveen Prem Inc	N	a16.23	17 5/8	+ 8.6	7.6
Nuveen Prem Inc 2	N	a15.04	14 3/8	− 4.4	N/A
Nuveen Prem Inc 3	N	a15.21	14 1/2	− 4.7	N/A
Nuveen Prem Inc 4	N	a14.23	13 7/8	− 2.5	N/A
Nuveen Prem Inc 5	N	14.24	14 1/2	+ 1.8	N/A
Nuveen Prem Ins Mu	N	a15.69	15 1/4	− 2.8	6.2
Nuveen Prem Mu Inc	N	a15.52	15 1/8	− 2.5	6.4
Nuveen Qual Inc Mu	N	a16.00	16 1/8	+ 0.8	7.1
Nuveen Sel Mat Mu	N	a11.83	12	+ 1.4	N/A
Nuveen Sel Mat Mu2	N	a11.87	12	+ 1.1	N/A
Nuveen Sel Qual Mu	N	a15.90	16 3/8	+ 3.0	7.3
Nuveen Sel TF Inc	N	a15.38	15 1/4	− 0.8	6.2
Nuveen Sel TF Inc2	N	a15.14	14 7/8	− 1.8	5.6
Nuveen Sel TF Inc3	N	a14.58	14 1/8	− 3.1	N/A
Nuveen Sel TF Inc4	N	a14.82	14 5/8	− 1.3	N/A
PaineWbr Prem Ins	N	15.22	14 7/8	− 2.3	N/A
PaineWbr Prem TxFr	N	16.48	15 1/2	− 5.9	N/A
Putnam Hi Yld Muni	N	N/A	10 3/4	N/A	7.7
Putnam Inv Gr II	N	N/A	15	N/A	N/A
Putnam Inv Gr Int	A	N/A	14 5/8	N/A	N/A
Putnam Inv Gr Muni	N	N/A	14 1/2	N/A	6.7
Putnam Mgd Mu Inc	N	N/A	11 1/8	N/A	6.9
Putnam Muni Opp Tr	N	N/A	14 1/2	N/A	N/A
Putnam Tx-Fr Hlth	N	N/A	14 3/4	N/A	6.2
Seligman Qual Muni	N	15.98	15 1/2	− 3.0	6.2
Seligman Sel Muni	N	13.20	13 1/4	+ 0.4	6.5
Smith Barney Muni	A	15.63	15 1/8	− 3.2	N/A
Smith Brny Int Mu	A	10.77	10 3/4	− 0.2	5.5
Van Kamp Mun Op II	N	N/A	N/A	N/A	N/A
VanKamp Adv Mu Inc	N	a16.59	15 3/8	− 7.3	N/A
VanKamp Inv Gr Mu	N	11.93	13 5/8	+ 14.2	7.0
VanKamp Mu Inc Tr	N	a11.07	12 3/8	+ 11.8	6.9
VanKamp Mun Opp	N	a16.88	16	− 5.2	6.4
VanKamp Muni Trust	N	a16.80	16 3/8	− 2.5	6.7
VanKamp Strat Sec	N	a14.68	14 5/8	− 0.4	N/A
VanKamp Tr Ins Mu	N	a17.49	16 1/2	− 5.7	5.7
VanKamp Tr Inv Gr	N	a17.40	16 5/8	− 4.5	6.4
VanKamp Value Mun	N	a15.68	14 7/8	− 5.1	N/A
Single State Muni Bond					
BlckRk CA Ins 2008	N	a15.52	15	− 3.4	N/A
BlckRk CA Inv Qual	A	14.23	15	+ 5.4	N/A
BlckRk FL Ins 2008	N	a15.59	15 1/8	− 3.0	N/A
BlckRk FL Inv Qual	A	14.25	15	+ 5.3	N/A
BlckRk NJ Inv Qual	A	14.16	14 3/4	+ 4.2	N/A
BlckRk NY Ins 2008	N	a15.71	15 1/8	− 3.7	N/A
BlckRk NY Inv Qual	A	14.22	15	+ 5.5	N/A
Dreyfus CA Mu Inc	A	9.81	9 3/4	− 0.6	6.2
Dreyfus NY Mu Inc	A	10.45	10 7/8	+ 4.1	5.6
InterCap CA Ins	N	14.32	15 3/8	+ 7.4	N/A
Minn Muni Income	A	c14.22	15 1/8	+ 6.4	N/A
Minn Muni Tm Tr	N	c10.95	10 3/4	− 1.8	5.7
Minn Muni Tm Tr II	A	c10.66	10 1/2	− 1.5	5.7
MuniVest CA Ins Fd	N	14.56	14 3/4	+ 1.3	N/A
MuniVest FL Fund	N	14.58	15 1/8	+ 3.7	N/A
MuniVest MI Ins Fd	N	14.52	15	+ 3.3	N/A
MuniVest NJ Fund	N	14.58	15 1/8	+ 3.7	N/A
MuniVest NY Ins Fd	N	14.53	15	+ 3.2	N/A
MuniYield CA	N	15.96	15 3/8	− 3.7	6.5

Source: *Wall Street Journal,* July 12, 1993, C-13. Reprinted by permission of *The Wall Street Journal,* © 1993 Dow Jones & Company, Inc. All Right Reserved Worldwide.

and 1992. Notice once again the extraordinary growth in bond funds and money market mutual funds (MMMFs). The number of taxable MMMFs increased by almost 200 during the period from 1987 to 1992. A short description of a few of the major types of investment funds is given below.

• Major Types of Mutual Funds in a Nutshell •

Income Funds

Income funds invest primarily in securities that pay high dividends or interest so that a high level of current income can be provided to investors. Income funds can be organized as equity funds, as bond funds, or as mixed funds that incorporate both equity and debt securities.

Growth Funds

Growth funds emphasize high capital gains as the primary investment objective. Most growth funds emphasize established companies, though some "high-growth" funds seek to identify new and smaller companies that have potential for extraordinary growth.

Global Bond and Equity Funds

These funds see international diversification as an important objective. Securities of multinational companies and securities traded on foreign markets are emphasized. Global funds offer an additional layer of diversification against foreign exchange rate changes, which is an important attribute to some investors.

High-Yield Bond Funds

These funds emphasize investment in lower-rated corporate debt, generally junk bonds. These securities typically bear high rates of interest, but have a substantially higher probability of default. Investors in these funds are willing to bear a higher level of risk for the potential of high interest income and capital gains.

Taxable Money Market Mutual Funds

Often referred to as "money funds," or MMMFs, these funds emphasize investments in commercial paper, banker's acceptances, bank CDs, U.S. Treasury bills, and other high-grade money market instruments. The objective of MMMFs is to provide a stable asset portfolio whose income is competitive with open money market rates.

Tax-Exempt Money Market Mutual Funds

Tax-Exempt MMMFs specialize in short-term municipal bonds and notes, usually with maturities of 90 days or less. Income from these securities is generally not subject to federal income tax.

Growth and Trends in the Mutual Fund Industry

The investment orientation of mutual funds has changed dramatically over the years. Until relatively recently, most mutual funds were oriented toward equity markets. During the past decade, however, the industry has placed relatively greater emphasis on debt securities and money market instruments. Figure 7-4 shows the mean net acquisition by U.S. mutual funds of three categories of securities over the past four decades. Notice that during the 1950s and 1960s, mutual funds acquired

Figure 7-3

Number of Mutual Funds Classified by Investment Objective

Source: 1993 Mutual Fund Fact Book, *Investment Company Institute, Washington, D.C. p. 33. Reprinted with permission.*

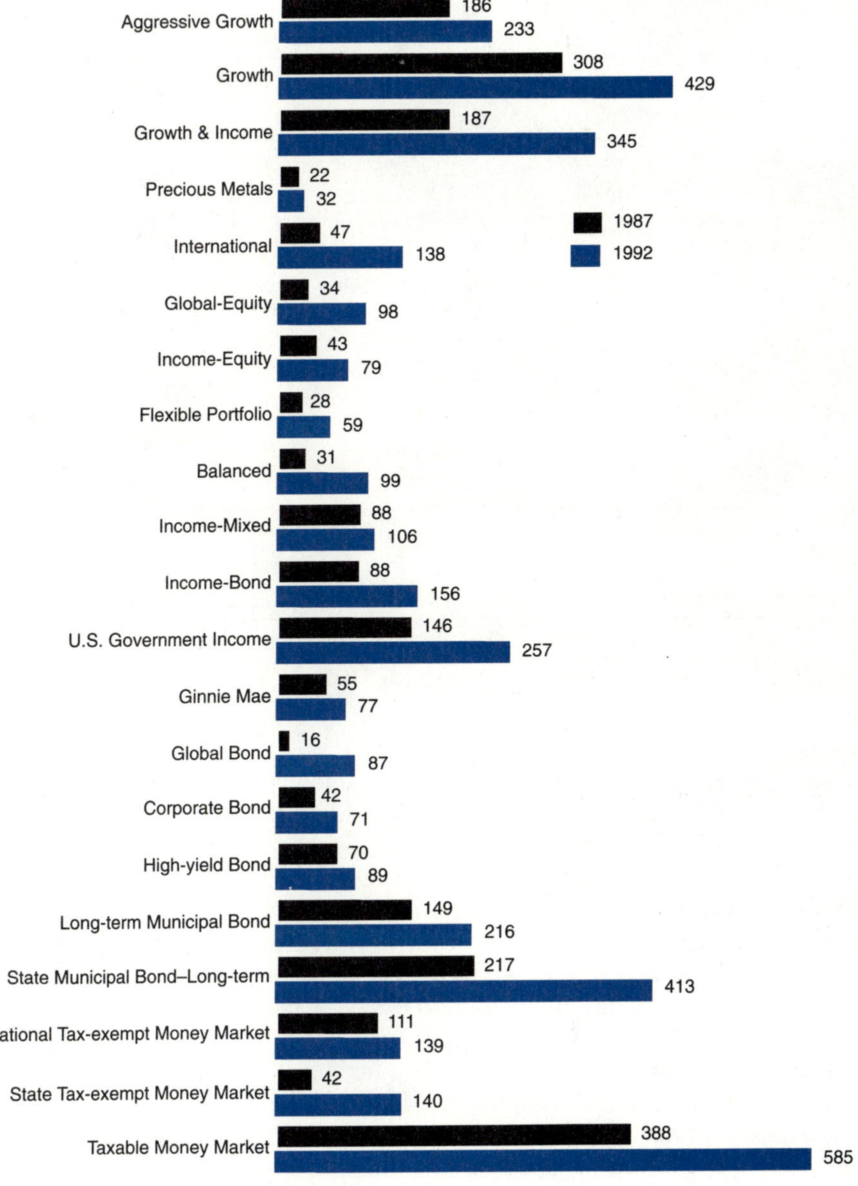

more stocks than bonds (MMMFs were not in existence until the early 1970s). During the 1970s and 1980s, net acquistion of bonds and money market instruments far exceeded net acquisition of stock.

Figure 7-4
Net Acquisition of Mutual Fund Assets

Source: "Changes in Financial Intermediation: The Role of Pension and Mutual Funds" by G. Sellon, Jr., Economics Review, *Federal Reserve Bank of Kansas City, 3rd Quarter 1992, pp. 53–70.*

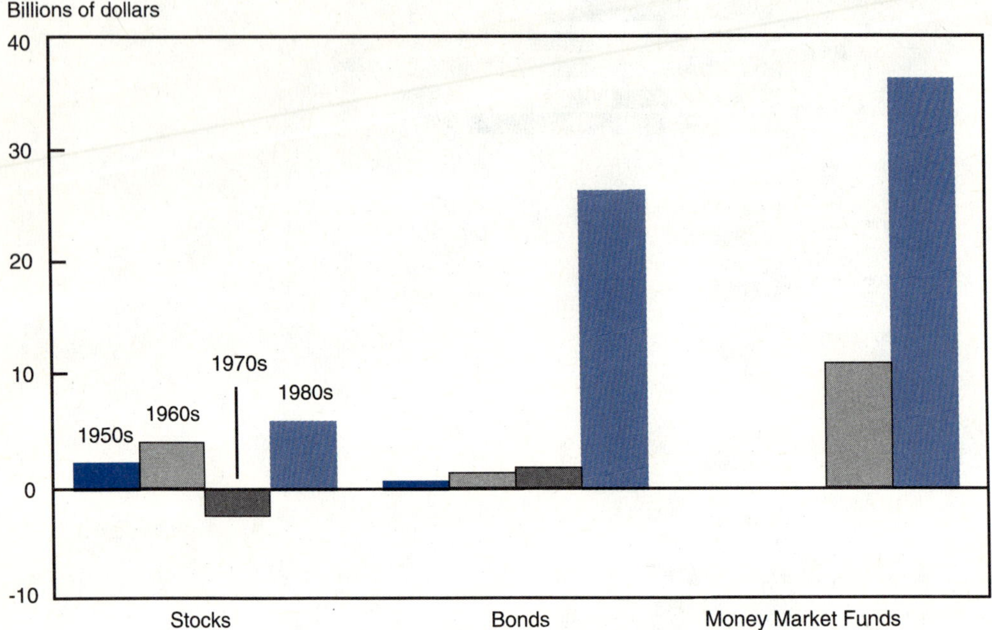

The trend toward mutual fund investment in money market instruments and bonds is further highlighted by Figure 7-5, which shows the percentage distribution of total mutual fund assets by four general categories of funds: equity, bond and income, taxable MMMF, and tax-exempt MMMF. The distribution is illustrated for years 1982 and 1992. Taxable MMMFs were in their heyday during the early 1980s, when they attracted billions of dollars of deposits away from more heavily regulated banks and savings institutions. Almost 70 percent of total mutual assets were concentrated in the taxable money funds during 1982. At the same time, equity funds held 17.1 percent of total assets, compared to 8.9 percent for bond funds. By 1992, the taxable MMMFs had lost ground to money market deposit accounts, shrinking the percentage of total assets in taxable MMMFs to 28 percent, almost equal to the share held by stock funds, 29.7 percent. The most significant change was due to the increase in percentage of total assets held in bond and income funds—36.3 percent. Thus, bond and income funds have grown most dramatically during the 1980s, to lead the mutual fund industry by percentage of total assets.

These illustrations reflect the dramatic growth in the number of mutual funds in operation during the past decade. In 1982, there were a total of 857 mutual funds in the United States, of which 539 were stock, bond, or income funds. The remaining

Figure 7-5
Percent Distribution of Total Net Assets by Type of Fund
Source: 1993 Mutual Fund Fact Book, *Investment Company Institute, Washington, D.C. p. 24. Reprinted with permission.*

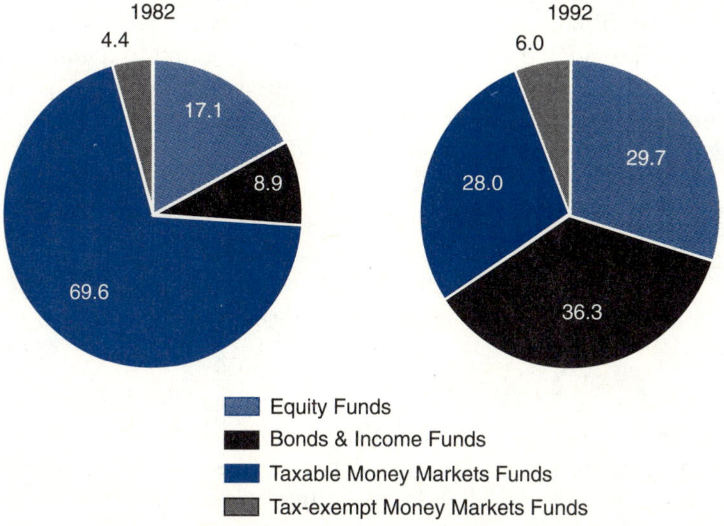

318 were MMMFs. By 1992, there were a total of 3848 mutual funds. Of that total, there were 2984 stock, bond, and income funds, and 864 MMMFs. During the year 1992 alone, sales in stock mutual funds were $142.8 billion and in bond funds $219.6 billion. By year's end 1992, total net assets in the mutual fund industry had reached $1.6 trillion, as compared with less than $1 trillion, just three years earlier, a three-year growth of over $600 billion.

Regulation of Mutual Funds

Regulations governing mutual funds require exhaustive disclosure to the SEC, state regulators, and fund shareholders. Mutual funds are among the most regulated entities in the securities industry. The Securities Act of 1933 was the first major legislation to set out regulations for mutual fund organizations. Under the 1933 Act, mutual funds were required to file a registration statement with the SEC that provided extensive information about the fund. The Act also requires the fund to give investors a current prospectus that discloses details of the fund's management, investment policies, and objectives. As is generally the case with all traded securities, the purchase and sale of mutual fund shares are subject to the Securities Exchange Act of 1934. The SEC and the NASD are responsible for regulating the distribution of mutual fund shares. Investment advisors to mutual funds are regulated by the Investment Advisors Act of 1940. The Investment Company Act of 1940 contains numerous provisions designed to protect investors in mutual funds. In particular, these provisions are intended to prevent abuses by managers of mutual fund assets such as self-dealing and other conflicts of interest. The Act is also designed to prevent funds from charging excessive fees for buying and selling shares.

As regards taxation, mutual funds are covered under Subchapter M of the Internal Revenue Code, which allows the fund income to be taxed only once, when received by the fund's owners. In order to qualify under Subchapter M, funds must typically distribute most of their income and capital gains to shareholders. An important aspect of this tax treatment is that the character of the distributions to owners is preserved. Owners must recognize income and capital gains distributed from the fund as such on their own tax returns. In order to qualify under Subchapter M, funds must meet certain requirements regarding asset diversification and sources of income and capital gains and must demonstrate that they distribute more than 90 percent of their taxable income to shareholders.

• Real Estate Investment Trusts Outperform the Market During 1992 •

Real estate investment trusts (REITs) are investment companies that specialize in real estate property. REITs can be viewed as a close relative to closed-end mutual funds. Both organizations raise money through the sale of a fixed number of shares of stock, but rather than investing the money in securities, as closed-end mutual funds do, REITs invest in real estate. The major advantages of REITs over direct investment in real estate properties are two. First, REITs spread investment capital out among a number of real properties, to give investors better diversification. While the benefit of diversification is common to both REITs and other closed-end investment companies, it can be especially important with regard to real estate investments. Real estate markets are especially prone to geographic downturns like the recent real ones in Texas and New England. REITs offer a mechanism to diversify real estate investment across different regional markets, offering better protection against devastating local downturns in prices. Another advantage associated with investment through a REIT is liquidity. REIT shares are traded over public security markets. This enables investors to sell off their investment more easily, and with lower transaction costs, than selling real estate property itself, which often involves a significant commission or brokerage fee.

The performance of REITs during 1992 was remarkable, especially considering how badly investments in real estate performed during the previous decade. In 1992, an index of REITs increased in value by 17 percent and outperformed the Standard & Poor's 500 by about 14 percent.[5] This is apparently due to some bargain hunting by REIT operators, which paid off. As the commercial real estate market bottomed out and the Resolution Trust Corporation auctioned off property of defunct savings and loans, REIT operators were able to pick up good property at relatively low prices. Some economists forecast that as the economy picks up, and rents of commercial properties of many REITs roll over at higher rates, REIT stock will continue to do well.

[5]See Weiss (1993) for detailed discussion.

Pension Funds

Pension funds are investment funds organized to provide retirement income to pension plan participants. Most pension plans are designed to receive contributions from individual participants (or their sponsors) during their income-earning years, to build a retirement fund. Fund assets are generally managed by professional investment managers. Once retirement age is reached, the fund is systematically liquidated, often in the form of an annuity, to provide retirement income to the participant.

In this section, we consider a variety of investment plans and organizations designed to provide retirement income to owners or participants. Though we may refer to these organizations broadly as "pension funds," we also include in our discussions a number of retirement plans that are not sponsored by employers, such as individual retirement accounts (IRAs) and Keough accounts.

Types of Pension Plans

All pension plans may be classified as either public or private plans. Public pension plans are those sponsored by a government agency. Many retirees from the federal government benefit from a federal employees' pension plan. In addition, most state governments offer pension benefits to their employees. For example, California has one of the largest public pension plans in the United States serving its state employees. Compared with the number of existing public pension plans, there are many more private pension plans, those provided by private companies to their employees. Most major companies offer pension benefits as a part of employee compensation.

Although employer pension plans vary in design, they can usually be classified into two broad types: defined-benefit plans and defined-contribution plans. The defined-contribution plan is the simpler of the two. Under a defined contribution plan, the employer or sponsor makes a predetermined contribution to an account held in trust in the employee's name. In a contributory plan the employee also makes a predetermined contribution. Contributions by the employer and the employee are usually specified as a fixed percentage of the employee's salary. For example, the employer might contribute 8 percent of the employee's salary while the employee contibutes 5 percent. As a result, a total of 13 percent of the employee's salary would be contributed to the employee's pension account during each year of employment.

The defined-contribution plan works like a tax-deferred retirement account. Contributions made by both the employer and the employee are deductible for computing their respective taxable incomes. In addition, taxes on earnings on the employee's account are deferred. At retirement, the employee receives a lump sum or an annuity, the amount of which depends on the accumulated value in the account. In most cases, the employee has some control over how the money in the account is invested that can affect the earnings growth in the account. That is, employees generally have some options on how much of the account is invested in bonds, stock, or money market instruments. At the same time, however, employees bear the investment risk associated with their selections.

Defined-benefit plans are slightly more complicated. Under a defined-benefit plan, the pension benefit is determined by a formula that takes into account the employee's history of service and salary. The major difference between the defined-contribution and the defined-benefit plan is that, under the latter benefits are defined and will not fluctuate with the performance of investments in the fund. Pension fund assets under defined-benefit plans typically are managed by a trustee, who often employs professional investment managers to handle the accounts in order to meet defined-benefit obligations.

Under most defined-benefit plans, the benefits are determined by the employee's salary during the last year, or last few years, of service. For example, an employee might receive 2 percent of her final annual salary for each year of service. An employee who earned \$80,000 per year at retirement with 25 years of service would receive \$40,000 in retirement benefits per year from the employer (0.02 × 25 × \$80,000). In this case, the employee receives 50 percent of final salary in retirement benefits. This percentage is often referred to as the "salary replacement rate." Most plans are designed to provide replacement rates of around 30 percent. Some "integrated plans," are designed in conjunction with Social Security benefits to provide employees with replacement rates from combined benefits of around 60 percent. In integrated plans, benefit payments from the private pension fund would be increased or decreased to offset changes in social security benefits.

While defined-benefit plans provide some protection against the investment performance of the fund, employees often must establish a minimum term of service to qualify for benefits. Such provisions are called "vesting requirements." For example, a new employee may have to satisfy a simple five-year vesting requirement in order to receive pension benefits from employer contributions. This implies that, during the first five years of employment, the employer will make normal pension contributions to the employee's account. Once the employee has worked five years, the benefits from these contributions are "vested"; that is, they are guaranteed regardless of whether the employee stays with the sponsoring company. If the employee leaves the firm before five years of service, the benefits may be lost.

Growth in Pension Funds

Though all types of pension plans have experienced strong growth during the past four decades, most of the growth has occurred in private pension funds. During the 1980s, however, the growth in private plans slowed somewhat, while growth in public pension funds accelerated. These trends are illustrated more clearly in Figure 7-6, which documents net financial acquisitions (financial assets purchased less financial assets sold) for private and public pension funds during each of the past four decades. Notice that net assets acquired by private funds are greater than those acquired by state and local pension funds for each of the decades of the 1950s, the 1960s, and the 1970s. In particular, by 1970, acquisitons by public funds were about \$44 billion while acquisitions by state and local funds were about \$24 billion. During the 1980s, however, net acquisitions by state and local plans were about \$45 billion whereas net acquisitions by public plans were about \$39 billion.

Historically, much of the increase in pension fund assets has been in equities. In 1952, pension funds held less than 1 percent of corporate stock outstanding. By

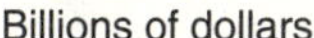

Figure 7-6

Growth of Private and Public Pension Plans

Source: "Changes in Financial Intermediation: The Role of Pension and Mutual Funds," by G. Sellon, Jr., Economics Review, *Federal Reserve Bank of Kansas City, 3rd Quarter 1992, pp. 53–70.*

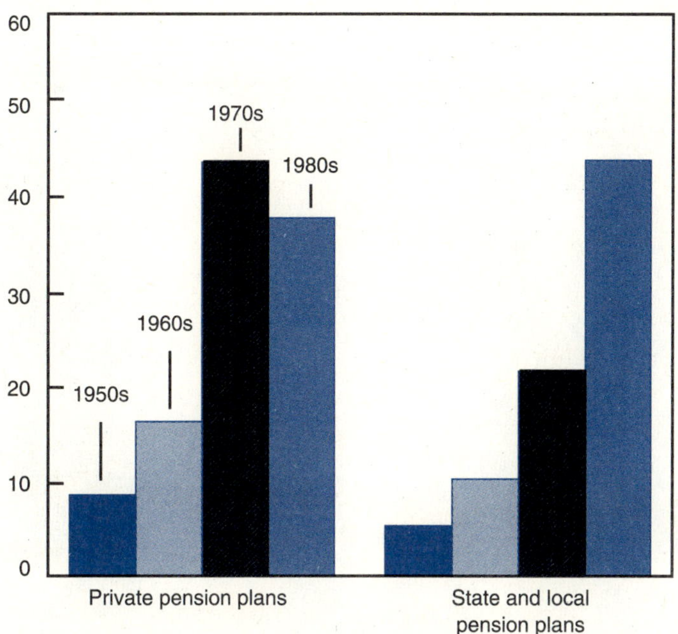

*Note: Mean net acquisition of real financial assets by decade.

1991, such funds held about 25 percent of outstanding corporate stock. The emphasis on stocks as a source of growth in pension fund assets was fueled largely by the relatively strong performance and higher returns of the stock market during the late 1950s and 1960s. By contrast, during the 1970s and 1980s investment by mutual funds swung away from equity securities to bonds. Since bonds provide fixed cash flows over long periods of time, they are natural investments to hedge future pension liabilities. The higher yields on most classes of bonds during the late 1970s and early 1980s made bonds the investment of choice for most pension plans. This shift in investment orientation is illustrated in Figure 7-7, which shows net asset acquisitions by private pension funds in stocks and bonds over the past four decades. Acquistions of stocks clearly dominated those of bonds during the 1960s, though during the 1970s net acquistions of stocks and bonds by private plans were nearly equal, about $15 billion each. During the 1980s, a period of high yields on most debt securities, acquisition of bonds was about $20 billion, compared to about $2 billion for stocks.

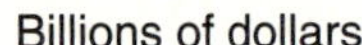

Figure 7-7.
Assets of Private Pension Plans
Source: "Changes in Financial Intermediation: The Role of Pension and Mutual Funds," by G. Sellon, Jr., Economics Review, *Federal Reserve Bank of Kansas City, 3rd Quarter 1992, pp. 53–70.*

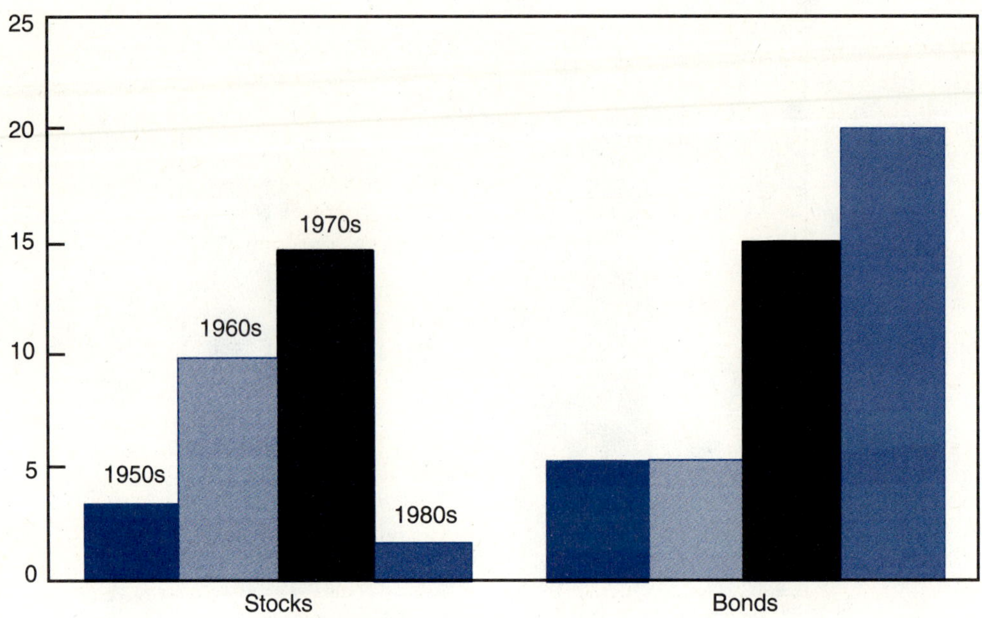

*Note: Mean net acquisition of real financial assets by decade.

Federal tax policy has been the principal reason for rapid growth in pension fund assets—from a relatively few plans during the early 1950s to more than 65,000 insured pension plans during the early 1990s. The tax-deductibility of pension contributions made pension benefits an attractive form of worker compensation for many employers. At the same time, pension funds provided employees the attractive combination of deferral of taxes on earnings and investment diversification.

Retirement Plans

Several types of retirement plans qualify for income tax deferment similar to that afforded to pension funds. In some cases, these plans are intended to provide a substitute retirement plan for individuals who are self-employed or who otherwise do not benefit from the tax-deferred savings opportunities of employer-sponsored pension plans. At the same time, however, these plans offer many persons a means of supplementing retirement income from sponsored plans and social security.

• *Types of Retirement Plans in a Nutshell* •

Individual Retirement Accounts

IRAs are one of the most common plans used by individuals to establish a tax-deferred retirement account. Any wage-earner under the age of 70 1/2 years may set up an IRA. Up to $2000 per year can be contributed to the account. Taxes on earnings of the account are deferred until they are withdrawn, usually after retirement. In addition, the amount contributed to the account may be wholly or partially tax deductible. Under the Tax Reform Act of 1986, all taxpayers covered by an employer-sponsored pension plan may take the full deduction for IRA contributions. Those who are covered by an employer-sponsored plan may currently take a deduction if the individual's income is below $25,000 (or $40,000 for married couples who file jointly). While IRAs do not provide individuals with higher incomes a tax deduction for contributions, they do shield the earnings on the account from taxation until they are withdrawn at retirement. If money is withdrawn from the account before age 59 1/2 the amount withdrawn is taxed as ordinary income and a penalty tax of 10 percent is applied. Amounts withdrawn after retirement are taxed as ordinary income. Finally, individuals are required to begin withdrawals by age 70 1/2 years.

Keough Plans

Keough plans, named after the sponsoring legislator, are retirement plans designed to provide self-employed workers with retirement savings opportunities similar to those available to participants in employer-sponsored plans and IRAs. Keough plans operate much the same as IRAs but may be established as defined-benefit or defined-contribution plans. The maximum contribution to the plan is 20 percent of profits up to a maximum of $30,000 per year. Contributions to the plan are tax deductible, and earnings accumulate tax sheltered. As with IRAs, early withdrawals (before age 59 1/2) are general subject to the 10 percent penalty tax in addition to taxation as ordinary income.

Section 403(b) and 401(k) Plans

Under Section 403(b) of the Internal Revenue Code, individuals employed by certain charitable organizations and public school systems may establish tax-sheltered retirement programs. 403(b) programs are similar to IRAs as regards tax benefits. Under Section 401(k), the IRS allows employees of a corporate or noncorporate sponsor to have a portion of their compensation contributed to a tax-sheltered plan. Amounts contributed to 401(k) plans accumulate tax free and and are often matched by contributions by sponsoring employers.

Employee Stock Option Plans (ESOPs)

ESOPs are a special type of defined-contribution plan in which employees of a company receive shares of the sponsoring company's stock. From the employer's standpoint, ESOPs provide two important advantages. First, ESOPs provide an important tax benefit to the employing firm in that contributions to the ESOP are tax deductible. Second, as employees become owners of the the firm's stock, ESOPs provide employees with incentives to be more productive. Ownership of the firm's shares aligns the interests of employees with those of other shareholders. ESOPs have one important drawback as well: when retirement benefits are received in the form of shares of stock, an individual's retirement account becomes concentrated in one investment. In other private pension funds, retirement contributions are ordinarily diversified among a number of different securities, which provides employees a reasonable degree of diversification.

Regulation of Pension Funds

Although pension funds have been regulated at both the state and federal level for many years, the major legislation governing the operation of pension funds was passed in 1974 as the Employee Retirement Income Security Act. One of the major components of ERISA was the creation of the Pension Benefit Guarantee Corporation (PBGC), a government corporation that insures defined-benefit pension obligations of participating pension funds. It operates much like the FDIC has done for banks for many years. The PBGC charges pension fund sponsors a fee each year to insure the benefits of the fund's beneficiaries (the employees). In the event a fund is terminated, the PBGC pays the accumulated pension obligations of the fund. As of 1992, more than 67,000 plans covering more than 41 million workers and retirees were insured by the PBGC. The accumulated liabilities of insured plans was about $900 billion.

The annual premium charged for PBGC insurance is $19 per insured participant. A surcharge of up to $53 per participant is attached to the basic premium, depending on the funding status of the plan. If a plan is "fully funded," meaning there are sufficient assets in the fund to meet future pension obligations, a surcharge is not required. If the plan is underfunded, however, a surcharge is imposed, the amount of which depends on the degree of underfunding. Under current premium limits imposed by the Congress the maximum annual premium the PBGC can charge is $72 per participant.

Recent deficits at the PBGC have caused some concern over the solvency of the insurance fund. A "deficit" refers to the extent to which the PBGC's liabilities exceed its assets. In 1991, the PBGC took over the failed plans of Pan American World Airways and Eastern Air Lines, causing the PBGC's deficit to increase by $2.5 billion. In 1992, the deficit increased by another $200 million. Some economists find the growing PBGC deficit reminiscent of the FSLIC, which became insolvent after enormous numbers of failures of insured S&Ls. To some extent, current difficulties at the PBGC may be due to its insurance pricing system. The premium pricing system employed by the PBGC is similar to that employed by the FDIC to insure the deposits of banks and savings and loans. As explained above, the premium charged varies only according to the funding status of the insured plan. No surcharge is applied to adjust the premium for the financial risk associated with the fund's assets. In other words, the premium is not adjusted for asset risk. As we discussed in Chapter 5, this was a fatal flaw in the deposit insurance–pricing system, which led to problems at the FSLIC, and which may hold the same dangers for the PBGC. It is widely believed that the fixed-premium insurance system operated by the FSLIC instilled in savings and loan managers incentives to take risks. If risky investments went sour, the FSLIC would pick up the tab; if they paid off returns would be high. Similar incentives are in place for sponsors of PBGC-insured pension plans. Pension funds pay the same premium to insure employee benefits, regardless of the risk of their investment portfolio. Thus, managers of pension assets have similar incentives to increase asset risk that is underwritten by the PBGC. Because premiums are not adjusted for risk, some believe that the federal goverment someday will face a bailout of the PBGC similar to the savings and loan debacle of the 1980s.

Other important components of ERISA are directed at the management of fund assets. Before ERISA, sponsoring firms were not responsible for the pension plans they initiated. Under ERISA, the ultimate responsibility for employee pension benefits resides with the employer. ERISA also established standards for management of fund assets. Generally, under these standards, fund managers are expected to operate under the so-called prudent man rule. Under this rule, managers act as a prudent, knowledgeable, disinterested professionals in managing the fund's investments. Essentially, managers who behave according to the prudent man rule make decisions that are in the best interests of pension beneficiaries. Other restrictions placed on pension fund managers under ERISA are designed to increase the amount of funds supporting future pension liabilities. Though ERISA does not ensure that every fund will be fully funded, it reduces the chance that a given fund will eventually be unable to meet pension claims. In 1981, 45 percent of the plans insured by the PBGC were fully funded. By 1992, 85 percent of insured defined-benefit plans were fully funded.

Finally, ERISA established a system of minimum vesting requirements. Employers are allowed to adopt one of two minimum vesting arrangements. The first is to give 100-percent vesting after five years with no partial vesting prior to five years' employment. The second alternative allows employers to phase in vesting over a period from three years of employment to seven years. Prior to ERISA, employers sometimes would fire employees after many years of service but prior to vesting, to avoid paying pension benefits. Minimum vesting requirements are designed to protect employees from such practices.

SUMMARY

This chapter has described and discussed the three major kinds of non-depository intermediaries: insurance companies, investment companies, and pension funds. Each provides distinct and important financial services to both individuals and business firms, and in so doing each serves as a conduit to channel individual savings to the money and capital markets. The primary service provided by insurance companies is the pooling and underwriting of risk. Insurance companies collect premiums from policyholders and invest in a variety of government and corporate securities. Investment companies provide a similar service in providing a economical means of diversifying investment risk. Investors in mutual funds receive a pro rata share of a portfolio of securities. Portfolios of mutual funds usually consist of corporate stocks, bonds, or money markets securities. Pension funds provide a means for individuals to save for retirement. Employer or employee contributions to a pension or retirement plan are invested in stocks, bonds, and other financial instruments.

The discussion in this chapter identified the major characteristics of each of the nondepository firms. Insurance companies can be classified into two general types: life and health insurers and property and casualty insurers. We discussed the basic types of policies offered by each type and provided a simple illustration of how insurance underwriters are efficient in pooling large numbers of risks. Investment companies may also be classified as two types: open-end and closed-end investment funds. The important aspects of investment in each type of fund were explained. The distribution and pricing of mutual fund shares were also described. There are also two important categories of pension plans: defined-benefit plans and defined-contribution plans. Advantages and disadvantages of each kind of plan to employees were discussed. The importance of ERISA in regulating pension plans was also explained.

QUESTIONS

1. Explain the difference between a mutual insurance company and a stock insurance company.
2. What is the difference between term insurance and whole life insurance? Explain the advantages or disadvantages of each.
3. Decreasing and increasing term insurance are specialized types of term insurance. Explain the specific objectives of each.
4. An insurance policy is written for $1 million to insure the life of a 40-year-old female executive of a medium-sized company. The policy is straight term insurance that may be renewed annually. The underwriter estimates the probability of death for a 40-year old woman to be 0.00075 during the next year. Administrative costs, overhead, and profit are charged to this category of policies at the rate of 4.5 cents per $1000 in insured value. Determine the annual premium charged by the underwriter in issuing this policy.
5. Explain and compare single-premium deferred annuities and guaranteed investment contracts.
6. Property-casualty insurance companies often maintain equity levels (as a percentage of assets) two to three times higher than comparable life and health insurance companies. Explain why.
7. Explain the difference between open-end and closed-end mutual funds. How is the value of a share in each type of fund related to the net asset value of the fund?
8. Explain the difference between defined-contribution pension plans and defined-benefit pension plans.
9. What are vesting requirements? What protection does ERISA provide pension participants regarding vesting provisions?

REFERENCES

Bodie, Z. "Pension Funds and Financial Innovation." *Financial Management* Autumn (1990), pp. 11–22.

Gottschalk,E. "Balanced Funds Don't All Weigh Alike." *Wall Street Journal,* May 20, 1993, p. C1.

Jereski, L. "Seized Insurer's Woes Reflect Perils of CMOs." *Wall Street Journal,* May 12, 1993, p. C1.

Jereski, L. and F. Rose, "Executive Life Bailout Springs Big Leaks." *Wall Street Journal,* April 2, 1993, p. C1.

Hardy, Q. "Pension Funds Rush to Japan." *Wall Street Journal,* February 4, 1993, p. C1.

Light, L., K. Holland, K. Kerwin, and S. Baker. "Many Unhappy Returns." *Business Week* May 31 (1993), pp. 76–77.

Roush, C. "The Weather Has Home Insurers Running Scared." *Business Week* April 5 (1993), p. 30.

Schroeder, M. "The Crying Game Over Pensions." *Business Week* April 5, (1993), pp. 70–71.

Smart, T., and C. Roush. "Insurer's Scramble to Spread the Risks." *Business Week* April 19, (1993), pp. 98–99.

Todd, R.M., and N. Wallace. "SPDAs and GICs: Like Money in the Bank." *Quarterly Review* [Federal Reserve Bank of Minneapolis] Summer (1992), pp. 2–15.

Weiss, G. "When Is It Un-Real Estate?" *Business Week* March 29 (1993), p. 79.

Wooley, S., and G. DeGeorge. "Why Insurance Rates Have Lost Their Old Bounce." *Business Week* May 10 (1993), pp. 52–53.

• Chapter 8
Global Financial Markets

As multinational corporations advanced into the international marketplace over the past three decades, a parallel development took place in the availability and sophistication of financial products and services offered worldwide. Certainly these developments are related. Expansion of commercial activity, domestically or abroad, involves a requisite increase in the support from all operating factors. As U.S. firms increased their activities in foreign countries the demand for financial services abroad increased as well. Thus, as individual economies continue to be integrated in a global economy, financial markets become ever more global in their orientation and operation.

It is useful to visualize the globalization of world financial markets as proceeding along two major dimensions. The first involves the expansion of commercial banking in the international marketplace to collect deposits, make loans, and carry out a variety of other banking services on a worldwide basis. International activities of commercial banks have grown most dramatically in recent years, owing to the substantial deregulation of banking markets around the world and advances in electronic data processing and communications technology that make possible foreign operations abroad.

The second dimension in the development of global financial marketplace concerns the securities markets. World securities markets are rapidly becoming interconnected through international operations of banks and securities firms, electronic communications networks and automated trading systems, cross-listing of securities on major international exchanges, and the use of after-hours trading sessions and 24-hour trading systems. The combination of technological breakthroughs and substantial financial deregulation worldwide has been directly responsible for significant integration of major markets in securities during recent years.

In the sections that follow we describe major developments in the globalization of financial markets. We begin with a general discussion of how the integration of financial markets worldwide confers benefits on both demanders and suppliers of funds. Opportunities for enhanced diversification and liquidity are discussed and contributing advances in market technology are identified. We then discuss the role of multinational banking in the global financial economy. Two important dimensions of international banking are explained: the operations of domestic banks in foreign markets, and the operations of domestic banks in the unregulated offshore markets—in particular, the Eurocurrency and Eurocredit markets. Then, we describe the internationalization of world securities markets. Specifically, we discuss integration of major stock and bond markets into the international environment.

• *Key Learning Concepts in Chapter 8* •

- Benefits of enhanced diversification, greater availability of funds, and increased liquidity created by globalization of financial markets
- Key characteristics of multinational banks
- Differences between the U. S. banking system and banking systems in other countries
- How securities markets have become globalized

The Globalizaton of Financial Markets

The globalization of financial markets involves numerous activities, innovations, and institutional changes that increase cross-borders access to financial markets. Historically, international financial activity has increased apace with international trade. As U.S. corporations began to extend themselves internationally, the need for trade and corporate financial services increased. Banks were among the first to respond to the international needs of their corporate clients by establishing a variety of operations, both at home and offshore, that assist in trade finance, international payments, and currency transactions. As the offshore financial markets developed, banks began to play a more important role in long-term financing activities of major customers. Banks serve as primary underwriters of international corporate debt, particularly in the syndication and placement of medium- and long-term debt issued in the Euromarkets. Finally, banks play a major role as intermediaries in markets for foreign currency, foreign currency options and forward contracts, and foreign currency and interest rate swaps.

The internationalization of financial markets and services has also been influenced by deregulation and the development of technology. Advances in data processing and telecommunications, liberalization of financial restrictions and regulations both in the United States and other countries, and greater competition from foreign countries have built up momentum leading toward further integration of world financial markets.

Benefits of Global Financial Markets

The integration of world financial markets provides significant benefits for both demanders and suppliers of funds. Investors are afforded more extensive investment alternatives and greater opportunities to diversify risk. Borrowers are afforded greater access to broader markets for funds. The integration of world financial markets provides the mechanism to allow funds to migrate toward their most efficient users, reinforcing incentives to save and invest and serving to enhance world productivity.

International Diversification

The benefits to investors associated with international diversification are evidenced in practice by the recent increase in the number of mutual funds that emphasize diversification in stock markets around the world. The benefits of international diversification have been understood for some time. Over the years, economists have extensively studied and compared the performance of domestic and international portfolios of stocks. The conclusion of these studies have consistently been that investors can significantly decrease risk by diversifying investment portfolios across international markets. This prospect is illustrated in Figure 8-1.[1]

A fundamental concept of investment theory is the notion of portfolio diversification which was introduced in Chapter 3. While we will not develop the concept fully in this chapter, diversification refers to the effect caused by dividing investments among several assets rather than concentrating investment in a small number of assets or in a single asset. If returns on alternative assets are not perfectly correlated, diversification of investments will reduce the variability, or risk, of the investment returns. In measuring the effects of diversification on investment portfolios, the most common measure of risk is the variance of the portfolio return on investment.

Figure 8-1 shows the variance of weekly returns of portfolios of randomly selected stocks traded on the NYSE for portfolios of increasing numbers of securities. For example, a U.S. portfolio of ten stocks was assembled by randomly picking ten companies from the list of all NYSE firms and computing the weekly stock returns for those companies over a five-year period. The equally weighted portfolio return was computed by simple averaging of the weekly return series. The risk, or variance, of the portfolio was then computed from the portfolio return series.

Two strategies are represented in Figure 8-1. In one strategy, only United States securities are included in it. The size of the portfolio is varied to show the effect of diversification as more stocks are included in it. Notice that when about 20 to 25 U.S. stocks are incorporated in the U.S. portfolio, the risk of the portfolio reaches its minimum, at about 26 percent, indicating the benefits of diversification have been exhausted.

The second strategy is identical to the first, except that international stocks are randomly included in the portfolio. Notice how the variability of portfolio returns decreases faster as the size of the portfolio increases. Again, when 20 to 25 stocks are included in the portfolio, its variance return bottoms out at 11.7 percent, less than half the risk of the domestic portfolio. This illustrates the incentive for investors to diversify their financial investments internationally. Similar incentives for diversification in other financial markets account for the variety of investment funds that are "globally oriented" to foreign equity and debt markets.

The potential benefits to investors from international diversification are underlined by the demand for membership by foreign brokerage firms on major stock exchanges. For example, after the "big bang" in the United Kingdom during 1986, which began deregulation of London financial markets, many U.S. securities firms

[1]Figure 8-1 is from Solnik (1974). The returns used in his study were collected over the period 1966–1971. Variance is computed from weekly returns on equally weighted portfolios.

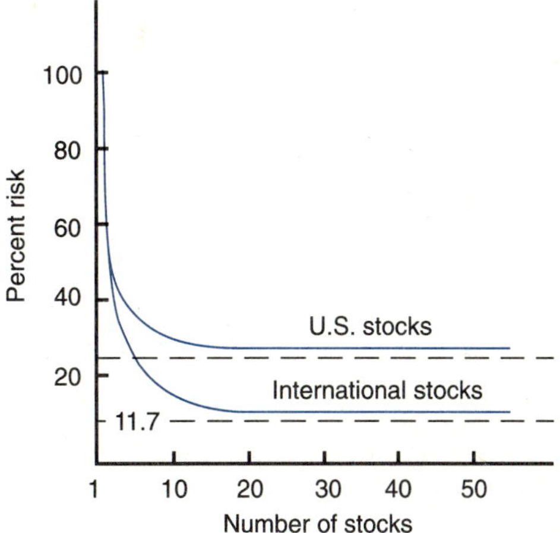

Figure 8-1

International Diversification. *Source: Reprinted, with permission, from* Financial Analysts Journal, *July/August 1974. Copyright 1974, The Financial Analysts Federation, Charlottesville, VA. All Rights Reserved.*

applied for seats on the London exchange. Deregulation in the United Kingdom significantly enhanced access to U.K. equity markets by U.S. financial institutions, which ultimately improved the efficiency of diversification to U.S. investors. Additionally, demand for international diversification is also evidenced by the practice of cross-listing. Cross-listing occurs when a company lists and trades its securities over several different exchanges or trading centers. For example, an American firm may list its stock on the London Stock Exchange as well as the NYSE.

Access and Liquidity

Another important benefit derived from the globalization of financial markets is the added depth and liquidity afforded by a broader and larger number of markets participants. A *liquid market* is one where the size of an order has a minimal effect on the transactions price. *Depth* refers to the number of participants in the market who are ready to transact at a given price. For a market to be sufficiently liquid, there must be sufficient depth that when an order arrives, say to buy securities, there are sufficient orders to sell that the market price is not moved drastically. Globalization of financial markets has increased market depth and contributed to liquidity in many circumstances. In turn, liquid markets become more attractive to investors, as they involve less risk when investments are converted to cash.

Increased liquidity of global financial markets has been the direct result of advances in communications technology that speed exchange of information among international trading centers and of the integration of major trading exchanges worldwide. Information about foreign firms is essential if domestic investors are to make timely investment decisions. Recent advances in information technology have increased the familiarity of investors worldwide with foreign corporations and opened up additional savings and investment opportunities for investment firms and individuals. Electronic communications and trade execution has been key in facilitating trading from foreign sources.

To a large extent, access to foreign markets has been facilitated by after-hours trading and automation. After-hours trading refers to special trading sessions that are organized by major securities exchanges after regular business hours. For example, the NYSE began limited after-hours trading sessions in 1991. Other major exchanges, including the American Exchange, the Philadelphia Exchange, and National Associaton of Securities Dealers Automated Quotation (NASDAQ) system have followed with plans to extend trading hours. A major motive for extending the trading day is to be able to make transactions during trading hours in other parts of the world.

Automated trading systems have been introduced in many of the world's markets, not only to expedite trading and introduce the economies of electronic clearing, but also to provide a 24-hour trading mechanism linking the world's markets. One of the first development in computerized market trading began in 1971 with the NASDAQ system, which provided price information for several thousand companies. By the early 1980s, the National Association of Securities Dealers (NASD) had developed the National Market System, providing investors with transactions data as they occurred. And by 1991, the Private Offerings, Resales, and Trading through Automated Linkages (PORTAL) system was developed, which enables users to trade in unregistered securities worldwide. NASD has also established an automated trading system that is linked to major stock exchanges in London and Singapore. This enables NASDAQ to provide cross-listing of foreign securities and automated trade execution, enhancing its position as a major market for domestic and foreign securities.

Another example of an automated system is Globex, an electronic trading system for futures trading recently designed by the Chicago Mercantile Exchange (CME). Globex was originated as an after-hours trading system that automatically matches and executes orders according to price and time priority. The CME uses Globex to provide access to the market after the close of business. The CME hoped to regain some of its market share recently lost to foreign exchanges. Yet another trend toward 24-hour trading is the practice of "passing the book," passing trading control from one trader to another, around the globe. For example, a currency trader may be waiting for a particular price at which to buy or sell foreign currency. When trading is closed in one market, say a U.S. exchange, the trader may "pass the book" to another trader where foreign currency markets are beginning to open, perhaps in Singapore. Trading instructions would be communicated from one trader to the next. This procedure enables the first trader to have the benefit of 24-hour trading involving a sequence of markets around the world and to execute the trade when the desired price first becomes available. The continued development of 24-hour electronic trading in world financial markets will improve access and diversification opportunities for investors and increase the liquidity of securities markets.

International Banking

The international banking market can be viewed as consisting of two segments. One is the foreign sector of the domestic market. From the perspective of a U.S. bank, this refers to the activities of U.S. banks competing in foreign countries. Depending on the country involved, the activities of foreign banks operating in these markets would be dictated by local regulations. The other segment of the international banking market refers to bank activities in the unregulated offshore market. Historically, most countries have been fairly protective of their local banking markets, imposing significant limitations on foreign banks attempting to compete with domestic banks. This is partly responsible for the growth of the unregulated offshore market for banking services. More recently, a strong trend toward deregulation of local banking markets has encouraged more direct competition by foreign banks. In the sections that follow, we describe how U.S. banks compete in each of these segments of the international banking market. International operations of U.S. banks are described first; then the activities of foreign banks in the United States are discussed.

International Operations of U.S. Banks

Just as nonfinancial corporations have expanded their activities into foreign countries to become global enterprises, U.S. commercial banks have established operations worldwide. Banks have sought new sources of funding from foreign countries and have often placed these funds with foreign borrowers. The international operations of U.S. banks play an important role in the financing of international trade, commerce, and investment. Beginning in the early 1960s the expansion of U.S. multinational corporations into foreign markets caused U.S. banks to "follow their customers" and provide needed banking services in new overseas markets. As a result, a variety of organizational forms evolved during the past three decades to provide overseas banking services. The structure of these organizations has been driven not only by the services needed by their domestic clients but also by the prevailing entry restrictions on foreign banks in various countries.

Several types of organizations have been used by U.S. banks to expand their services and activities into foreign markets. In most circumstances, the type of organization is dictated by the volume, location, and the nature of the business activity it is intended to support. Major forms of international operations by U.S. banks include Edge Act corporations, representative offices, shell branches, International Banking Facilities (IBFs), foreign subsidiaries and affiliates, and foreign branches. Each major form of international organization is described briefly below.

Edge Act Corporations

Often referred to as "Edge Acts," these corporations are subsidiaries of U.S. banks that are empowered by the Edge Act (1919) to engage in international banking under supervision of the Federal Reserve. Operating under a federal charter, Edge Act corporations are not subject to the banking regulations of the individual states in which they are located. There are a number of other very similar organizations, known as agreement corporations, that do operate under state charters and provide some, though not all, of the same services as Edge Act corporations. A major difference between Edge Act corporations and agreements corporations is that, while agreement corporations must engage principally in banking activities, Edge Acts can be involved in many nonbanking activities as well.

Edge Act corporations can be operated anywhere in the U.S. and are often located in centers of international trade and commerce such as New York or San Francisco.

Edge Acts enable any bank that can generate the necessary capital to establish an "international presence" and to compete for international business with other banks located more conveniently for such purposes. Another important feature of Edge Act corporations is that they can own subsidiaries of foreign banks. In 1979, the Federal Reserve relaxed restrictions over Edge Act corporations by allowing interstate branching. This resulted in many banks locating Edge Act offices in several cities around the United States. Branching by Edge Act corporations does not violate the McFadden Act, which restricts interstate branching, because these offices are organized to conduct international rather than domestic business.

Representative Offices

Representative offices are operated to locate new customers and to service the needs of existing customers. The term "representative" refers to the fact that the office cannot make loans or take deposits, per se. Loan and deposit clients are referred to the home office. The major function of the representative office is to find new business relationships for the bank and to put new clients in contact with the home office. Once new clients are located and relationships are established, the representative office acts as a servicing agent.

Shell Branches

Shell branches are offices of major banks located offshore, usually in the Bahamas or the Grand Cayman Islands, to carry on international banking business. These facilities are operated essentially as booking facilities located in countries with liberal regulations governing foreign currency transactions and banking practices, few if any local taxes, and a stable political environment. A major motive for establishing a shell branch is to provide a vehicle to attract Eurocurrency deposits and avoid domestic regulations. In addition, shell branches are one of the easiest and cheapest ways to enter foreign banking markets and are often an initial step that eventually leads to a full-service facility.

International Banking Facilities

International Banking facilities (IBFs) are a relatively new form of international banking organization. In 1981, the Federal Reserve authorized the establishment of IBFs to compete with foreign banks and shell branches for foreign deposits. The objective of Federal Reserve action was to bring more dollar-denominated deposits back to the United States. There was some concern at the time that foreign banking facilities drew loanable funds out of the United States and caused fewer loans to be made to domestic borrowers. IBFs are allowed to issue time deposits with minimum denominations of $100,000 to foreign nonbank residents. They are also allowed to offer time deposits to foreign banks or foreign offices of U.S. banks. Deposits are subject to some restrictions associated with minimum maturities but are not subject to reserve requirements or interest rate ceilings, which were in effect until 1986.[2]

---

[2]Interest rate ceilings under Regulation Q were in the process of gradual phase-out under the Deposit Institutions Deregulation and Monetary Control Act of 1980.

Given the lower perceived political risk associated with U.S. deposits compared to those in shell branches or Euromarkets, IBFs allow U.S. banks to attract deposits of foreign residents and foreign banks to the United States. An important feature of the IBF is that it does not constitute a separate office or location from the home office. Rather, an IBF consists of a set of computerized accounts showing flow of funds through credit and deposit accounts of foreign residents and foreign banks.

Subsidiaries and Affiliates

Under some circumstances, foreign governments do not allow U.S. banks to operate full-service branches. Large banks desiring to operate full-service banks in such countries have often taken an alternative approach—acquiring an existing bank operating under local authority. A foreign bank in which a majority interest is acquired is called a "subsidiary bank" of the U.S. parent. A foreign bank in which a minority interest is established is called an "affiliate bank." Each of these organizations continues to operate as a full-service bank, providing the U.S. parent access to both deposit and loan markets.

Full-Service Branches

Many United States banks operate full-service branches in foreign countries that are similar to their U.S. branches except as required by local regulations governing foreign branches. Full-service branches are generally located in more active trade centers worldwide, providing loan and deposit services to domestic customers and foreign trading partners. Because of their ability to raise U.S. dollar–denominated deposits, foreign branches are particularly important to their U.S. parents as a source of (less regulated) funding and as access to Eurocurrency markets.

Services Provided by Multinational Banks

Generally, U.S. banks have been allowed to engage in a wider variety of financial activities abroad than they have in the United States. For example, via their foreign operations U.S. banks have been allowed to make equity investments in nonfinancial companies and to underwrite securities in connection with their banking activities. In the United States, security underwriting and equity investment are prohibited under the Glass-Steagall Act of 1933. The reason why banks have been allowed to participate in a wider range of activities abroad is that most foreign banks are allowed a similar range of activities. To allow U.S. banks to be competitive internationally, U.S. regulators have relaxed regulations of U.S. bank operations abroad to an extent that they do not interfere with or undermine regulation of domestic activities. Generally, U.S. regulators have applied what is referred to as the "principle of mutual nondiscrimination," in forming public policy toward international banking. While allowing U.S. banks abroad to offer services similar to their foreign competition, foreign banks operating in the United States are allowed to offer the same services as U.S. banks domestically.

Euromarkets

Though the activities of United States banks in the international marketplace cut across almost all dimensions of retail and wholesale financial services, a considerable portion occurs in the unregulated offshore banking centers commonly referred to as "Euromarkets." Euromarkets, unlike the domestic markets, are virtually free of regulation. Euromarkets encompass the markets for Eurocurrency deposits and loans, and intermediate- and long-term Eurobonds, notes, and commercial paper.

A major source of funding by foreign operations of United States banks is obtained through Eurocurrency deposits, which have grown rapidly since the 1960s and now account for more than 80 percent of the foreign-owned deposits in U.S. banks. Eurocurrency deposits are created when international banks accept deposits denominated in currencies other than that of their home country. For example, London banks accept Eurocurrency deposits denominated in a variety of currencies, including Deutschemarks, U.S. dollars, French francs, and other major currencies. The Eurocurrency market began to grow in the 1950s, when European banks began accepting U.S. dollar–denominated deposits. Since that time, Eurocenters have developed throughout the world. Some countries with rather undeveloped financial markets, such as the Bahamas and the Grand Caymans, have become important Eurocenters because local governments have imposed very little regulation on the offshore activities of foreign banks. On the other hand, countries with well-developed financial systems, such as the United States, often provide very little in the way of offshore services. For example, the United States and Japan prohibited offshore banking facilities until 1981 and 1986, respectively.

Eurocurrency deposits play an important role in international trade as a source of currency to settle international transactions. The growth of the Eurodollar market—i.e., the Eurocurrency market for U.S. dollars—is also due to some extent to the difference between the reserve requirements. Reserve requirements for Eurodollar deposits in foreign branches or subsidiaries of U.S. banks have generally been lower (sometimes zero) than reserve requirements for similar domestic deposits. The reserve requirement differential made raising deposits in the Euromarket more attractive for U.S. banks over some periods of time.

Loans made by Euromarket facilities are commonly called Euroloans. Such loans usually carry relatively short maturities and charge a floating interest rate based on the London Interbank Offer Rate (LIBOR). Another feature of the Euroloan market is that loans are generally very large and are usually made only to the most creditworthy customers. In fact, it has been quite common during recent years for loans of this type to be highly syndicated. A syndicated loan would involve large multinational banks. Usually, one bank serves as the lead bank, which plays a key role in evaluating the borrower and organizing the syndicate. Smaller banks often participate in large Euroloans through members of the syndicate. The use of a syndicate in making large loans has two major advantages for participating banks. One is that larger loans *can* be made with a number of banks involved in the loan. The other is that the use of a syndicate and their subscribers spreads default risk more efficiently for participating banks.

Long- and Medium-Term Eurofinancing

Multinational banks provide a variety of services to their customers in the markets for long- and medium-term financing via Eurobonds and Euronotes. In these activities, banks may act not only as underwriters, but also as agents, and in some cases investors. Eurobonds and Euronotes are a growing segment of the international debt market, in which international investment banks and commercial banks play a key role. Eurobonds are long-term debt securities denominated in a currency other than that of the country (or countries) where the security is issued. Eurobonds are often issued by multinational corporations to raise money for foreign subsidiaries. One advantage of a Eurobond issue over a domestic issue is to afford the issuer access to bond markets in several different countries as part of a syndicated issue. Another reason is to denominate the bond so as to match currency in which debt service will be paid with the currency in which particular revenues will be received, say from a foreign subsidiary.

Multinational banks assist the issuer by creating an international network of banks and security brokers to underwrite the issue and deliver securities to ultimate investors. To place a Eurobond issue, a lead bank generally forms a consortium of international banks from several countries. Members of the consortium assemble a larger group of smaller banks and securities dealers, who agree to underwrite the issue. The consortium of banks earns a commission once the underwriting group establishes a firm price at which to purchase the bonds from the issuer.

Multinational banks also help corporate customers access the short- and medium-term market for Euronotes. In principle, this segment of the Euromarket operates like the Eurobond market in that a bank is involved in the process of placing the notes with investors. Generally, issuers gain access to this market through contractual arrangements with the bank, called a Note Issuance Facility (NIF). This segment of the Eurocredit market is less well-developed than the market for Eurobonds, but already it accounts for more than $200 billion of outstanding loans and securities. Together, Euronotes and Euroloans are the principal instruments of the short- and medium-term segment of the Euromarket. NIFs may or may not offer underwriting services. When underwriting is involved, banks are committed either to purchase any notes the borrower is unable to sell or to provide the issuer standby credit until the issue is sold.

When notes are issued under an NIF, the bank agrees to accept notes issued by the borrower throughout a period specified by the contract and to distribute the notes on either a fixed-margin or a best efforts basis. The underwriting arrangements under NIFs are similar to those for Eurobonds. The managing bank assembles a consortium of banks to assist in placing the issue. Under a best-efforts arrangement, the participating banks agree to place the note at the best available price; when a fixed-margin basis is used the banks receive a fixed percentage of the face value of notes when they are sold. In either case, a distinguishing feature of the NIF is that when all of the issue cannot be sold or placed under the terms of the contract, participating banks agree to do one of two things: (1) take up any notes that cannot be placed under the terms of the agreement or (2) provide short-term loans (standby credit) to the issuer in lieu of the unplaced notes.

Letters of Credit and Banker's Acceptances

Most banks enter the international banking markets to provide some form of trade financing. One source of activity is generated whenever domestic customers negotiate the terms of international trade. Under most circumstances, when goods are purchased overseas there is a considerable period of time between when goods are shipped by the exporter and when they are received by the importer. In such transactions the buyer (importer) generally does not pay for goods before they are received in good condition. The seller (exporter), on the other hand, is reluctant to ship goods without some security that payment will ultimately be made. In such situations, the importer often arranges for a letter of credit to be sent from its bank to the exporter. The letter of credit provides a standby guarantee to the exporter that in the event of a default of payment by the importer, the bank will pay any remaining obligation. If the bank is a well-known, credible institution, the seller's risk is minimal. However, if the seller is concerned about the soundness of the letter of credit, the seller may obtain a confirmation letter from its own bank, which guarantees payment in the event the importer *and* the importer's bank simultaneously default. The bank issuing the letter of credit charges the importing firm a fee for the service that is be based on the size of the credit and the default risk of the importing firm. Similarly, a fee for confirmation letters is based on the size of the loan and the default risk of the importer's bank.

Letters of credit are very closely related to another important form of trade finance called banker's acceptances or acceptance paper. As described earlier, banker's acceptances are basically dated bank drafts written on the importer's bank that are guaranteed by the bank. Say, shipment of the goods takes 30 days. The importer might write a draft on an account with its bank, payable to the exporter in 30 days. The draft becomes an acceptance when the bank stamps "accepted" across the face of the draft. The bank's stamp constitutes a guarantee that the draft will be paid by the bank, whether or not the importer has sufficient funds in the account on the date payment is due. Thus, the acceptance is similar to the letter of credit in that the accepting bank assumes the credit risk associated with the importer's obligation. In return, the importer pays the bank a fee, which, again, is based on the size of the payable as well as the creditworthiness of the importer.

While both instruments are essentially guarantees of payment by the importer's bank, there is one important difference between banker's acceptances and the letter of credit. The bankers' acceptance is a marketable instrument; that is, it is a claim that can be resold in a secondary market. Once the time draft is accepted, the default risk associated with the acceptance paper is easily evaluated by potential buyers, since the writer's promise to pay is guaranteed by a reputable and creditworthy bank. At that point, the acceptance becomes similar in risk to commercial paper issued by the accepting bank. In many cases, the exporter, upon receiving the acceptance, will immediately sell the paper at a discount to money market investors rather than wait for the paper to mature. The discount from face value reflects prevailing money market rates for short-term, liquid investments with low default risk. Of course, a key to the liquidity of the bankers acceptances is the soundness of the accepting banks. For this reason, the secondary market for bankers acceptances consists of paper guaranteed by larger, more reputable banks.

Foreign Exchange Services

Most banks offer customers access to markets for foreign currency by one means or another. Large banks operate foreign exchange departments to buy and sell foreign currency for customer accounts. Demand for foreign exchange transactions from customers of a bank occur for a variety of reasons, including settlement of payments in foreign trade, foreign tourism, and investments in foreign securities. Some banks operate as dealers in certain foreign currencies, generally currencies in which the bank does a significant amount of day-to-day business for its customers. Dealers operate in foreign currency markets much as they do in securities markets, quoting bid and offer prices for spot and forward delivery in various currencies on a continuous basis. Foreign currency desks at major banks make profits not only from buying and selling foreign currencies for customer accounts but also by trading on their own accounts. That is, they speculate on movements in the foreign currency exchange rates and try to make a profit by predicting such movements correctly. Foreign exchange speculation can be very risky, however, as there have been banks that have taken serious losses because of foreign exchange operations. One of the most famous bank failures in U.S. history was that of the Franklin National Bank during the 1970s, a failure precipitated by foreign exchange trading losses.

International Lending

No discussion of the activities of U.S. banks abroad would be complete without some mention of the recent difficulties of many U.S. banks that made loans to less developed Countries (LDCs). For various reasons, lending to foreign borrowers is potentially riskier than domestic lending. First of all, there are risks associated with foreign governments that are not encountered with domestic lending. This source of risk is often called "country risk"—changes in the economic or political environment of a borrower that would work to the detriment of the lender. For example, in many countries political regimes may change and new governments may confiscate private property and repudiate foreign debts. This represents an extreme circumstance, however. The refusal to honor outstanding obligations would greatly impair the ability of a foreign economy to attract capital from other countries in the future. More realistically, such political developments could precipitate other changes in taxes, price controls, or other restrictions that would diminish the ability of borrowers to make timely payments on their loans. These risks are significant in many parts of the world, particularly in LDCs.

The risks associated with loans to foreign countries, and in particular to LDCs, became all too clear during the 1980s, when U.S. banks were plagued by difficulties with loans to LDCs. In 1982, Mexico declared a moratorium on foreign debt payments that had widespread repercussions in the U.S. banking industry. Since the announcement by Mexico, more than 40 developing countries have rescheduled their debts with commercial banks. Rescheduling foreign loans typically involves the extension of the loan's maturity date, consolidation loan of balances, capitalization or forgiveness of unpaid interest, and many times the incorporation of third-party or government loan guarantees.

During the 1980s, the exposure of large U.S. commercial banks to troubled LDCs remained high, in part because rescheduling many loans involved capitalizing overdue interest payments. In 1978, the total exposure of nine U.S. money center banks to LDC loans was around $54 billion. In 1984, two years after Mexico declared its debt moratorium, total exposure at the same banks had peaked at about $56 billion. By 1987, exposure had dropped at these banks to $49 billion. During each year of the ten-year period, the nine money center banks accounted for more than half of the total exposure by U.S. banks to LDC credits.[3] Finally, during 1987, Brazil announced a moratorium similar to the one announced by Mexico five years earlier. This event triggered a sequence of loan write-offs by U.S. banks to recognize the likelihood that a large percentage of LDC debt would not be repaid. The first of these announcements was made by Citicorp in 1987, when a $2 billion write-down was announced. Other banks pioneered debt-for-equity swaps, in which they accepted shares of stock in certain overseas projects as a substitute for nonperforming loans. This innovation was aimed at replacing nonperforming assets with performing assets. Debt-for-equity swaps also provided more flexible funding arrangements for developing countries.

Another risk associated with international loans is currency risk. When loans are denominated in a foreign currency there is the risk that the currency may depreciate in value during the term of the loan, making loan payments worth less in terms of the lender's currency. For example, suppose a U.S. bank makes a loan to a customer in Germany when the exchange rate is 2.5 Deutschemarks (DM) per U.S. dollar. Assume the loan is to be repaid by a single payment of DM1 million, a year later. The U.S. dollar value of the debt payment is DM1,000,000 ÷ DM2.5/$ = $400,000. That is, when the DM1 million payment is received, if the current exchange rate does not change, the lender can convert the loan payment into $400,000. However, if the exchange rate changes over the year, the bank will receive more or less in U.S. dollars, depending on which way the exchange rate goes. If the rate turns out to be DM3.00 per U.S. dollar, the value of the loan payment will be $333,333. The value of the payment will be $500,000 if the exchange rate is DM2.00 per U.S. dollar in 1 year.

In our example, we assumed that the bank bore the exchange risk in the German loan. One way for the bank to avoid such risks is to write the terms of the loan so that promised payments are defined in U.S. dollars. That is the one-year payable would be stated as $400,000 rather than DM1 million. Then it is the borrower's problem to convert Deutschemarks to U.S. dollars before making the stipulated loan payment. Additionally, if the borrower's currency is actively traded in the foreign currency market, it is likely that such exposure can be effectively hedged in the forward or swaps markets, though currencies in LDCs frequently are not actively traded, making hedging ineffective. Another aspect of foreign currency risk has to do with exchange controls. Such controls have sometimes been established to prohibit movement of funds out of the country. Under exchange controls it becomes more difficult for lending banks to exchange payments into their own currencies.

---

[3]See James (1990) for a more complete discussion.

In addition to the political and currency risks is the usual risk of default, or credit risk. Most foreign borrowing by developing countries is either guaranteed by the borrower's government or is done directly by the government. To that extent, credit risk and country risk become one and the same. Nevertheless, it is highly likely that the evaluation and monitoring of credit risk is more difficult when borrower and lender are separated by great distances and come from different cultures.

Foreign Banks Operating in the United States

Just as the presence of U.S. banks in foreign countries has increased during the past few decades, so has the presence of foreign banks in the United States. The most important reason is so they can follow the business needs of their customers. For example, the large trade surplus enjoyed by Japan during most of the 1980s led to substantial direct investment by Japanese firms in the United States. By 1986 more than 700 Japanese firms had established manufacturing operations in the United States. As Japanese firms increased their business activities in the United States, especially in California, their needs for banking services in the United States increased as well. Rather than lose this potential source of business to U.S. banks, Japanese banks established various types of banking offices in the United States. There are other reasons why foreign banks entered U.S. banking markets. One is that the U.S. economy provides the world's largest market for loans and deposits. The sheer size of these markets presents an attractive opportunity for foreign banks seeking to raise deposits or place funds in money market instruments, investment securities, or loans. In fact, many foreign banks rely on American money markets as a source of liquidity that is not available in their domestic financial systems. Another attribute of the United States that is attractive to foreign banks is the stability of the U.S. political and economic environment. Compared to many foreign countries, the risk of financial losses to foreign banks operating in the United States. due to economic or political upheaval is very small. In general, the U.S. economy has experienced more stable economic growth and lower inflation and unemployment than most other developed countries.

Though the growth of foreign bank operations in the United States has not kept pace with the growth of U.S. banking overseas, there has been a substantial increase in the number and size of foreign offices in the United States during the past decade. The number of foreign bank offices in the United States by the end of 1991 was more than 550, whose total assets exceeded $570 billion. For many foreign banks, business in U.S. markets has grown faster than their own domestic business. Not surprisingly, the country with the largest number of offices is Japan, followed by France and Great Britain. Japan's banking expansion into the United States has been particularly pronounced in the state of California.

Entry by Japanese Banks into California

During the period 1982 to 1988, assets of Japanese-owned banking institutions in California increased nearly threefold, from $34.6 billion to $93.4 billion. As a percentage of the California bank market, this represents a sizable increase in the fraction of bank assets held by Japanese banks. At the end of 1988, Japanese banks owned a quarter of the banking assets and 30 percent of the business loans in the state.[4]

The dramatic increase in Japanese banking operations in California illustrates quite clearly the motives for domestic banks to expand worldwide. An important reason for the growth of Japanese banking in California is the growth of U.S. trade with Japan. California's location relative to Asian and Pacific Rim countries makes California an important point of entry for trade with those countries. As trade with Japan increased, the increased concentration of Japanese multinational companies in California was a powerful incentive for Japanese banks to follow.

Another factor that is responsible for the recent growth of Japanese banks in California is the large trade surplus Japan enjoyed through most of the 1980s. Providing an opportunity for investment abroad, these trade surpluses led to substantial increases in Japanese direct investment in California. Of 700 Japanese companies that had established manufacturing operations in the United States by 1986, about 25 percent of those were located in California.

The growth of Japanese banks in the United States, and particularly in California, can also be explained by the competitive funding advantage enjoyed by Japanese banks during recent years relative to their U.S. counterparts. Parent Japanese banks, by their size and credit standing, are able to raise capital more easily and more cheaply than many of their U.S. counterparts. This advantage is reinforced by the greater availability of funds enjoyed by Japanese banks owing to large trade surpluses during the 1980s.

Types of Foreign Banks in the United States

Foreign banks establish operations in the United States in organizational forms similar to those used by U.S. banks operating offshore. In many cases, foreign bank operations in the United States are less than full-service operations. There are several ways in which foreign banking operations are established in the United States. One is through the purchase of an existing bank. A foreign bank that buys a controlling interest in the stock of a chartered U.S. bank operates the bank as a subsidiary. The U.S. subsidiary bank continues to operate under U.S. regulations and is able to offer a full range of banking services. One of the advantages to foreign banks of entry by ownership of an existing U.S. bank is the ability to penetrate both retail and wholesale banking markets. Moreover, the U.S. subsidiary may also be funded by the foreign parent or affiliated institutions. Another way for foreign banks to establish a full-service bank in the United States is as a foreign branch operating in the United States. Branches of foreign banks in the United States operate, for the most part as their U.S. counterparts do, having a full range of banking powers. They can accept deposits and make loans. An important function of a full-service branch is to provide trade financing and money market services. Similar to subsidiary banks, branches of foreign banks can also be funded with borrowings from the parent.

---

[4]See the study by Gary C. Zimmerman (1989) for a complete discussion of the growth of Japanese banking in California.

Another vehicle used by foreign banks to gain entry to U.S. banking is an agency of the foreign bank. Just like agencies of U.S. banks abroad, foreign agencies in the U.S. offer more limited services than the full-service alternatives described above. Agencies cannot accept deposits but may accept credit balances. Generally, these institutions concentrate on trade financing and money market services for bank customers. Like subsidiaries, agencies can be funded by borrowings from the parent bank or bank affiliates. Foreign banks are also allowed to establish IBFs. Like IBFs of domestic banks, these operations are set up, not as separate entities, but as a set of accounts on the books of a subsidiary bank, agency, or branch. They may accept deposits from and make loans to foreign residents, the parent bank, and other IBFs. In addition, IBFs are not subject to U.S. reserve requirements.

Again, the recent activity of Japanese banks in the state of California provides a useful perspective on the extent of foreign acquisitions during the 1980s. During the period 1982 to 1988, 60 percent of the increase in Japanese bank assets resulted from acquisitions of three large foreign-owned banks by Japanese banks. California First (owned by Bank of Tokyo) acquired Union Bank in 1988 for $750 million. In 1986, Sanwa Bank of California acquired Lloyd's Bank California for $263 million. And, Mitsubishi paid $242.5 million to acquire BanCal Tri-State Corporation in 1984. By the end of 1988 ten Japanese-owned banks were operating in the state of California: eight were subsidiaries of Japanese banks, and two were Japanese-owned but not by banks headquartered in Japan. By asset size, four of these banks ranked in the top ten banks in the state. In addition, by the end of 1988 there were 22 foreign agencies and six foreign branches of Japanese banks, with combined assets of $58.1 billion. The agencies and branches provide commercial, money market, and trade-related banking services, either directly or through IBFs that serve only foreign residents.

Regulation of Foreign Banks in the United States

In many ways, the operation of foreign banks in the United States has been a source of irritation and concern for U.S. banks. The major reason was that, until quite recently, foreign banks were much less regulated than their U.S. counterparts. In particular, for most of the time since the banking reforms of the 1930s, U.S. banks have been subject to regulatory restriction in three major dimensions: (1) interest rate ceilings on deposit accounts under Regulation Q (1933); (2) interstate branching restrictions under the McFadden Act (1927); and (3) restriction from investing and underwriting corporate bonds and stocks under the Glass-Steagall Act (1933). During much of that time U.S. branches of foreign banks were not subject to these restrictions. In addition, foreign banks were not generally subject to the same reserve requirements as U.S. banks. In spite of the fact that U.S. bank expansion into foreign countries was proceeding at about four times the pace of entry by foreign banks into the United States, uneven regulation was held responsible for the "invasion" of foreign banks into the United States. During the late 1970s there was growing concern that these regulatory inequities might lead to some influence by foreign banks (or governments) over the U.S. economy, or that the presence of a significant population of unregulated banks might undermine the Federal Reserve's efforts to implement monetary policy. Responding to these concerns, Congress passed the International Banking Act in 1978. This legislation resulted in a substantially more equitable system of regulations for foreign branches, subsidiaries, and agencies operating in the United States. The intention of this legislation was to promote competitive equality between domestic and foreign banking institutions. As a result, while foreign banks were required to conform to essentially the same regulations as U.S. banks, they were also afforded many of the same benefits, such as deposit insurance and access to Federal Reserve services.

Even though recent legislation has substantially equalized regulations governing foreign and domestic banks operating in the United States, penetration of foreign banks into United States markets has proceeded at a surprising pace. Figure 8-2 compares the market share of foreign companies across several industries in the United States in 1988.[5] Foreign banks accounted for 28 percent of the wholesale banking market (banking services to business customers). Two reasons are often given for the continued growth of the market share held by foreign banks. The first is that foreign banks enjoy some advantages that allow them to underprice U.S. competitors. In particular, some economists argue that the cost of capital for many foreign banks is lower than for U.S. banks. This would allow them to quote better lending rates to their U.S. customers than U.S. banks can, and still earn a competitive profit.

Figure 8-3 shows the foreign share of the U.S. commercial lending market for 1980, 1984, and 1988.[6] Notice that the share of U.S. chartered banks owned by foreigners has remained fairly constant over the eight-year period, growing slightly from 4.4 percent to 6.3 percent. The market share of U.S. branches of foreign banks grew from 8.6 percent in 1980 to 14.4 percent in 1988. The most dramatic increase in commercial lending by foreign banks involved offshore loans by foreign banks. These are essentially loans by foreign banks to U.S. corporations that are booked in foreign offices not subject to the same regulations as domestic offices of the foreign banks. As indicated in Figure 8-3, this category of lending grew from 1.2 percent of total commercial lending to U.S. firms in 1980 to 7.6 percent in 1988. An important reason for the growth in offshore lending to U.S. banks is to avoid costly domestic regulation. This is due in part to the International Banking Act of 1978. Recall that legislation imposed the same reserve requirements on foreign banks operating in the United States as were required for U.S. banks. Reserve requirements impose costs on these banks that are passed on through higher loan rates. For example, if a bank raises $100 in new deposits with a 3 percent reserve requirement, only $97 can be used to make a new loan. The other $3 is tied up as non–interest-earning reserves. This means that, in order to earn annual interest of $10 on the new $97 loan, the bank would have to charge 10.31 percent annually ($0.1031 \times \$97 = \$10$). However, a bank with no reserve requirement could lend the entire $100 in new deposits and would need to charge only 10 percent to earn the same $10 interest. Some economists have referred to the difference in these costs as a "reserve tax."[7] Because

---

[5]Taken from Baer (1990), who provides a deeper discussion of market penetration by foreign banks and surrounding issues.

[6]Taken from Baer (1990).

[7]In theory, the reserve tax can be born by either depositors or borrowers. When depositors bear the tax, it takes the form of a lower deposit rate; when borrowers bear the tax, of a higher loan rate. Studies of loan and deposit rates for domestic U.S. banks support the hypothesis that the reserve tax is passed to borrowers in the form of a higher loan rate.

Figure 8-2

Foreign penetration of U.S. markets. *Source: H.L. Baer, "Foreign Competition in U.S. Banking Markets,"* Economic Perspectives *Federal Reserve Bank of Chicago, May/June 1990, pp. 22–32.*

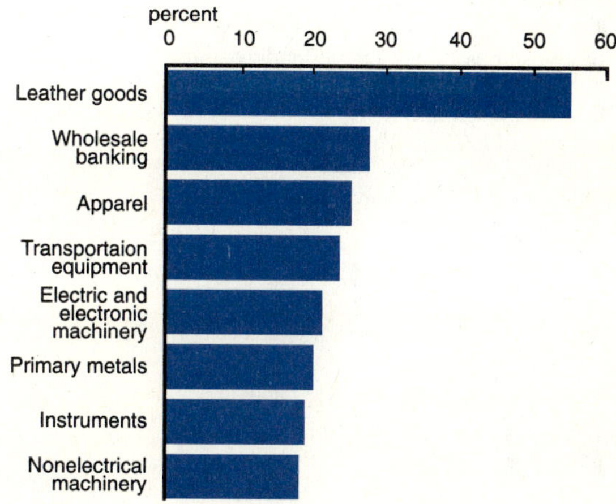

branches of foreign banks operating abroad are not subject to U.S. requirements they are able to make loans to U.S. companies at better rates because they avoid the reserve tax.[8] By going offshore, both the bank and the borrower can participate in the savings associated with avoiding the tax.

Foreign Banking Systems

In many ways, the manner in which foreign banks participate in the world financial system can be explained by the structure of their domestic banking system. The banking systems of many other countries are quite different from that of the United States. Many economists believe that the competitive position of U.S. banks in world banking markets is threatened by less regulated and more flexible banks, for example those in Germany, Switzerland, and Japan.

Probably the most apparent difference between banks in these countries and banks in the United States is their commerce powers. U.S. banks are prohibited from equity investment in commercial firms under the Glass-Steagall Act. In Germany, Switzerland, and a number of other countries, the practice of "universal banking" combines commercial banking with the underwriting of corporate securities and other investment banking activities. German banks maintain large shareholdings in industrial or commercial firms and effectively control the stock brokerage business. The effect of this combination is to confer a great deal of power to German banks over the decisions of their commercial customers. There are two reasons for this. First, the relatively large equity position established by universal banks gives them some voting control over management. Second, German law permits other shareholders to delegate voting authority to the brokerage firm in which their shares are deposited. Because German banks operate as securities brokers and

[8]The movement of activities such as lending to avoid costly regulations is often referred to as "regulatory arbitrage." See a complete discussion by McCauley and Seth (1992) on the growth of offshore lending to U.S. corporations.

Figure 8-3

Foreign share of commercial lending in the United States. *Source: H.L. Baer, "Foreign Competition in U.S. Banking Markets,"* Economic Perspectives *Federal Reserve Bank of Chicago, May/June 1990, pp. 22–32.*

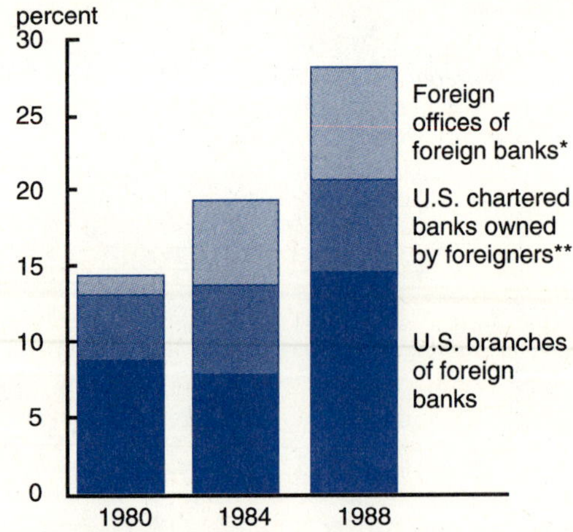

dealers their customer accounts are another source of voting control over commercial firms. These delegated voting rights enhance the ability of German banks to control risk in corporations with which they have loan relationships. In a real sense, they are able to directly control the risk of their credits by controlling the risk decisions of loan clients. For example, by having significant voting power in the borrowing firm, the bank may cause the management of the borrowing firm to choose lower-risk investments to the benefit of the bank's outstanding loan position.

Opponents of universal banking argue that such systems are anti-competition and promote dangerous concentration of economic power. When a bank holds a controlling interest in a firm's equity it can make loan decisions that may benefit the bank but not necessarily the firm's other shareholders. Again, consider the system in Germany. By controlling the economy's brokerage industry and having voting control over loan clients, universal banks in Germany are able to hold many companies, especially smaller firms, captive loan customers that are unable to issue equity or seek out alternative loan financing. Some economists contend this explains the dominance of bank lending as the primary source of commercial finance in Germany and the lack of well-developed equity markets. In the United States similar arguments were advanced against the combination of investment and commercial banking following the banking collapse of the early 1930s. At that time, many believed that the combination of lending and underwriting relationships between banks and commercial customers led to excessive risk taking, causing many banks to fail.

Similar patterns of stock ownership and control are found in Japanese banks. Japanese regulations are similar in many ways to those in the United States. This is a result of U.S. involvement in post–World War II reconstruction of the Japanese economy. Restrictions similar to the Glass-Steagall Act were imposed after the war. These restrictions are not very effective owing to the existence of the *keiretsu* industrial

Table 8-1
Within-Group Ownership of Equity and Debt

	Equity				Debt
	Nonfinancial firms' ownership of other firms in the same group		**Financial firms' ownership of other firms in the same group**		**Loans to other firms in the same group**
	(% of total shares)	(Number of companies owned)	(% of total shares)	(Number of companies owned)	(% of total loans)
Keiretsu					
Mitsui	22	69	11*	170	29
Mitsubishi	15	68	15	212	33
Sumitomo	22	72	12*	182	25
Fuyo	15	32	12	155	28
Sanwa	17	35	10*	142	23
Dai-Ichi	15	42	7*	86	19

*The percentage of equity owned by financial shareholders is different from that owned by nonfinancial shareholders at the 5 percent significance level.

Source: Genay, "Japan's Corporate Groups," *Economic Perspectives* Federal Reserve Bank of Chicago, January/February 1991, p. 23.

relationships, which concentrate a significant proportion of equity ownership in financial institutions. While Japanese banks are nominally limited to 5 percent equity posi-tions in nonbank corporations, through the *keiretsu* and cross-holdings with securities firms and other financial firms, banks control around 22 percent of all corporate equity in Japan.[9]

There are six major *keiretsu* in Japan. They are Mitsui, Mitsubishi, Sumitomo, Fuyo, Sanwa, and Dai-Ichi. Keiretsu are characterized by significant cross-holdings of equity by members. Members of the group have close ties to the main bank, which in turn provides members with a majority of their debt financing. Members also have close product market ties with each other. Table 8-1 shows the percentage of ownership of equity among nonfinancial and financial firms in each of the six major *keiretsu* groups during 1989. For each group, the percentage of ownership of other firms within the group by nonfinancial companies ranged from 15 percent to 22 percent. For financial firms, ownership of other firms within each group ranged from 7 percent to 15 percent. The differences in concentration of ownership between nonfinancial and financial firms in each *keiretsu* group are due to the 5 percent limitation on bank ownership. In addition, notice the large concentration of loans by financial firms to members of the groups. Besides being the major shareholders of group firms, affiliated financial institutions also are the single largest source for their group's loans. In 1989, *keiretsu* financial firms made between 19 percent (Dai-Ichi) and 33 percent (Sumitomo) of all loans made to their member firms.

Keiretsu have also established linkages among the large Japanese city banks and the big securities firms. The largest securities firms in Japan, commonly referred to as

[9]See Hale (1991).

the Big 4, are Nomura Securities, Yamaichi Securities, Daiwa Securities, and Nikko Securities. Each of these firms is linked to one of the large city banks—Nomura with Daiwa Bank, Yamaichi with Fuji Bank and International Bank of Japan, Daiwa Securities with Sumitomo Bank, and Nikko with Mitsubishi Bank. *Keiretsu* links between banks and securities firms are driven by the needs of their clients to access a broader range of financial services. Banks use their *keiretsu* links to build resources and expertise in securities activities. Banks provide their securities firms with financial support, including additional capital to meet licensing requirements, as well as personnel and introductions to corporate clients. In many cases, the *keiretsu* affords the bank a means to circumvent legal restrictions against the combination of investment and commercial banking, in particular in underwriting securities issues.[10]

Many economists and banking practitioners believe that to remain competitive in the international marketplace the U.S. banking system must adopt a system that relaxes the separation between investment and commercial banking. As financial markets continue to become more integrated, U.S. financial institutions will feel increasing competitive pressure from foreign financial institutions. From the standpoint of banking regulations, U.S. banks are at a distinct disadvantage relative to banks in many other countries. To remain competitive, U.S. regulations over banks and other financial institutions may have to be relaxed, to provide a level playing field against foreign competition.

Globalization of Securities Markets

During the decade of the 1980s the volume of international transactions across U.S. borders grew dramatically, as is evidenced by Tables 8-2 and 8-3.[11] Table 8-2 compares transactions volume in U.S. and foreign equity securities during the years 1980 and 1990. The table consists of two parts. The first shows the volume of transactions in U.S. equity securities involving buyers and sellers from five major foreign countries and all of Europe. The second part gives the volume of transactions involving U.S. buyers and sellers of foreign equity securities. The lower panel of the table provided annualized growth rates of aggregate transactions over the ten-year period.

During the decade of the 1980s, the growth rate of foreign transactions in U.S. equities was almost 17 percent per year over the ten-year period. Over the same ten-year period, the growth rate of U.S. transactions in foreign securities was more than 30 percent per year.

Similar, and even more dramatic evidence of the growth of international securities transactions is shown in Table 8-3, which shows the growth in transactions in long-term bonds involving the same set of foreign countries and the same time period. The volume of total foreign transactions in U.S. securities grew at an annual

[10]Relationships between securities firms and banks established by Japanese keiretsu are described in Kimura and Pugel (1992). This paper provides an in-depth discussion of the structure and performance of the Japanese securities industry and the effects of keiretsu arrangements.

[11]Tables 8-2 and 8-3 are from Abken (1991).

Table 8-2
Transactions Volume in Stocks

	Foreign Transactions in U.S. Securities				U.S. Transactions in Foreign Securities			
	Purchases[a]	Sales[a]	Aggregate Purchases and Sales[a]	Percentage Share of Market	Purchases[a]	Sales[a]	Aggregate Purchases and Sales[a]	Percentage Share of Market
				1990				
France	5.82	7.01	12.83	3.55	6.05	5.90	11.95	4.72
Germany	5.90	6.27	12.17	3.37	6.69	7.45	14.14	5.58
United Kingdom	44.94	48.07	93.,01	25.74	4.80	45.52	90.32	35.64
Total Europe	84.95	93.53	178.47	49.39	74.53	78.40	152.94	60.36
Japan	27.47	30.38	57.85	16.01	30.89	31.52	62.41	24.63
Canada	19.52	18.63	38.14	10.56	4.78	4.92	9.70	3.83
Total Worldwide	173.04	188.34	361.37	100.00	122.49	130.89	253.38	100.00
				1980				
France	2.73	2.24	4.97	6.60	0.47	0.67	1.14	6.36
Germany	2.75	2.56	5.30	7.05	0.24	0.22	0.46	2.57
United Kingdom	7.44	4.94	12.38	16.44	7.44	4.94	12.38	16.44
Total Europe	24.62	21.55	46.16	61.32	3.16	3.62	6.78	37.97
Japan	0.87	1.03	1.90	2.52	0.93	1.77	2.7	15.10
Canada	6.35	5.48	11.83	15.71	3.02	3.66	6.68	37.43
Total Worldwide	40.32	34.96	75.28	100.00	7.89	9.97	17.85	100.00

Compound Annual Growth Rate, 1980–1990
(percent)

	Foreign	U.S.
France	9.95	26.53
Germany	8.66	40.88
United Kingdom	22.35	41.81
Total Europe	14.48	36.56
Japan	40.73	36.92
Canada	12.42	3.80
Total worldwide	16.98	30.38

*In billions of U.S. dollars.

Source: Peter A. Abken, "Globalization of Stock, Futures, and Options Markets," Federal Reserve Bank of Atlanta *Economic Review* 76 (July/August 1991) 3,5, Tables 1 and 2.

rate of 41 percent over the decade of the 1980s. Over the same time period, the annual growth rate of U.S. transactions in foreign securities was almost 34 percent.

Notice also how the volume of transactions involving Japan has increased over the ten-year period. In 1980, transactions volume by Japan was $1.9 billion in U.S. equities and $6.81 billion in U.S. long-term bonds. As a percentage of total transactions volume from foreign countries for U.S. equities and bonds during 1980, this represents only 2.52 percent and 5.54 percent, respectively. By 1990, Japanese transactions in U.S. equity securities had grown to $57.85 billion, an annual rate of

Table 8-3
Transactions Volume in Long-Term Bonds[a]

	Foreign Transactions in U.S. Securities				U.S. Transactions in Foreign Securities			
	Purchases[b]	Sales[b]	Aggregate Purchases and Sales[b]	Percentage Share of Market	Purchases[b]	Sales[b]	Aggregate Purchases and Sales[b]	Percentage Share of Market
				1990				
France	13.47	12.78	26.24	0.68	14.67	15.50	30.17	4.65
Germany	45.31	39.87	85.18	2.21	15.91	18.23	34.14	5.26
United Kingdom	564.62	555.67	1,120.29	29.08	113.95	114.16	228.10	35.12
Total Europe	804.32	773.85	1,578.17	40.97	185.46	189.78	375.25	57.77
Japan	731.08	744.96	1,476.04	38.32	36.71	43.50	80.21	12.35
Canada	66.81	69.46	136.26	3.54	54.48	56.91	111.39	17.15
Total Worldwide	1,945.19	1,906.80	3,851.99	100.00	313.58	335.93	649.50	100.00
				1980				
France	0.71	0.45	1.16	0.94	0.66	0.62	1.28	3.64
Germany	2.54	5.21	7.75	6.31	0.45	0.43	0.88	2.50
United Kingdom	22.36	20.15	42.51	34.60	6.07	6.16	12.23	34.97
Total Europe	30.29	30.37	60.65	49.37	9.09	9.59	18.68	53.39
Japan	2.59	4.21	6.81	5.54	1.35	2.65	4.00	11.44
Canada	0.96	2.39	3.35	2.73	2.20	2.42	4.63	13.22
Total Worldwide	66.61	56.25	122.86	100.00	17.07	17.92	34.98	100.00

Compound Annual Growth Rate, 1980–1990
(percent)

	Foreign	U.S.
France	36.66	37.22
Germany	27.09	44.24
United Kingdom	38.70	33.99
Total Europe	38.53	43.99
Japan	71.24	34.96
Canada	44.86	37.46
Total worldwide	41.13	33.93

[a]Bonds having maturities of one year or greater.
[b]In billions of U.S. dollars.

Source: Peter A. Abken, "Globalization of Stock, Futures, and Options Markets," Federal Reserve Bank of Atlanta *Economic Review* 76 (July/August 1991) 3,5, Tables 1 and 2.

growth over the ten-year period of almost 41 percent per year. In addition, volume of Japanese transactions in U.S. bonds had increased to $1476.04 billion by 1990—an annual growth rate of 71 percent over the decade. This growth was driven by several factors. The most important, however, were the balance of payments surplus enjoyed by Japan during most of the 1980s and the dismantling of Japanese regulations to permit greater investment abroad. In particular, persistent U.S. deficits during the period led to significant growth in U.S. governments debt, much of which was purchased by Japanese investors.[12]

International Bond Markets

The international bond market consists of two major segments; the foreign bond market and the Eurobond and Euro–commercial paper market. The Euro–commercial paper market can be considered the short-term end of the Eurobond market. Foreign bonds are bonds issued in a foreign country with payments denominated in that country's home currency. For example, because many non-American firms need financing in U.S. dollars, perhaps to finance an investment by a U.S. subsidiary, they have an incentive to issue bonds in the United States. Such issues are often referred to as "Yankee bonds," or U.S. dollar–denominated bonds issued by foreign companies in the United States. Similar bonds issued by foreign companies in Japan and the U.K. are called "samurai bonds" and "bulldog bonds," respectively.

The relative importance of international issues (foreign bonds and Eurobonds) as compared to total publicly issued bonds is outlined in Table 8-4. International issues as a percentage of total public issues increased steadily from 1980 to 1988 for bonds markets in seven major currencies. Of the seven markets listed, international issues in the Swiss franc and the Australian dollar represent the largest fraction of total public issues. International bonds account for nearly half of all bonds denominated in the Swiss franc and more than a third of the bonds denominated in the Australian dollar. On the other hand, international bonds account for 10.5 percent and 5 percent of the total issues in the U.S. dollar and the Japanese yen. The substantial difference in the relative importance of international bonds in Table 8-4 is explained in part by the balance of payments surpluses experienced by Switzerland and Australia during the 1980s, especially relative to balance of payments deficits experienced by the United States. A balance of payments surplus resulted in slower growth in government debt in these countries, and therefore slower growth in total publicly issued bonds. In the United States, however, persistent deficits have resulted in more rapid growth of government debt, and international bonds are relatively less important as a fraction of total publicly issued bonds.

International bonds accounted for about 10 percent of all publicly issued bonds outstanding at the end of 1988. Figure 8-4 shows the relative importance of eight major bond markets with respect to total publicly issued bonds and total issues of international bonds at that time. Notice that the U.S. dollar bond market accounted for 46 percent of all publicly issued bonds and 48 percent of all international bonds. Japan is second in proportion of public issues with 23 percent. Taken together, the

[12]By the late 1980s, Japan had also established itself among the major issuers in world debt and equity markets. According to data collected by the World Bank, as of 1988, the value of world equity markets was \$9.6 trillion and the value of world bond markets was slightly greater at \$9.8 trillion. The United States, Japan, United Kingdom, and West Germany accounted for more than 75 percent of total publicly issued debt and equity. The United States and Japan alone issued more than two thirds of the world's total publicly issued debt and more than 70 percent of the value of world equity.

Table 8-4
International Shares of the World's Major Bond Markets

(Percent based on outstanding)

	1980	1985	1988
U.S. dollar	4.4	8.8	10.5
Japanese yen	1.6	3.2	5.0
German mark	12.6	11.2	14.2
U.K. sterling	0.9	9.4	21.3
Canadian dollar	3.1	5.5	13.7
Swiss franc	27.3	42.3	49.2
Australian dollar	n.a.	9.5	36.2

Source: Pavel/McElravey, "Globalization in the Financial Services Industry," *Economic Perspectives* Federal Reserve Bank of Chicago, May/June 1990, p. 3–21.

U.S. dollar, Japanese yen, U.K. pound sterling, and German mark account for more than three fourths of both total publicly issued bonds and total international bonds issued. One reason for the dominance of the United States and Japan in the public bond market is the large volume of government borrowing during the 1980s in both countries. As of 1988, more than two thirds of the bonds denominated in the U.S. dollar and the Japanese yen were government obligations.

In addition, it is interesting to note that among international issues Japan is the largest issuer of Eurobonds. According to World Bank statistics, Japanese companies issued 21 percent of the world's Eurobonds during 1988. The reason is that, historically, the Japanese government and Japanese securities firms have made domestic issues by Japanese companies very expensive. As a result, Japanese companies relied more on the unregulated Euromarkets as a source of funding. Beginning in 1984, the Japanese government began gradual deregulation of Japanese securities markets, in part to try to recapture some of the securities business formerly lost to the Euromarkets.

Equity Markets

In close parallel with bond markets, world equity markets are dominated by three countries: the United States, Japan, and the United Kingdom. At year's end 1988, the United States, Japan, and the United Kingdom accounted for three fourths of the capitalized value of world equity markets. Moreover, because equity has played a relatively minor role in the financial economies of many European countries, most of the value of world equity is concentrated in the United States and Japan. Figure 8-5 shows the total capitalized value of the world's equity markets at the end of 1988. Japan accounted for almost $4 trillion of the world's equity and the United States for slightly less than $3 trillion. The rest of the world accounted for about $3 trillion in equity.

While the world's equity markets become increasingly integrated, there remain substantial differences in the structure, operation, and importance of markets in different countries. For example, the largest and most active equity markets are in the United States, Japan, and the United Kingdom. These markets account for more than half of the equities listed on the world's stock exchanges. Yet, while the

Figure 8-4

Market shares of total publicly issued bonds: year-end 1988 (Based on outstanding). *Source: H.L. Baer, "Foreign Competition in U.S. Banking Markets,"* Economic Perspectives *Federal Reserve Bank of Chicago, May/June 1990, pp. 3–21.*

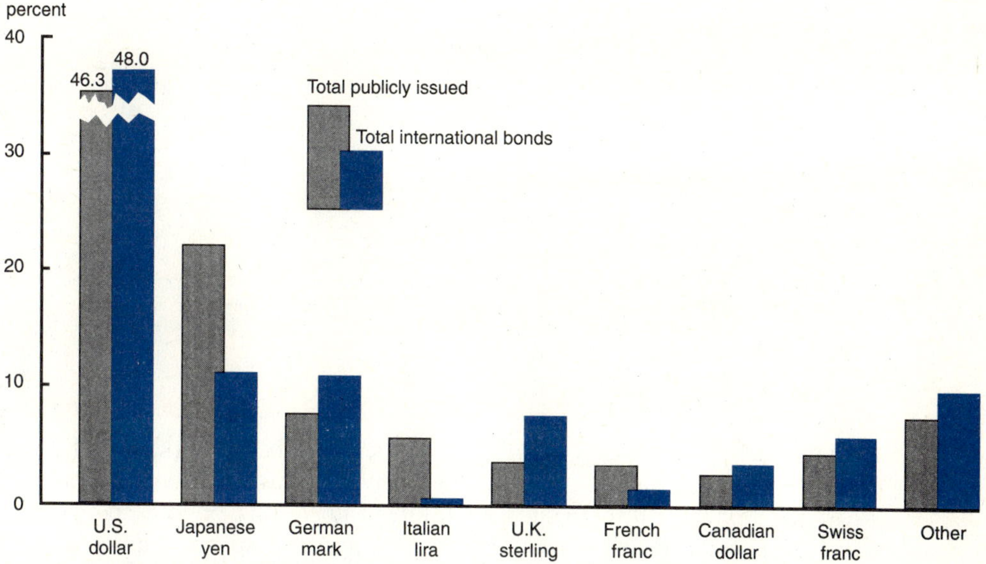

American and British markets have been open to foreign investors for some time, only recently has Japan begun to open its equity markets to foreign investors.

Table 8-5 provides a comparison across seven major countries of the relative importance of foreign trading in domestic equity securities. For the years 1985 and 1988 foreign transactions in domestic equity is given as a percentage of total transactions. Markets in France, the United Kingdom, and Canada had relatively more activity in foreign transactions; however the fraction of foreign transactions decreased for the U.K. and Canada and increased for France. In the other countries the fraction of foreign transactions in domestic equity was relatively lower. In particular, as we pointed out above, there is relatively little participation by foreigners in the Japanese equity market as compared to other equity markets.

Finally, with the exception of the United Kingdom, stock markets have played a less important role in the financial systems of most European countries. In Germany, for example, the structure of the banking system is responsible for a fragmented stock market that is of secondary importance to the German debt markets as a source of corporate financing. This is due partly to the practice of universal banking in Germany. As we discussed earlier, German banks have significant ownership positions in commercial firms and traditionally control the major stock exchanges and the brokerage business. As a result, German firms, under the control of the banks, have relied on bank credit and bond issues to finance growth. More recently, efforts to liberalize the German financial system have resulted in some integration of the German stock markets and an increase in the number and volume of issues traded on major exchanges.

Table 8-5
Foreign Transactions in Domestic Equity Markets: Share of Domestic Trading

(Percent of total volume)

	1985	1988
Japan	8.7	6.5
Canada	29.5	21.6
Germany	29.9	8.7
U.S.	9.7	13.1
U.K.	37.3	20.8
France	38.0	43.5
Switzerland	4.6	6.3

Source: Pavel/McElravey, "Globalization in the Financial Services Industry," *Economic Perspectives* Federal Reserve Bank of Chicago, May/June 1990, p. 3–21.

Derivative Markets

As the markets for equity and debt securities have become globalized, similar effects have occurred in markets for so-called derivative products such as Eurodollar futures and dollar options, foreign currency futures and options, options on cross-listed equity securities, stock index options and futures, and options and futures on governments securities. (We discuss derivatives in detail in Chapter 14 to 16.) Initially, the effects of globalization in derivative products affected U.S. markets primarily, as most of the trading in these products took place over U.S. futures and options exchanges.

As cross-border activity in the underlying assets increased around the world, demand from foreign countries for trading in their associated derivatives increased. For example, foreign investors in U.S. Treasury bills who desired to hedge their positions with T-bill futures might establish a position over the CME. In fact, the

Figure 8-5
World equity markets (Market Capitalization—1988). *Source: H.L. Baer, "Foreign Competition in U.S. Banking Markets,"* Economic Perspectives *Federal Reserve Bank of Chicago, May/June 1990, pp. 22–32.*

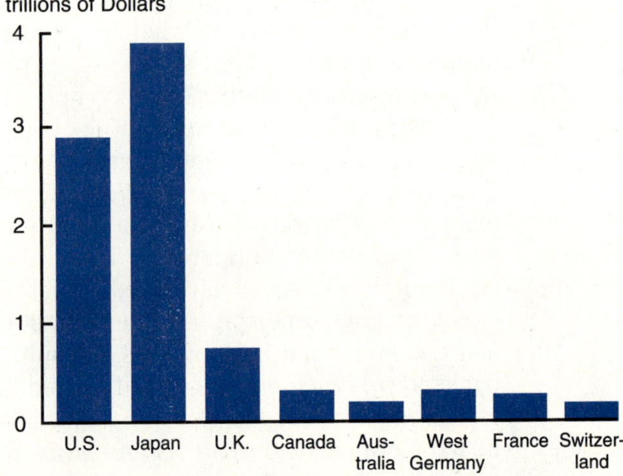

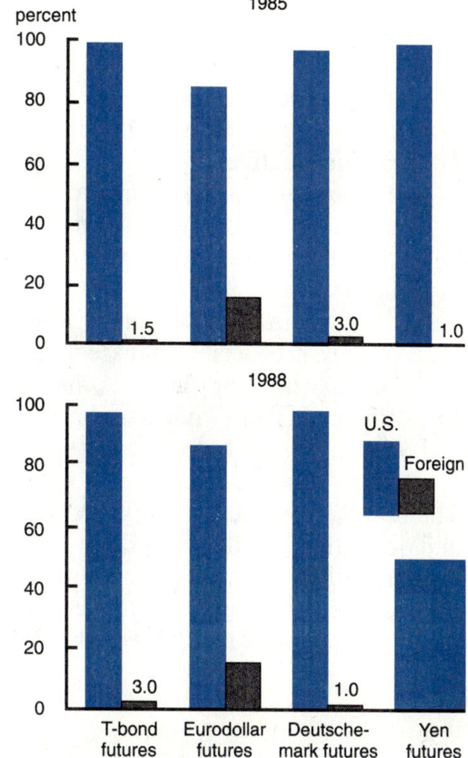

Figure 8-6
World competition for futures contracts (Market share of world volume).
Source: *H.L. Baer, "Foreign Competition in U.S. Banking Markets,"* Economic Perspectives *Federal Reserve Bank of Chicago, May/June 1990, pp. 22–32.*

extended trading sessions established by many exchanges were set up to accommodate such trades; though, as globalization progressed, foreign exchanges were established that would compete with U.S. exchanges in many derivative products, such as T-bond and Eurodollar futures.

The major competition from abroad for U.S. options and futures exchanges come from the London International Financial Futures Exchange (LIFFE) and the Singapore International Monetary Exchange (SIMEX). LIFFE competes with U.S. exchanges for trading in Eurodollar and U.S. Treasury bond futures and options. SIMEX competes in Eurodollar as well as Deutschemark and yen futures contracts. As shown in Figure 8-6, LIFFE has increased its share of trading in U.S. T-bond products from a 1.5 percent in 1985 to 3.0 percent in 1988. The strongest competition from LIFFE and SIMEX occurs in the market for Eurodollar futures and options (a combined share of 14 percent of trading volume) and in the market for yen futures and options, where the market share held by SIMEX is over 45 percent. This underlines the importance of organizing trading in derivatives in the same time zone as trading in the underlying asset.

While U.S. exchange holds the advantage in trading of most derivative products, the integration of financial markets worldwide makes the organization of foreign exchanges for derivatives more practical. In the futures and options markets, the number of exchanges established worldwide grew from 52 in 1985 to 72 in 1989, an increase in 20 exchanges over four years.

SUMMARY

The globalization of financial markets affords significant benefits for both demanders and users of funds. More integrated financial markets give investors better opportunities to diversify risk and access to broader markets. Borrowers gain access to foreign credit and capital markets, providing more efficient financing alternatives to support multinational operations.

In this chapter we described the evolution of the global financial marketplace in two major dimensions. First, the development of international banking was discussed. Activities of U.S. banks in foreign banking markets and in the unregulated offshore markets were discussed and the various organizational forms taken by multinational banking facilities abroad were described. The role of U.S. banks in trade finance, security underwriting, and foreign lending was explained. Finally, the activities of foreign banking in U.S. markets were explained and discussed.

Next we discussed the development and integration of world security markets. The relative importance and growth in the international markets for bonds, equities, and derivative products was described and explained. While the world security markets are still dominated by the United States and Japan, deregulation and advances in electronic communications have increased the competitiveness of smaller markets and exchanges in other countries.

QUESTIONS

1. Explain how the creation of a portfolio comprised of securities from various countries enhances diversification over that available from a portfolio invested in the securities of only one country.
2. What is an Edge Act corporation and how can it be used? What are the various ways in which a U. S. bank can establish operations abroad?
3. Explain the advantages of Eurodollar deposits and Eurobonds.
4. What is LDC lending? How has LDC lending affected commercial banks in the U.S.?
5. In the California banking industry, how important an element are Japanese banks? How have recent difficulties with capital levels affected Japanese banks?
6. What is universal banking? How is it practiced in Germany and Japan? Should the United States move toward a system of universal banking? Discuss the pros and cons.
7. Give an assessment of the importance of international transactions in the global equity and bond markets? What are some of the important forces responsible for recent trends in this area?
8. Do you believe that globalization of financial markets is a dangerous or advantageous development for the U. S. economy? Discuss the pros and cons.

REFERENCES

Abken, P. "The Globalization of Stock, Futures, and Options Markets." *Economic Review* [Federal Reserve Bank of Atlanta] (July-Aug) 1991, pp. 1–22.

Baer, H.L. "Foreign Competition in U.S. Banking Markets." *Economic Perspectives* [Federal Reserve Bank of Chicago] (May/June) 1990, pp. 22–32.

Genay, H. "Japan's Corporate Groups." *Economic Perspectives* [Federal Reserve Bank of Chicago] (Jan/Feb 1991) pp. 20–30.

Hale, D. "Learning from Germany and Japan." *Wall Street Journal* February 4, 1991.

James, C. "Heterogeneous Creditors and the Market Value of Bank LDC Loan Portfolios." *Journal of Monetary Economics* 25 (1990), pp. 325–346.

Kimura, Y., and T. Pugel. "The Structure and Performance of the Japanese Securities Industry." IMRI Working Paper, International University of Japan.

McCauley, R.N., and R. Seth. "Foreign Bank Credit to U.S. Corporations: The Implications of Offshore Loans." *Quarterly Review* [Federal Reserve Bank of New York] 17–1 (Spring 1992) pp. 52–65.

Pavel, C., and J. McElravey. "Globalization in the Financial Services Industry." *Economic Perspectives* [Federal Reserve Bank of Chicago] (May/June) 1990, pp. 3–21.

Zimmerman, G.C. "The Growing Presence of Japanese Banks in California." *Economic Review* [Federal Reserve Bank of San Francisco] 3(1989), pp. 3–17.

• Part II •

Interest Rates and Exchange Rates in a Global Economy

Interest Rates and Fixed-Income Securities in a Market Economy

Term Structure of Interest Rates

Exchange Rates and Capital Flows in the Global Economy

Government Policy and Interest Rates in a Global Economy

The Monetary Policy Debate

• *Chapter 9*

Interest Rates and Fixed-Income Securities in a Market Economy

In this chapter we focus on the determinants of the short-term interest rate in the economy and on the fundamentals of the risk structure of fixed-income securities. You may recall that we provided an introduction to the terminology used to describe the various rates of interest found in financial markets in Chapter 2. We use a number of those various definitions of the interest rate in this chapter. We begin with a treatment of our fundamental approach to valuation of fixed income securities. Then we examine the risk structure of interest rates. We break down the risk of fixed income securities into *four* components. The first three—market value risk, reinvestment risk, and prepayment risk—have to do with interest rate risk; the fourth is the risk of default. In the remainder of the chapter we concentrate on the basic determinants of the short-term interest rate. In Chapter 10 we examine the link between long-term and short-term interest rates. The key learning points in the chapter are listed below.

• *Concepts to Learn in Chapter 9* •

- How different types of interest rate risk affect the value of fixed-income securities
- How default risk influences interest rates
- What market forces determine real and nominal interest rates
- How you can and cannot forecast interest rates

The Nature of Risk in Fixed-Income Claims

In this section we identify and describe four forms or types of risk arising from uncertain timing of cash flows or uncertain interest rates and the risk of default on the payment of cash flows to a fixed-income security. The four forms or types of risk exposure are:

reinvestment risk
market value risk
prepayment or call risk
default or credit risk

Before we address these risks in fixed-income securities, let's spell out a simple approach to valuation that will be the foundation of everything else we will do.

The Valuation Framework

We need a basic approach to valuation of the simplest kinds of fixed-income securities. We begin with risk-free fixed-income securities. As we progress through the book we discuss how we can deal with various sources of risk. By risk-free cash flow we mean that the amount and the timing of the cash flow are certain. We also assume that, though we cannot predict the short-term interest rate that may prevail when a cash flow is to be received, we can observe interest rates today that apply to the time each cash flow in a security is to be received. The essence of the valuation of such a risk-free cash flow stream is to discount each individual cash flow in that stream by the zero-coupon interest rate pertaining to the date when that cash flow is to be received. Thus, we need to start by defining the zero-coupon yields and the yield curve. Recall that we have defined ${}_0r_N$ as the yield at time 0 on a zero-coupon instrument that pays a cash flow at time N. If we look to the set of such market interest rates, or yields to maturity, for a set of zero-coupon bonds with different maturities, then we can construct the zero-coupon yield curve. The yield curve portrays a set of such interest rates in a graph with the yield on the vertical axis and the maturity on the horizontal axis. We take up such yield curves in some detail in the next chapter. Henceforth, for simplicity of exposition, we drop the first subscript on r, as long as we are talking about the present time, or time 0. Only if we are dealing with observing r at some future or past date will we reinstate this first subscript.

Suppose we have a set of such yields observed at time 0: $r_1, r_2, r_3, \ldots r_{N-1}, r_N$. Also suppose we have a fixed income security with risk-free cash flows equal to C_1, $C_2, C_3, \ldots C_{N-1}, C_N$. The appropriate value of this instrument is equal to the present value of the cash flow stream when each cash flow, C_t, is discounted by the zero-coupon discount rate of the corresponding maturity:

$$\text{Present Value} = \Sigma_{t=1}^{N} \frac{C_t}{(1 + r_t)^t}$$

For example, suppose we had a bond with five cash flows to be paid one, two, three, four, and five years from now, respectively. Example cash flows and example values of the zero-coupon yields are presented in Table 9-1. Then, by our valuation equation the value of this bond would be:

Table 9-1

Cash Flows and Corresponding Zero-Coupon Yields

Year	**1**	**2**	**3**	**4**	**5**
Cash flow	\$100,000	\$125,000	\$150,000	\$175,000	\$200,000
Yield	6%	7.5%	9 %	10%	9%

$$\text{Bond value} = \frac{\$100{,}000}{1.06} + \frac{\$125{,}000}{1.075^2} + \frac{\$150{,}000}{1.09^3} + \frac{\$175{,}000}{1.1^4} + \frac{\$200{,}000}{1.09^5}$$

$$= \$567{,}847.$$

It is very important to distinguish between this basic valuation equation and the present value of the discount bond stated in Chapter 2, which we used to define the yield to maturity. Notice there are many interest rates or discount rates in this valuation equation. Each cash flow is discounted at a separate interest or discount rate that corresponds to that cash flow's maturity. If, by chance, all these discount rates were identical, then that discount rate would be equal to the yield to maturity. But this would be a very rare situation. Moreover, if we observe the price of the instrument, we can always compute the yield to maturity; it is simply the internal rate of return. But it is a very dangerous number because it is not the appropriate discount rate for any individual cash flow to which this security gives title.

Overview of the Types of Interest Rate Risk

Before we take up each of the four types of interest rate risk we mentioned earlier we must clarify the nature of the investment horizon of an investor in fixed-income securities and how this horizon influences his or her risk exposure. Suppose an investor buys a fixed-income security and holds it for a period of H years. There are any number of reasons why this investor might have a specific intended holding period, but in general the idea is that after H years this person is planning to use the proceeds from this investment for some kind of consumption. Suppose our investor buys a fixed-income obligation that has maturity equal to N years ($N > H$) that has a cash flow stream spread out over its life; that is, it is not a zero-coupon bond. Now we need to ask, What will cause the total proceeds this investor will have at year H to fluctuate, *or*, What are the sources of uncertainty about the value the investor will have at time H?

To answer this question we must define the sources of the total value the investor will have at year H. There are two sources of such value. One is that the investor will still own a fixed-income obligation with $N-H$ years to maturity. This means that our investor will have title to cash flows that we can designate, using our earlier notation, as C_{H+1}, $C_{H+2}, \ldots C_N$. The value of these cash flows will be determined by the discount rates prevailing in year H, applicable to these cash flows: ${}_Hr_{H+1}, {}_Hr_{H+2}, \ldots {}_Hr_N$. There is no reason to believe that these interest rates will be the same ones that prevailed at time 0 for these same maturity cash flows. Therefore, the value of these specific cash flows at year H may be quite different from what it would be using the interest rates at time 0. This market value risk arises because the discount rates at which cash flows are valued change over time.

The second source of uncertainty pertains to the accumulated value that our investor may realize from reinvestment of the cash flows received between time 0 and time H. For example, the cash flow received at time $1 (C_1)$ will be reinvested at time 1 and held until time H. At least that is reasonable behavior if our investor is using this security to fund consumption at time H, as we have assumed. While there is no uncertainty about the amount of the cash flow received at time 1, there is uncertainty about the amount of earnings that cash flow can generate between time 1 and time H. If at time 1 the investor reinvests that cash flow in an $H-1$ maturity security, then the value of the proceeds at time H will depend on the value or discount rates applicable at time 1 to that security. This is referred to as reinvestment risk.

Both of these sources of risk exposure are illustrated in Figure 9-1, which shows on a time line the cash flows to be received at each point. At time H, part of the value comes from reinvested cash flows received before time H; the other part comes from the present value of cash flows to be received after time H. Both are determined by the behavior of interest rates over time. You can see the nature of these risks most clearly if you imagine that the holding period was very short (i.e., H was very close to zero). Then, nearly all the risk exposure would be market value risk, as there would be very little reinvestment of cash flows. At the other extreme, imagine the holding period was nearly as long as the maturity of the bond (i.e., H is very close to N). Then, there is very little market value risk because the bond will be very close to maturity at time H. Thus, nearly all the risk is reinvestment risk.

Figure 9-1
Time line showing investor's total proceeds at time H.

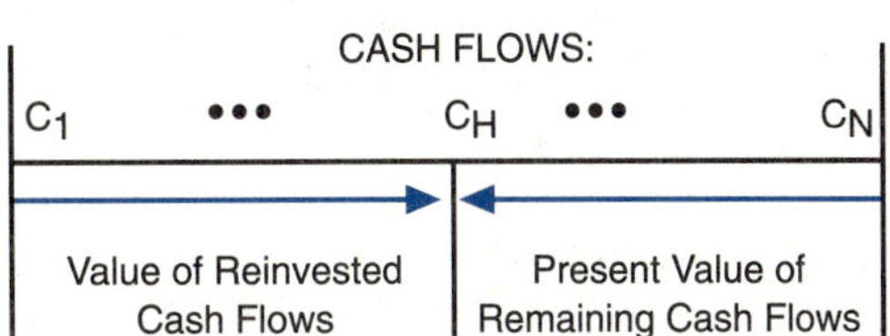

Thus far, our story has assumed that the cash flows themselves cannot change. Assuming the borrower that issued the security does not default, so that the cash flows cannot be diminished, the only question is whether their timing can be changed. But suppose the borrower can terminate the contract by making a lump-sum payment to the holder of the security. In a standard bond or mortgage, this would mean that the borrower paid off the principal, which would alter the cash flows. This would be harmful to the holder of the security if the value of the remainder of the cash flow stream, when it was paid off, was greater than the amount paid to terminate the contract. This is what is referred to as *prepayment* or *call risk.* We now explore each of the three sources of risk in more detail.

Reinvestment Risk

Reinvestment risk generally accrues to financial contracts that involve more than one cash flow. The yield on such securities depends in an important way on the reinvestment opportunities available for cash flows received before the contract matures. For example, investment in coupon bonds would involve some degree of reinvestment risk. The risk comes from uncertainty surrounding the interest rate at which intermittent coupon payments can be invested over the life of the bond. Some securities present no risks in this regard. Examples include zero-coupon bonds, single payment loans, and certain kinds of certificates of deposit, to name a few. These instruments deliver only one cash flow—on their maturity date—and so produce no intermittent cash flows that need to be reinvested.

The notion of reinvestment risk can be illustrated by a simple example. Consider a bank that makes a $100,000 installment loan to a commercial customer at an interest rate of 10 percent per year. The contract specifies that interest be compounded annually and repayment take place in three equal installments over the next three years. The annual installment payment necessary to amortize the loan is computed as follows:

$$\$100{,}000 = \left[\frac{1 - \frac{1}{(1.10)^3}}{0.10}\right] A$$

$$A = \$40{,}211.48$$

The annual cash flows and the associated reinvestment problem to the bank are illustrated in Figure 9-2. The cash flows of $40,211.48 are scheduled to be received by the bank at the end of years one through three, respectively. Assume the bank is concerned about the total accumulated earnings of its $100,000 investment over the three-year life of the loan. Each cash flow poses a different reinvestment problem to the bank. As Figure 9-2 shows, the total accumulation of cash flows to the bank over the three-year period of the loan depends on two uncertain interest rates: ${}_1r_2$, the interest rate at which, one year from now, the bank can reinvest money for one year, and ${}_2r_3$, the interest rate at which, two years from now, the bank can invest money for one year. The first cash flow must be reinvested for two years, first at ${}_1r_2$, and then at ${}_2r_3$. The second cash flow must be reinvested for one year at ${}_2r_3$. The third cash flow is received at the end of year three and does not have to be reinvested during the three-year term of the investment.

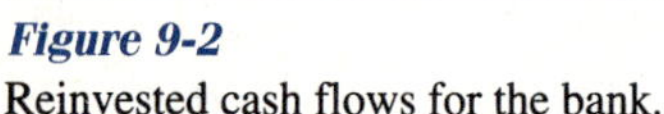

Figure 9-2
Reinvested cash flows for the bank.

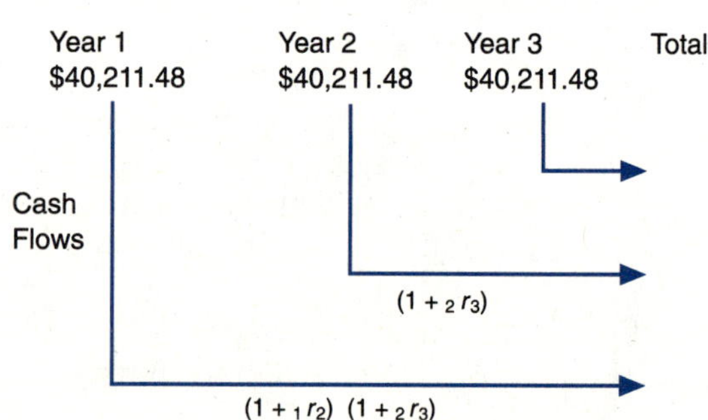

The total accumulation of cash flows over the three-year period is tabulated for three alternative interest rate scenarios: one of stable rates, where ${}_1r_2 = {}_2r_3 = 10$ percent; one of rising rates, where ${}_1r_2 = 11$ percent and ${}_2r_3 = 12$ percent; and one of declining rates, where ${}_1r_2 = 9$ percent and ${}_2r_3 = 8$ percent. (Table 9-2). Under each rate scenario, the three-year yield to maturity is computed. Notice how the behavior of interest rates over the life of the loan affects the bank's annual yield on the original $100,000 over the three-year period. While the original interest rate and the ex ante yield to maturity on the loan are 10 percent, the actual ex post three-year yield depends on the rates at which cash flows can be reinvested over the term of the loan. As we pointed out above, the ex-post annual yield on the investment equals

Table 9-2
Value and Holding Period Yield for Different Interest Rate Scenarios

Interest Rate Scenario	$_1r_2$ (%)	$_2r_3$ (%)	Total Accumulation	Holding Period Yield
Stable	10	10	\$133,100	10
Rising	11	12	\$135,239	10.59
Falling	9	8	\$130,977	9.41

the ex ante yield to maturity only when ex post reinvestment rates are equal to the original yield.[1]

Market Value Risk

The concept of market value risk can easily be explained by continuing our previous example. In this case we are concerned with how the value of the installment loan will be affected by changes in interest rates after the loan is made but before it matures.

For example, suppose the bank were to consider selling this loan to another bank at the end of year two. At that date, the bank buying the loan will be buying a claim providing one cash flow of \$40,211.48 in one year. In other words, in two years, when the loan is sold, the three-year installment loan that was originally booked will have already paid its first two cash flows and have only one more installment remaining. The value of the loan after two years, V_2, will depend on the prevailing interest rate on one-year loans, $(_2r_3)$ as follows:

$$V_2 = \$40{,}211.48/(1 + {_2r_3})$$

Now reconsider each of the interest rate pictures previously defined. The resale value of the loan, V_2, is tabulated in Table 9-3, for each value of $_2r_3$. Notice how the risk associated with market value is negatively correlated with risk associated with reinvestment. Higher rates were previously shown above to generate better reinvestment opportunities and higher overall yields. In this case, higher rates have just the opposite implication. When rates rise, the resale value of the loan is lower as the market applies a higher discount rate of 12 percent to value the promised cash flow of \$40,211.48. At the same time, when rates drop the lower required yield of 8 percent implies a higher resale value for the loan. Thus, when the three-year loan is sold after two years, changes in interest rates have both positive and negative implications for the investment yield.

---

[1]It may seem arbitrary to evaluate the yield on the loan over three years, and to assume that the bank would actually reinvest cash flows in the manner described; however, in order to evaluate the yield on any multiple–cash flow investment, some horizon must be chosen. This implies some reinvestment assumptions. The loan in the example above actually involves three "maturities": \$40,211.48 at the end of each of three years. A year-three investment horizon was chosen so as to describe the yield to maturity of the loan. To compute that yield, some assumption had to be made about the disposition of the first two cash flows.

Table 9-3
Value of Loan After Two Years

Interest Rate Scenario	${}_2r_3$	V_2
Stable	10%	$36,555.89
Rising	12%	$35,903.11
Falling	8%	$37,232.85

To illustrate this point more carefully, the total accumulation of cash flows to the originating bank after two years is outlined in Figure 9-3. As indicated by the left-hand arrow, the first cash flow is reinvested at ${}_1r_2$ for one year. The second cash flow is received at the end of year two and thus, has no associated interest rate risk. The third cash flow, indicated by the right-hand arrow, is in essence sold to the buying bank at its capitalized value determined by ${}_2r_3$. For the three interest rate scenarios the total accumulation of cash flows is demonstrated in Table 9-4.

The accumulated values at each of the indicated interest rates by the end of year two are given in parentheses. Once again, if rates remain stable at 10 percent, the actual cash flow over the two-year period yields a compound rate of return of 10 percent. In fact, if the loan were sold after one year, a similar result would obtain as long as rates stayed at 10 percent. The general message here is that under circumstances where interest rates remain unchanged—that is, the original yield to maturity is equal to reinvestment rates—the annual investment yield to the bank will be equal to the original yield, regardless of its investment horizon.

Also notice another important implication from the bank loan example. The possible yield fluctuations associated with the three- and the two-year horizons are very different. For the same system of interest rate scenarios, the three-year strategy provides a yield of 10.59 percent when rates rise and 9.41 percent when they fall, a range of 1.18 percent. On the other hand, the two-year strategy provides a yield of 10.12 percent when rates fall and 9.89 percent when they rise. The difference comes from the fact that in the case of the two-year horizon, reinvestment risk and market risk are at least partially offsetting. When rates rise, the first cash flow can be reinvested at a superior rate but the loan is sold at an inferior rate and a lower dollar price. When rates fall reinvestment returns are lower but the loan is sold at a higher price.

Figure 9-3
Reinvestment and market value risk at time 2.

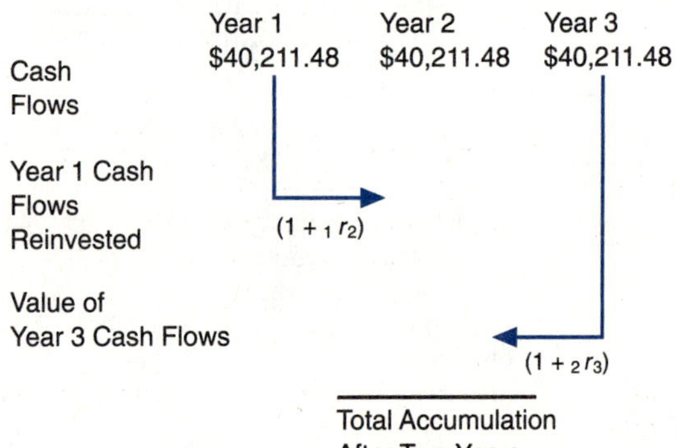

Table 9-4
Accumulated Cash Flows After Two Years

Interest Rate Scenario	${}_1r_2$ (%)	${}_2r_3$ (%)	Total Accumulation After 2 Years	2-Year Yield (%)
Stable	10 ($44,232.63)	10	$121,000	10.00
Rising	11 ($44,634.74)	12	$120,749	9.89
Falling	9 ($43,830.51)	8	$121,275	10.12

Prepayment or Call Risk

Prepayment risk arises when the borrower (the issuer) of a fixed income obligation has the option to prepay that obligation. In the context of bonds issued by corporations or governments, this is generally referred to as the "option to call the bond." In mortgages and mortgage-backed securities it is the "prepayment option." The prepayment problem is more complicated in the mortgage market than in corporate debt. Prepayment of mortgages can arise for one of two reasons. First, if the borrower moves to a new home, the mortgage is usually paid off when the home is sold. Second, if interest rates decline significantly relative to the interest rate on the mortgage, borrowers may prepay simply because they want to reduce their total debt burden. Since prepayment is at the borrower's discretion, the actual timing of prepayment on any given mortgage is uncertain. Thus, from the vantage point of the investor in either an individual mortgage or a security backed by mortgages, the prepayment option introduces uncertainty into the timing of cash flows from the mortgage. This source of uncertainty is not present in Treasury obligations, or even in most corporate obligations. Even if the corporate bond has a call provision, the timing of the exercise of a call on a corporate bond is generally determined by the financial cost of exercising the call option. Because the prepayment decision on a mortgage is determined by a larger number of factors, more uncertainty surrounds prepayment patterns on mortgages than call provisions on corporate bonds. This uncertainty has historically been a major drawback of residential mortgages as an investment vehicle, but it has also provided a stimulus for the development of innovative ways to manage this risk.

What makes prepayment risk such a problem for an investor in either mortgages or corporate bonds with call provisions is that prepayments tend to increase when interest rates are declining. This is the reinvestment risk problem. As either the corporate bonds or mortgages in a portfolio prepay, the investor in that portfolio must reinvest those prepayments. If interest rates decline, the holding period yield on the reinvested proceeds of the prepayments will decline, harming the investor. Moreover, as prepayments increase as interest rates fall, the magnitude of the reinvestment risk exposure is also sensitive to interest rates.

This is clearly evident in historical prepayment experience. During the 1980s prepayment rates on FHLMC and GNMA pass-through securities were lowest in 1981 and 1982 (approximately 2 percent) when interest rates were at their peak and rose significantly as interest rates declined during the rest of the decade. Most of this experience does not portray with sufficient clarity what happens when there is a significant decline in interest rates. Such an episode occurred in late 1991, when interest rates on 30-year fixed-rate conventional mortgages dropped to below 9 percent. The significant decline in mortgage rates in late 1991 paralleled a decline in other long-term interest rates, but the decline was not as steep as the fall in short-term rates in response to the Federal Reserve's repeated reduction in the discount rate and in the federal funds rate. As mortgage rates fell to the lowest level in over a decade, many borrowers with outstanding fixed-rate mortgages at higher rates or with floating rate mortgages were hoping to refinance those loans at the bottom of the interest rate cycle. Of course, in an efficient market, this is extraordinarily difficult to accomplish. Figure 9-4 shows monthly data on prepayment rates for Federal National Mortgage Association (FNMA) mortgage-backed securities for the year of 1991. Note that prepayments accelerated early in the year and then fell back somewhat as rates stabilized between 9 percent and 10 percent. Later, as mortgage rates fell below 9 percent prepayment rates again accelerated, to a little more than 17 percent.

Default or Credit Risk

To understand how the market factors default risk into the pricing of debt instruments, it is useful first to explain and illustrate (or redefine) three different definitions of the yield on a fixed-income claim: (1) the ex ante expected yield to maturity, (2) the ex ante promised yield to maturity, and (3) the actual, or ex post yield to maturity or holding-period yield. Recall that we first introduced the last two concepts in Chapter 2.

The *expected* yield to maturity is the yield based on the expected, rather than the promised, stream of cash flows associated with a financial claim. The market price of the claim can be viewed as the value of the stream of expected future cash flows, discounted at the expected yield to maturity. Alternatively, the expected yield can be

Figure 9-4

Prepayment rates in 1991. *Source:* Wall Street Journal, *January 17, 1992. Reprinted by permission of* The Wall Street Journal, © *1992 Dow Jones and Company, Inc. All Right Reserved Worldwide.*

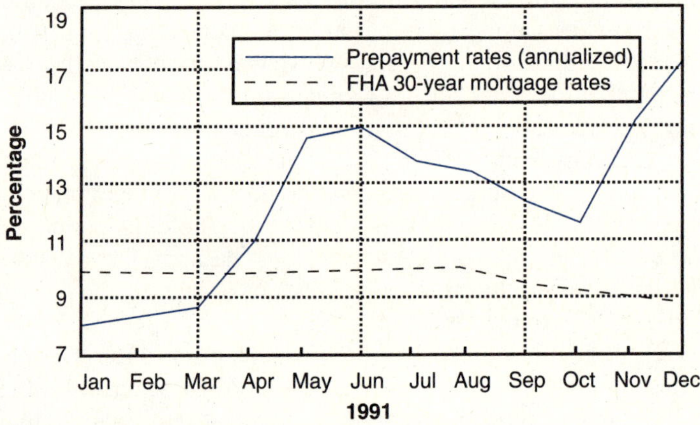

viewed as the ex ante required rate of return applied by the market in pricing the claim.[2] The level of the expected yield depends on the degree of default risk assessed by the market. Higher-risk claims—those having more uncertainty surrounding the level of future cash flows—are priced to yield higher expected returns. Thus, when a risky security is priced, the price is set so that the payment stream expected on the security provides the ex ante yield on invested capital necessary to compensate the investor for bearing risk.

The *promised* yield to maturity, R_p, is the yield on a financial claim assuming that all promised payments on the claim are paid in full and on schedule. At a given price, the promised yield is effectively the "no-default yield" on the claim. For a risky security, the promised yield is the highest yield that can be obtained over the remaining time to maturity. If default occurs on any of the remaining scheduled payments, the actual yield to maturity is less than the promised yield.

The *actual,* or ex post, yield to maturity, R_a, on a financial claim is the yield to maturity based on the actual payments made on the claim over the time remaining to maturity. Actual yields are computed from the historical price at which the claim is purchased and from succeeding payments, which are actually delivered during the remaining time to maturity. At a given price, the expected yield to maturity is the ex ante expectation of the actual yield to maturity, or $E(R_a)$.

To illustrate each of these concepts, consider the simple example of a pure discount, or zero-coupon, bond. Assume the bond has one year remaining to maturity and bears a redemption value, or face value, of $100. Also, assume that the bond is risky in the sense that the issuer may not be able to meet the promised payment in full. In pricing the bond, the market assesses the uncertainty surrounding repayment by the issuer according to the probability distribution illustrated in Table 9-5.

In this example, one of four possible economic states can obtain during the next year. Depending on the economic state, the issuer's ability to meet the scheduled $100 payment at year's end will vary. Under conditions of economic growth, the issuer will realize sufficient cash revenues to meet in full the scheduled debt payment of $100. Under three different scenarios of economic recession, however, the issuer will not be able meet the scheduled payment in full. C_1 is the amount *actually paid* by the issuer of the bond at maturity under each economic state. Prob $\{C_1\}$ is the probability that a given economic state will occur during the next year, and, therefore, the probability that the issuer will pay the amount, C_1, on the scheduled maturity date. The maximum the issuer will repay is the promised $100. As shown by the distribution above, there is a positive probability the issuer will pay an amount less than promised, which constitutes default. Thus, the bond market believes there is an 80 percent chance the issuer will meet the promised payment of $100 in one year. In addition, there is a 10 percent probability that the issuer will default in the amount of $5, a 5 percent probability of $10 default, and a 5 percent probability of $15 default.

[2]For multiple payment securities, like coupon bonds, expected cash flows scheduled at each date may be valued at different rates which depend on the timing of the payment and the risk surrounding the payment. The yield to maturity on such securities is a kind of complex average of the more fundamental rates applied by the market to the expected cash flows on risky debt.

Table 9-5
Probability Distribution of Payoffs on a One-Year, Pure Discount Bond

Economic State	Prob$\{C_1\}$	C_1
Growth	0.80	\$100
Mild recession	0.10	\$95
Moderate recession	0.05	\$90
Severe recession	0.05	\$85

Given the distribution of outcomes above, the expected payment due in one year is calculated as the probability-weighted sum of the four possible payoffs on the bond, or,

$$\mathrm{E}(C_1) = 0.8 \times \$100 + 0.10 \times \$95 + 0.05 \times \$90 + 0.05 \times \$85 = \$98.25$$

Thus, the bond market's expected payoff on the bond is \$98.25, which implies an expected shortfall, or expected dollar default of \$1.75.[3]

The *risk of default* associated with the bond is manifested in the variability of the payoff outcomes, especially those in which the promised payments are not made in full. Generally, the higher the probability of the more extreme default outcomes, or the more extreme the respective default outcomes, the more risky is the bond in the eyes of the market. Assuming the bond market is averse to bearing risk, the greater the perceived risk by the market the greater will be the market's ex ante required return for the bond. The adjustment made by the market for default risk can be conceptualized as follows,

$$E(R_a) = R_f + \Theta \tag{9.1}$$

where $E(R_a)$ is the ex ante required return set by the market in pricing the bond, R_f is the prevailing yield on default risk–free bonds with the same maturity, and Θ is the premium required by the market for bearing the default risk associated with this bond. Suppose the risk premium (Θ) required by the market for our pure discount bond described above is 2.5 percent. This premium represents market-determined compensation to the bondholder for bearing the default risk characterized in Table 9-5. Also, assume the default risk–free yield on one-year debt is 5 percent. Then, the risk-adjusted, ex ante required yield on the bond would be 5 percent + 2.5 percent = 7.5 percent. The market value of the bond, *V*, would then be determined as the discounted value of the *expected* redemption payment, or,

$$V = \frac{\mathrm{E}(C_1)}{1 + \mathrm{E}(R_a)} = \frac{\$98.25}{1.075} = \$91.40 \tag{9.2}$$

[3]The expected payoff of \$98.25 is not one of the possible outcomes defined by the distribution. The expected payoff defines the average tendency of the probability distribution. That is, if drawings from the distribution were to be repeated many times, the average outcome from those drawing would be \$98.25.

Equations 9.1 and 9.2 constitute a simple yet logical valuation model for risky debt. One difficulty with it is that it cannot be verified directly because we can never directly observe the expected redemption payment, $E(C_1)$, the risk-adjusted expected return, $E(R_a)$, or the market default risk premium, Θ. The only observable factors associated with bond valuation are the bond's current market price and its promised, or scheduled, payoffs. This implies the only ex ante observable yield is the *promised* yield to maturity, which for the pure discount bond is defined by,

$$V = \frac{\$100}{1 + R_p} \tag{9.3}$$

where, R_p is the promised yield to maturity. Note that this represents the conventional yield to maturity defined for more complex securities in Chapter 2.

The promised yield to maturity is the yield most commonly associated with fixed-income claims in the financial press. In our example of the bond in Table 9-5 we can use equation 9.3 to solve for R_p. At the market price of \$91.41, the promised yield to maturity for the pure discount bond is 9.41 percent. In other words, if the discount bond is purchased today for \$91.41 and \$100 is received (as promised) in one year, then the actual rate of return on the bond will be 9.41 percent. For another example, on 5 March 1992 the 12.75 percent coupon bonds maturing in 2002 issued by Inland Steel traded at 107 1/2. At this price, the implied yield was given as 11.13 percent.[4] The calculation of this yield is based on the assumption that Inland Steel would make its promised coupon and principal payments on schedule for the remaining time to maturity.

Promised yields are often used to represent the market's ex ante required returns on bonds. In so doing, the "default premium" for a bond is defined as the difference between the promised yield and the risk-free yield. In our example, this would be 9.41 percent − 5.00 percent or 4.41 percent. However, the ex ante risk premium above was 2.5 percent. In fact, for risky debt the promised yield to maturity always overstates the market's expected return. In the case of the discount bond, the promised yield is one of four possible *actual* yields to maturity that could be realized. At a given price, V, the actual yield for the discount bond is determined by the actual payoffs in Table 9-6 as,

$$V = \frac{C_1}{1 + R_a} \tag{9.4}$$

Given the current price of \$91.41, the distribution of actual yields across the four possible states of the economy is given in the final column of Table 9-6.

---

[4]This information was taken from the High-Yield Bond Report, *Wall Street Journal,* March 8, 1993, p.C15. Yields on corporate bonds are commonly quoted as the lower of the two, yield to maturity or yield to call.

Table 9-6
Actual Yields to Maturity for A 1-Year, Pure Discount Bond

Economic State	Prob $\{C_1\}$	C_1	R_a (%)
Growth	0.80	$100	9.41
Mild recession	0.10	$95	3.94
Moderate recession	0.05	$90	− 1.53
Severe recession	0.05	$85	− 7.00

R_a indicates the actual, or ex post, yield on the bond. Note also that the expected yield computed earlier, 7.5 percent, is the probability-weighted sum of the four actual yields to maturity given in Table 9-6.

To sum up our discussion so far, Figure 9-5 provides a graphic comparison of the three yields that are important for understanding how the financial market accounts for the risk of default in pricing debt instruments. This figure presents the probability distribution of actual yields to maturity generated at the market price of $91.41. The probability of each of the four possible states, or yields, is measured on the vertical axis and the level of each yield is measured on the horizontal axis in percent. The levels of the risk-free rate and the ex ante required rate of return are indicated by dotted lines at 5 percent and 7.5 percent, respectively. The risk premium, Θ, is indicated

Figure 9-5
Discrete yield distribution for discount bond.

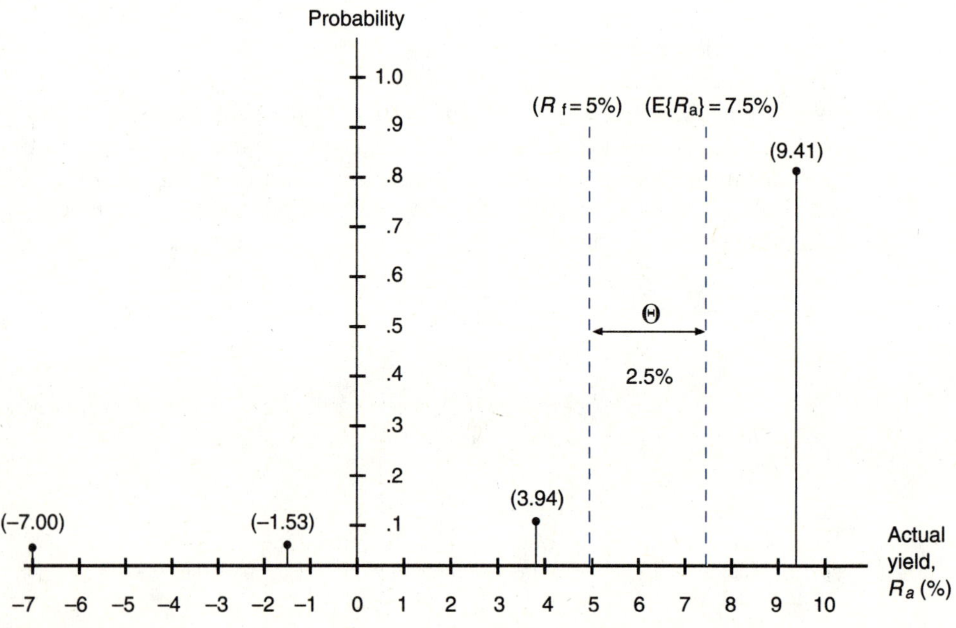

as the spread between R_f and $E(R_a)$. Notice that if the market were to increase the premium required to bear default risk, the market price of the bond would be lowered so as to generate a larger value for $E(R_a)$ and a larger value for Θ. This results in a shift in the entire distribution of actual returns. For example, the promised yield to maturity increases as the price of the bond decreases.

Obviously, our example of only four possible economic pictures is much simplified; however, the intuition of the result in Figure 9-5 can be generalized for claims with continuous distributions of payoffs and yields. Figure 9-6 presents continuous distributions of the actual yield to maturity for two risky bonds. The upper panel of

Figure 9-6
Continuous yield distribution for two risky bonds.

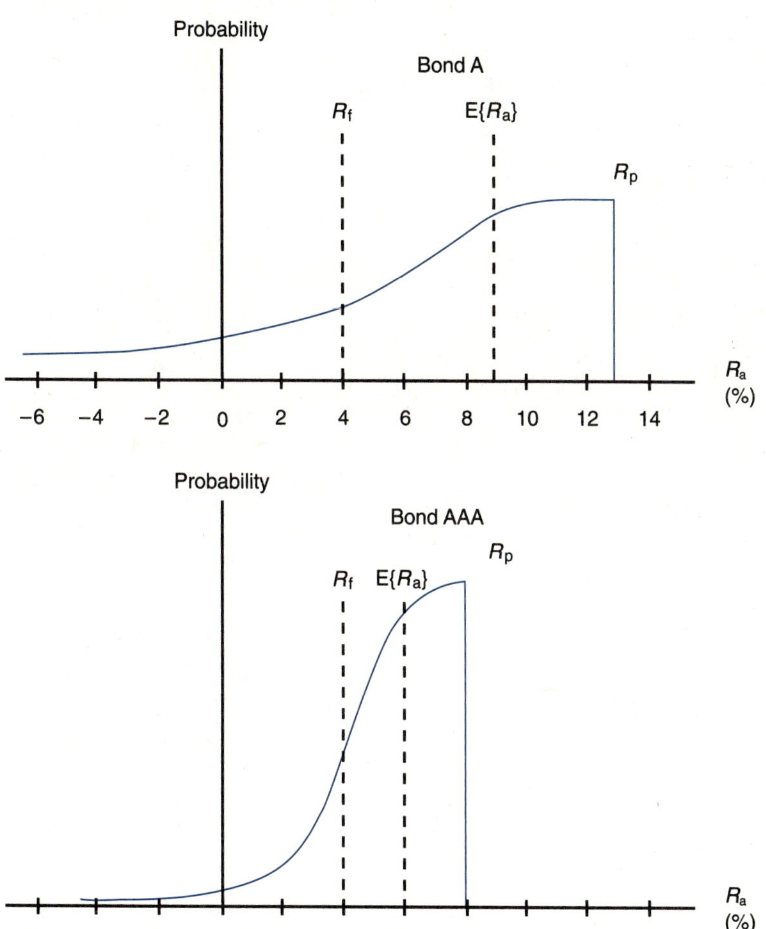

Figure 9-6 shows a hypothetical probability distribution for a "lower-rated" bond. At its current price, this bond has a promised yield to maturity of 12.5 percent. The bond has been priced to generate an expected yield of 8.5 percent with a risk premium of 4.5 percent. The second bond, with the yield distribution shown in the lower panel of Figure 9-6, is a higher-rated bond that is much less risky than the first one. This bond is priced to produce a lower expected yield of 6 percent, with a 2 percent default risk premium. Notice that, as the risk of the bond decreases, the yield distribution of the bond becomes less dispersed, or more compact; the spread between the risk-free yield and the expected yield to maturity, Θ, grows smaller; and the spread between the risk-free rate and the promised yield to maturity decreases. In the limiting case of a risk-free bond, the risk-free yield, the expected yield, and the promised yield are one and the same, or,

$$R_f = E(R_a) = R_p$$

One final point should be made. Bond markets often characterize the default risk on fixed-income instruments by the "yield spread." The yield spread is the difference between the risk-free rate and the promised yield to maturity. As we noted earlier, the yield spread does not directly represent the market's adjustment for default risk; the (unobservable) difference between expected yield and the riskless rate does. Nevertheless, the yield spread is consistent with the market premium for risk, in that as the risk premium increases so does the yield spread. In other words, larger yield spreads indicates larger underlying risk premiums.[5]

Basic Determinants of the Short-Term Interest Rate

A central message of the preceding discussion is the uncertain nature of future interest rates, both short- and long-term. Thus, we need to focus on the basic determinants of these rates. We now discuss some of the key market forces that drive the short-term rate and briefly characterize a stochastic process, or model for its random behavior. In Chapter 10 we turn to the connection between short-term and long-term rates, or the term structure of interest rates.

The Equilibrium Real Interest Rate

Our current understanding of the determinants of the real rate of interest dates back to the work of the famous economist Irving Fisher, who published a book in 1930 titled *The Theory of Interest.* His principal contribution was to examine explicitly the tradeoff between goods produced, purchased, and consumed in distinct time periods, based on individuals' preferences between goods consumed today and goods consumed tomorrow, as well as the production technology that permits investment in capital goods that are used to produce consumer goods for tomorrow. The basic problem is to

[5]We should also note that the bond literature refers to the difference between the promised yield to maturity and the expected yield as the "expected default."

determine an individual's optimal amount of investment in future goods and that person's amount of borrowing or lending with other participants in the market. An equilibrium rate of interest is then determined, where desired borrowing is equal to desired lending for all market participants.

You can think of the interest rate in the same way as you do any other price in the marketplace. There is nothing unique about the function of the interest rate as a price. The only distinction between it and prices in other markets is that the product involved is a little more abstract. We must, therefore, attempt to define precisely the product that is priced by the interest rate. One way to think of the interest rate is this: *It is the price of postponing payment.* This definition is still somewhat ambiguous because it is not the timeliness of the payment itself that is valuable; rather, it is what the payment can be used for—the opportunity cost of not having the funds available. An individual to whom a payment is due who agrees to postpone that payment forgoes the opportunity to consume it or to invest in an alternative investment. The interest rate can therefore be viewed as *the price of forgone consumption,* for the opportunity cost of delayed access to the funds is the postponement of consumption. More often we think of the interest rate as the *price of borrowing* or the price of credit. In effect, this is simply the more typical way of saying that the interest rate is the price of postponing payment or of forgone consumption.

In equilibrium, the real interest rate captures three important factors. It is, first and foremost, the rate at which borrowing and lending are in equilibrium. But, it is also equal to the marginal rate of return on productive investment for all participants in the market. Finally, it is equal to the marginal rate of time preference for market participants, the rate at which they desire to substitute current for future consumption. The real interest rate, therefore, reflects an equilibrium among all these important forces in the economy that determine the economic trade-offs across time. The real interest rate is the fundamental component of all the interest rates observed in the marketplace.

With the aid of Figure 9-7 it is possible to illustrate how the real interest rate is determined as a combination of investors' preferences for consumption, their opportunities to invest, and their ability to borrow and lend with each other. The horizontal axis in this figure measures the individual's current income and consumption, and the vertical axis measures income and consumption tomorrow. Assume that the individual starts with \$50 of current income, represented by the intersections of the II′ curve with the horizontal axis. The constraint this individual faces is defined by the set of investments available. The curved line labeled II′ represents the possible combinations of current and future income the individual can realize by investing his or her initial income in real goods or services. For example, by moving to point C with coordinates 32 and 52 on the line II′, the individual gives up \$18 of current income to invest in the future.

The rate of return or yield this individual receives on the investment can easily be calculated from curve II′. In this investment, which moved the individual from the initial point on the horizontal axis to point C, the rate of return is \$52/(\$50 − \$32) = \$52/\$18 = 289 percent. This is an exceptionally attractive return, but we can tell from the shape of curve II′ that as the individual continues to invest more current

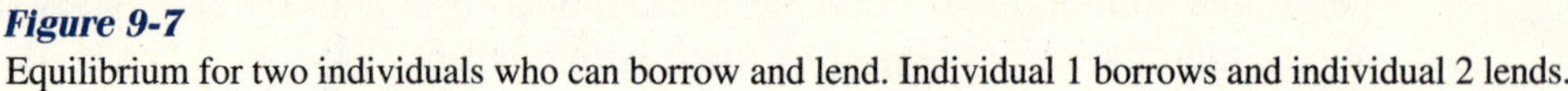

Figure 9-7
Equilibrium for two individuals who can borrow and lend. Individual 1 borrows and individual 2 lends.

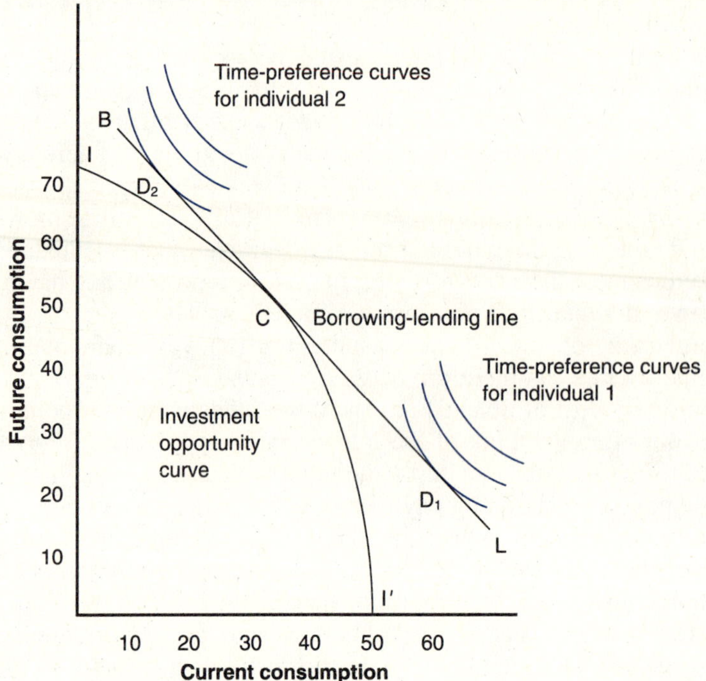

income, the rate of return will decline. If we consider an infinitely small investment, the rate of return is measured by the slope of a line drawn tangent to the curve II′ at that point of investment. This is illustrated by the tangent line at point C. We can see from the shape of the II′ curve that as we move farther up the curve, lines drawn tangent to the curve will have flatter and flatter slopes. This means that the more the individual invests, the lower the rate of return will be. Another way of saying this is that the individual receives diminishing marginal returns on investment.

The second ingredient in determining the real interest rate is each individual's attitude toward consumption today, as opposed to consumption tomorrow. The choice can be thought of as the choice between two distinct commodities. For example, there is a trade-off between days spent skiing at Snowbird, Utah, this year and days spent there next year, just as there is a trade-off between days spent skiing in Utah this year and days spent skiing in Wisconsin this year. Each is a distinct commodity in the sense that the typical skier is not indifferent about substituting one for the other.

The individual's attitude toward trade-offs between commodities, whether they are distinguished by time or other characteristics, can be represented with indifference curves, which show the combinations of commodities to which the individual would be indifferent. For example, a person might say that it didn't matter whether he or she had five days at Snowbird this year or seven days at Snowbird next year; either option would be equally satisfying. However, if the person had to give up one of the days this year, the only way the loss would be acceptable would be if he or she could have two days next year. This trade-off is illustrated with the two sets of curves in the upper left and lower right portions of the figure. This particular type of indifference curve, which is referred to as a "time-preference curve," is drawn to reflect the assumption that, as the individual is deprived of current consumption, ever larger amounts of future consumption are required to make him or her indifferent to the exchange. The curve is therefore drawn convex to the origin.

It is important to see that there will be an infinite number of indifference curves for each individual. The reason for this is that each curve represents the combination of present and future consumption that leave the individual equally satisfied. But it is always possible to come up with combinations that create either more or less satisfaction. For example, ten days at Snowbird this year and ten next year is obviously better than five this year and seven next year. It is also important to see that we have to have individuals in the marketplace who have different preferences to consume today versus tomorrow, in order for them to want to borrow and lend with each other. This is why we have two sets of indifference curves in Figure 9-7.

Finally, we need to introduce a way for our market participants to borrow from or lend to each other. The straight line in the figure represents the opportunity to borrow or lend. The slope of this straight line represents the interest rate at which the individual in the figure can borrow or lend. The fact that the line is straight means that the interest rate does not change with increases or decreases in the amount of borrowing or lending. We could draw any number of these straight lines in Figure 9-7, showing opportunities to borrow and lend, just as we can fill the figure with time-preference curves of an individual. But we will draw in only one of these lines, BL. This line has a slope of −1.1. This means it is consistent with an interest rate of 10 percent.

It will be optimal to invest until the investment opportunity curve is tangent to the line representing borrowing and lending opportunities, as indicated by point C on line BL. Then individual 1 can borrow until she reaches point D_1, which is the point of tangency with her time-preference curve. To see that this is optimal, notice that the individual can move to any position on BL by either borrowing or lending. A movement up and to the left sacrifices current income and is therefore a decision to lend; a movement down and to the right sacrifices future income for current income and is therefore a decision to borrow. By either borrowing or lending and moving along this line, the individual is able to move to a position that is tangent to a time-preference curve (at point D_1).

The second individual whose decision is illustrated in Figure 9-7 is also assumed to start with the same amount of current income, $50. The important distinction between the two is that the second individual chooses to lend rather than to borrow because his time-preference curve is tangent to the borrowing line above its tangency with the investment-opportunity curve at C. This individual finds it optimal to invest up to C and then lend at the prevailing interest rate. As a result, he will shift toward future rather than current consumption, whereas individual 1 borrowed to support current rather than future consumption.

Both of these individuals have an individual equilibrium in the sense that they have chosen a level of investment and borrowing or lending that allows them to achieve the highest possible time-preference curve. In this equilibrium, they equate the marginal rate of time preference, the marginal return on investment, and the interest rate on borrowing and lending. This follows because the straight line representing borrowing and lending opportunities is tangent to both the ll' curve and the time-preference curve. As a result, all three have the same slope. This means that the real interest rate is equal to all three of these alternative concepts of the rate of interest.

Real and Nominal Interest Rates

The real rate of interest is expressed without reference to prices. If the quantity of goods and services available for consumption in time periods 1 and 2 are represented by Q_1 and Q_2, respectively, then

$$\text{Real interest rate} = \frac{Q_2 - Q_1}{Q_1} \tag{9.5}$$

This means that the real interest rate is the real rate of growth in available goods and services or the real rate of growth in the economy. In the long run, the real rate of growth in goods and services is the only source of a real return to capital. Thus, in the long run the real rate of interest is driven toward this real growth rate in the economy.

The *nominal interest rate,* on the other hand, takes into account the change in the price of goods and services. It values the quantity of goods and services in each time period at their going price. If the aggregate price level of all goods and services is represented by P_1 and P_2 in periods 1 and 2, respectively, then the nominal interest rate can be expressed as

$$\text{Nominal interest rate} = \frac{P_2Q_2 - P_1Q_1}{P_1Q_1} \tag{9.6}$$

In addition, the rate of inflation between periods 1 and 2 can be defined as

$$\text{Inflation rate} = \frac{P_2 - P_1}{P_1} \tag{9.7}$$

A relationship between the real and the nominal rate follows directly from these definitions. The nominal interest rate can be expressed as the sum of the real interest rate, the rate of inflation, and the product of the real interest rate and the rate of inflation:

$$\frac{P_2Q_2 - P_1Q_1}{P_1Q_1} = \frac{Q_2 - Q_1}{Q_1} + \frac{P_2 - P_1}{P_1} + \frac{(Q_2 - Q_1)}{Q_1} \times \frac{(P_2 - P_1)}{P_1} \tag{9.8}$$

The nominal rate equals the real rate plus the inflation rate plus the product of these two rates. To see this, expand the right-hand side of equation 9.8 and cancel terms until this expression of the nominal interest rate reduces to the one on the left-hand side of the equation.[6]

A convenient simplification for this equation results in a simple and usable relationship between the nominal rate and the rate of inflation. The simplification relies on the fact that the last term is the product of two small fractions. As a result, it is likely to be so small that it can be harmlessly dropped. For example, suppose that the real rate is 3 percent and the inflation rate is 10 percent; the product of the two will be 0.003. Generally, this is simply too small to make much difference. Therefore, the simple expression for the nominal interest rate is that the nominal rate is approximately equal to the sum of the real interest rate and the rate of inflation:

$$r_N \cong r_R + \%\Delta P \tag{9.9}$$

where

r_N is the nominal rate, r_R the real rate, and $\%\Delta P$ the inflation rate.

For example, if the inflation rate is 10 percent and the real rate is 3 percent, the nominal rate is 13 percent.

Thus far, no economic hypothesis has been offered about the relationship between real and nominal interest rates. The expression just developed follows directly from the definitions of the real interest rate, the nominal interest rate, and the inflation rate. It says nothing about how financial markets respond to inflation. To develop a hypothesis about financial markets and inflation you must recognize that at any time the inflation rate is uncertain. The economic issue, then, is how anticipations of inflation affect the market.

It is exceptionally important to distinguish between anticipated and unanticipated inflation, or, stated another way, between the ex ante (expected) rate of inflation and the ex post (observed) rate of inflation. Irving Fisher offered a hypothesis some years ago about the relationship between nominal interest rates and the market's ex ante, expected inflation rate; that hypothesis is exceptionally relevant today. At first glance the hypothesis looks the same as equation 9.9, but it is not. Equation 9.9 followed directly from the definitions we specified when uncertainty about the inflation rate was ignored. Fisher's hypothesis can be stated as follows:

---

[6]We can rewrite equation 9.8, after expanding the final term, as follows:

$$\frac{P_2Q_2 - P_1Q_1}{P_1Q_1} = \frac{Q_2 - Q_1}{Q_1} + \frac{P_2 - P_1}{P_1} + \frac{P_2Q_2 - P_2Q_1 + P_1Q_1 - P_1Q_2}{P_1Q_1}$$

Next we multiply the numerator and denominator of the first term by P_1 and of the second term by Q_1. We then have

$$\frac{P_2Q_2 - P_1Q_1}{P_1Q_1} = \frac{P_1(Q_2 - Q_1)}{P_1Q_1} + \frac{(P_2 - P_1)}{P_1Q_1} + Q_1\frac{P_2Q_2 - P_2Q_1 + P_1Q_1 - P_1Q_2}{P_1Q_1}$$

After we cancel all the terms we possibly can, what remains is the expression for the nominal rate.

$$r_N \cong r_R + \%\Delta P^e \tag{9.10}$$

The nominal interest rate is equal to the ex ante real interest rate plus the market's ex ante expected rate of inflation, $\%\Delta P^e$.

The equilibrium nominal interest rate is such that lenders receive a compensation equal to the real interest rate plus an amount that perfectly offsets the expected rate of inflation. If the nominal interest rate provided less compensation than this, lenders would be expected to lose in real terms on financial transactions. Because, in equilibrium, lenders should not expect to lose on financial contracts, the nominal interest rate must rise to just cover the market's expectation of inflation plus the real interest rate.

Because the inflation rate is uncertain, the ex post or realized real return may be either more or less than the real interest rate demanded ex ante. To see this, let's examine a modified version of equation 9.10. Equation 9.11 says that the ex post real interest rate a lender actually receives, symbolized by r'_R, is equal to the nominal rate initially set for the financial transaction, r_N, less the actual inflation rate in the period in question, symbolized by $\%\Delta P'$:

$$r'_R \cong r_N - \%\Delta P' \tag{9.11}$$

In any given period the ex post real interest rate may be calculated from the actual nominal interest rate and the actual rate of inflation. But this ex post real interest rate is not the ex ante real interest rate of Fisher's theory. The ex post real interest rate reflects the market's errors in guessing the inflation rate. For example, we could look back at two quite distinct historical episodes (in fact, we choose these periods because they are so different), the ex post real interest rate earned by holding 90-day T bills in 1977 and 1985 shown in Table 9-7. These were computed according to equation 9.11. For example, in January 1977, r_N was 4.6 percent, and $\%\Delta P'$ was 10.2 percent, so that r'_R was –5.6 percent (4.6 percent − 10.2 percent). These returns reflect the actual returns, after inflation, from holding T bills during these years. They do not necessarily indicate the value of the ex ante real interest rate demanded by lenders. We simply do not see the ex ante real rate, in spite of its importance for lenders' decisions.

Actually, when we take into account that inflation rates are uncertain and investors are really interested in their real rather than their nominal return, we need to add uncertainty surrounding inflation to our list of the major forms of interest rate risk (market value, reinvestment, and prepayment risk) that we discussed earlier in the chapter. The risk arising from uncertain inflation rates is often referred to as *purchasing power risk.* It is important to understand the nature of the exposure generated by purchasing power risk. Anyone who is a net lender—that is, someone who lends more than he or she borrows—is hurt by unanticipated inflation. That is, unanticipated inflation drives down this investor's real return. Anyone who is a net borrower is helped by unanticipated inflation: unanticipated inflation increases his or her actual return. This means that lenders would want protection against increases in inflation while borrowers would want protection against decreases in inflation.

Table 9-7
Historical Ex Post Real Interest Rates

Panel A: Ex Post Real Returns on Three-Month T Bills for 1977				Panel B: Ex Post Real Returns on Three-Month T Bills for 1985			
Month Issued	**Three-Month Rate** (%)	**Subsequently Observed Inflation Rate[a]** (%)	**Ex Post Real Interest Rate** (%)	**Month Issued**	**Three-Month Rate** (%)	**Subsequently Observed Inflation Rate[a]** (%)	**Ex Post Real Interest Rate** (%)
January	4.6	10.2	−5.6	January	7.8	4.2	3.6
February	4.7	8.1	−3.4	February	8.2	5.1	3.1
March	4.6	8.3	−3.7	March	8.6	4.9	2.7
April	4.5	6.9	−2.4	April	8.0	4.4	3.6
May	4.9	6.1	−1.2	May	7.6	3.4	4.2
June	5.0	4.9	0.1	June	7.0	2.7	4.3
July	5.1	4.2	0.9	July	7.0	2.6	4.4
August	5.5	4.7	0.8	August	7.2	3.3	3.9
September	5.8	3.5	2.3	September	7.1	3.8	2.3
October	6.2	4.0	2.2	October	7.2	3.6	3.6
November	6.1	6.6	−0.5	November	7.2	3.6	3.6
December	6.1	8.2	−2.1	December	7.1	1.1	6.0

[a]This is computed from the three-month change in the Consumer Price Index; that is, for January this is the annualized change from January to April.

Behavior of the Ex Ante Real Rate and the Efficient Markets Hypothesis

At least two interesting and important questions should be asked about the observed behavior of the nominal interest rate on debt instruments or on assets that have returns fixed in money terms. The first question is, How much of a change in the nominal interest rate is due to a change in the real rate of interest as opposed to a change in the expected rate of inflation? The second is, Does the market efficiently use all available information in assessing the future inflation rate? The answers to these questions are not obvious. There is considerable disagreement, not only about the correct answers but also about how to determine the correct answers. Still, these questions are important and are worth considering, at least briefly, even if no definite answers can be provided.

Irving Fisher is widely perceived to have argued that the real rate of interest is essentially constant. According to Fisher, fluctuations in the nominal rate of interest basically represent changes in the expected rate of inflation. If correct, this implies that most interest rate risk is really inflation risk. It should be understood that the real rate of interest probably is never exactly constant. The argument is that fluctuations in the real interest rate are relatively small. This is because the real interest rate also represents the marginal rate of return on the economy's capital stock. That capital stock is very large and changes only very slowly. Therefore, when there are periods of fairly sizable changes in nominal interest rates, they should be attributed to changes in the expected rate of inflation.

The alternative view is that, for substantial periods of time, shifts in desired borrowing and lending, which influence the real interest rate in financial markets, can take place. Only in a very long-run equilibrium do these changes have to induce similar changes in the real rate of return on the economy's capital stock. This argument implies that the real interest rate in the credit market can move above or below the real return on capital for periods as long as a year or two. For the purpose of understanding monthly, quarterly, or annual changes in interest rates on financial contracts it is important to examine changes in the real rate of interest.

The second question, regarding market efficiency, is not quite as controversial. In this instance, the efficient markets hypothesis asserts that all available information is efficiently used by the market to assess future inflation rates. This seems easy enough to accept, but it is very difficult to verify because it is impossible to observe the market's expected rate of inflation directly—for the same reason that it is impossible to observe the market's ex ante real interest rate directly. It is possible to observe the ex post real interest and inflation rates, but these are not the direct subject of the efficient markets hypothesis.

Some conclusions can be drawn about market efficiency from the ex post real interest rate, however. One implication of the efficient markets hypothesis is that the market should not make systematic errors in guessing the inflation rate. For example, if there is some pattern in the way the actual inflation rate moves through time, then the market should figure out the pattern and it should not show up in the behavior of the market's ex post real return. If, for example, you looked at a graph of the ex post real interest rate, it should wander without any definable pattern.

This hypothesis has been examined extensively in the academic literature. One of the first and most important studies of the question was carried out by Eugene Fama.[7] Fama showed that there is an identifiable pattern in the behavior of the inflation rate and that when the real return on Treasury bills is computed the pattern does not show up there. He concludes that the market efficiently uses the information contained in the Consumer Price Index to assess future changes in that index. Other researchers have criticized some of Fama's methodology and have challenged his conclusions. This is a complex topic, and more definitive conclusions about the market's efficiency in this instance may be hard to come by.

• *So You Want to Try to Forecast Interest Rates?* •

Though it is important to have an understanding of what market forces drive observed nominal interest rates, many people want to take another step and try to build a model to simulate or forecast interest rates. One reason is to be able to formulate strategies and procedures for managing interest rate risk. It is sometimes useful in this effort to be able to characterize how we think interest rates fluctuate. This involves describing what is often called a "stochastic process"—a

[7]Eugene F. Fama. "Short-Term Interest Rates as Predictors of Inflation," *American Economic Review* vol 65–3 (June 1975), pp. 269–282.

process involving a random variable—for interest rates. The stochastic process we postulate for interest rates must be able to describe their behavior in a reasonable way. We specify here, as simply as we can, a model of the stochastic process for interest rates that is often used in industry. The model characterizes the way the short-term interest rate changes over time. The change in the short-term rate refers to how the rate for a short maturity changes from one date to another. Using our notation from earlier in this chapter, we can define the change in the short-term rate from today to tomorrow as

$$\Delta r = {}_1r_2 - {}_0r_1 \tag{9.12}$$

This model breaks down interest rates into two components. One specifies a deterministic, or nonrandom, reason why interest rates change. If this were the only component, this deterministic process would define a certain path for the interest rate. Of course, we know interest rates are not certain, so the second component relates interest rate changes to a statistical measure of random changes known as a "standard normal random variable." A standard normal random variable is a variable whose probability is described by a normal distribution with an expected value equal to 0 and a variance and standard deviation equal to 1. The equation for the stochastic process is as follows:

$$\Delta r = K(u - r) + \sigma\sqrt{r}\,\Delta Z$$

where u is a central tendency of r; Z is the standard normal random variable, σ is the standard deviation of the interest rate r; and K is a weight that fits the observed behavior of r.

This model has two important features that are consistent with the actual behavior of interest rates. In fact, that is the principal reason why this particular process is chosen. First, the rate has a tendency to move back toward the value u. This is called "mean reversion": the rate tends to revert toward the mean. To see why that occurs simply let ΔZ equal 0, so there is no random change in r. Then, the stochastic process says that the change in r is proportional to the gap between r and u, where the proportionality factor is K. This means r will move toward u. K determines the speed at which the rate returns to its long-term normal level. Second, the interest rate can never be negative. In fact, negative nominal rates make rather little sense and are not observed (though negative ex post real rates are). To see why the stochastic process gives this result, suppose the rate fell to 0. Then, since the random component includes the level of r, it must also be 0. Then the deterministic component tells us the rate would increase by Ku. Thus, if the rate ever actually hit 0, it would bounce back up toward its central tendency, u.

Figure 9-8 presents the results of some simulations of this stochast process, to illustrate how interest rates behave when they are governed by such a process. The examples in the figure are based on the assumption of values of K equal to 0.3 and 0.7 and a value for u of 5 percent. The initial value of the interest rate is assumed to be either 10 percent or 3 percent. Furthermore, it is assumed that σ is 0.7 percent. Notice that the simulated rates wander randomly around the assumed value of 5 percent. There are sometimes large changes in rates. These occur when the deterministic component of the change and the random change are both large and have the same sign or move the rate in the same direction.

While all of this may look quite formidable, if you learn to use a spreadsheet on a personal computer, it is relatively easy to program the spreadsheet to simulate interest rates with a stochastic process like this one. Some people even think it is fun.

Figure 9-8

Simulations of interest rates for alternative value of K and initial rates, *r*. All simulations assume u = 5 percent.

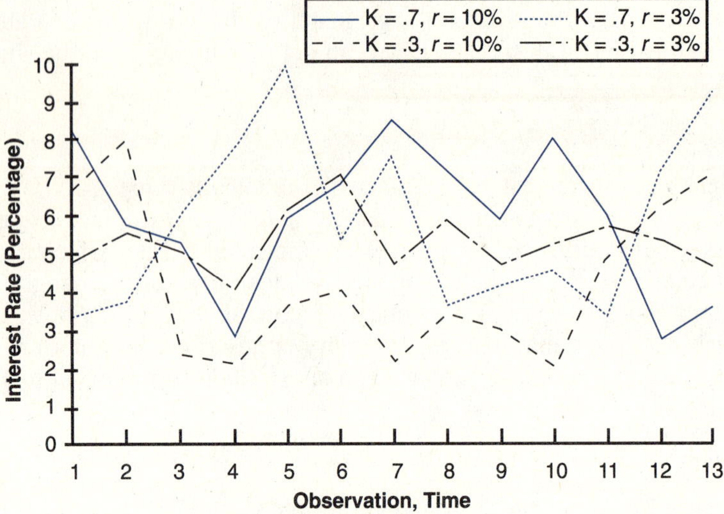

SUMMARY

In this chapter we built a foundation for understanding how interest rates are determined and how the risk of fluctuating interest rates creates the risk associated with fixed-income securities. We began by examining the risk structure of fixed-income securities. We postulated that the risk arises from the intention of an investor to hold the securities for some time, to provide funds for future consumption. Then we broke down the risk facing such an investor into four components. *Market value risk* is the risk of fluctuations in the value of cash flows remaining in a fixed-income security at the time when the investor wants to liquidate the security in order to consume. *Reinvestment risk* is the risk surrounding the rate at which cash flows received before the date of consumption can be reinvested in the market. *Prepayment risk* is the risk of fluctuations in the timing of cash flows arising from the option of the borrower in a fixed-income obligation to terminate the agreement or prepay the loan. We showed that all three of these sources of exposure are derived from uncertainty surrounding the underlying discount rates that are applicable to specific cash flows to be received at specific times. Finally, we considered *default risk,* the risk that the borrower will not meet scheduled cash flow obligations. These are the rates that should properly be used in any valuation of a fixed-income security.

Next we turned our attention to the basic determinants of the short-term interest rate. The basic theory of the real rate of interest is referred to as Fisherian interest rate theory, after Irving Fisher, the economist who developed the analysis of the real interest rate. It shows that in equilibrium the real interest rate must be equal to three distinct concepts: (1) the marginal rate of return on real investment projects, or the rate of return on real capital; (2) the marginal rate at which individuals choose to exchange present for future consumption, or the marginal rate of time preference; and (3) the interest rate on borrowing and lending.

This chapter also focused on inflation and interest rates. We learned that the nominal rate is equal to the sum of the real rate and the market's expectation of inflation. Therefore, in a time of high inflation there is a large difference between observed nominal rates and the underlying real rate. We focused on the distinction between the ex ante and ex post real interest rates. Though we can compute the ex post real interest rate, it is not generally a perfect measure of the ex ante real interest rate, which we believe determines nominal interest rates. Instead, the ex post real interest rate is determined both by the ex ante real interest rate and by the market's errors in guessing the actual inflation rate. We also evaluated some of the available evidence on the degree to which the market efficiently incorporates publicly available information regarding future inflation rates into nominal interest rates. Finally, because interest rate uncertainty is at the root of risk exposure in fixed-income obligations, we described a model of the stochastic process that determines the random short-term interest rate in the economy.

QUESTIONS

1. What is the difference between the ex ante and the ex post real interest rate? Why can we observe one and not the other? Why do many economists argue that the real interest rate is essentially constant? Do you think the real interest rate is just as likely to be constant in the very short run (a week, a month, a quarter) as in the long run? Give reasons for your answer.
2. What does it mean to say that the market efficiently uses available information about the future inflation rate in setting nominal interest rates? Why is it difficult to test whether this is true?
3. Explain why the ex post real interest rate should vary randomly. Should nominal interest rates vary randomly? Why or why not?
4. Suppose you buy a ten-year 8 percent coupon bond (semiannual payments) with a face value of $1 million. You intend to hold the bond five years. Suppose the zero-coupon interest rate for all maturities is the same and is equal to (a) 10 percent, (b) 8 percent, and (c) 6 percent over the entire holding period. Calculate the market value of your bond, the value of reinvested coupon payments, and the total value at year five, for the three interest rates.
5. Compute the values in question 4 for holding periods of one and nine years. Discuss how changes in length of holding period affect reinvestment and market value risks.

6. Suppose you hold a 12 percent mortgage with 20 years until maturity. Also suppose it costs you 1.8 percent of the mortgage balance as a fee to refinance the mortgage. At what interest rate does it pay for you to refinance if you expect to remain in your home seven years?
7. Suppose you are valuing a $100 million pool of 11 percent mortgages with 30 years to maturity. The expected life of the mortgages in the pool is 12 years. How would you value this pool if you assume all mortgages prepay after exactly 12 years?
8. Consider the stochastic process for interest rates defined at the end of this chapter. Using a spreadsheet program (e.g., Excel, Lotus) simulate the level of the interest rate for various values of K, u, σ, and the initial value of r. Choose your own values of these parameters and see what happens.

REFERENCES

Conrad, Joseph W. *Introduction to the Theory of Interest.* Berkeley: University of California Press, 1959.

Cox, John C., Jonathan E. Ingersoll, and Stephen A. Ross. "A Theory of the Term Structure of Interest Rates." *Econometrica* 53 (1985), pp. 385–407.

Fama, Eugene F. "Short-Term Interest Rates and Predictors of Inflation." *American Economic Review* 65–3 (June 1975), pp. 269–282.

Fisher, Irving. *The Theory of Interest.* New York: Macmillan, 1930.

Hirshleifer, Jack. *Investment, Interest and Capital.* Englewood Cliffs, NJ: Prentice-Hall, 1970.

Ingersoll, Jonathan E. Jr. *The Theory of Financial Decision Making.* Totowa, NJ: Roman & Littlefield, 1987.

• Chapter 10

Term Structure of Interest Rates

In this chapter we examine the relationship between the yield on fixed-income securities and their maturity, the "*term structure* of interest rates." Term structure has to do only with debt securities because only they have a stated maturity. In addition, the term structure refers to the relationship between maturity and yield for securities that are alike in all other respects—for example, in their risk and tax treatment. Therefore, the term structure is often applied to Treasury securities because of their high degree of homogeneity across maturities.

The term structure of interest rates contributes to a general understanding of financial markets and is one of the most critical financial considerations for any corporation. A financial manager of a company who is assessing whether to obtain funds with short-term or long-term debt will choose on the basis of the yields available at the alternative maturities. If the short-term interest rate is higher than the long-term rate, as it was in 1980 for 1- and 10-year maturities, for example, then he or she might conclude that long-term borrowing will be better. However, if the long-term rate is determined largely by the market's expectations of future short-term rates, the financial manager cannot expect to save by borrowing for the longer term because the rate is lower. We see why later in this chapter. Thus, an understanding of the term structure is of tremendous practical importance.

• *Concepts to Learn in Chapter 10* •

- How to define and compute forward interest rates
- The definition of the zero-coupon yield curve and how it is used
- How you can explain the shape of the yield curve
- How the yield curve helps forecast interest rates

Yield Curves and Forward Rates

The very first step in understanding the term structure of interest rates is to understand how a yield curve is constructed. The building blocks of the yield curve are what we call spot, or cash, interest rates, but the curve also gives us a picture of forward interest rates. So, as we learn about the yield curve we also focus our attention on spot (cash) and forward interest rates.

The yield curve shows the prevailing yield to maturity at a given point in time for bonds that differ only by maturity. As a result, a different yield curve or term structure exists at any such point. Different yield curves that have obtained at various times over the last 20 years are shown in Figure 10-1. The figure shows that the yield curve prevailing in September 1974 and December 1980 had a largely downward slope. A largely upward-sloping yield curve prevailed in May 1984 and in December 1991. The upward and downward slope mean, respectively, that short-term interest rates were below and above long-term interest rates at that point in time in the yield curve.

It is very common for short-term interest rates to be more volatile than long-term rates. This means that the yield curve tends to move around more in the range corresponding to short maturities than it does for long maturities. This pattern of relatively volatile short-term interest rates and less volatile long-term interest rates has become a common feature of business cycles in the United States. Though we can see this pattern in most of our history since World War II, it is useful to look back some years, to the recession of the mid-1970s, for a typical example. In September 1974 short-term interest rates reached record high levels, though that record was shattered in the early 1980s. For example, 90-day Treasury bill rates went as high as 10.33 percent in 1974. By comparison, long-term Treasury bond rates were not nearly as explosive, reaching a peak of approximately 8.5 percent. This is reflected in the shapes of yield curves observed at different points. At the peak of short-term interest rates in the 1974 recession, the yield curve was negatively sloped, as illustrated in Figure 10-1. Later in the recession, short-term interest rates fell relative to long-term interest rates, and the yield curve had a positive slope.

The basic reason that short-term rates are more volatile than long-term rates is that long-term rates reflect the market's expectations of what will transpire over a long period. Thus, these rates reflect an *average* of expected future events, but the short-term cost of credit is reflected directly in short-term rates. These rates rise and fall to reflect the equilibrium real rate and expected rate of inflation. Long-term rates would have patterns that are as volatile as short-term rates only if the market generally expected trends in short-term rates to continue. That is, if the market expected the short-term rate to increase and stay at the higher level, then long-term rates would make a similar adjustment. The volatility of short-term relative to long-term rates reflects the market's belief that, despite short-term changes, rates will return to a more normal level.

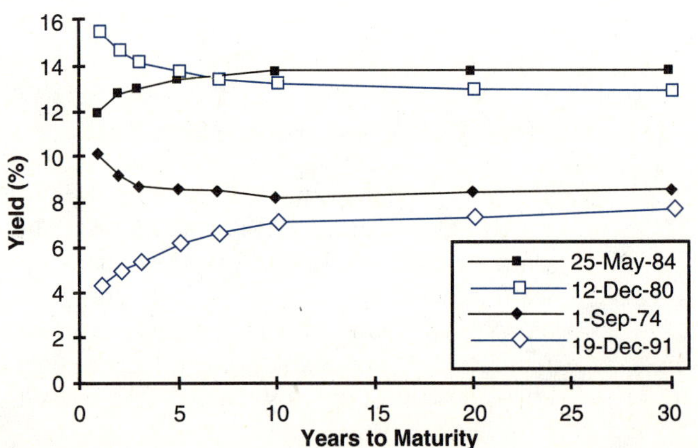

Figure 10-1
Yield curves for Treasury securities.

It is particularly interesting to examine the shape of the yield curve in late 1980, as illustrated in Figure 10-1. Short-term interest rates reached record high levels. Again, the yield curve had a negative slope because long-term rates were substantially below short-term rates. This was a time when the rate of inflation had accelerated sharply and was running in excess of 10 percent per year. It was widely perceived that short-term rates were rising to incorporate the expectations of inflation. But the fact that long-term rates were still substantially below short-term rates apparently reflected the market's belief that, in the long run, inflation rates would not remain at then-current levels. The only alternative explanation of such low long-term rates would be that the market was willing to accept an expected long-run negative real return.

Another interesting episode occurred in December 1991, when short-term interest rates were declining rapidly as the recession in the United States continued and the 1992 elections were approaching. The yield curve developed one of the steepest slopes ever recorded. There was pressure on long-term rates to remain relatively high as the market continued to be concerned about the prospects for a resurgence of inflation. However, the decline in short-term rates was so strong, and actual inflation as well as the entire economy so weak, that there was considerable speculation that long-term rates would have to fall farther. Steep slopes such as the one in December 1991 develop when short-term rates are changing rapidly and the bond markets have not yet "decided" whether these changes will be persistent or transitory. To see more precisely the way the market incorporates its expectations into the term structure we must understand forward rates.

Meaning and Computation of Forward Rates

The term structure of interest rates is the relation between the current long-term and short-term interest rates, but underlying this is really a relationship between the current long-term rate and the rates on current and future short-term loans. The market for future short-term loans, or the forward market, is the market where you can arrange for a loan to begin, say, one year from now and receive a promise today of the interest rate you would have to pay one year from now. Such rates are called "forward rates," and forward rates, or interest rates prevailing today for future loans, are an important part of the term structure relationship.

In order to understand the role of forward rates in the term structure, imagine a time line that begins today, time 0, and stretches *N* periods out into the future to time *N*. Then consider the choice between two types of debt contracts. One type is a long-term zero-coupon bond that yields a payment after *N* periods. Following the notation introduced in Chapter 9, the rate prevailing for such a contract today is symbolized by ${}_0r_N$. The r means that it is a cash, or spot, rate rather than a forward rate. The first subscript, 0, means that it is the rate that prevails at the present time, time 0; the second subscript, *N*, means that the loan matures at time *N*. This implies the loan lasts for *N* periods. For example, if the amount borrowed were \$1000, then the amount owed after five years would be \$1000 $(1 + {}_0r_5)^5$. The other contract involves *N* single-period zero-coupon loans that are set up in sequence or rolled over. The rate of interest in the first period is ${}_0r_1$, which is the rate for a single-period loan beginning today. The rates for loans in each future period that can be contracted for today are forward rates. A forward rate will be symbolized as ${}_1f_2$, where the f indicates it is a forward rate; the first subscript, 1, indicates it is a rate on a loan beginning at time 1, one period from now (now is time 0); and the second subscript, 2, indicates the loan matures at time 2, so that it is a one-period loan.

Figure 10-2 shows the time periods to which the forward rates and current rates apply in the case where N is 5. This figure illustrates there are four forward rates that apply to the four one-year-long intervals between the maturity of the one-year bond and the maturity of the five-year bond. For example, the forward rate ${}_2f_3$ measures the interest rate prevailing today for a one-year loan beginning two years from now.

The yield curve directly measures the prevailing rates today for current loans with different maturities, the rs. On the other hand, the forward rates, the fs, are not directly shown in a yield curve. Because we do not observe forward rates on a yield curve, the natural question is, Where do they come from? The answer is that we can compute forward rates from current spot rates of different maturities. To see how to do this we need to think about the choice between the two debt contracts just described, the long-term contract at a single interest rate and the alternative contract with a number of single-period future loans. We need to define the conditions under which the two contracts would have the same cost or the same future value. The two will have the same future value if the current and forward rates have the following relationship:

$$(1 + {}_0r_N)^N = (1 + {}_0r_1)(1 + {}_1f_2)(1 + {}_2f_3)\ldots(1 + {}_{N-1}f_N) \qquad (10.1)$$

Equation 10.1 means that the future value of the cash flows or the total amount owed will be the same for either debt contract. Another way of looking at this is to say that the long-term rate implies a sequence of forward rates, and equation 10.1 defines the relationship between them. For example, if the interest rate on a five-year bond is 12.8 percent and the rate on a one-year bond is 10 percent, then the following sequence of forward rates will satisfy equation 10.1:

$${}_1f_2 = 0.12 \qquad {}_2f_3 = 0.12$$

$${}_3f_4 = 0.15 \qquad {}_4f_5 = 0.15$$

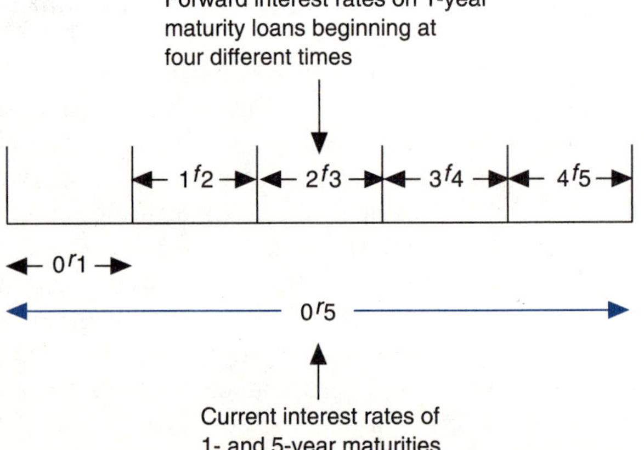

Figure 10-2
Illustration of the time periods covered by forward interest rates and current interest rates.

We can make sure of this by substituting them in equation 10.1. We find that both sides of the equation equal 1.82:

$$(1.128)^5 = 1.1 \times 1.12 \times 1.12 \times 1.15 \times 1.15 = 1.82$$

When we observe the current interest rates on bonds with different maturities at a given point, we can use equation 10.1 to solve for the forward rates these current rates imply. Suppose, for example, that we observe the current interest rate on nine-year bonds and ten-year bonds. We can use these to compute the forward rate for a one-year loan beginning nine years from now. It follows from equation 10.1 that the formula for the forward rate is as follows:

$$ {}_9f_{10} = \frac{(1 + {}_0r_{10})^{10}}{(1 + {}_0r_9)^9} - 1 \qquad (10.2)$$

We can satisfy ourselves that this is correct by moving the one to the left-hand side of equation 10.2 and substituting from equation 10.1 for the values of ${}_0r_{10}$ and ${}_0r_9$:

$$1 + {}_9f_{10} = \frac{(1 + {}_0r_1)(1 + {}_1f_2)(1 + {}_2f_3)\ldots(1 + {}_8f_9)(1 + {}_9f_{10})}{(1 + {}_0r_1)(1 + {}_1f_2)(1 + {}_2f_3)\ldots(1 + {}_8f_9)} \qquad (10.3)$$

The equation is satisfied because the first nine terms in the numerator and denominator cancel out. To see how this can be used in an example, suppose that ${}_0r_{10} = 0.12$ and ${}_0r_9 = 0.11$. Then we can solve for ${}_9f_{10}$ as follows:

$$ {}_9f_{10} = \frac{(1.12)^{10}}{(1.11)^9} - 1 = \frac{3.106}{2.558} = 0.21$$

So, the rate for a 1-year loan beginning 9 years from now is 0.21 or 21 percent.

Thus far we have dealt with forward rates that apply to future loans lasting only one period. In terms of our notation, the difference between the value of left-hand and right-hand subscripts on the forward rate has always been 1. There is no reason to deal only with single-period loans. In principle, we could contract for a future loan to last any number of periods. We can solve for the forward rate on such a loan from the rates on current loans just as we did for single-period forward rates. From now on we will refer to the length of the future loan as K periods.

The formula for the forward rate on a K-period loan is similar to equation 10.2, but with a complication introduced by the difference of K periods. If we observe current rates on an N-period bond and an $(N + K)$-period bond, then

$$ {}_Nf_{N+K} = \left[\frac{(1 + {}_0r_{N+K})^{N+K}}{(1 + {}_0r_N)^N}\right]^{1/K} - 1. \qquad (10.4)$$

To see why this is equal to the forward rate on a K-period loan, we need to examine the difference between the numerator and the denominator in this equation. Note that the numerator includes the last K forward rates for single-period loans, which are not included in the denominator. After cancelling terms in both the numerator and denominator, we are left with

$$\frac{(1 + {}_0r_{N+K})^{N+K}}{(1 + {}_0r_N)^N} = (1 + {}_Nf_{N+1})(1 + {}_{N+1}f_{N+2})\ldots(1 + {}_{N+K-1}f_{N+K}) \qquad (10.5)$$

But using the reasoning in Equation 10.1, the product of these rates on the right-hand side of the equation will be the same as the forward rate on a K-period loan, raised to the Kth power. That is,

$$(1 + {}_{N}f_{N+K})^{K} = (1 + {}_{N}f_{N+1})(1 + {}_{N+1}f_{N+2}) \ldots (1 + {}_{N+K-1}f_{N+K}) \qquad (10.6)$$

This means that the expression inside the brackets in Equation 10.4 is equal to

$$\frac{(1 + {}_{0}r_{N+K})^{N+K}}{(1 + {}_{0}r_{N})^{N}} = (1 + {}_{N}f_{N+K})^{K} \qquad (10.7)$$

Equation 10.3 follows readily from equation 10.7 in the special case where K is 1. The implication of this is that whenever we observe current rates with maturities that differ by K periods, we can compute the forward rate for a K-period loan that begins at the maturity of the shorter of the two bonds.

To illustrate these computations, suppose we observe a sequence of current yields to maturity on zero-coupon bonds with maturities of one to five years. An example of such rates is given in the left-hand column of Table 10-1. These current rates can be used to compute the equivalent forward rate on future loans over this 5-year period. For example, the current rates on one- and two-year bonds imply a forward rate for a one-year loan beginning one year from now of

$${}_{1}f_{2} = \frac{(1.11)^2}{(1.12)} - 1 = 0.10$$

Similarly, the current rates on three- and five-year bonds imply a forward rate for a two-year loan beginning three years from now:

$${}_{3}f_{5} = \left[\frac{(1.10)^5}{(1.105)^3}\right]^{1/2} - 1 = 0.09$$

Other forward rates that can be computed from the first column of Table 10-1 are presented in columns 3 and 4 of the table.

We can use our understanding of the forward rates implicit in the yield curve to calculate some actual forward rates from observed T-bill rates. Table 10-2 shows the T-bill rates listed in the *Wall Street Journal* of Friday, December 20, 1991. These

Table 10-1
Example of Spot and Corresponding Forward Interest Rates

Selected Spot Rates	Values of Spot Rates	Forward Rates Implied by Spot	Values of Forward Rates
${}_{0}r_{1}$	0.12	${}_{1}f_{2}$	0.10
${}_{0}r_{2}$	0.11	${}_{2}f_{3}$	0.095
${}_{0}r_{3}$	0.105	${}_{3}f_{4}$	0.095
${}_{0}r_{4}$	0.1025	${}_{4}f_{5}$	0.090
${}_{0}r_{5}$	0.10	${}_{1}f_{5}$	0.095
		${}_{2}f_{5}$	0.093
		${}_{3}f_{5}$	0.093

Table 10-2
T-Bill Prices, December 19, 1991

TREASURY BILLS					
Maturity	**Days to Mat.**	**Bid**	**Asked**	**Cg.**	**Ask Yld.**
Dec 26 '91	3	3.47	3.37	+0.08	3.43
Jan 02 '92	10	3.70	3.60	+0.05	3.66
Jan 09 '92	17	3.76	3.66	+0.08	3.73
Jan 16 '92	24	3.69	3.59	+0.01	3.65
Jan 23 '92	31	3.80	3.76	+0.04	3.84
Jan 30 '92	38	3.81	3.77	+0.04	3.85
Feb 06 '92	45	3.86	3.52	–0.01	3.90
Feb 13 '92	52	3.88	3.84	–0.04	3.92
Feb 20 '92	59	3.87	3.85	–0.07	3.94
Feb 27 '92	66	3.92	3.90	–0.05	3.99
Mar 05 '92	73	4.00	3.98	–0.06	4.08
Mar 12 '92	80	4.04	4.02	–0.08	4.12
Mar 19 '92	87	4.04	4.22	–0.08	4.13
Mar 26 '92	94	4.03	4.01	–0.09	4.12
Apr 02 '92	101	4.06	4.04	–0.10	4.15
Apr 09 '92	108	4.07	4.05	–0.09	4.17
Apr 16 '92	115	4.08	4.06	–0.08	4.18
Apr 23 '92	122	4.11	4.09	–0.07	4.22
Apr 30 '92	129	4.09	4.07	–0.08	4.20
May 07 '92	136	4.11	4.09	–0.07	4.22
May 14 '92	143	4.11	4.09	–0.07	4.23
May 21 '92	150	4.12	4.10	–0.06	4.24
May 28 '92	157	4.13	4.11	–0.06	4.25
Jun 04 '92	164	4.10	4.08	–0.05	4.23
Jun 11 '92	171	4.12	4.10	–0.05	4.25
Jun 18 '92	176	4.13	4.11	–0.06	4.27
Jul 02 '92	192	4.16	4.14	–0.05	4.30
Jul 30 '92	220	4.15	4.13	–0.05	4.29
Aug 27 '92	248	4.17	4.15	–0.04	4.32
Sep 24 '92	276	4.14	4.12	–0.05	4.29
Oct 22 '92	304	4.18	4.16	–0.07	4.35
Nov 19 '92	332	4.21	4.19	–0.04	4.39
Dec 17 '92	360	4.18	4.16	–0.05	4.37

Source: Reprinted by permission of *The Wall Street Journal*, © 1991 Dow Jones and Company, Inc. All Right Reserved Worldwide.

were the rates on Thursday, December 19. To see how to calculate forward rates for these pure discount instruments, we use the bills maturing on 26 March and 2 July 1992. These bills have maturities of 94 and 192 days, respectively. We continue to use the same equation we used above in our hypothetical examples, but now we will account for the daily compounding. This means that we will count time in days and annual interest rates will be divided by 365. The two relevant spot rates are ${}_0r_{94}$ (0.0412) and ${}_0r_{192}$ (0.043). The basic equilibrium equation, equation 10.1 is:

$$[1 + (0.0412/365)]^{94} [1 + ({}_{94}f_{192}/365)]^{98} = [1 + (0.043/365)]^{192}$$

Note that

$$[1 + (0.0412/365)]^{94} = 1.0106663 \text{ and } [1 + 0.043/365)]^{192} = 1.0228756$$

Then

$$[1 + ({}_{94}f_{192}/365)]^{98} = \frac{1.0228756}{1.0106663} = 1.0120804$$

This implies that

$${}_{94}f_{192} = [(1.0120804)^{1/98} - 1.0]\ 365 = 0.0447 \text{ or } 4.47\%$$

We could pick any two of the T-bill rates in Table 10-2 and perform the same calculations to determine the forward rates that cover the periods of time between these two spot rates.

Relationship Between Forward and Future Rates

Thus far we have made no attempt to relate the forward rates implicit in the term structure to the interest rates prevailing in the futures markets. In fact, this may be a little dangerous at this juncture, because we do not actually get into futures markets in a systematic way until Chapter 14. It may help to develop an understanding of forward rates, and eventually futures rates, if we take a little time now to draw the connection between the forward rates implicit in the yield curve and interest rates implicit in financial futures. Then we can return to this topic in Chapter 14. The connection is that futures rates obtained from the futures market and forward rates implicit in the cash market must be close to the same value. Actually, there are some important differences that pertain to the way the futures market operates and we will get into these issues in Chapter 14. The basic argument we are making is nevertheless correct (i.e., the forward rates we have developed out of the yield curve in the cash market are the same as the rates we can lock up through a futures contract). To see this relationship, suppose we consider two Treasury bills, one that matures in six months and one in nine months, as well as a futures contract with a six-month maturity. Suppose the price of the six-month bill is P_6 and that of the nine-month bill is P_9. We are interested in determining what the contract price of the futures contract will be if there are no profitable opportunities to substitute between the bills themselves and the futures contract. We represent this equilibrium price by the symbol P^*. Suppose that an investor buys the nine-month bill for the price of P_9 and then sells a futures contract to obtain a certain price for a three-month bill delivered in six months (P^*). She now holds what is the equivalent of a six-month bill. The only difference is that the certain payment to be received in six months is now P^* instead of the $10,000 face value of the six-month bill. Suppose that P^* is $9,750. If the annualized yield demanded by the market is, say, six percent, the value today of the six-month bill is determined according to the present-value equation as follows:

$$P_6 = \$10{,}000/(1 + 0.06/2) = \$9708$$

But the value of the nine-month bill sold in the futures market must be such that it gives the same six-month yield as the six-month bill:

$$P_9 = P^*/(1 + 0.06/2)$$

If the price in the futures market of the three-month bill to be delivered six months hence is set as in our example, at \$9750, then we can use this equation to determine the price of the nine-month bill today. It is

$$P_9 = \$9750/(1 + 0.06/2) = \$9466$$

Investors have two ways to invest their money in a risk-free asset with a six-month maturity. One way is to buy a six-month bill for P_6 and receive \$10,000 in six months. The second way is to buy a nine-month bill for P_9 and contract to sell it in six months for P^*. Two assets that promise risk-free payoffs at the same time must have the same rate of return. Otherwise there will be an arbitrage opportunity. Equality of rates of return requires that

$$\frac{\$10{,}000}{P_6} = \frac{P^*}{P_9}$$

This means that the price of the six-month bill must be in the same proportion to its maturity value as the price of the nine-month bill is to the price of the futures contract. If this were not true, there would be sure profits to be made by either buying or selling futures contracts and nine-month bills, depending on the direction of the imbalance. The profit opportunities ensure that, in equilibrium the market will price futures contracts according to our equation.

This relationship is only approximately true if there are costs involved in buying and selling T bills and futures contracts. Most empirical studies indicate that the actual prices of futures contracts in T bills conform reasonably closely to this relationship. For example, Rendleman and Carabini concluded there were some persistent but small opportunities for profitable trading between T bills and futures.[1] They found the opportunities were sufficiently small that if you included all of what they counted as the "indirect costs" for most market participants of conducting such trading, the opportunities would not be profitable. In other words, the equations we have developed here are a very close approximation of the actual relationship between T-bill prices and the prices of T-bill futures.

Thus far we have only the basic mechanics of the relationship between current interest rates on different maturities and the forward and futures rates with which they are consistent. Now we move on to examine the various theories about forward rates and current long-term rates. But before we do we need one more very important piece of information about yield curves and forward rates, the zero-coupon yield curve.

---

[1]See Rendleman, Richard J. Jr., and Christopher E. Carabini. "The Efficiency of the Treasury Bill Futures Market." *Journal of Finance* 34 (September 1979), pp. 895–914.

The Zero-Coupon Yield Curve

Thus far we have been using the yield curve in a way that camouflages a very important feature of long-term interest rates. It is finally time to get rid of this camouflage. From now on, when we speak of a yield curve or the term structure of interest rates we always use the *zero-coupon yield curve.* We need to see what the zero-coupon yield curve is and how we can compute this from the prices or yields to maturity of observed coupon-bearing bonds. Thus far, the yield curve we have been working with is generally called the "*par yield curve.*" It is defined using yields to maturity on coupon-bearing bonds, where the coupon rates are the same as the yield to maturity or, equivalently, where the bond is selling at par. From now on, unless we refer explicitly to the par yield curve, we are always using the zero-coupon yield curve.

The zero-coupon yield curve is constructed using interest rates that are the yields to maturity on zero-coupon instruments or bonds with only a single cash flow. Recall that we introduced these rates in Chapter 9 and used them in our basic valuation equation. We are going to reemphasize a few of the points we made when we introduced that valuation equation, to make sure you grasp and appreciate their importance. For example, consider a bond that promises to pay \$100,000 in exactly ten years and has no coupon payments. If the yield to maturity on this zero-coupon bond is 12 percent, then the price of the bond is

$$\$100{,}000/(1.12)^{10} = \$32{,}197$$

There is a certain lack of ambiguity in the calculation of the value of this bond, because we know there is a single cash flow. Therefore, the interest rate of 12 percent that we use in the present-value calculation applies directly to the ten years we will have to wait to receive the \$100,000. With this zero-coupon instrument we are always matching the timing of interest rates and the timing of cash flows.

Now suppose we had another instrument that promised to pay \$100,000 at maturity and also to pay \$10,000 after five years. We admit this is a rather strange instrument, but it will allow us to make our point simply. Suppose we are told that yield to maturity on this instrument is 12 percent. Then we know that we can compute its value by taking the present value of the two cash flows at 12 percent:

$$\$37{,}871 = \frac{\$10{,}000}{(1.12)^5} + \frac{\$100{,}000}{(1.12)^{10}}$$

Now, here is the crucial point. This is not generally the right way to do a present-value calculation. The right way is to discount each cash flow at each point in time by the interest rate that represents the appropriate opportunity cost for that point in time. It is not necessarily true that 12 percent is the right discount rate for each point in time. There are an infinite number of combinations of distinct interest rates, one for five years and one for ten years, that would give a present value of \$37,871. The only thing special about 12 percent is that it is the unique single interest rate that solves this present-value problem, for a price of \$37,871. But it is not necessarily the appropriate discount rate for cash flows received either five or ten years from now. In fact, it is an average of those two rates, whatever they may be. For example, two rates that would do the job are ${}_0r_5 = 3.51\%$ and ${}_0r_{10} = 13\%$:

$$\$37{,}871 = \frac{\$10{,}000}{(1.0351)^5} + \frac{\$100{,}000}{(1.13)^{10}}$$

Now what has this got to do with the yield curve? The answer is that if we are not careful we may simply take yields to maturity for coupon-bearing T bonds of different maturity and use them to construct a yield curve. Then, the interest rates on the yield curve would not necessarily be the interest rates that correspond to cash flows to be received on the dates stated on the horizontal axis of the yield curve diagram. In fact, it would almost be a miracle if they were. This is because coupon-bearing bonds have no single cash flows and therefore no single date when their cash flows are received. Therefore, any single interest rate, such as the yield to maturity, that might be attributed to them cannot be an interest rate that accurately measures the appropriate opportunity cost for any individual cash flow.

Ideally, the appropriate way to construct a zero-coupon yield curve would be to utilize only zero-coupon bonds. Then there would be no ambiguity about what point in time corresponds to a given interest rate. Zero-coupon bonds are now available as "strips." These are bonds that have been constructed by stripping the coupon payments from coupon-bearing T bonds and selling those coupon payments as zero-coupon bonds. Prices of such strips are now regularly quoted in the marketplace and can be found in the *Wall Street Journal,* but, if you like, you can also manufacture your own zero-coupon yield curve from prices and/or yields on coupon-bearing bonds. From now on, whenever we are talking about a yield curve, we always mean the zero-coupon yield curve or term structure. We may or may not always use the term "zero-coupon," but it will always be implicit. We just don't have any more use for yield curves that aren't zero-coupon. Now that we understand more about the yield curve and how it is used, we turn our attention to the various explanations for its shape.

• *So You Want to Construct Your Own Zero-Coupon Yield Curve?* •

The direct way to construct a zero-coupon yield curve from coupon-bearing bonds is to start with T bills, which are zero-coupon instruments, and use them to calculate the zero-coupon interest rates from progressively longer-maturity T bonds. The best way to see what we mean is with an example. Suppose we have a one-year T bill and a two-year coupon-bearing T bond. To keep the example simple, suppose the coupon rate on the bond is 10 percent and the face value is $10,000. Also suppose the coupon payments are made annually. Then the bond holder receives $1000 at the end of one year and $11,000 after two years. Finally, suppose the bond has a market value of $9900 and the bill a value of $9091. Now we can solve for the one-year zero-coupon rate for the bill ${}_0r_1$ directly from the present-value equation for the bill:

$$\$9091 = \frac{\$10{,}000}{1 + {}_0r_1}$$

so that ${}_0r_1$ is 10 percent. The value of the bond is the present value of the two cash flows, each discounted at their appropriate zero-coupon rate:

$$\$9900 = \frac{\$1000}{1 + {}_0r_1} + \frac{\$11{,}000}{(1 + {}_0r_2)^2}$$

Then we can plug in the 10 percent one-year rate we computed from the T bill and solve directly for ${}_0r_2$.

$${}_0r_2 = [\$11{,}000/(\$9900 - (\$1000/1.1))]^{1/2} - 1 = 10.6\ \%$$

Now we can continue to move up the maturity spectrum by plugging in both the rates we have just computed to the present-value equation for a three-year bond, and then proceed to a four-year bond, and so on. In this way we can compute the zero-coupon yield curve of interest rates for maturities of coupon bonds that are traded in the marketplace.

Classical Theories of the Term Structure of Interest Rates

Three classical theories attempt to explain the term structure of interest rates. The fact that they are "classics" means they have been around for quite a while. There is also a more recent, or "modern," theory of the term structure. We take up this more modern theory briefly, after we discuss the classical theories. The classical theories are called, respectively, the *expectations theory,* the *liquidity preference theory,* and the *preferred habitat theory.* Table 10-3 identifies the key characteristics of each of the three. We examine each one to see how it explains observed yield curves.

Throughout our investigation of each of these theories we rely on our understanding of yield curves and forward interest rates. Thus far we have looked at forward rates as interest rates contracted for today for loans that will actually take place sometime in the future. However, we can also use the forward rate to represent the expected interest rate on future spot or cash markets plus a premium or discount.

Throughout our discussion of the theories of the term structure we will consider an investor who is choosing between a sequence of zero-coupon bonds of various maturities. Moreover, we will assume that future interest rates are uncertain, so that this investor must decide which maturity of bond to purchase, given the existing uncertainty about the future course of interest rates. If the investor has a specific intended holding period, say five years, then he can choose among three basic

Table 10-3
Key Elements of Theories of the Term Structure

Expectations Theory	Preferred Habitat Theory	Liquidity Preference Theory
Borrowers and lenders are risk neutral	Borrowers and lenders are risk averse	Borrowers prefer long, lenders prefer short
Securities are perfect substitutes	Securities are substitutes at the market price of risk	Liquidity premium increases with maturity

strategies. The simplest option is to buy a zero-coupon bond with a five-year maturity. Then the maturity of the bond held is exactly the same as the maturity desired. However, the investor could buy a shorter-maturity bond (say one-year) and roll this over until he reaches the end of the holding period. As a result, he will earn the prevailing short-term interest rate in each future year. The investor's third alternative is to buy a bond with a maturity longer than five years, say ten years, and sell after five years. The first option—buying a five-year bond—is the simplest because the only transaction is the initial purchase. But without knowing the interest rate today and in the future, and ignoring any costs involved in making transactions, it is not apparent which alternative will turn out to be the most profitable investment.

The Expectations Theory

The expectations theory says this:

The expected one-year yield on all bonds, regardless of maturity, is the same as that of a one-year bond.

To see more clearly what this means, let's consider the value of a zero-coupon bond with a specific maturity at a given point in time. Suppose an investor considers buying a ten-year zero-coupon bond that pays $1000 at maturity. We designate the price of that bond today, at time 0, as ${}_0P_{10}$. Notice that the subscripts are identical to the subscripts used to characterize the zero-coupon interest rate for such a bond. That is, we have already learned we can write the price of this bond as

$$ {}_0P_{10} = \frac{\$1{,}000}{(1 + {}_0r_{10})^{10}} \tag{10.8} $$

Similarly, the price of the same bond one year later will be:

$$ {}_1P_{10} = \frac{\$1{,}000}{(1 + {}_1r_{10})^{9}} \tag{10.9} $$

The expectations hypothesis states that

$$ {}_0P_{10} = \frac{E_0({}_1P_{10})}{(1 + {}_0r_1)} \tag{10.10} $$

where E_0 means the expectation at time 0.

This says that the expected discounted value of the price of the ten-year bond prevailing one year from now should be equal to the price of that bond today. If this were not true, then an arbitrage opportunity would open up. For example, if the discounted expected value of the price one year from now were greater than the price today, it would pay to buy the bond today at its current price with the expectation of earning more than the one-year interest rate. Thus an investor could borrow at the one-year interest rate to buy the ten-year bond with the expectation of making a profit over the one-year holding period.

To see more precisely what this means let's consider a simple example of change in interest rates. Suppose that the current one-year rate, ${}_0r_1$, is 5 percent. Suppose that the uncertain future one-year rate can be either 7 percent or 3 percent but no value in between. Further, suppose that the rate changes from the current five percent to the new level of either 7 percent or 3 percent and will then remain there forever. This example of changes in interest rates is simple enough to capture the essence of the expectations theory, without being so complicated as to make it very difficult to compute values of zero-coupon bonds.

Now let's determine the actual value of the ten-year bond at time zero, given the relationship defined by the expectations theory of the term structure in equation 10.10. We have assumed that the one-year rate next year and every year thereafter will be either 7 percent or 3 percent, with equal probability. Therefore, at time 1, the nine-year spot rate will be either 7 percent or 3 percent. We can express the expected value, one year from now, of the zero-coupon bond maturing in year 10 as

$$
\begin{aligned}
E_0({}_1P_{10}) &= 0.5 \times \$1000/(1.07)^9 + 0.5 \times \$1000/(1.03)^9 \\
&= 0.5(543.93 + 766.42) \\
&= 655.18 \qquad (10.11)
\end{aligned}
$$

We can easily substitute this into 10.10 to obtain a specific solution for the value of the ten-year bond at time 0:

$$
\begin{aligned}
{}_0P_{10} &= E_0({}_1P_{10})/1.05 \\
&= \$655.18/1.05 \\
&= \$623.98 \qquad (10.12)
\end{aligned}
$$

The expectations theory tells us that we can use equation 10.8 to solve directly for ${}_0r_{10}$ as follows:

$$
{}_0r_{10} = [1000/623.98]^{1/10} - 1 = 1.6026^{1/10} - 1 = 4.83\%
$$

We have already mentioned that the classical theories of the term structure have been around for a long time. The way we stated the expectations theory is not the way it was always stated. It used to be stated in a way that is not quite correct. The old way said that the long-term rate is equal to the product of the expected future short-term rates. Suppose we use the forward interest rate to represent the investor's best guess of what the future short-term interest rate will be. Then the expectations theory was often written as the following relationship between the ten-year rate today and the corresponding forward rates:

$$
(1 + {}_0r_{10})^{10} = (1 + {}_0r_1)(1 + {}_1f_2)(1 + {}_2f_3)\ldots(1 + {}_8f_9)(1 + {}_9f_{10}) \qquad (10.13)
$$

plus

$$
{}_if_j = E_0[{}_ir_j] \qquad (10.14)
$$

These equations say two things. First, they say that the market expects to have the same long-term return, that is, over ten years, from buying the ten-year bond as it does from rolling over a sequence of short-term bonds. Second, each and every forward rate is equal to the corresponding expected future short-term rate. Unfortunately, neither of these statements is true, at least not in our modern economy. The problem is that contemporary interest rates are generally correlated over time or are correlated serially. This means that, historically, in the United States and in virtually every market economy in the world, a high or low interest rates on one date tends to be followed by high (low) interest rates on the next date. Put another way, the correlation coefficient between interest rates observed across time is generally positive, and definitely not zero. The problem this creates is that the only way equations 10.13 and 10.14 can be true is if the serial correlation of interest rates is zero. Only then is the expectation of a product equal to the product of expectations.

When interest rates have some degree of serial correlation there is only one completely accurate way to state the expectations theory of the term structure. This way equates the returns on investments in alternative maturity bonds, over one period. The presence of serial correlation in the interest rates drives a wedge between the forward rate and the expected future spot interest rate. We can capture this wedge in our concept of the term structure by introducing what is generally called a "term premium." The term premium captures the difference between the forward rate and the expected future spot rate:

$$ {}_{i}f_{j} = E_0({}_{i}r_{j}) + {}_{i}L_{j} \tag{10.16} $$

$$ {}_{i}L_{j} = \text{Term premium} $$

The term premium recognizes the fact that the forward rate may not be exactly equal to the expected future spot rate, possibly because of the serial correlation of interest rates. However, as we see shortly, we can also interpret the term premium as capturing compensation for bearing risk.

A useful way to interpret each of the theories of the term structure of interest rates that we deal with pertains to the shape of the yield curve. Each theory offers a different explanation for upward-sloping, flat, and downward-sloping yield curves. The expectations theory says long-term interest rates are determined largely by the market's expectations of future short-term interest rates and by any serial correlation. Therefore, this theory implies that the market's expectations largely account for the slope of the yield curve. For example, the expectations theory suggests that the upward-sloping par yield curve that existed in December 1991, shown in Figure 10-1, probably implies that the market expected future short-term interest rates to increase. By contrast, the downward-sloping yield curve observed in 1980 probably reflected expectations that short-term rates would decline.

The Preferred Habitat and Liquidity Preference Theories

The basic tenet of the expectations theory is that investors equate expected returns across a single period. They do not demand a premium for taking on risk, but it is quite possible that investors do demand some premium to accept risk. Moreover, the risk they take on may be determined by the length of the intended holding period.

The preferred habitat theory says that each investor has a preferred maturity or habitat at which he or she would like to borrow or lend. The maturity is determined by the nature of the investor's business. For example, if the investor wants to borrow money to build a factory with a long useful life, he or she will have a natural preference for a bond with a long maturity. Similarly, if a financial institution needs to obtain funds to lend to a customer for six months, it will generally seek to borrow for six months. The preferred habitat theory asserts that if the total amount of desired borrowing is equal to the total amount of desired lending at each maturity, then the term structure will be determined by the expectations theory. That is, there will not be any risk premiums. Because there is no imbalance between supply and demand at any maturity, investors at each maturity demand an interest rate that is fair, based on the market's expectation of future interest rates. All investors avoid risk because they are all borrowing or lending at their desired maturity; thus, no premiums for risk are reflected in the term structure.

It is unlikely, however, that total desired lending is very often exactly equal to desired borrowing at each maturity. More likely there are imbalances at almost all maturities most of the time. To see what happens when such imbalances arise, consider an investor who desires to invest for five years. That investor may demand to be paid a premium to move into a one-year investment to begin the arbitrage process that leads to the expectations theory of the term structure. If there are many such five-year investors they may bid that premium down very low. If there are very few, the premium may be very high.

The idea, under the preferred habitat notion, is that interest rates adjust until the investor in the example and the market as a whole are no longer willing to substitute between maturities. If investors are averse to risk, they will demand a premium to substitute between maturities. The interest rates on bonds of different maturities will adjust to a new equilibrium by which investors are compensated for bearing the risk of being out of their preferred maturity. The term or liquidity premium is the price demanded by the market to stretch its maturity some specified number of periods. These liquidity premiums are another way to interpret the term premiums we introduced in equation 10.16. In fact, we labeled the term premium in equation 10.16, L, in anticipation of this interpretation of the term premium. The liquidity premium represents the price demanded to stretch the desired maturity from time i to time j. Then the preferred habitat theory states that the expected total return from rolling over short-term contracts plus the liquidity premium is equal to the total return from a long-term bond.

The implication of the preferred habitat theory is that the yield curve does not necessarily give as clear a signal of the market's expectations of future interest rates as under the expectations theory. The preferred habitat theory implies that the yield curve is determined both by the market's expectations and by the imbalances in preferred habitats. If those imbalances are large, then premiums demanded to bring about an equilibrium will be also. If those imbalances are small, then the premiums will be small and the observed yield curve will be determined largely by expectations.

For example, suppose there is a pattern in the liquidity premiums such that the longer the maturity the larger the premium. The liquidity premiums would then satisfy the following inequalities:

$$0 < {}_0L_1 < {}_0L_2 < {}_0L_3 < \ldots < {}_0L_N \tag{10.17}$$

If liquidity premiums increased with maturity in this manner, the yield curve would tend to have a positive slope. This is illustrated in Figure 10-3, which shows typical upward- and downward-sloping yield curves and the curves that would prevail if the unbiased expectations theory of the term structure were accurate. Even if the market expected that short-term interest rates would remain constant and there was no serial correlation, the yield curve would slope upward to reflect the increasing liquidity premiums. While it is possible that liquidity premiums behave in the way we have just described, that is, they actually satisfy the inequalities in equation 10.17, we are not sure this is the case. Support for the pattern just described comes from the argument that lenders prefer to lend short rather than long. Therefore, larger premiums have to be offered to bear the additional risk of longer-maturity loans. This is the liquidity preference theory of the term structure. The liquidity premium is what must be paid to lenders to induce them to forgo some liquidity.

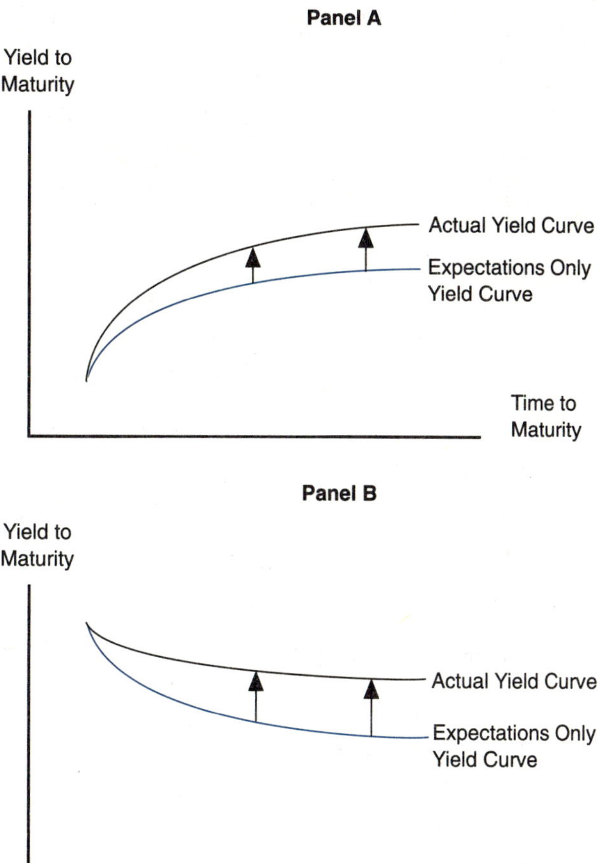

Figure 10-3
(*A*) Effect of liquidity premiums on yield curve when the market expects rates to increase. (*B*) Effect of liquidity premiums on yield curves when market expects rates to fall.

Most of the available evidence supports the view that there are term premiums in the term structure of interest rates. Some of the original tests for term premiums conducted during the 1960s left considerable doubt as to which theory was essentially correct. But, more recently, tests of the ability of long-term interest rates to forecast future short-term interest rates have made it almost impossible to escape the conclusion that term premiums do exist. However, there is little convincing evidence on their size and pattern over time.

Interest Rate Forecasts and the Term Structure

All of the classical theories of the term structure of interest rates include some role for the market's expectations of future short-term interest rates in explaining long-term rates. We know that the yield curve does not provide a perfect clue to the market's expectations as long as liquidity premiums are incorporated in the term structure. But it is fruitful to ask what we can learn about expectations by studying yield curves. We consider two aspects of this question. First, we examine whether the market efficiently incorporates information about future interest rates into long-term interest rates. Second, we explore how we can make practical use of yield curves as forecasts of future rates in financial decisions.

The Efficient Markets Hypothesis and the Term Structure

Any time the financial market incorporates a best guess of a future event into a price or interest rate, we can ask whether, in so doing, the market efficiently uses available information. Here we examine briefly the hypothesis that long-term interest rates efficiently incorporate all available information about the values of future short-term interest rates. The efficient markets hypothesis implies that if we try to forecast future short-term interest rates with forward rates computed from yield curves, these forward rates ought to provide the best forecasts we can find. There should exist no other mechanism, based on publicly available data, that provides a better forecast of future short-term interest rates. For if the market is efficient, then any such forecasting mechanism should be incorporated into the forecast in the yield curve.

Eugene Fama conducted a test of this hypothesis by comparing the forecasting ability of forward rates computed from the yield curve with alternative forecasts of short-term interest rates.[2] One very simple alternative is to assume that short-term interest rates are expected to remain constant for one period ahead or that the best forecast of tomorrow's short-term rate is today's short-term rate. Fama shows that the forward rates computed from yield curves provide forecasts inferior to the forecasts derived from this simple alternative forecast of the behavior of the short-term interest rate.

---

[2]See Fama, Eugene F. "Forward Rates as Predictors of Future Spot Rates." *Journal of Financial Economics* 3 (1976), pp. 361–377.

To develop more satisfactory tests of market efficiency, Fama attempted to measure the liquidity premiums present in the term structure of interest rates and extract those premiums from the forward rates to derive the market's true forecast of the future short-term interest rate. He compared this forecast to the simple alternative forecast of the future short-term rates based on the current short-term rate. Fama concluded from these types of comparisons that the forecasts of future short-term rates, which are embedded in the long-term rate, do as well as the simple alternative forecasting model. The performance of the term structure model is not noticeably superior to the performance of the alternative model with which it is compared. This is evidence, albeit weak, in favor of market efficiency. The fundamental difficulty here lies in deriving accurate measures of the liquidity premiums demanded by the market. Thus far, no very satisfactory measures of these premiums have been devised. Without better measures of liquidity premiums, it may well prove difficult to devise better tests of this dimension of market efficiency.

An alternative way to evaluate whether long-term interest rates efficiently incorporate information about future short-term rates pertains to the behavior through time of yields on debt securities with different maturities. The efficient markets hypothesis is often stated as implying that the past value of the price of a share of stock should be no clue to the future price level. That is, the best forecast of tomorrow's stock price is today's. The same argument applies to the yields on long-term bonds, such as 20-year U.S. T bonds, but it does not apply to short-term Treasury debt, such as 90-day T bills.

To see why this is true we need to examine the difference between long-term bonds and short-term bills. We can use 20-year and 90-day Treasury obligations as our example. Remember that what we observe in the market are the yields on both types of securities at discrete intervals. In terms of notation, we observe the yield on 20-year bonds at time t, then $t + 1$, then $t + 2$, and so forth. The interval between these dates is generally a week, month, or quarter, but it could be any interval you wanted to choose. In an efficient market, the yield on a 20-year bond at time t will incorporate all information known to the market about the next 20 years. The interest rate on the 20-year bond will not necessarily provide an efficient forecast of a 20-year rate observed at time period $t + 1$ because the periods of time these two rates cover do not overlap perfectly. This distinction between the time periods covered by two consecutive 20-year interest rates is illustrated in Figure 10-4. The figure shows that the periods covered by each rate differ by a single period at both the beginning and the end of the 20-year period.

The relevant question is whether this difference in periods of coverage influences the ability of the current interest rate to forecast the interest rate in the next period. If we are actually dealing with interest rates on 20-year bonds that are observed one month apart, then the lack of overlap amounts to two months out of 240 months in the total 20-year interval. In this case, the lack of overlap is a minor problem. But suppose we are talking about 90-day T bills. Out of the three-month maturity on two bills observed a month apart, there are only two months in common, or 60 out of 90 days. As a result, we would not expect the current 90-day bill rate to predict the future 90-day bill rate simply because, to a larger degree, each is covering a different time period.

Figure 10-4
Overlap in time included in the maturities of two 20-year bonds when the yields on these bonds are observed one year apart.

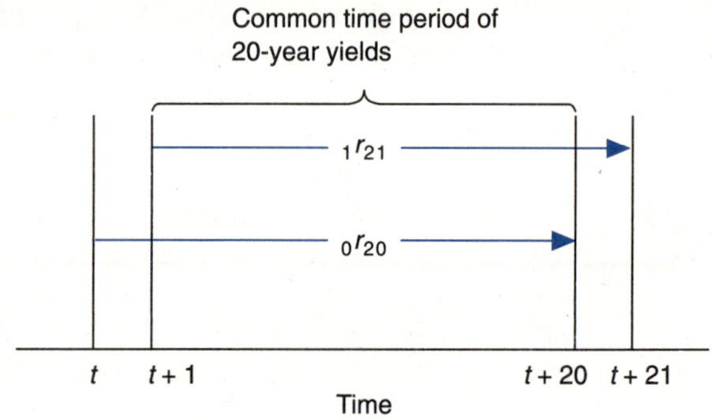

The actual empirical evidence on the predictive ability of 20-year bonds and 90-day bills confirms these arguments. If we try to predict future rates on 20-year bonds, we find that we cannot significantly improve the predictive ability of the current rate by adding past rates to the prediction, as the efficient markets hypothesis implies. But the current rate on 90-day T bills is not as good a predictor of the future 90-day T-bill rate. Here, past rates do add to the power of the current rate as a predictor, as our argument implies. The available evidence therefore suggests that, like stock prices, long-term interest rates efficiently incorporate publicly available information.

The Usefulness of the Yield Curve

The yield curve is often a rather maligned device because individuals ask too much of it. People often think that the yield curve is supposed to forecast future short-term interest rates—that individuals, business firms, or financial institutions can use the yield curve to construct estimates of future rates. We have learned that the forward rates in the yield curve are not directly equal to the expected future spot rate because they include term or liquidity premiums.

The nagging question this leaves is, Of what use is the theory of the term structure? First, and foremost, the zero-coupon yield curve provides the interest rates that we use in virtually all valuations of cash flows to be received in the future. It is the basic fundamental determinant of value. Therefore, understanding the yield curve as a basic ingredient of valuation is critically important. Can we also use the yield curve for forecasts of interest rates? Investors with their own forecast of future rates in hand can compute forward rates from the observed yield curve and compare them to their independent estimates of future rates. If the difference is large enough to compensate the investor for the risk perceived in betting on future rates, then an investment outside a preferred habitat will look profitable.

For example, suppose the forward rate on a 90-day loan beginning 90 days in the future, computed from current T bill rates, is 6.40 percent. Suppose your own forecast of the same 90-day rate is 6.00 percent. This means there is a 40–basis point liquidity or risk premium if your interest rate forecast is subtracted from the forward rate. You must decide whether the 40–basis point risk premium is enough to compensate for moving out of your preferred maturity. To see how this works, suppose you want to invest for three months and are choosing between 90-day and 180-day bills. If you buy 90-day bills, you have no risk. If you buy 180-day bills, you are hurt if interest rates increase significantly because there will be less appreciation in the value of your bills as you approach the time you will sell them, 90 days in the future. The question is, will the 40–basis point risk premium you anticipate be enough to compensate you to take on the risk?

• *So You Want to Do More Interest Rate Modeling?* •

As we mentioned, the so-called classical theories of the term structure have been around for quite a while. Therefore, it should come as no surprise that there is a modern approach to the term structure that has supplemented, and in some sense replaced, the classical theories. The only real drawback to the modern theory is that its full development requires a highly technical presentation. The modern theory posits that interest rates follow one or more stochastic processes, such as we defined at the end of the last chapter when we first introduced some modeling of interest rates. As in the last chapter, we assume there is a model or stochastic process for the short-term rate. This model of the term structure posits that the short-term interest rate is a random variable and changes in this rate from one period to the next, Δr, are determined by the stochastic process specified at the end of Chapter 9:

$$\Delta r = K(u - r) + \sigma\sqrt{r}\Delta Z \qquad (10.18)$$

where u is a central tendency of r, Z is the standard normal random variable, σ is the standard deviation of the interest rate r, and K is a weight determining how fast the interest rate is expected to move back toward its central tendency.

This view of the term structure does not really break out separate expectations or risk-premium components of the term structure. Instead, it simply relates the current observed level of the interest rate to the long-term central tendency (u) of interest rates specified in the stochastic process. Furthermore, the stochastic process contends that the interest rate is expected to track back toward its central tendency according to the parameter K. That is, if K is very close to one, then it is expected that the interest rate will move back toward u very quickly. However, note we have said that it is expected the rate will move back. This expectation comes from the first of the two components of the stochastic process, the deterministic component. The second component is the source of the random behavior in the changes in interest rates. Because this random behavior is based on a normal random variable, Z, and because a normal random variable has an expected value of zero, this random component has an expected value of zero. But the random component means that actual changes in the interest rate will not be equal to the deterministic component. The long-term rates must take this random behavior into account.

The modern model of the term structure develops an explicit equation for the price of long-term bonds and for the determination of long-term interest rates. Unfortunately, the mathematics involved is formidable. However, the basic conclusion about the nature of the term structure that results from this model is quite simple (see yield-curve diagram in Figure 10-5). The model implies there will be a long-term interest rate for bonds of infinite maturity (often called "consols"), r_∞. In the figure this value is assumed to be 5.4 percent. Notice this rate is

Figure 10-5

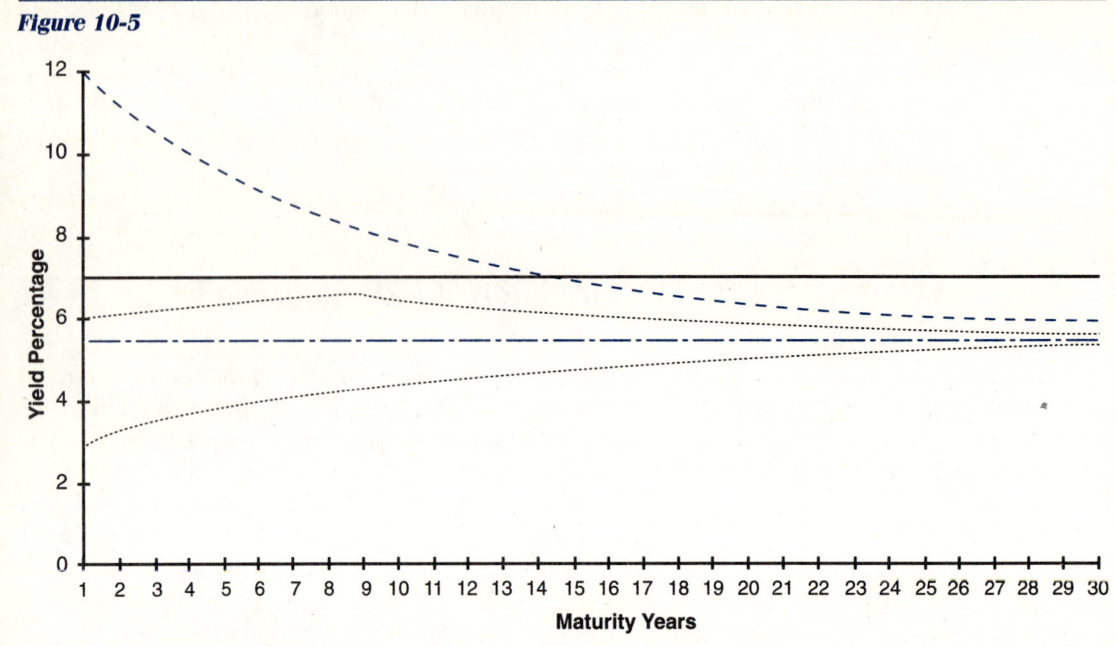

less than the central tendency of the short-term rate, u, which is assumed to be 7 percent in the diagram. Now consider alternative values of the current short-term rate, *r*. If *r* is greater than u, then the yield curve slopes downward from *r* to r_∞. If *r* is between u and r_∞, then the yield curve is humped. The hump develops because, for relatively short maturities the interest rate is drawn upward toward u, but as the maturity lengthens, it is drawn down toward r_∞. If *r* is less than r_∞, the yield curve slopes upward. Therefore, this model implies that the shape of the yield curve is determined by the spread between the current short-term rate and its central tendency and that the long-term rate will be below this central tendency.

SUMMARY

In this chapter we learned how fixed-income securities, that differ only by their terms to maturity, are priced. This relationship between fixed-income securities of different maturity is the term structure of interest rates. The classical view of the issue is that prices and yields of long-term securities are determined by the market's expectation of future short-term rates, the risk involved in betting on future short-term rates, and the amount of risk aversion of market participants.

We learned how to quantify the relationship between long- and short-term interest rates by relying on the use of forward interest rates. And we quantified the relationship between any long-term rate and the sequence of forward rates corresponding to the same time period. We learned to always use the zero-coupon yield curve and how to compute the zero-coupon yield curve from observed yields to maturity on coupon-bearing bonds. We also learned about the connection between the forward rates in the term structure and interest rates in futures markets.

Next we considered three classical theories of term structure that present distinct explanations of the relationship between long- and short-term interest rates. The first, the expectations theory, says that the expected one-year yields on bonds of different maturities are the same. This theory hinges on the hypothesis that investors will substitute between maturities until the expected return from all maturities is the same. The second theory argues that individuals will substitute out of their preferred maturities, but only if they are paid a sufficiently large premium to compensate for the risk they bear. The third theory says that, in the aggregate, people prefer to lend with short maturities and borrow with long maturities, so that the term premiums in the term structure increase with maturity.

All these theories are concerned with the ability of the market to forecast future short-term interest rates. It is natural then to ask how successfully the market does this and to inquire into how the market forms expectations. Evidence suggests that the market is efficient, but the difficulties involved in measuring liquidity premiums make it tough to evaluate the forecasting ability of the market.

Finally, we considered the more recent, or modern theories of the term structure that are based on stochastic processes for interest rates. We examined the basic structure of one of the modern models. We found that this model suggests a simple explanation of the shape of the yield curve based on the tendency of the short-term rate to revert to some central value. The long-term rate will be less than this value and the shape of the yield curve will depend on whether the current short-term rate is above or below the central value and the long-term rate.

QUESTIONS

1. What is the yield curve? What does it mean to say that the curve is upward- or downward-sloping? How does the yield curve usually change over the business cycle? What happened to the yield curve during 1980 and 1985? Why? (You won't find the answer to this last question here.)
2. Suppose you observed the following current rates from the yield curve: ${}_0r_{20} = 0.15$, ${}_0r_{15} = 0.14$, ${}_0r_{10} = 0.10$, and ${}_0r_5 = 0.05$. Compute all the forward rates you can from these current rates.
3. Now pick two pairs of rates from Table 10-2 and compute the forward rates for intervals in between these two spot rates.
4. The expectations theory of the term structure is often referred to as "the perfect substitution theory." Explain the connection between the ideas of perfect substitution and unbiased expectations. How does perfect substitution lead to unbiased expectations?

5. Compare the interpretations that would be placed on the slope of the yield curve if the expectations theory were correct. How would this interpretation change if the preferred habitat theory was correct?
6. In what way is the liquidity preference theory a special case of the preferred habitat theory? What does the liquidity premium measure, and how does it affect forward rates?
7. Suppose you observe the following par yield curve of yield to maturity on coupon-bearing T bonds. Note that each bond is priced at par. Also the yield to maturity on six-month T bills is 4.60 percent.

Maturity (yrs)	Yield (%)
1.0	5.4
1.5	6.3
2.0	8.8

   Construct the zero-coupon yield curve.
8. The efficient markets hypothesis says that long-term interest rates should make efficient use of public information about future short-term interest rates. What does this mean? Why is it difficult to devise a very satisfactory direct test of this hypothesis?
9. Suppose you have $100,000 to invest for retirement and you expect to retire in ten years. If you invest in a ten-year zero-coupon bond you will be able to lock in a return of 9 percent. A second alternative is to invest in a five-year zero-coupon bond and then reinvest your funds at the end of the five years. Suppose the five-year rate available today is 11 percent. Compute the total amount of money you will have under the second option if the five-year rate five years from now ranges from 6 percent to 12 percent. How would you decide which is the best investment?
10. Now suppose that instead of deciding between the ten-year and the five-year bonds in the previous question you are comparing a ten-year and a 20-year bond. The current ten-year rate is still 9 percent and the current 20-year rate is 8 percent. Compute the total amount of money you will have at the end of the ten years if you buy the 20-year bond and ten-year rates range between 6 percent and 12 percent. How would you decide which is the best investment in this situation?

REFERENCES

Brennan, Michael J., and Eduardo S. Schwartz. "A Continuous Time Approach to the Pricing of Bonds." *Journal of Banking and Finance* 3 (1979), pp. 133–155.

Cox, John C., Jonathan E. Ingersoll, Jr., and Stephen A. Ross. "A Re-examination of Traditional Hypotheses About the Term Structure of Interest Rates." *Journal of Finance* 36 (1981), pp. 769–799.

Cox, John C., Jonathan E. Ingersoll, Jr., and Stephen A. Ross. "A Theory of the Term Structure of Interest Rates." *Econometrica* 53 (1985), pp. 385–407.

Fama, Eugene R. "Forward Rates as Predictors of Future Spot Rates." *Journal of Financial Economics* 3 (1976), pp. 361–377.

———."Inflation, Uncertainty, and Expected Returns on Treasury Bills." *Journal of Political Economy* 84 (June 1976), pp. 427–448.

Modigliani, Franco, and Robert J. Shiller. "Inflation, Rational Expectations and the Term Structure of Interest Rates." *Journal of Political Economy* 81(February 1973), pp. 12–43.

———, and Richard Sutch. "Innovations in Interest Rate Policy." *American Economic Review* 56 (May 1966), pp. 178–197.

Rendleman, Richard J. Jr., and Christopher E. Carabini. "The Efficiency of the Treasury Bill Futures Market." *Journal of Finance* 34 (September 1979), pp. 895–914.

Roll, Richard. *The Behavior of Interest Rates: An Application of the Efficient Market Model to U.S. Treasury Bills.* New York: Basic, 1970.

• *Chapter 11*

Exchange Rates and Capital Flows in the Global Economy

This chapter deals with the international financial system. It focuses on the determination of foreign exchange rates and the relationships between interest rates and exchange rates in a competitive global economy. We begin by discussing the accounting system used to keep track of international trade and capital flows between countries. It is absolutely essential to have a basic understanding of the balance of payments and what it means for a country to have a deficit or surplus in either the current or capital accounts of its balance of payments. It is also important to see the connection between these measures of trade and capital flows and the economic policy issues regarding investment, saving, and budget deficits in a country. We focus on these important issues in the first half of this chapter. In the second half we turn our attention to the determination of exchange rates in a competitive global economy. First, we describe the market for foreign exchange, or foreign currency, and its organization. Most currency transactions are accomplished through large banks, which, to a great extent, make the market for foreign exchange. We explain standard spot and forward quotes and describe the process by which settlements are accomplished. We also discuss the relationship among interest rates, spot exchange rates, and forward exchange rates. Knowledge of these relationships is important to understanding how monetary policies affect changes in interest rates and foreign exchange, a topic we take up in Chapter 12. The key concepts to learn in this chapter are listed below.

• *Concepts to Learn in Chapter 11* •

- How the balance of payments accounting system works
- Pros and cons of government policy toward balance of payments deficits
- How the foreign exchange market is organized and how foreign exchange rates are measured
- Parity relationships for interest rates and exchange rates
- Connection between exchange rates, inflation rates, and interest rates

The Balance of Payments and International Capital Flows

The place to start in our exploration of financial conditions in the global economy is with the basic accounting system used to keep track of the flows of both goods and services and financial capital between countries. This accounting system is referred to as the "current and capital accounts of the balance of payments." We will explain the structure of the balance of payments in the United States, though we could assume the vantage point of any other country in the world and examine the balance of payments from its point of view. Statistics on the balance of payments are collected and published quarterly in the United States by the Department of Commerce. These statistics summarize all of the transactions between residents of the United States and those of all other countries.

The Current Versus the Capital Account

There are two basic categories of the balance of payments: the *current account* pertains to flows of goods and services, and the *capital account* to private investment and securities. The current account measures the balance between flows of goods, services, and transfers between one country, the United States for example, and the rest of the world. Services include investment income, such as interest and dividends, and fees for bank services, insurance, travel, or consulting. Transfers are any payments for which no services or goods are provided in exchange, such as pension payments. Table 11-1 illustrates some simple examples of the kind of items that show up on the current account of the balance of payments and the accounting treatment of these items. For example, suppose a U.S. company (Boeing) sells airplanes to Germany. This is recorded as a credit for the U. S. current account. This means it is a positive entry and raises our current account balance. Spending by tourists in the United States is also a credit for the U. S. current account. By contrast, when U.S. citizens buy autos from Germany or beer from Mexico then this is a debit, or a negative entry, on the U. S. current account balance.

The capital account measures the acquisition and liquidation of non-U.S. financial and real assets by U. S. citizens and corporations against such activity in U.S. assets by the rest of the world. Table 11-1 illustrates typical entries to the capital account of

Table 11-1
The Two Balance of Payments Accounts

Current Account	
Credit	**Debit**
Sale of Airplanes to Germany	Purchase of German autos
Spending by Japanese tourists in the U.S.	Purchase of beer from Mexico
Capital Account	
Purchase of U.S. securities	Loans to Poland by U.S. banks
Purchase of U.S. real estate by Japanese	Investment in new plants in Mexico by Ford

the U. S. balance of payments and the proper accounting treatment of these items. For example, if citizens of other countries purchase U. S. securities, this is recorded as a credit or a positive entry on the capital account of the United States. The same entry is made if foreign citizens purchase U. S. real estate. By contrast, if U. S. banks make loans to a foreign country, say Poland, then this is a debit or negative entry in the U. S. capital account. The same type of entry occurs when Ford makes an investment in a manufacturing plant in Mexico.

Table 11-2 shows the current and capital accounts for the United States for 1990 and 1991. Note that the United States had current account deficits of $92 billion and $8 billion in 1990 and 1991, respectively. Both exports and imports are broken down into categories covering merchandise, services, and income on U. S. or foreign assets. Transfers are shown on a net basis. The capital account shows net changes in U. S. assets abroad followed by net changes in foreign assets in the United States. A negative entry for either net change in U. S. assets abroad or net change in foreign assets in the United States means there was a capital outflow from the United States. The final item is the so-called statistical discrepancy. This is the gap between the computed balance on the current account and the balance on the capital account. In principle, these must be the same, but errors in estimating the individual components of each account make it impossible for the two sides of the balancc of payments to come out equal at any point in time. Notice that the statistical discrepancy was rather small in 1991, and much larger in 1990. Indeed, the size of the statistical discrepancy should alert you to the margin of error in the overall balance of payments accounts. Also, from now on we will use the measured current account balance as the appropriate indicator of both the current and capital account balance and avoid reference to the statistical discrepancy, unless it is particularly important.

Table 11-2
U.S. Balance of Payments Accounts

	1990	1991
Exports		
Merchandise	390	417
Services	133	145
Income on U.S. assets abroad	130	115
Total exports	653	677
Imports		
Merchandise	–498	–490
Services	–107	–109
Income on foreign assets in U.S.	–118	–106
Unilateral transfers	–22	20
Current account balance	–92	–8
U.S assets abroad, net change	–58	–68
Foreign assets in U.S., net change	86	80
Statistical discrepancy	64	–4

The statistical discrepancy notwithstanding, it is useful to see what happened in 1990 and 1991. Notice that the current account deficit was much smaller in 1991 than in 1990. In fact, the 1991 number is the smallest recorded in several years. You can see this if you look ahead to Figure 11-2. About half of the decline in the current account deficit is a result of a \$42-billion contribution from partners in Operation Desert Storm to reimburse the U. S. for the expenses of conducting that war. The remainder of the decline reflects a \$34.5-billion decrease in the merchandise trade deficit, or the excess of merchandise exports over merchandise imports, and a \$9.5-billion increase in the surplus on service transactions. The decline in the merchandise trade deficit was largely due to a decline in merchandise imports into the United States, as a result of the very weak economy in the United States during that year.

The Connection Between the Current and Capital Accounts

It is extremely important to have a clear understanding of the links between the two major categories of the balance of payments: they are not independent and they do not pursue lives of their own. The simplest way to appreciate the connection between the two accounts is to simply consider what must happen when a country runs a surplus on the current account. This surplus generally means that this country is exporting more goods and services than it is importing and therefore the amount of foreign currency it is receiving is larger than the amount of its own currency that it is exporting. The people within the country who are receiving foreign currency might simply hoard that currency, but this is an unlikely reaction. Instead they will turn around and invest the foreign currency in assets abroad. This means the country with the current account surplus will buy more foreign assets than it sells of its domestic assets. This is what it means for a country to have a deficit in its capital account. A country that runs a surplus in its current account must, by definition, run a deficit in its capital account. One is the mirror image of the other.

To see this consider what happens when a U.S. citizen buys a car made in another country, say a Toyota made in Japan. One possible route through the global financial system for the cash paid by the U.S. car buyer is illustrated in Figure 11-1. This figure shows that Toyota receives U. S. dollars for the car it sells in the United States and then converts those dollars into yen at a bank in Japan. Then the bank in Japan sells those U. S. dollars to some other party in Japan who uses the dollars to purchase equities or stock in some U. S. company, say Microsoft. The dollars initially flowed out of the United States to pay for a merchandise import from Japan to the United States, thus showing up on the current account of the balance of payments. But then that cash flowed back into the United States to pay for the purchase of assets that shows up on the capital account of the balance of payments.

We can summarize this relationship as follows:

A country has a surplus in its current account if
exports (credits) > imports (debits).
A country has a deficit in its capital account if
asset purchases abroad > asset sales abroad.
Surplus (deficit) on current account = Deficit (surplus) on capital account

Figure 11-1
Link between current and capital accounts of the balance of payments.

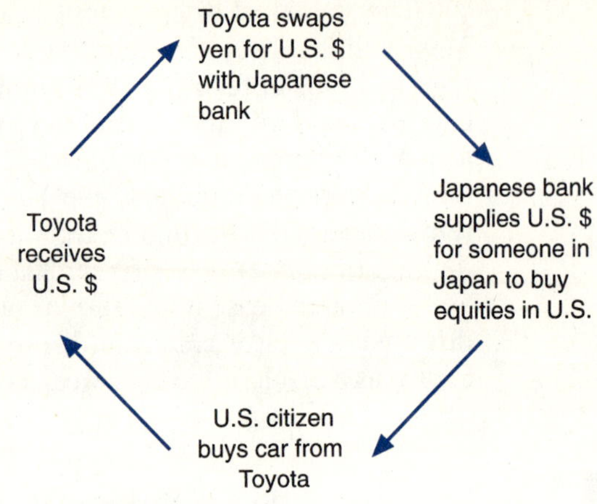

Another way to approach the connection between current and capital accounts requires some basic definitions of the level of income and expenditures in the entire U. S. economy. This approach is especially helpful because it allows us to make the additional connection between the balance of payments and savings and investment behavior in the U. S. economy. We can look at the total performance of the U. S. (or any) economy in two alternative ways, national income or national spending. Total national income (Y), or the income received in the United States for all goods and services produced here, can be divided into two parts, that sold here (Y_D) and that exported (E). We will represent this with a simple equation,

national income equals domestic income plus exports

$$Y = Y_D + E$$

We can divide up total national spending (D) in the same sort of way between spending within the United States, which must be the same as income within the United States (Y_D), and spending abroad or imports (M):

national spending = domestic spending + imports,

$$D = Y_D + M$$

Now we can link the relative balance of national income and national spending to a country's current account balance by combining the two equations above:

national income minus national spending equals exports minus imports,

$$Y - D = E - M$$

A country that has a current account surplus is a country that has more national income than it does national spending:

$$Y - D > 0 \text{ when } E - M > 0$$

Conversely, a country that has a current account deficit is a country that has less national income than it does national spending:

$$Y - D < 0 \text{ when } E - M < 0$$

Next it will be helpful to explore the connection between national income and spending and consumption (*C*), savings (*S*), and domestic investment (*I*). We have two basic choices we can make about how we will allocate our total national income: we can either spend it on consumption or we can save it. The proper way to conceive of savings is *foregone consumption*; savings is income we do not use up or eat in the current period. We have another basic allocation decision pertaining to our national spending. We can either spend on consumption goods, those assets that we use up completely during the current period, or we can invest in real assets that last more than one period. Such investment includes purchases of plant and equipment and research and development, but also purchases of "consumer durables" such as cars and refrigerators. We can express these two allocation decisions as follows:

national income equals consumption plus savings:

$$Y = C + S$$

and national spending equals consumption plus investment

$$D = C + I$$

By combining these two expressions we can see that national income minus national spending equals savings minus investment:

$$Y - D = S - I$$

This simply says that a country whose income exceeds its spending must be saving more than it is investing domestically. There is only one place for the excess of savings over domestic investment to go. It must go abroad. But recall that national income less national spending is also equal to the capital account surplus or deficit. This means that a country that has a surplus of savings over domestic investment and invests that surplus abroad will have a deficit on the capital account of its balance of payments. In fact, this excess of savings over investment is identical to the capital account surplus. Conversely, a country that is investing domestically more than it is saving domestically must be obtaining the additional financial resources from abroad. This is simply another way of saying that it must be running a capital account surplus.

But once again remember that a capital account surplus (deficit) is simply the mirror image of a current account deficit (surplus). Therefore, a country that is importing capital to fund domestic investment above the level provided by its domestic savings, is also a country that is running a current account deficit. That is, it is a country that is importing more goods and services than it is exporting. A country can't have a surplus in one class of its accounts without having a deficit in the other.

A Decade of U. S. Performance

The story we have been telling about the connections between the balance of payments and savings and investment is particularly important for the United States in the 1990s. Over the decade of the 1980s the United States shifted from having a surplus on its current account and a deficit on its capital account to the reverse. Simultaneously, a gap developed between domestic investment and savings. Moreover, much of the shortfall in savings, relative to investment, arose because of increases in the budget deficit of the U. S. government. After all, a government budget deficit is simply negative savings or dissavings.

The levels of domestic investment, total U. S. savings, and the U. S. capital account surplus from 1981 to 1991 are shown in Figure 11-2. Notice that domestic savings and investment were almost equal during the early years of the 1980s, but a gap between investment and savings developed as the decade progressed. It is no coincidence that the capital account surplus was negligible during the early 1980s and also grew with the deficit between investment and savings. In fact, we now know that there could not be a deficit between investment and savings if foreigners did not provide the necessary financial resources to fund that deficit. But recall that the capital account surplus mirrors the current account deficit, which also grew over the same years, at least through 1990. Recall that the capital account surplus declined in 1991, for several reasons that are unique to that period, we hope. Specifically, Operation Desert Storm prompted foreign governments to contribute in excess of $40 billion to the United States. This showed up as transfers to the United States. Furthermore, the recession in the United States decreased imports but it also decreased domestic investment, which declined by roughly 10 percent from 1990 to 1991. This reduced the need for foreign capital infusions during that year; however, when the U. S. economy recovers we may once again come to rely on infusions of capital from abroad.

It is also instructive to examine the major components of total savings. Figure 11-3 shows the level of private savings, or savings by individuals and corporations, as well as savings by the federal and state and local government sectors of the U. S.

Figure 11-2
U.S. domestic investment and savings.

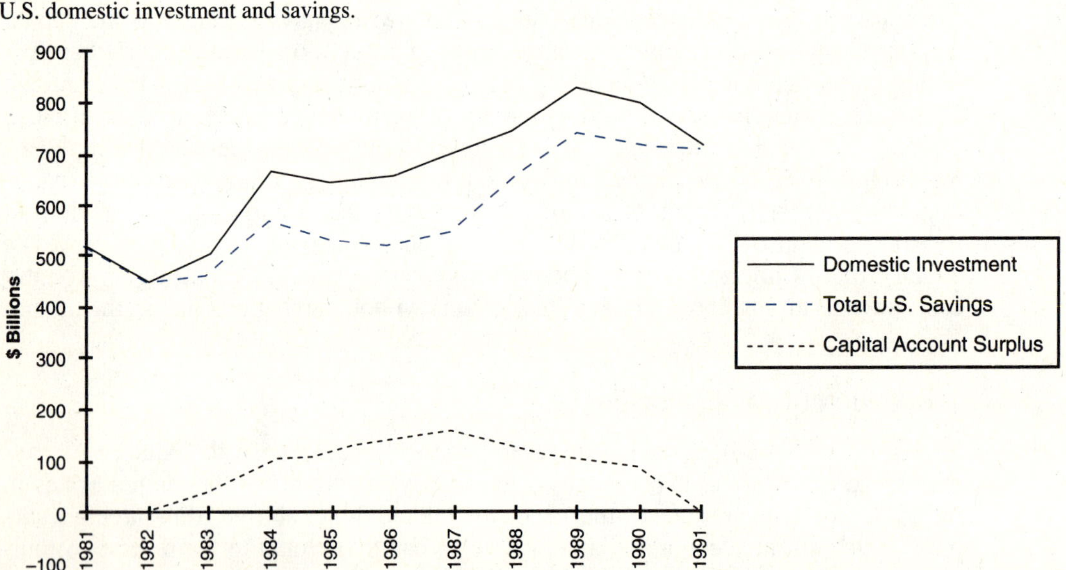

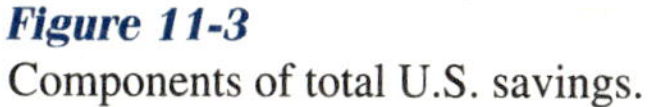

Figure 11-3
Components of total U.S. savings.

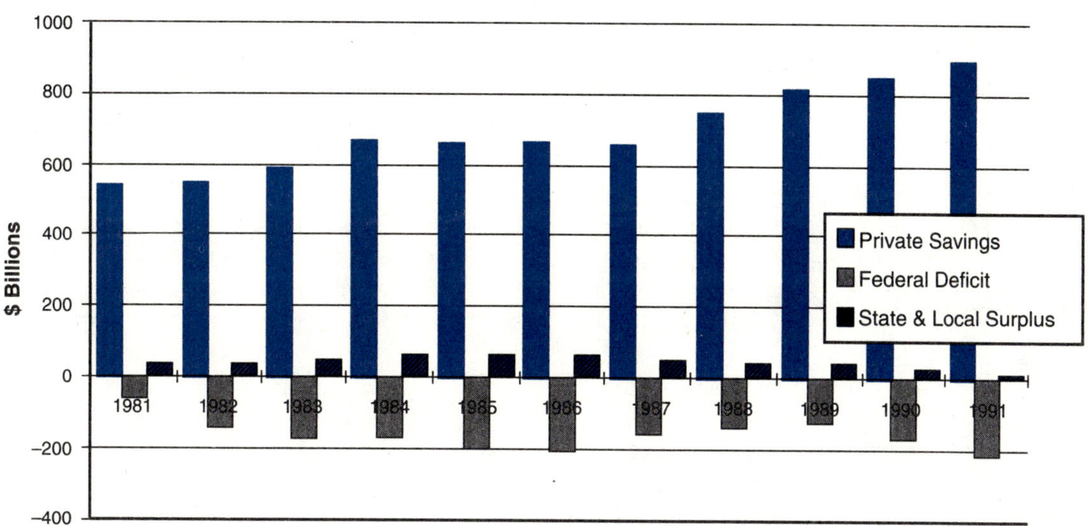

economy over the same period shown in Figure 11-2. Notice that the state and local sector consistently generated a small surplus. Most state and local governments are required to balance their budgets so that there cannot be large aggregate dissaving in this sector. Moreover, private savings has increased over most of this period. But there has been consistent dissaving by the federal government over the period. In fact, to put this in perspective, Figure 11-4 plots the level of the U. S. federal deficit against the capital account surplus. It is apparent from this figure that the capital account surplus has provided part of the resources to fund the U. S. budget deficit—without paying the price of curtailing domestic investment—over much of the 1980s.

Another interesting feature of recent current account deficits for the United States pertains to regions of the world where the United States has had a deficit as opposed to surplus. Table 11-3 shows the U. S. merchandise trade balance by area of the world. Notice that the United States had a merchandise trade surplus with Western Europe and Australia in 1990 and 1991 whereas it had a deficit with Asian countries, particularly Japan, and with oil producing and exporting countries (OPEC) and Latin America. Moreover, the largest part of the deficit with Latin American countries represents Venezuela, which largely exports oil to the United States. These data make clear that the key to the U. S. trade deficit is imports from Asia and imports of oil. It is also interesting to look more closely at the U.S. trade deficit with Japan. The major elements of both exports and imports from Japan to the U. S. are shown in Figure 11-5. The most striking element in this figure is the large amount of automotive and capital goods imports from Japan to the United States as compared to the almost negligible volume of automotive exports from the United States to Japan. In fact, the total merchandise trade deficit in autos in 1991 was $31.292 billion, which is 71 percent of the total merchandise trade deficit with Japan ($44,107 billion).

Figure 11-4
Federal budget deficit and capital account surplus.

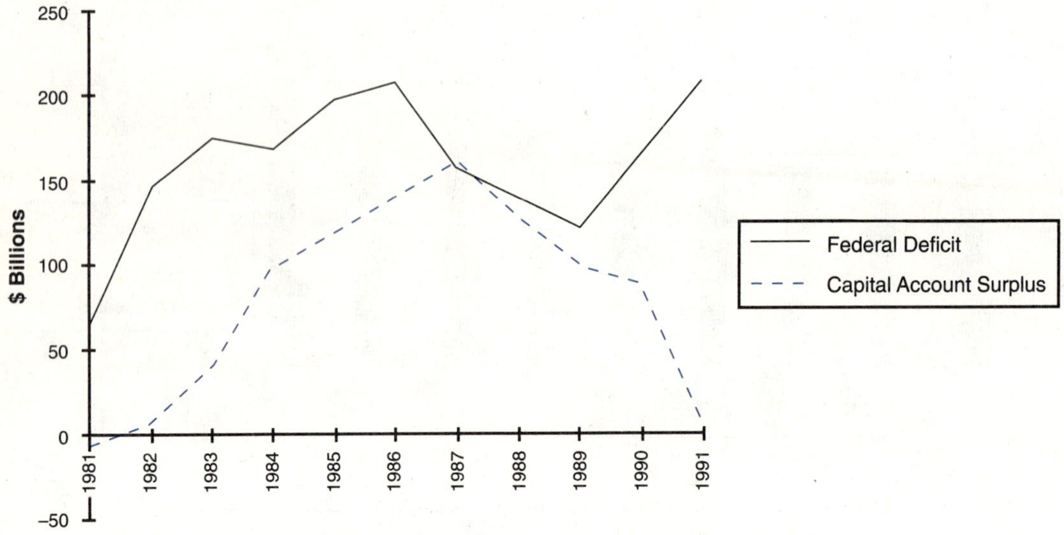

Which Deficits Should the United States Try To Fix?

Public policy debate in the United States often focuses on "fixing" one or more supposedly important deficits. The deficits that receive the most attention are the federal budget deficit and the trade deficit. Those who complain about the trade deficit argue that we must take action to stimulate exports to the point at which we no longer run a current account deficit; however, it should now be apparent that this can be a very dangerous policy. If we were to fix our current account deficit without also fixing our federal budget deficit or increasing private savings, then we would simply have to shrink our level of investment. In fact, if we believe there are attractive investments that should be undertaken in our economy, then it may be dangerous to focus specifically on fixing our current account deficit, as that will reduce the net amount of foreign capital available to fund U. S. domestic investment.

To decide which of the several important deficits facing the United States really needs fixing it is important first to identify the most important underlying problem. The deficits themselves are more like symptoms than diseases, and fixing symptoms can often be wasteful or dangerous. Let's briefly consider two possible interpretations of the underlying problems that are producing the symptoms. Both interpretations are based on the view that the basis for any action that fixes a deficit is to generate jobs for workers in the United States. The real question is whether the concern is for current or future workers.

Problem 1: We need to increase current employment. If you perceive the problem to be a lack of current jobs you may be enticed by the idea that we need to fix the trade deficit. If we can raise exports relative to imports, this may provide jobs for current workers. Because current workers are current voters, this reasoning is often politically attractive, but the focus on fixing the trade deficit has at least two drawbacks. First, actions taken to fix the trade deficit may end up driving down imports even if they succeed in driving up exports. For example, one supposed tactic to fix the trade deficit is to depreciate your currency so that your exports are cheaper to foreign buyers, but this strategy also makes other countries' imports more expensive. This is harmful to those who would like to consume those imports. Second, as we have already learned, fixing the trade deficit reduces the amount of foreign capital flowing into the country to fund domestic investment. This forces those who seek funding for such investment to compete more intensely for domestic savings and to attempt to offset the policies aimed at fixing the trade deficit. If this competition has the effect of driving up real interest rates, it makes many investments that looked attractive at lower interest rates look less attractive. In the end, if the fix-the-trade-deficit policy is successful, investment will fall, but that will be all right because it was presumed at the outset that the real problem was current employment.

Problem 2: We need to increase future employment. If you perceive that the important problem is future rather than current employment, you will be concerned about

Table 11-3
U.S. Merchandise Trade Balances by Area
[Balance of payments basis, millions of dollars]

	1989	1990	1991[P]
Total	−115,917	−108,115	−73,586
Canada	−9,277	−9,454	−7,976
Western Europe	−3,990	2,121	14,724
United Kingdom	2,381	2,999	3,186
Germany[1]	−8,280	−9,664	−5,340
Other	1,909	8,786	16,878
Japan	−49,669	−41,690	−44,107
Australia	4,246	3,893	4,269
Latin America	−10,594	−11,665	−819
Brazil	−3,670	−2,922	−669
Mexico	−2,450	−2,392	1,611
Venezuela	−3,795	−6,424	−3,597
Other	−679	73	1,836
Other Western Hemisphere	1,934	1,617	1,115
OPEC (non-Latin America)	−12,933	−17,528	−10,830
Asia (non-OPEC)	−39,280	−38,054	−34,595
Hong Kong, Republic of Korea, Singapore, Taiwan	−26,299	−20,622	−14,832
Other	−12,981	−17,432	−19,763
Eastern Europe	3,480	2,074	3,071

[P]Preliminary.

[1]Includes the former German Democratic Republic (East Germany) beginning at the fourth quarter of 1990. In earlier periods, the German Democratic Republic is included in Eastern Europe.

Source: U.S. Department of Commerce March 1992

Figure 11-5
U.S. exports to and imports from Japan for 1991

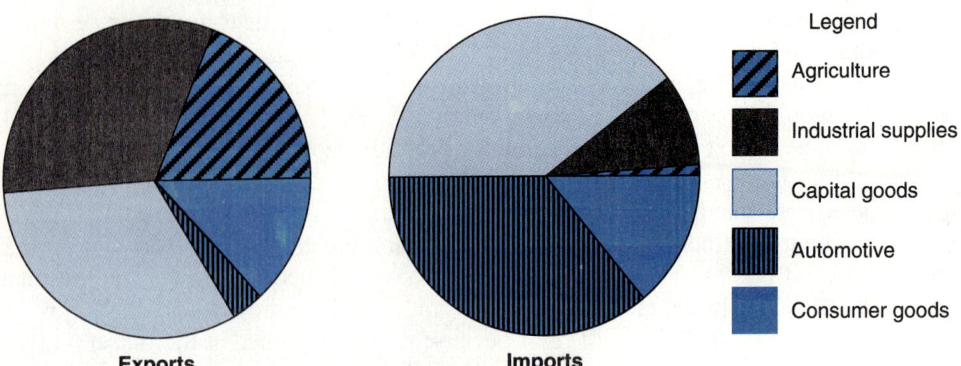

the level and productivity or quality of investing spending. More productive (positive net present value) investments make your economy stronger in the future. If your view is that future employment is the crucial problem, then you attempt to make sure that you do not inappropriately diminish incentives to carry out productive investments. As long as the federal government continues to run a significant budget deficit, you are compelled to ask whether you want to maintain an inflow of foreign capital to fund domestic investment. If you fix the trade deficit, you will imperil investment expenditures, but if you fix the budget deficit you may be able to free more domestic savings to fund domestic investment. The danger in fixing the government budget deficit is that you may also cause the entire economy to slow down, thus imperiling your objective. But, whatever the dangers of trying to deal with the government budget deficit, your objective is not served by trying to fix the trade deficit.

The Foreign Exchange Market

Now that we have some understanding of the way countries keep track of international trade and capital flows, as well as the importance of these flows for a country's domestic economic policy, we can turn our attention to the market where currencies are traded and exchange rates determined. First we describe the market for foreign exchange, or foreign currency, and explain its organization. Most currency transactions are accomplished through large banks, which to a great extent make the market for foreign exchange. We explain standard spot and forward quotes and describe the process by which settlements are accomplished. We also discuss the relationship among interest rates, spot exchange rates, and forward exchange rates. Knowledge of these relationships is important to understand how monetary policies affect interest rates and foreign exchange rates.

Organization of the Market

When foreign trade takes place, payment for goods generally involves a foreign exchange transaction. Most of the time, an importer, who buys goods, pays the exporter, who sells the goods, in the exporter's home currency. This requires the importer to accomplish a foreign exchange transaction that converts the importer's currency to the exporter's currency. A U.S. importer of German beer pays for the beer in Deutschemarks (DM). To obtain the necessary currency, the importer sells U.S. dollars ($) in return for Deutschemarks. The rate of conversion between the two currencies is called the "dollar–Deutschemark exchange rate." The market for such transactions is called the "foreign exchange market."

The foreign exchange market operates worldwide. It consists of two levels: the wholesale market, or dealer market, and the retail market. The wholesale market is dominated by large international money center banks and a few specialized brokers who are linked by a sophisticated communications network. Dealers and brokers obtain exchange rate quotes via video screens and accomplish transactions over the phone with other dealers. The retail market is able to monitor quotes made by major dealers via one or more of the leading electronic financial information systems, like Telerate or Reuters. Some of the large dealer banks make a market in specific currencies that are of special importance to their retail clientele. Such banks actually maintain an inventory in these currencies, to provide immediate availability for their customers. In addition they often trade on their own account to arbitrage, or speculate, in their specialized currencies. Other smaller banks trade in the wholesale market principally to accommodate their retail business. These banks are interposed between international investors, multinational firms, tourists, and so on, and the larger wholesale market.

An example of a spot transaction involving two U.S. banks is outlined in Figure 11-6. In this example, U.S. Bank A wants to buy DM500. A broker in the interbank market is able to locate another bank, Bank B, that wished to sell the Deutschemarks, and a price is agreed at DM 2.00 per dollar. The broker is paid a commission for bringing buyer and seller together. Subsequent settlement takes place in two days and is accomplished by transactions involving both German and U.S. banks. First of all, suppose that both banks maintain an account with a German bank. To transfer the DM500, Bank B authorizes the German bank by telephone or telex to transfer DM500 to the account of Bank A on the settlement day. At the same time, the German bank notifies Bank A that DM500 will be transferred to its German account. In the United States, Bank A pays for the Deutschemarks, at the rate of 2.00 per dollar, via a federal funds transfer at the New York Federal Reserve Bank of $250 from its account to the account of Bank B. Once completed, all transactions are confirmed by telephone or telex.

Transactions in the interdealer market are generally for multiples of $1 million in foreign currency; those in the retail market can involve amounts of any size. Most dollar-based transactions in the interbank market are facilitated through CHIPS, the New York–based Clearing House Interbank Payments System. This system allows for calculation of net obligations between banks on a daily basis and processes payments due by participating banks through the New York Federal Reserve Bank by 6:00 P.M. daily.

Figure 11-6
Spot transaction in foreign exchange.

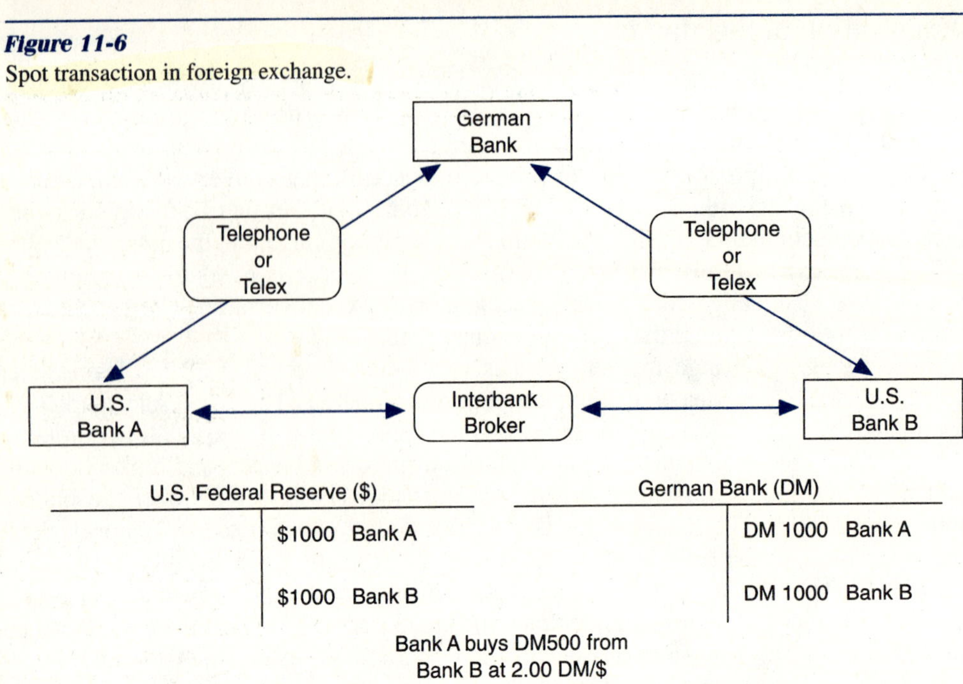

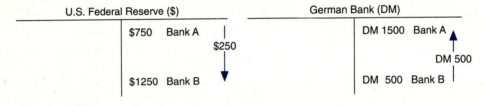

Foreign Exchange Rates

Exchange Rate Quotes

There are two types of transactions in foreign exchange: spot and forward. The spot exchange rate is the rate for buying and selling foreign exchange with a settlement in two days or less. Forward transactions involve a promise, or contract, to settle the transactions at some date more distant than two days. All major currencies are quoted against the U.S. dollar. Spot exchange rates can be quoted in terms of either currency. For example, the spot rate for Japanese yen in terms of U.S. dollars reported by the *Wall Street Journal* for January 8, 1992 was 124.15 yen per dollar. The same price can be stated in dollar per yen by computing the reciprocal, or 1/124.15:0.008055 dollar per yen.

Quotes can be stated in "direct" or "indirect" terms. A *direct quote* is one made from the perspective of the home currency. For example, U.S.-based direct quotes treat all other currencies as the commodity that is quoted and state the price (exchange rate) of the commodity in units of dollars. From the U.S. perspective, a direct quote on the yen is 0.008055 dollar per yen. That is, the yen is the currency being priced, and it costs 0.008055 dollars to buy one yen. An *indirect quote* on the yen would be in units of foreign currency per unit of home currency. From the U.S. viewpoint, the indirect quote on the yen is 124.15 yen per dollar. Just the reverse is the case if quotes are presented from the Japanese perspective. The direct quote on the U.S. dollar is 124.15 yen per dollar; the indirect quote on the U.S. dollar is 0.008055 dollar per yen. It is important to note that the definition of a particular quote depends on the country of reference. To eliminate this ambiguity, the New York bank dealers participating in the interbank market adopted *European terms* as a convention for making quotes. Under this convention, the U.S. dollar is used as the common currency against which all other currencies are quoted. Market quotes are made that give the price of U.S. dollars in terms of all other currencies—for example, yen per dollar, Deutschemark per dollar, French francs per dollar, and so on. The only exceptions to this convention come in the case of British sterling and other currencies now or formerly subject to the British monetary system (Ireland, Australia, New Zealand), where quotes are made on American terms, for example, dollars per pound sterling. The convention of quoting the British pound and other related currencies in American terms comes from the fact that these currencies were not formerly on a decimal system, making it easier to give U.S. dollar quotes in American terms.

Cross Rates and Intermarket Arbitrage

Another reason for quoting all other currencies against the U.S. dollar is that many pairs of currencies are infrequently traded with each other. Exchange rates on those currencies are determined by their relationship with an actively traded third currency. For example, the Australian dollar (A$) is infrequently traded with the Danish krone (DKr). But both currencies are actively traded with the U.S. dollar. Using the U.S. dollar–based quotes on the Danish krone and the Australian dollar, a *cross rate* may be calculated that provides the implicit quote for the Danish krone in terms of the Australian dollar. From the *Wall Street Journal,* for trading on January 8, 1992, here are the U.S. dollar quotes: on the Australian dollar: 1.3236 A$/U.S.$; on the Danish krone: 5.8625 Dkr/U.S.$. The implied cross rate can be determined by dividing the rate for the Danish krone by the rate for the Australian dollar. This gives the following cross rate for the Australian dollar in terms of Danish krone:

$$\frac{5.8625 \text{ Dkr/ U.S.\$}}{1.3236 \text{ A\$/ U.S.\$}} = 4.4292 \text{ Dkr/A\$}$$

Ignoring transactions costs, we could achieve the 4.4292 Danish krone per Australian dollar exchange rate by first buying U.S. dollars with Danish krones at 5.8625 Danish krone per U.S. dollar and then selling the U.S. dollars for Australian dollars at 1.3236 Australian dollar per U.S. dollar.

Cross rates are also important for recognizing opportunities for intermarket arbitrage. Suppose the following exchange rates obtained:

French francs per U.S. dollar: 5.1470 FF/$,

German marks per U.S. dollar: 1.5070 DM/$,

French francs per German mark: 3.5000 FF/DM.

The implied cross rate between French francs and Deutschemarks is 3.4154 francs per mark. The outright exchange rate between French francs and Deutschemarks is 3.5000 French francs per Deutschemarks. This implies a "triangular" arbitrage opportunity is available between the francs and the marks. The steps necessary to exploit the opportunity are explained via Figure 11-7.

Because the cross rate between French francs and Deutschemarks is less than the outright exchange rate between the two, it is cheaper to exchange French francs for Deutschemarks *through the U.S. dollar* than to exchange francs for marks directly. Beginning with FF100,000, Figure 11-7 shows how one can buy Deutschemarks at the lower rate and then sell the Deutschemarks for French francs at the higher rate. This procedure generates a profit of FF2477. Aside from the additional transactions costs associated with the steps involved, this represents an arbitrage profit that should be dissipated by market pressure on exchange rates. Intermarket arbitrage should ensure that outright exchange rates and cross rates are close to each other—that is, within transactions costs.

Bid-Offer Spreads

When quoting exchange rates, participants in the dealer market for foreign currency actually quote two rates: a bid quote and an offer quote. The *bid quote* is the number of units of foreign currency the dealer is willing to give in order to buy one U.S. dollar. The *offer quote* is similar to the ask price associated with other financial quotes. This quote is the number of units of foreign currency the dealer is willing to take in order to sell one U.S. dollar. In conventional European terms, the bid-offer exchange rates are the prices at which the dealer will buy and sell the U.S. dollar,

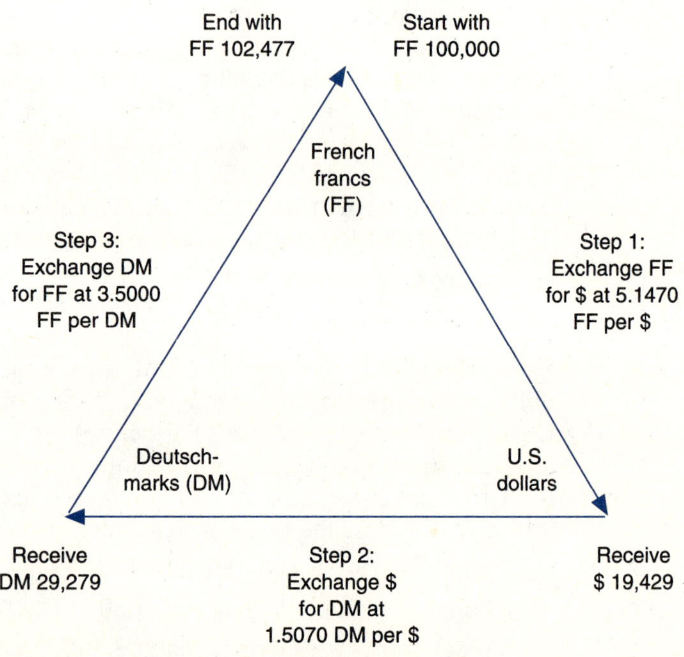

Figure 11-7
Cross rate and triangular arbitrage. The cross exchange rate implied by dollar exchange rates is FF3.4154 per Deutschemark, making it cheaper to exchange FF for DM through the dollar than to exchange francs for marks directly at FF3.5000 per Deutschemark.

where prices are expressed in a variety of other currencies. Table 11-4 provides a set of quotes for the Deutschemark.

Notice that at the spot rate, the bid is 2.5875 Deutschemarks per dollar and the offer is 2.5885 Deutschemarks per dollar. Thus, the dealer's spread is 0.0010 Deutschemarks per dollars. The difference between various quotes is often referred to as *points,* or *pips,* by traders, which means that the spread is ten points in this case. For every $1000 the dealer buys and resells at current spot rates, she makes DM 1 profit. Even though participants in the foreign exchange markets always encounter a bid-offer spread when buying or selling foreign currency, often the exchange rates are not quoted that way in the financial press. News sources like the *Wall Street Journal,* for example, generally publish the bid rate or the average of the bid and the offer rate. In Table 11-4 the average of the spot bid and offer rates is 2.5880 Deutschemarks per dollar. This number might appear in news sources as the most recent spot rate.

Table 11-4 also shows the one-, three-, and six-month forward exchange rates quoted for the mark. Two things are notable from the forward rates. The first is that the dealer's bid-offer spread increases with the time to settlement. The spread increases from ten points at the spot rate to 14 points for the one-month and the three-month forward rates, to 18 points for the six-month forward rate. Similar patterns are common across exchange quotes because positions in forward contracts are riskier the more distant the settlement date of the contract. Therefore, the market maker or dealer requires a greater spread to compensate for bearing more risk in making a market in forward contracts at more distant settlement dates.

The second thing to note about the quotes just cited is that the forward rates are lower than the spot rate. In other words, under forward agreements fewer Deutschemarks are required to buy U.S. dollars forward and fewer Deutschemarks are received from selling dollars forward. When this is the case, the dollar is said to be trading at a discount in the forward market. The premium or discount impounded in the forward rate is computed by subtracting the spot rate from the forward rate ($F - S$). A negative result indicates a discount and a positive one, a premium. In most cases, discounts and premiums are computed from the average of the bid and the offer rates at the various settlement dates. In Table 11-4, the average bid and offer rates are computed for the spot and for each forward rate. In addition, the discount is computed for each forward rate and is also provided in the table.

The fact that the dollar is trading at a 92-point discount in the one-month forward market means that it is worth less under the one-month forward contract than

Table 11-4

Computations in Foreign Exchange Quotes: Deutschemarks (DM/$)

	Bid	**Offer**	$\frac{\textbf{Bid + Offer}}{\textbf{2}}$	**Forward-Spot**
Spot	2.5875	2.5885	2.5880	———
1-Month forward	2.5781	2.5795	2.5788	–.0092
3-Month forward	2.5625	2.5639	2.5632	–.0248
6-Month forward	2.5382	2.5400	2.5391	–.0489

at the spot rate. Fewer Deutschemarks are required to buy the same number of dollars under a one-month forward agreement. (More dollars are required to buy the same number of Deutschemarks.) One interpretation of the forward discount is that the market expects the dollar to depreciate in value (in terms of Deutschemarks) over the period until the settlement date. Similar expectations are indicated by the discounts on forward dollars with three- and six-month settlement dates.

It is common to express forward discounts and premiums as a percentage of the current spot rate and to annualize those rates in order to compare them to discounts and premiums at alternative settlement dates and across alternative currencies. For example, the one-month forward discount on the dollar given in Table 11-4 is expressed as a percentage of the spot by dividing 0.0092 by the spot rate of 2.5880. This gives the percentage depreciation of the dollar over a one-month period at the current one-month forward rate. This rate is annualized by multiplying by 12, because there are 12 one-month periods in the year. In general, the annualized percent premium or discount can be computed as follows:

$$\left(\frac{F-S}{S}\right)\left(\frac{12}{n}\right)100\%$$

where F is the forward rate, S the spot rate, and n the number of months remaining to settlement on the forward contract. Table 11-5 computes annualized percentage discounts based on the quotes in Table 11-4.

The advantage of expressing the discount on one-month forward dollars as an annualized rate is that it is more easily interpreted and compared to other rates. For example, with respect to the spot and the forward rates, the dollar will lose value at the annual rate of 4.27 percent over the next month. At the same time, the three-month forward rate indicates a 3.83-percent rate of dollar devaluation annually. If forward rates are interpreted to represent expected spot rates, these rates imply that the value of the dollar is expected to fall most sharply over the next month, but its rate of depreciation will decrease during the following two months. More gradual depreciation is indicated over the six-month interval.

The Eurocurrency Market

The interbank market for foreign exchange is closely related to the Eurocurrency market. Though this market is sometimes called the "Eurodollar market," several other currencies, mostly European, are also traded. The Eurocurrency market is the interbank

Table 11-5

Forward Discounts on the Dollar: Deutschemarks (DM/$)

1 Month:	$\frac{-.0092}{2.5880} \cdot \frac{12}{1} \cdot 100\% = -4.27\%$ per year
3 Month:	$\frac{-.0248}{2.5880} \cdot \frac{12}{3} \cdot 100\% = -3.83\%$ per year
6 Month:	$\frac{-.0489}{2.5880} \cdot \frac{12}{6} \cdot 100\% = -3.78\%$ per year

market for short-term debt. Typically, banks quote bid and ask rates at which they are willing to borrow and lend in specific currencies and at different maturities, in amounts of $1 million or more. Table 11-6 provides an example of Eurocurrency rates for the U.S. dollar and for the Deutschemark as they might appear for a particular bank dealer.

These quotes represent the rates at which banks in the interdealer market are willing to borrow and lend to each other. For example, the quotes in our example indicate that the bank is willing to borrow dollars for six months at 12 percent per year. At the same time, the bank is also willing to lend dollars for six months at 12 1/4 percent per year. For Deutschemarks the bank quotes a rate to borrow at 8 percent and to lend at 8 1/4 percent. Retail customers of the bank would be quoted the same rates, but depending on their credit quality would be charged a premium on the ask rate and have to give up a premium on the bid. In other words, the bank would widen the spread quoted to the commercial customers. The more established and better-regarded the customer is, the narrower is the spread. For example, for better clients the bank might charge an "eighth" or 1/8 of one percent (annual). Then, the six-month quotes on the dollar to this customer would be 11 7/8 bid and 12 3/8 asked. Less creditworthy customers would encounter larger spreads from the bank to lend or borrow in Eurodollars. Similar adjustments would occur in other Eurocurrencies.

The Eurocurrency market and the forward foreign exchange market are closely integrated. At a given maturity, the difference between interest rates on the two currencies is directly related to the difference between spot and forward exchange rates in the two currencies over the same time to maturity. This relationship, known as the interest rate parity proposition, is explained in the following section.

Market Equilibrium and the Determination of Foreign Exchange Rates

Here we explain how the spot and forward exchange rates for a pair of currencies are related to the rates of interest in each currency and to the expected rate of inflation associated with each currency. We show that the forward premium (or discount) associated with a pair of currencies is directly related to two economic factors. The first is

Table 11-6
Eurocurrency Rates

	U.S. Dollar		Deutschemark	
	Bid (%)	**Ask (%)**	**Bid (%)**	**Ask (%)**
1 Month	$11\frac{7}{8}$	$12\frac{1}{8}$	$7\frac{7}{8}$	$8\frac{1}{8}$
3 Months	$11\frac{7}{8}$	$12\frac{1}{8}$	$7\frac{7}{8}$	$8\frac{1}{8}$
6 Months	12	$12\frac{1}{4}$	8	$8\frac{1}{4}$

the difference in interest rates between the currencies, a relationship commonly referred to as the condition of *interest rate parity.* The second factor is the difference in expected rates of inflation between the two currencies, the condition of *purchasing power parity.* These relationships show how equilibrium in the foreign exchange market requires the differential between forward and spot rates to be in a particular balance with differentials between interest rates and differentials between expected inflation rates in each currency.

Interest Rate Parity

An important perspective for understanding the relationship between interest rates and exchange rates is a proposition known as interest rate parity. *Interest rate parity* is a condition under which the rates of interest denominated in two different currencies provide equal returns, taking into account the spot and forward exchange rates between the two currencies. Consider, for example, the case of U.S. dollars ($) and British pounds (£). The Eurodeposit market provides an opportunity to invest in deposits denominated in either currency at competitive deposit rates. The definition of interest rate parity is as follows:

$$(1 + r_{\$}) = (1 + r_{£})\left[\frac{F_t}{S_o}\right] \qquad (11.1)$$

where $r_{\$}$ is the U.S. dollars–denominated rate of interest on deposits maturing in t months, $r_{£}$ is the pound–denominated rate of interest on investments maturing in t months, S_o is the current (time 0) spot exchange rate (expressed in dollars per pound), and F_t is the t-month forward rate of exchange.

The basic message of equation 11.1 is that, all else being the same, the returns on deposits at the dollar or the pound interest rate are equal. The intuition behind this result can be most easily seen by comparing two alternative investment strategies. The strategies are expressed from the viewpoint of a dollar investor, that is, one with dollar currency to invest. The first strategy is to simply invest one dollar in t-month, dollar-denominated deposits. The gross return from this strategy is given on the left-hand side of equation 11.1. The second strategy has three steps: (1) Exchange one dollar at S_o, giving $1/S_o$ in pounds; (2) invest the $1/S_o$ pounds at the pound interest rate; and (3) after t days, convert the pound deposit yields $(1 + r_{£})(1/S_o)$ in proceeds back to dollars at the forward exchange rate contracted earlier for time t. The return, given the forward rate for day t, F_t, is

$$(1 + r_{£})\left(\frac{F_t}{S_o}\right) \text{ expressed in dollars}$$

This is the same as the right-hand side of equation 11.1.

Notice that the key difference between the domestic and the foreign investment is that when investors make investments denominated in foreign currency, they actually make *two* investments: one in the foreign asset bearing interest at $r_{£}$ and the other in the pound currency itself, at the rate of return of $(F_t - S_o)/S_o$. If exchange rates were always constant, so that one currency would never appreciate (or depreciate) against the other, $F_t - S_0$ would equal zero and the effect of currency investment on interest rates would always be neutral. However, in an environment of floating exchange rates, the exchange rate is generally expected to change somewhat over the time of a foreign investment.

To illustrate interest rate parity consider the following example. Suppose the exchange rate between British pounds and U.S. dollars is $1.80 per pound. In addition, suppose that in the Eurocurrency market the annual interest rate on three-month dollars at bid is 12 percent and the annual interest rate on three-month pounds at bid is 16 percent. This means that a three-month investment in pounds will earn

$$(0.16)\left(\frac{90}{360}\right) = 0.04$$

or 4 percent over its three-month term. Similarly, the dollar-denominated investment will earn 3 percent over the same period. Interest rate parity implies that the forward dollar per pound exchange rate is determined by solving equation 11.1 for F_t.

$$(1.03)/(1.04) = F_t/1.80$$

so

$$F_t = .99038 \times (1.80\ \$/£) = 1.783\ \$/£$$

Finally, notice that if the interest rate parity condition did not hold there would be some incentive for investors to prefer investing in one currency over the other. For example, if the expected spot rate in three months was higher than 1.783 dollars per pound, there would be an incentive for U.S. investors to lend pounds rather than dollars. As money moves from dollar investments to pound investments, interest rates and the exchange rate adjust, tending toward the interest rate parity condition. The three-month dollar rate will be bid up, the three-month pound rate will be bid down, and the spot rate will be bid up (more dollars required to buy pounds).

• *So You Want to Arbitrage the Foreign Exchange Market?* •

To see how to uncover and take advantage of an arbitrage opportunity in foreign exchange let's modify our example of interest rate parity just a bit. Suppose that the three-month forward exchange rate is 1.79 dollars per pound rather than 1.783. This implies that the right-hand side of equation 11.1 is greater than the left, which means that a dollar investor could make more interest per dollar at the pound rate than at the dollar rate. Suppose you could invest $1 million. An investor can take the following steps to take advantage of this lack of interest rate parity:

1. Exchange $1 million at the spot rate of 1.8 dollars per pound for £ 555,556.
2. Invest £ 555,556 at the pound rate for three months at four percent.
3. Make a forward contract to exchange £ 577,778 for dollars in three months at the three-month forward rate of 1.79 dollars per pound.

In three months the following occurs:

1. The British pound–denominated deposit matures, delivering £ 555,556 × 1.04, or £ 577,778.
2. The £ 577,778 are sold under the forward contract for £ 577,778(1.79), or $1,034,222—an interest return in dollars of $34,222.

Alternatively, the dollar investor can invest the same $1 million at the dollar rate of 3 percent and earn $30,000 in interest. Thus, $4222 in additional interest is earned via the pound-denominated investment.

While the investment at the pound rate would be preferred by dollar investors and would likely be pursued instead of investments at the dollar rate, there has not been any pure arbitrage to this point. But if the dollar investor was able to borrow dollars at any rate of interest below 4 percent for three months, then some opportunity for pure arbitrage exists. For simplicity, imagine there is no bid-ask spread in the Eurocurrency market for dollars or pounds. This means that our dollar investor can also *borrow* dollars in the Eurocurrency market for three months at 3 percent. Actually, the dealer market in Eurocurrency provides quotes at bid and ask that generally vary by 1/8 to 1/2 of one percent (APR). Thus a three-month loan would likely be available at a three-month rate of 3 1/32 percent to 3 1/8 percent. Rather than put his or her own $1 million through the steps just outlined, the dollar investor borrows $1 million. After three months, the investor owes $1,030,000 to repay the loan but receives $1,034,222 from the covered pound-denominated investment. In essence, the left-hand side of equation 11.1 represents the loan repayment per dollar associated with raising dollars in the Eurocurrency market. The right-hand side of it gives the proceeds per dollar from the covered investment in pounds. Thus, $4222 is generated over three months with no equity capital invested—a *pure arbitrage profit.* This is called "*covered interest arbitrage*" because the investment is covered in such a way that there is no risk in this position.

Once markets respond to the arbitrage opportunity just described, the spread between interest rates should narrow. The process of borrowing dollars and reinvesting in pounds puts downward pressure on the pound interest rate and upward pressure on the dollar interest rate. In addition, the difference between the spot and forward exchange rates should increase. The forward rate is bid down from selling pounds forward and the spot rate is bid up from buying pounds on the spot. This tends to exaggerate the forward discount on the pound already reflected in the forward market. At some point, arbitrage ceases when prices and rates are sufficiently in conformance with the interest rate parity condition of equation 11.1 to eliminate profit opportunities net of transactions costs.

Purchasing Power Parity

Purchasing power parity is a proposition that resembles interest rate parity. It states that the difference between spot and forward exchange rates between two currencies is directly related to the difference in expected inflation rates of the two. The substance of the purchasing power parity proposition can be most easily explained in the context of a simple example.

Consider the currency of two countries, the United States (dollars) and Germany (marks). Let the current (at time zero) price of an identical bundle of real goods in each country be represented by $P^{\$}$, and P^{DM}, respectively. Ideally, these bundles would be comprised of a sufficiently broad cross section of goods so as to represent the general price level in each country. In addition, let the expected price of the same bundle of goods in each country at some future date, t, be $E_0(P^{\$}_t)$ and $E_0(P^{DM}_t)$, respectively. Finally, let the current spot exchange rate (Deutschemarks per dollars) be S and the forward exchange rate, with settlement date t be F_t (Deutschemarks per dollars). The price of the same bundle of goods should be the same in both countries at a given point in time. This is called "the law of one price." The law of one price holds that the same commodity or good should bear the same price on different markets. Otherwise, arbitrage between the two markets would drive prices to the same level. Obviously, there are some real-world frictions involved in buying in one market and reselling in another. In the case of markets for real goods, the costs of transportation, import tariffs, and other costs could allow for significant price differentials on the same goods. In addition, some transactions costs are associated with converting currencies, in the form of bid-ask spreads and broker's commissions, which would lead to price differentials. For simplicity, our discussion does not directly account for such frictions. In other words, a German buyer who compared the cost of buying goods in Germany with that of buying the same goods in the United States would find no difference in cost, as measured in Deutschemarks.

For a German buyer, buying the goods in the United States involves two purchases. The first is the purchase of dollar currency to buy the U. S. products, and the second is the purchase of the products themselves. The current price of the bundle of goods in the United States is $P^{\$}$. At the current exchange rate, the cost of the purchase in Deutschemarks is $P^{\$} \times S$. Thus for purchasing power parity to hold,

$$P^{\$} \times S = P^{DM} \tag{11.2}$$

To understand this idea, suppose the cost of goods was cheaper in the United States, so that

$$P^{\$} \times S < P^{DM}$$

There would be an immediate incentive for German buyers to import U.S. goods rather than continue buying the same goods made in Germany. Assuming production of goods remains constant, this results in the price of German goods being bid down and the price of U.S. goods being bid up. At the same time in the foreign exchange market, as Deutschemarks are exchanged for U.S. dollars, the price of dollars will be bid up (more Deutschemarks required to buy dollars). In terms of the purchasing power parity expression, prices would adjust thus:

$$\uparrow P^{\$} \times \uparrow S < \downarrow P^{DM}$$

until equation 11.2 is restored and there is no further incentive for a German buyer to prefer U.S. goods over German goods.

If equation 11.2 holds for *current* price levels and exchange rates, it should also hold for *expected* prices and *forward* exchange rates. In other words,

$$E_0(P^{\$}_t) \times F_t = E_0(P^{DM}_t) \quad (11.3)$$

The forward market allows the German buyer to lock up the cost of buying some number of dollars at date t. Based on current (time zero) expectations of the future price level at date t, buyers make the same comparisons as before. If the price of U.S. goods, based on both the expected price of U.S. goods and the forward price of dollars, is less than the expected price of German-made goods, or

$$E_0(P^{\$}_t) \times F_t < E_0(P^{DM}_t),$$

the German buyer will buy dollars forward, expecting to buy U.S.-made goods when date t arrives. Assuming expected future spot rates remain unchanged, by buying dollars forward, the forward price of dollars will be bid up as

$$E_0(P^{\$}_t) \times \uparrow F_t < E_0(P^{DM}_t)$$

until the equilibrium condition of equation 11.3 is restored.

The combination of the equilibrium conditions of 11.2 and 11.3 establish the relationship between expected price changes and foreign exchange rates, referred to as the purchasing power parity proposition. Dividing equation 11.3 by equation 11.2 gives

$$E_0(P^{\$}_t)/P^{\$} \times F_t/S = E_0(P^{DM}_t)/P^{DM}$$

which can be reexpressed as

$$(1 + E_0(\pi^{\$}))(F_t/S) = (1 + E_0(\pi^{DM}))$$

where the ratios of expected price level to current price level are recognized as 1 plus the expected rate of inflation, $(1 + E_0(\pi))$, in each currency, dollars and Deutschemarks. The preceding equation is the usual expression for the purchasing power parity proposition, but its logic can be made clearer by dividing both sides by $(1 + E_0(\pi^{\$}))$, to give

$$F_t/S = (1 + E_0(\pi^{DM}))/(1 + E_0(\pi^{\$})) \quad (11.4)$$

This expression shows that the percentage difference between the forward exchange rate, F_t, and the spot exchange rate, S—that is, the percentage premium or discount on the dollar—is directly related to the difference between expected inflation rates between the two currencies. Notice that if inflation in both currencies were expected to be the same over the time until date t, F_t would equal S, and no premium or discount would be priced into the forward rate.

Remember that the rate of price inflation is the rate at which a currency loses value or purchasing power over time. At the same time, exchange rates are a measure of the relative value of two currencies. If one currency depreciates in value faster than another, then the relative purchasing power of the two changes accordingly, and so must the exchange rate. This also applies to the effect of the expected rates of inflation on the expected spot exchange rate at date t. In turn, the forward rate of exchange must reflect the market's forecast of the future spot rate. In essence, the premium or discount in the forward rate represents the market's assessment of the expected change in the relative value of the two currencies, which is driven by the difference in the expected inflation rates in the two currencies.

For example, suppose the rate of dollar inflation is expected to be 0 percent over the period to date *t*. At the same time, the Deutschemark inflation rate is expected to be 100 percent. If the current spot rate is 2.50 Deutschemarks per dollar, from equation 11.4, the forward price at date *t* should be 5.00 Deutschemarks per dollar. The reason is that by date *t*, the mark is expected to buy half the amount of goods that it does currently. On the other hand, the purchasing power of the dollar is expected to stay the same. Certainly counterparties in the forward market for forward exchange will account for these expectations in setting the contract price for forward dollars. Because the DM is expected to be worth half as much by date *t* and the dollar is expected to be worth the same, the relative value of the dollar in terms of the Deutschemark has doubled. If the actual rates of inflation are as expected, it will take twice as many Deutschemarks to buy the same number of dollars. The forward market impounds this expected effect into today's forward rate.

Finally, it is worth noting that the purchasing power parity proposition set out by equation 11.4 lends a particular interpretation to the annual percentage discounts and premiums observed earlier in forward exchange rates. Given our discussion, there is a logical interpretation to these rates. In essence, a discount on the dollar indicates that the market expects the inflation rate in the U.S. dollar to be higher than that of the foreign currency. A premium indicates just the opposite. The market expects the foreign currency to depreciate at a greater rate than the dollar. The magnitude of the premium and discount indicate the expected difference in currency depreciation when projected over an annual period. Such information is often used as a market-based forecast of the strength of one currency against another.

The International Fischer Effect

To this point we have described three important propositions for understanding the determinants and behavior of exchange rates. Separately, we examined the relationship between expected spot and forward exchange rates, between interest rate differentials and exchange rates, and between expected inflation rates and exchange rates. One more proposition is useful in understanding how the various other propositions fit together. This proposition is commonly referred to as the "international Fisher effect": a simple extension of the Fisher effect, or the link between nominal interest rates and expected inflation rates described in Chapter 9, to a comparison of interest rates and inflation rates between countries.

Recall that the basic message of the Fisher effect described in Chapter 9 was that the nominal rate of interest is equal to the real rate of interest plus a premium to offset the expected rate of inflation. For default risk–free securities this can be expressed as

$$(1 + r_N) = (1 + r_R)(1 + \mathrm{E}_0(\pi))$$

The international counterpart to this relationship merely recognizes that a similar effect must hold for different countries and interest rates denominated in different foreign currencies. For the United States the Fisher effect is rewritten as

$$(1 + r^{\$}_{N}) = (1 + r^{\$}_{R})(1 + E_0(\pi^{\$})) \tag{11.5}$$

For similar securities in Germany, equation 11.5 can be restated as

$$(1 + r^{DM}_{N}) = (1 + r^{DM}_{R})(1 + E_0(\pi^{DM})) \tag{11.6}$$

If real rates of return on similar securities in the two countries are approximately equal, then by dividing 11.5 by 11.6 the following can be written:

$$(1 + r^{\$}_{N})/(1 + r^{DM}_{N}) = (1 + E_0(\pi))/(1 + E_0(\pi^{DM})) \tag{11.7}$$

Equation 11.7 summarizes the international Fisher effect. Basically, it says that differences in nominal interest rates between two countries are directly due to differences in expected inflation between the two countries.

Integrating Interest Rate and Purchasing Power Parity

The international Fisher effect is the link between interest rate parity and purchasing power propositions. Together, they provide an integrated equilibrium involving interest rates, exchange rates, and expected inflation rates. Figure 11-8 illustrates the three-way equilibrium combining each of the propositions identified earlier as interest rate parity, purchasing power parity, and the international Fisher effect. The figure uses Deutschemarks and dollars as example currencies.

In effect, three equations must hold at once if there is to be equilibrium among interest rates, exchange rates, and expected inflation. As is illustrated in Figure 11-8 this is more concisely stated as

Figure 11-8

An integrated equilibrium: exchange rates, interest rates, and expected inflation.

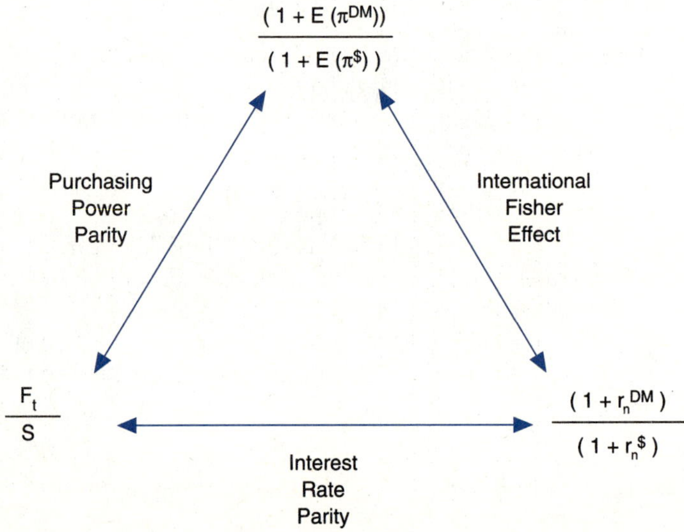

$$(1 + r^{\$}_{N})/(1 + r^{DM}_{N}) = (1 + E_0(\pi^{\$}))/(1 + E_0(\pi^{DM})) = (F_t/S) \qquad (11.8)$$

The important message from equation 11.8 is that both exchange rates and interest rates depend on expected inflation. As the expected rates of inflation for two currencies diverge, so do interest rates in the two currencies and their forward and spot exchange rates. A convenient way to interpret equation 11.8 is that the expected difference in inflation between two currencies simultaneously determines the equilibrium interest rate differential and the equilibrium differential between forward and spot exchange rates. The by-product of this joint equilibrium is that exchange rates and interest rates are in the appropriate balance as well. In that sense, it is natural to think of interest rate parity resulting from the combination of purchasing power parity and the international Fisher effect.

SUMMARY

This chapter is concerned with the trade and capital flows between countries and the markets for foreign exchange or the markets where the currencies of countries are priced. We began with a discussion of the balance of payments which focused on the current accounting system used in the United States to keep track of trade and capital flows with other countries. We emphasized the importance of having a basic understanding of this accounting system. We also delved into recent data for the balance of payments of the United States, and we explored the connections between balances on the current and capital accounts with investment and savings in the United States. We considered the public policy issue of how we might attempt to fix the deficit that the United States has run in recent years in the current account of the balance of payments. We emphasized that fixing the deficit would also mean reducing the surplus on the capital account, so that the United States would no longer have the benefits of foreign capital used to finance investments in this country.

Next, we turned our attention to the foreign exchange markets. We discussed the organization of the foreign exchange markets, the standard procedures for quoting foreign exchange rates, intermarket arbitrage, bid-offer spreads, and the Eurocurrency market. We placed considerable emphasis on the parity relationships that connect interest rates, spot exchange rates, and forward exchange rates. The first parity relationship, interest rate parity, states that the expected returns earned by investing in fixed-income obligations in different countries must be equal, taking into account the current spot and forward exchange rates between the currencies. We demonstrated how arbitrage would drive the marketplace toward such parity if it did not already exist. Then we considered purchasing power parity. This proposition holds that the difference between spot and forward exchange rates between two currencies is directly related to the difference in expected inflation rates between those currencies. Finally, we explained the international Fisher effect, which links nominal interest rates and expected inflation rates in each country around the world.

QUESTIONS

1. Distinguish between the current and capital accounts of the balance of payments. Explain the meaning of deficits and surpluses in both accounts.
2. Throughout most of the 1980s the United States ran a deficit on the current account of the balance of payments. Was this good or bad for the country? Why or why not?
3. What is the connection (if any) between the level of savings in one country and the level of investment in that country? How is this related to the balance of payments?
4. A large U. S. bank that functions a dealer in foreign currency is seeking to buy DM10,000,000 in the spot market. An interdealer broker locates another bank that states a bid price on DM10,000,000 of 1.5108 Deutschemark per U.S. dollar and an ask price of DM 1.5151.
   a. At which price can the bank acquire the needed Deutschemarks? Explain.
   b. Determine the cost of the purchase in United States dollars.
   c. Assuming the Deutschemarks are purchased at this price, describe how the transaction will take place. When will the transaction be completed?
5. Explain the difference between "American terms" and "European terms" as a convention for quoting exchange rates.
6. The spot exchange rate on the French franc is currently 5.1525 (French francs per dollar) and the 180-day forward rate is 5.5515 (French francs per U.S. dollar). Is the franc trading at a premium or a discount against the U.S. dollar? Explain. If the forward rate is an unbiased forecast of the future spot rate, what do these prices imply about the market's expectation of the future value of the U. S. dollar?
7. The current spot rate on the British pound sterling is 1.8835 (U.S. dollars per pound) and the current spot rate on the Deutschemark is 1.5121 (marks per U.S. dollar). Determine the cross rate for the Deutschemark and the pound. Suppose the spot rate for the pound against the Deutschemark is actually 2.837 (marks per U. S. dollar). Describe the arbitrage opportunity that results.
8. The current spot rate on the Japanese yen is 124.15 (yen per U.S. dollar) and the 180-day forward rate is 124.74 (yen per U.S. dollar). Suppose the U. S. Federal Reserve releases information indicating that inflation in the United States may be higher during the next six months than was previously anticipated. What should be the response in dollar rates on yen?

REFERENCES

Bach, Christopher L. "U. S. International Transactions, Fourth Quarter and Year 1991." *Survey of Current Business* (March 1992), pp. 51–74.

Fama, E. F. "Forward and Spot Exchange Rates." *Journal of Monetary Economics* 18 (1984), pp. 319–338.

Frenkel, J., and R. Levich, "Covered Interest Arbitrage: Unexploited Profits." *Journal of Political Economy* 83(April 1975), pp. 324–338.

Hekman, C. R. "A Model of Foreign Exchange Exposure." *Journal of International Business Studies* Summer (1985), pp. 85–99.

Shapiro, A. C. *Multinational Financial Management.* Boston: Allyn and Bacon, 1989.

• *Chapter 12*

Government Policy and Interest Rates in a Global Economy

This is the first of two chapters in which we explore the links between monetary policy, interest rates, and exchange rates in a global economy. We begin this chapter with the operation of the central bank in the United States, the Federal Reserve, and with the process of controlling the supply of money and interest rates. We explore how the Fed influences interest rates in the U. S. economy. We concentrate first on how the Fed affects domestic interest rates, holding aside the fact that the United States operates in a competitive global marketplace. Then we incorporate the impact of global competition into our discussion. Historically, the Fed had substantial latitude to conduct U. S. monetary policy without worrying about the monetary policies of other major countries in the world, but that is no longer true. Now, major countries cannot conduct a national monetary policy without paying attention to the policies of other countries that compete for capital in global financial markets. Thus, we also focus on the links between monetary policy, interest rates, and exchange rates in a competitive global economy. In the next chapter we examine how the Fed has conducted its policy in recent years. We start with a summary of the options open to the Fed in choosing the targets of monetary policy. These targets include interest rates, exchange rates, and some measure of the supply of money. We use this understanding of the policy tools open to the Fed to form the basis for a summary and examination of the conduct of U. S. monetary policy from the early part of this century up to the early 1990s. The key concepts to learn in this chapter are listed below.

• *Concepts To Learn in Chapter 12* •

- How the Federal Reserve is organized and how it operates
- Connections between monetary policy, money supply, and money demand
- How changes in monetary policy affect interest rates
- How changes in monetary policy affect exchange rates
- How to judge whether monetary policy is tight or loose

Operation of the Federal Reserve and Conduct of Monetary Policy

Organization and Structure of the Federal Reserve

The United States did not always have a central bank. In fact it was not until 1913 that Congress passed a law that created the U. S. central bank, the Federal Reserve. The Congress passed the Federal Reserve Act in response to the Panic of 1907, which constituted a serious liquidity crisis in the U.S. commercial banking industry. The Federal Reserve was created to function as a "lender of last resort," or a source of liquidity to the banking industry. Since 1913, the functions of the Fed, as well as our understanding of its proper role in the economy, have developed considerably. Today, the Fed not only serves its traditional role of providing liquidity to the banking industry; it also exerts control over the quantity of money in the economy and influences market interest rates. To understand how and why it has this power we need to know how the Fed is organized and how it conducts its business.

The Federal Reserve is controlled by a seven-member Board of Governors. Each board member is appointed for a 14-year term, and one member's term expires every two years. Appointments are made by the President with the consent of Congress and, because of retirements, are often made more frequently than the two-year interval. One of the seven members of the board serves as chairman. The chairman is selected by the President for a four-year term. Unlike almost every other agency in the federal government, the Federal Reserve does not have to go to Congress for a budget. The Fed is self-supporting and, in fact, generally returns billions of dollars to the Treasury each year from its earnings on its portfolio of government securities.

The formal independence of the Federal Reserve may overstate the reality of the matter, for the Federal Reserve's independence persists only with the consent of Congress and the President. There is always the possibility that the Federal Reserve Act will be modified to alter the Fed's accountability. The organizational structure and distribution of power within the Fed are the result of a number of compromises made over the life of the system. When the system was created, the offices of the Board were located in Washington but the country was divided into 12 districts that each had a Federal Reserve bank in. Considerable power was allocated to the district banks. Specifically, they had the power to grant loans and set terms for those loans to individual commercial banks in each district and to buy and sell United States government securities on their own accounts. In the 1930s this power was consolidated in Washington under the direction of a committee that maintained representation from the district banks. This committee, known as the Federal Open Market Committee (FOMC), remains the single most important decision-making body in the Federal Reserve system. It is composed of the seven members of the Board of Governors, the President of the Federal Reserve Bank of New York, and, on a rotating basis, four of the other 11 district bank presidents. The FOMC has the real responsibility for determining monetary policy.

The power of the FOMC results from its control of what are called "open market operations." Open market operations are the purchase or sale of U.S. Treasury securities by the Fed. This is the principal tool by which the Fed determines the money supply. The FOMC meets about once a month in Washington and on other special occasions to decide the future course of monetary policy.

Open Market Operations and Control of the Money Supply

Over the approximately 80 years it has been in business, the Federal Reserve has acquired a rather large portfolio of U.S. Treasury securities. As of December, 1992, the Fed owned $296 billion worth of Treasury securities, which represented approximately 7 percent of the total stock of such securities outstanding. The Fed doesn't buy such securities purely in order to make a profit. It is principally through the purchase of such securities that the Federal Reserve supplies reserves to the banking system. The FOMC sets the guidelines for the purchase and sale of such securities, and its operating arm, the Open Market Desk at the Federal Reserve Bank of New York (FRBNY), actually conducts the transactions, the open market operations.

The basic mechanics of open market operations are relatively simple. When the Open Market Desk, under the direction of the FOMC, decides that Treasury securities should be purchased, it calls up any of a number of dealers in such securities. The Fed maintains a list of commercial firms, usually large brokerage houses or banks, that continually make a market in Treasury securities, and for any given transaction it chooses some dealer on this list (see Chapter 2). The Federal Reserve then agrees to buy a certain volume of securities at the going price, say $10 million worth of securities. The FRBNY issues a check to the securities dealer for $10 million, and the Federal Reserve receives title to the securities. If the securities dealer is not a commercial bank, then that dealer has the check from the FRBNY deposited in its bank. The deposit balances of the dealer are increased by $10 million, and the deposits the commercial bank holds with FRBNY are increased by $10 million. This represents a net increase in the reserves of the banking system, for there is no offsetting decline in the deposits of any other bank.

Before we go any farther it is important to understand what reserves are. We in the United States operate in what is called a "fractional reserve banking system." Regulations require that banks and other depository institutions such as savings and loans hold reserves behind deposit accounts that function like demand deposits. One way these reserves are held is in the form of deposits with the various Federal Reserve Banks. Therefore, when the Fed purchases securities and the deposits of a commercial bank with the Fed increase, this is equivalent to increasing the amount of reserves held by the banking industry as a whole. When open market operations take place, the public as a whole merely exchanges one type of asset for another; that is, when the Federal Reserve buys securities, the public exchanges Treasury securities for demand deposits. As a consequence of this exchange the banking system acquires new reserves because they are the deposits of commercial banks with the Federal Reserve.

The net impact of the increase in reserves described above is illustrated in the following hypothetical balance sheet. The demand deposits of the commercial bank in question, which are a liability on its accounts, are increased by $10 million. Offsetting this is a comparable increase in reserves in the form of deposits with the Fed. This bank and the banking system now have $10 million in new reserves that did not previously exist.

Balance sheet of commercial bank

Assets	Liabilities and Net Worth
Reserves: + 10,000,000	Demand deposits: + 10,000,000

The unique and relevant characteristic of reserves is that they constrain the total supply of deposits the commercial banking system can make available to the public. If the required ratio of reserves to deposits is, say, 20 percent and the total stock of reserves is, say, $20 billion, then the maximum amount of deposits that can be issued by the banking system is $100 billion (20 percent of $100 billion is $20 billion). Therefore, when new reserves are created the banking system can let deposits expand. On the other hand, if the Federal Reserve withdraws reserves through open market sales of securities, the banking system must limit deposits to a smaller volume than it did previously. To more clearly see the links between reserves and the total volume of deposits we must examine what is called the multiple expansion process.

Defining Money

To establish the link between open market operations and the aggregate supply of money we need to have a workable definition of what constitutes money. To see how to define money it is necessary to understand the function money serves in an economy. Money is an asset that serves as a unit of account and medium of exchange. Money serves as the unit of account because the prices of all goods and services are denominated in money (e.g., in U. S. dollars). In this sense money is simply a measuring device, like inches, pounds, or liters. Moreover, the fact that we denominate the price of everything in money greatly simplifies the process of doing business. The alternative would be to state the price of every kind of goods in terms of every other kind, (e.g., the price of lamb chops in terms of Toyotas). It would be exceedingly difficult to carry out transactions, as this would essentially be a barter economy.

In our contemporary economy money also serves as a medium of exchange. People hold balances of money, which they exchange for goods and services they buy and sell. Thus, money is a commodity itself, not merely the unit of measure in an accounting system. In our world it is difficult to imagine conducting business without exchanging money. Regardless of what we purchase or sell, we are willing to accept money in exchange because we know it will be readily acceptable throughout the economy. As a result, we choose to use as money items that minimize the cost of executing transactions. We would, for example, find it difficult to use cows as money. The difficulties might not be overwhelming if we wanted to purchase something that cost exactly one cow. We would merely have to worry about transporting, feeding, and cleaning up after the cow. Suppose we wanted to purchase something that cost half a cow. Then we would have to worry about butchering and preserving the meat. If we started using cows for money, we would eventually wind up exchanging frozen meat. In effect, hamburger would drive out cows as a medium of exchange. Similarly, if some other asset were viewed as presenting lower costs of transacting, it would come to replace hamburger as a medium of exchange. The implication is that an economy will naturally evolve to using for a medium of exchange those assets that involve the lowest cost of transacting. These assets are characterized as the most liquid assets in the economy.

To see what serves as money today we can start with the assets that most clearly fit our concept of money. The first asset generally recognized as money is cash, or currency—the paper notes and metal coins issued by the Federal Reserve and the Treasury in denominations as small as a penny to as large as $1000. The second asset generally understood to be money is demand deposits. These are the balances in checking accounts held by individuals and corporations throughout the country. They are thought of as money because they are universally accepted as a medium of exchange. It is certainly true that checks drawn on deposit balances are not always accepted without some guarantee of payment, but this does not mean that the demand deposits themselves do not function as money. What it does mean is that a check itself does not guarantee that the demand deposit exists. If the reliability of payment of deposits were seriously enough impaired, they would cease to function as money. The sum of cash in the hands of the public, demand deposits at commercial banks, and other checkable deposits at nonbank depository institutions (as well as traveler's checks) is referred to as M_1. As of the end of 1992, the components of M_1 were as follows (in billions of dollars): currency, $293; traveler's checks, $9; demand deposits, $339; and other checkable deposits, $384.

There has been a long-standing debate about whether the money supply should also include time and savings deposits at commercial banks. Some argue that people substitute back and forth between these assets so closely that it is unreasonable to exclude them from the definition of the money supply. In fact, this has become the consensus view in recent years and this has meant that little attention is now paid to M_1. When these are included in the money supply, along with cash and demand deposits, the money supply is referred to as M_2. In addition, the Fed reports M_3, which also includes money market mutual funds.

Another possibility for defining the money supply, in comparison to M_1 and M_2, involves less rather than more aggregation. This alternative definition of money is called the monetary base or high-powered money. The monetary base (B) consists of cash in the hands of the public and reserves held by institutions that offer transactions accounts. Reserves include deposits held with the Federal Reserve by institutions with transactions accounts and cash held in the vaults of commercial banks. The base is called high-powered money because more aggregate measures of the money supply, like M_2, are multiples of the base. Therefore, if the base expands, M_2 expands by a multiple of the expansion in the base. The idea that the base represents money hinges on the argument that when transactions are made using demand deposits, banks exchange reserves. As a result, this high-powered money really underlies all other transactions. As long as there is a clearly definable, unique set of assets individuals and corporations use as a medium of exchange the base is a less attractive definition of money, but in today's financial environment, with a multitude of special types of liquid assets that are close substitutes for demand deposits, the concept of a distinct money other than the base is becoming more nebulous.

While it is not obvious which definition of the supply of money is most appropriate, it is necessary to choose one in order to proceed. We use M_2 in the remainder

Table 12-1

Alternative Definitions of Money

Designation	Amount in Billions of Dollars (1992)	Definition
B	351	Cash in the hands of the public plus reserves
M_1	1,024	Cash outstanding plus travelers checks, demand deposits with commercial banks, and checkable deposits with other depository institutions
M_2	3,504	M_1 plus time deposits at depository institutions

of this book; however, in the next chapter we also discuss some of the difficulties created for monetary policy by the ambiguity surrounding the appropriate definition of money. All three of the possible definitions of money, plus data on the levels of each in 1992, are summarized in Table 12-1.

The Multiple Expansion Process

To examine the link between reserves and deposits we utilize a simple example of a banking system with no cash and only one type of deposit, demand deposits. We will assume that all banks always try to hold exactly the amount of reserves that are required, as excess reserves are costly to banks, because they earn no interest income. The required ratio of reserves to demand deposits is represented by v, and it is assumed to be equal to 20 percent. We want to examine the impact on the total supply of demand deposits of an increase in reserves through an open market purchase of, say, $10,000.

Suppose that the initial purchase of Treasury securities by the Open Market Desk of the FRBNY is from a securities dealer named Jones & Henry. Jones & Henry has its demand deposit account with First Bank. When the transaction is made between Jones & Henry and the FRBNY, Jones & Henry has the payment made by the New York Fed credited to its demand deposit account at First Bank. Therefore, the demand deposit balances of First Bank increase by $10,000 and its reserves with FRBNY increase by an equal amount. The hypothetical balance sheet for First Bank before this transaction is this:

First Bank

Assets		Liabilities	
Reserves	$200,000	Deposits	$1,000,000
Loans	$800,000		

Before the Open Market purchase the actual reserves maintained by First Bank were exactly equal to the reserves required by the Fed—that is, 20 percent of its demand deposits. After the transaction the balance sheet looks like this:

First Bank

Assets		Liabilities	
Reserves	$210,000	Deposits	$1,010,000
Loans	$800,000		

Now First Bank has $8000 in reserves above what the Fed requires, which can profitably be used to fund new loans.

Suppose that First Bank extends a new loan to someone who wants to purchase a car. The car purchaser receives a check for $8000 from First Bank and presents it to the car dealer. The car dealer then deposits the check in his or her bank, say Second Bank. The accounts of First Bank are altered so that loans are increased by $8000 and reserves are decreased by the same amount. After extension of the new loan the balance sheet of First Bank looks like this:

First Bank

Assets		Liabilities	
Reserves	$202,000	Deposits	$1,010,000
Loans	$808,000		

Similarly, the books of Second Bank show an increase in reserves of $8000 and an increase in deposits of the same amount. Suppose Second Bank has exactly the required amount of reserves, 20 percent of deposits, before this transaction. This is its balance sheet before the automobile purchase:

Second Bank

Assets		Liabilities	
Reserves	$120,000	Deposits	$600,000
Loans	$480,000		

Once the car has been purchased, the $8000 addition to reserves and deposits will be reflected in the balance sheet of Second Bank as follows:

Second Bank

Assets		Liabilities	
Reserves	$128,000	Deposits	$608,000
Loans	$480,000		

Second Bank is now in the same position First was when it received the initial \$10,000 increase in reserves: it has excess reserves that it did not previously have. Its excess reserves is smaller than First's; they now represent 80 percent of \$8000, or \$6400. Second Bank may now extend a new loan and generate new deposits of \$6400 for some other bank and still meet its reserve requirements exactly. Another bank will then receive \$6400 in new reserves, and 80 percent of that will be in excess of what is required. The process will continue almost indefinitely until all reserves held in the system become required. As these reserves are distributed throughout the banking system and new loans are created, the total stock of deposits continually increases. Initially, when the Open Market Desk purchased Treasury securities from Jones & Henry, demand deposits increased by \$10,000. With the loan made by First Bank they increased another \$8000, and with the loan by Second, by \$6400. As more loans are made, demand deposits continue to increase, by \$5120, then \$4096, and so on. This multiple expansion process will lead to a total increase in demand deposits that can be represented as follows:

$$\Delta D = \Delta B + (1 - v)\Delta B + (1 - v)^2\Delta B + (1 - v)^3\Delta B + (1 - v)^4\Delta B + \ldots \quad (12.1)$$

where ΔD represents the total change in deposits and ΔB represents the initial change in the monetary base. (Recall, we have assumed cash is zero so the base and reserves are the same thing.) In this example, where the reserve requirement is 20 percent and the initial increase in reserves is \$10,000, this can be expressed thus:

$$\Delta D = 10{,}000 + 0.8 \times 10{,}000 + 0.8^2 \times 10{,}000 + 0.8^3 \times 10{,}000 + \ldots \quad (12.2)$$

Because equation 12.1 is a convergent series (i.e., the terms get smaller and smaller and converge, in this case, on zero), it is possible to rewrite it in much simpler form so that it is relatively easy to calculate the total increase in deposits. The simpler expression is[1]

$$\Delta D = \Delta B/v \quad (12.3)$$

In this example the total increase in deposits is five times the initial increase in reserves, or \$50,000 = (1/0.2) × \$10,000.

It is also interesting to see what happens if we change reserve requirements. In principle, the Fed could try to change the total volume of money in the economy by raising and lowering reserve requirements. As a practical matter, the Fed tends to leave reserve requirements alone and raises and lowers the total volume of money in the system by injecting new reserves. Suppose, however, the reserve requirement in our example were lowered from 20 percent to 15 percent. Now, \$10,000 of reserves will support \$66,667 rather than \$50,000 in total demand deposits. Thus, the 5 percent change in reserve requirements led to a \$16,667 increase in deposits.

---

[1]Equation 12.3 can be derived as follows. Multiply both sides of equation 12.1 by $(1 - v)$. Subtract the resulting equation from Equation 12.1. This yields

$$\Delta D - (1 - v)\Delta D = \Delta B.$$

This can be simplified to read

$$\Delta D v = \Delta B, \text{ or } \Delta D = \Delta B/v.$$

The idea behind the multiple expansion process is that reserves place a constraint on the total volume of deposits banks can issue. As a result, as the volume of reserves goes up or down the volume of deposits the system as a whole can support increases or decreases by a multiple of that amount. But the idea that the magnitude of the multiple expansion in deposits is equal to $1/v$ hinges on the assumption that all banks will increase deposits to the maximum extent and that there are no other leaks from the system. In the real world, however, there definitely are leakages.

Two principal types of leaks from this multiple expansion process tend to reduce the magnitude of the ultimate expansion of deposits, leakages into cash and into excess reserves. If people choose to convert part of each round of increase in deposits into cash, the expansion of the total amount of cash and demand deposits, tends to be smaller than it otherwise would be. Each time people choose to hold cash rather than demand deposits, the reserves of the banking system decrease, and with this goes a decrease in the stock of deposits the reduced volume of reserves can support. Increases in the public's cash holdings entail decreases in reserves because the total stock of reserves is composed of cash held in bank vaults and deposits with the Fed. As a result, when the public exchanges demand deposits for cash reserves decline, and so must the total supply of money or the sum of cash and demand deposits.

Another type of leakage takes place because banks choose to hold some excess reserves. In effect, some banks choose to hold more reserves than required as a cushion against a future deficiency. Banks incur a penalty if they run short of reserves, so there is incentive to avoid it. To the extent that banks hold excess reserves the size of the multiple expansion of an increase in reserves is decreased, just as when individuals choose to hold cash.

It is not obvious from our discussion of the Fed and the money supply process how interest rates affect the quantity of money supplied. The principal link is that higher interest rates encourage banks to lower their excess reserves, which leads to an increase in the money supply multiplier and the money supply. We therefore conclude that the quantity of money supplied is positively affected by the level of the interest rate. We can represent this in a diagram, (Fig. 12-1) where the nominal quantity of money supplied is on the horizontal axis and the nominal interest rate, *r*, on the vertical axis. We can represent an increase in open market purchases of securities by the Fed as a shift to the right in this curve. We will consider such changes in monetary policy after we introduce the demand for money.

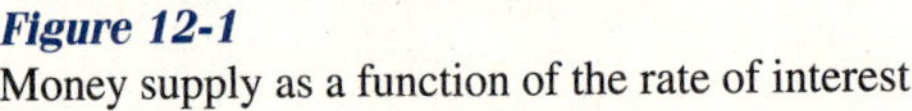

Figure 12-1
Money supply as a function of the rate of interest.

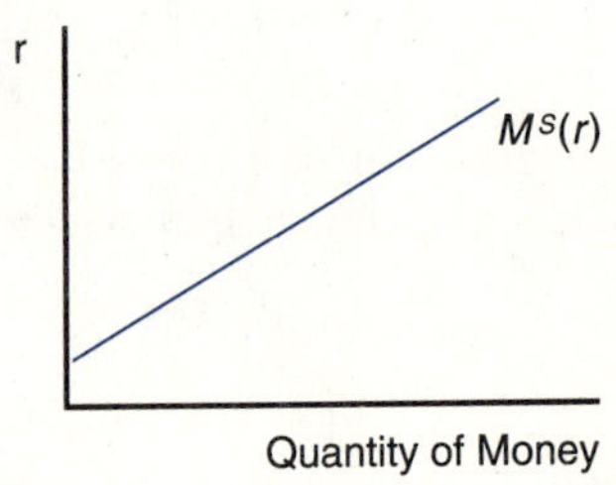

The Demand for Money

The next step in our analysis of the link between monetary policy and interest rates is to develop an understanding of the demand for money. We will then be able to put together the money supply determined by the Fed and money demand and define the link between monetary policy and interest rates. To understand the demand for money we need to identify the variables that influence people's desire to hold money and define the nature of their impact on the demand for money. Three factors influence the demand for money: the level of permanent income, the rate of interest, and the expected rate of inflation. Milton Friedman popularized the concept of permanent income as a basis for explaining aggregate consumption of all commodities, as well as the demand for money. Friedman's concept states that permanent income is the level of long-run income people expect they will average in the future. We will represent nominal permanent income with the symbol Y^p and real permanent income with the symbol y^p. The word "nominal" means that the variable is not adjusted for inflation or by the price level, whereas real means that the variable is inflation adjusted. Note that nominal permanent income is $Y^p = Py^p$ where P is the aggregate price level in the economy. The demand for money is positively related to permanent income, so that increases in permanent income cause increased money demand. The basis for this is that, in the aggregate, people have a stable notion of what portion of their total wealth, or permanent income, they want to hold in money balances. In general, people want to minimize their holdings of such balances because their return is fixed at zero. But as their wealth or their permanent income goes up they have more need to use money balances in their daily transactions and their desired holdings of these balances increases.

The next important determinant of the money demand function is the interest rate or the rate of return on assets other than money. As the return on alternatives to money increases the demand for money goes down. In effect, as it becomes more expensive to hold money people hold less of it. The final element affecting the return on money is the expected rate of inflation, P^e. Inflation penalizes those who hold their wealth in money, for the value of money holdings declines directly with the rate of inflation. Moreover, people's expectations of the future rate of inflation influence the rate of return they anticipate from holding money. Therefore, as the expected rate of inflation increases the demand for money decreases.

So we can summarize the money demand function as follows:

$$M_d = f(\overset{+}{Y^p}, \overset{-}{P^e}, \overset{-}{r})$$

The positive or negative sign over each variable influencing money demand indicates whether money demand increases or decreases, respectively, as the variable in question increases.

The money demand function is illustrated in Figure 12-2. Just as in Figure 12-1, the vertical axis in the figure measures the nominal interest rate, r, while the horizontal axis measures the nominal quantity of money demanded. The relationship between these variables is illustrated by the slopes of lines labeled M_d. These lines are drawn

Figure 12-2
Money demand as a function of permanent income and the rate of interest.

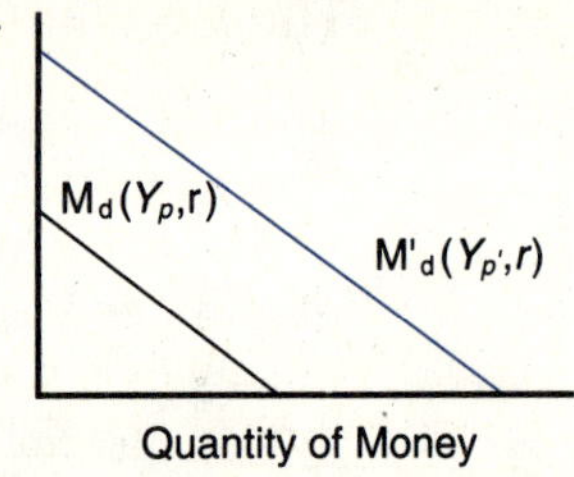

for two distinct values of Y^p: Y^p and $Y^{p\prime}$. Because increases in permanent income increase the demand for money, higher values of Y^p correspond to lines drawn farther to the right. For example, M_d' farther to the right represents the quantity of money demanded at different levels of the nominal interest rate if permanent income is $Y^{p\prime}$.

Monetary Policy, Interest Rates and Exchange Rates

Now that we have some understanding of the operations of the Fed and both money supply and money demand we can move on to examine the link between monetary policy and interest rates. We can also consider how monetary policy influences exchange rates in a competitive global economy. We need to consolidate our analyses of money supply and money demand in order to see how a country's domestic monetary policy influences interest rates. There are three separate effects of monetary policy on interest rates. They can be identified as follows:

1. **Liquidity effect:** The initial decrease in interest rates caused by an increase in the money supply.
2. **Income effect:** The tendency for the initial interest rate decrease to be moderated by the effect of increased income on money demand.
3. **Price anticipation effect:** The increase in nominal interest rates that results as money supply changes cause the market to expect higher rates of inflation.

We also need to take into account that monetary policy and interest rates in one country are tied up with interest rates in other countries and exchange rates between these countries. We need to try to decipher how monetary policy affects both interest rates and exchange rates in a global economy. To try to make sense of the complicated relationships here, we start with monetary policy and interest rates in a single country, as if it could operate in isolation from the rest of the world. Then we turn to the connection between monetary policy and exchange rates in a global economy.

Liquidity and Income Effects

To see how the separate effects of monetary policy on interest rates work we need to employ our notions of money supply and money demand. We can see directly from the money demand function that money demand depends on the interest rate. Moreover, we know that the relationship is negative, so, as the interest rate increases the quantity of money demanded decreases. Similarly, we know that the money

Figure 12-3
Money demand and money supply determine the equilibrium interest rate.

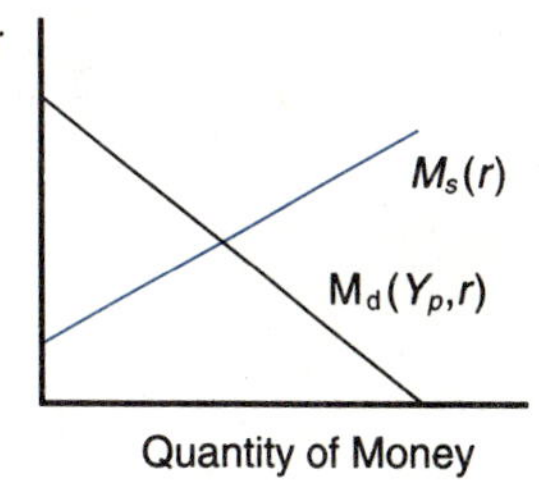

supply is increasing in the rate of interest. We have represented the relationships between the interest rate and the quantities of money supplied and demanded in Figure 12-3. The downwardly sloping curve represents the money demand function; the upwardly sloping curve represents the money supply function. This diagram shows how the equilibrium interest rate is determined at the point of intersection between the supply and the demand curves for money. The figure illustrates that, for a given level of permanent income there is a unique interest rate that equates the quantity of money demanded with the quantity of money supplied.

Figure 12-4 illustrates the liquidity effect of changes in monetary policy on the interest rate, holding the level of income constant. If the Federal Reserve purchases securities in the market, this leads to an increase in reserves and shifts the money supply function to the right, which increases M_s to M_s1 in Figure 12-4. To achieve a new equilibrium, so that the quantity of money demanded is equal to the new larger supply of money in the economy, something in the system has to change. If we hold income constant, and given that the quantity of money demanded is negatively related to the level of the interest rate, the interest rate falls until a new equilibrium is achieved. The new and lower equilibrium level of the interest rate is represented as r' in Figure 12-4. Only at the lower interest rate is the quantity of money supplied equal to the quantity demanded.

Under the income effect, the initial decrease in interest rates caused by the increase in the money supply makes income increase. The increase in income causes the money demand curve to shift to the right (Fig. 12-5). This in turn tends to moderate the initial decrease in interest rates caused by the increase in the money supply. Thus, the income effect tends to work in the opposite direction of the liquidity effect.

You might get the impression that the sole function of the rate of interest is to influence the money supply and demand functions. But we know that the interest rate serves a much broader role in the economy. The real interest rate is the price that allocates resources across time, and, in equilibrium it is the price that equilibrates both desired saving and investment and desired lending and borrowing. To relate the analysis of

Figure 12-4
Liquidity effect of monetary policy on interest rates.

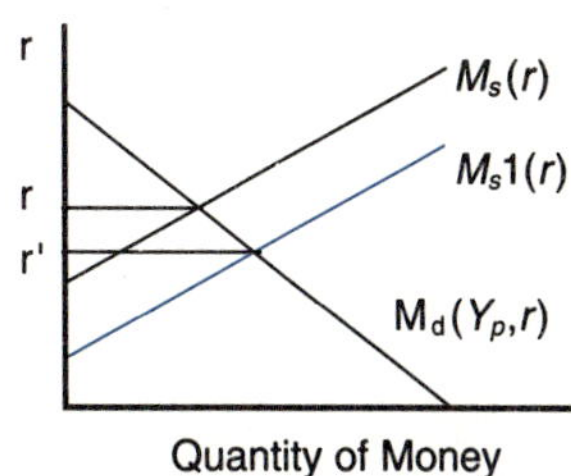

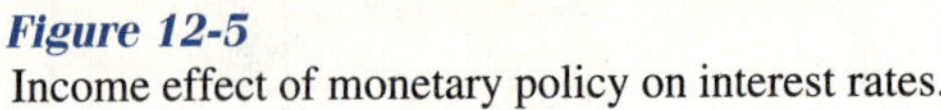

Figure 12-5
Income effect of monetary policy on interest rates.

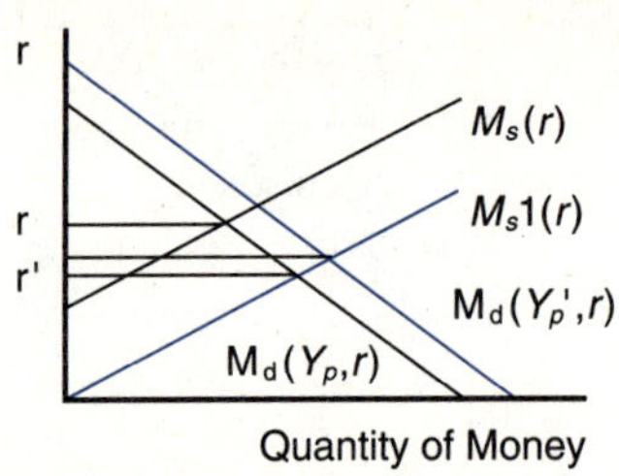

money supply and money demand to the analysis of the determinants of the real interest rate we need to examine the effect of changes in the supply of money on the market for borrowing and lending in the economy as a whole. To see the connection between demand and supply for money and borrowing and lending in the entire economy, we need to recognize that the supply of money is a source of lending. This means that increases in the volume of money in the economy represent increases in lending. As the quantity of money supplied is increased, this represents new lending in the economy as a whole. Thus, we can think of this as shifting the curve showing the total amount of lending at each level of the real interest rate to the right. This shift is illustrated in Figure 12-6. This curve, labeled *l,* indicates the supply of funds in the market, or the total desired amount of lending at each level of the real interest rate. A part of this desired lending is based on a given level of the money supply, *M*. If the Fed increases the money supply to a higher level, say, *M′*, this causes the supply curve to shift to the right, to *l′*. This, in turn, causes a decrease in the level of the real rate of interest. The new equilibrium is reached when the desired level of lending is equal to the desired level of borrowing, represented by the curve labeled D, at *r′*. The equilibrium rate of interest is the same as that that creates an equilibrium between money supply and money demand. The distinction between the analyses is that in the money supply and demand analysis we are implicitly assuming other factors that affect desired borrowing and lending remain unchanged, whereas when we examine the total market for borrowing and lending we are simply not according money supply and money demand any special significance. But a crucial factor is held constant in each analysis: with both approaches the equilibrium interest rate is determined with the level of nominal income held constant. If we also take into account the affect of interest rates on income and then, in turn, the effect of income on money demand, we can understand the income effect of monetary policy on interest rates.

Figure 12-6
Total borrowing and lending in the economy and the interest rate.

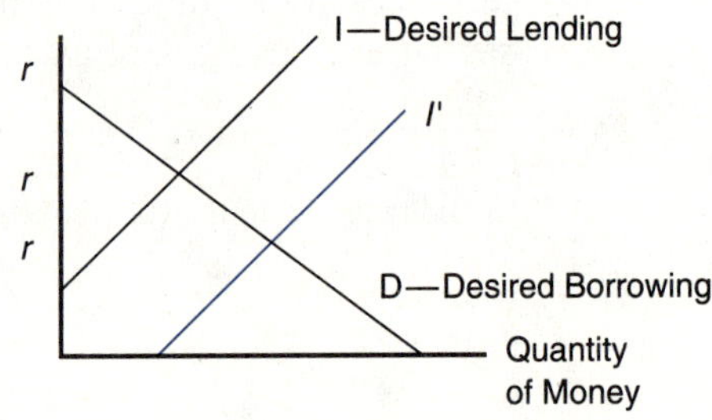

The Price Anticipations Effect

As we have examined the effect of changes in the supply of money on interest rates we have made the implicit assumption that the inflation rate in the economy remains constant. That is, we have assumed there is no link between monetary policy and inflation. Therefore, everything about the connection between monetary policy and interest rates we developed above pertains to the *real* interest rate, as the inflation rate was constant throughout our analysis. This is a terribly unrealistic assumption. There *is* a link between monetary policy and inflation, so now is the time to drop this assumption. Chapter 9 showed that nominal rates increase with increases in the expected rate of inflation. Therefore, if there is a positive link between monetary policy and inflation such that increases in the supply of money lead to inflation, it should also be true that increases in the supply of money will cause interest rates to increase as the market's expectations of inflation increase. This link between monetary policy and interest rates is the third effect described above, the price anticipation effect.

Monetary policy is argued to have a strong influence in determining prices and income. If the economy is near capacity, or full employment, high rates of change in the money supply generate expectations of inflation. These expectations of inflation increase nominal interest rates. Furthermore, if markets are efficient in incorporating information about future inflation rates, nominal interest rates rapidly and efficiently respond to high rates of growth in the money supply by incorporating the expected inflation rate that the money supply implies. This logic leads to the conclusion that increases in the money supply tend to increase, rather than decrease, observed nominal interest rates.

The historical evidence on the link between growth in the money supply and inflation documents a fairly strong correlation between the two. The evidence is basically of two types. One is the history of parallel movements in the money supply and inflation in individual countries, including the United States. Over long periods of time money supply and inflation move quite closely together in any individual country. The second type of evidence is the tendency for inflation rates and growth rates in the money supply to be highly correlated across countries. When a country experiences a high rate of inflation it almost always experiences a high rate of growth in its domestic money supply, too. An important caveat about this evidence should be taken into account. Evidence on a close correlation between inflation and money supply changes does not necessarily indicate that large changes in the supply of money cause inflation. There may be some other cause of inflation that also happens to be highly correlated with money supply changes. We need to be careful about inferring causation from high correlation.

Which Interest Rates Are We Talking About?

So far, the discussion has been devoted to explaining the effects of monetary policy on interest rates, but even after we understand the logic involved, it is sometimes difficult to pin down exactly what interest rate, or rates, we are talking about in the real world. It is therefore important to relate this discussion to the actual conduct of monetary policy and to observed behavior of both short- and long-term interest rates.

There are vast numbers of short-term interest rates, each one applying to a particular type of security or debt contract. Generally, when we speak of the short-term interest rate we mean all of these rates, because we think of a common interest rate that underlies them all. The factors unique to each security account for the differences between these rates.

Despite the generality of the concept of a short-term interest rate, the federal funds rate is of paramount practical importance, both because it has long been the focus of monetary policy and because it represents one of the shortest-term rates generally available in the market. The federal funds rate is the rate paid for loans that generally have a maturity of one day and are made between financial institutions. When the Federal Reserve engages in open market operations, it directly affects this interest rate. Expansionary open market operations immediately increase the supply of federal funds and drive down the federal funds rate. Rates on financial contracts with longer maturities are closely linked to the federal funds rate. The process of substitution between alternative financial contracts, if there is a profitable opportunity to do so, ensures this. If there are only limited barriers to substitution between financial instruments the federal funds rate cannot be driven down and held there without the rates on other financial instruments following a similar course. So, as the Federal Reserve puts pressure directly on the federal funds rate, this pressure soon affects other short-term rates as well, such as Treasury-bill rates, commercial paper rates, and even prime interest rates.

To link changes in monetary policy to changes in long-term interest rates we can return to the our understanding of the term structure of interest rates developed in Chapter 10. The theories that we examined in that chapter all argue that long-term interest rates are determined at least partially by the market's expectation of future short-term rates. As a result, to cause a change in long-term rates, Federal Reserve actions that affect today's short-term interest rate must be perceived as effecting a permanent change. If the market expects that a change in short-term rates will be reversed some months hence, then the effect on long-term rates will be slight. Because the long-term rate represents an average of a long period of expected short-term rates, a change in expectations for even a year or two will have only a limited effect. This does not mean that even relatively short-lived high short-term rates have no effect on the economy; rather, that the effect on long-term interest rates will be limited.

The idea that long-term rates are, at least in part, reflections of the market's expectations of future short-term rates suggests that short-term rates ought to be more volatile than long-term rates. For, while short-term rates may go up or down, only if the market expects that these rates will go up (or down) and stay there does the long-term rate change by a comparable amount. This prediction about the relative volatility of rates has been confirmed by experience. This type of pattern has been common to all business cycles in contemporary U.S. history. Moreover, the pattern emphasizes that it is more difficult for the Federal Reserve to alter long-term rates than short-term ones, because long-term rates reflect the market's expectations about the Federal Reserve's actions over an extended period.

Monetary Policy in an Open Economy

Most of our discussion until now has presumed that the Fed could conduct monetary policy for the United States without paying attention to the rest of the world. If that was ever completely true it is surely not true anymore. The U.S. economy is increasingly integrated with the economies of other countries. As a result, the exchange rate between the dollar and other currencies is tremendously important to the U.S. economy. In addition, the exchange rate is a barometer of the state of monetary policy in the United States. This is because the basic determinant of the exchange rate between two currencies is the relative level of prices of goods and services in those economies. We first encountered this relationship, known as purchasing power parity, in Chapter 11. We can summarize it in the following manner: let the price of goods in one country (say the United States) be $P^{\$}$ and the price level in any other country in the world (say Germany) be P^{DM}. Let the spot exchange rate between the two currencies be represented by S. Therefore, if you can buy two units of the other country's currency with your currency, S is 2.0. The exchange rate must be related to the prices of goods in the two countries thus:

$$P^{\$} \times S = P^{DM}$$

This is purchasing power parity as we developed it in Chapter 11. If it did not hold, it would be profitable to transport goods (with low transportation costs) from one country to the other for sale.

Now, if the United States follows a monetary policy that tends to drive up the prices of goods in the United States relative to prices in other countries, so that $P^{\$}$ rises while P^{DM} remains stable, the exchange rate between the two currencies must change so that the value of the dollar goes down. As a result, if the monetary policy of one country is expansionary, compared with that of another, so that the first country experiences more inflation than the other, the exchange rate between the two must adjust to satisfy purchasing power parity.

The fact that exchange rates are so closely linked to monetary policy means the Fed could use the exchange rate between the dollar and other major currencies, say, the Japanese yen or the Deutschemark, as its target of monetary policy. If the value of the dollar is rising, as it was in the early 1980s, this would indicate that monetary policy is tight, regardless of what might be happening to the money supply. Conversely, if the value of the dollar is declining, as it was in the late 1980s, this would indicate that monetary policy is loose.

There is another important implication of the relationship between monetary policy and exchange rates. Unless the Fed has extraordinarily good luck it cannot control both exchange rates and the supply of money. This is true for the same reason that, unless it is lucky it cannot control both domestic interest rates and the supply of money. Exchange rates, domestic interest rates, and monetary aggregates are all alternative measures of the impact of monetary policy. As a result, if a country attempts to operate with a system of fixed exchange rates, as did the United States and most of the world under the Bretton Woods Agreement from the end of World War II until 1971, it cannot pursue an independent course for the supply of money. This is readily apparent from the purchasing power parity equation. If the United States fixes S by having the Fed intervene in the foreign exchange markets, the relative level of prices between the United States and any other country must also be fixed. The intervention by the Fed in the foreign exchange market causes the U.S. money supply to change in a way that is sufficient to alter U S. inflation relative to foreign inflation to the point that purchasing power parity holds. That is, domestic monetary policy becomes a by-product of the effort to maintain the fixed exchange rate.

When Is Monetary Policy Tight or Loose?

There is ongoing debate about whether the Fed should focus on interest rates or the money supply in implementing monetary policy. Actually, the ultimate objective of monetary policy is full employment and price stability, but it is difficult to actually target these broad objectives in conducting monetary policy. If it is decided that the target should be the money supply, it is still necessary to figure out how to go about controlling that target. One view of how to control the money supply is to use the analysis in this chapter of the link between bank reserves and the money supply. From this view the Federal Reserve would conduct open market operations in a manner that leads to a desired change in the supply of money by altering the reserves at a certain rate based on an estimate of what the money supply multiplier will be. The problem is that if the multiplier changes, this alters the change in reserves needed to achieve a desired rate of change in the supply of money. As long as the money supply multiplier remains constant, if the Fed wants the money supply to change by, say, 6 percent, it has to increase the base by 6 percent. Therefore, the Fed must try to estimate what the multiplier is likely to be and try to change the base by an amount that leads to the desired increase in the money supply. As a result of the volatility of the multiplier and other problems involved in directly controlling reserves, the Fed can never precisely control the supply of money. So the question is, Can the Fed achieve control of the money supply within some reasonable margin of error?

However attractive this method of conducting monetary policy may seem, for much of its existence it was not actually the method followed by the Fed, which instead has focused more directly on its impact on interest rates, especially short-term rates such as the federal funds rate. It did so by standing ready to conduct open market operations—that is, buying or selling Treasury securities that increase or decrease reserves—and thereby to affect the supply of federal funds directly, and consequently the federal funds rate. If the Open Market Desk at the FRBNY observed that the federal funds rate started to rise above the target set by the Open Market Committee, it would buy securities or supply reserves to the market in order to drive the funds rate back down. This is illustrated in Figure 12-7, which shows a band within which the federal funds rate is allowed to vary. If the funds rate approaches the upper limit of this band, the Fed intervenes in the market to buy federal funds or Treasury bills and drive down the rate. If the funds rate approaches the lower end of the band, the Fed sells federal funds to drive the rate up. In this way the Fed has tried to keep the funds rate very close to its stated target or within a target range. It has always been difficult to measure directly how successful this policy has been because when it becomes difficult to maintain a given target rate it is always possible to change the target. Because

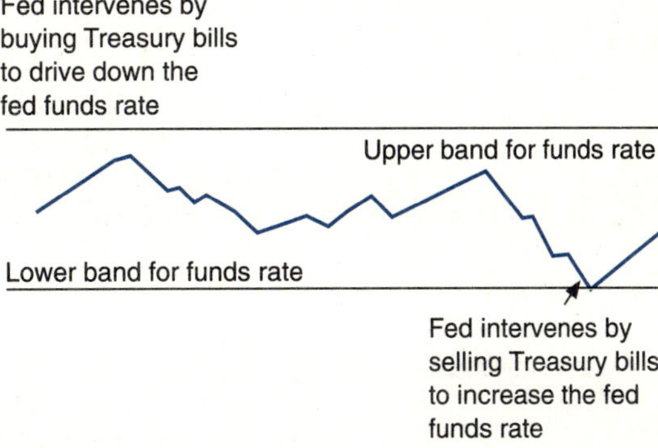

Figure 12-7
Monetary policy target of band around federal funds rate.

the Fed has chosen its federal funds target based on a long-run range for growth in the money supply, it was always possible to try to justify a change in the target. In any event, the target has never been explicitly stated ahead of time; rather, it always had to be inferred from the interest rate the Fed tried to maintain.

One result of this method of operation is that reserves increase or decrease by whatever amount is necessary to achieve the desired control of the federal funds rate. Depending on how the federal funds rate target is chosen, this may lead to large increases or decreases in the supply of money. Indeed, a major criticism of Federal Reserve policy in recent years is that it has allowed the money supply to grow at a fast rate when the economy is in a boom and has permitted its growth rate to decline when the economy is in a recession. Critics contend that if the Federal Reserve would follow a policy of more direct control of reserves, rather than interest rates, the problem could be avoided. In one form or another, this debate about monetary policy has been going on throughout the life of the Federal Reserve. To appreciate the significance of the issue it is useful to review the major episodes in the history of Federal Reserve policy. We will take this up in Chapter 13.

Based on discussion thus far in this chapter we can identify several possible targets for the conduct of monetary policy. The Fed might try to control interest rates, foreign exchange rates, or the supply of money. We might also try to judge whether monetary policy is tight or loose by evaluating what is happening to these potential targets. We can begin by asking how to judge whether monetary policy is tight or loose by looking at interest rates. You may have noticed a confusing point about the three effects of monetary policy on interest rates that we discussed above. The liquidity effect implies that increases in the money supply cause interest rates to decline. The other two effects indicate that increases in the money supply cause interest rates to increase. If you are perplexed about which of the three effects described above really explains how interest rates respond to monetary policy you are not alone. The fact that these distinct effects lead to opposite predictions about the direction of the link between monetary policy and interest rates is one of the major causes of a long-standing debate about how monetary policy should be conducted. Critics of U.S. monetary policy have often charged that the Federal Reserve cannot separate these three effects and therefore often gets confused about the impact of its policy decisions on the economy. Some critics argue that the Fed would be best served if it simply

Table 12-2
Alternative Targets and Measures of the State of U.S. Monetary Policy

	Loose Policy	**Tight Policy**
Real interest rate	Low	High
Nominal interest rate	High	Low
Value of U. S. $	Low	High
Change in M_2	High	Low

concentrated on trying to control the growth of money supply and did not worry about trying to influence interest rates or other prices of assets. This debate has gone on for some time and will probably continue in the future. Actually, given our discussion of the three effects of monetary policy on interest rates, we have to distinguish between real and nominal interest rates as two distinct possible targets of monetary policy. This is important because monetary policy that is expansionary, or loose, would have low real interest rates, possibly owing to a desire to stimulate the economy. But as that stimulation leads to inflationary pressure, it may cause observed nominal interest rates to rise. Thus, an expansionary or loose monetary policy can be associated with low real rates but high nominal rates.

The status of monetary policy can also be measured by its impact on the value of a country's currency. Many observers of monetary policy argue that monetary policy is loose when the value of the U. S. dollar is low or falling and tight when the value of the dollar is high or rising. This is because a tight monetary policy leads to low expectations of inflation in the dollar, which makes the dollar more valuable. Finally, many observers believe that the most direct measure of the state of monetary policy is the rate of growth in the supply of money, usually M_2. If the rate of growth in M_2 is high monetary policy is loose, whereas if it is low monetary policy is tight. These alternative measures of the state of monetary policy are summarized in Table 12-2.

SUMMARY

In this chapter we examined the links between monetary policy and interest in rates in a global economy. We began with a brief overview of the structure of the Federal Reserve system and the structure of power within the Fed. The FOMC is the most important decision-making entity within the Federal Reserve system because it decides on the volume of open market operations (purchases and sales of Treasury securities by the Fed). When the Fed purchases and sells securities, it increases and decreases, respectively, the volume of reserves in the banking system.

Next we learned that the total volume of reserves places a constraint on the total volume of deposits in the system or on the supply of money. Because reserves must be held at a fixed percentage of deposits, any increase or decrease in the volume of reserves increases or decreases the volume of deposits financial intermediaries can support. As a result, whenever reserves increase there is a multiple expansion in the volume of total deposits, and therefore in the supply of money. The idea behind the demand for money is that there is a stable and predictable relationship between the quantity of money people choose to hold, the level of permanent income, and the nominal interest rate.

We were also able to identify how monetary policy influences interest rates by combining our analyses of money supply and money demand. There are three effects of changes in the supply of money on market interest rates. The liquidity effect results from the fact that demand for money is negatively related to the level of interest rates. Therefore, as the supply of money is increased, interest rates must fall to maintain equilibrium between the demand and supply for money. The second effect, the income effect, refers to the fact that increases in income caused by increases in the money supply cause the demand for money to increase. This, in turn, causes interest rates to fall, partially mitigating the initial liquidity effect. Finally, the price anticipations effect pertains to the link between increases in the money supply and inflation. As increases in the money supply generate expectations of inflation, these expectations cause nominal interest rates to increase. Thus, increases in the supply of money can cause interest rates to either rise or fall, depending on the strength of the connection between money supply changes and inflation expectations.

We also focused on the conduct of monetary policy in a competitive open or global economy. In an open economy where the United States does not have fixed exchange rates with other currencies in the world, U.S. monetary policy also has an impact on the value of the dollar. An expansionary monetary policy tends to drive up inflation, which reduces the value of the dollar relative to other currencies. In a world without fixed exchange rates, monetary policy can be evaluated in part by its impact on the value of the dollar. In a world with fixed exchange rates, a country cannot conduct an independent monetary policy. In effect, its monetary policy must be used to maintain the fixed exchange rate.

QUESTIONS

1. What is the FOMC and what is its purpose? Why has it been described as the most important decision-making body within the Federal Reserve System?
2. Some argue that the Federal Reserve is virtually an arm of the executive branch of government; others argue it is independent. Evaluate the merits of each position.
3. Suppose there are no leaks in the multiple expansion process. Why is the multiplier then equal to l/v? How do leaks into cash and excess reserves influence the multiplier?
4. Suppose the FRBNY sells $100 million worth of Treasury securities. Trace the impact of this transaction through the banking system if reserve requirements are 15 percent.
5. Distinguish between the income effect and the liquidity effect. Why do they cause interest rates to change in opposite directions?

6. Some people argue that an expansionary monetary policy means low interest rates and others that it means high interest rates. How can you reconcile these two views?
7. What kind of evidence links money supply changes and inflation rates? Does this evidence imply that high rates of growth in the supply of money cause inflation?
8. What is the connection between the state of monetary policy and the value of a country's currency? How are these connected? Can we judge monetary policy by exchange rates? Why or why not?
9. Based on your understanding of the liquidity, income, and price anticipations effects of monetary policy on interest rates, analyze the viability of conducting monetary policy by creating a band around the federal funds rate. Under what types of economic circumstances is such a band likely to be (1) most and (2) least effective?
10. In 1986 and 1987 there was a significant decline in the value of the dollar relative to the yen, while earlier in the decade precisely the opposite occurred. What do these changes in exchange rates tell you about U.S. and Japanese monetary policies during these two periods?

REFERENCES

Friedman, Milton. *A Theory of the Consumption Function.* Princeton, NJ: Princeton University Press, 1957.

——— "The Quantity Theory of Money: A Restatement." in Milton Friedman, ed. *Studies in the Quantity Theory of Money.* Chicago: University of Chicago Press, 1956.

• *Chapter 13*

The Monetary Policy Debate

In this chapter we continue our examination of the conduct of monetary policy that began in Chapter 12. Chapter 12 dealt principally with the organization and operation of the Federal Reserve and with the connections between monetary policy and interest rates and exchange rates. We start this chapter by examining the debate about how monetary policy should be conducted. We describe the basic tenets of the main critique of the conduct of monetary policy, the monetarist critique, as well as some of the key elements of the rebuttal to the monetarists. Next we examine how monetary policy has been conducted in the past. We emphasize the historical record because we believe that if you don't have a good understanding of the history you may not realize that the contemporary debate about monetary policy is generally a repeat of some earlier debate on the same subject. The history provides important lessons that can be transferred to the present. We start our historical review with the conduct of monetary policy during the Great Depression and we work up to the early 1990s. Finally, we examine the connection between the conduct of monetary policy in the United States and in Europe and the recent attempts by the European countries to form a united Europe. The key concepts to learn in this chapter are listed below.

• *Concepts to Learn in Chapter 13* •

- Historical episodes in the conduct of monetary policy
- Principal arguments in the contemporary debate about how monetary policy should be conducted
- Advantages and pitfalls of creating a united Europe with a single monetary policy

The Monetarist Critique of Monetary Policy

The Key Elements in the Monetarist Argument

To really be able to appreciate the significance of the ongoing debate about the conduct of monetary policy it is important to have some understanding of the point of view of the so-called monetarists. While there have been many critics of the conduct of monetary policy from both sides of the political aisle, one of the most enduring and serious ones comes from the so-called monetarist camp and from its most articulate spokesperson, Milton Friedman. The monetarist view of monetary policy is associated with a long tradition of economics taught at the University of Chicago during the latter part of the nineteenth and the entire twentieth century.

The monetarists use the following simple equation as the vehicle for explaining their view of monetary policy:

$$MV \equiv Py \qquad (13.1)$$

where y represents real income or real gross domestic product, V is the velocity of money, M is the stock of money, and P is the price level. In fact, this equation is an identity, which means it is true by definition. We use the symbol $\equiv$ for an identity. The attractiveness of this identity lies in its simplicity and in the interpretation or usefulness of the concept of velocity. To understand the arguments of the monetarists we must understand their concept of velocity.

The monetarists argue that, within some limits, the Federal Reserve can make the money supply whatever it wants. Thus, we treat the money supply as being determined independently of the rest of the economy. In addition, monetarists argue that the money demand function is a very stable and predictable relationship. They contend that equilibrium in the economy can be represented by an equilibrium between the quantity of money supplied and the quantity of money demanded. This equilibrium condition can be represented as follows:

$$M_s = M_d = f(Y^P, r), \qquad (13.2)$$

where Y^P is nominal permanent income (see Chapter 12). Suppose that the level of nominal permanent income and the interest rate are such that this equilibrium condition is satisfied. At the existing level of income and interest rates people are willing to hold the quantity of money supplied by the Federal Reserve. Now suppose the Federal Reserve disturbs this equilibrium by increasing the supply of money so that

$$M_s > M_d \qquad (13.3)$$

Monetarists argue that people do not accept these excess money balances passively unless something determining money demand changes to restore equilibrium. If the money demand function is stable, which is to say that people do not willingly accept new money balances without some substantive inducement to hold them, then either nominal income or interest rates must change to bring about a new equilibrium. Furthermore, monetarists generally argue that the variable that does, in fact, change to bring about the new equilibrium is the level of nominal permanent income. They argue that the effect of interest rate changes on money demand is generally so small as to be inconsequential.

This monetarist explanation of the effect of money on income is usually made using velocity and equation 13.1. To see how the argument can be recast in this form, we need to alter equation 13.1 slightly by dividing through by M, so that we have velocity on the left-hand side:

$$V = Py/M \qquad (13.4)$$

Now, we can define velocity in two ways, just as we can approach the quantity of money in two ways: the quantity supplied and the quantity demanded. First, we will examine desired velocity, V_d. Typically, when monetarists refer to velocity, they are referring to desired velocity, for they argue that velocity is simply an alternative way of stating the demand for money. Desired velocity is simply the public's desired ratio of nominal income to nominal money balances:

$$V_d = \frac{Py}{M_d} = \frac{Py}{f(Y^p,r)} \tag{13.5}$$

However, just as there can be a disequilibrium between the quantity of money supplied and the quantity of money demanded, there can be a difference between desired and actual velocity. Actual velocity, V_a is the actual ratio of nominal income to nominal money balances:

$$V_a = \frac{Py}{M_s} \tag{13.6}$$

But in equilibrium, when the public's demand for money is equal to the quantity of money supplied, actual velocity must equal desired velocity:

$$V_a = V_d \tag{13.7}$$

We can summarize this equilibrium relationship by interpreting the M and V in the original equation 13.1 as the quantity of money supplied and the equilibrium-desired level of velocity, respectively:

$$M_sV_d = Py \tag{13.8}$$

The logic conveyed by this equation is as follows: Suppose the money supply is increased. To maintain equilibrium either velocity must decline or nominal income must increase. If nominal income changes to bring about an increase in the demand for money, then the right-hand side of equation 13.8 will adjust in the new equilibrium. But if people respond passively to changes in the money supply, so that income does not have to change for the demand for money to change, then a decrease in velocity may absorb the entire money supply increase.

Diagrammatically we can represent the monetarist interpretation of a change in the money supply as inevitably leading to a change in nominal income:

$$\uparrow M_sV_d = \uparrow Py$$

Conversely, a money supply change might simply be absorbed by a change in velocity:

$$\uparrow M_s \downarrow V_d = Py$$

This could happen either if the money demand function itself changes as the supply of money changes or if interest rates decline and that decline causes no change in income. The first possibility is usually characterized as a situation in which money demand, and hence velocity, is unstable.

Recently the velocity of M_2 has behaved in a rather unpredictable manner (we discuss this in more detail later in this chapter). If this sort of behavior continues, it makes it difficult reliably to predict what will be the consequence of a change in the supply of money. Nonetheless, the monetarists argue that such erratic behavior of M_2

is a response to changes in the financial system to a new institutional structure and that in the long run velocity exhibits a more stable pattern. Over the longer run, velocity has exhibited two fairly regular patterns. First, velocity has tended to increase over time, but it also had a procyclical pattern; that is, it has tended to rise and fall with the level of income.

The procyclical pattern in velocity can be explained in two ways. One explanation, advanced by Friedman, relies on the fluctuations of permanent income relative to nominal income in any given period. Because permanent income represents expected future long-run income, it changes less in any given period than does nominal income. Only if the change in nominal income were perceived to be permanent would permanent income change by the same amount. Most changes in nominal income are perceived to be transitory, so only part of the change is reflected in permanent income. If part of this perceived change in permanent income is allocated to money balances, the change in money must be less than the change in permanent income, which, in turn, must be less than the change in measured nominal income. This means that when nominal income changes the numerator in equation 13.5 is altered by a greater amount than the denominator; therefore, velocity tends to rise and fall with income.

An alternative explanation for the procyclical behavior of velocity relies on the observation that interest rates move procyclically. Because the quantity of money demanded is negatively related to the level of interest rates, an increase in interest rates leads to a decline in desired money balances. This tends to diminish growth in the demand for money caused by an increase in income, and velocity moves procyclically.

The Money Supply Rule

Monetarists argue that the money supply should be controlled directly by the Federal Reserve. Moreover, they argue that interest rates should be left free to fluctuate to whatever extent the market dictates. They believe that any attempt by the Federal Reserve to achieve short-run control over interest rates inherently sacrifices long-run control over growth in the quantity of money.

Monetarists also argue that monetary policy should be conducted according to what is called a "money supply rule." To see what this means we need to return to the basic equation of the monetarists stated in equation 13.1,

$$MV = Py$$

To use this equation to talk about the conduct of monetary policy we need to restate it in terms of the rate of change in each variable. If we let Δ stand for the change in a variable so that, for example, $\Delta M/M$ means the rate of change in the money supply from one period to the next, then equation 13.1 can be rewritten as follows:

$$\Delta M/M + \Delta V/V = \Delta P/P + \Delta y/y$$

This means that the rate of change in the money supply plus the rate of change in velocity must equal the rate of inflation plus the rate of change in real income.

The question the monetarists ask of this equation is, what should be the appropriate rate of growth in the money supply? To answer this question we alter the equation somewhat by moving velocity to the right-hand side:

$$\Delta M/M = \Delta P/P + \Delta y/y - \Delta V/V$$

To determine the rate of growth in the money supply we have to specify the values of the variables on the right-hand side of the equation. The logic of choosing these variables is as follows: From historical evidence we observe that velocity has a tendency to grow at a certain rate, say 1 percent. We observe from long-run historical evidence that real income tends to grow at a certain rate, say 3 percent. Therefore, if we expect that the long-run patterns of growth in velocity and real income will be the same in the future, then we can fill these in on the right-hand side of the equation. Given these future growth rates for velocity and real income, if we want the future inflation rate to be zero the rate of growth in the supply of money must be 2 percent.

$$2 = 0 + 3 - 1$$

The assumption underlying this conclusion is that changes in the growth of velocity and real income are not influenced by monetary policy in the long run. Rather, the influence of monetary policy is largely on the rate of inflation. Thus, we can extract our estimates of the growth of velocity and income from the historical evidence, and then choose the rate of growth in the money supply that will generate the desired rate of inflation. Presumably, this desired rate of inflation is zero.

Despite the fact that this argument is relatively simple, there are difficulties involved in estimating the actual future growth rates in velocity and real income. Arguments over the proper values of these estimates have persisted for some time, and it will never be possible to know these values with certainty. However, monetarists argue that, although it is impossible to determine precisely the rate of growth in the money supply that is best, a fixed rule is better than no rule at all.

The monetarists reached a peak of public awareness of their arguments and views in the 1970s and early 1980s, when inflation in the United States was high. Their message about controlling the supply of money to control the inflation rate found increasing acceptance in a variety of circles; however, as inflation rates in the United States have fallen the public eye has turned away from the monetarist view to some degree. Yet the message of the monetarists is not less true or relevant simply because it is getting less press. In fact, if the United States again experiences high inflation, we are willing to predict that the monetarists will once again find their phones ringing with calls from reporters eager to present their view in the popular media.

The Response to the Monetarist Critique

Throughout its history the Federal Reserve has been reluctant to try to conduct monetary policy in the manner described above. There appear to be at least three different categories of reasons why monetarist policy prescriptions have not been more popular within Washington. We label them political, practical, and philosophical. Let's start with the political issue. The monetarists argue that we should replace the judgment of officials of the Fed, and ultimately those in political power in Washington, with a simple rule. They argue that much of the activity and much of staff and much of the discretionary power of the Fed is actually unnecessary. Bureaucracies do not like to hear this kind of message and they often resist it. The Fed appears to be no exception.

We can identify at least three arguments that have been leveled against the monetarists that we think belong under the heading of practical arguments. All have to do with difficulties involved in complete reliance on the monetary aggregates and to directly targeting some measure of reserves. The first, and probably least serious in the long run, is that it is difficult to forecast the money supply multiplier and to know what reserves and the money supply really are from week to week. Thus, real, practical difficulties are involved in trying to directly control reserves in the very short run. Critics have argued that many of these difficulties were created by the Fed for itself and that they should not stand in the way of proper long-term control of the money supply. The second objection is that by attempting to control reserves the Fed will sacrifice control over short-term interest rates and cause serious problems in financial markets owing to additional interest rate volatility. The critics respond that it is generally impossible to control simultaneously both interest rates and reserves; therefore, if the Fed really seeks to control interest rates it loses control of the supply of money. Moreover, there is a serious question about whether the Fed should seek to provide the service of lowering interest rate volatility as the basis for its policy. The third objection to controlling the supply of money is the argument that the relationship between the supply of money and the level of nominal income that is the ultimate objective of monetary policy is unstable. Instability means that sometimes nominal income increases in response to changes in the supply of money and sometimes it does not. As we will see when we shortly turn our attention to the recent history of monetary policy, this contention has been made rather vigorously in some quarters in recent years as financial innovation in the banking system has led to major changes in the use of many different types of deposit accounts at commercial banks. If there is no predictable or stable relationship between money and overall economic activity, then targeting the money supply is not a particularly attractive approach to conducting monetary policy, but if our financial system reaches a point where there is such a stable relationship, the monetarist case will be harder to rebut.

• *The Politics of Monetarism* •

For many years the monetarist point of view was not taken particularly seriously by those who held power in Washington, D. C., especially from the post–World War II era until the later 1970s. The key economic fact that began to improve the political standing of monetarists was inflation. Monetarists argued that inflation was linked to monetary policy and could be cured by controlling the supply of money. When other methods for curing inflation did not appear to be effective more attention began to be focused on the monetarists' arguments.

Monetarists argued that by using a money supply rule, the economy would eventually settle down to a stable growth rate with very little inflation. Furthermore, they believed that without such a rule the Fed is forced to anticipate what will happen in the economy and to take actions to offset undesirable future economic fluctuations. Because we have rather imperfect knowledge of how and how quickly Fed actions influence the economy, its attempts to operate a countercyclical policy often backfire. In fact, one of the principal criticisms offered by monetarists such as Friedman is that monetary policy has tended to be procyclical; that is, the money supply tends to grow at a fast rate in an economic expansion and at a slow rate in an economic contraction. A money supply rule would force the Fed to abandon its allegedly misguided attempts to anticipate and offset future economic fluctuations.

A second reason monetarists advocate a money supply rule relates to the circumstances that govern modern international monetary arrangements. Until the middle of this century, the United States was on a gold standard. In other words, the government's money was backed by gold and, as a consequence, the supply of money was determined by the supply of gold. The disadvantage of this system is that the economy may grow faster than the gold supply, and deflation will result. The advantage of such a system is that the government is unable to increase the money supply at a rate that produces high inflation unless the supply of gold permits. The government's natural temptation to resort to inflationary increases in the money supply to support deficit spending is limited by the available supply of gold.

The discipline enforced on the government by a gold standard is arbitrary; that is, changes in the supply of gold may be unrelated to a given country's rate of economic growth. Thus, essentially by chance, there may be either inflation or deflation. For this reason, the gold standard was eventually abandoned, yet monetarists seek a mechanism that replaces the discipline of the gold standard, one that eliminates the government's temptation to inflate. Of course, politicians who seek power, even conservative ones, generally find such constraints unattractive. As a result of this, as well as of the rather erratic performance of the velocity, politicians only briefly embraced monetarism in the 1980s. Monetarism, and with a few exceptions monetarists, lost favor even in the Republican government of the 1980s. The monetarist point of view will always be around and will always have articulate advocates. Whether it will ever be in favor again in Washington is difficult to predict.

On a more philosophical level, those who oppose the monetarists often reject some of the basic precepts of the monetarist "model" of how the economy works. One point often made against the monetarist view is that the real link between monetary policy and economic activity is through the impact of monetary policy on the cost of borrowing or on the cost of credit. This is captured through market interest rates. So if the Fed is going to attempt to influence the level of economic activity, it needs to do so by affecting interest rates or the cost of credit. Thus, the counterattack to the monetarists is that by targeting monetary aggregates, the Fed is really using only a very indirect measure of its true target, the cost of credit. A second point made by those who reject the monetarist argument is that fluctuations in interest rates and financial conditions are often a result of speculative activity that creates excessive interest rate volatility. They argue that one of the Fed's responsibilities is to limit such volatility and maintain stability in the financial system. They view the money supply rule advocated by the monetarists as a device that would deprive the Fed of its ability to offset such unwarranted volatility.

We choose not to attempt to direct you toward a conclusion about whether the monetarists or their detractors are correct in this debate. We think you should form your own conclusions. But we do believe that you cannot gain a proper understanding of historical or current financial events without understanding these arguments. We turn to the historical record next.

A Brief History of Monetary Policy

The real importance of understanding the connections between monetary policy and interest rates and exchange rates, which we developed in Chapter 12, is to be able to make sense of what is happening in the global financial markets. We cannot review what is happening in the marketplace at the same time you are reading this book, but we can review the history of the conduct of monetary policy, to give you the background to evaluate current events. We begin with the events in the first few decades after the Fed was created.

Monetary Policy Until the Early 1950s

Probably the single most important episode in the first 40 years of the life of the Fed was the Great Depression of the 1930s. The Depression began after the stock market crash of 1929 and deepened in response to restrictive policies in international trade and restrictive monetary policies in the United States. The Fed pursued a passive policy that allowed the supply of money in the United States to decline by approximately one third between 1929 and 1933. While clearly concerned with the Depression itself, the Federal Reserve evidenced little direct concern for behavior of the money supply or of other aggregate measures of credit in the economy. The Board members simply did not perceive it to be their responsibility to try to influence these variables. Contemporary monetarist critics of the Federal Reserve, particularly Friedman, have argued that this passive policy, if it was not itself responsible for the Depression, was a principal contributing factor to its depth and longevity.

In his memoirs Herbert Hoover wrote rather disparagingly of this dominant view within the Federal Reserve system, one also held by then Secretary of the Treasury Andrew Mellon:

> [These people] felt that government must keep its hands off and let the slump liquidate itself. Mr. Mellon had only one formula: "liquidate labor, liquidate stocks, liquidate the farmers, liquidate real estate." He insisted that, when the people get an inflation brainstorm, the only way to get it out of their blood is to let it collapse. He held that even a panic was not altogether a bad thing. He said, "It will purge the rottenness out of the system. High costs of living and high living will come down. People will work harder, live a more moral life. Values will be adjusted, and enterprising people will pick up the wrecks from less competent people."[1]

At the time, the Federal Reserve's perception of its purpose was not to control the supply of money, contrary to the view espoused by modern monetarists. Instead, the Fed apparently thought its mission was to provide what has been referred to as an "elastic currency." This meant essentially that money and credit would be available to provide for the needs of trade and commerce rather than to maintain stable prices or pursue some other social purpose. This is known as the "real bills doctrine." The essence of the real bills doctrine incorporated two principles. The first

---

[1]The Great Depression, 1929–41, *The Memoirs of Herbert Hoover.* New York: Macmillan, 1952, p. 30. Reprinted by permission.

was that as the economy expanded the Federal Reserve's function was to ensure that enough money and credit were available so as not to hamper that expansion. The second was that the Fed was to discipline bankers so they did not engage in or finance what was judged excessive speculation. If the economy contracted, then money and credit should contract with it. The real bills doctrine meant that the Federal Reserve should assume a passive role as far as the money supply itself was concerned. In this view the money supply, or its rate of growth, was a by-product of economic events. This view implied that the Federal Reserve should allow the money supply to pursue whatever course the economy dictated.

The debate about the real bills doctrine dates back to the first few decades of the Fed's existence. Before the Great Depression of 1929 there was a struggle for power between the Board of Governors of the system located in Washington and the 12 regional Federal Reserve Banks spread throughout the country. This power struggle partly reflected a difference of opinion on the exact purpose of the system. Most of the district bank presidents believed that the Federal Reserve was to function as a banker's bank. They espoused the real bills doctrine. But throughout those years they were often dominated by the forceful president of the New York Federal Reserve Bank, Benjamin Strong. The New York bank was originally, and remains now, the most important bank in the system, in part because New York has long been the financial center of the country but also because the New York bank dealt directly with foreign banks and governments. Strong argued that the Fed should not be entirely passive but should use its powers to buy and sell government securities in order to influence reserves in a countercyclical manner. After Strong died in 1928, the view that the Fed should be a passive entity concerned with the stability of interest rates again became the dominant belief in the system as the country approached the Great Contraction of 1929. Of course, we cannot know what might have happen had Strong lived several more years, but the consensus of those who have analyzed the era is that the Fed failed to provide the liquidity needed to avert the Great Depression.

In the early 1940s the United States emerged from the Great Depression as it entered World War II. As the economy expanded to meet the production needs of the war, the problems of the Federal Reserve were also refocused on financing the war. The Fed agreed to help the Treasury finance it by pegging interest rates at the levels that had prevailed before the war. This was 3/8 of 1 percent on Treasury bills and 2 1/2 percent on long-term Treasury bonds. The Fed used these interest rates as their targets for monetary policy. If interest rates started to rise above these levels, the Fed would purchase Treasury bills or bonds and drive down interest rates; the Fed would sell Treasury bills or bonds if rates fell below these levels. Because the Treasury was selling a large volume of new debt, the Fed had to buy this debt to keep interest rates low, which led to a significant increase in the money supply. Because during wartime the U. S. economy operated under wage and price controls, inflation expectations remained low and the Fed was able to maintain control over interest rates and still inject a substantial amount of money into the economy.

The Fed continued to conduct monetary policy by pegging interest rates until 1951. Its decision to abandon its policy of pegging interest rates was prompted by the substantial increase in consumer prices that occurred during the Korean War.

During this period the U.S. economy was expanding rapidly, but there were no wage and price controls to hold down inflation. As a result, the policy of pegging interest rates at pre–World War II levels became untenable. In March 1951, the Fed and the Treasury agreed to abandon their previous policy, an agreement known since then as the Accord. The Fed did agree to prevent interest rates from increasing precipitously, and this continuing concern for control of interest rates has been an important feature of Fed policy ever since.

Monetary Policy from 1950 to 1979

From the early 1950s until 1979 the Federal Reserve aimed monetary policy at short-term interest rates. When it wanted monetary policy to be tight, it set out to raise short-term interest rates. On the other hand, when it wanted monetary policy to be loose, it set out to lower short-term interest rates. Moreover, it has always been concerned with preserving orderly conditions in financial markets—with ensuring that interest rates were not too volatile. This method of doing business began to face serious criticism in the mid-1960s. The principal objection was that concentrating on interest rates sacrificed control of the money supply. Critics argued that the real test of whether monetary policy was tight or loose was whether the money supply was growing at a fast or a slow rate.

In 1970 President Richard Nixon appointed Arthur Burns chairman of the Board of Governors. This appointment occurred at a time when interest rates and inflation rates were beginning to increase in the United States to levels not observed since the Korean War. Not surprisingly, this escalation of inflation and interest rates coincided with the Vietnam War, when the U. S. Treasury was attempting to fund relatively large federal deficits (by historical standards). Monetary policy was beginning to be the focus of increasing public attention and controversy as the concern for reducing inflation and interest rates increased. Moreover, as inflation began to increase it became more difficult to maintain the fixed exchange rates mandated in the Bretton Woods agreement. The United States was gradually forced to abandon its commitment to maintain a fixed exchange rate for dollars into gold and so accepted a system of fluctuating exchange rates.

In the early 1970s the Federal Reserve began to respond to its critics by concerning itself more directly with rates of growth in the money supply. In 1975, for the first time in its history, the Federal Reserve agreed to report targets for the future rate of growth in the money supply to Congress on a quarterly basis and to be accountable for meeting those targets. By this time there was general agreement that the Federal Reserve should seek to control the supply of money, but there was no agreement that the Fed should totally abandon attempts to tightly control short-term interest rates. The Fed continued to use the federal funds rate as its direct target for guiding monetary policy. The policy therefore attempted to control the long-run growth of the money supply by controlling the federal funds rate in the short run. The Fed would publicly announce a target range for the growth of the money supply, for example, of 3 percent to 6 percent for M_2. At the same time the Federal Open Market Committee would direct the Federal Reserve Bank of New York to conduct its trading operations to maintain the federal funds rate in a narrowly prescribed band, say 7 percent to 7.5 percent. Unfortunately, it would be pure luck if the target range for the federal funds rate turned out to be consistent with the intended range for the growth of M_2. Unless their luck held, and during the 1970s it generally did not, the Board of Governors and the Open Market Committee would continually be forced to choose between abandoning its publicly stated targets for M_2 and altering its private operating range for the federal funds rate. During much of the 1970s it appears that, more often than not the Fed stuck with the range for the federal funds rate in the short run and allowed M_2 to grow out of its range.

The basic problem here is that if the economy is booming and interest rates are rising, it will prove difficult for the Fed to maintain both types of targets effectively. If it attempts to maintain the federal funds rate target, this will lead to large increases in the supply of money. Increases in the money supply in a booming economy lead the market to expect inflation, and this tends to increase interest rates. This is the price anticipations effect operating. The increased pressure on interest rates makes it harder yet for the Fed to maintain its federal funds rate target. The opposite can happen if there is an unexpected decline in income and interest rates. Then, as the Fed tries to maintain its funds rate target it withdraws reserves from the banking system and the money supply declines. This can lead to a decline in inflationary expectations and a further decrease in interest rates. This kind of policy leads to a procyclical pattern of money growth; that is, the money supply tends to rise and fall with the economy rather than offsetting the fluctuations in the level of income. Critics of monetary policy in the 1970s argued that this was precisely what occurred.

On 6 October 1979, in the wake of growing pressure on financial markets, the new chairman of the Board of Governors of the Federal Reserve, Paul Volcker, who was appointed by President Jimmy Carter, formally abandoned the policy of trying to control the federal funds rate tightly. The Fed announced that it would try to control reserves directly, and through reserves the supply of money. Within a fairly wide range, it would allow the market to set the federal funds rate on a week-by-week basis. While there has been considerable disagreement about how much of the change was really cosmetic as opposed to substantive, this was probably the most dramatic alteration in the stated purpose of monetary policy in the history of the Federal Reserve system.

The change in monetary policy announced by Paul Volcker in October 1979 must be placed in context. The money supply had been growing at a rate slightly above 8 percent for several years. In addition, U. S. interest rates and inflation rates had reached unprecedented levels. In effect, Volcker's change in policy constituted an acknowledgement that, if the Fed continued to walk the tightrope of controlling both interest rates and the supply of money, it would not control either effectively or have any impact on inflation. The change in policy appears to have been designed to break market expectations of inflation by persuading the market that the Fed would seriously attempt to control the supply of money.

There is at least one other way to interpret Volcker's historic decision: that he wanted to raise interest rates enough to bring about a recession that would in turn reduce inflation. It would have been politically impractical to announce a policy of allowing interest rates to rise to such a level, so he chose to disassociate the Fed publicly from control of interest rates. By seeming to control the supply of money, he could really pursue a policy of allowing interest rates to rise. More specifically, he could abandon the policy of using the Fed to attempt to hold down interest rates.

Interest rates did increase significantly after October 1979. Figure 13-1 shows that Treasury-bill rates peaked in 1980 and the federal funds rate became substantially more volatile after October 1979. This seems to have been a direct response to the change in operating procedure. Once the Fed relaxed the band in which it had attempted to maintain the federal funds rate, the variance of the funds rate increased significantly.

By the fall of 1982 the Fed had begun to back away from its dramatic change in procedures for monetary policy. In part, this retrenchment seems to have been due to disenchantment within the Fed with its ability to control the supply of money effectively. Also, there was a perception that high interest rates that resulted from the new policy threatened to cause severe financial distress in the international economy because many loans from U. S. banks were denominated in dollars and pegged to U. S. interest rates. Interest rates in the United States had risen so high that many foreign borrowers were facing insolvency. The Fed backed away from its previous

Figure 13-1

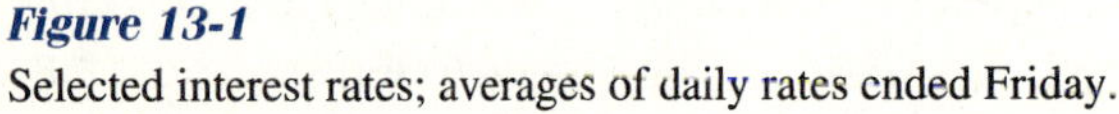

Selected interest rates; averages of daily rates ended Friday.

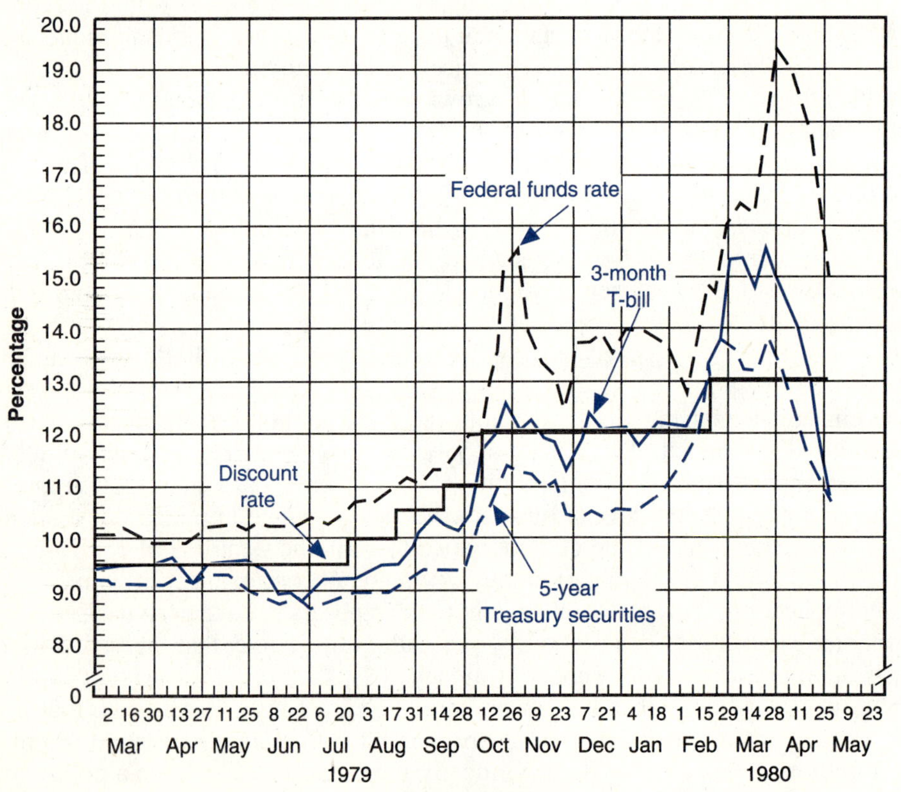

policy partly to avoid bankruptcy for many foreign borrowers. With all the immense changes in monetary policy that Paul Volcker put in place in 1979, it is difficult to say exactly what guided monetary policy during his tenure, that is, until 1987. Many observers of the Fed say that it followed a "*Volcker standard*" during this period, pursuing whatever course of action the Board Chairman thought appropriate.

Monetary Policy from the mid-1980s

During the late 1980s and early 1990s monetary policy became somewhat less visible to the public than it had been in the late 1970s and into the mid 80s, when inflation was a serious problem. In the early 1980s, when the Fed was focusing attention on the money supply, the financial press devoted extraordinary space to the technical details of the money supply and monetary policy and to the policy prescriptions of the monetarists. For example, publications such as the *Wall Street Journal* regularly published analyses of monetary policy that portrayed the Fed's target ranges for various monetary aggregates in terms of what were called cones and tunnels (Fig. 13-2). This example, taken from the 11 July 1986 edition of the *Wall Street Journal,* shows tunnels for M_1, M_2 and M_3, which graphically illustrate the possible ranges of these aggregates over time if their growth rates stay within their target ranges. A cone defines the level of the relevant monetary aggregate that would be consistent, at each point in time, with the announced target range of growth rates for that aggregate. A tunnel, as shown in Figure 13-2, shows the maximum or minimum level of the aggregate, at each point in time, that would keep the aggregate within its target range at the end of the horizon (November 1986 in this example) if it grew at the middle range of growth rates for the rest of the period. The topical importance in the financial press seems to have faded as the rate of inflation has declined and these cones and tunnels are now hard to find in major financial publications.

In the late 1980s and early 1990s, attention to monetary policy has focused more on how the Fed should help the economy escape recession. The Fed, under the leadership of Chairman Alan Greenspan, appointed in 1987, had the difficult job of deciding when to switch from fighting inflation to stimulating the economy. Many observers believe that the Fed responded too slowly to the threat of recession. The case against the Fed in this regard has been made by focusing on both interest rates and the money supply as the target of monetary policy.

Part of the problem for the conduct of monetary policy in the late 1980s and early 1990s derives from the apparent instability that appears to have developed in the behavior of M_2. As we already emphasized, if any particular measure of the supply of money is to be a useful target for conducting monetary policy, there must be a reasonably stable and predictable relationship between the level of that measure of the money supply and the level of nominal income, or between the growth of the money supply and the growth of nominal income or gross domestic product. However, in the late 1980s and the early 1990s, the growth rate in M_2 slowed appreciably relative to earlier years. Moreover, the relationship between nominal income and M_2 measured as the velocity of M_2,

$$\text{Velocity} = \frac{\text{Nominal income}}{M_2}$$

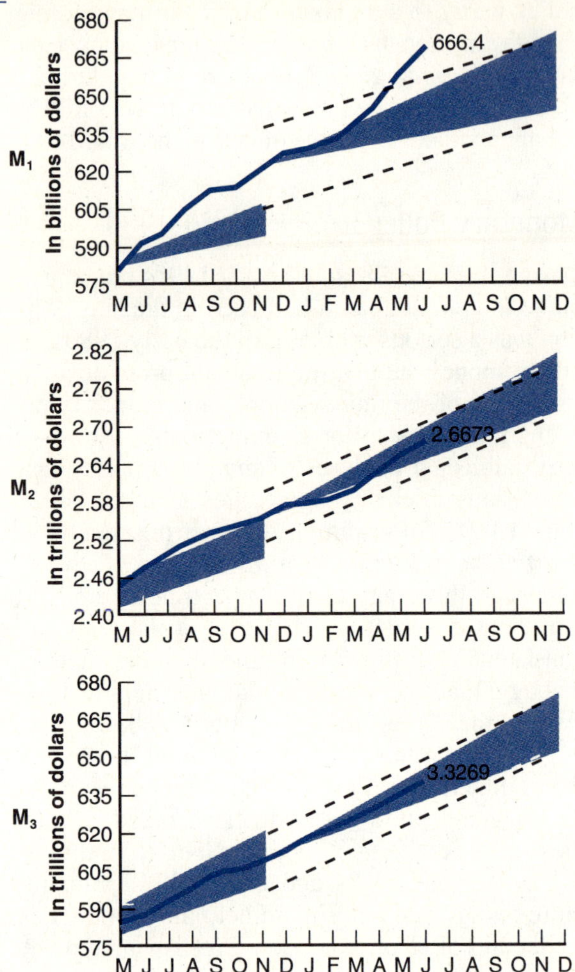

Figure 13-2

Tunnels for monetary aggregates. *Source:* Wall Street Journal, *July 11, 1986, p. 34.*

was also exhibiting fairly erratic behavior (Figs. 13-3, 13-4). Figure 13-3 shows the rate of growth of M_2 from 1961 through the middle of 1992. Notice that the annual rate of growth of M_2 slipped from roughly 9 percent in 1986 to slightly less than 3 percent by mid-1992. After 1989 this reduction in the growth rate of M_2 is partly due to a slowdown in economic growth in the U. S. as the economy entered a recession. But this does not seem to account fully for the behavior of M_2. This is more evident if we examine the behavior of the velocity of M_2 which is shown in Figure 13-4, from 1960 through 1991. While the growth rate in M_2 was declining in the late 1980s, income declined less sharply, so that velocity went up relative to the long-term trend. Note that velocity in this figure is a standardized measure, so the actual amount of measured velocity is meaningful only in comparison to velocity in another period. The standardization is accomplished by subtracting the actual measure of velocity in

Figure 13-3

M_2 Growth (Eight-quarter average). *Source: Board of Governors of the Federal Reserve System.*

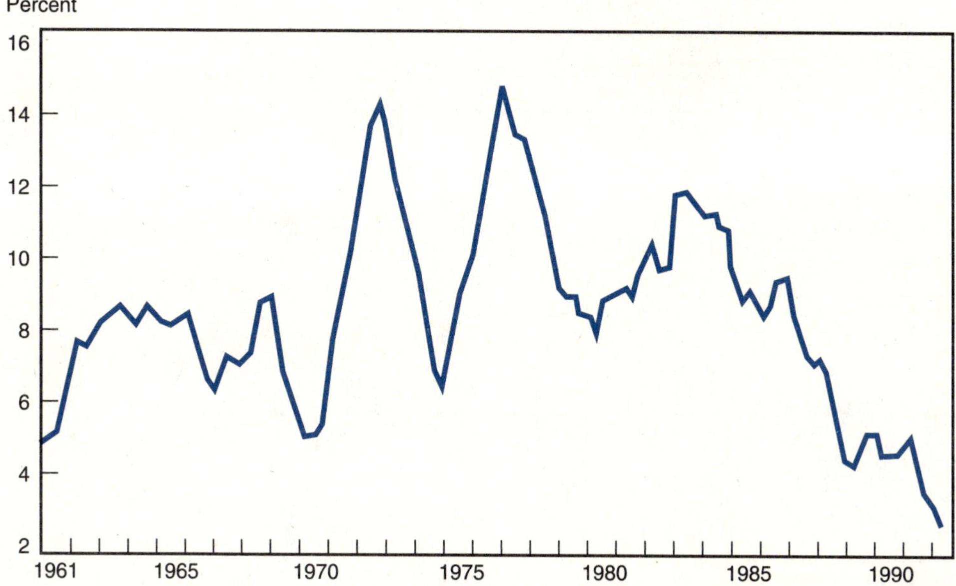

any period from the average for the whole time period in the figure and dividing that difference by the standard deviation of velocity computed over the whole period. The figure shows that velocity started increasing in 1985 from a low point but has persistently remained above average since then.

To see why the behavior of M_2 has apparently been changing, it is instructive to break M_2 down into two parts. One part includes all so-called time deposits, or interest-bearing accounts of various duration excluding demand deposits at banks and thrifts, and all other components of M_2. Figure 13-5 shows the behavior of growth rates of these components of M_2. It is apparent from this figure that time deposits have been falling while the other components of M_2 have not. What is driving this behavior of time deposits? The only explanation that seems to be persuasive to us is that depositors are increasingly being attracted away from banks and thrift institutions and are placing their funds in other forms of investments. This relative decline in the share of the total financial pie going to banks and thrifts shows up more clearly in time deposits than in other forms of bank and thrift liabilities. Some observers of the system believe that any target for monetary policy should not be especially sensitive to these sorts of shifts between various sectors of the financial marketplace. As a result, they advocate moving away from using M_2 as the target for monetary policy.

As in past debates about monetary aggregates, there are at least three points of view about how to respond to the problems with M_2. One view is to use a broader

Figure 13-4

M_2 Velocity and Interest Rates. *Sources: Board of Governors of the Federal Reserve System and the Department of Commerce, Bureau of Economic Analysis.*

Note: The series are standardized by subtracting from a given value in a series the mean of the series and dividing the result by the standard deviation of the series.

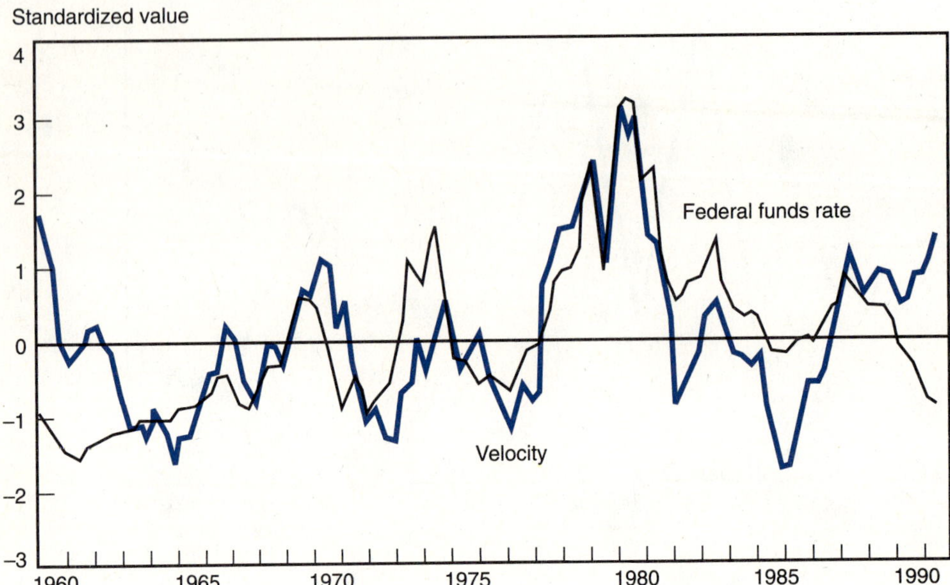

aggregate that includes claims on other types of institutions to which time deposits have been shifting. Another is that a narrower aggregate should be used, essentially eliminating time deposits from M_2. The third is that the aggregates are too unreliable to be used at all, at least until their behavior becomes more stable. Indeed, this appeared to be the view of Chairman Greenspan, in 1992. Erratic behavior of M_2 compelled the Fed to follow a more eclectic policy that emphasized interest rates and monetary aggregates. It also has encouraged efforts to see if other measures of the money supply might be more reliable. However, the behavior of M_2 documented here has also provided evidence for those who believe the Fed did not respond quickly enough to stop the recession of the early 1990s. They believe that the Fed inappropriately allowed the growth of M_2 to fall below its target range and that this slow growth of the supply of money in part caused or prolonged the recession.[2] These critics of recent Fed policy argue that the Fed focused too much on setting a target for short-term interest rates, particularly the federal funds rate, rather than placing their emphasis on M_2 and its growth rate. While the federal funds rate fell precipitously in 1990 and 1991 in response to actions by the Fed, the critics contend this was too little and too late. This debate about the proper targets and conduct of

[2]See James M. Buchanan and David I. Fand. "Monetary Policy: Malpractice At the Fed." *Wall Street Journal,* December 21, 1992.

monetary policy has been going on for some time through various historical episodes. It seems likely that the same issues will continue to be debated and the same problems will arise throughout the 1990s.

Monetary Policy and European Unity

While U. S. monetary policy in the early 1990s was focused on fighting recession, the Europeans were attempting to build an integrated economic community that would ultimately have a single European currency. The monetary policies pursued by the countries of Western Europe during the late 1980s and early 1990s were heavily influenced by the historic agreement, known as the Maastricht Treaty, to create a unified Europe. A central objective of this treaty is to create a free-trade zone within Western Europe where goods and services can be exchanged across national boundaries without tariffs or duties. An important element of the process of integration is the movement toward a common monetary policy for the countries of Europe. In the 1980s the major Western European countries took an important step in this direction by agreeing to a system of managed exchange rates known as the exchange rate mechanism (ERM) by which currencies are allowed to float within agreed-on bands. A common way to view the system puts the strongest member of the mechanism, Germany, at the center and views all exchange rates of other countries relative to the Deutschemark.

Figure 13-5

Growth of Components of M_2. *Source: Board of Governors of the Federal Reserve System.*

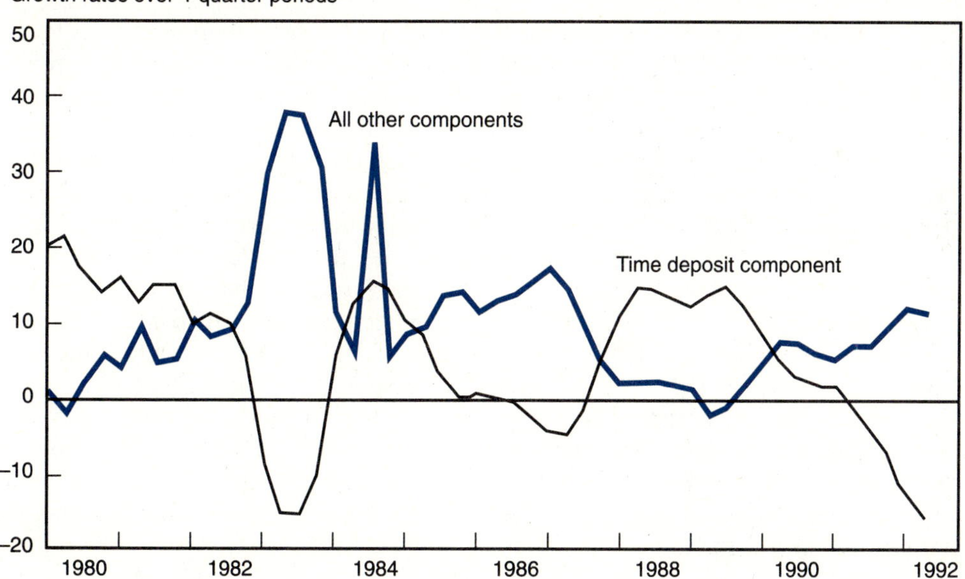

Actually, some observers have referred to the ERM as more of a pseudo–fixed exchange rate system, or a fudged exchange rate system. To see why these adjectives have been applied, it is important to contrast the ERM with a gold standard as followed by many of the same countries during the nineteenth and early twentieth century. The key feature of a gold standard, indeed the very reason for its adoption, is that it has an automatic self-correction mechanism. A country on the gold standard agrees to convert its currency to gold at a fixed exchange rate. If two countries are both committed to exchange their currencies for gold at fixed prices, then this directly implies that the exchange rate between their currencies is also fixed. If a country on the gold standard pursues a highly inflationary policy that makes holding its currency less attractive, then the country is obligated to exchange gold for its currency. Thus, gold acts as a disciplining device on the policies pursued by a country's government. By contrast, the ERM recently employed in Europe relies on the political willingness of participating countries to carry out economic policies that maintain the relative values of their currencies. Failing that, they must agree to periodic "realignments" or revaluations by which the agreed exchange rates between currencies are adjusted to new economic realities.

As we discussed in Chapter 12 when describing the conduct of monetary policy in an open economy, if a country is going to target or maintain a specific exchange rate with another currency the two countries cannot pursue contradictory monetary policies. That is, their inflation rates must be roughly comparable. This is particularly applicable to the European countries involved in the ERM. To make sure this is clear, suppose that two countries that were attempting to maintain a fixed exchange rate between their currencies had significantly different inflation rates. Let's take France and Britain for example. Suppose that the British have twice as high an inflation rate as the French, say, 10 percent and 5 percent. If this much difference in inflation rates is allowed to persist by a more expansionary monetary policy in Britain than in France, interest rates in Britain must rise to a level that is higher than in France. In fact, we would predict that interest rates in the two countries would have to differ by approximately 5 percent, assuming that real rates in both countries were approximately the same. If, however, the two countries commit to maintain a fixed exchange rate between their currencies, their interest rates must also be roughly the same. Otherwise an arbitrage opportunity will arise because speculators who know that France and Britain will maintain a fixed exchange rate, can move back and forth between financial instruments in the two countries without worrying about the consequences of changes in exchange rates. That is, they do not face any exchange rate risk. Therefore, investors in France could enter the foreign exchange market and buy British pounds, then buy short-term, say one-year–maturity, British government securities. Recall that these British securities are paying 5 percent more than they can earn in France. Knowing that the exchange rate will remain fixed, they can simply wait until the British securities mature and convert their earnings in pounds back into French francs at the fixed exchange rate. This arbitrage operation will put upward pressure on short-term British security prices or downward pressure on British interest rates, and it will tend to drive up the price of the pound, forcing the British government to intervene to attempt to maintain the fixed exchange rate.

We hope it is apparent that this situation cannot persist too long. Something has to give. If the relative inflation rates in the two countries do not change, then it is almost inevitable that the fixed exchange rates between the countries must be abandoned. The bottom line in the operation of a system of fixed exchange rates is that if the economic fortunes of the participating countries diverge significantly, it is extremely difficult to maintain a managed, fixed, fudged, or pseudo-fixed exchange rate system. This lesson has been learned and relearned in economic history. But one of the more interesting such lessons occurred in late 1992.

In late 1992 precisely the situation we just described developed in Western Europe with the countries in the ERM. The problem arose principally because Germany had to make a choice about how it was going to finance its policy of rebuilding East Germany. The decision by the German central bank, the Bundesbank, to use monetary policy to protect against a rise in inflation as the rebuilding of East Germany proceeded, was motivated, in part, by Germany's disastrous experience with high inflation during the 1930s. The Germans could either print more money or sell bonds to finance the rebuilding. Because the benefits of rebuilding stretch into the future, it seems reasonable that the cost should similarly be spread into the future through the interest rates on bond issues. The alternative of printing money would mean that current citizens would be exposed to the cost of higher inflation as a way to pay for rebuilding East Germany. The Bundesbank raised short-term interest rates in Germany to roughly 9 percent when German inflation was running at roughly 4 percent. This provided monetary discipline within Germany and helped attract foreign capital to Germany to finance the rebuilding effort under way. However, other Western European countries faced serious problems if they allowed their interest rates to follow Germany's in order to maintain fixed exchange rates. For example, the British were in the midst of a serious recession in 1992 and needed relatively low interest rates to stimulate their economy.

The problems with the ERM became acute in September 1992, when speculators around the world became convinced that many Western European countries would have to devalue their currencies relative to the Deutschemark. The governments of many of these countries went to extraordinary efforts to attempt to maintain the fixed exchange rate system. For example, Sweden raised overnight interest rates as high as 75 percent for a short time, to thwart the speculators. The political problem was particularly acute in Britain, where there had long been a strong political debate about whether Britain should be a member of the European Economic Community and the ERM. British Prime Minister Major reportedly took the position that participation in the ERM was in British interests in large part because fixed exchange rates would pressure British industry to restructure to be more competitive in a global economy. Reportedly, he was concerned that reliance on devaluation of the pound to stimulate the British economy would provide a quick fix without addressing underlying problems about the competitive position of the British economy. Thus, he attempted to maintain Britain's position in the ERM if at all possible. However, on 16 September 1992 Britain reversed its position and withdrew from the ERM. They simply did not have the resources to maintain the stated exchange rate in the face of widely held belief that the pound would have to be devalued.

Throughout this crisis, the Bundesbank maintained its position that a tight German monetary policy was in the interest not only of Germany but all of Europe. It appears that the German economy is too strong for other European countries to attempt to maintain fixed exchange rates with the mark without also aligning their economic and monetary policies with those in Germany.

It is of some interest to briefly compare the problems Western European countries are having in coordinating monetary policies with the historical situation in the United States. The United States was originally formed as a union of separate states that had a large degree of sovereignty. One of the historic rights of a sovereign state is control of its own monetary policy. Individual states in the United States gave up this right gradually, and not without a fight. Indeed, part of the issue at stake in the U. S. Civil War revolved around fiscal and monetary sovereignty. We take it for granted now that Arkansas, California, and Montana cannot all choose separate monetary policies. Instead, we all accept a common currency. While the Western Europeans could adopt a similar system, individual countries within that system give up separate political power or sovereignty in the process. The United States' evolution toward a single currency took roughly a century and it was extremely difficult. It is highly unlikely that the European experience will be any smoother than our own.

Through the late 1980s and early 1990s the United States has maintained floating exchange rates with other currencies in the world; however, the events in western Europe are of crucial importance for the United States. Rebuilding East Germany has radically changed the financial needs of Germany. While it was an exporter of capital (running a capital account deficit) throughout much of the 1980s, reunification of the two Germanys transformed the combined country into an importer of capital. This portends a period of intense competition for capital in a competitive global marketplace. Germany's decision to run a tight monetary policy means that it will not finance its internal rebuilding program with inflation. This will undoubtedly lead to a stronger Germany in the long run, but it will require other countries to adapt to the polices of this important part of the global economy. Other countries that want to obtain capital will have to be prepared to compete with Germany in the global capital markets of the 1990s.

SUMMARY

We began this chapter by examining the principal modern critique of the conduct of monetary policy, monetarism. We defined the basic tenants of the monetarist positions and described the monetarists' prescription for the conduct of monetary policy, a money supply rule. We emphasized that one of the strongest cases for the money supply rule is that it takes the discretion regarding the conduct of monetary policy away from the government and thus denies it the tool of inflation to deal with political problems.

Next, we turned our attention to an account of the history of U. S. monetary policy. We discussed the evolution of monetary policy over the life of the Federal Reserve. During the early years of the Fed there was an internal debate about its obligations and objectives. One view was that it should simply provide an elastic currency, allowing credit to expand and contract with the economy. This view appears to have dominated as the Depression began, because the Fed did not attempt to prevent the decline in the money supply that occurred. As World War II began, the Fed shifted to a policy of pegging interest rates motivated by a desire to accommodate the Treasury's need to finance the war without driving up interest rates. This policy continued until 1952.

From the early 1950s until the 1970s the Fed principally used interest rates and general economic conditions as its target for monetary policy. In the 1970s, as inflation increased in the United States, there was increased pressure on the Fed to switch to monetary aggregates as targets for monetary policy. The Fed gradually paid more attention to the aggregate supply of money during this period. In October 1979, Federal Reserve Chairman Paul Volcker announced that the Fed would abandon interest rates as targets of monetary policy and switch to the money supply. This policy lasted until 1982, when conditions in financial markets convinced the Fed once again to adopt a more eclectic policy of focusing on both targets. We also focused attention of U. S. domestic monetary policy in the 1980s, as the Fed had to switch from fighting inflation to dealing with an economy in recession. We summarized the criticisms of the Fed's conduct of policy during this period.

Finally, we turned our attention to the recent experience of Western European countries operating under a system of fixed exchange rates known as the exchange rate mechanism. We argued that a system of fixed exchange rates requires that these countries have coordinated monetary and economic policies; however, recent events have dictated precisely the opposite. Germany has chosen a tight monetary policy to prevent inflation as it attempts to rebuild East Germany. Other western European countries have faced recession and have wanted to avoid the high interest rates maintained in Germany. We emphasized that this created an environment where fixed exchange rates could not be maintained.

QUESTIONS

1. How did the Fed conduct monetary policy from the early 1950s to the late 1970s?
2. What happened on 6 October 1979, and what is its significance?
3. What is the real bills doctrine? How did this influence the policy of the Federal Reserve during the 1930s?
4. How should the decrease in the value of the dollar relative to the yen in 1986–1987 affect U.S. interest rates? How can and should the Fed respond to these changes in exchange rates in its conduct of monetary policy?
5. How do the monetarists explain the long-run pattern of the behavior of velocity?
6. Why is velocity simply a restatement of the demand for money?
7. What is the "money supply rule"? What is the main case for this rule?
8. What is the principal difficulty in trying to create a single monetary policy for a group of distinct political states?

REFERENCES

Buchanan, James M., and David I. Fand. "Monetary Policy: Malpractice at the Fed." *Wall Street Journal,* December 21, 1992.

———. "The Quantity Theory of Money: A Restatement," in Milton Friedman, ed. Studies in the Quantity Theory of Money. Chicago: University of Chicago Press, 1956.

Higgins, Bryon. "Policy Implications of Recent M_2 Behavior." *Economic Review* [Federal Reserve Bank of Kansas City] (Third Quarter 1992), pp. 21–36.

Hoover, Herbert. The Great Depression, 1929–41. *The Memoirs of Herbert Hoover.* New York: Macmillan, 1952.

Sease, Douglas R. "Pound Crisis Shakes World Currency Markets." *Wall Street Journal,* September 17, 1992, p. C1.

Walters, Alan A., and Steve H. Hanke. "End of the Exchange Peg." *Wall Street Journal,* September 18, 1992, p. A10.

• *Part III* •

Innovation in Financial Markets

Forward and Futures Markets

Options

Swaps

Risk Management Strategy

Securitization

• Chapter 14

Forward and Futures Markets

This chapter introduces the markets for forward and futures contracts. These contracts are similar in many ways, especially in their potential use for speculation on or hedging of financial risks. The markets in which these instruments are traded are quite different from each other. We examine the nature of forward and futures contracts and the operation of the markets where they are traded. We explain the distinctions between the operations of these markets and describe the essential features of each type. We also explain the factors that determine prices of forward and futures contracts. More specifically, we discuss how the futures or forward price is related to the current spot price and the expected future spot price. The discussion shows how futures (forward), spot, and expected spot prices are linked together in equilibrium by the interaction of hedgers, speculators, and arbitrageurs.

• Concepts to Learn in Chapter 14 •

- Definitions and structure of futures and forwards contracts
- How futures markets operate
- How to compute payoffs on positions in futures contracts
- How futures markets provide standardization and liquidity
- How futures prices are determined

Forward Contracts

A forward contract is an agreement between a buyer and a seller—normally referred to as the "*counterparties*" to the agreement—to execute a trade at some date in the future. That is, buyer and seller agree on the quantity and price of the commodity or instrument to be traded. The difference between a forward and a spot transaction concerns the timing of the trade. In most spot transactions, the asset to be exchanged is transferred and payment is made immediately or within a two-day settlement period after the agreement is reached. In many markets, and financial markets in particular, spot transactions are seldom "cash" transactions wherein cash is transferred immediately after the agreement is reached. Some time usually must pass for transfer of ownership of commodities or securities, and some time is also necessary to make payment and transfer funds. In most financial markets, two business days is assumed to be sufficient time to accomplish such transfers. Two-day settlement, sometimes referred to as "skip-day settlement," is often used to distinguish between spot and forward transactions. That is, forward trades (and forward contracts) are defined as agreements to trade that have settlement dates later than two days after the agreement to trade is reached (contract date).

Forward contracts specify a settlement date, or the time the trade will actually take place. When the settlement date arrives, the buyer initiates payment for the asset at the previously agreed price and the seller transfers (ownership to) the asset in the specified quantity. On the settlement date, sellers satisfy their obligation in one of two ways: either by decreasing their own inventory of the asset or by buying the asset in the spot market. Owing to the pending obligation at the settlement date, the seller under the contract is often referred to as the short side of the contract. The term "short" implies a future obligation to deliver an asset whereas "long" implies an obligation to purchase or take delivery of an asset. The obligation faced by the short side of the forward agreement is similar to that encountered by short sellers in the stock market where the asset is borrowed and sold for cash. Short sellers must later repay their debt by replacing the security out of their own inventory or by purchasing it on the spot market. The terms long and short are often used interchangeably with buyer and seller, respectively, in the context of forward contracts or agreements.

One of the easiest ways to understand a forward contract is to draw a picture of the payoffs from taking long and short positions in such a contract. Figure 14-1 is such a picture. The spot price of some underlying asset is shown on the horizontal axis and the gain or loss on a forward contract is shown on the vertical axis. The upwardly sloping line portrays the payoff on a long forward contract. This payoff is defined as the difference between the spot price, P, and the forward contract price, F, or $P - F$. Conversely, the payoff on a short forward contract is simply the reverse of the long position, or $F - P$. We will give you several examples with some numbers shortly.

Although they are pervasive in modern economies, forward contracts can actually be traced back to medieval Europe, when it was commonplace for merchants to enter into them to buy goods and materials. Most people have been party to one form of forward agreement or another—perhaps without being aware of it as such. Various purchases of consumer products or real estate are often accomplished with sales agreements that are types of forward contracts. In order to freeze the future price involved in the sale, these contracts often require a deposit by the buyer as security against reneging. Forward contracts are fundamental to financial markets. Many more complex securities are comprised of bundles of forward contracts. As we show later, interest rate and currency swaps can be viewed as being comprised of a series of forward contracts to exchange interest-contingent cash flows, or currencies.

Forward Markets in Foreign Currency

Modern markets for forward contracts vary widely in their volume and degree of organization. One of the most organized forward markets exists in the market for foreign currency. Most of the major dealers in foreign currency, including most large banks, have a "*forward desk*" in their foreign exchange trading rooms. The forward desk regularly quotes prices and quantities to customers to buy and sell foreign currencies at various forward settlement dates (e.g., 30 days, 90 days, 180 days). Table 14-1 contains an excerpt from the *Wall Street Journal* that provides a good example of forward and spot prices in the foreign currency market. This information appeared in the 9 January 1992 edition, with quotes from trading in Japanese yen (¥) collected on 8 January 1992.

These prices represent exchange rates quoted for $1 million or more in the interbank market in foreign currency at 3:00 P.M. on 8 January. Two columns of prices are provided. The first gives the price in dollars per yen; the second the same price in yen per dollar. The first row gives the spot price. Thus, at the time and date reported, the dollar was trading for 124.15 yen over the spot market. The other three rows of prices identify quotes for *forward* contracts in yen with 30-, 60-, and 180-day settlements. In the case of the 30-day settlement, a contract could have been made on 8 January for, say $1 million, which would sell dollars to receive yen at a rate of 124.26, with the exchange to take place 30 days later. Then on 6 February, the settlement date, the buyer of ¥ would pay $1 million and receive ¥124,260,000. By contrast, if $1 million were exchanged for yen at the (8 January) spot rate, ¥124,150,000 would be received.

Forward Markets in U. S. Government Securities

Another well-organized forward market exists in U.S. government securities. Several dozen securities firms, many of them primary dealers in U.S. government securities, quote prices to buy and sell U.S. government and agency bonds, usually in amounts of $1 million (face value) or more, at various forward settlement dates. In the foreign currency market, there is an interdealer market in U.S. government securities in which brokers play an important role in bringing compatible buyers and sellers together. Major dealers are connected to an automated quotation system that allows them to make quotes to buy and sell U.S. government instruments both on the spot and forward and to see quotes made by competing dealers. These systems are provided by what are called "*screen brokers,*" like Garban, Ltd. or FBI. In many markets, brokers operate by making phone calls to various dealers to collect information about bids and offers. After receiving a bid (offer to buy) on an issue, a broker often contacts several other dealers about the offer, trying to find someone willing to sell at the same price. Screen brokers speed up this process substantially

Table 14-1
Forward Rates for Yen

	U.S. $ Equivalent	Currency Per U.S. Dollar
Japan (yen)	.008055	124.15
30-Day forward	.008048	124.26
60-Day forward	.008033	124.48
180-Day forward	.008017	124.74

by allowing numerous potential sellers to see the bid simultaneously over the screen. Any particular dealer who wants to accept the bid seen on the screen calls the screen broker and offers to sell at the quoted price. The broker brings both sides of the transaction together and charges both a commission.

Forward Rate Agreements

Forward rate agreements, or FRAs, are forward contracts on interest rates. The market for FRAs is closely tied to the foreign exchange market. Many of the same banks that make the interdealer market in the foreign exchange also make the market in FRAs. FRAs can be made in most major currencies, and quotes for FRAs are communicated among the major traders via electronic quotation systems such as Reuters.

The FRA evolved from what is called the "forward forward contract." Forward forwards are agreements, made most of the time between large banks, in which one bank agrees to deposit money in the other. These agreements are essentially forward contracts in deposits. The amount of the deposit, the interest rate on the deposit, the term of the deposit, and the future date on which the deposit is to take place are all stipulated by the agreement. When the settlement date is reached, the agreement requires the depositor to actually deliver by depositing the agreed amount in the borrowing bank.

FRAs are a simplified version of the forward forward agreement because they do not require physical delivery of the deposit money. Rather, a value settlement is made on the scheduled deposit (or value) date, which reflects the difference between the agreed rate and the market rate. The settlement process can be best understood by a simple example. Suppose Bank A enters into a forward rate agreement with Bank B to borrow U.S. dollars "three versus six" at 6 percent, on a notional amount of $1 million. The term "*three versus six*" refers to the three-month interest rate that will be observed in the market three months from now on agreements, bearing a maturity date six months from now. Most FRAs are tied to the London interbank offer rate (LIBOR) because most of the trading occurs over the London market. This means that settlement of the FRA in this case will be based on the value of three-month LIBOR on U.S. dollars, three months from now. The contract rate on the agreement is 6 percent (annual). If LIBOR is greater than 6 percent on the settlement date, the borrowing bank, Bank A, will *receive* a net cash flow based on the notional amount and the difference between actual three-month LIBOR and 6 percent. If LIBOR is less than 6 percent, Bank A will *pay* a net settlement to the lending bank.

Suppose LIBOR turned out to be 8 percent, three months from now. Bank A will receive a net cash payment from Bank B, based on the 2 percent (annual) spread between LIBOR and the FRA contract rate. The three-month equivalent of this spread is

$$(90/360) \times (2\%) = 0.5\%$$

On the notional amount of $1 million, the interest settlement is

$$(\$1{,}000{,}000)(0.005) = \$5000$$

Because FRAs are based on deposits that would mature three months later, like the original forward forward agreement, this $5000 payment represents an interest differential (between the contract and actual market rates) that would be received in three more months time. Because a deposit will not actually be made under the FRA, the contract is settled as the discounted value of the interest due in three months at the actual three-month market rate (three-month LIBOR or 8 percent), or,

$$\frac{\$5000}{\left(1 + \frac{90}{360}(.08)\right)} = \$4902$$

There is a simple link between the FRA and the forward interest rates described in Chapter 10: The forward rates impounded in the term structure of interest rates should be approximately equal to the rates quoted on FRAs over the same forward intervals of time. The forward rate in the term structure of Eurodollar rates for the interval from three months to six months from now should represent (approximately) the market's forecast of the three-month Eurodollar rate in three months. In fact, such information is key to the formation of market quotes in FRAs by dealer banks. Dealers in FRAs use the spot yield curve to price forward rate agreements. If the spot yield curve is upward sloping, the contract rate for FRAs with later settlements is higher.

The most important way in which FRAs are used by financial managers is as a hedge against interest rate risk. FRAs can be used to offset losses associated with unexpected increases in borrowing costs or decreases in investment yields. For instance, in the example just outlined Bank A may have entered into the FRA with Bank B to hedge against increases in the cost of borrowing $1 million in the short-term market in three months. As LIBOR increased from 6 percent to 8 percent during the ensuing three-month period, the FRA paid Bank A $4902 to offset the higher interest rate on borrowing $1 million in the spot market.

Contracting Problems in the Forward Market

As we shall see shortly, a futures contract is a highly standardized form of a forward contract that is traded on an organized exchange. To understand why both futures and forwards exist, it is essential to consider some of the problems that develop in forward markets. To some extent, the evolution and development of futures markets can be attributed to a variety of contracting problems that are encountered in forward markets, particularly concerning the participation of smaller, anonymous traders. In general, forward markets are directly accessible only to very large, well-established traders whose reputation and credibility are well-known or easily determined. Smaller, less established parties may participate in forward markets indirectly, through customer relationships with dealers in the market. The inability of many to participate directly in the wholesale forward market is due to some, if not all, of the following factors:

Contract Dimensions: Size and Settlement Date

One of the contracting problems associated with using forward markets concerns the ability of counterparties to agree on the size or amount to be delivered and on the settlement date. Suppose that on 7 January a buyer wanted to make a contract to buy *exactly* 1.23 million Deutschemarks for delivery 45 days later on 21 February. In principle, on 7 January a forward contract could be negotiated with a seller that is specifically tailored to purchase exactly 1.23 million Deutschemarks on 21 February. In fact, any number of marks or any settlement date could be fixed under the right circumstances. The problem is finding the other side of the contract, a counterparty to the contract who is willing to sell *exactly* the same number of Deutschemarks on *exactly* the same date. In organized forward markets, like the market for foreign exchange, brokers play a key role in locating compatible counterparties to buy and sell currency forward, and also in bringing prospective buyers and sellers to negotiate the size, settlement date, and price of their offers when they are sufficiently close to each other. However, brokered transactions are generally for large amounts involving institutional counterparties. Thus, though forward contracts are more flexible with regard to the size and settlement date and can be tailored to suit individual needs, it is this flexibility that causes difficulty in finding a suitably matched counterparty.

Default Risk

Another problem encountered with forward contracts is the risk of default. When the spot price changes relative to the forward contract price, one side of the contract gains while the other side loses. Suppose in our example a contract was made to buy Deutschemarks at 66 (cents per Deutschemark) deliverable on 21 February. For convenience suppose the spot price in Deutschemarks is currently also at 66. If the spot price of Deutschemarks on 21 February turns out to be 65, it would have been better for the buyer to buy them on the spot rather than via the forward contract. At the spot price of 65, the buyer could save one cent per Deutschemark, a total of $12,300. Certainly, there would be a strong monetary incentive to renege on the agreement, refuse to buy the Deutschemarks, and save $12,300 by purchasing the Deutschemarks in the spot market. Of course the virtue of using the forward contract to begin with is to avoid the opposite prospect. If the price of Deutschemarks were to increase to 67 cents, there would be an equivalent savings relative to the February 21 spot price. It is under those circumstances that the seller has an incentive to default on the agreement, since Deutschemarks could be sold at a better price on the spot than under the forward agreement.

The incentives to default are illustrated in Figure 14-1. The spot price of the commodity deliverable under the contract is represented on the horizontal axis as P; the settlement price under the forward contract by F. The gains or losses, relative to the spot price, are shown for each counterparty by the diagonal profiles. Notice that the profiles are symmetric. For a given spot price, the gain to one counterparty is matched by an equal but opposite loss to the other. Unless P equals F on the settlement date, there will always be some incentive to default on the contract by one side of the agreement or the other. The prospect of default becomes particularly troublesome when prospective

Figure 14-1
Gains and losses to the buyer and seller in a forward contract. Schedules show the gain or loss to parties of a forward contract having a forward delivery price of *F*. Gain or loss is the difference between the spot price of the underlying commodity and the forward price, or, $F - P$ for the buyer and $P - F$ for the seller.

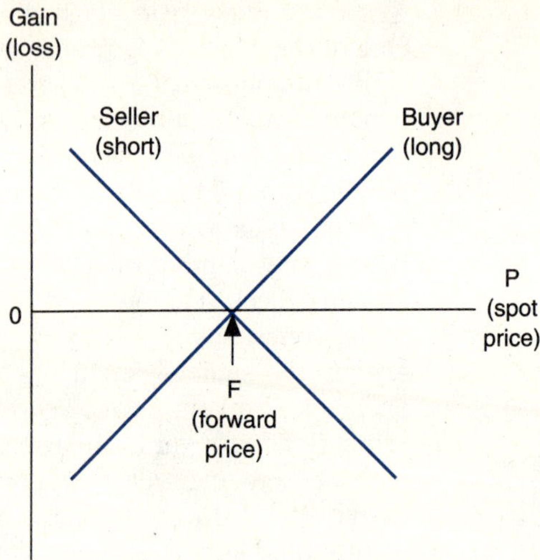

counterparties are anonymous, that is, when the creditworthiness of one counterparty cannot be easily evaluated by the other. To some extent, this is why the forward markets for foreign currency and U.S. governments are dominated by large financial institutions with established reputations. They are "bonded" by the potential loss of future business in the market if they renege on an agreement.

Liquidity

Still another difficulty encountered in forward contracts concerns their *liquidity,* the ability of a counterparty to unwind her obligation to the contract. Returning to our previous example, recall the buyer who entered into a forward contract to buy Deutschemarks 1.23 million at 66 cents per Deutschemark with settlement on 21 February. Suppose that 1 week later, on 14 January, the buyer learns that the Deutschemarks will no longer be needed. To avoid potential losses in reselling DM 1.23 million purchased under the contract on 21 February, the buyer would like to get out of the contract now. Three courses of action are available to the buyer:

1. *Assignment of the obligation to another party.* Another party could agree to accept the obligation under the contract. This could involve some compensation to the new party who will assume the original obligation. It would also require the approval of and/or compensation to the other counterparty, since such rearrangements may increase default risk.
2. *Cancellation of the contract.* The buyer could arrange with the seller to agree to cancel the contract. This generally involves compensating (via a cancellation fee) the seller, who may then be faced with renegotiating a similar contract with a different counterparty.
3. *An offsetting position.* Under this alternative, the buyer under the first contract would enter into another contract to sell DM 1.23 million on February 21. As a result, on the settlement date, there would be two equal and offsetting obligations to buy and sell the same amount of Deutschemarks. Of course there may

be some difference in settlement prices on the long and short positions, which could impose a gain or a loss. In addition, there will also be default exposure to *two* counterparties, rather than one. Finally, some difficulty will likely be encountered in finding another counterparty, given the size and settlement date of the offsetting contract.

In all cases, unwinding an outstanding obligation is likely to involve recognition of some accumulated gain or loss (as in Figure 14-1) on the contract as of 14 January. More important, however, under any of the alternatives just outlined some costs will be associated with liquidating the obligation.

Futures Contracts

Evolution of the Futures Market

A convenient way to define futures contracts is that they are highly standardized forward contracts that are based on a relatively small number of commodities, standard contract sizes, and a limited number of settlement dates. From a structural standpoint, a futures contract can be viewed as a specialized kind of forward contract. The reverse is not the case, though: there are many types of forward contracts that should not be considered futures contracts.

Trading in financial futures contracts on organized exchanges is a relatively recent innovation. Trading in foreign currency futures dates back to 1972. Beginning in October 1975 the Chicago Board of Trade (CBT) introduced a futures contract in GNMA mortgage–backed securities. Within a few months new contracts on both Treasury securities and commercial paper had also been introduced. There is now active trading in futures contracts on a variety of financial instruments, including U.S. Treasury bills, U.S. Treasury notes and bonds, prime quality commercial paper, and bank certificates of deposit (CDs). In addition, there are now futures contracts on market indices such as the Standard & Poor's 500 index, the New York Stock Exchange (NYSE) index, and a municipal bond index. Moreover, financial futures contracts are traded over several different exchanges: the Chicago Board of Trade (CBT), the International Money Market of the Chicago Mercantile Exchange (IMM), the Amex Commodities Exchange (ACE), the Commodity Exchange (COMEX), and the New York Futures Exchange (NYFE).

Though trading in futures contracts on financial instruments is a relatively recent phenomenon, futures contracts on commodities have been traded for many years. In fact, the first four of the five exchanges just listed began as exchanges for commodity futures. Only the NYFE, which is a part of the NYSE, has grown specifically to trade financial futures. Financial futures, including futures on indexes, now generally account for more than 50 percent of aggregate trading volume on these exchanges.

Futures on commodities evolved principally to protect farmers from the risk of price fluctuation in the commodities they produced. Farmers incur most of their costs during the growing season, without knowing what the selling price of their crop will be after harvest. If prices are low, the farmer may lose money. By selling corn futures, a corn farmer would realize a profit on the futures when corn prices fall. Ideally, the profit from corn futures would cover the losses from lower prices when the crop is sold. On the other hand, if prices were high after harvest, the sale of corn would generate profits that would cover losses on the futures position. By choosing the short position carefully, a farmer could stabilize profits and reduce the risk of his operation. Being centrally located in the farm belt, Chicago was a natural place for the development of the commodity futures markets. Once these markets were in place, it was a natural extension of their traditional function to innovate in developing financial futures.

The futures exchanges are regulated by the Commodity Futures Trading Commission (CFTC), which has many of the same oversight responsibilities for futures markets as the Securities and Exchange Commission (SEC) does for the securities markets. However, the CFTC also has responsibility for approving the introduction of new futures contracts. For a futures contract to be approved, it must be demonstrated that it will serve some useful economic purpose, such as making possible hedging of some risk. This requirement is apparently motivated by a concern that futures markets do not become simply a vehicle for speculation. The CFTC also regulates procedures on the trading floor and settles limits on allowable daily price fluctuations.

The CFTC, long a controversial agency, was involved in a long dispute with the SEC over jurisdiction over options trading. In addition, the CFTC has generally had very meager funds allocated to carry out its responsibilities, so it has relied on self-regulation to a much greater extent than the SEC. In recent years it has not been particularly concerned with insider trading. The futures exchanges utilize procedures that do not currently include automated records of transaction. As a result, it is difficult to conduct the kinds of trade investigations that have led to identification and prosecution of insider trading by the SEC.

Introduction to Financial Futures Contracts

U.S. Treasury-Bill Contracts

Table 14-2 presents a sample of financial futures prices taken from the *Wall Street Journal.* Panel A contains data reported on 9 January 1992 for trades that took place on 8 January 1992 in U.S. T-bill futures contracts.

The heading of the table indicates the contract being traded, the exchange on which it is traded (in parentheses), the dollar amount per contract, and the units in which the price is stated. For example, the T-bill contracts are traded over the IMM of the Chicago Mercantile Exchange (CME). The denomination of T bills traded per contract is $1 million (face value), and the maturity of the deliverable bills is 90 days. This means that the seller (short) of a March futures contract is obligated on the settlement date to sell $1 million in 90-day U. S. T bills to the buyer of the contract.

In practice, because of the substantial liquidity of the futures market, very few contracts ultimately involve delivery. It is generally much cheaper and easier to "even the position up," or cancel the obligation out with an offsetting transaction, than to go through the costly process of delivery. In some contracts, in particular U.S. T-bond futures, the option to deliver different coupon securities against the obligation can convey value to the short side of the contract. In those cases, the prospect of actual delivery taking place is more important.

Table 14-2

Panel A: Treasury-Bill Futures
Treasury Bills (IMM)—$Mil; Pt. of 100%

						Discount		
	Open	**High**	**Low**	**Settle**	**Chg**	**Settle**	**Chg**	**Open Interest**
Mar	96.43	96.43	96.39	96.39	+.01	3.61	−.01	38,869
Jun	96.37	96.37	96.33	96.33	. . .	3.67	. . .	11,163
Sep	96.15	96.16	96.13	96.14	+.01	3.86	−.01	1,804
Dec	. . .	. . .	. . .	95.75	−.01	4.25	+.01	425

Est vol 5,261; vol Tues, 11,162; open int 52,283 + 3,102.

Panel B: Treasury-Bond Futures
Treasury Bond (CBT)—$100,000; Pt. 32nds of 1%

						Yield		
	Open	**High**	**Low**	**Settle**	**Chg**	**Settle**	**Chg**	**Open Interest**
Mar	105–07	105–15	104–27	105–01	−7	7.510	+.021	305,071
June	104–02	104–11	103–24	103–30	−7	7.613	+.020	22,660
Sep	102–28	103–07	102–23	102–28	−7	7.716	+.022	5,683
Dec	102–00	102–09	101–25	101–28	−7	7.813	+.021	4,081
Mr93	101–00	101–14	100–29	101–00	−7	7.900	+.022	1,515
June	100–05	100–05	100–05	100–05	−8	7.984	+.025	187

Panel C: Stock Index Futures
S & P Index (CME) 500 Times Index

	Open	**High**	**Low**	**Settle**	**Chg**	**High**	**Low**	**Open Interest**
Mar	417.70	422.60	416.50	419.20	−.25	422.60	372.90	140,920
June	419.20	423.75	417.90	420.60	−.25	423.75	374.50	3,328
Sep	422.00	425.00	419.30	421.80	−.35	425.30	376.25	236

Est vol 59,129; vol Tues 48,887; open int 144,507, + 1,215.
Indx prelim High 420.23; Low 415.02; CLose 418.10, + .70

The headings of the first four columns provide the important prices for trading on January 8: the opening price, the high price for the day, the low price for the day, and the settlement price. The next column gives the change in the settlement price from the previous day (January 7). The next two columns under *Discount* show the settlement discount and the change in the discount from the previous day. The settlement discount is merely 100.00 minus the settlement price, or for the March contract, 100.00 minus 96.39, or 3.61. Obviously, the two "Change" columns will always have the same value with opposite signs. Normally, a discount is the difference between the price of a security and its face value. In the case of T-bill prices, however, the discount is annualized. For example, the March T-bill discount shown reflects the product of the actual discount and the annualization factor (360/90). The factor (360/90) assumes a 360-day year. The 360-day convention is the norm in expressing interest rates and discounts in most money markets; though when yields, or returns to investment, are concerned a 365-day year is used for annualizing. This annualization procedure is useful for expressing discounts and rates on instruments of different maturities on a common annual basis so that their interest, or earning power, can be more fairly compared. To deannualize the discount for March T bills we need only to multiply the stated discount 3.61 by (90/360):

$$3.61(90/360) = 0.9025$$

This means that the actual discount on the 90-day instrument is 0.9025 percent at the settlement price, and that the actual settlement price in dollars is

$$\$1{,}000{,}000(1 - 0.009025) = \$990{,}975$$

Therefore, at the current settlement price the seller is obligated to sell $1 million in 90-day T bills at a price of $990,975 when the March delivery date arrives.

Notice that under the T-bill futures contract the deliverable instrument is *always* a 90-day T bill, regardless of the contract delivery month. Delivery of T bills is scheduled to take place by the Thursday following the third U.S. T-bill auction of the delivery month. To facilitate delivery in available maturities of T bills, alternative maturities of 91 days and 92 days are also accepted to satisfy delivery under the IMM contract. To cover the delivery obligation, sellers must provide $1 million (face value) in 90-day T bills to the buyer under each contract. This implies that a change in the contract price of one decimal point (0.01) will result in the same change in the dollar value per contract, regardless of the settlement date. In other words, for each change in the price of 0.01 percent, or one basis point, the change in the value of one T-bill contract is

$$\$1{,}000{,}000\left[0.0001\left(\frac{90}{360}\right)\right] = \$25.00$$

For example, our information indicates that the settlement price of the March contract changed by +0.01 from the previous day. This implies that the dollar change per contract was an increase of $25.

The final column of the table shows the "Open Interest" in each contract. Open interest refers to the number of bilateral contracts between buyers and sellers currently outstanding for the various settlement months. For example, at the March settlement date there are currently 38,869 contracts outstanding, which means there are 38,869 separate $1 million obligations at the March settlement date, in 90-day T bills.

From the same issue of the *Wall Street Journal* information is also provided for trading in the U.S. T-bond contracts traded over the CBT on 8 January 1992 in Panel B of Table 14-2.

One of the most obvious differences between the T-bill and T-bond contract is their size. In the case of T bonds the standard denomination of one contract is

$100,000 (face value) in bonds. For T-bond futures, the same open, high, low, and settlement prices are presented. The change in the settlement price from the previous day is also given. For T-bond contracts the yield-to-maturity is also given at the settlement price, and the change in the yield from the previous day's settlement price is provided. Finally, the open interest in the various contracts is given again in the last column. The standard instrument deliverable under this contract is the 8-percent coupon U. S. Treasury bond with at least 15 years remaining to maturity, or until the nearest date when the bond can be called. In addition, T-bond issues with alternative coupon rates can be delivered under the terms of the contract.

Because the convention for quoting bonds is different than the one for quoting T bills, there is an important difference in interpreting the prices. Bond prices are given as a percentage of face value, with the decimals indicating 1/32s of 1 percent. Therefore, the settlement price for the March contract corresponds to a dollar value of

$$\$100{,}000\left(\frac{105+\frac{1}{32}}{100}\right)=\$105{,}031.25$$

This means that the buyer under the March contract is entitled to receive $100,000 (face value) in U.S. T bonds (standard 8-percent coupon) in March at a price of $105,031.25. Also note that a price move of 00–01, or 1/32 of one percent of face value results in a dollar change per contract of $31.25.

Notice another important difference between the T-bill and the T-bond contracts: The number of contracts, or delivery months, offered in T bonds is greater than the number of T-bill contracts. This can be explained as a difference in demand from market participants. Market demand in a particular contract is indicated by the level of open interest. When open interest is too low, market interest in a particular contract is too low to generate sufficient economies to justify centralized trading. As more distant contracts are offered by the exchange, there comes a point at which there is not enough additional interest by the market—either in hedging or in speculating at more distant dates—to make trading in that particular contract worthwhile. This point is clearly reached for T-bond contracts with the June 1993 contract, which has open interest of only 187 contracts. As of January 1992, the June 1993 contract is settled almost a year and a half in the future. Apparently there is little desire on the part of hedgers and speculators in the T-bond market to take positions to be settled any farther out than 18 months. Similarly, market interest in T-bill futures drops off to 425 contracts for contracts with settlement dates 15 months in the future.

Stock Index Futures

One of the more important futures contracts introduced in the last few years is the stock index future, a futures contract written on a stock market index. Four stock index futures based on U.S. market indices are actively traded: S & P 500 (CME), the NYSE Composite (NYFE), the Value Line Index Kansas City Exchange (KC), and the MMI (CBT). Quotes on the prices of S&P 500 futures contracts for 8 January 1992 are provided in Panel C of Table 14-2. The heading of the table indicates that the S&P 500 index futures contracts trade over the CME. To find the value of an index contract, price must be multiplied by some dollar amount. In the case of the S&P 500 contract, the heading also indicates that the price should be multiplied by $500 to determine the contract price. Therefore, the settlement price for the March contract of 419.20 translates to a dollar value of $209,600. Also a change of 1.00 in the contract price obviously implies a change of $500 in the value of one contract. One difference between the quotes for the S&P 500 contract and those previously discussed is that the lifetime high and low prices are given for each contract in the columns closest to open interest.

A special characteristic of stock index futures is that the underlying asset is never delivered to close out the obligation. Because the index itself is not an asset, delivery could only be arranged with the portfolio of assets used to construct the index. In the case of the S&P 500 index, this would involve 500 stocks. Actual delivery of this portfolio would be impractical and would reduce the liquidity of the contract. Instead of delivery "in kind," index futures impose cash settlement at the delivery date. That is, all positions are closed out at maturity and a final cash settlement is made based on the value of the index at that date.

Organization of Futures Trading

The futures exchanges utilize a trading process called an "open outcry auction," which processes orders to buy and sell futures contracts through brokers. Brokers contact their agent, known as a *"pit broker,"* on the floor of the exchange. The pit broker verbally arranges the trade with another pit broker; thus the term "open outcry." (Actually, because of the noise from a large number of pit brokers simultaneously screaming orders at each other, a system of hand signals has evolved for order communication.)

The distinguishing feature of the open outcry system is that any offer to buy or sell a futures contract must be made to all of the traders in the pit where that contract is traded. This is very different from the system of specialists that prevails on the NYSE, where all trading in a particular security takes place through a specialist in that stock. The specialist holds an inventory in order to be able to buy and sell with anyone, but sellers and buyers can execute trades only through that specialist. On the futures exchange, anyone in the pit can bid on any contract. Once a verbal agreement has been made between two individuals in the pit, they report the trade to the clearinghouse, and the transaction is then between the clearinghouse and the buyer or seller of the contract.

As trading in financial futures has increased, considerable pressure has developed to change the open outcry system of trading. One complaint is simply that the existing system of verbal agreements and hand signals followed by written records of orders is too slow and inefficient. As a result, the CBT and the CME are considering installing electronic order routing and execution systems. Another difficulty with the existing system is that pit brokers are allowed to trade simultaneously for their customers' and their own accounts. Critics contend that this creates an inherent conflict of interest. In the current system, it is difficult if not impossible to spot many potential types of abuse, since the exchanges have no electronic record of transactions. It is difficult to determine to what extent the open outcry process actually requires pit brokers to offer trades to all those in the pit. It is alleged that pit brokers often arrange trades with just a few others in the pit without seeking widespread bidding on the transaction.

Another problem is that futures exchanges do not currently allow block trading of futures contracts. Block trading involves trades of large numbers, or blocks of contracts. The desire for it is directly related to the growth of trading in stock index futures. With the growth in trading has come increased participation in the futures market by Wall Street firms that are used to trading other types of securities, particularly equities, where block trading is now commonplace.

Comparison of Forward and Futures Contracts

As with forwards, futures contracts involve two counterparties: the buyer, or long side of the contract, and the seller, or short side of the contract. The buyer agrees to buy a certain amount of the commodity on the settlement date, at the settlement price, *F.* The seller agrees to sell the same amount of commodity on the same date at *F.*

As we noted before, one motivation for the recent development and growth of futures markets is the variety of contracting problems associated with negotiating forward contracts, particularly as smaller, relatively less active participants in futures or forward markets are concerned. Several important characteristics of futures markets, outlined in Figure 14-2, are important in mitigating these problems. The most important difference between forward and futures markets is the existence of an exchange for trading futures contracts. The futures exchange enables anonymous traders to buy and sell futures contracts without specific knowledge of who takes the other side of a particular contract. The exchange also centralizes trading in particular futures contracts, improving the chances that contract counterparties can be matched up in a reasonably short time. In addition, the exchange provides a desirable level of liquidity to the market, which enables futures counterparties to unwind their obligations more efficiently than when using forward contracts.

Standardized Contracts

Several aspects of futures contracts and futures trading contribute to the successful operation of an exchange. The first is the standardization of contracts. In order for trades to occur over an organized exchange there must be regular arrival of matching orders to buy and sell. In other words, there have to be compatible buyers and sellers for commodity, size, and settlement date. Exchange-traded futures ensure that there will be reasonable arrival of compatible orders to buy and sell futures contracts by restricting the dimensions of the contracts that are traded to a relatively few specifications. Settlement dates are generally restricted to fall in the months of March, June, September, and December. There are other contracts that employ a more frequent settlement rotation; the one-month LIBOR contracts use a monthly rotation, that is, January, February, March, April, and so on. The rotation interval determines not only how often contracts are settled, but also how frequently new ones are offered. Once the nearby contract (the one closest to delivery) ceases to trade, another contract with the most distant settlement month is introduced and trading begins in that contract. And the size of the contract, or amount to be delivered, is standardized. In general, the objective of contract standardization is to *force* counterparties to agree on compatible terms. This promotes higher order volume in

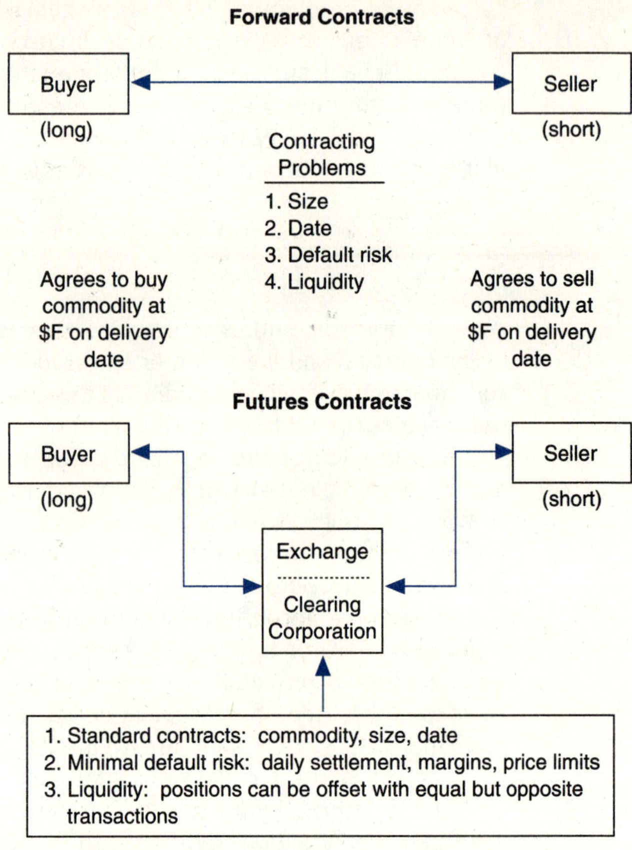

Figure 14-2
Comparison of forward and futures contracts.

a smaller number of contract types. Without standardized contracts, orders would seldom match up, and the exchange would provide little advantage or economy over a less centralized trading system.

It is for the same reason that contracts are restricted to trade in a relatively few differentiated commodities. Contracts that are too similar in the commodity delivered fragment market demand and make centralized trading less efficient. For example, the IMM does not provide a contract in 180-day T bills. The reason is that the 90-day T-bill contract is sufficient to satisfy most demand for hedging short-term interest rate risk. While some demand may exist for such contracts, it will likely be small and may serve only to draw business away from the 90-day T bills. In determining what new contracts to offer, the exchange would be more interested in identifying new risks that customers may want to hedge that are not effectively provided for by existing contracts.

Control of Default Risk

Another important feature of futures markets is the operation of a clearing corporation. On most exchanges, the clearing corporation is owned by the exchange itself or its members. Its primary function is to act as the opposite counterparty to all contracts on the exchange. The clearing corporation is interposed between the buyer and seller of every contract, so that neither has an obligation to the other. All obligations are between the respective counterparties and the clearing corporation. This arrangement is important for two reasons. First, it removes any concern on the part of individual traders to determine the default potential of the other side of the contract. Orders to buy and sell from anonymous counterparties are matched through the exchange process where, in effect, the clearing corporation underwrites the default risk of every contract. Second, it enables counterparties to more easily unwind, or "liquidate," open positions by establishing equal but opposite positions in the same contract. If a counterparty *bought* 5 December Deutschemark contracts in June, he or she could unwind the position anytime before December by *selling* 5 December Deutschemark contracts. The clearing corporation would recognize that the counterparty had the obligation to buy and sell the same number of Deutschemarks on the December settlement date, and would cancel out both positions.

By interposing itself in the settlement process, the clearing corporation assumes the risk of default associated with all open positions. In order for the clearing corporation to manage its exposure to default risk of individual counterparties successfully, a number of requirements are imposed on individual counterparties when they engage in futures contracts over the exchange. The first is to establish an account and a margin deposit. The account is usually established with a broker who initiates the counterparty's order on the exchange. Gains and losses realized on the futures position over time are recognized with increases and decreases to the account balance. A margin deposit is merely a deposit into the account that acts as security against potential defaults. If a counterparty defaults on a futures obligation, the account balance is used to offset accumulated losses and insulate the clearing corporation against loss.

Another requirement imposed to limit default risk is daily settlement, which requires individual accounts be *"marked to market."* This means daily changes in the value of the account, which reflect changes in the market price of the underlying futures contracts, are recognized each day. The procedure of daily settlement is demonstrated by an example presented in Table 14-3 that focuses on the purchase of one T-bill futures contract (traded over the IMM of the CME). On May 12 the position is established at a settlement price of 93.43. The settlement price is the price to which contracts are marked from day to day. Most exchanges have what is called a settlement committee, whose job it is to set settlement prices at the end of each trading day. In most cases this price is the closing price that occurs over the exchange, though for contracts that are not traded frequently, the settlement price may be set by the exchange at a level intended to reflect "market value." An initial margin deposit of $2000 is required to establish the position. After one day, the settlement price on T-bill futures has increased to 93.93. This represents an increase in the value of the account of $1250. This is put into the account so that by the end of the day on May 13, the balance in the account is $3250. Similar changes in account value are recognized through May 19, at which time the account balance would be $5375, assuming no withdrawals are made by the accountholder in the meantime.

In each contract, the exchange specifies an initial margin deposit and a maintenance margin. The initial margin is the amount, either in cash or Treasury securities, that must be deposited in the account to open a position in one contract. In the case

Table 14-3

Daily Settlement Procedure (Marking to Market)

On May 12, a T-bill futures contract is purchased over the IMM at the settlement price of 93.43. The table documents the changes in the value of that position on a mark-to-market, or daily settlement, basis.

May	Settlement Price	Implied $ Price/Contract	Adjustment to Acct. Balance
12	93.43	$983,575[a]	–
13	93.93	$984,825	+ $1,250
14	94.03	$985,075	+ $250
15	94.26	$985,650	+ $575
16	94.27	$985,675	+ $25
17	94.68	$986,700	+ $1,025
18	94.28	$985,700	–$1,000
19	94.78	$986,950	+ $1,250
			+ $3,375

[a]The May 12th price of 93.43 reflects the annualized rate of discount of a 90-day T bill: 100 – 93.43 = 6.57% annualized discount from face value; (0.0657)(90/360) = 0.016425 (1.6425%) actual discount; ($1,000,000) × (1 – 0.016425) = $983,575.

Note: A change of .01 in the price = (0.0001)(90/360)($1,000,000) = $25; Or, each basis point change is the equivalent of a $25 change in the value of one T-bill futures contract.

of T-bill futures, the initial margin is $2000. If losses occur to the account—say, over several days—the account balance is reduced on a daily basis as those losses occur. When the balance reaches the maintenance margin, which is some level below the initial margin requirement, the account holder receives a *"margin call."* In general in futures markets, the account holder meets a margin call by making an additional deposit, called *"variation margin,"* in the account to bring the balance back to the initial margin level. If the account holder does not meet the margin call, the account is closed out by executing an offsetting transaction and the remaining balance is returned to the account holder.

The combination of daily settlement and margin requirements serve to protect the clearing corporation from default on a given contract. To see this more clearly, return to Table 14-3 and imagine that the initial position was a short position rather than a long one. On May 12 the account holder sold one contract at 93.43. For every price change from May 12 to May 19 the dollar adjustment to the account is the same but with the opposite sign. Therefore, at the end of the day on May 13 the account would be reduced to $750. The maintenance margin for T-bill futures is $1500, so a margin call would occur after the first day. The account holder would have to deposit $1250 into the account to hold it open for another day's trading. Notice how this forces the account holder to recognize losses on a daily basis. For the prices given in Table 14-3, the short position would have to meet margin calls on each day where the account balance fell below $1500—May 13, May 15, and May 17. If daily adjustment were not made to the account, by May 19 the account would be –$1375. In effect, this settlement system is designed to avoid negative balances.

One other feature of futures markets enables the exchange to manage its default risk exposure successfully: the imposition of daily price limits. In our previous example, if the entire price change from 93.43 to 94.78 were to occur in one trading day, then the daily adjustment procedure would fail to protect the clearing corporation from a default on the account. The one-day loss of $3375 would exceed the available margin deposit and result in a negative balance. For T bills the maximum price change allowed during one trading day is 0.60, or 60 basis points. If trading were to cause a 60-point move during a particular day, trading would be stopped by the exchange to prevent a larger price change. Notice that a 60-point move would change the value of one contract by $1500. Because the maintenance margin is also $1500, this ensures that for any given day, there is enough money in each account so that the balance cannot become negative.

Liquidity

Another problem resolved by the futures market that can arise when using forward contracts is that of liquidating, or unwinding, obligations. As we discussed earlier, some difficulty or cost can be associated with liquidation of a forward contract. In futures markets, however, the existence of a clearing corporation and the facility of trading over the exchange conveys substantially more liquidity to the market. For example, suppose that Counterparty A put in an order through her broker to buy 2 March T-bill futures contracts over the IMM on 8 January. The order was executed as another order to sell 2 March T-bill contracts arrived on the trading floor on behalf of another trader, Counterparty B. At the end of the day on 8 January, Counterparties A and B have equal but opposite obligations to the clearing corporation of the exchange. That is, A has an obligation to buy $2 million in T bills in March and B has an obligation to sell $2 million in T bills in March.

Suppose that on January 10, Counterparty A decides to unwind her position. Does Counterparty B have to be convinced to do the same? No. Counterparty A merely initiates another order to *sell* 2 March contracts on 10 January. Sometime during that day, another order arrives at the exchange to buy 2 March contracts, say from Counterparty C. The orders match up and the transaction is completed. At the end of the day on January 10, Counterparty C has an obligation to the clearing corporation to buy $2 million in T bills in March. Counterparty B has done nothing and still has his original obligation to sell $2 million in T bills in March. Counterparty A, however, has obligations to *both buy and sell* $2 million in T bills in March to the clearing corporation. Moreover, under daily settlement procedures, both of these obligations will be at the same settlement price by the end of the day on January 10. Therefore, A's obligations to the clearing corporation are a wash, and once settlement takes place they may be canceled out. In effect, when Counterparty A executed the offsetting transaction to unwind her position, Counterparty C replaced Counterparty A's position in balancing out the total obligations against the clearing corporation.

The existence of an exchange makes it quicker and easier to execute the offsetting transactions necessary to unwind a given position. The clearing corporation facilitates the process, making it unnecessary to break contracts between counterparties, because all obligations are between respective counterparties and the clearing corporation.

Determinants of Futures Prices

In this section we explain the relationship between spot (cash) and futures markets. There are two important ways in which futures and spot prices for a particular asset should be linked to each other. First, the futures price should be related to the spot price expected by the market on the settlement date. This does not mean that the futures price *must be equal* to the expected spot price. But if the futures price was sufficiently different from the spot price expected on the settlement date, speculation in the futures market should take place that would drive the two prices closer together. The following discussion explains the market forces that not only contribute to, but also moderate, any difference between the futures and the expected spot price.

From a second perspective, the futures price should also be related to the *current* spot price. This view holds that the difference between the current spot and futures prices should reflect the cost of holding, or carrying, the deliverable asset until the settlement date. The forces of market arbitrage ensures that futures and spot prices do not diverge by more than the "cost of carry." In the discussion that follows, we further explain the ways in which futures, spot prices, and expected spot prices are linked together. In equilibrium, a simultaneous balance exists among the futures price, the spot price, and the expected spot price.

An overview of the equilibrium is presented in Figure 14-3. Consider an asset that at the present, or time 0, trades over the spot market at a price of P_0. Also at time 0, a futures contract, with settlement at time K, trades at the settlement price, $F_0(K)$. Time K

Figure 14-3

Futures prices and cash prices.

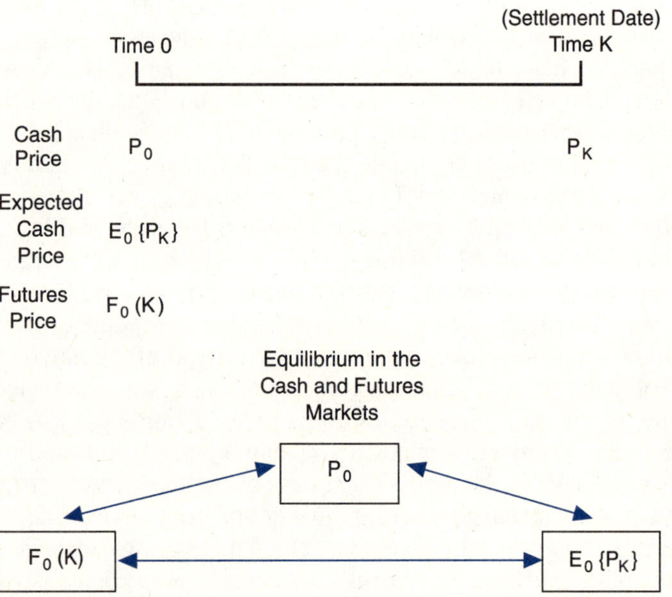

indicates the date at which K periods of time will have passed from time 0. When time K is reached, the spot price observed then is defined as P_K. Also at time 0, the market expects the spot price at time K to be $E_0(P_K)$, where $E_0(.)$ means expected value. In other words, $E_0(P_K)$ represents the market's current forecast of the future spot price, P_K. In the discussion that follows, we identify three logical pairwise relationships that should hold between P_0, $F_0(K)$, and $E_0(P_K)$ for any equilibrium system of spot and futures prices. As is shown in Figure 14-3, it is convenient to visualize a triangular, or simultaneous, balance among the three variables. None of the three can change in isolation from the other two. For example, if something were to cause a change in $E_0(P_K)$, changes in $F_0(K)$ and P_0 must occur that would maintain three-way equilibrium.

In the discussion that follows we are not as directly concerned with the relationship between P_0 and $E_0(P_K)$ as we are with the other two sides of the triangle. These are the relationships that are important in understanding *how* P_0 and $E_0(P_K)$ determine the futures price.

Spot Prices and Futures Prices: The Cost of Carry

The *cost of carry* condition defines the relationship that should hold between spot and futures prices in a particular asset or instrument. Basically, the condition says that the difference between these two prices is determined by the "cost of carrying" the asset. If the condition does not hold, arbitrage will result that will restore it. The cost of carry condition can be defined by the following equation:

$$F_0(K) = P_0[\,1 + {}_0r_K]^K \tag{14.1}$$

This condition says that the futures price of an asset should reflect the spot price of the asset plus the carrying cost to finance the purchase of the asset and hold, or store, it until the settlement date, K periods away. Here, ${}_0r_K$ is the zero-coupon interest rate over the period from time 0 to time K, or the K-period interest rate. The right-hand side of equation 14.1 is the debt service due at time K to finance the time 0 purchase of the asset at price, P_0.

There is one special case where condition 14.1 can be simplified. That is, when the settlement date is reached, $F_0(K)$ must equal P_0. You can see this in equation 14.1, as, at the settlement date K becomes 0. Intuitively, the futures and spot transactions become identical on the settlement date. If the prices were different on that date there would be an immediate arbitrage response. The property of the futures and spot prices moving toward each other as the settlement date approaches is referred to as the "property of convergence." Arbitrage (see below) ensures that futures and spot prices converge as settlement nears.

The cost of carry condition has slightly more complicated implications for financial instruments than for commodities. The difficulty arises because most financial contracts have a finite life or maturity. That is, suppose you compare the price of T-bill futures to the current spot price of 90-day T bills. Obviously, today's 90-day T bills cannot be delivered against any T-bill futures contract. When someone buys silver today, it can be stored and delivered against silver futures contracts months later. However, when someone buys a 90-day T bill, it becomes an 89-day T bill the next day. What comparisons should be made between the spot and futures markets regarding the cost of carry condition? The correct comparison to make is not between the current price of the 90-day T bills implied by the term structure at some future date and the T bill futures with the same settlement date.

• *So You Want to Arbitrage Futures Markets?* •

The process of arbitrage drives the prices of futures and spot contracts toward the equilibrium described in equation 14.1. This process is often mystifying to newcomers to finance, and we want to provide some examples that will make the process of arbitrage fairly clear. Let's begin with the case where we have arrived at the settlement date of a futures contract. Now suppose, in contradiction of equation 14.1, that $F_0(K) < P_0$. It would now be possible to buy the future and take immediate delivery of the commodity at a price of $F_0(K)$ and then to immediately resell the commodity over the spot market at P_0. The profit of $P_0 - F_0(K)$ would be quickly dissipated as such transactions would bid up the futures price and bid down the spot price.

Similar arguments show why equation 14.1 should hold in equilibrium at all points in time before the settlement date. Consider first, the following *disequilibrium* condition:

$$F_0(K) > P_0[1 + {}_0r_K]^K$$

If this condition exists, there is incentive for arbitrage in which the futures contract is sold and the asset is purchased (and the purchase is financed) at time 0. This strategy is implemented through the transactions at time 0 and time K that are shown in Panel A of Table 14-4.

The sequence of transactions at time 0 result in no net cash flows. At time *K*, the amount $F_0(K) - P_0[1 + {}_0r_K]^K$ represents pure arbitrage profit. In effect, when $F_0(K) > P_0[1 + {}_0r_K]^K$, the asset is trading at a premium in the futures market relative to the spot market. One captures that premium by selling the asset forward at the higher (futures) price. One economically covers the delivery obligation at time *K* via the spot market by buying the asset at time 0, holding it until time *K*, and delivering it against the contract at time *K*. As futures contracts are sold and the commodity is purchased over the spot market, pressure will result on spot and futures prices that eventually restores the condition in equation 14.1. As futures contracts are sold, the futures price is bid down. And as the asset is purchased, the spot price is bid up. This continues until the arbitrage profit is eliminated, which implies that condition 14.1 is restored.

Now consider the other possibility. When $F_0(K) < P_0 [1 + {}_0r_K]^K$, a similar arbitrage opportunity arises. In this case the asset is trading at a premium in the *spot* market. To capture the premium one should short-sell the asset on the spot market and cover the position at time *K* by buying the asset via the futures contract. A short sale is accomplished by borrowing the asset, usually through a broker, and selling it over the spot market. This leaves a debt that must eventually be repaid. The short obligation is usually covered by purchasing the asset over the spot and delivering it to the lender's account. The arbitrage can be accomplished by following the sequence of steps laid out in Panel B of Table 14-4. Again, these transactions will precipitate changes in spot and futures prices. As buying pressure occurs, futures prices are bid up, and as the asset is sold, the spot price falls. Arbitrage continues until condition 14.1 is again restored and there is no future arbitrage profit available.

Now let's consider a numerical example of the arbitrage process. Suppose the zero-coupon yield curve presently shows the two-year yield to be 12 percent and three-year yield to be 10 percent. Suppose also that a futures contract is traded that delivers a $100 (face value) zero-coupon bond with one year to maturity. The delivery date on the contract is two years from now and the price of the futures contract is $93.45.

The one-year yield implied by the zero-coupon yield curve for the period starting two years from now is computed in the left-hand column of Panel C of Table 14-4. In the right-hand column, the implied futures yield for a contract settled in two years is also computed. The implied futures yield is the yield to maturity on the deliverable instrument at the current futures settlement price. In essence, if at the settlement date a one-year zero was purchased at $93.45 and held to maturity, the yield to maturity would be 7 percent.

Notice that the forward yield implied by the term structure and the futures yield are not the same. The forward price of the one-year zeros implied by the yield curve is $94.25 and that given by the futures market is $93.45: an 80-cent difference. The basic principle of the cost of carry condition is that the cost of delivering an asset at the settlement date should be the same whether through the futures market or through the spot market. In this case, the price of buying a one-year zero-coupon bond via a futures contract is less than that implied in the spot market. To exploit this opportunity, a strategy can be established that buys the zero-coupon bond in the futures market and simultaneously sells the bond at the better price in the cash market. The strategy is outlined in Panel D of Table 14-4.

Notice that the strategy involves no net outlay of cash at the present. A three-year zero-coupon bond is sold at $75.13 and the proceeds are invested for two years at 12 percent. At the same time, one futures contract (settled in two years) is purchased at a settlement price of $93.45.

In two years, the investment matures, providing $94.25. The futures contract is settled by purchasing a one-year zero-coupon bond at the contract price of $93.45. Thus the net cash flow after two years is $0.80. After three years, the zero-coupon bond purchased one year earlier matures, paying $100, and the three-year debt matures, costing $100. Thus, no net cash flows occur after three years.

The overall result is that $0.80 is received in two years' time with no capital invested. This represents a pure arbitrage profit that can be exploited until prices respond. As more futures are purchased, the price of futures increases, causing the futures yield to decrease from 7 percent. At the same time, two things will happen in the spot market that will cause the implied forward rate to increase from 6.106 percent: (1) selling pressure on three-year bonds will drive their prices down, and (2) buying pressure on two-year bonds will drive their prices up. Naturally, as forward and futures rates approach each other, the arbitrage profit will vanish and the futures and spot prices will be in equilibrium.

Table 14-4

Panel A

Time 0	*Time K*
1. Sell future at $F_0(K)$ 2. Borrow P_0 at ${}_0r_K$ for K days 3. Buy asset at P_0	1. Deliver asset against future for $F_0(K)$ 2. Repay loan amount $P_0(1+{}_0r_K)^K$
(no net $ cash flows)	$F_0(K)-P_0(1+{}_0r_K)^K$

Table 14-4 (continued)

Panel B

Day 0	*Day K*
1. Buy future at $F_0(K)$ 2. Sell asset (short) at P_0 3. Lend P_0 at ${}_0r_K$ for K days	1. Take delivery of asset for $F_0(K)$ 2. Cover (repay) short position 3. Receive $P_0(1+{}_0r_K)^K$ from loan
(no net cash flows)	$P_0(1+{}_0r_K)^K - F_0(K)$

Panel C

Spot Market	*Futures Market*
${}_0r_2 = 12\%$ ${}_0r_3 = 10\%$ ${}_2f_3 = \frac{(1+{}_0r_3)^3}{(1+{}_0r_2)^2} - 1$ ${}_2f_3 = .06106$	$F_0(2) = \$93.45$ ${}_2z_3 = \frac{\$100}{\$93.45}$ ${}_2z_3 = .07000$

Panel D

Now	*Two Years*	*Three Years*
Borrow \$75.13 at 10% for three years		Pay off debt obligation \$100
Lend \$75.13 at 12% for two years	Receive loan payment \$94.24	
Buy one futures contract at \$93.45 (settled in two years)	Buy one year security at futures price \$93.45	Receive maturity of security \$100
Net cash flow = 0	Net cash flow = \$0.80	Net cash flow = 0

Futures Prices and Expected Spot Prices[1]

A common perception among observers of futures markets is that futures prices represent market-based forecasts of the future prices of the underlying assets. In other words, the price of a futures contract with a settlement at time *K* is equal to the market's expectation of the spot price at time *K*. Under such circumstances, futures prices would be actuarially fair in the sense that, at the time of the contract there is equal probability that the spot price will be above or below the contract price on the settlement date. While this interpretation certainly has intuitive appeal, it is probably almost never exactly correct. The reason is that many parties to futures contracts

[1]The analysis in this section follows an exposition by Kenneth Garbade. *Securities Markets.* New York: McGraw-Hill, 1982, pp. 321–353.

would not require the price of the contract to be "fair" in the sense just described. Many of those who buy or sell futures contracts do so to avoid risk, or to hedge. The need to hedge often arises because of a need to buy or sell a commodity at some date in the future. Futures contracts written on that commodity, settled at that date, would lock up a future price at the settlement date. Being averse to risk, such hedgers are willing to accept a certain price (i.e., the futures contract price) that is lower or higher than the expected spot price (at time K) to avoid the risk associated with a spot transaction.

Of course hedgers on each side of the contract have similar but opposite incentives to avoid risk. One counterparty may need to buy the commodity at some date in the future. The other counterparty may need to sell the commodity on the same date. Thus, they have an opposite exposure to the same risk: fluctuations in the spot price of the commodity. To avoid risk, a buyer agrees to a price higher than the expected spot price, whereas a risk-averse seller agrees to a price lower than the expected spot price. At the margin, the question of whether the contract price ends up above or below the expected spot price depends on which counterparty is *most* risk averse, or which has the greatest need to hedge.

Let us look at this in just a little more detail. Suppose the futures market consisted of only two groups: short hedgers and long hedgers. Short hedgers are the ones with a "seller's risk," the need to sell the commodity in the future. Long hedgers are those with a "buyer's risk," who need to buy the commodity at some future date. The demand for long positions by long hedgers can be represented by a downwardly sloping demand curve, as shown in panel A of Figure 14-4. In this illustration the futures price with settlement time K, $F(K)$, and the spot price expected at time K, $E(P_K)$, are shown on the vertical axis. The expected spot price is shown as a horizontal line. The horizontal axis measures demand as the number of long positions in futures contracts.

Notice that as the spread between $F(K)$ and $E(P_K)$ narrows, the number of contracts demanded by long hedgers increases. This is because the "cost" of hedging is the price concession, $F(K) - E(P_K)$, the *expected* loss the long hedger accepts to avoid uncertainty and lock up the futures price. As this "cost" decreases, more hedgers will emerge, in order of decreasing degree of risk aversion, at the margin to hedge their risk at the prevailing futures price. When the cost is nil, all long hedgers should have hedged. This is the point where the demand curve becomes vertical.

The supply of long positions is actually the demand for short positions. Whenever a counterparty takes a short position in a futures contract, he in effect *sells* a long position. As a result, it is convenient to recognize the demand for short positions as an upward sloping supply curve for long positions, realizing all the while that this represents the demand for futures contracts from short hedgers. Notice in panel B of Figure 14-4 that the cost of hedging to the short hedger is now $E(P_K) - F(K)$. As the spread between $E(P_K)$ and $F(K)$ narrows, the cost of hedging decreases and more hedgers are drawn into the market. Again, when the cost of hedging is zero, or $E(P_K) = F(K)$, all short hedgers have hedged their risk and the supply curve for long positions turns vertical.

Figure 14-4
Demand and supply of futures contract.

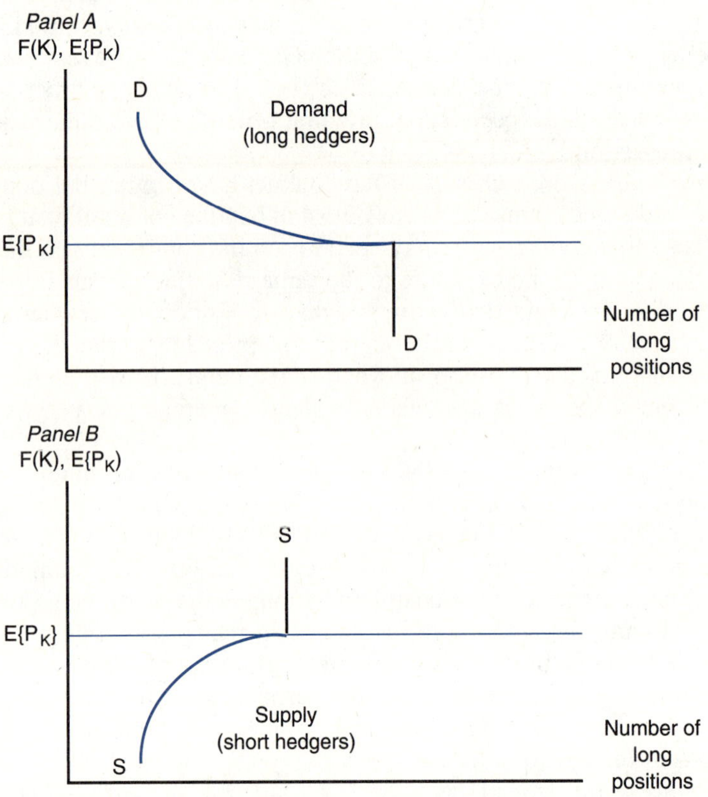

The interaction of the supply and demand for long positions can produce a futures price that is equal to, greater than, or less than the expected spot price. The outcome depends on the predominance (if any) of short or long hedgers. Suppose that, for some reason, the market was dominated by long hedgers. That is, there is more exposure to buyer's risk than to seller's risk overall, and as a result, more demand for long positions than short positions. The implications of such conditions are illustrated in Panel A of Figure 14-5. The resulting equilibrium futures price is higher than the expected spot price. Only a portion of the demand for long positions is satisfied in equilibrium. At $F(K)$, Q contracts are made, representing the amount of open interest. The remaining demand is unmet. In effect, the unmet demand represents long hedgers who are unwilling to pay the expected premium of $F(K) - E(P_K)$, instead choosing to remain unhedged. Implicitly, these hedgers are the ones who are the least risk averse and more willing to leave their risk exposure unhedged.

The result that $F(K) > E(P_K)$ has another implication for the behavior of futures and spot prices. As time passes and the maturity date of the contract approaches, the futures price approaches the spot price from above. This is called the "theory of contango," which predicts that, because of the dominance of long hedgers in the market, the futures price will *decrease* toward the spot price over time. The opposite case is presented in Panel B of Figure 14-5. In this case, there exists an excess supply for long positions (excess demand for short positions) from short hedgers. This results in a kind of "discount" being received by long hedgers with the expected value of $E(P_K) - F(K)$ on the settlement date. Again, Q contracts are created in equilibrium, and the prevailing futures price lies below the expected spot price, or $F(K) < E(P_K)$. Thus, the predominance of short hedgers would cause the futures price to *increase* toward the cash price over time. This is called the "theory of normal backwardation."

One final situation should be considered. It is possible that the supply and demand for long positions could be equal at $F(K) = E(P_K)$. If this were the case, the futures price *would* represent a forecast of the future spot price. Notice that each of the three

Figure 14-5

Interaction of supply and demand of future contracts.

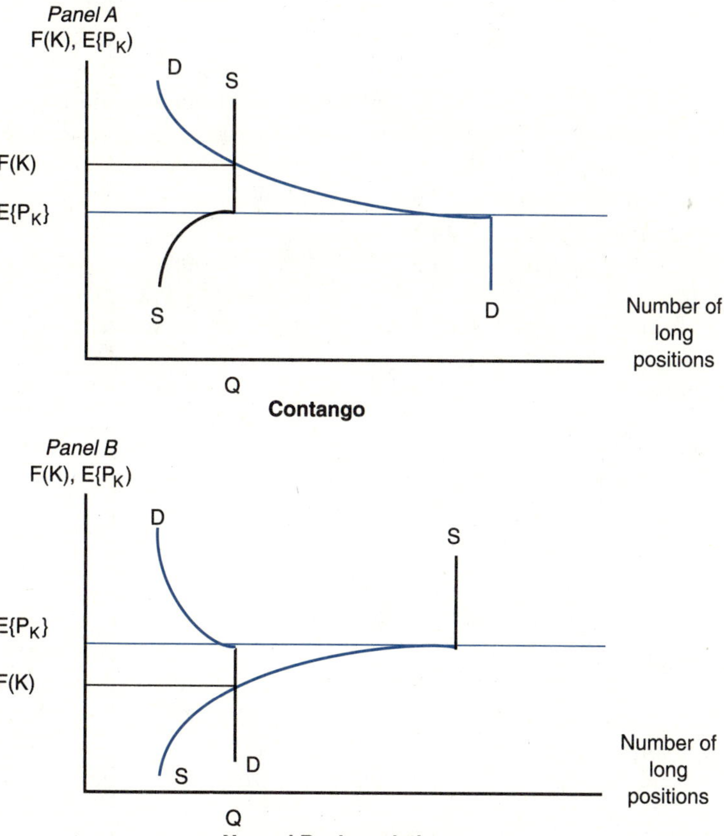

theories are essentially statements about the relative dominance and persistence of short versus long hedgers in the market. None is correct or incorrect, as it is possible that over time that this balance might change. It is possible to make some inference about which influence is at work from the observed behavior of prices over time.

SUMMARY

This chapter provided an overview of the markets for financial forward and futures contracts. In many ways, these contracts are similar. In fact, it is useful to think of the futures contract as a specialized forward agreement. At the same time, however, forwards and futures have important differences that are crucial to understanding their practical advantages and limitations as instruments to hedge or speculate in financial markets. Forward and futures contracts are traded on a variety of financial commodities—in fact, in many of the same commodities. Most important, futures contracts differ from their forward counterparts by being traded over an organized exchange. The feature of an organized exchange requires that futures contracts have highly standardized dimensions. At the same time, the exchange allows for the interaction of anonymous buyers and sellers and provides substantial liquidity to the futures market as compared to the market for forward contracts.

In general, the prices of forward and futures contracts should be determined by the same system of conditions. We showed how futures prices are influenced by the spot price of the underlying commodity and by the expected future spot price on the settlement date of the contract. The cost of carry condition defines a relationship between spot and futures prices that should be enforced by arbitrage. The interaction of hedgers and speculators determines the relationship between the expected future spot price and the current futures price. The existence of a discount or premium in the futures price was shown to be determined by the relative dominance of short (versus long) hedgers in the futures market. The size of the premium or discount was shown to be determined at the margin by the activity of speculators.

QUESTIONS

1. One of the most important differences between futures markets and forward markets pertains to the liquidity of the contracts. Explain the major difficulties that may be encountered when attempting to "liquidate" a forward contract.
2. A speculator in U.S. T-bill futures (IMM) sold 15 June contracts on 1 October. On 3 October the speculator bought 20 June contracts. Then on 5 October the speculator sold 5 June contracts. If the market price of the June contract from 1 October through 5 October is as given below, what will be the speculator's gain or loss over the five-day period?

Date	Price
Oct. 1	92.35
Oct. 2	92.58
Oct. 3	92.43
Oct. 4	92.16
Oct. 5	92.01

3. Why are futures contracts standardized for the commodity traded, the amount of the commodity traded, and the settlement date of the trade?
4. How are margin requirements, price limits, and the process of daily settlement important to making trading in futures contracts viable?
5. A commodity currently sells in the spot market at $100 per unit. A futures contract on the same commodity, with settlement date in six months, trades at $105 per unit. Each contract is for 100 units of the commodity. If the current borrowing and lending rate is 12 percent per year (compounded semiannually), are the futures and spot markets in equilibrium? (If not, describe the arbitrage process that will restore equilibrium.)
6. Suppose the price of 52-week U.S. T bills is 90.25. In addition, the price of T bills with 270 days remaining to maturity is 90.45. What should be the equilibrium price of U.S. T-bill futures contracts with nine months remaining to settlement?
7. The spot price of a commodity expected in K days will be greater or less than the price of a futures contract on the commodity deliverable in K days, depending on whether the futures market is dominated by short or long hedgers. Explain how the absolute difference between the expected spot price and the futures price depend on the following variables:
   a. the variance of the spot price;
   b. the risk aversion of speculators in the futures market;
   c. the size of K.
8. Discuss the merits of the following propositions:
   a. The futures price is equal to the market's expectation of the future cash price on the settlement date.
   b. The futures price is an unbiased forecast of the futures cash price on the settlement date.

REFERENCES

Black, Fisher. "The Pricing of Commodity Contracts." *Journal of Financial Economics* 3 (1976), pp. 167–179.

Cox, John C., Jonathan E. Ingersoll, and Stephen A. Ross. "The Relationship Between Forward Prices and Futures Prices." *Journal of Financial Economics* 9 (1981), pp. 321–346.

Garbade, Kenneth. *Securities Markets.* New York: McGraw-Hill, 1982.

Kane, Edward J. "Market Incompleteness and Divergence Between Forward and Futures Interest Rates." *Journal of Finance* 35 (May 1980), pp. 221–234.

Kolb, Robert W. *Understanding Futures Markets.* Glenview, IL: Scott, Foresman, 1985.

Phillips, Susan M. "Regulation of Futures Markets," in Y. Amihud, T. Ho, and R. Schwartz, eds. *Market Making and the Changing Structure of the Securities Industry.* Lexington, MA: Lexington, 1985.

Scarf, Douglas. "The Securities and Commodities Markets: A Case Study in Product Convergence and Regulatory Disparity," in Y. Amihud, T. Ho, and R. Schwartz, eds. *Market Making and the Changing Structure of the Securities Industry.* Lexington, MA: Lexington, 1985.

• Chapter 15

Options

In the 1970s and early 1980s the markets for options and futures—or contingent claims on financial instruments—came of age. Before 1972 there were no such organized markets. Today there is a wide variety of options and futures on stocks, bonds, currencies, commodities, and even on stock indexes. In fact, daily trading volume for stock options on the Chicago Board Options Exchange (CBOE) often exceeds trading volume on all stock exchanges in the country except the New York Stock Exchange (NYSE).

It is no accident that the growth in options and futures occurred during this particular period. One of the forces behind the growth in these financial instruments appears to be the increased riskiness of the underlying assets to which these options and futures apply. In the 1970s inflation increased the level and volatility of market interest rates on most fixed-income obligations. The demise of fixed exchange rates between the dollar and other currencies led to increased exchange rate risk for many participants in the financial markets. The decline in the stock market in the mid-1970s also apparently led to increased desire for mechanisms to hedge the risk of investments in stocks. In addition, increased volatility in many financial markets led to a demand on the part of many market participants for new vehicles by which they could leverage their investments in financial instruments. Both in principle and in practice, futures and options satisfy all of these demands.

Because futures and options have become such an important part of the financial markets in the United States, a basic understanding of how these instruments work has become essential for anyone who intends to participate in the market. It is important to understand these instruments, not simply because it may be profitable to use them but also because they are a critical part of a major transformation of the financial marketplace in the United States. During much of the U.S. postwar era many of the risks involved in financial transactions were shifted to various types of financial intermediaries, particularly the risk of fluctuations in market interest rates, but as the volatility of interest rates has increased and financial institutions have changed, their risk-bearing role has been altered. Options and futures represent new vehicles for redistributing risks so that the risks can be borne more efficiently.

This chapter presents an introduction to how options and options markets work and how risks are priced in these markets. This complements the material on futures in Chapter 14. However, the material presented here is only a very modest introduction to this fascinating but complicated topic. Options and futures are a growth industry in finance. They will be more, rather than less, important in the future.

• *Concepts to Learn in Chapter 15* •

- Definitions and structure of option contracts
- How option markets operate
- How to compute payoffs on positions in option contracts
- How options can be used
- How option prices are determined

How Options Work

Definition of Terms

First of all let's define our terms. A "*contingent claim*" is a financial claim whose price depends on or is contingent on the price of another underlying asset. One example of a contingent claim is a futures contract. As we learned in Chapter 14, a futures contract constitutes a commitment to provide or deliver a specific asset at a prespecified price and time. In principle, if this commitment is to be honored, the asset involved would have to be purchased (or sold) at the market price prevailing when the commitment expires. Thus, a futures contract is a bet about the prevailing market price of the asset in question. A futures contract involves an obligation rather than an option. The obligation in the contract must be honored at its maturity or bought out for an appropriate price before its maturity.

By contrast, an "option" on a financial instrument provides a choice to the holder of the option. The choice depends on whether you have purchased the right to buy the underlying asset, referred to as a "call option," or the right to sell it, referred to as a "*put option.*" The price at which the option may be exercised is called the "*exercise*" or "*strike price.*" Options are limited to a specific time period or maturity. Some options may be exercised only at maturity. These are known as "European options." Other options may be exercised at any time before maturity. These are known as "American options."

The value of a call option, for example, derives from the fact that the holder may be able to exercise the option at a time when the value of the underlying security is greater than the strike or exercise price. For example, suppose you hold a European call option on a bond with an exercise price of $50. If at maturity the value of the underlying asset is greater than $50, then the gross proceeds you will receive from the exercise of the option will be equal to the difference between the value of the underlying asset and $50:

$$\text{Proceeds from exercise} = \text{Value of the asset} - \$50$$

If the value of the asset is $75, you have earned $25. On the other hand, if the value of the underlying asset is less than $50 at maturity of the option, then the option is worthless. As a result, the value of the call option at maturity is equal to the difference between (1) the value of the underlying security and (2) the exercise price or zero, whichever is greater. This is illustrated in Panel A of Figure 15-1. The vertical axis illustrates the value of the call option at maturity; the horizontal axis shows the value of the underlying security at maturity. The line in Figure 15-1 shows what we term "gross payoff." This means the gain taking into account only the price of the underlying asset at maturity and the exercise price of the option. It ignores the price that the holder of the option paid for the option when it was acquired. We introduce that into the story shortly.

Once you understand how a call option works, it is relatively simple to understand a put option. The put represents an option to sell rather than to buy the asset. If the value of the underlying asset is less than the exercise price at maturity, then the pay off on the put option is equal to the difference between the exercise price and the value of the underlying security. Conversely, if the value of the underlying security exceeds the exercise price, then the put option is worthless. For example, if the exercise price of a put option is $50 and the price of the underlying security at maturity is

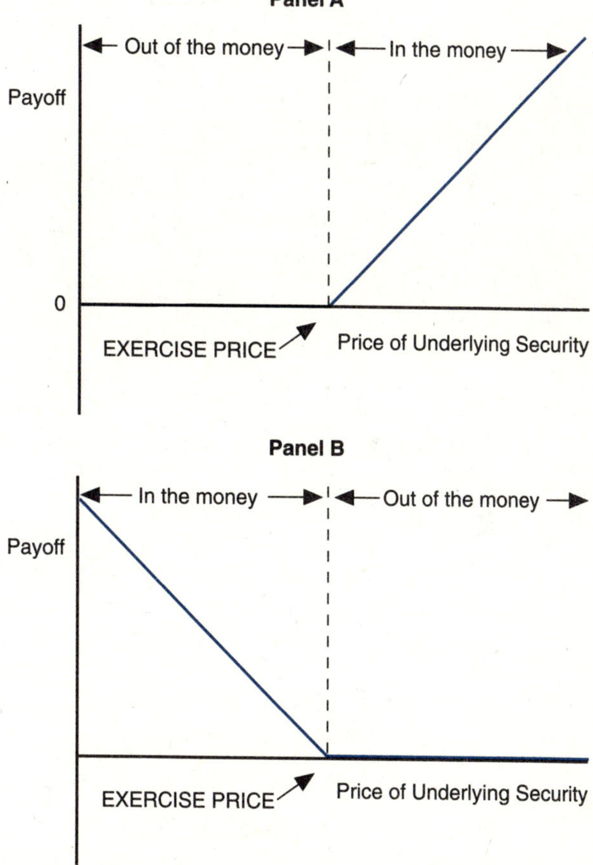

Figure 15-1
Panel A: Payoff on call option.
Panel B: Payoff on put option.

$30, the put option is worth $20 at maturity. This is because the holder of the option has the right to sell the underlying security for $50, yet it can be bought for $30 in the marketplace. The relationship between the value of the put at maturity and the value of the underlying security is illustrated in Panel B of Figure 15-1.

Figure 15-1 illustrates that the proceeds from an option always take the form of the maximum of either zero or, in the case of a put, the difference between the exercise price and the price of the underlying asset. Thus, the proceeds from an option are never negative. This is inherent in the definition of an option, for the holder of the option can always choose not to exercise if the proceeds from so doing would be negative. By contrast, the proceeds from either a long or a short position in a futures contract may well be negative, as the futures contract represents a commitment to deliver a financial instrument at a prearranged price and time. The payoff on long and short futures, respectively, is illustrated in Panels C and D of Figure 15-1.

If an option can be exercised for a positive gross payoff, at or before maturity, then it is said to be "*in the money,*" and if it cannot it is said to be "*out of the money.*" This is illustrated in Panels A and B of Figure 15-1. Notice that the call is

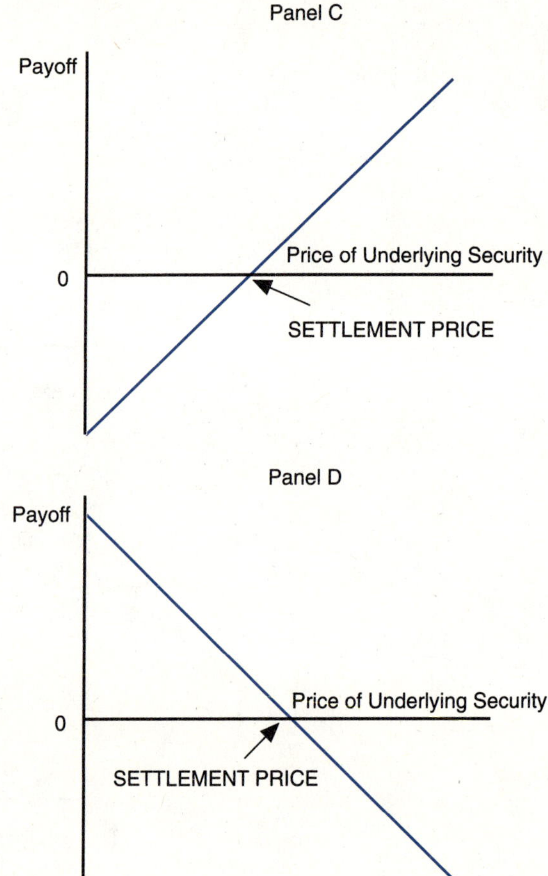

Figure 15-1 (continued)
Panel C: Payoff on long future.
Panel D: Payoff on short future.

in the money if the value of the underlying security is greater than the exercise price of the option, whereas the put is in the money if the price of the underlying security is less than the exercise price.

Long Versus Short Positions in Options

Thus far we have focused solely on the payoff of a person who buys an option. This person is said to be "long" the option. Now we have to look at the payoff of the person on the opposite side of the transaction, or the person who "writes," or is "short" the option. The easiest way to understand what it means to write an option is to note that the combined payoffs received by the purchaser and the writer of an option always net out to zero. That is, the owner's gain is the writer's loss and vice versa. To see this, suppose we return to the call option with an exercise price of $50. If the value of the underlying security at maturity is $75, then the option will be exercised by its owner for a gain of $25. This gain occurs at the expense of the writer of the option whose loss is equal to $25. The payoffs to the writer of the call option are illustrated in Panel A of Figure 15-2. The solid line in the figure shows that as long as the price of the underlying asset is equal to or less than the exercise price of the option, the writer of the call receives a payoff of zero. If the price of the underlying asset at the maturity of the option is greater than the exercise price, then the loss incurred by the writer of the option is equal to the difference between the value of the underlying security and the exercise price.

The same relationship holds between the owner and the writer of a put option. The owner of a put chooses not to exercise if the price of the underlying asset exceeds the exercise price. In this case the payoff to both the owner and the writer of the put is zero. If the market price of the underlying asset is less than the exercise price, then the owner of the put will choose to exercise, and her gain will be exactly equal to the loss of the writer of the put. The gross payoff to the writer of the put is illustrated by the solid line in Panel B of Figure 15-2.

It is apparent from Figure 15-2 that the writer of either a put or a call can never have a positive gross payoff as a result of the exercise of an option. Therefore, no rational investor will ever write an option without being paid to do so. The price for an option will be set so that the writer believes that the net payoff from writing that option represents a fair gamble. The *net* payoff received by the writer of an option is the sum of the price initially paid to the writer for the option plus the gross payoff just described. The nature of the net payoff to the writer of a call and a put are illustrated by the dashed lines in all four panels in Figure 15-2. The dashed lines are derived by adding the initial price, or the initial value of the call or the put, to the payoff illustrated by the solid line in each Panel. Panels C and D in the figure show the gross and net payoff to the holder of a call and a put option. For example, suppose the price paid for the call option were $5. Then the net payoff to the writer of a call with an exercise price of $50 would be $5, as long as the option matured out of the money. If the price of the underlying security at the maturity of the option were, say $60, then the writer's net payoff would be –$5. This loss is illustrated by the dashed line in Panel A of Figure 15-2.

Figure 15-2
Net payoffs on options.

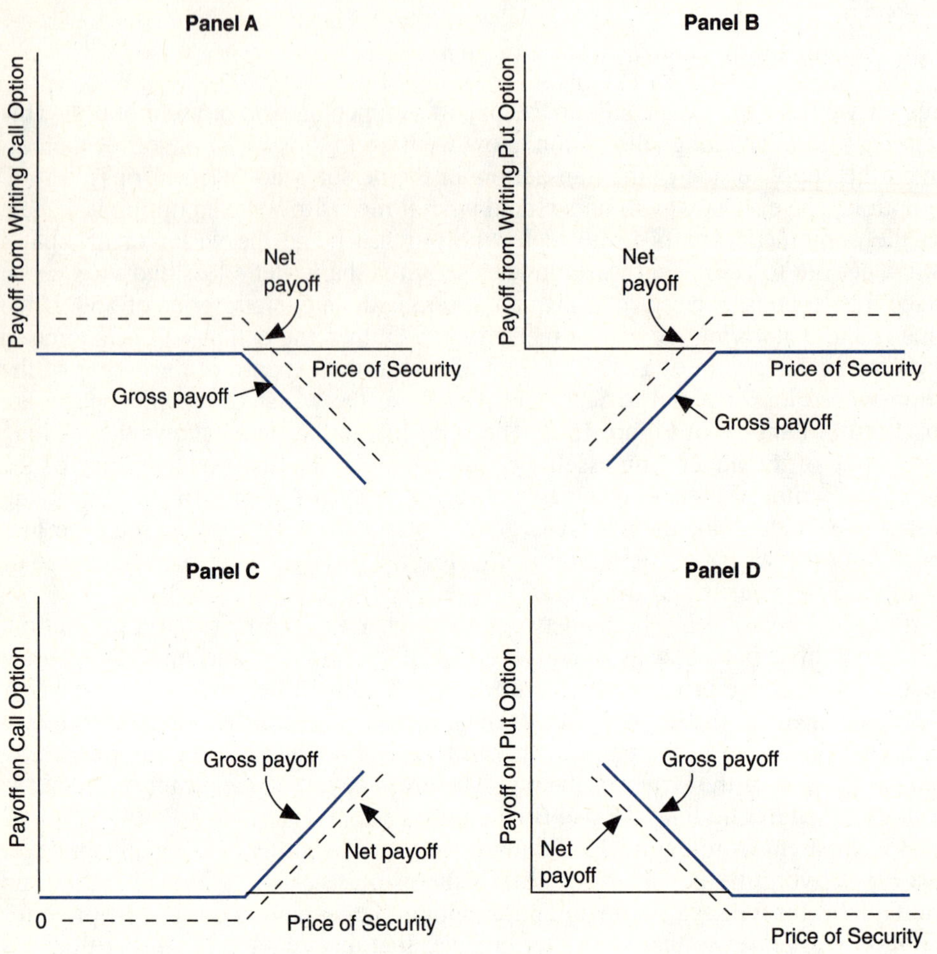

An Example of Payoffs on Options

To understand how options work it is very helpful to work through an example of the gains and losses that might result from changes in the value of the underlying security for each of the four basic possible positions in options contracts. The four positions include buying (long) or writing (short) either a put or a call. We will enumerate these as follows:

Position 1: Buy (long) a call.

Position 2: Write (short) a call.

Position 3: Buy (long) a put.

Position 4: Write (short) a put.

Suppose we are considering an option on Deutschemarks (DM) on the Philadelphia Stock Exchange. Suppose puts and calls are available with an exercise price of $0.62 per Deutschemark. The price of the call is 0.75 cent per Deutschemark and the price of the put is 1.75 cents per Deutschemark. Deutschemark option contracts on the Philadelphia Stock Exchange are written for DM 62,500. Therefore, if you buy a call, for example, you will have to pay the writer of the call $0.0075 times 62,500, or $468.75 when the call is purchased. We want to see what your payoff will be when the price of the underlying security is greater and less than the exercise price of each of the four positions described. Therefore, we consider three possible values for the underlying security at the maturity date of the option: $0.58, $0.62, and $0.64 per Deutschemark. Table 15-1 defines the net payoffs—the gain or the loss when the option is exercised—plus the value paid or received when the option was written, for each of the combinations of positions and prices of the underlying asset at the maturity of the option. Let's start with the case where the price of the underlying asset is $0.62.

Case A: Price = $0.62

In this case neither the put nor the call option can be exercised for a profit. As a result, the purchasers of both the put and the call allow the option to expire at maturity. They are out the initial cost of the option, 0.75 cent for the call and 1.75 cents for the put. This is the price per Deutschemark. Therefore, the price of one contract is 0.75 cent times 62,500, or $468.75. The purchaser's loss is the writer's gain, so the writer of the call experiences a net gain of 0.75 cent and the writer of the put experiences a net gain of 1.75 cents.

Case B: Price = $0.58

In this case the call option cannot be exercised for a profit, so the owner of the call will allow it to expire. The net payoff for the purchaser and the writer of the call is identical to his or her payoff in Case A, where the price at maturity was $0.62. The put option does have value because the exercise price exceeds the current price of Deutschemarks by $0.04 per Deutschemark; this means the put option can be exercised for a gain of $0.04. The net gain to the purchaser of the put is the difference between $0.04 and the price initially paid for the option of 1.75 cents. Thus the net gain is 2.25 cents. Once again, the gain for the purchaser of the put is the same as the loss for the writer of the put, so the writer loses 2.25 cents.

Table 15-1

Options Payoffs at Various DM Prices (All in Cents/DM)

	Price of Underlying Asset at Maturity		
Position	**58¢**	**62¢**	**64¢**
1. Buy call	−.75	−.75	1.25
2. Write call	.75	.75	−1.25
3. Buy put	2.25	−1.75	−1.75
4. Write put	−2.25	1.75	1.75

Note: Each contract is for 62,500 DM.

Case C: Price = $0.64

In this case the put option has no value at maturity, just like the call option in case B. Therefore, the owner of the put allows it to expire and incurs a net loss of 1.75 cents. The writer of the put will have a net gain of 1.75 cents. On the other hand, the call option has a value at maturity of $0.02. Therefore, the purchaser of the call experiences a net gain of $0.02, less the initial cost of the call of 0.75 cent, or 1.25 cents. Once again, the purchaser's gain on the call must be the same as the writer's loss, so the writer's net loss is also 1.25 cents. For DM 62,500, this represents $0.0125 times 62,500, or $781.25.

This example shows how investors in long and short positions in both calls and puts determine their net payoffs. The payoffs here are identical to those illustrated in Figure 15-2. Understanding the numbers and how to use the diagrams shown in Figures 15–1 and 15–2 is extremely important. If you master these ideas, options will become an important element in your knowledge of modern finance.

The Market for Exchange-Traded Options

Like futures contracts, options are traded on a number of U.S. exchanges, including the CBOE, the American Stock Exchange (AMEX), the Philadelphia Stock Exchange (PHLX), the Pacific Stock Exchange (PSE), and the NYSE. It is important to learn how these options markets operate and compete for business. We address this issue next.

Structure of Options Contracts

Let's start by examining how options and futures are described each day in the financial press. Table 15-2 contains examples of option and futures prices. Panel A of Table 15-2 contains quotes from the CBOE on options on various NYSE stocks; Panel B contains quotes on currency options from the PSE as well as options on currency futures; Panel C contains quotes on options on futures on various fixed-income securities and on currencies on a collection of exchanges.

Note that many of the options in Table 15-2 are actually options on futures contracts rather than options directly on the underlying security of the future. For example, there are options on Treasury-bond futures rather than Treasury bonds. The principal reason for this is that there is greater liquidity, and therefore more frequent and reliable price information, on Treasury-bond futures than on the Treasury bonds themselves. Recall that the futures are traded on an organized exchange while the bonds themselves are traded in an over-the-counter secondary market. Because generally more futures contracts are available than there are specific maturity Treasury bonds that could be used as the underlying security in an option, option contracts written on the futures contract generally have fewer problems than contracts written directly on the bonds themselves. This also helps minimize the chance that a short squeeze will develop in the underlying security. See Chapter 2 for a discussion of a short squeeze in the Treasury market.

Table 15-2

Panel A: Options on Stocks

Option/Strike				Vol	Exch	Last	Net Chg	a-Close	Open Int
Elan	Apr	30	p	250	CB	2⅛	+ ⅞	31⅝	159
Elan	Feb	35	p	110	CB	4⅝	+ 1⅝	31⅝	500
Elan	Jan	40	p	200	CB	6¾	+ 6¾	31⅝	...
Epitpe	Jan	15	p	93	CB	5/16	+ 1/16	17¾	891
Epitpe	Jan	15	p	382	AM	5/16	+ 1/16	17¾	891
Epitpe	Jan	17½	p	512	CB	⅞	− ⅛	17¾	1,492
Epitpe	Jan	17½	p	93	AM	⅞	+ ¼	17¾	1,492
Epitpe	Apr	17½	p	400	CB	3	+ ½	17¾	89
Epitpe	Jan	20	p	148	AM	2¼	− ¼	17¾	1,284
Epitpe	Apr	20		79	AM	1 9/16	− 7/16	17¾	1,148
Epitpe	Apr	20		86	CB	1½	− ⅝	17¾	1,148
Equifx	Jan	20	p	75	PC	½	+ ½	20	...
Ethyl	Jan	30		97	PC	⅜	+ ¼	29⅞	1,413
Exxon	Jan	55		100	CB	7⅛	+ ⅛	61¾	1,692
Exxon	Jan	60		112	CB	2	− ⅛	61¾	6,941
Exxon	Apr	65		95	CB	9/16	− ⅛	61¾	1,893
Exxon	Apr	70		108	CB	⅛	− 1/16	61¾	753
F N M	Jan	70		229	PB	7¼	...	77¼	2,884
F N M	Jan	75		190	PB	2½	− ⅝	77¼	4,117
F N M	Feb	75		150	PB	3⅜	− ⅞	77¼	168
F N M	Feb	80		346	PB	1 1/16	− ½	77¼	504
FHLB	Jan	45		165	AM	3	− ½	47⅞	3,011
FHLB	Feb	45	p	270	AM	⅞	+ 3/16	47⅞	320
FHLB	Jan	50	p	185	AM	2⅜	+ ¾	47⅞	342
FHLB	Feb	50		175	AM	13/16	− 1/16	47⅞	240
FHLB	Feb	50	p	150	AM	3⅛	+ 11/16	47⅞	287
FM Cop	Mar	25		200	PB	½	...	21⅝	745
FedDSt	Jan	17½		230	CB	2⅞	+ 5/16	20	604
FedDSt	Jan	20		103	CB	⅜	+ ⅜	20	739
FishPr	Mar	22½		135	AM	3¾	+ ⅜	25	238
FishPr	Jan	25		280	AM	¾	+ 3/16	25	737
FleetC	Feb	15		130	CB	6½	+ 1½	21¼	90
Fluor	Feb	40	p	331	CB	1¼	+ ⅜	40½	31
Ford	Jan	40		186	CB	4⅞	+ ¼	44¾	2,804
Ford	Mar	40		274	CB	5½	+ ⅜	44¾	3,658
Ford	Jun	40		114	CB	6⅜	+ 1⅛	44¾	826
Ford	Feb	45		396	CB	1 9/16	+ 1/16	44¾	1,923
Ford	Mar	45		634	CB	2⅛	+ ⅛	44¾	4,193
Ford	Jun	45		102	CB	3¼	+ ¼	44¾	922
Ford	Mar	50		245	CB	9/16	+ ⅛	44¾	476
FostWh	Apr	25	p	100	PC	⅝	+ ⅛	27⅞	28
FrptMc	Aug	17½		250	CB	1 7/16	− ⅛	18⅛	63
-G-H-I-									
G M	Jan	30		290	CB	3⅞	+ ½	34	1,384
G M	Jan	30	p	120	CB	1/16	...	34	2,245
G M	Feb	30	p	112	CB	¼	− ⅛	34	258
G M	Mar	30		225	CB	4½	+ ⅜	34	6,902
G M	Mar	30	p	75	CB	9/16	− ⅛	34	7,670
G M	Jan	35		1,348	CB	5/16	+ ⅛	34	8,191
G M	Jan	35	p	106	CB	1 7/16	− 7/16	34	1,492
G M	Feb	35		775	CB	1	+ 3/16	34	2,125
G M	Mar	35		443	CB	1 7/16	+ 3/16	34	12,153
G M	Jun	35		235	CB	2½	+ ¼	34	6,217
G M	Mar	40		242	CB	⅜	+ ⅛	34	11,347
G T E	Jan	35		201	AM	⅛	− 1/16	34⅝	2,297
G T E	Feb	35		444	AM	⅝	+ ⅛	34⅝	1,360
G T E	Mar	35		109	AM	¾	+ ⅛	34⅝	8,272
G T E	Jun	35		156	AM	1¼	+ ¼	34⅝	1,275
GMills	Jan	60		100	PC	8⅜	− 2⅛	68⅛	7
GMills	Apr	60		314	PC	9¼	− ⅛	68⅛	234
GMills	Jan	70		102	PC	½	...	68⅛	1,503
GSignl	Jan	65		140	PB	5/16	+ 5/16	62	...
GaPac	Jan	60		123	PB	2¼	+ ¼	61½	1,664
GaPac	Feb	65		125	PB	1¼	+ ¼	61½	59
Gap	Jan	30		179	CB	2⅛	− ⅝	32⅝	744
Gap	Jan	30	p	427	CB	¼	− 1/16	32⅝	1,362
Gap	Feb	30		182	CB	3⅜	− ⅛	32⅝	227
Gap	Mar	30	p	135	CB	1⅜	+ ⅛	32⅝	722
Gap	Jan	35		827	CB	¼	...	32⅝	4,476
Gap	Jan	35	p	551	CB	2⅞	...	32⅝	1,809
Gap	Feb	35		106	CB	1	+ 1/16	32⅝	767
Gap	Mar	35		768	CB	1⅜	+ 1/16	32⅝	2,660
Gap	Jun	35	p	200	CB	5	+ ½	32⅝	220
Gap	Jan	55	p	400	CB	22¾	+ 1¾	32⅝	...
Gen El	Mar	80	p	94	CB	1⅛	+ ⅛	86	1,763
Gen El	Jun	80	p	127	CB	2½	+ ⅛	86	774
Gen El	Jan	85		293	CB	1 11/16	− 5/16	86	4,520
Gen El	Feb	85		120	CB	2⅞	− ⅛	86	1,132
Gen El	Feb	85	p	85	CB	1⅜	+ ⅛	86	324
Gen El	Mar	85		112	CB	3½	− ½	86	5,900
Gen El	Jun	85	p	102	CB	4¼	+ ¾	86	106
Gen El	Jan	90		210	CB	⅛	− ⅛	86	1,145
Gen El	Feb	90		100	CB	13/16	− ⅛	86	309
GenRe	Feb	120		150	AM	1½	+ ¼	115	75
Gensia	Mar	25		97	CB	2¾	− ⅞	24¼	405
Gentch	Feb	35		535	PC	3½	+ ¼	37⅞	5
Gentch	Jul	35	p	74	PC	1⅝	+ 1⅝	37⅞	...
Gentch	Feb	40		133	PC	13/16	+ 3/16	37⅞	304
GerbPd	Apr	32½		260	AM	⅝	− ⅛	30½	333
GerbPd	Apr	32½	p	240	AM	3¼	...	30½	241
Gillet	Mar	50		135	AM	5½	− 1⅜	55	663
Gillet	Jan	55		90	AM	⅝	− 1	55	207
Gillet	Feb	55		104	AM	1¼	− 1	55	55
Gillet	Mar	55	p	82	AM	2⅜	+ ⅞	55	605
Gillet	Feb	60		570	AM	¼	− ⅛	55	1,053
Gillet	Mar	60		160	AM	¾	− ¼	55	1,236
Glaxo	Jan	22½		243	AM	11/16	− 7/16	22¾	2,541
Glaxo	Jan	22½	p	110	AM	5/16	+ 1/16	22¾	1,225
Glaxo	Feb	22½		353	AM	1 5/16	− ¼	22¾	6,201
Glaxo	Feb	22½	p	100	AM	13/16	+ ⅛	22¾	4,295
Glaxo	May	22½		81	AM	2⅛	− ⅜	22¾	1,789
Glaxo	May	22½	p	73	AM	1 9/16	+ 3/16	22¾	2,570
Glaxo	Jan	25		600	AM	1/16	− 1/16	22¾	19,974
Glaxo	Jan	25	p	211	AM	2¼	+ ½	22¾	5,647
Glaxo	Feb	25		487	AM	7/16	− ⅛	22¾	8,202
Glaxo	Feb	25	p	93	AM	2⅜	+ ⅜	22¾	4,524
Glaxo	May	25		494	AM	1⅛	− ⅛	22¾	5,306
Glaxo	Aug	25		112	AM	1⅝	− ¼	22¾	231
Glaxo	Feb	30		467	AM	1/16	...	22¾	6,741
Glaxo	May	30		104	AM	5/16	− 1/16	22¾	3,745
GlfStU	Aug	15		1,000	NY	2¼	+ 2¼	16⅜	...
GlfStU	Aug	17½		1,000	NY	½	+ ½	16⅜	...
Goodyr	Jan	65		101	AM	5	+ 1⅝	69⅞	628
Goodyr	Jan	70		77	AM	1⅛	+ ¼	69⅞	1,609
Grace	Jan	40		127	AM	9/16	+ 1/16	39½	386
Grace	Feb	40		140	AM	1	− ⅛	39½	2,717
Grace	May	45		100	AM	½	...	39½	900
GrenTr	Jan	50	p	165	CB	2 11/16	+ 11/16	47⅝	188
GrenTr	Feb	50	p	185	CB	3⅝	+ 3⅝	47⅝	4
GtLCh	Jan	70		195	CB	¼	− ¼	67⅝	507
GtLCh	Feb	70		100	CB	1 5/16	− 11/16	67⅝	30
Gtech	Jan	40		92	CB	3⅜	+ 1 13/16	43¼	453
HCA	Feb	17½		150	CB	3⅞	+ ¾	21¼	...
HCA	Jan	20		200	PB	1¼	+ ½	21¼	594
HCA	Feb	22½		140	CB	7/16	+ 7/16	21¼	...
HCA	Mar	22½		200	PB	¾	...	21¼	557
HCA	Mar	22½		75	CB	13/16	+ ¼	21¼	557
HMO Am	Jan	17½		75	CB	4½	+ ⅝	22¼	139
HMO Am	May	20		208	CB	3⅜	+ 1¼	22¼	121
HMO Am	Jan	22½		80	CB	⅝	+ ¼	22¼	5
HMO Am	Feb	22½		363	CB	1	+ 5/16	22¼	34
HeartT	Jan	17½		183	CB	2 7/16	+ 1⅜	19	200
HeartT	Jan	20		85	CB	¾	+ ½	19	350
Hecla	Jun	7½		102	AM	1⅛	+ ⅛	7½	159
Heinz	Jan	50	p	150	CB	5⅞	+ 5⅞	44	...
HelmP	Mar	25		130	NY	⅜	− 7/16	23	389
Hewlet	Aug	60	p	223	CB	1⅝	− 7/16	72¾	210
Hewlet	Jan	65		250	CB	7⅞	+ 2⅞	72¾	3,070
Hewlet	Feb	65		199	CB	8⅝	+ 2	72¾	3,211
Hewlet	Feb	65	p	687	CB	9/16	− 7/16	72¾	1,707
Hewlet	May	65		243	CB	10⅝	+ 2¾	72¾	1,142
Hewlet	Jan	70		566	CB	3⅛	+ 1 11/16	72¾	2,200
Hewlet	Jan	70	p	274	CB	7/16	− 1 5/16	72¾	343
Hewlet	Feb	70		795	CB	4¾	+ 1¾	72¾	4,595
Hewlet	Feb	70	p	385	CB	1¾	− 2	72¾	1,006
Hewlet	Aug	70		405	CB	8⅜	+ 2⅛	72¾	366
Hewlet	Jan	75		192	CB	9/16	+ ¼	72¾	235
Hewlet	Feb	75		455	CB	2¼	+ 15/16	72¾	1,323
Hewlet	May	75		216	CB	4⅜	+ 1½	72¾	50
Hilton	Jan	45		169	PC	¾	+ 5/16	44¾	743
Hilton	Feb	45		147	PC	1 13/16	+ ¾	44¾	105
HomeDp	Jan	55		259	PB	9	− 1¾	63½	2,890
HomeDp	Feb	55		87	PB	10⅛	− 1⅝	63½	3,773
HomeDp	Feb	55	p	88	PB	⅜	+ ⅛	63½	1,840
HomeDp	May	55	p	130	PB	1⅜	+ ⅜	63½	413
HomeDp	Jan	60		845	PB	3⅞	− 2⅜	63½	1,772
HomeDp	Jan	60	p	255	PB	⅜	+ ¼	63½	2,023
HomeDp	Feb	60		303	PB	5¼	− 2⅜	63½	3,783
HomeDp	Feb	60	p	768	PB	1½	+ 11/16	63½	2,329
HomeDp	May	60		151	PB	7¼	− 2	63½	2,364
HomeDp	May	60	p	247	PB	3⅛	+ 1	63½	1,031
HomeDp	Jan	65		1,799	PB	¾	− 1¼	63½	2,919
HomeDp	Jan	65	p	1,795	PB	2⅛	+ 1 5/16	63½	2,147
HomeDp	Feb	65		568	PB	2 7/16	− 1 3/16	63½	2,955
HomeDp	Feb	65	p	613	PB	3½	+ 1¼	63½	1,212
HomeDp	May	65		827	PB	4¾	− 1¼	63½	4,962
HomeDp	May	65	p	541	PB	5¼	+ 1¼	63½	432
HomeDp	Jan	70		1,054	PB	1/16	− ⅛	63½	3,187
HomeDp	Jan	70	p	75	PB	6¼	+ 2¼	63½	496
HomeDp	Feb	70		1,222	PB	¾	− ¾	63½	2,470
HomeDp	Feb	70	p	116	PB	7	+ 2	63½	397
HomeDp	May	70		191	PB	2⅞	− ⅞	63½	1,349
HomeDp	Feb	75		105	PB	¼	− ⅛	63½	331
HomeDp	May	75		338	PB	1⅜	− ½	63½	743
HomeDp	Aug	75		100	PB	3⅛	− ½	63½	331
Homstk	Jan	10		162	CB	¾	+ ⅛	10⅝	2,118
Honwll	Feb	30	p	102	CB	¼	− ¼		956
Honwll	Feb	35		78	CB	⅞	+ 7/16		1,096
Humana	Jan	20		75	CB	⅜	− ⅛	20½	424
Humana	Aug	22½		300	CB	1½	+ 1½	20½	...
I B M	Jan	45		1,230	CB	3½	− ¾	48	1,784
I B M	Jan	45	p	5,118	CB	7/16	...	48	14,052
I B M	Feb	45		1,543	CB	4⅜	− ½	48	1,399
I B M	Feb	45	p	2,993	CB	1⅜	+ 1/16	48	6,087
I B M	Apr	45		282	CB	5⅜	− ⅝	48	1,110
I B M	Apr	45	p	1,046	CB	2⅜	+ 3/16	48	3,205
I B M	Jul	45		93	CB	6½	− ⅞	48	376
I B M	Jul	45	p	319	CB	3⅝	+ ⅛	48	1,799
I B M	Jan	50		7,410	CB	9/16	− 7/16	48	15,038
I B M	Jan	50	p	6,975	CB	2 7/16	+ 5/16	48	15,557
I B M	Feb	50		3,221	CB	1⅞	− 7/16	48	5,286
I B M	Feb	50	p	666	CB	4	+ ¼	48	2,684
I B M	Apr	50		1,652	CB	3	− ½	48	5,133
I B M	Apr	50	p	493	CB	5⅛	+ ⅜	48	5,678
I B M	Jul	50		753	CB	4¼	− ½	48	2,179
I B M	Jul	50	p	188	CB	6⅛	+ ⅜	48	2,873
I B M	Jan	55		3,110	CB	⅛	− 1/16	48	29,667
I B M	Jan	55	p	1,231	CB	7	+ ¾	48	7,159
I B M	Feb	55		1,763	CB	11/16	− 3/16	48	6,393
I B M	Feb	55	p	103	CB	8½	+ 1⅛	48	507
I B M	Apr	55		826	CB	1 11/16	− 5/16	48	12,724
I B M	Apr	55	p	196	CB	8¾	+ ¾	48	4,098
I B M	Jul	55		394	CB	2⅝	− ⅜	48	2,404
I B M	Jul	55	p	161	CB	9¾	+ 1	48	1,592
I B M	Jan	60		3,449	CB	1/16	...	48	18,868
I B M	Jan	60	p	255	CB	12⅛	+ ⅞	48	6,340
I B M	Apr	60		598	CB	13/16	− 3/16	48	11,442
I B M	Apr	60	p	88	CB	13⅛	+ ⅞	48	4,041
I B M	Jul	60		142	CB	1⅝	− 3/16	48	2,704
I B M	Apr	65		396	CB	7/16	− ⅛	48	7,841
I B M	Apr	65	p	126	CB	17¾	+ 1¼	48	2,780
I B M	Apr	70		275	CB	5/16	− 1/16	48	10,697
I B M	Jul	70		97	CB	¾	− 1/16	48	1,705
I B M	Apr	75		252	CB	3/16	− 1/16	48	5,291
I B M	Jan	80		157	CB	1/16	...	48	10,636
I B M	Apr	80		194	CB	3/16	+ 1/16	48	5,087
I T T	Mar	75		103	CB	1⅛	− ⅛	71¾	200
I T W	Feb	70		100	PB	⅞	− ⅛	67¾	15
IGame	Jan	22½		200	AM	28	+ 1⅛	50⅝	26
IGame	Jan	45		119	AM	5⅛	+ ½	50⅝	1,249
IGame	Jan	45	p	75	AM	3/16	− 1/16	50⅝	809
IGame	Jan	50		154	AM	1½	+ ⅜	50⅝	2,833
IGame	Feb	50		84	AM	3¼	+ ¼	50⅝	535
IGame	Jan	55		145	AM	⅛	...	50⅝	1,447
IllCtr	Feb	25		80	PB	¾	...	24⅝	20
ImunRs	Aug	15		192	CB	6½	− ½	18	120
ImunRs	Feb	20		140	CB	1 5/16	+ 1/16	18	670
In Flv	May	110		145	CB	2½	− 2¼	104⅝	107
Inco	Apr	25		800	AM	1	+ ⅛	23	61
Infrmx	Feb	25		300	CB	11⅛	+ 1	36¼	459
Intel	Jan	65		82	AM	34½	+ 11½	98⅝	2,159
Intel	Jan	80		109	AM	18⅞	+ 7⅞	98⅝	2,391
Intel	Jan	80	p	1,673	AM	1/16	− ⅛	98⅝	2,780
Intel	Apr	80	p	108	AM	¾	− 1⅝	98⅝	276
Intel	Jan	85		755	AM	13½	+ 7⅜	98⅝	2,982
Intel	Jan	85	p	181	AM	⅛	− 5/16	98⅝	2,300
Intel	Feb	85		784	AM	14¼	+ 6⅛	98⅝	978
Intel	Feb	85	p	136	AM	11/16	− 1 5/16	98⅝	764
Intel	Apr	85		187	AM	15	+ 5	98⅝	1,605
Intel	Jan	90		2,468	AM	8½	+ 5½	98⅝	3,898
Intel	Jan	90	p	1,719	AM	3/16	− 1 11/16	98⅝	689
Intel	Feb	90		307	AM	10⅛	+ 5⅛	98⅝	992
Intel	Feb	90	p	169	AM	1 9/16	− 2 3/16	98⅝	222
Intel	Apr	90		119	AM	11¾	+ 4½	98⅝	612
Intel	Apr	90	p	88	AM	2¾	− 4¼	98⅝	170
Intel	Jul	90	p	74	AM	5¾	− 2½	98⅝	179
Intel	Jan	95		3,247	AM	4¾	+ 3⅞	98⅝	1,156
Intel	Jan	95	p	1,427	AM	1	− 6½	98⅝	...
Intel	Feb	95		826	AM	6¾	+ 3¾	98⅝	551
Intel	Feb	95	p	347	AM	3	− 6¾	98⅝	24
Intel	Apr	95		231	AM	8¾	+ 3¾	98⅝	413
Intel	Jul	95		75	AM	11½	+ 3⅝	98⅝	126
IntelE	Jan	12½		83	CB	1 3/16	+ 1/16	13½	2,046
IntelE	Mar	12½		162	PC	1⅞	− ⅛	13½	1,172
IntelE	Feb	15		75	CB	7/16	− 1/16	13½	360
IntrDig	Jan	7½		142	PC	2¼	+ ¾	9¾	714
IntrDig	Jan	10		293	PC	⅜	+ ¼	9¾	743
Itel	Apr	25		1,000	CB	1⅞	+ 1⅞	24	...
IvaxCp	Jan	25		146	CB	1 5/16	− 1½	26⅜	40
IvaxCp	Feb	25	p	110	CB	1⅛	+ ⅜	26⅜	20
IvaxCp	Mar	25		73	CB	2¾	− 1¼	26⅜	474
IvaxCp	Mar	25	p	83	CB	1¾	+ ⅜	26⅜	508
IvaxCp	Feb	30		90	CB	⅝	− ⅝	26⅜	527
IvaxCp	Feb	30	p	120	CB	4⅞	+ 1½	26⅜	122
IvaxCp	Mar	30		100	CB	1 9/16	− 3/16	26⅜	1,222
IvaxCp	Mar	30	p	164	CB	4⅜	+ 1⅜	26⅜	640
-J-K-L									
JohnJn	Jan	40		187	CB	6¾	− 2⅛	46⅞	3,336
JohnJn	Jan	45		154	CB	2½	− 1	46⅞	1,834

Reprinted by permission of *The Wall Street Journal,* © 1993 Dow Jones and Company, Inc. All Right Reserved Worldwide.

Table 15-2

Panel B: Options on Currencies

Option & Underlying	Strike Price	Calls—Last Jan	Calls—Last Feb	Calls—Last Mar	Puts—Last Jan	Puts—Last Feb	Puts—Last Mar
50,000 Australian Dollars-European Style.							
ADollr	70	r	r	0.19	r	r	r
67.43	72	r	0.03	0.06	r	r	r
67.43	74	r	r	0.03	r	r	r
67.43	75	0.01	r	r	r	r	r
50,000 Australian Dollars-cents per unit.							
ADollr	66	r	r	r	r	0.60	0.71
67.43	67	r	r	r	r	r	1.25
67.43	68	r	0.38	0.64	0.82	1.56	1.85
67.43	69	r	r	r	r	r	2.22
67.43	73	r	r	r	r	r	6.06
31,250 British Pound-German Mark cross.							
BPd-GMk	248	r	r	r	r	r	2.20
252.02	252	r	r	4.15	r	r	r
252.02	254	r	r	3.23	r	r	r
252.02	256	r	r	2.40	r	r	r
31,250 British Pounds-European Style.							
BPound	152½	r	r	4.10	1.00	r	3.75
155.14	157½	0.60	1.70	r	r	r	r
155.14	160	r	1.34	r	r	r	r
155.14	147½	r	r	r	r	0.70	r
31,250 British Pounds-cents per unit.							
BPound	140	r	r	r	r	r	0.46
155.14	147½	r	r	r	r	1.00	1.35
155.14	150	r	r	6.50	0.23	r	2.81
155.14	152½	2.18	3.65	4.42	1.10	r	3.90
155.14	155	1.05	2.29	3.38	2.25	r	5.00
155.14	157½	0.45	r	2.65	r	r	r
155.14	160	0.18	0.82	1.55	r	r	r
155.14	162½	0.15	0.92	r	r	r	r
50,000 Canadian Dollars-European Style.							
CDollar	77½	r	r	r	0.09	r	r
50,000 Canadian Dollars-cents per unit.							
CDollr	77	r	r	r	r	0.42	r
78.32	77½	r	r	r	0.14	r	r
78.32	78	r	r	r	0.31	0.84	r
78.32	78½	0.22	r	r	r	r	r
78.32	79	0.08	r	r	r	r	r
78.32	79½	r	r	0.30	r	r	r
78.32	80	r	r	0.15	r	r	2.30
78.32	83	r	r	r	r	r	5.00
78.32	83½	r	r	r	r	r	5.50
78.32	84	r	r	r	r	r	6.00
62,500 European Currency Units-cents per unit.							
ECU	114	r	r	r	0.08	r	r
120.46	122	r	r	r	2.70	r	r
250,000 French Francs-10ths of a cent per unit.							
FFranc	17	r	r	r	r	r	1.96
180.47	17¼	r	r	r	r	r	2.70
180.47	17½	r	r	r	r	r	3.94
180.47	17¾	r	r	r	r	r	4.90
180.47	18	r	r	r	r	r	6.56
180.47	19	r	r	r	11.50	r	r
62,500 German Mark-Japanese Yen cross.							
GMk-YJn	73	r	r	r	r	r	0.55
76.80	75	r	r	r	r	r	1.20
76.80	76½	r	r	r	r	r	1.90
76.80	81	r	r	0.23	r	r	r
62,500 German Marks-European Style.							
DMark	57	r	4.15	r	r	r	r
61.59	59	r	r	r	r	r	0.78
61.59	59½	r	2.10	r	r	r	r
61.59	60½	r	r	1.55	r	r	1.40
61.59	61	0.50	r	r	0.55	r	r
61.59	61½	0.32	0.83	r	0.82	r	r
61.59	62½	r	r	0.75	r	2.15	r
61.59	63½	0.04	r	r	r	r	r
61.59	66	0.02	0.08	0.16	r	r	r
61.59	68	r	r	0.06	r	r	r
62,500 German Marks-cents per unit.							
DMark	56	r	r	5.26	r	r	0.21
61.59	57	r	r	4.30	r	r	r
61.59	58	r	r	r	r	0.26	0.54
61.59	58½	r	r	r	r	0.36	r
61.59	59	r	r	r	0.06	0.37	0.80
61.59	59½	r	r	r	r	0.52	0.98
61.59	60	r	r	1.86	0.18	0.75	1.24
61.59	60½	r	r	r	0.33	0.94	1.45
61.59	61	0.56	r	1.34	0.56	1.20	1.67
61.59	61½	0.35	r	r	0.57	r	1.81
61.59	62	0.24	0.61	0.91	1.14	1.73	2.20
61.59	62½	0.12	r	0.87	1.40	2.15	r
61.59	63	0.07	r	0.59	2.10	r	3.04
61.59	63½	r	0.32	r	r	r	r
61.59	64	r	r	0.36	3.02	r	3.79
61.59	70	r	s	r	r	s	9.16
6,250,000 Japanese Yen-100ths of a cent per unit.							
JYen	77	r	r	r	r	0.09	r
80.21	78	r	r	r	r	0.19	r
80.21	79	r	r	r	r	r	0.71
80.21	80	0.34	r	r	0.40	r	r
80.21	80½	r	r	r	0.72	r	r
80.21	81	r	r	0.79	r	r	r
6,250,000 Japanese Yen-European Style.							
JYen	78	r	r	r	r	0.18	r
80.21	82	0.02	r	r	r	r	r
80.21	85	r	r	0.10	r	r	r
62,500 Swiss Francs-European Style.							
SFranc	65	r	r	r	r	r	0.95
67.99	67	r	r	r	r	r	1.74
67.99	73	r	0.10	r	r	r	r
62,500 Swiss Francs-cents per unit.							
SFranc	65	r	r	r	0.07	r	0.75
67.99	66	r	r	r	0.23	0.80	1.31
67.99	66½	r	r	r	r	0.78	1.31
67.99	67	r	r	1.65	0.64	r	1.91
67.99	67½	r	r	2.12	r	r	r
67.99	68	0.30	r	1.39	1.26	r	2.30
67.99	68½	0.23	r	1.03	1.52	r	r
67.99	69	r	r	r	1.90	r	3.10
67.99	69½	0.10	r	r	r	r	r
67.99	70	r	r	r	3.02	3.06	3.86
67.99	71	r	0.21	r	3.70	r	r
67.99	72	r	r	0.34	5.02	r	5.17
50,000 Australian Dollar EOM-cents per unit.							
ADollr	68	r	0.58	r	r	r	r
31,250 British Pound EOM-cents per unit.							
BPound	157½	1.12	r	r	r	r	r
155.14	160	r	1.28	r	r	r	r
62,500 German Marks EOM-cents per unit.							
DMark	60	r	r	r	r	0.92	r
61.59	61	r	r	r	r	r	1.79
61.59	62	r	r	1.03	r	r	2.42
62,500 Swiss Franc EOM-cents per unit.							
SFranc	69	r	r	r	r	2.77	r
Total Call Vol	18,541			Call Open int	441,007		
Total Put Vol	16,456			Put Open int	480.456		

Panel A of Table 15-2 shows prices prevailing on January 6, 1993 for the most actively traded options on selected equity securities, listed in alphabetical order. Note that the *Wall Street Journal* reports options on equities for only the most actively traded options. Other options are often available on the stocks shown reported. The first column in the table identifies the company on which the option is traded. The next two columns show the month in which the option matures and the exercise or strike price of the option. The next column indicates whether the option is a put or a call. If nothing is shown in this column then the option is a call, whereas a "p" is shown if it is a put option. The next two columns show the volume of contracts traded

Table 15-2
Panel C: Options on Futures

FUTURES OPTIONS PRICES

CURRENCY

JAPANESE YEN (IMM)
12,500,000 yen; cents per 100 yen

Strike	Calls—Settle			Puts—Settle		
Price	Jan	Feb	Mar	Jan	Feb	Mar
7900	0.89	1.22	1.56	0.03	0.36	0.70
7950	0.43	....	....	0.07	0.54	0.91
8000	0.13	0.63	1.01	0.27	0.77	1.15
8050	0.06	0.44	0.80	0.70	1.08	1.44
8100	0.03	0.30	0.62	1.17	1.44	1.75
8150	0.01	0.19	0.48	1.65	....	2.11

Est. vol. 1,754;
Tues vol. 1,188 calls; 1,415 puts
Op. int. Tues 19,566 calls; 18,193 puts

DEUTSCHEMARK (IMM)
125,000 marks; cents per mark

Strike	Calls—Settle			Puts—Settle		
Price	Jan	Feb	Mar	Jan	Feb	Mar
5950	1.15	....	....	0.05	0.53	0.89
6000	0.71	1.29	1.66	0.12	0.72	1.08
6050	0.37	1.02	1.40	0.28	0.94	1.32
6100	0.16	0.79	1.17	0.67	1.20	1.58
6150	0.06	0.60	0.97	0.98	1.52	1.87
6200	0.01	0.45	0.80	1.43	1.86	2.20

Est. vol. 13,624;
Tues vol. 7,223 calls; 8,962 puts
Op. int. Tues 146,350 calls; 151,646 puts

CANADIAN DOLLAR (IMM)
100,000 Can.$, cents per Can.$

Strike	Calls—Settle			Puts—Settle		
Price	Jan	Feb	Mar	Jan	Feb	Mar
7650	....	....	1.51	.0000	0.19	0.39
7700	0.65	0.96	1.19	0.03	0.34	0.56
7750	0.25	0.66	0.90	0.12	0.53	0.77
7800	0.04	0.42	0.66	0.41	0.79	1.03
7850	.0000	0.25	0.45	0.87	1.12	1.33
7900	.0000	0.14	0.31	1.37	1.50	1.67

Est. vol. 396;
Tues vol. 356 calls; 315 puts
Op. int. Tues 4,174 calls; 6,306 puts

BRITISH POUND (IMM)
62,500 pounds; cents per pound

Strike	Calls—Settle			Puts—Settle		
Price	Jan	Feb	Mar	Jan	Feb	Mar
1475	5.82	6.60	7.36	0.04	0.84	1.62
1500	3.46	4.74	5.66	0.18	1.48	2.42
1525	1.46	3.22	4.24	0.68	2.44	3.48
1550	0.40	2.06	3.08	2.12	3.76	4.78
1575	0.14	1.24	2.18	4.36	5.44	6.36
1600	0.04	0.72	1.48	6.76	....	8.16

Est. vol. 1,762;
Tues vol. 1,827 calls; 1,810 puts
Op. int. Tues 11,668 calls; 9,462 puts

SWISS FRANC (IMM)
125,000 francs; cents per franc

Strike	Calls—Settle			Puts—Settle		
Price	Jan	Feb	Mar	Jan	Feb	Mar
6550	....	....	....	0.04	....	1.04
6600	1.00	....	....	0.11	0.83	1.24
6650	0.63	....	....	0.24	1.04	....
6700	0.35	1.16	1.60	0.46	1.27	1.71
6750	0.17	0.94	1.38	0.78	1.55	1.99
6800	0.08	0.76	1.18	1.19	1.87	2.28

Est. vol. 3,222;
Tues vol. 2,697 calls; 3,583 puts
Op. int. Tues 18,267 calls; 20,509 puts

MARK/YEN CROSS RATE (CME)
125,000 marks; yen per mark

Strike	Calls—Settle			Puts—Settle		
Price	Jan	Feb	Mar	Jan	Feb	Mar
7500	....	....	....	....	....	....
7550	....	....	....	....	....	....
7600	....	....	....	....	....	....
7650	....	....	....	....	....	....
7700	....	....	....	....	....	....
7750	....	....	....	....	....	....

Est. vol. 0;
Tues vol. 0 calls; 0 puts
Op. int. Tues 50 calls; 27 puts

U.S. DOLLAR INDEX (FINEX)
1,000 times index

Strike	Calls—Settle			Puts—Settle		
Price	Jan	Feb	Mar	Jan	Feb	Mar
92	2.21	2.69	3.10	0.01	....	0.90
93	1.35	2.00	2.47	0.06	....	1.26
94	0.52	1.42	1.92	0.31	1.22	....
95	0.09	0.97	1.46	0.92	1.76	....
96	0.02	....	1.08	....	....	....
97	0.01	....	0.78	....	....	....

Est. vol. 81;
Tues vol. 130 calls; 33 puts
Op. int. Tues 1,477 calls; 316 puts

INTEREST RATE

T-BONDS (CBT)
$100,000; points and 64ths of 100%

Strike	Calls—Settle			Puts—Settle		
Price	Feb	Mar	Jun	Feb	Mar	Jun
102	....	3-41	3-32	0-03	0-18	1-22
104	1-37	2-07	2-22	0-16	0-47	2-10
106	0-28	0-62	1-28	1-04	1-38	3-15
108	0-04	0-21	0-52	....	2-60	4-39
110	....	0-05	0-29	....	4-43	6-14
112	....	0-01	0-16	....	6-40	....

Est. vol. 55,000;
Tues vol. 37,690 calls; 22,661 puts
Op. int. Tues 207,195 calls; 176,607 puts

T-NOTES (CBT)
$100,000; points and 64ths of 100%

Strike	Calls—Settle			Puts—Settle		
Price	Feb	Mar	Jun	Feb	Mar	Jun
105	....	2-43	2-21	0-04	0-17	1-14
106	1-36	1-57	1-49	0-10	0-31	1-42
107	0-53	1-14	1-20	0-27	0-52	2-11
108	0-22	0-46	0-60	0-60	1-20	....
109	0-07	0-25	0-42	....	1-61	3-32
110	....	0-12	0-29	....	2-49	....

Est. vol. 13,000;
Tues vol. 6,712 calls; 6,652 puts
Op. int. Tues 51,742 calls; 74,304 puts

MUNICIPAL BOND INDEX (CBT)
$100,000; pts. & 64ths of 100%

Strike	Calls—Settle			Puts—Settle		
97	1-02	1-05	....	0-53	1-50	....
98	0-39	0-46	....	....	2-26	....
97	1-02	1-05	....	0-53	1-50	....
98	0-39	0-46	....	....	2-26	....
99	0-20	0-30	....	2-06	3-10	....
100	0-10	....	....	2-58	....	....

Est. vol. 0;
Tues vol. 6 calls; 1 puts
Op. int. Tues 3,651 calls; 3,050 puts

5 YR TREAS NOTES (CBT)
$100,000; points and 64ths of 100%

Strike	Calls—Settle			Puts—Settle		
Price	Feb	Mar	Jun	Feb	Mar	Jun
10600	....	1-48	1-42	0-03	0-18	1-10
10650	....	1-24	1-24	0-07	0-26	1-24
10700	0-46	1-03	....	0-15	0-37	....
10750	0-27	0-49	0-61	0-28	0-51	....
10800	0-14	0-35	....	....	1-04	....
10850	....	0-24	....	....	1-25	....

Est. vol. 3,000;
Tues vol. 5,985 calls; 980 puts
Op. int. Tues 14,695 calls; 17,878 puts

EURODOLLAR (IMM)
$ million; pts. of 100%

Strike	Calls—Settle			Puts—Settle		
Price	Mar	Jun	Sep	Mar	Jun	Sep
9600	0.45	0.32	0.25	0.04	0.28	0.64
9625	0.25	0.20	0.16	0.09	0.41	0.80
9650	0.11	0.11	0.10	0.20	0.56	0.99
9675	0.03	0.06	0.06	0.37	0.75	1.19
9700	0.01	0.03	0.04	0.59	0.97	....
9725	.0004	0.02	0.03	0.84	....	....

Est. vol. 38,533;
Tues vol. 24,637 calls; 23,464 puts
Op. int. Tues 402,921 calls; 401,570 puts

LIBOR – 1 Mo. (IMM)
$3 million; pts. of 100%

Strike	Calls—Settle			Puts—Settle		
Price	Jan	Feb	Mar	Jan	Feb	Mar
9625	0.48	0.45	0.35	.0004	0.01	0.07
9650	0.24	0.22	0.17	0.01	0.03	0.14
9675	0.03	0.05	0.08	0.05	0.11	0.30
9700	0.01	0.02	0.03	0.28	0.33	0.50
9725	.0004	....	0.01	0.52	....	0.73
9750	....	....	....	....	....	....

Est. vol. 1,337;
Tues vol. 85 calls; 65 puts
Op. int. Tues 3,635 calls; 1,997 puts

TREASURY BILLS (IMM)
$1 million; pts. of 100%

Strike	Calls—Settle			Puts—Settle		
Price	Mar	Jun	Sep	Mar	Jun	Sep
9625	0.58	0.42	0.34	0.01	0.14	0.39
9650	0.34	0.27	0.21	0.03	0.23	0.51
9675	0.13	0.16	0.13	0.07	0.37	0.68
9700	0.04	0.08	....	0.22	0.53	....
9725	0.01	0.03	....	0.43	0.73	....
9750	....	....	....	0.68	....	....

Est. vol. 102;
Tues vol. 197 calls; 8 puts
Op. int. Tues 720 calls; 1,206 puts

EURODOLLAR (LIFFE)
$1 million; pts. of 100%

Strike	Calls—Settle			Puts—Settle		
Price	Mar	Jun	Sep	Mar	Jun	Sep
9600	.46	.33	.26	.05	.30	.64
9625	.26	.21	.17	.10	.43	.80
9650	.12	.12	.10	.21	.59	.98
9675	.04	.07	.06	.38	.79	1.19
9700	.02	.04	.03	.61	1.01	1.41
9725	.01	.02	.01	.85	1.24	1.64

Est. vol. Wed, 0 calls; 0 puts
Op. int. Tues, 3,335 calls; 2,972 puts

LONG GILT (LIFFE)
£50,000; 64ths of 100%

Strike	Calls—Settle			Puts—Settle		
Price	Mar	Jun	....	Mar	Jun	....
99	2-27	3-56	....	0-23	0-56	....
100	1-43	3-13	....	0-39	1-13	....
101	1-06	2-38	....	1-02	1-38	....
102	0-40	2-04	....	1-36	2-04	....
103	0-22	1-39	....	2-18	2-39	....
104	0-11	1-15	....	3-07	3-15	....

Est. vol. Wed, 1,754 calls; 1,628 puts
Op. int. Tues, 11,259 calls; 14,663 puts

INDEX

S&P 500 STOCK INDEX (CME)
$500 times premium

Strike	Calls—Settle			Puts—Settle		
Price	Jan	Feb	Mar	Jan	Feb	Mar
430	6.75	10.30	12.45	1.50	5.05	7.25
435	3.25	7.05	9.40	3.00	6.80	9.15
440	1.20	4.55	6.80	5.95	9.30	11.50
445	0.40	2.65	4.70	10.15	12.40	14.35
450	0.10	1.45	3.05	14.80	16.10	17.70
455	0.05	0.65	1.90	....	....	21.50

Est. vol. 7,546;
Tues vol. 3,465 calls; 2,703 puts
Op. int. Tues 35,860 calls; 71,131 puts

that day and the exchange from which the option price is taken. The next two columns show the option price for the last trade of that option during the day and the net change from the price at the end of the previous day. The next column shows the price of the underlying security at the close of the day. Finally, the last column shows open interest or the total amount of outstanding contracts for that particular option. The price of stock options is quoted on a per share basis so that to determine the price of one option contract for 100 shares, the listed price must be multiplied by 100.

Panels B and C of Table 15-2 contain quotes for options on currencies and options on futures. These options are generally presented in a different format in the *Wall Street Journal.* The first column of the options in Panels B and C of Table 15-2 shows the closing price of the underlying security or currency. The second column shows the various strike or exercise prices for which option contracts are trading in that security or currency. The next three columns show the prices of call options for various maturity dates corresponding to each exercise or strike price. The final three columns show the prices of put options for various maturity dates corresponding to each exercise or strike price. The options prices shown represent the last trade of the day. If the letter "r" is shown the option is available for trading but did not trade that day.

In specifying an option contract a number of terms must be clearly defined, including the identity of the underlying security, the maturity date, and the strike or exercise price. Options can have a variety of maturity dates, depending on the exchange on which they are traded and the nature of the underlying security. You can see from Table 15-2 that there are various maturity months for the different options quoted in the three Panels of the table. Option contracts always expire on the Saturday immediately following the third Friday of their expiration month.

Each of the exchanges chooses the strike prices for which it will offer options for a particular underlying security. Regarding options on equities, their freedom is restricted by rules established by the Securities and Exchange Commission (SEC). Allowable strike prices are in integers divisible by five, plus or minus 2.5 points for stocks where the underlying price is less than $100 and five points if the price is over $100. The exchange may use larger intervals if it chooses. The total number of options available for a particular security are essentially determined by the market demand to acquire and trade those options. For securities with a large outstanding volume and active trading and where there is a perception that the price variance of the underlying security is large, more options may be listed. For example, you can see that many more options are quoted in Table 15-2 for the Deutschemark than for the Australian dollar.

Options contracts on stocks are generally for round lots of 100 shares of the underlying security. This means the option contract represents a right to buy or sell 100 shares of the underlying security. The underlying stock must meet a number of requirements: it must be traded on a national exchange and meet minimum standards for number of shares outstanding and volume of trading, and it must have a minimum stock price of $10 and a record of not defaulting on debt obligations. Options on currencies and fixed-income instruments are also set up for standardized volumes. For example, as we indicated above, each option on the mark traded on the Philadelphia Exchange is for DM 62,500. Since these standardized units vary by contract and exchange, you have to look into how the contract is set up on a given exchange before you venture into buying or selling that option.

Options Trading

The procedures for trading options used on the various exchanges differ to some degree, so we will concentrate on procedures used on the CBOE. To see how the trading process works, suppose you want to purchase a call on IBM. Suppose you do not have a position in the underlying security. Then you are called "naked in the option." If, for example, you owned the stock and bought a put on it, you would have what is called a "*covered position in the put.*" If the price of the underlying security falls below the exercise price, the potential gains from the put are offset by the loss in value of the stock itself. If you also have no short position (i.e., you have not already written a call option in the same security), then your purchase of the call is an opening purchase transaction, which means you are buying a call that you have not already written.

To purchase the call you will need to go to a broker, who takes your order and transmits it to a floor broker. The floor broker, a member of the CBOE, goes to the place on the exchange floor (the "post") where IBM call options are traded and acts as your representative in attempting to obtain the best price for your purchase of the IBM call. The floor broker may trade with an order book official, a market maker, or another floor broker. An order book official is an exchange official who trades only for public customers (that is, she does not maintain an inventory in her own name or trade on a personal account). A market maker is an exchange member who trades only for his own account and does not trade for public customers. The floor broker and the other party with whom he trades on the exchange floor execute a verbal agreement and record the transaction with the exchange at the end of the day.

Orders can take either of two forms: a market order or a limit order. A floor broker who receives a market order is instructed to fill the order at the best price as soon as possible. A floor broker who receives a limit order is instructed to fill the order only if it is possible to do so at a prespecified price or better. In addition, both types of orders can have a variety of different contingencies attached.

When an option is purchased the investor must put up the entire purchase price of the option. At first glance, this seems like a heavy restriction on the amount of margin involved in the purchase. With regular stock purchases, current regulations require at least 50 percent of the purchase price to be paid with cash; this represents a 50-percent margin requirement. By purchasing a call option on a stock, you are indirectly acquiring the stock itself. In effect, you have equal claim on all increases in the price of that stock above the exercise price, just as if you owned it. In addition, the value of the option is generally far less than the value of the stock itself. For example, consider the call options on General Electric in Table 15-2. The January call on GE at a strike price of $85 sells for $1 11/16, while the price of the underlying stock is $86. Thus, you can acquire access to nearly all the increases in the future price of the stock through the maturity date in January for a very small fraction of its purchase price. When writing an option it is necessary to make a deposit against the prospect that a loss will be incurred, but the price paid by the option purchaser can be used as part of this deposit, and Treasury bills can be deposited as well. Therefore, the deposit is an interest-bearing asset for the option writer.

When a transaction in options is executed by the floor broker, the transaction is then cleared at the end of the day through the Options Clearing Corporation (OCC), which handles all options trades on the CBOE, AMEX, PHLX, and PSE. In order for an exchange member to clear trades, she also must become a member of the OCC, which imposes a minimum capital requirement and payment of fees. Members must put up margin to the OCC for options where it represents the writer. In addition, deposits must be made with the OCC at least equal to the amount of the purchase price of every option purchased on the exchange until that transaction is cleared by the exchange. These two requirements of margin and deposits protect the OCC against defaults on transactions, both at the time of purchase and when the option writer has to pay the purchaser if the option is exercised.

The procedure for executing trades on the CBOE and on the PSE, involving market makers and order book officials, resembles the open outcry auction process on the commodity exchanges. The CBOE pioneered development of exchange-traded options and followed the lead of the commodity exchanges in a number of respects. By contrast, the AMEX and PHLX utilize a system closer to the specialist system used on the NYSE, where a single specialist makes the entire market in a given security. The various options exchanges compete with respect to product development and the nature of the exchange process. The CBOE was the pioneer in developing exchange-traded options, and it remains the principal exchange, accounting for more than half of all options trading. The tremendous growth of exchange-traded options in general has provided an environment in which a number of exchanges can successfully participate in this market. It is not at all clear how many separate exchanges will continue to operate if and when the growth of options trading materially slows down.

We can identify at least four major advantages of exchange-traded options over the over-the-counter form of trading that prevailed before exchange trading developed. They are:

1. Liquidity is provided by highly standardized options contracts.
2. Increased efficiency in managing credit risk results from introduction of the OCC.
3. Improved disclosure and surveillance of trading activities are afforded by centralized auction markets.
4. Reduced transactions costs drive the efficient trading process on the options exchanges.

While we have emphasized exchange-traded options in our discussion, many financial institutions are now offering over-the-counter option contracts as well. The advantage of these contracts is that they can be structured to meet the precise needs of a particular client. The drawback is that the lack of standardization implicit in such contracts limits their liquidity and raises their price. We will encounter what amounts to over-the-counter options when we take up interest rate swaps in Chapter 16.

The Relationship Between Options and Futures

Next let's consider the relationship between options and futures contracts. The most important distinction between an option and a future is that there is a symmetrical payoff with a futures contract but an asymmetrical payoff with an option. The nature of the symmetry refers to the pattern of payoffs around the exercise price for the option or the settlement or contract price for the future. This symmetry was apparent in Figure 15-1. There is no kink in the line describing the payoff for a futures contract. The owner of a (long) future gains if the market price at maturity is above the settlement price and loses if it is below. With an option, the owner of either a put or a call never has a negative (gross) payoff. Thus, the payoff is not symmetrical around the exercise price.

This difference in symmetry between options and futures suggests that it might be possible to combine options in such a way that the payoff to a futures contract can be perfectly mimicked. In fact, this is quite easy to do. Suppose we consider a put, a call, and a futures contract on the same underlying asset, all with the same exercise or settlement price and maturity date. By inspecting Figures 15-1 and 15-2 we can see how to combine the put and the call to duplicate the payoff of the futures contract. If we buy the call, we will have duplicated the payoff to the futures contract if the market price of the underlying asset is above the exercise price at maturity. If we write the put, we will have duplicated the payoff to the futures contract if the market price of the underlying asset is below the exercise price at maturity. Therefore, if we buy a call and simultaneously write a put with the same exercise price, we will have a payoff that is identical to a long futures contract. For example, Table 15-3 shows the payoffs to each of these contracts for alternative values of the market price of the underlying asset where the exercise price is $50. The table illustrates that the difference between the payoffs from the call and the put are equal to the payoffs from the futures contract. We can summarize this relationship as follows:

$$\text{Payoff on a call} - \text{Payoff on a put} = \text{Payoff on a (long) future}$$

A similar relationship holds for a short position in a futures contract—a commitment to sell an asset at a prespecified price and time. A short position in a futures contract is the opposite of a long position in that the payoff in the long position is simply the negative of the payoff in the short position. Therefore, the payoff to the short futures contract can be duplicated by buying a put and writing a call or:

$$\text{Payoff on a put} - \text{Payoff on a call} = \text{Payoff on a (short) future}$$

If the payoffs on two assets are the same, then their values should also be the same. Therefore, we can write these equations not only for the relationship between the payoffs on options and futures but also for the relationship between the values or prices of options and futures:

$$\text{Value of call} - \text{Value of a put} = \text{Value of (long) future}$$

$$\text{Value of put} - \text{Value of a call} = \text{Value of (short) future}$$

Table 15-3
Payoff on Contingent Claims with an Exercise Price of $50

Price of Security	Call	Put	Future (long)
100	50	0	50
90	40	0	40
80	30	0	30
70	20	0	20
60	10	0	10
50	0	0	0
40	0	10	−10
30	0	20	−20
20	0	30	−30
10	0	40	−40
0	0	50	−50

There is another important distinction between futures and options, in addition to the difference in symmetry of the payoffs. This distinction is a result of the way futures and options contracts are structured. The market determines an equilibrium settlement or contract price for each futures contract at each point in time, and that is the only such price available. By comparison, in the options market a variety of exercise prices are generally available for each security on which options are traded. Then, for each exercise price the options market determines the equilibrium "price" or value of the option today.

To really understand this it is essential to look closely at how options and futures prices are quoted. Therefore, we need to return to Table 15-2. The price of the call options shown in this table are prices of the right to buy the underlying security at the specified exercise prices. There is no directly comparable price for futures contracts. Futures contracts trade at only one contract price, whereas options trade at a variety of distinct exercise prices, as the options quotations shown in the table illustrate. For example, there are six different exercise prices for options on Treasury bill futures on the IMM in Table 15-2 and the prices of the calls decrease as the exercise price increases.

Given this difference in the way futures and options are structured, it might not appear to make sense to say the value of a call less the value of a put is equal to the value of a long future. The problem here is that the value of the futures traded in the market is implicitly always zero. To take a position in the futures market you do not have to pay a positive (or negative) price for the futures contract. Other than commissions or transactions costs, it doesn't cost anything. Your broker will require that you deposit funds in an account with the brokerage house to cover future losses if they occur. But the cost of the future the day you buy it is still zero. The futures market is setting a settlement price so that the fair value of the future today is zero. The next day the market will set a new settlement price that may be higher or lower than the prevailing one. If you have a futures position and the price moves against you, you will have to settle your loss on a daily basis; this means that you must put up enough cash to cover your loss; however, once again, the cost of acquiring the futures position that day is still zero.

We can see from the relationship between futures and options that, at the equilibrium contract price for the future the value of the call must equal the value of the put because their difference must equal zero. There will always be an exercise or settlement price for which this is true. But options may be traded at any exercise price, not necessarily this particular one, whereas futures are traded at only one settlement price. Therefore, the settlement price quoted in the market for a futures contract has a special significance that the exercise price on an options contract does not have. The significance is that the settlement price contains the market's best forecast of the future price of the underlying security; that is, it is the settlement price where there is no incentive for the market as a whole to switch from a short to a long position or vice versa. If there were put and call options on the same Treasury bill where there is a futures contract, the settlement price on the Treasury-bill future would be the exercise price on the options where the price of the put would be exactly the same as the price of the call.

Viewing Assets Through the Options Framework

Many financial instruments that at first glance might not appear to be options actually turn out to be so under close examination. This is one reason the topic is so interesting and useful. Once you recognize that a financial instrument is an option, it often helps you understand this instrument better.

Debt and Equity as Options on the Assets of the Firm

We will examine only one example of an asset that turns out to be an option here, but this may be the most important example. The most obvious and widely used options are options on equity shares or stock of companies. However, the equity shares themselves are also options. They are options on the assets of the firm. More specifically, equity shares are *call options* on the assets of the firm. The exercise price of this call option is the amount borrowed from debtholders. If, at the maturity date for this debt, the value of the assets of the firm exceeds the obligation to debtholders, then the option will have a value equal to this difference. On the other hand, if the value of the firm's assets is less than the outstanding obligations to debtholders, then the option will expire worthless.

Using what we have already learned about options, we can also describe the position of debt holders. One way to view debt is to consider that debt holders own the assets of the firm but have written a call on the firm to the stockholders. Therefore, the value of debt is equal to the value of the assets of the firm less the value of the call held by stockholders.

The debt holders' claim on the firm is illustrated in Figure 15-3, which uses the options diagram employed throughout this chapter to illustrate how debt can be described with options. The three panels in the figure illustrate the two alternative ways in which you can get to the same conclusion, shown in Panel A. This Panel describes the payoff from a debt instrument, a bond or a loan, in terms of the option diagram used in earlier figures in this chapter. In this case the underlying security shown on the horizontal axis is the value of the assets controlled by the firm. The exercise price is represented by the point labeled P on both axes. If the value of the

Figure 15-3
Debt as an option on a firm's assets.

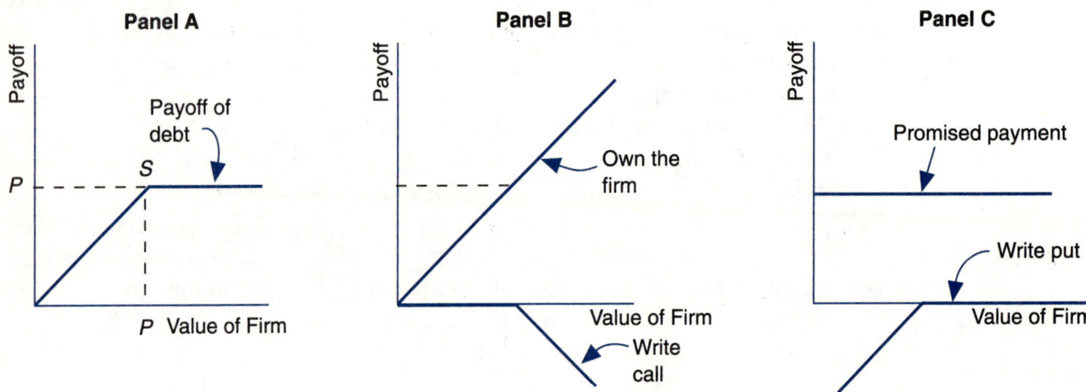

assets is less than the payment promised to lenders, then the firm is bankrupt. In this event the lenders have the entire firm, so the value of their claim moves up and down the 45-degree line in Panel A of the figure. This is the value of debt at any value of the underlying assets less than *P.* If the value of the assets is greater than the promised payment to debt holders, then the debt holders still get only *P.* This is illustrated by the horizontal line emanating from point *S* in the figure. Therefore, the kinked line starting at the origin and going to point *S,* then becoming horizontal, defines the payoff to bondholders for all possible values of the assets of the firm.

There are two ways to get to the conclusion shown in Panel A of Figure 15-3 using options and the basic equilibrium relationship between puts and calls we defined earlier. One way is to notice that the payoff described in Panel A is equivalent to the payoff from owning the firm and writing a call with an exercise price equal to the promised payment to debt holders. These two claims are illustrated in Panel B. One line shows the payoff to the writer of a call, just as in Figure 15-2. The other line shows the payoff to owning the underlying asset directly. When you add these two together you end up with Panel A. Therefore, one way to view claims held by debt holders is that they own the assets of the firm but have written a call to stockholders with an exercise price equal to the promised payments from those stockholders.

There is another way to view the claims of debt holders using options. This alternative is shown in Panel C. Debt holders also have a risk-free promised payment and have written a put option at an exercise price equal to the promised payment to debt holders. The risk-free payment is represented by the horizontal line in Panel C. The other line in this Panel is the payoff from writing a put. When these two are added together we also arrive at Panel A.

Viewing Lockheed's Debt Issue as an Option

The securities of almost any company could be used to illustrate the idea that debt and equity can be viewed as options on the underlying assets of a company. Let's consider Lockheed as an example. On 30 September 1986, Lockheed had 49,095,000 shares of common stock outstanding. The closing price of Lockheed stock on that date was \$44 1/8, so the total value of Lockheed stock was \$2.166 billion. This represents the value of a call option on Lockheed's assets. In order to know what the exercise price of this call option was, we have to identify the book value of the outstanding Lockheed debt. We use book rather than market value because we want the actual obligation to debt holders. It is not always so easy to determine this, for many companies have a lot of different debt obligations outstanding with different provisions and maturity dates. In Lockheed's case we can simplify the matter by assuming that its total short-term assets just about offset its total short-term liabilities. Then we can count the book value of Lockheed's long-term debt as the exercise price of the option. The book value of long-term debt for Lockheed in September 1986 was approximately \$500 million. Therefore, the exercise price for the call option represented by Lockheed's common stock was approximately \$500 million.

Is the call on Lockheed's assets represented by its common stock very far in the money? One important clue is that the market value of Lockheed's outstanding long-term debt was virtually identical to its book value. This implies that, at this point in time, the market rated Lockheed's probability of bankruptcy as very low. If we view the value of debt as the value of the promised payment less the value of the put option on Lockheed's assets, this suggests that the market is placing a very small value on this put option. Another way of saying this is that the call option represented by Lockheed's common stock is a deep-in-the-money option on Lockheed's assets. This is illustrated in Figure 15-4. This figure is just like Panel A of Figure 15-3. It shows the payoffs to the debt holders depending on the values of Lockheed's assets and the exercise price of \$500 million. We have also drawn in a probability distribution for the value of Lockheed's assets. This is a subjective distribution because it merely guesses

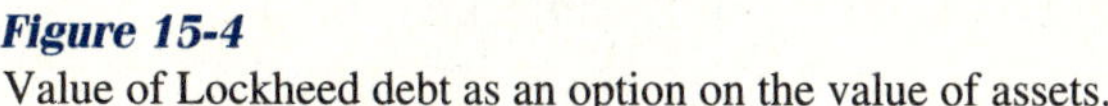

Figure 15-4
Value of Lockheed debt as an option on the value of assets.

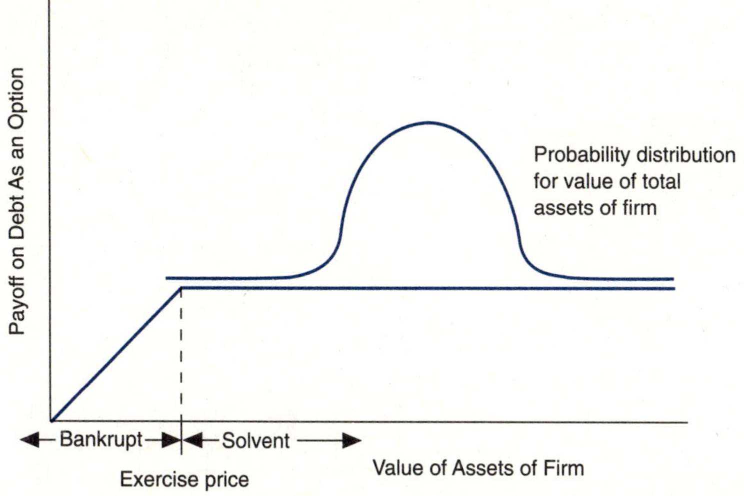

at what the market expected for Lockheed in 1986. It is drawn so there is a very small chance that the value of the assets will be less than $500 million; this is what is meant when we say the call represented by Lockheed common stock is deep in the money.

Uses of Options

We have already noted that options and futures markets have experienced tremendous growth in the last decade. Apparently options and futures increase the alternative ways in which risk may be redistributed in society. But why are options and futures useful? We started addressing this issue in the last chapter dealing with futures. Here we look more specifically at options.

Acting on Specific Information

It appears that one of the greatest uses of options contracts available in the United States is as a mechanism to speculate on the movements in prices of securities. They allow an investor to take positions that are otherwise difficult or impossible to construct. The advantage arises from the asymmetrical nature of the option relative to the futures contract. This asymmetry is valuable if you have some specific information or belief about the direction of change of the price of an asset. An option provides a direct mechanism for placing a bet on a specific direction of change in the asset price or even a specific range of the asset price. For example, if you think the price index of a class of bonds such as five-year Treasury notes has a good chance of being greater than a specific value, say $80, you can purchase a call with an exercise price of $80.

If you look closely at what types of investment positions you can take with options, you can construct ways to make almost any specific kind of bet you can imagine about the future performance of the value of an asset. For example, suppose you believe that the price of the five-year note would be close to $80 six months from today; that is, you think the chance is very low that the actual price will be either much higher or much lower than $80. Then you could take a position that reflects this view. You would want a short straddle or you would write a straddle. What you would do is write both puts and calls on the note at an exercise price of $80. The payoff you would receive is illustrated in Panel A of Figure 15-5. If you are right and the price of the note is exactly $80, then neither the put nor the call will be exercised at maturity, and you will get to keep the full price of both the put and call that you were paid for writing the options. But if the price of the note is anything but $80, then one or the other option will be exercised against you. If the price goes either up or down more than the amount of the two option prices you were paid, you lose money. Here you have made a bet that the price of the note would not change very much, or on low volatility. You could make exactly the opposite bet by setting up a long straddle, or by buying both a put and call. Then you make money if the price of the note goes either up or down by more than the prices of both options. This is illustrated in Panel B of Figure 15-5. You should notice that the long straddle, shown in Panel B, has one distinct advantage over the short straddle. If you are wrong, the most you can lose is the

Figure 15-5
Panel A: Short straddle.
Panel B: Long straddle.

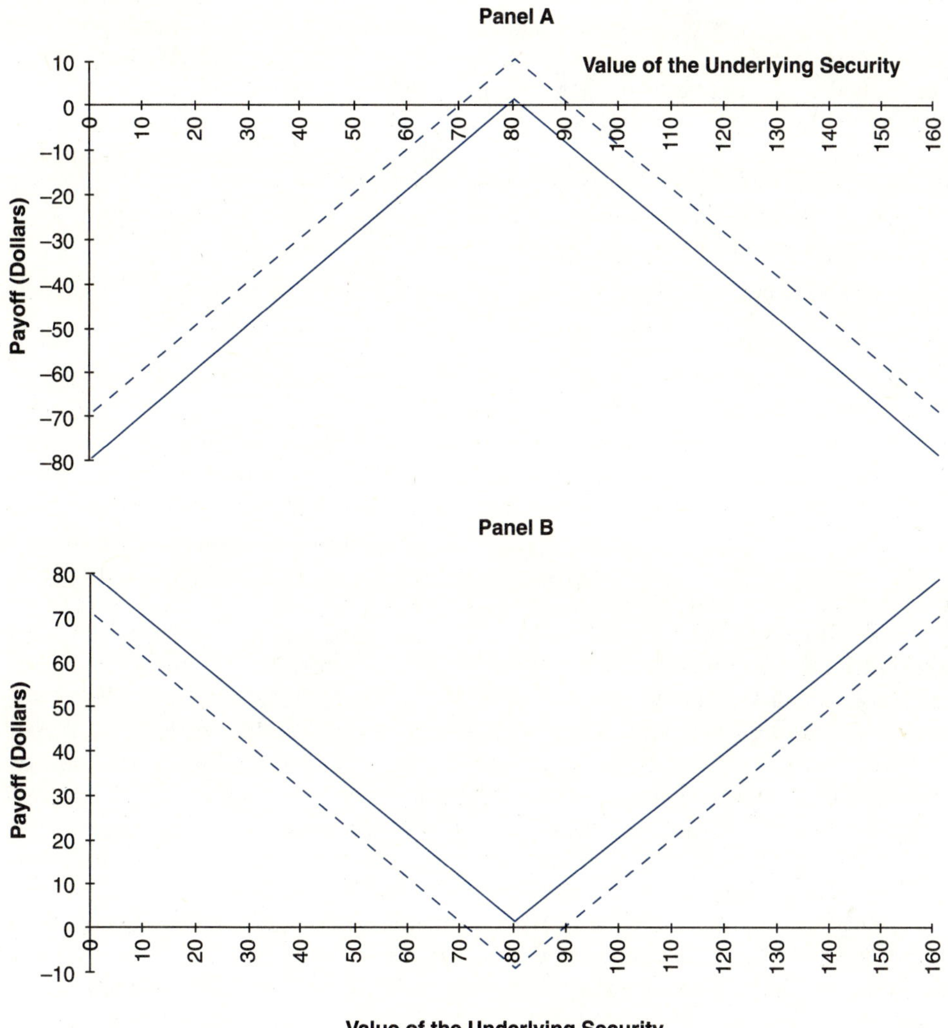

amount of the two option prices you paid up front. In the short straddle your losses are virtually unlimited if the price of the underlying security takes a big move in either direction. This is an important distinction whenever you take a long versus a short (that is, write) position in options. Writing options can be very dangerous. This example is only one of a wide range of possibilities.

For a financial market, options add to what economists call the market's "completeness." To understand what a complete market is, imagine a market in which every possible investment outcome had an individual security associated with it. For example, there would be a security with a payoff of, say, \$1 if the price of AT&T

stock were precisely $112 one year from today and no payoff if the price assumed any other value. Such a security is called a *primitive security.* If a primitive security actually existed for every conceivable event or state of the world we could imagine, then the market would be complete. The attraction of a complete market is that every conceivable opinion or piece of information an investor might possess could be acted upon in the market with the available primitive securities. Real-world markets will never actually be complete. In fact, like any other product, new securities develop when demand for them is sufficient. New securities are demanded when people want to make bets or act on information in ways that are not feasible with the available securities. Another way of putting it is that new securities arise because of a desire for a more complete market. Options accomplish precisely this purpose.

Limiting Risk with Options

One of the most important uses of both futures and options is to hedge risks or to sell off risks to another party. Futures markets in commodities have been used for many years by various commodity producers to limit the risks of price fluctuations in the product they will have available for sale in the future. For example, a farmer who has planted a wheat crop may use futures markets to contract for a price when his wheat is ready for harvest. Without futures markets his profits would depend on the uncertain price of wheat at harvest time. Using futures markets he can shift that uncertainty to investors in the futures markets who are interested in speculating on the future price of wheat.

While futures markets have been used for many years to hedge the risk of commodity prices, only in the last two decades have futures and options on financial instruments been widely used to hedge financial risks. Because later chapters are devoted to hedging financial risks, we consider only one example here.

Consider an investor who has a position in T bonds. Suppose that the bonds are currently valued at $50 each. This investor is particularly averse to risk and does not want to accept the prospect that there might be large fluctuations in the price of the bonds. Suppose the investor decides that she does not want to be exposed to more than a 20-percent fluctuation in the price of the bonds. The way to accomplish this is to buy put options with an exercise price of $40 and write call options with an exercise price of $60. The results are illustrated in Figure 15-6. Panel A shows the payoff from holding the bonds. Once again the payoff in this figure is gross rather than net return, as in Figure 15-1. Panel B shows the payoffs from buying the put and writing the call. Panel C shows what happens when these distinct payoffs are combined. The solid line in Panel C defines the payoff when the three positions are added together. The figure shows that if the price of the underlying asset is equal to or less than $40, then the payoff to the combined positions is $40. The payoff is exactly equal to the payoff from holding the bond if the bond price is between $40 and $60. If the price of the bond exceeds $60 the payoff is only $60. Panel D illustrates both the loss exposure and the potential gain that have been eliminated by buying the put and writing the call.

The investor in this situation has purchased insurance against substantial declines in the price of the bond by buying the put. In effect, the price of the put can

Figure 15-6
Panel A: Payoff on holding bond.
Panel B: Payoff from buying put and writing call options.
Panel C: Payoff from combined positions.

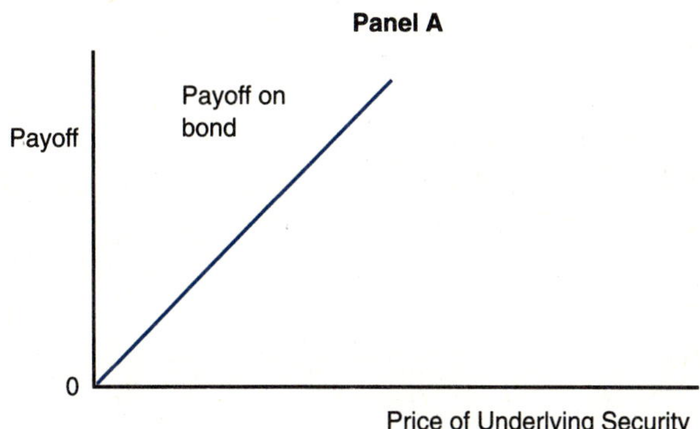

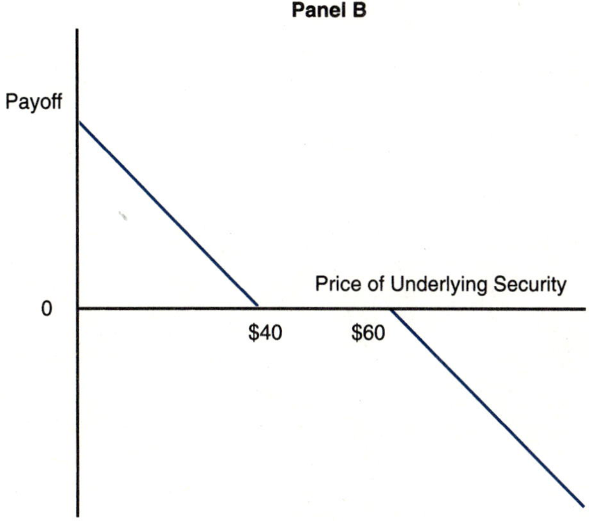

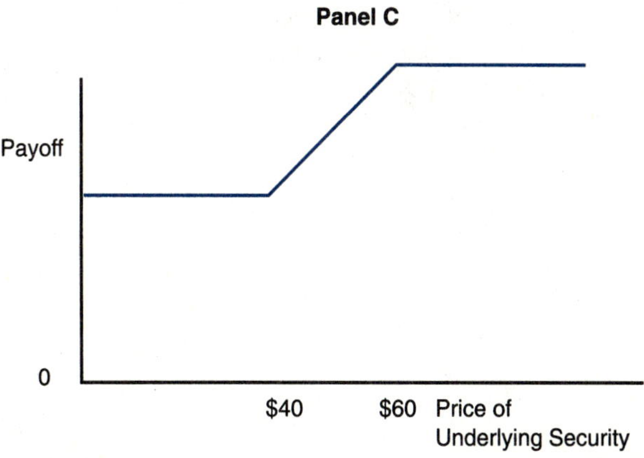

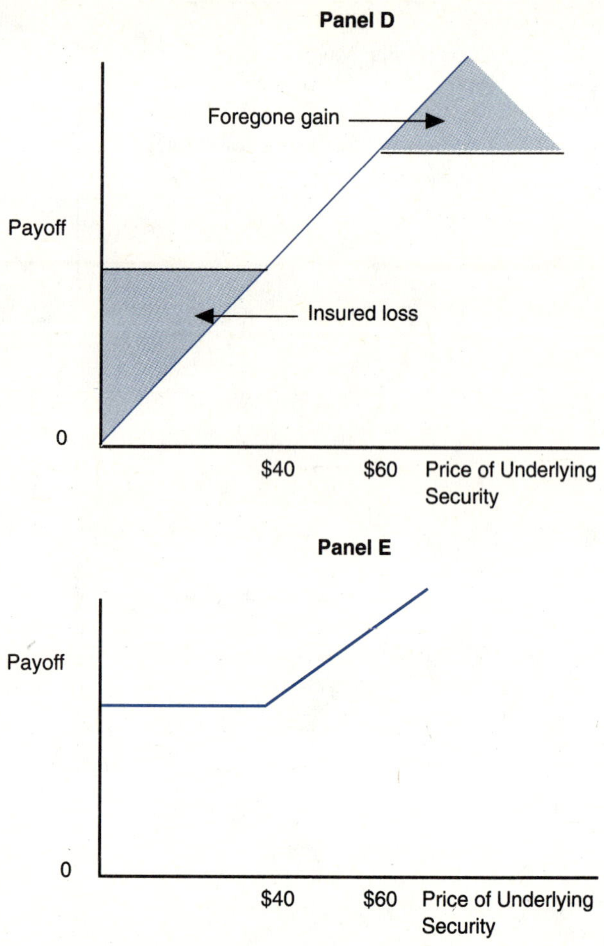

Figure 15-6 (continued)
Panel D: Insured loss and foregone gain from combined positions.
Panel E: Payoff from combination of underlying security and put option.

be thought of as an insurance premium. At the same time, using the call, she has sold off the prospect for substantial appreciation in the price of the bond. For this transaction she receives, rather than pays, a price. There is no reason why an investor has to engage in both of these transactions simultaneously. An investor might simply want to purchase insurance against substantial declines in the price of the bond. The payoff from this transaction, which includes holding the bond and buying a put, is illustrated in Panel E of Figure 15-6. Once again, the solid line shows the payoff without taking account of the price of the put.

Determinants of Options Prices

It is no simple task to figure out how an option should be valued. In fact, while options have been of interest for many years it was only recently that somebody came up with a satisfactory analysis of how to value them. In 1973 Fischer Black and Myron Scholes advanced a model for pricing options. Their contribution was quickly recognized as a major breakthrough, and their insight is now referred to as the Black-Scholes model. In the remainder of this chapter we examine the principal determinants of options prices. We start with options on equities, as shown in Panel A of Table 15-2. Then we move on to options on fixed-income securities. Options on fixed-income securities present some special problems in valuation that do not develop with options on stock. The problems pertain to the fact that the interest rate cannot be taken as given with bonds because changes in interest rates are what drive bond prices. Therefore, we first discuss how options on equities, or on anything where we can take the interest rate as given, are priced. Then we discuss some of the procedures employed to deal with options on fixed-income securities.

There are five principal variables that influence the price of an option. We explore why and how call option prices are influenced by each of these variables. Table 15-4 summarizes the qualitative relationship between the value of a call option and each of the five independent variables itemized in the table. That is, the table indicates whether an increase in the independent variable causes the price of a call option to increase or decrease.

Current Price of the Underlying Security

Let's return to the call option on a share of stock with an exercise price of $50 that we considered earlier. How will the value of an American call option be influenced by changes in the current price of the underlying stock? To answer this question, suppose that the current price of the stock is above the exercise price, so that the option is in the money. The value of an American call option that is in the money must be at least equal to the difference between the current price of the stock and the exercise price. Furthermore, an option can never have a negative value, since the payoff from an option will never be negative; this establishes a minimum value for the option for any value of the underlying security. This minimum value is illustrated in Figure 15-7 by the line identical to the one in Figure 15-1 that shows the payoff from a call option. We also know that the option can never be more valuable than the underlying security itself because the payoff from the stock will always exceed the payoff from the option.

The relationship between the value of the underlying security and the value of a call option on that security hinges on the impact of changes in the price of the asset

Table 15-4

Determinants of Option Prices and Direction of Effect

Determinant of Option Price	Direction of Price Change
Current price of underlying security	Positive
Exercise price of option	Negative
Variability of the underlying security	Positive
Time to maturity of option	Positive
Risk-free interest rate	Depends on security[a]

[a] The effect of interest rates is positive for options on stocks but is generally negative for options on bonds.

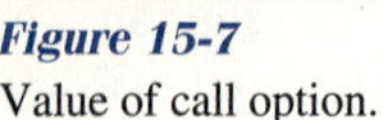

Figure 15-7
Value of call option.

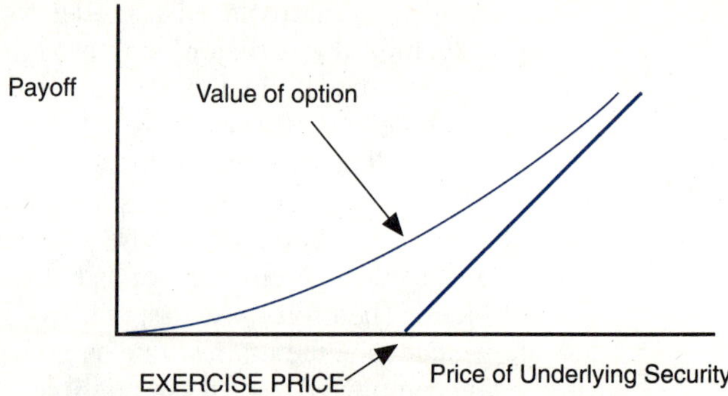

on the probability distribution of payoffs from the option. If the current price of the security increases, there should be a better chance of greater payoffs. This is apparent when the option is in the money, as the gain from an increase in the current share price could be realized by exercising the option immediately. But it is also true when the option is not in the money, as an increase in the current price of the asset in this case must increase the chance the option will be in the money at maturity. Therefore, regardless of whether the option is in the money, the higher the price of the security the higher the value of the call option should be.

If the price of the underlying asset is very high relative to the exercise price, the probability is also very high that the option will be exercised. As a result, the value of the option must be very close to the value of the underlying asset less the exercise price of the option. This is illustrated in Figure 15-7: A solid curve shows the value of the option as a function of the price of the underlying security. This line is increasing throughout, which shows that an increase in the price of the underlying security leads to an increase in the price of a call option. The value of the option line also approaches the line that shows the payoff to the option, or the value of the stock less the exercise price for an in-the-money option, as the stock price increases. The slope of this curve is known as the option "*delta.*" It measures the sensitivity of the price of the option to changes in the value of the underlying security.

Exercise Price of the Option

A simple extension of the relationship just discussed will show how a change in the exercise price of an option influences its value. A decrease in the exercise price has the same effect as an increase in the current price of the underlying asset. For an in-the-money option it increases the payoff if it is exercised immediately. For an out-of-the-money option it increases the chance it will be in the money in the future. Therefore, a decrease in the exercise price must lead to an increase in the value of the option. This is illustrated in Figure 15-8, which presents curves representing the value of two options that differ only by their exercise prices. One has an exercise price of $30 and the other an exercise price of $50. The figure shows that the option with the lower exercise price has a higher value for any value of the underlying security. It is also evident in the options prices shown in Table 15-2. For example, the price of March call options on Gillette decreases from 5 1/2 to 3/4 as the exercise price increases from 50 to 60.

Figure 15-8
Value of options at two exercise prices.

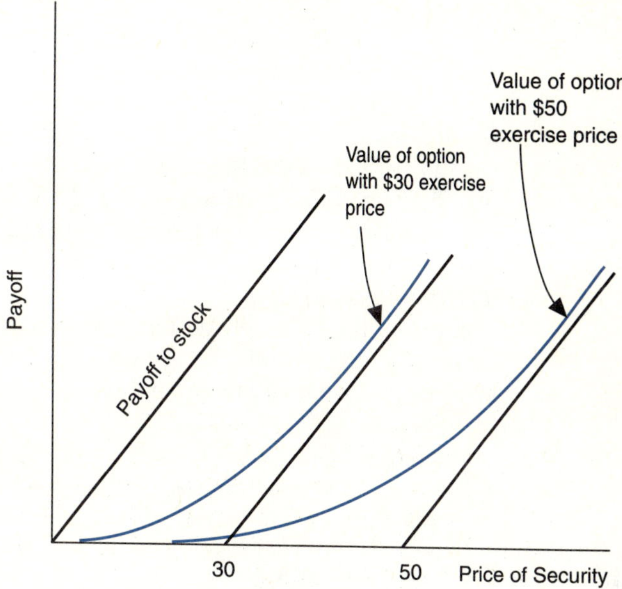

Variability of the Price of the Underlying Security

The next variable that can influence the value of an option is the variability of the price of the underlying security. Imagine identical call options on two different stocks, both having a current value of $50. The first stock has a 50-percent chance that the price will either increase or decrease by $25; the second stock has only a 25-percent chance of a comparable increase or decrease. The call option on either stock will be worthless if the stock goes down in value (assuming a $50 exercise price); however, the first stock has a greater chance of large positive payoffs than the second. Therefore, the call option on this stock should be more valuable than the option on the second stock.

The probability of a large change in the price of a stock in any given period is determined by the variance of the stock price. Therefore, a call option on a security with a high variance should have a higher value than a call option on a security with a relatively low variance.

Time to Maturity

The fourth variable that determines the price of an option, the time to maturity, also influences the probability that there will be large increases in the value of the underlying security. This is because the chance that there will be a large increase in price prior to maturity depends on the variance applicable to the entire time until maturity. The variance of an asset is generally measured for a unit of time, such as a day. Therefore, the variance applicable to the period until maturity increases as the length of the period to maturity increases.

The Risk-Free Interest Rate

The final variable that determines the price of an option is the risk-free interest rate. To see why this is important, compare investing in a call option on a stock with a levered investment directly in that stock. With either investment you are exposed to the same possible payoffs. If the risk-free interest rate increases, the cost of borrowing to finance the purchase of the stock will increase. This makes the call option more attractive, and its value must rise relative to the value of the stock. The implication is that increases in interest rates cause call options to increase in value. For this relationship to be correct, changes in interest rates must not directly cause changes in the value of the underlying asset. For options on equities this may be a reasonable assumption, but for options on bonds it is not. Here the relationship can be reversed. We take this up in more detail shortly.

• *So You Want to Price Options?* •

Binomial Approach to Option Pricing

Thus far we have developed only some intuition about how an option should be priced. This intuition is extremely important, and we don't want to underestimate its value, but it would be helpful if we could also actually see how to compute the price of an option. Thanks to Fischer Black and Myron Scholes we now have a formula for computing the value of European options. We'll get to the Black-Scholes formula shortly, but we want to approach it gradually, starting with a relatively simple option-pricing problem. We construct an artificial option that has an important simplifying characteristic: It has only two possible payoffs, thus the name "binomial" approach to pricing. You can value the simple option by using a no-arbitrage condition. We duplicate the payoff on the option by taking a leveraged position in the underlying asset. This means we borrow money to buy the underlying asset. If we can duplicate the payoff on the option, then the price we must pay for the leveraged position in the underlying asset and for the option itself must be the same, otherwise there would be an arbitrage opportunity, or what is often called a money machine. The fundamental underlying hypothesis in this approach to pricing an option is that such money machines don't exist, or at least not for very long. If they are uncovered, people move from the option to the levered position in the underlying asset (or vice versa) until the arbitrage opportunity is eliminated.

Consider an option on a debt instrument—you can think of this as an option on a T bond, though T bonds don't have binomial outcomes like the ones we describe—where the underlying security has two possible payoffs at the end of six months. Let these payoffs be $117 and $83 (like the market quotes on Treasury securities, we are expressing these prices per $100 of initial face value of the bond). We will rule out outcomes other than these two. Let the maturity of a call option on this bond be six months and let the exercise price on the call option be $100. Finally, suppose that the price of the bond in the cash market is $90 and that the interest rate in the economy (the zero-coupon rate for six-month maturities) is 7.5 percent.

Now let's consider two alternative ways in which we might try to take a position in the bond. One possibility is to buy call options in the bond with the terms we have just identified. If we buy two call options we will have a (gross) payoff that depends on the payoffs on the bond as follows:

Payoff on Two Options

Value of bond	$83	$117
Payoff on two call options	$0	$34

Now let's consider how much we could borrow to buy this bond if our leveraged position is going to be viewed as riskless and assuming we don't subsidize this transaction by pledging some other resources to reduce the risk to the lender. That is, our borrowing has to be riskless, taking into account only our investment in this particular bond. Given that the interest rate is 7.5 percent and that we are dealing with a six-month loan and that the most we can promise to repay is $83, the maximum amount we can borrow is $83/1.0375, or $80. This means that we will have to put up $10 of our own money to buy the bond at the going price of $90. Now our payoff on this levered investment will turn out to be the same as the payoff we computed for our two call options:

Payoff on Levered Position in Bond

Value of bond	$83	$117
Repayment of debt	−$83	−$83
Total payoff	$0	$34

Notice that the payoffs from the levered investment in the bond and the two call options are identical. This means that the value of the two investments to an investor must be identical:

Value of two call options = Value of bond − $80 loan

We have already specified that the value of the bond is $90. This means that the value of the six-month call option on that bond must be $5. Any other value would create an arbitrage opportunity. If, for example, writers of call options were asking $10, they would find that anyone considering how they might take a position in the underlying bond would choose to use the levered direct investment over the option. Only if those potential writers of calls dropped their price to $5 would they find any takers. Moreover, if they dropped the price even a little below $5 they would be swamped with takers. Another way to see the same thing is that if the price of the call were greater than $5 it would be profitable to write calls and unwind or hedge the resulting risk exposure by taking the levered position in the underlying security we have just described. Thus, $5 is the only sustainable price for the call option.

There is at least one other thing to notice about this example. We needed two call options to replicate the payoffs on the levered investments. The technical way to say this is that the option delta is 1/2. The option delta, or the hedge ratio of the option, is the number of units (shares for equities) of the underlying security that are needed to replicate the behavior of one call option. Here we need half of a bond for each call option on that bond.

This is a very simplistic example. We do not actually see options on bonds where the bond has only two possible payoffs. However, the restriction of two possible payoffs is not really as big an obstacle as it might seem at first glance. Remember we said there were two possible payoffs in six months and none in between. We might suppose, instead, that there were two possible payoffs in three months and then, for each of those payoffs, two more possible payoffs in three more months. We could value these options as sequences of two payoff options identical to the one we just considered. But we can keep cutting the time interval indefinitely—each three-month interval can be divided in half and then in half again, ad infinitum—and valuing the resulting sets of two payoff options. This may sound unduly messy, but it is relatively simple to program a computer to do this sort of thing.

As you keep breaking the length of the period into finer and finer subintervals, you begin to approach continuous time or time measured continuously. This is the realm of the Black-Scholes option-pricing model. That is, one way to view the Black-Scholes model is simply as the limiting case of the binomial approach we just went through (for a very simple case) when the interval between payoffs becomes arbitrarily small. Fortunately, you don't have to know much about how Black and Scholes actually developed their model to use it. That is one of its virtues. It is enough to understand the binomial case and see that the Black-Scholes model generalizes the insights of this simple case.

The Black-Scholes Model

Black and Scholes developed their pricing formula for European options by doing a careful comparison of the alternatives of investing in a call option and making a leveraged investment directly in the underlying asset[1]. Their actual analysis is quite formidable, and well beyond the scope of this book, but the basic idea is just an extension of the binomial approach we have just discussed. The key is to attempt to replicate the position taken through an option by a leveraged position in the underlying asset on a continuous basis and then to recognize that the two positions cannot have different values. In the Black-Scholes approach we must constantly adjust the hedge position, or the delta of the option, or else we may find we are not creating a perfect arbitrage position. If we actually tried to make these adjustments continuously, and if we recognize that there are transactions costs to be dealt with in performing these adjustments, it would become infinitely costly to construct the proper arbitrage positions. So, in practice, we need to balance these transactions costs against the gains from adjustments in our hedge ratio. The Black-Scholes formula can be written as follows:

$$\text{Value of a call option} = PN(d_1) - Ee^{-m} N(d_2)$$

where

$$d_1 = \frac{\log(P/E) + rt + \sigma^2 t/2}{\sigma\sqrt{t}}$$

$$d_2 = \frac{\log(P/E) + rt - \sigma^2 t/2}{\sigma\sqrt{t}}$$

[1]See F. Black and M. Scholes. "The Pricing of Options and Corporate Liabilities." *Journal of Political Economy* 81 (May-June 1973), pp. 637–654.

$N(d)$ is the cumulative normal probability density function (the probability that a normally distributed random variable will be less than or equal to d), E is the exercise price of the option, t is time to maturity, P is the current price of the underlying asset, σ^2 is the instantaneous variance of the rate of return on the underlying security, and r is the risk-free interest rate (continuously compounded).

Fortunately, you do not have to understand this equation thoroughly to use it. Many participants in the options markets use the equation because it can be programmed into a hand-held calculator quite easily. You may notice that the formula can be interpreted in terms of the arbitrage position we constructed in the simpler binomial case. The formula tells us that the value of a call is equal to an investment of $PN(d_1)$ in the underlying security less borrowing of $Ee^{-rt}N(d_2)$. The option delta in the Black-Scholes model is $N(d_1)$. This measures the sensitivity of the stock price to changes in the value of the underlying security. The process of creating a hedge in the Black-Scholes arbitrage process involves the adjustment of this delta over time as P changes.

It is important to introduce a major qualification of the Black-Scholes model: It applies directly to European rather than American options, that is, to options that can be exercised only at maturity. It is not as big a limitation as it might seem at first glance. If an American option is on an underlying security that provides no intermediate cash flows, such as dividend payments for stocks or coupon payments for bonds, then it is *never* optimal to exercise the American option before maturity. If you hold an American option and you think it is optimal to exercise it, you can always do better by selling the option. If you exercise it early you will give up part of the value of the option. Therefore, the Black-Scholes model applies directly to American options in this situation, but if the underlying asset for an option pays significant dividends or coupon payments it can sometimes be optimal to exercise early in order to get access to those cash flows. Here, the Black-Scholes model must be modified. We caution you to be careful about these situations.

The Black-Scholes option pricing model is specifically applicable to options on stocks where the short-term interest rate in the economy is taken as given or is constant and the price of the stock is random or uncertain. Part of the reasoning behind the model posits that it is possible to duplicate the payoff on an option by borrowing money, at the known interest rate, to finance a levered investment in the underlying security. The returns on the option and on the levered investment with identical payoffs cannot be different. This leads to the price of the option. It is not possible to extend this idea of formulating a replicating investment with bonds when interest rates are uncertain without specifically taking into account the nature of the uncertainty about interest rates. (By the way, this is a shortcoming of our binomial example of the pricing of a bond option presented earlier.) This requires some model of the term structure and some model for interest rates. It is important to note that many types of bonds include some kind of option on the interest rate as a part of the bond. Bonds with call provisions or mortgages with prepayment provisions have such options embedded in them. In addition, convertible bonds, or bonds convertible into stock, include such options. Therefore, it is tremendously important to have a practical mechanism for pricing such options. Though this problem is sufficiently complicated that we cannot directly take it up here, we will consider some of the implications of the special problem of options on bonds when we deal with prepayment risk in Chapters 21 and 22.

If you intend to use this or any other model for pricing options, it is important to know when the equation is applicable and when it can be misused. A few references about the equation are listed at the end of the chapter.

SUMMARY

Options represent the right or option to buy or sell an asset at a prespecified time and price. We examined how options work and learned that the holder of a call option, the option to buy a security, receives a payoff that cannot be less than zero. If the price of the underlying asset is greater than the exercise price of the option, then the holder of the call option will earn a profit equal to the difference between these two prices. We learned about the operation and growth of the exchanges on which options are currently traded in the United States.

We examined the relationship between options and futures and the underlying securities on which they are claims. The value of a call option less the value of a put option is equal to the value of a futures contract on that asset. We also explored how an equity claim on a company is simply a call option on the assets of the firm. The value of the debt of the company can be characterized in terms of the value of options.

In exploring the actual and potential uses of options we found that options allow market participants to act on specific information or to make specific bets that are otherwise unavailable in the marketplace. In this way options add to the completeness of the market; but options and futures also allow market participants to redistribute risk. Finally, we explored how prices of options are determined in organized markets. The price of a call option is determined by the exercise price, the current price of the underlying security, the variance of the price of the underlying security, the time to maturity, and the risk-free interest rate. We also examined the binomial option pricing model and the formula for the Black-Scholes option-pricing model, which relates the price of an option to these variables, and the recent empirical evidence on its effectiveness. Finally, we briefly compared the Black-Scholes model to option-pricing models developed explicitly for bonds with uncertain interest rates.

QUESTIONS

1. Distinguish between being long and short in both puts and calls. What are the payoffs in each position? How can they be illustrated graphically?
2. Explain the difference between a futures and an option contract. Why is there only one "contract price" for a futures contract when there are many exercise prices with options?
3. What is a complete market? How do options help to complete a market?

4. How can equity and debt securities issued by a firm be characterized as options? What is the underlying asset in these options?
5. What is an in-the-money option? When is a call versus a put in the money?
6. Suppose a firm is planning to borrow from a bank to finance some new inventory. The loan is going to be taken down in three months in the amount of $10 million. The bank is willing to commit to an interest rate for this future loan. However, the borrower is unsure whether she is getting a good price. How can the borrower use futures or options markets to accomplish the same guarantee as the banker provided? How can she check if the banker is providing a good price?
7. Why is it true that as the variance of an option increases its value must increase? Does this conflict with the idea that variance measures risk and that value should go down as risk increases? Why or why not?
8. Suppose you had the job of approving the introduction of new options and futures contracts on the exchanges in the United States. How would you evaluate whether an option contract should be allowed to be traded on the exchange?
9. Consider a call and a put on the same stock with the same maturity date and an exercise price of $72. Suppose the current value of the stock is $75, so that the call is in the money. Suppose the current price of the call is $4.50 and the current price of the put is $1.50. Calculate the net payoffs to the purchaser and writer of both calls and puts if the value of the underlying security at the maturity of the option is $70, $72.50, $75, $77.50, and $80.
10. Suppose you owned 1000 shares of GE stock and the current value of the stock and options available on that stock were as reported for GE in Table 15-2. Suppose you wrote 10 February puts with an exercise price of $85. Define the net payoffs you would have from both your stock position and your options if the price of GE stock varied from $75 to $95 at the maturity date of your options.
11. Return to the call and put options on GE in Table 15-2. Now suppose you purchased both one February call and one February put on GE at $85, but you hold no stock. Define the payoffs you would have for alternative values of GE stock at maturity. When would you be interested in taking this type of position using options?
12. Suppose you are comparing the values of two call options on different underlying assets. Both assets have the same exercise price, and the current prices of both assets are the same. However, the first asset has a higher variance than the second and its maturity date is shorter. Which of the two assets would you expect to have the higher value? Explain why.

REFERENCES

Black, F., Emanuel Derman, and William Toy. "A One-Factor Model of Interest Rates and Its Application to Treasury Bond Options." *Financial Analysts Journal* 46 (Jan-Feb 1990), pp. 33–39.

Black, F., and M. Scholes. "The Valuation of Option Contracts and a Test of Market Efficiency." *Journal of Finance* (May 1972), pp. 399–417.

———. "The Pricing of Options and Corporate Liabilities." *Journal of Political Economy* 81 (May-June 1973), pp. 637–654.

———. "Fact and Fancy in the Use of Options." *Financial Analysts Journal* 31 (July-August 1975), pp. 36–41, 61–72.

Bookstaber, R., and R. Clarke. *Option Strategies for Institutional Investment Management.* Reading, MA: Addison-Wesley, 1983.

Brennan, Michael J., and Eduardo S. Schwartz. "Savings Bonds. Retractable Bonds and Callable Bonds." *Journal of Financial Economics* 5 (1977), pp. 67–88.

Geske, R., and R. Roll. "On Valuing American Call Options with the Black-Scholes European Formula." *Journal of Finance* 39 (June 1984), pp. 443–455.

Giddy, I. "The Foreign Exchange Option as a Hedging Tool." *Midland Corporate Finance Journal* 1 (Fall 1983), pp. 32–42.

Goodman, L. "New Options Markets." *Federal Reserve Bank of New York Quarterly Review* 8 (Autumn 1983), pp. 35–47.

• Chapter 16
Swaps

This chapter is devoted to swaps, both interest rate and currency swaps. Interest rate swaps were one of the most important growth businesses in the financial markets of the 1980s. They grew from virtually zero to an estimated volume of almost $1 trillion worldwide. It is rather difficult to provide a precise estimate of the total outstanding volume of swaps because no centralized reporting agency collects accurate data, but there is no doubt that swaps have experienced tremendous growth. In this chapter we want to develop an understanding of why and how the swaps market has become so important and grown so rapidly and to see how swaps can be used. Swaps are now integrated with all sorts of other more traditional financial arrangements. No company can seriously look at its financing today without considering whether it should utilize a swap as a part of its financial structure. Thus, not only do the treasury staffs of companies have to be well-versed in swaps, but the bank officers who call on those people also have to understand how swaps can be used to help companies accomplish their financial objectives. In this chapter we seek to develop enough understanding of swaps to see how and why companies can use them effectively.

• *Concepts to Learn in Chapter 16* •

- Definition and characteristics of a swap agreement
- Why swaps have become important instruments
- How swaps can be used in many situations
- How swaps are priced

The Nature of Swaps

The single most important thing to understand about a swap is that it is very similar to a portfolio or collection of forward contracts. This is true whether the swap is a currency swap, an interest rate swap, a combination of both, or even a commodity swap. Recall that a forward contract is a commitment to buy (long) or sell (short) an underlying asset at a prespecified price and time. For example, we might engage in a forward contract in the yen-dollar exchange rate, where we could commit to buy yen at a prespecified or contract price denominated in dollars at a specific future date, the maturity date for the contract. A swap is almost identical to a sequence of forward contracts at different maturity dates.

Because forward contracts are not highly standardized it is easier to draw a direct comparison between swaps and the close relative of the forward contract, the future. Table 16-1, which contains a summary of the key features of both swaps and futures contracts, emphasizes that whereas futures are highly standardized swaps are quite flexible. They can vary in maturity from as short as a month to 20 years. They can be for virtually any amount. They can include settlement or payments on any date desired. They can be bought out or unwound without having to worry about delivery of an underlying asset. They are also available from a variety of market-makers or intermediaries, including both commercial and investment banks.

As our first introduction to swaps, let's begin with an example of a yen-dollar currency swap. Just as in a forward contract, there must be two parties to the swap. Here they are called *counterparties.* The two counterparties might agree to exchange yen for dollars at a predetermined exchange rate on a sequence of dates in the future. Suppose the current date is 1 January 1992 and the swap involves commitments to exchange yen for dollars every six months for ten years, beginning 1 July 1992. Suppose also that the agreed-upon exchange rate is 130 yen-dollar and the contract is written for $100,000. This means one counterparty would agree to pay the spot exchange rate prevailing on each of the 20 dates. Let's call him Counterparty 1. Simultaneously, the other counterparty would agree to pay the contract exchange rate. Let's call her Counterparty 2. For example, suppose that the applicable spot yen-dollar exchange rate on 1 July 1994, is 140. Then, per dollar of the contract, Counterparty 1 would pay 140 ¥ and receive from Counterparty 2, ¥130. A simpler way to settle this would be for Counterparty 1 to simply pay Counterparty 2, ¥10, though on the total contract amount of $100,000, the actual payment made by Counterparty 1 to Counterparty 2 would be ¥10 × 100,000, which equals ¥1 million.

Of course the settlement we have just described would also be perfectly applicable to a forward contract in the yen-dollar exchange rate. The event we described for 1 July 1994, literally is a forward contract, but the swap entails 20 forward contracts, all agreed to on 1 January 1992 with settlements based on the spot exchange rate prevailing at six-month intervals for ten years. Thus, the swap is a portfolio of forward contracts. The currency swap in our example is illustrated in Figure 16-1, where the basis for the settlement between the counterparties is identified over the life of the swap.

Table 16-1

Comparison of Swaps and Interest Rate Futures

	Futures	**Swaps**
Maturities	Up to 2.5 years	1 Month to 20 years
Costs	Margins and commissions	Broker's fees
Size	Standard contracts	Any amount over $10 million
Settlement dates	Fixed quarterly cycle	Any dates
Difficulty of management	Complex	Simple
Termination of positions	Closed out with opposite contract	Reversed or bought out
Transactions completed	Organized exchange	Commercial and investment banks

Figure 16-1

Currency swap of yen for dollars where fixed payment is 130 yen and floating obligations are equal to spot exchange rate. Bars show floating payments on each settlement date. Line at 130 yen shows fixed payments.

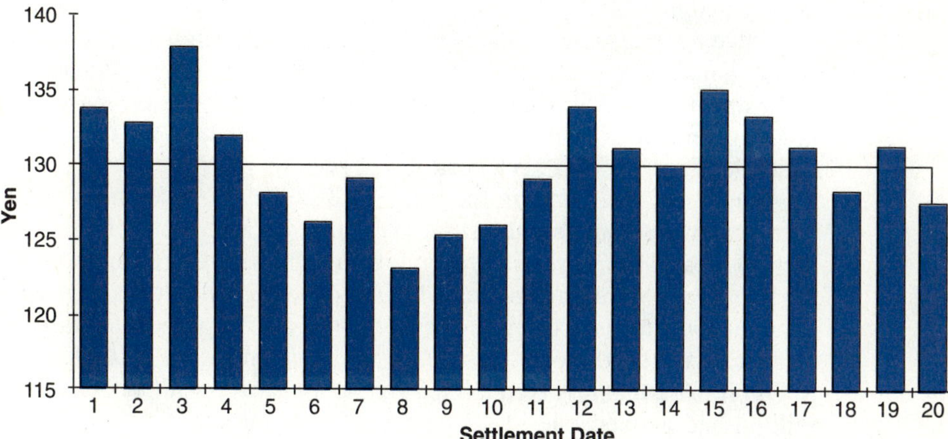

Notice that a sequence of 20 forward contracts would not all be priced at the same contract exchange rate, ¥130 per dollar in our example. Instead, the forward or the futures markets would set a distinct settlement price for each contract. The normal procedure in the swaps market is to set one exchange rate, or one interest rate in an interest rate swap, that determines one side of the swap obligation for all settlement dates of the swap, but this need not be the case. A swap could be arranged with any desired sequence of agreed fixed exchange rates or interest rates.

The arrangement we have just described for a currency swap applies equally to an interest rate swap. An interest rate swap is simply a portfolio or collection of forward contracts or forward rate agreements on an interest rate. To see what we mean let's examine a simple example of a so-called fixed-for-floating interest rate swap. We consider more detailed examples throughout this chapter. This one is stripped down to its essentials to illustrate the basic idea. Suppose that on 1 January 1994 Company 1 agrees to pay a fixed interest rate to Company 2 every six months for two years, just as in our currency swap example. Suppose the fixed interest rate is 12 percent so that 6 percent would be paid every six months. Also suppose that the amount of the principal involved is $10 million. This is called the *notional principal.* The word notional is used because the $10 million never actually changes hands. Company 1 is said to "pay fixed" and "receive floating"; Company 2 is said to "pay floating" and "receive fixed." The floating rate could be any market interest rate we might pick, but a common rate used in the market is the London interbank offer rate (LIBOR). This is the rate prevailing for short-maturity loans among financial institutions around the world. Now suppose that on 1 July 1994, LIBOR is 8 percent. This rate will determine the payment six months later, on 1 January 1995. Counterparty 1 has agreed to pay 12 percent × 1/2 × $10,000,000 to Counterparty 2; Counterparty 2 has agreed to pay

8 percent × 1/2 × $10,000,000 to Counterparty 1. (The 1/2 reflects the fact that settlement takes place every six months.) The simplest way to settle this exchange is for Counterparty 1 to pay Counterparty 2 4 percent × 1/2 × $10,000,000, or $200,000 on 1 January 1995. Hypothetical payments used to determine the actual amount of cash that changes hands on each settlement date are illustrated in Figure 16-2.

Once again, just as in the case of the currency swap, the exchange between the two counterparties on 1 July 1994 is virtually identical to that which would take place under a forward contract with a contract interest rate of 12 percent. But a swap is an agreement to a series of such contracts, stretching out over two years in this example. Thus, the swap is a portfolio of such forward contracts.

Swaps got their start in the early 1980s. The most common early swaps were currency swaps. But as interest rate volatility became more of a concern to companies all around the world, interest rate swaps became more common. The first interest rate swaps were arranged as what are called parallel loans. *Parallel loans* entail simultaneous loans executed between two counterparties. To see how such an arrangement would work, let's return to the example we introduced and illustrated in Figure 16-2 that involved a fixed-for-floating swap with a notional amount of $10 million and a fixed rate of 12 percent. We could duplicate the cash flows in this swap if one counterparty lent $10 million to the other at a fixed rate and the other counterparty lent the first $10 million at LIBOR, with the same maturity as the swap and with payments due every six months. The only difference would be that the parties would each have to pay the other the amount of the loan and make the loan payments every six months. The swap improves on this arrangement by requiring that only the net amount due at each settlement date actually be paid and by never exchanging the amount of the loan or the notional principal of the swap.

Reasons for the Growth of the Swaps Market

There appear to be five basic reasons for the growth of the interest rate swap market. The first four can be lumped under the heading of demand-side reasons for the growth of swaps. They pertain to ways in which swaps can help companies manage risk or lower total funding costs. Some of these reasons are controversial, and we try to lay out the arguments and provide our own critique of these arguments. The fifth reason we believe the swaps market has grown so large is the efficiency of the market makers, or intermediaries in the swaps market, as risk managers. That is, we believe that swaps and swaps market makers provide relatively efficient hedging of risk. We call this a supply-side consideration, to distinguish it from the first four factors.

Demand-Side Reasons for the Growth of the Swaps Market

1. Interest rate swaps are a convenient and flexible way for companies to manage balance sheets and limit the mismatch between the maturities of assets and liabilities.

Figure 16-2

Payments on settlement dates for 2-year $10-million swap with fixed rate of 12%.

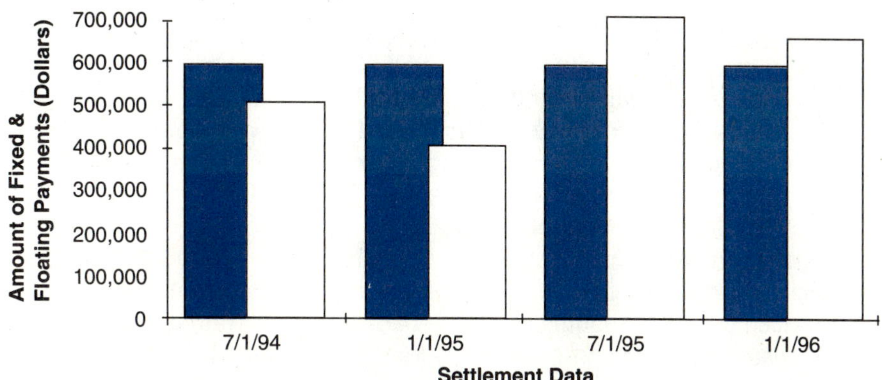

2. Interest rate swaps create a link between distinct markets or firms with differential access to fund sources.
3. Interest rate swaps provide a way to reduce the total funding cost for debt.
4. Interest rate swaps can minimize the costs of regulation and tax laws.

Using Swaps for Interest Rate Risk Management and Linking Distinct Markets

Swaps provide a relatively straightforward vehicle by which companies can control the amount of mismatch in timing or maturity of the assets and liabilities on their balance sheets. This may not have been apparent in our simple example of a fixed-for-floating swap because the counterparties' balance sheet positions were not introduced into the example. Let's return to this example and consider the structure of the balance sheets of the counterparties to the fixed-for-floating swap.

Suppose one counterparty to an interest rate swap already has an obligation on its balance sheet to make interest payments that are tied to a short-term interest rate. Let this counterparty also have long-term assets on its balance sheet, so that it has a mismatch of excess long-term assets relative to liabilities. Suppose the other counterparty has an excess of long-term debt on its balance sheet, relative to its assets, so that it has virtually the opposite kind of mismatch. If the first party would prefer a long-term obligation and the second party would prefer a short-term obligation, then it makes sense for them to swap interest payments. This simple desire to exchange existing positions was one of the greatest forces that led to the emergence of the swaps market in the early 1980s.

Like interest rate swaps, currency swaps can also arise because of a desire to alter the exposure a company already has on its balance sheet or in its existing business. Suppose, for example, that two companies each have fixed-interest rate obligations on outstanding debt, but Company A has debt denominated in dollars while

Company B has debt denominated in Deutschemarks. The two companies could swap their obligations so that Company A has a Deutschemark-denominated interest rate obligation while Company B has a dollar-denominated obligation. Actually, a more common variety of currency swap might well include some change in the nature of the interest obligation as well. That is, Company A might have a floating-rate dollar-denominated obligation, and Company B might have a fixed-rate Deutschemark–denominated obligation. Then a swap would entail changes in both the currency and the interest rate maturity used to determine the obligation. This is often called a currency-coupon swap.

Let's look more closely at the desire to restructure balance sheets by considering the situation facing a typical U.S. bank or savings and loan that generates significant funds from short-term deposits, such as money market certificates that are repriced every six months. The U.S. bank has a portfolio mismatch problem because its customers prefer to borrow for long maturities, say through mortgage loans. It needs to find a way to minimize the risk inherent in the mismatch of maturities. One way is to offer variable-rate loans, but the demand for these loans is considerably less than the demand for long-term fixed-rate loans. So, while the U.S. bank pursues this option vigorously, this is not enough to solve its problem.

At the same time the U.S. bank has more short-term liabilities than assets, a bank in Europe has exactly the opposite problem. It has access to a large volume of long-term fixed-rate funds through the Eurobond market. It has a sizable demand for loans with variable rates matched to LIBOR. In large part this is because long-term fixed-rate mortgages were never widely available in Europe, and most Europeans have become accustomed to loans with shorter maturities and more frequent repricing of interest rates.

This is an accurate description of the situation that faced many financial institutions during the early 1980s, when short-term interest rates hit their postwar peak in the United States and the yield curve was steeply inverted. U.S. banks and savings and loans were eager to find new ways to deal with their interest rate exposures, and this need led, in part, to the growth of the swaps market.

Both of the banks in our example can meet their objectives by using an interest rate swap. To illustrate, suppose the United States and Eurobank agree to a $10 million interest rate swap. Also suppose that the U.S. bank agrees to pay a fixed interest rate of 12 percent every six months for five years on a notional principal of $10 million. At the same time, the Eurobank agrees to pay the U.S. bank LIBOR on the same notional amount over the same period. As we have already noted, the two banks will not actually exchange cash equal to the total amount of the promised interest payments; instead, they will exchange the net difference between these obligations. Therefore, if LIBOR is 11.0 percent during one six-month period, then the U.S. bank would pay the Eurobank $50,000 (1 percent times $10 million per year or 1/2 percent times $10 million for six months). This transaction is illustrated in Panel A of Figure 16-3.

There is generally a market maker in an interest rate swap, so the counterparties may not be aware of each others' identity. The market maker acts as a settlement agent, collecting and paying obligated cash flows when they are due. The market maker generally takes on the obligation to pay the cash flows due, so it also acts as

Figure 16-3

Panel A: Fixed-for-floating swap between U.S. banks and Eurobank where United States pays fixed and receives LIBOR while Eurobank pays LIBOR and receives fixed.

Panel B: A market maker serves as counterparty to both sides of the swap and collects 15 basis points for its services.

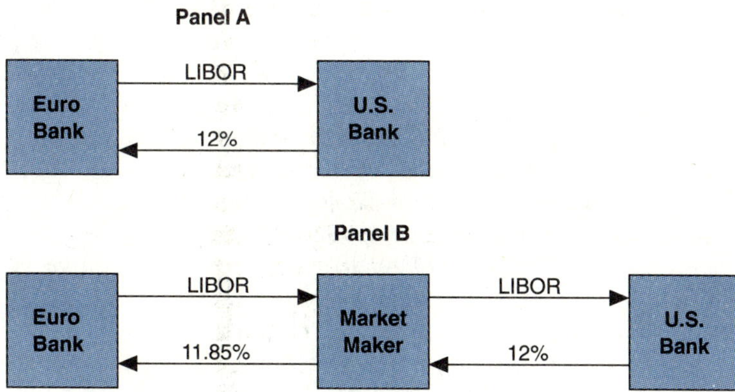

a guarantor in the swap. The market maker also arranges the transaction and acts as a settlement agent. Panel B of Figure 16-3 illustrates how the swap works if a market maker is involved. Both counterparties settle directly with the market maker, who extracts a fee for the services. For example, the fixed-rate payer, the U.S. bank, might pay 12 percent to the market maker, who would pass along only 11.85 percent to the floating-rate payer, keeping 15 basis points for compensation. We look more closely at the role of the market maker later in this chapter.

The interest rate swap in this example is an attractive alternative for two reasons. First, it is a relatively flexible way to alter the nature of the maturity mismatch on the books of both banks. It might be possible to accomplish the same thing with interest rate futures; however, the swap transaction can be tailored to meet the specific needs of individual parties to the transaction. The standardization of the futures contract has made it possible to create highly liquid instruments with active secondary markets, but this standardization means that the futures contract cannot be highly flexible. This creates the opportunity for the swap transaction.

Second, the swap is valuable because it creates a link between the European market or bank and the U.S. bank. In effect, the swap links institutions operating in different markets or with different access to funds, creating internationalization or globalization of financial markets. This process of arbitraging otherwise segmented markets was probably an important element in the growth of the swaps market in the 1980s. To a significant extent, the market for debt instruments in the United States and the Eurobond markets were quite distinct rather than integrated markets. U.S. companies that did not have high visibility in Europe found it difficult if not impossible to sell their debt successfully directly into the Euromarket, but the swap provided indirect access to this market. By swapping interest payments (often in different currencies) with a European company, a U.S. company could tap the Eurobond market.

This example of a U.S. company gaining indirect access to the Eurobond market by using swaps is one example of a more generalized phenomenon that is often said to be an important reason for the growth of swaps. The more general argument is that some firms have a comparative advantage in financing in a particular portion of the capital markets. In our present example the comparative advantage lies in access to the Eurobond market, but there could be other forms of comparative advantage, and, indeed, we will encounter another—relating to better access to longer-term financing. Regardless of the specific example, the general point is that some firms have a comparative advantage in access to attractive sources of funding. This concept of comparative advantage has been borrowed from international trade theory, where it is argued some countries or regions may have comparative advantages in particular types of products. This comparative advantage leads to efficient specialization, which in turn leads to an advantage to trade. Reasoning by analogy, the same advantage to trade is said to be at work in the swaps market.

It is important to note that the key to the idea of comparative advantage in international trade is that there are significant cost barriers that make it inefficient for other countries to come directly to the country with a particular comparative advantage and duplicate its production activity. For example, if South Africa has high-quality diamond mines, it is difficult for people from other countries to either attempt to produce diamonds in their own country or move into South Africa and acquire diamond production rights without paying dearly for them to those who already own the diamond mines. In the language of international trade theory, "comparative advantage requires factor immobility."

It seems highly debatable whether there are highly immobile factors in financial markets. Capital appears to be one of the most highly mobile entities in the world, and countries have to take extreme measures to inhibit the mobility of capital effectively. Therefore, we recommend great skepticism in the face of any argument about comparative advantage for any firm or group of firms that has access to specific forms of financing as a long-run phenomenon. Instead, in the case of access to the Eurobond market, we suspect that swaps have helped to break down any barriers that may have existed to capital flowing through the global capital markets and that this process of arbitraging segmented markets has effectively reduced any comparative advantage that may have existed at one time.

Using Swaps to Reduce the Cost of Debt

An often cited advantage of interest rate swaps is the potential for reducing the *total* financing cost for the two counterparties. The opportunity for cost reduction apparently arises from differences in risk premiums between high- and low-quality borrowers using short- versus long-maturity debt. Before we get into this argument it is important to point out that it is not at all clear that some versions of the explanation we are about to embark on for reducing the cost of borrowing actually make sense. The least plausible arguments here (to us at least) rely heavily on persistent sources of comparative advantage, but the argument is an important part of the history of the swaps market and we must take up this point to provide the complete story. We also scrutinize this explanation for swaps fairly carefully and try to sort out the underlying story that we believe does make sense.

The argument begins with the observation that, in both the short-term or floating-rate market and the long-term bond market, borrowers with higher perceived probability of default have to pay higher premiums to borrow. Evidence indicates that the premiums are substantially higher in the long-term market than in the short-term market for a borrower of a given quality. Figure 16-4 presents the level and spread between Baa- and Aaa-rated 20-year fixed-rate corporate bonds from 1981 to 1990, the period

Figure 16-4

Panel A: Corporate bond yields 1981–1990.

Panel B: Quality spread between Baa and Aaa corporate bonds 1981–1990.

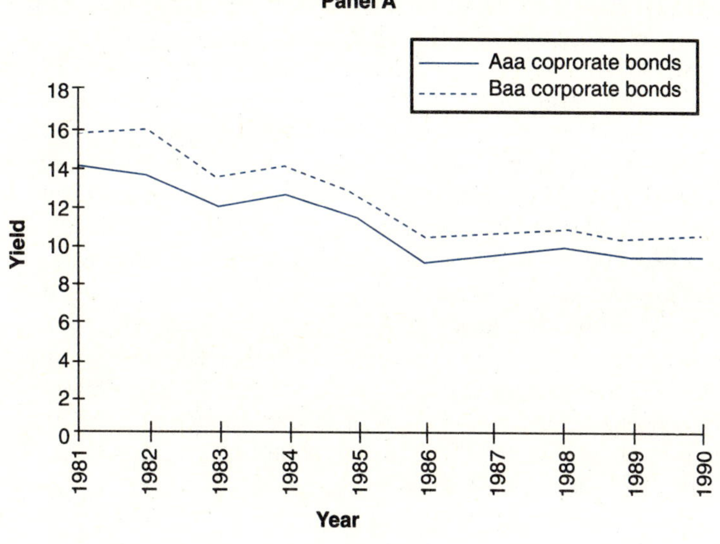

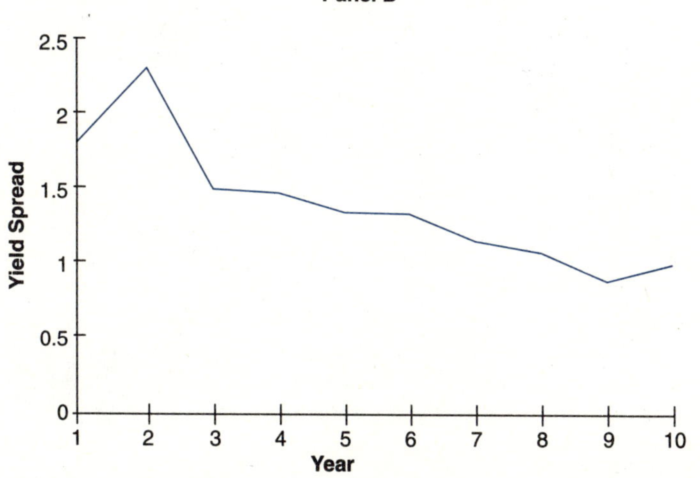

when the swap market was rapidly evolving. During the same time, the average spreads for comparable quality issues in the short-term floating-rate market were in the neighborhood of 50 basis points. Some observers argued that the interest rate swap market was created largely as a device to take advantage of, or arbitrage, this spread.

To see how a swap can be used in this way, let's consider an example of a Baa-rated firm that can borrow in the short-term market at a rate equal to the T-bill rate plus 50 basis points and an Aaa-rated firm that can borrow at Treasury plus 25 basis points. This example is illustrated in Figure 16-5. We also assume that in the long-term bond market the spread between the rates charged, or the quality spread, is 150 basis points for a five-year bond. If the high-quality firm had to pay 11.5 percent for a new five-year bond issue, then the lower-quality firm would have to pay 13 percent. The idea behind the swap in this situation is for the high-quality borrower to issue a five-year bond (though it would prefer a shorter-maturity issue) then to swap the cash flows with the lower-quality firm that issues a short-maturity obligation. The cost savings for the lower quality firm is then shared between the two firms, and both come out with a lower cost of funds than they would otherwise. To complete the example, suppose the Aaa firm issues a bond of $100 million at 11.5 percent, then swaps with the Baa firm issuing short-maturity debt at the T-bill rate plus 50 basis points. The Baa firm agrees to pay the Aaa firm 12 percent and receives the six-month T-bill rate in exchange. The Aaa firm incurs a net cost of the Treasury rate less 50 basis points. Had it simply gone directly to the short-term market it would have paid the T-bill rate plus 25 basis points. Therefore, it saved 75 basis points in total financing cost.

The Baa firm reduced its cost of borrowing through the swap: It will receive the T-bill rate from the Aaa firm and it will pay out 12 percent. Because it borrowed in the short-term market at the T-bill rate plus 50 basis points its net cost will be 12.5 percent for a five-year fixed-rate loan. Had it gone directly to the long-term market, it would have paid 13 percent. As a result, it reduced its cost of funds by 50 basis points. The combined savings of 125 basis points was split between the Aaa firm and the Baa firm, 75 and 50, respectively.

The example makes clear that the aggregate savings in borrowing cost is generated because of differences in pricing default risk in short-term and long-term markets for debt. Does this discrepancy represent some kind of mispricing or inefficiency in the market? One possibility is there is some kind of segmentation between short-term and long-term markets. According to this view, the interest rate swap is a device

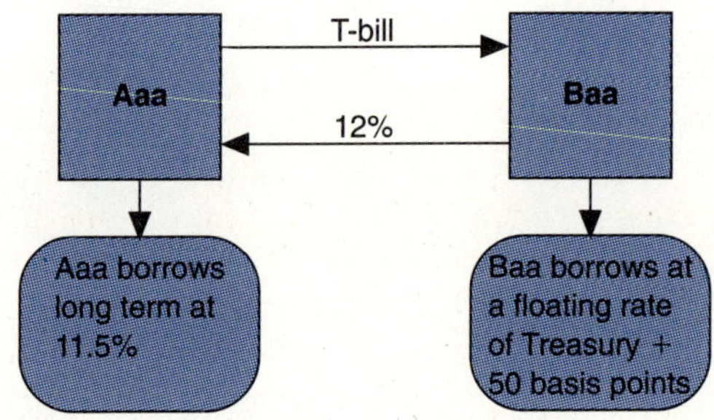

Figure 16-5
Firms of differential credit quality engage in fixed-for-floating swap in order to lower total borrowing cost.

for arbitraging away that mispricing by bridging the gap between the two markets. Another possibility is that some of the Baa firm's default risk has been shifted from the financial markets to the Aaa firm in the transaction, though the Aaa firm is never obligated to pay off the principal of the loan incurred by the Baa firm. If the Baa firm defaults on its obligation to pay 12 percent to the Aaa firm, the swap is terminated and the Aaa firm is left with long-term debt rather than the short-term obligation created through the swap. (You might want to read the discussion of default risk in swaps in Chapter 20.) Thus, each counterparty faces the potential risk that a default on the agreement will force it to accept the interest rate obligations to which it is committed in public markets. The perception of the nature and extent of this risk may affect the initial swap terms or pricing.

Even this explanation carries with it a little lack of realism about how the market actually works. In nearly all swaps a market maker is interposed between any two counterparties like the Aaa and Baa firms in our hypothetical example. Therefore, it is the marketmaker or intermediary that is exposed to the default risk of both counterparties. In turn, the counterparties are exposed to the default risk of the market maker. As a result, as long as the market maker is not being fooled by some sort of shell game, she must perceive that the risk of swapping with Baa is less than the risk to which any long-term lender or purchaser of long- term bonds from Baa would be exposed.

A slightly different way to look at the issue recognizes that by issuing short-term floating-rate debt and swapping this for fixed payments, the low-rated firm has unbundled the interest rate risk of its borrowing from the credit risk of its borrowing. Why might it want to have those priced separately in the credit markets? One very real possibility is that the managers of the firm have quite different expectations than their lenders about both the future course of short-term interest rates and the future prospects of the firm, and therefore the credit spread the firm is likely to have to pay.

Suppose the borrower thinks that short-term interest rates will rise. Then, he will want the protection afforded by a fixed rate. Suppose, however, that he also thinks that his firm's credit situation will improve so that its risk premium will fall. Then he does not want to lock in the risk premium that goes with long-term financing. Such a borrower will want to unbundle the level of general interest rates and its risk premium in its borrowing. By borrowing at floating rates and swapping that borrowing so that he obtains a fixed rate, the borrower is protected against increasing interest rates without locking in the risk premium on his debt. This unbundling perfectly fits his expectations of the future.

One other explanation of the gain in this example claims that this is an apples and oranges problem. This argument starts with the observation that most fixed-rate debt includes a prepayment option that allows the borrower to prepay the debt and refinance if interest rates decline. Though such prepayment options are available in swaps (see the discussion later in this chapter), they are not standard features of fixed-for-floating swaps. Therefore, the apparent attractiveness of the fixed-for-floating swap to firms with different credit quality may be due to a failure to recognize this prepayment option. That is, the yield to maturity on the long-term borrowing may actually be higher than it otherwise would be if it did not include the prepayment option. Therefore, it is really the value of this prepayment option that accounts for part or all of the apparent gain from the swap.

The final explanation of the true source of the gain in this example, and the one we find most attractive, relies on the concept of *agency costs* of debt. Before we take up this explanation we need to spend a little time discussing agency costs. Agency costs pertain to problems within organizations generated by conflicts of interest between managers and shareholders or between equity holders and debt holders. Let's focus on one particular conflict that can easily arise between debt holders or lenders and the equity holders of a firm. Suppose the firm borrows money or sells debt before it has completely decided how those funds are to be spent, so that it has some discretion about what type of investment projects it might finance with the new debt. It is important to notice that such discretion is virtually assured if the firm sells long-term public bonds. With this type of financing it is difficult for bondholders to include convenants that tightly restrict the activities of the firm, and since the bonds have a long maturity, over the life of the bonds the firm will surely encounter opportunities of the type we are about to describe. Now suppose that after the firm sells its bonds, it discovers (actually it might have secretly known about this all along) an opportunity to engage in some highly risky venture. You might think of investing in real estate as an example, as this is a fairly good description of how many savings and loans operated in the 1980s. While the lenders might not have initially perceived that the equity holders intended to use the funds obtained from them to pursue such a risky investment, once the equity holders have those funds they might not be able to be stopped. Now the attractiveness of this kind of scheme to equityholders and managers depends on how healthy their firm is to begin with. If the firm is already in a fairly precarious state, the prospect of going after the very risky investment with the new funds is likely to look more attractive than if the company is not already so badly off. Thus, firms with lower credit ratings are more likely than firms with higher credit ratings to take new debt and go after what we might term risky negative net-present-value investments. If those projects pay off handsomely, the equity holders get the gain; and if they do not, the loss falls on the lenders, since the equity holders have rather little to lose in the first place. In this example, "agency costs" are the cost imposed by this potential conflict between debt holders and equity holders.

The relevance of agency costs to the swaps market relies on the observation that low–credit quality firms are often likely to have higher agency costs of using long-term debt than are high–credit quality firms. If this is true, then a sensible strategy for low–credit quality firms that want long-term financing is to borrow short term and then swap the floating-rate obligation for a fixed-rate obligation with a fixed-for-floating swap. Notice that the agency costs have been fundamentally changed by this strategy, under which no one is lending funds to the low-rated firm for the long term without having any way to call the loan. Since the low-rated firm must continually come back to the credit markets to replace its borrowing, it will not have as great an opportunity to engage in the kind of suboptimal investments we have just described. This lowers the agency costs of debt and results in real savings for the low–credit quality firm.

Using Swaps to Avoid Regulation

A final motivation for swaps is to avoid costs of regulation and tax laws. In some circumstances swaps are desirable because simpler vehicles that accomplish the same thing are restricted by regulation or have undesirable tax consequences. One often-cited example pertains to the Japanese government's restrictions on the ability of Japanese pension and investment funds to diversify internationally. To avoid such restrictions, a class of instruments known as dual currency yen-dollar issues have been introduced, where interest payments are in yen but the principal repayment is in dollars. This type of bond has been exempt from Japanese government restrictions, though the issuer might not want exposure to the risk of changes in the yen-dollar exchange rate. To protect its position, the issuer could also issue a yen-denominated zero-coupon bond with the same maturity date as the principal in the dual currency bond. Now the issuer can offset its obligations to make payments in yen, which consist of both principal and interest, by swapping those into a dollar obligation. It is left with fixed-rate debt obligations, one a zero-coupon and one coupon bearing, solely in dollars. However, it has benefited from a relatively attractive cost of the dual currency bond that arises because of regulations on diversification historically imposed by the Japanese government. These dual currency bonds generally have had lower yields because they were one of the few avenues open to Japanese investors for international diversification. The issuer of the dual currency bond generally has been the beneficiary of this lower yield.

Market Makers and Efficient Hedging

The essence of the supply-side argument for the growth of swaps is that the market makers in the swaps market have developed highly efficient technology for hedging risks that can be applied to a wide variety of problems by using swaps. We use the word "*market makers*" to refer to the various commercial and investment banks that make a market in swaps and hold significant portfolios of swap contracts. While this market began to a large degree with innovations by investment banks, many of the major market makers are now commercial banks such as Citicorp, Chase, Chemical Bank, Bankers Trust, and Bank of America. One of the major reasons for this, as we see when we discuss the default risk of swaps in Chapter 20, is that the market maker is absorbing the default risk of each counterparty. The commercial banks are already in the business of analyzing the financial condition of prospective counterparties and have the infrastructure and systems in place to make credit decisions. Thus, they are well-positioned to operate as effective intermediaries in this market.

The efficiencies that arise through market making result from economies in the fixed and variable transactions costs that counterparties would incur if they attempted to hedge or manage their risks on their own. In addition, by creating portfolios of swaps, market makers are able to diversify away the residual risk that cannot be readily eliminated using futures or other markets for hedging. Because the swaps market maker knows that its hedging technology will be applied to a number of different counterparties, it has an incentive to seek more efficient hedges than would any individual counterparty. This means that a counterparty may be able to obtain a hedge in publicly available instruments but that this hedge would be either more costly to construct and monitor or less effective than she could obtain through the intermediary at the same cost. By contracting with a swap market maker, counterparties can also reduce the variable transactions costs or brokerage fees incurred in implementing a hedge. This saving arises from the fact that the marketmaker need hedge only the net exposures that result when individual counterparties' exposures are combined in a portfolio, taking account of the "natural hedges," or offsetting positions, among counterparties within the portfolio.

The argument about the gains from avoiding fixed setup costs is similar to what happens with intermediate processors in the commodities market, such as Cargill and Archer Daniels Midland. Growers of agricultural commodities often arrange forward contracts with an intermediate processor rather than hedging their positions directly in the futures markets. They do this in order to avoid the fixed costs of learning about the appropriate futures-hedging strategies. The intermediate processor then uses futures markets to hedge its combined positions with growers.

Varieties of Swaps

The interest rate swaps we have discussed so far are essentially fixed-for-floating swaps, what we might term "plain vanilla" swaps. As you might imagine, the market has come up with a wide variety of different types of swaps that go way beyond the simple ones we have covered so far. We like to say that swaps now come in a wide variety of flavors. Table 16-2 presents a catalog, or profile of alternative types of swaps. There are three essential ways to change the basic structure of a swap, and these correspond to the three headings in Table 16-2. The first way to alter a swap is to change the timing or contingency of when the swap begins or ends. The second pertains to the notional principal of the swap. The third refers to the index or financial instrument to which the swap is tied. We describe and illustrate the various forms that swaps can take. You will find more examples of various types of swaps later in the book.

Timing and Contingency

One of the simplest ways that swaps differ is their maturity schedules. Swaps with relatively short maturities, generally less than three years, are called "money market swaps." Those with longer maturities are called "term swaps." While there are no aggregate data on swaps that allow us to document the volumes at different maturities, swaps often involve longer maturities than can generally be found on futures or options contracts traded on organized exchanges. In fact, one of the advantages of swaps is that a market maker can tailor a swap to fit the needs of a particular counterparty, whereas standardization is the key to the success of exchange-traded instruments. Therefore, swaps have evolved in part to serve the needs of specific longer-term risk management problems.

Table 16-2
Profile of Alternative Types of Swaps

Label	Description
Timing-Contingency	
Money market swap	Maturities of 3 years or less
Term swap	Maturities of 3 years or more
Spot-start swap	Starts 2 days after verbal agreement
Delayed-start swap	Starts up to 1 year after verbal agreement
Forward swap	Starts 1 year or more in future
Option on swap	Counterparty buys option on terms of swap
Swaption	Counterparty has option to alter swap
Buyout	Swap is closed and settled at current price
Index	
Fixed-for-floating	Fixed interest rate is exchanged for floating rate
Basis swap	Two floating interest rates are exchanged
Off-market swap	Fixed rate is not equal to swap market rate
Zero-coupon swap	Fixed rate is zero
Notional Principal	
Amortizing swap	Notional principal declines with time
Uneven cash flows	Notional principal takes on any pattern

Generally, swaps begin two business days after the swap has been agreed to by the counterparty and the market maker. Swaps that commence according to these terms are called "spot-start swaps." Sometimes a swap may start more than two days after the verbal agreement but still within the next year. These are called "delayed-start swaps." Swaps that begin more than one year in the future are called "forward swaps." Sometimes they are even referred to as "forward-forward swaps." Notice that any swap that begins some time in the future can really be thought of as a "*forward contract on a swap*"; that is, the market maker is providing a commitment or a contract today on the terms, such as the fixed-pay interest rate, on a swap that begins at some future date. This is virtually a forward contract. If we can have a forward contract on a swap we can also have an "*option on a swap.*" That is, a market-maker can write an option to a counterparty to take out a swap at a future date on prespecified terms. Of course, the counterparty will have to pay a premium for such an option, just as would be the case with any of the more standard exchange-traded options we discussed in Chapter 15.

Finally, a swap can have an option embedded in it for a counterparty to terminate the swap according to some prespecified terms, generally with no penalty for the counterparty. This is generally referred to as a "*swaption.*" For example, suppose a counterparty agreed to pay fixed in a fixed-for-floating swap that lasted five years, but the swap also includes the option for the counterparty to terminate the swap after three years. Notice that the counterparty has an option on the fixed rate in fixed-for-floating swaps with two-year maturities on a date three years out in the future. That is, the underlying security in this option is the cash or spot rate on new fixed-for-floating swaps with two-year maturities. Now, consider the alternatives open to this counterparty three years hence. Suppose the original 5-year swap began on 1 January 1991 and included a fixed rate of 10 percent. Then suppose the fixed rate on new two-year swaps on 1 January 1994 turns out to be 12 percent. The existing swap is relatively cheap compared to the cost of a new swap. The option to terminate the swap has matured out of the money, and it will be allowed to expire unexercised. Suppose, however, that the fixed rate on the new two-year swap is 8 percent. Now the option to terminate is in the money. If the counterparty still wants to participate in a fixed-for-floating swap for two more years, he should exercise his option to terminate the existing swap and replace it with a new swap at the more attractive rate of 8 percent. If he does not want the swap anymore, he should simply exercise his swap and do nothing more. This is illustrated in Figure 16-6.

A final characteristic of swaps that affects their timing refers to the "*buyout*" of a swap. Buying out a swap simply means paying the appropriate price to terminate the swap. Let's return to our example of the counterparty who agreed to a five-year fixed-for-floating swap with a fixed rate of 10 percent, but let's drop the assumption that this swap includes an option to terminate. Again, suppose three years has passed and the fixed rate on a new swap with a two-year maturity is 8 percent. Suppose the counterparty who is paying fixed wants to terminate the swap. She tells the market maker she wants to buy out the swap. The market maker wants to be compensated for the loss he will incur from early termination of the swap. The alternative open to the market maker is the rate on two-year swaps, or 8 percent. Therefore, the market maker stands to lose 200 basis points on the outstanding notional principal over two years. Because this is a fixed payment, the amount of the cash flow is subject only to the risk of default by the counterparty. If this risk is negligible, we can determine the amount of the buyout by taking the present value of the cash flow, equal to the 200 basis points times the notional principal, over the remaining two years of the swap, discounted at the risk-free rate. When market makers determine the amount of the buyout, they are quite precise about consulting the appropriate zero-coupon interest rate for each cash flow when calculating the present value. To keep the calculations in this example as simple as possible, let's suppose that the date is 1 January 1994 and that the zero-coupon yield curve is perfectly flat at 7 percent. Also, let's suppose that the notional principal of the swap is $10 million and, as is standard procedure, that the swap specifies settlement every six months. Then, a buyout of the swap in

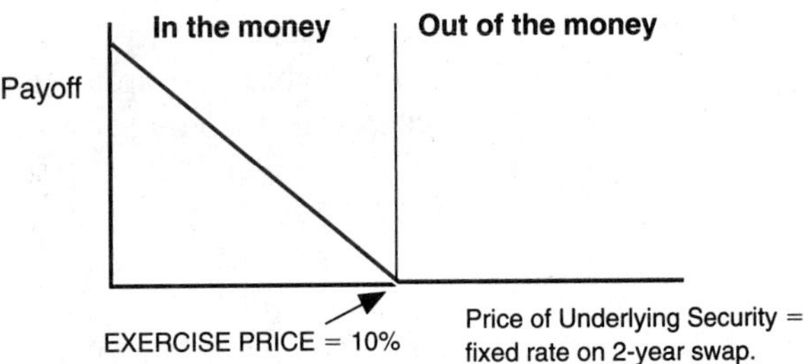

Figure 16-6

Swaption represents a 10 percent fixed-pay swap with option to terminate after three years.

our example would mean that the market maker would lose cash flows of $100,000, or 1 percent of the notional principal, every six months for two years.

The calculations for the buyout of this swap are shown in Table 16-3. The first two columns show the date and amount of each cash flow. The next two columns show the discount factor applied to that cash flow. The final column shows the present value as of 1 January 1994 for those cash flows. The total present value or amount of the buyout is shown in the lower right-hand corner of the table. These calculations tell us that the buyout in this example would cost the counterparty $367,307. Notice that if the interest rate on a new two-year fixed-for-floating swap on 1 January 1994 were 12 percent rather than 8 percent, the amount of the buyout would still be $367,307, but now the counterparty could sell his swap for this price instead of having to pay this price to the market maker to terminate the swap. The reason for this is simply that the counterparty now owns an asset that has gone up in value because the current rate for fixed-for-floating swaps is now 200 basis points higher than the one in the five-year swap initiated in January 1991.

Index

Now let's consider the various ways in which the index or the interest rate on a swap can be changed. Thus far we have considered solely fixed-for-floating swaps. Another common form of swap is called a basis swap. A *basis swap* involves swapping one floating rate index for another; it is essentially a floating-for-floating swap. For example, consider once again the two banks, the U.S. bank and Eurobank, in the example we dealt with above. The U.S. bank agreed to pay fixed and receive LIBOR in a swap with Eurobank. The U.S. bank was interested in such a swap because it had large volumes of floating rate liabilities on its balance sheet and it was looking for a way to replace these liabilities with more long-term fixed-rate liabilities; however, its short-term liabilities are not likely to be tied to LIBOR. Because these are mostly consumer deposits they will be tied to domestic rates like the Treasury bill rate or the 90-day certificate of deposit (CD) rate. Therefore, the U.S. bank is still exposed to fluctuations in the spread between the CD rate and LIBOR. If it wants to eliminate this exposure, it can engage in a swap where it pays LIBOR and receives the CD rate. This will give it precisely the kind of protection against fluctuations in its cost of funds that it wants. Now you may ask why it did not initially engage in a fixed-for-floating swap with the CD rate as the floating rate. That's a good question.

Table 16-3

Buyout of a Fixed-for-Floating Swap

Date	Amount	Discount	Discount	Present Value
6/30/94	$100,000	1/1.035	.96618	$96,618
12/31/95	$100,000	$1/1.035^2$	.93351	$93,351
6/30/95	$100,000	$1/1.035^3$	.90194	$90,194
12/31/96	$100,000	$1/1.035^4$	.87144	$87,144
Total				$367,307

It is possible that the U.S. bank might get better terms by shopping around among market makers for two distinct swaps. It is also possible that a market maker might find it cost effective to seek separate counterparties for a fixed-for-floating and a basis swap and yet bundle them together in one swap for a U.S. bank. The best approach will be the one that is least expensive.

Another way we can change the interest rate on a swap is to take all or part of the fixed payments in a fixed-for-floating swap and make them in one lump sum. For example, suppose we have a fixed-for-floating swap with LIBOR as the floating rate and the going rate on such swaps is 10 percent fixed. Now a prospective counterparty who would be paying fixed does not want to incur the cash flow obligations of 10 percent fixed right away. Rather, he wants them deferred. The swap could be restructured to be set up at a lower rate of, say, 5 percent and then include a lump-sum payment at the end. This is called an "off-market swap." The lump sum would be equal to the value of the deferred obligations by the fixed-pay counterparty at the end of the swap. We can figure out these obligations the same way we determined the amount of the buyout of the swap earlier in this chapter. For example, if the notional principal of the swap were $20 million, then the 500–basis point reduction in the fixed-pay obligation would create an annuity of payments of $500,000 every six months over the life of the swap, assuming the swap entailed settlement every six months. The future lump-sum payment required to give this swap the same value as the straight fixed-for-floating swap would be the future value at the end of the swap of a $500,000 annuity discounted at the interest rate that reflects the risk of the counterparty to the swap. Of course, if we can defer some of the fixed payments in the swap to the maturity date of the agreement we can also accelerate them to the first day of the swap. That is, the counterparty could prepay part of the fixed payment obligations at their present value.

An extreme version of the off-market swap is called a "*zero-coupon swap,*" where all of the fixed payments are paid in one lump sum. This single payment could take place at any point in time over the life of the swap. Of course, the amount of the payment would reflect the appropriate present value, depending on when the payment was made.

Notional Principal

The final major way in which the structure of swaps can be changed is by altering the notional principal. In all the swaps we have discussed so far the notional principal of the swap remains the same over the life of the swap. In many cases, however, counterparties to a swap have a need for the notional principal to change over the life of the swap. For example, suppose a company is engaging in a swap to restructure its balance sheet without actually getting rid of the on–balance sheet liabilities it has outstanding. Suppose it currently has an amortizing fixed-rate loan. It wants to replace the fixed interest rate with a floating rate, but it will keep its actual balance sheet intact. Here it will engage in a swap by which it will receive fixed and pay LIBOR. If its outstanding debt is at 11 percent it will want to receive 11 percent fixed to cover its existing fixed obligation. Before we take up the issue of notional principal, note that it will be able to obtain exactly these terms, without making any other payments, only if the going rate in the swaps market on fixed-for-floating swaps against LIBOR is exactly 11 percent, which is highly unlikely. If it wants the swap to be at 11 percent it will have to arrange an off-market swap, but then, as we have just learned, it would either receive or make a lump-sum payment to the market maker, depending on whether the going rate on the fixed-for-floating swap was below or above 11 percent.

Now lets suppose that the existing long-term fixed rate debt on its balance sheet currently has an outstanding balance of $20 million, but a payment of principal of $4 million is due at the end of each year for the next five years. Then the amount of the outstanding loan would decline, in steps of $4 million, from $20 million to zero over five years. This pattern is illustrated in Panel A of Figure 16-7. A swap market maker would have no difficulty arranging a swap with a notional principal that declined in precisely the manner illustrated in the figure. It would simply write a contract with a declining notional principal. This particular variety of swap is called an "*amortizing swap.*"

It is important to notice that an amortizing swap can be constructed out of a sequence of swaps with constant notional principal but different maturity dates. Each of these alternative swaps would be for $4 million. The first one would last for one year, the second two years, then three, four, and five years. Each swap corresponds to one step in the diagram in Panel A of Figure 16-7. This highlights the important fact that swaps can be broken down into component parts and combined in whatever way best suits the needs of prospective counterparties.

Now let's consider another example of how the notional principal of a swap can vary to suit a company's financing needs. Suppose a company that is building a new manufacturing facility is gradually going to be drawing down funds in a financing package for that project. The total financing is for $100 million, but the borrower expects to take down the loan or use the funds in increments of $20 million every six months. It has arranged the loan so that it has a floating interest rate, but it wants to swap this for a fixed rate to protect itself against fluctuations in its cost of borrowing. It would be interested in a fixed-for-floating swap in which the notional principal increases rather than decreases over time. This is illustrated in Panel B of Figure 16-7. A market maker can arrange such a swap directly with the counterparty, or the counterparty could choose another alternative that provides the same result. Notice that a swap in which the notional balance increases over time is equivalent to a sequence of swaps in which the first one is a spot start swap but the remaining ones are forward swaps. In this example, the company with the construction project could arrange for a spot start swap of $20 million and also for a sequence of forward swaps, each with a notional principal of $20 million but with starting dates that begin six months in the future and continue out for two years. You can see by inspecting Panel B of Figure 16-7 that this sequence of forward swaps is identical to one swap with notional principal that increases by $20 million every six months until a total of $100 million is reached.

Figure 16-7

Panel A: Amortizing swap. *Panel B:* Swap with increasing notional principal.
Panel C: Notional principal for a seasonal swap.

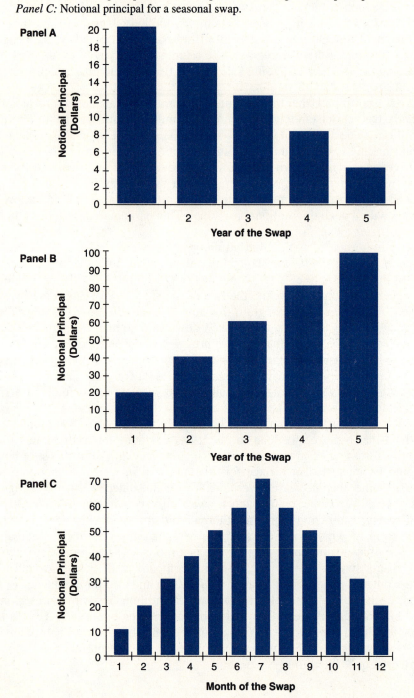

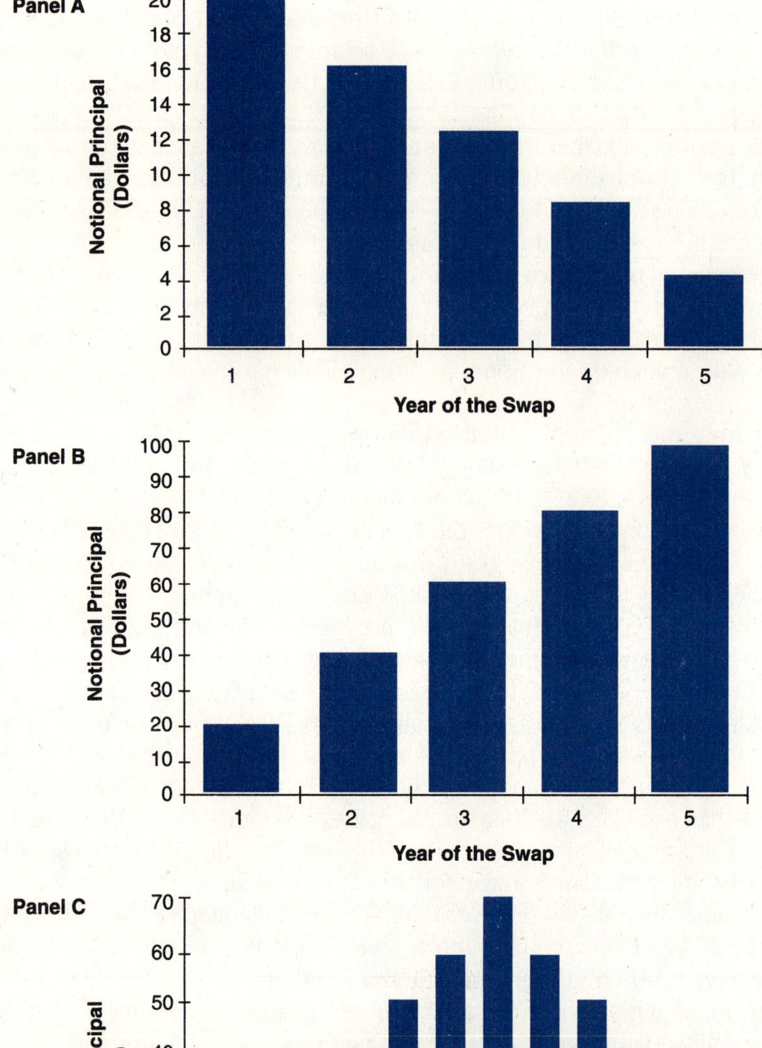

Yet a third way in which the notional principal can vary over the life of a swap is shown in Panel C of Figure 16-7. Consider a firm that has a large seasonal borrowing need. Firms that produce consumer goods with large sales during the Christmas season generally have financing needs that peak as their finished goods inventory accumulates toward the end of the year and their financing needs decline sharply after the Christmas holidays. If such a firm is using swaps to change the interest rate risk structure of its financing, it will need swaps whose notional principal varies with its financing needs. Swap market makers can readily provide swaps with any pattern of varying notional principal to satisfy the needs of firms like this one.

Pricing Swaps

The Pricing Convention

We have not yet addressed the question of how swaps are priced. It is important to clarify the convention the market uses for quoting prices on fixed-for-floating swaps. Interest rate swaps originated as parallel loans between two counterparties, and the periodic payments are comparable to coupon payments on loans (though a swap differs from two loans since the notional principal never changes hands). The pricing convention relates the fixed interest rate on a fixed-for-floating swap to the coupon rate on a T bond of comparable maturity. For example, a five-year swap with a fixed interest rate of 8 percent is expressed relative to the coupon rate on a five-year T bond selling at par. Since the T bond is selling at par, the coupon rate is also the yield to maturity on the bond. If the yield or coupon rate on the five-year Treasury were 7.30 percent, the price, or fixed interest rate, on the five-year swap would be stated as five-year Treasury plus 70 basis points. A price sheet (see Table 16-4) for swaps of various maturities would normally list the T-bond rate corresponding to each maturity and a markup over the Treasury rate for the fixed rate on a swap against a floating rate, say LIBOR. Notice that the swap includes any premiums in the fixed-rate side of the transactions, so that the floating rate is commonly quoted as LIBOR "flat," when LIBOR is the floating rate in the swap. In this example, prices are quoted relative to Treasury yields at five maturities. Two prices are shown for a swap market maker. The first is the price the market maker would pay fixed to a counterparty who received fixed and paid floating; the second is the price the market maker quotes to receive fixed and pay floating. The spread between the two represents the market maker's compensation for its services, including acceptance of default risk of the counterparty in question. The size of this spread depends on the creditworthiness of the counterparty. In the example in Table 16-4, it is around 15 basis points, an appropriate value for counterparties of relatively high credit quality, but higher than the spread that would prevail for swaps engaged in by two market makers with each other or for swaps in the interbank market.

Table 16-4
Sample Price Structure for LIBOR Swap

Treasury Maturity (yr)	Market Maker Pays	Market Maker Receives
2	Treasury + 60	Treasury + 74
3	Treasury + 65	Treasury + 79
5	Treasury + 65	Treasury + 78
7	Treasury + 62	Treasury + 77
10	Treasury + 63	Treasury + 79

The fact that swap prices are generally stated relative to Treasury bonds of different maturities can easily give the impression that swaps are priced using the Treasury par yield curve. However, the actual determination of the appropriate rate to charge uses the zero-coupon yield curve, just as we cautioned we should always use in Chapters 9 and 10. Once the appropriate fixed payments are determined using the zero-coupon yield curve, it is conventional to state those prices relative to the Treasury par yield curve, as illustrated in Table 16-4. So it is important not to get fooled by this use of the Treasury par curve into thinking it is the appropriate tool for pricing swaps—or any other financial instruments. We will stick with the zero-coupon approach.

• *So You Want to Price a Swap?* •

Now we can address the question of how the market determines the price or the fixed interest rate on a fixed-for-floating swap. We break the problem down into three steps:

Step 1: Determine the best guess of the floating rate applicable to each future settlement date in the swap.

Step 2: Use the zero-coupon yield curve to calculate the present value of the expected future floating-rate payments under the swap.

Step 3: Calculate the annuity that has the a present value equal to that determined in step 2.

The strategy outlined in these three steps involves determining the present value of expected future floating-rate payments from the swap. Then, if the swap market is competitive, the price or the fixed rate on the swap will be driven down until the present value of the fixed-rate payments must equal the present value of expected floating-rate payments. The present values must be determined using the appropriate zero-coupon yield curve. Moreover, since the fixed payment on the swap is constant over the life of the swap, it is an annuity. Therefore, once the present value of the expected floating-rate payments has been determined, it is necessary to solve for the annuity payment that provides the same present value. We'll use as an example a five-year swap of fixed against LIBOR flat. Assume that the notional principal in the swap is $10 million. Also note that in a standard swap of fixed-for-floating against LIBOR flat, each floating payment is based on the LIBOR rate prevailing six months prior to the settlement date in question. We use the zero-coupon yield curve in column 2 of Table 16-5.

Table 16-5
Break-Even Pricing of Swap

Time	Zero-coupon rate	Floating index	Floating payment	Present value
1	5.00	5.00	$250,000	$243,902
2	5.20	5.40	$270,010	$256,498
3	5.45	5.95	$297,546	$274,489
4	5.70	6.45	$322,591	$288,294
5	6.20	8.21	$410,609	$352,481
6	6.75	9.52	$476,104	$390,130
7	7.10	9.21	$460,624	$360,824
8	7.60	11.13	$556,698	$413,086
9	8.00	11.23	$561,394	$394,428
10	8.20	10.01	$500,434	$334,842
Total present value				$3,308,974

Step 1

There is no way we can know with certainty the spot rate at each settlement date, but we know that the market's best guess of these rates is embedded in long-term rates or in the yield curve. We can extract from the yield curve the implied forward rate for each settlement date. We know that the forward rate contains the market's best guess of the future spot rate, though it may also contain a liquidity premium. We also learned how to compute these forward rates. We have utilized the procedure described in Chapter 10 to compute forward rates for the swap in our example.

There is an important point to consider about the zero coupon yield curve before we begin. Ideally, the yield curve we use to calculate the implied forward LIBOR rates should be the LIBOR yield curve, but generally the LIBOR market does not include long-maturity loans. We must construct longer-term rates from some other market, generally the U.S. Treasury market, and then use this yield curve both to estimate implied forward rates and to discount back the cash flows accruing at each settlement date. We are assuming that this is the appropriate zero-coupon yield curve for both purposes. In practice it is possible to compute a variety of different yield curves using rates in different markets each of which reflects differential risks and other factors of that market. If we switch from one market to another we must make adjustments based on the expected spreads between markets.

Column 3 of Table 16-5 contains the forward rates computed from the zero-coupon yield curve in column 2. We can interpret these forward rates as being close to an estimate of the expected future spot rates if we are willing to accept the expectations theory of the term structure, though we know that this is an approximation. Alternatively, these forward rates may also include liquidity premiums. To verify the calculations in the table, consider the forward rate corresponding to time 2. Recall the swap requires that the floating payment due on the second settlement date, one year after the start of the swap agreement, is based on the LIBOR rate observed on the first settlement date, six months earlier. The forward rate we are interested in for this payment is the rate observed today for a six-month loan beginning on the first settlement date of the swap. If the swap begins on 1 January 1994, this would be 1 July 1994. This forward rate would contain the best guess of the six-month LIBOR to be observed on that date. The first entry in the first column is the current six-month LIBOR, which began 1 January 1994. The rest of the spot rates pertain to maturities that increase by six-month intervals that correspond to the settlement dates in the swap. We can compute the first forward rate—and all the rest of the entries—as follows using the procedure we explained in Chapter 10:

$$_1f_2 = \left[\frac{(1.0260)^2}{(1.025)} - 1\right]2 = 5.4\%$$

Step 2

The estimated floating payment at each settlement date is equal to the corresponding forward rate multiplied by one half and by the notional principal. For example, the estimated floating rate payment for the second settlement date, time 2 in the table, is determined by the estimate of the LIBOR rate to be observed six months earlier, or 5.4 percent. Then the estimated payment is

$$\$270{,}010 = 0.054 \times 0.5 \times \$10{,}000{,}000$$

The present value of this expected cash flow, using the corresponding time-2 zero-coupon rate as the discount rate, is $256,498. Finally, the sum of all the present values of floating rate payments in the swap is $3,308,974.

Step 3

The fixed interest rate in the swap is determined by solving for the annuity that has the same present value we just determined for the floating-rate payments, $3,308,974. Let r_F designate the fixed interest rate in the swap and C designate the annuity amount or the cash flow. Then this cash flow in the annuity, is equal to

$$C = r_F \times 0.5 \times \$10{,}000{,}000$$

Also let z_t represent the zero-coupon interest rate corresponding to cash flows occurring t periods in the future. Recall that the values of z_t in our example are shown in the second column of Table 16-5. For the present value of an annuity of C to be equal to the present value of the expected floating-rate payments it is required that

$$\sum_{t=1}^{10} \frac{C}{\left(1 + \frac{z_t}{2}\right)^t} = \$3{,}308{,}974$$

Now we can factor C out of the annuity and solve for it directly. Note that, using the zero-coupon yields in Table 16.5, the annuity factor is equal to 8.317.

Then we can solve for r_F directly as follows:

$$\sum_{t=1}^{10} \frac{1}{\left(1 + \frac{z_t}{2}\right)^t} = 8.317$$

$$r_F = \frac{\$3{,}308{,}974 \times 2}{8.317 \times \$10{,}000{,}000} = 7.96\%$$

This tells us that the expected payoffs from both the floating and the fixed sides of the swap against LIBOR will be close to the same if the fixed interest rate on the swap is 7.96 percent, given that the expectations theory of the term structure is correct. If the forward rate includes a liquidity premium, then the present value of the floating side of the swap includes those liquidity premiums.

SUMMARY

We began by outlining the structure of some basic interest rate and currency swaps. We defined a swap and learned some of the terminology of the swaps market, including notional principal, counterparties, and a fixed-for-floating swap. Then we turned to the evolution of the swaps market. We noted that originally swaps were more often currency swaps, but as interest rates became more volatile in the late 1970s and early 1980s, demand increased for vehicles to manage interest rate risk. Swaps grew up, in part, in response to this demand.

We also identified a number of specific explanations for the origins of the swaps market. We examined how swaps can be a convenient way for companies to manage interest rate risk and looked at an example of a swap between financial institutions in Europe and the United States to see how swaps can bridge some of the barriers between financial markets in different parts of the globe. We examined the way swaps can reduce borrowing costs. We looked at a sequence of arguments about how swaps between counterparties of differential credit quality can reduce the total cost of credit of both counterparties. We found there may be advantages to unbundling the timing of when the risk premium is set and when the general underlying interest rate is adjusted. We also focused on the idea that the agency costs of debt can be reduced by shortening the interval between dates when the risk premium is adjusted. Finally, we examined how market makers in the swaps market have become relatively efficient at hedging interest rate and foreign exchange risk. This suggests that one of the continuing reasons for the popularity of swaps comes from the cost savings generated by using market makers to set up swaps that are tailored to the needs of a given customer. We referred to this as the supply-side reason for the growth of the swaps market.

Next we turned our attention to the many different types of swaps available from market makers. We divided the swaps in the marketplace into three categories: timing-contingency, index, and notional principal and examined the different swaps in each category. The general message of the discussion is that swaps are tremendously flexible tools for managing risk. A market maker can construct a swap that is perfectly tailored to almost any conceivable kind of risk management need a company might have. This can include variations in notional principal, different indexes, options or forward contracts on the terms of a swap, and options to terminate a swap. All of this flexibility has made the swap market a critical part of modern financial markets.

Finally, we examined the question of how a swap should be priced. We based our analysis of pricing on the idea that the present value of the fixed and floating sides of a swap should be equal. We divided the process of pricing the floating side of a swap into three steps: estimating the expected future payments or the expected values of the floating index at future settlement dates; using the zero-coupon yield curve to determine the present value of those floating payments; and determining the fixed interest rate on the swap as the determinant of the annuity payment on the fixed side of the swap that has the same value as the floating side of the swap estimated in the first two steps. We learned to apply this procedure to a simple example of a standard fixed-for-floating swap.

QUESTIONS

1. Explain the difference between a parallel loan and a fixed-for-floating interest rate swap.
2. Consider a fixed-for-floating LIBOR swap with notional principal of $100 million and a fixed rate of 9 percent. Suppose the date the swap is established is indexed time 0 and six-month intervals ahead are indexed time 1, 2, and so on, so that time 2 is one year from the date the swap is set up. Suppose LIBOR at time t turns out to be

t	LIBOR %
0	6.25
1	7.3
2	7.9
3	8.4
4	6.9
5	6.0
6	5.4

   What would be the net payments between the two counterparties on each of the six settlement dates?
3. Suppose a market maker makes a $100 million loan and engages in a $100 million swap to receive fixed with a firm. What is the difference in the default risks of these two contracts?
4. What are agency costs? Can you construct an example in which a borrower would prefer a negative over a positive net-present-value investment project because the firm is funded with debt as opposed to equity?
5. Explain why agency costs of debt are relevant to the swaps market. Be sure to include an explanation of unbundling and why it may be valuable.
6. Consider a buyout of a fixed-for-floating $10 million LIBOR swap with a 9 percent fixed rate. Suppose that swap had three years before maturity. Now suppose the fixed rate on new three-year swaps was 7 percent and then 10 percent. Suppose the zero-coupon yield curve is flat at 9 percent. What amounts would the fixed-rate payer, respectively, pay and receive to buy out the swap?

7. Explain the differences between the following types of swaps: forward swap, option on a swap, swaption.
8. Swaps with varying notional principal can be equivalent to either a sequence of forward swaps or a sequence of spot-start swaps with different maturities. Explain.
9. Suppose a prospective counterparty wants to swap fixed for floating to receive the CD rate for five years. You have the following swap prices:

A five-year fixed against LIBOR:	12 percent
A five-year fixed against CD rate:	11.35 percent
A basis swap, pay LIBOR and receive CD rate:	CD + 50 basis points

   What are the costs of alternative ways in which the counterparty can accomplish its objective?
10. Suppose you observe the following zero-coupon yield curve (note that the time period involved is six months):

$_0r_1 = 5.5\%$
$_0r_2 = 5.7\%$
$_0r_3 = 6.0\%$
$_0r_4 = 6.2\%$
$_0r_5 = 6.4\%$

   Suppose you are considering a 2 1/2-year LIBOR swap with semiannual settlement. Estimate the current value of the floating side of this swap per $1000 of notional principal.

REFERENCES

Arak, M., A. Estrella, L. Goodman, and A. Silver. "Interest Rate Swaps: An Alternative Explanation." *Financial Management* 17 (Summer 1988), pp. 12–18.

Bicksler, J., and A. Chen. "An Economic Analysis of Interest Rate Swaps." *Journal of Finance* 41 (1986), pp. 645–655.

Brown, K., and D. Smith. "Recent Innovations in Interest Rate Risk Management and the Reintermediation of Commercial Banking." *Financial Management* 18 (1988), pp. 45–58.

Campbell, T., and W. Kracaw. "Intermediation and the Market for Interest Rate Swaps." *Journal of Financial Intermediation* 3 (Dec 1991), pp. 362–384.

Cooper, I. A., and A. S. Mello. "The Default Risk of Swaps." *Journal of Finance* 46 (June 1991), pp. 597–620.

Hirshleifer, D. "Risk, Futures Pricing, and the Organization of Production in Commodity Markets." *Journal of Political Economy* 96 (1988), pp. 1206–1220.

Loeys, J. "Interest Rate Swaps: A New Tool for Managing Risk." Federal Reserve Bank of Philadelphia *Business Review* (May/June 1985), pp. 17–25.

Myers, S. "Determinants of Corporate Borrowing." *Journal of Financial Economics* 5 (1977), pp. 147–176.

Smith, C., C. Smithson, and L. Wakeman. "The Evolving Market for Swaps." *Midland Corporate Finance Journal* 3 (1986), pp. 20–32.

Turnbull, S. "Swaps: A Zero-Sum Game?" *Financial Management* 15 (1987), pp. 15–21.

Wakeman, L. M. "The Portfolio Approach to Swaps Management." Unpublished manuscript. Chemical Bank Capital Markets Group, May 1986.

Wall, L. "Interest Rate Swaps in an Agency Theoretic Model with Uncertainty Interest Rates." *Journal of Banking and Finance* 13 (1989), pp. 261–270.

Wall, L., and J. Pringle. "Alternative Explanations of Interest Rate Swaps: A Theoretical and Empirical Analysis." *Financial Management* 18 (1989), pp. 59–73.

Whittaker, J. G. "Interest Rate Swaps: Risk and Regulation." Federal Reserve Bank of Kansas City *Economic Review* 72 (March 1987), pp. 3–13.

• Chapter 17

Risk Management Strategy

In this chapter we take a look at the process of financial risk management. We assess the best way for a company or an individual to analyze and solve risk management problems. We address how a company, whether a commercial bank or an industrial firm, can develop effective solutions to its risk management problems. We begin with a simple five-step process useful in choosing the appropriate risk management strategy. After we describe our recommended approach to the process, we summarize the product set for risk management and discuss the pros and cons of each instrument. Most of these products should be familiar to you by now because they were covered in the last few chapters, but we want to see how to choose among them when confronting specific risk management problems. Finally, we take up the question of hedging strategy and the management of *basis risk.* This is the crucial issue underlying all of the strategic issues of risk management. Moreover, an essential determinant of choosing an appropriate risk management strategy boils down to selecting the most cost-effective way to manage basis risk. So it is important to understand basis risk and how it can be controlled. All of this is important for any type of company in managing financial risk, but since financial firms are often in the business of selling risk management services to other companies, as well as using such services themselves, it is especially important to financial firms such as commercial banks. This chapter lays a foundation for the topics on management of financial institutions that we take up in Part IV.

In the financial markets of the 1990s are many firms that specialize in selling the instruments that comprise the risk management product set. These companies prosper to the extent that they understand and can control the basis risk of instruments they use. One of the great advantages of having a large number of specialists in this market is that we do not all have to acquire their level of expertise. In fact, it would be wasteful and silly for us all to attempt to duplicate their skills. These people compete with one another to develop products that help their clients solve their risk management problems in a simple way with little expense. Vigorous competition in this process is essential. Without it we would not be able to compare risk management products and prices across the various purveyors. We would then really have to become experts in risk management strategy to avoid being at the mercy of the specialist in this area. This chapter will help you become a good comparison shopper in the risk management market and will prepare you to provide these services. The key concepts to learn in this chapter are listed below.

• Concepts to Learn in Chapter 17•

- How to formulate a risk management strategy
- How a perfect hedge works and what is required for a perfect hedge
- How to measure basis risk
- How to design a hedging strategy
- When and how to hedge using options

Designing a Risk Management Process

We begin our discussion of risk management strategy by examining why risk management is important to any company. Then we turn our attention to a five step process for risk management.

Why Is Risk Management an Important Part of Corporate Strategy?

Before we examine the details of risk management strategy for a company we need to ask (and answer) a fundamental underlying question: Why should a company seek to manage risk? At first glance this might appear a somewhat silly question. Obviously, if a company has foreign exchange exposure, for example, and if foreign exchange rates change significantly in the direction that hurts the company, this can cause severe losses. Shouldn't the company always hedge or insure such an exposure so that this bad scenario cannot come to pass? While it might seem that the answer to this question is yes, the issue is more subtle than it might appear.

The stakeholders in a modern publicly held corporation include, at least, the managers, other employees, suppliers, customers, the community where the company operates, stockholders, and bond holders. Is it always in the interests of all of these parties for the managers to pursue an active risk management program? Let's start with the stockholders, since they have a claim on the residual risks of the company after all the other parties take their portion of the pie. In a fundamental sense, they have the largest risk exposure, but it is here that the case for risk management is most subtle. The problem is that shareholders have other avenues for reducing their risk exposure to the company. In fact, one of the fundamental purposes of capital markets is to spread the risks of ownership in a company across the market as a whole. This is why most ownership of corporate stock is now diversified. This means that the stockholders of most companies have already taken advantage of the risk management function of the stock market to limit their risk exposure. In the language of modern finance, they are exposed solely to the systematic risk, rather than to the entire risk (systematic plus unsystematic) of the company's performance. It might appear that the only value of corporate risk management to the stockholders would be if the risk that is managed at the corporate level is a systematic risk, but even then the corporate risk management program would have to be able to sell off systematic risk on more attractive terms than the same risk is bought and sold in the capital markets. This seems highly unlikely.

By contrast it is much easier to see why other stakeholders in the modern corporation would see value in a risk management program carried out by corporate management. Corporate managers themselves are one of the most obvious constituents in favor of such programs. The key difference between almost any stakeholder and equity shareholders of the company lies in their ability to shift or redistribute the company's risks. Few stakeholders have the capability to redistribute their exposure to the company the way stockholders do. This means that most stakeholders have an exposure to the unsystematic risk of the company as well as the systematic risk. For example, managers as well as other employees have their careers tied up in the company. If the company does poorly, especially so poorly as to be liquidated, they will lose that portion of their total human capital that is tied to the company. It is harder for employees to diversify their human capital than it is for stockholders to diversify their financial claims on the company. In fact, in order to provide managers and other workers with appropriate incentives in the corporation, it is even desirable to force them to have their future tied in tightly to the company's performance. This is how employees are motivated to work both hard and smart, but this feature of incentive compensation schemes means that the managers are exposed to substantial risk that stockholders can diversify.

The same is true of various other stakeholders in a company. At least it is true if the company is not selling a highly standardized or commodity product for which there are many substitutes. If there are close substitutes, then consumers lose little if a specific company does poorly; they simply purchase from another supplier of an identical product. Similarly, if a company's suppliers have close substitute purchasers for their products they are not so concerned about the risk exposure of one specific customer, whereas a company that sells a unique product or a product part of whose value derives from some intangible features should be very concerned about risk management. To illustrate what we mean, consider the value of a product like a specific kind of computer system, for example Apple Macintosh. Part of the value of the Apple Macintosh derived from the perception in the market of the enhancements and of the software that would be developed for the computer in the future. Suppose that Apple, or a supplier of software for Apple computers, is perceived as having substantial financial risk exposure. The chance that they will face some adverse event that will prevent them from carrying out their intended product enhancements will be a real concern to the purchasers of the Apple Macintosh. This will affect the willingness of consumers to buy their product and the price they are willing to pay. For this reason, companies that derive a significant part of their value from noncommodity products, where perceptions about future viability of the company are important, should be especially concerned about risk management. Such companies generally view financial leverage as a very dangerous form of financing, for exactly the same reason.

The same kind of effect develops even for companies that are selling commodity products, if they are financed with risky debt. This is simply because a serious risk exposure might mean that the company could experience financial distress. Such distress entails substantial dead weight, or extra costs, including loss of tax write-offs and extra legal or administrative expenses. All of these costs can be avoided by effective risk management. Risk management is important as a device that limits the chances of losses that interfere with the implementation of a company's business strategy.

A second source of real gain for a company deriving from risk management pertains to the effect of risk management on the incentives of managers and other workers or suppliers in the organization. Managers must make investment decisions about how the firm's resources are to be employed in the future. Workers must make decisions about whether to invest their own time and energy in learning to be more effective parts of the organization or in acquiring firm-specific skills. Suppliers must make the same investment decisions about both financial resources and time and energy. If the company is exposed to substantial financial risks, both managers and employees may be very reluctant to invest the kind of time and resources necessary for the company to succeed. As a result, risk management can limit the chances that adverse financial events will develop and thereby create a better environment or incentive structure for the organization's workers and suppliers.

We can summarize the reasons for a corporation's engaging in risk management simply. Risk management can benefit the modern corporation with diversified shareholders by

1. reducing the prospect of losses which will interfere with the execution of the company's business strategy and
2. allowing managers to focus directly on shareholder value as an objective in decision making.

Structuring the Risk Management Process

We divide the process of managing financial risk into five steps. The first four outline the preparation necessary to make the proper risk management decision. The last step constitutes the action that must be taken. It is important to understand that these steps pertain to the setup or selection of the right risk management strategy. They are not guides to executing a particular strategy or guides to the details of, say, designing an appropriate hedge. We get to that kind of more technical question after we lay out the key elements of the risk management process. Here are the five steps:

Step 1: Identify the source of the risk exposure.

Step 2: Quantify the exposure.

Step 3: Assess the impact of exposure on business and financial strategy.

Step 4: Assess your capability for operating your own hedging or insurance program.

Step 5: Select the appropriate risk management products.

Step 1: Identify the Source of the Risk Exposure

The first step seeks to develop a clear understanding of the nature of the risk exposure. Often the simplest and most direct way to do this is to draw a picture of the exposure, much like the pictures we drew of payoffs on futures and options contracts in Chapters 14 and 15. By forcing yourself to draw the picture or the profile of the risk exposure, you can usually sort out the true nature of that exposure. There are three principal things to identify about the exposure. First, you want to identify the economic factors that create the exposure, like exchange rates or interest rates. For example, the risk management problem may pertain to an exposure to changes in exchange rates for a company that produces a product in one country and sells it in another. Second, you want to determine the direction of the exposure, for example, whether an increase in a specific exchange rate is good news or bad news. Third, you want to determine whether the exposure is contingent on some other event. For example, a company may have an exposure that is contingent on winning some contract. This means that the exposure has elements of an option and probably requires a different risk management approach than an exposure that is not contingent. We examine contingent and noncontingent exposures later.

Step 2: Quantify the Exposure

In step 2 you measure the sensitivity of the company's performance to the source of risk. Generally, this involves some kind of simulation of what would happen to the company if the source of risk, for example interest rates or exchange rates, changed and the company had done nothing to manage its exposure. For example, in Chapter 21 we explain how to construct a simple "GAP" report to quantify the impact of changes in interest rates on a company's financial performance. Such a report focusing on the impact on accounting performance of changes in interest rates, might conclude that if interest rates increase by, say, 200 basis points, then the company for which the GAP report is prepared would experience an increase in interest expense over interest income of, say, $7 million over the next year. This kind of statement provides a clear quantitative assessment of the significance of the risk exposure. Of course, such simple assessments are often based on crucial simplifying assumptions that need to be spelled out and understood. We look at this closely when we take up the GAP report later.

Step 3: Assess the Impact of Exposure on Business and Financial Strategy

This step actually is designed to make the managers of a firm ask themselves why they want to manage risk. The key question is, How will this risk management process benefit the company and its shareholders? As we just discussed above, it is not obvious that the shareholders of a company are better off if all the sources of exposure are completely hedged or insured. If a risk management process is going to consume resources, either directly through fees or indirectly through use of management's time, then it is important to understand how controlling the risk will prove beneficial.

Step 4: Assess Your Capability for Operating Your Own Hedging or Insurance Program

The most important decision in formulating a risk management system amounts to a make-or-buy decision, or a choice between two broad classes of risk management strategies. One strategy relies on a financial intermediary to provide a tailormade solution to the risk management problem. The second involves the purchase of exchange-traded instruments like futures and options or over-the-counter products like forward contracts and the construction of your own risk management implementation capability. This involves constructing and implementing the correct hedging or insurance system and the monitoring and adjustment of the necessary positions over time. We delve into exactly what is required here a little later. As we have already emphasized, in today's marketplace many banks are eager to provide tailormade solutions to risk management problems. The management of every company needs to decide whether it can afford to directly manage its risk exposure or whether it should hire one of these firms.

Step 5: Select the Appropriate Risk Management Products

In the ultimate action that must be taken in the risk management process you have to choose the appropriate product from the available set. The elements of this set have been covered (with the exception of caps and collars, which we introduce in Chapter 22) in earlier chapters. So now it is simply necessary to highlight their pros and cons as a part of a risk management strategy. Table 17-1 summarizes the advantages and disadvantages of the key elements of the product set. Note that the first set of products includes cash, or spot market instruments like loans or bonds. These are useful for directly managing interest rate risk. Generally, for every interest rate risk management problem facing a company there is a solution that involves direct rearrangement of the balance sheet, or use of cash or spot market instruments. We will explain why many corporate managers see a variety of disadvantages in this approach to the problem. The principal advantage of all exchange-traded products lies in the liquidity that derives from standardization. Liquidity means that hedges established using futures and options can be unwound easily and at little cost. The

Table 17-1

The Risk Management Product Set

	Element of Product Set	Advantages	Disadvantages
Cash market products	Loans, bonds	Simplicity	Realization of gain or loss, issue cost, tax consequences
Exchange-traded contingent claims	Options, futures	Liquidity and efficiency of pricing	Inflexibility and basis risk, monitoring costs
Over-the-counter products	Swaps, forwards, caps, collars, options	Flexibility	Potential illiquidity

disadvantage is that standardization can lead to a significant mismatch between a company's specific exposure and the exchange-traded instruments that could be used to manage it. This can lead to substantial basis risk and to expensive monitoring and implementation problems. The alternative—purchasing a tailormade product from a commercial or investment bank is attractive since the seller of the product takes responsibility for managing the exposure, though at a cost. Moreover, if circumstances change and it is necessary to unwind the position it can easily be more expensive to do so than if you had used an exchange-traded instrument. This trade-off between the advantages of liquidity and the disadvantage of standardization is the key issue in setting up a risk management strategy. There is no simple or direct guide to what constitutes the best approach for a given company. You have to go through the five steps and try to weigh the costs and benefits of the alternatives.

Setting Up a Hedge

To make an informed choice among the products in Table 17-1 for any specific risk management problem, you must understand what is involved in developing your own risk management strategy, or what we call your own "hedging strategy." Our next task is to see to how to construct a hedge. This is a relatively simple problem when circumstances make it possible to create what is called a "perfect hedge." Unfortunately, perfect hedges are not achievable very often. The problem that gets in the way of constructing a perfect hedge is basis risk, but before we address managing basis risk we need to start with hedging.

The Basic Idea of Hedging

The basic idea behind constructing a hedge is to identify the exposure you face, measure that exposure, and then construct another position that has the opposite exposure. The combined positions will then be offsetting. If it is possible to construct a position that is exactly the opposite of your exposure you will have a perfect hedge. Sometimes the hedging problem can be addressed effectively with futures (or forward) contracts; in other situations hedging involves options. It is also important to distinguish hedging from insurance. Hedging involves offsetting the entire exposure to a source of risk, whereas insurance involves purchasing protection solely against adverse movements in the source of risk. For example, if the source of risk is fluctuations in the cost of borrowing, a hedge would replace an uncertain future cost of borrowing with a specific fixed cost. On the other hand, insurance involves replacing the uncertain borrowing cost with a fixed cost solely for increases in the cost of borrowing above some prespecified rate. We hope you see that hedging a risk like changes in the cost of borrowing requires a symmetric offsetting position, as in a futures contract, whereas insurance requires an asymmetric position, as in an options contract. We develop these ideas in more detail later.

In any number of situations a market participant might want to hedge an exposure that arises in the cash market. A depository financial institution that writes a loan, intending to fund that loan with future short-term deposits, might want to hedge the risk of future changes in the cost of those deposits. A mortgage broker who holds an inventory of mortgage-backed securities before they can be resold in the secondary mortgage markets might want to hedge the risks of changes in the value of that portfolio. A manufacturing firm may know that it needs to borrow from a bank in the future and may attempt to arrange a loan commitment from the bank. If the firm believes the bank is not offering attractive terms, it may attempt to lock in financing terms by hedging in the futures market. A company that produces products in one country and sells them in another generally wants to hedge its exposure to foreign exchange rates. Finally, a company that either produces or uses a commodity, such as oil, may want to hedge fluctuations in its price.

In order to understand the basic idea of hedging and the fundamental elements of constructing a proper hedge, let's consider an example of a multinational firm that sells products denominated in a number of different currencies. Let's assume this company has its production facilities in Japan, the country in which it is domiciled. Suppose also that this company's business involves a relatively steady volume of sales of Japanese-manufactured products in a number of countries. While the volume of production and sales is quite steady, substantial production time is involved.

Suppose the Japanese company decides to use exchange-traded products rather than the others listed in Table 17-1. Then it would find it optimal to use futures contracts to hedge the prospect of fluctuations in the exchange rate between the yen and the currencies in which products are sold. If the magnitude of the ultimate sales volume, and hence the amount of the currency that needs to be hedged, is known with certainty or is subject to little risk, then all the company needs to worry about is hedging the value of its dollar-denominated sales when the income is converted back into yen. A futures contract can be written in the amount of goods to be sold in the currency of each country where the firm has sales. If the price of currency in the country where the goods are sold declines, the firm will gain on its futures contract, but it will suffer from the changes in the exchange rate. Exactly the opposite happens if the price of the foreign currency increases. In this case the firm experiences a loss on its futures contract, but it is able to sell products for a higher price denominated in its home currency. As a result it has hedged its risk of fluctuations in foreign exchange rates.

To see more precisely how this would work, suppose the Japanese company expects to sell 10,000 units of its product in the United States in one year for $10 each so that it will have $100,000 in revenue. If the exchange rate between yen and dollars was 120, then the revenue in yen would be ¥12 million. This exposure is illustrated in Figure 17-1, which shows the payoff to the firm on the vertical axis and the yen-dollar exchange rate on the horizontal axis. It is always a good idea to draw a picture of the exposure and of the hedge position whenever you are facing a hedging problem. To insure this level of revenue, the Japanese company could sell (short) futures, say at a settlement price of 120, in the amount of $100,000 (see Fig. 17-1). The idea behind the hedge is that if the value of the dollar denominated in yen declines or, equivalently, if the yen-dollar exchange rate declines, the company will earn a profit on its hedge. Some sample payoffs from the hedged position are defined in Table 17-2. The table illustrates that if the exchange rate declines the firm will earn profits on the futures contracts, but the value in yen of the goods sold will decline. On the other

Figure 17-1
Exposure and hedge for Japanese firm.

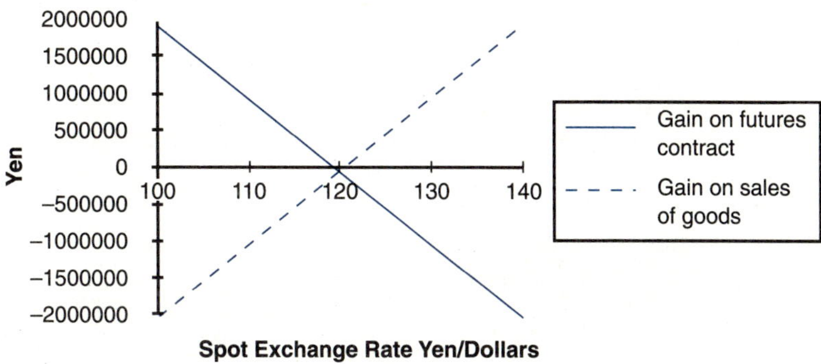

hand, if the exchange rate increases exactly the opposite will occur. The final column illustrates that the net proceeds from the hedged position are always the same, regardless of the exchange rate. This is precisely the purpose of a hedge.

Constructing a Perfect Hedge

In the foreign exchange example we just considered we did not take into account many of the difficulties usually involved in constructing a perfect hedge. Instead, we just assumed that a perfect hedge was available. Often, particularly in managing interest rate and commodity price risks, this is not the case, so now we consider an interest rate example where we encounter an imperfect hedge. First, we assume there are futures contracts available that will allow us to construct a perfect hedge. Then we consider the key reasons why we probably could not implement such a hedge in practice, or why it would probably be imperfect. The fact that we are able to construct a perfect hedge means we will be able to *completely eliminate* all of the risk exposure. We have constructed this example so that will work out. Such are the advantages of textbook examples.

Table 17-2
Gain on Short Futures Contract for \$100,000 in Yen with a Contract Yen-Dollar Exchange Rate of 120

Future exchange rate (¥/\$)	Gain on futures in yen (in millions)	Value of goods sold in yen (in millions)	Net proceeds sales and from futures (in millions)
100	2	10	12
110	1	11	12
120	0	12	12
130	-1	13	12
140	-2	14	12

A manufacturing firm wants to hedge the risk of changes in its cost of credit. The firm knows it will be purchasing materials for inventory in one month, and it will need a three-month loan to finance the inventory. It has approached its bank for a current commitment on the rate on the loan, but it suspects the bank rate is not in line with the market's estimates of future interest rates. We assume that the future cost of borrowing from the bank is tied directly to the interest rate on 90-day Treasury bills. Therefore, the manufacturer decides to hedge its risk in the futures market for 90-day T bills.

The appropriate position for the firm to take is to short futures on 90-day bills. Then, if interest rates increase, prices of 90-day bills will fall and the firm should make a profit from its futures position. At the same time, the increase in interest rates will cause its cost of credit from the bank to increase. If the hedge works perfectly these should be exactly offsetting. The time frames of the loan and the perfect hedge are illustrated in Figure 17-2. The firm faces its hedging problem at time 0, and it intends to take out its loan after 30 days, at day 30 in the figure. The loan will last 90 days, until day 120. If a futures contract is available that matures on day 30, then, as we shall see, a perfect hedge will be available. The figure also shows that we might instead use a futures contract that matures on day 60, though, if we are forced into this alternative we have an imperfect hedge.

Table 17-3 illustrates how a perfect hedge would work in this example. The firm attempts to lock in the rate on a discount loan beginning 30 days from now and the forward rate on 90-day T bills in the futures market is 3 percent. It also assumes that the amount of the loan is \$10 million, which is the same as the amount of ten T-bill futures contracts. Since the loan is a discount loan, the firm does not actually receive \$10 million. (See Chapter 2 for a discussion of discount loans and Treasury-bill pricing.) Rather, it promises to pay \$10 million after three months. It will receive the present value of that \$10 million discounted at the 90-day rate applied to the loan. For example, if the 90-day rate is 3 percent, the firm will borrow \$10,000,000/[1 + 0.03(90/360)], or \$9,925,558.

Table 17-3 shows the cost of borrowing and the gain or loss on the futures contract for five different levels of interest rates prevailing when the loan is to begin, that is, after one month. Because the forward rate for 90-day Treasury bills one

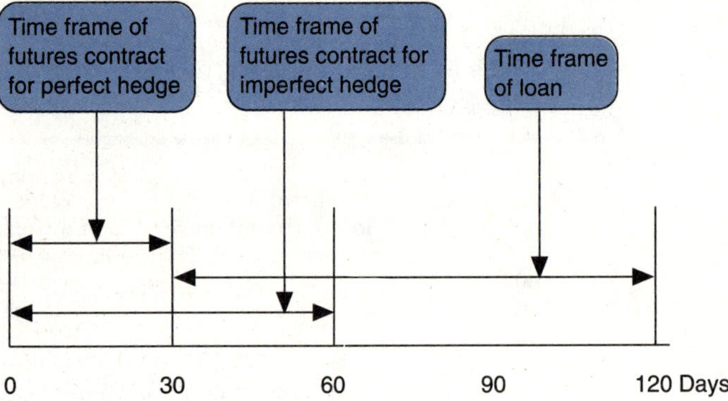

Figure 17-2
Time frame of loan and futures contracts.

Table 17-3
Hedging the Cost of Bank Credit

Interest Rate (%)	Cost of $10-Million Loan ($)	Increase in Borrowing Cost Over 3% Forward	Value of Future at Maturity[a]	Gain on Future[b]	Net Cost of Credit
3.5	86,741	12,299	9,913,259	12,299	74,442
3.25	80,595	6,153	9,919,405	6,153	74,442
3	74,442	0	9,925,558	0	74,442
2.75	68,281	-6,161	9,931,719	-6,161	74,442
2.5	62,112	-12,330	9,937,888	-12,330	74,442

[a]If 90-day rate is 3% value of future is $10,000,000/[1 + .03(90/360)].
[b]Short position with contract price per contract of $992,555.8

month from now is assumed to be 3 percent, the range of interest rates in the table is centered on 3 percent. The first column shows the alternative interest rates; the second column the cost of borrowing through a discount loan for alternative interest rates; the third column the increase or decrease in the cost of credit over the cost at 3 percent; and the fourth column the value of the futures contract on 90-day bills at maturity for different levels of the prevailing 90-day bill rate. Note that the contract price is the value of the futures contract if the prevailing interest rate is 3 percent. That is, the contract price for one contract is $992,555.80. The fifth column shows the gain or loss on the short futures position used in the hedge. If interest rates fall, there is a loss on the short position. The gain is simply computed by taking the difference between the price of ten contracts at the prevailing interest rate and the contract price of $9,925,558 for ten contracts. The final column in the table shows the net cost of credit, including the gain or loss on the futures contracts. The table illustrates that this cost is always the same, regardless of the level of interest rates. This is the result of a perfect hedge. The increase in the cost of borrowing (column three) is always offset by the gain or the loss on the futures contracts (column five).

Thus, this example is a perfect hedge. It was possible to completely offset the risk of changes in the cost of borrowing by using T-bill futures. The loan contract was directly tied to Treasury bills, so that the correlation between changes in Treasury-bill rates and changes in the cost of the loan is perfect.

In practice, a perfect hedge generally is not attainable. Two problems can make a hedge less than perfect. Both generate what is called "basis risk." Basis risk occurs whenever there is less than perfect (negative) correlation between the price of the hedging instrument and the price of the asset being hedged. When the maturity or desired length of the hedge does not coincide with the maturities of futures contracts available in the market this leads to what is called "delivery basis risk." The second problem arises when no hedging instrument exists that is perfectly correlated with the asset being hedged, even when maturity dates are perfectly matched. In this case it is necessary to construct what is called a "cross hedge." Because the key to hedging strategy is managing basis risk we need to look at basis risk quite closely.

Basis Risk

The Nature of Basis Risk

When the treasurer of the firm in our example attempts to hedge that firm's risk exposure, the first thing she might notice is that there are only four delivery dates for financial futures: March, June, September, and December of each year. (See Chapter 14 for the structure of futures markets.) As a result, it probably would not be possible to execute the hedge we described exactly as shown in Table 17-3. Unless the date that the treasurer wanted to take out a loan corresponded with one of the four delivery dates, it would not be possible to write a futures contract that would mature on the precise date the treasurer prefers. Therefore, she could not close out the hedge by delivering a 90-day T bill. Instead, it would be necessary to write a futures contract for one of the four delivery dates and close it out prior to maturity. This would be accomplished by buying back (since the hedge involved a short position in futures) the futures contract at the end of the hedge period but before it matured. Returning to Figure 17-2, if the nearest dated futures contract matured on day 60 there would be a 30-day gap between the maturity date of the futures contract and the date the treasurer wanted to hedge T-bill rates.

This creates a problem. The prevailing price of the futures contract when it must be closed out may differ from the price that would yield a perfect hedge. In the context of the example in Table 17-3, the gain or loss on the futures contract may not exactly offset the change in the cost of borrowing as shown in the final column. The gain or loss on the futures contract will still be equal to the difference between the futures price when the hedge is initiated and the price of the contract used to close out the futures position, but in this case the latter price would be the price at the end of the hedge period of the same futures contract. In theory that price should be determined by the market's best guess of what interest rates will be when that futures contract matures. It will not be determined by the spot (cash) 90-day T-bill rate prevailing when the contract is closed out.

For example, suppose that the futures contract used in the hedge described had two months to maturity when it was initiated (i.e., that it matured on day 60). We continue to assume that the maturity of the hedge is one month. Therefore, the futures contract must be closed out with one month remaining to maturity in order to close out the hedge. When the futures contract is closed, it will be a one-month contract. The price or interest rate on the futures contract when it is closed should contain the market's best guess of spot T-bill rates that will prevail in one month, at the maturity of the futures contract. If the forward rate prevailing for one-month futures is 3.5 percent, the price that must be paid to close out the ten contracts in the example in Table 17-3 is $9,913,259. The gain on the futures contract from the date of purchase would be $9,925,558 − $9,913,259, or $12,299, as shown in Table 17-3. The cash 90-day T-bill rate will not necessarily be 3.5 percent when the contract is closed. It could easily be any other value. Table 17-4 shows what would happen to the net cost of credit if the spot T-bill rate went from 3.50 percent to 2.50 percent while the rate in the futures market was fixed at 3.50 percent. For example, the table shows

Table 17-4
Hedging the Cost of Bank Credit When Futures Contract is Closed at 3.5%

Interest Rate (%)	Cost of $10-Million Loan ($)	Increase in Borrowing Cost Over 3% Forward	Value of Future at Maturity[a]	Gain on Future[b]	Net Cost of Credit
3.5	86,741	12,299	9,913,259	12,299	74,442
3.25	80,595	6,153	9,913,259	12,299	68,296
3	74,442	0	9,913,259	12,299	62,143
2.75	68,281	-6,161	9,913,259	12,299	55,982
2.5	62,112	-12,330	9,913,259	12,299	49,813

[a]If the 90-day rate is 3.5 percent value of future is $10,000,000/[1 + .035(90/360)].
[b]Short position with contract price per contract of $992,555.8

that if the cash rate were 3 percent the net cost of borrowing would be $62,142. This is the difference between $74,442, the cost of borrowing at 3.0 percent, and the gain on the futures contract of $12,299. As a result, the net cost of borrowing is no longer constant, as in Table 17-3. Instead, it depends on the difference between the price of the futures contract when it has to be closed (the forward rate) and the value of 90-day T bills at the same point in time. This, in turn, depends on what the market expects to happen to T-bill rates over the next month. The greater the difference between these two, the larger the variation will be in the net cost of credit.

The example presented in Table 17-4 is not constructed as a cross hedge because it was assumed that the cost of borrowing is directly tied to the Treasury-bill rate. Suppose that, instead, the cost of borrowing was tied to the bank's prime rate and the prime rate was not specifically tied to any market interest rate. This is actually a more realistic description of bank borrowing terms. The problem facing the borrower in this case is that there are no futures contract on the prime rates of banks. There are futures contracts on commercial paper that might be used for such a hedge. But regardless of whether commercial paper or Treasury-bill futures were used, there would still be basis risk because the prime rate could diverge from the interest rate in the future's contract.

It is also important to note that our example does not take account of the fact that the treasurer would be required to settle up daily based on daily changes in settlement prices on the futures contract (discussed in Chapter 14). This means that the transaction would not be quite as simple as we portrayed it, even if it were possible to construct a perfect hedge. Daily settlement could require the firm to commit sizable amounts of cash over the course of the hedge, even though the hedge is perfect and those losses would be recouped as the maturity date approached. This would be costly because the firm would incur the opportunity cost of any cash it had to commit to pay losses on daily settlement, even though those losses would be offset at maturity.

Measuring the Basis

It is helpful to step out of our example of the company hedging its future borrowing costs and to examine the basis in a hedge from a more general perspective. The basis of a hedge refers to the spread between the value of the hedge position, which we assume to be a futures contract, and the value of the asset being hedged, or the cash position. Let C_t and F_t be the value of the cash and futures positions, respectively, at time t. Then the basis at time t is simply the spread between C_t and F_t:

$$\text{Basis}_t = C_t - F_t$$

There is a very important feature of a futures contract that we can state in a simple way using the basis. At the maturity of the futures contract, the market will force the price of the future (that is, the settlement price at maturity) to be equal to the cash price of the underlying security. That is, if we designate the maturity date as $t = m$, then

$$C_m - F_m = 0$$

If this were not true there would be a perfect arbitrage opportunity in the futures market whereby you could buy or sell futures contracts with a right to buy or sell the underlying security immediately at a price that differed from the cash price of that security (the property of convergence described in Chapter 14). Returning to our example in Tables 17-3 and 17-4, we can now see why the T-bill futures contract that matured on day 30 provided a perfect hedge. On that day, we know that the basis must be driven to zero. Notice, however, that we do not have this assurance on any other day before the maturity of the futures contract. On any other day, the price of the futures contract contains the market's best estimate of the cash price of the underlying security on the maturity date of the future. This can differ from the current cash price by any amount, though as we approach the maturity date the likelihood of significant differences in the futures price and the contemporaneous cash price gets smaller and smaller. Thus, the basis normally gets smaller and smaller as we approach the maturity of a futures contract.

This phenomenon is illustrated in Figure 17-3. Panel A shows a simulation of the level of cash and futures yields. Purely for simplicity of exposition we have used yields rather than prices here. Normal procedure is to use prices, since futures and options contracts are denominated in prices rather than yields. But it is often easier to understand an exposure or a risk management problem related to interest rates by working in yields. The horizontal axis of both panels of the figure shows the number of days remaining to maturity on a futures contract that starts with 30 days to maturity. Panel A shows the two yields; Panel B shows the delivery basis, or the spread between the yields. When the futures contract is far from maturity the basis can be fairly large, and it wanders around randomly, reflecting differences between the current cash rate and the market's estimate of the cash rate at maturity. As the maturity date approaches, however, the spread between the two yields, or the delivery basis, narrows until it reaches zero at maturity.

The problem in an imperfect hedge arising from delivery basis risk can be seen directly in either panel of Figure 17-3. If you pick any of the 30 days in the figure before maturity, you cannot be sure that the basis will be zero. The basis is random and could be positive or negative. You can expect that the basis will decline until it

Figure 17–3

Panel A: Cash and futures interest rate over life of future. *Panel B:* Basis between future and cash.

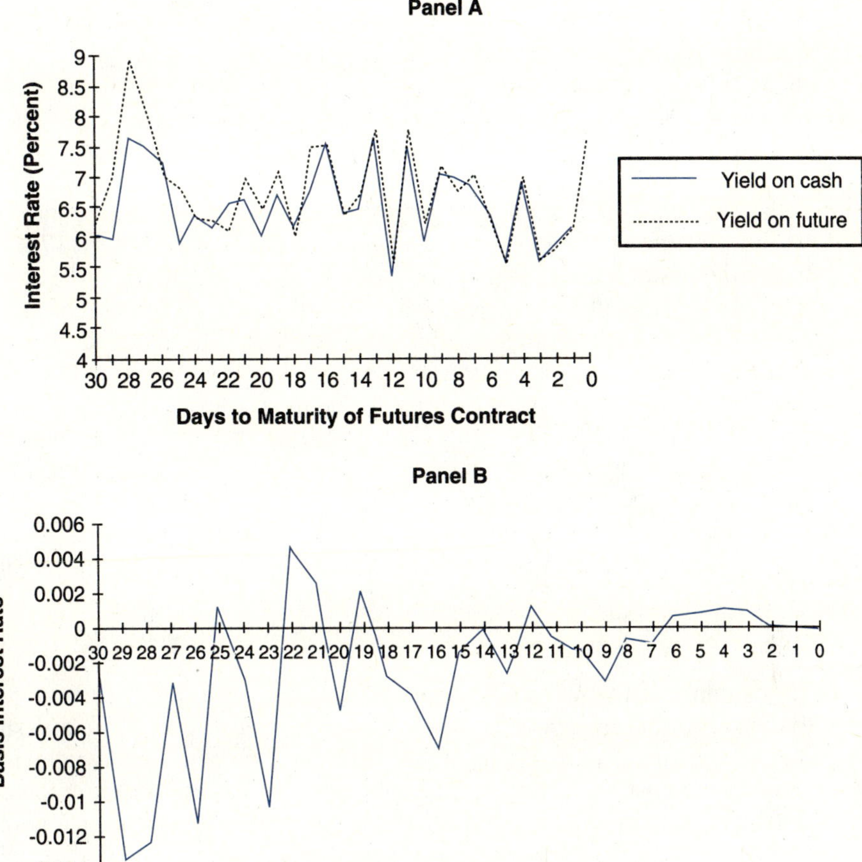

reaches zero at delivery, but unusual events can cause large changes in the basis even near maturity, though this is not normal.

Hedging Strategy

The central strategic problem involved in hedging is to design a hedge so that you achieve a desirable combination of expected return and risk. In this sense, the hedging decision is like any investment decision: it requires balancing expected return and risk. Two specific decisions are involved in designing a hedging strategy:

(1) choosing the appropriate hedging instrument to use for the hedge and
(2) choosing the appropriate volume of that instrument to acquire, or the appropriate hedge ratio.

To keep things simple, we still generally assume that we are considering futures contracts as our hedging instruments, though in many applications we might use other instruments.

These decisions are simple when a futures contract that generates no basis risk is available. Such a contract is the one to use for the hedge. The choice of how many futures contracts to acquire is illustrated in Panel A of Figure 17-4. This figure shows expected return and risk in a portfolio of assets. In this case the portfolio consists of our cash and our hedge positions. The vertical axis in the figure shows the total expected return from the sum of the cash position and the futures position, depending on how large a futures position is taken. The horizontal axis shows the variance of the portfolio of cash and futures. Panel A of Figure 17-4 is constructed under the assumption that there is no basis risk. When this is the case it is always possible to reduce the variance of the portfolio to zero by taking a futures position exactly equal in magnitude to the cash position. The fact that a perfect hedge is available means that the correlation coefficient between the two assets in the portfolio is -1. The zero variance or perfect hedge position corresponds to the vertex of the triangle in Panel A of Figure 17-4. The diagonal lines emanating from the origin to form this triangle define the feasible combinations of expected return and variance, or the opportunity set.

Another way to describe the second choice is to say that it is necessary to choose the appropriate hedge ratio. The hedge ratio, *H*, is defined as follows:

$$H = -\frac{\text{Quantity of futures held}}{\text{Quantity of cash position}}$$

For example, if the investor is short the futures contract in an amount exactly equal to the size of his cash position, then the hedge ratio is one. If the investor has a short futures position half the size of his cash position, the hedge ratio is one half. In hedging the cost of borrowing in Table 17-3 the perfect hedge involved purchasing ten futures contracts of $1 million each to match the discount loan with a face value of $10 million. This amounted to a hedge ratio of one. The hedge ratio is equal to one in Panel A of Figure 17-4 at the point where the variance of the portfolio is

Figure 17-4

Optimal and minimum variance hedge ratios.

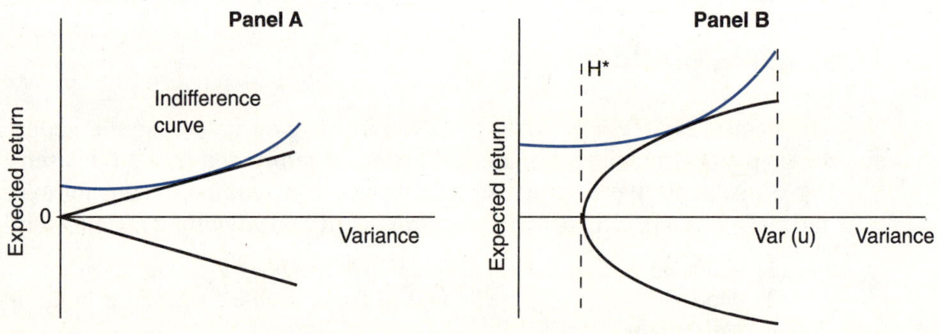

zero. Therefore, when there is no basis risk a hedge ratio of one results in a perfect hedge, or a portfolio with zero variance.

Let's reconsider both of the decisions involved in hedging strategy if there is basis risk in all the futures contracts that might be used for a hedge. This means no futures contract is available that will generate a perfect hedge. It is then necessary to choose the best instrument from available alternatives and to choose the best hedge ratio for that instrument. The best futures contract is the one whose price is best correlated with the price of the cash position, or the asset to be hedged. The degree to which the futures contract is correlated with the asset to be hedged is called the "effectiveness" of the hedge.

To see how to measure effectiveness we have to consider the *minimum-variance hedge ratio.* The minimum-variance hedge ratio for a particular futures contract is the ratio that eliminates as much risk of the cash position as possible using that futures contract for the hedge. This is illustrated in Panel B of Figure 17-4, which shows what combinations of risk and expected return are attainable in a hedge with basis risk. To understand what is represented in this figure it is useful to compare Panels A and B. The line showing the opportunities that can be created by combining the two assets, the efficient frontier, is now a smooth curve rather than a triangle. In addition, the minimum variance that can be achieved is no longer 0. While it is not evident from an inspection of the figure, the minimum variance, shown by the tangency of the dashed line labeled H^* with the opportunity curve, no longer occurs when H is 1. In fact, the value of H that minimizes variance, H^*, could assume any value.

An effective hedge is one where it is possible to eliminate a large part, relative to other available alternatives, of the variance of the cash position. In terms of Figure 17-4, this would mean that the minimum variance would be close to the origin. One way to measure this is to measure the distance between the vertical axis and the dashed line representing H^* and to divide that by the distance between the vertical axis and the dashed line through the point on the horizontal axis labeled Var(U). This point represents the variance of a completely unhedged cash position. This measure of the effectiveness of a hedge, which we label e, can be defined as follows:

$$e = 1 - \frac{\text{Var}(R^*)}{\text{Var}(U)}$$

where Var(R^*) is the variance of the portfolio comprised of the cash position and a futures position with a hedge ratio of H^*, or the minimum-variance portfolio. Though we will not get into detail here, it can be shown that

$$e = \frac{(\sigma_{CF})^2}{\sigma^2_C \sigma^2_F}$$

where σ_{CF} is the covariance of rates of return on cash and futures positions and σ^2_C and σ^2_F are variances of the rate of return on cash and futures positions, respectively. This is the coefficient of determination, or the square of the correlation coefficient between the returns on the cash and futures investments.

Another way of looking at the problem of selecting the proper hedge ratio is that it amounts to the estimation of a regression equation, where the price of the asset to be hedged is regressed on the price of the futures contract used in the hedge. In effect, we are asking what expected change in the value of the asset to be hedged is generated by a given change in the price of the futures contract. This is measured by the slope coefficient in a regression of the price of the cash position on the price of the future where H^* is the slope coefficient:

$$C_t = H^*F_t + u_t$$

In the regression equation, C_t and F_t represent observed historical values of the price of the cash and futures positions, and u_t is the error term in the regression. Thus, the most effective hedge ratio for eliminating risk depends on the relationship between the rates of return on cash and futures investments. This makes sense because it is this relationship that determines the extent of the basis risk. Similarly, the effectiveness of the hedge is simply the R^2 of the regression, that is, the percentage of the variation in the cash price that is explained by the variation in the futures price.

Now we can return to the question of how to choose the best futures contract for a hedge. It is necessary to evaluate the effectiveness using the measure *e* for each futures contract that might be used to hedge the risk of a specific asset. The futures contract with the highest measure of effectiveness will be the best instrument for the hedge, in the sense that it will introduce the least basis risk. Once it has been decided which of the available futures contracts is most effective it is necessary to choose the appropriate hedge ratio. One possible answer is to choose the minimum-variance hedge ratio. While we have focused our discussion on the minimum variance that can be achieved by a hedge, it is not obvious that the best solution to any risk management problem is to minimize risk. As with all investment decisions, the appropriate approach is to balance risk against expected return. The investment opportunity curve shown in Panel B of Figure 17-4 shows the opportunities for trading risk against expected return provided by the futures market. The optimal portfolio, and therefore the optimal hedge ratio, depends on the risk aversion of the person making the decision, which can be represented by the indifference curves in Panel B. The tangency between the indifference curve and the opportunity curve for the hedge illustrates the optimal solution for the investor pictured here. The indifference curve simply represents the judgment management must make about how much risk should be retained in the business and how much should be sold off. Recall our discussion of this point at the beginning of this chapter. There is no simple or general answer to this question.

Evidence on Hedging Effectiveness

A number of researchers have computed measures of *e* and H^* for various types of hedges where the basis risk arises because of different maturities of the hedge and of the futures contract used in the hedge. By studying these measures we get a clear impression of how useful the futures markets actually are for hedging. Shortly after futures markets on financial instruments were first introduced in the mid-1970s,

Table 17-5

Estimates of Hedging Effectiveness and Minimum-Variance Hedge Ratios

Futures Contract	Hedge Length	Estimated *e*	Estimated H^*
8 % GNMAs	2-week	0.664	0.801[a]
	4-week	0.785	0.848[a]
90-Day T bills	2-week	0.686	0.698[a]
	4-week	0.661	0.669[a]
Wheat	2-week	0.898	0.864[a]
	4-week	0.918	0.917
Corn	2-week	0.649	0.915
	4-week	0.725	1.021

[a]Significantly different from one at 5 percent level.

a number of researchers estimated the effectiveness of these new instruments as hedging vehicles. Charles Franckle estimated measures of effectiveness, the values of *e,* for two-week and four-week hedges in corn, wheat, 90-day T bills, and Government National Mortgage Association securities (GNMAs) carried out during 1977.[1] For example, the two-week hedge of T bills involved the purchase of a 90-day bill and a short futures position that was closed out in 14 days. The 90-day bill, then a 76-day bill, would be sold. Similarly, at maturity in a four-week hedge the original 90-day bill would then be a 62-day bill. Table 17-5 shows Franckle's estimates of H^* and e in each futures market. Notice that these estimated hedge ratios tell you how many futures contracts you would want to buy, per dollar of exposure to the cash price, for each contract. While the estimates all are different from 1, these estimates do not tell us the true or actual values of H^*. As in any statistical estimation problem the true value of the variable you are estimating cannot be known, though you can estimate the probability, given your estimate of H^* and the estimate of its variance, that the true value differs from 1. The data in Table 17-5, taken from Franckle's results, tell us that for both the two- and the four-week hedge, the values of H^* are significantly different from one at the 0.05 percent level in each of the four cases for financial futures, but only one of four cases for commodity futures. The table indicates that the lowest measure of hedging effectiveness in all four markets is 0.65. Moreover, hedging effectiveness of financial futures appears to be roughly comparable to the effectiveness in commodity markets.

Commodity futures have been used to redistribute risk for many years, so basis risk is not an insurmountable obstacle to the practical use of financial futures. Nevertheless, understanding basis risk is critical to understanding how useful financial futures are in practice.

[1]See Charles T. Franckle. "The Hedging Performance of the New Futures Market: Comment." *Journal of Finance* 35 (December 1980), pp. 1272–1279.

• *Understanding the Limits of Statistical Estimates of Hedge Ratios* •

The procedure we have just described for estimating the minimum-variance hedge ratio and the expected effectiveness of the resulting hedge relies on historical data, so these estimates are only as reliable as the historical record in predicting what may happen. If something happens to change the relationship between the cash price you are trying to hedge and the futures price you are using as the hedging instrument, then the estimates derived from historical data may be very far off. As a result, there can still be very large losses (or gains) on a position that seems to have low basis risk if the value of the hedging instrument and that of the security being hedged move in widely different directions.

A dramatic episode during the late 1980s illustrated how things can go wrong. We think this example is highly instructive about the shortcomings of any hedging strategy. The episode occurred in the mortgage markets in April 1987 when there was a significant increase in interest rates, owing largely to the fact that the Federal Reserve took steps to protect the value of the dollar, which had been falling against other major currencies. The rate increase caught many investors by surprise and was very painful to those who were not fully hedged.

The April 1987 change in interest rates led to one of the largest trading losses ever reported—approximately $275 million incurred by Merrill Lynch & Co. Merrill Lynch blamed the loss on unauthorized trading in securities backed by mortgages. Shortly after announcing the loss, the firm fired one of its senior mortgage-backed-securities traders, Howard A. Rubin, whom it blamed for much of the loss. Merrill Lynch claimed Rubin had accumulated a large unauthorized position in a new type of mortgage-backed security that was particularly risky. When interest rates went up in April these securities experienced a significant decline in value. Figure 17-5 shows the level of mortgage interest rates and the value of mortgage-backed securities issued by the Federal Home Loan Mortgage Corporation for April 1987. There was a significant decline in the value of these securities during a very short period. It has been estimated that Wall Street investment banking firms had approximately $5 billion of this type of security in their inventories when the significant price decline occurred. Apparently, Merrill Lynch had the largest exposure of all the participants in the market.

To protect themselves against precisely this type of interest rate change, many market participants had implemented hedges using options or futures on 7- to 10-year T bonds, which were chosen because the basis risk was believed to be rather low, or the hedging effectiveness high. It appeared, however, that a large number of market participants had failed to hedge their positions completely. In effect, many participants were accepting at least some of the interest rate risk themselves. One might also argue that they were speculating somewhat that interest rates would fall rather than rise and so had chosen very small hedge ratios or none at all. Beginning on April 10, when interest rates started to increase dramatically, people with unhedged positions apparently attempted to dump their securities to protect themselves against further increases in rates. This drove down the prices of mortgage-backed securities and drove up their yields relative to U.S. Treasury securities. This further increased the losses of unhedged investors in mortgage-backed securities. As a result, the basis between mortgage-backed securities and hedges using Treasury securities of investors who had been hedging, increased; that is, their hedges became less effective than market participants thought they would be. This is an example of how the yield spread between two instruments can diverge in an unexpected way and seriously harm the effectiveness of a cross hedge. This particular episode represented a serious setback to many mortgage market participants.

Using Options to Hedge Risk

The Role of Options in Hedging

Thus far we have approached the problem of risk management as if the appropriate choice from the product set presented in Table 17-1 is always a futures or a forward contract. This is because the exposures we have considered have all been symmetric as in Figure 17-1. Futures are the simplest types of instruments that can be used to hedge such an exposure. It is often possible to construct hedges using options that are virtually identical, except for transactions costs and margin requirements, to the interest rate hedges constructed using futures markets, so in many instances options can be used as a substitute for futures. But the attractiveness of options derives not simply from the ability to duplicate the kinds of hedges we have already examined. More flexible tools than futures or forwards for managing risk, options are most valuable in two ways. First, some types of risk exposure are contingent on some event. In these cases, options rather than futures are best suited to constructing a hedge. Second, many times the manager who has to choose a risk management strategy is actually interested in insuring against the prospect of losses arising from an exposure and wants to retain the opportunity for gains in that exposure. Options are the natural device for purchasing insurance rather than hedging. In order to develop these two points let's consider a sequence of examples.

Consider the example of a mortgage lender who has a cash position in GNMAs. This lender might hedge its cash position by shorting a futures contract on T bonds. The exposure and the hedge are illustrated in Panel A of Figure 17-6. To see how to use options to construct the same hedge, recall from Chapter 15 that if you buy a call and write a put option with the same exercise price, the payoff will be the same

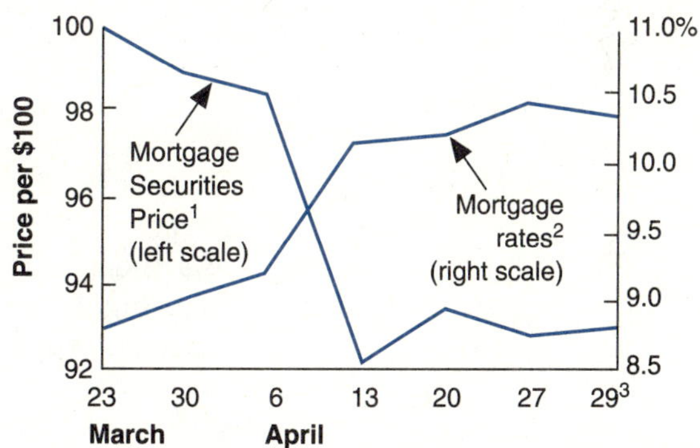

Figure 17-5

Mortgage-backed securities prices and yields in April 1987. *Source:* Wall Street Journal, *April 30, 1987, p. 2. Reprinted by permission of* The Wall Street Journal *©1987 Dow Jones and Company, Inc. All Right Reserved Worldwide.*

[1]Price of Federal Home Loan Mortgage Corp 8 1/2% 30-year mortgages sold in secondary market.
[2]Net yields required by Federal Home Loan Mortgage Corp. for 60-day delivery of 30-year mortgages.
[3]11 A.M. EDT.

Figure 17-6

Panel A: Exposure to GNMA prices of mortgage lender. *Panel B:* Using options to hedge exposure.

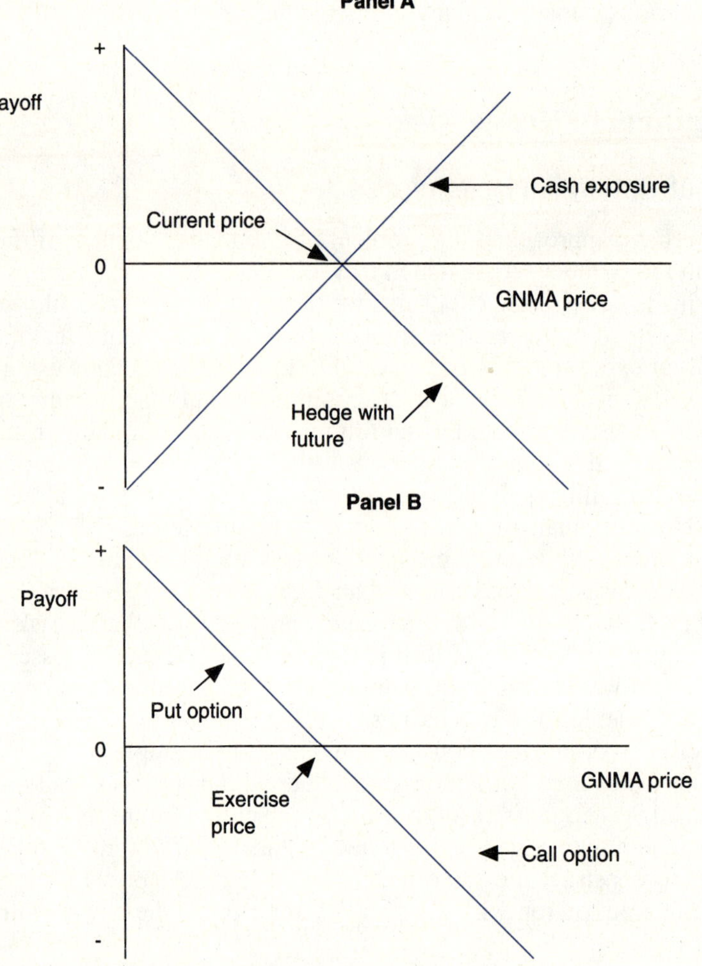

as if you had a long forward contract in the same underlying asset. By using the put and the call we are creating what is often called a "*synthetic security,*" in this case a synthetic forward contract. Therefore, the appropriate option position to take to hedge a cash position in an asset is simply to buy a put and write a call in that asset. This will be the equivalent of a short futures contract. In our GNMA example, we have to pick another asset that is highly correlated with GNMA or is effective as a hedging vehicle. A prominent candidate is a T-bond option or T-bond futures option. Panel B of Figure 17-6 illustrates the construction of the synthetic forward using puts and calls. We can always seek to construct hedges of symmetric exposures by combining options to mimic the behavior of a future or forward contract.

Hedging a Contingent Exposure

The other important use of options arises when the exposure to be managed is asymmetric, like the payoff on an option, or when the exposure is contingent on some event. Return to the Japanese firm selling its products in the United States that we examined at the beginning of this chapter. Recall that this firm was concerned about the foreign exchange risk of a product it produced in Japan and sold in the United States. Suppose it has a second type of product that involves sizable special orders from a variety of countries. Each order involves a substantial level of production, but it is uncertain how many orders might be received.

While it is preferable to use the futures market to hedge the foreign exchange risk in the steady and certain type of production we considered earlier, this would not be so with the second type of production. The fact that the futures contract makes a firm commitment to trade currency at a future price makes it less attractive than an option in this situation. Let's compare what happens to the company in our example if it uses an option rather than a futures contract and if no contract for production is signed. If the firm had originally hedged with futures—that is, before it knew whether a contract would be signed—it would face the symmetrical payoff characteristic of a futures contract. It would have unlimited gains if the price of the foreign currency declined but it would also have unlimited losses if the price of the foreign currency increased. If the firm's production contract is not signed, then there would be no sales of goods in that currency to offset these gains or losses. The company would have assumed a speculative, rather than a hedged, position.

On the other hand, if it had utilized an options contract, it would have an asymmetric rather than a symmetric payoff pattern. The appropriate option would have been to purchase a put on the foreign currency. Then, if that currency fell below the exercise price, it could exercise the put option for a profit. If a production contract had been signed, then this profit would offset losses due to the change in the exchange rate. If a production contract were not signed, exercising the put option would yield a profit. Had the foreign currency increased in value, the put option would be worthless and would remain unexercised, and the firm would lose only the price it had paid for the option. In this situation, had the firm used the futures contract it would have been exposed to an unlimited loss. The moral of the story is that the options contract provides greater protection when the exposure is contingent.

For another example, consider the situation facing a bank or a construction lender that offers fixed-rate lines of credit. These commitments to lend in the future at fixed interest rates are commonly used in commercial and construction lending. A lender who offers fixed-rate lines of credit has, in effect, written a put option. If the cost of credit increases, or the price of fixed-income obligations falls, borrowers are likely to increase their borrowing on fixed-rate credit lines, to take advantage of the relatively attractive interest rate. The lender loses because, unless it has hedged its position it will have to pay market interest rates to attract funds to support these loans. The lender receives a commitment fee for providing this credit line, which is analogous to the price of the put option that has been indirectly written by the lender.

A lender who has written a put option in providing a line of credit can hedge its risk by acquiring an offsetting put option in the options market. A futures contract does not achieve the same end because of its symmetrical payoff. With a futures contract the lender would gain or lose depending on the price of the underlying security. On the other hand, by buying a put option the lender can simply offset the loss exposure created by the fixed-rate line of credit.

The position taken by the lender if the fixed-rate credit line is hedged with a put option as opposed to a futures contract is illustrated in Figure 17-7. The figure is constructed on the assumption that the lender receives a fee for providing a fixed-rate line of credit. Panel A illustrates the magnitude of the losses incurred by the lender if interest rates increase and borrowers make use of their line of credit. The price of the underlying security shown on the horizontal axis is stated in terms of an interest rate, representing the cost of credit in the marketplace rather than a dollar price. This will reverse the illustration of payoffs on put and call options in our figure. The interest rate might be represented by a 90-day T-bill rate. If rates do not rise above a critical level, represented by r_e, then the lender incurs no losses and, therefore, receives a gain equal to the fee paid for the credit line, or the commitment fee. Here, r_e is the exercise price of the put option written by the lender, stated in terms of an interest rate rather than the price of the bill.

Panel B of the figure shows the payoff for the lender from a short position in T-bill futures with an exercise price, stated in terms of yield, of r_e. The line representing the payoff has a positive slope for a short position in the futures market for 90-day T bills simply because the exercise price is stated in yield rather than in price of the T bill. Panel C shows the net payoff to the lender if he attempts to hedge the risk of the credit line with the futures acquisition represented in Panel B. It is apparent from Panel C that utilizing the futures market has not enabled the lender to eliminate the risk inherent in the line of credit. The risk has simply shifted so that losses are incurred if interest rates fall (rather than rise).

Panel D shows the net profit from purchasing a put option on T-bill futures. If interest rates are below r_e, then the put will not be exercised and the lender will lose the price of the put. If interest rates are above r_e, the put will be exercised at a gain. When the payoffs in Panels A and D are combined (that is, when the line of credit is hedged with an option), the resulting payoff is constant. It is equal to the difference between the fee received by the lender for offering the line of credit and the price of the put option on 90-day T bills. The spread between these two prices is the risk-free return earned by the lender. This is illustrated in Panel E.

The option markets can also create more flexible hedges against interest rates than the one illustrated in Figure 17-7. To illustrate one possibility, suppose the lender who offers a linc of credit is willing to accept a limited amount of interest rate risk but prefers to be protected against large increases in interest rates. Protection of this type can be arranged using options by purchasing a put with an exercise price, stated in terms of yield, equal to r_e*, which is greater than r_e. The net payoff from hedging the line of credit with this option is represented by the dashed line in Panel F of Figure 17-7. Since the exercise price, measured in yield, is higher than the one illustrated in Panel D, this option should command a lower price. Therefore, the spread between the fee earned on the line of credit and the price of the option should be larger than that shown in Panel E. If interest rates are below r_e* the lender will

Figure 17-7
Hedging with options.

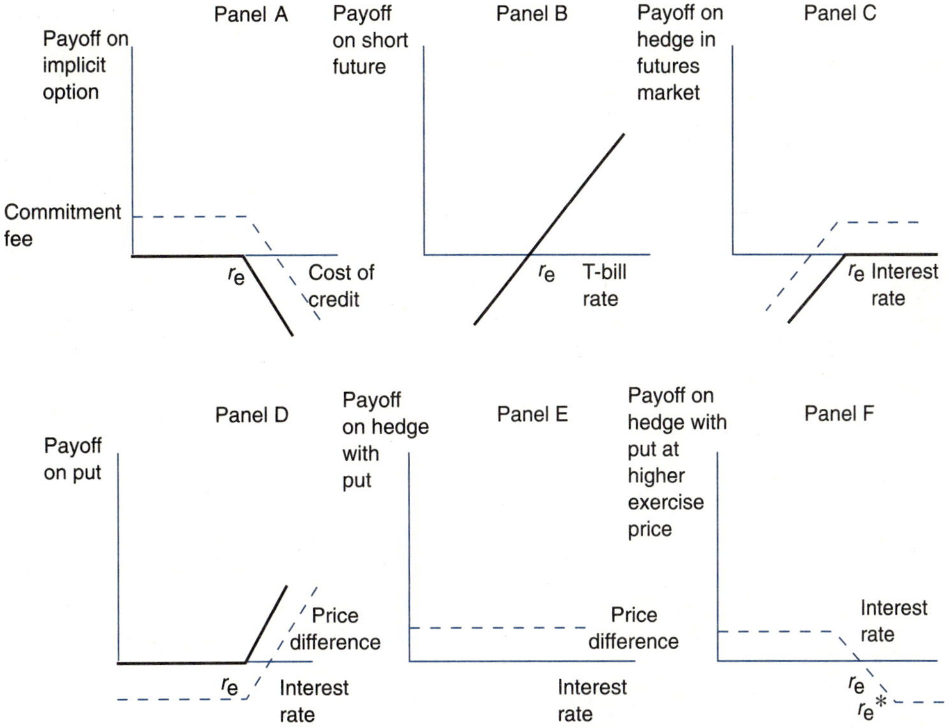

Panel A
Payoff on implicit option
Commitment fee
r_e
Cost of credit

Panel B
Payoff on short future
r_e
T-bill rate

Panel C
Payoff on hedge in futures market
r_e Interest rate

Panel D
Payoff on put
Price difference
r_e
Interest rate

Panel E
Payoff on hedge with put
Price difference
Interest rate

Panel F
Payoff on hedge with put at higher exercise price
Interest rate
r_e
r_e*

receive this spread, but if they are between r_e and r_e*, borrowers will utilize their lines of credit and the lender will incur some losses, though he will not exercise the put option purchased in the market. If interest rates exceed r_e*, the put option will be exercised and risk will be hedged, but the return will be lower than that earned in the risk-free hedge illustrated in Panel E.

SUMMARY

We began this chapter by discussing some of the issues involved in formulating an effective risk management program. We summarized a simple five-step program: (1) identifying the sources of exposure, (2) quantifying exposure, (3) clarifying the impact of exposure on the company's overall business strategy, (4) assessing the capability for managing the exposure internally as opposed to utilizing a specialist in risk management, and (5) selecting the appropriate risk management products. A company that is going to manage its own exposure internally must understand hedging strategy.

The basic idea behind a hedge is to take a position in one asset that will have a payoff that is the opposite of the payoff generated by the asset or position you already hold. Hedging has a number of practical applications for both financial and nonfinancial firms: a bank may want to hedge the future cost of deposits; a manufacturing firm may want to hedge the future cost of borrowing; a firm operating in more than one country may want to hedge future exchange rates between currencies.

Basis risk occurs whenever it is not possible to construct a perfect hedge, that is, whenever the price of the asset being hedged does not coincide perfectly with the price of the hedging instrument. There are two sources of basis risk. The first is failure of the maturity of the risk being hedged to coincide exactly with the maturity of the instrument. This can occur quite easily with hedges using futures since contract standardization limits the number of maturity dates for futures. The second source of basis risk is unavailability of a hedging instrument that is identical to the asset to be hedged. Then a cross hedge must be established.

Whenever there is basis risk in a hedge—whenever the hedge is not perfect—a strategic element is involved in hedging. The strategy involves choosing the best futures contract for the hedge and the appropriate hedge ratio. A hedging instrument can be selected by comparing measures of the effectiveness of a hedge. We also learned how to compute the minimum-variance hedge ratio, which yields the lowest attainable level of risk, though this may not be viewed as the best hedge, which is a matter of personal preference or a choice of the appropriate trade-off of risk and return.

We also reviewed the available empirical evidence on the effectiveness of financial futures with respect to the mismatch of maturities of the asset being hedged and the futures contract. According to this evidence, financial futures on T bills appear to be about as effective in limiting risk as commodity futures contracts such as corn and wheat.

Next we turned our attention to the use of options as hedging devices. We can always create the equivalent of a long futures contract by buying a call and writing a put with an exercise price equal to the contract price of the futures contract. Thus, if we are to find a special role for options as hedging devices it must be because we can use them to split up a futures contract. Some types of risks in the marketplace might inherently be like options and might have asymmetrical payoffs. For example, a bank that has written a line of credit has implicitly written an option. For the bank to attempt to hedge the risk of that commitment with a future, it would simply trade one kind of risk exposure for another. It can hedge its risk by acquiring an option that offsets its risk exposure.

QUESTIONS

1. Describe the basic idea behind a hedge using futures markets.
2. What is basis risk? How does a cross hedge create basis risk? How does a mismatch in maturities between the asset being hedged and the futures contract in the hedge create basis risk?

3. Suppose you are managing a savings and loan with a portfolio of mortgage-backed securities that earn 10 percent on a current market value of $800 million. You are funding half of this portfolio with long-term deposits matched with the maturity of your loan portfolio and half with 90-day deposits priced at the T-bill rate plus 50 basis points. You consider hedging the risk of changes in the cost of your 90-day deposits with T-bill futures. The T-bill rate implied by current futures contracts with three-month maturities on 90-day T bills is 7 percent and the current 90-day bill rate is 6.5 percent. Compute the profits and losses on your portfolio over the next year if you hedge your risk in the futures markets as opposed to accepting the risk of fluctuations in futures interest rates on T bills. Allow T-bill rates to vary from 5 percent to 8 percent in your computations.
4. Reconsider the problem in question 3. Recalculate your profits and losses with hedge ratios of 0.5 and 1.5. Remember, you are hedging half of the $800 million portfolio. How would you select the best hedge ratio?
5. How do you measure the effectiveness of a hedge? What is the relationship between the effectiveness of a hedge and the R^2 in a regression equation?
6. What does the evidence say about the effectiveness of financial futures as hedging devices compared with commodity futures?
7. Why would you ever use an option rather than a future in a hedge? Suppose you were a bank making a loan commitment. How would using a future contract simply exchange one type of risk exposure for another?
8. The solution to the hedging problem presented in Table 17-3 ignored the impact of daily settlement of futures contracts. How would recognition of such daily settlement change the results described in Table 17-3?

REFERENCES

Campbell, Tim S., and William A. Kracaw. "Corporate Risk Management and the Incentive Effects of Debt." *Journal of Finance* 45 (Dec 1990), pp. 1673–1686.

Smith, Clifford, and Rene Stulz. "The Determinants of a Firm's Hedging Policies." *Journal of Financial and Quantitative Analysis* 20 (1985), pp. 391–403.

Duffie, D. *Futures Markets*. Englewood Cliffs, NJ: Prentice Hall, 1989.

Ederington, Louis H. "The Hedging Performance of the New Futures Markets." *Journal of Finance* 34 (March 1979), pp. 157–170.

Franckle, Charles T. "The Hedging Performance of the New Futures Market: Comment." *Journal of Finance* 35 (Dec 1980), pp. 1272–1279.

Rendleman, Richard J. Jr., and Christopher E. Carabini. "The Efficiency of the Treasury Bill Futures Market." *Journal of Finance* 34 (September 1979), pp. 895–914.

• *Chapter 18*

Securitization

Securitization refers to the transformation of an asset that once had no secondary market into a tradeable security that can be traded in a secondary market. Another way to look at it is that securitization is the transformation of an intermediated market into an over-the-counter market, and ultimately an auction market. A number of assets that once were funded largely through financial intermediaries that functioned as portfolio lenders, issuing debt or deposit claims and holding loans on their books until maturity, are now becoming securitized. The market where securitization has gone farthest is the residential mortgage market, but almost every form of consumer receivable, as well as leases, commercial mortgages, and commercial bank loans, have now been securitized. Moreover, commercial paper and junk bonds are essentially securitized alternatives to bank loans. Securitization is one of the most important forms of innovation to develop in the financial markets of the 1980s. We also believe it may be one of the most enduring innovations.

In this chapter we examine the process of securitization. We begin by defining what it is and how it evolved. We explore some of its important precursors and some new forms of securities that are close, but not identical, to securitized assets. We will identify what we call "the six steps of the securitization process" and use these steps to identify the key skills or core competencies that are important for firms that plan to compete in a securitized market. We call these six steps and the competencies they require "the value chain in a securitized market." Then we evaluate the costs and benefits of securitization and its potential pitfalls. We provide a simple analytical framework for determining when securitization makes sense and when it does not. Finally, we examine some of the major markets in which securitization is now a common financing option. We look first at the mortgage market, since this is where securitization has progressed farthest, and focus on the development of the quasigovernmental agencies that package mortgages for sale as mortgage-backed securities. (We will return to this topic in Chapter 22 when we deal with the design of securities to deal with interest rate risk.) We also consider securitization of consumer receivables. The key concepts to learn in this chapter are listed below.

• *Concepts to Learn in Chapter 18* •

- The structure of the securitization process and the value chain in a securitized market
- The benefits of securitization
- The costs of securitization
- How securitization has revolutionized mortgage finance
- How securitization is used in a wide variety of debt markets

Origins of Securitization

If we turn the clock back roughly 30 years to the early 1960s we encounter a financial world where depository institutions in the United States functioned essentially as portfolio lenders. This means that they made loans to both corporations and consumers with the intent of holding loans until they matured or were paid off. The loans were funded principally by issuing deposits, and sometimes by issuing marketable securities. Any securities sold by the bank were direct obligations of the bank, rather than claims on its assets. This world of portfolio lenders has gradually been changing. It has now changed to the point that no bank or savings and loan, or even a finance company such as General Electric Credit Corporation, can afford to view itself exclusively as a portfolio lender. Virtually every type of loan or receivable a lender might consider holding can now be packaged or combined with other loans and sold into the securities markets. To understand this process we begin with a description of what securitization entails.

What Is Securitization?

Securitization is the transformation of a collection or portfolio of loans into a debt security that is tradeable in some form of market. The key difference between a loan and a debt instrument is its liquidity. By and large, loans are not liquid—they cannot easily be sold—whereas debt securities have greater liquidity. Securitization involves the creation or enhancement of liquidity. The debt instruments into which loans are transformed are often referred to as "asset-backed securities" (ABSs) since they are backed by specific assets, or collateral. Unlike regular debt obligations they are not general obligations of their issuer and they do not commit the issuer to provide cash to the security holder except through specific contractual commitments that are part of the legal agreement that comprises the security.

An ABS is a security in the legal sense and it must satisfy the various relevant statutes. This means that if the security is publicly distributed (and if it has a maturity longer than 270 days) it must be registered with the Securities and Exchange Commission (SEC) under the 1933 Securities Act and public disclosure requirements must be satisfied. Some ABSs are sold as private placements, and these do not have to be registered, but since private placements have less liquidity than publicly distributed obligations this option is generally not very attractive. In addition, securities backed by commercial paper are exempt from SEC registration since commercial paper itself is exempt owing to its short maturity. Loans or other assets can also be sold without transforming them into a security. These sales are often referred to as "whole loan sales" or "participations," depending on whether the entire interest in a loan or group of loans or only a part of the interest is sold. For many years, commercial banks have actively bought and sold participations in loans, particularly commercial and industrial loans. Strictly speaking, this is not securitization because no security is created. Moreover, such trading of participations does not provide increased access to a wider class of investors for commercial banks. Instead, it tends to redistribute risk of loans throughout the banking community.

To develop a more complete understanding of securitization it is useful to examine what is involved in structuring an ABS. Figure 18-1 illustrates the basic structure of a typical ABS. Four distinct participants in the securitization process are illustrated in this figure. At the top of the figure is the originator of the asset. This party creates or extends the loan and often services it as well. Servicing involves the collection and processing of payments (generally monthly). This originator contributes a set of loans or assets to be placed in an ABS. These assets are sold to a special-purpose entity or corporation that, in turn, issues the ABS. This special-purpose entity is often a distinct legal corporation or trust that is organized solely for the purpose of issuing ABSs. The issuing entity may be a subsidiary of the originator or it may be created by an investment bank that specializes in structuring ABSs. For example, First Boston has created a distinct entity called Asset-Backed Securities Corporation, which issues ABSs. In addition, Citicorp has created subsidiaries that acquire loans or

Figure 18-1
Basic structure of an asset-backed security.

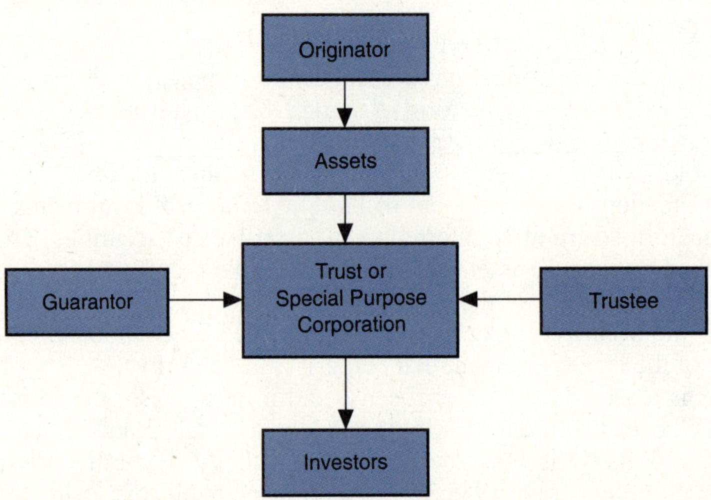

receivables from Citicorp and then issue debt directly on those subsidiaries. In many cases the preferred legal structure is to use a trust rather than a corporation for issuing the securities. The principal advantage of a trust is that it is immune from taxes and reduces liability for the issuer and originator. The issuer of the securities sells them directly to investors, who receive the cash flows from the underlying assets. The trustee handles the collection of cash flows, including both principal and interest payments, on the underlying assets from the servicer and disbursement of cash to the investors. The investors and the issuer generally cannot make a claim directly on the originator of the assets, beyond any stipulations in the legal agreement, if the loans are sold without recourse. A separate party, generally a bank or an insurance company, often guarantees to make payments to the trust in the event of defaults so that the promised payments can be made to investors as scheduled.

In the ABS market almost all securities sold have either a double-A or a triple-A rating from one of the rating agencies (Moody's or Standard & Poor's) unless the assets have a default guarantee from the U.S. government. In the case of mortgages, many of the securities are guaranteed by agencies of the U. S. government, so ratings are not obtained. High ratings are viewed as important for all securities that are not guaranteed by such agencies. One reason ratings are used is that many potential investors, including insurance companies and pension funds, are required by regulation to purchase only investment-grade securities. Another reason is that these private ABSs must compete with ABSs that have government agency guarantees. High ratings appear to be important in that competition, but the most compelling explanation seems to be that the purchasers of ABSs do not find it economical, on their own, to carry out the kind of detailed inquiries into the quality of the security that would be necessary if those securities could not be rated. Finally, when high ratings are commonplace, any issuer who attempted to distribute an ABS without a rating would be raising a red flag indicating some potential problem with the security. Thus, for all practical purposes ABSs are highly rated instruments.

To provide a high rating, rating agencies require that the assets be of sufficient quality that the promised cash flows will be paid in all but the most extreme or disasterous scenario. This often involves the commitment of additional reserves by the issuer or a guarantee against default by a highly rated third party. This "credit enhancement" can take a number of forms. The issuer itself can provide limited recourse or a form of self-insurance, but this often defeats part of the purpose of the transaction for many issuers, since they want to eliminate the obligation to cover any losses generated by the assets that are securitized. A bank can provide a letter of credit, a promise by the bank to make payments in the event of default. A financial insurance policy, or surety bond, can be purchased from an insurance company. A reserve account or allocation of assets can be set up by the issuer to ensure that resources are available in the event of defaults on the underlying loans. Finally, the security can be overcollateralized. This means that additional loans can be contributed to the ABS by the originator so that the extra loans provide sufficient cash flow to cover the obligations to investors if some of those loans default. All of these methods require the scrutiny of the rating agencies to ensure that sufficient resources are available to produce for investors the obligated cash flows in all but a disaster scenario.

The approach generally taken by the rating agencies is to stipulate a scenario of losses that the security must be able to sustain without defaulting on payments to investors. For the highest (AAA) rating, the agencies generally require that the security be able to withstand an experience comparable to that that occurred in the Great Depression of the 1930s. For example, the rating agency might determine that the type of asset under consideration had a default rate of say 6 percent per year for four years. This means that 6 percent of the assets in a given pool defaulted each year for four years. Moreover, the rating agency would have to determine the loss experienced on those assets. A defaulted asset might experience a loss of say 40 percent in value. Then, if a pool of assets experienced a 6 percent default rate and a 40 percent loss, this would amount to a loss of 2.4 percent in the value of the assets each year. If this default rate continued for four years the total loss experience would be 9.6 percent of the assets in the pool. Moreover, this ignores any loss due to delays in collecting cash flows due to lost interest. The rating agencies examine the historical experience for the specific type of asset being securitized and develop assumptions, like those described above, that characterize an adverse scenario. They then require that there be sufficient resources, including any third-party guarantees, to continue to make scheduled payments to investors in such a scenario.

Most of the originators of assets that become securitized have debt outstanding that does not have a triple-A rating, particularly commercial banks and thrifts, very few of which have high ratings. An issuer who wants to obtain a rating that is higher than the rating of the originator must obtain an opinion from a reputable law firm that the assets have truly been sold for bankruptcy purposes. This means that, if the originator files for bankruptcy, the assets that have been securitized cannot be legally claimed by any creditors of the bankrupt originator. This characteristic of the trust or the special-purpose subsidiary set up for the securitization is referred to as its being "bulletproof."

Antecedents of Securitization

The essence of securitization is that a market that once operated with financial institutions that act as portfolio lenders, holding assets until maturity, is replaced with an alternative market where assets are no longer originated, funded, and held by intermediaries. When a market is securitized, the intermediaries that once acted as portfolio lenders can still participate if they can compete in any portion of the securitization process. In some financial markets the traditional intermediaries have been driven out almost entirely.

Two examples of this kind of transformation of a market include the markets for commercial paper and for junk bonds. Recall that commercial paper constitutes short-term (less than 270 days to maturity) debt obligations of corporations, generally marketable securities that do not require expensive SEC registration owing to their short maturity. For a company issuing commercial paper the principal alternative is to arrange bank loans. If we look back to the mid 1960s, most corporations relied largely on bank loans as their principal source of short-term financing, but by the mid 1970s that had begun to change. By that time, commercial paper had begun to develop as a viable alternative to bank lending. This occurred principally because corporate borrowers found that it was cheaper to directly access the commercial paper market than to pay banks for their cost of funds plus the costs of the bank regulatory system. Banks simply could not compete with the low costs relatively highly rated companies could obtain by accessing short-term investors directly through the commercial paper market. Once the market began to grow the base of companies that could access that market expanded as banks began to provide guarantees of funding through letters of credit. This commitment from the banks made it possible for less highly rated issuers to obtain the backup support to directly access the commercial paper market. The success of the commercial paper market is documented in Table 18-1.

A similar story of the evolution of a product that has been a successful competitor of lending through financial intermediaries is that of junk bonds. Junk bonds are debt obligations that are distributed without industrial-grade ratings from one of the major rating agencies (see Chapter 2). Junk bonds emerged in the 1980s as a potent competitor to financing from banks and insurance companies. Companies that issued junk bonds found that more attractive financing could be had through junk bonds than through a portfolio lender that funded and generally held a loan to maturity. The key to the success of the junk bond market was the perception that, though there would be some losses on individual junk bonds, there would be enough winners in a portfolio of junk bonds to more than cover those losses. Moreover, the issuers of junk bonds often included relatively loose covenants in those bonds, so that borrowers had considerably more freedom from close scrutiny from the lender than was usually the case with loans from traditional intermediaries such as banks and insurance companies. These features made junk bonds a tremendously attractive form of financing for companies whose credit risk was perceived as less than the highest quality.

The emergence and success of junk bonds as an innovative form of financing constitutes a phenomenon closely related to securitization. Like commercial paper, junk bonds competed successfully with bank and insurance company loans and provided an alternative to the intermediated form of market. Instead of loans being originated and held by banks and insurance companies, marketable securities were originated by investment banks and distributed throughout the capital markets. In the end, some of the banks and insurance companies that might have made loans to junk bond issuers acquired those bonds as investments, though they were driven out

Table 18-1
Outstanding Amount of Commercial Paper for Selected Years, 1960–1991

Year	Outstanding Amount ($ Billions)
1960	4.5
1965	9.3
1970	33.4
1975	48.4
1980	124.4
1985	298.9
1990	566.9
1991	528.3

of the origination function. Both junk bonds and commercial paper are therefore important innovations in capital markets that were driven by some of the same forces that are driving securitization.

Stages of the Securitization Process

We can divide the securitization process into a sequence of six steps or actions to be taken by the various parties. As we discuss these steps we will use a mortgage as an example of the type loan being securitized. The six stages in the securitization process are:

- origination of the asset
- servicing of the asset
- collection of assets and creation of securities
- distribution of securities
- guarantee of cash flows
- provision of liquidity

The first stage, origination of the asset, involves the initial creation of the loan or security agreement that requires funding. In the case of a mortgage it involves arranging the loan with the original borrower, who is purchasing or refinancing a home. The second stage involves the collection and processing of payments from the borrower. This generally requires monthly processing of payments, maintenance of records of those payments, pooling of the payments, and distribution of the cash to investors. The third stage involves creation of a portfolio of loans out of individual loans, which must be combined in a way that effects diversification of default risk. In the case of mortgage loans, loans from different originators are generally combined into a pool so that they have sufficient *geographic* diversity. While the loans are being formed into pools that have the proper characteristics they fluctuate in value with changes in market interest rates, so it is important to be able to hedge the risk of changing interest rates until a complete portfolio can be formed and a security can be issued that is backed by the loans in the portfolio. The fourth stage, distribution or sale of the securities to investors, generally is handled by an investment bank that has ongoing relationships with institutional investors such as insurance companies and pension funds. The fifth stage entails the splitting off of specific risks and the sale of those risks to specialized investors or guarantors. An insurance company or a bank, for example, may write a guarantee against default on the assets that back the security. This is common practice with mortgage-backed securities. The final step is provision of liquidity through maintenance of an active secondary market. This is the dealer's traditional role in a secondary market, to provide liquidity by maintaining a market in the security.

In an intermediated market, some of these activities are eliminated and the remainder are internalized within each institution active in the market. The origination process is not affected significantly by securitization. The debt contract must still be executed, though in an intermediated market securities are not formed and distributed, since the institution that originates the loan holds that loan in its portfolio. The fifth function, that of providing a guarantee, is present in both an intermediated and an over-the-counter market. The distinction lies in whether the guarantee is internalized. In an intermediated market, the bank or other type of portfolio lender provides a guarantee to depositors when it issues deposits to fund a loan. For regulated and insured banks and savings and loans there is also a guarantee by the Federal Deposit Insurance Corporation (FDIC). In a securitized market the guarantee may be provided by the same institution that originates the asset or loan, but generally it is not. It may be provided by another firm that also originates its own loans, or it may be provided by a distinct type of institution, generally an insurance company, that is not involved in the origination process. Finally, the last stage in the process, that of providing liquidity, is not a part of an intermediated market. When loans are held in portfolio until maturity (or prepayment), so that a secondary market does not develop, there is no liquidity for the investor and no service to be provided by a dealer.

In an over-the-counter market each of these six distinct functions may be provided by a different type of firm. For example, a commercial bank may originate a loan. The loan may be acquired by another bank and placed in a portfolio. An investment banking firm may create and distribute a security backed by that portfolio of loans. A separate bank or insurance company may provide a guarantee against default on those loans. Finally, a number of investment banking firms, as well as other types of institutions, may operate as dealers in the market for these securitized loans. Moreover, the specific arrangements utilized for any particular type of asset, such as mortgages or commercial loans, or even auto loans, vary from case to case. There is no standard or uniform way of structuring securitized financing that applies to all types of assets.

The Value Chain in a Securitized Market

One of the potential advantages of securitization is that it forces financial intermediaries to break their business into component parts and to ask fundamental questions about the sources of value in each part of the business. Instead of taking it for granted that they will perform all the functions that a portfolio lender must provide, an intermediary in a securitized market is compelled to carefully decide where it can compete successfully. Using the language of modern corporate strategy, it must ask where its core competencies lie and how to take advantage of those core competencies. (See Chapter 19 for a discussion of the core competencies.) A map or schedule of the core competencies that are necessary to compete at each point in the process of securitization defines the "*value chain*" in a securitized market. Modern financial intermediaries must understand that value chain, and they must understand where they have the competencies to compete in that chain.

Now we ask the following question about each stage in the securitization process: What does a firm have to do well in order to compete effectively in this part of a securitized market? Put another way, the question asks what type of core competency is required for success in each of the six stages of a securitized market.

Origination of the Asset: Consumer Marketing Skills

Origination of the asset involves the retail marketing function of attracting loan customers and persuading them to take out a loan through your institution rather than through some competitor. At one time, this marketing function essentially involved establishing branch offices of a bank or thrift in convenient locations and then waiting for customers to walk into that branch, at least in states that allowed branch banking. To a very large degree this is no longer the case. Instead, the retail marketing function has come to require all the marketing skills essential for any other type of consumer marketing, whether it is ready-to-eat cereal or consumer electronics. Retail marketing involves establishment of brand names through use of advertising, the development of mechanisms to listen to what customers want, control of the distribution channels to keep competitors at a disadvantage, management of the product development cycle so that new products are continually introduced, and provision of timely and high quality service to customers. Historically, commercial banks had no need to develop these particular skills in their organizations, since regulation provided protected geographic markets. To a large degree this is no longer true, so banks must develop retail or consumer marketing skills to maintain a competitive position in the origination market.

Servicing the Asset: Economies of Scale in Operations

Servicing the asset involves maintenance of payment records, collection of payments of interest and principal from borrowers, and distribution of cash flows to security holders. This is a so-called backroom operation that is heavily data processing–oriented. The necessary skill for success in this type of operation is the capability to process large volumes of transactions as quickly and cheaply as possible. This requires a continuing investment in computer technology and development of a technically capable work force that can process payments efficiently. There is substantial evidence that there are economies of scale in this servicing function. For example, at one time in the mortgage market (where most thrift institutions once operated as portfolio lenders) they often did their own processing. As the mortgage market has become securitized the servicing function is now often sold to a separate company that maintains a large servicing portfolio, beyond its own origination capability. By expanding the volume of servicing beyond a minimum level related to a lender's origination capability, it is possible to drive the cost of servicing a given loan down, at least over some range of servicing volume. Thus, the key to success in loan servicing is to have enough servicing volume, regardless of how much origination capability you may have, to generate the scale economies necessary to compete in this portion of the market. The same thing is now happening with credit cards and other payment processing.

Collection of Assets and Creation of Securities: Financial Risk Management

The third stage of operation of a securitized market involves the collection of loans from originators who function in separate regions of the country and the creation of diversified portfolios. Often referred to as the "conduit function," this stage of the securitization process is generally required by the fact that many originators are not geographically diversified so that they cannot create portfolios that have geographic diversification of default risk. This means that to properly diversify default risk it is necessary for some entity to collect loans from distinct originators and pool them in such a way that they satisfy acceptable standards for diversification. This is essentially a clerical function that does not provide many opportunities for specialization or for application of some core competency, but any company that collects loans for the creation of securities inherently finds itself holding a portfolio of loans or warehousing loans until a security is ready to be issued. It is essential that the risk of this portfolio be managed effectively while the loans are warehoused. This means that the conduit must be competent at the financial risk management skills described in detail in Chapters 21 and 22.

Distribution of Securities: Institutional Marketing

The fourth stage in a securitized market involves the distribution of securities to investors. Since most of the investors in asset-backed securities are institutions—insurance companies, banks, thrifts, pension funds, corporate treasurers—this function involves marketing to institutions. It is important to realize that a financial intermediary could develop tremendous retail marketing skills that make it excellent at retail origination of loans yet have little or no capability to market securities to institutional investors. Though both are marketing, they are very different kinds of marketing. Marketing to institutions requires a talented and sophisticated sales force that can provide the information required by institutional investors. Investors are keenly interested in two features or characteristics of the ASBs they buy. They want to understand the timing of the cash flows they will receive and they want to understand the credit risk. Institutional marketing requires clear and persuasive analyses of these sources of risk.

It is important to emphasize another aspect of marketing of securities. Investors are not particularly interested in the type of loan that has been originated and included in an ABS. Investors are buying *cash flows* rather than specific loans such as mortgages or auto loans, so an institution that has developed the marketing capability to sell, say, mortgage-backed securities is well prepared to move into selling other ABSs such as auto loans or credit card receivables. Investors look at the cash flows generically. As long as the seller of the securities can make a persuasive case for the timing and default risk characteristics of the cash flows, its institutional marketing capability can be applied to an unlimited variety of distinct types of loans. This is why the Wall Street firms that market mortgage-backed or auto-backed receivables characterize and approach these products from the more generic standpoint of ABSs. Notice that this drives a wedge between the origination and the distribution function. Originators may well be specialized in mortgage loans or auto loans. Indeed, relationships with automobile retailers or real estate brokers may be very important for building the retail marketing capability that is important in origination. However, the institutional marketer of securities can obtain loans from originators with a variety of different specialties in originating different types of loans.

From the vantage point of institutional marketing, these loans are all raw materials, or simply a "product," that is used to create cash flows with different characteristics for particular investors. This feature of the marketplace is making it very difficult for financial intermediaries to successfully integrate vertically across all the six stages of the securitized market.

Guarantee of Cash Flows: Low Cost of Capital

The fifth stage in a securitized market is to guarantee investors against default risk on the securities. A company that provides this service, whether it is a commercial bank or an insurance company, is placing at risk its own capital rather than the capital of the asset's originator. For this to be economically attractive the guarantor must have a lower cost of capital, which requires a higher credit rating, than the originator. Over the last decade, there have been very few, and sometimes no, AAA-rated commercial banks in the United States. Table 18-2 shows the ratings of the top nine U.S. commercial banks in 1983 and 1992 as determined by Standard & Poor's. The table shows the deterioration in ratings over the ten years and the fact that, as of 1992, there was only one AAA-rated U.S. bank, JP Morgan. This means that U.S.–based commercial banks have been precluded from directly pledging their overall credit rating as a vehicle to obtain a triple-A rating for an ABS issue. It is possible for a bank to either create a separate subsidiary to guarantee a loan and capitalize the subsidiary sufficiently, or to overcollateralize an ABS in order to obtain a high rating. We discuss all of these presently. The central question is still whether it is relatively cost effective for such a firm to use its own capital in this way or to obtain a guarantee from a separate entity. During the late 1980s a few European banks and a number of Japanese ones seemed to grab much of the global market for commercial bank-provided guarantees. This appears to stem from their desire to gain a foothold in the U.S. marketplace and from relatively lax regulation in their countries. In fact, one of the key determinants of which class of firms has a lower cost of capital is the type of regulatory system imposed on those institutions. We argued in Chapter 5 that regulation for commercial banks is making it difficult for them to compete in many aspects

Table 18-2

Credit Ratings of the Top Ten U.S. Banks

	1983	**1992**
Citicorp	AA +	A −
BankAmerica	AA −	A
Chemical Banking Corp.	AA +	A −
NationsBank	A	A
JP Morgan	AAA	AAA
Chase Manhattan	AAA	BBB +
Bankers Trust	AA +	AA
Wells Fargo	AA −	A −
First Chicago	AA −	A

of the financial marketplace. Regulation that makes capital expensive for banks tends to drive them out of this fifth stage of the operation of a securitized market.

Provision of Liquidity: Trading Skills

The final stage of the operation of a securitized market is the provision of liquidity for the ABSs that have been issued. We will argue later in this chapter that the most important hypothesized benefit of securitization is probably the advantage provided by liquidity of securitized assets. For this to be a reality, issuers of securities, or other parties, must maintain a secondary market where purchasers of assets can resell them. As a practical matter, operation of a trading desk generally goes hand in hand with institutional marketing of securities. These functions are often combined in Wall Street firms that participate in the ABS marketplace. Maintenance of a trading function requires the technological capability to monitor market prices and trade effectively, but it also requires the capital to hold a portfolio of ABSs and monitor and manage the risk of that portfolio. This involves the same risk-management skills that are crucial to performing the conduit function, and it is closely linked to the institutional marketing function. Firms that participate in institutional marketing also tend to participate in the conduit and the trading functions of the market.

The most important feature of the value chain (Table 18-3) is that any company that intends to be successful in this market must carefully decide where it has the capacity to compete and where it does not. It is very difficult to compete effectively across the entire value chain. A company that hopes to be so vertically integrated must have competency in retail marketing, institutional marketing, financial risk management, and backroom operations, and it must have a low cost of capital. All of these are rather difficult to accomplish simultaneously. A company that cannot compete across the board in these competencies must choose where it will compete based on its competencies. The reality for many traditional commercial banks and thrifts appears to be that they cannot compete in the latter stages of the value chain. They simply have no chance to compete with Wall Street in financial risk management skills, institutional marketing, or access to capital, so they have to develop competence in either retail marketing or operations. This is a substantial challenge for many commercial banks. It will be interesting to see how it works out over the coming years. We will explore the strategic issues facing commercial banks in more detail in Chapter 19.

Table 18-3

Value Chain in a Securitized Market

Stage	Core Competency
1. Origination of the asset	Retail marketing
2. Servicing the asset	Economies of scale
3. Collection of assets and creation of securities	Financial risk management
4. Distribution of securities	Institutional marketing
5. Guarantee of cash flows	Low cost of capital
6. Provision of liquidity	Trading capability

Benefits and Costs of Securitization

Once you develop an understanding of what is happening in a securitized market, you may ask what is actually driving market participants to securitize assets. What are the benefits and costs of securitization?

Benefits of Securitization

We can identify six distinct reasons that firms may find it attractive to securitize assets that would otherwise appear on their balance sheets. Some of these reasons apply to any type of firm, whether it is a regulated intermediary such as a commercial bank or a firm not subject to this type of regulation, such as Sears or General Motors Acceptance Corporation (GMAC). A few of them pertain only to commercial banks and savings and loans, since they deal with the government regulatory treatment of these types of institutions.

Increase the Economic Efficiency of the Market

One of the most important potential benefits of securitization is a reduction in the cost of operating the market. That is, it effects a gain in efficiency that should lower the cost of funds or the interest rate for a given type of financing. To see how securitization can do this we need to refer to the six components of the securitization process described above. Recall that in an intermediated market each of these stages of the process is either internalized in one institution or is eliminated. When they are internalized, each institution that operates in the market must be vertically integrated to the extent that it provides the entire range of services, from origination through provision of guarantees to depositors. This limits opportunities for specialization that might increase efficiency. Securitization provides an opportunity for, and even fosters, specialization, which can lead to a more cost-effective system for funding an asset. In addition, securitization allows financial institutions to make separate choices about how much interest rate risk versus credit risk they want to bear. Securitization lets them specialize in one area of risk bearing or another, and this allows them to take advantage of specialized capabilities or knowledge.

In addition, the regulatory system for commercial banks and savings and loans in the United States has traditionally sheltered these institutions from competition with other types of firms. One way this has been accomplished is by enforcing a separation between banking and commerce and by creating specialized or segmented financial institutions. These institutions are not as diversified as they might be without regulation. In addition, restrictions on geographic expansion have made it possible for many small institutions to survive that might not be viable in a less restrictive regulatory environment.

It is important to evaluate the benefits of securitization in light of the impact of current regulatory restrictions on financial intermediaries. Securitization can become attractive simply as a way of avoiding the inefficiencies induced by regulation. Were it not for costly regulation, intermediaries might be able to provide financing at a cost that is competitive with a securitized form of funding. That is, there may be no inherent reason why a securitized market is more cost effective than an intermediated market. Rather, securitization may provide a way to escape or arbitrage the undesirable effects of regulation.

This argument suggests that securitization may be more attractive to regulated depository intermediaries than to unregulated firms, since they bear substantially different costs of regulation. For example, one observer of the securitization process has estimated that the cost of intermediating a mortgage-backed security—including underwriting costs, market-making costs, and issuing costs (lawyers, accountants, rating agency fees)—averages about 1/4 of 1 percent per year over the life of the security. By contrast, the cost of holding that loan in the portfolio of a bank, including equity costs, income taxes, reserve requirements, and insurance (but excluding the cost of deposits or other debt to fund the loan) averages about 1.5 percent.[1] Even if this spread is overestimated, it still communicates the essential message. Regulated institutions operate with substantial regulatory costs that can be partially avoided through securitization.

Increase Liquidity of Instruments

It seems important to single out one of the elements of securitization for special treatment—provision of liquidity. Participants in the market often argue that the main benefit of securitization is that it provides institutions in the market with liquidity. Lenders who previously had no option but to hold assets until they matured can sell them in the market if they need to do so. In addition, institutions can add to their asset portfolio not only by originating new loans, but also by acquiring loans from others. The options to buy and sell assets in the market may be valuable for a number of reasons. For example, an institution may have difficulty attracting deposits to fund existing assets and may therefore need to liquidate assets. It may find new and more attractive investment opportunities that can best be funded by liquidating existing assets. It may change its operating strategy and want to alter the type of assets it holds. It may have more deposit liabilities than it can profitably invest in loans it can originate on its own. When there is no secondary market for its assets, none of these options are available.

Satisfy Bank Capital Requirements

In Chapter 5 we noted that at the end of 1992 commercial banks and thrifts had to satisfy new capital requirements based on the perceived risk of bank assets. Many banks found themselves in the position of having to make significant adjustments to meet these new requirements. There are basically only two ways to satisfy an increased capital requirement: one is to add more capital and the other is to reduce the volume of assets. For example, consider a bank that has $10 billion in assets and that needs to raise its capital-asset ratio by 1 percent, from 3 percent to 4 percent of assets. One possibility is to attempt to enter the market and raise $100 million in new equity. This may be difficult to accomplish or it may be quite costly. The cost

---

[1]Lowell L. Bryan. "Introduction," in *The Asset Securitization Handbook.* New York: Dow Jones Irwin, 1989.

depends on how optimistic the management of the bank is about its future earnings, relative to the equity market's perception of those earnings. If the bank management feels the market is too pessimistic it may not want to sell equity, since it will be giving that equity away at what it believes to be too cheap a price. By contrast, suppose the bank chooses to shrink its asset base by securitizing and selling assets. It determines that if it reduced its assets to $7.5 billion, its capital base of $300 million would provide the necessary 4 percent capital ratio; thus, it must securitize and sell $2.5 billion. If many banks are making the same sort of decision simultaneously, this will create a boom in securitization. U. S. banks have used both the sale of assets and the acquisition of new capital to come into compliance with the 1992 requirements. In fact, it is difficult to determine how much of the total volume of securitization that took place from 1989 to 1992 was generated by a perception that securitization entailed fundamental advantages of cost or liquidity as opposed to the practical reality that assets had to be taken off the balance sheet to satisfy more stringent capital requirements. Even if a large part of recent activity was motivated by the drive to increase capital ratios, the increased volume of ABS that was generated may enhance the liquidity in the market to the point where securitization is now inherently more attractive than it would otherwise be.

Take Advantage of Mispriced Deposit Insurance

Commercial banks and savings and loans have their deposits insured by the Federal Deposit Insurance Corporation. This insurance has long been provided at a price that is not related to the risk of individual banks. In effect, historically a bank has paid the same price for insurance for its depositors regardless of whether it is highly risky or not very risky at all. This amounts to providing a subsidy to take on excessive risk, since insurance for high-risk activities is underpriced. The addition of risk is particularly attractive if the bank does not have to increase its assets, and, therefore, does not need more deposits to support those assets. A bank can accomplish this by originating assets and then securitizing them. It is difficult to determine how powerful an incentive this has been or may be in the future in driving banks toward securitization. At a time when banks are striving to satisfy capital ratios this may not be a powerful force compelling securitization, but, in another environment, much like the one faced by savings and loans in the early and mid-1980s, when there was very little capital and savings and loans were funding a variety of risky ventures, it might be a very important force.

Develop Alternative Funding Sources

A reason for securitizing assets often given by executives of companies, other than regulated depository intermediaries that are actively involved in this process, has to do with diversification of sources of funding for a company. Many large companies with significant ongoing funding needs are acutely interested in making sure that they will have ongoing access to the capital markets. Access can be limited if a company experiences financial difficulties and the capital markets become concerned about potential problems for that company down the road. A company that experiences such difficulties may find that there are fewer buyers for its commercial paper and that its banks are less willing to provide additional credit than they would be in less strenuous times. One task of the financial officers of the company is to develop sources of funding that will minimize the funding problems that the company will encounter should its performance deteriorate. Securitization provides a source of funding for some assets on the company's balance sheet that is separate from the other activities of the company or that does not rely on the credit quality of the whole company. For example, this reasoning was cited by the vice president of GMAC after it issued over $8 billion of asset-backed auto receivables in 1986. He said, securitization "adds to our flexibility by decreasing dependence on other forms of financing. ABSs access new investors or a different pocket within the same institution. By reducing demand for credit from other sources at the margin, GMAC should be able to pay less for traditional sources. An added benefit is the ability to sell receivables to third parties such as the ABSC, thereby accessing the market with an entirely new name, and often a different class of credit."[2]

Reduce the Cost of Funding Low Risk Assets

The final reason that companies find securitization attractive, and we think one of the most compelling, is that securitization can reduce the cost of funding assets that are of relatively low risk, compared to the companies' other investments or lines of business. By securitizing relatively low-risk assets a company is insulating the parties who provide financing for those assets from the uncertainties that are inherent in the rest of the company's businesses. It is also preventing existing creditors of the firm from benefiting from new low-risk assets, which reduces the chance that they will experience a loss on their loan to the company. By securitizing low-risk assets, a firm can literally make it financially attractive to invest in those assets when otherwise it would not be. We think that this point about the cost of funding low-risk assets is sufficiently important that we want to explore it in some detail.

How Securitization Can Affect Subsidies Between a Firm's Creditors

One of the most important aspects of securitization of assets is the effect it has on the claims of existing debtholders of a firm. This applies not only to securitization of assets but to any use of collateral where specific assets of a firm are pledged to specific debt holders, rather than all debt holders having general claims on all the assets of the firm. When debt holders have general claims on all assets of the firm, conflicts of interest can arise if the firm seeks to undertake new investments that have quite different risk than do existing investments. By collateralizing debt, or by securitizing assets, such conflicts can be minimized or avoided. One such conflict arises when uncollateralized debt is used to finance low-risk investments (with positive net present value). Such uncollateralized debt represents a claim against all cash flows of the firm, not just those from the low-risk investment it may be funding. As a result, its yield will be based on the average risk characteristics of the firm's assets. This implies that the yield on the new debt will be priced higher than if it were collateralized by the low-risk assets.

---

[2]See Phillip L. Zweig. "The Corporate View," in *The Asset Securitization Handbook.* New York: Dow Jones Irwin, 1989.

The addition of low-risk assets financed by unsecured debt has three implications for the firm. One, it subsidizes existing debtholders, since they share pro rata in the improved (lower-risk) characteristics of the firm's cash flows. That is, the new investment lowers the risk of outstanding debt. Two, that subsidy comes at the expense of the firm's equity holders, since they are not able to capture all of the positive net present value of the new investment. Three, the combined effects of the subsidy to existing debt holders and the relatively high required yield on new unsecured debt (owing to the risk of existing assets to which new debt holders are exposed) increase the chance that the investment will be turned down by equity holders. Under these circumstances the equity holders are better off without the positive net present value project than with it. This loss of opportunities to increase value is often referred to as an agency cost of debt. Notice that the entire problem derives from the fact that the firm has debt financing outstanding on an existing base of assets that has very different risk characteristics than new assets being considered. If the firm had not initially been financed with debt no problem would arise when the new low-risk opportunity is being considered.

• *The Effects of Unsecured Financing on Risky Investments: The Case of Diversified Holdings* •

To appreciate the problem associated with unsecured financing of low-risk investments it will be helpful to consider an example of a firm that has in place high-risk investments financed by risky debt and that encounters a new opportunity to invest in a relatively low-risk asset. Therefore, consider the case of a hypothetical firm called Diversified Holdings (DH). DH's balance sheet, described in Table 18-4, shows that it has two distinct types of assets, which we have labeled low-risk and high-risk. No company actually prepares a balance sheet with these types of labels, but we want to emphasize the crucial difference between the assets DH holds. In our example, DH has an equal book value of both the low-risk and high-risk assets of $1 million each. You might imagine that the low-risk assets are accounts receivable and various forms of equipment that could be used by other companies if DH had to liquidate, whereas its high-risk assets are highly proprietary high-technology equipment that is being used in a risky venture under development at DH. If this project is unsuccessful, the assets will be worth less than their book value. We can be more specific about the possible future values or payoffs on the two types of assets that appear on DH's balance sheets. First, suppose that both types of DH's assets have a payoff in one year. Suppose that the low-risk assets have a certain payoff of $1.1 million and the risky assets have a fifth-fifty chance of a payoff of either $0.8 million or $1.4 million. This means that the combined payoffs on both types of assets will be a 0.5 probability of a payoff of $1.9 million and a .5 probability of a payoff of $2.5 million. Furthermore, we assume that DH has already invested in the high-risk assets and is now considering investing in the low-risk asset. Therefore, the asset side of the balance sheet in Table 18-4 portrays DH's position if it proceeds with the new, low-risk investment.

Before we can consider how DH might finance the new investment, we need to see how the original assets of the firm are financed. We will assume that DH has chosen a capital structure, or mixture of debt and equity financing, that includes 90 percent debt and 10 percent

Table 18-4
Balance Sheet
Diversified Holdings

Assets	
High risk	$1,000,000
Low risk	$1,000,000
Total assets	$2,000,000
Liabilities and Net Worth	
Original debt	$900,000
New debt	$900,000
Net worth	$200,000
Total liabilities and net worth	$2,000,000

equity. For an industrial company, this would be extremely high leverage, but for a financial firm such leverage is not unusual and for a commercial bank it is extremely conservative, or low leverage. To complete the ingredients for our example we assume that debt holders, whether they are the old debt holders financing the existing assets or new debt holders financing the new, low-risk assets, demand an expected return of 5 percent. The balance sheet shows that the amount of debt outstanding for the original high-risk assets is $900,000. It shows a separate debt for the low-risk assets, also equal to $900,000. Finally, it shows the book value of equity as $200,000. It is important to recognize that this balance sheet shows all values at historical cost, and therefore does not really reflect the economic (net present) value of the firm's investments.

The original debt was initially priced without any knowledge that the firm would later consider a new, low-risk investment, so it was priced using the payoffs on the high-risk investment. If the creditors of the firm expected to break even and receive exactly a 5 percent expected return, they would choose a contract interest rate for the $0.9 million of debt, r, so that they would expect to earn a 5-percent return. This requires:

$$1.05 \times \$900{,}000 = 0.5 \times \$800{,}000 + 0.5 \times (1 + r) \times \$900{,}000.$$

This states that the loan amount ($900,000) times one plus the expected return (5 percent) must equal the expected payoff to debt holders, taking into account the payoffs on DH's risky assets. If the payoff is $800,000, the debt holders receive the entire payoff, since the firm is bankrupt. If the payoff is $1 million the debt holders receive (one plus) their contract interest rate times the amount lent ($900,000). If we solve for the contract interest rate, r, we find that it is 21 percent. That is,

$$\$945{,}000 = 0.5 \times \$800{,}000 + 0.5 \times (1.21) \times \$900{,}000.$$

The question facing DH is, how it should finance the new low-risk assets. Let's first consider the alternative of issuing more unsecured debt on DH. DH will need $900,000 in new debt, and equity holders will contribute $100,000. The first thing we might ask, before we attempt to determine how new debt holders would price the new $900,000 in debt, is what happens to the expected payoff to the old debtholders who initially financed the firm. The value of their claim has been changed since they will have a pro rata share of the total payoff to DH. Suppose DH is unlucky and its total payoff is \$1.9 million. The original debtholders demand a payment of 1.21 × \$900,000, or \$1,089,000. As long as the new debtholders demand any positive interest rate at all, they will ask for an amount greater than \$900,000 as payment. This means that the amount owed to debt holders will exceed the \$1.9 million DH will receive, if it is unlucky and gets the lower payoff. DH will then be bankrupt, and the debtors will split the \$1.9 million so that the old debt holders' payoff in this event will be \$1,900,000/2, as each class of debt holders contributed \$900,000. If DH is lucky and earns \$2.5 million the original debt holders will receive their contractual payment of 1.21 × \$900,000 = \$1,089,000. This means that the new expected payoff to the original debtholders is

$$0.5 \times \$1{,}900{,}000/2 + 0.5 \times \$1{,}089{,}000 = \$1{,}019{,}500$$

But recall that, before DH acquired the low-risk assets, its existing debt holders' expected payoff was only \$945,000. This means that debt holders expected payoffs went up by \$1,019,500 − \$945,000, or \$74,500.

It should be apparent by now that DH has just enriched its existing debt holders by acquiring new assets that were less risky than the existing ones. Where did the gain experienced by old debt holders come from? One answer is that it surely cannot come from new debt holders. They will price their claim so that they expect to earn 5 percent, just as the old debtholders did. This means that they will end up taking \$45,000, or 5 percent, for providing \$900,000 of debt. Recall that the payoff on the low-risk investment was \$1,100,000 and the cost was \$1,000,000, leaving a profit of \$100,000. Notice that this low-risk investment has now become unprofitable for the equity holders, who will end up paying out the following amounts to debt holders out of their total gain from the low-risk assets:

Gain from low-risk assets	\$100,000
Increase in payoff to old debt holders	−\$74,500
Return demanded by new debt holders	−\$45,000
Net gain to equity holders	−\$19,500

The problem here is that the financing of the new, low-risk investment provides a subsidy for DH's existing debt holders. That subsidy is so great in this situation that it makes the entire low-risk investment unattractive to DH. It must find a way to finance its new assets in a manner that preserves the positive net present value for equity holders rather than transferring it to existing debt holders. The way to do this is to collateralize or securitize these new assets. By securitizing the new assets DH is, in effect, creating two separately financed sets of assets. The existing debt holders continue to finance the risky asset. New debt holders finance the new, low-risk assets, without taking on the obligation of indirectly financing the old, high-risk assets. Therefore, securitization is very close to creating two separate companies for separate classes of assets.

While we have posed the example of DH as if it originally had high-risk assets and was considering a new investment in low-risk assets, it is important to recognize the variety of ways in which such combinations are encountered in practice. DH might have had both sets of assets on its books and might have attempted to spin off one set or the other. Say it paid off some of the debt holders and then securitized the low-risk assets. This would take away some of the protection that the remaining bond holders thought they had. These bond holders might well have initially included restrictions or covenants in the debt to prohibit precisely this kind of action.

That is often why new assets, rather than old ones, are securitized. Conversely, it might have had low-risk assets on its books and wanted to acquire high-risk ones. Debt holders who lend to a company for what they think are low-risk investments are generally interested in attempting to prevent the company from changing its assets to higher-risk ones. If equity holders could do this, they would be able to take wealth away from, rather than subsidize, existing debt holders. Once again, debt holders will try to utilize covenants to protect themselves against such actions.

Costs of Securitization

While securitization has some important benefits, it also has some potential costs. The costs pertain largely to the incentives for monitoring and controlling the risk of default in debt instruments and to the prospect that some economies derived from intermediaries' acting as portfolio lenders might be lost. Two distinct types of incentive problems can arise when debt contracts are securitized. These problems are called "adverse selection" and "moral hazard." Let's consider adverse selection first.

Adverse selection is common in many types of insurance arrangements. The problem occurs when one party to a transaction has better information about the nature of its risk than the other party. In the case of securitization, adverse selection can occur when the originator of a loan has better knowledge of the quality of individual loans than investors who might acquire those loans in a secondary market. If the originator has no stake in the outcome of the loans once they are sold in the secondary market, then he or she will have an incentive to keep the loans known to be of relatively low default risk and to sell those known to be of high default risk. If the market as a whole perceives that lenders have an incentive to behave in this way they are not likely to acquire loans from these lenders. If no way can be found to limit the originator's incentive to distribute only low-quality loans, the secondary market will fail to function at all.

The general nature of the solution to the adverse selection problem is for the loan originator to maintain a stake in their ultimate disposition. A simple way for this to happen is for the originator to offer a guarantee of their credit quality or the ultimate purchaser of the securitized loans to have recourse to the originator. A less formal way is for originators to develop a reputation for eschewing adverse selection. Reputable originators are perceived to have an incentive to distribute only high-quality loans. Their reputation arises from the fact that if they engage in adverse selection they may be denied future access to the market.

The moral hazard problem is similar but not identical to the adverse selection problem. Moral hazard refers to an originator's incentive to expend effort or resources to reduce the risk of default. This can apply both at the time the loan is originated and throughout its life. In many types of loan agreements, particularly business loans, continual monitoring of the borrower's performance over the life of the loan is as important as good underwriting when the loan is originated. If the originator can sell the loan to another party, then his or her incentive to continue to monitor the loan is eliminated. The apparent way to induce the originator to monitor the loan effectively is to insist that he or she continue to have a significant stake in the loan's outcome. As a result, an originator of loans that require continual monitoring may sell participations in those loans rather than selling the entire loan in a secondary market. Thus, the secondary market for corporate or business loans tends to function as a market for participations, for this reason.

Another way to deal with both moral hazard and adverse selection is for a special class of institutions to monitor the originators. Both rating agencies and private guarantors or insurers of securitized debt provide this service. Since these guarantors are legally obligated to pay off if a loan they guarantee defaults, they have a strong incentive to monitor the origination process of lenders whose loans they guarantee, so that adverse selection and moral hazard are limited. In addition, rating agencies also evaluate the guarantors so there is an additional layer of scrutiny of the credit evaluation process.

In determining whether a market can be successfully securitized, it is necessary to evaluate both the costs and the benefits of securitization. The benefits are essentially gains in efficiency, including benefits provided by liquidity, as well as a possible reduction in the regulation costs. The costs pertain to reduction of the incentives to evaluate and monitor risks properly. In addition, there may be some efficiencies within some markets from intermediaries being vertically integrated across the stages of the securitization process. If these kinds of economies are significant, they will present a barrier to securitization. In any specific market these costs and benefits may be quite different. Thus, securitization might be quite successful in one market and might not progress very far in another.

Securitization of Just About Everything

In the last few years almost every kind of asset that has been financed with debt has been securitized to some degree. Securitization of some assets has met with more success than others. The most successful example is mortgages, but various types of other receivables, including auto loans, credit card balances, leases, bank loans to businesses, and commercial mortgages have been securitized to some degree. Moreover, securitization has so far been more successful in the United States than abroad. To give some flavor for the securitization of specific products, we describe the process of securitization of mortgages and credit card receivables. We also talk about aspects of securitization of specific products throughout the rest of this book. In particular, in Chapter 22 we focus on how the cash flows in mortgage-backed securities are often restructured to deal with interest rate and prepayment risk.

Securitization of the Mortgage Market

As we have already indicated, the portion of the capital markets where securitization has progressed farthest is the residential mortgage market. There seem to be three basic reasons that securitization of mortgages has been so successful. First, the largest traditional mortgage originators, the savings and loans, are not geographically diversified. This means that default risk needs to be diversified by creating regionally diversified mortgage portfolios. Securitized mortgage portfolios drawn from a geographic cross-section of mortgage originators provides that diversification. Second, the savings and loans became relatively inefficient providers of mortgage finance, in large part because the poor regulatory system forced them to operate as highly segmented financial institutions. (See Chapters 4 through 6 for a discussion of the problems with savings and loans.) Third, a set of quasi-governmental agencies with the ability to sell federal Agency debt created a market for mortgage-backed securities that carried the credit guarantee of the U.S. government. These agencies provided a subsidy to the development of the market and a form of standardization for the types of mortgage-backed securities, which helped establish the liquidity of the market. To understand how this process of securitization has worked in the mortgage market it is essential to have some understanding of the quasifederal agencies that have dominated the market.

Two of the quasifederal agencies, the Federal Housing Administration (FHA) and the Veterans Administration (VA), provide loans at attractive interest rates to borrowers and guarantee those loans against default. In addition, three agencies either provide guarantees of credit quality on privately issued securities backed by mortgages or acquire and hold mortgages. These three agencies are the Federal National Mortgage Association (FNMA or "Fannie Mae"), the Federal Home Loan Mortgage Corporation (FHLMC or "Freddie Mac"), and the Government National Mortgage Association (GNMA or "Ginnie Mae"). These agencies are referred to as quasigovernmental because, to varying degrees, they have been transformed into privately owned companies with a government mandate and some form of government backing and control. Each has some form of public supervision and is constrained to pursue public policy objectives. Moreover, they issue or guarantee their own securities, known as agency securities. Agency securities are issued by agencies of the federal government other than the U.S. Treasury.

The oldest of the three quasifederal agencies, Fannie Mae, was originally created in the late 1930s to assist the home mortgage industry by purchasing mortgages insured by the FHA. Freddie Mac was established in 1970 to do essentially the same thing but with conventional mortgages, that is, mortgages not backed by FHA. Both of these agencies initially operated by selling agency securities in the market and using the funds to purchase mortgages directly. Fannie Mae historically has operated much like a traditional savings and loan in issuing debt securities with specified maturities, usually shorter than the maturity of the mortgages it was purchasing. Hence, it bought mortgages and funded them with shorter-maturity debt and, as a result, accepted substantial interest rate risk. By contrast, Freddie Mac has traditionally issued securities that simply obligated it to pass through the cash flows received from mortgages to the securities' holders. In addition, Freddie Mac guaranteed to pay the promised cash flow if the mortgage was delinquent or in default. Hence, Freddie Mac did not accept the interest rate risk inherent in funding mortgages with short-term liabilities; the only risk it assumed to any large extent was default risk.

Throughout the 1960s and 1970s one of the basic purposes of these quasi-governmental mortgage agencies was to act as a countercyclical source of funds in the mortgage industry. During this period the housing industry tended to experience a

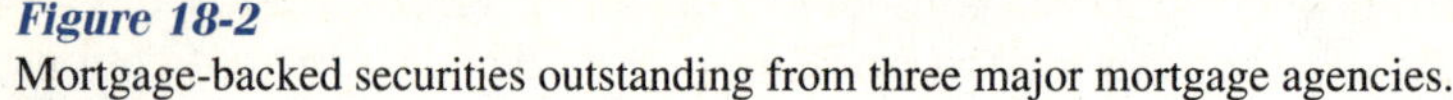

Figure 18-2
Mortgage-backed securities outstanding from three major mortgage agencies.

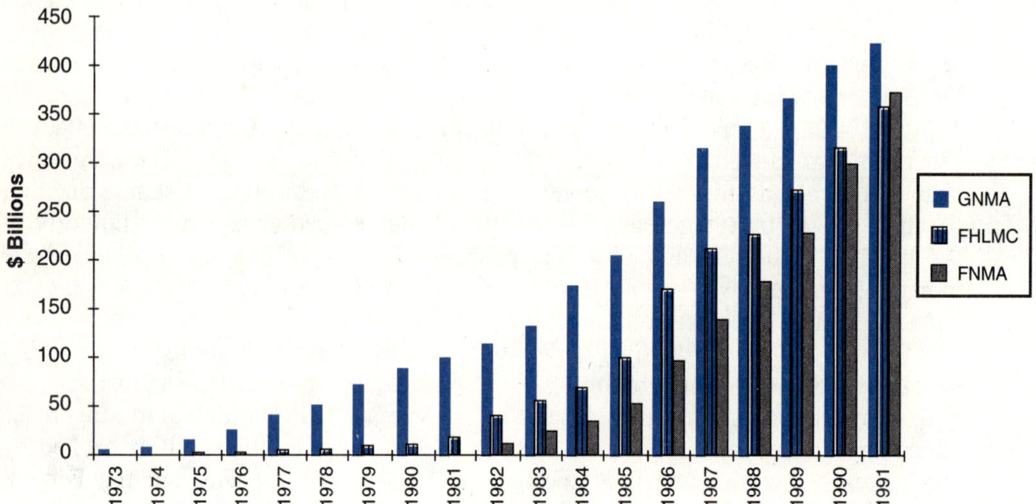

pattern of activity determined by fluctuations in market interest rates. When market interest rates rose above the deposit account ceilings enforced by Regulation Q, depositors shifted funds out of savings and loans and into other forms of investments, a process known as "disintermediation." This limited the availability of funds for mortgage financing, since the housing industry was dependent largely on the savings and loan industry. The secondary mortgage markets emerged during the 1960s and 1970s, as the major alternative source of funds for mortgage financing when savings and loans or thrifts became illiquid.

Figure 18-2 shows the volume of securities backed by mortgages issued by the three major agencies from 1973 until 1992. GNMA and FHLMC issue virtually all claims as mortgage-backed securities. However, FNMA has a large volume of debt as well as mortgage-backed securities outstanding, so the table understates the total participation of these agencies by the amount of FNMA debt. In December 1991, FNMA had debt outstanding of $129 billion. It is apparent from the table that these agencies represented a very small portion of the total mortgage market in the early 1970s but the situation had changed dramatically by the early 1980s, when the mortgage-backed securities market had become one of the largest portions of the world's capital markets.

The process of securitizing a mortgage can probably be best understood by considering an example of an individual borrower and how the process of structuring and selling that borrower's loan takes place. One example is provided by a Southern California couple, the Vogels,[3] who purchased a $160,000 home in August of 1987 with a 25 percent down payment and a 30-year fixed-rate loan for $120,000 at 10 5/8 percent interest from First Federal Savings of San Gabriel. While at one time First Federal might

---

[3]See George Anders. "How a Home Mortgage Got into a Huge Pool That Lured Investors." *Wall Street Journal,* August 17, 1988.

have lent the Vogels the money for their home with the intention of keeping that loan on their books, by 1987 they were planning on selling most of the loans they originated. The Vogels' loan was purchased by Freddie Mac and placed into Freddie Mac Pool No. 360018, which included $443 million of fixed-rate loans from throughout the United States. Part of the mortgages in this pool were purchased by First Boston Corporation and placed into a real estate mortgage investment conduit, or REMIC. Then shares in the REMIC were distributed by First Boston to a variety of different investors. The creation and distribution of this security is illustrated in Figure 18-3. Once the mortgage-backed security has been created, the investor is not particularly interested in the identity of the underlying loan. Instead, investors are interested in the default risk and timing of cash flows in the loan. The quasigovernmental agencies that dominate the mortgage-backed securities markets have established standardized procedures to document and control the timing and default risk of mortgages, and therefore of the securities they back. It is these characteristics of the cash flows that investors are concerned about and that drive the securitization process.

Figure 18-3

How one mortgage crisscrossed the U.S.

Source: Reprinted by permission of The Wall Street Journal *©1988 Dow Jones and Company, Inc. All Right Reserved Worldwide.*

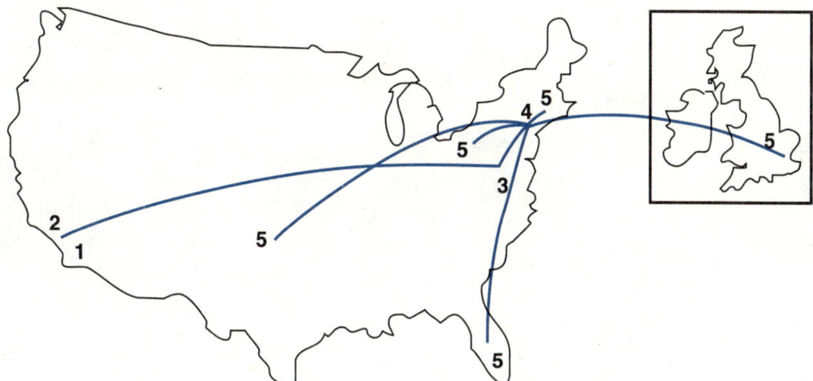

STEP 1 *September 1987.* Jim and Erica Vogel buy a four-bedroom home in San Dimas, Calif. They get a $120,000 mortgage from First Federal S&L of San Gabriel.

STEP 2 *December 1987.* First Federal sells the Vogels' mortgage to the Federal Home Loan Mortgage Corp., known as Freddie Mac.

STEP 3 *December 1987.* In Reston, Va., Freddie Mac puts the Vogels' mortgage into a giant pool with more than 6,000 other mortgages.

STEP 4 *May 1988.* Part of that pool is bought by First Boston Corp. in New York. The pool goes into a $550 million offering of mortgage-backed securities.

STEP 5 *May/June 1988.* In Hartford, Conn., Cigna Investments Inc. buys $10 million of the REMIC for its pension accounts.

May/June 1988. In El Reno, Okla., Globe Savings Bank buys $66 million of the REMIC to expand its loan portfolio.

May/June 1988. In Florida, an S&L buys $40 million of the REMIC as an interest rate hedge.

May/June 1988. Other buyers of the REMIC range from a Pittsburgh S&L to a London commercial bank to a Florida S&L.

The overall process for creating mortgage-backed securities is summarized in Figure 18-4, which diagrams how borrowers initially take out mortgages from some originator, such as a mortgage banker. The mortgage banker sells the mortgage to one of the quasigovernment mortgage agencies but may also retain the servicing. Then securities are issued to the mortgage market with a guarantee from a mortgage insurer or from an agency of the federal government.

Credit Card Backed Securities

Another successful form of securitized asset is the credit card-backed security, which constitutes a claim on a pool of receivables from a credit card, such as Visa or Mastercard. These receivables have many of the same features of mortgages that make them amenable to standardization and avoid the moral hazard and adverse selection problems that plague some other types of assets, but they pose some substantial difficulties because the cash flows are generally much shorter than with mortgages and because the outstanding balance on a revolving charge card like a Visa card is potentially quite volatile. As a result, Wall Street firms have worked hard to document and control the cash flow risks involved in credit card receivables.

One of the most direct ways to acquire an understanding of how securitization of credit card receivables works is to examine the structure of a specific transaction.

Figure 18-4
Organization of the secondary market for mortgage credit.

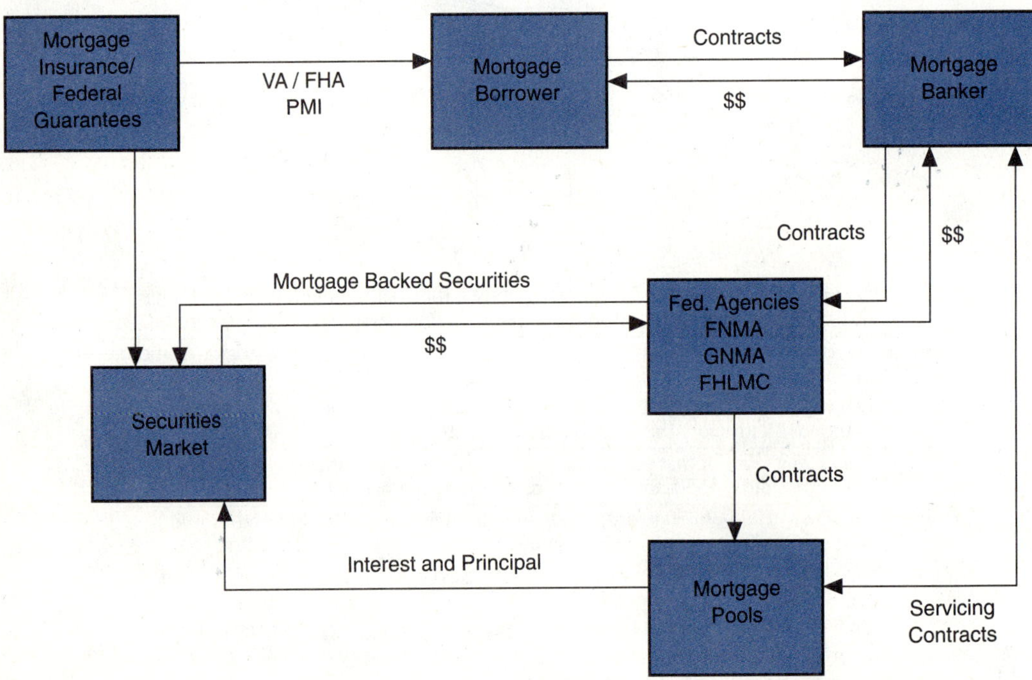

We will examine one of the first securities backed by credit card receivables, an issue created by Bank of America in 1987.[4] At this time Bank of America was having substantial financial difficulties and it was looking for ways to sell assets to improve its capital position. Securitization of credit card receivables provided a potentially attractive but challenging new opportunity. The attraction is the large volume of credit card receivables outstanding in the United States, but the challenge was the short maturity and the volatility of the outstanding balance in any particular account, as compared to mortgages. Special procedures have been developed to manage the unique features of credit card receivables.

Bank of America issued what they called the California Credit Card Trust 1987-A, consisting of $400 million of Classic Visa card receivables drawn from their northern California accounts. Bank of America structured this trust so that the outstanding amount that investors would hold would be fixed at $400 million. The trust was given the authority to purchase all receivables generated by a selected group of Visa accounts over the life of the trust. This means that the total value of the trust would fluctuate with the outstanding balance in these accounts. Bank of America retained ownership of assets in the trust over the $400 million held by investors. The objective of the management of the trust was to make sure that the value of the public investment in the trust does not fall below $400 million. Thus, the total amount of receivables acquired by the trust would generally exceed the $400 million.

Investors in the trust received protection against losses through defaults by a letter of credit issued by the Union Bank of Switzerland. Union Bank of Switzerland has been an active participant in the market for securitized assets, providing guarantees for a significant number of issues. In fact, it provided the guarantees on the initial large securitized automobile receivables issued by GMAC in 1986. Union Bank of Switzerland had an upper limit on its liability for losses in this trust equal to 15 percent of the initial balance of $400 million, or a liability limit of $60 million.

The 1987-A Trust was designed to last two years. The scheduled cash flows are illustrated in Table 18-5. The outstanding balance in the trust was scheduled to remain at $400 million until the last four months of the two-year period and then the principal would be repaid to the investors in the trust. The trust was priced so that investors would receive a 6.9 percent return. This means that for each month that the outstanding balance was $400 million the investors received an interest payment of $2.3 million. Bank of America charged the borrowers using Visa cards an interest rate of 18.5 percent on their outstanding balance. This represents a monthly finance charge of $6.17 million. A servicing fee for collecting the payments and managing the cash flows amounted to $1,433,333 per month, or 4.3 percent per year of the outstanding balance. A monthly fee of $31,250 was also paid to Union Bank of Switzerland to partially cover the cost of the guarantee against default. In addition, all finance charges paid by the borrowers above the 6.9 percent paid to investors and the 4.3 percent servicing charge were paid to the guarantor, Union Bank of Switzerland. This

[4]This Trust is described in detail in "Securitizing Credit Card Receivables," prepared by the Asset Finance Group, First Boston Corporation and published in *The Asset Securitization Handbook,* New York: Dow Jones Irwin. 1989.

Table 18-5

Sample Credit Card ABS Cash Flow

California Credit Card Trust 1987-A
6.9% Asset Backed Certificates
Investor Cash Flow Report

Month	Beginning Investor Amount	Investor Principal Distributions	Investor Earned Finance Charges	Additional Paymment by the LOC Bank	Investor Servicing Fee	Guaranty Fee	Payment to the LOC Bank	Investor Interest Distributions	Total Investor Distributions
	(A)	(B)	(C)	(D)	(E)	(F)	(G)	(H)	(I)
3/87	$400,000,000	$ 0	$6,170,000	$0	$ 1,433,333	31,250	2,405,417	2,300,000	2,300,000
4/87	400,000,000	0	6,170,000	0	1,433,333	31,250	2,405,417	2,300,000	2,300,000
5/87	400,000,000	0	6,170,000	0	1,433,333	31,250	2,405,417	2,300,000	2,300,000
6/87	400,000,000	0	6,170,000	0	1,433,333	31,250	2,405,417	2,300,000	2,300,000
7/87	400,000,000	0	6,170,000	0	1,433,333	31,250	2,405,417	2,300,000	2,300,000
8/87	400,000,000	0	06,170,000	0	1,433,333	31,250	2,405,417	2,300,000	2,300,000
9/87	400,000,000	0	06,170,000	0	1,433,333	31,250	2,405,417	2,300,000	2,300,000
10/87	400,000,000	0	06,170,000	0	1,433,333	31,250	2,405,417	2,300,000	2,300,000
11/87	400,000,000	0	06,170,000	0	1,433,333	31,250	2,405,417	2,300,000	2,300,000
12/87	400,000,000	0	06,170,000	0	1,433,333	31,250	2,405,417	2,300,000	2,300,000
01/88	400,000,000	0	06,170,000	0	1,433,333	31,250	2,405,417	2,300,000	2,300,000
02/88	400,000,000	0	06,170,000	0	1,433,333	31,250	2,405,417	2,300,000	2,300,000
03/88	400,000,000	0	06,170,000	0	1,433,333	31,250	2,405,417	2,300,000	2,300,000
04/88	400,000,000	0	06,170,000	0	1,433,333	31,250	2,405,417	2,300,000	2,300,000
05/88	400,000,000	0	06,170,000	0	1,433,333	31,250	2,405,417	2,300,000	2,300,000
06/88	400,000,000	0	06,170,000	0	1,433,333	31,250	2,405,417	2,300,000	2,300,000
07/88	400,000,000	0	06,170,000	0	1,433,333	31,250	2,405,417	2,300,000	2,300,000
08/88	400,000,000	0	06,170,000	0	1,433,333	31,250	2,405,417	2,300,000	2,300,000
09/88	400,000,000	81,529,941	6,170,000	0	1,433,333	31,250	2,405,417	2,300,000	83,829,941
10/88	318,470,059	81,529,940	4,912,401	0	1,141,184	31,250	1,908,763	1,831,203	83,361,143
11/88	236,940,118	81,529,941	3,654,801	0	849,035	31,250	1,412,110	1,362,406	82,892,346
12/88	155,410,178	81,529,941	2,397,202	0	556,886	31,250	915,457	893,609	82,423,549
01/89	73,880,237	73,880,237	1,139,603	0	264,738	31,250	418,250	424,811	74,305,049
02/89	0	0	0	0	0	0	0	0	0
Totals		$400,000,000	$129,334,007	$0	$30,045,177	$718,750	$50,358,051	$48,212,028	$448,212,028

Notes:
(A) Outstanding certificate principal balance.
(B) Investor principal liquidations plus payments under the guaranty minus principal reinvestment.
(C) Investors' share of portfolio finance charges.
(D) Any additional payments by the Letter of Credit Bank, Union Bank of Switzerland (UBS), to protect the certificate yield.
(E) Investors' share of the servicing fee paid to servicer.

Source: Philip L. Zweig, *The Asset Securitization Handbook.* New York: Dow Jones/Irwin, 1989.

totals $2,405,417 per month during the period when the outstanding balance on the trust was $400 million. Union Bank of Switzerland held these payments in a reserve account throughout the life of the trust and used the reserves to pay investors for any losses arising from defaults on the receivables in the trust. Thus, investors had two sources of security in the trust. First, they had access to the reserve accumulations generated by the finance charges paid by borrowers. Second, if these reserves should be exhausted, they had access to the assets of Union Bank of Switzerland, up to the limit of $60 million. At the end of the two-year life of the trust, any reserves generated by finance charges held by Union Bank of Switzerland that have not been paid out to investors to cover defaults are returned to the originator, Bank of America.

The reserve accounts are particularly important in a securitized issue such as the California Credit Card Trust, since the underlying cash flows are volatile and defaults are hard for investors to predict. The maintenance of a reserve account funded by finance charges from the borrowers provides the security necessary to persuade investors that the security deserves a high rating. To the extent that there is competition in the pricing of credit card receivables, originators such as Bank of America are under pressure to reduce total finance charges to be competitive. This means that the originator's total profit depends on the ultimate default experience of a particular pool of receivables, because that determines the amount of any reserves that may ultimately be returned to the issuer at the maturity of the trust.

Securitization Abroad

Many financial innovations of the last decade have become important and popular financial products throughout the world, particularly futures, options, and swaps. Securitization seems to be a form of innovation that is much less popular in other countries than it has been in the United States. Because no aggregate data is collected on securitized assets it is hard to develop a precise estimate, but there appear to be far fewer securitized assets in Europe and Asia than in the United States. It seems there are three basic reasons for this international difference in the use of securitization.

First, the volume of securitizable assets outside the United States seems to be smaller than that within. In Europe and Asia, the per capita level of consumer debt such as credit card receivables is lower than in the United States. Moreover, mortgage borrowers in most other countries have not become accustomed to having access to the long-term fixed-rate mortgages that have become common in the United States. Therefore, there simply is not as large a volume of underlying assets that can profitably be securitized. If this were the only reason, it probably would not adequately explain the apparent differences.

The second reason is that there are fundamental differences between the structures of financial institutions in the United States and those in most other countries. We can identify at least two that bear on securitization. In most European countries, a modest number of depository institutions are involved in originating consumer receivables, particularly mortgages. These institutions often have the implicit support of their governments. Most other countries do not have the large numbers of local depository institutions with limited regional markets that we have in the Unites States, so there is less need to reach outside the originating institutions for regional diversification than in the United States. In addition, institutions outside the United States did not evolve with the same set of problems related to large-scale mismatches between the maturities of assets and liabilities as did the savings and loans in the United States. There was no compelling need to restructure the system by relying heavily on securitization as there was in the United States, since institutions in other countries did not incur the massive losses that have plagued U. S. mortgage lenders in the last decade.

Third, the regulatory systems in most other countries are significantly different from that in the United States. Since we have such a large number of independent banks and savings and loans, we have relied on a regulatory system that emphasizes capital requirements and monitoring of the riskiness of bank investments. As we have tightened capital requirements on banks in recent years, they have been compelled to securitize assets in order to comply with these requirements. Similar problems have not occurred in the banks in those countries. Moreover, regulations in some countries, such as in Britain, where accounting rules have required some securitized assets to still be maintained on a bank's balance sheet, have tended to hamper securitization. Whether securitization will blossom abroad depends, to a large degree, on whether some classes of institutions that can generate profits by originating assets will find it unattractive to hold those assets on their balance sheets and whether the regulators will allow them to securitize assets as a way of dealing with these problems.

SUMMARY

In this chapter we have focused on the process of securitization of financial assets. Securitization is the creation of tradeable securities using various forms of loans or accounts receivable. It also involves the transformation of an intermediated market (where intermediaries function as portfolio lenders, originating loans and holding them in their portfolios until maturity) into an over-the-counter one, and ultimately into an auction market.

We began the chapter by describing the securitization process and the various participants in a securitized market or the market for ABSs. We identified four distinct participants: the originator of assets, the servicer of the assets, the issuer of the security, and the trustee of the cash flows. We also discussed the role of rating agencies as monitors of the structure of ABSs. We noted that rating agencies require that a security issue have sufficient resources to withstand a given historical level of adverse default experience. The Depression level experience of the 1930s is the benchmark for a triple-A rating. We also described the various types of guarantees, including bank letters of credit and financial guarantees from insurance companies in ABSs. We broke down the securitization process into six steps: origination, servicing, collection of assets and creation of security, distribution of securities, guarantee of cash flows, and provision of liquidity in the secondary market.

We used the six steps to describe the *value chain* in commercial banking, the set of core competencies a company must have in order to compete successfully in all of the phases of a modern financial market. We explored the core competency that a company must possess to compete successfully in each stage of the market and noted that a company must possess all of these core competencies to be successful in vertically integrating across all stages, something it is very difficult for most companies to do. Companies that are not going to be vertically integrated must choose where in the value chain they can compete. Traditional commercial banks generally are being pressured by Wall Street investment banks from the bottom of the value chain, where the core competencies pertain to institutional marketing, financial risk management, and operation of a trading room. If a bank cannot compete effectively in these areas it must focus either on retail origination or servicing. This means it must develop economies of scale in servicing and it must develop the ability to control the retail distribution system for its products.

Next we turned our attention to the benefits and costs of securitization. The six specific benefits of securitization are an increase in the economic efficiency of the market, an increase in liquidity of instruments, satisfaction of bank capital requirements, a means of taking advantage of mispriced deposit insurance, development of alternative funding sources, and reduction of the cost of funding low-risk assets.

We took special note of the last item and explored it in some detail. We examined an example of a company with both high- and low-risk assets. We demonstrated that when a company does not securitize or collateralize its debt, undertaking investments with distinctly different levels of risk than that of existing assets can cause wealth to be shifted between the company's lenders and equity holders. If the company has existing assets that carry high risk and are funded by risky debt and then seeks to invest in relatively low-risk assets, some of the value of the new investment will accrue to its existing debt holders. This occurs because the investment in the low-risk assets reduces the risk of default, so the outstanding debt becomes less risky, and therefore more valuable. This problem can often be a sufficiently severe to deter a firm from undertaking otherwise profitable investments in low-risk assets, but if those assets are financed separately through securitization, the problem is alleviated.

We also focused on the costs of securitization, which involve the adverse incentives created when originators of assets no longer hold them over their life. We divided these problems into two broad categories. *Moral hazard* is the diminished incentive to take care to maintain the quality of a loan over its life that can occur when the loan is securitized. Adverse selection is the incentive to sell off only the low-quality loans and to represent them as being of high quality when a group of loans is securitized. Both of the problems are perceived to be more serious for some types of loans than for others, particularly commercial and industrial loans and commercial real estate loans.

Next we turned our attention to two important markets where securitization has been quite successful, the residential mortgage market and the market for credit card receivables. Securitization of the residential mortgage market has been facilitated by the activities of several large quasigovernmental entities that acquire mortgages and issue mortgage-backed securities. The presence of these companies in the marketplace has created large-volume standardized forms of securities that have allowed the market to generate substantial liquidity. We examined the structure of a specific credit card-backed security using Visa receivables originated by Bank of America in 1987. We examined the details of how this particular issue was structured and how the security holders were provided guarantees against default risk in this issue.

Finally, we examined the various reasons why securitization has been more successful in the United States than in the rest of the world. These include the fact that there are relatively fewer assets amenable to securitization outside the United States, the fact that there important structural differences in the financial institutions in other countries compared to those in the United States, and the fact that regulations in many other countries have hampered the development of securitization.

QUESTIONS

1. Define securitization. How does it differ from portfolio lending?
2. How does a rating agency evaluate the credit risk of an ABS? What requirements must be satisfied for an ABS to receive a triple-A rating?
3. Describe the stages or functions involved in a securitized market. How does the operation of this market differ from a traditional market with portfolio lenders?
4. Is commercial paper considered an ABS? How does it differ and what is the significance of the differences?
5. Describe how securitization might increase the efficiency of a financial market. How is regulation involved in the issue of the efficiency of securitization?
6. Suppose a bank that is considering how it might satisfy a new capital requirement has outstanding assets of $4 billion and capital equal to 4 percent. Consider two alternative ways of satisfying a higher capital requirement—securitizing assets and raising more capital. Calculate how much new capital would have to be raised versus how many assets would have to be securitized to satisfy capital requirements of 5 percent, 6 percent, 7 percent, 8 percent, 9 percent, and 10 percent.
7. Return to the situation facing Diversified Holdings company described in this chapter and illustrated in Table 18-4. Suppose that, instead of the situation illustrated in the chapter, DH initially had low-risk rather than high-risk assets and is now considering a new investment in high-risk assets, just as illustrated in Table 18-4. How would the acquisition of the high-risk assets affect the position of outstanding creditors of the firm who originally funded the low-risk assets? Calculate the gain (loss) to outstanding creditors and equity holders if DH acquires the high-risk assets, assuming the existing creditors do not have securitized or collateralized debt.
8. Discuss how collateral changes the risk of outstanding debt holders in situations such as that of DH, as portrayed either in the chapter or in the previous question. What is the distinction between collateral and securitization?
9. Explain the concepts of moral hazard and adverse selection. Can you come up with some examples of these types of problems beyond the area of securitization?
10. It can be argued that a wedge is driven between the origination of loans and the distribution or securities backed by those loans by the fact that investors are interested in "generic cash flows" rather than in the specific nature of the collateral behind individual loans. Generic cash flows are defined by the timing and default risk of the cash flows. How does this lack of concern with the nature or type of collateral of loans affect the strategy of companies considering vertical integration across the stages of a securitized financial market?

11. Describe the major quasigovernmental agencies in the mortgage markets. How do you think the presence of these agencies has affected the structure and operation of the market? As a matter of national policy, should we encourage or limit the growth of these types of agencies?
12. Two distinct sources of security against default risk are provided to the holders of the California Credit Card Trust 1987-A documented in Table 18-5. Describe both and explain how they work in as much detail as possible.

REFERENCES

Anonymous. "Stunted Securitization." *Economist* November 2, 1991, p. 71.

Albert, Howard W. "Asset Securitization: Benefits for All Banks," *The Bankers Magazine* (Nov/Dec 1991) pp. 16–20.

Benston, George J. "The Future of Asset Securitization: The Benefits and Costs of Breaking Up the Bank." *Journal of Applied Corporate Finance* 5 (1992), pp. 71–82.

Anders, George. "How a Home Mortgage Got Into a Huge Pool That Lured Investors," *Wall Street Journal* August 17, 1988.

Asset Finance Group, First Boston Corporation, "Securitizing Credit Card Receivables," in *The Asset Securitization Handbook.* New York: Dow Jones Irwin, 1989.

Bryan, Lowell L. "Introduction," *The Asset Securitization Handbook,* New York: Dow Jones Irwin, 1989.

James, Chris. "The Use of Loan Sales and Standby Letters of Credit by Commercial Banks," *Journal of Monetary Economics* 22 (Nov 1988), pp. 395–422.

Kavanagh, Barbara, Thomas R. Boemio, and Gerald A. Edwards, Jr. "Asset-Backed Commercial Paper Programs," *Federal Reserve Bulletin* (Feb 1992), pp. 107–116.

Stulz, Rene M., and Herb Johnson. "An Analysis of Secured Debt," *Journal of Financial Economics* 14 (1985), pp. 501–421.

Wittebort, Suzanne. "Asset-Backeds Come of Age," *Institutional Investor* (Dec 1991), pp. 77–80.

Zweig, Phillip L. "The Corporate View," in *The Asset Securitization Handbook,* New York: Dow Jones Irwin, 1989.

• Part IV •

Management of Financial Firms

Creating Value in Financial Firms

Managing Credit Risk

Managing Interest Rate Risk

Innovations in Managing Interest Rate Risk

Managing Foreign Exchange Risk

• *Chapter 19*

Creating Value in Financial Firms

This chapter is concerned with how financial companies can find ways to distinguish themselves in the competitive global marketplace of the 1990s and, in the process, achieve high rates of return for their shareholders. This is an extremely important topic for the managers of any type of company, and what we have to say in this chapter applies to virtually any company, but our concern in this book is somewhat more narrowly focused on financial companies.

We begin this chapter by outlining various approaches to corporate strategy that focus on the development of power in the markets in which a company operates. "Market power" is valuable, because it allows a firm to charge prices that generate excess returns, so-called monopoly rents. Market power can come from barriers to entry that either exist naturally or can be erected by clever managers who thoroughly understand their markets, but it is not easy to erect barriers to entry, and many barriers to entry cannot be sustained very long. An alternative approach to creating value focuses more attention on building a superior organization within a company. A company that has a superior organization competes effectively because it conducts its operations in a way that is smarter or at a lower cost than its competitors. Organization-based sources of advantage are likely to be more important in the future, as our world becomes more competitive, so we think this approach to creating value is very important. If a company can create a superior organization, it may be possible to attempt to expand that organization to a variety of different types of businesses. But companies must be careful here. They must understand what they are good at—where their core competencies lie—and not stray too far away. We will explore some of the main sources of organizational competitive advantage. Finally, we take a look at the strategies pursued by three major U.S. banks in recent years, Banc One, Bankers Trust and BankAmerica, to see if we can assess how financial firms are actually creating value in today's highly competitive financial services marketplace.

In the remaining chapters of this book (Chapters 20 through 23) we discuss three specific aspects of the management of financial firms. All include management of the various forms of risk that financial firms face. In fact, we view financial institutions as being essentially providers of services based on risk management. This does not mean that all of what a financial firm does is risk management. As our list of competencies in the last chapter makes clear, financial firms are also engaged in marketing and in the management of operations, but given the financial focus of this book we will concentrate on the financial management aspects of financial firms. We divide these into management of credit risk, interest rate risk, and foreign exchange risk. In this chapter we lay the foundation for this treatment of risk management by providing an overall strategic context for the management of financial firms.

• *Concepts to Learn in Chapter 19* •

- The various forms of barriers to entry and their probable effectiveness in the market for financial services
- The key types of organization-based sources of competitive advantage
- The strategies that are being pursued by some successful banks

Competitive Advantage the Old-Fashioned Way: Product by Product

We want to start our search for competitive advantage in financial firms by focusing on products or services. That is, we start with the products and the markets for those products rather than with the organization that produces and sells them. This basic idea is to find ways to build competitive advantage, or monopoly power, in the markets in which a company operates. By "monopoly power" we do not mean that the objective is to act illegally with respect to the antitrust laws. The objective is to find ways to insulate products and services from competition to the maximum extent possible, in order to generate "rents." The points we have to make about finding ways to protect products or services from competition are necessary steps along the way to competitive advantage. In the intensely competitive markets in which most companies presently operate, we think it turns out to be very hard to find sustainable sources of competitive advantage that are based on protecting a market, but these sources of advantage are the ones to look for first, the ones to identify and take advantage of if you can. Those who find them and can use them for very long are the fortunate ones.

Know Your Customers and Your Competitors

Before a company can even begin to plot a strategy to generate competitive advantage it is absolutely essential for that company to develop a clear understanding of the market in which it operates. In fact, there is virtually no substitute for success in this arena. The marketing gurus tell us: Know your customer! We put it a slightly different way. Understanding who your customers are and what they want is a necessary, but not sufficient, condition for success. Many companies have gotten in trouble because they misunderstood the needs of their customers. Examples abound, but one of the most interesting is the computer industry. In this business, with rapid technological progress, customers quickly switch to new products and to suppliers who can provide better products and services at lower prices. A number of traditional computer companies, particularly IBM, thought they had a source of competitive advantage in large-scale mainframe computers, but the advent of personal computers, the growth of work stations, and the movement toward parallel processing has fundamentally changed the marketplace. Many of the older computer companies did not appreciate how the true needs of their customers could be adequately served at lower prices with new technology. The problem was not a failure in the technical arena. It was not a failure to understand the scientific aspects of the new technology. It was a failure to understand the match between that technology and the customers' needs. It was a failure really to understand the customer.

A closely related prerequisite for the formulation of any competitive strategy is to have a clear understanding of who your competitors are and who they may be in the future. An unnecessarily narrow concept of the competition is that competitors are simply the firms currently serving your target customers or the other firms that currently make up the industry. New entrants into an industry can often be bigger threats than established competitors. At one time, each of the Big Three auto makers in the United States viewed the other two as their only real competition. Of course, we all know that the real threat to the Big Three came from new market entrants, especially from Japan. New entrants may be producing the same product in some other part of the world and expanding their geographic market, as Japanese auto companies did. New entrants can also be companies that move across product lines to provide a new way to satisfy customers' real needs. An excellent example in financial services is provided by the growth of money market funds. In the early 1980s, commercial banks faced a completely new entrant into the market for provision of low-risk liquid investments to consumers. Money market mutual funds, which were created as a joint venture between securities firms regulated by the Securities and Exchange Commission (SEC) and commercial banks, provided diversified investments in low-risk short-term marketable securities bundled with check-writing privileges. Customers could use them without ever having to go to a physical location or branch of the fund. They caught on because banks were prevented from competing for their customers' investments with high interest rates by regulation designed to protect the banking industry. This included Regulation Q, which directly restricted the level of interest rates that banks could offer on deposit accounts, but that protection turned out to provide an opportunity for a very effective new competitor to enter the market.

Another form of competition, sometimes an unexpected form, may be a company's suppliers. As our financial markets become more technologically sophisticated in the years ahead, financial service companies will become more dependent on technology, especially computer and communications technology. Companies providing financial services are forced to compete to an increasing degree on the basis of how effectively they can manage technology. This puts them in the difficult position of being dependent on the relationships and the knowledge they can develop with the suppliers of that technology. This interplay between technology and the suppliers of technology and competitive advantage in financial services will be of critical importance in coming decades.

Erecting Barriers to Entry

Barriers to entry are impediments or obstacles that stand in the way of current or potential competitors and make it difficult for them to compete effectively in a specific market. Barriers to entry may arise naturally, or they may be created by clever managers. Sometimes luck puts a company in a position where it has a barrier to entry. This can happen most easily in markets for natural resources, where discovery of a particularly rich endowment of such a resource conveys an inherent advantage. South Africa has had such advantages in diamonds and gold; Saudi Arabia in oil. Of course, the control of these products must be protected, sometimes politically and militarily. Since natural barriers to entry are hard to come by in financial services, it is very important to learn how to go about erecting one. We identify at least six distinct types of barriers to entry[1]:

Economies of Scale and Scope

Scale economies refer to advantages in the cost of producing a product that are derived from large-scale production. A company has scale economies when the average cost of producing a product is declining with the volume of production. The idea behind scale economies as a barrier to entry is illustrated in Figure 19-1, which shows the average cost of producing a product as a function of the volume of production, where volume of production is expressed as a percentage of the total output of a product, or as market share. Notice that the firm illustrated in Figure 19-1 has scale economies up to the point where it has a 60 percent market share. That is, the average cost of producing the product declines until the market share reaches 60 percent and only then do costs begin to rise. Now suppose that one firm already in the business depicted in Figure 19-1 is producing at the minimum level of average cost; it has a 60 percent market share. Notice that any other firm that has a smaller market share has higher average costs than our dominant firm with the 60 percent share. The dominant firm may well be able to price its product in such a way that the other firms with smaller shares make a profit, but not as large a profit as the dominant firm. The scale economies enjoyed by the dominant firm provide a barrier to entry, though not necessarily an impenetrable one. Competitors must perceive that they can displace the dominant firm in order to obtain the profits that come from these scale economies. The dominant firm will try to protect its position and persuade potential competitors that it will not be displaced easily.

Economies of scope, closely related but not identical to economies of scale, are advantages that arise from producing or marketing multiple products that have some kind of connection between them. The connection often arises from a common technological base in the production and design of the product, but it can also arise from connections between the marketing of similar products. For example, scope economies arise in the marketing of products to consumers through grocery chains. Proctor and Gamble invests in developing relationships with supermarket chains

[1]This rendering of alternative barriers to entry closely follows the structure outlined by Michael E. Porter. "How Competitive Forces Shape Strategy." *Harvard Business Review* (Mar-Apr 1979) pp. 137–145.

Figure 19-1
Scale economies.

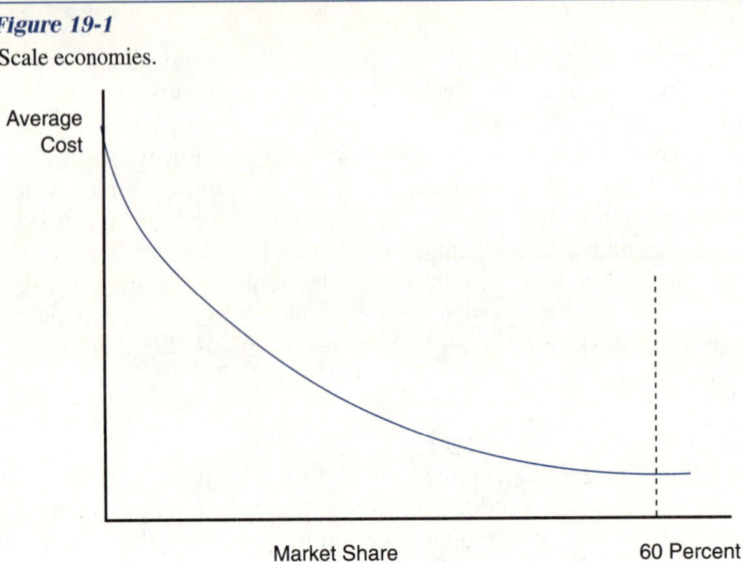

throughout the United States and pushes a wide variety of products through that distribution system. Once it develops the distribution network, it has the knowledge and capability to increase the number of products marketed through that distribution network. A similar phenomenon may develop in the marketing of financial services, to the extent that regulations are relaxed to allow financial institutions to diversify across a wider variety of products. An investment or commercial bank that develops a distribution capability for selling mortgage-backed securities can take advantage of the economies of scope inherent in that distribution network to sell a wider variety of securities, such as securities backed by cash flows on credit card receivables. The key insight is that customers are interested in the timing and riskiness of cash flows rather than the specific nature of the collateral that generates that cash flow. Therefore, there are natural economies of scope in marketing securities that represent different types of borrowing.

In the financial services marketplace there has long been a belief that there are some economies of scale, particularly in backroom, or data-processing, operations. The perception that scale and scope economies are important has led a number of researchers to statistically analyze the extent of such economies using data on costs and output of commercial banks. Because these institutions are regulated and must report a wide variety of information to regulators, many data are available that can be used in such inquiries. Some of the most recent work in this area indicates that the total scale and scope economies in banking amount to roughly three percent of total costs. This does not seem like a very significant number. Recall that in the last chapter we argued that scale economies are important in the backroom operations or loan servicing business. Even if scale economies are important here, this may not be a large enough part of the total cost of a bank so that it creates a significant volume of scale economies for the typical bank taken as a whole.

Cost Advantages and Disadvantages

Sometimes companies have some kind of advantage or disadvantage in cost that is unrelated to economies of either scale or scope. This is particularly prevalent in natural resources, where access to a high-quality or inexpensive source of raw materials conveys an advantage, or in high technology, where patent protection coveys some cost advantage. For example, patent protection of specific drugs, such as Amgen's Epogen, used to treat infection in kidney dialysis patients, prevents competitors from duplicating that product for some time. The actual protection provided by a patent is often much less substantial than the nominal protection stated in patent laws, since it is often difficult to enforce patent infringement and since patent laws are not recognized in all countries in the world. Cost advantages and disadvantages are more apparent in natural resources industries such as oil or copper or gold mining. Saudia Arabia's and Kuwait's advantages in quality and volume in the oil industry are legendary. Indeed, the loss to Gulf Oil corporation of Kuwait's oil reserves in 1975 when they were nationalized by the government of Kuwait was an almost crippling blow for Gulf.

Oftentimes, competition takes the form of trying to acquire or control the major low-cost assets in a line of business. For example, competition in the marketing of both gasoline and financial services historically has involved attempts to acquire the best physical locations for bank branches or service stations. In the 1960s and 1970s, when government regulations prohibited direct competition for consumer deposits with interest rates, banks were virtually compelled to compete by providing more convenient services. This meant acquisition of the best sites for branch locations. Indeed, often one of the key jobs in a bank in high-growth areas such as California involved the selection of future sites for branches. The bank that had the best branch network had a substantial cost advantage that was hard for competing banks to duplicate.

The aggregate data on bank costs do suggest that, though aggregate scale and scope economies may be modest, there are significant differences in aggregate costs across banks. This means that some banks are considerably more efficient than others at managing their costs. Banks that have learned to manage their costs most effectively have a significant advantage over those that are not so accomplished. The data on these cost differences are summarized in Figure 19-2. Panels A and B show the variation in average costs for 13 size classes of banks in branching and unit banking states. The curves in the figure show average costs computed as total interest expense plus operating costs per dollar of assets. The lines shown are the average costs for the lowest-cost bank in each size class (AC_{MIN}), the mean average cost for the lowest-cost quartile (AC_{Q1}), the overall mean average cost (AC_{MEAN}), and the mean average cost for the highest-cost quartile (AC_{Q4}).

The figure shows much variation in average costs, even for banks of one size class, which offer roughly the same mix of products and services. Notice that the dispersion of costs across quartiles is striking by comparison with variation among size classes within a quartile. For banks in branching states, the costs for the highest-cost quartile (Q4) are 33 percent higher on average than for the lowest (Q1), while the maximum difference in costs across size classes (taken from the AC_{MEAN} curve) is only 8 percent. For banks in unit states, Q4 costs are 31 percent higher on

Figure 19-2

Average costs by bank asset size class and cost quartile, 1984. (Key: M, million; B, billion.)

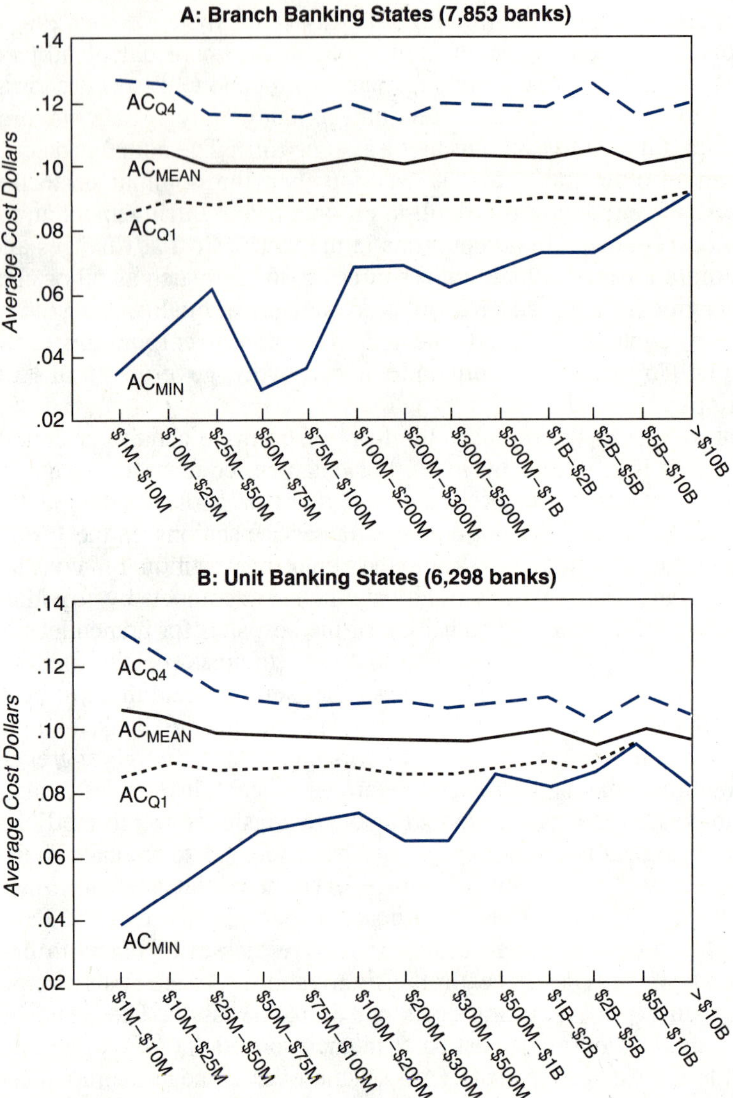

average than Q1, and the maximum difference across size classes is 12 percent.[2] These data suggest that there are significant differences in efficiency of banks within a given size class. Such efficiency differences afford some banks a clear source of competitive advantage over less efficient ones.

---

[2]See Allen N. Berger and David B. Humphrey. "The Dominance of Inefficiencies Over Scale and Product Mix Economies in Banking." *Journal of Monetary Economics* 28 (1991) pp. 117–148.

Product Differentiation

One of the key distinguishing features of a perfectly competitive marketplace, one without barriers to entry, is homogeneity of the products sold in that market. Such a market is often referred to as a commodity business. The polar opposite of a commodity business is a business in which competing products sold by firms in the industry are highly differentiated. In many cases, that differentiation is consciously engineered by the managers of the company. A highly differentiated product is one that is difficult for the competition to copy. It commands a higher price. The differentiation and difficulty of copying creates a barrier to entry. Examples of differentiated products include such items as Levi's. Indeed, "Levi's" is a brand name for a more generic product, jeans or cotton denim pants. However, Levi's 501 jeans are a highly differentiated product that other companies find it very difficult to copy. This type of product differentiation is often created through advertising and positioning of a product as a unique item in the mind of the consumer. Sometimes it seems hard to identify a real distinction that can justify that status. For example, there is reportedly virtually no difference between generic aspirin and branded aspirin such as Bayer, but Bayer aspirin has a sizable market share and commands a price premium over its generic competitors. There appears to be a perception in the mind of the consumer of some important distinction between aspirins. This distinction creates a barrier to entry for any competitor that does not already have a branded product.

It seems extremely difficult to find ways of differentiating many financial products. Most financial innovations are easy for competitors to replicate. Most of the innovative financial products we discussed in Chapters 12 through 16 are products that can be provided by any company that has sufficient technical expertise. It is difficult to establish market power through differentiation of financial products, as it is not, say in the market for cereals or luxury automobiles.

Access to Distribution Channels

Distribution channels constitute the avenues or means by which products are sold to ultimate customers. In many lines of business, access to such channels is fought over fiercely. Grocery stores provide the main distribution channel through which producers of food products sell their goods, and competing producers of specific products fight hard to get shelf space in grocery stores. They stock the shelves for the supermarket and provide services that select the appropriate placement of products on the shelves, based on computerized forecasts of sales volume. Oftentimes these computer forecasts are based on advertising expenditures for those products, which in turn have substantial economies of scale (as we discussed above). A similar distribution channel issue faces airlines, which must sell most of their tickets through travel agents. The airlines realized long ago that a critical weapon in their competitive struggles involved controlling the ticket agent. American Airlines reaped substantial benefits from being the first to successfully implement a computerized airline reservation system for travel agents. By controlling the distribution of flights that would appear on a travel agent's computer screen, American achieved significant advantage in managing this distribution channel. Distributors can also generate substantial power if they effectively control the marketing of a product. The balance of power between distributors and auto manufacturers has always been a major issue facing the automobile companies. Because auto dealers are a virtually exclusive distribution channel for the products of auto manufacturers, the manufacturers are particularly interested in making sure that the dealers do not obtain too much control over the whole auto-marketing function. If dealers were to obtain too much power they could literally dictate the division of profits between retailing and auto manufacturing.

We believe that much of the competition in the 1990s in commercial banking, particularly in the retail portion of the business, will take the form of attempts to control distribution channels. Part of this battle pertains to branch locations—physical sites where customers can come to do business with their bank. Competition will include the locations, design, quality of service, and variety of products that can be distributed through branch networks. Competition in new forms of delivering financial services will also increase. Banks already compete intensely through the placement of automated teller machines. In the future, increased emphasis will likely be placed on telecommunications as a mechanism of providing financial services. Companies that find ways to gain control over new forms of distribution, or that acquire dominant branch networks, will have one of the few sources of barriers to entry into financial services.

It will be particularly important for banks to generate a significant market share in a specific regional market, in order to have a chance to manage the distribution channels in that market. The importance of market share in a regional market has become increasingly apparent to all banks that have been seeking to expand to other regions of the country. A striking example of this is provided by Citicorp's decision to withdraw from the market in Arizona. In February 1993, Citicorp announced that it would sell its Arizona bank to Norwest Corporation of Minneapolis. Previously Citicorp followed a strategy of aggressive expansion in many parts of the country, but in Arizona it indicated that it did not perceive its fourth position in market share to be the basis for a profitable operation. The three largest market shares in 1992 were reportedly held by Banc One, BankAmerica Corporation, and First Interstate Corporation of Los Angeles. Norwest already operates a large number of banks, principally throughout midwestern states, and at the time of the announcement of the acquisition from Citicorp it had 32 financial services locations throughout Arizona. These included several small banks and mortgage and finance company subsidiaries.[3]

Government Policy

Possibly the most important form of barrier to entry in the United States in the entire post-World War II era has been government policy. Government regulation of airlines, trucking, pharmaceuticals, and financial services, to name some of the most conspicuous examples, created sizable barriers to entry in each business. Indeed, much of our discussion of regulation of financial firms in Part I of this book focuses on the role of government regulation in creating financial services markets that are segmented by product and geography. This amounts to explicit creation of barriers to entry. Without such protection, it is hard to imagine that we would have the large

---

[3]See "Citibank is Selling Arizona Unit to Norwest For Undisclosed Sum." *Investor's Business Daily,* February 4, 1993.

number of small banks that we do in the United States. Virtually no other country has a similar sort of size structure of financial firms. Government regulation is often motivated by some seemingly justifiable social purpose, but the reality is that regulation that limits entry to an industry creates market power for those who have government-protected franchises. It is possible for the government to scrutinize the activities of these protected competitors in such a way that their market power is dissipated, though we suspect that this is more often the exception rather than the rule. If this conclusion is right, the search for barriers to entry can be most successful if it is possible to persuade the government to create those barriers through well-intended protection.

Are Barriers to Entry Sustainable?

One question we need to ask of all of the forms of barriers to entry we have been discussing is whether they are sustainable. Do scale economies or cost advantages or government protection persist? Our judgment is that few barriers to entry can be maintained very long. The most important exceptions are probably cost advantages arising from access to high-quality raw materials and, in some cases, government protection. Some competitive advantage due to sources of raw materials, such as oil in Saudi Arabia, clearly last many years. Government protection of relatively small banks in the United States has lasted much of this century. Government protection of the insurance industry from competition from commercial banks has also lasted most of this century. That is a rather long time for a commercial marketplace. Industries where barriers to entry are probably most fleeting are ones where the technology of the industry is changing rapidly. This limits the life of differentiated products, alters the economies of scale and scope of production, and makes cost advantages transitory. Indeed, if we think of the major branded consumer products that are highly differentiated and have been around a long time, they are generally very low-tech products such as Marlboro cigarettes or Rice Krispies. Technological progress is often the enemy of barriers to entry. Indeed, rapid technological progress is the enemy of the entire approach to competitive advantage that is based on riding some barrier designed to protect a product. We suspect that organizations that are searching for products with which they can "coast" on a barrier to entry are not easily focused on trying to move faster than the pace of technology. That is why we want to turn our attention now to sources of advantage that are grounded in organizations rather than focused on specific products.

Building Competitive Advantage Through Superior Organization

We believe there are three fundamental approaches to building a superior organization. They emphasize, respectively, core competencies, time, and hustle. We will describe each of these briefly. Keep in mind that companies that can successfully erect barriers to entry may not have to rely on strategies that focus on organizational advantages. The real question facing the competitors in any given market is whether they are so lucky as to have an opportunity to erect a barrier to entry. If not, they need to refocus on building competitive advantage through superior organization. Our judgment is that in financial services barriers to entry will be difficult to erect and maintain. As a result, we think companies involved in financial services will be compelled to rely increasingly on organization-based forms of competition.

Core Competencies

A core competence is a skill or a capability—something you do well. Core competencies are often based in technology. In that context, a core competency is an understanding of and ability to apply a specific kind of technology to produce and distribute products. For example, Canon is widely recognized as a successful Japanese manufacturer of copiers. In the United States, it is known for its competitive challenge to Xerox in the copying business Xerox long dominated. But a more revealing way to view Canon is as an expert in at least three core technologies: optics, imaging, and microprocessor controls. These technologies turn out to be essential to the success of a seemingly diverse set of products, including not only copiers but laser printers, cameras, and image scanners. A second example is provided by Honda, another Japanese company that has been extremely successful in the United States. Honda was once known as a motorcycle manufacturer, but its true identity was based on its core competencies in engine and drive train design and manufacturing. Those core competencies allowed Honda to compete successfully, not only in the market for motorcycles, but also in lawn mowers, generators, small tractors, and ultimately automobiles.

Figure 19-3 shows how to picture the organization of a multiproduct company that is focused on core technologies rather than on strategic business units.[4] The company pictured in Figure 19-3 asks what it is good at—how its basic competencies can be developed, nurtured, and expanded. It is constantly looking for ways to apply core competencies in the form of basic or core products, such as various sizes and types of engines in the case of Honda. Finally, it is seeking alternative ways to apply its competencies in diverse businesses. Compared to a company whose structure is based on strategic business units, a company that focuses on core competencies seems to be positioned to find quickly the opportunities to create new products in existing markets and develop new products and markets. It is constantly focused on the connections between basic competencies and technologies and marketable products. A focus on core competencies can force a company constantly to take inventory of the things it does well and the things it should be able to do well, and to match that inventory with opportunities for growth in a broad variety of products.

In Chapter 18 we identified what we believe are the key core competencies in a securitized financial markets. Most apply equally well to a financial market that is not securitized. Companies that intend to be successful in the financial services marketplace of the future will have to carefully select the products and portions of the markets where they believe they have the capabilities or competencies to compete. Having a realistic understanding of your competencies will be extremely important.

---

[4]This figure is taken from C.K. Prahalad and Gary Hamel. "The Core Competence of the Corporation." *Harvard Business Review* (May-June 1990) pp. 79–91.

Figure 19-3

Links between end products and core competencies. *Source:* Harvard Business Review, *May-June, 1990. Reprinted by permission of* Harvard Business Review. *An exhibit from "The Core Competencies of the Corporation" by C.K. Prahalad and Gary Hamel, May-June 1990. Copyright © 1990 by the President and Fellows of Harvard College; all rights reserved.*

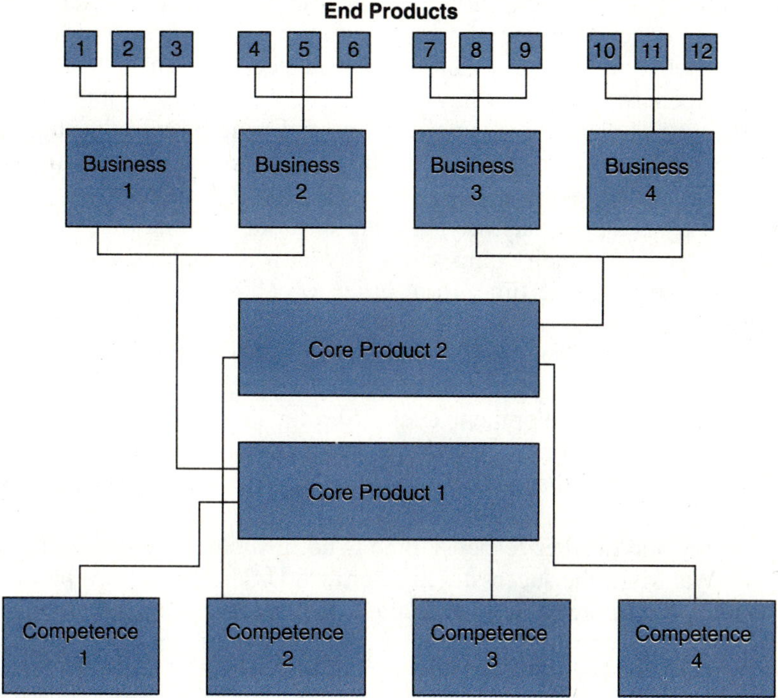

Timing

Another approach to establishing competitive advantage that derives from how a company is organized involves concentrating on time. It is a truism of finance that time is money, but we mean something more important than simply the fact that cash received sooner is more valuable than cash received later. Time as a competitive advantage involves flexibility in design and manufacturing, rapid response to customer needs, and speed in innovation. A manufacturing company that has a time-based advantage has developed a flexible system for identifying and responding to customer needs. That flexibility must make it possible to build and deliver the product the customer wants quickly. This speed of response provides an edge for companies that cannot respond in the same way. Moreover, the flexibility and speed with which a company can deliver a specific product that closely meets the customers needs make it possible to charge a higher price than it could for a slower response and a more standardized product. This applies just as much to financial services as it does to manufacturing.

It is important to recognize that, for many companies, the time-based approach to competitive advantage is diametrically opposed to traditional approaches that emphasize scale economies and standardization to achieve low costs. Scale economies and standardization have been the cornerstone of the approach to large parts of U.S. manufacturing industries. The premise has long been that standardization generates scale economies and leads to lower costs of production; however, Japanese auto companies, particularly Toyota, have made it all too apparent that they can achieve lower costs by using a manufacturing process that has fewer employees who work in teams, lower inventories, and shorter production runs to generate more products that satisfy consumer needs more rapidly and with lower costs than firms can achieve that rely on traditional manufacturing based on scale economies and standardization.[5]

Many Japanese companies have been leaders in forging competitive advantage based on time. Toyota, for example, pioneered time-based advantage by moving toward flexible manufacturing and just-in-time inventory. Success in this approach to the market required the technological capability to change the manufacturing process quickly and inexpensively, in order to produce small runs of a wider variety of products than could their competitors. Toyota was fabulously successful in reducing the response, or cycle time, from order to delivery of a specific automobile—from time formerly measured in weeks to only a few days. Indeed, the ultimate bottleneck was delays in the sales and delivery process as much as in the manufacturing process. A similar level of success has been achieved in reducing the length of the new product development cycle. Shorter new product development cycles mean that new innovations can be introduced more frequently and into more products. The conclusion is that a time-based advantage creates an accompanying advantage in a higher rate of innovation.

Flexibility and quicker response time is not a strategy limited to the manufacturing sector. Wal Mart, the successful high-growth U.S. retailer, owes part of its success in competing with more traditional retailers such as Sears to a system of flexibility in response to customer needs that includes quicker turnover of inventory and fewer intermediaries between the manufacturer and the Wal Mart store. This has meant for Wal Mart not only faster response but also lower inventory levels, which have reduced the financing and storage costs of the products it sells relative to its competitors. The message is that the time-based advantages can be important across a wide variety of businesses. We believe that the same sorts of changes that have taken place in manufacturing and in retailing may well be developing soon in financial services.

Hustle

Movement toward increased flexibility and quicker response time is creating a virtual revolution in manufacturing, as this approach is replacing mass production based on economies of scale and low costs for standardized products. Some lines of business, generally service businesses, do not have the sorts of problems that are inherent in manufacturing, ones that derive principally from the need for large amounts of fixed assets and plant and equipment that are used in the manufacturing process. Moreover, in many service businesses, other than product differentiation,

[5]See James P. Womack, Daniel T. Jones, and Daniel Roos. *The Machine That Changed the World.* New York: Rawson Associates, 1990.

there are few potential sources of competitive advantage based on barrier to entry. The real question becomes whether and how a company can differentiate its product or distinguish itself from other suppliers of a service when the essential features of that service can be easily duplicated. One possible way to establish such a difference has been referred to as "hustle."[6] Hustle is closely related to the time-based advantage that is becoming so important in manufacturing.

Companies that hustle are quick to spot changes in the preferences and desires of their customers and to change their products in response to those needs. They are quick to spot new technological opportunities and to move to incorporate that technology in their products. They build their organizations around the principle that there is nothing proprietary in their corporate strategy, nothing that needs to be hidden from the competition. Instead, they concern themselves with their ability to respond and change more quickly than their competitors. As a source of competitive advantage hustle relies heavily on the quality of the people in the organization. They must thrive on constant change and on the search for continuous improvement in the company's products and services. They must not be focused on the alternative of establishing a barrier to entry that can provide extra returns without continuous innovation. The key idea behind hustle is that high profits stem largely from superior execution and a focus on innovation, rather than from the erection of barriers to protect an established market or product from competition. A company that is focused on hustle need not concern itself as much with the strategies of competitors. Just as it is not so concerned if its own strategies are public knowledge, it expects to gain little by learning the strategies of competitors. Instead, a company that relies on hustle focuses on harnessing and promoting the creative strengths of its employees and on carefully monitoring the needs of its customers. To be successful, the strategy of hustle requires that companies understand their costs and direct the energies of their people to the most profitable opportunities it can identify. Thus, an effective information system is essential for a company that succeeds through hustle.

Profiles of Innovative Financial Competitors

In the remainder of this chapter we describe the basic strategies and operations of three innovative banking firms in the United States. Each has been successful in different ways in the financial services marketplace. We have chosen these three from the many U.S. banks and nonbank financial firms to illustrate different strategies being pursued by companies with different histories and market positions. The first company, Banc One, is a regional bank holding company that operates principally in the Midwest. Banc One has consistently been one of the most successful banks in the United States in recent years by focusing on retail banking and middle market business lending. The second company, Bankers Trust, has positioned itself as more of a merchant bank, concentrating on various financial services to corporations and on trading activity. The third company, BankAmerica, has one of the largest retail

[6]See Amar Bhide. "Hustle as Strategy." *Harvard Business Review* (Sept-Oct 1986) pp. 59–65.

Table 19-1
Performance and Efficiency Measures of Three Bank Holding Companies—Five-Year Averages 1988–1992 (Percent)

	Banc One	Bankers Trust	BankAmerica
After-tax margin	18.24	9.93	8.44
Return on equity	14.08	10.24	10.89
Annual growth in earnings	12.38	192.79	8.59
Volatility of earnings	1.80	87.29	4.30

Source: Bridge Information Services.

and commercial lending franchises in the United States. It operates principally in California but has expanded into a number of other western states. Our objective is to explain how these companies compete in the financial marketplace of the 1990s.

Data on the financial performance of each of these three companies is presented in Table 19-1 and in Figures 19-4 and 19-5. Table 19-1 shows five-year averages, ending in 1992, of various measures of operating efficiency. These measures of efficiency include after-tax margin (on revenues), return on equity, annual growth rate in earnings, and volatility of earnings. Figures 19-4 and 19-5 present data on the stock price performance of the three companies and the performance of two banking industry portfolios, one comprised of money center banks and the other of major regional banks. Figure 19-4 shows the stock price performance of each of the three banks and indices of money center banks, regional banks, and the Standard & Poor's 500. All

Figure 19-4
Performance of bank stocks and bank portfolios (January 1983 = 100).

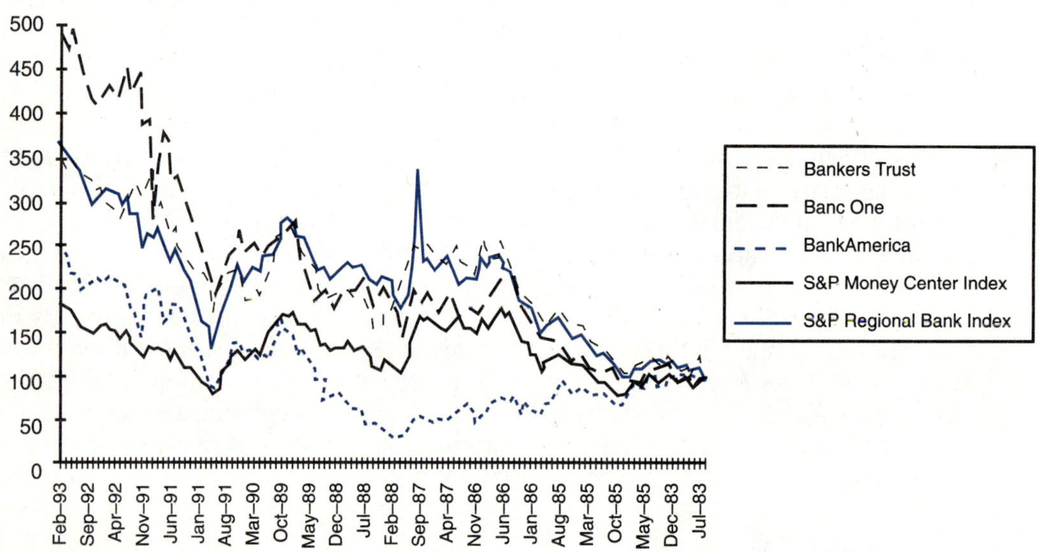

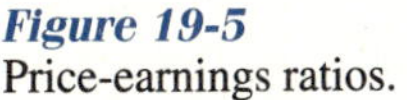

Figure 19-5
Price-earnings ratios.

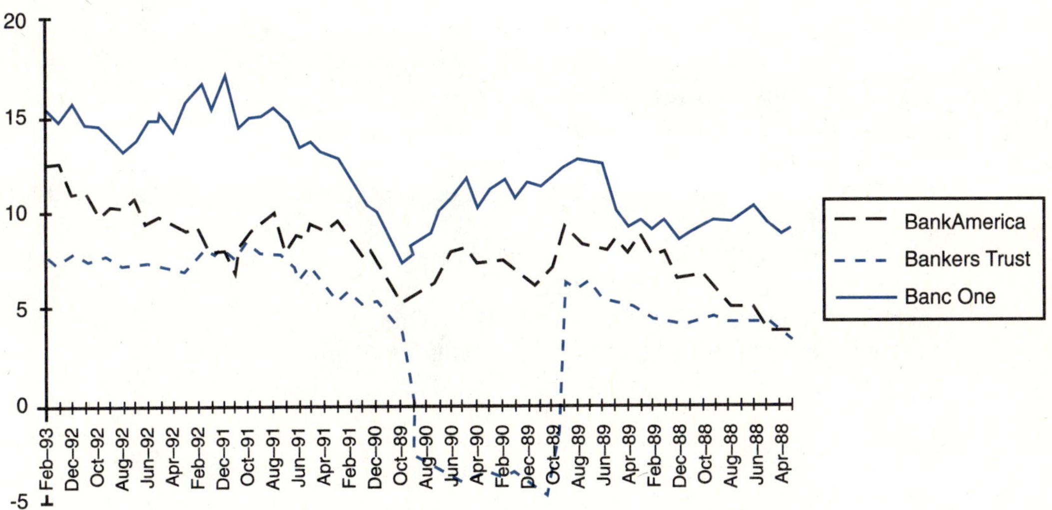

data are monthly data expressed as indexes starting with 100 in January 1983. This method of presenting stock price performance over time makes it easy to compare the performance of different companies and portfolios of companies. Figure 19-5 shows monthly price-earnings ratios for each of the three banks from 1988 to early 1993.

Before we launch into this discussion, it is informative to see what Figures 19-4 and 19-5 tell us about the banks' performance. First, notice that the prices of all three banks and the indices of bank stocks, particularly major regional banks, increased dramatically in the early 1990s. This appears to reflect increased profitability of banks as interest rates declined and an increased perception in the market that many banks are developing better strategies for operating in a highly competitive marketplace. The major regional bank stocks consistently outperformed the money center bank stocks throughout the entire ten-year period. In the first half of the ten years shown in Figure 19-4, Bankers Trust had the best stock performance; however, Banc One's stock price passed Bankers Trust in 1991 and outperformed all others by a significant margin after that. The worst individual performer, BankAmerica, experienced significant problems in the mid-1980s that were reflected in its poor performance relative to the others in the figure until 1988. Then its stock began to rebound and outperformed the money center index for the rest of the period. It is also interesting to note that if one had been able to invest $100 in a ten-year bond paying 10 percent interest at the beginning of the period shown in Figure 19-4, the value at the end of the ten-year period would have been $270. Notice that only BankAmerica and the money center bank index performed below this standard, though that was largely the tremendous appreciation in the last two years of the period that enabled the other three performers to significantly outperform such a bond.

Figure 19-5 documents the price-earnings ratios of the three banks we will examine. Notice that Banc One had the highest price-earnings ratio of the three throughout the entire five-year period shown in the figure. On the other hand, Bankers Trust had the lowest price-earnings ratio for most of the time. Bankers Trust also had a negative ratio for a while, during 1990 when the company reported negative earnings as a result of recognizing loan losses. Once this period passed, Bankers Trust rebounded to roughly its historical relationship between price and earnings. It is important to recognize that a company's stock price is based partly on the market's perception of the management of assets presently in place and partly on perception of growth opportunities. We will find, as we move into our discussion of these three banks, that Bankers Trust has been perceived by the market as having a risky long-run position in the marketplace. Thus, it is awarded a lower price-earnings ratio than other banks. By contrast, Banc One has been very successful in managing the market's perception of its long-run growth opportunities.

Banc One

Banc One is a regional bank holding company based in Columbus, Ohio. As of the end of 1992, Banc One had approximately $75 billion in total assets, taking into account recent acquisitions in Texas and Arizona. This means that it now is in or near the top ten in total asset size for all the bank holding companies in the country. Banc One is unique in several respects. First, it has consistently been among the best performers, measured in return on assets (ROA) of the 50 largest banks in the United States. In fact, for six of ten years in the 1980s Banc One had the highest ROA of the top 50 banks. From 1981 to 1990 Banc One's average annual ROA and return on equity (ROE) were 1.34 percent and 17.14 percent, respectively. That compares to a median of 0.73 percent and 13.1 percent, respectively, for the 50 largest U.S. banking firms in the same period. This accomplishment is all the more remarkable given the rapid growth that Banc One experienced. Between 1967, when the holding company was formed, and 1991, its total assets grew more than 63 times. This level of growth combined with a consistently high return on assets is very hard to accomplish. In fact, Banc One is such an interesting company precisely because it has been able to combine rapid growth with consistently high profits. We can learn a lot by looking closely at how this was accomplished.

History and Culture

To understand Banc One's success it is important to have a sense of the history of the bank and of the banking markets in which the company has historically been competing. The holding company currently called Banc One was founded in 1967 from City National Bank (CNB) of Ohio. It was initially named First Bank, and the name was changed to Banc One in 1979. The unusual spelling of the word bank was employed because Ohio law forbids a holding company to be called a "bank." Like many states in the United States, Ohio had laws for branch banking that prohibited banks from expanding beyond their home county. This meant that there were numerous small banks throughout the state. The ultimate mechanism for circumventing these restrictions on bank ownership entailed the formation of a bank holding company and the acquisition of small regional banks. This was the path that Banc One pursued.

The management style at Banc One appears to be a reflection of the personal style of its chief executive. Three generations of John McCoys have held this job. John H. McCoy, the first McCoy to be Chief Executive Officer of CNB, died in 1958. He was succeeded by his son, John G. McCoy. John G. McCoy began the process of rapid growth for the bank and created the holding company in 1967. His son, John B., continued the rapid expansion. There appears to be a culture maintained within the bank that derives from long-standing traditions instituted by the McCoys. This has been an important part of the strategy of dealing with rapid growth. One reported anecdote seems to capture this culture: Employees are not allowed to drink coffee in their offices. This apparently dates back to John G. McCoy, who thought that coffee would be spilled on the carpeting and otherwise make the bank's offices look less than tidy. Therefore, he forbade drinking coffee outside specific areas in the bank.

As Banc One has grown by acquisition, a part of the strategy in those acquisitions has been to instill the Banc One culture into the newly acquired banks. At the same time, existing management of newly acquired banks is generally retained and given substantial license to manage their banks, at least as long as performance targets are met. Top executives of the Banc One affiliated banks meet regularly to exchange information and review a variety of performance measures of these affiliated banks. Furthermore, executives of affiliated banks are expected to keep up with new ideas and so-called best practices throughout the Banc One system. Such best practices are regularly identified and distributed to the affiliated banks in Banc One.

Strategy

We think important elements in Banc One's strategy include these:

- Concentrate on retail and middle market business lending, where there are high profit margins.
- Grow patiently through acquisitions where the Banc One culture can be effectively instilled.
- Manage risk through centralized systems, but maintain local decision making.
- Control costs and invest in information technology.

Banc One has consistently focused its lending activities on retail or consumer lending and lending to small to medium-sized businesses. It has avoided lending activities that were attractive to many of its larger competitors: foreign lending, lending to large corporations, and lending for large commercial real estate. In 1991 roughly 50 percent of Banc One's loan portfolio consisted of consumer-related assets. In effect, Banc One operates like a local or small regional bank that just happens to operate in a number of different locations. It understands that local banks generally face less competition and are able to price their products in a way that generates attractive margins. Thus, it has attempted to grow by maintaining a focus on these high-margin portions of the market but increasing the volume of local markets that it can serve. The historical disadvantage of local banks that have served such high-margin customers is that they have not be able to develop the professional expertise, variety of modern products, and competitive cost structures of large banks that have large urban markets. Banc One has tried to put both of these advantages together.

In order to succeed with this strategy, Banc One must find ways to maintain local autonomy. Local bank executives must be closely tied to their communities to maintain the relationships that generate high margins. Within Banc One, affiliate bank officers have a substantial degree of control over prices, marketing, and credit decisions; on the other hand, they are supported with a modern and centralized information system and other support from the holding company. This approach combines the best features of high-margin local markets with the sophistication of a larger organization.

The acquisition process at Banc One has also been carried out with some degree of patience and care. Banc One reportedly follows several rules in pursuing acquisitions. First, they stay focused on regions of the country where they can attract the high-margin local business. Second, they focus on acquisitions that are not too large. This is important if they are to instill their culture into the acquired institution. Third, they take time to instill that culture into an acquired bank before launching a new large acquisition. Generally, installing the systems and culture into an acquired bank takes about two years. Fourth, they try not to pay too much for acquisitions. Finally, the bank seeks acquisitions where they can be number one or two in the local market. If their market penetration is too low, it is too difficult to maintain the high-margin business. The key to the acquisition strategy is the expansion of distribution channels in order to achieve economies of scale in the centralized and back-room operations of the bank.

The decentralization inherent in the Banc One strategy extends to credit decisions made by affiliated banks. The holding company establishes rules and guidelines for the affiliated banks' portfolios, but, individual credit decisions are left largely up to local bank officers. This means that some mistakes are always likely to be made, but they are not likely to be large mistakes from the standpoint of the entire holding company. By contrast, a centralized credit approval system could result in an environment where consistent bad decisions by the centralized system could threaten the overall viability of the entire company.

Finally, Banc One has consistently been a leader in the application of computer and information technology to banking. In fact, its entire strategy relies on modern communications technology to maintain the traditional culture of the organization as it grows. When Banc One was a relatively small institution it was technically feasible to have all of the CEO's of affiliated banks report directly to John McCoy. As more acquisitions were made, this became less and less practical. At one time, John B. McCoy had 22 executives reporting directly to him. The structure was changed so that there would be one bank chairman in each state who reported directly to John B. McCoy. At the same time Banc One invested in developing more sophisticated communications and information systems to link the increasing number of affiliate banks. Without this linkage, it is difficult or impossible to communicate down from the holding company to the affiliated banks the strategies and ideas that are crucial to continuing excellent performance of the entire organization.

Technology has always been an important focus of Banc One. Technology has not only been central to Banc One as a communication and information system among the affiliated banks, but investment in data processing technology has been a key strategy in developing economies of scale in backoffice operations. In fact, Banc One attracted considerable attention in the early 1980s, when it was awarded a contract by Merrill Lynch to do the data processing for its cash management account (CMA). Though Merrill Lynch moved this processing function in house in 1984, Banc One had by then developed the capability to find new customers for its backoffice capabilities. By focusing on building better data-processing capability Banc One positioned itself to have the economies of scale and information systems capability to integrate acquisitions into its management system.

Overall, it appears that Banc One has done an excellent job of managing its performance to date. It has managed existing assets in a superior manner, earning a high rate of return on assets and on equity, but it has also managed the markets perception of its future growth opportunities with much skill. It has articulated and executed a good strategy for expansion and it has communicated that strategy to the marketplace. This has led to the extraordinary stock price performance documented in Figure 19-4 and the high price-earnings ratio shown in Figure 19-5.

Bankers Trust

Bankers Trust is one of the major New York money center banks. In 1992 it was the seventh largest U.S. bank, as measured by total assets. In 1991 Bankers also had the highest return on equity of any of the top 50 banks in the U. S. Bankers' strategy is radically different from Banc One's. Bankers concentrates on trading and on originating loans, but not necessarily on holding them. This means that, perhaps more than any other U. S. commercial bank, Bankers concentrates its operations in the products described in Part IV of this book, which deals with financial innovation. Bankers is a market maker in various types of derivative securities, including futures, options, and swaps. It has also organized itself to take advantage of securitization of financial assets by concentrating on originating loans, especially corporate loans, and then selling those off rather than holding them until maturity. In addition, Bankers has no domestic retail operations. This is in stark contrast to some of its other large competitors, such as Citicorp and BankAmerica, which have concentrated to a great degree on large-scale retail operations.

The unusual nature of Bankers' operations is indicated by the data in Figure 19-6, which shows the major categories of assets on Bankers' balance sheet as of mid-1992 and the same categories for the average of the ten other largest U.S. banks, expressed as a percentage of total assets. Note that, at the typical large commercial bank in the United States loans account for 57 percent of total assets. Investments and trading accounts make up another 12 percent and 6 percent, respectively. At Bankers, the situation is virtually the opposite. There, loans are only 19 percent of total assets, and trading accounts and investments comprise a total of 51 percent. Moreover, resale agreements and federal funds account for 19 percent of Bankers' assets, nearly four times as much as at the typical large commercial bank.

Figure 19-6
Assets for Bankers Trust as of 30 June 1992.

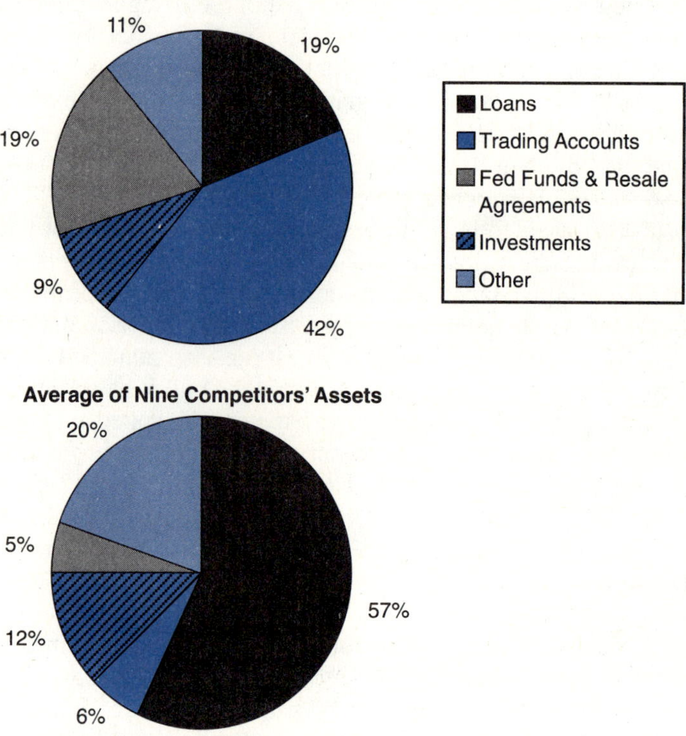

The structure of the balance sheet at Bankers is a result of its assessment of where it has a potential source of competitive advantage. First, Bankers Trust is a wholesale, rather than a retail, bank. This means that its history, franchise, and expertise are in dealing with corporate clients rather than consumers. As a result, it has no access to consumer deposits (often called "core deposits"). The bank's strategy, as articulated by its chairman, Charles S. Sanford, Jr., results from its lack of such core deposits. Such deposits are perceived to be cheaper than so-called purchased deposits attracted from money managers and corporate treasurers. Thus, the bank's management indicates that, given its lack of core deposits, it is inappropriate to allocate the bank's capital to the function of holding loans in its own portfolio. Given this assessment of the cost of holding loans, Bankers is virtually driven to look elsewhere for a source of competitive advantage.

Bankers has consistently invested in building the capability to operate a profitable trading operation. Bankers was one of the first major U. S. commercial banks to emphasize its risk management capabilities and to cultivate a market for risk management products and services throughout the world. That is, it got into this business early and it has continued to focus on it. Bankers, like any other commercial bank, has a potential advantage in this business over nonbank institutions as a result of its access to emergency assistance from the Federal Reserve. In addition, it may have the advantage of being viewed as too big to fail, so that the Federal Deposit Insurance Corporation and the Fed would be forced to bail it out, should it experience serious difficulty. Bankers' position in the market for derivatives has not precluded competitors from the ranks of other commercial banks and investment banks from actively competing in this market. In fact, this has been one of the highest-growth and most intensely competitive portions of the financial markets of the late 1980s and early 1990s. Nonetheless, thus far Bankers has been very profitable in this portion of its operations.

Bankers has also been a major competitor in the market for highly leveraged debt. It was an early lender to many takeover specialists in the 1980s and provided substantial funding for leveraged buyout companies such as Kohlberg, Kravis and Roberts (KKR). Bankers' management estimated that its peak year of fees for originating and syndicating so-called highly leveraged transactions was 1989 and that these fees total $229 million or 15 percent to 20 percent of pretax profits. Bankers' strategy of choosing to sell off many of these loans has proved somewhat controversial with its clients. Major clients such as KKR prefer to retain the ability to renegotiate a loan with the originator or lead bank. When the loan is sold entirely to other banks, the task of renegotiation with these other players, should it be necessary, can be considerably more difficult than if the loan were held largely by the originator.

One of the most important problems facing Bankers Trust in carrying out its strategy is communicating that strategy to the marketplace. Bankers has consistently suffered from a price-earnings ratio that is substantially lower than many of its major competitors'. This is clearly evident in Figure 19-5. The market seems to be far more skeptical about Bankers' ability to maintain its earnings than it is about Banc One or BankAmerica, apparently because trading profits, which are a key part of Bankers' earnings, are both risky and hard for an outsider to understand. Rather than having a clear strategy that provides an understandable source of advantage, Bankers relies on the continuing need for sophisticated risk management products *and* on its capability of satisfying that need profitably as the source of its current and future profitability. The market has trouble understanding how it is possible to build a sustainable source of attractive earnings here, and therefore it appears to be less optimistic about future profits than it is in the case of Banc One.

BankAmerica Corporation

BankAmerica Corporation is one of the most interesting and important bank holding companies in the United States. As of 1992, it became the second largest bank holding company, with total assets of roughly $190 billion in 1992, second only to Citicorp (assets approximately $217 billion). In 1992 Bankamerica acquired the second largest bank in the western United States, Security Pacific. Both institutions had large branch networks in California and had expanded by acquiring institutions in other major western states, principally Washington, Arizona, and Nevada. Each bank had large retail franchises that covered much of the populated portions of the western United States. BankAmerica is also interesting because it has staged such a dramatic turnaround. Between 1985 and 1987 it lost $1.8 billion as a result of sour loans, abroad and in California. Evidently, the bank's internal credit evaluation system had apparently made major mistakes. It was widely considered to be a serious possibility that BankAmerica would be taken over by regulators or forced to merge with another bank with regulatory assistance. By 1992, that situation was completely reversed. BankAmerica was searching for merger targets to enhance its retail franchise and reduce costs through consolidation with other competing institutions in its traditional markets. Bank analysts and observers often argue that BankAmerica is better positioned than any other institution to be the first bank to operate nationwide.

BankAmerica has long been a dominant force in California banking and has long sought avenues to expand its market, in terms of products and geography. In fact, BankAmerica was once a part of a financial conglomerate called Transamerica. Regulators forced BankAmerica and Transamerica to separate into two companies operating in the banking and insurance businesses, respectively. Since BankAmerica regained its financial health after the serious losses of the mid-1980s it has consistently sought to expand its distribution network to other parts of the country. Even before its period of major losses ended, BankAmerica acquired the largest independent bank in the state of Washington, Seattle First National Bank. In 1990, it entered Arizona by acquiring the failed thrift institutions MeraBank Savings and Western Savings. BankAmerica also attempted to expand its franchise to the east coast by bidding for the failed Bank of New England, but the attempt failed.

The acquisition of Security Pacific by BankAmerica constitutes one of the largest, and possibly most important, bank mergers in U. S. history. Security Pacific was a large regional bank based in California that tried to function as a money center and global merchant bank. In the 1980s Security Pacific aggressively expanded beyond its base of retail and business lending in California by participating in leveraged buyouts, international lending, and securities brokerage. It acquired brokerage firms in Britain and Canada and established a merchant banking unit to manage its investment banking and international operations. In addition, Security Pacific, attempting to expand its regional franchise to other states in the western United States, encountered great difficulties in the process. It purchased a commercial bank in Arizona for $480 million in 1985, shortly before there was a serious decline in the Arizona economy and in real estate prices there. In 1992 it was forced to declare a write-off totalling $650 million on loans in Arizona and Australia.

BankAmerica seized the opportunity to acquire Security Pacific in 1991, when Security Pacific was having serious difficulties. The merger was attractive to both banks for a number of reasons. First, it combined two of the most important competitors in many of the regional financial markets throughout the western United States. This gave the merged entity greater market share in all of these markets. In fact, it has been estimated that BankAmerica would gain first place in four fifths of California's specific markets and in Washington and Nevada. In addition, it became among the country's four largest credit card issuers. Second, it allowed substantial consolidation of operations and reduction in costs. Recall, from our discussion earlier in this chapter, that there are significant differences among banks in costs or in efficiency of conducting similar operations. BankAmerica and Security Pacific realized that consolidation of their operations could lead to substantial savings. In fact, BankAmerica publicly estimated that it would achieve savings of $1.2 billion a year within three years.

Finally, Security Pacific's financial problems and its failed strategy might be managed better by the BankAmerica management team than by trying to continue on its own.

BankAmerica's aggressive expansion through the acquisition of Security Pacific did not come cheap. BankAmerica paid a premium of 40 percent over Security Pacific's market price shortly before the merger. In addition, BankAmerica has taken substantial restructuring charges as a result of the bad loans carried by Security Pacific. Possibly more important, BankAmerica was threatened with the prospects that constraints would be imposed on its expansion in a number of markets, to satisfy both antitrust requirements and state legislatures in Washington and Arizona. It has been forced to divest roughly 200 branches and $9 billion in deposits to satisfy antitrust rules. On the human side, achieving the cost savings that BankAmerica is seeking requires large-scale reduction of the combined workforces of the two banks. This can seriously test the ability of a large company to motivate its workforce.

In comparing all three of the banks we have been discussing, it is apparent that, thus far Banc One has been the most successful. Each of the three banks has implemented dramatically different strategies for establishing competitive advantage. In large part, these alternative strategies grow out of the historical origins of the three companies. It would be very difficult for Bankers Trust and Banc One to attempt to copy each other's approaches to the marketplace. Of the three, BankAmerica is the one that has probably had the greatest flexibility to pursue alternative strategic objectives. It appears to be focusing on building a large retail and commercial banking franchise throughout as much of the United States as it believes it can profitably manage. It will be interesting to see how this works out.

SUMMARY

In this chapter we have concentrated on the strategies open to commercial banks, and implicitly to other types of firms, in the financial services marketplace, to establish competitive advantage. We began our search for competitive advantage with six sources of barriers. We argued that there are probably few opportunities to create barriers to entry in financial services. We emphasized that though there has long been a perception that there are significant scale economies in banking, recent evidence indicates that such economies probably do not account for more than about three percent of the total cost of banking services. A more dramatic cost differential seems to exist between the most and least efficient banks in a given size class. This points toward difficulties in the less efficient banks exiting the industry; though we also argued that in specific aspect of banking, specifically backroom operations, scale economies may be very significant, though this may still not represent a sizeable advantage when measured as a percentage of the total cost of all banking services. We also emphasized that control of distribution channels and the use of government policy are still important ways to attempt to erect barriers to entry.

Next we described what we call organization-based sources of competititive advantage. These are skills developed within organizations that allow them to compete effectively. Organization-based sources of advantage include the development of specific competencies in an organization, often called core competencies. They also include the ability to outhustle your opponent or achieve shorter time to market with products and services.

Finally, we provided profiles of the recent operations of three major U.S. commercial banks that have distinct histories and have pursued very different strategies. Banc One has focused on middle-market commercial and retail lending, principally in the Midwest. It has grown through acquisitions but has concentrated on integrating acquired banks into its particular culture or way of doing business. It has consistently avoided investing in areas that have attracted many money-center banks but where *it* has little expertise, such as loans to less-developed countries. It has been among the most successful and faster-growing banks in the United States over the decade ending in 1992.

The second bank we examined, Bankers Trust, is virtually the opposite of Banc One. It has focused on trading securities and on originating, but not selling, loans. It has also been extremely active in developing and selling risk management products throughout the world. We emphasized that, while Bankers has been successful in recent years, the financial markets seem to be somewhat skeptical about whether its strategy can be sustained or that it has a sustainable source of competitive advantage. This is the inference we draw from the fact that Banc One has consistently outperformed Bankers Trust in the stock market.

The third bank we examined, BankAmerica, is in some sense a hybrid of Banc One and Bankers Trust. It successfully rebounded from serious losses in the mid-1980s that threatened its survival as an independent institution. BankAmerica has expanded its franchise both inside and outside of California by acquiring institutions in other western states and by acquiring one of the other major California banks, Security Pacific. BankAmerica now has one of the best and largest consumer and middle-market lending capabilities in the United States. Many believe it has the best position to become the first truly nationwide bank in the United States. The market has rewarded BankAmerica with increased share prices as it has improved its performance and positioned itself to have a dominant market position throughout much of the western United States.

Each of these banks provides examples of different strategies or different choices about where to positions themselves in the value chain we described in Chapter 18. We hope it is apparent that this marketplace will be very competitive in the next decade. The successful companies will have to continue to focus on improving their competencies and managing with an eye to good execution and control of costs.

QUESTIONS

1. Distinguish between economies of scale and economies of scope. How do these create barriers to entry?
2. What is product differentiation? Can you give some examples of differentiated products in the finance area?
3. What are the core competencies of a company? How should a company organize itself to take advantage of its core competencies?

4. How are "time" and "hustle" sources of competitive advantage? Can you give some examples of companies or markets in which these sources of advantage may be important?
5. How important do you believe economies of scale may be in commercial banking? How do scale economies compare with cost differentials across banks?
6. What are exit barriers in an industry? Do you think there are exit barriers in commercial banking? How do you think this affects the state of competition in the industry?
7. How important do you think control of distribution channels will be for commercial banking in the years ahead? What can banks do to obtain better control over distribution of their products?
8. Suppose you were going to operate a bank that originated loans and sold them but retained their servicing. Discuss the competencies that you believe you would have to maintain within your organization to be successful with this strategy.
9. Compare the strategies pursued by Banc One, Bankers Trust, and BankAmerica. Are the strategies interchangeable in the sense that it would make sense for Bankers Trust and Banc One to switch to the other's strategy? Which strategy do you think promises to be the most successful?
10. What do you think that Bankers Trust could do to achieve a price-earnings ratio closer to that commanded by Banc One?
11. Pick a bank other than the three we profiled in this chapter and examine its strategy. Can you find a successful one that is pursuing a strategy completely different from that of any of the three we have discussed here?

REFERENCES

Berger, Allen N. and David B. Humphrey. "The Dominance of Inefficiencies Over Scale and Product Mix Economies in Banking." *Journal of Monetary Economics* 28 (1991), pp. 117–148.

Bhide, Amar. "Hustle as Strategy." *Harvard Business Review* (Sept-Oct 1986), pp. 59–65.

Cocheo, Steve. "What's So Good About Banc One?" *ABA Banking Journal* (July 1991), pp. 54–58.

Furlong, Tom. "The Curtain Falls on Security Pacific." *Bankers Monthly* (Nov 1991), pp. 15–17.

Loomis, Carol J. "A whole new way to run a bank." *Fortune* September 7, 1992, 76–85.

Patterson, Gregory A., and Francine Schwadel. "Sears Suddenly Undoes Years of Diversifying Beyond Retailing Field." *Wall Street Journal,* September 30, 1992, p. A1.

Porter, Michael E. "How Competitive Forces Shape Strategy." *Harvard Business Review* (Mar-Apr 1979), pp. 137–145.

Prahalad, C. K., and Gary Hamel. "The Core Competence of the Corporation." *Harvard Business Review* (May-June 1990), 79–91.

Taylor, John H. "A Tale of Two Strategies." *Forbes* August 31, 1992, pp. 40–41.

Teitelman, Robert. "The Magnificent McCoys: Running America's Best Bank." *Institutional Investor,* July 1991, pp. 47–56.

Womack, James P., Daniel T. Jones, and Daniel Roos. *The Machine That Changed the World.* New York: Rawson Associates, 1990.

• *Chapter 20*

Managing Credit Risk

The remaining four chapters of this book deal with risk management issues facing financial institutions. We view risk management as the key service underlying all the other more obvious services that financial institutions provide their customers. This has long been the view of many key players in the financial services marketplace. Walter Wriston, the retired chief executive officer of Citicorp, was recently quoted in an article in the *Economist* on international banking: "The fact is that bankers are in the business of managing risk. Pure and simple, that is the business of banking."[1] This is precisely the view that underlies the approach taken in these final four chapters. We divide the risks facing financial institutions into three categories: credit (or default) risk, interest rate risk, and exchange rate risk. We have laid the foundations for each of these areas of risk throughout the book. Now we devote some time to each of the three.

One of the major functions of financial intermediaries is to evaluate and manage credit, or default, risk. The very nature of financial intermediation creates a need to manage default risk on both sides of the balance sheet. As intermediaries raise funds by issuing financial liabilities, they must be sensitive to their own credit standing in the money and capital markets. And as they invest those funds in financial assets they must be sensitive to the credit quality of those claims, as well. Credit risk is also an important determinant of the prices of publicly traded debt instruments. This chapter provides an introduction to the management of credit risk. We approach the topic of credit risk management from two perspectives: its pricing and its control. Most financial intermediaries are involved in both types of activities. First, they must evaluate and price the risk they determine to be present in a given debt instrument or loan. Second, they can try to control or limit credit risk, and thus reduce the price that must be charged.

Our approach to the topic of credit risk should also be viewed in the context of the value chain that we outlined for financial institutions in Chapter 18. There, we pointed out that one of the key skills, or core competencies, that is important in the financial marketplace is the ability to provide a guarantee against loss in the event of default. A guarantor is responsible for both of the functions we will deal with in this chapter, pricing and control of credit risk. We want to emphasize here the same point of view we emphasized in Chapter 18. Credit risk management may be bundled together with the other functions provided by portfolio lenders or vertically integrated financial intermediaries, or it may be provided by a separate guarantor, as in securitized markets. The particular way this function is handled in a specific market depends on the relative efficiency of vertical integration versus unbundling, including the costs imposed by regulation. In fact, a

[1]See "A Survey of International Banking." *Economist,* April 10–16, 1993.

key message of this chapter is that all risky claims can be conceptualized as a combination of a riskless claim and a financial guarantee. This concept is key to understanding how credit risk is managed in modern financial institutions, and it provides a useful framework for understanding the roles of public and private guarantors. The key concepts to learn in this chapter are listed below.

• *Key Concepts to Learn in Chapter 20* •

- How fixed-income instruments can be decomposed into a risk-free component and a financial guarantee
- How guarantors and rating agencies assess credit risk
- Basic mechanisms used to limit or control credit risk
- How credit risk is handled in derivative securities

The Historical Record on Credit Risk

"Credit risk" is the risk of loss from default on a financial contract, usually a debt instrument. Default occurs on a debt instrument when a scheduled payment of interest and/or principal is not paid in full. The loss that occurs in default involves any scheduled payments that remain uncollected by the lender, costs incurred in carrying out legal proceedings against the borrower, the opportunity cost of payments made late but without sufficient late penalties, and legal and administrative costs associated with recontracting, or restructuring, debt. We begin our discussion of credit or default risk by providing a brief overview of the historical record. There are a variety of different ways we might examine the historical record on default experience and returns on fixed-income securities. We have chosen two examples that we think are both interesting and revealing. The first deals with the loss experience of commercial banks.

Loan Losses at Commercial Banks

The provision for loan losses is a device used by banks to recognize in a timely fashion impending losses on troubled loans. For banks, the loan loss reserve is generally similar to the reserve for bad debts set aside for uncollectable accounts by nonbank firms. Banks recognize that some portion of the loans they make will default and that some accounts will go uncollected. Under some circumstances, defaults occur in clusters, as is the case for consumer and real estate loans during a local economic downturn. Recognizing a large loan write-off all at once may cause a serious decline in earnings that the bank might wish to avoid. The provision for loan losses provides a means for smoothing out loan losses so as to protect and stabilize the earnings stream. Figure 20-1, which shows loan loss provisions of U. S. commercial banks from 1983 to 1991 as a percentage of total assets, indicates that losses hit their peak

Figure 20-1

Loss provisions divided by total assets for all commercial banks.

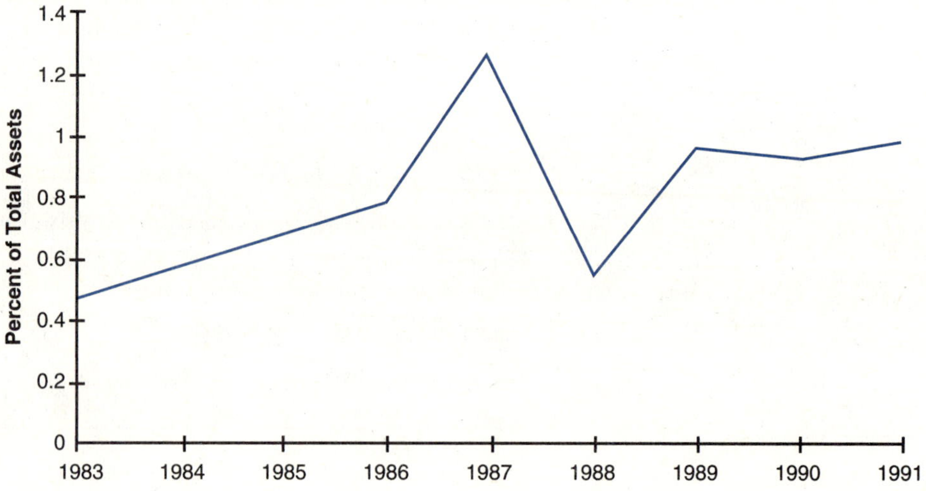

in recent experience in 1987. That was the year when many banks chose to recognize major losses on loans to less developed countries, so-called LDC loans.

It is important to note that the process of setting aside reserves for future loan losses has no direct consequences for the cash flows to the bank. It is merely an accounting transaction that reduces the statement of current earnings for some portion of an anticipated loss. As loans are actually charged off, the reserve account is reduced accordingly. Before the Tax Reform Act of 1986, banks enjoyed an important advantage that derived from this procedure. The benefit occurred as banks were allowed to make liberal provisions for loan losses, which directly reduced their taxable income. From 1965 to 1986 banks could make an addition to reserves (deductible against current income) in an amount equal to 2.4 percent of eligible loans. The 1986 Tax Reform Act required banks to recognize loan losses as a direct charge to operating income (net of recoveries) during the current period for tax purposes. This generally eliminated the tax incentive for loan loss reserves. The loan loss provision at banks is not a perfect indicator of the value of banks' outstanding loans, since, historically, banks have been allowed to carry loans at original values and then write off losses when they deemed it appropriate or when regulators forced them to do so. Increasingly, banks are being compelled to record the market value of loans, reflecting both credit and interest rate risk. We will discuss this further in the next chapter.

The provision for loan losses at major U. S. banks has been the subject of much attention during the past decade. One of the most significant events of the 1980s in the U. S. banking industry was an announcement made by Citicorp chairman John Reed on 19 May 1987 that Citicorp would add $3 billion to its reserve for loan losses to cushion the bank against bad loans. Note that 1987 was the peak year for loan losses as indicated in Figure 20-1. This action resulted in a $2.5 billion loss to Citicorp for the quarter and a loss of about $1.1 billion for the year. Reed's announcement came as the result of the deteriorating position of the bank's loans to LDCs, in particular in Latin America.

Five years before Reed's press conference, Mexico had announced a moratorium on repayment of foreign debt. In February 1987, Brazil announced a suspension of interest payments on its sovereign debt. As economic conditions in Latin American countries continued to worsen in the mid-1980s, it became increasingly clear that American banks would experience serious losses from their foreign loan portfolios. By mid-1987, Latin America's five biggest debtors reportedly owed U. S. banks more than $70 billion. Table 20-1 shows the total bank debt for each of the five major Latin American borrowers and the amounts owed by each to U. S. banks as of mid-1987, when the crisis was at its peak.

The exposure to Latin American debt was particularly serious for Citicorp. On 31 December 1986 Citicorp had loans outstanding to Brazil of $4.6 billion and to Mexico of $2.8 billion. The combined lending to these two countries represented about 55 percent of Citicorp's primary capital at that time.[2] Citicorp's 1987 announcement of massive new reserves for losses on its LDC debt was generally received as good news by the capital markets, as measured by the fact that Citicorp's stock price increased by 10 percent during the week immediately following the announcement. This positive response to Citicorp's action indicated that the capital market was looking beyond the decrease in current profitability at Citicorp to the potential for improved position in managing its risk exposure in the future. Furthermore, most other large banks soon followed Citicorp's lead and announced increases in their loan loss reserves for LDC debt. Unfortunately for Citicorp, facing up to its losses in LDC debt did not bring about the needed revitalization of the company, and Citicorp has continued to experience serious problems for a few years.

Junk Bonds

A second interesting and important example of specific experience in defaults deals with so-called junk bonds. Recall from Chapter 2 that junk bonds are merely bonds whose ratings are below investment grade (below BBB). Traditionally, most junk bonds occurred as "fallen angels," investment grade bonds that are downgraded by Standard & Poor's or Moody's to a speculative rating because of deterioration in the financial condition of the issuer. During the late 1970s and 1980s original issue junk bonds became widely used, in large part to finance takeovers, leveraged buyouts (LBOs) , and other corporate restructuring.

The proliferation of junk bond issues during the 1980s can be traced to the innovative marketing by the investment banking firm of Drexel Burnham Lambert. Drexel basically "created" the original issue market for junk bonds by acting as a dealer for the bonds in secondary transactions. Before Drexel became involved

---

[2]*Primary capital* is defined as total equity plus loan loss reserves plus notes and debentures subordinated to deposits.

Table 20-1A

Latin America's Five Biggest Debtors (1987) ($ billions)

	Total Bank Debt	Amount Owed U.S. Banks
Brazil	$77.9	$22.1
Mexico	71.8	23.7
Argentina	26.6	8.5
Venezuela	25.1	9.4
Chile	13.4	6.5
Total	$214.8	$70.2

Table 20-1B

Amount Owed to Five Biggest U.S. Banks ($ billions)

	Total Debt	% of Bank Equity
Citicorp	$10.4	149%
Bank America	7.5	186%
Manufacturers Hanover	7.5	199%
Chase Manhattan	7.0	143%
J.P. Morgan	4.6	89%
Total	$37.0	

Source: Bartlett S., and W. Glasgall. "A Stunner from the Citi." *Business Week.* (1987) pp 42–43.

many investors were leery of junk bonds, in part because they were not actively traded in any secondary market and, thus, were not very liquid. The dealer activity of Drexel alleviated that problem. During this period, Drexel was very active in buying and reselling high-yield debt to securities clients. Once there was perceived to be liquidity in junk bonds, they became a more attractive investment opportunity for a variety of large institutional investors. In many cases, firms that originally issued their own junk bonds through Drexel later invested in the junk bonds of other firms, supporting Drexel's efforts to sustain a secondary market in junk debt. As a result of these efforts, the primary (original issue) market for junk bonds grew rapidly.

Many economists explain the growth of the junk bond market as part of a process of securitization that affected commercial banks during the 1980s. For lower-quality firms in particular, junk bonds provided the only alternative to bank loans, which were issued primarily on short-term, floating rate terms. Because these same firms preferred longer-term financing as a better maturity match with long-term projects, junk bonds posed a better financing vehicle than traditional bank financing. This precipitated an exodus of lower-rated firms from bank loan markets to the junk bond market.

The demand from investors for junk bonds was fueled primarily by financial institutions such a savings and loans, life insurance companies, pension funds, and investment funds. Investment in junk bonds was attractive at the time, because it was argued that junk bonds would out-perform investments in higher-rated bonds and

U.S. government securities, owing to the high promised interest rates on the bonds relative to the projected number of defaults on junk issues. In part, the performance of junk bonds was enhanced by the general expansion of the U.S. economy during the 1980s and the more extensive use of leverage for financing corporate growth and restructuring. When the economic expansion of the 1980s began to wind down during 1989 and 1990, the number of defaults began to increase. Losses from junk bond investments are now being blamed for financial difficulties in many financial institutions and for playing a major role in the savings and loan debacle.

An important—and hotly contested—issue surrounding junk bonds was whether they promised sufficiently high rates of return to compensate for the risk to which investors were exposed. When original issue junk bonds first appeared, their promoters argued that they were attractive investments, but it was necessary to compile some historical experience before that argument could be subjected to serious scrutiny. Since the recession of the early 1990s hurt sizable numbers of companies that had relied on junk bond financing, the recession drove down the performance of junk bond investments. One analysis contends that the average ten-year total return ending 30 June 1991 on high-yield bond funds was 174.6 percent while the returns on U. S. government bond funds and A-rated corporate bond funds over the same period were 189.2 percent and 224.1 percent, respectively.[3] At this point the economy had started a serious downturn. As a result, if you had chosen an earlier period, say ending in 1988, the junk bond investment would have looked much better.

Since many of the junk bonds issued in the 1980s were used to finance leverage buyouts of companies, where the company's public stockholders were bought out using debt financing, it is instructive to look to the performance of LBOs to understand the fate of junk bond investments. One particularly revealing study of LBOs indicated that the ones completed in the early 1980s were generally well-structured transactions that helped the companies involved improve performance and produced attractive returns for investors. As more people observed the process and went looking for ways to imitate these successes, however, the risk of the LBOs increased tremendously, and the fees charged by investment banks increased as well. As a result, LBOs completed between 1986 and 1988 were structured with very little room for a downturn in performance of the company or for error in estimates of what company assets would command if sold.[4] These LBOs might not have fared so well even in a booming economy, but since shortly thereafter the economy fell into recession, many of them experienced serious difficulties, and the junk bonds the companies issued performed poorly.

Now that we have examined how the market prices credit risk and some examples of the actual performance of specific types of loans, it is important to consider how banks and guarantors attempt to manage their exposure to credit risk.

---

[3]See Edmund Faltermayer. "The Deal Decade: Verdict on the '80s." *Fortune,* August 26, 1991. Data provided by Lipper Analytical Services.

[4]See Steven Kaplan and Jeremy Stein. "How risky is the debt of highly leveraged transactions?" *Journal of Financial Economics* 30 (1990), pp. 215–246.

Pricing and Control of Credit Risk

A Review of the Basics of Credit Risk and Interest Rates

Now that we have some sense of the historical record on credit risk in commercial banking and in traded debt issues, we can begin to focus on the pricing and control of credit risk. Recall that we first considered the connection between credit risk and observed interest rates in Chapter 9, when we discussed the basic determinants of market interest rates. There we focused on the distinctions between (1) the ex ante *expected* yield to maturity, (2) the ex ante *promised* yield to maturity, and (3) the *actual,* or ex post, yield to maturity. The ex ante expected yield to maturity is based on expected cash flows rather than promised cash flows and is therefore always less than the ex ante promised yield to maturity. The promised yield to maturity is the highest yield that a fixed-income instrument can possibly earn or the highest possible ex post actual yield. We generally think of the ex ante expected yield to maturity as being determined by the risk-free interest rate plus a premium demanded by the party that bears the risk to cover the expected losses and any compensation for bearing the risk. For example, if the expected cash flow ($E\{C_1\}$) from a very simple single-period bond with a face value of \$100 is \$98.25, the risk-free interest rate is 5 percent, and if we assume that the market attaches a premium of 2.5 percent measured in additional expected return demanded for this loan, we can express the price of this loan as:

$$V = \frac{E\{C_1\}}{1 + E\{R_a\}} = \frac{\$98.25}{1.075} = \$91.40. \qquad (20.1)$$

Here, the expected yield-to-maturity, $E\{R_a\}$ is expressed as

$$E\{R_a\} = R_f + \Theta \qquad (20.2)$$

where R_f is the prevailing yield on default risk–free bonds with the same maturity (5 percent in the example), and Θ is the premium required by the market for bearing the default risk associated with the bond (2.5 percent in the example).

There are two important lessons to be learned from this basic relationship about default risk and interest rates. First, the promised yield to maturity, which is readily observable in the financial markets, is always higher than the expected yield to maturity, which is not directly observable. Second, expected losses from defaults drive up both expected and promised yields to maturity. This means we should expect more risky instruments to be priced with higher ex ante yields, and this is precisely what we see in the marketplace. This is evident in Figure 20-2, which shows the spreads (or differences) between yields to maturity on AAA and BAA corporate bonds and comparable maturity Treasury bonds over the last decade. Notice that the spreads between BAA bonds and Treasury bonds are consistently larger than the spreads between AAA bonds and Treasuries.

Figure 20-2
Yield spreads between AAA and BAA corporate bonds versus treasury bonds.

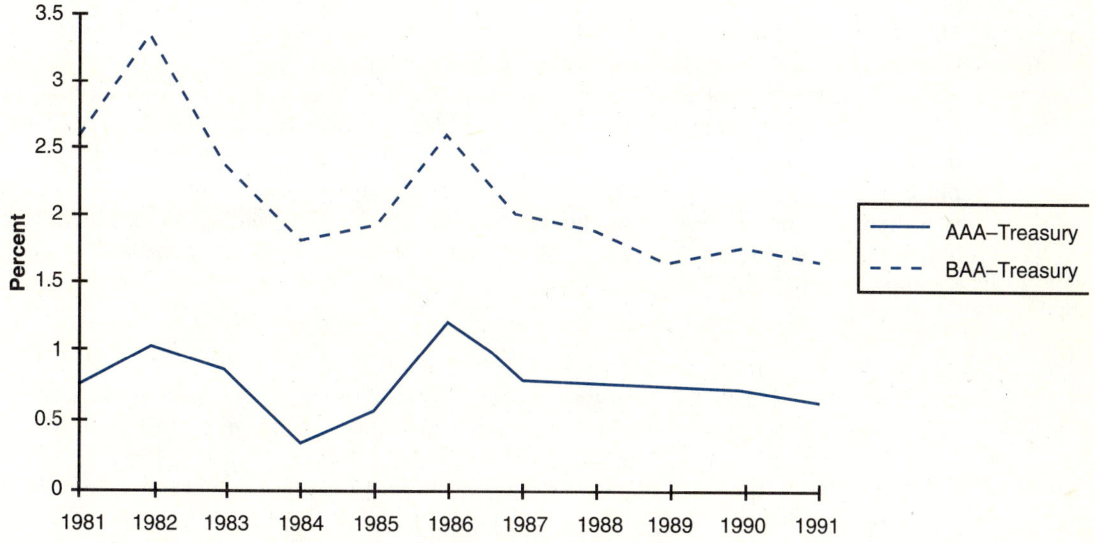

Pricing Credit Risk and Financial Guarantees

We mentioned at the beginning of the chapter that we would approach the issues of pricing and controlling credit risk from (1) the standpoint of a financial intermediary that acts as a portfolio lender and (2) from the standpoint of a financial guarantor. Financial guarantees occur in a variety of ways. In many circumstances, they occur as stand-alone products, or explicit guarantees, which are generally provided by financial intermediaries to "enhance" the credit standing of risky financial claims. For example, third-party guarantees are common in the municipal bond market. Prominent suppliers of such insurance are American Municipal Bond Assurance Corporation (AMBAC) and Municipal Bond Insurance Association (MBIA). Many institutional investors are restricted to investing in "investment grade" securities, that have been given at least the minimum acceptable credit rating by the major rating agencies. Thus, it is advantageous for a municipal issue to be rated as investment grade, as it is then marketable to these large institutional investors. Municipal bond insurance is also attractive to individual investors, and they have become increasingly important purchasers of municipal bonds in recent years.

Another example of a financial guarantee is the letter of credit issued by many banks in conjunction with foreign trade. In the course of financial transactions with foreign companies, a domestic firm often negotiates a letter of credit with its bank. The letter of credit guarantees payment for a specific obligation, usually the purchase of imported goods. The letter of credit specifies that if the importer defaults (fails to make payment), the bank stands ready to make up the shortfall. In return for this guarantee, the domestic company pays the bank a fee. In addition to the many private sources of financial guarantees, in many instances the federal government provides financial guarantees in conjunction with government-assisted loan programs. Residential mortgage, farm, and student loan programs are examples of financial obligations guaranteed by the U.S. government.

While explicit and independent guarantees are very important, it is important to recognize that most guarantees are *implicit.* Indeed, implicit guarantees are manifested throughout debt markets, since virtually all forms of lending can be viewed as taking place in two stages, (1) the purchase of a guarantee and (2) the taking of a loan. More specifically, a default risk–free loan can be assembled by combining a risky loan with a loan guarantee. Accordingly, the value of the risk-free loan can be stated as

$$V_f = V_r + V_g \tag{20.3}$$

where V_f is the value of the default risk–free loan, V_r is the value of the risky loan, and V_g is the value of the loan guarantee. Alternatively, a risky loan can be viewed as a risk-free loan where the borrower pays the value of the guarantee back to the lender—a kind of "rebate" for bearing default risk.

To illustrate this idea, return to the example of the pure discount bond illustrated above. Recall that the value of the bond was determined to be V_r = \$91.40. Given the risk-free rate of 5 percent, the value of a one-year *default risk-free* bond with redemption value of \$100 is

$$V_f = \frac{\$100}{1.05} = \$95.24$$

This implies that the market value of the guarantee to insure the loan against default, as given by equation 20.3 is,

$$V_g = V_f - V_r = \$95.24 - \$91.40 = \$3.84$$

The bond could be viewed as a risk-free bond of \$95.24 with an embedded "rebate" of \$3.84 to the bondholder for bearing default risk. Alternatively, suppose the bond were guaranteed by a third party, say through bond insurance. The bond market would value the insured bond at \$95.24 to yield the risk-free rate of 5 percent, and the bond issuer would pay \$3.84 to guarantee the bond through the third-party insurer. In either case the bond issuer would receive a net cash flow from issuing the bond of \$91.40.

It is important to reemphasize the idea that all risky debt instruments can be viewed as the equivalent of the purchase of a default risk–free contract plus the issue of a guarantee on the contract. The purchase of a risky claim can be viewed as taking place in two stages. In the first stage, the lender buys a risk-free claim. In the second stage, one of two things happens. Either the borrower buys a financial guarantee on the contract which in fact makes the claim risk-free to the lender, or the borrower pays the lender an amount equal to the value of the guarantee. In the case of a AAA-rated bond, the value of the implicit guarantee is relatively small. In the case of a B-rated bond, however, the value of the implicit guarantee is relatively larger.

• So You Want to Apply Options to Financial Guarantees? •

A financial guarantee can be viewed as a put option on the underlying financial contract, written by the guarantor. The put (guarantee) gives the holder the right to sell the guaranteed contract to the guarantor at the exercise price (guaranteed value). If the obligation is guaranteed in full, the exercise price will be the promised value or payment associated with the guaranteed asset. As a put contract, the value of the guarantee on the expiration date is Max $\{0, E-C\}$, where E is the guaranteed value of the underlying contract and C is its actual value on the date payment is due. A graphic profile of the guarantee's payoffs to the holder of the guarantee on its expiration date is provided in Figure 20-3. The horizontal axis measures the actual payment, C, or value associated with the underlying (or guaranteed) contract. E is the guaranteed value of the payment and is effectively the exercise price of the implied put option. $E-C$ is the amount the guarantee is in or out of the money at maturity. Finally, P is the cost of the guarantee or implied premium of the implied put option. Usually the premium is directly or indirectly borne by the beneficiary of the guarantee. For example, in the case of a guaranteed loan, the lender may bear the cost of the guarantee by making a risky loan and buying its own insurance or guarantee against asset loss. Alternatively, the lender may require the borrower to buy the guarantee. In that case, the value of the guarantee would be reflected in a lower interest rate on the loan.

As an example, suppose the discount bond described in Table 20-2 was guaranteed by a third party. In return for the premium to write the guarantee the guarantor promises to pay the bondholder any shortfall occurring under the default states on the bond. This amounts to writing a put option to the bondholder with an exercise price equal to the redemption value of the bond, or $100. The payoffs on the bond and on the guarantee are outlined below in Table 20-2.

Obviously, the exposure to loss by the guarantor is affected directly by changes in the distribution of the guaranteed cash flow. For example, as the probability or magnitude of the default states on the bond increase, the value of the guarantee increases. This is a common characteristic of options. As we showed in Chapter 15, holding everything else constant, the value of an option increases with the variance of the value of the underlying asset, and, since the value of the guarantee represents a liability to the guarantor, the guarantor has obvious incentives to manage its exposure.

Table 20-2

Payoffs on the Financial Guarantee for a Pure Discount Bond

Economic Picture	**Probability $\{C_1\}$**	**C_1 (\$)**	**$E - C_1$ (\$)**
Growth	0.80	100	0
Mild recession	0.10	95	5
Moderate recession	0.05	90	10
Severe recession	0.05	85	15

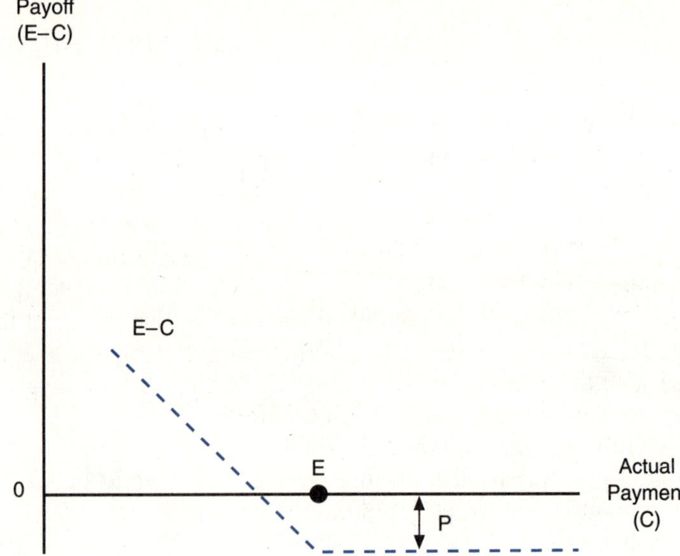

Figure 20-3
Payoff profile of financial guarantee
Source: *Financial Management, Summer 1992, p.84.*

Mechanisms to Control Credit Risk

The traditional approach to evaluating credit risk has been to start with an assessment of the ability of a borrower to repay a loan. Historical financial statements are analyzed to determine the financial health of the borrower and to project how the borrower's financial condition will evolve in the future. For loans to businesses, pro forma sources and uses-of-funds statements are used to project cash flows accruing to the borrower throughout the term of the proposed loan contract. Cash flow forecasts are used to determine the likelihood that the firm will be able to meet scheduled payments of interest and principal. The condition of the borrower's industry, and the strength of economic conditions are also important to the lender in assessing the advisability of a new loan. Lending officers who evaluate individual loan requests are generally specialists in one or more particular industries. In reviewing a loan application, the loan officer is informed about market conditions, competition, potential demand, and other factors that are important in evaluating the feasibility of a loan proposal. While the determination of the borrower's financial condition or capacity defines the firm's vulnerability to an economic downturn, the general assessment of economic conditions helps determine what economic conditions will obtain during the term of the loan.

Both portfolio lenders and independent guarantors are intensely interested in devising mechanisms to control credit risk. At least four considerations are important in controlling credit risk:

1. maintaining a diversified portfolio of risks,
2. collateral and capital requirements,
3. monitoring and covenants, and
4. the character of the borrower.

Diversification

Diversification of risk is a fundamental element in all financial risk management. We first introduced diversification as a way to reduce risk in equity securities in Chapter 3, but diversification of risk is crucial in all types of investments, whether the risk pertains to price fluctuations (as in equities) or to both price fluctuations *and* the ultimate prospect of default (as with bonds). We also emphasized that a lack of geographic diversification is one of the forces that has led to securitization of many financial instruments, particularly mortgages, since much of the risk of default on many instruments is determined by local economic conditions. Therefore, it is particularly important to construct portfolios that are diversified both geographically and with respect to other factors that create nonsystematic risk. Commercial banks and other portfolio lenders generally have guidelines for risk exposures in specific industries as well as regions in order to maintain proper diversification of their credit risk exposure.

There is substantial evidence that many banks have done a rather poor job of developing systems that ensure that their portfolios are well-diversified. The record of loan losses described in the previous section gives substantial indications that many banks followed each other into dangerous loans, particularly loans abroad, during the 1980s. Moreover, most commercial banks are not regionally diversified, and many types of default risk are driven by the performance of a particular region, particularly loans related to real estate.

The need for diversification is also an important determinant of whether credit risk will be borne and managed by the originator of a loan or by a separate guarantor. Consider the situation in the mortgage market. On mortgage loans in which the home buyer borrows more than 80 percent of the appraised value of the home, mortgage lenders often turn to other guarantors to manage exposure to default risk. For instance, mortgage lenders often require the borrower to purchase what is called private mortgage insurance (PMI). Mortgage insurance guarantees repayment of the loan to the lender in the event of a default on the mortgage. For example, suppose a $100,000 home is financed with a 95-percent mortgage ($95,000 loan). Also suppose that in two years, the value of the property falls by 10 percent and the remaining loan balance is $94,000. Then, if the borrower defaults, the lender stands to lose $4000, though if the lender originally requires the borrower to buy PMI in order to receive the loan, the $4000 shortfall is paid by the mortgage insurance company. The mortgage insurer normally charges around 0.5 percent (per annum) of the loan balance to insure the loan. This constitutes the price of the financial guarantee on the mortgage.

The interesting issue surrounding the management of financial guarantees against default concerns the following question: Why does the mortgage insurance company find it advisable to underwrite the default risk of the 95 percent loan whereas the mortgage lender does not? Presumably, the mortgage lender could charge the same insurance premium to underwrite the risk, or embed the premium in the loan via a higher interest rate, or higher loan fees. The answer lies, in part, in the economics of diversification. Recall that the risk-reducing benefits of diversification are generated when investment is divided among many risky assets whose returns have less than perfect positive correlation with each other. The less correlated the returns are with each other, the greater are the opportunities for reducing risk through diversification.

A typical mortgage lender serves a relatively small geographic market. Under most circumstances, changes in the local economy will have a strong influence on the default prospects for the typical mortgage. If a local economy experiences a downturn, business sales may drop off, firms may lay off employees, real estate values may decrease, and mortgage borrowers will find it more difficult to meet mortgage obligations. Thus, there is a strong positive correlation among defaults in a small geographic area. This limits the mortgage lender's ability to diversify default risk. When defaults occur, they have some tendency to occur in bunches, and diversification cannot reduce the portion of risk that stems from systematic factors like economic fluctuations.

A mortgage insurer typically underwrites mortgage default risk on a national, rather than a local, level. For the mortgage insurer, the opportunities for diversification of default risk are much improved, since the risk of the portfolio of guarantees is not driven by the fortunes of any one local economy. In a nationally diversified portfolio, financial guarantees are diversified over many local economies, improving the opportunities for risk reduction. This is the major economic advantage enjoyed by mortgage insurers that allows them to underwrite mortgage default risk more efficiently, and charge lower premiums, than local mortgage-lending institutions. In fact, the fact that most mortgage lenders have not had diversified credit risk exposure led regulators to require that they obtain mortgage insurance for relatively highly-leveraged loans. Remember, ultimately it is the taxpayers, through the Federal Deposit Insurance Corporation (FDIC), who are responsible for the risk in this system.

Capital and Collateral Requirements

An important way to control the risk of loss on a loan is for the borrower to pledge collateral for it. This means that the lender has a claim on a specific asset in the event the borrower defaults. Most personal loans to individuals are collateralized by homes or cars or other assets, and many loans to corporations are collateralized. The value of collateral derives principally from the fact that, in the event of default, the lender does not have to determine the value of the borrower's other assets as long as the collateral is sufficient to cover the amount owed on the loan. Moreover, the lender does not have to absorb the expense of dealing with other general creditors who also may have claims on the borrowers other assets. Collateral thus reduces the costs of dealing with the actual process of default, though if collateral is to be pledged, the lender must investigate the collateral to determine if it is in good condition, to establish its value, and to determine whether or not it is encumbered by other obligations of the borrower, as by being pledged against other loans. During the term of the loan a variety of measures may be employed by the lender to ensure that collateral remains in place and in good condition. One common to commercial loans is called "warehousing." Under a warehousing arrangement, collateral (usually finished goods or product) is physically secured in a warehouse or other location so that the borrower cannot move or tamper with it while the loan is in force. Under other circumstances, monitoring collateral may be much easier. In some situations a loan can be secured by marketable securities. The value of the securities is easily observed in the capital markets, and necessary adjustments in the level of collateral are easily identified.

A lender is also interested in the total level of capital of a borrower. A sufficient capital cushion is important to the lender, to ensure that the borrower can absorb temporary or short-term losses without becoming insolvent or declaring bankruptcy. Capital requirements can serve as a kind of substitute for collateral in circumstances in which marking the value of collateral to market (and requiring infusions of collateral) may be difficult or costly. Difficulties in marking the value of collateral to market may occur when collateral is not easily available to observe or if market prices are observed infrequently. In the case of the futures market, margin accounts are easily observed by the exchange and market values of the accounts are available daily, so collateral works well to control the risk of guarantees to counterparties. In other markets, however, it may be difficult to observe the value of collateral frequently and to require the appropriate adjustments. Take the example of a deposit insurance system like the FDIC, which insures deposits of individual accounts at member institutions up to $100,000. As security against its guarantee to depositors, the FDIC employs the assets of the institution as collateral, though it is difficult for the FDIC to monitor the value of the collateral on a very frequent basis. As a result, the capital cushion serves as an alternative device for risk control. If the capital account is sufficiently large, relative to the value of insured claims against assets, the FDIC can afford to inspect assets less often. Potential losses in the value of collateral (assets) between examinations can be absorbed by equity holders.

To see how capital influences risk, consider the situation of a standard residential mortgage contract. The borrower signs a lien against the property, which the lender holds until the loan is repaid. In the event of default on the loan, the lien gives the lender claim against the value of the property up to the extent of the outstanding balance on the loan. In effect, the home acts as collateral on the mortgage loan. As with any loan, if the value of the collateral falls below the outstanding balance, the lender is exposed to loss in the event of default. That is why, under "standard" terms on new loans, mortgage lenders normally finance as much as 80 percent of the appraised value of the property. This means the borrower must put at least 20 percent equity capital into the home purchase. In the event of a default, the equity cushion protects the lender against changes in the value of the property up to 20 percent of the original value. For example, suppose a home is purchased for $100,000 and financed by an $80,000 mortgage loan and $20,000 equity. Two years later, suppose the remaining balance on the loan is $79,000 (assuming repayment of principal of $1000) and the market value of the property has fallen by 10 percent to $90,000. If the borrower defaults, there is still sufficient liquidation value in the home to insulate the lender from loss. In this case, the lender stands to lose money only if the value of the property has fallen by more than $21,000. And, as the loan continues to be paid down, the lender's position improves, since the outstanding balance decreases over the term of the loan. Thus, the exposure to default risk of 80-percent loans is relatively small. Mortgage lenders often choose to bear the default risk of these loans by retaining the loans in their portfolios without third-party insurance.

Monitoring and Covenants

Covenants associated with most loans and financial guarantees include a number of restrictions designed to control changes in risk that would increase the liability of the guarantor. For example, if a company borrows money via a guaranteed loan, the guarantor may require that the borrower conform to a number of conditions designed to maintain, or improve, the borrower's financial stability. Such constraints could include minimum levels of liquid assets or working capital, maximum limits on dividends, or conditions required to maintain the quality of assets pledged as collateral. To ensure that the covenants associated with the guarantee are observed, the guarantor must monitor the borrower frequently enough to protect itself. When the guarantor detects violations in the covenants, it must seize collateral or accomplish other remedies to control its exposure to future liabilities to the guarantee's beneficiary.

In collateralized loans, restrictions are often placed on the collateral itself and on how it may be managed. These restrictions are intended to ensure that the value of collateral does not deteriorate during the term of the guarantee. In some circumstances, guarantees enjoy what is called "perfected collateral," the circumstance in which the value of collateral posted by the guaranteed party is always sufficient to cover potential liabilities to the guarantor. An example of perfect collateral is the maintenance of margin accounts involved in trading futures contracts over organized futures exchanges. Recall from Chapter 14 that, in order to facilitate futures trading among anonymous counterparties the futures exchange interposes itself between the two sides of the futures contract and assumes all default risk associated with both sides. In effect, the futures exchange issues a financial guarantee to both of the counterparties, insuring them against default by the other counterparty. To protect itself against default against either counterparty, the exchange requires both counterparties to post collateral in the form of a margin deposit. Recall also from Chapter 14 that to ensure that this collateral is sufficient to cover any default exposure the exchange does three things:

1. The exchange imposes daily settlement on outstanding positions and marks individual accounts to market on a daily basis.
2. The exchange imposes margin calls when the account balance falls below a minimum level (maintenance margin).
3. The exchange limits daily price changes to ensure that account balances are always sufficient to absorb maximum daily losses.

A similar system is used by major options exchanges to manage guarantees of performance on options contracts bought and sold over the exchange.

Often, loan agreements specify covenants that are designed to protect or sustain the capital level of the firm. Such covenants could limit the payment of dividends during the life of the loan or prohibit risky ventures that might generate operating or capital losses. In addition, in more recent years loans have incorporated requirements that the borrowers limit their exposure to interest rate or other forms of market risk during the loan. For example, some bank loan agreements require the borrower to hedge exposures to interest rate risk, which might impair the firm's ability to meet bank loan payments. Required hedging might include positions in interest rate options, futures, or swaps to control interest rate risk exposure.

Character

Finally, *character* of the borrower is an important determinant of the overall risk of a potential loan relationship. "Character" refers to the sense of moral responsibility a borrower has toward repayment of debts. In most circumstances, a borrower's reputation is built up over time as part of a long-lasting banking relationship. New loan clients that are small companies or individuals are often screened by asking for character references or recommendations. Credit checks are also performed to learn if a potential borrower has a good credit history with other lenders. Larger companies' credit reputations are often visible in the capital markets. For example, if a company has publicly traded debt, the debt rating assigned by Standard & Poor's or Moody's serves as an evaluation of the firm's credit risk. In addition, the prevailing yield or other measures of the cost of outstanding debt provides a market-based evaluation of the firm's credit risk. A lower required rate of return on unsecured debt (yield to maturity) indicates that the debt market has a more favorable evaluation of the credit risk of the issuer.

• *Marriott Drops a Bombshell with Its Spinoff Proposal* •

An important and interesting example of how bonds can change value as a result of actions taken by a corporation's management, and of the potential value of covenants in protecting against such changes, is provided by Marriott Corporation. For many years Marriott has been in the business of developing, owning, and operating hotels. In the early 1980s Marriott decided to begin to change its business strategy in the direction of deemphasizing hotel ownership and concentrating on management contracts for hotels and on development of hotel properties. This decision was motivated in large part by the large capital requirements necessary to own all the hotels that Marriott could manage and by the relative profitability of the hotel management business as compared to hotel ownership. Through the late 1980s and into the early 1990s Marriott still owned a substantial volume of hotel properties. In October 1992 the company announced that it intended to split the existing Marriott Corporation into two parts, and it accomplished this spinoff one year later, in October 1993. One part, called Host Marriott, owns the bulk of the hotel properties, including 141 Marriott lodging properties and 16 retirement communities. It was been reported that, in 1991, had it been a separate enterprise, Host Marriott would have had sales of about $1.7 billion and operating cash flow of more than $350 million. In addition, Host Marriott retains $2.9 billion of Marriott's long-term debt or all but $20 million of the total Marriott long-term debt outstanding before the proposed spinoff. The other part of Marriott is called Marriott International, Inc. This company manages hotels, provides food and facilities management for health care, business, and educational institutions, and operates retirement communities. Had Marriott International been a stand-alone company in 1991, it is estimated that it would have had revenue of $7.4 billion and operating cash flow before interest and taxes of nearly $500 million.[5] The spinoff was accomplished through a special dividend to existing Marriott stockholders of shares

[5]See Robin Goldwyn Blumenthal. "Marriott to Split Its Business into 2 Entitites." *Wall Street Journal,* October 6, 1992.

in the new enterprises. The Marriott family retained roughly a 25-percent ownership position in both companies, about the same proportion they owned in the existing Marriott Corporation.

Marriott management made a strong case for the efficiencies to be gained by splitting the company into two parts, but existing stockholders there also clearly stood to gain by changing the risk exposure of the long-term bond holders in Marriott. Under the change, Marriott bond holders have claims on the cash flows and assets of Host only, which includes the hotel properties. You can see, from the figures cited above, that most of the cash flow or earning power in Marriott came not from the properties per se, but from the management contracts operated by Marriott. Indeed, it is easily argued that the total value of the intangible assets represented by the management contracts are larger than the tangible assets of real estate, though the intangible assets of management contracts do not appear on the company's balance sheet.

The stock and bond markets responded rather strongly to the Marriott announcement. The *Wall Street Journal* reported that the day after the announcement the price of Marriott stock rose by 12 percent, though the stock market as a whole declined that day. During the same time period, the value of Marriott's outstanding bonds declined by roughly 30 percent. This decline reflected the bond market's perception that the risk of the bonds had increased since the capacity and capital of the company supporting those bonds had declined as a result of the proposed spinoff.

Investors in Marriott bonds responded to the proposed spinoff and the resulting decline in bond values in at least two ways. First, they took legal action to block the spinoff. Second, they pressured the investment banking community, who sells them bonds, to stop this action. In fact, Merrill Lynch, the lead advisor to Marriott in the proposed spinoff, chose to withdraw from the transaction in response to the pressure that bond investors placed on their bond traders and salespeople. In addition, Marriott management has adjusted the terms of the proposed spinoff to cushion the blow to the bond holders to some degree.

Some observers believe that the actions of Marriott's management may be both illegal and unethical, but it appears that the case for either point is not as strong as it might be. On the legal front, bond holders are free to include covenants that place restrictions on management that are designed to prevent actions that much reduce the credit quality of outstanding bonds. If they choose not to use those covenants, as the Marriott bond holders chose not to do, they are exposed to this type of risk. One commentator on the issue cited the case of *Katz v. Oak Industries* (1986), where the Delaware Chancery Court wrote, "the terms of the contractual relationship agreed to, and not broad concepts such as fairness, define the corporation's duty to bond holders."[6]

You might well ask why bondholders did not impose covenants that could have made it difficult or impossible for Marriott to change the risk of outstanding bonds to such a degree. One such covenant would have been a covenant on unusual dividends, since the proposed transaction involves such a dividend. Of course, we cannot know for sure why covenants were excluded, but we know that Marriott management had a strong reputation for integrity. It is highly likely that at least some bond holders view this action as unethical and, to the extent that they do, Marriott's reputation with these investors will be tarnished. We leave it to you to judge whether this was a wise management decision.

[6]See Kenneth Lehn. "The Lessons of Marriott." *Wall Street Journal,* March 11, 1993, p. A–14.

Quantification of the Credit Evaluation Process

Now that we have some understanding of the factors that influence credit risk, we want briefly to turn our attention to the quantitative procedures currently in use to assess credit risk. One reason to do so is that in 1993 an important issue regarding regulatory policy toward banks was whether the increased regulatory standards imposed by FIDICIA (see Chapters 5 and 6) have compelled banks to rely less on the more intangible criteria for evaluating credit risks and to rely strictly on more concrete standards captured by capital and collateral.

Increasingly, most lenders and independent guarantors are relying more on statistical and quantitative screening or credit scoring systems to evaluate credit risk. Once a credit score or evaluation is obtained, the borrower is generally assigned a credit category (prime credit risks, low-risk, intermediate-risk, high-risk credits, or unacceptable credits). In each category, the lender would design more or less standard terms of lending for qualifying firms that would specify available rates of interest, term limits, collateral requirements, and protective covenants.

One of the pioneers in the development of such methods has been Professor Edward Altman of New York University. In the late 1960s, Professor Altman performed an extensive statistical evaluation of companies that experienced financial distress. His objective was to determine which, if any, financial characteristics of the firm could reliably predict financial distress leading to bankruptcy. Altman developed a model that measured, or scored, firms for the likelihood that they would experience financial distress. The measure, commonly called Altman's Z score, is a function of five important financial ratios:

1. the ratio of sales to assets (a measure of "asset turnover");
2. the ratio of market value of equity to book value of debt (a "leverage" measure);
3. the ratio of earnings to assets (a measure of "return on assets");
4. the ratio of retained earnings to assets (another "leverage" ratio); and
5. the ratio of working capital to assets (a "liquidity" ratio).

Altman's Z has been the basis for systems used by commercial banks principally in their commercial lending operations. The model has two important applications. First, it is used in conjunction with other screening techniques to classify new loan clients. Second, and probably more important, it is used to monitor the financial health of outstanding loan clients. For example, commercial borrowers are regularly required to submit financial information to the lender to maintain their credit lines and to have their credit standing routinely evaluated. Altman's model can be used to help detect important changes in the financial condition of commercial clients and to provide early warning of problem loans.

An important limitation of Altman's model is that it was developed using information about financial distress and bankruptcy for larger firms (for which financial data was available). Thus, it cannot be applied reliably to other classes of borrowers such as consumers or small business. Nevertheless, it is significant that important factors associated with the model (e.g., leverage, return on assets, and liquidity) are factors that obviously are essential to an effective risk evaluation of almost all classes of lending.

How Effective Are Credit Risk Evaluations?

An obvious question we might want to ask is, how effective are the systems in place for evaluating credit risk? This is difficult to determine from the performance of financial intermediaries other than by inference from their actual losses on loans. A more direct measure of the effectiveness of evaluation techniques can be based on the historical record of the debt-rating agencies.

In evaluating the default risk of publicly traded debt, the market relies to a great extent on information provided by two major rating agencies that operate to assess the default risk of specific corporate and municipal debt bond issues, Standard & Poor's and Moody's. As we indicated in Chapter 2, when we first introduced these rating agencies, they evaluate new and outstanding bond issues and provide a default risk rating that summarizes the risk of default associated with each issue. Many factors are taken into account in establishing a bond rating, including the capacity of the issuer to meet scheduled interest and principal payments, the seniority of the issue with respect to other obligations of the issuer, the protection afforded by debt insurance or other financial guarantees provided by third parties, among others.

The major rating categories established by Standard & Poor's to classify corporate and municipal bond issues are listed in Table 20-3. Bonds rated in categories from AAA to BBB are referred to as "investment grade" bonds. Those rated below BBB are regarded as "speculative" to varying degrees. To most issuers, a rating of BBB or higher is important, since many institutional investors are restricted to investing only in investment grade securities. Institutional investors represent a rather large segment of the bond market. Thus, an investment grade rating can be an advantage in selling a new issue.

The ability of Standard & Poor's to anticipate defaults and to rate bond issues accordingly has been documented by Altman (1992). For 556 issues that defaulted during the period from 1970 to 1991, Altman determined the original rating on the issue, the rating one year before the default, and the rating six months before the default. The results of his observations are reproduced in Table 20-3.

Of the 556 issues that eventually defaulted, 146 issues (26.3 percent) were originally investment grade, and 410 (73.7 percent) were originally speculative grade (so-called junk bonds, which were discussed earlier). The table also shows that the proportion of issues that were still rated as investment grade one year before default and six months before default were 9.7 percent, and 7.7 percent, respectively.[7] This documents the agency's ability to correctly detect likely defaults as the actual default approaches. Notice that, though these proportions may appear high to some people, the proportion of defaults that are still investment grade grows smaller as default becomes imminent. Altman also notes that none of the issues were rated as investment grade at the time of default. This evidence is cited by some, including Standard & Poor's, as support for the overall accuracy of their ratings.

---

[7]Altman also note that only 3.2 percent of defaulting issues would be rated as investment grade six months before default, if defaulting issues from *one company* (23 issues by Columbia Gas System) were excluded.

Table 20-3
Rating Distribution* of Defaulted Issues at Various Points Prior to Default, 1970–1991

	Originating Rating		Rating One Year Prior to Default		Rating Six Months Prior to Default	
	Number	**Percentage(%)**	**Number**	**Percentage (%)**	**Number**	**Percentage (%)**
	5	0.9	0	0.0	0	0.0
AA	19	3.4	0	0.0	0	0.0
A	60	10.8	2	0.4	2	0.4
BBB	62	11.2	45	9.3	36	7.3
Total investment grade	146	26.3	47	9.7	38	7.7
BB	59	10.6	47	9.8	29	5.9
B	266	47.8	238	49.4	199	40.4
CCC	81	14.6	137	28.4	198	40.2
CC	4	0.7	10	2.1	25	5.1
C	0	0.0	3	0.6	3	0.6
Total noninvestment grade	410	73.7	435	90.3	454	92.3
Total	556	100.0	482	100.0	492	100.0

*Based on Standard & Poor's bond ratings.

An interesting additional question pertains to whether the rating agencies are able to generate any information about future default rates that hasn't already been figured out by investors in the rated bonds. One way to address this question is to ask whether changes in ratings on outstanding bonds by the bond-rating agencies cause a significant reaction in the prices of the bonds of the companies that are experiencing the rating change. A number of academic studies have been carried out to test this rather interesting question. The general consensus is that rating changes are largely anticipated by the market. That is, the rating agencies really aren't any smarter or quicker than investors in figuring out what is happening to change the risk of companies with publicly traded bonds. So when the rating agencies announce rating changes, it is generally taken as old news. It is important to see that this does not mean that the rating agencies perform no useful function. Indeed, the rating agencies have made a profit charging companies for ratings for many years and have therefore passed the relevant market test. But we suspect that their real value is in the screening of new issues, rather than in the monitoring over time of the risk of outstanding issues.

Managing Default Risk in Swaps and Derivative Securities

Many financial institutions, including commercial and investment banks, are heavily involved in providing a variety of "off–balance sheet" financial products to customers, including derivative securities such as interest rate swaps, financial futures and options, and interest rate caps and floors. In many cases, larger commercial and investment banks act as market makers in over-the-counter derivatives. These activities present a different set of credit risk exposures that are similar to those associated with implicit guarantees in risky assets and liabilities.

In making a market in over-the-counter derivatives, banks or other financial firms act as counterparty to the derivative product. For example, commercial banks are actively involved as market makers in the market for interest rate swaps. In making a market for swaps, the bank quotes prices at which it will take either the fixed-pay or variable-pay side of a swap. Once a swap deal is made, the bank acts as the counterparty to the swap and assumes the risk associated with default by the opposite counterparty. Even when individual swap agreements are set off against each other, so that the bank is not exposed to interest rate risk, the bank still acts as a credit intermediary and bears the credit risk on both swap counterparties in a matched transaction. Next we want to turn our attention to the credit risk to which these institutions are exposed. We want to start by discussing the default risk involved in a swap and then move on to various methods that market makers in the derivatives and swaps markets have used to limit and manage their risk exposure.

What Causes a Default on a Swap?

The single most important thing to understand about the default risk of swaps is that it is *not* the same as the default risk for a loan of the same amount and maturity and to the same counterparty. This was a common source of confusion in the early years of the swap market and it is still the source of much mischief. To understand the distinction between default risk of a loan and default risk of a swap, recall that the notional principal of a swap never changes hands. For example, a market maker who takes the floating side of a swap for $50 million has not lent the counterparty to that swap $50 million, and therefore, is not exposed to the potential loss of $50 million and does not have to charge a price to compensate him for this loss. By contrast, if that market maker made a regular loan to the same firm for $50 million, he could lose the $50 million and would have an incentive to price the loan accordingly. There is no reason to expect the price extracted from a counterparty by a market maker—say a spread in the range of 10 to 15 basis points—to be comparable to the price that might be charged to the same customer for a loan of the same amount and maturity, possibly 100 or 150 basis points. It is therefore erroneous to infer that, because spreads on swaps are much less than risk premiums on loans, swaps are underpricing the default risk in these instruments. Of course, they may be underpricing this risk, but the analogy to loan pricing provides no evidence of such behavior.

The key to understanding the default risk of a swap is to recognize that two events must occur simultaneously if there is to be a default on a swap. First, one counterparty in the swap must experience financial distress, even file for bankruptcy. Second, the price of the swap must be such that from the vantage point of the counterparty in distress, the swap is under water. This means that this counterparty would have to pay some amount, rather than be paid, to buy out the swap. To see why both of these conditions are necessary, let's consider them one at a time. Suppose the second condition applied. Let's make this more concrete by considering the example we introduced in Chapter 16 of a firm known as Baa that is paying fixed and receiving floating in a swap that we will assume has two years remaining. Let the current date be March 1, 1994. Recall that Baa is paying 12 percent fixed. Now suppose that the going price on two-year London interbank offer rate (LIBOR) swaps is only 10 percent. This means that the best the market maker could do if it tried to replace Baa on this swap is receive 10 percent rather than 12 percent. If Baa wanted out of the swap without defaulting, it would have to buy out the market maker by paying the present value of the 200–basis point spread multiplied by the notional principal over two years. Would Baa walk away or default on this obligation? Firms that expect to avoid being sued or want to maintain good relationships with those with whom they do business do not default on such obligations simply because the price has moved against them. Unless this firm is experiencing financial distress and is considering defaulting on many or all of its financial obligations, it will honor the swap agreement.

Now suppose the firm does get into financial distress and even declares Chapter 11 bankruptcy. Suppose also that the price on new two-year LIBOR swaps is 14 percent rather than 10 percent. Would the counterparty default on the swap? Notice that the swap is now a valuable asset to Baa and to those who are handling its bankruptcy. It now has a value equal to the present value of the 200–basis point spread multiplied by the notional principal over two years. Baa would no more default on this obligation than it would abandon any other valuable asset on which it has a claim. Thus, the default risk to the market maker in a swap depends on both a counterparty experiencing financial distress and the right (or wrong, depending on your point of view) movement in interest rates.

The Expected Loss on a Swap

Probably the most direct way to think about the default risk on any fixed-income instrument is to divide the expected cost of default into two parts. The expected loss or cost is determined both by the probability of default and by the expected loss if default occurs. That is,

$$\text{Expected loss from default} = \text{Probability of default} \times \text{Expected loss with default}$$

In a traditional loan, the expected loss if default occurs depends on how much of the loan amount can be recovered. This, in turn, depends on the quality of the borrower's assets or its viability as a going concern. In a swap, the expected loss, given that a default occurs, is not really an issue with regard to the quality of the counterparty's assets, or its business at all. Instead, this conditional expected loss is entirely a matter of interest rate risk, that is, in what direction and how far the swap price has moved away from the price of the existing swap. Of course, the kind of events that can trigger financial distress for a borrower or counterparty, and so create a situation where a default might occur, are exactly the same for a regular loan and for a swap. But that is as far as the similarity can be carried.

The questions of exactly how large the risk of default on swaps may be and how to determine the appropriate price for a swap are topics that have been of keen interest to the market makers in the swaps market, their customers, and the bank regulators who oversee the commercial banks who act as market makers. Research work in this area has involved simulations of the likely performance of a swap given possible future paths for interest rates. The plausibility of alternative paths for interest rates can be gauged by using as a guide the historical variability of interest rates. A number of such simulation experiments have been conducted, by independent researchers and by regulators, in the United States and Europe. Many of these studies are in the public domain, so their procedures and findings can be scrutinized. One study reports that the expected loss if a default occurs takes the values reported in Table 20-4. This study assumed that the relevant volatility of the underlying interest rate was 23 percent, which to some observers is a bit high. The table indicates that the expected loss on, say, a three-year swap would be 1.79 percent of the notional principal. This still doesn't tell us the expected loss on the swap, because we have to weight it by an estimate of the probability of default, or in effect by the probability of distress. That is, the expected loss is the product of the expected cost of buying out the swap and the probability of default. If we use estimates of default probability that reflect the experience of industrial firms in the United States, we end up with substantially lower estimates of prices for default risk on swaps than those on comparable regular debt. So it should not be surprising that we see premiums extracted by market makers in the swaps market that are substantially smaller than those same market makers would demand for a loan of the same amount as the notional principal of a swap to the same counterparty.

Managing Credit Risk for Market Makers in Derivative Securities

Banks that participate in the over-the-counter derivatives market are concerned not only with their own default exposure to customer counterparties but with their own credit rating. If the bank's liabilities are perceived by the market to be too risky, it will find it difficult to participate in the over-the-counter swaps market. Recently, the bankruptcy of several major market makers, including Drexel Burnham Lambert, have created increased credit sensitivity in the derivatives market. That is, the credit standings of many major participants have been downgraded, and some companies have limited their exposure to AAA- or AA-rated counterparties. Having realized that a high-quality credit rating is essential to a continued presence in the derivatives market, some market makers have taken steps to enhance their credit

Table 20-4
Estimates of Conditional Expected Loss as Percentage of Notional Principal by Maturity of Swap

Maturity (yr)	**1**	**3**	**5**	**7**	**10**
Conditional expected loss (%)	0.43	1.79	3.15	4.45	6.74

Source: J. Greg Whittaker. "Interest Rate Swaps: Risk and Regulation." *Economic Review,* [Federal Reserve Bank of Kansas City] (March 1987), pp. 3–13.

standing in the market.[8] We discuss some of the more important solutions to these problems that have been pursued recently.

Special-Purpose Vehicles

One mechanism that has been used recently to enhance the credit standing of derivative operations is to isolate the derivative business from the rest of the firm as a separate entity or subsidiary. Such entities are called special-purpose vehicles (SPVs). This is very similar to the arrangement discussed in Chapter 18, by which special-purpose companies are created for securitized assets. The objective of establishing an SPV is chiefly to achieve a higher credit rating than the parent's. In the early 1990s, both Goldman Sachs and Merrill Lynch have established SPVs to improve their derivative products capabilities. In each case the parent contributed significant capital to the SPV. Both SPVs received AAA ratings, whereas the parent firms had A + ratings on senior unsecured debt.

The credit market risk associated with the SPV's business is limited by setting certain limits designed to contain default risk—minimum credit ratings, maximum limits on aggregate exposure to a single client, limits of exposure to certain countries, among others.

Bilateral Netting

Another mechanism used to control credit risk in derivative markets, bilateral netting, allows two counterparties to collapse the outstanding obligations of several contracts or agreements against each other, restating those agreements as one net obligation. Bilateral netting works much like a clearinghouse for interbank settlements. The following example illustrates the idea. Suppose a bank, say Bank A, is owed a present value of $100 million on interest rate swaps by Bank B. At the same time, Bank B is owed $50 million by Bank A in currency swaps. Notice that these numbers are not the notional principals of outstanding swaps but the present value of the cash flow streams due to each counterparty. The notional principals would be much larger than these amounts. By netting the obligations, the credit exposure of Bank A could be cut in half and the credit exposure of bank B could be cut to zero.

To see this, suppose there were no netting arrangement and Bank B went into default. The $50 million obligation owed by A to B cannot be immediately applied against the $100 million owed by B to A. They are different contracts between the firms, involving different products. In a bankruptcy, Bank A's $50 million obligation is but one of the assets of Bank B against which all general creditors of the firm have a claim. At the same time, Bank A's $100 million claim against Bank B means only that A is but one of many general creditors against B's assets. Thus, while Bank A still owes the full $50 million associated with the currency swap, it likely will not receive full value for the interest rate swap. Suppose Bank B's assets (including A's obligation) are liquidated and distributed to creditors on a prorata

[8]See Behof (1993) for a detailed discussion.

basis at 50 cents on the dollar. Bank A receives $50 million on its $100 million claim against Bank B. In that case, Bank A's claims and obligations on the two swaps wash out—$50 million apiece. Bilateral netting can make a substantial contribution toward reducing credit exposure, especially if it is carried out across products, as in the example above. If the two swaps had been netted out prior to the insolvency of Bank B, Bank A would have shown a net claim against Bank B of $50 million, which, at 50 percent liquidation value, would have paid Bank A $25 million. Moreover, it would have owed nothing, so it would have come out with a net of $25 million. This is $25 million more than before the netting took place. Also notice that Bank B would have no credit exposure against bank A after the netting though it would have had an exposure of $50 million without the netting.

Pledging Collateral

Many participants in the interbank derivatives market have used the pledging of collateral to manage risk of default between themselves and in agreements with corporate counterparties. These arrangements can be either unilateral or bilateral agreements in which cash or securities are pledged against the outstanding obligation. For example, in the case of a swap agreement, the counterparties may have different credit ratings, say an AAA-rated counterparty and an A-rated counterparty. To make the agreement, the AAA counterparty may require an A-rated firm to pledge collateral in the form of cash or marketable securities as security against default. Or, in an agreement between two A-rated firms, both counterparties may agree to pledge collateral.

The role played by collateral in over-the-counter swap agreements or other derivatives is similar that of the margin deposits that must be established for exchange-traded derivative products like futures and options. In fact, it is common for over-the-counter agreements to require the amount of collateral to change as the value of the obligation changes. This is the functional equivalent of the practice of marking positions to market and imposing margin calls, which is a standard characteristic of exchange-traded derivatives. For example, in a bilateral collateral agreement, say on an interest rate swap, each counterparty would pledge collateral at the inception of the swap. Suppose Counterparty A agrees to receive fixed from, and pay variable to, Counterparty B. Being of the same A-rated credit standing, both agree to pledge the same initial collateral. Suppose interest rates go up. This causes A to have a net obligation to B. As interest rates continue to increase, the bilateral agreement may require A to post *additional* collateral to insure that future payments will be made to B. At the same time, B may be allowed to recover some of its pledged collateral. This process is almost identical to that of marking positions to market in futures markets and the maintenance of margin deposits.

Mark to Market Cash Settlements

Another mechanism for managing credit risk in over-the-counter derivative markets involves periodic cash settlement of the value of net position. This procedure is similar to the one above that involves collateral, but in this case no explicit collateral is pledged to guarantee future settlement. In this case, counterparties to an agreement such as an interest rate swap would agree to periodically mark the value of the agreement to market by accomplishing a cash settlement between counterparties. This eliminates the accumulation of a large obligation that might precipitate default, and in the event of default, it ensures that the implied loss will not have grown too large at any point in time.

To illustrate this technique, recall the example above for a swap involving counterparties A and B. As interest rates rise during the course of the swap, the fixed payer, Counterparty B, becomes the receiver of net cash flows. As interest rates continue to rise, the risk of default by Counterparty A increases. To moderate credit risk, the swap agreement may specify that the agreement be periodically marked to market with an associated cash settlement. In our example, A would pay B a cash sum equal to the net value of B's position (e.g., the present value of net payment over the remaining term of the swap). This is tantamount to A buying itself out of the existing swap. At the same time the terms of the swap would be marked to market. That is, the fixed rate received by A would be increased to the market rate on new swaps. Then the process starts over again, with either counterparty having the same chance to accumulate a net cash payment from the other, depending on whether rates continue to go up (in B's favor) or go down (in A's favor).

Other Credit Enhancement Techniques

Other credit enhancement techniques are employed to reduce the exposure to over-the-counter products. Most of the remaining techniques currently in use involve some form of third-party support or financial guarantee. Sometimes, a counterparty to an agreement such as a swap contract purchases a third-party guarantee from a bank or other intermediary. The guarantee may be in the form of a letter of credit, guaranteeing payment of a future obligation. Other forms of guarantee occur as credit insurance or private portfolio insurance. In each case, the credit-enhanced counterparty pays the intermediary a fee to underwrite the credit risk associated with the contract. To manage its exposure to the guarantee, the intermediary sometimes requires collateral or compensating balances (cash deposits by the counterparty) against the value of outstanding obligations.

SUMMARY

A major function of modern financial intermediaries is the evaluation and management of credit or default risk. The very nature of financial intermediation creates the need to manage such risks on both sides of the balance sheet. In this chapter, we introduced the basic concepts of default risk and credit risk management. We started by focusing on the connection between market interest rates and default risk. We reviewed the basic relationship between default risk and interest rates, which we originally introduced in Chapter 9. Then we emphasized that all risky loans can be viewed as a combination of a risk-free loan and a financial guarantee. We also examined this relationship using our understanding of options. Then we examined the historical record on loss experience of commercial banks. In recent years losses as a percentage of total assets peaked in 1987. As a result, we examined some of the actions of major U. S. commercial banks to deal with LDC debt, which was so serious in 1987. We also examined the recent performance of junk bonds and discussed the role of LBOs in junk bond returns.

We moved on to consider systems or processes for managing credit risk in private and public debt markets. We considered several specific mechanisms banks and other bond investors use to control credit risk, including diversification, monitoring and covenants, collateral and capital requirements, and character of the borrower. For the public bond market, we explained how bond-rating agencies are important in rating the default potential of publicly traded issues and we discussed the predictive power of ratings.

We also examined the default risk of swaps and other derivatives. The key here is to understand that the default on a swap involves two distinct events. First, the counterparty must experience financial distress so that it will default on it liabilities. Second, swap prices must have moved against this counterparty, so that its swap is under water. If the swap goes into default, the loss on it is not the same as that would be on a loan of the same notional principal. Instead, the loss is determined by the amount of the deviation between the price on the swap and current prices on new swaps that have the same characteristics. Thus, the risk of default on a swap is very different from the default risk in traditional lending. Finally, we discussed methods that are now being used in swap and derivative markets to limit credit exposure, including special-purpose vehicles, bilateral netting, pledging collateral, and market-to-market cash settlements.

QUESTIONS

1. XS Corporation, a large manufacturer of luggage and travel accessories, has just made an issue of five-year, noncallable notes for $50 million. The notes are scheduled to pay 8 percent coupon interest per year and were sold at par. Given XS's financial position, Standard & Poor's gave the issue a BAA rating. On the issue date, the yield on five-year non-callable Treasury debt was 6 percent. XS's debt issue can be viewed as being composed of two claims: a risk-free debt issue sold by the issuer to the borrower, plus a financial guarantee on the issue sold by the borrower to the issuer. Determine the value of each of these components and show how they comprise the total value of XS Corporation's debt.
2. Discuss the economic importance of an announcement by a commercial bank of its intention to increase its reserve for loan losses. Why was Citicorp's announcement of a $3 billion addition to loan loss reserves in 1987 accompanied by an increase in their stock price?
3. Describe the major mechanisms used by banks and other institutional lenders to control the credit risk of their loan portfolios.

4. Why have Special Purpose Vehicles (SPVs) recently become a popular way for investment banks to provide derivative products to their customers?
5. Explain how default on a swap obligation has different implications for the counterparties involved than does default on a bond with a similar maturity.
6. How does bilateral netting reduce the exposure to loss associated with two counterparties engaged in multiple swaps?
7. Assess the performance of the major public debt rating agencies in assessing the credit risk of public debt issues. Do the rating agencies appear to have access to special financial information which the market does not? Why or why not?
8. A zero-coupon bond with ten years to maturity is priced to give a promised yield-to-maturity of 10 percent. According to the market's assessment of the issuer's credit risk, the expected payoff from the security at maturity is 85 percent of the face value (par value) of the security. What is the (ex ante) expected yield-to-maturity?
9. Suppose you estimate the probability that a typical counterparty will experience financial distress by the end of the next year at 1 percent. Also suppose you think the chance swap prices will go down below current levels at the end of one year is as follows for the increments listed:

100 basis points	25 percent
200 basis points	10 percent
300 basis points	5 percent

Suppose you are receiving fixed in a new $10 million fixed-for-floating swap with a two-year maturity. Suppose the zero-coupon yield curve is specified as in problem 10 in Chapter 16. Estimate the expected loss due to default risk from the typical counterparty at the end of year one as a percentage of notional principal.

REFERENCES

Altman, E.I. "Revisiting the High-Yield Bond Market." *Financial Management* 21 (Summer 1992), pp. 78–92.

Altman, E.I. "Financial Ratios, Discriminant Analysis and the Prediction of Corporate Bankruptcy." *Journal of Finance* 23 (Sept 1968), pp. 589–611.

"A Survey of International Banking." *The Economist,* (1993).

Becketti, S. "The Truth About Junk Bonds." *Economic Review,* [Federal Reserve Bank of Kansas City] 75 (July/Aug 1990), pp. 45–54.

Behof, J.P. "Reducing Credit Risk in Over-the-Counter Derivitives." *Economic Perspectives* [Federal Reserve Bank of Chicago] 17 (Jan/Feb 1993), pp. 21–31.

Benston, G.J. "The Furure of Asset Securitization: The Benefits and Costs of Breaking Up the Bank." *Journal of Applied Corporate Finance* 5 (Spring 1992), pp. 71–82.

Cooper, I. A., and A. S. Mello. "The Default Risk of Swaps." *Journal of Finance* 46 (June 1991), pp. 597–620.

Kaplan, S., and J. Stein. "How Risky is the debt of highly leveraged transactions?" *Journal of Financial Economics* 30 (1990), pp. 215–246.

Merton, R.C "On the Pricing of Corporate Debt: The Risk Structure of Interest Rates." *Journal of Finance* 29(May 1974), pp. 449–470.

Merton, R.C., and Z. Bodie. "On the Management of Financial Guarantees." *Financial Management* 21 (Winter 1992), pp. 87–109.

Randall, R.E. "Can the Market Evaluate Asset Quality Exposure in Banks." *New England Economic Review* [Federal Reserve Bank of Boston] (July/August, 1989), pp. 3–24.

Rosengren, E.S. "The Case for Junk Bonds." *New England Economic Review* [Federal Reserve Bank of Boston] (May/June 1990), pp. 40–49.

Simons, K. "Measuring Credit Risk in Interest Rate Swaps." *New England Economic Review* [Federal Reserve Bank of Boston] (Nov/Dec 1989), pp. 29–38.

Whittaker, J. G. "Interest Rate Swaps: Risk and Regulation." *Economic Review* [Federal Reserve Bank of Kansas City] 72 (March 1987), pp. 3–13.

• *Chapter 21*

Managing Interest Rate Risk

This chapter and the next one deal with the management of interest rate risk. We have already discussed interest rate risk a number of times throughout this book. Here, we want to concentrate on the analytical tools and techniques that can be used by financial institutions to manage such risk. Recall that in Chapter 9 we introduced three sources of risk for fixed-income securities: market value risk, reinvestment risk, and prepayment risk. In this chapter and the next we explore these sources of interest rate risk in more detail and provide an analytical framework for identifying, measuring, and controlling exposure to interest rate changes. In this chapter we focus on the connection between maturity and the value of a fixed-income security and introduce the concept of duration. We start by examining what is called the "coupon effect." We show how duration can be used to measure the sensitivity of the value of a security to interest rate changes. (Duration has its limitations, which we discuss.) We also describe how to prepare a GAP report, in order to quantify the magnitude of the mismatch between the interest rate exposure on the asset and liability sides of a firm's balance sheet. Then we examine how changes in the duration of assets and liabilities affect the duration of the equity of a company. Finally, we see how, using duration, to immunize a portfolio of fixed-income securities against changes in interest rates. Management of the risk of fixed-income securities has increasingly become a crucial element of the business of financial institutions, particularly commercial banks. All of the techniques we discuss in this chapter and the next are an essential part of the tool kit of modern financial management.

• *Concepts to Learn in Chapter 21* •

- How interest rate changes influence bond prices for different maturities
- How to measure and use duration
- The limitations of duration
- How to construct a GAP report
- How to immunize a bond portfolio

Coupon Effect and Duration

Let's begin by focusing on the connection between maturity and interest rate risk. Everything else being the same, the longer the term to maturity on a fixed income instrument, the more sensitive the instrument is to a given change in interest rates.

For example, suppose the zero-coupon yield curve is flat at 12 percent. Consider two zero-coupon bonds that have the same price. The first—call it Bond A—pays $1762.34 in five years; the second, Bond B, pays $3105.85 in ten years. Given these two rather peculiar maturity values, both bonds are currently priced at $1000:

Bond A	Bond B
$P = \$1{,}000 = \dfrac{\$1{,}762.34}{(1.12)^5}$	$P = \$1{,}000 = \dfrac{\$3{,}105.85}{(1.12)^{10}}$

What happens to the price of each bond if the zero-coupon yield curve shifts up to 14 percent? Substituting 14 percent into our calculation for each bond implies a price for Bond A of $915.30; a 14-percent yield on Bond B implies a price for B of $837.78. For the same 2-percent increase in market yield, the price of A dropped by $84.70 whereas the price of B dropped by $162.22.

The important difference between the two bonds was their term to maturity. The term to maturity of Bond B was twice that of Bond A. At the same time, the price of Bond B dropped by roughly twice as much as that of Bond A. Thus, the general implication seems to be that the longer the bond's term to maturity, the more sensitive is the bond's price to changes in yield. Moreover, the difference in price changes appears to be proportional to the difference in term to maturity. Indeed, it turns out that these implications are generally true for zero-coupon bonds out; the connection between term to maturity and price risk is more complicated than we have so far demonstrated. In particular, with more complex securities, term to maturity is not an effective index of price sensitivity or risk. To see why we need to explore the coupon effect.

The Coupon Effect

The coupon effect is a characteristic of coupon-bearing bonds that pertains to differences in price sensitivity, which derive from differences in coupon rate. We show here that two bonds with identical maturities produce different changes in price when the same change in the discount rate is applied to their cash flows. This contradicts the general implications just defined for the price sensitivity of zero-coupon bonds and is directly attributable to differences in coupon rates among bonds.

Tables 21-1 and 21-2 illustrate the coupon effect by comparing the price sensitivity of two bonds to changes in a common discount rate. Note that we are assuming here that we can apply a single common discount rate to all cash flows for both bonds. Table 21-1 illustrates the effect of yield changes on the price of a 6 percent coupon bond. This table tabulates the price of a 6 percent bond for alternative annual discount rates of 4 percent, 6 percent, and 8 percent and alternative maturities of 20, 10, 5, and 1 year. The prices calculated assume a $1000 face value. For each combination of term to maturity and discount rate the price is the present value of the stream of $30 semiannual coupon payments plus the present value of $1000

Table 21-1
Price Sensitivity of 6 Percent Coupon Bond (Semiannual Interest Payments)

n \ r	8%	6%	4%	Price Range
40	$802	$1000	$1273	$471
20	$864	$1000	$1163	$299
10	$919	$1000	$1089	$170
2	$981	$1000	$1019	$37

P = $30[PVA; r/2; n] + $1000[PVF; r/2; n]; n = number of semiannual payments remaining; r = annual yield-to-maturity

face value, all discounted at the semiannual yield (annual yield divided by two). Or, letting P equal the price of the bond,

$$P = 30\left(\frac{1-\left[\frac{1}{(1+r/2)^n}\right]}{r/2}\right) + \$1000\left[\frac{1}{(1+r/2)^n}\right] \tag{21.1}$$

where r is annual yield-to-maturity and n is the number of semiannual periods remaining to maturity.

The prices tabulated in Table 21-1 demonstrate that the impact of a change in the yield on the price of the bond depends in an important way on the term to maturity of the bond. Notice the effect of a 2-percent swing in interest rates on the 20-year bond (n is 40). If rates go up by 2 percent, the price falls to $802—almost a $200 loss. If rates go down by 2 percent, the price increases to $1273—a gain of $273. The difference between these two outcomes is $471. Thus, the range of prices spanned by an interest rate change of plus or minus 2 percent is $471. At the other end of the maturity spectrum, if the same bond had only one year remaining to maturity, the same swing in interest rates would produce a range of price shifts of only $37.

It is clear from this example that the price sensitivity of the 6 percent bond, with respect to changes in yield, increases with maturity. This can be easily visualized in

Figure 21-1
Price, yield, and maturity of 6-percent coupon bond.

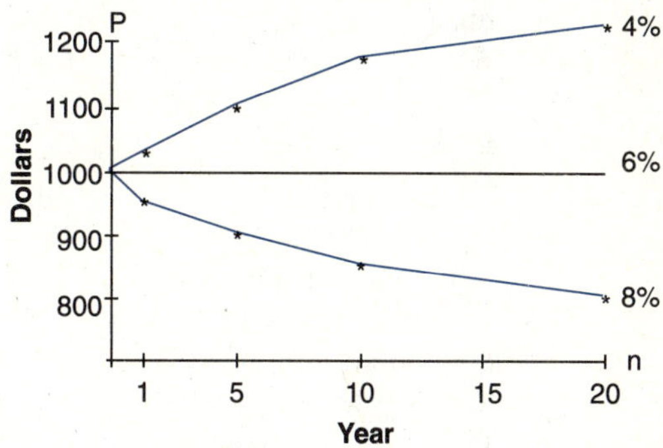

Table 21-2

Price Sensitivity of 8 Percent Coupon Bond
(Semiannual Interest Payments)

n \ r	10%	8%	6%	Price Range
40	$828	$1000	$1231	$403
20	$875	$1000	$1149	$274
10	$923	$1000	$1085	$162
2	$981	$1000	$1019	$38

P = $40[PVA; r/2; n] + $1000[PVF; r/2; n]; n = number of semiannual payments remaining; r = annual yield-to-maturity.

Table 21-1 and Figure 21-1. In Figure 21-1, the price of the bond is plotted against the number of years remaining to maturity (*n*) for each of the alternative yields. The difference between the 4- percent and the 8-percent schedule replicates the *Price Range* column in Table 21-1. The results here are similar to those found in the case of the zero-coupon bond discussed earlier. As term to maturity increases, price sensitivity of the coupon bond increases, though in contrast to the case of zero-coupon bonds, the relationship is not proportional. From the shapes of the schedules in Figure 21-1 it is clear that the *difference* between bond prices at the 4-percent and 8-percent yields *increases* at a *decreasing* rate. For example, an increase in maturity from 10 years to 20 years, doubling the term to maturity, causes the range of prices between the 4-percent and 8-percent yields to go from $299 to $471, an increase in interest sensitivity of only 58 percent.

Table 21-2 provides an analysis similar to that of Table 21-1, except that the bond is an 8 percent coupon bond rather than a 6 percent bond. Calculations in Table 21-2 are identical to those in Table 21-1, with two important exceptions. First, the semiannual payment involved is $40 per period rather than $30. Second, the bond sells at par, or $1000, when the discount rate is 8 percent rather than 6 percent. To explore the implications of a 2-percent swing in yields for this bond, we evaluate the price of the bond at 6-percent and 10-percent discount rates.

The important implication of Table 21-2 is provided in the last column, which calculates the range of prices generated by a swing in yields of 2 percent around the coupon rate of 8 percent per year. Notice that, for each term to maturity, the range of prices is smaller than it was for the 6-percent coupon bond. This implies that the price of the 8-percent bond is less sensitive to yield changes than the price of the 6-percent bond. That is, as regards market value risk, the higher-coupon bond is less risky. This fact is highlighted by Figure 21-2, which once again maps the prices of the two bonds against the term to maturity for three yield regimes: yield equals coupon rate, yield equals coupon rate plus 2 percent, yield equals coupon rate minus 2 percent. The resultant schedules are scaled around yield-equals-coupon rate, so that a relative comparison can be drawn between the two bonds. This diagram shows graphically that, at every term to maturity, the price of the lower-coupon security is more sensitive to yield changes than that of the higher-coupon security. In some sense, the higher-coupon bond carries less risk of potential capital losses (or gains). Thus, term to maturity itself is not sufficient basis for ranking the market value risk of alternative-coupon bonds.

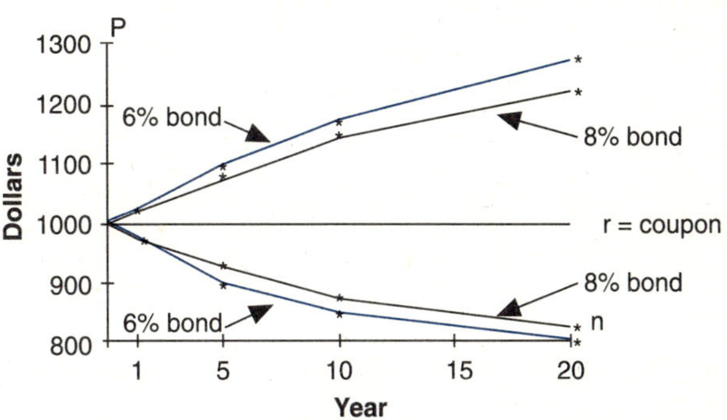

Figure 21-2
Price, yield, and maturity for 6-percent and 8-percent coupon bonds.

This property of coupon bonds has frequently been referred to in finance as the "*coupon effect.*" In general, all other factors being held constant, the higher the coupon rate, the less sensitive will the bond's price be to changes in yield. The coupon effect is due to the nearness of cash flows associated with higher-coupon bonds. That is, the important difference between the 6-percent and the 8-percent bond that drives their difference in price sensitivity is that the 8-percent bond delivers more of the value of its total cash flows sooner than the 6-percent bond. In fact, time to maturity *is* key to understanding the price risk of fixed-income claims, but not maturity in the usual sense. Rather, coupon bonds and other complex securities have as many maturities as they have different cash flows. A different maturity is associated with each cash flow scheduled at a different date during the term of the bond. In the case just described, a greater portion of the 8-percent bond "matured" sooner, causing its price sensitivity to be less than that of the 6-percent bond.

Generalizing the Coupon Effect: A Comparison of Loan Contracts

The properties just described are more general and apply to other securities besides coupon-bearing bonds. In fact, the coupon effect operates for all fixed-income claims and generally becomes more pronounced the more different are the cash flow patterns of the securities involved. This point is illustrated in another comparison of two loan contracts (Table 21-3). The example shows how the choice of loan terms affects the market risk to the borrower and lender in circumstances in which the contract might be repurchased or resold.

In this example, imagine that a bank offers two alternative loans to a customer. The first (outlined in Part *a*) is a discount loan. The contract promises to pay the bank a future payment (F = \$1000) in ten years. The loan is initially valued at a rate of 10 percent, the interest rate charged by the bank over the term of the loan (compounded annually). In return for this payment this means the borrower receives \$385.54, which is also the market value of the loan, P (i.e., its resale value to the lending bank). If the market rate on a ten-year discount debt immediately decreases by 2 percent, the value of the loan increases to \$463.19. This means the bank can resell it for a gain of \$77.65. The borrower, on the other hand, has realized an increase of \$77.65 in the value of her liabilities. Assuming the market value of the borrower's assets remain constant, this implies a decrease in the value of the borrower's equity

Table 21-3
Generalizing the Coupon Effect

Example: A Discount Loan vs. An Installment Loan

a. Discount loan ($F = \$1000$; $r = 10\%$, $n = 10$ yr.)

$P = \$1000\,[1/(1.10)^{10}] = \$385.54$	@$r = 10\%$
$P = \$1000\,[1/(1.08)^{10}] = \$463.19$	@$r = 8\%$
$P = \$1000\,[1/(1.12)^{10}] = \$321.97$	@$r = 12\%$

b. Installment Loan ($L = \$385.54$; $r = 10\%$; $n = 10$ yr.)

$\$385.54 = A[\text{PVA @ } r;\ 10]$	
$A = \$62.74$	@$r = 10\%$
$P = \$62.74\,[\text{PVA @ } r;\ 10]$	
$= \$420.99$	@$r = 8\%$
$P = \$62.74\,[\text{PVA @ } r;\ 10]$	
$= \$354.49$	@$r = 12\%$

Summary of Changes:

Discount Rate	+ 2%	− 2%
Value of Discount Loan	$63.57	$77.65
Value of Installment Loan	$31.05	$35.45

of the same amount. From another perspective, as a result of the decrease in market rates of 2 percent, the cost to the borrower to buy back the loan from the bank has increased by $77.65, unless there are other provisions in the contract for the borrower to buy back the loan which may involve substantial penalties and assuming the bank is willing to sell at the going market rate. On the other hand, when the market rate increases to 12 percent, similar but opposite windfalls are realized by borrower and lender. The lender finds the value of the loan has decreased by $63.57 while the value of the borrower's liabilities decreased by the same amount. From either the bank's or the loan customer's perspective, the risk of a 2-percent fluctuation in the market yields implies a substantial risk to their financial positions. This exposure, under the discount terms, is summarized at the bottom of Table 21-3.

Now consider the second set of loan terms outlined in part *b* of Table 21-3. We refer to these terms as "installment terms." Assuming an equal amount of money is loaned (borrowed) as in the preceding discount loan arrangement, $385.54 is paid off, or amortized with ten equal annual installments over the ten-year term of the loan. The equal installment payment, *A,* is determined as the solution to an ordinary annuity with a present value of $385.54, using the initial interest rate of 10%.[1] This implies that the contract purchased by the bank promises ten equal payments of $62.74 per year for ten years. The impact of an immediate change in market rates for the amortized loan is shown in the table. When rates decrease, there is a $35.45 increase in the market value of the loan. When rates increase, there is a $31.05 decrease in the value of the contract. The changes in value for both types of loans are summarized at the bottom of Table 21-3.

[1]The notation [PVA @ *r*; 10] refers to the annuity discount factor with a discount rate of *r* and ten equal payments.

Notice the dramatic difference in the effect of yield changes on the value of the two contracts. The risk associated with the loan under discount terms is more than twice that associated with the installment terms. Under both arrangements, the amount loaned, the term of the loan, and the contract rate are the same. The important difference was in the timing of cash payments under the two contracts. Under discount terms, all cash flows ($1000) are delivered after ten years. Under installment terms, cash flows are spread out over the ten-year period in equal installments of $62.74 per year. Ignoring other factors that may impact the decision of the borrower or the lender, the installment loan provides the best protection against exposure to market risk. Finally, note that the coupon effect identified in comparisons between coupon-bearing bonds is generic to all fixed-income claims. Moreover, the more different are the cash flow patterns between two financial contracts, as we highlighted in the bank loan example, the more exaggerated the effect will be.

Duration: A More Effective Measure of Market Risk

As we demonstrated in the previous sections, the timing of cash flows of financial claims has an important bearing on the exposure of market value to changes in yields. We also argued that among different claims, the important characteristic in explaining differences in the sensitivity of market value to changes in yield is the maturity of *individual* cash flows, and not merely their term to maturity per se. In this section, we present a measure to account for differences in the timing of cash flows for alternative financial claims. The measure is *duration,* of which there are several versions. We use the *Macaulay duration,* named for the person who first derived the expression, but we also discuss the pros and cons of this specific measure of duration and of the entire concept of duration.

Macaulay's duration is defined as follows:

$$D = \frac{\sum_{t=1}^{n} \frac{C_t}{(1+r)^t}(t)}{\sum_{t=1}^{n} \frac{C_t}{(1+r)^t}} = \sum_{t=1}^{n}\left(\frac{PV(C_t)(t)}{\sum_{t=1}^{n} PV(C_t)}\right) \qquad (21.2)$$

where D is duration, t is the number of time periods in the future, C_t is cash flow to be delivered t periods in the future, n is the number of periods to final cash flow (term to maturity), r is the yield to maturity, and PV is present value. At first, Equation 21.2 seems rather complex. Acutally, it is simpler than it first appears. Basically, duration represents an average of the maturities of all of the cash flows promised by the financial claim. This "average" is a little special, in that it is a weighted average of the time to receipt of all cash flows. The weights used in computing the average are the present values of each respective cash flow expressed as a percentage of the present value of all of the cash flows, or the value of the claim as a whole.

A simple example will illustrate the mathematical procedure more clearly. Consider a $1000 installment loan, amortized by two equal annual installments at an

Table 21-4

Duration of an Installment Loan

Time		0	Payments 1		2
			\$522.61		\$522.61
PV of Payments	=		$\frac{\$522.61}{(1.03)^1}$	+	$\frac{\$522.61}{(1.03)^2}$ = \$1000
PV of Payments	=		\$507.39	+	\$492.61 = \$1000
Duration	=		$\frac{\$507.39}{\$1000}[1]$	+	$\frac{\$492.61}{\$1000}[2]$
Duration	=		[.50739][1]	+	[.49261][2]
Duration	=		1.493		

interest rate of 3 percent per year. The annual payment, calculated as an ordinary annuity, is \$522.61 per year for two years. The duration of the loan contract is computed in Table 21-4.

The diagram at the top of Table 21-4 shows the pattern of cash flows delivered under the contract. Installment amounts of \$522.61 are scheduled in one and two years. The present values of the respective cash flows are \$507.39 and \$492.61, which, taken together, equal the present value of the contract, or \$1000. At the current yield of 3 percent, the first cash flow represents 50.739 percent of the value of the contract; the second cash flow represents 49.261 percent of the value of the contract. In computing the duration of the contract, these weights are used to average the time to delivery of each cash flow. The duration on this contract is 1.493 years.

The loan outlined in Table 21-4 can be viewed as a composite of two simple securities similar to zero-coupon bonds, each paying a single cash flow of \$522.61 at maturity: a one-year bond costing \$507.39 and a two-year bond costing \$492.61. Quite simply, the first bond has a duration of one year and the second has a duration of two years. The duration of the composite security, the two-year loan contract, is merely the average duration of the two simpler securities, though the average is not merely the simple average of the respective durations (maturities), 1.5 years. Of the total \$1000 value of the composite loan, more value accrues from the first cash flow than from the second (\$507.39 versus \$492.61). Therefore, in calculating the average duration of the component "bonds," the duration of the first is given proportionately more weight.

The definition of duration proposed and illustrated above is only one of a number of possible ways to measure duration. The Macaulay duration has a major advantage over other versions of duration. As shown here, it provides a relatively simple measure of the relationship between the percentage change in the price of a fixed-income claim and its percentage change in yield or the unique discount rate applied to the cash flows:

$$\frac{\left(\frac{\Delta P}{P}\right)}{\left(\frac{\Delta r}{r}\right)} = -D\frac{r}{1+r} \tag{21.3}$$

where, P is the price or market value of the claim, D the duration, and r the single discount rate or yield-to-maturity on the claim. Note that the yield-to-maturity is expressed as a rate compounded over the same units of time in which duration is defined. If duration is expressed in terms of semiannual intervals, r is a semiannual yield-to-maturity. In turn, it is most convenient to define duration in terms of the intervals of the cash flows. That is, if cash flows occur annually, duration and yield in equations 21.2 and 21.3 are most easily defined in annual units—for example, a duration of 2.5 years. If cash flows occur quarterly, duration and yield are more conveniently defined in quarterly units—for example, ten quarters.

Another, slightly simpler version of this expression is obtained by multiplying both sides of the equation by $\Delta r/r$:

$$\frac{\Delta P}{P} = -D\left(\frac{1}{1+r}\right)\Delta r \tag{21.4}$$

$$= -D^*\Delta r$$

where $D^* = D/(1 + r)$

and D^* is known as *modified duration.* For relatively low yields, the term in brackets is approximately equal to 1.0 and the expression can be simplified further:

$$\frac{\Delta P}{P} \approx -D\Delta r \tag{21.5}$$

Modified duration has the attractive interpretation that it measures the sensitivity of the financial claim's price to unit changes in the single interest rate. Notice also that the percentage change in price is *inversely proportional* to the change in market yield. For example, recall from our previous illustration of a two-year installment loan that its duration was computed to be 1.493. If the yield on such loans was to immediately change to 4 percent, an increase in yield of 1 percent, the percentage change in the market value of the loan should be approximately, $-1.493 \times 1\% = -1.493\%$. To verify this result we recalculate the value of the installment contract at a discount rate of 4 percent:

$$P = \frac{\$522.61}{(1.04)^1} + \frac{\$522.61}{(1.04)^2} = \$502.51 + \$483.18 = \$985.69$$

This represents a change in the value of the contract of \$1000 − \$985.69 = \$14.31, or −1.43%.

Notice that the change we computed with duration is only approximately correct. The actual percentage change in the price of the loan differs from that predicted by the duration equation by 0.063 percent. This discrepancy is due to two factors. First, the final version of the equation used to compute the anticipated change in price assumed away the factor $[1/(1 + r)]$, which in this instance is equal to 1/1.03, or 0.971. If this is accounted for, the anticipated percentage change in price, $\Delta P/P$, is 1.45 percent, which is closer to the observed price change of 1.43 percent. The second reason is easiest to see by inspecting Figure 21-3, which portrays the relationship between the price of a bond and its yield. Notice that this curve is drawn convex to the origin. This means that changes in price generated by changes in yield are increasing in the level of price, or the curve gets steeper at higher levels of price. The relationship we developed in equation 21.4 represents the slope of this curve at a specific point on the curve, or the slope of a straight line drawn tangent to the curve at a point, as illustrated in Figure 21-3. This may be more apparent if we rewrite equation 21.4 as follows:

$$\Delta P = -\mathrm{D}\left(\frac{P}{1 + r}\right)\Delta r$$

If we use the slope of such a line to estimate the change in price for very small changes in yield, we get a very accurate answer, but the larger the change in yield we are dealing with, the worse is the approximation. This is simply because the slope of the curve is changing as we change the yield.

One final illustration demonstrates the superiority of duration over maturity as a measure of market risk. Table 21-5 provides a comparison of three debt contracts, each having two-year maturities. In each case the amount loaned under the contract is \$1000 and the contract rate is 3 percent. The first contract is the simple installment loan described earlier, which provides payments of \$522.61 in each of the two years on the contract. The second is a discount loan that promises \$1060.90 at the end of two years. The third, identified as a "balloon" contract, is similar to a coupon bond. It provides interest of 3 percent after each of the subsequent two years and return of principal (\$1000) after two years.

In the lower portion of Table 21-5, a tabulation is provided of the impact of a 1-percent increase or decrease in the yield on the value of each instrument. Notice that for the range of yields from 2 percent to 4 percent, the fluctuation in the value of the contracts can be rank ordered by the duration of each contract. The most volatile contract is the discount loan with a duration of 2.0 years; the next

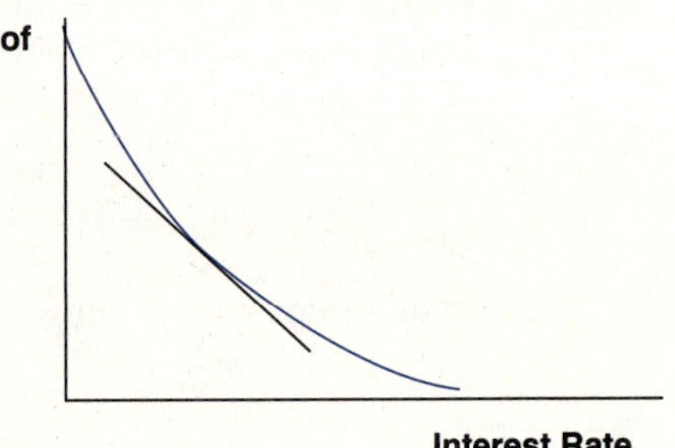

Figure 21-3
Convex relationship between the interest rate and price of a bond.

Table 21-5

Duration as an Index of Interest Rate Risk

Three loans plans are offered by a commercial bank. Each loan is priced to yield 3 percent. The loan amount is $1000, and the term is two years under each plan. The loan plans are outlined as follows:

1. Installment terms: Level payments at the end of each year.
2. Discount terms: Single payment of interest and principal at maturity.
3. Balloon payment terms: Interest paid each year and repayment of principal at maturity.

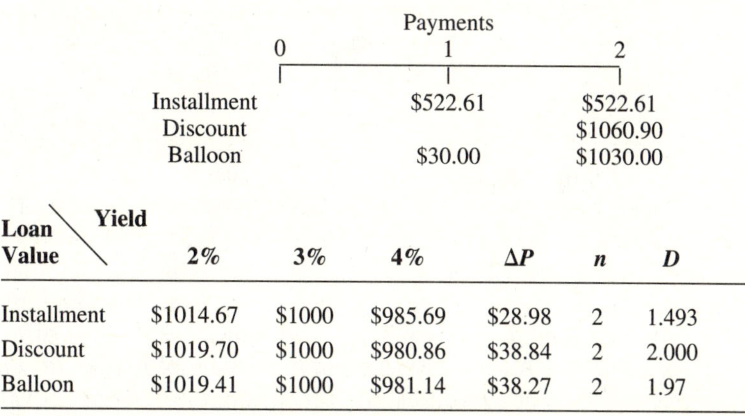

Payments	0	1	2
Installment		$522.61	$522.61
Discount			$1060.90
Balloon		$30.00	$1030.00

Loan Value \ Yield	2%	3%	4%	ΔP	n	D
Installment	$1014.67	$1000	$985.69	$28.98	2	1.493
Discount	$1019.70	$1000	$980.86	$38.84	2	2.000
Balloon	$1019.41	$1000	$981.14	$38.27	2	1.97

most volatile contract is the balloon loan with a duration of 1.97 years; and the least volatile contract is the installment loan with a duration of 1.493 years. Also note that the relative magnitude of the price fluctuations across contracts is equal to the relative magnitude of their durations. That is, the change in the value of each contract in response to a change in yield is directly proportional to its duration. This is the central message of the preceding equations.

There is one more issue about the relationship between the price and the yield of a bond that is worth pointing out before we move on. This pertains to how the relationship we developed does and does not apply to bonds that have call (prepayment) provisions. A bond or a mortgage with a call or prepayment provision is equivalent to a bond without such a provision plus an option on the interest rate. The underlying straight bond behaves exactly as we have just described, but the total relationship between yield and price also includes the option. If we draw a picture of the relationship, as we did for the straight bond in Figure 21-3, we will not get a convex curve throughout. It will be convex, just like the straight bond, for high levels of interest rates where prepayment is unlikely, but when the interest rate reaches a level where prepayment is likely, then the curve bends back, as portrayed in Figure 21-4. The decline in price represents the fact that the bond is prepaid and the funds must be reinvested at lower interest rates. This characteristic of callable bonds or bonds with prepayment provisions is often referred to as "negative convexity."

Figure 21-4
Negative convexity in the relationship between the interest rate and price of a callable bond.

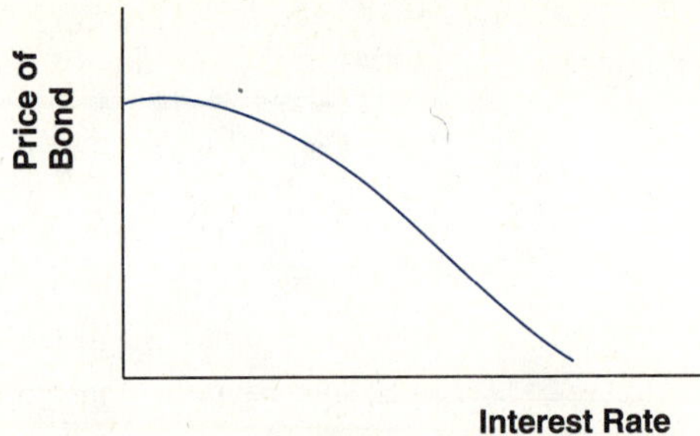

Limits of Duration

We emphasized throughout our previous discussion that we were using a specific duration measure, the Macaulay duration. The virtue of the Macaulay duration is its simplicity, but it has a serious drawback. The relationship we defined in Equation 21.4 between duration and yield changes is appropriate only in circumstances where there are *parallel* changes in yields; that is, parallel shifts in the yield curve. This means that yields at all terms to maturity change by the same absolute amount. This was implicit in the formulation of equation 21.4, since we were dealing with only one yield applicable to cash flows at different maturities. When yields change by different amounts at different maturities, the changes in the discounted values of different cash flows are sensitive to how those individual interest rates change. This is not captured in the Macaulay duration. The Macaulay duration is often interpreted as measuring the sensitivity of the price of a bond to changes in its yield to maturity, but the price of the bond is not determined by its yield to maturity. Instead, yield to maturity and price are two alternative ways of stating the same thing. As we first emphasized in Chapter 9, the variables that logically determine the price, and therefore the yield to maturity, of a bond are the market interest rates that apply to different maturities, that is, the zero-coupon term structure of interest rates. Once the bond price has been determined by the cash flows to the bond and by the term structure of interest rates, we can use the price and the cash flows to solve for the yield to maturity by solving for the single interest rate that satisfies the present value equation for the bond. We can define the Macaulay duration with respect to this rate, but it is not very meaningful to ask how the price of a bond changes as this yield to maturity changes. Therefore, the Macaulay duration is limited to situations where the yield curve experiences parallel shifts. Unfortunately, the yield curve often changes shape. Indeed, we know that short-term rates have greater fluctuations than long-term rates. For example, recall the various yield curves and their very different shapes (see Figure 10-1). For many applications, the Macaulay duration is not a sufficiently accurate tool to provide a proper basis for valuation or for constructing a risk management strategy. Whenever greater accuracy is desired, it is necessary to specify and validate a model for interest rates or design a hedging procedure that will accommodate a wide variety of fluctuations in the yield curve.

Asset-Liability Management

Now that we have learned some of the tools of interest rate risk management we are going to turn our attention to measuring and controlling the interest rate exposure a firm has on its balance sheet. We start by exploring how to measure the interest rate risk exposure and how to construct a simple GAP report.

Interest Rate Risk: Future Earnings Versus Present Value

There are two general perspectives from which to evaluate exposure of a company to interest rate risk. One approach identifies the effects that interest rate changes will have on future financial flows such as cash flows, net interest income, or earnings. In most cases this perspective emphasizes the differential effects of interest rate changes on interest income and interest expense. For example, consider a bank or savings and loan that makes a three-year auto loan at 10 percent and funds the loan by issuing a one-year certificate of deposit (CD) at 8 percent. The bank is assured of a 2-percent interest rate spread on the loan for the first year. If rates remain unchanged over the term of the loan, one-year CDs can be used during the second and third years at 8 percent again, and a 2-percent spread can be earned in those years as well. Unless the loan is prepaid, however, there is the prospect that deposit rates may rise during the term of the loan. If the bank must borrow in the CD market at 9 percent for the second year of the loan, the spread is cut in half and the interest income net of interest expense, or net interest income (NII) is affected accordingly. Moreover, there is the possibility that the spread could become zero or negative during the second or third year of the loan if interest rates were to rise fast enough. The most popular approach to organizing and evaluating the exposure of NII to interest changes over time is commonly referred to as interest rate GAP analysis. Basically, GAP analysis projects the interest income (NII) over several operating periods, under alternative interest scenarios and alternative asset and liability strategies.

The second perspective focuses on the impact of interest rate changes on market value. In this case, the primary concern is not directly with how rate changes will affect future financial flows. Rather, emphasis is placed on how changes in interest rates will affect the *current value* of future cash flows or profits, typically measured as the market value of the firm, or the value of owners' equity. Here, the notion of duration is often used to quantify the sensitivity of assets and liabilities to fluctuations in rates. In certain situations it is also possible to construct a measure of the interest rate sensitivity of owners' equity–or the duration of equity–which defines the risk of shareholders' wealth to changes in interest rates. In our example of the auto loan, this approach would focus on how current changes in rates would affect the values of the loan and the CD and on the residual effect on shareholder wealth. Suppose, for instance, that the duration of the auto loan was longer than one year (the duration of the CD). If rates were to increase during the first year of the loan, the value of the loan would decrease by more than the value of the CD, causing a decrease in the value of equity.

Obviously, these two conceptual approaches to identifying interest rate risk exposure are related to each other, since the market value of a firm can logically be viewed as the present value of its future cash flows. There are differences between the two that should be understood, particularly if we are going to evaluate how alternative risk management strategies may affect the interests of shareholders. We want to examine these approaches to managing interest rate risk more carefully and note their similarities and differences.

Interest Rate GAP and GAP Management

The notion of an interest rate GAP can be best explained using the illustration provided in Figure 21-5. The GAP is defined by classifying financial assets and liabilities as being of two types: those that will be repriced within a specified interval, called the GAP interval or GAP maturity, and those that will be repriced later. An asset or liability is repriced, either when it matures and must be reissued at a competitive contract

Figure 21-5
The simple interest rate gap.

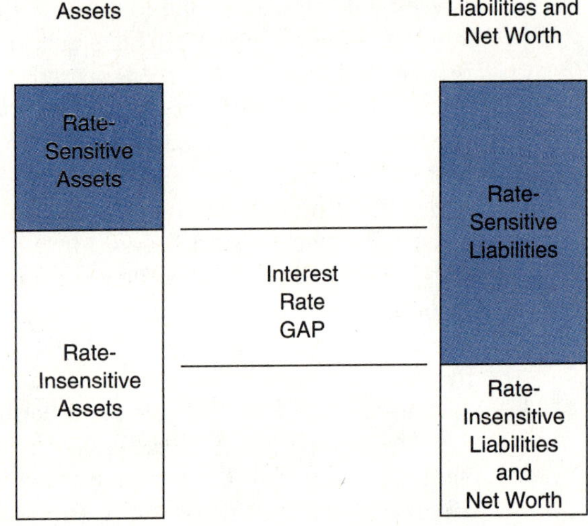

GAP = RSA minus RSL

Interest Rate Movement	Net Interest Margin (Interest Income minus Interest Expense)	
	GAP > 0	GAP < 0
Increase	Increase	Decrease
Decrease	Decrease	Increase

rate or when its contract rate is reset periodically before maturity (as in the case of a variable-rate loan). In some sense, financial claims are classified as being short-term or long-term. However, there may be instruments that are very long-term contracts, such as a variable-rate mortgage, that are classified as interest sensitive, since the contract rate may be reset within the GAP period when interest rates change. Assets and liabilities that are repriced within the GAP interval are called "rate-sensitive assets" and "rate-sensitive liabilities," or RSA and RSL, respectively. Figure 21-5 represents a balance sheet in which RSA and RSL are represented by the shaded areas. The difference between RSA and RSL (RSA minus RSL) is equal to the GAP.

The GAP is the dollar amount of assets and liabilities that are mismatched. That is, in Figure 21-5 the GAP is negative, indicating there are more interest-sensitive liabilities than interest-sensitive assets on the sheet. Essentially, the GAP measures the volume of fixed-rate assets (fixed over the GAP interval) that are financed with variable-rate liabilities. Thus, if rates rise, the interest cost on that volume increases whereas the interest income does not. This causes the net interest margin to decrease. The lower panel of Figure 21-5 tabulates how increases and decreases in interest rates affect the net interest margin, depending on the sign of the interest rate GAP. The magnitude of these effects depends on the magnitude of the GAP. Notice that, as shown by Figure 21-5, increases in rates can increase the net interest margin of a firm. This is not generally the case in most financial intermediaries that generally run negative GAPs. The most visible effects of interest rate increases have been the difficulties of savings and loan associations, the depositories with the most extremely negative GAPs.

In both financial and nonfinancial firms it is often helpful to prepare a GAP report to assess the magnitude of the difference between RSA and RSL. An example of a simple GAP report is presented in Table 21-6 for a hypothetical company called Imaginary, Inc. The GAP report for Imaginary, Inc. covers a one-year horizon, though a GAP report could cover any period you wish. The interval is broken down into periods of overnight, 1 to 30 days (or less than 30 days), 30 days to 60 days (or less than 60 days), less than 90 days, less than 180 days, less than 270 days, and less than 1 year. These intervals correspond to the columns in the table. The rows in the table pertain to assets and liabilities that reprice at different points over the year. Imaginary, Inc. has other assets that reprice beyond the one-year horizon in this report, but they are not considered here. Also notice that this report pertains to financial assets for which it is possible to define the repricing in a clear way. Other types of assets, such as inventory and accounts receivable and payable, may also have terms that adjust with current market conditions and might be included as well, if the repricing can be readily calculated and if they are perceived to affect the firm's earnings directly. This is often a difficult judgment call for management preparing this kind of report. Imaginary, Inc. has three distinct types of financial assets that reprice during the year: T bills, CDs, and federal funds. Notice that federal funds have overnight maturities whereas the T bills have maturities spread throughout the year. Imaginary, Inc.'s CDs mature between 30 and 60 days from the date of the report. Similarly, Imaginary, Inc. has three types of interest-sensitive liabilities whose repricing is distributed throughout the year. The report shows total

Table 21-6
Sample Gap Report
Imaginary, Inc.
$ Millions

	Overnight	<30 days	<60 days	<90 days	<180 days	<270 days	<1 year
T bills	5.00	10.00	10.00	10.00	10.00	10.00	10.00
CDs			20.00'				
Fed fds	10.00						
Tot RSA	15.00	10.00	30.00	10.00	10.00	10.00	10.00
CP	0.00	30.00		50.00			
Banks lns			50.00		60.00		20.00
Notes							50.00
Total RSL	0.00	30.00	50.00	50.00	60.00	0.00	70.00
RSA - RSL	15.00	−20.00	−20.00	−40.00	−50.00	10.00	−60.00
RSA/RSL		0.33	0.60	0.20	0.17		0.14
Cum RSA	15.00	25.00	55.00	65.00	75.00	85.00	95.00
Cum RSL	0.00	30.00	80.00	130.00	190.00	190.00	260.00
CRSA/CRSL		0.83	0.69	0.50	0.39	0.45	0.37
Fraction of year in which interest is earned							
	1.00	0.92	0.83	0.75	0.50	0.25	0.00
Interest income - expense generated by each exposure							
	0.30	−0.37	−0.33	−0.60	−0.50	−0.05	0.00
Interest income - expense year-to-date:							
	0.30	−0.07	−0.40	−1.00	−1.50	−1.45	−1.45

RSA and RSL for each interval over the year. This report is structured to compute the difference and the relative amount of RSA and RSL and to cumulate RSA and RSL over the year. Imaginary Inc. has a surplus of RSA over RSL overnight, but generally more RSL than RSA throughout the rest of the year.

The report also estimates the effect on Imaginary, Inc. of a change in interest rates. Specifically, this report assumes that interest rates immediately increase by 200 basis points and that every RSA and RSL reprices at a 200–basis point increase over the year. This means that the report shows only the impact of a change in interest rates from current levels, not the total impact of repricing if interest rates do not change. For example, suppose existing CDs are earning 4 percent, current rates are 6 percent, and the 200–basis point increase will push those rates to 8 percent. The GAP report would only show the impact of the 200–basis point increase to 8 percent, yet when the CD repriced, it would actually earn 400 basis points more. It is not too hard to prepare a GAP report that would show the 400–basis point increase, but this requires storing and using the history of rates on all existing RSA and RSL. As an exercise, you might try using a spreadsheet program to prepare such a GAP report.

The report then shows the effect on net interest income of the 200–basis point change at each interval and for the year as a whole. This report shows that the 200-basis point increase would cost Imaginary, Inc. $1.45 million over the course of the year. Notice that this computation uses the fraction of the year over which the repricing applies for each time interval. For example, the column for *<60* applies for 0.83 of the year. This is simply 300/360.

While the GAP report in Table 21-6 can be a useful management tool for Imaginary, Inc., it is a very simple and crude measurement of the company's interest rate exposure. Its virtue is its simplicity; its principal drawback is that it focuses only on the impact of interest rate changes on accounting measures of performance, rather than on market value. It also ignores default risk. Moreover, it is important to remember that it does not show what is happening to assets and liabilities that do not actually reprice. The market value of these assets and liabilities is sensitive to interest rates even if they do not show up on this GAP report. This influences the equity value of the company, as we see shortly. Thus, the simple GAP report will be helpful to managers if it does not blind them to the larger effects of interest rate changes.

• *Banks and Insurance Companies Are Being Forced to Tell the Truth About Market Values of Securities* •

For many years banks and insurance companies have been governed by accounting rules that protected them from having to inform investors of the true market value of securities they held. The accounting rules essentially said that banks and insurance companies could report the values of securities at the either book value or market value and that they were not required to report market value until a bond was sold. This had at least two big disadvantages. First, it simply did not tell the market the truth about the value of a bank's assets. Investors had a more difficult time than they otherwise would have, trying to figure out what the real value of a bank actually was. Second, it provided an incentive for banks to game the system in managing investments. In particular, there was an incentive to engage in so-called "gains trading," where bonds that went up in value were sold and bonds that declined in value where retained in order to drive up reported accounting earnings. Not surprisingly, many managers of banks and insurance companies liked these rules, because it made their reported earnings and the reported value of their assets appear less volatile than they really were. Some even believed that the lower reported volatility provided an incentive for banks to invest in longer-maturity securities or create more of an interest rate GAP than they would if they had to tell the truth about their investments. Bankers and insurance company managers also have argued that, to the extent that these financial institutions act as portfolio lenders that hold assets until maturity, the fluctuations in the market value of assets are not really a relevant risk to which they are exposed. Indeed, the American Bankers Association, the Savings & Community Bankers of America, and the Council of Life Insurance all have opposed movements to market-value accounting.

One person who consistently has advocated modifying the system to introduce market-value accounting was the Chairman of the Securities and Exchange Commission during the Bush Administration, Richard Breeden. He consistently argued for accounting and disclosure rules that compelled all financial institutions to report the market value of assets. In April 1993 he won a considerable victory in this struggle. The Financial Accounting Standards Board (FASB) voted five to two to compel banks and insurance companies to follow new reporting requirements that moved them much closer to telling the complete truth. The rules adopted by FASB require that banks and insurance company bond portfolios be divided into three categories. Bonds that are held until maturity can still be held at original cost. Bonds available for sale, which may or may not actually be traded before maturity, are to be marked to market with any reduction from original cost taken from shareholders' equity. Finally, bonds held only for trading purposes must be marked to current market prices, with any unrealized gains or losses charged against earnings.[2]

FASB's actual decision was a compromise relative to an earlier proposal that would have required changes in the value of bonds that are either available for sale or held for trading to be charged against earnings. We would not be surprised if this original proposal is ultimately adopted by FASB, perhaps maybe by the time you read this.

A few of the effects of the new accounting proposal are relatively easy to discern. Bank and insurance company asset levels and earnings will be more volatile than they would have been before the change, assuming asset holdings are not changed toward investments in inherently less volatile or shorter-duration securities. Second, the increase in volatility will be greater for asset values than for earnings. Beyond this, it is difficult to be sure whether these changes will have a significant impact on the actual behavior in the industry. If bankers and insurance company managers had been successfully hiding risks from the investment community via the old accounting rules, these changes may have a big effect as those risks are disclosed. It is possible, however, that the market had figured out the values of banks' assets pretty well even without the new accounting rules. And it is possible that bankers and insurance company managers believed that the market pretty much knew what they were up to, though if this *were* the case, why was the movement to market-value accounting so controversial? Our best guess is that the banks and insurance companies will be forced as never before to closely examine the interest rate risk they undertake.

Immunization

The GAP report we have described provides a tool with which to assess a company's exposure to interest rate risk. Now we want to describe a procedure for protecting any party who holds fixed-income securities from being exposed to risk of fluctuating interest rates. This procedure applies to an investment with a specific time horizon. An investor who holds fixed-income securities may often have in mind a specific time horizon. Say, for example, that an investor wants the proceeds from her investment in ten years to fund her retirement. Ideally, it would be advantageous to lock in the value of the fixed-income investment ten years from now. One way to do this is to buy a zero-coupon bond. Another way may be to try to make a fixed-income portfolio that is not composed of zero-coupon bonds behave as if it were. Designing a fixed-income portfolio of coupon bonds so that it behaves like the equivalent of a zero-coupon bond with a maturity equal to the decision maker's investment horizon is called "immunization."

[2]See Lee Berton, "FASB Votes to Make Banks and Insurers Value Certain Bonds at Current Prices," *Wall Street Journal,* April 14, 1993.

Recall that a coupon bond involves two types of risks. First, it has the risk of price changes that will be realized if it is liquidated before maturity. Second, it has the risk of changes in the interest rate at which coupon payments can be reinvested. These risks respond in opposite directions to changes in market interest rates. The idea behind immunizing a portfolio is to make these two risks fully offsetting, so that the bond value plus the accumulation of reinvested coupon payments will be the same at the end of the investment horizon, regardless of the level of interest rates.

The way immunization works is illustrated in Figure 21-6. The horizontal axis shows time; the vertical axis shows the value of the portfolio, including reinvested coupon payments. The length of the investment horizon is represented by n. The solid line in the figure emanating from point V_0 on the vertical axis shows the value of the portfolio, including reinvested coupon payments, if there are no changes in interest rates. The value of the portfolio at the end of the investment horizon when it follows the solid line is labeled V_n. If interest rates fall in time 0, that is, if the whole term structure shifts down, then the value of the portfolio will increase. At this new level of interest rates, the value of the portfolio, including reinvested coupon payments, will follow a new path over time defined by the dashed line above the solid one in the figure (to the left of V_n). This line starts from a higher initial portfolio value. The value of the portfolio appreciates at a slower rate, owing to the lower level of interest rates, which means lower reinvestment income. Thus, at each point in time the slope of the dashed line is lower than the slope of the solid line below it. Conversely, if interest rates increase at time 0, then the value of the bonds in the portfolio will decline initially, but the higher interest rates will mean the reinvested coupons will appreciate at a higher rate. This is represented in the dotted line below the solid one. At any point in time, this line has a higher slope than the solid line.

All three of the curves in Figure 21-6 are drawn so they intersect at one point, which represents the value of the portfolio at the end of the investor's investment horizon, V_n. The figure was not constructed this way by accident. The fact that they

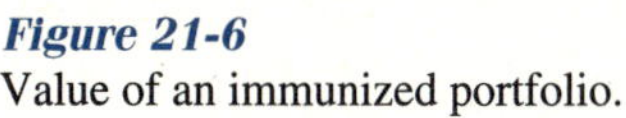

Figure 21-6
Value of an immunized portfolio.

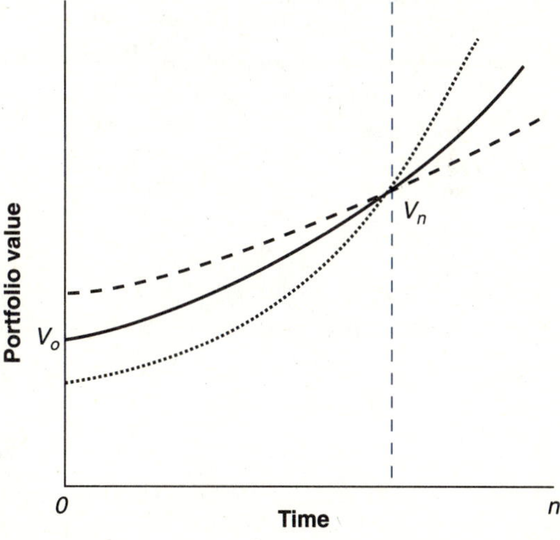

intersect at this point means the portfolio will always have the same value at time *n*, regardless of how interest rates change at time 0. The way to construct a portfolio so it will behave like this is to choose the portfolio's duration so that it equals the length of the investment horizon, *n*. It can be shown that when the duration is equal to the length of the investment horizon, changes in reinvestment income caused by changes in interest rates offset changes in the price of the portfolio in such a way that the total proceeds realized at time *n* cannot decrease.

To look into this more carefully, let's consider an example of a portfolio of bonds with $100 million in face value. This means that, at maturity, these bonds will pay $100 million. Let's assume that as the investor we can choose among a variety of such bonds, all with different coupon rates but with a common maturity of ten years. As the coupon rate goes down, we know the price of the bond will go down. This is illustrated in Table 21-7, which shows bond values and durations of bonds with coupon rates ranging from 3 percent to 12 percent. All the durations are computed using a discount rate of 10 percent, assuming that the current yield curve is flat at 10 percent. Next, suppose that the investor who is considering the purchase of these bonds has a seven-year holding period. She can immunize her investment by purchasing a bond with a coupon payment that yields a seven-year duration. Notice that Table 21-7 tells us the coupon rate that generates a seven-year duration is 8.27 percent. Also notice that this bond will have a current value of $89,369,898.91.

Now consider what would happen if interest rates were to change immediately and remain constant at the new level for seven years. Table 21-8 shows the impact of such an immediate and long-lasting shift in the yield curve. The change in rates would have two effects. First, coupon payments would no longer be reinvested at 10 percent; lower interest rates would mean lower reinvestment income. Second, lower rates would mean that the value of the bonds at year seven would go up, and vice versa. These two effects are documented in the first two columns of the table. Here, "reinvestment income" refers to the accumulated value of coupon payments received up to

Table 21-7
Duration for $100 Million Portfolio with 10 Percent Yield and Various Coupon Rates

Coupon Rate	Maturity	Value of Bond	Duration
0.03	10	$56,988,030.26	8.29
0.04	10	$63,132,597.37	7.95
0.05	10	$69,277,164.47	7.66
0.06	10	$75,421,731.58	7.42
0.07	10	$81,566,298.68	7.22
0.08	10	$87,710,865.79	7.04
0.0827	10	$89,369,898.91	7.00
0.09	10	$93,855,432.89	6.89
0.1	10	$100,000,000.00	6.76
0.11	10	$106,144,567.11	6.64
0.12	10	$112,289,134.21	6.54

year seven and "bond value" refers to the value of the bond at year seven. The total value is the sum of these columns at various discount rates. Finally, the holding yield is the holding-period yield for the seven years the bond has been held; that is, it is the internal rate of return for the given coupon payments and reinvestment income they generate plus the value of the bond at year seven.

The effect of immunization is apparent in Table 21-8. Recall that the discount rates that prevailed when the bond was acquired and the rate used to compute the duration of seven years was 10 percent. Table 21-8 shows that the total value of reinvestment income and the bond value at year seven is at a minimum of $174,156,650 if rates remain at 10 percent. Similarly, the holding-period yield is at a minimum of 10 percent if rates remain unchanged, though, if rates either increase or decrease, the total value of the investment at year seven increases slightly; it never goes down. This is the effect of immunization.

This effect of the change in the discount rate on holding-period yield is illustrated diagrammatically in Figure 21-7. The solid line in the figure plots holding-period yield as a function of the discount rate for the 8.27 percent coupon or seven-year duration bond. Notice, the line is slightly U-shaped, reflecting the fact that changes in the discount rate cause the holding-period yield to increase but never decrease. It is important to recognize that this relationship between holding-period yield, or total value, and the discount rate requires the duration of the bond in question to be equal to the holding period, seven years in this example. If we picked a bond with a shorter or a longer duration, the resulting relationship would no longer plot as a U-shaped curve. Figure 21-7 demonstrates this for 5-percent and 12-percent coupon bonds or bonds with durations of 7.66 and 6.54 years, respectively (see Table 21-7). The holding-period yield for the 5-percent bond is a decreasing function of the discount rate, while the reverse is true for the 12-percent coupon bond. This occurs because the reduced reinvestment rates resulting from a decrease in the market interest rate takes a bigger toll on the total value of the bond with a

Table 21-8

Value and Holding Period Yield After Seven Years on Bond with 8.27 Coupon or Seven-Year Duration at 10 Percent Discount Rate

Discount Rate	Reinvestment Income	Bond Value	Total Value	Holding Yield
0.06	$69,417,037	$106,067,737	$175,484,774	0.101194
0.07	$71,568,754	$103,332,881	$174,901,636	0.100671
0.08	$73,791,584	$100,695,816	$174,487,400	0.100298
0.09	$76,087,595	$98,152,155	$174,239,750	0.100075
0.10	$78,458,904	$95,697,746	$174,156,650	0.1
0.11	$80,907,677	$93,328,659	$174,236,336	0.100072
0.12	$83,436,127	$91,041,169	$174,477,296	0.100289
0.13	$86,046,518	$88,831,748	$174,878,266	0.10065
0.14	$88,741,164	$86,697,048	$175,438,212	0.101153
0.15	$91,522,429	$84,633,895	$176,156,324	0.101796

Figure 21-7

Yield at seven years on bond portfolio with various coupons and discount rates.

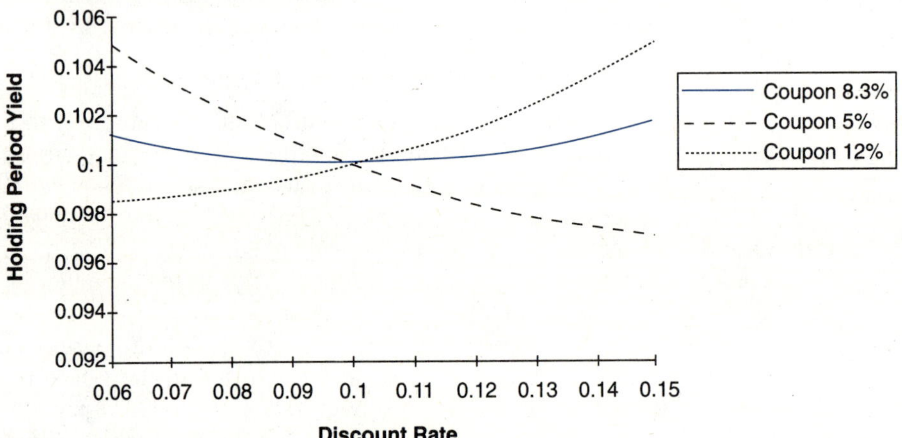

higher coupon, since more of total value comes from the reinvestment of that higher coupon. The bottom line here is that only the bond with a duration equal to the intended holding period can immunize the total value of all proceeds from holding that bond at the end of that holding period against changes in market interest rates.

As we did earlier in this chapter, we have used duration as a tool for interest rate risk management. Duration is a very useful element in the set of tools that can be employed, particularly for immunization; however, as we emphasized earlier it has its drawbacks. At least two practical difficulties are involved in setting the duration of a portfolio equal to the investment horizon. First, as time passes, both the investment horizon and the duration of the portfolio decrease, but they do not decrease at the same rate. Therefore, the portfolio must be altered as time passes to keep the duration equal to the remaining horizon. Adjustments must be made constantly in the portfolio if it is to be immunized perfectly.

Second, the duration that yields perfect immunization is the "true" duration of the portfolio, defined with respect to the entire term structure of interest rates. In general, this is not the Macaulay duration. As we mentioned in this chapter, the true duration depends on the underlying model of interest rates. If we can identify the model that determines interest rates with certainty, we can derive a measure of duration that corresponds to that model. However, we cannot know the model with certainty. We can empirically evaluate how effective various models are in explaining the observed historical patterns of interest rates, but we will always be left with a residual, or basis, risk if we use any given duration. An alternative approach is to view the risk management problem as a hedging problem. It is necessary to pick the appropriate hedging instruments and the appropriate hedge ratios for those instruments, in order to hedge all of the individual cash flows in a portfolio, just as we described in Chapter 17.

• So You Want to Manage the Risk of Equity? •

During recent years, there has been increased attention paid to the effects of interest rate changes on the value of equity or shareholder wealth. In large part, this attention has been motivated by the experience of savings and loans during the 1980s, and to some lesser extent, many commercial banks. In the early 1980s, when interest rates skyrocketed, the effect on the savings and loans industry was devastating. The traditional business of savings and loans has been to borrow money via short-term deposits and lend money via long-term fixed-rate mortgages. For the typical savings and loans, the increase in market rates affected the asset portfolio much more dramatically than deposits. In particular, while the market value of mortgages plummeted the value of deposit claims was virtually unchanged. The reason why is simple. The duration of the mortgage portfolio for a typical savings and loans was somewhere between 7 and 12 years. The duration of most deposit liabilities, for practical purposes, was less than one year. Obviously, when rates rose, the assets of the savings and loans would decrease much more than the value of liabilities. This implies a large loss in the market value of equity.

Of course, as we have already mentioned, historically such losses on outstanding loans for savings and loan's did not have to be recognized until they are sold. If assets (and liabilities) had been required to be periodically "marked to market"—as has been frequently recommended in proposed financial reforms—these losses would have been recognized and written off against equity. Had that been the case, many savings and loans would have been driven to insolvency during the early 1980s. As it was, many of these firms carried the hidden losses for many months or years, and in many cases their situation became much worse.

Obviously, it is important for financial managers to be cognizant of the impact of interest rate exposures on the value of shareholder interests. The experience of the savings and loans shows us how an outsized mismatch between the durations of assets and liabilities places the value of equity at great risk when rates increase. In the discussion that follows, we provide a framework for evaluating the exposure of the asset-liability position of a firm to changes in market rates and suggest alternatives for correcting such exposures.

Our framework is based on the relationships discussed earlier in this chapter between duration and the price sensitivity of financial claims to yield changes. Recall that the rate of change in the price of an asset is equal to the product of its modified duration and the change in the (unique) discount rate or yield to maturity (see equation 21.5), or approximately

$$\Delta P/P \approx -D\Delta r$$

Imagine a simple firm composed entirely of financial assets with market value A, financial liabilities with value L, and equity with market value of $E = A - L$. The change in the value of equity in response to a change in market yields can be expressed as follows:

$$\Delta E = \Delta A - \Delta L$$

and substituting from 21.5,[3]

$$\Delta E = (-AD_A\Delta r) - (-LD_L\Delta r)$$

$$\Delta E = -(AD_A - LD_L)\Delta r, \qquad (21.6)$$

where D_A and D_L are the durations of A and L, respectively. Moreover, the implicit duration of equity can be defined by,

$$ED_E = AD_A - LD_L$$

or

$$D_E = (AD_A - LD_L)/E \qquad (21.7)$$

The intuition behind equation 21.6 is that, for a given change in market yields, equity will realize greater losses when D_A is large relative to D_L. This was the case for the savings and loans industry during the 1980s. In addition, since the decrease in the value of liabilities associated with a rate increase partially offsets asset losses, the change in the value of equity, E, will depend on the initial imbalance between assets and liabilities, or A and L. This is most easily seen if we allow the durations of both assets and liabilities to equal 1.0. Then the change in equity will depend purely on $A - L$, the initial level of equity. Equation 21.7 is based on the idea that equity has no duration in the usual sense. It is not a fixed-income claim by definition, though in this case, the cash flows to equity are entirely determined as the residual of cash flows to two other fixed-income claims. Therefore, equity behaves, regarding the effects of yield changes, like a fixed-income claim with the duration defined in equation 21.7. This perspective is useful to conceptualize how equity responds to changes in rates and to formulate appropriate hedging strategies to protect equity from losses due to changes in market yields.

An important implication of equation 21.7 concerns the proper financial structure necessary to hedge against movements in market yields. This is easily seen by solving it for the case where D_E is zero, which requires that the following condition hold:

$$AD_A = LD_L \qquad (21.8)$$

For the firm as a whole, positive equity requires that A be greater than L; so, to hedge the market value of equity, the requisite condition is that D_L be greater than D_A. At the margin, however, new assets may be entirely funded by debt. In that case, to hedge the impact (at the margin) of new assets and liabilities on the interest rate exposure of existing equity, $D_L = D_A$.

A final numerical example will illustrate and further clarify the relevance of this point. Consider a simple financial firm that makes three-year fixed-rate loans at 10 percent (annual) and funds those loans with five-year deposits at 8 percent and with equity. Assume that loans and deposits pay interest semiannually, with principal due at maturity. The initial balance sheet and pro forma income statement are shown in Panel A of Table 21-9. Notice that net earnings

[3]Remember that equation 21.5 is an approximation of equation 21.4. The term $1/(1 + r)$ is assumed to be close to unity. Our derivation of equation 21.6 also assumes that changes in the yields on both assets and liabilities will be equal. A more precise but more complicated version of equation 21.6 can easily be developed that relaxes both assumptions. We use the simpler version here to facilitate and clarify the exposition.

are hedged for a period of three years. Additionally, the interest rate GAP over the first three years is zero. From that perspective the firm is not exposed to interest rate changes until the loan must be rolled over after three years. However, the value of equity is not hedged over the first three years. The exposure of equity to changes in market yields during that time can be determined by applying equation 21.6.

Durations (measured in half years) for loans and deposits are determined as shown in Panel B of Table 21-9. These calculations imply:

$$D_A = 5.32 \text{ or } 2.66 \text{ years}$$

$$D_L = 8.44 \text{ or } 4.22 \text{ years}$$

The implied duration of equity is computed according to equation 21.7 as

$$D_E = \frac{AD_A - LD_L}{E} = \frac{\$300(2.66) - \$275(4.22)}{\$25} = -14.5 \text{ years}$$

Table 21-9

Panel A: Balance Sheet and Income Statement

Balance Sheet				Pro Forma Income Statement	
Assets		Liabilities and Net Worth			
3-Year loans (10%)	\$300	\$275	5-year deposits (8%)	Interest Income	\$30
		\$25	Equity	Interest Expense	\$22
	\$300	\$300		NII	\$8

Durations (measured in half years) for loans and deposits are determined as follows:

Panel B: Duration Values

Loans

$$D_A = \frac{\frac{\$15}{1.05}(1) + \frac{\$15}{1.04^2}(2) + \frac{\$15}{1.04^3}(3) + \frac{\$15}{1.04^4}(4) + \frac{\$15}{1.04^5}(5) + \frac{\$315}{1.04^6}(6)}{\$300}$$

Deposits

$$D_L = \frac{\frac{\$11}{1.04}(1) + \frac{\$11}{1.04^2}(2) + \frac{\$11}{1.04^3}(3) + \ldots + \frac{\$11}{1.04^9}(9) + \frac{\$286}{1.04^{10}}(10)}{\$275}$$

This result implies that, as regards changes in market yields, the value of equity will respond as if it were a short position in a fixed-income security with a duration of 14.5 years. In other words, equityholders' exposure to interest rate risk is the same as if they held a short position in a zero-coupon bond with a maturity of 14.5 years. This risk is considerably greater than you might have initially expected. The impact of a 1-percent decrease in rates is to change the value of equity by

$$\Delta E/E = D_E \Delta r = 14.5\%$$

$$\Delta E = -ED_E \Delta r = \$3.625 \text{ loss}$$

This means that the value of equity would change from \$25 to \$21.375 as a result of the 1-percent interest rate change. Note finally that, in some sense, the effect of the 1-percent decrease in yields on the value of equity "foreshadows" the ultimate changes in cash flows that will take place if the rate change is permanent. The net interest income (NII) will become \$5 during years four and five when loans are rolled over at 9 percent after three years.

This procedure is useful not only to identify and quantify the exposure of equity to interest rate risk but also to suggest appropriate actions to modify the situation, either to eliminate such exposures or to bring interest sensitivity of equity to a more acceptable level. For example, suppose the objective of management of our firm was to eliminate as much exposure to interest rate risk as possible. What alternatives might be pursued to do so? One approach is to alter the durations of assets and /or liabilities so that the condition in equation 21.8 holds more closely. This involves some combination of shortening the duration of liabilities and lengthening that of assets. Thus, the firm's management may not be able to correct the imbalance quickly by altering the maturities of instruments on the sheet. Loans may have to be sold and new loans may have to be made to lengthen maturities. This would have to be done selectively, and there may be some costs to consider. At the same time it may also be difficult to call deposits and reissue at shorter maturities unless higher rates are offered. Another alternative is to offset the interest rate sensitivity with an appropriate position in futures contracts. A sufficiently long position in interest rate futures could be used to offset the exposure associated with equity.

SUMMARY

We began this chapter with a treatment of duration and the coupon effect in fixed-income instruments. We examined how changes in interest rates and maturity influence the value of bonds with different coupon rates. We constructed a variety of examples to illustrate the effects of interest rate and maturity on price and found that we needed a measure of the overall maturity of cash flows accruing to a bond. The measure we employed to capture maturity of many cash flows is the Macaulay duration. We showed how to compute it and demonstrated how it captures the relationship between a bond's price and a common discount rate applied to its cash flows. We also discussed some of the shortcomings of duration.

Next we focused on asset and liability management. We described the nature of the potential mismatch between assets and liabilities on a company's balance sheet and how a GAP report could be prepared to show the impact of changes in interest rates on accounting measures of performance. We showed how to simulate the impact of a shift in the yield curve on interest income net of interest expense, or NII. This simple tool has tremendous practical value, but its simplicity should be kept in mind. It does not measure how interest rate changes influence the market value of assets and liabilities and therefore does not show the sensitivity of the value of equity to interest rates. Next we addressed the topic of immunization, strategies that can fix the value of a portfolio of cash flows accruing at different times or a portfolio of bonds at a point in time. This entails structuring that portfolio so that fluctuations in reinvestment income generated by early cash flows offset fluctuations in the market value of the portfolio at a specific point in time. We learned it is possible to pick an immunized portfolio by structuring it so that the duration of the cash flows in it equals the horizon or the time interval at which we would like to fix the portfolio's value. We gave an example of immunization and found that when the portfolio is structured in this way the total value at the intended investment horizon will not decrease as a result of changes in interest rates. The limitation of using duration for immunization or for other purposes in managing interest rate risk is that the immunization strategy we described works using the Macaulay duration only for parallel shifts in the yield curve. Next, we examined how to measure the duration of equity as a function of the durations of assets and liabilities. Using this approach we showed how equity responds to interest rate changes.

QUESTIONS

1. Consider a $100,000 bond that pays on 10-percent coupons semiannually. Calculate the value of the bond for combinations of the following maturities and zero-coupon yields for all maturities (flat yield curve): maturities of 5, 10, 15, and 20 years; interest rates of 8 percent, 10 percent, 12 percent, and 14 percent.
2. Consider the results of question one. Describe how maturity and discount rate affect the value of a coupon-bearing bond. Explain these effects in as much detail and with as much intuition as you can.
3. Compute the duration of the following bonds, all with face value of $100,000, that differ by their coupon and maturity. Assume coupon rates of 8 percent, 10 percent, 12 percent, and 14 percent. Consider maturities of 5, 10, 15, and 20 years, and assume the yield curve is flat at 9 percent.
4. Notice that the duration of a bond decreases as the coupon increases, for a given maturity. Also notice that the duration of a zero-coupon bond is equal to its maturity. Explain these properties of duration as thoroughly as you can.
5. Why is duration better than maturity as a measure of the timing of cash flows of a bond?
6. In question 3, you calculated duration of a 10-percent ten-year bond. Suppose the zero-coupon yield curve is flat and changes from 9 percent to 8 percent. How can you use duration to predict the change in the bond price that will result? Will you be exactly correct or only approximately correct? Why?

7. What are *convexity* and *negative convexity?* Why are they important?
8. The Macaulay duration is only one possible measure of duration. It has some serious drawbacks. Explain the limits of this measure of duration as thoroughly as you can.
9. Suppose a financial firm has the following balance sheet as of 31 December 1992:

Assets	($ Millions)
Treasury bills[a]	80
Mortgages	140
Credit card receivables[b]	60
Commercial loans[c]	120
Leases[d]	60
Total assets	460
Liabilities and Equity	
CDs[e]	60
Commercial paper[f]	120
Banks loans[g]	80
Notes payable[h]	140
Equity	60
Total liabilities and equity	460

[a]$20 matures at the end of each quarter over the next year.
[b]At a fixed rate.
[c]Reprices semiannually.
[d]Reprices monthly.
[e]Reprices in six months.
[f]Three-month maturity.
[g]One-year maturity.
[h]Three-year maturity.

Prepare a GAP report with a one-year time frame for this company. Estimate the impact of selected interest rate changes on the company.

10. Explain the idea of duration of the equity of a company. Assuming a company has positive equity, what is required for the duration of equity to be zero? What does it mean for the duration of equity to be zero? Is this good or bad for the company?
11. Immunization involves the balancing of reinvestment and market value risk. How can these be balanced? Explain the basic idea here with as much intuition as you can.
12. Suppose you want to buy a bond and hold it five years. The yield curve is flat at 8 percent. You can select from a set of seven-year and ten-year bonds with the following coupons:

    Seven-year: 0 percent, 2 percent, and 4 percent coupons

    Ten-year: 14-percent, 12-percent, and 8-percent coupons

    Which would you choose, assuming all are fairly priced? Why?

13. Given your choice in question 12, show what would happen to the total value of your investment at year five if interest rates (i.e., the zero-coupon yield curve) shifted to 4 percent and to 12 percent.
14. How would your choice in problem 12 be affected if you thought there was a 20-percent chance you might need the money after three years rather than five years?

REFERENCES

Bierwag, Gerold O. *Duration Analysis: Managing Interest Rate Risk.* Cambridge, MA: Ballinger, 1987.

Berton, Lee. "FASB Votes to Make Banks and Insurers Value Certain Bonds at Current Prices." *Wall Street Journal,* April 14, 1993.

Macaulay, Frederick R. *The Movement of Interest Rates, Bonds, Yields, and Stock Prices in the United States Since 1865.* New York: Columbia University Press, 1938.

• *Chapter 22*

Innovations in Managing Interest Rate Risk

In this chapter we explore additional methods for managing interest rate risk. In the first half we concentrate on how securities have been designed to facilitate better management of interest rate risk. This constitutes an additional avenue through which innovation has affected financial markets, in addition to those discussed in Part III. We start be examining the pricing of prepayment risk in mortgage-backed securities. Then we look at some of the ways fixed-income securities, particularly mortgage-backed securities, have been restructured or redesigned in recent years to make them more attractive to investors. In the second half of the chapter we return to the product set for risk management that we developed in Part III of this book, that is, futures, forwards, options, and swaps. We complete our description of the product set by describing caps, collars, and floors. Then we work through a sequence of problems that companies often face in structuring new, current, and future financing and in restructuring their balance sheets. The examples we consider could apply to either financial or nonfinancial firms. They illustrate how the various risk management products can be used to solve a variety of problems. Because an important role of financial firms is to provide risk management services to nonfinancial firms, it is just as important for the managers of financial institutions to understand how to apply these tools to their customer's problems as it is to apply them to their own financial management.

• *Concepts to Learn in Chapter 22* •

- How to create a synthetic zero-coupon bond
- How IOs, POs, and CMOs work
- How floors, caps, and collars work
- How to use swaps, floors, caps, and collars to restructure a balance sheet

Security Design and Product Innovation

One of the most important approaches to managing interest rate risk involves restructuring cash flows, or designing securities that are suited to the tastes or interests of particular investors. During the 1980s a large number of new types of securities were introduced into the marketplace with exactly this purpose in mind. The underlying reason for such innovation is that it is often advantageous for the issuers to try to construct securities in such a way that the risk management problem facing the investor is minimized. Probably the area of the capital markets where this restructuring to facilitate risk management has progressed farthest is mortgage-backed securities, and more generally, asset-backed securities. As we learned in Chapter 18, asset-backed securities are backed by a wide variety of consumer or commercial receivables, including auto, boat, and credit card (e.g., Visa) receivables, or leases. Here the magnitude of the prepayment problem and the sheer size of the total mortgage and receivables market created a critical need for new and effective ways to deal with interest rate risk. In this chapter we describe just a few of the key innovations in this area and how they help solve the interest rate risk management problem. We first examine prepayment risk in mortgage-backed securities; then we turn to the process of security design, beginning with the creation of synthetic discount or zero-coupon instruments, or what is called coupon "stripping." Then we discuss CMOs and other forms of asset-backed securities.

Managing Prepayment Risk

Prepayment risk has taken on tremendous importance in the U.S. capital markets because of the large volume of mortgages and mortgage-backed securities that now exist and because the volatility of interest rates over the last decade has led to considerable volatility in prepayment rates. The prepayment option in a mortgage is similar to the call option in a corporate bond. The issuer of the mortgage, the borrower, has the right to pay off the mortgage by prepaying the principal any time over the life of the loan. As we discussed in Chapter 9, this might occur because the borrower moves or because better terms become available on new mortgages. If interest rates on new mortgages fall below the rate on a borrower's existing mortgage, it may be in her interest to prepay, though since substantial costs are involved in taking out a new mortgage, it is not wise to refinance whenever the current mortgage rate falls just a little below the rate on one's existing mortgage. In general, given the normal level of transactions costs involved in taking out a new mortgage, a spread of nearly 200 basis points is required before the present value of the savings from refinancing is expected to cover the transactions costs of taking out a new mortgage.

In order to be able to value a portfolio of mortgages or evaluate a potential mortgage investment, it is exceptionally important to be able to predict prepayment rates. As a result, considerable resources have been expended in recent years, both on Wall Street and in academia, in attempts to construct statistical models that can explain prepayment patterns. The early studies of prepayments and early pricing systems for mortgages simply assumed that mortgages would prepay according to the historical experience of the Federal Housing Administration (FHA). FHA experience is important since Government National Mortgage Association (GNMA) mortgage pools are comprised largely of FHA-guaranteed mortgages. In addition, the largest data base on prepayment experience is for FHA mortgages. Table 22-1 shows the prepayment experience of the FHA for mortgages originated from 1957 to 1977 (what are called section 203 30-year home mortgages).

Table 22-1

1957–1977 FHA Experience—Survivorship Levels for FHA-Insured Section 203 30-Year Home Mortgages

Policy Year	Survivors at Beginning of Policy Year	Terminations During Policy Year	Prepayment Rate (%)
1	100,000.0	836.9	0.84
2	99,163.1	3,100.0	3.13
3	96,063.1	4,170.8	4.34
4	91,892.3	4,603.7	5.01
5	87,288.6	4,908.9	5.62
6	82,379.7	4,955.3	6.02
7	77,424.4	4,668.4	6.03
8	72,756.0	4,398.6	6.05
9	68,357.4	4,093.3	5.99
10	64,264.1	3,783.7	5.89
11	60,480.4	3,595.3	5.94
12	56,885.1	3,399.6	5.98
13	53,485.5	3,240.9	6.06
14	50,244.6	3,126.9	6.22
15	47,117.7	3,055.4	6.48
16	44,062.3	3,028.4	6.87
17	41,033.9	3,036.8	7.40
18	37,997.1	3,057.2	8.05
19	34,939.9	3,073.5	8.80
20	31,866.4	3,105.0	9.74
21	28,761.4	2,953.7	10.27
22	25,807.7	2,793.1	10.82
23	23,014.6	2,624.8	11.40
24	20,389.8	2,450.0	12.02
25	17,939.8	2,270.8	12.66
26	15,669.0	2,089.0	13.33
27	13,580.0	1,906.6	14.04
28	11,673.4	1,725.5	14.78
29	9,947.9	2,181.3	21.93
30	7.766.6	7.766.6	100.0

Source: Actuarial Division, U.S. Department of Housing and Urban Development.

The FHA experience can be used in at least two ways to value a mortgage portfolio. The simpler way is to compute the average life of the mortgages based on FHA experience and then assume that all of them in a specific portfolio will prepay at precisely that point in time. The FHA experience documented in Table 22-1 indicates that the average life of a mortgage during this period was between 14 and 15 years. We could use the assumption that mortgages will prepay at the end of 15 years to value a specific mortgage portfolio. For example, suppose we had a portfolio of 9-percent mortgages. Also suppose we applied a 14-percent interest rate to all of the cash flows in those mortgages. The value of this portfolio would be $70.25 per $100 of face value of the mortgages. This is the present value of scheduled interest and principal payments over 15 years and 100-percent prepayment at year 15, all at a discount rate of 14 percent.

A second, and presumably more accurate, method is to assume that the mortgages prepay in a pattern like that defined by FHA experience. This means that FHA prepayment rate in each year would be applied to the total mortgage portfolio so that it would be assumed to prepay gradually. For the same 9-percent mortgage portfolio discussed above, if the 14-percent discount rate were used, it would generate a value of $74.54. This is higher than the value generated using the average-life assumption above. The price based on the weighted-average life of a loan will always understate the value of a mortgage portfolio computed by applying the whole schedule of prepayment rates.

In this example we have computed the value of a mortgage portfolio for a given assumed prepayment pattern and with a single discount rate applied to all of its cash flows, but it is important to see that the risk of the prepayment pattern also affects the yield or price of a mortgage portfolio. In this example, we assumed that the relevant discount rate to apply to the assumed cash flow stream from the mortgages was 14 percent. A more sophisticated way to approach the mortgage pricing problem is to take into account the value of the option to prepay the mortgage. This has become a topic of tremendous importance in contemporary capital markets because of the large volume of mortgage-backed securities where the mortgage borrowers have this option.

Unfortunately, valuing the option to prepay a mortgage is a very complex problem. The essence of the difficulty is that mortgage borrowers do not prepay simply to minimize the cost of borrowing. Instead, as indicated above, many prepayments reflect the decision to move to a new home. Moreover, it is costly to exercise the option, since considerable fees must be paid to the lender to originate a new mortgage. Thus, the borrower has to determine whether it is worthwhile to refinance a mortgage; given the level of interest rates, the intended length of time that the borrower expects to remain in the residence, and his or her expectations about interest rates in the future. This problem is sufficiently complicated that prepayments probably will always have a considerable random component that is impossible to predict. It has been demonstrated, using historical data on prepayments as the basis for predicting future prepayments, that the value of mortgage-backed securities exhibits the negative convexity shown in Figure 22-1. This is the same as that illustrated in Chapter 21 in Figure 21-4. Recall that negative convexity means that, rather than exhibiting a negative relationship between the price of a bond and the interest rate, in some range of relatively low rates, the price of the bond actually decreases with falling rates. This is because at falling rates the option to prepay the bond is exercised so frequently that the value of the bond declines.

Since prepayment risk has become so important in recent years, Wall Street has become intensely interested in finding ways, not only to manage prepayment risk, but also to structure securities so that all forms of interest rate risk are easier to manage. This has led to the creation of a variety of new types of instruments. In order to explain these new securities, we begin with one of the earlier forms of innovations in security design, which does not deal directly with prepayment risk. Then we move on to innovations in mortgage-backed securities that are concerned with prepayment risk.

Figure 22-1
Negative convexity in the relationship between the interest rate and price of a bond with a prepayment option.

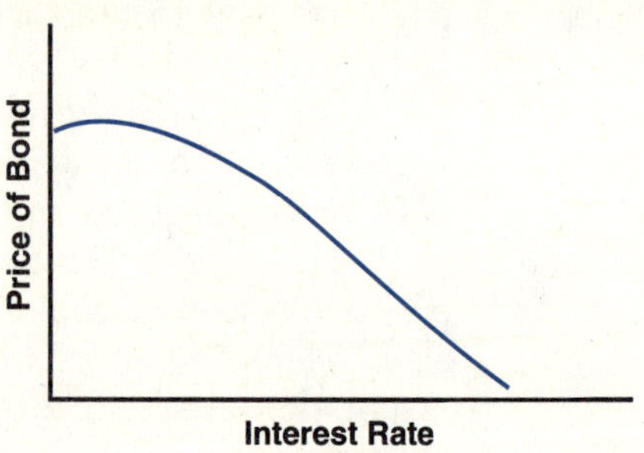

TIGRs, CATS, and Other Zeros

Recall that one of the key elements of interest rate risk is reinvestment risk. An obvious and seemingly simple way for many investors to deal with reinvestment risk is to avoid securities where either the cash flows are spread out over many periods or where the timing of cash flows is uncertain. This would mean avoiding traditional coupon-bearing bonds and the pass-through form of mortgage-backed securities. Instead, an investor who knew that he wanted to invest for, say, five years could buy a zero-coupon bond with a five-year maturity. If he could not find a zero-coupon bond he might try a deep-discount bond or an original issue discount (OID) bond. An OID bond is a bond issued with a coupon rate below the going market interest rate for a bond of the same maturity. The zero-coupon bond is simply the limiting case of an OID, since the coupon rate for such a bond is zero.

Historically, OID and zero-coupon bonds were rather rare financial instruments. Neither the U.S. government nor private corporations issued them. Private corporations did not do so because a corporation financed entirely with zero-coupon debt has no obligation to provide cash flows to bondholders until maturity. Since insolvency is determined by ability to meet cash obligations, an OID bond and particularly a zero-coupon bond provides substantial latitude to corporate borrowers. A corporation financed largely with zero-coupon debt does not have to answer to debt holders for a long time, a situation viewed as very risky for debt holders. However, as the level and volatility of interest rates increased in the late 1970s and 1980s, corporations began to issue OID bonds. Originally, the issuance of OID bonds was also enhanced by their tax treatment.

When they first began to appear in 1980, OID bonds had some very attractive tax advantages. The principal one was that the Internal Revenue Service allowed the issuer to amortize the interest expense over the life of the bond based on a straight-line prorating procedure. A straight-line procedure means that the present value of the tax-deductible interest expense will be larger for a discount bond than for a comparable bond without a discount. The risk reduction and tax advantages of OID bonds led to a virtual flood of such bonds into the public U.S. bond market, beginning in March 1981 and ending in 1982. The first publicly issued OID bond was issued by Martin Marietta Corporation in March 1981. Before that time all OID bonds were privately issued and generally of poor credit quality. After the Martin Marietta issue there were 21 publicly placed high–credit quality OID bonds issued by July 1981, raising a total of $2 billion. It was not until 1982 that the first corporate zero-coupon bond was issued, by PepsiCo, for $850 million. The net borrowing cost for this issue was almost 4 percent, or 400 basis points below the prevailing yield at that time on comparable maturity Treasury bonds. But the Tax Equity and Fiscal Responsibility Act of 1982 (approved 3 September 1982) changed this situation. It dropped the tax advantages by eliminating the straight-line prorating of taxes. Issuers of OID bonds would have a tax advantage only if these bonds could be sold to tax-exempt investors. Domestically, the most important tax-exempt investors who had a desire to avoid reinvestment risk were pension funds, though there was also a significant market for OID bonds in Japan, since Japanese investors had no taxes on capital gains and appreciation of OID bonds was considered at that time a capital gain in Japan. Therefore, the 1982 tax changes in the United States created a market for zero-coupon Eurobonds.

While major U.S. corporations were issuing OID bonds to take advantage of their tax treatment and gain from the risk reduction they provided investors, investment bankers were busy searching for a way to add to the supply of zero-coupon bonds. One possible way was to attempt to transform coupon-paying bonds into zero-coupon bonds. Investment bankers at Merrill Lynch were the first to capitalize on this opportunity. They introduced a new security they called Treasury income growth receipts, or TIGRS. TIGRS were created by acquiring coupon-paying T bonds and stripping the coupons. This means that the coupon-paying T bonds were broken into parts; coupon payments or cash flows due on a specific date were combined from a number of distinct T bonds. These cash flows were then used to form a new security with a single cash flow due on the same day as the coupon payment for all of the underlying T bonds. A separate security was created for each of the coupon dates on the underlying T bonds. These new securities were then zero-coupon bonds. They had the added advantage of being free of default risk, since all of the cash flows were obligations of the U.S. Treasury. The issuer of the new securities placed the T bonds in a trust, so that investors could be certain that the cash flows would be available as promised.

This example of financial engineering involves the creation of a new security that is perceived to be more valuable to the market than the existing securities from which it is created. The new security adds value, since it provides real opportunities for risk reduction not previously available. To the innovator of such a product the benefits can be short lived. Once Merrill Lynch created the first stripped zero-coupon bond, it took very little time for other investment bankers to create their own out of T bonds and to market them under their own names. For example, Salomon Brothers introduced their own zero-coupon bonds formed by stripping T bonds and labeled them CATS, certificates of accrual on treasury securities. As a result, zero-coupon bonds are often generically referred to as *"cats."* Another version created from municipal bonds were called MCATS. The profits earned by an originator of zero-coupon bonds depends on the difference between the selling prices of the zero-coupon bonds created from T bonds and the prices at which those T bonds must be acquired. If real value is added to the market and if there is only one issuer of these zero-coupon bonds, as was the case for a short time with Merrill Lynch, then the issuer reaps the benefit of the spread between the value of the zero-coupon bonds and the value of the underlying T bonds. As new issuers enter the market, however, they drive down the price of zero-coupon bonds until the benefits accrue to those bond purchasers simply as a result of the competition in the market for creating or issuing zero-coupon instruments.

• *LYONs Give Merrill Lynch a Reason to Roar* •

A particularly interesting example of zero-coupon bond created by Wall Street firms in recent years is known as a LYON (for liquid yield option note). LYONs were created by Merrill Lynch & Co. in 1985, and they have been responsible for underwriting roughly 80 percent of all the issues of this form of security since that time. LYONs, and their competitors from other firms, are zero-coupon bonds that are convertible into the stock of the issuing company or possibly into some other security. The appeal of LYONs to the companies that issue them is that they can deduct the interest each year from their taxable income, even though they don't actually have to make interest payments until the bonds mature. This is the case for an issuer of any zero-coupon bond. If LYONs are converted into stock, the companies may never actually have to pay that interest expense, since the holders of the bond have chosen to hold stock instead. Of course, the issuers have still received their tax deduction.

LYONs have been one of the most successful and profitable innovations Wall Street, and particularly Merrill Lynch, has come up with in some time. As of the end of 1991, $38.85 billion face amount of such securities had been issued in the United States. This resulted in total proceeds for the issuing companies of $11.7 billion, since these zero-coupon bonds are sold at a deep discount relative to face value.[1] Figure 22-2 documents the total annual proceeds from new issues of LYONs and the fees earned by Merrill Lynch on theirs. It is particularly interesting to note that Merrill Lynch has been so successful in maintaining its market share for so long and in installing their particular brand name as the generic label for this class of securities.

Restructuring Mortgage Cash Flows: Interest-Only and Principal-Only Securities

Coupon stripping to create zero-coupon securities devoid of reinvestment risk is not possible in the mortgage market, owing to the prepayment risk. While it is feasible to separate the interest payments from the principal payments, the resulting instruments are not risk free. It is possible to construct instruments with very different risk exposures. This prospect has led to the emergence of what are referred to as interest-only (IO) and principal-only (PO) securities. It is important to understand

---

[1]See Randall Smith, "Tax Status of LYONs, One of Street's Hottest Products, Gets IRS Challenge," *Wall Street Journal,* December 17, 1991.

Figure 22-2

Annual proceeds from new U. S. issues of Liquid Yield Option Notes, in billions.

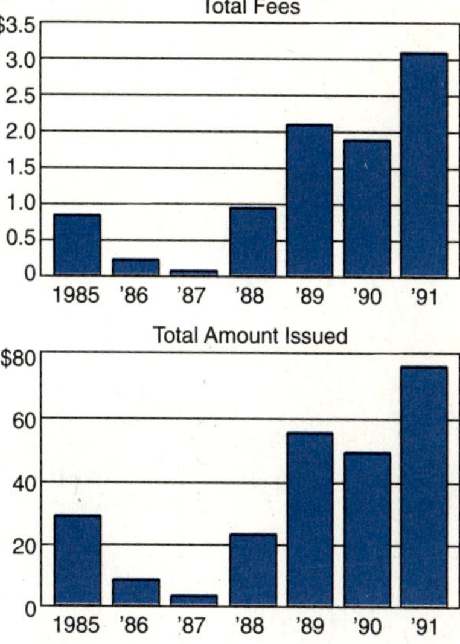

Annual Merrill Lynch Fees For Lyons issues sold in the United States, in millions.

Source: Reprinted by permission of The Wall Street Journal © *1992 Dow Jones and Company, Inc. All Rights Reserved Worldwide.*

the differences in the effect of prepayment on these two portions of the mortgage cash flow. Prepayments do not affect the total cash flows accruing to the PO, but they do affect their timing. As prepayments increase, the duration of the PO decreases. The same cannot be said for the IO, however. As mortgages are prepaid, the cash flow stream accruing to the IO is reduced.

Since we know how changes in interest rates are likely to affect the cash flows to the IO and PO, we can trace the connection between interest rates and the values of each. To understand this, let's consider an example of a very simple mortgage with an initial value of \$10,000, four years to maturity, an amortization schedule of one payment per year, and an interest rate of 12 percent. The annual payment from the borrower will be an annuity, *A*, that solves the following present value problem:

$$\$10{,}000 = A\left[\frac{1 - (1/1.12)^4)}{0.12}\right]$$

The amortization schedule for this loan is shown in Panel A of Table 22-2. If we knew there would be no prepayments, then the value of the IO would be the present value of interest payments shown in Table 22-3. Discounting at the rate of 12 percent, this yields a value of \$2527.34. Similarly, the value of the PO under the same assumptions is \$7472.65. Notice that the combined value is \$10,000, the value of the entire loan.

Now suppose the loan prepays at the end of year three. Panel B of Table 22-2 shows the modified cash flows that would now accrue to the IO and the PO. Notice that if we discount these new cash flows at the same interest rate of 12 percent the new values of the two cash flow streams are as follows:

Value of IO = \$2303.15

Value of PO = \$7696.84

Table 22-2
Cash Flows for Amortizing Loan With and Without Prepayment

Panel A: Cash Flows Without Prepayment

	1	2	3	4
Interest portion	$1200.00	$948.92	$667.71	$352.75
Principal portion	$2092.34	$2343.42	$2624.63	$2939.59
Principal remaining	$7907.66	$5564.24	$2939.61	0

Panel B: Cash Flows from a Loan That Prepays in Three Years

	1	2	3
Interest portion	$1200.00	$948.92	$667.71
Principal portion	$2092.34	$2343.42	$5564.24
Total	$3292.34	$3292.34	$6231.95

The value of the IO has declined by $224.19 while that of the PO has increased by the same amount. This reflects the fact that the cash flows on the PO have simply been accelerated while the cash flows on the IO have been reduced.

Next let's see what happens to the value of the IO and the PO if interest rates change. We assume that the yield curve shifts either up or down by 200 basis points, so that interest rates are either 10 percent or 14 percent. We want to separate the effect of the changing discount rate on the value of the two cash flow streams from the effect of the prepayment that the declining interest rate may generate. Table 22-3 illustrates both effects. The table shows the value of both the IO and the PO at the 10-percent and 14-percent interest rates, both with and without prepayment. Note that the table highlights what we call the most likely scenarios. This means that if the interest rate increases to 14 percent, prepayment is not likely, whereas if it decreases to 10 percent prepayment is likely. Notice that if no prepayment occurs a decline in

Table 22-3
The Effect on the Value of IO and PO Streams of a Change in Rates of 2 Percent

Prepayment experience	Yield scenario	Value of IO portion	Value of PO portion	Value of total
No prepayment	$R = 10\%$	$2617.72	$7818.25	$10,435.96
No prepayment	$R = 14\%$	$2442.35	$7150.59	$9,592.93
3-year prepayment	$R = 10\%$	$2376.79	$8019.34	$10,396.13
3-year prepayment	$R = 14\%$	$2233.48	$7394.27	$9,627.75

*The likely scenarios are enclosed by the heavy line.

interest rates causes the values of both securities to increase. If that decline precipitates a prepayment at year three, the prepayment causes the value of the IO to decline while it causes the value of the PO to increase farther. In this example, the combined effect of the decrease in interest rates and the prepayment at year three means that the value of the IO declines as interest rates fall to 10 percent while the value of the PO rises. The fact that the IO can react directly rather than inversely to changes in interest rates means that the IO security has a very unique feature relative to other forms of fixed-income securities. This makes it valuable as a hedging instrument. Also, notice that the value of the PO is more volatile because the direct effect of interest rates and the indirect effect through changing prepayments reinforce each other. The value of the IO is less volatile because the two effects oppose each other.

This behavior of the value of the PO and IO with respect to interest rate changes is illustrated in Figure 22-3. Panel A shows the value of the IO and Panel B the value of the PO, corresponding to interest rates of 10 percent, 12 percent, and 14 percent. Both figures assume that prepayments occur only at 10 percent. Notice that as interest rates fall from 14 percent to 12 percent, both the IO and the PO increase in value,

Figure 22-3

Panel A: Value of IO with and without prepayment at 10 percent. *Panel B*: Value of PO with and without prepayment at 10 percent.

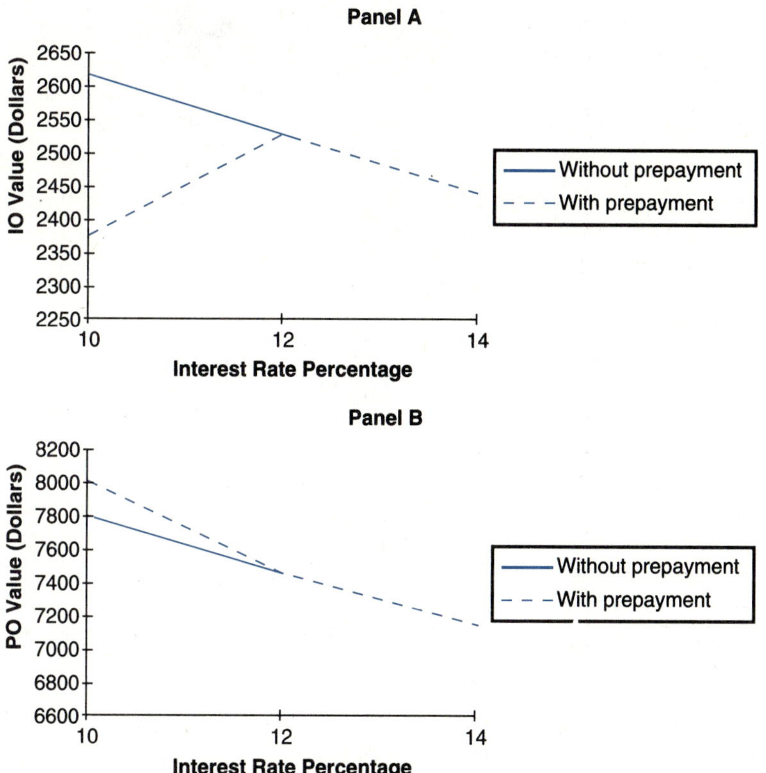

but then the effect of prepayment and the direct effect of the decline in rates are relevant for the drop in rates to 10 percent. Notice that the value of the IO declines while the value of the PO increases even more, as a result of the effect of prepayment.

The Advent of the Collateralized Mortgage Obligation

IOs and POs are only one possible way to restructure cash flows in mortgages to deal with prepayment risk. Probably the most important form of restructuring is the collateralized mortgage obligation (CMO). The CMO splits the cash flows generated by a pool of mortgages into separate categories and issues securities with claims to the specialized cash flows generated by an entire pool of mortgages. This kind of innovation is useful, because security holders with preferences for specific maturities can purchase a claim on the cash flows from a pool of mortgages that has been constructed to satisfy specific maturity preferences. The investor need not accept a pro rata share of all the cash flows from all mortgages. Instead these cash flows can be carved up in such a way that early cash flows are concentrated in one class of security holder while later ones are concentrated in another class who prefer a longer maturity.

The CMO creates tranches, or classes of securities. *"Tranches"* are claims to principal payments generated by the mortgage pool in order of priority. For example, one possible structure would entail four tranches, where the first tranche has title to all of the principal payments until the securities in that tranche are retired. The second tranche would have a claim on all principal payments generated after the first tranche is retired or paid off. Then the third tranche would have a claim on all of the subsequent cash flows until retired. The fourth tranche would receive the final payments. Throughout the life of the pool all three tranches would accrue interest at the rate specified in the mortgages in the pool, though as principal payments flowed in they would be allocated to a specific tranche.

This structure is illustrated in Figure 22-4.[2] Panel A of this figure shows how the cash flows generated by the pool over time are allocated among four tranches, plus a residual. Each of the four tranches is divided into two parts, corresponding to the principal and interest payments to that tranche. For example, AI refers to the interest payments to tranche A; BP refers to the principal payments to tranche B. Notice that the first three tranches are referred to as tranches A, B, and C; the final tranche is labeled tranche Z. The figure shows that during the first few years of the life of these securities all four tranches receive their interest payments, but tranche A receives all principal payments up to some prespecified limit. If there are principal payments over that limit, they accrue to the residual. After tranche A has been completely paid off, then prepayments are allocated to tranche B until it is paid off, and so forth. Panel B of the figure shows the time distribution of cash flows that would accrue from the presumed pattern of prepayments. Notice that fluctuations in

[2]This way of portraying the tranches in a CMO is extracted from A. Hess and C. Smith, "Elements of Mortgage Securitization," *Journal of Real Estate Finance and Economics* 1 (1988), pp. 331–346.

Figure 22-4

Allocation of cash flows to tranches of a CMO.

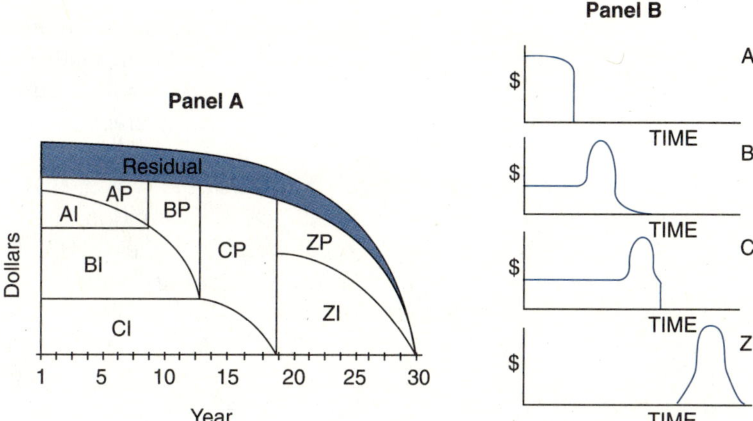

the level of prepayments are absorbed first by the residual, so that the specific tranches are protected from much of the prepayment risk. This means that the residual is a very risky instrument; it is sometimes referred to as "nuclear waste."

The CMO structure incorporates risk regarding the timing of cash receipt, just as there is in the traditional pass-through security; however, that risk has been split up and allocated to specific securities. The CMO reduces the timing uncertainty associated with principal repayments by directing principal to each class of security in order of priority. In addition, the issuer often guarantees a minimum prepayment rate to further reduce the uncertainty of cash flows. This is the residual in Figure 22-4. Because of the more predictable cash flows, the higher-priority CMO securities are like short-term coupon-bearing bonds and the lower-priority securities like intermediate and long-term coupon-bearing bonds. Furthermore, the CMO may make semiannual or quarterly payments rather than monthly ones, as with most pass-through securities. Because CMOs were made more like coupon-bearing bonds, a broader class of investors have developed a preference for mortgage-backed securities via the CMO.

The difference between the CMO and the standard pass-through is important. With the standard pass-through, every security holder in a given issue receives a pro rata share of all cash flows generated by a pool of mortgages. Therefore, every investor has an equivalent share of the total prepayment risk for that pool. In a CMO, specific tranches bear all of specific parts of the prepayment risk for the entire pool of mortgages. This risk partitioning is valuable to the market if there are clienteles who want cash flows with specific maturities that can be matched with a tranche. These investors may be willing to accept some risk that corresponds to a tranche of the CMO though they would be willing to accept the entire prepayment risk that is inherent in the traditional pass-through only if they were paid a very high price to do so. By limiting the magnitude of specific portions of the prepayment risk, the CMO structure can add value to the market.

In the first few years that CMOs were issued, investors and issuers were keenly interested in evaluating the prepayment patterns and life of these new instruments. By 1986, $36 billion in CMOs had been issued. This was enough volume to begin to analyze their behavior. Table 22-4 provides some data on the number of tranches used in the first $36 billion of CMOs. More than 80 percent of the CMOs utilize four tranches, and a little more than half utilize quarterly cash distributions.

Figure 22-5 shows what is called the mean weighted-average life of the tranches in the CMOs described in the previous table. The *mean weighted-average life* measures the expected maturity, or life, of each tranche of the typical CMO. In order to calculate this number it is necessary to make some assumption about prepayment patterns on the mortgages that provide collateral for the CMO. One possible assumption is that the mortgages will prepay according to the FHA experience described earlier. The assumption underlying Figure 22-5 is that mortgages will prepay according to the experience recorded by the Public Securities Association, whose experience differs from that of the FHA. Figure 22-5 shows the mean weighted-average life for CMOs with three, four, and five to ten tranches.

Once the mean weighted-average life of a particular tranche of a CMO has been calculated, as in Figure 22-5, it is possible to compute the estimated yield on this tranche of the CMO and compare it with the yield on a comparable maturity Treasury instrument. The yield on each tranche of the CMO is calculated as the internal rate of return, given the assumption about prepayments used to compute the mean weighted-average life and the observed price of that tranche of the CMO. Figure 22-6 compares the yields on specific tranches of CMOs with the corresponding maturity Treasury for all CMOs issued by February 1986. The figure indicates that the spread between CMO yields and corresponding maturity T bonds increases with maturity. For example, the average spread was 76 basis points when the reference Treasury had three years to maturity, but it increased to 81 basis points for the seven-year maturity, 95 basis points for the ten-year, and 111 basis points for the 20-year one.

The spread between the yield on CMO and corresponding maturity Treasury instruments represents a compensation to the investor for the CMO's prepayment risk. Because the vast majority of CMOs are backed by mortgages guaranteed against default by the government (either GNMA or Federal Home Loan Mortgage

Table 22-4

Number of Tranches and Periodicity of Bond Payments

Number of Tranches	Cases	%	Periodicity	Cases	%
3	16	9.9	Monthly	17	10.6
4[a]	133	82.6	Quarterly	86	53.4
≥5	12	7.5	Seminannual[b]	58	36.0

[a]There is one case of two tranches plus serial bonds.

[b]In one case interest was semiannual and principal was quarterly.

Source: Richard Roll. *Collateralized Mortgage Obligations: Characteristics, History, Analysis.* (New York: Goldman Sachs & Company, April 1986.)

Figure 22-5

Mean weighted-average life by number of tranches in CMO. *Source: Richard Roll.* Collateralized Mortgage Obligations: Characteristics, History, Analysis. (*New York: Goldman Sachs & Company, April 1986.*)

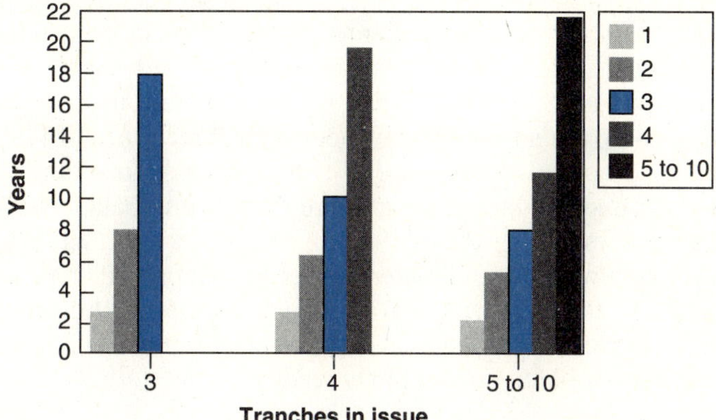

Corporation [FHLMC] mortgages), the yield spread shown in Figure 22-6 should not include a significant premium for default risk. The fact that the spread between CMO yields and Treasury yields increases with maturity indicates that the market perceives a higher prepayment risk for longer maturity tranches of the CMO. Since this figure represents a composite of what happened over a three-year period, it obscures the fact that the spreads between yields on each tranche of a CMO and the corresponding maturity Treasury instrument tend to rise and fall with the level of interest rates, a logical consequence of the relationship of prepayment risk to interest rates.

Figure 22-6

Yield spread versus Treasury maturity and frequency of use. *Source: Richard Roll.* Collateralized Mortgage Obligations: Characteristics, History, Analysis. (*New York: Goldman Sachs and Company, April 1986.*)

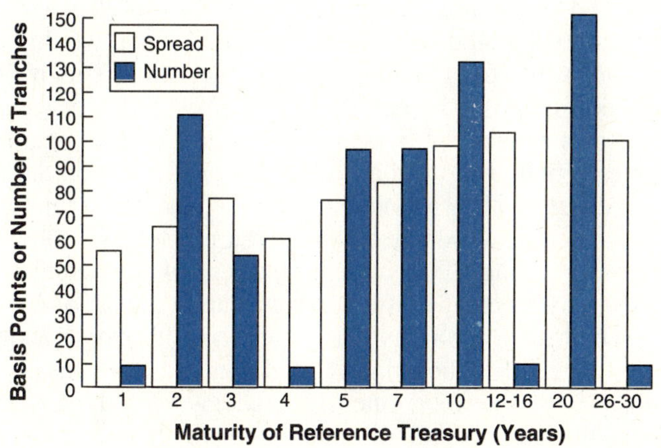

Using the Risk Management Product Set

Now we turn our attention to the practical problems that companies face when they are trying to manage their interest rate risk exposure. Our objective is to explore how what we have called the risk management product set can be used to solve various types of interest rate risk management problems. Recall that the product set includes cash market instruments, futures, forwards, options, swaps, caps, collars, and floors. We want to assess the alternative ways these various instruments can be used to structure a company's financing. We consider three types of financing problems often faced by corporations: the need for new current financing, the need for new future financing, and the need to restructure the existing balance sheet. We consider alternative ways in which the risk management product set can be used to solve problems in each of these three arenas. Before we proceed, we need to complete our description of the product set. We have spent quite a bit of time on most of the products in the set in earlier chapters, but we have yet to discuss caps, collars, and floors. We have the tools to do this fairly readily.

Caps, Collars, and Floors

A *cap* is simply a ceiling or upper bound on a specified interest rate; a *floor* is simply a lower bound on a rate. The easiest way to understand caps and floors is to think of them as being packaged with a loan, though this is somewhat dangerous, since they can easily be unbundled and sold or traded separately. Suppose a company arranges for a floating-rate loan from a bank, say at the London interbank offer rate (LIBOR) plus 50 basis points. The company is concerned that LIBOR might increase in the future, and it wants some protection against that increase. Suppose the loan reprices every three months and lasts three years. This means there would be 12 settlement dates. This company could also buy a cap from the bank to place an upper bound on the interest rate it would pay. If the cap were at 8.5 percent, then it would never pay an interest rate greater than that, regardless of what happened to LIBOR over the life of the loan. For example, suppose that on the fourth settlement date, one year from the beginning of the loan, LIBOR was 9 percent. Then the appropriate rate for the loan would be 9.5 percent, but the loan would be capped at 8.5 percent, so the borrower would be saving 100 basis points. This is illustrated in Figure 22-7, which shows a possible path for LIBOR over the three-year life of the loan. The horizontal axis is indexed by settlement dates, or by three-month intervals. The figure portrays both a cap and a floor on the index rate on the loan, ignoring the 0.5 percent markup. A floor would work just like a cap, except that it would set a lower bound on the rate. A borrower who had arranged for a floor of 6.5 percent would never pay less than 6.5 percent, regardless of the actual LIBOR rate. While it is easy to see why a borrower might want a cap, it is not so obvious why he might want a floor. The reason is simply that he will have to pay to acquire the cap while he will be paid to acquire the floor. If he thinks the compensation is worthwhile, he may choose to use the floor. Once you understand both caps and floors, it is simple to understand a collar. A collar is simply the simultaneous use of a cap and

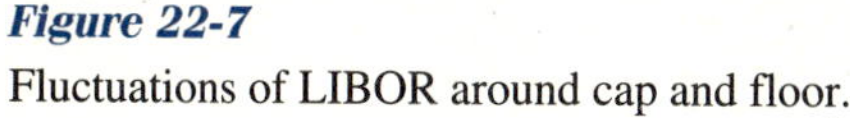

Figure 22-7

Fluctuations of LIBOR around cap and floor.

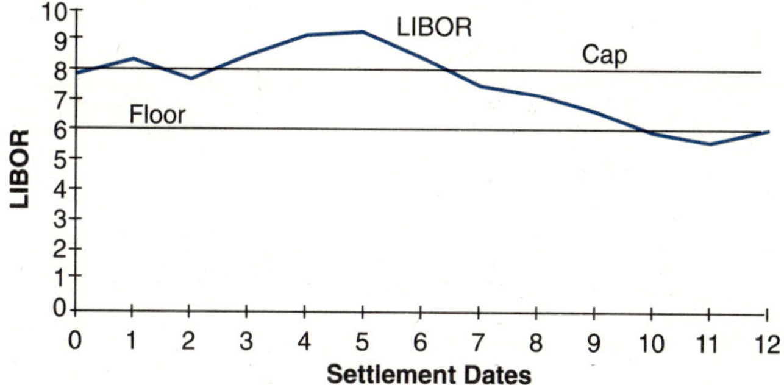

a floor. If the borrower in our example uses both an 8.5 percent cap and a 6.5 percent floor, he knows that his borrowing cost will fluctuate by no more than 200 basis points, regardless of what happens to LIBOR. Moreover, the price he has to pay for the cap will be partially offset by the price he is paid for the floor.

To see more clearly what we mean by the price of the cap or the floor, let's examine the connection between caps and floors and options. A cap on LIBOR at a specific settlement date is a put option on Eurodollars or on LIBOR. It is a put rather than a call, because options are defined in terms of prices rather than yields. The payoff on the option increases with LIBOR for values above 8 percent, so this is a put. The borrower who acquires the cap is long that put. This is illustrated in Figure 22-8, which shows the payoff on a cap, a floor, and a collar for a specific settlement date, as a function of LIBOR observed on that date using the standard option payoff diagram introduced in Chapter 15. Notice that the cap has a payoff like a call, since the axis is defined in terms of LIBOR. The floor taken by the borrower is equivalent to a short call, or a payoff like a put when stated in terms of the LIBOR rate. The borrower has written the option for the floor, since he is agreeing to pay the bank if LIBOR drops below 6 percent. The figure illustrates that the collar is defined by the difference between the exercise price, stated in terms of yield, of the cap and the collar. Notice that if the borrower obtained both a cap and floor at the same exercise price, say 7 percent for example, this would be equivalent to a fixed rate on the loan, or a forward rate agreement. Therefore, as the size of the collar shrinks, it approaches the equivalent of a forward rate for a specific settlement date.

The payoffs illustrated in Figure 22-8 pertain to only one of the 12 settlement dates in the loan in our example. There would be a similar set of payoffs for each of the 11 other settlement dates. The cap, floor, and collar generally describe a commitment to a sequence of settlement dates or a bundle or portfolio of options such as we just described. Notice that this structure parallels the structure of swaps (see Chapter 16). Recall that a swap is nearly identical to a portfolio or bundle of forward contracts, since a swap is an agreement to exchange cash flows at a sequence of future dates. Actually, a collar in which the floor and the cap are written at the

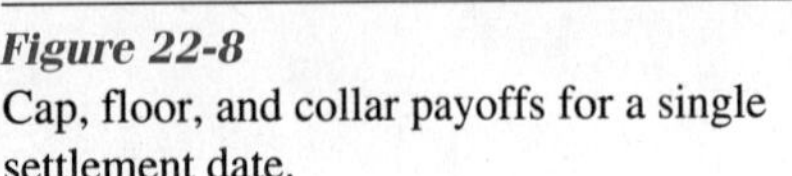

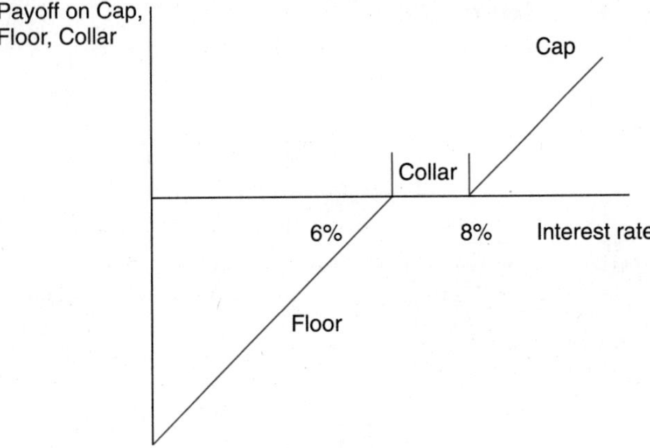

Figure 22-8
Cap, floor, and collar payoffs for a single settlement date.

same yield or exercise price, is identical to a swap, since the agreement in the collar is to a sequence of forward contracts.

Caps, collars, and floors have become attractive risk management tools for the same reasons swaps have. Essentially, it is relatively more efficient for many market participants with risk management problems to obtain a cap, floor, or collar from a financial intermediary than it is to attempt to structure the same sort of transaction on their own. The intermediary has the problem of managing the basis risk that arises in most applications, which spares the borrower from having to solve that problem. Notice that, just as with other forms of hedging discussed in earlier chapters, since a floor or a cap can be broken down into a sequence of options, it is technically possible for a prospective borrower to construct her own floor from positions in the options markets. Of course, if the borrower has timing needs that do not match up with the available options contracts, she faces a substantial problem in constructing the appropriate positions and adjusting them over time to manage basis risk effectively. The financial intermediaries who offer caps, floors, and collars have specialized in developing the hedging capability to manage this type of basis risk at minimum cost.

Now that we have acquired some understanding of caps, collars, and floors, our risk management product set is complete. We can use this product set to structure alternative solutions to common financial problems faced by both financial and nonfinancial corporations around the world.

Alternative Approaches to Current Financing

Consider a firm that is evaluating alternative ways to engage in new current fixed-rate financing of a new investment project or new plant and equipment or new financial assets. Suppose this firm is concerned about future fluctuations in interest rates and wants protection against interest rate changes over the next five years. It has, at least, the following alternative ways to accomplish its objective using the risk management product set.

Alternative 1: Private or Public Bond Issue

Suppose this firm is a medium-sized one that would normally turn to the private placement market for long- and medium-term debt. Also suppose that it is quoted an interest rate equal to the five-year Treasury rate plus 110 basis points for a private placement of five-year debt. If the five-year Treasury rate is 8.4 percent, then its private placement cost is 9.5 percent. This solution is the simplest way a company can often arrange its financing. If alternatives using the risk management products are to prove more attractive, they must have a lower all-in cost or provide other advantages relative to this cash market alternative.

Alternative 2: Fixed-for-Floating Swap with LIBOR-based Loan for Five Years

Suppose the firm can obtain a floating-rate loan tied to LIBOR at LIBOR plus 40 basis points and that the five-year fixed-for-floating swap is priced at five-year Treasury plus 70 basis points. The cost of the swap will be as follows:

5-year Treasury	8.40 %
70–basis point swap spread	0.70 %
40–basis point spread over LIBOR	0.40 %
All-in rate	9.50 %

If the price of the swap is anything less than five-year Treasury plus 70 basis points, the swap will have a lower rate than the private placement. In Chapter 16 we discussed the prospect that swap prices might often be low enough that the all-in cost of alternative two can be lower than alternative one for firms that are perceived to have substantial risk over the long term.

Alternative 3: LIBOR-based Loan with a Cap

The firm can undertake the LIBOR-based floating-rate loan at LIBOR plus 40 basis points and then choose a cap with the desired protection against increases in interest rates. Suppose LIBOR is currently 6 percent and five-year cap prices for LIBOR at different levels of the cap are as follows:

Cap Limit	Cap Price (in Basic Points)
8%	65
9%	40
10%	28

These prices are stated in terms of the additional interest rate that must be paid per year on the loan rather than in terms of a portion of the loan balance to be paid when the loan is taken down at the beginning of the five-year period. If the firm chooses the 8-percent cap, it would pay either LIBOR plus 105 basis points or 8.65 percent, whichever was larger. The 105–basis point premium represents the combined cost of the 40–basis point spread over LIBOR and the annual cost of the cap.

Alternative 4: Fixed-for-Floating Swap with LIBOR-Based Loan for Ten Years That the Counterparty Can Call After Five Years: Sell a Swaption

This alternative is similar to alternative two, except that now the firm has obtained a longer swap than it would prefer but has written an option to the counterparty, the intermediary, to call the swap after five years. This means that the swap will terminate after five years only if the intermediary chooses to allow it to do so. The bank will exercise its option to terminate if the fixed rate on new five-year fixed-for-floating swaps is higher in five years than the rate set on this ten-year swap. Suppose the rate on the ten-year swap is 90 basis points over the five-year rate but the price of the option to call the swap in five years is 55 basis points per year over the first five years of the swap. Then, the all-in cost to the borrower for the first five years of the swap is as follows:

5-Year Treasury	8.40%
90–basis point swap spread	0.90%
Less 55–basis point option price	–0.55%
40–basis point spread over LIBOR	0.40%
All-in rate	9.15%

This rate is lower than that in alternative three, because the borrower has written an option to extend the swap five more years. The payment for that option reduces the borrowing cost over the five years of the loan, but it exposes the borrower to the risk of this option at the end of the five years.

Alternative 5: Buy an Option on a Swap or a Collar

Suppose the managers of the firm decide they want to fix the interest rate for three years and after that they want to be able to take advantage of decreases in interest rates, should they occur, but have protection against increases in interest rates. The firm engages in a three-year fixed-for-floating swap and then buys an option on a two-year swap beginning three years from now. Equivalently, the firm could engage in the initial three-year swap but also purchase an option on a two-year cap with a maturity date three years from now. In either case, the interest rate is fixed at the current fixed rate on the three-year swap, plus 40 basis points for three years. Then it will be capped at the exercise rate in the cap or the fixed rate in the two-year swap. In addition, the borrower must pay the option premium.

Alternative Approaches to Future Financing

Next consider a firm that is considering alternative ways to fund a future investment. Suppose the firm is planning to make an acquisition in one year. Moreover, it is sure that the acquisition will be made and it is sure of the acquisition price. It has decided that when it makes the acquisition it will need five-year funding, and it wants protection against changes in the cost of financing over the five years when it will be financing the acquisition. Moreover, it is also concerned that over the next year, before the acquisition is made, interest rates may increase to a level where the acquisition is no longer attractive. Thus, it wants protection today against increases in the cost of borrowing over the next year.

Alternative 1: Hedge the Five-Year Rate One Year from Now

This alternative involves taking a short position in the futures market for Treasury notes. Futures contracts on five-year Treasury notes are available on the Chicago Board of Trade. Thus, it is a straightforward transaction to purchase sufficient Treasury-note futures contracts to offset the exposure to the cost of obtaining five-year funding in one year. Two potential sources of basis risk are involved in taking such a position. First, the timing of the financing of the acquisition may not coincide with the maturity of the futures contract. Since the exact timing of the acquisition may not be known, this risk is unavoidable. Second, the spread over the five-year Treasury rate that may be demanded for five-year funding, in one year, is uncertain. However, the futures position will protect the firm against most of the fluctuation in the cost of financing its acquisition. Because the firm is sure of the acquisition price, it knows with certainty how much exposure it needs to hedge. Moreover, since it is sure that the acquisition will be made, it knows that if it were to take a futures market position it would not be left with a hedge without an offsetting risk exposure.

Alternative 2: Put Option on the Five-Year Treasury Note with One-Year Maturity

This alternative is similar to the first one, except that here the firm buys insurance against increases in the five-year rate rather than hedging both increases and decreases in that rate. The option requires the payment of a price for the option or for that insurance. It is necessary to choose the desired exercise price. This entails deciding whether to obtain a deep out-of-the-money option that provides protection only against large increases in interest rates, or an in-the-money or near-the-money option that provides greater protection. The greater the degree of protection, the greater the price demanded for the option. Both of the first two options are straightforward, in that they require merely the purchase of a standardized exchange-traded instrument from a broker. Since the risk exposure is uncomplicated, the hedging problem is relatively simple and an exchange-traded instrument can be attractive if it provides the least cost.

Alternative 3: Forward Five-Year Fixed-for-Floating Swap Against LIBOR and Borrow at LIBOR

This alternative entails arranging a forward contract on a fixed-for-floating swap so that the fixed rate on the swap is fixed today. This hedges the future cost of obtaining the swap. Then it is necessary to enter the market for short-term funding one year from today and borrow at LIBOR plus whatever spread is required. Moreover, this exposes the firm to the risk of changing spreads in the short-term market over the five years of the financing. If the management of the firm is optimistic about its creditworthiness over this period, it may be attractive to roll over such short-term financing. This approach may offer an advantage over alternative one or two, if the firm's credit worthiness when the acquisition is made is likely to be more suspect than it will be over the subsequent five years as the acquisition is absorbed. Thus if the firm chooses alternative 3 it is betting in part on an increase in credit quality over time after the acquisition is made, as compared to alternatives one and two.

Alternative 4: Obtain an Option on a Five-Year Fixed-for-Floating Swap with a One-Year Maturity

This alternative has the same attraction relative to alternative three that alternative two has relative to alternative one. That is, the option provides protection against increases in the fixed rate on the five-year swap over the next year. If, however, the fixed rate on such swaps declines over the next year, the firm can take advantage of that decline. This option also means that the firm is intending to absorb the risk of changing creditworthiness over the life of the intended swap. Of course, under this option, the firm must pay a price for the option on the swap, whereas with a forward contract on a swap, as in alternative three, no such premium is required.

Alternative 5: Obtain a One-Year Forward Contract on a Five-Year Cap on LIBOR

This alternative locks in the price of a cap on the cost of short-term borrowing. Under this arrangement the firm intends to roll over short-term borrowing over the five-year financing horizon, but it places a ceiling on the short-term rate that it will have to pay. In effect, it purchases a sequence of options on LIBOR, corresponding to the five-year horizon over which it will be borrowing. Here it chooses to place a ceiling on actual borrowing costs and to gain from reductions in those costs, so it chooses the level, and the corresponding price, of that ceiling. In addition, it locks in the cost of obtaining that ceiling, rather than purchasing an option on that cost or exposing itself to the risk of that cost over the next year.

Alternative 6: Obtain an Option on a Five-Year Cap on LIBOR with a One-Year Maturity

Here the firm obtains an option rather than a forward contract on the five-year cap. It still is committing to roll over its actual financing at the current LIBOR rate over five years and to expose itself to fluctuations in the spread over LIBOR, but now it is buying one-year protection against the cost of that ceiling increasing over the next year. It must choose both the level of protection against increases in the cost of the cap over the next year and the level of the ceiling. The price of its one-year option will increase with increases in either level of protection.

Now let's modify our assumption about this company's planned acquisition. Suppose the management is no longer certain that the acquisition will take place. They now want protection against the cost of financing if the acquisition does take place. Notice that alternatives one, three, and five create an exposure for the firm if the acquisition does not proceed. For example, consider alternative one. If the firm takes a short position in Treasury-note futures and the acquisition does not proceed, then its hedge will become a risk exposure to the price of five-year notes. If the price of five-year notes rises above the contract price on the futures contract, it will incur a loss. If it had still been hedging the cost of the acquisition financing, this loss would have been offset by the reduction in that cost. Without the acquisition, the hedge position becomes a risk exposure. This is not the case with alternatives two, four, and six, that is, alternatives involving options on a Treasury note, a fixed-for-floating swap, or a cap. For example, under alternative four, suppose the firm obtained an option on a five-year swap with a fixed interest rate of 10 percent. Also suppose that that option cost 90 basis points. The worst possible scenario for the firm under these assumptions is that the acquisition does not take place and the cash price for five-year swaps one year from now turns out to be less than 10 percent. In this case the firm does not actually use the five-year swap, so it does not benefit from the relatively low fixed rate on the swap. In addition, it loses the 90 basis points it paid for its option, since the option matures out of the money. While it can lose the 90–basis point option price, it does not have the downside risk exposure that would occur had it used futures or forwards to hedge its contingent exposure created by the acquisition opportunity.

Restructuring the Balance Sheet

Often, companies are interested in restructuring their balance sheets to rearrange or redistribute interest rate risk exposure or to change the timing of interest payments. There is usually a direct way to do this through cash or spot market transactions. This may entail selling an existing asset, paying off or calling debt and replacing it with a new obligation. There are a variety of reasons why companies sometimes want to avoid such direct methods of restructuring balance sheets. Some of these reasons are appropriate and some are not. The appropriate ones include the avoidance of transactions costs associated with issuing new securities or retiring old ones. The not so legitimate ones pertain to the use of off–balance sheet transactions to camouflage the precise nature of the intended changes. We avoid moralistic or other commentary on the merits of some motives and methods of balance sheet restructuring, but we do want to provide some examples of how balance sheets can be restructured using the risk management product set. We consider two examples of such restructuring: the first example involves realizing the gain or loss on an existing swap and the second, redistributing the timing of interest rate expenses.

Realizing the Gain or Loss on an Existing Swap

Suppose a company has outstanding an existing swap by which it receives fixed and pays LIBOR. Let the swap have a notional principal of \$10 million, three years to maturity, and a fixed rate of 10 percent. Suppose the current fixed rate on three-year swaps is now 8 percent. Also suppose that management has decided it would like to realize the gain generated by the decline in swap rates. There are two ways this can be accomplished. One is to terminate or sell the swap. The other is to engage in a new swap that offsets the existing one. If the firm terminates the swap, it will receive a fixed payment equal to the present value of the 200–basis point spread between the 10-percent and 8-percent fixed rates. This will be computed on a \$10 million notional principal over a life of three years with semiannual settlement dates. If the zero-coupon yield curve is flat at 6 percent, this implies that the value of the swap will be

$$\text{Value of swap} = \$541{,}719 = \sum_{t=1}^{6} \frac{\$100{,}000}{1.03^t}$$

As an alternative, the firm could agree to a new three-year swap in which it pays fixed 8 percent and receives LIBOR. This would offset its existing swap so that, netting the two swaps out, it would receive 2 percent of the $10 million notional principal for three years with certainty.

Redistributing the Timing of Interest Rate Expense

Suppose a company has outstanding bonds with a face value of $10 million that commit it to interest payments of 15 percent over five years. These bonds were issued some years earlier, when interest rates were higher, but the bonds have no call provision. This company wants to reduce the payments and spread them over a longer time. It also wants to avoid any increased current cash obligations or expenses, and it cannot call the existing debt, so that debt will have to remain in place. The company can use a form of swap often called a "blend and extend swap." For example, it might want to restructure its obligations so that it spreads its payments over ten years, rather than five years. It wants to know what interest rate it can get on such an obligation, given current swap prices. Suppose this rate turns out to be 12 percent. We'll explain this shortly. Then it will agree to a swap with the following characteristics. For the first five years of the swap, the firm will receive 15-percent fixed and pay 12 percent fixed. It will receive enough to pay its current 15-percent obligation on its outstanding debt. Then it ends up paying 12 percent, though from years 6 through 10 it will still pay 12 percent fixed, will receive LIBOR. For years 6 through 10, the firm has a fixed-for-floating swap against LIBOR at 12 percent fixed. Assuming that it will continue indefinitely to need the financing provided by its existing debt, it will enter the short-term debt market at the end of year 5 and borrow at LIBOR plus whatever is the required spread. Its net cost in years 6 through 10 will be the 12-percent fixed rate provided through the swap plus the spread demanded to borrow short term. This arrangement is spelled out in Table 22-5.

How could we determine that the swap price should be 12 percent? Notice that this swap is essentially a five-year forward start on a five-year fixed-for-floating swap, but, in addition, a cash flow stream of 3 percent per year times the notional principal is paid from the market maker to the counterparty, each year for five years until the start of the swap. These cash flows over the first five years can be converted to a lump sum at the beginning of year 6 by computing their future value using the zero-coupon year curve prevailing today. For simplicity, assume that the yield curve is flat at 6 percent. Also assume semiannual settlement. This cash flow stream will be $150,000 every six months for five years. We can estimate today that this stream would have a future value at the beginning of year six equal to

$$\$1{,}719{,}581 = \sum_{t=1}^{10} \$150{,}000(1.03)^t$$

Then, the current fixed rate on a forward start fixed-for-floating swap will have to be increased by an amount that is sufficient to ensure that the value of the swap at the end of year five is also equal to $1,719,581. That is, the fixed rate on the swap

Table 22-5
Payoffs in Blend and Extend Swap

	Debt Payment	Receive in Swap	Pay in Swap	Net Cost
Year 1–5	15%	15%	12%	12%
Year 6–10	LIBOR + spread	LIBOR	12%	12% + spread

would have to be marked up by an amount, *k,* such that the following present value equation is satisfied:

$$\$1{,}719{,}581 = \sum_{t=1}^{10} \frac{(k/2)(\$10{,}000{,}000)}{1.03^t}$$

If we solve for *k* in this equation we find that *k* is approximately 4 percent. So, if the five-year forward rate on a five-year fixed-for-floating rate swap is 8 percent, the blend and extend swap will be fairly priced at a 12 percent fixed rate over its ten-year life.

SUMMARY

In this chapter we focused on applying the tools we acquired in previous chapters to risk management problems faced by financial and nonfinancial companies. We began by examining how securities have been redesigned in recent years to deal with interest rate risk. We discussed so-called coupon stripping of coupon bonds to create synthetic zero-coupon bonds. Wall Street firms have developed a large volume of such synthetic zero-coupon bonds to provide investors with specific maturity preferences, securities that have very low interest rate risk. We examined how the interest and principal portions of a bond or mortgage have distinct risk structures and how dividing these cash flows into their respective parts, IOs and POs, can be valuable. A more extensive process of innovation has been applied to mortgage-backed securities in order to deal with prepayment risk. The structure of CMOs has been invented to allocate cash flows from mortgages to distinct classes of security holders rather than to compel all holders of a particular mortgage-backed security to have a pro rata share of all the cash flows accruing from the mortgage backing that security.

The second half of the chapter analyzed a selection of practical interest rate risk management problems encountered by corporations in their ongoing financial management. We explored how the risk management product set could be used by companies to structure current and future funding. These examples are designed to show that there are a variety of ways to solve the same financing problem if we draw on futures, options, swaps, caps, floors, and collars. The best solution depends both on the preferences and strategic objectives of the management of the firm and on the relative costs of the alternative instruments at any point in time.

QUESTIONS

1. What are stripped zero-coupon bonds and OID bonds? Why are OID bonds fairly rare?
2. Explain IOs and POs and how prepayments affect their values. Also explain how the effect of prepayments either reinforces or damps the effect of interest rate changes on values of IOs and POs.
3. Explain tranches in a CMO. How are prepayments alloted in the typical CMO? Why do you think CMOs have been so successful?
4. What is the difference between a collar and a "plain vanilla" fixed-for-floating swap? What would have to be true about each to make them identical?
5. Suppose you are the chief financial officer of a company searching for new $50 million financing. You are told you can get LIBOR plus 40 basis points short term and Treasury plus 120 long term. You are considering a fixed-for-floating swap. What price would you need in the swap market to make the swap attractive relative to long-term borrowing?
6. Suppose you expected your company was going to have some financial difficulty down the road that was not currently anticipated in the market. How would this influence your answer to question 5?
7. Suppose a company wants a new swap at 11 percent fixed for five years but current rates are 13 percent. How much would this company pay in a lump sum up front or at the end of the term of the swap to make the transaction work?
8. Reconsider the blend and extend swap in Table 22-5. Suppose the firm in this example wanted to extend only three years. Solve for the fixed rate on the swap that would prevail for this maturity. Now suppose the firm wanted a 10-percent rather than 12-percent rate. How long would the swap have to last to make this feasible?

REFERENCES

Einzig, Robert. "Swaps at TransAmerica: Analysis and Applications." *Journal of Applied Corporate Finance* 2 (Winter 1990), pp. 48–59.

Dunn, Kenneth B., and John J. McConnell. "Valuation of GNMA Mortgage-Backed Securities." *Journal of Finance* 36 (June 1981), pp. 599–616.

Finnerty, John D. "Zero Coupon Bond Arbitrage: An Illustration of the Regulatory Dialectic at Work." *Financial Management* 14 (Winter 1985), pp. 13–17.

Fisher, Lawrence, Ivan E. Brick, and Francis K. W. Ng. "Tax Incentives and Financial Innovation: The Case of Zero-Coupon and Other Deep-Discount Corporate Bonds." *The Financial Review* 18 (November 1983), pp. 292–305.

Goodman, Laurie S. "The Use of Interest Rate Swaps in Managing Corporate Liabilities." *Journal of Applied Corporate Finance* 2 (Winter 1990), pp. 35–47.

Hess, A., and C. Smith. "Elements of Mortgage Securitization." *Journal of Real Estate Finance and Economics* 1 (1988), pp. 331–346.

Macaulay, Frederick R. *The Movement of Interest Rates, Bonds, Yields, and Stock Prices in the United States Since 1865.* New York: Columbia University Press, 1938.

Roll, Richard. *Collateralized Mortgage Obligations: Characteristics, History, Analysis.* New York: Goldman Sachs & Company, April 1986.

Schwartz, Eduardo S., and Walter N. Torous. "Prepayment and the Valuation of Mortgage-Backed Securities." *Journal of Finance* 44 (June 1989), pp. 375–392.

Waldman, Michael. *Mortgage Securities: 1972–1984 Historical Performance and Implications for Investors.* New York: Salomon Brothers, Inc., March 1985.

Waldman, Michael, March Gordon, and Steven Guterman. *The Salomon Brothers Prepayment Model: Impact of the Market Rally on Mortgage Prepayments and Yields.* New York: Salomon Brothers, Inc., 1985.

• *Chapter 23*

Managing Foreign Exchange Risk

The simultaneous increase in the volatility of foreign exchange rates and the expansion by U.S. firms into the international marketplace during the 1970s and 1980s has forced U.S. managers to adapt to ever-increasing exposures to foreign exchange rate risks. To a large extent, the successful management of modern corporations depends on the ability of managers to recognize and manage exposures to foreign exchange rate changes and to anticipate their impact on their firms. Moreover, commercial and investment banks are the principal sources of expertise for corporations that seek to design and implement foreign exchange risk management programs. As a result, the capability to manage foreign exchange risk is an integral part of the operations of banks that deal with business customers. This chapter presents basic principles governing the recognition, evaluation, and management of exposure to foreign exchange risk.

We discuss three basic sources of exposure to foreign exchange risk: transaction exposure, translation exposure, and economic exposure. Each manifests itself, to some degree, in virtually all multinational companies. The role of the financial manager is to decide which, if any, exposures to risk are important to hedge, and to determine the best tools and strategies for doing so. Various strategies are explained that involve transactions in spot, forward, futures, and options markets. We cover the markets for foreign currency options, futures, and forward contracts and provide a perspective on how each instrument may be used to hedge against changes in foreign exchange rates. The important concepts to learn in this chapter are listed below.

• *Concepts to Learn in Chapter 23* •

- Alternative types of foreign exchange exposure
- How to structure balance sheet and money market hedges
- How to use forward and futures contracts to manage foreign exchange risk
- How to use options to manage foreign exchange risk

Exposure to Foreign Exchange Risk

The Basic Nature of Foreign Exchange Risk

Foreign exchange risk occurs as the result of changes in the rate of exchange between two currencies. During the period from 1945 to 1973 foreign exchange risk in most major currencies was minimal, owing to the Bretton Woods Agreement, a system established after World War II to maintain stable, or "pegged," exchange rates. When the Bretton Woods Agreement was abandoned in 1973, exchange rates between various currencies were allowed to float. The impact of allowing exchange rates to float is readily apparent in Figure 23-1, which shows the exchange rates of four major currencies against the U.S. dollar from 1960 through 1990. The exchange rates illustrated in the figure are expressed in units of foreign currency per U.S. dollar, except for the British pound sterling, which, by convention is in dollars per pound. Notice that the during this period, the value of the U.S. dollar generally weakened against the Deutschemark, and the Japanese yen while it strengthened against the pound. The French franc shows no clear tendency or trend, up or down. In fact, a general appreciation in the values of most major currencies against the U.S. dollar was one of the main reasons why the system of pegged exchange rates was eventually abandoned.

During the early 1970s, changes in "fundamentals"—real factors such as productivity and trade flows—made it increasingly difficult for monetary authorities to maintain pegged exchange rates. In particular, as the volume of international trade grew during the 1960s and early 1970s, it became clear that the adjustments necessary to maintain pegged exchange rates would be increasingly costly. The impact of abandoning the Bretton Woods agreement on exposure of multinational corporations to foreign exchange risk is illustrated in Figure 23-1. Until 1973 there was little fluctuation in each of the four exchange rates shown. Under the Bretton Woods Agreement, exchange rates among the major currencies were largely stabilized. After 1973, however, foreign exchange rates exhibited significant volatility.

It is during the latter exchange rate regime that exposure to foreign exchange risk became a much more important concern for multinational firms. Two factors contributed. First, the expansion of multinational companies into foreign markets was responsible for an increase in their level of exposure to foreign exchange risk generally. As more of their business was conducted abroad, their demand for foreign currency transactions grew. Given the larger scale of international operations, any change in the relevant exchange rate would have greater implications for the cash flows of the multinational firm. In effect, even if the risk or variability of foreign exchange rates themselves had remained constant, the *exposures* of multinationals to this source of risk increased with the growth of international business. The second contributing factor was the abandonment of Bretton Woods, which led to an increase in the risk itself—that is, to greater exchange rate volatility. For any volume of foreign currency transactions, greater risk was introduced under the regime of floating exchange rates. Thus, the expansion of multinational firms into foreign markets simultaneously increased their exposure to foreign exchange risk and contributed toward increasing the magnitude of the risk itself through the downfall of the Bretton Woods system.

Figure 23-1

Nominal U.S. Dollar Exchange Rates, 1960–90 (Annual average). *Source: Vikram Kumar, and Joseph A. Whitt, "Exchange Rate Variability and International Trade," Federal Reserve Bank of Atlanta* Economic Review, *77 (May/June 1992): 19, Chart 1.*

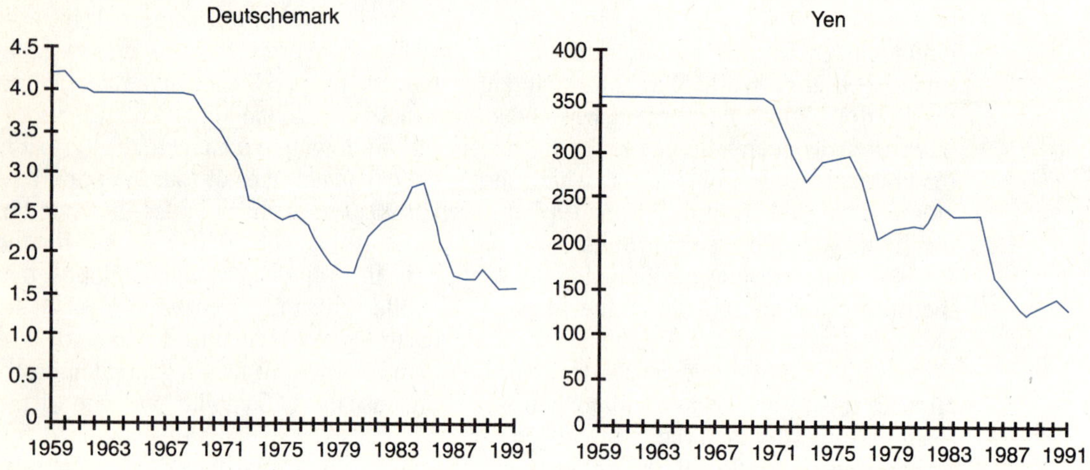

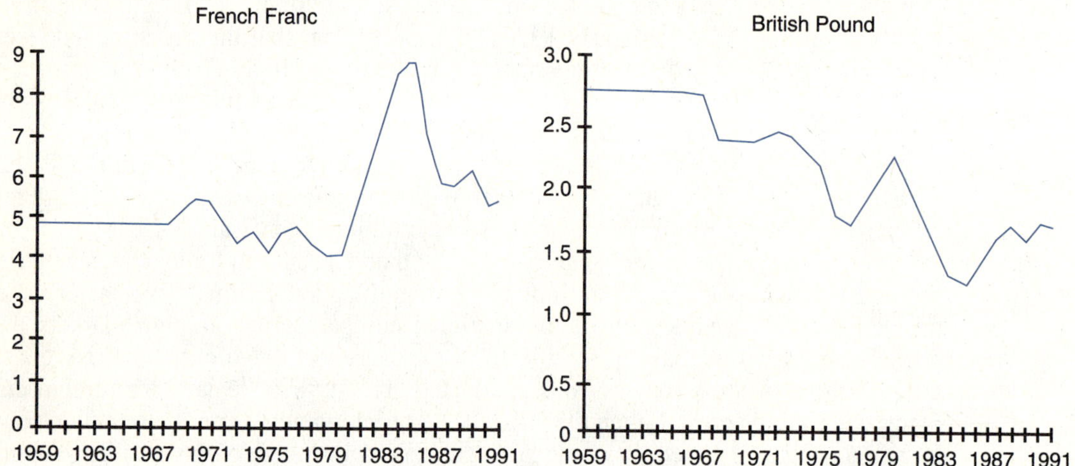

Note: All rates are expressed in units of foreign currency per U.S. $, except the British Pound, which is expressed in U.S. $ per pound.

Exposure to foreign exchange risk occurs in a variety of ways. Anyone who has traveled abroad can appreciate the effects of foreign exchange rate changes on the costs of meals, transportation, entertainment, and hotel accommodations in the foreign countries they visit. When the U.S. dollar *appreciates* against a foreign currency—when $1 buys more units of the foreign currency—foreign travel becomes more affordable for U.S. tourists (assuming consumer prices remain constant as the exchange rate changes). Suppose for example, that the exchange rate for Deutschemarks is DM2.50 per U.S. dollar and the price of a room in a Berlin hotel is DM500 per night. At the given exchange rate, the cost of the room to a U.S. tourist is $200 per night (DM500 ÷ DM2.50 = $200). Then assume that the hotel rate remains constant in DM but the exchange rate increases to DM4.00 per U.S. dollar. The cost to the U.S. tourist for the same room is $125 per night. When the dollar *depreciates* against the foreign currency, the opposite effect is observed. U.S. tourists find hotel room rates and other costs of foreign travel to be more expensive in U.S. dollar terms. If the exchange rate changes to DM2.00 per U.S. dollar, the dollar cost of the Berlin hotel is $250 per night. This is why the depreciation of the U.S. dollar against major foreign currencies during some recent periods has made foreign travel more expensive for U.S. tourists and at the same time more affordable for foreign tourists visiting the United States.

The exposure to risk associated with exchange rate movements comes not so much from changes in the exchange rate per se (and the attendant changes in equivalent dollar costs) as from *unexpected* changes in exchange rates. Certainly, U.S. travelers understand that exchange rates may change so as to make their trips more costly in terms of dollars, and those expectations are factored into the plans themselves (i.e., length of trip, countries to visit, choice of hotels). The forward markets for foreign currencies provide market information about *expected* movements in exchange rates, though some debate remains as to whether the forward rates provide *unbiased* forecasts of future spot exchange rates. Given the expectation that exchange rates will increase or decrease over time, the effects of such rate changes can be accounted for when plans are made. For example, suppose that in July a U.S. tourist plans a vacation to Germany in September. In July the mark-dollar exchange rate is DM2.50 per dollar. The U.S. tourist expects, however, that the exchange rate will decrease to DM2.00 per dollar during the next two months, increasing the German expenses 20 percent by September in U.S. dollar terms. Anticipating this result, the U.S. tourist can budget for the trip accordingly. Exchange rate risk is two sided. The actual September exchange rate may be higher or lower than was anticipated in July. The "down side" of this risk for U.S. tourists is that the mark-dollar exchange rate will be lower than expected (i.e., lower than DM2.00 per dollar) when the hotel bills and other expenses are realized.

In the remainder of this chapter, we explain how exposures to foreign exchange risks should be measured and conceptualized. We also describe various strategies for hedging or managing the risks associated with exchange rate movements. In some circumstances, such strategies are relatively simple. For example, foreign currency can be purchased in advance of the date on which it is needed, to avoid adverse changes in rates. Or forward contracts can be employed that lock up a price in advance of the actual transaction date. Owing to the usually small size of their currency transactions, neither of these alternatives is very practical for tourists like the one described above, but they are commonly used by U.S. companies that are likely to trade for relatively large amounts of foreign currency. These companies often turn to their banks to trade in both spot and forward markets in foreign exchange, so foreign exchange risk management is an important part of the services modern banks provide their corporate customers.

Most companies, especially multinational ones, realize major effects from movements in foreign exchange rates. For multinational firms, exposures to foreign exchange risk are more extensive and complex than we have described so far. For these companies it is useful to describe possible sources of exchange risk as falling into three basic categories: transactions exposure, translation exposure, and economic exposure. We describe each of these sources of risk below.

Transactions Exposure

Transactions exposure occurs when future transactions, either payments or receipts, will be settled in a foreign currency and require exchange of foreign currency for domestic. This source of exposure is similar to the problem of the U.S. tourist described above, in which dollars will have to be exchanged for marks at an uncertain exchange rate two months hence. For corporations, similar exposures could arise when a U.S. company operates a foreign subsidiary. Operations of subsidiaries in foreign countries require a variety of transactions that are denominated in foreign currency, such as purchases or sales of goods and materials, financial transactions, and capital investments and divestitures. It is often necessary for the parent company to convert revenues in one currency (perhaps the home currency) into another currency in order to meet a foreign subsidiary's obligations. For example, if a U.S. company operates a manufacturing plant in a foreign country that employs local labor, wages must be paid in the local currency rather than the manufacturer's home currency. At the same time, it is possible that goods produced in the plant are shipped elsewhere for sale, perhaps back to the manufacturer's home country. If so, this means that while labor costs are incurred in one currency the revenues produced are incurred in U.S. dollars.

This is the essence of a transactions exposure. In the example above, the U.S. dollar cost of wage expenditures rises as the dollar depreciates against the foreign currency, requiring more dollars to meet the same foreign wage payroll. At the same time, if the foreign subsidiary ships its goods back to the United States for sale, the dollar revenues associated with foreign production remain constant. The combined effects result in lower dollar profits from operation of the foreign subsidiary. On the other hand, if the dollar appreciates against the foreign currency, the dollar value of foreign wage expenditures decreases, resulting in higher dollar profits. To some extent, this particular source of risk can be hedged by selling the goods in the country where they are produced, causing revenues to be received in the same currency in which production costs are paid, but even when foreign subsidiaries operate independently of the parent company, so as not to rely on the parent company as a source of cash, they ultimately remit dividends to the parent in the home currency. Once again, this transaction requires eventual conversion of foreign currency to domestic currency and thus involves some exposure to exchange rate risk.

An example of the adverse consequences of transaction exposure concerns a British company named Laker Airlines, which during the late 1970s was expanding rapidly to accommodate a growing demand, primarily from British vacationers traveling to the United States. Laker purchased several DC-10s at that time, financing the investment with U.S. dollar–denominated debt. The problem was that Laker's revenues from ticket sales were primarily in pounds sterling. At the same time, the debt service associated with its purchase of new aircraft was denominated in U.S. dollars. When the dollar strengthened against the pound in 1981, two things happened. First, travel to the United States became more expensive for British tourists, as it took more British currency than previously to buy a given number of dollars. Thus, demand from British vacationers for travel to the United States decreased. Second, the pound cost of Laker's U.S. dollar–denominated debt went up: it took more British currency for Laker to make the same dollar-denominated debt payments. Lower revenues combined with higher interest costs meant lower profits. By 1982 Laker Airlines was bankrupt.

Translation Exposure

Translation exposure occurs in multinational corporations that have foreign subsidiaries whose assets and liabilities are denominated in foreign currency. Translation exposure occurs because the value of these accounts must eventually be stated in U.S. dollar terms in reporting financial statements. In general, as exchange rates change the home currency value of the foreign subsidiaries' assets and liabilities does also. Such changes can result in translation losses or gains, which will be recognized in financial statements. The nature and structure of the subsidiaries' assets and liabilities determine the extent of translation exposure to the parent company.

To some extent, the effects of exchange rate changes for translation purposes will be offsetting. For example, suppose a U.S. firm has a German subsidiary that has a German bank deposit of DM1 million and an account payable of DM1 million. Suppose also that the exchange rate between marks and dollars is DM2.00 per dollar. The dollar value of the subsidiary's position in these two accounts is $500,000 in both cases. If the dollar were to suddenly appreciate against the mark, say to DM2.50 per dollar, both the asset and the liability accounts would lose dollar value by the same amount. Both would be revalued in dollars at $400,000. There would be no loss to the U.S. parent, however, since the dollar loss on the bank deposit is exactly offset by the dollar gain on the payable. In essence, these two accounts hedged each other from translation exposure to exchange rate changes.

While our example is fairly straightforward, the treatment of other types of assets and liabilities for translation purposes is more complex. Accounting standards have varied over time with regard to how different types of assets and liabilities should be translated in constructing accounting statements. One of the most difficult issues concerns whether current assets and liabilities should be treated differently than long-term assets and liabilities when recognizing exchange rate changes. Under previous rules, the values of long-term assets, which were primarily real assets, were considered to be independent of exchange rate changes and were therefore translated at historical exchange rates. Current assets, viewed primarily as financial assets, were considered to be exposed to changes in exchange rates and were translated at contemporary exchange rates. Similar distinctions were applied to long-term and current liabilities.[1]

Under presently accepted standards, defined by the Financial Accounting Standards Board (FASB) 52, companies use what is referred to as the "current method" for translation. According to this method, all assets and liabilities are translated at the current exchange rate on the balance sheet date. Equity accounts are translated at historical rates. Income statements are translated either at the prevailing rate on the date of a particular transaction or a weighted average of exchange rates for a period involving a system of transactions. In addition, translation gains and losses generally are not recognized in the income statement until an account is liquidated. Instead, gains and losses are accumulated as a separate equity account until they are realized.

Economic Exposure

Economic exposure, often referred to as "operating exposure," is concerned with the response of the firm's real operating cash flows to changes in *real* exchange rates. Changes in real exchange rates are essentially deviations from the condition of purchasing power parity. Recall from Chapter 11 that purchasing power parity is based on the proposition that changes in exchange rates are driven by differences in the inflation rates of two currencies. When exchange rates change, they should do so at a pace that reflects the change in relative prices for goods in the foreign, versus the domestic, market. Such changes, referred to as "nominal changes" in exchange rates, convey no net advantage to buying goods in the domestic versus the foreign market. In units of domestic currency, the price of goods in the domestic market remains equal to the price of the same goods in the foreign market, after accounting for the change in the price of foreign currency. An exchange rate change that deviates from the condition of purchasing power parity is called a "real change," implying a change in relative price for the same goods between two countries. Empirical evidence shows that purchasing power parity is a good description of exchange rate movements only in the very long run. Over shorter periods, real exchange rate movements are commonplace and give rise to economic exposure of real cash flows in the multinational setting.

To see how changes in the real exchange rate will impact operating cash flows, consider the example of a U.S. firm that exports a substantial amount of its product to France. Suppose the firm competes with a number of firms in France for its share

---

[1]Before 1976, the "current/noncurrent" method was used for translating balance sheet and income statement accounts. This method translated current assets and liabilities at current exchange rates and noncurrent assets and liabilities at historical exchange rates. Income statement items were translated at average exchange rates for the accounting period except in cases where the item was related to a balance sheet account (e.g., depreciation), in which case the item was translated in the same manner as the balance sheet account. In 1976, FASB 8 defined the "temporal" translation method, which was used until FASB 52 took effect in 1982. Under the temporal method, financial assets and liabilities were translated at current exchange rates quarterly and gains and losses were recognized quarterly on the firm's income statement. Real assets were translated at historical rates. FASB 8 was very controversial, since quarterly recognition of exchange rate changes contributed greatly to volatility in earnings.

of the French market. Also, for simplicity, suppose that the inflation rates in France and the United States are equal and that the exchange rate between the franc and the United States dollar is 6.00 francs per dollar. If the U.S. dollar strengthens against the franc, causing the exchange rate to increase to 7.00 francs per dollar, what will be the implications for the U.S. exporter? First of all, if the exchange rate change is purely the result of an increase in the inflation rate in France, the effect on sales revenues is purely nominal. A price increase commensurate with the new rate of inflation in France will leave the dollar equivalent of French sales unchanged. For example, if the unit price of goods sold in France is FF60 per unit, at an exchange rate of FF6.00 per dollar the U.S. dollar equivalent of each unit sale is, FF60 divided by FF6.00, or $10. If inflation in France forces the price up to FF70 per unit, and the exchange rate goes up to FF7.00 per dollar, the U.S. dollar equivalent of each unit sale is again, FF70 divided by FF7.00/$, or $10. This is the prediction of purchasing power parity. Changes in exchange rates reflect changes in the relative price of goods.

On the other hand, if the increase in the exchange rate is a real shock—as it is when inflation rates remain unchanged—there will be implications for the real cash flows to the U.S. firm. Faced with an appreciating dollar, and no concomitant increase in French prices, the U.S. company can react in one of two ways. It can raise the franc price of its exports to compensate for the depreciation of the franc. If each franc earned on French sales will produce fewer dollars under the new exchange rate, a higher franc price could be used to offset this effect. Using the example above, an increase in the exchange rate from FF6.00 to FF7.00 per dollar would reduce the dollar equivalent of unit sales from $10 to $8.57 (FF60 per unit ÷ FF7.00 per dollar). To offset the decrease in the dollar equivalent price, the U.S. company could increase the unit price to FF70 to maintain the $10 per unit U.S. equivalent. The problem with this strategy is that the unit price increase is not part of a general inflationary trend in France, and the result is a difference between the FF price of goods produced in the United States and the same goods produced in France. If the U.S. firm charges a higher price for its exports, competition from other producers in France will surely lead to a loss of sales, and thus to a loss of dollar revenues from France. On the other hand, if the firm chooses instead to leave its price set, in order to continue to compete against French firms, the dollar value of its sales will depreciate with the value of the franc. Either way, the change in the real exchange rate results in a real loss of market share and revenue from French operations.[2]

Changes in real exchange rates can also cause difficulties for U.S. firms competing with foreign companies in the United States. During the early 1980s the appreciation of the U.S. dollar against the Japanese yen caused problems for many U.S.

[2]Needless to say, the effects of exchange rate changes may stimulate other reactions by consumers, competitors, and government officials that will complicate the simple picture in our example. For example, the strengthening dollar of the 1980s was responsible in part for increased competitiveness of Japanese products in the United States. The effects of this phenomenon in the United States, both politically and economically, are far reaching and may result in new policies regarding import competition and foreign ownership of U.S. assets.

companies competing with Japanese firms in the United States and abroad. One example involves Caterpillar, a U.S. producer of heavy equipment, and Komatsu, a Japanese company and one of Caterpillar's chief competitors in the U.S. market. As the dollar grew stronger against the yen, the dollar price of equipment produced by Komatsu fell relative to the dollar price of Caterpillar equipment. The change in relative prices gave Komatsu a competitive advantage, which led to loss of market share for Caterpillar both in the United States and in international markets.

More recently, the reverse has been the case. In 1993 the Japanese yen reached its strongest position ever against the dollar. The stronger yen made imports from Japan more expensive for U.S. buyers. At the time, the Japanese were concerned that the strength of the yen would contribute to or prolong the prevailing recession in Japan. They had hoped that strong foreign export sales would continue, pulling the Japanese economy out of the recession. As the value of the yen rose against the U.S. dollar, the dollar cost of Japanese imports in the United States increased. Many Japanese companies, like Toyota and Sony, had based their business plans on the assumption that the yen would go no lower than ¥120 per dollar. As the yen dropped below ¥120 per dollar, serious losses in revenues occurred for Japanese firms. It was reported that during the last three months of 1992 Sony Corporation lost an estimated ¥43 billion ($343 million) in revenue owing to appreciation of the yen against other major currencies and that for every ¥1 appreciation in the value of Japanese currency, Sony would lose about ¥5 billion annually.[3]

Hedging Foreign Exchange Risk

In this section we provide some perspective on the tools and techniques employed to measure and manage exposures to foreign exchange risks. In the discussion that follows we describe four tools commonly used by financial managers to manage foreign exchange risk:

(1) balance sheet or internal hedges,

(2) money market hedges,

(3) forward and futures contracts in foreign currency, and

(4) foreign currency options.

Uses of these tools are discussed in the context of a simple example of a U.S. manufacturer that relies on raw materials imported from Germany. We focus on one particular exposure to foreign exchange risk. The U.S. company has agreed to buy raw materials costing DM500,000, with payment to be made in six months. The terms of the agreement specify that payment for the purchase is to be in Deutschemarks. Currently, the spot exchange rate (ignoring bid-ask spreads) is 1.50 Deutschemarks per dollar. This implies that the current dollar cost of the import is $333,333. Since payments are specified in marks, the U.S. firm bears the risk of fluctuating

---

[3]See Chandler and Bussey (1993) for a more complete discussion.

exchange rates. If the Deutschemarks per dollar increases (the dollar strengthens), the dollar cost of the materials decreases. On the other hand, if the exchange rate decreases (the dollar weakens), the dollar cost of the import increases. Exposure to the latter prospect is the one the firm would like to reduce. In each of the following sections, specific strategies are discussed that are directed at reducing the U.S. firm's exposure to decreases in the marks per dollar rate over the next year.

Balance Sheet Hedges

Recall from Chapter 17 that there is generally a cash market solution to most risk management problems. Under most circumstances a position in a risky asset can be hedged by taking an appropriate position in another asset. For example, a long position in one asset can be hedged with a short position in another, similar asset. Alternatively, the long position could be hedged by issuing a financial liability with similar risk characteristics. In general, such solutions can be referred to as "balance sheet hedges," since they imply some rebalancing of the overall financial position.

In our particular example, one way the U.S. company can reduce its exposure to future payments in Deutschemarks is to generate offsetting receipts in marks. For example, if the U.S. firm were to sell its products in the German market and the sales were denominated in marks, the firm's Deutschemarks receipts could be used to make the necessary payments for raw materials. Alternatively, the firm may operate a subsidiary in Germany that will generate profits in marks. In any case, there may not be sufficient Deutschemarks available from operations in Germany to exactly hedge the amount and timing of the six-month payable, though there may be some substantial reduction in the extent of the original exposure due to accounts receivable denominated in Deutschemarks. At a minimum, the firm should begin its analysis of exposure to the Deutschemark by netting out all contractual payments and receipts denominated in Deutschemarks over the next six months.

In addition, while the U.S. firm may not generate enough Deutschemarks to offset the German payable in six months, the firm may generate foreign revenues in other foreign currencies that are more stable against the Deutschemarks. Suppose, for example, that the dollar depreciates against the Deutschemark while the French franc remains stable, or even appreciates, against the Deutschemark. If the U.S. firm has revenues from operations in France that can be exchanged for Deutschemarks to meet the six-month payable, the German exposure could be hedged via French franc revenues. In fact, multinationals that have operations in several foreign countries benefit from a kind of "global currency diversification." With revenues and expenses occurring in many foreign currencies it is likely that, in terms of their dollar equivalents, exposures in one foreign currency can be partially hedged by exposures in another. This diversification effect occurs because movements in foreign exchange rates are not perfectly correlated. In effect, the multinational corporation can diversify itself through foreign direct investments in a variety of foreign countries by generating cash flows in a variety of different foreign currencies. In fact, this diversification happens in two ways. First, the diversification of total returns occurs by dividing an investment among a number of assets whose returns are less than perfectly correlated. This results in a reduction in the risk (e.g., standard deviation) of total returns. The second dimension of diversification, which is rather unique to international investments, is the diversification of foreign currency risk that is accomplished by investing in assets denominated in a variety of foreign currencies. When foreign exchange rates are less than perfectly correlated, foreign exchange risk is reduced as well.

In many circumstances, there is not sufficient opportunity for multinational companies, or other, smaller firms, to diversify foreign exchange exposures. As in our example there may be only one exposure, a six-month payable in Deutschemarks, that must be managed. Under these circumstances, there is a more proactive way in which the balance sheet can be used to manage the firm's exposure, that is, to take an offsetting position in another instrument or asset to balance out the effect of the mark-denominated payable. For example, the U.S. importer could move cash from U.S. dollar bank deposits to a German bank deposit with a maturity and amount necessary to match the timing and amount of the maturing payable. If the rate of interest on Deutschemark-denominated deposits at the six-month maturity is 12.000 percent (annually), the dollar deposit necessary to hedge the six-month payable is determined as follows (assuming semiannual compounding): Six-month deposits: DM500000/(1 + .12/ 2) × \$(1/ 1.5)/ DM = \$314,465. At the stated interest rates, these amounts provide the required Deutschemark cash flows in six months—DM500,000. As we show in the following section, this strategy is similar to a money market hedge, except that the firm must divest itself of a dollar-denominated asset in order to hedge with a Deutschemark-denominated asset. In some circumstances, liquid assets may not be available in sufficient amounts to acquire the necessary deposit. Finally, the cost associated with the "internal" hedge just described can be viewed as the interest income foregone by spending dollars now on a Deutschemark-based deposit. In some sense, the firm is spending dollars now to cover a future payable and is "parking" the cash in the German deposit until it is needed. By giving up the interest that would have been earned on the amount, the firm avoids future uncertainty about the future spot exchange rate.

Money Market Hedge

A money market hedge is a system of transactions involving borrowing in one currency and lending in another in order to construct a pair of future transactions in the two currencies similar to a forward exchange. In the case of our U.S. importer, this could be accomplished by borrowing dollars today for six months, exchanging the dollars for marks, and investing the marks for six months in a Deutschemark-denominated instrument. In six months the maturing U.S. loan will require repayment in dollars while the maturing German investment will provide Deutschemarks.

To see more clearly how the money market hedge works, suppose that the six-month dollar-borrowing rate for the U.S. importer is 6.5 percent (annual). Recall the six-month deposit rate in Deutschemarks is 12.0 percent (annual). Figure 23-2 outlines the following steps that should be taken today to hedge the firm's six-month payable in Deutschemarks:

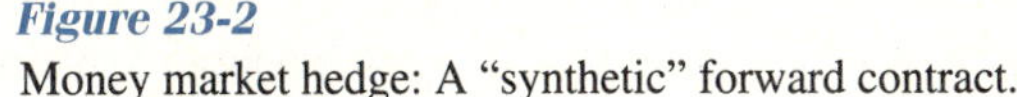

Figure 23-2
Money market hedge: A "synthetic" forward contract.

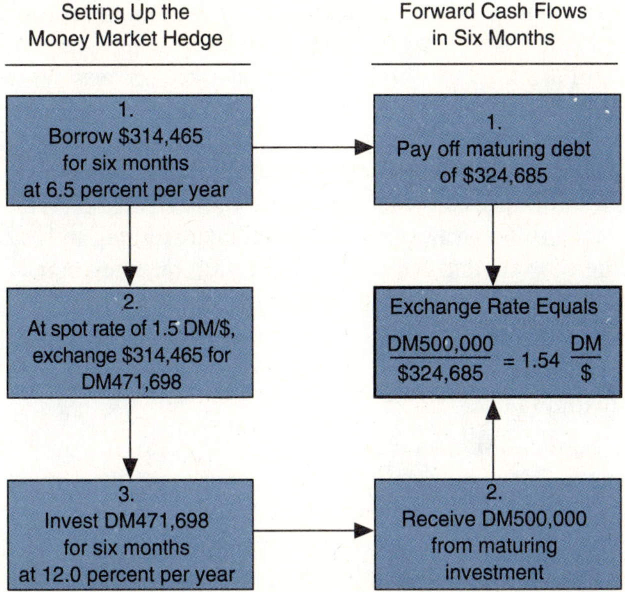

1. Borrow $314,465 at 6.5 percent for six months.
2. Convert the proceeds to Deutschemarks at the spot rate, 1.5 marks per dollar.
3. Invest the resulting DM471,698 at 12 percent for six months.

Notice these steps result in no net cash outlays today. In six months time the following will occur:

1. The Deutschemarks-based investment will mature, yielding DM500,000.
2. The dollar-based liability will mature and require payment of $324,685.

The net result is to create a "synthetic" forward contract under which $324,685 is paid to receive DM500,000. Of course this does not create a forward contract per se. Contracts are actually made with two different parties during the course of borrowing and relending, but the resultant cash flows provide the same kind of hedging protection as an outright forward.[4]

The "synthetic" forward rate created by the money market hedge is (DM500000/$324685), or 1.54 Deutschemarks per dollar. Notice that this rate could

[4]There will be obvious differences in credit risk that attend financial contracts between different counterparties; however, the differences are likely to be very small, since in most cases the parties involved are likely to be large banks. A forward contract will generally be made with a dealer bank, and the debt contract and investment involved in the money market hedge will likely be with a large bank, or with an even better credit risk, as when domestic or foreign government securities might be employed.

not be very different from the outright forward rate quoted by dealers in foreign currency or an arbitrage opportunity would result. In fact, the proposition that the synthetic forward will be equal to the outright forward rate is essentially a restatement of the interest rate parity proposition in Chapter 11. For example, if the outright forward rate was 1.52 Deutschemarks per dollar at the six-month settlement, an arbitrageur would sell dollars forward via the money market process just described at the synthetic forward rate of 1.54 marks per dollar. At the same time, the arbitrageur would arrange under a forward contract to buy the dollars forward at 1.52 marks per dollar. For every dollar turned around on the six-month settlement date the arbitrageur would make DM0.02. These are the same transactions described earlier as *covered interest arbitrage.* Arbitrage will rebalance interest rates and exchange rates to levels at which the outright and the synthetic forward rates are equal. This is also the circumstance where interest rate parity holds.

Forwards and Futures

The markets for forward and futures contracts in foreign currency were discussed at some length in Chapter 14; examples of hedges using these instruments were presented in Chapter 17. Here we describe in more detail how these contracts can be used to manage exposure to exchange rate risk, in particular the risk exposure to marks faced by our fictional U.S. manufacturer. A useful starting point for analyzing how these contracts can reduce risk is first to describe the exposure of the firm conceptually. Recall from Chapter 17 how the exposure to risk can be presented as a gain-loss profile (see Figure 17-1). A similar gain-loss profile for the case of our U.S. importer is presented in Figure 23-3.

Exchange rates are reexpressed in American terms to be consistent with the way prices are quoted in futures (and later options) contracts. As a result, the present spot exchange rate of 1.5 marks per dollar is restated as 0.667 dollars per mark, or 66.7 cents per Deutschemark. Similarly, the six-month forward rate of 1.54 Deutschemarks per dollar becomes 64.9 cents per Deutschemarks in American terms. Notice that the gain-loss profile (CC in Figure 23-3) slopes downward to the right. This is typical of a "short" exposure to the future spot rate. The importer must buy DM 500,000 in six months; therefore, the importer is *short* Deutschemarks. If the price decreases during the next six months, the importer gains the difference between the current spot rate and the eventual spot rate. This gain is shown on the left-hand axis in cents saved per Deutschemark, for the upper portion of the gain-loss profile. Losses would be indicated again on the left-hand axis for the lower portion of the profile. A loss is incurred if the spot rate increases over the next six months.

The six-month forward contract in Deutschemarks can be used to hedge the exposure to changes in the spot rate over the next six months. DM500,000 would be purchased forward at the rate of 64.9 (cents per mark). The effect of this transaction can be visualized in Figure 23-4, where the gain-loss profile for the "long" forward position is incorporated into Figure 23-3. The gain-loss profile for the forward contract slopes up and to the right, as will generally be the case for a "long" position. Gains will be realized on the contract if the spot rate ends up above 64.9 cents per

Figure 23-3
Gain and loss profile for changes in spot exchange rate (cents per Deutschemark).

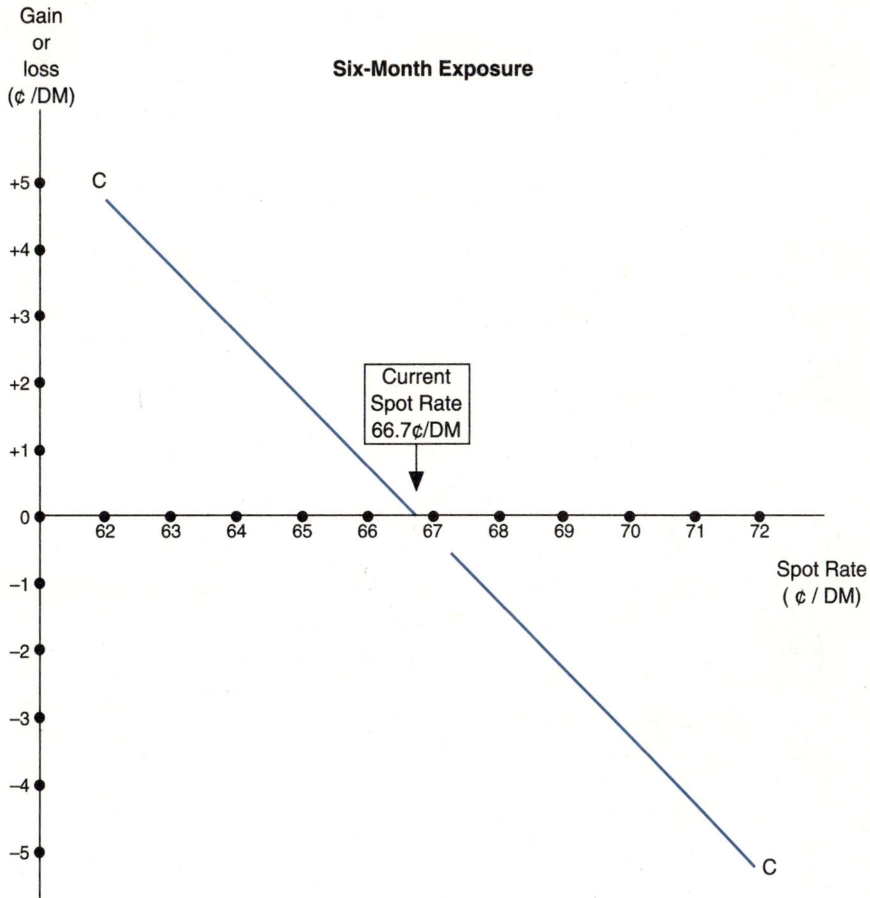

Deutschemark, since the contract locks up a cheaper price. On the other hand, if in six months the spot rate ends up below 64.9 cents per Deutschemark, the forward contract will lose money because the contract price will be higher than the spot rate.

The reason why the long forward position hedges the risk associated with the mark purchase is indicated by the opposite slopes of the two profiles. When one position gains, the other loses; the amounts are offsetting. By adding the two profiles together for every spot rate on the horizontal axis, the overall effect of the forward hedge can be seen. This is represented in Figure 23-4 as the heavy line XX. Notice this line is horizontal at a value of +1.8 (cents per marks). Regardless of the spot rate in six months, the firm will gain 1.8 cents per Deutschemark against the current spot rate by hedging through the forward market. Obviously, this savings is secured by contracting now to buy the needed marks in six months at 64.9 cents per Deutschemarks—a savings of 1.8 (cents per Deutschemark) as compared to the

Figure 23-4
Gain and loss profile for changes in spot exchange rate (cents per Deutschemark).

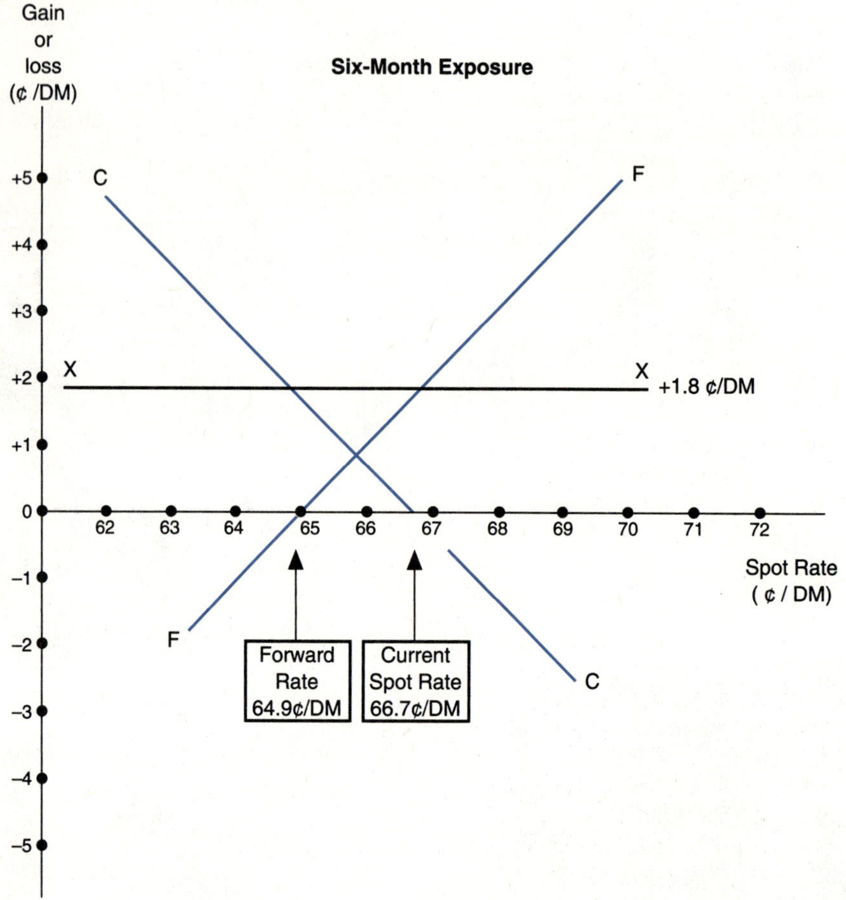

current spot rate of 66.7 (cents per Deutschemark). The forward contract allows the firm to lock up this price now rather than bear risk that the price will increase. Of course, if the price of marks decreases below 64.9 (cents per Deutschemark) in six months, the firm will not realize any additional savings.[5]

---

[5]The fact that the forward rate is less than the spot rate reflects the market's expectation that the spot rate will decrease over the next six months. If the forward rate represents an unbiased forecast of the future spot rate, then the market expects the spot rate to be 64.9 ¢/DM in six months. This may be a better benchmark than the current spot rate for computing gains and losses. The 1.8 ¢/DM gain we calculated represents a savings the firm should *expect* over the next six months relative to the current spot rate. The forward contract allows the firm to lock up this rate and avoid the risk associated with an eventual spot rate above or below 64.9 ¢/DM.

The operation of a futures hedge is similar to that of a forward contract. We can construct the same kind of graphical perspective to visualize how the futures position hedges the firm's risk. For the six-month exposure, the firm should again *purchase* futures contracts on the Deutschemark. The standard denomination on this contract, traded over the International Money Market (IMM) of the Chicago Mercantile Exchange, is DM125,000. The firm should buy (go long) four contracts with a six-month settlement. Four contracts will give the firm an obligation to buy a total of DM500,000. Suppose the firm buys four contracts with six months remaining to settlement. In six months, if the firm were able to take delivery on the Deutschemarks, the hedge would work entirely like the forward contract. However, it is more likely that the firm will close out the futures position prior to the settlement date by selling five contracts, and then buy the needed DM500,000 on the spot market. Ideally, the gain or loss associated with liquidating the futures position would offset losses associated with a higher-than-expected spot exchange rate, and vice versa.

To see how this works, suppose that the settlement price of the six-month futures contract is equal to 64.9 (cents per Deutschemark), the same rate as the forward contract. Futures and forward prices should not necessarily be equal, but they will be similar for the same settlement dates. Under this assumption the profile of the futures position is the same as that of the forward contract in Figure 23-4. Here, however, we must also measure the settlement price of the futures contracts on the horizontal along with the spot exchange rate. The profile for the long position in Deutschemark futures is again represented by FF. In this case, the gain or loss on the futures position depends on the settlement price in six months, when the futures position is closed out. If the futures price goes up over the next six months, there will be futures gains defined by the upper portion of FF. If the futures price goes down over the next six months, losses are defined by the lower portions of FF.

Because the futures and the spot rate must approach each other (converge) as the delivery date approaches, the futures hedge should also result in a gain of 1.8 cents per Deutschemark. This is because the basis, or the difference between the futures and spot prices, is 1.8 cents per Deutschemark when the hedge is put on. As the settlement approaches, the basis must approach zero; otherwise there would be arbitrage between the futures and spot markets. Given that fact, regardless of whether the exchange rates go up or down over the next six months the overall result will be that 1.8 (cents per Deutschemark) gain. For example, suppose the spot rate did not change over the next six months. The gains and losses on the spot and futures positions are outlined as follows:

	Futures Position	**Spot Position**
Now	Buy four contracts at settlement price of 64.9 (¢/DM) with six months to settlement.	Need to buy DM500,000 in six months. (spot = 66.7¢/DM)
In six months	Sell four contracts at settlement price *66.7 (¢/DM)*	Buy DM500,000 on the spot at *66.7 (¢/DM)*
Gain or loss	1.8 ¢/DM (gain)	None

A gain of 1.8 cents per Deutschemark on DM500,000 is a savings of $9000 on the cost of the marks acquired in six months. As long as the spot and futures prices converge on the settlement date, the same result will be obtained.

As we discussed in Chapter 17, the preceding result will occur only when the futures contract matures on the same date as the exposure to risk. If, for example, the available futures contract had eight months to settlement, and that contract was used to hedge the six-month risk, the spot and the futures price would likely *not* be equal when the futures position is closed out and the Deutschemarks are purchased. However, because the spot and futures rate should be highly correlated over the six-month period, gains and losses against the current spot rate should largely be hedged by the futures position. That is, if the spot rate was to go up dramatically during that time, so should the futures settlement price. Any remaining uncertainty concerns what the basis will be after six months, though as in the previous case, the basis should become smaller as settlement approaches, conveying some but perhaps not all of the 1.8 cents per Deutschemark to the firm when the position is closed out and Deutschemarks are purchased. The following table illustrates one possible outcome:

	Futures Position	**Spot Position**
Now	Buy four contracts at settlement price of 64.9 (¢/DM) with six months to	Need to buy DM500,000 in six months. (spot = 66.7 ¢/DM)
In six months	Sell four contracts at settlement price *69.5 (¢/DM)*	Buy DM500,000 on the spot *70.0 (¢/DM)*
Gain or loss	Gain: 4.60 (¢/DM)	Loss: 3.30 (¢/DM)

In this case, the additional cost of Deutschemarks is 3.30 cents per Deutschemark. However, the gain associated with the futures hedge is 4.60 cents per Deutschemark, leaving the firm with a saving of 1.3 cents per Deutschemark, or $6500.

Foreign Currency Options

Options on foreign currency provide different hedging characteristics than forward or futures contracts. As we discussed in some detail in Chapters 15 and 17, the difference is because the option contract allows the buyer to participate in the good side of the risk, while insuring against the bad side of the risk. In the case of the U.S. importer who needs to buy Deutschemarks in six months, the foreign currency option may be used to hedge against a rising (dollars per Deutschemark) exchange rate while it allows the firm to take advantage of decreases in the exchange rate. By contrast, in the case of the forward and the futures hedge, both sides of the risk were hedged. The forward contract allowed the firm to lock up a certain exchange rate of 64.9 cents per Deutschemark. As a consequence, the firm could not take advantage of a dramatic decrease in the exchange rate, or be subject to a dramatic increase either. The option contract, on the other hand, allows the holder to exercise the option when it is in her interest to do so.

To demonstrate the foreign currency option as a risk management tool, imagine that the firm is able to buy a call option on DM 500,000, with an exercise price of 68 cents per Deutschemark and a six-month exercise date, at a premium (price) of 1/2 cent per Deutschemark. A payoff profile can be constructed to show the hedging characteristics of the option. The profile, similar to those described in Figures 23-3 and 23-4, is represented in Figure 23-5 as of the exercise date in six months. The schedule, 00, indicates the net payoff of the option in cents (gained or lost) per mark purchased on the exercise date. The payoff is expressed net of the option premium of 1/2 cent per Deutschemark. Therefore, in the range of spot exchange rates where the option will not be exercised—that is, for spot rates equal to or less than 68 cents per Deutschemark, the payoff is a −1/2 cent per Deutschemark, indicating purely the cost of the option.[6] In the range above 68 cents per Deutschemark, the option will be exercised, and for spot rates above 68.5 cents per Deutschemark, the option will make a profit net of the option premium.

When the unhedged foreign exchange exposure represented by Figure 23-3 is combined with Figure 23-5, the effect of the long call position on the unhedged risk is easily seen. Adding the unhedged profile to that for the long call position generates the heavy line, XX, shown in Figure 23-6. Notice that for exchange rates above a certain level, the call provides complete protection. The exercise value of the call exactly compensates for the additional cost of exchange rates above the exercise price, 68 cents per Deutschemark. At 68 cents per Deutschemark, the option has no exercise value, the spot price has increased by 1.3 cents per Deutschemark, and the option premium of 1/2 cent per Deutschemark has been paid. For rates above 68 cents per Deutschemark, the increase in the exchange rate beyond the exercise price is exactly offset by an equal payoff on the option. This results in a "floor" in the combined, or hedged, profile, which occurs at −1.8 cents per Deutschemark. This means that with the call in place the worst outcome the firm could face is an increase in cost of the needed marks of 1.8 cents per Deutschemark, as compared to the current spot price.

For prices less than the exercise price of the option, the hedged profile increases one-for-one with decreases in the spot price. In effect, because the option will not be exercised in this range, the firm will realize any benefits (savings) from decreases in the spot rate, less the cost of the option. At exchange rates below 66.2 cents per Deutschemark, the firm will begin to realize savings net of the option price. The upper portion of the hedged profile, XX, shows the savings in the cost of marks that the firm will capture for further decreases in the spot rate.

Other options with different exercise prices should also be considered. In particular, if greater protection against exchange rate increases is desired, a call option with a lower exercise price should be chosen. This would cause the option to give more immediate protection as the exchange rate increases. For example, if a (67) call

---

[6]The option premium must be paid when the option is purchased, six months before the exercise date. Therefore the option cost should include the opportunity cost of the option premium. For simplicity, we ignore adjustments for the time value of the option premium.

Figure 23-5
Payoff profile for the (68) call option (cents per Deutschemark).

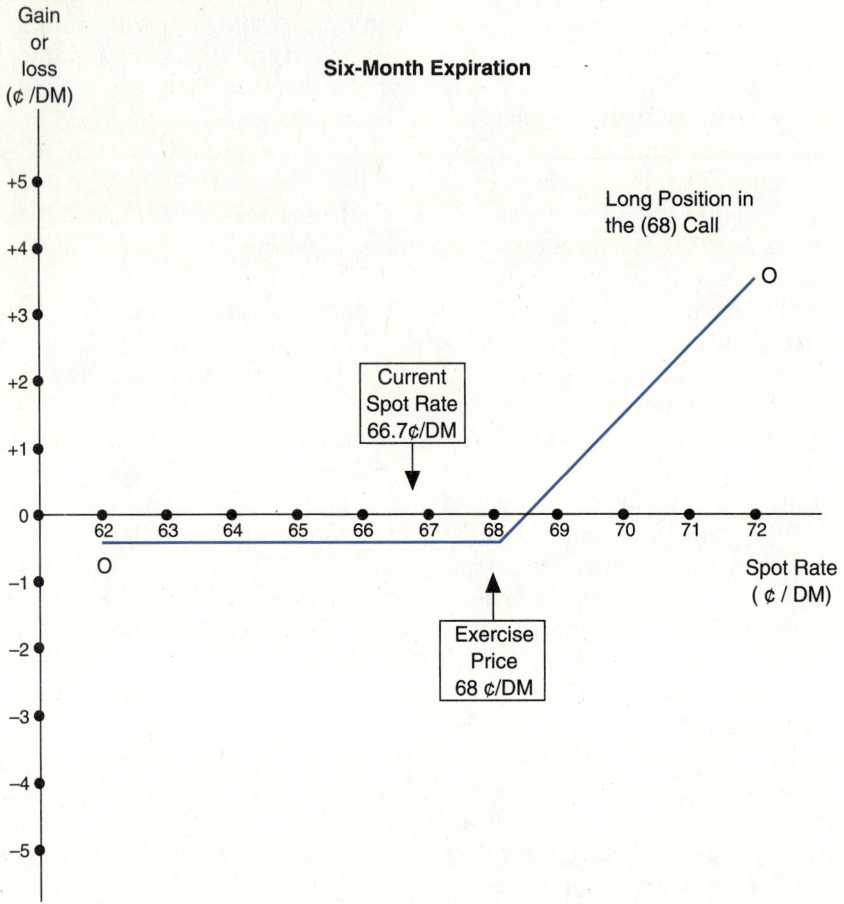

option were used, once the exchange rate reached 67 cents per Deutschemark, the option would begin to hedge any further increases in the rate one-for-one. At the same time, however, call options with the lower exercise price will have larger premiums. Therefore, though the "insurance" protection afforded by the (67) call is greater, the cost of that protection is also greater. Suppose the price of the (67) call option is 1.0 cent per Deutschemark. A hedged profile similar to that in Figure 23-6 can be derived. At a rate of 67 cents per Deutschemark a "floor" of −1.3 cents per Deutschemark is reached. Further increases in the exchange rate are hedged. This provides better protection against rising exchange rates than the (68) call option, which limits losses to −1.8 cents per Deutschemark. At the same time, the cost of the (67) call is greater than that of the (68) call. A comparison of the two option strategies is made in Figure 23-7. The heavy lines represent the *hedged* profiles under each of the options; that is, the options payoff schedules are netted against the unhedged profile of the exchange rate exposure.

Figure 23-6

The hedged profile using the (68) call option (cents per Deutschemark).

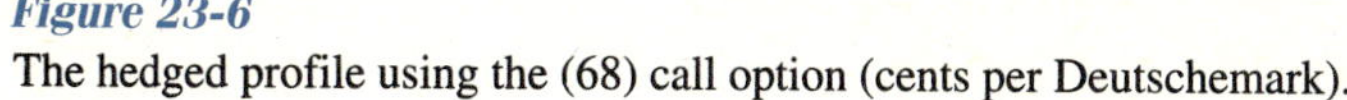

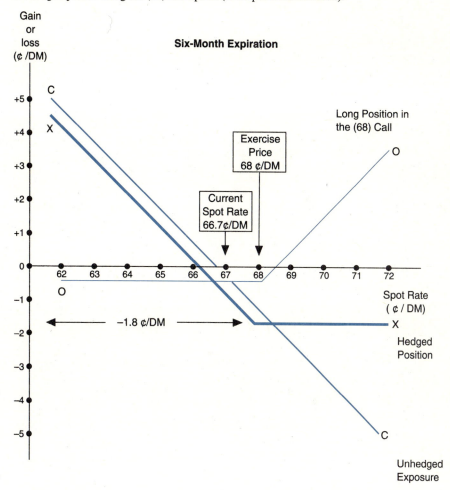

Notice the tradeoff between the two alternatives. When exchange rates decrease, the (68) call strategy dominates because the premium is less. When exchange rates increase, the (67) call strategy dominates, owing to the greater protection (lower exercise price) afforded by the option. In essence, the more expensive option gives up more of the upside potential, or cost savings, when exchange rates fall over the next six months. But when exchange rates rise, this option provides the greater protection.

Finally, the availability of options that expire at the six-month exposure date is also a concern. Exchange-traded options are generally available that have expiration dates over the next three months. Options with more distant expiration dates are more difficult to obtain. However, for a fee, dealer banks in the foreign exchange market offer tailor-made options to their clients that have the needed dimensions (exercise price, date, denomination).

Figure 23-7
A comparison of the (67) and the (68) call options (cents per dollar).

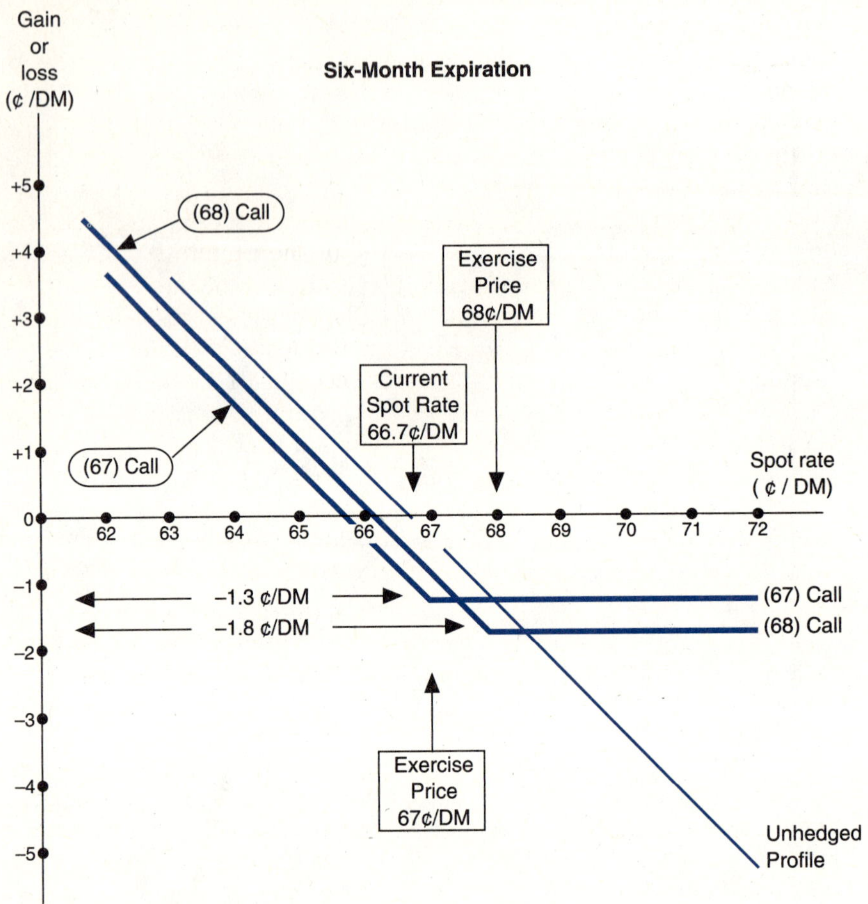

Dynamic Hedging

Thus far the hedging process we have described has been entirely static. That is, you could get the impression that once you have set up the hedge there isn't anything more to do. Sometimes this is close to correct, but often it is not. There are several reasons why the hedge may have to be adjusted over its life. The first is that the hedging strategy may involve rolling over a futures contract. This occurs when the exposure you want to hedge is dated so far in the future that there are no futures contracts with maturity dates that match the exposure. For example, consider an interest rate hedging problem where you would like to use Eurodollar futures contracts with a four-year maturity. The problem here is that you cannot generally obtain such long-dated Eurodollar futures on an organized exchange. You may be able to get a forward contract over the counter, but if you intend to use a futures contract you will have to take a position on a contract that matures before your exposure date and then roll over that contract into a new future one or more times.

The second reason hedges often need to be adjusted is that the nature of the exposure can change. For example, suppose a company is hedging the foreign exchange exposure of its sales in another country. When sales occur, the company intends to convert foreign currency into U.S. dollars. To hedge the risk that the dollar may appreciate against the foreign currency involved, the firm sells futures contracts on the foreign currency in a total denomination equal to the expected volume of future sales. Once the future position is in place, the firm may find that its expected sales volume changes over the life of the hedge. If expected sales volume increases, the firm may want to increase the number of short futures positions to maintain the hedge. If its sales volume declines, it may want to eliminate some short positions. In addition, the company's policy toward risk management may change, or its financial position and ability to withstand adverse developments may change. In effect, it may want to accept more risk rather than to protect against it, though this can be a dangerous aspect of hedging. Oftentimes, senior operating managers of a company may see either a loss or a gain on a hedge position and may want to either realize that gain early or close out a losing position for fear it might get worse. That is, they may succumb to the temptation to begin to use the risk management instrument as a speculative device rather than as a mechanism for controlling risk. It is important that management have a clear philosophy about risk management, so that these changes from risk avoidance to speculation do not happen without just cause.

The final reason that many hedges must be monitored and adjusted over time derives from the technical aspects of the hedging problem rather than from managerial problems of risk management policy. As time goes on, you may acquire new information about the effectiveness of a hedge or about the appropriate hedge ratio. That is, using new information, the estimated hedge ratio may change. In some cases, the hedge itself may depend on observed values that change through time. This occurs regularly with hedges that use options. To understand why such adjustments may be needed, let's return to the discussion of options contained in Chapter 15. Recall that the delta of an option is the change in the price of an option as a result of a change in the value of the underlying security. This means that the delta represents the hedge ratio, relative to the underlying security, that will eliminate risk of fluctuations in the price of the option. For example, if we have a call option on a stock with a delta equal to one half, then if we short one share of the stock for every two options we hold we will have perfectly hedged the price of the option. The problem with this characterization of the hedging problem is that, as we hope you recall, the delta of an option changes with the value of the underlying security. An option that is far out of the money has a delta very close to zero; one that is far in the money has a delta close to one. Therefore, as the price of the underlying security changes, so does the delta, or the minimum-variance hedge ratio. This means that if we really wanted perfectly to hedge the risk of fluctuations in the value of an option, we would need to adjust the hedge ratio with changes in the price of the underlying asset constantly. Of course, if transactions costs are incurred when you change the hedge ratio constant adjustments of that ratio will be infinitely costly and, so unattractive. Short of that extreme situation, it is still necessary to monitor the changes in the price of the asset and to decide when to make adjustments to the hedge position. This kind of monitoring requires an ongoing commitment to the hedging process rather than a one-time decision about the best hedge.

The fact that foreign exchange hedges must often be monitored and adjusted over time is one important reason why financial intermediaries often provide risk management services to their corporate customers. Banks that make markets in foreign exchange and sell forward, futures, and options contracts are in a good position to help their clients manage the entire foreign exchange risk management process.

• *Speculation Versus Hedging: The Case of Dell Computer* •

In various places throughout this book we have emphasized the point that companies that are engaged in hedging risks, whether those risks arise from interest rates or foreign exchange, should be careful to make sure that they are actually hedging, as opposed to speculating. A company that hedges is offsetting exposures that arise in its basic business. A company that is speculating is taking positions that are unrelated to its exposures in its basic business or that increase those exposures.

This question of whether a company is hedging or speculating is important, not simply because speculation is risky, but also because it can sometimes be possible for a company to attempt to use gains from speculation in foreign exchange to convince investors that its basic underlying business is more profitable than it might actually be. To successfully play these kinds of games with investors, it must be possible to make profits from speculation look as if they are actually profits from other parts of a company's business.

Partly to limit the ability to engage in such misleading activities, accounting rules stipulate that companies must include gains and losses on currency speculation in their earnings immediately, whereas gains and losses on hedging activities can be deferred over a number of future quarters. This reporting requirement makes it especially important to draw a clear distinction between what constitutes hedging and what constitutes speculation. We have made a fairly clear distinction in principle; that is, speculation entails activities that increase risk exposure or activities that are unrelated to a company's basic line of business. It is not always easy, however, to determine whether a specific activity fits the definition of speculation or hedging, particularly by the information most companies disclose about their currency hedging activities.

A particularly interesting recent case of this problem involved Dell Computer in 1992. Dell, one of the most successful retailers of computers, specialized in mail-order distribution of its products. It had been recording record earnings growth in 1992, and its stock price had been increasing dramatically. The financial markets were acutely interested in what was going to happen to Dell's profits in the future. Dell reported, in a footnote to its second-quarter 1992 financial statement, that it had incurred an unreported loss on currency hedging activity of $38 million. This represented more than half of Dell's pretax profits for the first half of fiscal 1992, so it was a pretty large number. Some people began to wonder whether Dell was really engaging in hedging or whether it was, instead, speculating.

As it turned out, the *Wall Street Journal* reported that directors of Dell had been told at a board meeting in August 1992, "Dell's treasury department was convinced it could make money, not just protect the company from exposure, by trading currency options...." It was also reported that Dell directors ordered an external audit by Price Waterhouse to make sure the company was complying with all accounting rules pertaining to its currency trading and that orders were given to "cut out the speculative trading." Thus, the independent audit seemed to confirm that there had not yet in fact been speculative trading, despite the belief by the company's treasury staff that they could speculate profitably.[7]

What constitutes speculation here is difficult to determine from the publicly available information. Dell had disclosed that it had sold currency option contracts worth $435 million as of 2 February 1992, the end of the company's fiscal year, but its international sales were only $200 million that year. On the surface, this made it appear that Dell had indeed been speculating, since its outstanding options were substantially in excess of its exposure during the previous year. Dell officials reportedly responded with two arguments. First, they pointed out that international sales were expected to be much larger in the future than in past years and that this was the basis for the hedging needs of the company. Second, they argued that a large portion of the $435 million in written options was actually offset by options that had been purchased, so that Dell's net position was actually much smaller than $435 million.

This entire episode was very costly for Dell, in a number of respects. First, the stock price was driven down in the short term by at least 10 percent as a result of questions raised by outside analysts about Dell's activities. Second, senior management had to divert attention from the management of the company's primary business of computers to concentrate on convincing the investment community that no inappropriate actions had been taken and that they were able to manage the currency hedging program properly. Given that Dell was in the middle of an epic battle for market share in the computer business, this was a costly distraction for senior management. Dell's primary or core business was computers, not currency speculation, and the financial markets were investing in Dell because of their perception of Dell's future profits from selling computers. It was very important that the market not be confused about the actual source of Dell's profitability.

SUMMARY

The simultaneous increase in the volatility of foreign exchange rates and the expansion by U.S. firms into the international marketplace during the past three decades has thrust the managers into a financial environment where they must adapt to ever increasing exposures to foreign exchange risks. During the 1990s, the successful management of foreign operations and exposures of domestic operations to foreign exchange risks will be crucial to the performance of U.S. corporations. A key to the

[7]See Kyle Pope and Anita Raghavan. "Dell Computer at War With Analyst Critical of its Currency Trades," *Wall Street Journal,* October 30, 1992.

successful management of financial and nonfinancial corporations in the future lies in the ability to recognize and manage exposures to foreign exchange rate changes and to anticipate their impact on the firm. The role of the financial manager in dealing with foreign exchange risk is to decide which exposures to risk are important to hedge and to determine the best tools and strategies to employ.

This chapter introduced basic principles of the recognition, evaluation, and management of exposure to foreign exchange risk. Three basic sources of such risk were identified and explained: transaction exposure, translation exposure, and economic (or operating) exposure. Each type manifests itself to some degree in virtually all multinational companies. As multinational corporations have expanded into international markets, exposure to these risks has increased. As a result, the demand for products and strategies with which to manage foreign exchange risk has grown. Foreign currency futures, forwards, options, and other derivative instruments have evolved as a response to this demand. This chapter explained how these instruments are used to effectively manage risk exposure associated with changes in foreign currency exchange rates.

QUESTIONS

1. Explain how a stronger U.S. dollar affects the inclination of U.S. citizens to travel abroad. When the dollar strengthens against another country's currency, is it more or less expensive for U.S. citizens to buy goods and services in that country? Explain why.
2. List and explain three types of exposure to foreign exchange risk most multinational corporations encounter.
3. A certain French wine costs FF900 per bottle. If the exchange rate between French francs and U.S. dollars is FF7.50 per dollar, what is the dollar cost of the wine per bottle? Suppose the French franc appreciated against the dollar by 10 percent (i.e., the French franc per dollar exchange rate fell by 10 percent). What would the dollar cost of wine be then? Explain.
4. A U.S. company makes ball bearings for a variety of manufacturing firms. A major customer is located in Japan. Shipments to Japan are handled through a subsidiary in Japan, and payments are received in Japanese yen. Describe potential risks to the U.S. exporter associated with changes in the yen-dollar exchange rate.
5. Suppose the U.S. company in problem 4 were to receive payment from Japanese buyers in U.S. dollars. Are there any remaining risks to the U.S. firm associated with exchange rate changes? In particular, suppose the U.S. company faces competition from Japanese ball bearing producers.

REFERENCES

Adler, M. "Exposure to Currency Risk: Definition and Measurement." *Financial Management* (Summer 1984), pp. 41–50.

Chandler, C., and J. Bussey. "Yen's Surge Against Dollar Taxes Japan, Burdening Recession-Weary Exporters." *Wall Street Journal* February 23, 1993, p. A12.

Dufey, G., and S. L. Srinivasulu. "The Case for Corporate Management of Foreign Exchange Risk." *Financial Management* (Winter 1983), pp. 54–62.

Fieleke, N.S. "Foreign Currency Positioning by U.S. Firms: Some New Evidence." *Review of Economics and Statistics* (February 1981), pp. 35–42.

Hekman, C.R. "A Model of Foreign Exchange Exposure." *Journal of International Business Studies* (Summer 1985), pp. 85–99.

Kumar, V., and J. Whitt. "Exchange Rate Variability and International Trade." *Economic Review,* Federal Reserve Bank of Atlanta, 77 (May/June 1992), pp. 17–32.

Pope, Kyle, and Anita Raghavan. "Dell Computer at War with Analyst Critical of its Currency Trades." *Wall Street Journal* October 30, 1992.

Rodriguez, R. M. "Corporate Exchange Risk Management: Theme and Aberrations." *Journal of Finance* 36 (May 1981), pp. 427–438.

Shapiro, A. C. "International Corporate Finance: A Survey and Synthesis." Tampa, FL: Financial Management Association, 1986.

Index